JAPANESE LEGAL SYSTEM: TEXT AND MATERIALS

Cavendish
Publishing
Limited

JAPANESE LEGAL SYSTEM: TEXT AND MATERIALS

Meryll Dean, JP, BA, LLM (Cantab), Barrister
Lecturer in Law
Sussex University

Cavendish
Publishing
Limited

First published in Great Britain 1997 by Cavendish Publishing Limited,
The Glass House, Wharton Street, London WC1X 9PX
Telephone: 0171-278 8000 Facsimile: 0171-278 8080

British Library Cataloguing-in-Publication Data A catalogue record for this book is available from the British Library.

Dean, M
Japanese Legal System: Text and Materials
I Title
345.2

ISBN 1 85941 192 4

Printed and bound in Great Britain

For my mother and in memory of my father

PREFACE

This book is the culmination of nearly 10 years of work which started when my husband was posted to Tokyo and came to fruition, as a book, through the planning and design of undergraduate and postgraduate courses on the Japanese legal system. As a comparative lawyer whose main interest had been in Europe, the move to Tokyo provided an unparalleled opportunity to familiarise myself with a different legal system and culture. To that extent I owe a debt of gratitude to James Capel & Co who, unknowingly, started what was to become an enduring relationship with Japan and her people, which was eventually to develop into the focus for my research.

The aim of the book is to provide a distinctive contribution to the study of comparative law by presenting a wide-ranging account of a legal system which is often overlooked, is certainly difficult to access, yet belongs to a nation which influences, leads and shapes political, commercial and industrial developments throughout the world. Although this book is in one sense a culmination it is, in another, only the beginning. By providing a relatively comprehensive account of the modern Japanese legal system, I hope that a wider audience will be given a timely introduction to a fascinating and different legal culture which will undoubtedly be at the forefront of global developments as we enter the 21st century.

Japan is a country about which the words homogeneous and unique are often used, but it is all too easy to be misled, if not persuaded, by stereotype and misconception. By using a diversity of academic sources, from political scientists, anthropologists, sociologists and historians through to lawyers, it is hoped that the reader will gain an insight into the Japanese polemic. The issues of uniqueness and homogeneity are challenged through the medium of comparative discourse, as opposed to textual judgment. Each chapter offers an outline of the subject matter and introduces the issues, but leaves the reader to develop their own critique through the materials. On occasion, what might seem repetitive may in fact be a presentation of culturally opposing views on the same topic, or represent analyses by writers from different academic disciplines. In short the book provides a cross-cultural, multi-disciplinary approach to the Japanese legal system.

During my research I became aware that it was more challenging to obtain even the simplest piece of information on the Japanese legal system than to find the most complex about almost any other country in the developed industrial world. Japan is a country of contradictions, at once familiar and alien, accessible yet inaccessible, a conundrum which has been reflected in the compilation of this book. The diversity of sources has led to insights as well as inconsistencies. These range from simple things such as the difference between American and English spelling and the difficulty of translating Japanese words and names, to the more fundamental problems of dates and terminological inexactitudes. I have not attempted to rationalise these inconsistencies, rather, where possible, to explain them. It is hoped that taken as a whole, the book will provide a sufficient understanding of the basic structures and essential differences between other legal cultures and that of Japan.

Whilst researching and writing this book I have been helped in a variety of ways by more people than can be named here. However, I owe a particular debt of gratitude to Professor Takashi Maruta without whose inspiration and encouragement this work would never have been started and whose support has at all stages been invaluable. My time at Konan University as Visiting Professor was particularly productive and gave me the opportunity both to reflect and research. I would like to thank all colleagues and friends who helped and contributed during my stay. I am also indebted to Professor Masayuki Murayama whose interest in, and comments on, earlier work helped me to believe that a project of this sort was both important and possible. Research for this book was carried out in Japan and England and I wish to thank Judge Katsumi Chiba of the Supreme Court of Japan for providing much needed material and Machiko Konno for her hospitality and help with negotiations during my visits to Tokyo. Thanks must also go to Joan Benning of Sussex University Library who performed miracles in obtaining information from all over the world. Richard Vogler's advice and comments on early drafts were most helpful. Throughout the project I have received invaluable support from Beverley Walker. Her eagle eye and incisive comments kept me on my toes and in general she lifted my spirits and provided much appreciated encouragement. Finally, thanks are due to my husband, David, whose culinary skills have sustained me and computer wizardry saved me on a number of occasions. His infinite patience, sense of humour and wise counsel provided the support and encouragement which made it all possible.

Meryll Dean
February 1997

ACKNOWLEDGMENTS

Grateful acknowledgment is made for the following:

Abe, H, Shindo, M and Kawato, S, *The Government and Politics of Japan* (University of Tokyo Press, 1994)

Akita, G, *Foundations of Constitutional Government in Modern Japan 1868–1900* (Harvard University Press, 1967)

Ashibe, N, 'Human Rights and Judicial Power' in *Constitutional Systems in Late 20th Century Asia*, Beer, LW (ed) (University of Washington Press, 1992)

Beer, LW, 'Law and Liberty' from *Democracy in Japan*, Takeshi Ishida and Ellis S Krauss, *Democracy in Japan* © 1989 by University of Pittsburgh Press. Reprinted by permission of the University of Pittsburgh Press

Beer, LW, 'The Present Constitutional System of Japan' in *Constitutional Systems in Late 20th Century Asia*, Beer, LW (ed) (University of Washington Press, 1992)

Benedict, R, *The Chrysanthemum and the Sword: Patterns of Japanese Culture* (Routledge, 1967)

Buckley, R, 'The British Model: Institutional Reform and Occupied Japan' in *Modern Asian Studies* 16: 234–240 (1982) (Cambridge University Press)

Danelski, DJ, *The Political Impact of the Japanese Supreme Court* Volume 74, Issue 5, *The Notre Dame Lawyer* June (1974) 955–980 reprinted with permission. © by Notre *Dame Law Review*, University of Notre Dame

Danelski, D, *The Supreme Court of Japan: An Exploratory Study* © Schubert, G and Danelski, D, 1996 from *Comparative Judicial Behaviour* used by permission of Oxford University Press Inc

Dean, M, 'Administrative Guidance in Japanese Law: A Threat to the Rule of Law' *Journal of Business Law* (Sweet & Maxwell, 1991)

Guide to the Family Court, Supreme Court of Japan (revised for publication, 1995)

Henderson, DF, *Conciliation and Japanese Law: Tokugawa and Modern* 2 Vols (University of Washington Press, 1965)

Ishii, R, A *History of Political Institutions in Japan* (University of Tokyo Press, 1980)

Ito, M, 'The Modern Development of Law and Constitution in Japan' in *Constitutional Systems in Late 20th Century Asia*, Beer, LW (ed) (University of Washington Press, 1992)

Itoh, H, *The Japanese Supreme Court: Constitutional Policies* (Markus Wiener, 1989)

Iwasaki, K, 'ADR: Japanese Experience with Conciliation' from *Arbitration International* 1994 Vol 10 91–97 © LCIA (London Court of International Arbitration: reprinted by permission of Kluwer Law International)

Kigawa, Susan Sayuri 'Gaikoku Bengoshi Ho, Foreign Lawyers in Japan: The Dynamics Behind Law' 66, 62 *Southern Californian Law Review* 1489–1521 (1989), reprinted with permission of the *Southern California Law Review*

Krauss, ES, 'Politics and the Policymaking Process' from *Democracy in Japan*, Takeshi Ishida and Ellis S Krauss (eds), *Democracy in Japan* © 1989 by University of Pittsburgh Press. Reprinted by permission of the University of Pittsburgh Press

Lehmann, J, *The Roots of Modern Japan* (Macmillan, 1982)

Maki, J, *Japan's Commission on the Constitution: The Final Report* (University of Washington Press, 1980)

© Matsushita, Mitsuo 1993. Reprinted from *International Trade and Competition Law in Japan* by Mitsuo Matsushita (1990) by permission of Oxford University Press

Miyazaki, A, 'The Judicial System' from *The Japanese Legal System* Tanaka, H (ed), (University of Tokyo Press, 1976)

Noda, Y, *Introduction to Japanese Law* (University of Tokyo Press, 1976)

Okudaira, Y, *Forty Years of the Constitution and its Various Influences* from *Japanese Constitutional Law*, Luney, P and Takahashi, K (eds) (Tokyo University Press, 1993)

Oppler, AC, *Legal Reform in Occupied Japan – A Participant Looks Back* © 1976 by Princeton University Press. Reprinted by permission of Princeton University Press

Outline of Criminal Justice in Japan, Supreme Court of Japan 1993 (revised for publication 1995)

Outline of Civil Trial in Japan (revised for publication 1995)

Shindo, M, *Administrative Guidance: Securities Scandals Resulting from Administrative Guidance* Japanese Economic Studies 1992 reprinted by permission from M E Sharpe Inc, Armonk, New York

Stockwin, JAA, 'Political Parties and Political Opposition' from *Democracy in Japan*, Takeshi Ishida and Ellis S Krauss, *Democracy in Japan* © 1989 by University of Pittsburgh Press. Reprinted by permission of the University of Pittsburgh Press

Tanaka, Hideo 'Legal Equality Among Family Members in Japan: the Impact of the Japanese Constitution of 1946 on the Traditional Family System' 53 *Southern Californian Law Review* 611–43, reprinted with permission of the *Southern California Law Review*

Upham, FK, *Law and Social Change in Postwar Japan* (Harvard University Press, 1989)

Urabe, N, 'Rule of Law and Due Process – A Comparative View of the United States and Japan' from *Japanese Constitutional Law*, Luney, P and Takahashi, K (eds) (Tokyo University Press, 1993)

van Wolferen, K, *The Enigma of Japanese Power* (Macmillan, 1990)

von Mehren, AT (ed), *Law in Japan: The Legal Order in a Changing Society* (Harvard University Press, 1963)

Ward, R (ed), *Political Development in Modern Japan* © 1968 by Princeton University Press. Reprinted by permission of Princeton University Press

Young, MK, 'Judicial Review of Administrative Guidance Governmentally Encouraged Consensual Dispute Resolution in Japan' 84 *Columbia Law Review* 1984, reprinted by permission

Acknowledgments

Grateful acknowledgment to the *American Journal of Comparative Law;* to the Regents of the University of California Press for extracts from *Asian Survey;* to *Comparative International Law Journal of South Africa*; to *Harvard Law Review Association* and *Harvard College* respectively for extracts from *Harvard Law Review* and *Harvard International Law Journal;* to the Institute for International Legal Information for extracts from the *International Journal of Law Libraries*; to the *Journal of Japanese Studies;* to the *Journal of Legal Education*; to Duke University School for Law for extracts from *Law and Contemporary Problems*; to the Japanese-American Society for Legal Studies for extracts from *Law in Japan*; and to the Academy of Political Science for extracts from *Political Science Quarterly*. Extracts from *Law and Society Review* are reprinted by permission of the Law and Society Association.

Every effort has been made to trace all the copyright holders but if any have been inadvertently overlooked the publishers will be pleased to make the necessary arrangement at the first opportunity.

CONVENTIONS AND COMMENTS

Due to the range of sources referred to in this book, a number of contradictions may appear. In the text, every attempt has been made to be consistent, but the materials may be at variance. Thus, the following conventions have been observed in the text:

1 Where direct translation is used the source is *Kenkyusha's* New Japanese-English Dictionary, Editor in Chief, Koh Masuda, 4th edn, 1974, 16th impression, 1987.

2 The text of the Codes and the 1946 Constitution are taken from the official English translation published from time to time by Eibun Horei Sha Inc as EHS Law Bulletin Series – *Roppo.*

3 Japanese names are written in Western order, with the personal name first and surname second. It should be noted that some materials adopt the Japanese order of surname first followed by personal name.

4 In texts containing Japanese words it is the practice to include macrons to aid pronunciation. However, due to technical difficulties and for the sake of consistency all macrons have been removed.

5 English spelling has been used in the commentary but where American source material has been used no changes have been made. Due to variations in translation some discrepancies may exist, eg Shimpei or Shinpei, the forename of Minister of Justice Ito during the Meiji era (see Chapter 2) and Kenpo, or Kempo as the word for Constitution.

6 References to the two modern Constitutions may vary. The Meiji Constitution was promulgated in 1889 and came into effect in 1890. The 'new' or Showa Constitution was promulgated in 1946 and came into effect in 1947. Throughout the text reference is made to the Meiji Constitution and the 1946 Constitution however, as will be apparent in the materials, practice may vary between authors.

7 Where there is reference to a statute, the word 'Law' is used rather than 'Act'.

8 Footnote and bibliographic references have been taken out of materials unless specifically requested by the publishers. Similar editing has taken place at the request of publishers in relation to quotations within certain materials.

CONTENTS

TABLE OF MATERIALS

CHAPTER 1

INTRODUCTION

At first glance the Japanese legal system seems familiar. It has a written constitution, legal Codes and recognisable institutions of government and parliamentary democracy. Closer inspection reveals that, in very broad terms, the constitution was influenced by America. The parliamentary system is a mixture of Anglo-American ideas and the French and German legal systems provided the models for the Japanese Codes. Whilst it is natural to start by looking for what is familiar, it is also rather dangerous since this approach is likely to entail ethnocentric assumptions and generalisations. Moreover, the Japanese legal system is a cornucopia of contradiction derived from the synthesis of indigenous and extraneous influences, which makes the process of analysis extremely complex.

The standard texts on comparative law rely upon categories such as common law, civil law, religious law and socialist law, which oblige the reader to view a particular country's legal system as part of a 'tradition' or 'family'.[1] Although they provide a lifeline to something recognisable, these concepts, unless used with care, can be theoretically and practically problematic, as well as confusing and inadequate.[2] Furthermore, since a legal system is much more than a mere collection of laws and institutions, it is necessary to consider ideas of culture and identity.[3] In relation to this, it is useful to bear in mind Lawrence Friedman's theory that it 'ought to be possible to classify and compare legal systems by means of their cultures'.[4] He defines 'legal culture' as the 'attitudes, values, and opinions held in society, with regard to law, the legal system, and its various parts' and goes on to say:

> So defined, it is the legal culture which determines when, why, and where people use law, legal institutions, or legal process; and when they use other institutions, or do nothing. In other words, cultural factors are an essential ingredient in turning a static structure and a static collection of norms into a body of living law. Adding the legal culture to the picture is like winding up a clock or plugging in a machine. It sets everything in motion.[5]

---

1 David, R and Brierley, JEC, *Major Legal Systems in the World Today,* 3rd edn, 1985, Stevens, group national legal systems into four major 'families' (1) Roman-Germanic (2) Common Law (3) Socialist (4) Religious and Traditional. See also Merryman, JH, *The Civil Law Tradition,* 2nd edn, 1985, Stanford University Press; Watson, A, *Legal Transplants: An Approach to Comparative Law,* 1974, Scottish Academic Press; 2nd edn, 1993, University of Georgia Press; Zweigert, K and Kötz, H, *An Introduction to Comparative Law,* 2nd rev edn, 1992, Oxford University Press.

2 Friedman, L, *Law and Society,* 1977, Prentice-Hall, at p 76 argues that the traditional classification of legal systems is 'helpful in many ways' but without an understanding or knowledge of legal culture their structures and substance are merely 'lifeless artefacts'.

3 This is vital to understanding the Japanese legal system and is illustrated by the use of cultural anthropology to understand the concept of *giri* in the work of Ruth Benedict *infra,* n 23. It is also important to consider the cultural content in Kawashima's work on Japanese 'legal consciousness', in particular his recent adoption of the concept of *mentalité, infra,* n 16. On the nature of legal culture in general see the work of Lawrence Friedman, in particular *Law and Society,* Chapter 7, 'Systems and Cultures of Law'.

4 Friedman, at p 76.

5 *Idem.*

Thus, whilst this book maps the creation of the modern Japanese legal system with reference to the influence of foreign legal systems, these cannot be separated from the cultural context into which they were transplanted, adopted, developed and in which they now function. Ultimately, the search for interrelated ideas and influences is more productive and useful when considering the Japanese legal system, than the pursuit of analogies through the use of such imperfect theoretical tools as the categories of 'family' or 'tradition'.[6]

The diversity of Japanese history, together with the synthesis of various foreign influences, has ensured that the modern Japanese legal system is a 'laboratory of operative comparative law.'[7] However, within that laboratory the contradictions create formidable challenges to understanding how the system operates. As one writer has put it:

> Westerners who seek to enter the way of law in Japan often are frustrated by what appears to be a house of mirrors. Texts that seem to speak clearly and directly are routinely evaded. On the other hand, when the law is silent, behaviour still conforms (or is expected to conform) to the accepted norm.[8]

The problem for anyone wishing to study the Japanese legal system is the struggle to understand the difference between what is seen and unseen, said and unsaid. Moreover, as a result, that which appears to be the same often turns out to be manifestly different, whilst that which seems alien is reflected within one's own system of law.[9] A major part of that difference, which is not

---

6 Friedman *idem* states that, 'using the traditional classification makes Haiti and France close kin, and France and England unrelated. One wonders how true a picture this gives of legal life, in the broadest sense, within these countries'. It is interesting to note the views of Pierre Legrand in relation to comparative law in general, which he summarises in a review article: 'I have argued that the time has come for comparative legal studies to realise that it is chiefly concerned with the matter of the intellectual interconnectedness between discrepant legal and cultural experiences in a context where we who compare are *of* the connections and not outside them. The comparatist must accept that the focus on categories and rules will produce a persistent miscognition of the experiences of legal order under scrutiny and of the symbolic modes and interpretative performances through which these legal orders are expressed, perceived and accomplished by members of the legal and lay worlds.' 'Comparative Legal Studies and Commitment to Theory' (1995) 58 MLR 262 at 272.

7 Itoh, H and Beer, LW, *The Constitutional Case law of Japan: Selected Supreme Court Decisions, 1961–1970*, 1978, p 9, University of Washington Press. Although this comment was made in connection with the 1946 Constitution and the 'intermingling' of American common law approaches and Japanese civil law methods, the idea is equally appropriate for the entire Japanese legal system.

8 Rosen, D, 'The Koan of Law in Japan' (1991) 18 *Northern Kentucky Law Review* 367. A *koan* is a teaching device used in Zen Buddhism. Using the *koan* as a metaphor, the author argues that for a Western student to emerge from the 'house of mirrors' it is necessary 'to look for the meaning behind the meaning, and not the superficial comprehension of the literal words.' Furthermore, that instead of clinging to known signposts, it is necessary to see the Japanese legal system in its own terms and not attempt to force it into Western categories, at p 368. Interesting background reading on the Japanese way of thinking is provided in Random, M, *Japan: Strategy of the Unseen. A Guide for Westerners to the Mind of Modern Japan*, 1987, Crucible.

9 It is possible to argue that the Japanese legal system is unique and it may well be that the arguments for this view, as opposed to it being a hybrid, are compelling (on traditional categorisation see *supra* n 1, but note the views of Friedman, *supra*, n 4 on legal cultures). However, a conclusion that the Japanese legal system is unique requires that it be put in the context of the broader belief of the Japanese in their 'uniqueness'. This widely held view ...

specifically dealt with elsewhere in this book, is the place of law in Japanese society.[10] The purpose of this chapter is to provide a brief introduction to certain aspects of this subject, which will be examined more fully in the materials.

A convenient focus for this purpose is the debate concerning Japanese 'legal consciousness'.[11] Although the term was used earlier, it is generally taken to have been introduced by Takeyoshi Kawashima in an article in 1963 entitled 'Dispute Resolution in Contemporary Japan'.[12] In this he used 'legal consciousness' (*ho-ishiki*) as a cultural factor to explain the low levels of litigation in a society which had experienced rapid industrialisation.[13]

---

9 ... concerning the special and superior nature of 'Japaneseness' is expressed in the word *Nihonjinron*, of which former Prime Minister Nakasone was a very public supporter. At one level it represents racial purity and nationalism; at another, it is the social and cultural cohesion which binds the people together and has an immense psychological power. More importantly, it represents a defensive ideology against foreign influence and intervention and in this sense is relevant to the discussion of Article 9 (the Peace Clause) of the constitution. See Chapter 7. A further area where it illuminates the debate is in the case of the *Burakumin*, Japanese 'outcasts' or 'untouchables'. In dealing with these people reference is made to their racial difference, although the real origin of their status seems to have more to do with their occupations as executioners, butchers, tanners, etc see Upham, FK, *Law and Social Change in Postwar Japan*, 1987, Harvard University Press, Chapter 3. A detailed account of the whole subject is given in Dale, PN, *The Myth of Japanese Uniqueness*, 1986, Croom Helm. For a general overview see Reischauer, EO, *The Japanese Today: Change and Continuity*, rev edn 1988, Harvard University Press, Chapter 39; van Wolferen, K, *The Enigma of Japanese Power*, 1990, Macmillan, Chapter 10.

10 However, Chapter 6 'Alternative Dispute Resolution' touches on a number of matters relevant to this discussion.

11 The focus of this debate has been civil law and contracts in particular, although the material illustrates the broader relationship between law and society. Nevertheless, constitutional law and criminal law illustrate that relationship from an alternative perspective. The problem of 'rights and duties' in a group oriented and relatively homogeneous society is explored in Chapter 7 on the Constitutional Framework. Whilst it is not possible to cover the criminal law, it is worth bearing in mind that, in this area at least, the generally accepted view of Japanese law and society is true. It has the lowest crime rate in the world. Significant features are the traditional social structures and hierarchies and their relationship to authority and the state. In particular it is interesting to study the role of the police in Japanese society. See Ames, W, *Police and Community in Japan*, 1981, University of California Press. For an accessible and generalist view see van Wolferen *supra* n 9, Chapter 7 'Nurses of the People' in which he characterises the role of the police in Japanese society as 'Nannies, monitors and missionaries'. However, it is important to reflect that in this well ordered and safe society, when the law is forced to intervene in criminal matters there is a 99.7% conviction rate of which 86% are based on confession evidence (*Hanzai Hakusho*, 1990, White Paper on Crime and *Hoso Jiho*, 1991, Lawyers' Association Journal). As Haley (1982) *infra* n 15 at p 269 observes: 'Confession, repentance, and absolution provide the underlying theme of the criminal justice process. At every stage, from initial police investigation through formal proceedings, an individual suspected of criminal conduct gains by confessing, apologising, and throwing himself upon the mercy of the authorities.' For a thorough analysis of confession and apology in Japanese criminal law, see Bayley, D, *Forces of Order: Police Behaviour in Japan and the United States*, 1976, University of California. (NB New edition, 1991, published as *Forces of Order: Policing Modern Japan*); Wagatsuma and Rosett, *infra*, n 25, p 483.

12 In von Mehren, AT (ed), *Law in Japan: The Legal Order in a Changing Society*, 1963, Harvard University Press. Kawashima developed his ideas further which were published (in part) in English as 'The Legal Consciousness of Contract in Japan' (1974) 7 *Law in Japan: An Annual* 1.

13 'Litigiousness' has been defined by Ehrmann as 'the propensity to settle disputes through the judicial process'. See Ehrmann, HW, *Comparative Legal Cultures*, 1976, p 83, Prentice-Hall.

According to his thesis, the traditional Japanese 'legal consciousness' viewed resort to the formal legal system as anathema. In other words, Japan must be seen as a litigation averse society in which any use of the laws and institutions of the formal legal system is seen as a threat to social harmony.[14] Kawashima's work fuelled a vociferous debate, led by the American John Haley, as to whether the Japanese are in fact non litigious and if so, whether this might result from cultural preference and social forces.[15] However, it is interesting to note that although the term is now common currency amongst writers, Kawashima found the translation of *ho-ishiki* as 'legal consciousness' to be inadequate. He later expressed a preference for the French translation of the term as *mentalité*, which he felt more accurately reflected the socio-cultural aspect of his theory.[16] Certainly if the Japanese Legal System is to be considered as more than a 'static structure' it is important to recognise the cultural context in which its institutions function.[17] Understanding the place of law in society is

14 Following Friedman's definition of legal culture *supra* n 2 at p 76 as (*inter alia*) the attitudes, values and opinions which determine when, why and where people use law, or choose to do nothing, the idea of 'legal consciousness' could be seen as another term for the same concept. However, note Kawashima's more recent preference for the term *mentalité*. See *infra* n 16. A short and interesting comparative perspective of legal culture is provided by Fujikura, K, 'A Comparative View of Legal Culture in Japan and the United States' (1983) 16 *Law in Japan* 129.

15 Haley, JO, 'The Myth of the Reluctant Litigant' (1978) *Journal of Japanese Studies* 359; Haley 'Sheathing the Sword of Justice in Japan: An Essay on Law Without Sanctions' (1982) *Journal of Japanese Studies* 265. The debate has now been taken up by others. See Upham *supra* n 9 at p 2 who states that the primary purpose of his book is 'to demonstrate that the assumption of law's insignificance is fundamentally incorrect'. Ramsayer, JM, 'Reluctant Litigant Revisited: Rationality and Disputes in Japan' (1988) *Journal of Japanese Studies* 111; Ramsayer, JM and Nakazato, M, 'The Rational Litigant: Settlement Amounts and Verdict Rates in Japan' (1989) 18 *Journal of Legal Studies* 263. See also Haley, JO, *Authority Without Power: Law and the Japanese Paradox*, 1991, Oxford University Press. Kim, C and Lawson, CM, 'The Law of the Subtle Mind: The Traditional Japanese Conception of Law' (1979) 28 *International and Comparative Law Quarterly* 491 stand out as maintaining the 'myth' and ideas of Kawashima. Their account has been criticised by Upham *supra* n 9 at p 2 for resorting to 'mystical abstractions' to support their claim that the cold rationalism of litigation is unsuited to the subtle and aesthetic Japanese mind (a view put forward by Noda *infra* n 20). However, there is no doubt that in increasingly litigious Western societies, there is a growing interest in alternative dispute resolution. This has revived interest in litigation rates in Japan and focused attention on methods of dispute resolution in Japan. See Chapter 6. A slightly different appraisal of the Kawashima-Haley debate is given by Takashi Maruta. He suggests that there is a need to reconstruct the traditional model of legal consciousness and consider the issue of claims consciousness from an empirical and structural perspective, something which he says that younger Japanese scholars are beginning to do. Maruta, T, 'Japanese Claims Consciousness: Are the Japanese Still Reluctant Litigants?' in Blankenburg, E, Commaille, J and Galanter, M (eds), *Disputes and Litigation* (Oñati Proceedings, No 12, 1991). See also Miyazawa, S, 'Taking Kawashima Seriously: A Review of Japanese Research on Japanese Legal Consciousness and Disputing Behaviour' (1987) 21 *Law and Society Review* 219.

16 Miyazawa *idem* at p 219 notes that in a 1982 Japanese publication Kawashima opposes the translation of *ho-ishiki* as 'legal consciousness'. Kawashima 'meant to include subconscious as well as conscious elements of psychological phenomena' and that his concept was based on 'sociology of culture or anthropology'. Thus because *ho-ishiki* was merely a convenient term he felt responsible for the misleading translation and in fact preferred *mentalité*. Miyazawa at p 221 also comments that 'legal consciousness' is another term for 'legal culture' as defined by Friedman, *supra* n 3, p 76.

17 Friedman, *supra*, n 3.

an important part of that context.[18] The essence of that is caught by Kawashima who likened law in Japan to an heirloom samurai sword: there to be treasured but not used.[19]

However, the presence of law as an object of interest, even reverence, rather than an instrument actively to be used, implies the existence of some other rules for the management of society and settlement of disputes. In broad terms these are the rules of *giri*. These are difficult for a Westerner to understand, but involve ideas of the individuals' obligation and duty to the group (community), as well as encompassing notions of reciprocity.[20] Furthermore 'they are rules of conduct, and do not presuppose the existence of any relationship of clearly defined and quantitatively delimited rights and duties between subjects whose conduct they regulate.'[21] Sanction, such as it exists, is psychological and is illustrated by such things as concern about 'honour' and 'loss of face'.[22] This reflects the theory that Japan is a 'shame culture' and not a 'guilt culture', a description of Japanese society that was first presented to Western readers by Ruth Benedict in her book *The Chrysanthemum and the Sword*.[23] Using her skills as a cultural anthropologist, she draws a distinction between guilt cultures which have 'an internalised conviction of sin', whereas shame 'is a reaction to other people's criticism.'[24] She concludes that shame (*haji*) 'is a potent sanction'. Thus, in Japanese society, to maintain harmony (*wa*), whether in the family or the community, it is preferable to ignore a person's mistake than to seek official (formal) sanction, since an individual's shame is the group's shame.[25] A more recent description of these informal structures of social restraint is provided in the following assessment:

> Contemporary Japan remains a place where the family, neighbourhood, the work place yield formidable sanctions over the behaviour of individuals. Loyalty, obedience, deference to authority, acquiescence, and group identity are powerful deterrents to misbehaviour. Though informal, the penalties are stringent, for this is a society in which the incurring and repayment of obligations in a carefully

18 An interesting historical and cultural perspective is provided by Haley, 'The Role of Law in Japan: An Historical Perspective' (1984) 18 *Kobe University Law Review* 1. Some of the ideas Haley discusses are more fully developed in his book *Authority Without Power: Law and the Japanese Paradox*, 1991, Oxford University Press, in particular on law without sanctions and social control see Chapter 8.

19 Cited by Haley, 1982, *supra*, n 15 and from which he takes inspiration for the title of that article.

20 For a detailed explanation see Noda, Y, *Introduction to Japanese Law*, 1976, pp 174–83, University of Tokyo Press. In general see Fukutake, T, *The Japanese Social Structure: Its Evolution in the Modern Century*, 1989, University of Tokyo Press.

21 Noda, *idem*, p 174. He goes on to comment that 'the rules of *giri* are of a singular nature, and it is very difficult to explain them in an entirely satisfactory fashion'.

22 The higher a person's social status, the more demanding the sense of duty (*giri*), but the demands in terms of sanction may be no less severe. Thus the duty of a student or pupil is to pass their exams and in some cases failure results in suicide.

23 *The Chrysanthemum and the Sword: Patterns of Japanese Culture*, 1946, Houghton Mifflin; 1967, Routledge.

24 *Idem*, 1967, at p 157. Haley, 1982, *supra*, n 15, p 275 discusses 'substitute sanctions' such as loss of face and damaged reputation through adverse publicity and threat.

25 In this context it is necessary to understand the role of apology as a method of dispute resolution, see Wagatsuma, H and Rosett, A, 'The Implications of Apology: Law and Culture in Japan and the United States' (1986) 20 *Law and Society Review* 461.

> calculated network of human relations characterise the lives of all but its most marginal members.[26]

In such a culture, law has a limited function and becomes one small part of the mechanisms for social control. Where there are conflicts or disputes, resort to formal law and institutions is not the first course of action. Traditionally, the Japanese have used alternative forms of dispute resolution, such as conciliation and mediation.[27] These procedures have been preserved and developed over centuries and form an extremely important part of the modern legal system.[28] Formal law serves as *tatemae,* a body of guiding principles, which control social behaviour as well as having a coercive effect.[29] In a society where the group is the most important unit of reference, an individual would not expect to be protected by legal institutions; instead, disputes would be the subject of mediation and legal protection would not be at the forefront of an individual's concern.[30] Moreover, in so far as the law is a device aimed at achieving certain social goals and on occasion administering sanctions, it is something which is the responsibility of the State. Thus, the individual's role in the legal process is neither expected, nor encouraged.[31] Whilst there is no doubt about the importance of alternative dispute resolution and its attraction to those from other countries, some care needs to be taken in assessing its place in Japanese society. As Dan Henderson, the leading authority on the subject, has commented:

> Although few experienced observers would doubt that the Japanese have an unusually pronounced tendency to avoid litigation and, conversely, an equally pronounced tendency to obtain settlements informally, nevertheless the informal and confidential handling itself makes such a process very illusive to the investigator.[32]

Furthermore, even greater caution needs to be taken in view of what Henderson observed to be 'the coercive character of didactic conciliation' resulting from the social differences between participants in the process, in addition to the lack of appeals and alternative remedies.[33] In view of this, he wondered whether the

26 Smith, RJ, 'Lawyers, Litigiousness, and the Law in Japan' (1984) 11 *Cornell Forum* 53 at 54.

27 On alternative dispute resolution, see Chapter 6.

28 Henderson, DF, *Conciliation and Japanese Law: Tokugawa and Modern,* 2 vols, 1965, University of Washington Press.

29 Haley, 1991, *supra,* n 15, Chapter 8.

30 Fukutake, T, *The Japanese Social Structure. Its Evolution in the Modern Century,* 1989, University of Tokyo Press.

31 Tanaka, H and Takeuchi, A, 'The Role of Private Persons in the Enforcement of Law: A Comparative Study of Japanese and American Law' (1974) 7 *Law in Japan* 34. The authors' comment that one of the characteristics of Japanese law is 'the marked inclination for giving the governmental agencies a predominant role in the enforcement of law' with the result that little, if any, thought was given to the need to encourage private actions. Furthermore 'there is a marked tendency in Japanese law to emphasise the criminal and administrative methods of sanctions – both to be exercised on the state's initiative – and to neglect the role of others to be exercised on private initiative' at pp 36–37.

32 Henderson, *supra,* n 28, Vol 2, p 191.

33 Henderson, DF, 'Law and Political Modernisation in Japan' in Ward, RE (ed), *Political Development in Modern Japan,* 1968, p 410, Princeton University Press.

conciliation process 'did not serve well the established authority of the community and tend to perpetuate tradition.'[34] Although Henderson was commenting on the Tokugawa Period (1600–1867), the idea of a tradition creating and reinforcing hierarchical and establishment power structures is supported in other areas.[35] First, at the time of Western inspired law reform in the late 19th century, there was a clear attempt to preserve 'the Japanese attitude of looking upon law merely as a tool for the ruler'.[36] The consequence was that little effort was made then, or subsequently, to 'make the machinery of justice more easily understandable or available to the people'.[37] Second, if the law is inaccessible, unavailable, even unnecessary, then there need be few lawyers.[38] But if there are few lawyers, access to the processes of formal law is impossible and again, a tradition of non-litigiousness becomes reinforced.[39] Questioning authority by attempting to enforce constitutional rights through resort to formal law and challenging the establishment through direct litigation is discouraged. The tradition of non confrontation and alternative dispute resolution is thereby preserved by restrictions on access to the law and the lack of lawyers.

This *circulus inextricabilis* is the result of a confrontation between the traditional and revisionist views of law in Japanese society. The former are represented by Kawashima and Noda, the latter by the (mainly American) empiricist Japanologists led by Haley and Ramsayer.[40] The so-called 'traditionalist' explanation of the failure of the Japanese to engage with formal law and to litigate claims, is that any form of litigation threatens the fundamental concern for consensus and harmony in Japanese society. Litigation is seen as a threat to social order because the public nature of the disagreement makes compromise difficult. Furthermore, formal law represents a head-on confrontation with traditional cultural structures and therefore the Japanese choose to avoid the courts. These views are reinforced by statements such as the following from Professor Noda:

---

34 *Idem.*

35 Henderson, *supra*, n 28, Vol 2, p 183 notes the change in the character of Japanese conciliation from the pre-war didactic form to present-day voluntary conciliation.

36 Tanaka and Takeuchi, *supra*, n 31, p 38.

37 *Idem.* See also comments on the place of law in Japanese thought in the 19th century in Maruyama, M, *Thought and Behaviour in Modern Japanese Politics*, 1963, Oxford University Press, in particular, the consequences, in law, of the failure of political theory to distinguish between the public and private domains at p 6.

38 See Chapter 5. In 1995 there were only 15,450 lawyers registered with the Japan Federation of Bar Associations. A fascinating insight into the Japanese legal profession is provided by a collection of four articles published in (1995) 25 *Law in Japan* 104–34. Although written by journalists, rather than lawyers, they provide useful accounts of the day-to-day lives of lawyers in 'ordinary' practice – as opposed to those in large international firms in Tokyo or Osaka. A further insight is provided by the symposium papers and additional articles published in (1988) 21 *Law in Japan* as a result of the change in the law on foreign lawyers practising in Japan.

39 See comments of Tanaka and Takeuchi, *supra* n 31, p 36.

40 *Supra*, n 15. However, in the area of contracts, significant empirical work has been conducted in Australia. See most recently Taylor, V, 'Continuing Transactions and Persistent Myths: Contracts in Contemporary Japan' (1993) 19 *Melbourne University Law Review* 352.

> To an honourable Japanese the law is something that is undesirable, even detestable, something to keep as far away from as possible. To never use the law, or be involved with the law, is the normal hope of honourable people. To take someone to court to guarantee the protection of one's own interests, or to be mentioned in court, even in a civil matter, is a shameful thing; and the idea of shame ... is the keystone to the system of Japanese civilisation. In a word, the Japanese do not like law. There is no wish at all to be involved with justice in the European sense of the word.[41]

It has been the aim of the revisionists' analysis to deconstruct this persuasive and pervasive view.[42] The suggestion is that the cultural antipathy toward law is merely a manifestation of the failure of the modern legal system. Japanese people do not resort to law because it is costly, ineffective and in terms of outcome, unsatisfactory. Moreover, it is sometimes suggested that the legal profession in Japan is a cartel whose aim is to control access to law in order to maintain high prices.[43] By controlling and limiting the numbers entering the profession it is possible to preserve an elite which in turn protects the established order.[44] In short, it is a system that does not work.

The actuality is probably somewhere between the two extremes and involves an empirical analysis beyond the scope of this book. However, in relation to civil actions, alternative explanations have emerged which suggest that the reason people do not go to court is not because they are 'reluctant litigants' as the traditionalists would have it; neither is it, as the revisionists claim, due to the failure of the system, or an establishment conspiracy aimed at self perpetuation. Instead, the parties settle disputes out of court because they are able to agree in advance how the courts might determine the matter and what type of awards would be made. In other words, potential litigants are

41 Noda, *supra*, n 20, p 159.

42 Although Kawashima's paper was titled 'Dispute Resolution in Contemporary Japan' it is clear that in that paper and 'The Legal Consciousness of Contract in Japan' *supra*, n 12, he was talking of *traditional* attitudes to contract. At the very least, it is necessary to acknowledge that the law is not static, that the legal culture must have moved forward and developed. However, the broader implications of Kawashima's thesis, when combined with statements such as Noda's *idem* have created and perpetuated the 'traditionalist' view point, which can be both misleading and dangerous for the lawyer or businessman working in Japan.

43 Ramsayer, JM, 'Lawyers, Foreign Lawyers, and Lawyer-Substitutes: The Market for Regulation in Japan' (1986) 27 Special Issue *Harvard International Law Journal* 499 at 514. 'The regulatory scheme in the Japanese legal services industry ... constitutes the classic cartel: a framework for excluding competitive outsiders and charging monopoly prices.' This article was written at a time when there was much debate about the exclusion of foreign lawyers from practice in Japan. The law was changed in 1987 and a detailed account can be found in (1988) 21 *Law in Japan*. See also, Chapter 5.

44 Ramsayer, *idem* at p 507 comments: 'Of all aspects of the regulatory programme in the Japanese legal services industry, the entry barriers, advertising restrictions, and fee schedules potentially carry the most severe consequences. Among these three, perhaps the most Draconian are the barriers to entry.' The paucity of 'rights' litigation and constitutional challenges are seen as examples of an unwillingness to challenge authority. This is true both of individuals and lawyers, although some significant changes in attitude and approach have taken place in the last 20 years. In general, see: Gresser, J, Fujikura, K and Morishima, A, *Environmental Law in Japan*, 1981, Massachusetts Institute of Technology; Upham, F, *Law and Social Change in Postwar Japan*, 1987, Harvard University Press. On the legal profession, see Chapter 5.

rational, even utilitarian, in their approach to litigation.[45] Another, rather neat, explanation of the polarity and ambiguity of the debate is that 'Japanese claims consciousness is not characterised solely either by traditional norms or by defects of the legal system. Their attitudes change in accordance with human relations; sometimes extremely traditional and sometimes surprisingly legalistic'.[46]

The 'legal consciousness' debate illustrates the broader difficulties of studying another legal culture. There are degrees of difference, problems of perception and ethnocentric interpretations, all of which seem to provide an explanation of what is otherwise unfamiliar. For those wishing to familiarise themselves with the Japanese legal system, it is particularly important to be aware of these difficulties. Nonetheless, it is a fascinating legal culture, but one where there is a temptation to be misled by exotic stereotypes and persuaded by theories of Japanese uniqueness. It is hoped that this book will provide a sufficient insight to enable the reader to go beyond that.

Benedict, R, *The Chrysanthemum and the Sword*, 1967, pp 94–101, 102–06, 156–59, Routledge and Kegan Paul

'*Giri*,' runs the Japanese saying, is 'hardest to bear'. A person must repay *giri* as he must repay *gimu*, but it is a series of obligations of a different color. There is no possible English equivalent and of all the strange categories of moral obligations which anthropologists find in the culture of the world, it is one of the most curious. It is specifically Japanese. Both *chu* and *ko* Japan shares with China and in spite of the changes she has made in these concepts they have certain family likeness to moral imperatives familiar in other Eastern nations. But giri she owes to no Chinese Confucianism and to no Oriental Buddhism. It is a Japanese category and it is not possible to understand their courses of action without taking it into account. No Japanese can talk about motivations or good repute or the dilemma which confront men and women in his home country without constantly speaking of *giri*.

To an Occidental, *giri* includes a most heterogeneous list of obligations ... ranging from gratitude for an old kindness to the duty of revenge. It is no wonder that the Japanese have not tried to expound *giri* to Westerners; their own all-Japanese dictionaries can hardly define it. One of these renders it – I translate – 'righteous way; the road human beings should follow; something one does unwillingly to forestall apology to the world'. This does not give a Westerner much idea of it but the word 'unwillingly' points up a contrast with *gimu*. *Gimu*, no matter how many difficult demands it makes upon a person, is at least a group of duties he owes within the immediate circle of his intimate family and to the Ruler who stands as a symbol for his country, his way of life, and his patriotism. It is due to persons because of strong ties drawn tight at his very birth.

45 Ramsayer, JM and Nakazato, M, 'The Rational Litigant: Settlement Amounts and Verdict Rates in Japan' (1989) 18 *Journal of Legal Studies* 263. The theory is based on empirical evidence of outcomes in traffic disputes. Rationality is an important ingredient in the model and is used to rebut the idea that 'the Japanese people to a large degree lack a sense of logic', Noda, *supra*, n 20, p 163. Moreover, Taylor, *supra*, n 40, argues that, in relation to contracts, there is a misconception as to how the law operates and that dynamic changes in law and practice have resulted in broad generalisations about contracts being of little use.

46 Maruta, *supra*, n 15, p 60.

However, unwilling specific acts of compliance may be, *gimu* is never defined as 'unwilling'. But 'repaying *giri*' is full of malaise. The difficulties of being a debtor are at their maximum in 'the circle of *giri*'.

Giri has two quite distinct divisions. What I shall call '*giri* to the world' – literally 'repaying *giri*' – is one's obligation to repay on to one's fellows, and what I shall call '*giri* to one's name' is the duty of keeping one's name and reputation unspotted by any imputation, somewhat after the fashion of German 'honor'. *Giri* to the world can roughly be described as the fulfilment of contractual relations – as contrasted with *gimu* which is felt as the fulfilment of intimate obligations to which one is born. Thus *giri* includes all the duties one owes to one's in-law's family; *gimu*, those to one's own immediate family. The term for father-in-law is father-in-*giri*; mother-in-law is mother-in-*giri*, and brother- and sister-in-law are brother-in-*giri* and sister-in-*giri*. This terminology is used either for spouse's sibling or for sibling's spouse. Marriage in Japan is of course a contract between families and carrying out these contractual obligations throughout life to the opposite family is 'working for *giri*'. It is heaviest toward the generation which arranged the contract – the parents – and heaviest of all on the young wife toward her mother-in-law because, as the Japanese say, the bride has gone to live in a house where she was not born. The husband's obligations to his parents-in-law are different, but they too are dreaded, for he may have to lend them money if they are in distress and must meet other contractual responsibilities. As one Japanese said, 'If a grown son does things for his own mother, it is because he loves her and therefore it couldn't be *giri*. You don't work for *giri* when you act from the heart'. A person fulfils his duties to his in-laws punctiliously, however, because at all costs he must avoid the dreaded condemnation: 'a man who does not know *giri*'.

The way they feel about this duty to the in-law family is vividly clear in the case of the 'adopted husband', the man who is married after the fashion of a woman. When a family has daughters and no sons the parents choose a husband for one of their daughters in order to carry on the family name. His name is erased from the register of his own family and he takes his father-in-law's name. He enters his wife's home, is subject 'in *giri*' to his father- and mother-in-law, and when he dies is buried in their burying ground. In all these acts he follows the exact pattern of the woman in the usual marriage. The reasons for adopting a husband for one's daughter may not be simply the absence of a son of one's own; often it is a deal out of which both sides hope to gain. These are called 'political marriages'. The girl's family may be poor but of good family and the boy may bring ready cash and in return move up in the class hierarchy. Or the girl's family may be wealthy and able to educate the husband who in return for this benefit signs away his own family. Or the girl's father may in this way associate with himself a prospective partner in his firm. In any case, an adopted husband's *giri* is especially heavy – as is proper because the act of changing a man's name to another family register is drastic in Japan. In feudal Japan he had to prove himself in his new household by taking his adopted father's side in battle, even if it meant killing his own father. In modern Japan the 'political marriages' involving adopted husbands invoke this strong sanction of *giri* to tie the young man to his father-in-law's business or family fortunes with the heaviest bonds the Japanese can provide. Especially in Meiji times this was sometimes advantageous to both parties. But resentment at being an adopted husband is usually violent and a common Japanese saying is 'If you have three *go* of rice (about a pint), never be an adopted husband'. The Japanese say this resentment is 'because of the *giri*.' They do not say, as Americans probably would if we had a like custom, 'because it keeps him from playing a man's rôle.' *Giri* is hard enough anyway and 'unwilling' enough, so that 'because of the *giri*' seems to the Japanese a sufficient statement of the burdensome relation.

Not only duties to one's in-laws are *giri*; duties even to uncles and aunts and nephews and nieces are in the same category. The fact that in Japan duties to even such relatively close relatives do not rank as filial piety (*ko*) is one of the great differences in family relations between Japan and China. In China, many such relatives, and much more distant ones, would share pooled resources, but in Japan they are *giri* or 'contractual' relatives. The Japanese point out that it often happens that these persons have never personally done a favor (*on*) for the person who is asked to come to their aid; in helping them he is repaying *on* to their common ancestors. This is the sanction behind caring for one's own children too – which of course is a *gimu* – but even though the sanction is the same, assistance to these more distant relatives rates as *giri*. When one has to help them, as when one helps one's in-laws, one says, 'I am tangled with *giri*'.

The great traditional *giri* relationship which most Japanese think of even before the relation with in-laws, is that of a retainer to his liege lord and to his comrades at arms. It is the loyalty a man of honor owes to his superior and to his fellows of his own class. This obligation of *giri* is celebrated in a vast traditional literature. It is identified as the virtue of the samurai. In old Japan, before the unification of the country effected by the Tokugawas, it was often considered a greater and dearer virtue even than chu, which was at that time the obligation to the Shogun. When in the twelfth century a Minamoto Shogun demanded of one of the *daimyo* the surrender of an enemy lord he was sheltering, the *daimyo* wrote back a letter which is still preserved. He was deeply resentful of the imputation upon his *giri* and he refused to offend it even in the name of *chu*. 'Public affairs,' he wrote, '(are a thing) over which I have little personal control but *giri* between men of honor is an eternal verity' which transcended the Shogun's authority. He refused 'to commit a faithless act against his honored friends'. This transcendent *samurai* virtue of old Japan suffuses great numbers of historical folktales which are known today all over Japan and are worked up into *noh* dramas, *kabuki* theater and *kagura* dances.

One of the best known of these is the tale of the huge invincible *ronin* (a lordless *samurai* who lives by his own wits), the hero Benkei of the twelfth century. Entirely without resources but of miraculous strength he terrorizes the monks when he takes shelter in the monasteries and cuts down every passing *samurai* in order to make a collection of their swords to pay for outfitting himself in feudal fashion. Finally he challenges what appears to him to be a mere youngster, a slight and foppish lord. But in him he meets his match and discovers that the youth is the scion of the Minamotos who is scheming to recover the Shogunate for his family. He is indeed that beloved Japanese hero, Yoshitsune Minamoto. To him Benkei gives his passionate *giri* and undertakes a hundred exploits in his cause. At last, however, they have to escape with their followers from an overwhelming enemy force. They disguise themselves as monkish pilgrims travelling over Japan to collect subscriptions for a temple and to escape detection Yoshitsune dresses as one or the troop while Benkei assumes its headship. They run into a guard the enemy has set along their path and Benkei fabricates for them a long list of temple 'subscribers' which he pretends to read from his scroll. The enemy almost lets them past. At the last moment, however, their suspicions are aroused by the aristocratic grace of Yoshitsune which he cannot conceal even in his disguise as an underling. They call back the troop. Benkei immediately takes a step which completely clears Yoshitsune from suspicion: he berates him on some trivial issue and strikes him across the face. The enemy is convinced; it is beyond possibility that if this pilgrim is Yoshitsune, one of his retainers should lift his hand against him. It would be an unimaginable breach of *giri*. Benkei's impious act saves the lives of the little band. As soon as they are in safe territory, Benkei throws himself at Yoshitsune's feet and asks him to slay him. His lord graciously offers pardon.

These old tales of times when *giri* was from the heart and had no taint of resentment are modern Japan's daydream of a golden age. In those days, the tales tell them, there was no 'unwillingness' in *giri*. If there was conflict with *chu*, a man could honorably stick by *giri*. *Giri* then was a loved face-to-face relation dressed in all the feudal trimmings. To 'know *giri*' meant to he loyal for life to a lord who cared for his retainers in return. To 'repay *giri*' meant to offer even one's life to the lord to whom one owed everything.

This is, of course, a fantasy. Feudal history in Japan tells of plenty of retainers whose loyalty was bought by the *daimyo* on the opposite side of the battle. Still more important, as we shall see in the next chapter, any slur the lord cast upon his retainer could properly and traditionally make the retainer leave his service and even enter into negotiations with the enemy. Japan celebrates the vengeance theme with as much delight as she celebrates loyalty to the death. And they were both *giri*; loyalty was *giri* to one's lord and vengeance for an insult was *giri* to one's name. In Japan they are two sides to the same shield.

Nevertheless the old tales of loyalty are pleasant day-dreams to the Japanese today for now 'repaying *giri*' is no longer loyalty to one's legitimate chieftain but is fulfilling all sorts of obligations to all sorts of people. Today's constantly used phrases are full of resentment and of emphasis on the pressure of public opinion which compels a person to do *giri* against his wishes. They say, 'I am arranging this marriage merely for *giri*'; 'merely because of *giri* I was forced to give him the job'; 'I must see him merely for *giri*.' They constantly talk of being 'tangled with *giri*,' a phrase the dictionary translates as 'I am obliged to it'. They say 'He forced me with *giri*', 'he cornered me with *giri*', and these, like the other usages, mean that someone has argued the speaker into an act he did not want or intend by raising some issue of payment due upon an *on*. In peasant villages, in transactions in small shops, in high circles of the Zaibatsu and in the Cabinet of Japan, people are 'forced with *giri*' and 'cornered with *giri*'. A suitor may do this by taxing his prospective father-in-law with some old relationship or transaction between the two families or a man may use this same weapon to get a peasant's land. The man who is being 'cornered' will himself feel he must comply; he says, 'If I do not hold the shoulder of my *on*-man (man from whom I received *on*), my *giri* is in bad repute'. All these usages carry the implication of unwillingness and of compliance for 'mere decency's sake', as the Japanese dictionary phrases it.

The rules of *giri* are strictly rules of required repayment; they are not a set of moral rules like the Ten Commandments. When a man is forced with *giri*, it is assumed that he may have to override his sense of justice and they often say, 'I could not do right (*gi*) because of *giri*'. Nor do the rules of *giri* have anything to do with loving your neighbor as yourself; they do not dictate that a man shall act generously out of the spontaneity of his heart. A man must do *giri*, they say, because, 'if he does not, people will call him "a person who does not know *giri*" and he will be shamed before the world.' It is what people will say that makes it so necessary to comply. Indeed, '*giri* to the world' often appears in English translation as 'conformity to public opinion', and the dictionary translates 'It can't be helped because it is *giri* to the world' as 'People will not accept any other course of action.'

It is in this 'circle of *giri*' that the parallel with American sanctions on paying money one has borrowed helps us most to understand the Japanese attitude. We do not consider that a man has to pay back the favor of a letter received or a gift given or of a timely word spoken with the stringency that is necessary in keeping up his payments of interest and his repayment of a bank loan. In these financial dealings bankruptcy is the penalty for failure – a heavy penalty. The Japanese, however, regard a man as bankrupt when he fails in repaying *giri* and every contact in life is likely to incur *giri* in some way or other. This means keeping an account of little words and acts Americans throw lightly about with no thought of incurring obligations. It means walking warily in a complicated world.

There is another parallel between Japanese ideas of *giri* to the world and American ideas of repaying money. Repayment of *giri* is thought of as repayment of an exact equivalent. In this *giri* is quite unlike *gimu,* which can never be even approximately satisfied no matter what one does. But *giri* is not unlimited. To American eyes the repayments are fantastically out of proportion to the original favor but that is not the way the Japanese see it. We think their gift giving is fantastic too, when twice a year every household wraps up something in ceremonious fashion as return on a gift received six months earlier, or when the family of one's maidservant brings gifts through the years as a return on the favor of hiring her. But the Japanese taboo returning gifts with larger gifts. It is no part of one's honor to return 'pure velvet'. One of the most disparaging things one can say about a gift is that the giver has 'repaid a minnow with a sea bream (a large fish)'. So too in repaying *giri.*

Whenever possible written records are kept of the network of exchanges, whether they are of work or of goods. In the villages some of these are kept by the headman, some by one of the workparty, some are family and personal records. For a funeral it is customary to bring 'incense money'. Relatives may also bring colored cloth for funeral banners. The neighbors come to help, the women in the kitchen and the men in digging the grave and making the coffin. In the village of Suye Mura the headman made up the book in which these things were recorded. It was a valued record in the family of the deceased for it showed the tributes of their neighbors. It is also a list which shows those names to which the family owes reciprocal tributes which will be honored when a death occurs in other families. These are long-term reciprocities. There are also short-term exchanges at any village funeral just as at any kind of feast. The helpers who make the coffin are fed and they therefore bring a measure of rice to the bereaved family as part payment on their food. The rice too is entered in the headman's record. For most feasts also the guest brings some rice-wine in part payment for the party drinks. Whether the occasion is birth or death, a rice-transplanting, a house-building or a social party, the exchange of *giri* is carefully noted for future repayment.

The Japanese have another convention about *giri* which parallels Western conventions about money repayment. If repayment is delayed beyond due term it increases as if it drew interest. Doctor Eckstein tells a story of this in his dealings with the Japanese manufacturer who financed his trip to Japan to gather material for his biography of Noguchi. Doctor Eckstein returned to the United States to write the book and eventually sent the manuscript to Japan. He received no acknowledgement and no letters. He was naturally troubled for fear something in the volume might have offended the Japanese, but his letters remained unanswered. Some years later the manufacturer telephoned him. He was in the United States, and shortly afterward he arrived at Doctor Eckstein's home bringing with him dozens of Japanese cherry trees. The gift was lavish. Just because it had been held in abeyance so long it was proper that it should be handsome. 'Surely', his benefactor said to Doctor Eckstein, 'you would not have wanted me to repay you *quickly*'.

A man who is 'cornered with *giri*' is often forced into repayments of debts which have grown with time. A man may apply for assistance to a small merchant because he is the nephew of a teacher the merchant had as a boy. Since as a young man, the student had been unable to repay his *giri* to his teacher, the debt has accumulated during the passing years and the merchant has to give 'unwillingly to forestall apology to the world'.

...

Giri to one's name is the duty to keep one's reputation unspotted. It is a series of virtues – some of which seem to an Occidental to be opposites, but which to the Japanese have a sufficient unity because they are those duties which are not repayments on benefits received; they are 'outside the circle of *on*'. They are those acts which keep one's reputation bright without reference to a specific previous indebtedness to another person. They include therefore maintaining all the miscellaneous etiquette requirements of 'proper station', showing stoicism in pain and defending one's reputation in profession or craft. *Giri* to one's name also demands acts which remove a slur or an insult; the slur darkens one's good name and should be got rid of. It may be necessary to take vengeance upon one's detractor or it may be necessary to commit suicide, and there are all sorts of possible courses of action between these two extremes. But one does not shrug off lightly anything that is compromising.

The Japanese do not have a separate term for what I call here '*giri* to one's name', They describe it simply as *giri* outside the circle of *on*. That is the basis of classification, and not the fact that *giri* to the world is an obligation to return kindnesses and that *giri* to one's name prominently includes revenge. The fact that Western languages separate the two into categories as opposite as gratitude and revenge does not impress the Japanese. Why should one virtue not cover a man's behavior when he reacts to another's benevolence and when he reacts to his scorn or malevolence?

In Japan it does. A good man feels as strongly about insults as he does about the benefits he has received. Either way it is virtuous to repay. He does not separate the two, as we do, and call one aggression and one non-aggression. To him aggression only begins outside 'the circle of *giri*'; so long as one is maintaining *giri* and clearing one's name of slurs, one is not guilty of aggression. One is evening scores. 'The world tips,' they say, so long as an insult or slur or defeat is not requited or eliminated. A good man must try to get the world back into balance again. It is human virtue, not an all-too-human vice. *Giri* to one's name, and even the way it is linguistically combined in Japan with gratitude and loyalty, has been a Western virtue in certain periods of European history. It flourished mightily in the Renaissance, especially in Italy, and it has much in common with *el valor Español* in classic Spain and with *die Ehre* in Germany. Something very like it underlay duelling in Europe a hundred years ago. Wherever this virtue of wiping out stains on one's honor has been in the ascendant, in Japan or in Western nations, the very core of it has always been that it transcended profit in any material sense. One was virtuous in proportion as one offered up to 'honor' one's possessions, one's family, and one's own life. This is a part of its very definition and is the basis of the claim that these countries always put forward that it is a 'spiritual' value. It certainly involves them in great material losses and can hardly be justified on a profit-and-loss basis. In this lies the great contrast between this version of honor and the cut-throat competition and overt hostility that crops up in life in the United States; in America it may be that no holds are barred in some political or financial deal but it is a war to get or to hold some material advantage. It is only in exceptional cases, as, for instance, in the feuds of the Kentucky Mountains, where codes of honor prevail which fall in the category of *giri* to one's name.

Giri to one's name and all the hostility and watchful waiting that accompany it in any culture, however, is not a virtue that is characteristic of the Asiatic mainland. It is not, as the phrase goes, Oriental. The Chinese do not have it, nor the Siamese, nor the Indians. The Chinese regard all such sensitivity to insults and aspersions as a trait of 'small' people – morally small. It is no part of their ideal of nobility, as it is in Japan. Violence which is wrong when a man starts it out of the blue does not become right in Chinese ethics when a man indulges in it to requite an insult. They think it is rather ridiculous to be so sensitive. Nor do they react to a slur by resolving by all that is good and great to prove the aspersion baseless. The Siamese have no place at all for this kind of sensitivity to insult. Like the Chinese they set store by making their detractor ridiculous but they do not imagine that their honor has been impugned. They say 'The best way to show an opponent up for a brute is to give in to him.'

The full significance of *giri* to one's name cannot be understood without placing in context all the non-aggressive virtues which are included in it in Japan. Vengeance is only one of the virtues it may require upon occasion. It includes also plenty of quiet and temperate behavior. The stoicism, the self-control that is required of a self-respecting Japanese is part of his *giri* to his name. A woman may not cry out in childbirth and a man should rise above pain and danger. When floods sweep down upon the Japanese village each self-respecting person gathers up the necessities he is to take with him and seeks higher ground. There is no outcry, no running hither and thither, no panic. When the equinoctial winds and rain come in hurricane strength there is similar self-control. Such behavior is a part of the respect a person has for himself in Japan even granted he may not live up to it. They think American self-respect does not require self-control. There is *noblesse oblige* in this self-control in Japan and in feudal times more was therefore required of the *samurai* than of the common people but the virtue, though less exigent, was a rule of life among all classes. If the *samurai* were required to go to extremes in rising above bodily pain, the common people had to go to extremes in accepting the aggressions of the armed *samurai*.

The tales of *samurai* stoicism are famous. They were forbidden to give way to hunger but that was too trivial to mention. They were enjoined when they were starving to pretend they had just eaten: they must pick their teeth with a toothpick. 'Baby birds,' the maxim went, 'cry for their food but a *samurai* holds a toothpick between his teeth.' In the past war this became an Army maxim for the enlisted soldier. Nor must they give way to pain. The Japanese attitude was like the boy soldier's rejoinder to Napoleon: 'Wounded? Nay, sire, I'm killed.' A *samurai* should give no sign of suffering till he fell dead and he must bear pain without wincing. It is told of Count Katsu who died in 1899 that when he was a boy his testicles were torn by a dog. He was of *samurai* family but his family had been reduced to beggary. While the doctor operated upon him, his father held a sword to his nose. 'If you utter one cry,' he told him, 'you will die in a way that at least will not be shameful.'

Giri to one's name also requires that one lives according to one's station in life. If a man fails in this *giri* he has no right to respect himself. This meant in Tokugawa times that he accepted as part of his self-respect the detailed sumptuary laws which regulated practically everything he wore or had or used. Americans are shocked to the core by laws which define these things by inherited class position. Self-respect in America is bound up with improving one's status and fixed sumptuary laws are a denial of the very basis of our society. We are horrified by Tokugawa laws which stated that a farmer of one class could buy such and such a doll for his child and the farmer of another class could buy a different doll. In America, however, we get the same results by invoking a different sanction. We accept with no criticism the fact that the factory owner's child has a set of electric trains and that the sharecropper's child contents itself with a corncob doll. We accept differences in income and justify them. To earn a good salary is a part of our system of self-respect. If dolls are regulated by income that is no violation of our moral ideas. The person who has got rich buys better dolls for his children. In Japan getting rich is under suspicion and maintaining proper station is not. Even today the poor as well as the rich invest their self-respect in observing the conventions of hierarchy. It is a virtue alien to America, and the Frenchman, de Tocqueville, pointed this out in the eighteen-thirties in his book already quoted. Born himself in eighteenth-century France, he knew and loved the aristocratic way of life in spite of his generous comments about the egalitarian United States. America, he said, in spite of its virtues, lacked true dignity. 'True dignity consists in always taking one's proper station, neither too high nor too low. And this is as much within the reach of the peasant as of the prince.' De Tocqueville would have understood the Japanese attitude that class differences are not themselves humiliating.

'True dignity', in this day of objective study of cultures, is recognized as something which different peoples can define differently, just as they always define for themselves what is humiliating. Americans who cry out today that Japan cannot be given self-respect until we enforce our egalitarianism are guilty of ethnocentrism. If what these Americans want is, as they say, a self-respecting Japan they will have to recognize her bases for self-respect. We can recognize, as de Tocqueville did, that this aristocratic 'true dignity' is passing from the modern world and that a different and, we believe, a finer dignity is taking its place. It will no doubt happen in Japan too. Meantime Japan will have to rebuild her self-respect today on her own basis, not on ours. And she will have to purify it in her own way.

Giri to one's name is also living up to many sorts of commitments besides those of proper station. A borrower may pledge his *giri* to his name when he asks for a loan; a generation ago it was common to phrase it that 'I agree to be publicly laughed at if I fail to repay this sum'. If he failed, he was not literally made a laughing-stock; there were no public pillories in Japan. But when the New Year came around, the date on which debts must be paid off, the insolvent debtor might commit suicide to 'clear his name'. New Year's Eve still has its crop of suicides who have taken this means to redeem their reputations.

All kinds of professional commitments involve *giri* to one's name. The Japanese requirements are often fantastic when particular circumstances bring one into the public eye and criticism might be general. There are for instance the long list of school principals who committed suicide because fires in their schools – with which they had nothing to do – threatened the picture of the Emperor which was hung in every school. Teachers too have been burned to death dashing into burning schools to rescue these pictures. By their deaths they showed how high they held their *giri* to their names and their *chu* to the Emperor. There are also famous stories of persons who were guilty of a slip of the tongue in ceremonious public readings of one of the Imperial Rescripts, either the one on education or the one for Soldiers and Sailors, and who have cleared their names by committing suicide. Within the reign of the present Emperor, a man who had inadvertently named his son Hirohito – the given name of the Emperor was never spoken in Japan – killed himself and his child.

...

In anthropological studies of different cultures the distinction between those which rely heavily on shame and those that rely heavily on guilt is an important one. A society that inculcates absolute standards of morality and relies on men's developing a conscience is a guilt culture by definition, but a man in such a society may, as in the United States, suffer in addition from shame when he accuses himself of gaucheries which are in no way sins. He may be exceedingly chagrined about not dressing appropriately for the occasion or about a slip of the tongue. In a culture where shame is a major sanction, people are chagrined about acts which we expect people to feel guilty about. This chagrin can be very intense and it cannot be relieved, as guilt can be, by confession and atonement. A man who has sinned can get relief by unburdening himself. This device of confession is used in our secular therapy and by many religious groups which have otherwise little in common. We know it brings relief. Where shame is the major sanction, a man does not experience relief when he makes his fault public even to a confessor. So long as his bad behavior does not 'get out into the world' he need not be troubled and confession appears to him merely a way of courting trouble. Shame cultures therefore do not provide for confessions, even to the gods. They have ceremonies for good luck rather than for expiation.

True shame cultures rely on external sanctions for good behavior, not, as true guilt cultures do, on an internalized conviction of sin. Shame is a reaction to others people's criticism. A man is shamed either by being openly ridiculed and rejected or by fantasying to himself that he has been made ridiculous. In either case it is a potent sanction. But it requires an audience or at least a man's fantasy of an audience. Guilt does not. In a nation where honor means living up to one's own picture of oneself, a man may suffer from guilt though no man knows of his misdeed and a man's feeling of guilt may actually be relieved by confessing his sin.

The early Puritans who settled in the United States tried to base their whole morality on guilt and all psychiatrists know what trouble contemporary Americans have with their consciences. But shame is an increasingly heavy burden in the United States and guilt is less extremely felt than in earlier generations. In the United States this is interpreted as a relaxation of morals. There is much truth in this, but that is because we do not expect shame to do the heavy work of morality. We do not harness the acute personal chagrin which accompanies shame to our fundamental system of morality.

The Japanese do. A failure to follow their explicit signposts of good behavior, a failure to balance obligations or to foresee contingencies is a shame (*haji*). Shame, they say, is the root of virtue. A man who is sensitive to it will carry out all the rules of good behavior. 'A man who knows shame' is sometimes translated 'virtuous man,' sometimes 'man of honor.' Shame has the same place of authority in Japanese ethics that 'a clear conscience,' 'being right with God,' and the avoidance of sin have in Western ethics. Logically enough, therefore, a man will not be punished in the afterlife. The Japanese – except for priests who know the Indian *sutras* – are quite unacquainted with the idea of reincarnation dependent upon one's merit in this life, and – except for some well-instructed Christian converts – they do not recognize post-death reward and punishment or a heaven and a hell.

The primacy of shame in Japanese life means, as it does in any tribe or nation where shame is deeply felt, that any man watches the judgment of the public upon his deeds. He need only fantasy what their verdict will be, but he orients himself toward the verdict of others. When everybody is playing the game by the same rules and mutually supporting each other, the Japanese can be light-hearted and easy. They can play the game with fanaticism when they feel it is one which carries out the 'mission' of Japan. They are most vulnerable when they attempt to export their virtues into foreign lands where their own formal signposts of good behavior do not hold. They failed in their 'good will' mission to Greater East Asia, and the resentment many of them felt at the attitudes of Chinese and Filipinos toward them was genuine enough.

Individual Japanese, too, who have come to the United States for study or business and have not been motivated by nationalistic sentiments have often felt deeply the 'failure' of their careful education when they tried to live in a less rigidly charted world. Their virtues, they felt, did not export well. The point they try to make is not the universal one that it is hard for any man to change cultures. They try to say something more and they sometimes contrast the difficulties of their own adjustment to American life with the lesser difficulties of Chinese or Siamese they have known. The specific Japanese problem, as they see it, is that they have been brought up to trust in a security which depends on others' recognition of the nuances of their observance of a code. When foreigners are oblivious of all these proprieties, the Japanese are at a loss. They cast about to find similar meticulous proprieties according to which Westerners live and when they do not find them, some speak of the anger they feel and some of how frightened they are.

No one has described these experiences in a less exacting culture better than Miss Mishima in her autobiography, *My Narrow Isle*. She had sought eagerly to come to an American college and she had fought down her conservative family's unwillingness to accept the *on* of an American fellowship. She went to Wellesley. The teachers and the girls, she says, were wonderfully kind, but that made it, so she felt, all the more difficult. 'My pride in perfect manneredness, a universal characteristic of the Japanese, was bitterly wounded. I was angry at myself for not knowing how to behave properly here and also at the surroundings which seemed to mock at my past training. Except for this vague but deep-rooted feeling of anger there was no emotion left in me.' She felt herself 'a being fallen from some other planet with senses and feelings that have no use in this other world. My Japanese training, requiring every physical movement to be elegant and every word uttered to be according to etiquette, made me extremely sensitive and self-conscious in this environment, where I was completely blind, socially speaking'. It was two or three years before she relaxed and began to accept the kindness offered her. Americans, she decided, lived with what she calls 'refined familiarity'. But 'familiarity had been killed in me as sauciness when I was three'.

Miss Mishima contrasts the Japanese girls she knew in America with the Chinese girls and her comments show how differently the United States affected them. The Chinese girls had 'self-composure and sociableness quite absent in most Japanese girls. These upper-class Chinese girls seemed to me the most urbane creatures on earth, every one of them having a graciousness nearing regal dignity and looking as if they were the true mistresses of the world. Their fearlessness and superb self-composure, not at all disturbed even in this great civilization of machinery and speed, made a great contrast with the timidity and oversensitiveness of us Japanese girls, showing some fundamental difference in social background'.

Miss Mishima, like many other Japanese, felt as if she were an expert tennis player entered in a croquet tournament. Her own expertness just didn't count. She felt that what she had learned did not carry over into the new environment. The discipline to which she had submitted was useless. Americans got along without it.

Once Japanese have accepted, to however small a degree, the less codified rules that govern behavior in the United States they find it difficult to imagine their being able to manage again the restrictions of their old life in Japan. Sometimes they refer to it as a lost paradise, sometimes as a 'harness' sometimes as a 'prison', sometimes as a 'little pot' that holds a dwarfed tree. As long as the roots of the miniature pine were kept to the confines of the flower pot, the result was a work of art that graced a charming garden. But once planted out in open soil, the dwarfed pine could never be put back again. They feel that they themselves are no longer possible ornaments in that Japanese garden. They could not again meet the requirements. They have experienced in its most acute form the Japanese dilemma of virtue.

Noda, Y, *Introduction to Japanese Law*, 1976, pp 174–83, University of Tokyo Press

THE RULES OF GIRI

The Japanese manner of thinking clearly favors neither the formation nor the functioning of law as a conceptually arranged system of rights and duties. This does not, however, mean that there is no rule of conduct which functions for the maintenance of the social order. Before the modern system of state law was established, a system of social rules of a non-legal nature directed the lives of Japanese, and that system continues to operate today, side by side with the more clearly defined system of state law. Whether this fluid system be called 'custom' or 'non-law' its rules play a very important part in Japanese social life. The system of a purely legal nature is penetrating gradually deeper into the life of Japan and the system of the past will eventually disappear, but the evolution will be slow and difficult because the ethnic character of the Japanese both facilitates the survival of the former system and compromises the proper functioning of the modern one. In addition, there is the conservatism of government which supports the natural inclination of the people.

The traditional rules that the Japanese obey are called the rules of *giri*. They are rules of conduct, and do not presuppose the existence of any relationship of clearly defined and quantitatively delimitable rights and duties between the subjects whose conduct they regulate. The rules of *giri* are of a singular nature, and it is very difficult to explain them in an entirely satisfactory fashion.

The word *giri* is difficult to define, even in Japanese, because it evokes many ideas which are difficult to group together into one general notion. Attempts have been made to define it in a coherent manner, but any such undertaking encounters almost insurmountable difficulties. A Japanese sociologist who studied the problem in detail sees a similarity between the notion of *giri* and that of *potlatch*. Such a comparison undoubtedly defines the notion of *giri* to a certain degree, but does so at the risk of excluding from it certain of its essential elements. It is therefore necessary to be satisfied with listing some of the characteristics of *giri* without worrying too much about conceptualization. *Giri* (*gi*, just or right; *ri*, reason or reasonable behavior) means the manner of behavior required of one person to others in consequence of his social status. More specifically:

1. *Giri* is a duty or the state of a person who is bound to behave in a prescribed way toward a certain other person. The content of this duty or obligation varies greatly according to the situation in which the subject of the duty is placed and of the person toward whom the duty is owed. There is the *giri* of a child to his parents, that of the student to his teacher, that of a beneficiary to his benefactor (*onjin*), that of one friend to another, and so on.
2. The person toward whom the duty is owed has no right to demand its fulfillment from the subject of the duty. He must wait for the latter to fulfill it voluntarily. Anyone who does not satisfy his *giri* in the desired manner is seriously dishonored, but the other party must avoid applying pressure to oblige him to fulfill his duty. If the beneficiary of the duty applies pressure for performance of the duty, he in his turn violates *giri*. Usually the beneficiary of the duty is himself bound by another *giri* relationship of which the content is determined by the special link which unites him to the person bound in his regard, and the two subjects of the rules are thus placed in a condition of reciprocal obligation. This relationship does not, however, constitute a synallagmatic contract sanctioned by the exception *non adimpleti contractus*, as that would presuppose that the two parties had entered into the arrangement of their own free will.
3. The relations of *giri* are perpetual. They are not extinguished, even when a duty deriving from *giri* has been performed by the 'debtor'. *Giri* relationships are maintained outside time limitations and are continually giving rise to duties. Even between a merchant and his customer the relationship tends to be permanent. If the *giri* relationship has been established between them, the customer who buys from another merchant is considered as failing in his *giri*. In return for continuing custom a merchant gives his customer advantages of both a material and general kind.
4. *Giri* relationships are founded on feelings of affection. They have an emotive quality. The relationship must not be conceived of as being in consideration of an interest or profit that is anticipated, though in practice there are many cases where feelings of *giri* are mixed with selfish desires. Japanese people are, however, bound to behave, at least in appearance, as if they act for reasons of affection coupled with feelings of duty. This feeling of affection is called *ninjo* (natural human affection). The two feelings of *giri* and *ninjo* are so closely related that they are often referred to by the compound *giri-ninjo*. No one wants to be regarded by others as a person who acts only in his own interests, and it is said of a person who does act in that way that 'he does not know his *ninjo*', and he is considered abnormal from the social point of view. For this reason few people in Japan would consider entering into a marriage contract or take time to think about matrimonial property regimes. Everyone believes that conjugal relations must be exclusively ruled according to *ninjo* and that they are by their nature incompatible with monetary preoccupations. A fiancé who would think of regulating the future matrimonial property relationship before marriage would be considered by his future spouse as *mizukusai*, a person who 'smells of water', a person whose affection is likely to be submerged by material preoccupation. The force of this attitude is shown by the small number of marriage contracts that have been concluded since the promulgation of the Civil Code, and also by the number of articles in the Japanese Civil Code dealing with matrimonial property regimes, the number of which is very limited by comparison with the French Civil Code.

5. *Giri* relationships are imbued with principles of a hierarchical order characteristic of feudalism. *Giri* duties are derived from the social status of the subject of the duty, and in the feudal hierarchy of Japan until the Restoration of 1868 the station in society of each person was strictly determined. To remain faithful in his *bungen* was the chief virtue required of a Japanese in feudal society. It follows that the content of the *giri* of a socially inferior person toward his superior is not the same, even where there is a relationship of reciprocal duties, as that of the *giri* of the superior to the inferior. For example, in the relationships between merchants and their customers, which are governed by the principles of a hierarchy, the customers are always considered superior to the merchants for the sole reason that they are clients. In the case of a sale, therefore, there is not just a simple legal relationship existing between the seller and the buyer. Of course, the merchant has the duty to deliver the thing sold to his client, but he may not fulfill this duty in just any manner. He must conform to his *giri*. He must show his client the deference appropriate to indicate his own inferiority. A large shop in Tokyo instructs its employees: 'We have from time immemorial called our clients Sir and Madam *Zenshu* [former master] to express our feelings of respect toward them. The manner of behaving in front of our clients cannot be democratic.' The departmental head of a company has not fully acquitted his *giri* toward his subordinates if he has only given them directions, however perfect, for their professional activity. A good head knows his *giri-ninjo* and always has a concern for the personal and domestic affairs of his inferiors. In return, those inferiors must be ready to help their head of department in his private affairs. For example, when he is involved in a house-shifting operation they must assist him gratuitously.
6. The rules of *giri* are not imposed by means of a system of public constraint but are sanctioned simply by a feeling of honor. Those who fail in their giri are seriously dishonored in the eyes of those around them. They lose face; they will say, 'I cannot look the world in the face'. Everyone in Japan is very sensitive about his honor; there is an effort to save face at any cost. It is this feeling of shame which prevents a person from acting immorally, or doing any act contrary to giri. Restraint is exercised because it is known that if a certain act is committed, a feeling of shame will follow.

Ruth Benedict distinguishes two types of civilization: one founded on the idea of shame and the other on the idea of sin. In the second the non-observance of a moral rule is considered a sin. The feeling of sin weighs heavily on the conscience of the individual. Each person in this type of civilization tries to avoid doing evil, simply because he does not wish to have to suffer pangs of conscience. What others think does not matter. In a civilization based on shame, however, people refrain from doing wrong to avoid being criticized by others. Consequently, if there is no one to see the commission of a wrongful act, a person in the latter civilization will readily do it because he will not be likely to suffer dishonor for it. Therefore, in those places where the idea of shame dominates, people are continually concerned about the attitude of others even in regard to the most trivial events of private life. It is because of this psychological sanction that the rules of giri are observed scrupulously.

INFLUENCE OF THE RULES OF GIRI

Generally speaking, where the rules of *giri* dominate, the rules of a purely legal nature have difficulty penetrating; the emotional excludes the legal. The nature of the rules of *giri* does not favor the invasion of their domain by the notion of subjective rights, because if this happened social relationships would be regulated in a clear-cut manner by norms with a defined area of relevance, and duties would lose their emotive aspect; they would be qualitatively and quantitatively delimited, and execution would no longer depend on the mental attitude of the person under the obligation. People would take notice of the equality of all subjects before the law, and that would destroy the hierarchical order. It is therefore quite natural that those who are concerned with the maintenance of the social order do their best to create conditions which favor the survival of the rules of *giri*. Even after the reception of modern legal thought, state law, which was founded on rational principles incompatible with the idea of *giri*, was unable to regulate the social life of the Japanese people, and social conflicts have been and still are regulated for the most part outside the state law system. Even the courts operate less as instruments of judgment than as organs of conciliation.

In rural areas, where a community conscience remains, resistance to modern law is very strong. There the relationship between owners and farmers, for example, has for a long time been regarded as resting on *giri*. The farmers can cultivate the land thanks to the *go-on*, or favor, of the owners and not because they have rights under any contract of lease. They do pay rent for the use of the land, but this is in execution of their duty of *giri*, which is owed toward the owners, and not in execution of a contractual duty. The owners in their turn are not simply parties to a lease. They are superiors *vis-à-vis* the farmers in the hierarchical order of the peasant community. In these conditions the lessees must perform their part not only by paying the rent but also by fulfilling other duties that their social position imposes upon them *vis-à-vis* the landlords, their superiors. In return the latter grant them material and moral favors of various kinds. These relationships can be assimilated very readily to those that exist between parents and children, where human affection (*ninjo*) must dominate. To ask for the satisfaction of one's rights in this type of circumstance would be shameful. According to Kawashima, a peasant who filed a plaint in court to have a joint ownership dispute settled was condemned by the inhabitants of his village, and for three generations he and his descendants were refused the right to take a spouse from among the villagers.

Although the Japanese Civil Code regulates the obligations of contractors in almost the same way as the French Civil Code, in practice these contracts are not regulated as in France. The practice is for the contractor to write to the principal requesting him to fulfil his duties. At the level of pure law the principal must fulfil his contractual duties even without any letter, but in the world of *giri* the contractor, who is hierarchically inferior to the principal, hopes that by this letter future conflicts between the principal and himself will be regulated not in a legal manner but through the grace or special favor of the principal. Parties very rarely appear in court for the enforcement of their rights, and though only a specific type of contract has been mentioned the position is the same for almost all other contracts.

In the field of obligations the Japanese legal solutions to problems do not differ greatly from those of the European legal systems, but Western jurists are often surprised to notice that the average number of court cases in this field of law is very much higher in their own countries. When a person suffers loss in Japan he reacts in a special way. Characteristically:

1. Japanese have difficulty in distinguishing the legitimate exercise of rights from extortion. It is regarded as extortionary, if not avaricious, to bring a claim for damages before the courts, even when the claim is against the author of the damage suffered.

2. Japanese seek to avoid altering their personal relationship with the author of any injury suffered. They do not bring an action, because to do so would seriously affect the feelings and honor of the defendant.
3. The Japanese are not greatly sensitive to the damage which they suffer. Having been continuously exposed over the years to natural and human scourges, such as earthquakes, typhoons, fires, civil wars, and despotic governments, they are accustomed to accepting with submission the results of external forces, which they regard as inevitable. They readily resign themselves to their fate and do not seek to improve their lot by recourse to the law. The most frequent means of resolving a damage case is for the victim of the injury to renounce his right to indemnity. Usually what happens is that the author of the damage comes to offer his apologies and at the same time offers a sum of money. The sum is frequently much less than the extent of the damage suffered by the victim, but the victim is quickly moved by a more or less sympathetic attitude on the part of the author of the injury. It is not the amount of the indemnity but the sincere attitude worthy of *giri-ninjo* on the part of the offender which is the important thing to the victim. Sometimes the victim is so moved by the sincerity of the author of his loss that he does not accept the sum offered to him. Exceptionally, the victim may seek reparation from the author of his loss, but even in this case he does not want to go to court. He resorts rather to the authority of some person such as a notable in the community or a police officer who has influence over the person who has injured him. More rarely the victim even proceeds to court, but this is only done in order to achieve an amicable settlement of the dispute through the good offices of the court. Such extrajudicial procedures are considered more honorable and desirable than the judicial. They save face for both parties.

The cases that are brought to court mostly concern relationships between large enterprises which are competing with each other for purely economic interests, or between moneylenders and their debtors. Nevertheless, even big companies do not seek a legal answer to their problems when the enterprises concerned are those between which there exists a close business link. People in the business world say that a client who has an obligation toward an enterprise should not be called a debtor, because the very use of the word might leave an unfavorable impression with the client. Even in the business world, therefore, relationships are imbued with *giri-ninjo*.

THE FUTURE OF *GIRI*

The manner of thought and behavior of a people is not something static. It is dynamic and constantly changing, even though there always remains in the spirit of a people a central core which permits them to retain their individuality notwithstanding the continuing transformation. It is particularly important to bear this dynamic quality in mind because all that has been said of the mental outlook of the Japanese people is concerned only with the present attitude, the present outlook, which, though formed by a thousand years of development, in no way precludes the possibility of great development in the future. Indeed, the Japanese state of mind is changing at a rapidly increasing rate. The traits described here as those most characteristic of the Japanese mental outlook are much less marked among the younger than among the older members of the community, and young Japanese do not know the full detail of the rules of *giri* even though they may have the same mental outlook as their elders. The older generation often complain that the young do not know how to behave according to *giri-ninjo*, that they are too hard and calculating.

Present indications are that the Japanese attitude to law will continue to become more Westernized but that the Japanese outlook will not necessarily come to be identical with that of the West. Japan has often adopted European ideas which have enriched the Japanese spirit greatly, particularly with respect to rationality and objectivity, but this has never prevented the Japanese spirit from retaining its congenital characteristics. The Japanese spirit will change in the course of time, but it will always be Japanese.

Upham, FK, *Law and Social Change in Postwar Japan*, 1987, pp 16–20, 209–16, Harvard University Press

The identification of litigation as a threat to the political and social status quo is implicit in all writing on Japanese law and society, and recent scholarship argues persuasively that self-interest has led the Japanese elite to take deliberate steps to discourage litigation.

Whether these legal and institutional measures were taken out of self-interest or out of a sincere desire to preserve unique cultural values and avoid the economic and social cost of litigation is less important for our purposes than the fact that, though effective in a quantitative sense, these measures have failed to prevent litigation from playing an important social and political role in contemporary Japan.

What elite hostility has done, however, is to influence the development of litigation's role in such a way that it has evolved in directions largely different from either of our Western models. The process of that influence and the resulting form and role of litigation in Japan will be presented in detail throughout the case studies that constitute the bulk of this volume. For now it will suffice to sketch from selected perspectives a necessarily tentative and partial view of what one might call the Japanese model of litigation. Though heavily influenced by the data of the case studies and therefore more descriptive of an actual legal system than rule-centered or judge-centered law, this model, which I shall call bureaucratic informalism, is also meant to serve as an intellectual reference point to guide the reader through the detail of the following chapters. It is not meant, however, to explain or account for all that occurs within Japanese law and society.

Central to the Japanese model of law generally and of litigation in particular is the elite's attempt to retain some measure of control over the processes of social conflict and change. The vehicle for that control is a skilled and dedicated bureaucracy, itself one branch of Japan's tripartite elite coalition, which has a long history of active intervention in Japanese society. But social control, even the indirect control favored by Japanese governments since the Tokugawa Period, is extraordinarily difficult in democratic societies. Japan enjoys not only representative government but also a high degree of social and economic mobility, a vigorous and irreverent press, and an independent and respected judiciary and private bar. Even if the bureaucracy wished to exercise direct social control – and there is no reason to believe that the bureaucrats are any less committed to democratic values than any other segment of Japanese society – it would be impossible to do so.

Given these limitations, the bureaucracy does retain a surprising degree of control over the pace and course, if not the substance, of social change in Japan, and one of its major instruments for such control is the manipulation of the legal framework within which social change and its harbinger, social conflict, occur. The institutional barriers to litigation already well documented by recent scholarship are part of this framework, but they are only the beginning of the story; they cannot help us understand the nature and the role of the litigation that nonetheless occurs nor explain why there is so little demand, except perhaps among American social scientists and legal professionals, for more effective access to formal processes. For answers to these inquiries, one must analyze the way in which litigation is used today in Japan and the legal aspects of the governmental reaction to it in particular and to social conflict in general.

Unless one assumes that Japanese cultural traditions preclude the possibility, one will not be surprised to learn that litigation with elements of the rule-centered and judge-centered models occurs with some frequency in Japan, especially in politically charged areas such as freedom of speech, defense policy, or electoral malapportionment in the Diet, where opposition parties, particularly the Japanese Communist Party, are constantly searching for political leverage against the Liberal Democratic Party. It also occurs in less ideologically polarized social conflict among groups and under circumstances with only ambiguous political implications. In varying degrees, litigation or potential litigation with strong elements of these models has arisen in each of the four areas of social life that will be examined in the case studies, but in each instance, using various doctrinal and institutional devices and with varying degrees of success, the Japanese government has attempted to prevent the development of litigation into an effective and ongoing vehicle for social change.

One consistent Japanese response to social conflict in any form is the creation of institutional mediation. Although recent empirical work has cast doubt on its accuracy, the conventional wisdom has been that disputes are usually resolved by the informal intervention of a trusted third party, most typically an older person of higher status. Whether or not such spontaneous intervention occurs successfully on a regular basis in contemporary Japan, the continuing belief that it does makes it politically easier for the government to establish bureaucratically controlled mediation schemes whenever informal means fail to prevent serious social conflict.

Such was the case in two of the case studies presented here, where litigation played a large role in the articulation of conflict. In the antipollution case, victims of air pollution and toxic substance poisoning eventually became dissatisfied with what informal dispute-resolution methods could achieve and filed suit against the polluting companies. This litigation, which was known as the 'Big Four Pollution Suits', became the focus for a social and political movement that ended the conservatives' rule in many local governments and threatened their majority in the National Diet. The lawsuits, which were all won by the plaintiffs, also spawned a second generation of environmental litigation that focused on government and business development policy and threatened to narrow the bureaucracy's discretion by formalizing the development process in a way that was inimical to the interests of both business and the bureaucracy.

The Japanese government responded in three ways. First, the bureaucracy drafted and the Diet passed a series of statutes that constitute a pollution control regime as strict as any in the world. Second, it established a polluter-financed but government-administered scheme to compensate officially certified pollution victims. Third and perhaps most significant for the present discussion, the government created a bureaucratically administered and staffed system of identifying and mediating pollution disputes. Since it began operating in 1971, the system has handled thousands of disputes of various kinds and degrees of complexity.

Whether each dispute mediated by the government is a lawsuit forgone – even whether the creation of alternative avenues for grievance articulation decreases litigation at all – is unclear, but the creation of the system and its staffing with competent and conscientious bureaucrats have combined with the compensation system and a dramatic decrease in urban pollution levels to defuse the antipollution movement and to return the locus of Japan's environmental and development policy making from the courts to the bureaucracy. In doing so, the government succeeded in avoiding the continued development of litigation into a regular tactic of the environmental movement. Litigation is of course still available to potential plaintiffs – indeed, the antipollution regulatory scheme and the doctrines judicially developed in the Big Four and other early cases have arguably made pollution litigation easier doctrinally – and it does occur occasionally. But what appeared as a real threat in the early 1970s – that courts applying new pro-plaintiff norms would become the general arbiters of pollution disputes and that judges would increasingly intervene in environmental policy making in pivotal cases of national importance – never materialized.

The official response to successful sex-discrimination litigation was not dissimilar, despite substantial differences in the nature of the litigation and its social and political context. In the mid-1960s Japanese working women began to sue their employers for what were initially blatantly discriminatory practices. In spite of daunting doctrinal problems, the plaintiffs attacked progressively more subtle and indirect methods of discrimination. This process gradually accelerated through the seventies, and at the end of the decade the Ministry of Labor began enforcing bureaucratically the most firmly established of the judicially developed norms. The process culminated in 1985 when the Diet passed without serious amendment the bureaucratically drafted Equal Employment Opportunity Act, which statutorily prohibits a wide range of practices already clearly prohibited judicially. The Act, on the other hand, left the Ministry wide discretion in devising and enforcing policy in areas that the courts had not yet fully developed, areas that, perhaps not coincidentally, are the most threatening to the fundamental employment practices of Japanese firms. Simultaneously, the Act created a system administered and staffed by the Ministry for mediating employment discrimination disputes.

It is too early to tell whether these measures will be as successful in recapturing the initiative in the antidiscrimination area as similar steps were in pollution. In the former area, substantially alleviating the underlying cause of discontent – the conflict between the rising aspirations of Japanese women and the fundamental structure of current employment patterns – may be much more difficult than it was in the case of pollution. Nor is there a clear national consensus for eliminating discrimination as there was for improving the environment. On the contrary, the nature and scope of equal-employment legislation was a matter of considerable partisan debate, and labor and management took opposite positions on various aspects of the bill. The Ministry of Labor is therefore likely to be criticized no matter what position it eventually takes on the issues deliberately left ambiguous in the statute. As a result, women may eschew government mediation and continue to sue at a greater rate than have environmental plaintiffs, particularly if the opposition parties decide to support such suits in a systematic manner.

...

There are many ways of interpreting the insistence of the Japanese that their legal system functions on the basis of harmony, consensus, and compromise rather than legally binding rights and duties. One is to take each instance of rhetoric and analyze it in terms of the speaker's self-interest, what one might call the negation of Japanese legal imagery. Thus one would point out, *inter alia,* that as a retired MITI bureaucrat Amaya would naturally argue for weakening his former ministry's major rival in the setting of industrial policy; that, however high-minded were the stated goals of the Big Four plaintiffs, they did in fact ask for and receive large sums of money as a direct result of their supposedly selfless actions; and that the replacement of legal sanctions with moral suasion in statutes like the Special Measures Law for Assimilation Projects or the Equal Employment Opportunity Act precisely suits the interests of the Liberal Democratic Party and Japanese industry.

This mode of interpretation is not wrong – indeed, it is necessary to a complete understanding of the rhetoric and the law – but it can only partially capture their true meaning because it assumes that the images that the law evokes in statutes and court decisions and that citizens evoke in their discussion of law can be separated from the 'real' motivations and consequences of social action. It denies the interdependence of legal consciousness and social action, a relationship that moved Clifford Geertz to describe law as society's way of 'imagining the real'. To approach the full meaning of law in Japanese society, one must combine the instrumental analysis of power relationships and social results with an awareness that what people say and believe they are doing is part of social behavior. Thus a full analysis needs to recognize and examine the interdependence between the legal imagery of harmony, consensus, tradition, and litigation and its concrete influence on and role in the management of social conflict and change.

Cultural predispositions notwithstanding, it does not make sense to discuss these concepts, particularly the ideal of consensus, as if they somehow pre-exist law. In a liberal democracy like Japan, law determines what the power relationships within the group will be by defining who will be in the decision-making group and the kind and degree of sanctions available to them to achieve consensus. Since the decision rule is unanimity, the group must be carefully selected and managed: members must either share fundamentally complementary interests, or those with opposed interests must be excluded or suppressed. Given the preference for the appearance of harmony in Japan, exclusion is preferred to overt suppression, but quiet pressure on members' unrelated outside interests is entirely appropriate.

A simplified review of the industrial policy process, perhaps the area where Japanese consensus and harmony are most frequently celebrated in the West, can illustrate how legal doctrine establishes concrete parameters for policy making. As was true in the Sumitomo Metals incident of 1964–65, the formation of the ill-fated oil cartels of 1973–74, and the 'naphtha war' of the 1980s, policy formation begins with informal discussions among MITI bureaucrats and representatives of the leading firms in the immediately concerned industry. When the problem cuts across many industries, this process may take place within a framework of subcommittees and study groups established by the appropriate *shingikai*. Once the basic problem is analyzed and a tentative solution identified, the group is broadened to include suppliers, customers, other affected industries, and related divisions of MITI and other ministries. Once an acceptable compromise is worked out at this level, the full *shingikai* is convened to ratify a formal proposal for MITI action, perhaps a draft statute or criteria for cartelization.

The time-consuming consultation in policy formation lays the groundwork for implementation because by the time a final detailed plan has been worked out, everyone with a recognized interest has had a chance to influence the result or at least to register his complaint. In those relatively rare occasions when circumstances change or one firm is recalcitrant, the group is not without means to compel compliance. In extreme instances like the Sumitomo Metals incident, publicly coordinated bullying by the trade association backed up by threats of indirect legal action by MITI may be necessary, but in the vast majority of cases pressure can be brought quietly on the dissident firm's *keiretsu* allies as well as on the firm itself.

As long as the pressure remains private, the power relationships within the process are disguised by the culturally laden rhetoric of consensus. Even when the use of power becomes overt, the underlying role of law in structuring the consensus and then protecting it from dissidents' attacks remains unspoken and unevaluated. But without statutes meticulously drafted to avoid both the creation of private causes of action and clear criteria for administrative discretion, the consensus makers could not maintain the virtual monopoly over the substance of policy making and interpretation that they now enjoy; and without the careful nurturing of legal informality in administrative processes, partially through the threshold doctrines of standing and justiciability and partially through the avoidance of procedural formality in statutory drafting, the informality necessary to mask political and economic power would be impossible.

The result of opening up the process of industrial policy, it is imperative to note, would not necessarily be a change in its content. By and large, the substance of current policy enjoys broad support within Japanese society, especially by those most directly concerned, and there is no reason to think that exposing the political choices involved would lead to an immediate rejection of heretofore accepted policies. What would change, however, is the rhetoric of industrial policy: what had formerly appeared through the rose-tinted lens of consensus as the natural result of custom and culture would have to be discussed as the accommodation of conflicting interests. Reasoned accounts would have to be made for what would now emerge as conscious political decisions, and the application of indirect sanctions would have to be defended against charges of bureaucratic overreaching. In the long run the shift in formal legal power, whose initial effect would likely be limited to the power to question, would affect the way in which participants and observers thought about the industrial policy process and might eventually influence the substance of economic policy itself.

More important, however, such a shift would weaken the domination of legal discourse now exercised by the ideology of consensus. This ideology is at the heart of informality throughout the Japanese legal system. Industrial policy and MITI provide highly visible examples on a grand scale, but the same processes are at work in the mediation of environmental disputes and the compensation of pollution victims; the toleration of forceful tactics like denunciation and direct negotiations and the intensive bargaining that they foster in areas like affirmative action grants or superlegal tort compensation; and the attempt through the EEOA to remove employment discrimination from the public forum of the courts to the informality and unaccountability of Ministry of Labor mediation. In any of these or many other areas across Japan's legal landscape, recourse to formal processes, even if the substantive result remained constant, would mean that the management of social conflict would openly contradict the dominant Japanese vision of their society as harmonious and conflict-free. Any weakening of that vision or of the similar and interdependent vision of their legal system as informal and consensual would be much more destabilizing to Japanese society than any substantive changes in, for instance, the amount of tort compensation for pollution victims or the status of women in the workplace.

The essential paradox of consensus is that the better the process functions to control human behavior, the less important it becomes. Because unanimity is required, consensus works best when interests are complementary or when dissidents leave or are suppressed. When such actions are attempted on a social level in a democracy, there are severe limits to the effectiveness of exclusion and suppression. The more parties are excluded from the decision group, the smoother the process and the more complete the consensus, but the less likely it becomes that the result can be effectively extended to the rest of society. If those excluded are powerless or unaware of their exclusion, of course, it does not matter, but in Japan they frequently are neither, and both litigation and limited instrumental force are often available to refute the consensus, demand inclusion, or simply pursue one's own interests.

Whether one views the applicable consensus as the 1959 mediation agreement that reestablished 'harmony' in Minamata or the postwar national consensus for economic growth, the Big Four cases demonstrate the potential of litigation in attacking consensus. They exposed the government's neglect of its most fundamental obligations and played a role reminiscent of the Tokugawa *ikki* and Ashio protest marches. The subsequent suits demanding legal accountability and procedural safeguards in environmental management, however, had no place in either the neo-Confucian ideology that animated Tokugawa Japan or the consensus model that had become its contemporary analogue. These suits were asking not for benevolent concern on the government's part, but for an enforceable right to participate in government policy making and implementation according to a formal and legally defined procedure. These later plaintiffs were asking for legal checks on the process as well as the substance of government behavior rather than assurances of official concern. The government is willing to give sincere avowals of the latter; it abhors the former. The result was the series of legislative and administrative steps that at once reaffirmed government's concern, maintained procedural informality, and marginalized the environmental movement in Japan.

MITI's response to the Oil Cartel cases, as well as the process of economic policy making in general, repeats the pattern of bureaucratic concern for the preservation of procedural informality in the face of judicial intrusions. The threat posed by the High Court opinions to the informal and vertical nature of industrial policy was effectively countered, at least for the immediate future, by the widening of the consensus group to include the Fair Trade Commission and its avoidance of direct legal coercion in the cartelization process. Although the FTC's inclusion and the generally increasing power of Japanese industry may mean some changes in substantive policies, this seems to have been of less concern to MITI than the maintenance of informal policy making.

The Structurally Depressed Industries Law institutionalized and legitimated the continued use of *shingikai* and their myriad subcommittees and study groups, which give the impression of consideration of a wide variety of public concerns and interests while avoiding any loosening of control over the process of policy making. As with the mediation and compensation systems in the pollution context, problems in industrial policy are heard and dealt with on an informal and bilateral basis. Interest groups play a major role in the form of the industry associations, economic federations, and so on, but the role is cooperative and informal rather than formal and adversarial. Equally important, the nature and number of participating groups are entirely within the bureaucracy's hands. As with the later environmental litigation, a major factor in MITI's ability to control both the participants and the process of participation is Japanese administrative law. Statutes like the SDIL combine with the doctrines of standing, justiciability, and so forth to enable the ministries to maintain control over the policy making process and force participants, even industry representatives, into supplicatory roles. The process works smoothly because both the bureaucracy and business recognize their symbiotic identity of interest and because potentially disaffected parties are hindered in forming politically effective groups and denied any legal right to independent participation in the decision-making process.

When we compare the Burakumin and employment discrimination case studies with the pollution experience, the fit is somewhat more ambiguous. Both groups are pursuing norms which, if realized, could destabilize the corporate workplace, the perceived source of Japan's postwar social and economic success. In this sense they pose a greater potential threat than even the antipollution movement despite their current meager popular support; their goal of equal access and equal opportunity would mean a substantial restructuring of Japanese society. In spite of the clear constitutional norms supporting equality, contemporary social practice and government policy leave little room for equality for either women or minorities, not necessarily because of sincere beliefs that either group is unable to perform well but because the diversity and flexibility introduced into the workplace by women and minorities threaten to destroy the social and psychological basis of Japan's political stability and economic success. It is in this context that we should understand the tactics of denunciation and litigation and the government's response to them.

Although in both cases the process is incomplete and the outcome uncertain, the government response seems to be aimed at maintaining control over the process of social change rather than at preventing it. In this sense, tacit toleration of denunciation is understandable. In the middle and late 1960s two paths were open to the Buraku liberation movement: a path toward full integration with majority society through equal opportunity, or one toward the improvement of material conditions for Burakumin and a 'separate but equal' type of material equality. The two paths are not mutually exclusive, but denunciation as a tactic is extremely limited in achieving integration, and the Buraku Liberation League has not even tried to use it in that direction in any consistent manner. The result has been continued insulation of the mainstream from the Buraku movement, which remains directed at local governments and incremental material advances within the current social and economic structure. To the extent that denunciation limits the BLL's ability to appeal effectively to the norm of equal opportunity, it is natural for the government to prefer it to litigation – it achieves incremental social progress without threatening the particularistic norms of justice that underlie the government's mode of social control. As long as the BLL is directing its energy and protest against the bureaucracy through denunciation rather than against basic public and private policies through the courts, the government can be sure of continued control over the pace and nature of the movement.

The Ministry of Labor's response to the women employees' litigation is consistent with this interpretation. Although adroit manoeuvering by corporate personnel departments has managed to maintain discriminatory employment practices in the years since the *Sumitomo Cement* decision, most observers agree that bureaucratic measures against early retirement and similarly discredited practices are, though belated, effective and in good faith. This may not be true of the Ministry's response to demands for equal access to management track positions. Even here the official rhetoric is one of eventual equality, but the EEOA leaves the definition and enforcement of equality up to the Ministry. As with the Special Measures Law in the Buraku context, the EEOA may have been politically significant, but it leaves legal control squarely in government hands. Greater equality may result, but it will be on the bureaucracy's terms. This does not leave total discretion to the government; working women and their supporters will continue legal and political pressure and will influence the pace and nature of change through lobbying, participation on consultative bodies, and litigation, but the government will attempt mightily to keep the forum for the ultimate battles out of the courts and within the bureaucracy.

Maintaining control in this context, however, may not be so easy. The government may not be willing to meet the demands of the women's movement for completely equal opportunity to the extent that they have met those of pollution victims or Burakumin, and thus there will remain a larger number of dissatisfied potential plaintiffs to continue to push the legal norms in the direction of equality. Whether such plaintiffs will be successful is of course unclear at present, but if they are, we may see litigation continue to play the role that it has in the last fifteen years – that of reflecting and contributing to changing social norms and simultaneously forcing the pace of the government's response to such changes. Such continued success is uncertain, but even if it occurs, the limitations in popular support and judicial remedies, neither of which will have been strengthened by the passage of the EEOA, will mean that the ultimate forum for substantial change will likely remain bureaucratic, rather than legislative or judicial.

Kawashima, T, 'Dispute Resolution in Contemporary Japan' in von Mehren, AT (ed), *Law in Japan: The Legal Order in a Changing Society,* 1963, pp 41, 43–48, Harvard University Press

There is probably no society in which litigation is the normal means of resolving disputes. Rarely will both parties press their claims so far as to require resort to a court; instead, one of the disputants will probably offer a satisfactory settlement or propose the use of some extrajudicial, informal procedure. Although direct evidence of this tendency is difficult to obtain, the phenomena described below offer indirect support for the existence of these attitudes among the Japanese people.

...

Traditionally, the Japanese people prefer extrajudicial, informal means of settling a controversy. Litigation presupposes and admits the existence of a dispute and leads to a decision which makes clear who is right or wrong in accordance with standards that are independent of the wills of the disputants. Furthermore, judicial decisions emphasize the conflict between the parties, deprive them of participation in the settlement, and assign a moral fault which can be avoided in a compromise solution.

This attitude is presumably related to the nature of the traditional social groups in Japan, which may be epitomized by two characteristics. First, they are hierarchical in the sense that social status is differentiated in terms of deference and authority. Not only the village community and the family, but even contractual relationships have customarily been hierarchical. From the construction contract arises a relationship in which the contractor defers to the owner as his patron; from the contract of lease a relationship in which the lessee defers to the lessor; from the contract of employment a relationship in which the servant or employee defers to the master or employer; from the contract of apprenticeship a relationship in which the apprentice defers to the master; and from the contract of sale a relationship in which the seller defers to the buyer (the former being expected in each case to yield to the direction or desire of the latter). At the same time, however, the status of the master or employer is patriarchal and not despotic; in other words, he is supposed not only to dominate but also to patronize and therefore partially to consent to the requests of his servant or employee. Consequently, even though their social roles are defined in one way or other, the role definition is precarious and each man's role is contingent on that of the other. Obviously this characteristic is incompatible with judicial decisions based on fixed universalistic standards.

Second, in traditional social groups relationships between people of equal status have also been to a great extent 'particularistic' and at the same time 'functionally diffuse.' For instance, the relationship between members of the same village community who are equal in social status is supposed to be 'intimate'; their social roles are defined in general and very flexible terms so that they can be modified whenever circumstances dictate. In direct proportion with the degree to which they are dependent on or intimate with each other, the role definition of each is contingent upon that of the other. Once again, role definition with fixed universalistic standards does not fit such a relationship.

In short, this definition of social roles can be, and commonly is, characterized by the term 'harmony'. There is a strong expectation that a dispute should not and will not arise; even when one does occur, it is to be solved by mutual understanding. Thus there is no *raison d'être* for the majority rule that is so widespread in other modern societies; instead the principle of rule by consensus prevails.

It is obvious that a judicial decision does not fit and even endangers relationships. When people are socially organized in small groups and when subordination of individual desires in favor of group agreement is idealized, the group's stability and the security of individual members are threatened by attempts to regulate conduct by universalistic standards. The impact is greater when such an effort is reinforced by an organized political power. Furthermore, the litigious process, in which both parties seek to justify their position by objective standards, and the emergence of a judicial decision based thereon tend to convert situational interests into firmly consolidated and independent ones. Because of the resulting disorganization of traditional social groups, resort to litigation has been condemned as morally wrong, subversive, and rebellious.

On the other hand, there were, even in the traditional culture, disputes in which no such social relationship was involved. First, disputes arising outside of harmonious social groups, namely *between* such social groups, have a completely different background. Such disputes arise, so to speak, in a social vacuum. Since amicable behavior from the other party is not to be expected in such a context, both parties to the dispute tend to become emotionally involved to a great extent, and the traditional culture contains no fixed rules of behavior to indicate the acceptable course of action. Yet, even in the absence of a specific tradition of harmony and in spite of strong emotional antagonism, disputes of this type are often settled by reconciliation. If one disputant apologizes, it is postulated by traditional culture that the other party must be lenient enough to forgive him, and, as a matter of fact, emotional involvement is usually quite easily released by the apology of an enemy. Occasionally disputes, usually antagonisms of long standing, are settled because the disadvantage of continuing disagreement outweighs the price of concession. These agreements are usually achieved through the mediation of third parties and are similar in nature to peace treaties. Until and unless such a peaceful settlement is made, sheer antagonism and the rule of power, very often of violence, prevail. Disputes of this kind are also settled when one party can impose a fait accompli by force. In other words, superiority in power establishes a new social order. The only way in which the weaker party can escape from this rule of power is through the lawsuit. For this reason, a large number of suits relating to the 'right of common' (*iriaiken*) in land recorded in the law reports of the prewar period were disputes between village communities.

A second class of disputes, those between a usurer and his debtor, lacks from the very beginning a harmonious relationship comparable to that normally found between lessor and lessee or master and servant. Usurers never fail to be armed not only with nonlegal means with which to enforce the factual power situation but also with means founded upon law that enable them to resort to the courts. Since the Meiji era (1867–1912), long before industrialization was under way, official statistics have shown a surprisingly large number of cases involving claims of this sort.

In short, a wide discrepancy has existed between state law and the judicial system, on the one hand, and operative social behavior, on the other. Bearing this in mind, we can understand the popularity and function of mediation procedure as an extrajudicial informal means of dispute resolution in Japan. This attitude is also reflected in the customary characteristics of contracts. Parties to a contractual agreement are not expected to become involved in any serious differences in the future. Whenever they enter such a relationship, they are supposed to be friendly enough not to consider eventual disputes, much less preparation for a lawsuit. Parties do not, or at least pretend that they do not, care about an instrument or other kinds of written evidence and rather hesitate to ask for any kind of written document, fearing that such a request might impair the amicable inclination of the other party. Even when written documents are drawn up, they do not provide machinery for settling disputes. The contracting parties occasionally insert clauses providing that in case of dispute the parties 'may' (instead of 'must') negotiate with each other.

...

This emphasis on compromise has produced its own abuses. A special profession, the *jidan-ya* or makers of compromises, has arisen, particularly in the large cities. Hired by people having difficulty collecting debts, these bill collectors compel payment by intimidation, frequently by violence. This is of course a criminal offense, and prosecution of the *jidan-ya* is reported from time to time in the newspapers. But their occupation is apparently flourishing. Furthermore, public opinion seems to be favorable or at least neutral concerning this practice; even intimidated debtors thus compelled to pay seem to acquiesce easily and do not indicate strong opposition. This attitude is doubtlessly due to some extent to the delay and expense of litigation, but at the same time the traditional frame of mind regarding extrajudicial means of dispute resolution undoubtedly has had some influence on public opinion toward the *jidan-ya*. The common use of the term *jidan-ya* seems to suggest that extrajudicial coercion and compromise are not distinctly differentiated in the minds of people.

Finally, the specific social attitudes toward disputes are reflected in the judicial process. Japanese not only hesitate to resort to a lawsuit but are also quite ready to settle an action already instituted through conciliatory processes during the course of litigation. With this inclination in the background, judges also are likely to hesitate, or at least not seek, to expedite judicial decision, preferring instead to reconcile the litigant parties, ... which shows the number of lawsuits actually settled by reconcilement. Complaint about delay in reaching judicial decisions is almost universal, particularly in recent years, and the reasons for the delay are diverse. But one reason may be this judicial hesitancy to attribute clear-cut victory and defeat to the respective parties. It is, though, interesting to note that the percentage of judicial decisions has tended to rise since 1952, while the percentage of judicial proceedings terminated by compromise and successful mediation has tended to fall. It would be incautious to conclude hastily that these figures indicate a popular shift from the traditional attitude to a more individualistic one, but the beginning of such a tendency may be suggested.

Haley, JO, 'The Myth of the Reluctant Litigant' (1978) 4 *Journal of Japanese Studies* 359–61, 366–68, 371–73, 378–80, 389–90

The belief that the Japanese are an exceptionally nonlitigious people is remarkably pervasive. Commentators, both within and without Japan, are almost unanimous in attributing to the Japanese an unusual and deeply rooted cultural preference for informal, mediated settlement of private disputes and a corollary aversion to the format mechanisms of judicial adjudication. As a result, they say, Japanese do not take advantage of the available mechanisms for formal dispute resolution. These attitudes, they commonly add, are bolstered by a peculiar Japanese penchant for compromise, distrust of clearcut 'all or none' solutions and distaste for both public quarrels and their public resolution. As explained by Kawashima Takeyoshi, one of Japan's leading legal sociologists and most articulate exponents of this belief, the endurance of a traditional concern for preserving cooperative personal relationships makes unwanted any definitive delineation of rights and duties through litigation. Bringing a lawsuit has meant issuing a 'public challenge and provoking a quarrel'.

The importance of this notion is difficult to exaggerate. Most critical, upon it rests the conventional evaluation of the role of the judiciary within Japan's political and social order. The standard introductory works in English on Japanese government, for instance, uniformly dismiss the courts as politically insignificant on the basis of this perceived unwillingness of the Japanese to litigate. Without cases the courts cannot act. Unlike other arms of the state, the courts do not apply or enforce laws on their own initiative. They must wait passively for controversies to be brought before them for decision. This notion of the nonlitigious Japanese raises obvious doubts as to the efficacy of the postwar legal reforms, which were premised on an active, American-styled judiciary. Yet even as optimistic an observer as Alfred C Oppler, who was among those who contributed most to the Occupation's efforts to realize a judiciary capable of implementing the ideals of the postwar constitution, accepts it without question.

The dilemma posed by the institutional ideal of an active judiciary in a nonlitigious society is surmounted at least in pan by those, such as Kawashima, who view Japanese aversion to litigation as a gradually fading, 'traditional' response. Indeed, the literature is replete with observations on rising litigation rates in postwar Japan, which some take as a convenient index to measure Japan's progress toward a 'modern' society.

Despite the ubiquity of these ideas few have bothered to appraise their accuracy or, more important, to analyze with care their implications, particularly as to the role of law and the courts. Even the most basic question has not been fully answered. Are the Japanese, in fact, unusually loath to resort to court? The common retort is to pose another question: If not, then how does one explain the apparent lack of litigation in Japan relative to the United States and the failure of the judiciary to exert a more positive influence on the political process?

...

The Myth Reconsidered

Is there, then, any evidence of an unusual Japanese aversion toward lawsuits that leads a party to accept a settlement less beneficial than one he anticipates he would gain by suing? The answer, I believe, is negative. What little evidence there is suggests the opposite – that most Japanese are willing to go to court in such circumstances. The recent pollution cases and the thalidomide case are illustrative.

A recently published inquiry into the decisions to litigate in the pollution cases documents a variety of cultural factors causing the litigants to hesitate to sue. These included a sense of 'shame' for physical and mental deformity, constraints on individual initiative and 'selfish' behavior imposed by the demands of community unity and group consciousness, and hostility against an association with what was perceived to be – correctly, I believe – a leftist, antigovernment cause reflected in the politics of the lawyers who dominated the conduct of these trials. This experience was paralleled in part in the thalidomide case, where the apparent reason for reluctance to sue was a fear of public exposure of the children's deformities. 'In a society strongly prejudiced against deformity,' one of the plaintiffs' lawyers wrote, 'it took considerable courage to sue'. In each of these cases the plaintiffs filed suit only reluctantly and as a last resort. The reluctance, however, was based on a variety of factors related to the particular circumstances and nature of the disputes, not an unwillingness to sue in general.

The one arguable exception was the attitude that bringing an action for damages reflected socially unacceptable 'selfishness'. At first blush this would appear to be a cultural barrier to litigation in general. It was overcome in these instances, however, by justifying the lawsuit as a means of bringing wrongdoers to justice, coupling compensation with a desire to prevent others from inflicting similar harm. But such justifications are among the principal policies behind damage awards and private tort actions, and few plaintiffs would find similar rationalization of their motives difficult. Moreover, the success of the initial suits in these cases has produced others as well as a significant change in the standards being applied in private settlements of similar disputes.

The few direct surveys of Japanese attitudes that have been made provide further support for rejecting the orthodox view. For example, in the survey by Sasaki Yoshio cited by both Dan F Henderson and Kawashima, when asked, 'What would you do if a civil dispute arose and despite discussions with the opposite party you could not settle it?' 64% of the 2,098 respondents replied that they would willingly go to court.

...

Although, at least since the middle of the Meiji Period and perhaps even earlier, the Japanese in general may not have been unusually reluctant to litigate, the evidence points to the conclusion that to do so was offensive to some – that is, those who wished to maintain a paternalistic order based on a hierarchical submission to authority. As Henderson has detailed in his often cited (but apparently seldom read) study of conciliation in Japanese law, Tokugawa officialdom had constructed a formidable system of procedural barriers to obtaining final judgment in the Shogunate's courts. The litigant was forced each step of the way to exhaust all possibilities of conciliation and compromise and to proceed only at the sufferance of his superiors. We can only marvel at the endurance and perseverance of those who eventually prevailed. Conciliation was coerced – to use Henderson's phrase 'didactic' – not voluntary. Yet, as Henderson tells us, litigation increased.

The modern analogues to Tokugawa conciliation are equally revealing. Formal conciliation proceedings (*chotei*) were not instituted until enactment of the Land Lease and House Lease Conciliation Law in 1922. This measure was followed in succession by the Farm Tenancy Conciliation Law of 1924, the Commercial Affairs Conciliation Law of 1926, the Labor Disputes Conciliation Law of 1926, the Monetary Claims Temporary Conciliation Law of 1932, the conciliation provisions added to the Mining Law in a 1939 amendment and to the Placer Mines Law in a 1940 amendment, the Agricultural Land Adjustment Law of 1938, the Personal Status Conciliation Law of 1939, and finally the conciliation provisions of the Special Wartime Civil Affairs Law of 1942.

...

The Reality of Institutional Incapacity

If the Japanese are not particularly averse to litigation, how then can we explain why they appear to use their courts far less frequently than do Americans and perhaps others? Why has litigation decreased since the war (and continues to do so)? Also, what accounts for the pervasive acceptance by Japanese themselves that they are unusually 'nonlitigious'? And how do such explanations relate to the efficacy of the judicial model in Japan? To answer these questions, we should first reconsider the paradigm process of dispute resolution.

Typically, the parties to a dispute will move through stages – from direct negotiation, to third party mediation and finally to litigation as a result of failure in the preceding stage to agree to an acceptable resolution. In this process, a relative lack of litigation can be explained by several factors.

One is the effectiveness of third party intervention. The availability of suitable third parties who are willing and able to perform this role reduces the need to invoke formal judicial intervention. At the outset, mediation requires the presence of persons who, because of position or personal relationships, command respect and are able to exercise some measure of authority. In other words, to be effective, the mediator must be someone who can command the parties' trust and their obedience to the settlement.

One would thus anticipate that suitable third parties are more readily available in a stable, closely-integrated and hierarchical society like Japan, than in a more geographically mobile, less cohesive society like the United States in which individual autonomy and social equality are emphasized. Societal expectations and habits are equally relevant. The role of the mediator becomes increasingly legitimate for both the mediator and the parties to disputes where there is repeated reliance on third parties to settle disputes. A contrast in police attitudes in Japan and the United States pointed out by David H Bayley is especially interesting in this respect. Japanese commonly rely on the police for assistance in settling disputes. But despite similar popular demand in the United States, 'what is different,' says Bayley, 'is that American police organizations have not adapted willingly to perform this function'. Another Japanese example is the mediating service some companies provide for employees involved in traffic accidents. In short, the Japanese may be more successful in avoiding litigation because of social organization and values more conducive to informal dispute resolution through mediation.

The tendency of the Japanese to mediate does not necessarily impair the effectiveness of the judiciary, however. As we have seen, the judicial model does not depend on the actual frequency of litigation, but rather the influence of the perceived outcome of the litigation on the mediated settlement.

Resort to court is, however, reduced by another set of factors that do inhibit or enhance the utility of the judicial model as a vehicle for social control and development.

First, for courts to have an impact through decisions in individual cases beyond those persons immediately affected in those cases, information about the courts and these decisions must be disseminated in order that parties to similar disputes are sufficiently aware of the legal norm for it to influence informal resolution of their disputes. This does not mean the judicial model cannot work unless people are fully aware of what the courts will do. But people must be generally cognizant that the courts do provide an available option and they must have the means to become informed about what the probable outcome will be in the specific case. Thus in societies where illiteracy rates are high or little is communicated about the courts, the judicial model will be less successful. A lack of law trained persons and the absence of published reports of court decisions, for example, are serious barriers to the effectiveness of the judiciary.

There must also be meaningful access to the courts. Access can be denied directly by jurisdictional barriers that prevent the courts from adjudicating certain types of disputes altogether. Bond posting requirements that may place an intolerable burden on the parties seeking relief illustrate another form of conscious policy designed to prevent resort to courts. Limited institutional capacity also inhibits access. There must be a sufficient number of courts, of judges and lawyers, to insure that the costs and delays of litigation do not preclude lawsuits as a realistic option.

A third factor is the capacity of the courts to provide adequate relief. Courts must have available a range of remedial measures and forms of relief to suit the variety of controversies that arise. An award of monetary damages or declarations of the rights and duties of the parties will not always help the aggrieved party. In addition especially in cases where the legal norm and thus the outcome is reasonably certain, filing suit may evidence a recalcitrant party against whom coercive measures have become necessary. Indeed many of the cases courts handle each day do not involve any real controversy of fact or law, but simply a last resort to force the other party to perform an acknowledged legal duty. For relief to be adequate the courts must be able to provide a remedy that fits the case and have the capacity to enforce its judgments.

...

Conclusion

Few misconceptions about Japan have been more widespread or as pernicious as the myth of the special reluctance of the Japanese to litigate. In emphasizing this peculiar Japanese response, most commentators ignore the distaste for litigation and preference for informal dispute resolution common to most societies. As noted at the outset of this article, censure of litigation is arguably as much a part of the traditional Christian heritage as it is a legacy of Confucianism. What distinguishes Japan is the successful implementation of this interdiction through institutional arrangements. When we disregard the shared nature of these attitudes, we also fail to note applicable lessons from the Japanese experience. By increasing the number of judges to reduce our court delays, for instance, we may simply spur more litigation and greater social disintegration.

The myth also directs attention away from factors that may help us to understand better some of the dynamics of Japanese life and hides from view relationships that we might otherwise profitably explore. Does the failure of the courts to provide adequate relief explain, at least in part, such apparent social abnormalities such as gangsterism and recurrent bouts of violence in Japan's otherwise remarkably crime-free society? On the other hand, does limited access to the courts also have the effect of promoting beneficial forms of mediation and other mechanisms for disputes resolution? What is the relationship between the number of lawyers and litigation in other societies?

Finally, attributing a relative lack of litigation in Japan to pervasive cultural – and thus more immutable – causes, provides justification for continuing intended and unintended barriers to a more effective judiciary. It hinders inquiry into what the proper balance should be between the need to assure adequate judicial relief and the need to maintain social harmony. 'Why should we have more judges' a Minister of Finance preparing the budget might ask, 'since we are not a very litigious people'.

Haley, JO, 'Sheathing the Sword of Justice in Japan: An Essay on Law without Sanctions' (1982) 8 *Journal of Japanese Studies* 266–71, 273–78

I. The Lack of Formal Sanctions

Few meaningful sanctions or effective legal remedies exist at all in Japanese law. Although other jurisdictions share some of the limitations of Japanese law, none share so comprehensive a failure to provide effective sanctions or remedies for violation of legal norms. In civil cases in Japan, as elsewhere, the ultimate formal sanction is to attach property. The propertyless or those who are able to hide what they have – for instance, by false registration of land – are thus beyond the law's reach. Even those with accessible assets, however, are not easily subjected to legal compulsion. For example: in Japan as in other civil law jurisdictions, such as Germany and France, the general remedy for a breach of contract is a court order to the breaching party requiring performance. In the case of a sale of personal property, say a painting, should the seller violate his duty to deliver the painting, in theory the buyer can obtain a court decree ordering the seller to hand it over. Only if the buyer, as plaintiff, knows where the painting is actually located and can direct the bailiff there without interference can the court order be effectively enforced. Otherwise, the buyer is able only to recover damages to compensate for the monetary loss, which must be proved and can be enforced only if the seller has property that can be attached. A sale of land is easier to enforce. All land is registered and a court judgment effecting the prerequisites for a registry transfer of title is possible. To force an obstinate seller off the land even after title has been transferred can be a costly and time-consuming effort. What on the surface appears to be an effective remedy may in reality be of little avail.

Nor do the government and other public authorities in Japan have more effective means to enforce the law. Several years ago at a dinner in Tokyo with several former students and other University of Washington graduates, I happened to sit next to a Japanese lawyer whose father is a prominent psychiatrist. Our conversation turned to the topic of his father's practice: he mentioned that it was tax audit time and thus his father was exceptionally busy. 'I suppose,' I said, 'that quite a few taxpayers seek psychiatric relief.' 'Oh no,' he quickly responded, Psychiatrists are busy with tax collectors not taxpayers.' My surprise showed, so he went on to explain. In the case of small firms, more often those that belong to trade associations affiliated with one of the opposition parties, especially the Communist Party, tax auditors are frequently barred from even entering the premises by members of the association and others who surround the building and block the entrances. Incredulous I asked, 'What do the auditors do?' 'See their psychiatrists,' he replied.

The civil process offers little help. Civil fines may be provided as a sanction for violation of an administrative order or regulation, but collection will depend upon attachment or registry transfers – in other words, the private party's capacity to pay or willingness to abide by the court order despite refusal to obey the agency order.

In contrast, in the United States and most other common law jurisdictions, the courts' contempt powers make available in the civil process both the threat of prompt imposition of a fine of unlimited amount or imprisonment for an indefinite term, or both. By failing to obey a court order to deliver a painting, vacate land, or to obey an administrative order, the defendant faces the possibility that he will be fined whatever amount the judge believes will provide sufficient compulsion, or that he will be jailed until he complies. Although in many cases judges may be reluctant to resort to contempt, its threat is ever present, and its importance should not be underestimated. Judicially enforced subpoenas to compel disclosure of documents or other information provide only one of many examples of the critical role contempt plays in American public law enforcement. Moreover, since agencies do not have contempt powers under American law, the courts perform an important supplementary role in administrative law enforcement. An agency anticipating that a party may disobey an agency order will seek an enforcing court order. Both orders will be identical in legal effect both requiring the same conduct and both equally binding as a matter of law. The only difference is that the court order is backed by contempt. The importance of contempt is thus illustrated each time an American agency seeks a judicial enforcement order. Lacking contempt powers, Japanese courts have no role in civil enforcement of administrative regulations except in terms of appeals from agency actions. One consequence is that the Japanese judiciary tends to be less sympathetic to the government.

Judicial contempt is also unknown in other continental legal systems. It is viewed as too dangerous a power to place in the hands of the least accountable branch of government and as inconsistent with fundamental notions regarding the need for certain and legislatively-fixed penalties. Nonetheless, German law at least has an analog to contempt. Under the German Code of Civil Procedure, court injunctions can be enforced either through a fire up to 500,000 DM (approximately $250,000) or confinement up to two years. Moreover, administrative officials have the authority in most instances to enforce administrative orders by levying fines or attaching property without resort to the civil process or criminal proceedings. There are no similar provisions in Japanese law.

Until the Allied Occupation and the postwar reform of Japan's legal system, administrative officials in Japan could resort to an extensive variety of sanctions under special legislation, repealed in 1947 without effective substitute. Moreover, the police had broad jurisdiction to adjudicate cases involving infractions defined as 'police offenses'. Today, however, the Japanese must rely almost completely on criminal prosecution for enforcement of court orders and of almost all public law. Most Japanese regulatory legislation, for example, includes provisions at the end for criminal penalties, both fines and imprisonment. These may appear to be adequate, yet in reality, they are rarely invoked. In over thirty years of antitrust enforcement, for example, there have been only six criminal prosecutions. Three were begun in 1949. The successful prosecution on September 26, 1980 of Japanese oil companies and their executives for illegal price-fixing in the Tokyo High Court was thus an extraordinary event. One culls the statistics and records in vain to find more than a handful of prosecutions under other statutes. This dearth is only in part explained by limitations in applying criminal sanctions to economic misconduct found in most other jurisdictions or institutional barriers to effective enforcement, described below: it is also a product of the inherent incapacity of the Japanese legal system to rely effectively on criminal sanctions.

Confession, repentance, and absolution provide the underlying theme of the Japanese criminal process. At every stage, from initial police investigation through formal proceedings, an individual suspected of criminal conduct gains by confessing, apologizing, and throwing himself upon the mercy of the authorities.

The experience of a long-time American resident of Tokyo is illustrative. His *besso* or vacation home was destroyed by arson late one Sunday evening an hour or two after he and his family had left to return to the city. Learning that a few weeks earlier he had increased the insurance on the house, the local police asked him to meet with them the next day. Upon his arrival the police ushered him into a room reminiscent of an early James Cagney film – small table, uncomfortable wooden chair for him on one side, two or three policemen sitting or standing at ease on the other, glaring light overhead. What made the scene uniquely Japanese were the three portraits, at either side and facing him but tilted slightly to insure direct vision from where he sat. They were of Buddha, the Emperor, and Christ. Then in a somber but pleading voice the principal investigator said: 'Now, Mr – , why don't you just confess.'

Such incidents illustrate the significance attached by the Japanese authorities to confession and apology. I should note quickly that the confession does not provide a shortcut to conviction as in the United States. It does not save the police and prosecutor the time and effort of obtaining other evidence to prove guilt. There is no guilty plea in criminal cases in Japan: there is no plea bargaining. In every case brought, the prosecution must prove that a violation was committed by the defendant. A summary procedure that avoids oral hearings and defense is available and much used at the discretion of the prosecutor if there is confession, but for each case that goes to court the prosecutor must marshal evidence other than the confession to prove the accused guilty.

Held out to each suspect, however, is the promise of absolution if he does confess and apologize, and Japanese authorities respond in predictable fashion. Under Article 248 of the postwar Code of Criminal Procedure (Article 279 of the prewar code) the procurator may suspend prosecution after taking into consideration three factors: (1) the age, character, and environment of the offender, (2) the circumstances and gravity of the offense, and (3) the circumstances following the offense. The first two do not necessarily surprise us. To treat leniently a case involving a minor first offense would not be unusual in any legal system. In Japan, however, the third is equally, if not more, important. For the Japanese prosecutor the accused's attitude – in other words his willingness to confess and apologize – is critical to the decision whether to prosecute or not. In 1972, 94% of all persons formally charged with a crime admitted guilt, and in approximately 33% of all cases involving non-traffic offenses prosecution was suspended.'

Judges repeat the pattern. The rate of conviction in the cases that do go to trial is currently 99.99%. In less than 3%, however, do the courts impose a jail sentence: and 87% of these are terms of less than 3 years. Moreover, the courts regularly suspend more than two-thirds of all jail sentences. In 88% of all cases, all with confessions, the prosecution availed itself of the summary procedures described above. The penalty in such instances is restricted by law to 200,000 yen. In 65% of these cases, however, the fines were less than 50,000 yen. Consequently, the overwhelming majority of offenders in Japan confess and are either not prosecuted or are penalized by a fine of less than 250 US dollars.

The determinative factor for the judge, as for the prosecutor, in deciding the sentence to impose or whether to suspend sentence is the attitude of the offender. Confession is demanded and repentance rewarded. Japanese judges tell of a veteran of the bench who refused to permit convicted defendants to leave the courtroom even after sentencing until they had confessed and apologized. A primary purpose of trials in Japan, Japanese judges emphasize, is to correct behavior, not to punish. Nor, one might infer from the conviction rates, to determine guilt.

...

II. Institutional Barriers to Effective Law Enforcement

Added to the lack of formal sanctions, however, are a variety of institutional barriers that diminish the efficacy of those that do exist. In all but a few cases the imposition of sanctions is a judicial task. An obstructive debtor can, in most instances, force formal adjudication of even the strongest claim. Yet even to enforce instruments, such as notarial deeds, that do not require a preliminary judgment or to collect a court award or an administrative fine may require further judicial assistance. No court can fulfill such tasks adequately unless it is accessible and can act promptly and efficiently.

On these counts the state of the judiciary in Japan is woeful indeed. Governmentally imposed restrictions limit total entry into the legal profession – private attorneys, government lawyers and judges – to less than 500 persons a year. As a result Japan has fewer lawyers and judges per capita today than it did in the mid-1920s. The number of judges has remained almost constant since 1890. Today there is approximately one judge for every 60,000 persons in Japan as compared to one judge for every 22,000 persons in 1890. This is not, I must emphasize, the result of any lack of demand. Japanese judges handle caseloads that would stagger an American judge – nearly double the number of cases decided by judges in 'litigious' California and five times that of the Federal bench.

Often overlooked is a similar lack of government lawyers – or procurators. All cases – civil, criminal, or administrative – in which the government of Japan or any public agency is a party requires involvement if not direct representation by the procuracy. (In the case of most minor local government cases, private attorneys are retained.) Yet there are only about 2,000 procurators. For purposes of comparison, Los Angeles County alone has more than 400 lawyers in its district attorney's office.

The comparison with Germany is even more revealing. With less than two-thirds of Japan's population, Germany has nearly six times as many judges as Japan (approximately 15,500 to 2,700) and the ratio of judges to the population has steadily decreased: from one judge to 6,080 persons in 1911, to one judge to 4,840 persons in 1951, and to one judge to 3,963 persons in 1979. There are also nearly three times as many private attorneys (approximately 28,800 to 10,000) in Germany today as in Japan, and a third more procurators (approximately 3,330 to 2,100). It should be noted, however, that the German procurator (*Staatsanwalt*) handles only criminal cases. In administrative and civil cases the government is represented by private attorneys.

Aside from the shortage of judges, lawyers, and procurators, there are other obstacles to prompt and efficient justice in Japan. The continental system of disconnected hearings, trials *de novo* upon first appeal, the appeals of right to the Supreme Court rather than by court discretion, filing fees, bond posting requirements, stringent requirements of evidentiary proof, the unwillingness of judges to discipline lawyers for unnecessary delays – all combine to foreclose the courts as a viable means of obtaining relief. 'The litigation of a small claim,' say two of Japan's leading civil procedure scholars, 'tends to be an economic disaster.' What is remarkable about the Japanese legal system is not that people are reluctant to sue but that they sue at all. Despite these hurdles, the demand for legal relief, for sanctions, strains the legal resources of Japan to their limits.

III. Substitute Sanctions

The dearth of formal sanctions is balanced by an enduring set of informal, extralegal means of compulsion. The most persuasive is loss of face or damaged reputation. Japanese explaining why the apology works as a means of inducing conforming behavior, almost invariably say that to apologize in public carries with it the stigma of loss of reputation.

Examples of threats to reputation as an effective sanction abound. Antitrust enforcement provides one example. Firms will, agree to Japanese Fair Trade Commission recommendations tacitly admitting their violation and subjecting themselves to possible damage actions, rather than prolonging the case because of fears of a damaged company reputation. This, however, may reflect more the weakness of the formal sanction – no damage action has been successful – than the strength of adverse publicity. A better example is found in the pollution and drug cases, where the primary hurdle delaying settlement was the plaintiffs' uncompromising demand for public apologies by the presidents of the firms involved. It was far easier apparently to reach agreement on the amount of damages than for the defendants to comply with such a demand. In the SMON litigation, the one case involving a foreign party, I am told by the attorneys that the officers of the company were incredulous at this attitude by the Japanese plaintiffs and defendants. It was as if the amount of damages – over 100 million US dollars – was of no consequence compared with the apology.

Adverse publicity is a tool of law enforcement in most countries. The threat of public condemnation is often the most effective means to force compliance that is available to an administrative agency. 'Jaw-boning' by the President of the United States to keep a firm from raising prices, or labor from demanding wages in excess of a benchmark figure, is often little more than an exercise in the persuasive effect of adverse publicity. Officials enforcing antitrust laws in both the United States and Germany agree that adverse publicity is their most effective sanction. Yet upon close scrutiny, where effective, a tangible financial loss rather than mere reputation is usually at stake. It is easy to understand why the threat by the Food and Drug Administration or the Department of Agriculture to release a report that a certain drug or food product may be hazardous is apt to cause consternation and a rapid, positive response by the manufacturers. Reputation is important because its loss involves other types of deprivation. Although the same argument may be said to apply to Japan, the role of reputation in Japan appears to be a more subtle and complex matter.

IV. The Social Impact of Sanctionless Law

Few of the many enigmas of Japan are as acute as the paradox it presents of a society so free from crime, rule-abiding and cohesive with such overt thuggery, widespread flouting of law, and virulent conflict. Although not the complete or even certain answer, such riddles begin to unravel by viewing Japan as a society of law without sanctions.

A legal order without effective formal sanctions need not grind to a halt. Legislators, bureaucrats, and judges may continue to articulate and apply, and thus legitimate, new rules and standards of conduct. The norms thus created and legitimized may have significant impact. To the extent no legal sanctions apply, however, their validity will depend upon consensus and thus, as 'living' law, become nearly indistinguishable from nonlegal or customary norms. As to those norms the community accepts as necessary or proper, the absence of legal sanctions is likely to produce extralegal substitutes and to reinforce the viability of preexisting means of coercing behavior. Thus the legal order relies increasingly upon community consensus and the viability of the sanctions the community already possesses. The evolution of Japanese law exemplifies this process.

The coincidence of Neo-Confucian values and the demands of polity ensured that Tokugawa justice remained as inaccessible as possible. The fragile equilibrium of the early Tokugawa settlement made indirect rule and local autonomy a necessity. Each unit of the society, the lesser communities and the whole – whether han, village, guild, or family – were left alone so long as taxes were paid and outward order maintained. This was in stark contrast with Angevin England where the monarchy achieved dominion by extending the king's justice, through greater access to the king's courts and by fashioning new and more effective remedies. In England the consequence was a common law for the nation and a vigorous judiciary as well as a central monarchy. In Japan, community autonomy and weak government remained hidden behind a veil of ritualized deference to authority.

It is unlikely that the draconian penalties that adorned the *ritsuryo* codes and that appalled nineteenth-century Europeans were ever as important as the simple group sanction of ostracism and expulsion, especially when joined to the notion of vicarious liability. Social control develops new dimensions when landlords are made responsible for the conduct of their tenants, community leaders for the activities of its members, or parents for the conduct of their children, and when expulsion from the community and its resources is an ever present threat.

The absence of formal sanctions in modern Japanese law has had direct impact on both the retention of these earlier forms of social control as well as the creation of new ones. Boycotts, refusals to deal, and other forms of modern *murahachibo* are among the most prevalent means by which social order is maintained. The Japanese financial clearinghouse, for example, has a rule that no bank is allowed to transact business of any type with any individual or firm that defaults twice on promissory notes or checks. Since no firm could long stay in business without at least a bank account, promissory notes in Japan are almost as secure as cash (and indeed are used as collateral).

The combination of refusals to deal and other forms of ostracism with vicarious liability produces an even more effective deterrent to nonconformity. One of the first graduates of a new university to be allowed even to apply for employment with a large Japanese manufacturer turned down an offer by a foreign firm, that in monetary terms amounted to more than he could ever expect to make, at least in part because he feared that such a display of 'disloyalty' to the Japanese firm would result in its refusal to hire another graduate of that university.

Community or group cohesion is inexorably intertwined with such informal sanctions. Ostracism is not effective in a mobile society in which the benefits of membership in one group can be easily had by independence or by joining another. However, where one of the primary benefits of the community is its capacity to maintain stability and order, its ability to sanction reinforces its cohesion. Independence becomes a risky alternative and access to other groups becomes more difficult. Clientage too is the product of a demand for security by those who are unable to fend for themselves and whom the general community is unable to protect. In any society where the state fails to secure its citizens against lawlessness by those who exercise physical, economic, and social powers, there may be no choice but to attach oneself to those who can. The inability of the formal legal system in Japan to provide effective relief, to impose meaningful sanctions, thus tends to buttress the cohesion of groups and the lesser communities of Japanese society and to contribute to the endurance of vertical, patron-client relationships. The use of private mediators, the procuracy, and police in dispute settlement, the role of the yakuza and organized crime, the reliance on banks and other large enterprises, all fit this pattern of conduct.

Miyazawa, S, 'Taking Kawashima Seriously: A Review of Japanese Research on Japanese Legal Consciousness and Disputing Behaviour' (1987) 21 *Law and Society Review* 223–27, 230–31, 234–35

Since Kawashima's works appeared, the dominant form of analysis of the Japanese legal consciousness has been anecdotal. A critical problem with this approach is that, given the complexities of any society, one can always find some episodes that apparently support one's thesis. As part of their broader criticism of this method, for instance, Sugimoto and Mouer (1982: chap 11) could easily find examples that suggest a description of Japan which is opposite from the standard stereotype and is instead an individualistic society where people are always engaged in dry calculation and are exposed to constant controls from the powerful.

Of course, to be persuasive, any analysis must explain our daily experiences of the real world. What we need, then, are representative data that provide a context in which anecdotal data can be properly evaluated. Questionnaire surveys have been conducted to collect such data about dominant culture. What distinguishes the Japanese surveys on legal consciousness is that, unlike their foreign counterparts (eg Podgorecki et al, 1973; Curran, 1977; Gibson and Baldwin, 1985), they have been expected to provide information on something more general than knowledge, opinions, and demands about the existing legal system.

Major surveys on legal consciousness have been conducted by the Nippon Bunka Kaigi (Japan Culture Forum) (1973; 1982), the Osaka Bengoshikai (Osaka Bar Association) (1977), the Kyoto Daigaku Hogakubu (Kyoto University Faculty of Law) (1978), and the Nihon Bengoshi Rengokai (Japanese Federation of Bar Associations) (1986). The last survey is particularly large (a national sample of 2,315) and rich (402 questions). However, its data have not yet been fully examined. Therefore, I cite samples of questions and response distributions from the Nippon Bunka Kaigi (NBK) and the Kyoto Daigaku Hogakubu (KDH) projects.

The first study by the NBK was the earliest large-scale sample survey on legal consciousness in Japan. It was conducted in 1971 and based on a representative sample of 1,053 Tokyo area residents. In 1976 NBK conducted a follow-up survey of the same area with 1,080 respondents. Table 1 presents some of the data.

The results of the surveys were ambiguous. Apparently contradictory patterns appear for Questions 15 and 16. On the one hand, notwithstanding the stereotypes about Japanese legal behavior, an overwhelming majority of respondents indicated that they preferred detailed contracts. On the other hand, a majority also indicated a rather relaxed view about the bindingness of a contract, a result consistent with the stereotype. Apparently contradictory results were also obtained for other areas, including the administration of criminal justice, and the project reporters interpreted these results to mean that the Japanese hold strict views about the formal legal system as an institution but at the same time expect flexible enforcement. They also interpreted the responses to Questions 32 and 33 to indicate flexibility.

*Table l. Selected Questions from the Nippon Bunka Kaigi Surveys (in percent)**

	1971 (N = 1,053)	1976 (N = 1,080)
Question 15: What would you do if a contract became unsuited to the actual situation a few years after it was made?		
1. However unsuitable, a contract is a contract, and I would abide by it.	31.6	31.7
2. I would discuss with the other party whether the contract could be ignored.	64.3	61.7
3. Don't know/no answer.	4.1	6.6
Question 16: Which statement most closely reflects your opinion?		
1. Because a contract is a formality, it is better to make written contracts as simple as possible and descriptions in it as flexible as possible.	8.5	6.3
2. It is better to include as many details and concrete descriptions in a contract as possible so that a dispute will not arise.	89.5	89.1
3. Don't know/no answer.	2.0	4.7
Question 32: Which statement most closely reflects your opinion?		
1. Laws should enable us to live more comfortably with each other.	54.5	49.5
2. Laws should realize justice in the world.	42.0	39.8
3. Don't know/no answer.	3.5	10.7
Question 33: Do you agree with the statement that 'We should abide by the law of the country even if we believe it to be unjust'?		
1. Agree.		28.9
2. Do not totally agree.		59 0
3. Totally disagree.		7.0
4. Don't know/no-answer.		5.1
Question 42: Would you consider suing if your rights were violated?		
1. Immediately.	22.8	11.1
2. Occasionally.	24.0	23.7
3. No, unless the matter were extremely really grave.	49.9	60.6
4. Don't know/no answer.	3.3	4.5

Question 43: Do you agree with the statement that 'Litigation is expensive and time consuming, and even when you win, you will usually lose money'?		
1. Agree.	58.8	59.6
2. Disagree.	27.1	21.6
3. Don't know/no answer.	14.2	18.7
Question 44: Which statement most closely reflects your opinion?		
1. If you think it is better to sue, you may do so.	8.6	8.1
2. Suing is not the most desirable action, but you may use court-sponsored mediation or formal discussion as much as you wish.	39.7	42.7
3. You should try to avoid bringing suit whenever possible and instead work to resolve the matter through private discussions.	46.6	41.3
4. Don't know/no answer.	5.0	7.8

* *Unfortunately the authors of these studies have not provided tests of significance of differences in these data.*

More relevant to the conventional understanding of Japanese legal culture as nonlitigious may be Questions 42, 43, and 44. Only a minority of respondents to Questions 42 and 44 gave positive responses regarding the use of litigation, a result supportive of the stereotype. However, the response to Question 43 also suggests a calculative basis for this aversion to litigation. What the researchers most emphasized was the drastic decline in the most positive response to Question 42 between 1971 and 1976, as its percentage fell by one-half.

Several methodological problems in these surveys have been noted (Rokumoto, 1983a). Some questions were so abstract that the respondents were asked about matters most of them had never considered. Others, such as Question 43, encompassed more than one issue. These projects often used only one question for a very broad issue (eg Question 42 for the violation of rights and Question 44 for the use of courts) on which different responses could be expected under specific conditions. Certain questions also had response categories that were not mutually exclusive. For instance, among the answers to Question 32, a comfortable life (*guai no yoi seikatsu*) and the realization of justice (*seigi no jitsugen*) may coexist. In short, we may be sceptical about the validity of the results.

There is also a problem of reliability. Consider Question 42, for example. While the second survey repeated the same question to a representative sample in the same area only five years after the initial survey, the percentage share of the first response category became one half. Considering the very general character of the question, this change may raise doubts about the reliability of the entire project. Should we believe that the Japanese became more conservative so abruptly?

Most importantly, these two NBK projects are not directly relevant to our renewed interest in Kawashima's concept of legal consciousness, namely what Rokumoto called legal conception and rights conception. According to Rokumoto's explication, we have to measure the general normative framework that forms the basis of, for example, relaxed views on the bindingness of contracts or unwillingness to sue. This is not a fault of the NBK projects, which were planned before Rokumoto's explication. But it is nonetheless a problem we must face.

...

V. INDIVIDUAL ATTITUDES AND BEHAVIOR IN DISPUTE RESOLUTION

No one has seriously explored legal consciousness as an attitudinal factor of individual behavior in empirical research. This is somewhat surprising since even in Japan longitudinal studies on the relationship between attitudes and behavior are no longer unusual. Indeed, such studies are quite common in the research on political behavior, particularly voting behavior, conducted by political scientists who are, at most Japanese universities, members of law faculties.

I do not mean, however, that there have been no major empirical studies of individual behavior in dispute resolution. In fact, I would like to summarize three examples. Sasaki's book on mediation in the court (1974) was probably the first attempt by any Japanese scholar to criticize the stereotype of Japanese legal behavior. The first edition of his book appeared in 1967, when Kawashima's *Nihon-jin no Ho-ishiki* [The Japanese Legal Consciousness] was also published. From 1958 through 1961, Sasaki conducted mailed questionnaire surveys of 2,034 residents of Shimane prefecture and 2,411 city residents of Osaka prefecture; examined the records of all civil mediation cases processed in 1957 by a district court in Shimane (441 cases) and a district court and a summary court in Osaka (2,944 cases) and conducted mailed questionnaire surveys of the par ties of those cases (384 in Shimane and 1,811 in Osaka); and conducted mailed questionnaire surveys of 74 volunteer mediation commissioners in Shimane and of 82 in Osaka. It is easy to criticize the use of mailed questionnaires that do not guarantee the identity of respondents. However, because these surveys were carried out almost thirty years ago in Japan about a subject considered confidential, they were quite a heroic effort.

... Rural residents were more afraid of the reactions of party and neighbors than were urbanites, a result that might be taken as support for both the conventional view as well as for my proposal that we initiate interregional comparative studies of activities of the formal legal system.

However, the main point of these findings is that the most frequent reasons given for avoiding litigation concerned the costs involved rather than beliefs rooted in the traditional consciousness. The issue is how disputes can be resolved if litigation is not used; court-sponsored mediation may be one means. In other words, the public may see mediation as a substitute for litigation in realizing legally justifiable interests rather than as a mechanism for realizing conventionally assumed purposes such as restoring harmonious social relationships.

The data on complaints heard from the parties who had actually been involved in mediation might be cited to support this interpretation. These parties sought mediation expecting both more involvement from the judge, who is nominally the chairman of the mediation commission, and binding resolutions based on more complete investigations of the facts (for similar observations regarding family court mediation, see Bryant, 1984). The reality of mediation, however, is that most cases are handled only by lay commissioners and that the commission does not have authority to make a binding decision Presented this way, Sasaki's project should have attracted more attention as a study on individual attitudes and behavior in dispute resolution.

Unfortunately, Sasaki did not ask the involved parties their specific reasons for choosing mediation. We cannot be sure to what extent we can infer the existence of a high degree of interest consciousness behind behavior seeking mediation. The first attempt to reconstruct individual dispute processes retrospectively did not occur in Japan until 1968, when Rokumoto conducted his dissertation research (1971).

Rokumoto wanted to discover the factors that determined the degree of the legalization of social ordering in Japan. He defined legalization as the process through which society comes to rely increasingly on the formal legal system to maintain order. He first sent a card asking a representative sample of 2,013 residents of the Bunkyo ward of Tokyo if they had been involved in automobile accidents or housing disputes. He then interviewed 103 of the 226 respondents who answered affirmatively. Rokumoto reported data on forty-five accident cases and forty housing cases. Only three of the accident cases reached a court, while eleven of the housing cases went to litigation and another eleven went to mediation. Attorneys were used in only three accident cases but in thirty housing cases. Seemingly against the conventional view of the role of local officials in Japan, local politicians and police did not play any significant role in these cases. Instead, particularly in accident cases, non-attorneys who were nevertheless specialists in automobile accidents, such as insurance agents and accident managers of taxi companies, figured conspicuously as agents for parties, thus raising the possibility that these specialists sometimes engaged in the arbitrary manipulation of legal rules, exploitation of ignorant opponents, or deceit. The outcomes of these cases indicated that the parties who retained attorneys or specialists could expect favorable results.

Rokumoto's main argument is that the chance to obtain the assistance of attorneys and specialists and hence to mobilize the formal legal system to one's advantage is unevenly distributed in society. The people with the greatest advantage are those who are by occupation repeat users of legal specialists, most notably professional landlords (a result that reminds us of Mayhew and Reiss's work [1969] to which Rokumoto in fact refers). Those with the second greatest advantage belong to natural networks that include legal specialists. For those outside these groups, it is difficult to obtain legal counsel in Japan. Even when one is able to retain legal representation, parties without a previous relationship with the specialists, however indirect, will often find it hard to receive full, personal service.

As for legal consciousness, even mediation is a deliberate attempt to enforce one's legally protected interests. In some cases, mediation is used to block the use of litigation by the other party, whose legal basis may be much stronger. In contemporary Japan, at least in urban areas, parties use both mediation and litigation to pursue their own interests. These results apparently differ from a commonsensical version of the Kawashima thesis.

However, Rokumoto does not regard such interest-mindedness as the truly modern legal consciousness. Instead, he implies that this thinking lacks internalization of universalistic standards, acceptance of the reciprocity of right-duty relationships, and reliance on the court as an objective adjudicator. Indeed, the mobilization of law does not necessarily reflect legal consciousness, even in the sense of interest-mindedness. After all, if one happened to be in one of those networks mentioned above, the assistance of legal specialists would naturally be provided. In light of this argument, it seems logical that

Rokumoto tries to resurrect Kawashima's conception of legal consciousness through his explication.

Wagatsuma, H and Rosett, A, 'The Implications of Apology: Law and Culture in Japan and the United States' (1986) 20 *Law and Society Review* 463–67, 469–70, 471–73, 475–77, 478–79, 488–89, 492

I. APOLOGY AND CULTURE

Apology is an objective act that can be observed and measured, but its primary significance is in the social context. In every culture people have a common way of defining interpersonal relationships and attributing significance to social actions. These definitions vary, but, for a person operating in a specific context, these attributions seem so real that the meaning of the situation cannot be otherwise. Members of different societies attribute different significance to social behavior because their assumptions about the world and themselves are different. In a previous article (1983) we considered contract law in Japan and the United States in light of our hypothesis that the Western insistence on protecting the rights of the weak against the powerful is based on the illusion that individuals are autonomous and free to choose their social commitments rationally, just as the Japanese perspective on enforcing promises is based on the *tatemae* of *wa*, the illusion that social life reflects a strong order hierarchically connecting individuals and groups and that the aim of law is to realize the inherent harmony among the parts. These motifs of individual autonomy and social harmony describe realities found in both societies, but their significance is affected by cultural assumptions that overstate or downplay their role in a particular situation.

This study of the implications of apology in Japanese and American law is motivated by our recognition that the behavioral differences we posit are connected to the processes by which serious disputes and accusations are resolved. This kind of study is inherently problematic, and our conclusions are therefore stated with full recognition of their tentative nature. In a real sense, all attempts to describe the factors contributing to cultural differences are reductionist and denature the essence of cultural coherence. No single contributing factor can be isolated from the rest without distorting the image of the whole. The evidence reported in this essay is incomplete and anecdotal. We believe, nonetheless, that there are real differences in the incidence of apologetic behavior by Japanese and Americans faced with a serious claim that they have injured another. We are even more confident, however, that there are differences in the significance that is likely to be attached to apologetic behavior or the failure of a person to apologize. These differences in significance are expressive of important cultural assumptions that influence many forms of social interaction and that form a central part of the foundation supporting the structure of the legal system. Studying them should reveal significant information about the formal and informal operation of both the Japanese and American legal systems and about the connections between culturally influenced behavior and the legal processes used to resolve disputes.

We would agree, for example, with Haley's recent suggestion (1982: 275) that apology in Japan is one of a number of social behaviors that compensate for the weakness of the formal enforcement sanctions of the law. Haley's point also can be turned inside out. The availability of social restorative mechanisms like apology obviates formal legal sanction in many cases. In the United States, the relative absence of recognition of apology may be related to the observed tendency of American society to overwork formal legal processes and to rely too heavily on the adjudication of rights and liabilities by litigation. Alternative means of dispute resolution accordingly receive less attention and social support. The relative absence of apology in American law may also be connected to the legal system's historic preoccupation with reducing all losses to economic terms that can be awarded in a money judgment and its related tendency either not to compensate at all or to award extravagant damages for injuries that are not easily reducible to quantifiable economic losses. Finally, the small role of apology or any other personal contact between criminal and victim also seems related to the disquieting tendency in American law to ignore and even abuse the victim during the formal process of criminal prosecution (eg President's Task Force on Victims of Crime, 1982; Hall, 1975; Geis, 1975).

Haley persuasively connects the absence of effective sanction in Japanese law with the Japanese emphasis on group cohesion, conformity, and the maintenance of strong social sanctions against those who disturb the order and harmony of the community (1982: 275–79). Young offers a comparable explanation of the operation of 'administrative guidance' that dominates governmental control of Japanese economic life when he describes it in terms of the weakness of the Japanese notion of rights (1984: 968–78). Traditional Japanese social norms emphasize harmonious interpersonal relations and group solidarity. Interpersonal and group conflict can be found in many forms in Japan as elsewhere, but in Japan many forms of self-assertion are strongly discouraged while great emphasis is placed on the sacrifice of personal needs and individual emotional self-expression to avoid confrontation with the group (see Steinhoff, *et al* 1984; Lebra, 1976: chaps 2, 4). Japanese tend to make a sharp distinction between in-group and outgroup, or between those they know very well and those they do not know at all (Nakane, 1970: chap 2). Within a group, maintenance of harmonious and smooth interpersonal relations, interdependence, and mutual trust are of utmost importance. At the same time, vague animosity, competition, suspicion, or at least indifference is strong between groups. In-group solidarity and out-group hostility are two sides of the same psychodynamic coin. Aggressive feelings that are generated but not allowed to be expressed inside a social group are often directed outward in the form of hatred focused at a specific scapegoat or suspicion toward outsiders. The more the group insists that aggressive self-assertion and confrontation within the group be avoided, the more likely it becomes that these tensions will be directed outward. Consequently, the stronger the emphasis on in-group harmony and solidarity, the more intense the outgroup enmity can be. Japanese are taught to accept such tensions and feelings of frustration as a natural consequence of social life, although they may not openly acknowledge the fact.

Japanese describe a person's stated reasons or opinion as *tatemae* and his real intention, motive, or feeling as *honne*. These two terms describe two sides of a single reality; there can be no *tatemae* or public character to behavior, without its linked *honne* or private connotation (Doi, 1973b; 1986). *Tatemae* is that which one can show or tell others, while *honne* is that which one should not or had better not tell others. At the conversational level, *tatemae* may be an indirection in discourse, while *honne* is a more candid message underneath. Yet *tatemae* is more than conventional evasiveness. It can be the expression of one's commitment or compliance to the demands of social norms, while *honne* may be the expression of one's sense of frustration, unwillingness, or the feeling that the demands of the group are unreasonable or impractical. When Japanese recognize that there is a normative way of doing something and say that they do that thing in the normative way, this is an expression of *tatemae*. At the same time, they know and may confide to a friend that it is impossible for them to do the thing that way. The admission of this frustration is *honne*. Ames makes this point nicely in describing the conflicting expectations regarding law enforcement that operate in the work of a rural Japanese policeman (*chuzai san*):

> There is a certain amount of tension in the role of a *chuzai san* enforcing the law within a social setting that stresses closeness between him and the surrounding community. Police officers by the nature of their job must formally intervene occasionally and invoke legal sanctions when violations of the law occur. Yet this can be at odds with the idea of rapport and understanding between the *chuzai san* and his tightly knit village neighbors. His dilemma is solved by the distinction between *tatemae* and *honne*. ... The formal *tatemae* is that he enforces the law evenhandedly and rigorously, but in reality (the *honne*) the villagers neither expect nor want him to do so (1981: 28).

Disparity between operating by the rules (*tatemae*) and operating by pragmatic judgment (*honne*) is familiar to Americans also. Yet the typical American emphasis on internal emotional consistency makes it difficult for many Americans to understand the Japanese attitude toward *tatemae* and *honne*. It is said that when Americans feel positively and negatively toward the same object, they tend to repress one of their feelings so as to establish internal consonance in their minds (Festinger, 1957). Americans find it harder to live with the cognitive dissonance of ambivalent emotions than Japanese. They tend not to admit their ambivalence, to identify it with hypocrisy and insincerity, and to avoid it by repression. One might say that Japanese have a greater tolerance for ambiguity and ambivalence, which at times may appear as even a preference for the ambiguous. In a society that emphasizes group membership as a basis for personal identity, it is important to maintain the sense of 'insideness' after a rupturing conflict. There must be a ceremony of restoration to mark the reestablishment of harmony. The process of 'conciliation' (*chotei*) and 'compromise' (*wakai*) and the show of benevolence by the insulted superior party are important, but an apology, and best of all a mutual apology, are even better as the explicit acknowledgment of commitment to future behavior consonant with group values.

...

II. THE ELEMENTS OF APOLOGY

Apology becomes important when it provides significant evidence of the state of mind of the apologizer. From a Westerner's perspective the ambiguities of apology are therefore intimately tied to the uncertainties of human intention and their potential for manipulation. Apology relies too heavily on inferring from an external act the presence of a state of mind – remorse or non-hostility – and therefore seems to be too subject to manipulation by deceitful people who say they are sorry but do not mean it. Even when there is no conscious intention to deceive, the formal aspect of the act of apology inevitably tends to convert it into a conventional or stereotyped ceremony. Some of the more flowery forms of apology in English, for example 'I *beg* your pardon', or 'Oh, I'm *terribly* sorry', are used most commonly in precisely those minor social situations in which the literal meaning of the words are very unlikely to express the actual state of mind of the person saying them. Conventionality can erode the content of the concept and obscure its meaning. From a Western point of view, these features make apology a dangerous foundation upon which to build an important legal structure.

One way to retrieve the essential connotations of the concept is to ask what constitutes a meaningful apology. For instance, one may ask whether a person can meaningfully apologize without acknowledging that:

1. the hurtful act happened, caused injury, and was wrongful;
2. the apologizer was at fault and regrets participating in the act;
3. the apologizer will compensate the injured party;
4. the act will not happen again; and
5. the apologizer intends to work for good relations in the future.

III. APOLOGY AS AN ADMISSION OF THE ACT

At first glance the simplest sincere apology appears to be, 'I'm sorry it happened'. A logical distinction exists between an expression of sympathy or regret and an apology, but contextually the distinguishing element of admission by the speaker of responsibility for the object of regret is strongly inferred in most cases (Coulmas, 1981: 76). It is hard to imagine in the American context a sincere apology that does not acknowledge that the act occurred and caused injury. However, several well known Japanese cases indicate that while remorse, a strong intention to avoid repetition of the act, and a willingness to compensate the injured party may be present in an apology, it may be very difficult for the apologizer to admit that the events occurred or that he did them. Disassociation from the wrongful act can be used to maintain a coherent sense of self; for instance, one can accept such acts only by insisting that some external force, rather than the person apologizing, was primarily responsible.

...

IV. APOLOGY AS AN ADMISSION OF THE WRONGFULNESS OF THE ACT

Apologizing for an act, without admitting the act itself, may be rare, but a person is more likely to apologize for acts that she does not recognize as wrongful, although she may regret the harmful consequences of her behavior. These uncertainties of apology are reflected in English in the two conflicting connotations of the word *apology* itself. Its original, now less common, meaning is derived from the Greek root of the word and denotes a defense, explanation, or justification (*Oxford English Dictionary*, sv 'apology;' *Webster's Third New International Dictionary*, sv 'apology'). *Apology* in the Socratic sense of a legal defense passed on to the Roman tradition and ultimately into English, where it can be seen in such examples as *Apologie of Syr Thomas More, Knyght, made by him, after he had geven over the Office of Lord Chancellor of England* of 1533, Philip Sidney's *Apology for Poetry* of 1595, or John Henry Newman's *Apologia pro vita sua* of 1865 (Peterson, 1985: 300). Its second, and now more common, definition suggests confession, expression of remorse for injury, and acceptance of responsibility for wrong, rather than defense of the act. Socrates' *Apology* is anything but a confession of wrongdoing, although it is a statement of acceptance of moral responsibility for acts. These two branches of the idea coexist in Western thought and to a degree characterize the differences between American and Japanese apologies. Nagano's survey of Japanese and American students (1985) indicates that in minor social situations, Japanese apologize by acknowledging their fault, while Americans believe that a statement of explanation or justification of their behavior is an appropriate apology.

Many Japanese seem to think it is better to apologize even when the other party is at fault, while Americans may blame others even when they know they are at least partially at fault. Americans, as a group, seem more ready to deny wrongdoing, to demand proof of their delict, to challenge the officials' right to intervene, and to ask to speak to a lawyer (Bayley, 1976: 145). Japanese criminal offenders are said to be more ready than Americans to admit their guilt and throw themselves on the mercy of an offended authority. Only when an individual 'sincerely' acknowledges his transgression against the standards of the community does the community take him back.

An apology in the Japanese cultural context thus is an indication of an individual's wish to maintain or restore a positive relationship with another person who has been harmed by the individual's acts. When compensation or damages are to be paid to the victim, it is extremely important that the person responsible expresses to the victim his feeling of deep regret and apologizes, in addition to paying an appropriate sum. If a person appears too willing to pay the damages, that willingness may be taken as the sign of his lack of regret. He may be regarded as thinking that money can settle anything and as not being sincerely interested in restoring a positive relationship with his victim. In dealing with those who have offended them, the cultural assumption of social harmony would lead the Japanese to accept the external act of apology at face value and not to disturb the superficial concord by challenging the sincerity of the person apologizing. The act of apologizing can be significant for its own sake as an acknowledgment of the authority of the hierarchical structure upon which social harmony is based. At a deeper psychological level, the restoration of a harmonious relationship is attained by the denial of one's self-serving and self-preserving tendencies. In this context, the external act of apology becomes significant as an act of self-denigration and submission, which of itself is the important message. Then the internal state of mind of the person who tenders the apology is of less concern. Conversely, if an offender is too willing to offer reparation without indicating his repentance and expressing apology, the response of other Japanese is likely to be unaccepting.

Sincerity of apology thus has different connotations in the two cultures, with the Americans preoccupied with the problematics of wholeheartedness and the Japanese focused on the more attainable externality of submission to order and return to harmonious relationship. Thus it appears that the Japanese view an apology without an acceptance of fault as being insincere, while an American is more likely to treat an exculpatory explanation as the equivalent of an apology at least to the extent that it is accompanied by a declaration of non-hostile intent in the future.

...

V. APOLOGY AND DISASSOCIATION

The sincerity of an apology is connected with personal coherence and ambivalence on two distinct levels. An apology suggests change in attitude when the apologizer expresses remorse for past hurt and the commitment that future behaviour will not be hostile and will make up for the rupture in relationship created by the hurtful act. Apology thus is Janus-like, with one face looking back remorsefully on the hurtful deed and the other looking forward hopefully to a better future. As Goffman has observed (1971: 113), an apologizing individual splits herself into two parts, the part that is guilty of an offense and the part that disassociates itself from the delict and affirms a belief in the offended rule. In this way apology is likely to involve a disassociation from that part of the self that committed the unacceptable act.

This disassociation can be accomplished in a variety of familiar ways. The bad behavior might be attributed to some external agency; it may be said to have been unintentional, unwitting, or otherwise not the work of the conscious self; or the individual might claim to be a new and different person who is no longer chargeable with the delicts of his old self. 'Oh, I'm sorry, I didn't mean it!' is a typical American apology. The biblical sacrificial rite of atonement involved a confession of wrongdoing accompanied by the claim that the sins of the people were unwitting (Num, 15: 26). Later

Christian practice adopted the rite of baptism, during which the sinner is reborn and washed clean of the faults of the old self. Many traditions project bad behavior externally on the influence of devils and demons. The defense of temporary insanity in modern American criminal-procedure reflects the same inclination to attribute bad behavior to something outside the actor's personality for which she is not responsible. The modern Japanese salaried worker is freed from the rigid hierarchical structures of the work world and can tell his boss just what he thinks without fear of punishment by means of the excusing ingestion of alcohol. Japanese workers and bosses often drink together after work, and it is widely reported that on such occasions matters can be raised that would be impermissible during the workday. Yet custom requires that what is said at such time be attributed to the influence of the drink and not be held against the speaker.

The Japanese word *mushi* literally means 'worm' or 'bug', but it is used in a number of idioms to describe some internal force distinct from the rest of the personality that influences feelings and emotions. When a person is depressed, he or she is said to be possessed by the 'worm of depression' (*fusagi no mushi*). When someone is in a bad temper, the worm is said to be in the 'wrong place' (*mushi no idokoro ga warui*). When a person persists in anger, it is said to be because 'the worm in her abdomen has not calmed down' (*hara no mushi ga osamaranai*). When a man is tempted to have an extramarital affair, it is explained as the effect of the 'worm of fickleness' (*uwaki no mushi*). If a child has temper tantrums, his mother may take him to a shrine to have the 'worm of tantrum sealed off' (*kan no mushi*). A selfish individual who expects much of others without reciprocating is described as a 'person with too good a worm' (*mushi ga yosugiru*). Impulsive behavior thus is attributed to an external agent, that is, the worm, that has found its way into the human's body. People acting according to their true selves would have to be condemned as disruptive members of society. However, since people are merely victims of their *mushi*, the worm can be 'sealed off,' thus permitting people to return to their true selves and to be restored to the community without guilt.

This view affirms a Japanese belief in basic human goodness and expresses an expectation that once relieved of the dire influence of the worm, people will return to a normal life. This view also suggests that, in dealing with those who behave badly, the appropriate attitude is one of 'nurturant acceptance' (*amayakashi*) that does not hold them fully responsible for their impulsive behavior. This cultural assumption of basic goodness also suggests a belief that each individual has innate capacity for eventual self-correction. Japanese thus not only believe that human character is mutable, but they also view an excessively bad person as 'nonhuman' (*hito de nashi*). When such persons reform, they are seen as 'returning to being a real human' (*ma-ningen ni kaeru*).

Disassociation also exists on another level. The notion of sincere apology assumes that human feelings have a coherence and wholeheartedness that is not common in an emotionally charged conflict situation. When someone has hurt us (or when we have hurt someone), we are likely to have conflicting feelings at the moment of apology. Almost all apologies are insincere in the sense that the person apologizing probably continues to entertain at some level, certain hostile thoughts toward the other. Those tolerant of such ambivalence may admit while offering an apology that they do not completely mean what they are saying. Those intolerant of such ambivalent states of mind will insist that their apology is wholehearted and sincere. Western ideology places a higher value on the need to maintain internal consistency and has difficulty simultaneously holding ambivalent feelings. A common resolution of this ambivalence is to repress one feeling and insist that the other is genuine (Festinger, 1957).

...

VI. LEGAL ASPECTS OF APOLOGY

Despite the obvious social and moral significance of apology, its legal implications are somewhat uncertain both in Japan and the United States. These uncertainties arise at several levels. At a formal level, the norms of substantive rights and liabilities announced in the codes and court decisions rarely treat apology as a significant factor. In American civil law, for example, we found no clear instance in which apology serves as a defense to a cause of action. A person is not relieved of liability for causing harm because he or she has apologized for the injury. The closest instance to the use of apology as a defense is the doctrine, now largely embodied in statute, that a retraction or apology mitigates damages in a defamation suit. If the retraction or apology is effective, the plaintiff is permitted to recover only actual damages, which in the vast majority of cases leaves the plaintiff with a moral victory but no substantial monetary recovery. Thus in states with such a statute or common law rule, an apology is a practical bar to a libel action, although the law does not quite say that. A somewhat similar situation exists in criminal law. Apology is not a defense to a criminal charge, but in both Japan and the United States the codes and rules permit apologetic behavior to be considered in mitigation of punishment. In distinction to the defamation law example, however, there is little reason to believe that those who apologize for serious offenses receive no punishment.

Uncertainty regarding the legal consequences of apology arises at two other levels as well. The procedural and evidentiary legal structures of Japanese and American law treat apology quite differently, although an apology is likely to have an impact on the outcome of a case in both systems. In American law, a statement that meets the standards of a sincere apology discussed above might also be characterized as an admission of liability admissible against the utterer. As we shall suggest, the law of evidence in America is torn between the pull to encourage compromise settlement of disputes by a process that is likely to include an apology and the countervailing attraction to a common lawyer of an admission, that 'queen of proof,' which can be used to prove the claim despite the hearsay rule and other artificial strictures that make proof at common law so complex. Such rules of evidence do not play a role in the judge-centered Japanese trial. As in the United States, few Japanese lawsuits are resolved by judgment after a full judicial trial. In both countries the slowness, expense, and uncertainty of the court process are used to motivate the parties to settle. What is notably different in Japan is the extent to which the court process includes and may actually require that the parties undertake to resolve the dispute by 'conciliation' (*chotei*) and 'compromise' (*wakai*).

In such a process, the tender of an apology is a crucial step toward resolution and has important practical consequences, even if the provisions of the civil code that define the legal obligations of the parties say nothing about apology.

...

VII. FORMAL APOLOGY AND *SHIMATSUSHO*

A striking difference in apologetic behavior in the two legal cultures is the frequency with which a formal, ceremonial apology is tendered in Japan, often by an abject public apology by the senior official of an organization responsible for injury or by a written letter of apology (*shimatsusho*). For example, following the crash of a Japan Air Lines DC-8 caused by a mentally unstable pilot in 1982, the president of the airline personally called on the bereaved families of the crash victims and was pictured in the press on his knees, bowing in remorseful apology. The ceremony was accompanied by a large cash payment, which apparently obviated litigation of the legal claims arising from the accident. By contrast, American executives whose enterprise has been accused of injury or wrongdoing are thought to be more likely to deny or evade charges of any responsibility and to avoid direct contact with the victims. They are less likely to acknowledge publicly any responsibility and remorse, and even less likely to call on the victims personally and apologize tearfully. The behavior of Union Carbide officials after the Bhopal disaster in 1985 combined an attempt to meet promptly the human problems engendered by the corporation's operations with a desire to avoid admissions of unlimited legal liability. The efforts appear to have satisfied no one.

Although its origins are not clear, it has long been the custom in Japan that a person who breaks a rule should express regret by writing a *shimatsusho*, or 'letter of apology', in lieu of facing official punishment. These letters are a common and significant aspect of Japanese apology. The practice suggests the use of a formal, written apology as the basis for relieving a wrongdoer from the legal consequences of the misbehavior. A number of examples suggest the range of ways in which a shimatsusho may serve the needs of both the wrongdoer and, equally important, the injured person or the official interested in resolving the hurtful situation without recourse to formal legal sanctions.

For example, it is common in Japanese schools and government offices for teachers or officials to work occasional night duty in rotation. In a family court being studied by one of us, an officer forgot that it was his turn for night duty and went home as usual. The clerk of the General Affairs Department of the court called on the negligent officer and 'asked' him to submit a *shimatsusho*. The officer wrote that he had neglected his duty on a certain date, which he regretted deeply, and pledged himself never to repeat his dereliction. The *shimatsusho* was filed with others in the General Affairs Department, but not in the personnel file of the officer. The clerk explained that it was only a 'customary procedure'. It was the officer's impression that his supervisor never officially examined the *shimatsusho* of those working in his unit. It would have been unusual if he did, because a Japanese supervisor is expected to know in intimate detail the character and family circumstances of individuals working under him. That he had to look through a bundle of *shimatsusho* to find out which workers were neglectful of their duties would suggest that he was unqualified to be a supervisor.

Bayley describes many instances in which people were required to write *shimatsusho* at the police station and indicates that sample letters are kept on file for future writers to copy (1976: 134–37). He also points out that the practice of writing apology letters is reported in popular fiction of the pre-Second World War era (Ito, 1962: 258). Interestingly enough, in response to our inquiries officers in the juvenile and patrol divisions of several prefectural police headquarters said that they did not ask people to write *shimatsusho* and that they did not have standard forms to guide those writing such letters. Our findings thus appear different from those of Bayley, who reports that Japanese police are open about their exercise of discretion, in contrast to what he found to be the denials by American police that they exercise similar discretion (1976: 138). We suspect that the responses we received were the 'official' statement of the *tatemae*, namely that there is no legal procedure in the code for the writing of such letters, which therefore cannot be officially acknowledged as a police action. We believe that the fact, or *honne*, is that police do obtain *shimatsusho*, although we have no way of knowing how many of them do so or how often. The letters are received by the officers as their 'private' act, although it is probable that most citizens who write the letters do not know that they are not official documents.

...

VIII. CONCLUSION

We said earlier that there are real differences in apologetic behavior in Japan and the United States. We are even more confident that there are differences in the significance that is attached to such behavior or to the failure to apologize in each nation. Americans attach greater significance and legal consequence to the perceptions of autonomy and internal coherence, thus making apology important as an expression of self. This leads apologetic behavior to be accompanied by a justification or an emphasis on the acceptance of liability along with responsibility. The act of apology must accordingly spring from internal motivations, not from the request of external authority, and must not be weakened by mixed motives. In Western eyes, ambiguity and ambivalence detract heavily from the worth of an apology. Sincerity in an apology means internal coherence and wholeheartedness.

In contrast, the Japanese concept of apology attaches primary significance to the act as an acknowledgment of group hierarchy and harmony. Less concern is expressed for paying the damages and more on repairing the injured relationship between the parties and between the offending individual and the social order that has been disturbed. Sincerity therefore be comes less a function of the internal mental state of the person apologizing and more a matter of performing the correct external acts that reaffirm submission to that order. The presence of internal ambivalence is expected and accepted as not threatening.

Tanaka, H and Takeuchi, A, 'The Role of Private Persons in the Enforcement of Law' (1974) 7 *Law in Japan* 37–40

Law is a social device for achieving various goals by resort to one or several methods of sanction if necessary. Such methods of sanction are usually divided into two major groups, criminal and civil. Under the Japanese law the former includes 'capital punishment (*shikei*), imprisonment with labor (*choeki*), imprisonment without labor (*kinko*), fine (*bakkin*), petty fine (*karyo*), detention in jail (*koryu*) and criminal forfeiture (*bosshu*)'. The latter includes various sanctions, eg awarding damages, enjoining certain acts, refusing to give legal effect to an act, or creating certain legal effects. In not a few instances, the law also tries to achieve a desirable result by asking a private person to do an act or to refrain from doing an act, with a provision for some disadvantage to be imposed on those who do not obey a court's order or legislative demand. In addition to this, there are a group of methods of sanctions labeled 'administrative,' as, for example, requiring a license for certain acts and refusing to grant a license or suspending or revoking a license once given.

There seems to be a marked tendency in the Japanese law to emphasize the criminal and administrative methods of sanctions – both to be exercised on the state's initiative – and to neglect the role of others to be exercised on private initiative. Such characteristics of the Japanese law are to be best illustrated through comparison with American law as we will discuss in this article.

Differences in historical background would account for much of the difference between the two legal systems. While American law, though having received much of the English legal systems and techniques, is in large part a result of the people's efforts from the colonial period to develop an official scheme for solving disputes among themselves, Japanese law is basically a means developed by the rulers to rule the people. That is, when the Japanese leaders tried to modernize their country after the Meiji

Restoration in 1867, establishment of an entirely new legal system on the Western model was an immediate need. Indeed, such law reform was widely believed as a first prerequisite for Japan's negotiating the amendment of treaties with Western powers concluded in 1850's and 1860's which recognized extraterritoriality to foreigners. When the then Japanese government insisted that foreigners who had committed a crime in Japan should be tried in a Japanese court instead of by the consulate of the mother country of the suspected, the answer it received was always that they cannot hand their nationals to courts under an undeveloped system of law. Thus law reform, more particularly adoption of codes based upon the Western models, became one of the first things for the Japanese government to do. They sent young scholars to England, France and Germany, and adopted a number of codes in 1890s. They also had to create a new group of people capable of administering the new system. With a limited period of time, they had to bring up a group of elites who could supervise the working of the entire system through bureaucratic channels. It was indeed remarkable that they succeeded in training a sufficient number of judges and public procurators within two decades. But they could not go as far as to develop a corresponding number of practising lawyers. This process of law reform was historically almost inevitable for Japan. But it had much to do with preserving the Japanese attitude of looking upon law merely as a tool for the ruler, which had been nurtured during the feudal age. Under these circumstances, enforcement of law has been virtually monopolized by the 'rulers'.

Under this setting, law was apt to be regarded merely as a scheme for giving redress to the ruled who happened to suffer from injustices, and the court merely as a machinery for the ruler to rule the people, by giving protection to them from injustice. There had seldom been the notion that the law should equally bind the ruler as well as the ruled, consequently no idea that the court was a forum for the people to rectify wrongs committed by the ruler as well as their fellow citizens. Hence little effort has been made to make the machinery of justice more easily understandable by and more available to the people, nor to adopt such substantive rules of law as to give the people incentives to participate in the enforcement of law. The people were regarded, to use grammatical terms, as 'objects' to be governed, not 'subjects' expected to exercise positive efforts for achieving justice and maintaining order among themselves. Had they been regarded as such 'subjects', their resort to the judicial process should have been encouraged as showing their preference for solving problems through the official channels.

Needless to say, not all lawsuits are motivated by the plaintiff's sense of justice. There are certainly cases brought for the primary purpose of vexing others, or with the hope of getting some money out of a frivolous claim. It should also be noted that a greater number of lawsuits does not necessarily mean a higher stage of development of that society, nor better welfare enjoyed by the people living therein. All we wish to mention here is that the resort by private persons to courts for remedies should not be looked upon merely as a means of affording redress to them but also as a device for letting them cooperate in the enforcement of law. We, therefore, doubt the wisdom of the legislative policy (as is sometimes to be found in Japanese statutes) of building various barriers to private litigation in order to exclude ones brought by 'bad motives'. And by 'bad motives', it is often meant 'with intent to get some extra money', a sort of windfall. We believe that it is one of the peculiarities of the Japanese society that realizing pecuniary gain out of a lawsuit is *ipso facto* looked upon with highly suspicious eyes. The absence of multiple damage provisions in the Antimonopoly Law, efforts to discourage shareholders' derivative actions and the relatively small amount of damages awarded for defamation or invasion of privacy ail seem to reflect such an attitude by laymen toward lawsuits and lawyers. But if we see the positive value in private lawsuits, ie cooperation in enforcing law, the matter should be looked upon from an entirely different angle. Since it is not practicable to suppress only the 'abuses', the above-mentioned policy of law may easily result in discouraging private litigation in general. This, in turn, is to put almost the total burden of law enforcement on the shoulders of public officials. But isn't such attitude very near to treating the people merely as the governed?

(3) The fact that the Japanese law relies heavily on the initiative of governmental agencies for its enforcement and fails fully to utilize other means of law enforcement to be exercised by private initiative, seems to point out two major problems to be discussed by the Japanese legal profession.

(a) First, it should be questioned whether Japanese lawyers have paid enough attention to the problem of what the most effective means of enforcement of a particular law is. Thus we find too little analysis made on how law really functions in a particular field, the primary concern of legal scholarship still being to expound on statutes and to comment on cases without paying full attention to the actual working of the law, and to build up a magnificent 'system' of one's own theories. This is not limited to the sphere of substantive law. In the field of procedure as well, study of judicial administration became the subject of common interest only about a decade ago.

Such characteristics of Japanese legal scholarship, we believe, are largely responsible for the deficiencies in the means of law enforcement.

CHAPTER 2

HISTORICAL DEVELOPMENT

The focus of this book is the modern Japanese legal system, the starting point of which could be placed in the latter part of the 19th century, beginning with the main process of legal codification signalled by the introduction of the Criminal Code and Code of Criminal Instruction of 1880. However, not to refer to the history and development of previous centuries would be to ignore an important element in understanding the current legal system and in particular the sociolegal, political and cultural context of its operation. Even a short account of all periods of Japanese legal history would be beyond the scope of this chapter, but some background is necessary and will be provided here, whereas the main focus in the materials will inevitably rest upon the years following the Meiji Restoration (1868) and the Occupation Reforms (1945–50).

The tendency of historians is to divide time into periods which accord with their own preferences and historical agenda.[1] Throughout this book the periods most frequently referred to are the Tokugawa (1600–1867), Meiji (1868–1912), Taisho (1912–26) and Showa (1926–89).[2] These are periods which are commonly referred to in a variety of texts. However, a leading Japanese legal historian, Professor Ryosuke Ishii, eschewed the usual periodisation of historians and put forward a useful alternative, based upon his idea that 'the course of historical development proceeds in a wave like motion'.[3] In this paradigm 'the flow of historical time is taken to be a series of fluctuations, and one such "wave" is understood to constitute a single period'.[4] Each period contains a distinctive feature which, like any wave, has a beginning during which the special feature is developed, a middle when it reaches its peak and an end, when it declines. Based on this, Ishii divides Japanese legal history into six periods. First, the Archaic period (*circa* 250 BC–603 AD) characterised by 'law of uniquely Japanese origins', a time when religious influence was particularly strong and foreign influence nil.[5] The next three periods, the Ancient (603 AD–967 AD),

---

1 See in general, *The Cambridge History of Japan*, 6 ed vols, 1989, Cambridge University Press, and compare with Storry, R, *A History of Modern Japan*, rev edn, 1982, 1960, Penguin; Beasley, WG, *The Rise of Modern Japan: Political, Economic and Social Change since 1850*, 2nd edn, 1995, Weidenfeld and Nicolson.

2 Since October 1868 when Emperor Mutsuhito announced the commemorative name (*nengô*) for the period of his rule, the reign of each Emperor has been given a single commemorative name thereby defining each period in modern Japanese history. Prior to this there could be more than one *nengô* per reign. Thus Meiji meaning 'enlightened rule' was the name given by Emperor Mutsuhito to govern his period of reign (1868–1912); Showa, meaning 'brilliant harmony' was the era-name for the reign of Emperor Hirohito (1926–89). The current era-name for the reign of Emperor Akihito (1989–present day) is Heisei, meaning 'achieving peace'. Japan adopted the Western calendar in 1872. However, in formal documents, the year of the Emperors reign is used. This can give rise to complications in translation and on occasion can account for errors in texts. This may be particularly so in years when one Emperor dies and another ascends the throne. Thus 1988 was straightforward Showa 63, but Emperor Hirohito died in January 1989 thus Showa 64 became Heisei 1.

3 Ishii, R, *A History of Political Institutions in Japan*, 1988, p vii, University of Tokyo Press. See also the useful Chronological Table pp 133–53.

4 *Idem*.

5 *Idem* p 91. See also Noda, Y, *Introduction to Japanese Law*, 1976, p 21, University of Tokyo Press.

Medieval (967–1467) and Early Modern (1467–1858) were heavily influenced by Chinese law. The foundations for this were laid in the Ancient period when Japan was very much a satellite of China, whose culture, political and legal systems were to have a lasting influence over Japan long after any direct influence had ceased.[6] The Modern period (1858–1945) was when the law of a few European nations had an overwhelming influence on the content of Japanese law and the shape of the legal system, particularly in the form of monarchical constitutionalism. Finally, the Contemporary period from 1945 onwards has been a period determined by the events of the defeat and surrender of Japan in 1945 followed by the Allied Occupation.[7]

Following this analysis, it is clear that prior to the reception of Western law in the 19th century, the Japanese legal system was shaped by the effect of two main influences. First, there was the overwhelming influence of the Chinese legal tradition and second, the indigenous and essentially feudal political and social order. The common element was Confucianism which had flourished in China and went to the heart of the Chinese system of law, shaping the legal and administrative structures which Japan adopted and which found a natural home in the feudal structure of Medieval and Early Modern Japanese society. The essential coherence of these influences, combined with the fact that Japan was a closed country for over 200 years, meant that the totally alien ideas and structures of Western law and government, which Japan was forced to consider adopting in the mid-19th century, represented a major challenge of unprecedented proportions.

The need to confront Western ideas and laws arose out of the Japanese desire to stop what was perceived as Western encroachment of their land and to reassert themselves after signing the 'unequal treaties' in 1858. From the 1630s onward, Japan had pursued a policy of national isolation which led to the description of the country as being 'closed'. In effect this meant that Japanese were prohibited from leaving the country, missionaries were prevented from entering and trade was limited to a northern port and conducted with China and Holland alone.[8] Thus Japan was not part of the international political order and for two hundred years was able to develop a social, political and legal order without any 'outside' or alien influences interfering with the cultural coherence of that growth. Unusually, given the European interest in East Asia in general, it was the Americans who 'opened up' Japan. Whilst the Russians had tried to establish trading relations in the early 19th century, this had not been successful

6 The Ancient period is sometimes referred to as the *Ritsuryo* era because a number of codes were introduced which were imitations or adaptations of Chinese T'ang Dynasty. See Ishii, *supra*, n 3 p 19; Noda, *idem*, p 22.

7 An interesting division of Japanese legal history into distinct periods is suggested by one writer in the following way: 'Tokugawa Japan had aspects of a decentralised rule-by-man (or rule-by-status) based on its Confucian philosophy; Meiji Constitutionalism had a rule-*by*-law and post-World War Japan has a genuine rule-*of*-law, although its social bite is limited by a lingering tradition of Confucian ideas and the strengths of entrenched bureaucratic elitism.' Henderson, DF, 'Japanese Law in English: Reflections on Translation' (1980) *Journal of Japanese Studies* 119.

8 Storry, *supra*, n 1, Chapter 2; Beasley, WG, *Great Britain and the Opening of Japan 1834–1858*, 1951, Luzac; Beasley, WG 'The Foreign Threat and the Opening of the Ports' in *The Cambridge History of Japan*, Vol 5, 1989, p 259.

and eventually, the British started to show an interest in opening up the ports as part of their global trading network.[9] However, it was the Americans, whose whaling fleet argued for the Japanese ports to be opened, who were to force the issue.[10]

In 1853 Commodore Matthew Perry was successful in delivering a letter from President Fillimore requesting permission for American ships to call at Japanese ports for supplies and suggesting the setting up of trading relations between the two countries. Previous attempts to establish relations with Japan had been rejected, but the arrival of Perry and his four 'black ships' (steam ships) conveyed the strength of the American resolve to open Japan.[11] Promising to return within a year, Perry left the Japanese to consider their reaction to his demands, described by one writer as 'panic'.[12] When he returned with eight 'black ships' in 1854 Perry, by means of this blatant gunboat diplomacy, was able to extract agreement to the opening of two ports, the residence of a consul in one of the ports and the establishment of a most-favoured-nation status.[13] The Treaty of Kanagawa was signed on 31 March 1854 and was soon followed by similar treaties with Britain, France, Russia and Holland. Extracted in the face of overwhelming military power, these 'unequal treaties' not only set up a system of unilateral customs agreements, but established the principle of extraterritoriality for the Western nations, to be administered through consular jurisdiction.[14] It was this, more than any other feature of the treaties which created fear of colonisation. More importantly it generated a desire for Japan to reassert its national authority, which in turn was to create a need for national unity. In the simplest terms, the ensuing struggle for power and search for an answer to the 'barbarian invasion' and possible colonisation of Japan was eventually to lead to the fall of the Tokugawa

9 Storry, *idem*, Chapter 3, pp 83–85.

10 Lehmann, J-P, *The Roots of Modern Japan*, 1982, p 136, Macmillan, comments that there can be few greater ironical twists in modern history to rival the fact that Japan was opened in the name of free trade as a result of pressure from American whalers, yet 120 years later had to face American protectionism and 'a hysterical outburst against her whaling activities'.

11 In 1846, Commodore Biddle had arrived off Japan with two warships but failed to achieve his objective, which was then passed to Perry. In the same year, following a British Naval survey of the Ryuku Islands, a missionary was allowed to settle on Okinawa. Interestingly enough, Perry was later to propose that if the Japanese did not accede to the American demands, they should annex Okinawa because it would be a good base for military operations. See Storry, *supra*, n 1.

12 Lehmann, *supra*, n 10, p 137.

13 Throughout the Tokugawa period there had been good relations with the Dutch and in 1716 the ban on Western books was lifted. In reality this resulted in the importation and study of Dutch works and Lehmann, *idem*, p 136 notes that at the time of negotiating the Treaty of Kanagawa 'the *lingua franca* was Dutch, hence negotiations and memoranda were translated from English into Dutch into Japanese and *vice versa*'.

14 Japan was in no doubt about the power of Western nations since it was aware that China had been forced to sign various treaties at the end of the Opium Wars in 1842 and had ceded Hong Kong to the British.

Shogunate and the establishing of a centralised imperial government in the form of the Meiji Restoration of 1868.[15]

Vital as this episode in Japanese history was, it would be a mistake to conclude that the opening of Japan was the event which alone resulted in a search for a new legal system. The process was more subtle than that.[16] The development of law, in particular through the codes of the Tokugawa and early Meiji periods, was to lay the foundation for the reception of Western law in the late 19th century. Whilst the events of the 1850s prompted certain action amongst the ruling elites and gave the search for a new legal and political order an urgency in the minds of some, the eventual acceptance of Western law was arguably not necessitated by that event alone.[17] Instead, it was the start of a new wave prompted by unforeseen developments, but for which the ground had been laid, first by the Chinese influence and the feudal government and administration of Tokugawa Japan, but second by the work of Japanese scholars in the early Meiji era.

During the Tokugawa period (1600–1867) Japanese law developed under the influence of Chinese scholarship founded on Confucian values.[18] Decentralised local government based on feudal structures and supported by status based customary laws and rules formed the essential character of the system.[19] Traditionally law and government were closely related, but only in the sense that 'law' was really the exercise of an administrative and bureaucratic function

15 Storry, *supra*, n 1, p 82 notes that 'among the educated classes in Japan there was already, by the 1850s, a mental climate prepared for a return of the emperors to the centre of the stage. There was also – though this was much less apparent – a half conscious readiness among a few people to abandon the national policy of exclusion'. In general see Jansen, M, 'The Meiji Restoration' *The Cambridge History of Japan*, Vol 5, p 308 and Beasley, 'The Foreign Threat and the Opening of the Ports', *supra*, n 8, p 259.

16 Although the Western powers had made law reform a precondition to revision of the 'unequal treaties' and there can be no doubt that this acted as a major factor in stimulating legal reform, it would seem that the external pressure resulted in the Meiji authorities looking for a solution beyond its national boundaries rather than codifying Japanese customary laws. See discussion below.

17 The unequal treaties caused some to doubt the legitimacy of the Tokugawa government and added further to the power struggles in the late Tokugawa period. To put Japan on an equal footing with the Western powers and stop what was perceived as creeping encroachment, if not colonisation, national unity and strength was needed and this would require institutional change. The ensuing power struggle led to the 1867–68 crisis which resulted in the fall of the Tokugawa government and the restoration of direct, centralised Imperial rule. Vlastos, S, 'Opposition Movements in early Meiji, 1868–1868' *The Cambridge History of Japan*, Vol 5, p 367.

18 Hiramatsu, Y, 'Tokugawa Law' (1981) 14 *Law in Japan* 1; The author notes the importance of the *ritsuryo* system based on the Chinese legal scholarship of the T'ang period. Also, the Tokugawa Confucian scholars were very much aware of the modifications and revisions which took place during the Ming and Ch'ing period. In general see Wigmore, JH (ed), *Law and Justice in Tokugawa Japan*, 20 Vols, 1967–86, University of Tokyo Press; Hall, J and Jansen, M (eds), *Studies in the Institutional History.of Early Modern Japan*, 1968, Princeton University Press.

19 Hall, JW, 'Rule by Status in Tokugawa Japan' (1974) 1 *Journal of Japanese Studies* 39; Hall, J, 'From Tokugawa to Meiji in Japanese Local Administration' in Hall and Jansen (eds), *idem*, p 375.

and therefore was a set of social rules for the ordering of society.[20] Nowhere was this more clearly illustrated than in the *Kujikata Osadamegaki* which was drawn up in 1742.[21] Issued to administrators only, the *Osadamegaki* was a manual akin to a modern day set of bureaucratic rules, not least since justiciable law and 'rights' in the modern and Western sense did not exist. Instead 'justice', in the Tokugawa sense, rather than 'law' in the Western sense, was administered by the Shogunate (*Bakufu*) through its officials.[22] The *Osadamegaki* was therefore not a code in the sense of promulgated law, but an administrative manual consisting of Book 1 which listed the rules, or directives and Book 2, listing the penalties.[23]

The Tokugawa period was in many ways a laboratory of social ordering in which a variety of influences merged and grew into a coherent whole, but which, when confronted with Western demands, was forced to adapt and adopt in order to survive. However, the foundation it provided for the evolution of

---

20 Henderson, 1980, *supra*, n 7 and (1987) *infra*, n 26, notes the difficulty of the use of the word 'law' in the Tokugawa period. During the Tokugawa period, Japan had a decentralised system of local government based, in large part, upon autonomous units which consisted of villages. However, central government, such as it was, could use these units to exercise power when necessary. See Harumi, B, 'Village Autonomy and Articulation with the State' (1965) 25 *Journal of Asian Studies* 1. As will be seen later, the Meiji Restoration resulted in a breaking down of traditional structures. In the process of constructing a modern, centralised system of government, it had to address the issue of relations between the old decentralised system of government and the new, centralised structure. See Steele, MW, 'From Custom to Right: The Politicisation of the Village in Early Meiji Japan' (1989) 23 *Modern Asian Studies* 729. See also Ishii, *supra*, n 3, Chapter 4. However, centuries-old structures endured, for although there would be central bureaucratic control of local government, social control would still be exercised through the old semi-feudal status system. It is also interesting to note that the Meiji Constitution contained no reference to local government at all, whereas the 1946 Constitution devoted a whole chapter to the authority of local governments. See Abe, H, Shindo, M and Kawato, S, *The Government and Politics of Japan*, 1994, Chapter 7 and 8, University of Tokyo Press; MacDougall, T, 'Democracy and Local Government in Postwar Japan' in Ishida, T and Krauss, ES, *Democracy in Japan*, 1989, University of Pittsburgh Press.

21 Another area illustrating the function and operation of Tokugawa society is provided in Henderson, DF, *Village Contracts in Tokugawa Japan*, 1975, University of Washington Press; Henderson, DF, 'Contracts in Tokugawa Villages' (1974) 1 *Journal of Japanese Studies* 51.

22 Hiramatsu, *supra*, n 18, p 48 describes Shogunal law of the Tokugawa period as 'a law of advanced control and discipline'. This was in line with the Confucian-inspired Chinese legal tradition which Japan had embraced, whereby general administration was inseparable from the administration of justice. Furthermore, if there was no system of 'rights' a judiciary and legal profession as we know it was otiose; thus, 'judicial officers, as distinguished from administrative officials, did not exist'. Hattori, T, 'The Legal Profession in Japan: Its Historical Development and Present State' in von Mehren, AT (ed), *Law in Japan: The Legal Order in a Changing Society*, 1963, p 111, Harvard University Press; see also Rabinowitz, RW, 'The Historical Development of the Japanese Bar' (1956) 70 *Harvard Law Review* 61 who discusses the role of *kujishi* as the forerunner of the lawyer. See Chapter 5.

23 Henderson, 1980, *supra*, n 7 notes the difficulty of translating 'law' and the need to use equivalents to modern terms in order to convey the concept. He refers to particular problems with the *Osadamegaki* which was based on the *ritsuryo* of the 8th century; *idem*, pp 152–54. In view of this it is understandable why the *Osadamegaki* is referred to by some writers (incorrectly) as a code. Book 1 of the *Osadamegaki* was translated into German by Otto Rudorff, a German legal adviser to the Meiji Government, but a complete analysis in English had to wait until Henderson, *infra*, n 26. However, an English translation of Book 2 was made in 1912; see Hall, JC, 'Japanese Feudal Laws: Tokugawa Legislation' (1913) 41 *Transactions of the Asiatic Society of Japan* 683.

the modern Japanese legal system cannot be underestimated; it continued to shape the thinking of Japanese legal scholars through the period of the reception of Western law and into the contemporary period.[24] The challenges and difficulties which the Tokugawa system posed for Westerners arriving in the 19th century and which still form much of the bedrock of legal culture and jurisprudence in modern Japan, are well illustrated by Dan Henderson in his conclusion to a study of the *Kujikata Osadamegaki*:

> Our modern institution of 'law', implying the whole apparatus of justiciability – a judiciary separate from administration, a bench, a bar, substantive rules and procedural protections for equal individuals – was not congenial to the basic concepts of Tokugawa governance. In Edo[25] the concepts rested more on officially sponsored and societally rooted morality (perhaps 'natural law') of Confucian derivation. The vehicle of governance was the superior ('moral') man; his 'morality' was defined in terms of hierarchical status. This rule-of-status was not merely an incidental aspect of Tokugawa justice. It was the essence of justice, administered not by law but by men, who derived superior authority from their status. It was justice-above-the-law, perhaps comparable to the oft-stressed *li* and *fa* relationship in Chinese tradition. In Edo, it was a clear jurisprudential preference, an alternative to our rule of law, or justice-under-the-law. We must identify this Tokugawa position as such, to understand the Osadamegaki, which existed only to reinforce this 'natural' order. It would be a mistake, therefore, to suppose that a lack of 'law' meant a lack of justice in terms of the philosophy of the system here presented.[26]

Throughout the pre-Meiji era there were identifiable elements of formal, or written law, some going back to the 7th century, so that by the end of the Tokugawa period it could be said that there was an identifiable jurisprudence, perhaps even, in certain areas, an emerging body of justiciable law.[27] However, the 1868 watershed provided by the Meiji Restoration meant that there has been a tendency to see this period of Japanese legal history in terms of two discreet periods. In consequence, most sources tend to hop from Tokugawa Law to the Western Reception in 1880 without any, or due, regard to the intervening

---

24 This can be seen most clearly when it comes to alternative dispute resolution *infra* Chapter 6. See Henderson, DF, *Conciliation and Japanese Law: Tokugawa and Modern*, 2 Vols, 1965, University of Tokyo Press.

25 The Tokugawa period is also known as the Edo period because the capital moved to Tokyo (Edo).

26 Henderson, DF, 'Introduction to the *Kujikata Osadamegaki* (1742)' in *Ho to Keibatsu no Rekishiteki Kosatsu* (Historical Considerations of Law and Punishment) Memorial Essays in Honour of Dr Hiramatsu Yoshiro (1987) *Nagoya Daigaku Shuppankai* 489–544.

27 One of the first examples of formal, or written, law is the so-called constitution of the Seventeen Articles. Promulgated in 604 AD by Prince Shotoku, it was not a constitution in the modern sense, but was nevertheless used to establish a set of principles to guide officials and people alike, and outlined the political authority and legitimacy of the imperial throne. See Ishii, *supra*, n 3, p 18. For further examples of written law/codes of these periods see Hiramatsu, *supra*, n 18. On the issue of judiciable law during the Tokugawa period see Henderson, DF, 'Law and Political Modernisation' in Ward, RE, *Political Development in Modern Japan*, 1968, p 405, Princeton University Press. See also Noda, *supra*, n 5, who at p 36 notes that in addition to the various codes (eg the *Kujikata Osadamegaki*) there were several collections of law. 'Five collections of penal judgments, of which the first four are extant' and on the civil side 'a collection of judgments in 45 volumes, of which only two volumes have survived.' As noted by Hiramatsu, *supra*, n 18, p 48, most documentation from the period was lost in the great Tokyo earthquake of 1923.

period.[28] In fact the post-Restoration and early Meiji period involved a complex balancing act between continuity and discontinuity, between Japanese culture and tradition and Western influence and pressure. The magnitude of the effect which the reception of Western law had on the future of the Japanese legal system, explains the focus on the period leading up to the introduction of the Criminal Codes in 1880 and the constitution in 1889.

This focus on modernisation and Westernisation has resulted in a gap in scholarship.[29] The consequence of this has been twofold; first, the importance of the work of the early Meiji codification movement has been underestimated and second, the lasting influence of the Chinese legal tradition, from which that movement took its inspiration, has been diminished. Indeed, reading most texts on Japanese law, it is possible to believe that no codes existed before the Western inspired codes of the 1880s, when in fact four major examples from the early Meiji codification movement existed. These were the Provisional Criminal Code (*Kari Keiritsu*), the Essences of the New Code (*Shinritsu Koryo*), the Statutes and Substatutes as Amended (*Kaitei Ritsurei*) and the Draft of Statutes and Substatutes as Revised (*Kosei Ritsurei Ko*); all but the last was promulgated.[30] Their historical importance lies in having provided an ideological and practical foundation in codification work which prepared the way for the reception of the Western inspired codes. The *Shinritsu Koryo* and the *Kaitei Ritsurei* remained in force until the end of 1881 and even then, following dissatisfaction with the Western inspired Criminal Code, there was a suggestion that the former should be reactivated to take its place.[31] Thus, even in the face of the Meiji leaders' wish to develop a modern and more Western oriented legal system, the importance of these codes in the minds of scholars and jurists of the time should not be underestimated. Although the trend in learning Western law was to gather pace, particularly following the appointment of Shinpei Eto as Minister of Justice in 1872, the influence of the Chinese legal tradition and early Japanese legal principles remained significant. Thus the early indigenous codification movement provided a bridge between the legal tradition of the Tokugawa era and the late Meiji modernisation movement which led to the adoption of Western inspired codes.[32]

28 Even Noda makes no mention of this period. Having dealt with the Tokugawa period he moves to the Meiji Restoration and the Japanese government's preoccupation with translation of the French codes, *supra*, n 5, Chapter 3.

29 Until relatively recently the only work to consider this period was a translation and adaptation by William Chambliss of a work in Japanese by Ryosuke Ishii, published as *Japanese Legislation in the Meiji Era*, 1958, Panpacific Press. The only other appraisal of the period is Ch'en, P, *The Formation of the Early Meiji Legal Order*, 1981, Oxford University Press. Even in Japanese there has been only one significant publication covering that period (cited in Ch'en, *idem*, p xxi). Mention is made of this period of legal history in Ishii, *supra*, n 3, Chapter 5.

30 Ch'en, *idem*, Chapter 1.

31 Takayanagi, K, 'A Century of Innovation: The Development of Japanese Law 1868–1961' in von Mehren (ed), *supra*, n 22, p 5 at p 20.

32 Ch'en, *supra*, n 29 argues that with a Confucian background and training it was natural for Japanese jurists and officials to incline in favour of the Chinese legal tradition and to adapt the Chinese codes. However, the transformation of society from 1868 onwards, combined with intensive contact with Western ideas and values meant 'the reception of Western ideas became greater as Japan intensified her effort to secure independence from Western political intervention and to abolish the so-called "unequal treaties" between Japan and the Western powers' at p xix.

Following a period of internal upheaval and a brief civil war, on 3 January 1868 the formal declaration of restoration was issued and the new Emperor installed along with an administrative structure supporting imperial rule.[33] Later that year on 6 April the Emperor issued the Charter Oath of Five Articles which set out the guiding principles through which he would transform the former feudal nation into a modern state.[34] Political, administrative and legal modernisation were essential if Japan was to establish sovereignty by revising the unequal treaties. Although the transformation of the legal system was, in a sense, precipitated by antagonism to Western power, it was nevertheless to be primarily influenced by their legal systems. The legitimacy of the search for a 'modernised' legal system came from Article 5 of the Charter Oath which stated that 'knowledge from all over the world' should be sought in order to strengthen the foundation of the Empire.

In 1871 the Ministry of Justice was established and immediately set about seeking knowledge of other legal systems by sending students to Europe and the United States.[35] The enthusiasm of the Minister of Justice, Shinpei Eto, was a significant feature in generating the research into foreign legal systems and in this he was ably assisted by the work of Rinsho Mitsukuri who first translated the French Criminal Code and was then encouraged to translate the Civil Code, followed by the remaining Napoleonic Codes, a task which he completed by 1873.[36] The gathering strength of the new wave of Western inspired scholarship was given a boost by the arrival of two French scholars, Georges Bousquet in 1872 and Gustave Boissonade in 1873. Together with the Germans, Hermann Roesler, Hermann Techow and Otto Rudorff, these five European jurists were to make a particularly significant contribution to the transformation of the Meiji legal system and ensure the Western civilian tradition formed the basis of the

33 Lehmann, *supra*, n 10, Chapter 5; Storry, *supra*, n 1, Chapter 4; Vlastos, *supra*, n 17. A fascinating account of the period is given by Sir Ernest Satow in *A Diplomat in Japan*, 1921, Seeley Service, which he sub-titles: *The Inner History of the Critical Years in the Evolution of Japan When the Ports were Opened and the Monarchy Restored, Recorded by a Diplomat who took an Active Part in the Events of the Time with an Account of His Personal Experiences During that Period*. Satow was resident in Japan from 1862–82 and was Secretary to the British Legation. Chapter 23 deals with the fall of the Shogunate and Chapter 24 covers the outbreak of the Civil War.

34 The Five Articles were as follows: (1) Deliberative assemblies shall be established on an extensive scale and all measures shall be determined by public discussion. (2) High and low shall unite in carrying out the nation's plans with vigour. (3) All classes shall be allowed to fulfill their just aspirations and be content. (4) Base customs of the past shall be discontinued, and just and equitable principles of nature shall become the basis of our policy. (5) Knowledge shall be sought throughout the world in order that the welfare of the empire may be promoted. See Ishii, *supra*, n 3, p 98.

35 The rise of the Ministry of Justice to a position of influence within the Japanese power structure is illustrated in Yasko, R, 'Bribery Cases and the Rise of the Ministry of Justice in Late Meiji and Early Taisho Japan' (1979) 12 *Law in Japan* 57. A collection of essays covering the institutional and policy modernisation of this period is published in Ward, RE (ed), *Political Development in Modern Japan*, 1968, Princeton University Press. See also Wilson, RA, *Genesis of the Meiji Government of Japan 1868–1871*, 1957, University of California Press.

36 Noda, *supra*, n 5, p 43. Ch'en, *supra*, n 29, p 19 notes that 'under Eto's leadership the Meiji codification movement achieved a significant leap forward.' However, although his contribution is recognised now, his work was cut short due to his being sentenced to death in 1874 for a political crime.

modern Japanese legal system.[37] The English Common Law system was considered to be 'far too complicated and diffuse to be understood and incorporated within the short period of time desired by the government' and although English and American scholars were in Japan at this time, their contribution was mainly through teaching and diplomacy.[38] Whilst the French legal tradition was particularly influential in the development of the codes, and the German (Prussian) influence at its greatest in relation to the constitution and court organisation, at the core of all reforming activities were the Japanese scholars.

The various influences of Western law found different institutional homes. First, in 1871 under the auspices of the Ministry of Justice the *Meihoryo* (Bureau for Illuminating the Law) was established for the purpose of drafting legislation. It also provided legal training in French and was given by French jurists, including Boissonade. Eventually this was replaced in 1875 by the Ministry of Justice Law School which continued until 1884 when it came under the Ministry of Education and was known as Tokyo Law School, later to be renamed Tokyo Imperial University.[39] Since it supplied the administrative officials for the Ministry of Justice, it is not surprising that French law played such an important role in the transformation of the Meiji legal system. Although English Law had been taught at the Imperial University since the beginning of the Meiji era, the pre-eminence of French law was to remain with the establishment of the French Law Section in 1885.[40] However, German Law was

---

37 Boissonade was to have the most important influence on the Criminal Codes as well as working on the Civil Code. Bousquet worked on the Civil Code, but his greatest influence was through his work teaching French law at the Ministry of Justice. Roesler was responsible for the Commercial Code, and another German, Hermann Techow, drew up the Code of Civil Procedure. Rudorff, who is incorrectly referred to in Noda, *supra*, n 5, p 54 as Rudolph, was responsible for the court organisation. Their work is often singled out, but there were many others who made important contributions; see Henderson, DF, 'Law and Political Modernisation' in Ward, RE (ed), *Political Development in Modern Japan*, 1968, pp 430–31, Princeton University Press.

38 Lehmann *supra*, n 10, p 254. Noda, *supra*, n 5, p 43 also comments that the Common Law system 'appeared too complicated'. Henderson, DF, 'Law and Political Modernisation' in Ward (ed), *idem*, p 387 at p 433 says that 'the American and English common laws, as well as Japanese customary law, were not in sufficiently coherent form to enable the Japanese to adapt them as solutions to their urgent diplomatic or systemisation problems'. At p 431 he comments on the contribution of Americans, Henry Terry, John Henry Wigmore and Henry Dennison. In addition the American EH House made an important contribution which is assessed in Daniels, G, 'EH House, Japan's American Advocate' (1980) 5 *Proceedings of the British Association for Japanese Studies* 3. The Englishman, Francis Pigott, also made an important contribution in the drafting of the constitution; see Piggot, F, 'The Ito Legend: Personal Recollections of Prince Ito' (1910) 57 *Nineteenth Century and After*. For an assessment of the British contribution to this period; see Daniels, G, 'The Japanese Civil War 1868: A British View' (1967) 1 *Modern Asian Studies* 241; Daniels, G, 'The British Role in the Meiji Restoration: A Re interpretative Note' (1968) 2 *Modern Asian Studies* 291. For an account of British diplomatic life see the memoirs of Sir Ernest Satow, *supra*, n 33.

39 See Chapter 5. The development of the law schools and the complex change in names between the universities is explained by Toshitani, N and Mukai, K, 'The Progress and Problems of Compiling the Civil Code in the Early Meiji Era' (1967) 1 *Law in Japan* 25, n 27. See also Hattori, T, 'The Legal Profession in Japan: Its Historical Development and Present State', in von Mehren (ed), *supra*, n 22, p 111, n 8 and n 127.

40 Noda, *supra*, n 5, p 48, n 14.

to play an increasingly important role in Japanese legal development with the setting up of the German Law Department at the Imperial University in 1887 and the start of translation of German works around the same time.[41] It was against this background that the leading Japanese scholars embarked upon creating the new legal order.[42]

First came the Criminal Code and the Code of Criminal Instruction of 1880.[43] Although Boissonade was central to their compilation, they were not simply 'adopted' without discussion or revision. Indeed, although the Imperial Diet under the Meiji Constitution did not yet exist, in line with the modernisation of the new era, in 1875 a council of elders, or senate (*Genro-in*) was established to 'enact laws for the Emperor'.[44] Abolished in 1890, without becoming a legislature in the modern, democratic sense, it nevertheless had significance as a forum for discussion even though the government could pass a law without such discussion.[45]

Both codes were brought into effect on 1 January 1882, by which time Boissonade had started work on a Civil Code.[46] However, there was little controversy or difficulty in their being accepted. On the one hand, for the government and rulers, they represented a return to the *ritsuryo* antecedents of ancient Imperial Japan, whilst on the other, there was no popular debate or dissent since the Japanese people 'had no knowledge of the principle of legality in crime and punishment until the codes drawn up by Boissonade were promulgated'.[47] The introduction of these two criminal codes was a pivotal point in the transformation from a feudal legal system to the modern, code based order. Since the process of codification involved a transplantation of ideas and values from alien legal cultures and traditions, it cannot be described as either a natural process, or part of an organic growth. Instead, it marks the end

41 *Idem,* p 50, n 19. See also Rabinowitz, R, 'Law and the Social Process in Japan' (1968) 10 *Transactions of the Asiatic Society of Japan* 11, in which the author focuses on the difficulties of adopting alien principles through an analysis of the 'dispute' surrounding the Civil Code. In doing this he touches upon the conflicting schools of thought and tradition between, in particular, the French and German, as illustrated by the debate which took place in the Law Scholars Society.

42 Under the influence of the second Minister of Justice appointed in 1873, Takato Oki, Boissonade started his work on the Criminal Code. Noda, *supra,* n 5, p 45. However, it was in relation to the Civil Code and the constitution that the Japanese had the greatest profile. Hirobumi Ito is referred to as the author, or 'chief architect' of the Meiji Constitution of 1889; see Akita, G, *Foundations of Constitutional Government in Modern Japan,* 1967, p 1, Harvard University Press. The influence of Kowashi Inoue, particularly as an advocate of the so-called 'Prussian-school', was important prior to the arrival of Roesler in 1878, as was the work of Miyoji Ito and Kentaro Kaneko. Thus Akita, *idem,* at p 63 concludes that 'the constitution was essentially drafted by five men – four Japanese and one foreigner'. In relation to the Civil Code the contribution of Nobushige Hozumi, Kenjiro Ume and Masaaki Tomii stood out. See Ishii, *supra,* n 3, p 118.

43 Great Council of State Decrees No 36 and No 37 of 1880.

44 Hackett, R 'Political Modernisation and the Meiji *Genro*' in Ward (ed), *supra,* n 35, p 65 at p 68.

45 Noda, *supra,* n 5, p 45, n 7.

46 Noda, *supra,* n 5, p 45; Takayanagi, *supra,* n 31, p 5, p 19.

47 Ishii, *supra,* n 3, p 92; Noda, *supra,* n 5, p 46. For comparison see Hiramatsu, Y, 'Summary of Tokugawa Criminal Justice' (1989) 22 *Law in Japan* 105.

of one particular era of transformation which was relatively smooth, as compared with the challenges and demands of introducing the Constitution and the Civil Codes.[48]

Described as 'epoch-making', the 1880 Criminal Code was certainly enduring and operated for 25 years before it was revised.[49] During that time German legal science came to the fore and was to influence Japanese legal thinking in a fundamental way. Boissonade's adaptation of what was, by comparison, the relatively liberal Napoleonic Code was replaced in 1907 by a German inspired revision which was more authoritarian in style.[50] The 1880 Criminal Code introduced the inquisitorial system which was common to much of Western Europe as well as the concept of personal, as opposed to collective, guilt.[51] Furthermore, it adopted the French classification of offences as *'crime' 'délit'* and *'contravention'*, but, most important of all, it introduced the principle of *nullum crimen, nulla poena sine lege* (no crime, no punishment without law). This left little room for judicial discretion, but allowed for certainty and justice, in line with its guiding French jurisprudential antecedents.[52] In contrast, the 1907 Criminal Code did away with the classification of offences but, most significantly, abolished the principle of *nullum crimen* thereby allowing for subjective judicial discretion.[53] Following the Occupation it has undergone some minor revision; for example, an amendment of the chapter on crimes against the Imperial family so as to take account of the principle of equality before the law and the new status of the Emperor. In the 1950s the Ministry of Justice started work on a wholesale revision of the Criminal Code with the Legislative Advisory Committee eventually recommending it be completely

48 Ishii, *idem*, Chapter 5 argues that the Modern period (1858–1945) can be divided into three phases, the beginning phase (1858–81), the middle phase (1881–1931) and the final phase (1931–1945). Henderson, *supra*, n 26, p 419 states that these two codes 'became a great watershed in Japanese law, marking the end of massive Chinese influence in Japanese law'.

49 Lehmann comments, *supra*, n 10, p 256 that whilst the Criminal Code 'met with significant approval both in Japan and indeed abroad for its progressive character, it should not be forgotten that the government simultaneously retained an impressive array of extra-judicial powers which enabled it to promulgate a whole series of ordinances for specific purposes, covering such matters as public meetings, the press, censorship, libel and so on'. For a list of these special regulations see Henderson, *idem*, p 419, who also notes that under the Peace Preservation 'law' 600 political figures were banished from Tokyo on 26 December 1887. This demonstrates the authoritarian control of dissenters or democrats and was used with even greater force during the 1920s in accordance with the Peace Preservation Law 1925. See Ito, M, 'The Rule of Law: Constitutional Development' in von Mehren (ed), *supra*, n 22, p 205 at p 222, n 50 and Hirano, R, 'The Accused and Society: Some Aspects of Japanese Criminal Law' in von Mehren, *idem*, p 276 at p 293.

50 Law No 45 of 1907.

51 Boissonade's original draft had provided for a jury, but this was deleted by the Japanese. Takayanagi, *supra*, n 31, p 21. A Jury Law was promulgated in 1923 and came into effect in 1928, only to be suspended in 1943. On this and the modern debate on the jury see Dean, M, 'Trial by Jury: A Force for Change in Japan' (1995) *International and Comparative Law Quarterly* 379.

52 Takayanagi, *supra*, n 31, p 15.

53 Takayanagi, *idem*, p 18 notes the debate concerning this omission and in particular the fact that some viewed its inclusion as unnecessary since Article 23 of the Meiji Constitution provided that 'no Japanese subject shall be arrested, detained, tried, or punished, unless according to law'.

amended. However, the draft revised code was the subject of severe criticism by academics and lawyers alike with the result that the 1907 Criminal Code remains substantially unchanged to this day.[54] The Code of Criminal Instruction was revised in 1922 to become the Code of Criminal Procedure, albeit retaining the German influence. It was revised once more under the American Occupation in 1948, thereby giving it Anglo-American adversarial characteristics and resulting in a system which is described as 'semi-inquisitorial'.[55] Thus, the modern criminal justice system is a rather unusual mixture of the Western civil law tradition, combined with an Anglo-American common law influence.[56]

The introduction of the Civil Code and the Code of Civil Procedure was to prove more complicated and controversial leading to what became known as the Codification Disputes which led to the postponement of implementation of the Civil and Commercial Codes. Boissonade had started work on drafting a civil code in 1879, but in this area of law the wholesale transplantation and adoption of a Western code proved particularly problematic.[57] First, there was a need to take account of Japanese custom and tradition which had developed through the Tokugawa era and the early Meiji years with the result that a foreign code could not simply be transplanted and the indigenous system overlaid with an alien set of rules. Second, from 1886 onwards, as a prerequisite to revision of the unequal treaties, there was pressure on the Japanese to produce a codified system which was acceptable to the foreign powers.[58] Boissonade had been working on a draft civil code since 1879, but his work was subject to revision and redrafting by the Civil Code Drafting Bureau which was set up in 1880. However, as a result of the pressure to renegotiate the treaties, the adoption of a civil code became associated with foreign policy objectives and was placed under the control of the Law Investigation Committee of the Ministry of Justice.[59] The French inspired Civil Code was ready for

---

54 Meyers, H, 'Revisions of the Criminal Code of Japan During the Occupation' (1950) 25 *Washington Law Review* 104 (also published in 1977 (Special Edition) *Washington Law Review* p 66). On the revision debate see Hirano, R, 'The Draft of the Revised Penal Code: A General Critique' (1973) 6 *Law in Japan* 49. Amendments to the Code have taken place from time to time, eg on computer fraud in 1987. However, in 1990, the Ministry of Justice started a programme of revision, its main aim being to modify the style and writing of the earlier Code. A revised Criminal Code was introduced in 1995. See Criminal Code of Japan (1996) EHS Law Bulletin Series, promulgated on 12 May 1995, implemented on 1 June 1995.

55 Takayanagi, *supra*, n 31, p 23; Hirano, *supra*, n 49, p 274. On the American Occupation revision, see Oppler, AC, *Legal Reforms in Occupied Japan: A Participant Looks Back*, 1976, Chapter 9 and 10, Princeton University Press. For a detailed account of the process, see Appleton, R, 'Reforms in Japanese Criminal Procedure under Allied Occupation' (1949) 24 *Washington Law Review* 401 (also published in 1977 (Special Edition) *Washington Law Review* p 36.

56 In general see: Dando, S, *Japanese Criminal Procedure*, 1965, Rothman & Co; Castberg, AD, *Japanese Criminal Justice*, 1990, Praeger; Hirano, R, 'Diagnosis of the Current Code of Criminal Procedure' (1989) 22 *Law in Japan* 129; Kim, C, *Selected Writings on Comparative and Private International Law*, 1995, Chapter 7, 'The Criminal Trial in Japan', Rothman & Co.

57 Rinsho Mitzukuri had already translated the French Civil Code by 1875 and Boissonade's brief was to redraft, taking into account a wider range of factors.

58 Rabinowitz, *infra*, n 62.

59 Jansen, M, 'Modernisation and Foreign Policy in Meiji Japan' in Ward, RE (ed), *Political Development in Modern Japan*, 1968, Princeton University Press.

promulgation by 1890, to take effect on 1 January 1893.[60] However, the first signs of open discord among the various factions emerged with the publication of a paper in a legal journal demanding an open debate on the code.[61] This was the start of the Code Dispute which in turn led to the postponement controversy and had two main strands of debate.[62] First, there was an ideological struggle between the French, German and English schools of law as represented by the three main Japanese protagonists in the drafting process, together with the Ministry of Justice and university faculties.[63] Second, there was the strongly held belief which had stimulated the debate on the 1890 draft that it was an attack on established Japanese social structures which, in particular, threatened the traditional family and status relationships which were the root of all private law matters; moreover it represented an assault on the Emperor system itself.[64] In the event, the supporters of postponement won the day and a bill delaying implementation of the 1890 code until 1896 was passed in the Diet.[65]

A Codification Committee was set up in 1893, chaired by the Prime Minister and consisting of six members who represented the postponement faction and six from the implementation faction. In the event Hozumi, Tomii and Ume emerged as the leading protagonists and drafters of the new Code, the former two having been in favour of postponement and the latter enforcement. Working separately and then submitting their work to the committee, they produced a new draft Civil Code which came into operation on 16 July 1898. Unlike the 'old' code which had its origins in the French Civil Code, the 1898 Civil Code was heavily influenced by the German Civil Code and perhaps more importantly, paid due regard to traditional customs and family structures.[66]

60 Takayanagi, *supra,* n 31, p 27.

61 Rabinowitz, *infra,* n 62; Lehmann, *supra,* n 10, p 257.

62 For a comprehensive account of the Civil Code postponement controversy see: Rabinowitz, RW, 'Law and the Social Process in Japan' (1968) 10 *Transactions of the Asiatic Society of Japan* 11; Mukai, K and Toshitani, N, 'The Progress and Problems of Compiling the Civil Code in the Early Meiji Era' (1967) 1 *Law in Japan* 25, also Kitagawa, Z, 'Theory Reception – One Aspect of the Development of Japanese Civil Law Science' (1970) 4 *Law in Japan* 1. See also Haley, JO, *Authority Without Power*, 1991, pp 75–77, Oxford University Press.

63 The three leading Japanese scholars who contributed to the Civil Code, *supra,* n 42 came from diverse educational backgrounds. Hozumi had studied in Berlin and qualified as a barrister in England; Tomii was educated in France and Ume studied in Lyon and Berlin. On the rivalries of these protagonists of the postponement movement, see Takayanagi, *supra,* n 31, p 30.

64 The importance of the family went beyond the social structures and was a symbol of power in a more general and important sense. As Lehmann observes, *supra,* n 10, p 258: 'The family, in legal terms, was an autocratic, hierarchically structured unit. The power of the head of the household, was virtually absolute over both his children and his wife. In this respect the family represented the microcosm of what the oligarchy desired should be the total nature of the Japanese state. The power of the head was a reflection of the power that the *tenno* should exercise over his children, namely the subjects of the Japanese Empire.'

65 Takayanagi, *supra,* n 31.

66 The complexities and importance of the (family) system are explained in Fukutake, T, *The Japanese Social Structure*, 1989, Chapter 3, University of Tokyo Press and Hendry, J, *Understanding Japanese Society*, 2nd edn, 1995, Chapter 2, Routledge. See also Mukai and Toshitani, *supra,* n 62, p 43.

Although minor revisions have taken place and the chapters on family and inheritance law underwent a major revision in 1947, the essential structure and content of the Civil Code today is that which came in to effect on 16 July 1898.[67]

Meanwhile, the Commercial Code which had been drafted by Hermann Roesler and promulgated on 27 April 1890 was similarly engulfed by the code controversy.[68] Unlike the 1890 Civil Code, parts of this Commercial Code were put into effect, but in the main it was subjected to the revision and redrafting process of the Codification Committee.[69] It was finally completed and promulgated in 1899 and came into effect on 16 June that year. Originally consisting of five books, major economic and industrial advancement necessitated frequent revision, with the result that the current code now consists of four books.[70]

Against this background of controversy it might be reasonable to suppose that the Code of Civil Procedure was beset by a similar fate: it was not. Instead, although there had been French inspired laws on civil procedure during the early Meiji period, in line with the increasing influence of German legal thinking during the 1880s, the German, Hermann Techow, was invited to draft a Code of Civil procedure.[71] In 1877 a new German Code of Civil Procedure had been introduced and Techow, who started work in 1884, not surprisingly based his draft on that formula. Promulgated in 1890, it proved to be the least controversial code at the time, escaping the postponement debate and coming into effect on 1 January 1891. In so doing, it created one of the ironies of Japanese legal history in that the procedural code was in place before the code containing the substantive provisions. Not unnaturally, therefore, it did not accord with the new Civil Code of 1898 and consequently underwent a major revision in 1926. When it was further amended under the Occupation, the essentially German character of the code remained but, as with the Code of Criminal Procedure, important elements of the Anglo-American adversarial trial system were introduced.[72]

---

67 On the general structure of the code see Noda, *supra*, n 5, p 197. Oppler, *supra*, n 55, p 111 comments that 'The objectives of the Occupation did not call for a change in the first three books of the Civil Code, namely General Provisions, Real Property and Obligations ... It was only in the fields of family and inheritance law covered by the fourth and fifth books that fundamental changes were required to have constitutional principles such as dignity of the individual, equality of the sexes, free choice of marriage partner and freedom of movement implemented.'

68 Noda, *supra*, n 5, p 53 comments that whilst Roesler was German, his draft was based principally on the French Commercial Code. In contrast, Takayanagi, *supra*, n 31, p 31 states that 'Roesler's draft was eclectic and not exclusively French, since German and English law were also taken into account'.

69 The three Japanese scholars whose work on the redrafting of the Commercial Code stands out, are Kenjiro Ume, Keijiro Okano and Kaoru Tabe. Takayanagi, *idem*, p 32.

70 The original Book 4 deal with bills of exchange and cheques, which due to the requirements of international convention was removed and dealt with by specific statutes. See Noda, *idem*, p 202; Takayanagi, *idem*, p 32.

71 On the early Meiji French influence on civil procedure, see Noda, *supra*, n 5, p 54.

72 Noda, *idem*, p 204.

It had been a major policy objective of the Meiji government to renegotiate the unequal treaties, but adoption of legal codes had become a pre-condition set by the foreign powers for that to happen.[73] At this time, foreign policy in general was problematic and on treaty revision the Japanese were no less divided on how best to deal with the matter.[74] There were those who took a conservative view and argued that to revise Japanese law to accord with Western demands was an affront to national dignity and independence. On the other side, there were those who took a pragmatic approach and argued that the trading and economic advantages accruing to Japan as a result of treaty revision would far outweigh any loss of national pride.[75] Indeed, the political climate during the 1880s was extremely volatile; not only was the government divided on this and other issues, but there was strong public opposition to some of the plans for revision.[76] This eventually resulted in a bomb attack on Foreign Minister Okuma in 1889 and led to the temporary cessation of negotiations.[77] However, by this time the precondition on the introduction of legal codes had all but been met. Although the postponement controversy had delayed implementation of some of the codes, in effect the five main codes had been drafted and were in place by 1890. Although the Government was still engaged in a struggle over foreign policy matters, both with the opposition and public opinion, in 1893 Foreign Minister Mutsu reopened negotiations in London on treaty revision.[78] In July 1894 a treaty was signed with Britain which effectively abolished the unequal clauses. It provided for the ending of extraterritoriality once the Civil Code was introduced, although this did not happen until 1899. It gave foreign merchants access to the whole of Japan (not just the treaty ports) and instituted a new tariff agreement. Similar revision treaties were entered into with other countries, although none came into effect until 1899.

Although the codes were fundamental to the modernisation of Meiji Japan, so too was the introduction of a constitution. However, whereas the codes have lived on in amended form into the 20th century, the Meiji Constitution of 1889 was replaced by the 1946 Constitution.[79] Its development and introduction was no less significant as marking the change from feudal rule by right and might,

73 Rabinowitz, *supra*, n 62, n 32.

74 On the difficulty over foreign policy and on the treaties in particular, see Jansen, *supra*, n 59.

75 Nish, I, *Japanese Foreign Policy 1869–1942*, 1977, Routledge; Akita, G, *Foundations of Constitutional Government in Modern Japan 1868–1900*, 1967, Harvard University Press.

76 On the political background at the time, see Beasley, WG, *The Rise of Modern Japan: Political, Economic and Social Change Since 1850*, 2nd edn, 1995, Weidenfeld and Nicolson.

77 Popular dissatisfaction had been fuelled by a Japanese Press translation of a report in *The Times* concerning the negotiations which were being conducted in various Western capitals. The bomb was thrown by a nationalist and although Okuma survived, he lost a leg. Storry, *supra*, n 1, p 125. Akita, *supra*, n 75, p 64 comments that there was 'vigorous public opposition to Inoue's and Okuma's treaty revision attempts in the years 1887–1889' but that 'the failure to revise the treaties can be explained as much by looking at the conflicts within the government as by focusing on external pressure'.

78 Akita, *supra*, n 75, pp 113–17.

79 Article 73 of the Meiji Constitution provided for future amendment, as a result of which there has been some considerable debate as to whether the 1946 Constitution is a new constitution which replaced the Meiji Constitution, or whether it was an amendment. See Chapter 7, n 13.

to constitutional monarchy. In the same way that there was a significant Western influence on the codes, this was also true of the Meiji Constitution. The difference was that whereas with the codes the Westerners were very often the authors, in the case of the constitution this was not so and the Western influence came, in the main, through the research and scholarship of the Japanese.

The Meiji Constitution was essentially drafted by four Japanese – Kowashi Inoue, Miyojo Ito, Kentaro Kaneko, and led by the man who became the first Prime Minister, Hirobumi Ito.[80] He had earlier travelled to Europe and studied the Prussian and Austrian constitutions. The teachings of Rudolf von Gneist, Albert Mosse and Lorenz von Stein were particularly influential on his thinking.[81] However, during the actual drafting process one Westerner, Hermann Roesler, had a significant input. In fact it was he, together with Kowashi Inoue, who mainly drafted the constitution.[82] Even so, the Meiji Constitution 'bore Ito's unmistakable imprint' and it was he who defended the draft from a series of attacks from within the Government and steered the constitution to promulgation on 11 February 1889.[83] Titled 'The Constitution of the Empire of Japan', it came into effect on 29 November 1990 and consisted of a mere 76 articles (the 1946 Constitution has 103 articles).

Although, with the benefit of hindsight, it is easy to criticise the Meiji Constitution as conservative, essentially undemocratic and mere window dressing, it was a remarkable, even revolutionary, document.[84] In a quantum leap forward, it achieved the aim of moving the country from a feudal state to one of constitutional monarchism. At the same time it preserved a balance between tradition, as symbolised by the Emperor's divine right to rule, and

80 Akita, *supra*, n 75, p 63. Ito was appointed head of the Imperial Household Ministry in March 1884 and because he was the leading councillor he was effectively the 'prime minister' although he is not formally acknowledged as having become Prime Minister until 22 December 1885. Another senior government official Tomomi Iwakura had been sent to Europe to study various constitutions and on his return drew up a set of principles together with a commentary supporting a Prussian style monarchical constitution. It was on his recommendation that Ito studied with Gneist, Mosse and Stein. Ishii, *supra*, n 3, p 113.

81 Described as 'a pilgrimage to the fountainhead of constitutionalism' Akita, *supra*, n 75, p 61, Ito acknowledged the importance of these scholars when he wrote to a colleague: 'Thanks to the famous German scholars Gneist and Stein, I have come to understand the essential features of the structure and operation of states. In the most crucial matter of fixing the foundations of our imperial system and of retaining the prerogatives belonging to it, I have already found sufficient substantiation.' Cited *idem*.

82 One Japanese writer, Osatake, made the following assessment of their work: 'Inoue sounded out Roesler's views on every conceivable matter. It would thus not be an exaggeration to say that our constitution was really drafted with Inoue listening in one ear to Roesler.' Cited in Akita, *idem*, p 63, n 38.

83 Akita, *idem*, p 65.

84 Noda, *supra*, n 5, p 57 cites a leading Japanese historian as concluding that 'what was assured by the Constitution was ... only apparent constitutionalism'. See also Takayanagi, *supra*, n 31, p 6 who notes that 'it is now the fashion of the day to criticise severely this constitutional document' but that 'in view of the practical problems that the statesmen of the Meiji era had to tackle, it is at least debatable whether Japan was not wise in taking a conservative course rather than the progressive or radical line advocated by many Japanese politicians at the time'. In general see Pyle, K, 'Meiji Conservatism' in *The Cambridge History of Japan*, Vol 5, 1989, p 674.

modernity, as represented by the new structures of government.[85] Central to the document was the fact that sovereignty rested with the Emperor and all else flowed from that. It was therefore inevitable that the powers of the Diet (parliament) were very limited. Legislative power was exercised by the Emperor. The courts and judiciary, under the control of the Ministry of Justice, were merely a branch of the executive, the supremacy of which was guaranteed in the constitution. Whilst it was clearly authoritarian and absolutist in origin and ideology, the Meiji Constitution was the start of an evolutionary process of modernisation and democratisation. As one writer has concluded:

> the Meiji Constitution provided a very substantial degree of political innovation and at the same time installed a type of government calculated to maximise national unity, stability, and strong political leadership. These are very impressive accomplishments in the annals of political development that should not be discounted lightly.[86]

As we know, the Meiji Constitution did not prevent the rise of nationalism, the destruction of constitutional monarchical government and war.[87] Although there was a period of liberalisation and the development of a democratic political movement during the Taisho period (1912–26), the forces of nationalism and militarism prevailed. By 1930 Japan was on the path which would lead to war, defeat, surrender and occupation, although ultimately a new democratic legal order would emerge. The rise of militarism is reflected in the fact that between May 1932 and August 1945 eight out of the 11 heads of government were drawn from the armed forces.[88] In 1938 the National Mobilisation Law removed even symbolic power from the Diet and the dissolution of political parties in 1940 was the final act in handing complete authority to the military.[89] Only with the surrender of Japan in 1945 at the end of the Pacific War was the legal vacuum brought to an end.

85 Ward, RE, 'Epilogue' in Ward (ed), *supra*, n 35, p 587 comments that the system established under the Meiji Constitution was 'remarkably well adjusted to both the political capacities and needs of modernising Japan' and that 'it was probably superior in modernising efficiency to any practicable alternative at the time'. See also Beasley, WG, 'Meiji Political Institutions' in *The Cambridge History of Japan*, Vol 5, 1989, p 618.

86 *Idem*.

87 For general background, see Iriye, A, 'Japan's Drive to Great-Power Status' in *The Cambridge History of Japan*, Vol 5, 1989, p 721. Also see Beasley, WG, 'The Edo Experience and Japanese Nationalism' (1984) 18 *Modern Asian Studies* 555 which traces the early origins of nationalism and concludes at p 565 that by the end of the Tokugawa period the 'principle ingredients of Japanese nationalism had been brought together, though the Meiji era was to see them more fully integrated and developed'.

88 There were four admirals and four generals: Admiral Saito (1932–34), Admiral Okada (1934–36), General Hayashi (1937), General Abe (1939–40), Admiral Tonai (1940), General Tojo (1940–44), General Koiso (1944–45) and Admiral Suzuki (1945). The three civilians who served in-between the military consisted of two former bureaucrats, Hirota (1936–37) and Hiranuma (1939) and a court nobleman, Konoe, who served twice (1937–39 and 1940–41).

89 On the National Mobilisation Law and dissolution of political parties, see Ishii, *supra*, n 3, pp 123–26; for general background to this period, see Beasley, 1995, *supra*, n 1, Chapter 11.

The Allied Occupation of Japan was from 1945–52 and has been described as 'an experiment in directed political change'.[90] Central to its success was the new constitution which was promulgated on 3 November 1946 and came into effect on 3 May 1947. The background to this 'new' constitution is considered later in Chapter 4 and Chapter 7. However, equally important was the programme of legal reform undertaken by the Courts and Law Division of the Government Section and later, the Legislation and Justice Division of the Legal Section, Supreme Commander for the Allied Powers (SCAP).[91] Though there were many contributors, the person who played the most prominent and significant role in legal and judicial reform at this time was Alfred Oppler.[92] A refugee from Nazi Germany who had held various positions in the Prussian judiciary, Oppler arrived in America in 1939, and by 1944 had joined the Federal Government service from where he was posted to the Government Section of general MacArthur's Tokyo Headquarters.[93] Unlike the other members of the Government Section of SCAP, he did not come from the Anglo-American Common Law tradition and as head of the Courts and Law Division, his familiarity with the civilian tradition that had shaped the laws and constitution of Meiji Japan was particularly useful.[94] Moreover, his vision of the Occupation staff as 'mentors' and 'midwives' encouraging rather than imposing the reform

90 Steiner, K, 'Forward' p vii in Oppler, *supra,* n 55. See also Williams, J, *Japan's Political Revolution Under MacArthur: A Participant's Account,* 1979, University of Georgia Press; Ward, RE, 'Reflections on the Allied Occupation and Planned Political Change' in Ward (ed), *supra,* n 35.

91 The abbreviation SCAP is used to indicate both the person of General MacArthur and, more often, as shorthand for the Headquarters of the Occupation forces. SCAP Headquarters was divided into 13 sections, the most important of which, for reform of the legal and political system, were the Government Section and the Legal Section. See Oppler, *idem.*

92 Many of those who took part in the reform process published contemporaneous accounts of their work: Blakemore, TL, 'Post-war Developments in Japanese Law' (1947) *Wisconsin Law Review* 623; Appleton, RB, 'Reforms in Japanese Criminal Procedure under Allied Occupation' (1949) 24 *Washington Law Review* 401; Oppler, AC, 'The Reform of Japan's Legal and Judicial System Under Allied Occupation' (1949) 24 *Washington Law Review* 290; Meyers, H, 'Revisions of the Criminal Code of Japan During the Occupation' (1950) 25 *Washington Law Review* 104; Steiner, K, 'Post-war Changes in the Japanese Civil Code' (1950) 25 *Washington Law Review* 286; Steiner, K, 'The Revision of the Civil Code of Japan: Provisions Affecting the Family' (1950) 9 *Far Eastern Quarterly* 169; Wagatsuma, S, 'Democratisation of the Family Relation in Japan' (1950) 25 *Washington Law Review* 405; Wagatsuma, S, 'Guarantee of Fundamental Human Rights under the Japanese Constitution' (1951) 26 *Washington Law Review* 145. (The contributions in the *Washington Law Review* have been reprinted in a Special Edition of the journal published in 1977.)

93 Oppler was born in 1893 in (German) Alsace-Lorraine and went on to study law at the universities of Munich, Freiburg, Berlin and Strasbourg. After army service in the First World War he moved to Berlin and joined the German judiciary, rising to become associate judge of the Supreme Administrative Court and vice-president of the Supreme Disciplinary Court. The fact that he was Jewish meant that with the rise of Hitler he was deprived of his job and citizenship and forced to flee to America.

94 Oppler was eventually joined by the Austrian jurist, Kurt Steiner. The other significant person in the Courts and Law Division was Thomas Blakemore who was an American lawyer, but the only one who had command of the written and spoken Japanese language and had studied the Japanese legal system. See Chapter 5, n 70.

and birth of a new legal order, was to be influential in preventing the wholesale 'Americanisation' of Japanese law.[95]

The enduring nature of the reforms which Oppler and his colleagues supervised, is testimony to their insight and skill in bringing together American constitutional principles and Western European-derived institutions and legal concepts.[96] However, it would be wrong to explain the Japanese legal system solely in terms of developments since 1945. Whilst the current legal system quite clearly has a strong American content it has to be contextualised as part of a process of continuing development. Over at least nine millennium there has been a teleological evolution creating a fundamental core. At various times this has been subjected to 'foreign law' transplants, namely Chinese, Western European and American. Their reception and consequent adaptation mean that any attempt to categorise the system as civilian, hybrid, or even 'unique' is ultimately self defeating.[97] Furthermore, it would be wrong to see the Japanese legal system merely as the sum of its historical parts. Instead one must accept the whole in its historical context and acknowledge that the answer is probably as elusive as it is unnecessary.

Noda, Y, *Introduction to Japanese Law*, 1976, pp 20–38, University of Tokyo Press

FIRST ERA: EARLY SOCIETY

From the third to the fourth centuries the social life of Japan came under strong religious influence. Law at that stage was not distinguished from other social rules, and in particular was not distinguished from religious rules. According to the *San-kuo Chih*, Himiko was considered a pontiff and governed the cult of ancestors. Traditional Japanese religion considers ancestors as gods; hence Himiko served the gods and the foundation of her political power was religious. Through prayer she knew the will of the ancestor gods and pronounced oracles which were law. As evidence of this, the old Japanese words describing political matters are very closely linked to religion. For example, 'to govern' was *shiroshimesu* or *shirasu*. Both these words mean 'to know' (*shiru*), and the main object of politics consisted in knowing the will of the gods. Politics in Japanese is *matsurigoto*, which means religious cult; law is called *nori* and *noru*, the verbal form of *nori*, means 'to declare.' Thus, law was the will of the gods as declared by

95 His views are well summarised in a memorandum he sent pointing out the enormity of the task of implementing the principles of the new constitution, which stated *inter alia* that certain legal reforms: 'desirable though they might appear to the Western mind, should not be imposed by SCAP ... We should promote gradual development toward long-range objectives by inspiration and advice rather than by pressure ... Although we may be inclined to consider the Anglo-Saxon legal system superior to the Continental, we should resist any temptation to replace hastily one by the other. The Japanese would not be able to work an artificially imposed system which differed fundamentally from what they have practised up to the present time.' *supra*, n 55, p 83.

96 Oppler comments on his task and this fusion thus: 'A constitution is only a blueprint of pious principles and will remain ineffective as long as these are not implemented in the law of the land; ... and even the most progressive laws are of no avail unless they are willingly respected, vigorously enforced, and become an ingredient of the social fabric.' *idem*, p 65.

97 Pierre Legrand argues that 'the focus on categories and rules will produce a persistent miscognition of the experiences of legal order under scrutiny' 'Comparative Legal Studies and Commitment to Theory' (1995) 58 *Modern Law Review* 272.

the person interceding between the gods and the people. The person interceding was almost always a woman, and it could even be said that in this first era the 'woman-king' was the rule rather than the exception. The fact that the most important divinity in Shinto is the goddess Amaterasu strengthens this opinion. It is interesting to note, however, that Himiko did not herself execute the will of the gods, although she declared it. It was her brother who undertook the execution of the divine will. Himiko therefore reigned but did not govern. This fundamental principle was observed for a long time with only a few exceptions.

The governmental institutions of the era were not influenced in any way by foreign civilization and in them is reflected the manner of thinking that is peculiar to the Japanese people. For example, the old-time Japanese considered delicts as blemishes or blots that the gods detested but that could be cleansed by religious ceremonial. Condemned persons had to present offerings to the gods. The priest said prayers for purification, and sometimes there was a washing of the bodies of condemned persons. Delicts came under the notion of *tsumi,* which dealt at the same time with illness and plagues. People's manner of thought was non-rigorous and simple, and they were by nature optimists. The *San-kuo Chih* shows us that Japanese morals were very strong and that there were few crimes or trials.

SECOND ERA: THE REGIME OF RITSU-RYO

During the preceding era the imperial power had become more and more laicized and was continually being threatened with overthrow by the powerful clans. Partisans of the imperial family sought to stabilize the situation by concentrating all state powers in the government of the emperor. This method was also necessitated by the external political situation. There was a highly centralized government in China, and in order to defend itself against possible invasion the national cohesion of Japan became a matter of great importance. By the beginning of the seventh century, Japan had a state organization of a centralized type along the lines of the Chinese model. The task of centralization was a difficult one because the powerful clans resisted it, but from the Taika Reform of 646, the basis of the imperial government was gradually strengthened, and a strongly centralized and bureaucratic state emerged. The emperor governed personally, following the model of the despotic Chinese emperor, and all the Chinese political institutions were transplanted to Japanese soil.

Similarly, in the field of law several codes drawn up on the model of the Chinese ones were promulgated and put into practice. This legal system is called the system of *ritsu-ryo* because the codes were made up of two parts, the *ritsu* and the *ryo. Ritsu* is a body of penal rules and ryo a body of admonitory rules. The laws had a strong moral character, closely linked to the Confucian doctrine according to which the *ritsu-ryo* had as its mission either the encouraging of people to do good or the punishing of them for doing wrong. The aim of the laws was to educate ignorant men and lead them toward the Confucian ideal. Since the education of the people was under the control of public officials, rules of administrative law occupied a very important place in the system of *ritsu-ryo*. The criminal laws that made up the *ritsu* were also important, but there were few rules of civil law.

During this era several *ritsu-ryo* codes were promulgated and all fairly faithfully imitated the codes of T'ang, the powerful Chinese dynasty of the time. The language used in these Japanese codes was Chinese, with the result that it is difficult for present-day jurists who have no special knowledge of the history of Japanese law to understand them. The *ritsu* is a replica of the Chinese ritsu except that the punishments described were mitigated in the Japanese code. The *ryo* on the other hand is very much simplified, for account was taken of the customs and social conditions peculiar to Japan. Of these codes that known as the *Taiho Ritsu-ryo*, promulgated in the first year of the Taiho era (701), is the most famous, but regrettably it is no longer extant. The one of which the greatest part is still extant is the *Yoro Ritsu-ryo*. It was promulgated in the second year of Yoro (718) and came into force thirty-nine years later. In this code the *ritsu* is divided into twelve books and the *ryo* into thirty. The code was amended and complemented by particularized laws (*kyaku*), and rules (*shiki*) were promulgated to facilitate its application.

Since the aim of the codes was the education of the people, it was necessary that they be made known, and so a faculty of law known as *myo-bo-do* was set up in the *daigaku* under the control of the Ministry of *Shikibu* (the ministry with responsibility for the examination and education of public officials). The *daigaku* had about 400 students and was the national administrative college set up to educate state functionaries. Apart from it there were provincial schools called *kokugaku*, which had the same aim. It is said that legal knowledge was very much respected throughout this era, a phenomenon exceptional in Japanese history. Studies on the *ritsu-ryo* were carried out with great zeal and many commentaries were published. Among them are two important books that are still extant: *Ryo-no-gige* (Commentary on the *Ryo*) and *Ryo-no-shuge* (Collection of Theories on the *Ryo*). The first is an official commentary on the *Yoro Ryo*. It was drawn up by twelve scholars and published with the force of law in 833. The second is a private collection of doctrinal writings on the *ryo* drawn up about the beginning of the tenth century by Koremune Naomoto, a doctor of *myo-bo*, and is said to contain a comparative study of the Japanese and Chinese codes.

The system of *ritsu-ryo* did not stay in favor for long. The cultural milieu of Japan differed considerably from that of China, which made it difficult for the laws to be assimilated. Most of the provisions soon fell into disuse, and around the legislative texts more and more usages of an administrative or judicial nature developed, with the result that the basic text soon became obscure or was forgotten. Though the *ritsu* admitted capital punishment, there is no case of an execution in the three and a half centuries between 810 and 1156. However it must not be forgotten that these laws were never formally abrogated and some of them were even applied after the 1868 Restoration.

By means of the *ritsu-ryo* system the imperial government succeeded in concentrating all state powers in its hands. The political powers of the big clans were closely related to the ownership of land, and these powers they lost to the imperial government. The legal and political position of the emperor came very close to that of the Chinese *tenshi*, who was a despotic monarch. In order to imbue his powers with religious authority the cult of the emperor was invented. He was held to be a living god (*aki-sukami*). At the beginning of the Taika Reform, the emperor proclaimed, in accordance with the Confucian ideal, that all land and all persons were in direct submission to imperial authority. Public offices and land were from that time distributed by the imperial government according to the rules of the *ritsu-ryo*. A certain amount of land, as determined by a law which distinguished several categories of persons, was given for life to every person of six or more years of age. This was an agrarian system with socialistic tendencies, but the main aim was to assure the state of its taxes. As far as public offices were concerned they appear to have been open to everyone, but in practice those who were given high offices belonged almost exclusively to the noble class.

The Confucian ideal was quickly neglected. In the ninth century a definite tendency toward appropriation of public offices and land can be seen. The estates obtained by means of usurpation, hoarding, and accepting offers of those who wanted to submit themselves to the patronage of the strong grew little by little and were known as *sho* or *shoen*. Though illegal and aimed solely at increasing wealth, private property of this kind gradually acquired an official character, and its owner (*honjo*) was given immunities. He was exempt from taxes and had the right to prevent the provincial governors (*kokushi*) from entering his sho to collect tax. This law was negative in effect at the beginning but was later accompanied by prerogatives in the legislative, administrative, and jurisdictional fields exercised within the framework of the *sho*.

Parallel to this development a military class was emerging. Under the *ritsu-ryo* system the army was composed of professional officers and soldiers recruited from among the people. Military service was considered an unpleasant duty because the soldiers were obliged to provide arms and supplies at their own cost and because the officers used the soldiers as their servants. As a result, the system was suppressed at the end of the eighth century and replaced by an army consisting of members of the powerful families from the provinces. For this reason the powerful provincial families came to form a new social class – the *samurai*.

With the weakening of the central government the military class increased its power in the provinces. The Taira (or *Heike*) and Minamoto (or *Genji*) clans became particularly important. In the twelfth century the Taira succeeded in gaining political control in the imperial government, and its head, Kiyomori, was named *dajo-daijin* (prime minister). But the Taira clan was soon defeated by the Genji clan, and in 1185 the head of the Genji, Yoritomo, set up a military government at Kamakura, a town near Tokyo. The emperor continued to reign, but he no longer ruled.

This form of military government lasted till 1868. From the legal viewpoint, the change meant that the centralized *ritsu-ryo* system gave way to feudalism. This feudal system developed in two separate stages, dual feudalism and unitary feudalism.

THIRD ERA: DUAL FEUDALISM

The feudal regime of this era is characterized by a dualist nature, a mixed regime of feudalism and *sho*. Under it the *sho* continued to exist but were used as the economic basis of the feudal system. All Japan was not immediately subjected to feudalism. It was only the domain of the *bushi* that it governed. The domains of the *kuge* (courtiers of the imperial court) and of the *honjo* remained from the earlier systems, though the influence of the *bushi* was felt more and more.

This era is divided into the Kamakura period, during which the central government (*Bakufu*) of the *bushi* was established at Kamakura, and the Muromachi or Ashikaga period, during which the *Bakufu* dominated by the Ashikaga military clan was set up in 1338 at Muromachi, a suburb of Kyoto. Between these two periods there was the short-lived Kemmu restoration of the emperor in 1334.

After the victory of Yoritomo over the Taira clan, all the *bushi* came under Yoritomo, and a hierarchical order was established with Yoritomo at the top. In this order the inferior owed his superior a duty of devoted service and the latter gave the former some benefits by way of reward. The bond of vassalage had a marked familial character, and each group of *bushi* linked by a blood relationship constituted a coherent unit directed by its head (*katoku*). The head had the right and the duty to receive obedience from the members of his group. When the *Bakufu* wished to call the *bushi* together, it had only to give the order to the clan heads.

The bond of vassalage was constituted by a contract in the broad sense between the suzerain and his vassal, but its content was not given precision by agreement between the parties. The vassal owed his overlord an absolute duty of fidelity but had no legal right to ask for the fulfillment of the overlord's duties.

Thus the suzerain's duty was not a legal one, though the vassal was bound legally in his duties toward his lord. In this characteristic, it is said, is the essential difference between vassalage in Japanese feudalism and Western feudalism.

The benefices the lord gave his vassals in reward for their services were of a varied nature and had the general name of *on* or *go-on* while the act by which the lord deigned to grant a benefice to his vassal was called *onkyu*. The system of *onkyu* has many points of similarity with the *beneficium* of European feudalism, and it is possible without too great a degree of inaccuracy to translate *onkyu* as *beneficium*. The *onkyu* is literally an act of beneficence on the part of the lord that he was in no way legally bound to perform because by law the vassal could not demand it of him. In practice, however, the lord could not wait for the performance of a suitable act of service by one of his vassals before distributing him due benefice, and the vassals themselves were not slow in seeking the *go-on* from their lord.

The link of *onkyu* was originally created in connection with the *sho*. The lord of a *sho* gave benefices to a person who owed him services and duties, whether of a military or non-military type. Most frequently it was land which was the object of the *onkyu*, but as time went on the masters of *sho* more and more frequently appointed their servants to positions which obliged the servants to conduct the business of the *sho*, and the master simply received land revenue from it. Such an appointment was called *shiki*, and as this sort of office was always accompanied by certain rights of enjoyment over the land of a *sho*, the word *shiki* came to represent the right of enjoyment itself.

After his victory over the Taira clan, Yoritomo confiscated all the land that had belonged to that family and distributed it to his vassals. He then required that the imperial court appoint him as chief *jito*, which meant that he could send his vassals to each *sho* in his capacity as *jito* and allow them to enjoy the *shiki* corresponding to his office. The *jito*, an officer of the *sho*, was also the official of the *Bakufu* who had responsibility for police and judicial activities in the *sho* to which he was sent and, as Jouon des Longrais says, 'It was by this means that Yoritomo could place *jito*, who were warriors, even on manors (*sho*) that did not belong to him. Once in this position these new military officials quickly took on a leading role.' Many very violent conflicts arose concerning the rights given to the bushi and those of the masters of the sho. Moreover, the *jito* frequently usurped the *sho* by using their military and political influence. In spite of the efforts of the *Bakuru* to find a balance between the interests of the two parties, the rights of the *bushi* increasingly exceeded those of the lords of the manors, and in the last half of the era under discussion the sho regime had largely come to an end. The development was hastened by the promulgation of a law by the Muromachi *Bakufu* called *Hanzei-ho* (law on the payment of half), under which each lord of a manor was ordered to set aside half his taxes from the sho for the bushi for military provisions.

Apart from the feudal dualism there was pluralism on the legal side, too, and the coexistence of the following three systems can be seen:

1. *Kuge-ho*. At the end of the *ritsu-ryo* era the administrative and judicial customs constituted a system of customary law based on the *ritsu-ryo*. The *ritsu-ryo* itself continued to apply even in this period in the field reserved to imperial authority. During the Kamakura era the *kuge-ho* was still in theory common law, but in practice it was increasingly being limited in application and had little importance in the Muromachi period. The imperial court often promulgated laws, but they were mostly of a moral character. They aimed at encouraging a moderate way of life and exhorted people to improve their morals. It is to be noted, however, that the opinions of jurists who gave solutions to problems posed by the government authorities according to the rules of *ritsu-ryo*, constituted an important source of customary law.
2. *Honjo-ho*. The customary law that applied to all the private manors was called *honjo-ho*. It varied greatly in content from region to region, but it is possible to distinguish the custom peculiar to a given *sho*, that common to the region, and that common to the whole country. The *honjo-ho* was a variant of *ritsu-ryo*.
3. *Buke-ho*. The moral rules or customs peculiar to the *bushi* class formed gradually with the class. They were called *bushido*, the body of rules of conduct for *bushi*, and can be likened to a code of chivalry. Based on them to a certain extent and supported by the *honjo-ho* for the rest, this third system was established to regulate relationships between the *bushi*. It was mainly a customary system but contains some written law which was known at the time as *shikimoku* or *shikijo*. The most important of these written laws was that promulgated in 1232 and called *Goseibai-shikimoku*, or *Joei-shikimoku*. The object of this law, according to the draftsman, was to inform the public of the nature of the law of *Bakufu* so that the administration of justice would be impartial. This law contained only fifty-one articles, but its influence on the laws that followed was very great. The code was, of course, applicable only to the *bushi* class, and was based on reason rather than positive legal principles.

Generally the law of the era is of a customary nature, and morality occupies an important place in it. The law of the *buke* in particular is distinguished from others in this respect. The system of morality of the *bushido* rests in Confucianism but, in contrast to the moral concepts of the preceding era when Chinese ideas were followed blindly, the *bushido* was formed in a spontaneous manner in the daily life of the *bushi*. However, it must not be forgotten that the Kamakura period was one in which Japanese Buddhism flourished. Buddhism had spread throughout Japan in the preceding era under state patronage, and its influence had been limited to the nobility. In the Kamakura period Buddhism penetrated into the daily life of the people, and its influence was very great on the *bushi*.

FOURTH ERA: UNITARY FEUDALISM

The power of the Kamakura *Bakufu* shifted in the fourteenth century to the *Bakufu* of Muromachi (1338–1573). The dualist nature of the social structure remained intact under the Muromachi reign, but as the power of the *Bakufu* weakened, the sho regime broke down rapidly. In place of the owners of the sho and the public officials appointed by the Bakufu or by the imperial court for the administration of the *sho*, there arose local lords who banished others in order to seize political power over the conquered lands. The *sho* disappeared one by one, and by about the end of the fifteenth century small independent states were emerging here and there. The ruler of each such state or province was called *sengoku daimyo* (lord of the period of the private wars) by historians. These *sengoku daimyo* fought among themselves, each seeking to gain political power over the whole of Japan, and at the end of a long period of violence and after the short-lived hegemony of Hideyoshi, Tokugawa Ieyasu succeeded in 1603 in establishing a solidly based unitary feudal regime. Thanks to the skillful political handling of Ieyasu and to the form of politics known as *sakoku* (closure of the country) this period, known as the Tokugawa or Edo period, lasted until 1868.

The new regime was purely feudal; all of Japan was *bushi* dominated. The head of the central government, still known as the *Bakufu*, was just one of the *daimyo*, who was the strongest and greatest of them and had the title of *shogun* (*generalissimo*). He had the greatest domain, *tenryo* (literally, the heavenly domain), which he governed directly, and all the other land was divided into fiefs among the big and small *daimyo* and the direct vassals of the *shogun* who were not *daimyo*. Even the imperial court was under the *shogun*'s surveillance, but the emperor remained the symbol of national unity. All *bushi* were attached by a bond of vassalage to their immediate superiors. The vassals of the *shogun* were the *daimyo, hatamoto*, and *gokenin*. The rest of the *bushi* were vavasors as far as the *shogun* was concerned. In order to maintain the hierarchical order as long as possible the *Bakufu* took very strict measures, which it enforced pitilessly, and adopted Confucianism as the official ideology in order to use it as moral support for the hierarchical order that existed. The *Bakufu* tried to convince the people that the established order was an immutable natural order. The result was that authoritarian ideology was deeply rooted in the heart of the nation. Japanese society at that time was characterized by a rigid and extremely detailed system of superiority and subordination in all social relationships. Not only was the bond of vassalage dominated by this principle but so too were the relationships between master and servant, parent and child, husband and wife, and among persons outside the *bushi* class.

The classes making up society were the *kuge* (nobles of the imperial court), the *buke*, the clergy (Buddhist and Shinto), the commoners, and pariahs. The court nobles were not bound by any bond of vassalage to the shogun, but they were under the strict control of the *Bakufu*. Commoners were divided into three categories, which were, in order of their social standing, peasants, artisans, and merchants. The peasants had the highest status among the commoners, but they had extremely heavy burdens to bear in the form of levies and service. They were therefore obliged to live extremely frugally and to work from dawn to dusk. A book published in 1720 said that the peasants were treated by a pitiless government like domestic animals and were borne down by heavy taxes and demanding service. Further they were not allowed to change their place of residence or their occupation. They were almost serfs. In a word the peasants, 80% of the population, were persons of abject condition. Another book published anonymously in 1815 describes their misery in the following manner:

> In order to supplement their meager diet they earned some money, using any leisure time they had by working as day laborers or performing other manual tasks. But even this was not enough to enable them to live comfortably. Thus they knew no rest for their body or their mind. They were not allowed to look after a relative who was kept in bed by illness nor were they able to provide him with medicines. The whole family suffered in summer from fleas and mosquitoes and in the winter from the cold because they had no heating. They did weaving but since they had to pay the price of materials in advance they were at the mercy of the merchants who exploited them on any number of pretexts, and so

> they made no profit. For this reason farmers are called *mizunomi-byakusho* [peasants who only drink water], but they could not even get enough water.

The *chonin*, or city dwellers, were no better off. They were involved in artisan's work and in commerce, but they were allowed to do so only by the grace of the *bushi*, and many restrictions were imposed on them to prevent them from exceeding their *bungen*. This word *bungen* is very important in understanding the hierarchical order. Literally it means the line of demarcation. Each social level is separated from the others by an impenetrable barrier; each individual belongs from birth to a given social status which imposes on him a manner of life adapted to that status. As Stoetzel says, 'It was forbidden to change class. Class distinctions were rigidly maintained and moral, social, and customary practices appropriate to each class were carefully codified.' A regulation put out by the Tokugawa government directed to the peasants stated:

1. It is henceforth forbidden for the head of the village and any peasant to build a house out of proportion to their status.
2. As far as clothes are concerned the village chief, his wife, and his children can wear silk or cotton, but the peasants can wear only cotton, and they may not use other materials even for the collar or the belt.
3. It is forbidden for a village chief or any peasants to dye their clothes violet or red. They can use all other colors but without pattern.
4. As far as food is concerned everyone must eat cereals other than rice. Rice can be eaten only on special occasions.

This hierarchical morality was strongly inculcated in all persons of the era. A book published in 1721 instructed peasants that 'everything which is above is called heaven and all that is below earth. The heaven is high and noble, the earth is low and humble. Peasants are destined to the earth. Therefore it is their heaven-ordained duty to busy themselves with agriculture and remain very humble.' Another book counseled merchants: 'Never, never desire the *bungen* that does not suit your rank. However intelligent you may be, you cannot attain a higher rank by your intelligence or talent, for our fate is determined by heaven from birth.' Besides this the arrogance of the *bushi* was almost quixotic. They despised the lower classes only because they were not *bushi* and disdained commerce in particular, as the following extract from a letter written by a high *Bakufu* official at the beginning of the nineteenth century shows: 'There is a custom among the barbarians to deliberate day and night on commercial dealings, and, even in a letter embellished with the royal seal and addressed to a foreigner, to mention openly an interest in commerce without feeling shame. This is a custom of the barbarians, but it is nonetheless detestable.' Another book of the period shares this opinion of commerce: 'In the barbarian countries of the West the kings and generals are all a type of rich merchant and have no cares for their honor or for honesty. There is no distinction between knights and merchants because distinguished persons sail the world to do business with strangers. They have no feeling of shame.' Fukuzawa Yukichi, a brilliant liberal of the Meiji era, recounts an interesting fact in this connection. As a boy he studied under a private teacher who taught him arithmetic. Fukuzawa's father, who was a *samurai*, found this unworthy of his son and withdrew him from the school, saying, 'It is unpardonable that you should teach my young boy arithmetic.'

Such was the social order of the Edo period. As for the law of the period, it was not unified and custom was dominant in every domain. Each *hun*, that is to say, each of the territories that had been divided up among the *daimyo* into fiefs, enjoyed political and legal autonomy and had its own law. The law of *Bakufu* applied in principle only in the area governed directly by the *shogun*. Nevertheless, since the *Bakufu* exhorted each *han* to follow the model of the *shogunate* law and as each of the *han* willingly did so, the laws of the *han* came to resemble those of the shogunate. Diversity of laws did, however, continue to exist until the Restoration of 1868, and Voltaire's statement that, when traveling in France one changed customs as often as horses, very aptly described the situation in Japan too. This system, which is called *baku-han taisei* by Japanese historians, was made up of two elements: a strong central power and autonomous *han*, which, though always different from it, gradually came to govern in a manner similar to the central power.

Alongside customary law, legislation (*hatto*) was promulgated by the *Bakufu* and by each of the *han*. This legislation dealt mostly with matters concerning the feudal regime. In 1742 a very important code was drawn up. It was called *Kujikata Osadamegaki* (Written Rules of Procedure) and was commonly known as *Osadamegaki-hyakkajo* (The Hundred Written Rules). This code has one hundred and three articles and is divided into two volumes. Volume I contains eighty-one regulations of various sorts, and volume II rules relating to both criminal and civil procedure. The civil law dispositions are not numerous and although called a code it is not so much a code as a series of directives addressed to judicial authorities. The text could only be consulted by the three *bugyo*, the top magistrates of the three important *Bakufu* courts.

Apart from these codes, several official collections of *Bakufu* law were made. Five collections of penal judgments, of which the first four are still extant, were also made. On the civil side there was a collection of judgments in forty-five volumes, of which only two volumes have survived. The jurisdictional setup of the period was very complicated, but the judgments collected all concern the *Hyojo-sho* jurisdiction of the central government.

The law of the period was strongly influenced by Confucianism, and in this respect it resembles the *ritsu-ryo* system. There was a basic difference between the two systems. Under the *ritsu-ryo* system the object was to control and educate the people in order to make them cognizant of the law for the purposes of maintaining public security and assuring the receipt of revenues. The government of the Edo period, on the other hand, wanted to attain the same objects by constraining the people to obey silently like domestic animals. The more ignorant and docile the people were, the easier it seemed for the *Bakufu* to realize its political objective. This attitude is expressed very clearly in the Tokugawa political motto: 'Let the people know nothing, but make them obey.' Under such conditions it was quite natural that the rights of individuals were not respected. Everything useful and necessary according to *Bakufu* politics was justified by reasons of state, and there was no possible way of criticizing the government. The government imposed its will pitilessly on the people, menacing with, and even executing, inordinately severe punishments for disobedience.

In a book written by a famous Confucianist of the time there appears the following dictum: 'According to the old theory, you must not censure the rulers of the country in which you live. If you do not occupy a position which gives you competence, you must not criticize state policy. It is contrary to loyalty and fidelity that an inferior should criticize his superior.' In the accusation against Oshio Heihachiro, who provoked an insurrection because he felt sorry for the plight of the populace, one reads: 'The accused did wrong to criticize policy because he was only a man of humble origin.' Yoshida

Shoin, one of the precursors of the Meiji Restoration, was condemned to capital punishment for a similar reason: 'Whereas the accused who is only a person of low rank was wrong to have criticized important state policies ...'. Furthermore, the imposition of penalties was not submitted to a procedure that guaranteed the dignity of the individual against the caprice of the judges. Since the confession of the guilty party was frequently the only means of proof, torture was officially admitted, and the legitimacy of its use to obtain a confession was not even questioned for a long time. It was Gustave Boissonade, when he arrived in Japan in 1873, who advised the government to abolish it.

From what has just been said it is clear that the law for most Japanese meant little else than the means of constraint used by the authorities to achieve government purposes. Powerless before the government might, the people could only obey, but because they were not convinced they developed a complex (*menju-fukuhai*) which became part of their psychological make-up.

In the Edo period doctrinal writings developed very little. There was no special law school corresponding to the faculty of law instituted in the *daigaku* under the *ritsu-ryo* regime, there was no class of professional lawyer such as formed early in French and English history, and judicial offices were not distinguished from other public offices. The *bugyo*, who enjoyed an important position in the field of justice, was a public official whose competence covered all public matters within his territorial jurisdiction, just like a bailiff of the French middle ages. He was therefore far from being comparable to the *Conseillers au Parlement* in pre-Revolutionary France. There were no barristers, no notaries, and no *ministère public*, and in the plays of the era there is nothing comparable to the advocates and notaries who often played an important part in Western dramas.

This state of affairs continued almost unchanged for two hundred years and contributed greatly to the formation of the Japanese conception of law. Isolated and confined to their small islands and forced to put up with wretched living conditions, the Japanese people quickly lost all sense of initiative. A quotation from a book of the period speaking about the immobility of the peasants represents accurately the mentality of the nation during that time: 'They did not easily accept new ideas. Imbued with the moral outlook and the customary practices of their province, they refused to consider other manners of behavior. They obstinately maintained their traditional agricultural methods in everything from the setting out of the rice paddies to the sowing of seeds. They did not wish to change the known pattern for a better method even if it was found to be suitable.' The Japanese outlook was dominated by one concern – personal security. 'Don't get involved' was the sad maxim of the greater part of the population. Even at the beginning of the following era, Fukuzawa was able to write:

> The Japanese people are so concerned with their own security that they have no desire to distinguish between the closed circle of their personal life and public life. All political business is left to the government. Millions of men with millions of different attitudes withdraw into themselves. Outside his home the Japanese feels at a loss and has no interest in anyone else. Since this is so, no one would consider the repairing of a community well, and the repair of public roads was even further from his thoughts. Seeing a dead person in the street the Japanese moves away as quickly as possible, and he turns away when he sees dog excrement in his path. This happens because everyone is trying to avoid what is called *kakariai*, being implicated in embarrassing matters. In such circumstances how could it be hoped that important matters would be discussed in public? Habits followed for so long have come to be rooted deep in the life of the Japanese of today.

Lehmann, JP, *The Roots of Modern Japan*, 1982, pp 166–78, Macmillan

The determinant force in Japan's transformation to modernity was her absorption into the world economy and the international relations which evolved in the course of the latter part of the nineteenth and early twentieth centuries. Japan was wrenched from the quiescence of *sakoku*, even from the comparative tranquillity of the traditional East Asian order, into the turbulence of the European-dominated international setting. In the period 1870 to 1914 there occurred the most significant and momentous changes which the world had ever witnessed. Western economic development was well fortified by numerous revolutionary advances in science. Scientific supremacy and technological applications in transportation, communication and, of course, armaments led to the continents of Asia, Africa and Latin America being carved up into colonies or spheres of influence by the major Western powers. Europe and the United States expanded in all directions. Traditional peasant economies were either uprooted or made to serve the economic needs and interests of the metropolitan powers: beef from the Argentine, cocoa from Ghana, silk from China were ferried in bulk to Marseilles, Liverpool, Rotterdam, New York. In order to secure readier access to sources of raw materials and markets for manufactured goods, greater political, military and financial control was exerted by the industrialised powers over the rest of the world.

Following the Treaty of Vienna internal European peace was maintained for a century, in spite of the occasional hiccup, as in the Crimean and Franco-Prussian wars. European rivalry was projected on to the continents of imperial expansion. While the geography of the non-European world was changing and various degrees of external sovereignty imposed, the balance of power in the West, however, was equally shifting in perceptible fashion. The supremacy of Britain was being challenged economically, militarily and in terms of international influence. The newly unified Germany particularly was accelerating the pace of change and the shift in the centre of gravity.

While this was an age of nationalism and imperialism, it was also an age in which the European political order was being militantly challenged by the dissemination of revolutionary ideas and the resort to means of direct action: socialism, communism, syndicalisrn, anarchism counted vociferous apostles and an increasing number of disciples. Indeed the prologue to this period was the Commune, its epilogue the October Revolution.

While political orthodoxy was being undermined, so were hitherto accepted social and cultural values. The growth of feminism is one illustration of this phenomenon. While movements such as the suffragettes may have been primarily concerned with achieving political ends, others were concerned with a radical re-evaluation of prevailing European sexual mores. Both birth control and free love were passionately advocated in certain quarters. In the arts radicalism featured prominently. The drama of Henrik Ibsen (1828–1906) evoked contemporary philosophical and social themes in direct challenge to the bourgeois conscience. Claude Monet (1840–1926) launched the school of Impressionism with his painting 'Impression, soleil levant' (1874). The naturalism of Emile Zola (1840–1902) created a powerful genre whose influence spread throughout Europe and beyond. Claude Debussy (1862–1918) caused a furore in musical circles. These new tendencies, to cite only a few of the more obvious examples, illustrated the cultural revolution which Europe was in the process of experiencing – while the gyrations of Isadora Duncan (1878–1927) vividly reflected a mood of hedonistic escapism.

Japan's absorption into the European-dominated world meant that not only was she heavily influenced, indeed motivated to action, by the major economic and imperialistic trends of the time, but she was also subjected to the whole range of Western intellectual, political, social, cultural and sexual contemporary ideas. In the Meiji era (1868–1912) Japan experienced and expressed nationalism and imperialism, but she was also penetrated by socialism, syndicalism, anarchism, feminism; advocates of birth control and free love could also be found in Meiji Japan. All aspects of Japanese culture were deeply impregnated by Western art forms and thought.

The only area in which European influence, albeit present, was not fundamental was religion. There is no doubt that Western missionaries did their best to achieve conversion and it is also true that for a while at least they did strike a responsive chord; ultimately, however, their efforts reaped a meagre harvest. It is perhaps somewhat of an irony that Japan, the most advanced, thus hitherto designated as occidentalised, nation of the modern era, was one of the least christianised countries. There are many reasons for this phenomenon. One, however, refers back to the European scene in the modern age. While on the one hand Pope Pius IX (1792–1878) proclaimed papal infallibility, on the other Europe witnessed the growth and indeed ascendancy of secularism, anti-clericalism and atheism. The power and influence of the established Churches were among the many orthodoxies being undermined in the Europe of the modern age.

Japan's absorption into the modern world, however, was not limited to the West. For the purposes of the period under review here, Africa, Latin America and the Middle East need not figure prominently. Africa, in fact, can be totally ignored. Latin America seemed to provide in certain cases possible areas for Japanese colonisation, in terms of exporting surplus population. While, so far as the Middle East was concerned, and especially Egypt, the Japanese found here a situation which they must endeavour to avoid. It is instructive that as early as the 1870s Japanese government officials were analysing the dangers confronting Japan in relation to the Western powers by making references to developments occurring in that part of the world. Although China was a more obvious negative model, the internationalisation of the official Japanese outlook on world affairs is well illustrated by this phenomenon.

Among the features which radically altered the international landscape in the late nineteenth and twentieth centuries was the emergence of newly industrialised, internationally influential powers. As indicated earlier, Britain's paramountcy, with France in second place, was challenged not only by Germany but also by the United States and Japan. By the early part of the twentieth century Japan had joined the exclusive club of the world powers Britain, France, Germany, the United States, Russia. Yet while Japan was achieving this exalted status, there was also an ambivalence in her international position – one which, to a degree, has been retained to this day. although Japan came to be with Europe, she was not part of Europe. Japan's ambivalent position in the international setting, namely that of a world power associated with the West in one sense, but situated in East Asia, racially and culturally part of East Asia, created a confusion, indeed a contradiction which gave rise to tensions and frustrations. This ambivalence remained a constant source of perplexity, indeed anxiety, throughout the course of Japan's transformation to modernity. It heavily influenced the direction of Japan's relations both with the Western powers and her East Asian neighbours and indeed had a significant impact on more underlying socio-psychological factors, all of which can perhaps be subsumed under modern Japan's quest for a national identity.

In terms of an understanding of Japan's transformation to modernity it is, therefore, essential that the context of Japan's relations with the West be properly understood. This exercise involves far more than simply economic or diplomatic relations. Here we are not so much interested in the chronological development of these relations as in their more general characteristics. This context must be perceived from two angles: that of the West and that of Japan. While this may appear to be stating the obvious, it is important that the two perspectives be properly appreciated for an understanding of the propelling forces of Japan's transformation to modernity.

In terms of the Japanese perspective, the first point which needs to be stressed is that Japan was obsessed with the West; the West was by no means obsessed with Japan. Indeed, apart from the odd occasion when Japan would temporarily figure prominently on the international scene, as in her wars against China in 1894–95 and against Russia in 1904–05, generally speaking there was only marginal Western interest in Japan. From the start, therefore, there existed a significant imbalance. Japan's obsession with the West operated at different levels. Throughout the period of transformation to modernity what may rather loosely be termed the superiority of the West was recognised by the Japanese. This superiority was clearly manifested in economic, technological, scientific, generally political and military terms and, of course, in the West's predominant position in the world. The West was feared. The Japanese had only to look round them to see what the West was capable of. All of Asia, apart from China and Thailand, was colonised and China was in a Western stranglehold. While Western power and the arrogance which it bred were undoubtedly resented, much of Western civilisation tended to be respected, admired and emulated.

The respect, admiration and desire to emulate were particularly strong in the seventies and eighties. By the nineties, for a variety of reasons, the adulation of the earlier period waned. The national mood was more assertive, more defiant. This was partly due to the fact that by this time Japan after all could boast not insignificant successes on both the economic and military fronts, partly due to the fact that the treaties, especially the more injurious clauses of extra-territoriality, had been revised. A major turning point, however, was the Triple Intervention of 1895, whereby three Western powers – Russia, Germany and France – ganged up on Japan in order to deprive her of her fruits of victory in the war against China.

In the preceding decades, however, the internal and external policies of the Japanese government were completely dominated by the country's relations with and position vis-à-vis the West. In fact, the early part of Japan's transformation to modernity could be written in two words: treaty revision. It is not simply that in order to try to convince the West that Japan was achieving 'civilised status', that is by Western standards, that the whole indigenous jurisprudential system had to be radically overhauled and developed along Western lines, but that even such innocuous customs as mixed bathing were officially frowned upon in order to cater to Western susceptibilities. As the West played the tune, Japan danced. The fact that it became increasingly apparent that the melody was frequently made to change in order to suit Western tastes not unnaturally led to bitterness.

So far as general European policies and attitudes towards Japan are concerned, a few factors need to be borne in mind. Policies were elaborated, needless to say, by considerations of economic and geopolitical factors. European resistance to treaty revision, for example, was motivated not simply by pig-headedness, but because

Europeans perceived that their economic interests were better served by maintaining a relationship based on inequality. The Triple Intervention, so injurious to both Japanese interests and susceptibilities, was determined by geopolitical strategies. The policies of the various Western powers towards Japan were established and developed according to contemporary rationality in the field of international affairs. An addendum to this general proposition is that if Japan perceived the Western powers as a monolithic force, this was not necessarily a misconception.

There were, of course, intense rivalries between the occidental powers. In the Far East, however, all efforts were directed towards minimising these, though in the case of Russia not necessarily successfully. The operative system of Western international relations in the Far East throughout most of the nineteenth century was what was called the Concert of Powers. The intention was that the Western powers should share in a common, reasonably harmonious, exploitation of the opportunities afforded by Far Eastern markets and sources of raw materials. The most-favoured-nation clause was an important instrument devised to achieve this end. Although as the century advanced, European imperialistic rivalries in diverse parts of the world, though initially mainly over the disintegrating Ottoman Empire, came to be reflected in the Far East, it was in fact Japan's defeat of China which shattered the Concert of Powers; it was occasionally resurrected, such as in the allied intervention in China at the time of the Boxer uprising (1900–01) – with, however, Japan as one of the allies – but in real terms it was moribund. Japan's defeat of China (1895), the German-initiated 'slicing of the Chinese melon' (1897–98) – whereby the Western powers appropriated to themselves spheres of influence in China in a manner reminiscent of the earlier partition of Africa – the US victory over Spain and the former's acquisition of the Philippines (1899), the Anglo-Japanese alliance (1902) and the spectacular victory of Japan over Russia (1905) heralded an entirely new age of international relations in the East Asian sector of the globe. Following 1905 the Concert of Powers was until the 1914–18 war briefly reduced to a quartet and, following Germany's exit from the scene, to a trio composed of Japan, Great Britain and the United States; that particular age in the history of East Asia came to an end in 1945.

While Western policies towards Japan may have had their own internal logic, based, as has been stated, on economic and geopolitical considerations, there were also other factors, less tangible perhaps but no less important, which were influential in terms of both European actions and Japanese reactions. Among the various 'isms' mentioned earlier in regard to Europe of the late nineteenth/early twentieth centuries another very important one needs to be added: racism. It is of course true that European racism was by no means a feature solely of this period; it is, needless to say, still very much with us today. The point is, however, that racism in this period of European history enjoyed philosophical and scientific respectability. It was a subject about which biologists, ethnologists, anthropologists, philosophers and all manner of literary amateurs did not hesitate to pontificate. On the continent of Europe the major figure was undoubtedly Joseph-Arthur de Gobineau (1816–82), whose four-volume work, *Essai sur l'Inégalité des Races Humaines*, was translated into numerous languages and heavily influenced scores of writers on the subject. In the Anglo-Saxon world the predominant theory of race was found in that rather loose body of doctrine known as Social-Darwinism, namely the application of Darwin's biological theories to ethnology and anthropology, with as its most articulate and prolific exponent Herbert Spencer (1820–1903).

The use of the term 'racism', however, implies a degree of ideological conformity which was markedly not in evidence. Rather, perhaps, one should speak of 'racisms'. For while racial theories ran rampant throughout the West, there were not just a few self-contradictory elements in this particular period piece. For the purposes of Japanese history only two need to be noted. On the one hand, social theories derived from Darwinism postulated that the inferior species were doomed either, in an extreme case, to extinction, or, alternatively, to a perpetual status of absolute inferiority. The races were inherently unequal. Nothing could be done to alter this situation, or indeed this truism. On the other hand, consciousness of the European's superiority dictated in some quarters a responsibility for educating, and elevating to the standards at least approximating those of the West, the inferior peoples. There was, therefore, a paternalistic quality evident in a great deal of European rhetoric and indeed policy. This applied mainly to Christian missionaries. The sense of a civilising mission, of the proverbial white man's burden, however, was by no means exclusively limited to missionaries, but motivated many men and women of diverse persuasions to bring enlightenment to the unenlightened. In her period of transformation to modernity, especially the early decades following the revolution of 1868, Japan by no means lacked advice from these do-gooders. These Europeans, however, whether Christian or atheist, with very few exceptions, never questioned, indeed accepted as axiomatic, the inherent and eternal superiority of the West. A paternalistic attitude necessarily implies that others are perceived as children. Herein lies a second contradiction of European racism, dramatically visible as it was projected on to Japan in the early part of the twentieth century. That is, while the non-European races were held to be inferior, once they did manage to challenge, indeed contradict, this proposition, then they became threatening. In the course of her transformation to modernity, especially when a measure of success, on both economic and military fronts, was at hand, Japan became the victim of European racial discrimination.

Racism as an important element in modern Japanese history cannot be underestimated. As Japan was increasingly opened to the West, as contacts between Japanese and Europeans, both in Japan and in Europe, as Japanese officials, the press, and hence the populace, came to a greater appreciation of the nature and motivations and underlying tenets of Western policy, the Japanese became not only aware, but indeed acutely conscious of European racism.

While realisation of this phenomenon and resentment against it began developing in the course of the earlier decades, the crunch undoubtedly came with the Triple Intervention of 1895. The national mood changed. The conversion of hitherto pro-Western ideologies from liberalism to social-Darwinism, in certain cases *à outrance,* is testimony of the Japanese reaction to Western racism. Japanese people came to accept the principles of the struggle of survival, something which only the fittest would achieve. In spite of numerous vagaries in the course of subsequent Japanese political, social and cultural history, this perception, indeed obsession, of a potential racial conflict certain to be translated into actuality in the future remained a significant and increasingly loud leitmotiv in the ensuing decades of the twentieth century. Counter-factual speculation is not a particularly fruitful exercise. In all probability, however, the course of modern Japanese political and military history would have been substantially different had the Japanese not been repeatedly faced with, and humiliated by, European racist barriers. Western racism has a lot to answer for; its eradication is perhaps the greatest challenge in this twilight of the twentieth century.

Having noted this *leitmotiv* of Western racism and Japanese consciousness, of and reaction to it, it should be made clear that by no means was it the only theme in Japan's transformation to modernity. Similarly, while Japanese nationalism developed, and indeed was fuelled by success, atavistic xenophobia remained in certain quarters, but very much in the background. Japanese reaction towards the West tended to be positive in that throughout the period of transformation the West continued to be perceived as a model which should be emulated, not necessarily in lock-stock-and-barrel fashion, but by careful selection and adaptation, though that too frequently proceeded on a trial and error basis.

II

Earlier it was stated that Japan's transformation to modernity took place under Western domination. The question which may be asked is: what does this mean? Alternatively, what was the role of the West in the course of Japan's modernisation? First, as was made clear in the former chapter, the West was initially perceived above all else as a menace – a menace to Japanese sovereignty. This perception induced fear, and fear concentrates the mind. In that sense the West acted as a catalyst. Political and administrative centralisation, military modernisation, concentration and rationalisation of the means of production, the widespread diffusion of literacy and numeracy by means of a national education system, scientific research, importation and integration of modern technology in the mode of production, broadening of the national intellectual horizon, were all policies or pursuits embarked upon out of a sense of necessity, indeed urgency, in the face of the Western peril. All of these measures were implemented with a reasonable degree of success and ultimately popular approval because of the rising tide of Japanese nationalism. Japanese nationalism, generally credited with providing the motive force of modernisation, was the offspring of the Western challenge. The roots, as seen in earlier sections, were there; the West provided the impetus to grow.

In the manner described above, the role of the West can be defined as impersonal and indirect. Japan's transformation, however, also occurred under more direct Western tutelage. On the part of the Japanese there was, undoubtedly a strong desire that their society should be transformed to the extent of reaching Western standards. Desire, however, albeit representing a great deal, was not everything; the necessary extra input was the material wherewithal.

Capital is one obvious, indeed essential, element in the recipe for modern transformation. The Japanese case in terms of industrialisation and foreign investment of capital is generally presented as exceptional in that Japan is credited with having been successful in generating her own capital; in other words she was not dependent on foreign loans. This is not an altogether acceptable view of Japanese economic development. A certain chronological sequence must be borne in mind. In the period covering roughly the three decades following the 1868 revolution, no foreign loan capital was imported into Japan with the exception of five million yen borrowed from Britain in 1871 in order to construct the railway between Tokyo and Yokohama. This was a track of some eighteen miles; the fact that two decades later railway track mileage had expanded more than a hundred times is an indication of what the Japanese were capable of doing without foreign capital investment – and certainly a stark contrast with the situation in China (and in Russia for that matter) where railway construction was almost exclusively financed by foreign capital. In so far as these decades are concerned, however, three factors need to be borne in mind. First, Japan was not a particularly attractive market to

Western financiers; China was much more interesting and perceived as far more lucrative. Secondly, the Japanese government's decision not to depend on foreign capital was taken mainly for political, rather than economic, reasons. As has been repeatedly pointed out, the Japanese were not only acutely conscious of what was happening in China in terms of spiralling foreign indebtedness, but more than dimly aware of comparable developments in places such as Egypt and Turkey. Thirdly, however, a good deal of Japanese initial industrial capital was fiduciary. For that reason, among others, although industrialisation was undoubtedly taking place and proceeding at an accelerating pace, its fiscal foundations were far from sound.

Japan's take-off into sustained modern economic growth occurred in the final years of the nineteenth century and the first decade or so of the twentieth. It was precisely during this period that external capital flowed into Japan. A good deal of it, admittedly, came from China; the reparations imposed following the victory of 1895 and the Japanese share of the Boxer indemnity provided a welcome fillip to industrial development and the further laying of the social infrastructure necessary for industrialisation – for example, part of the Boxer settlement was invested in education. At the same time, however, Western capital began pouring into Japan. The Japanese government required external funds in order to pursue military ventures, particularly against Russia. The country's obvious economic success and viability made it a more attractive market for Western financial investment. Similarly, from the Japanese government's viewpoint, the country's military and diplomatic (thanks to the Anglo-Japanese Alliance) security of the early twentieth century meant that borrowing from the West involved far fewer risks than had been the case when Japan was in a more vulnerable position. Foreign capital, therefore, undoubtedly played a significant role; indeed as the First World War broke out foreign capital represented a quarter of the country's GNP. The importation of foreign capital is one thing, the intelligent absorption and application of it is a different matter; in the latter sense, the Japanese were eminently skilful in a way that the Argentines, the Brazilians, the Egyptians, the Chinese were not.

Another vital element of the material wherewithal for industrialisation was modern technology. Throughout the period of transformation, and indeed until recently, Japan was almost totally dependent on Western technology. All industrialising societies, not excluding Britain, have depended on imports of foreign technology. Between the various Western European countries and the United States, however, there was a greater degree of reciprocity in terms of exchange of inventions. Also, migration patterns within the Western hemisphere disguised the degree of foreign dependence, thereby giving an impression of greater national self-reliance. It remains the case, however, that throughout her period of transformation to modernity Japan was a beneficiary rather than a benefactor of major scientific and technological inventions.

This phenomenon can be explained by a number of factors. First, there is the element here of the latecomer, perforce reliant on the pioneering efforts and advances of others. Secondly, Japan's geographical situation must be borne in mind. In Western Europe not only was there a tradition of scientific enquiry which had existed for centuries, but the short geographical distances and close intellectual affinities between the centres of learning and those who were actively engaged in the pursuit of knowledge provided a European-wide atmosphere conducive to fruitful research. This atmosphere was completely lacking in East Asia. Thirdly, in spite of significant advances when compared to other non-European societies, Japan remained, as has already occasionally been pointed out but needs to be frequently emphasised, backward by comparison with

Western Europe and the United States. In adopting an ambitious policy of modernisation, the Japanese government was in effect attempting a great leap forward. Emphasis had to be placed on a rapid achievement of ends rather than in a patient pursuit of causes.

A third prerequisite in terms of material wherewithal for industrialisation was that of expertise. It is undoubtedly here that Japan's initiatives are the most impressive. By the end of the century the country possessed a highly capable, efficient, modern elite. Japanese medical doctors, professors of the various disciplines, school teachers, technicians and scientists, foremen of skilled workers, bureaucrats, army and navy officers, industrial managers and financiers provided the high-quality human resources necessary for the country's development and self-reliance. This, needless to say, did not occur overnight. Here again the debt to the West was substantial. While a trickle of Japanese had gone abroad to study in the *bakumatsu* period, following 1868 this temporary academic migration to the West assumed the proportion of a steady flow – never that of a flood, emphasis generally being placed more on the quality of the expatriate students rather than the quantity. Also, whereas, as we have seen in the former chapter, the *bakufu* had inaugurated the policy of importing Western expertise, the Meiji government not only continued, but indeed significantly increased, the allocation of national revenue to this (expensive) exercise. Experts were invited mainly from Britain, Germany, France and the United States, but also from other countries, such as the Netherlands, Italy, Switzerland, Belgium, Russia, Sweden, Austria, Canada, and so forth. Throughout the first two decades of the Meiji era there was an average of approximately one thousand Western experts per annum engaged either by the government or by the private sector. While the emphasis was not unnaturally placed in areas of greatest national relevance in terms of industrial and military development, even more erudite activities such as painting and music were not deprived of foreign tutelage.

On the surface Western nations would appear to have been most generous in terms of provision of expertise. Both on the part of the governments and the individuals concerned there undoubtedly was a certain element of altruism. This motivation was very much in keeping with the consciousness of Europe's civilising mission mentioned above. This in turn – as is made clear from the memoirs of those foreign experts who chose to bequeath their thoughts to contemporaries and posterity – provided those individuals with a sense of moral self-satisfaction. They were, after all, not only providing enlightenment but were also highly respected, indeed flattered, for doing so. In Europe their intellectual capacities would not necessarily gain the degree of recognition and admiration that they were able to command in Japan. These comments should not be interpreted as belittling the qualities of the individuals concerned; there were inevitably a number of charlatans, of self-seekers, but there were also many men of integrity and dedication, indeed a few of whom associated themselves strongly with Japan's endeavours at modernisation and obtaining respectability in Western eyes, including, for example, advocating the revision of the treaties. To paraphrase Cecil Rhodes, however, while altruism may be fine, altruism plus 5% is even better. There was also a not insignificant financial incentive. As far as the individual Western experts were concerned, they were very handsomely paid. For the governments the provision of expertise also had economic implications in that it was hoped that the Japanese would purchase capital goods and technology from the countries of origin of the experts.

As was indicated in the case of the importation of foreign capital, similarly in that of foreign expertise, it is not the importation which is significant, but the use made of it. Japan succeeded in forming an indigenous élite capable of leading and sustaining the country's progress to modernisation in a manner of which the Argentinians, Brazilians, Egyptians, Turks, Siamese and Chinese were incapable. Why?

It cannot be the purpose here to analyse the problems which the various nations listed above encountered in terms of creating a modern indigenous elite. Certain features specific to the Japanese experience, however, should serve the purpose of indicating those contrasts which did exist. Perhaps the most fundamental element is that in the new society which began emerging in the course of the first decade or so following 1868 there were no major contending elites in Japan. In other words, certainly by the early 1880s, the elite was almost entirely composed of the modern sectors of society: the bureaucrats staffing the new ministries, military officers, the liberal professions, managers of industry, financiers, scientists. Increasingly in the course of the period of transformation, a common element among all these components of the elite was that they had obtained a modern, Western-inspired education. Japan, in spite of being a late developer, nevertheless quite quickly entered into at least an embryonic form of the age of the technocrat. In the early period of transformation, Japanese landlords provided a local elite, not a national one. This situation changed, much to the country's detriment, but the important point to note for the present is that in this initial spurt towards modernisation the élite was concentrated, reasonably homogeneous, educated and modern-orientated. In most other societies, including those mentioned above, the elite was still closely associated with and indeed derived from the possession of land and/or religious station: bishops and latifundists in Latin America, nawabs and mullahs in the Ottoman empire, the Confucianist Chinese scholar-gentry, all retained privileged and highly influential positions in all domains of society for which there were no Japanese counterparts. There were progressive doctors of medicine, skilled scientists, modern military officers – *hic nascent* the Young Turks – etc in all of these countries, but their status was inferior to traditional elites and in many cases their livelihood insecure. Japan is not rich in natural resources, nor, as we have seen, was she endowed with capital at this stage of her history. Her economic development had a great deal to do with the skilful exploitation of the capital she had at her disposal or that she fabricated. Workers and peasants, as will be seen in the following chapter, were exploited; the former provided cheap labour, the latter a high percentage of government revenue in the form of taxes. The élite, on the other hand, tended to be well remunerated. Narrow national income differentials, a prominent and indeed highly admirable feature of contemporary Japan, represent a very recent development. Material incentives, therefore, undoubtedly played a significant role among Japan's modern élite.

For all that, however, and again in stark contrast with the other societies mentioned above, it is the comparative absence of conspicuous consumption among the Japanese élite that represents a marked feature of this period of transformation to modernity. Profits and savings were reinvested into production. The *samurai* ethic of frugality may have had something to do with this, but that particular proposition should not be pushed too far; there cannot be many 'ethics' which actually encourage profligacy. The behaviour of the Japanese élite can be attributed – even if it cannot be satisfactorily explained – to the national atmosphere, however intangible such variables may be, one which in the early stages of modernisation was expressive of a national will to achieve ambitious ends irrespective of the sacrifices. In terms of motivation, therefore, once again, one turns to nationalism, but a nationalism which encapsulated a high degree of determination and singularity of purpose among the elite; that element was lacking in the other would-be modernising nations.

Ishii, R, *A History of Political Institutions in Japan*, 1980, pp 112–16, 121–26, University of Tokyo Press

1. The Making of the Constitution and the Beginning of Parliamentary Government

In 1881, an imperial edict stated that a parliament would be opened in 1890. Ito Hirobumi was sent to Europe in 1882 to study the constitutions of other countries. In 1881, Iwakura Tomomi, the *udaijin*, had drawn up a set of general principles and a commentary supporting a monarchical constitution like that of Prussia. His recommendations were almost all adopted in the Meiji Constitution. Ito, according to Iwakura's recommendation, studied with R von Gneist and A Mosse of Germany, and with L von Stein of Austria. When he returned to Japan in 1883, Okuma had resigned and Iwakura had died, leaving Ito the sole major figure on the political scene. In 1884 he established the Seido Torishirabe Kyoku (Institutions Research Bureau), and became its director. With the assistance of Inoue Kowashi, Ito Miyoji, and Kaneko Kentaro, he made preparations in secret for drawing up the constitution and supplementary laws. In the same year, in anticipation of the opening of an upper house, the *Kazoku Rei* (Law of Nobility) was promulgated, establishing the five aristocratic titles of prince, marquis, count, viscount, and baron. In 1885, the *dajokan* was abolished and its authority transferred to a cabinet (*naikaku*) on the European model. Under the *dajokan* system, the *dajodaijin*, together with the *sadaijin* and *udaijin*, were seen as assisting the emperor in the conduct of state affairs, and the various ministry heads as mere bureaucratic subordinates. The new cabinet was a collegial decision-making body made up of a prime minister and ministers of foreign affairs, home affairs, finance, army, navy, justice, education, agriculture and commerce, and communications. In the cabinet, all these ministers took part in making national policies, and outside it, each discharged the duties of his specific branch. The new system also institutionalized a clear distinction between the government and the imperial court itself. An additional ministry, of the imperial household (*kunai*), was established outside the cabinet, and Sanjo Sanetomi, who had been *dajodaijin*, was named minister (*naidaijin*). Sanjo was thus in charge of liaison between the court and the government. A large amount of state property was also transferred to the imperial household at about the same time. The office of prime minister was assumed by Ito Hirobumi. The elevation of Ito, a man of lower rank *samurai* origins, to this post amazed the people of the time.

As the government carried out these preparations for the promulgation of the constitution, corresponding political movements were in progress among the people. The Liberal Party (*Jiyuto*) was founded in 1881 and the Constitutional Imperial Rule Party (*Rikken Teiseito*) in 1882. These parties, however, were dissolved in 1883 and 1884, respectively, as several conditions made it difficult for parties to survive. The government repressed political movements, both directly and indirectly, using both pressure and persuasion. The parties themselves engaged in internecine power struggles. Most important, Liberal Party headquarters was unable to restrain its local members from participating in riots by poor farmers, which broke out in several areas due to the unfavorable economic conditions created by the government's deflationary policies. Even though the parties could not continue, however, riots by local liberals went on. In

1887, great numbers of people memorialized the government on such topics as treaty revision, freedom of speech and assembly, and reduction of taxes. Goto Shojiro and others revived the party movement by organizing the opposition into a 'Great Coalition' (*Daido Danketsu*). Disorder in the capital followed, and in the same year, the Peace Preservation Law (*Hoan Jorei*) was promulgated, enabling the government to expel people's rights advocates from Tokyo, requiring them to remain at a distance of more than three *ri* (about 12 kilometers) from the capital.

In 1888, the Privy Council (*Sumitsuin*) was established. Ito Hirobumi was appointed its president and started examining the draft constitution that had been in preparation since the end of 1885. In anticipation of the promulgation of the constitution, local autonomy was established through a system of *shi* (cities) and *cho-son* (towns and villages), enacted in 1888 and one of *fu-ken* (prefectures) and *gun* (counties), enacted in 1890. On February 11, 1889, the constitution was promulgated. It was, as we have seen, a monarchic constitution, based on Iwakura's principles and opinions. The drafting was mainly the work of Inoue Kowashi and KFH Roesler, a German.

The constitution went into effect on November 29, 1890, the day the First Imperial Diet was convened. It comprised 76 articles in seven chapters. It was a monarchic constitution in the Prussian style, but it was simply worded and was characterized by elasticity. It stated that the Japanese empire was to be ruled by the emperor (of lineage unbroken through the ages) according to the articles of the constitution. All three branches of the government – executive, legislative, and judicial – were to be presided over by the emperor. A great many things were included in the imperial prerogative and therefore did not require the consent of the Diet. An especially severe restriction on the Diet's fiscal authority was imposed by the rule stipulating that the previous year's budget went into effect automatically if the Diet failed to approve a new one. Laws could not be passed without Diet approval, but constitutional amendments could be proposed by the emperor alone. The ruler was also given broad powers to issue special emergency ordinances (*kinkyu meirei*), independent supplementary ordinances (*dokuritsu meirei*) and ordinances delegating his authority to subordinates (*inin meirei*). The constitution also laid down rules concerning the rights and duties of the people, but these dealt only with the relation of the people to the nation, and ideas of fundamental human rights were not strongly articulated. Instead, the freedoms granted were nearly all made subject to whatever limitations the law might determine. The Imperial Diet was bicameral, consisting of the House of Representatives, elected by the nation at large, and the House of Peers, made up of *kazoku* (nobility), who were the bulwarks of the Imperial House, and officially nominated members. Except for the priority recognized for the House of Representatives in the debates on the budget, the two houses had equal rights. The judicial power was independent, but the right to appoint or dismiss judges was held by the Minister of Justice. Supreme command of the army and the navy rested with the emperor and, in accordance with earlier tradition, was placed outside the scope of the ministers' power to advise the ruler; this practice was ultimately to lead to military dictatorship.

Since this Meiji Constitution was characterized by elasticity, it admitted of different interpretations, and many changes should be noted in the history of its operation. For instance, in the minds of the original makers of the constitution the formation and continuation of the Cabinet depended on the emperor's confidence and were to have nothing to do with the Diet. Later, however, it became customary for the Cabinet to be formed by political parties. Also, the draftsmen had intended that there should be property restrictions on voting, but the constitution relegated the matter to law and contained no clear article on it, thus enabling the nation to win universal male suffrage in 1925.

Together with the constitution, the Imperial House Law (*Ko-shitsu Tenpan*) and such supplementary laws as the Diet Law, the House of Representatives Election Law, and the Imperial Ordinance on the House of Peers were issued.

In 1890, the members of the nobility elected their representatives to the House of Peers, and additional representatives were nominated by the emperor. A general election for the House of Representatives was held, and in November of that year the First Imperial Diet was opened. A majority of the elected members of the House of Representatives were from either the Liberal Party *(Jiyuto)* or the constitutional Reform Party (*Rikken Kaishinto*), and thus stood to some degree in opposition to the government. The government was represented by the Cabinet under Yamagata Aritomo. The first Diet session ended in comparative peace.

The Matsukata (Masayoshi) Cabinet that followed Yamagata's engaged in wide-scale bribery and intimidation before the general election of 1892. This became the pattern for the Satsuma-Choshu clique cabinets in dealing with the political party opposition: combining repression and harassment with conciliation. For their part, the parties attacked the government in the only way open to them: by drastically cutting government budgets in the House of Representatives.

...

From the Manchurian Incident to the China Incident

Prime Minister Hamaguchi was shot in 1930 and died the next year. Ignoring the government's policy of non-proliferation of warfare, the military forces in 1931 took over the whole of Manchuria and established the entity called Manchukuo in March of 1932. In May of the same year, a group of naval officers and noncommissioned officers, with the aim of establishing a military government, assaulted the official residence of the prime minister and killed Inukai Tsuyoshi, premier and president of the *Seiyukai,* in what is known as the May 15 Incident. The incident brought an end to party government, and Admiral Saito Makoto became prime minister in the first of a series of so-called 'National Unity' cabinets not based on political parties.

The League of Nations, in answer to an appeal from the Chinese government, sent a survey team to Manchuria. The team declared the actions of Japan in Manchuria to be aggressive, and stated that the foundation of Manchukuo was not (as Japan claimed) a voluntary movement for independence. It concluded that, although Japan's special interests in Manchuria should be recognized, all its armed forces should be withdrawn. This report was supported by the League's general session of 1933, and so Japan decided to withdraw from the League, of which it had been a member since its establishment.

Japan pursued an independent course in foreign policy and became more and more isolated internationally. In 1934 the effective period of the Washington Naval Treaty expired, and Japan announced its abrogation. At the naval disarmament conference held in London at the end of 1935, Japan insisted on possessing a navy equal in size to those of Britain and the US; when its demands were not met, Japan withdrew from the conference.

Saito Makoto was followed as prime minister by Admiral Okada Keisuke. These men and their cabinets were fairly liberal in policy; some military officers, dissatisfied with them, resorted to violence to sweep away the liberalistic tendency in politics. About a dozen officers of the army's First Division, leading more than a thousand soldiers, rose in rebellion in 1936, attacked the prime minister's official residence and other places, and occupied the central area of Tokyo. Premier Okada narrowly escaped death, but several other high officials, including Saito Makoto, then *naidaijin*, were assassinated. The attack is known as the February 26 Incident.

This uprising was soon put down, but the militarists took advantage of it to expand their influence and role in the government. At the end of the year, in response to pressure from the army, an anti-Comintern pact was concluded with Germany; it professed a joint defense against communism, in order to resist the threat of the Soviet Union. In 1937, this part was expanded to include Italy.

The Kwantung army, encouraged by its success in Manchuria, extended its war front from North China to Central China and then to South China, despite the government's localization policy. This undeclared war is known as *Nisshi jihen*, or the China Incident.

2. The National General Mobilization Act and the Imperial Rule Assistance Association

With this expansion of the battle front, the munitions industry became increasingly active. The embargo on the export of gold, lifted by the Hamaguchi Cabinet in 1930, was revived in 1931. Japan's exports increased, and the economy thrived at first, but the prolonged warfare began to take its toll financially and brought about a shortage of goods. Wartime control more and more affected the life of the nation.

The government, in an effort to accomplish its war objectives at whatever cost, issued a declaration of a New Order in East Asia in 1938, and demanded the 'total mobilization of the national spirit' by issuing the National General Mobilization Act, which in effect deprived the nation of the freedom of speech. This law endowed the government with the power to mobilize the total power of the nation, in wartime and in times of emergency equivalent to war, without having to obtain the approval of the Imperial Diet. It was a law practically nullifying the function of the Diet. There were protests against this virtual nullification of the function of the Diet from both the *Seiyukai* and the *Minseito*, but the demurring voices were suppressed by the high-handedness of the militarists, and the Diet passed the measure without amendment. In 1939, the Personal Service Drafting Law (*Choyo Rei*) was issued.

With the outbreak of the Second World War in 1939, the Abe (Nobuyuki) Cabinet declared that Japan would not interfere with the war in Europe. Under the next cabinet, however – that of Admiral Yonai Mitsumasa – the army insisted on concluding a strong military alliance with Germany. The prime minister and the navy objected to it, but a military alliance with Germany and Italy was formally concluded by the second Konoe (Fumimaro) Cabinet in 1940. In the same year, Foreign Minister Matsuoka Yosuke declared the establishment of the Greater East Asia Co-Prosperity Sphere (*Daitoa Kyoeiken*).

Konoe in October 1940 established the *Taisei Yokusan Kai* (Imperial Rule Assistance Association) and became its president. This was the outcome of the movement for a new order which had been evolving around Konoe since June of that year. All the political parties – *Seiyukai, Minseito, Kokumin Domei, Shakai Taishuto* – were now dissolved. With the formation of the *Taisei Yokusan Kai*, the ultra-partisan national movement desired by the militarists had materialized, and the political parties, which had relinquished their right to deliberate on state affairs in the Diet by their passage of the National General Mobilization Act, had lost their own *raison d'être.* constitutional government – that is, governments formed by the parties – had disappeared, and the Meiji Constitution had lost its function as fundamental law. All labor unions were dissolved, and the *Dai Nihon Sangyo Hokoku Kai* (Japanese Association of Industrialists' Service to the State) was formed to take their place.

Finally, in December 1941, with the attack of the Japanese navy on Pearl Harbor, Hawaii, the Pacific War began. The Japanese armed forces fared well in the beginning, but suffered a serious setback in the sea battle off Midway in June 1942. In May 1945, Germany, Japan's ally in Europe, surrendered unconditionally to the Allied Powers. In June, all the land forces in Okinawa were destroyed. While the militarists were announcing the imminence of the decisive battle on the mainland of Japan, the Potsdam Declaration was published on July 26, 1945, by the United States, Britain, and France (later joined by the Soviet Union); the Declaration prescribed the final conditions for Japan's surrender. The Japanese government at first ignored it, but after the aerial attacks on Hiroshima (August 6) and on Nagasaki (August 9), in which atomic bombs were used, and the sudden declaration of war on Japan by the Soviet Union followed by the Soviet invasion of North Manchuria and northern Korea, the Suzuki (Kantaro) Cabinet notified the Allied forces on August 14 of Japan's decision to accept the Declaration. On August 15, 1945, the emperor's recorded message on the termination of the war was broadcast to the nation. On August 30, General Douglas MacArthur of the US arrived at Atsugi Airport, and the occupation of Japan by the Allied Powers began.

3. Economic Control

When the China Incident occurred in 1937, the government saw the urgent need to increase munitions production and made all resources, funds, and imports subservient to the arms industry. The sudden growth of the munitions industry caused inflation, and prices began to rise. With the outbreak of the Second World War in September 1939, the government, using the powers given it by the National General Mobilization Act, enforced price-control regulations in an attempt to check the rise of prices. Commercial and industrial syndicates were formed all over the nation, and all enterprises were placed under government control.

The Pacific War began under these circumstances. After the United States became Japan's main enemy, all materials, funds, and labor were made to serve the fighting power of Japan. Private enterprises were suppressed, and a number of semi-governmental, semi-private companies were created. Since Japan had limited resources for a war of this scale, ordinary consumption was greatly restricted, and strong controls were applied, even to food and clothing.

4. Decay of Constitutional Monarchy

In terms of political institutions, the fourteen years from the Manchurian Incident (1931) to the end of the Pacific War (1945) was a period marked by the decay of constitutional monarchy.

The emperor was held in awe as a divinity incarnate (*arahito-gami*), and was used by the militarists as a shield against criticism of their wrongful and illegal acts. But since the Meiji Constitution was still in effect, the emperor was in fact the ruler of the nation, and his termination of the Pacific War in 1945 by his own decision was the last and greatest glory achieved by the emperor system under the Meiji Constitution.

The Meiji Constitution, although it did not anticipate the growth of party cabinets, expected the Diet to function properly as a legislative organ. From the middle of the Taisho era to the early Showa years, party cabinets were formed one after another, but after 1932 the party system ceased to function, and the National General Mobilisation Act deprived the Diet of much of its right to deliberate on state affairs. After 1942, when the *Yokusan Seiji Kai* (Political Assistance Association) was formed, and *yokusan giin* (cooperative Diet members) were elected, the Diet became a puppet legislature which applauded every move of the government. Freedoms of speech, assembly, and publication guaranteed by the Meiji Constitution were taken away; security of ownership was disregarded; and under the controlled economy, freedom to enter into contracts was severely restricted.

Thus, the Meiji Constitution still existed, in name only, during the war years. However, even the militarists did not try to abolish the constitution. They had no need to do so, for anything could be accomplished by invoking the emperor's authority. By making full use of the prerogative of supreme command acknowledged by the constitution, the militarists could have their own way.

Takayanagi, K, 'A Century of Innovation: The Development of Japanese Law 1868–1961', in von Mehren, AT (ed), *Law in Japan: The Legal Order in a Changing Society*, 1963, pp 6–12, 15–23, 27–33, Harvard University Press

The Meiji Constitution of 1889

The Meiji Constitution was drawn up with the utmost secrecy and promulgated as a gift of the Emperor to his subjects. Sovereignty resides in the Tenno, the hereditary monarch, not in the people. The constitution takes scrupulous care to guarantee executive supremacy, which had been the policy of the Meiji government since the Restoration, by recognizing broad imperial prerogatives. This will strike the present generation of Western observers as highly antidemocratic, and political realists are apt to see in the document a selfish attempt to perpetuate, behind a Western constitutional facade, the political power of the oligarchs. The constitution is certainly conservative; but, compared with the Japanese political regime prior to the Restoration, it was definitely a step forward in the direction of democratizing Japan. It provided for a Diet, including a Lower House, composed of elected representatives. It provided for the usual bill of rights, though 'under reservation of the law'. It provided for an independent judiciary, though its province was strictly limited, in conformity with the French and Continental traditions, to the trial of civil and criminal cases, and administrative matters were outside its jurisdiction. If it was not the rule of law in the English sense of the term, at least justice according to law was guaranteed.

It is now the Japanese fashion of the day to criticize severely this constitutional document as compared with the more democratic constitution of 1946. In view of the practical problems that the statesmen of the Meiji era (1867–1912) had to tackle, it is at least debatable whether Japan was not wise in taking a conservative course rather than the progressive or radical line advocated by many Japanese politicians of the time. There were two major tasks to be performed. The first was to create a sovereign state out of the chaos of a feudal state, a task similar to that faced by sixteenth-century European statesmen who had to create a strong centralized government to combat feudal anarchy. The Meiji statesmen had also to take account of the modern democratic developments that had occurred in Europe after the French Revolution – if for no other reason than to ensure the abolition of consular jurisdiction. The two exigencies were, in a sense, antagonistic to each other, and the statesmen of that day chose the more conservative line.

The views of prominent European and American scholars of the time respecting the Meiji Constitution are interesting. After promulgation of the constitution, Kentaro Kaneko, a graduate of the Harvard Law School who had assisted Prince Ito in the drafting, was sent abroad with the English translation of Ito's Commentaries on the constitution to obtain the criticisms of eminent political scientists and constitutional lawyers. In England, Kaneko met and heard the views of Herbert Spencer, James Bryce, Henry Sedgwick, William Anson, and Albert Dicey. In Germany, Rudolf von Gneist, who had lectured to Prince Ito, was too ill to give his opinion, but Kaneko met with Rudolf von Ihering. In Austria, Lorenz von Stein, to whose lectures Ito had listened with much admiration, was visited. Kaneko also journeyed to France and there talked to Le Bon, professor of constitutional law at the University of Paris. In the United States, comments were furnished by Professor James Bradley Thayer of the Harvard Law School and Oliver Wendell Holmes, Jr, then Chief Justice of the Supreme Judicial Court of Massachusetts.

Spencer approved both the respect shown by the draftsmen of the constitution for Japanese historical traditions and their conservative course, which avoided a progressive policy that would be incompatible with the stage of social development in Japan. He observed that European constitutions were all historical products and that it would be a mistake to expect the same results in Japan by translating and enforcing one of these constitutions. He also sounded the warning that, although wisdom and assiduous endeavors of a select few could make a constitution, its enforcement affected the people in general. Consequently, it was several times more difficult to operate a constitution well than to draft a satisfactory document. Specifically citing the case of Irish members of the House of Commons, Spencer opined that participation in public affairs must be conditional on the payment of taxes, for otherwise the discussions of the Diet could degenerate into the mere expression of impractical and irresponsible views.

Bryce favored the conservative policy of concentrating political power in the hands of the Emperor and of separating the executive from the legislature. He felt that changes implicit in the adoption of English cabinet government would be too abrupt for a nation long used to despotic rule. He and Professor Sedgwick took up specifically a number of articles and drew attention to troubles, from the standpoint of the ideal and custom of the English constitution, which might arise under those articles. Sedgwick, then over seventy, had been preparing his *Elements of Politics* and was eager to scrutinize the Japanese constitution in connection with his forthcoming work.

Dicey approved the decision of the drafters to take the German and not the English constitution as their model for the relation between the executive and the legislature. He also advised the adoption of a limited franchise. In addition, he expressed his well-known prejudice against *droit administratif,* saying that the constitution wrongly adopted the Continental system of administrative courts and that all legal matters should be left to ordinary courts.

Anson expressed his view of a written constitution as nothing more than 'a textbook of strategy', whose practical application was to be likened to actual warfare that did not necessarily follow the prescriptions laid down in the textbook. He stressed the importance of political facts rather than of constitutional theories. In his opinion, once a parliamentary system was established, no government could be conducted without the support of political parties, so that, even under the constitution, Japan might develop a party government. Anson also warned the Japanese government against the danger of relying too much on the Upper House as the bulwark of the government and of minimizing or antagonizing the Lower House.

Ihering said that he was a student of the Roman law, not a constitutional expert; however, his clear logic and his lucid eloquence, as well as his erudition in constitutional lore, seem to have impressed Kaneko deeply. He not only explained in detail the practical working of the Prussian constitution of 1850, but also cited a number of political events in other European countries to support his points. He stressed that, though the Lower House naturally tends to be radical, the government must, lest the state of affairs in Japan lapse into chaos, stick to a conservative policy. Approving the composition of the Upper House, as provided in the House of Peers Order, Ihering recommended that a system of 'imperial nominees' be utilized. They should be chosen by the government, to check, as the parliamentary atmosphere suggested, either the ultraconservatism of the nobility or the radicalism of the elected representatives. He also explained Bismarck's way of 'managing' the Lower House without any resort to dubious methods.

Holmes approved the conservative spirit in which the constitution was drafted. In introducing constitutional government into Japan, the constitution should be so drafted as to confine popular participation within narrow limits, with the view, however, of gradually extending this participation. Holmes said that there was no universal principle as to how much popular participation ought to be granted, this being a matter depending on the history of each nation. Although the establishment of constitutional government in Japan was, Holmes believed, a wise step, the Emperor should bear in mind that he himself could not change it at will. Moreover, the constitution was an ax which would cut the country into several compartments, dividing the people into political parties. Finally, Holmes stressed that the success or failure of the constitution depended on the political education of the Japanese nation and on the political genius of the Japanese leaders.

Thayer believed that the constitution could be a success only if Diet members maintained a conservative spirit and refrained from expressing radical opinions. He reminded Kaneko that, immediately after the enactment of the constitution of the United States, Washington became president and his official family consisted of such outstanding men as Jefferson, Adams, and Hamilton – all of whom had served with distinction the cause of American independence – together with other first-rate statesmen; these men followed the policy of gradual progress. In the same way, the first cabinet under the new Japanese constitution should consist of outstanding statesmen who had rendered meritorious services in the Meiji Restoration and who had enjoyed high prestige in the eye of the entire nation. Kaneko was not a stranger to Thayer and Holmes. Thayer had taught Kaneko constitutional law at Harvard. He was fond of proudly telling American visitors to Japan that Justice Holmes had been his private tutor during his student days in Cambridge.

Thus, all these prominent men of the Western world approved the conservative policy adopted by the Meiji statesmen in drafting the constitution. English constitutional lawyers did not recommend their own cabinet government. Perhaps they approved the more conservative approach embodied in the constitution because their historical knowledge indicated that the development of constitutional government was most successful in England and other countries in which the powers of the parliament had originally been limited and only gradually extended. They probably felt that thrusting wide responsibility on parliamentarians before they learned the technique of popular government would be inimical to the sound development of constitutional government. Indeed, the institution of popular government might itself be discredited. The holders of these views were not reactionaries in politics but wise men who never lost historical perspective.

Some of the fundamental institutional arrangements established by the constitution were soon tested in operation. Perhaps the first to be decisively tried was the independence of the judiciary. Before the Meiji Constitution, the Japanese judiciary had not enjoyed independence; and, just about one year after the constitution came into effect, the newly guaranteed right was given an acid test.

On May II, 1891, a policeman made an attempt in Otsu on the life of the Russian crown prince who was then traveling in Japan. The news threw the whole nation as well as the government into consternation, and there was fear of 'grave consequences'. Since the Penal Code then in force did not specifically regulate offenses against members of a foreign royal household, no penalty heavier than imprisonment for life – the maximum punishment for an ordinary attempt at murder – was available under the code. The government wanted to have the death penalty meted out to the prisoner by an analogous application of provisions concerning offenses against the Japanese imperial household. Great political pressure was brought to bear on Iken Kojima, President of the Great Court of Judicature (the prewar supreme court), as well as on the judges of that court who went to Otsu to conduct the trial. Rejecting the arguments of the Procurator-General, the court imposed a sentence of penal servitude for life, not the death penalty. Thus the judges dramatically guarded their independence, rejecting all governmental pressure. Kojima did not preside at the trial. Some historians censured him for having himself infringed judicial independence, considering his urging of the trial judges to reject political pressure an interference with the judicial process. However, Kojima is today looked up to by the Japanese people in general as the embodiment of the spirit of judicial independence.

In a sense, the Otsu affair and its legacy contradict the basic thesis advanced by the Western scholars interviewed by Kaneko; the inclusion in the constitution of an institution quite foreign to the Japanese scene provided the foundation on which a tradition of judicial independence very quickly emerged. The Otsu judgment remains the most valuable tradition of the Japanese judiciary. Whatever their shortcomings, Japanese judges since then have scrupulously guarded their independence, and the nation has reposed implicit confidence in their integrity and their freedom from corruption, although of course not everyone always likes their decisions.

In another area – the relation between the executive and the legislature – the several predictions of Anson did indeed come true.. The relation between the two branches of government did not develop along the lines, strictly conceived, laid down in the constitution. Once Western institutions and thinking had acquired a basis within the formal structure of Japanese society, they were able to develop in ways quite incompatible with traditional Japanese thinking and feeling. Unfortunately, however, what had given promise of being a healthy development was cut short in the 1930s.

The draftsmen of the Meiji Constitution envisaged a strong bureaucracy, consisting of civil and military branches, with social prestige and honors emanating from the semidivine emperor. The Diet was not to be allowed any direct control, and even in matters of legislation and finance its authority was to be limited by imperial retention of comprehensive prerogative powers. The conception was a minimum recognition of

Western institutions and practices of government while retaining, as far as possible, traditional Japanese institutions and practices.

Yatsuka Hozumi, who occupied the chair of constitutional law at Tokyo Imperial University, interpreted the constitution in conformity with the intent of its authors, and his interpretation was regarded for some time as authoritative. He made the distinction between *kokutai* (form of state), which is unchangeable, and *seitai* (form of government), which is subject to change. The sovereignty of the Tenno constituted the *kokutai* of the Japanese state that could not be changed. But this theory was challenged by his junior colleague Tatsukichi Minobe, who rejected this metaphysical distinction and adopted the theory, then prevailing among German publicists, that sovereignty resided in the state, of which the Tenno was but an organ, though undoubtedly the highest organ. Although the controversy was an academic and theoretical one concerning the position of the Emperor in the Japanese constitutional system, it concealed a political controversy between proponents of executive supremacy and of legislative supremacy. Hozumi's mantle fell on Shinkichi Uesugi, his successor at the university. Uesugi came to represent the conservative and Minobe the progressive wing of Japanese constitutional theory. If Uesugi could be characterized as a strict constructionist, true to the legislative intent, Minobe was a liberal constructionist, his interpretation being more in conformity with the emerging trend toward parliamentary government. Minobe occupied the chair of constitutional law at the university much longer than his younger rival, and his theory became more influential in the 1920s. However, when political reaction set in with the military ascendancy in the 1930s, his 'organ theory' was severely attacked as heretical by, among others, ultranationalistic politicians in the Diet.

The statesmen who drafted the constitution felt, with George Washington and eighteenth-century European statesmen, that political parties were immoral. A similar motive to that which gave rise to political parties in eighteenth-century England – the desire for patronage – stimulated the organization of parties and the mobilization of parliamentary powers. The government endeavored to suppress the opposition by force, but in vain. After the First World War, indications were strong that Japan would evolve a party cabinet of the British type. 'Transcendental cabinets', which included men of divergent political beliefs, were discredited in the public mind. By 'protection of the constitution' (*goken*) was meant in fact a movement to establish cabinet government. In 1925, the popular basis of Japanese parliamentarism was widened by the adoption of universal suffrage. When the London Naval Treaty was being ratified in 1930, the liberal Prime Minister, Hamaguchi (nicknamed 'the Lion'), forced the conservative Privy Council to yield to his iron will. There were even some signs that civilian supremacy might be realized in due course. This, however, proved to be the wishful thinking of Japanese liberals, for a reign of what an English journalist called 'government by assassination' ensued.

At first, the interest in parliamentary affairs was mostly limited to fief leaders, just as in eighteenth-century England active interest in parliamentary government was confined almost entirely to the gentry. The major political parties in Japan, the Seiyukai and the Minseito, were, like the Tories and the Whigs in eighteenth-century England, simply factions within the ruling aristocracy. After the First World War, when Japanese capitalism made huge strides, the industrialists headed by the *zaibatsu* interests, like the Mitsui and the Mitsubishi, entered the political arena using the political parties to promote their own interests. A little later, a political consciousness began to emerge among urban working men and the first proletarian parties were organized. The process of the widening of the popular basis of parliamentarism seen in nineteenth-century England was being repeated in Japan.

This normal development in Japan was checked in the 1930s by the capture of political power by army extremists and by the renewal of bureaucratic absolutism. Following the Great Depression, executive supremacy seemed to be a world-wide trend. Its development in Japan, however, assumed peculiar traits that are little known in advanced Western countries: the use of assassination to express dissatisfaction with the policy of the government or the political opinions of leading statesmen and a gradual erosion of military discipline, which took the form of *gekokujo* (overpowering of seniors by juniors). Indeed, the period between 1934 and 1941, characterized by murderous conspiracy at home and unchecked aggression abroad, was most unpalatable to those Japanese liberals who looked forward to the gradual and peaceful development of constitutional democracy. This period has fairly been styled that of the 'Dark Valley' (*kurai tanima*).

The political situation in Japan during the Second World War followed the course which was taken everywhere else: national unity for success in war. Although the Meiji constitution was in force until May 3, 1947, when the new constitution took effect, the political parties had been dissolved, and the Diet in its sittings did nothing but rubber-stamp government-sponsored measures, though it sometimes showed independent judgment in refusing to pass a bill in its original form. A tolerable number of parliamentarians refused to belong to totalitarian parties. Only the judiciary continued to maintain its independence. In that respect the government of Japan was perhaps not as thoroughly totalitarian as that of Nazi Germany.

The text of the constitution was never amended during the half century of its existence. Japanese political life did not proceed in conformity with the 'textbook of strategy' as penned by the Meiji statesmen. The prophesy of William Anson in 1889 proved true.

...

The Old Penal Code

The Penal Code of 1880 was based on a draft made by Boissonade. Before coming to Japan in 1873, Emile Gustave Boissonade de Fontarabie had assisted Ortolan in teaching criminal law at the University of Paris. Both men belonged to the neoclassical school. This school followed, in the main, the classical retaliatory doctrine of De Maître and Kant, incorporating, however, the social-defense idea of Beccaria and Bentham. Boissonade himself expressly stated that his *Projet révisé de code pénal pour l'empire du Japon* (1886) was not based solely on the doctrine of absolute justice or solely on the utilitarian doctrine, but on the idea that an act which was both a *mal moral* and a *mal social* was to be made a punishable crime. He aimed at a combination of two basic ideas, 'justice' and 'utilité'. The most 'revolutionary' provisions of the code, as far as Japan was concerned, were the following two articles:

> *Article 2. Nulle action ou omission ne peut être punie, si ce n'est en vertu d'une disposition expresse de la loi.*
>
> *Article 3. La loi pénale n'a pas d'effet rétroactif sur les infractions commises avant sa promulgation. Toutefois, les dispositions plus douces d'une loi nouvelle sont immédiatement applicables.*

These two articles embody the well-known principle of *nullum crimen, nulla poena sine lege* and the principle of banning punishment by an *ex post facto* law. Although expressed in Latin, these are by no means time-honored principles in Continental Europe, and, as far as the judicial process is concerned, they are not honored without exception in contemporary England. They were products of the French Revolution, and nineteenth-century Continental Europe regarded them as fundamental to a civilized concept of justice. These principles were 'revolutionary' in Japan because no such general principles were known in the administration of criminal justice in feudal Japan. The Tokugawa statesmen, under the influence of the Confucian conception of government, believed that their primary duty was to teach the governed how to behave according to morality as defined in the feudal period and that the administration of criminal justice was something secondary. Thus orders such as the famous Code of a Hundred Articles (*O-Sadamegaki Hyakkajo*) of 1742 took the form of instructions to officials. The texts of the orders were not published. Of course, the people were not kept entirely in the dark regarding punishable conduct, but it was considered a wise policy to keep the correspondence between offenses and penalties an official secret. The new code definitely abandoned this policy.

The code was also revolutionary in establishing the principle of equality before law. The feudal criminal law was an elaborate system. What conduct constituted a crime and what penalties were to be meted out varied according to the social class to which the accused belonged and also according to his family standing and other social relations. The new code swept away all these feudal complexities.

The code established, as its third great innovation, the individualistic principle that guilt was personal. Collective criminal responsibility and guilt by association, which had characterized feudal justice, were abolished. It may be noted that to contemporary Japanese jurists *actus non facit reum, nisi mens sit rea* is not, as in some Western countries, a mere maxim to which lip service is paid. These jurists use a subjective rather than an objective test regarding *mens rea*. Presumptions as to knowledge or belief are unknown to Japanese criminal jurisprudence. Incidentally, a heavy burden of proof is thus put on the public procurator, which accounts, in some measure, for the procurator's tendency to employ inquisitorial methods in the examination of suspects. Punishment for negligent crimes is still today exceptional and cannot be imposed in the absence of an express statutory provision. Although *mens rea* is based on intent, negligence which presupposes lack of intent is treated as similar to *mens rea*, the subjective test also being adopted in determining whether the accused was negligent. Most Japanese lawyers consequently find it difficult to swallow the Anglo-Saxon doctrine of conspiracy, which reminds them of feudal justice. As is well known, rapid industrialization and the related influx of the rural population into large cities in Western countries is giving rise to 'public-welfare offenses,' punishable without any reference to *mens rea*. However, the influence of the doctrine that guilt is personal, introduced by the Penal Code of 1880, is still so strong that Japanese lawyers experience difficulty in adapting themselves to the era of 'eclipse of *mens rea*,' to the growing tendency to import strict or absolute liability into the field of criminal justice.

Finally, it is interesting to note that the code introduced the category of offenses against the imperial household. When, in 1869, a new criminal code was being drafted, the draftsmen provided for the offense of high treason. Upon reading this draft provision, Taneomi Soyejima expressed his indignation and immediately ordered its deletion, saying that such an inauspicious event would never occur in this country. Soyejima's thinking may remind the reader of the ancient Greeks, who refrained from providing for parricide, and of the ancient Persians, who adopted the fiction that any person who committed parricide was born on the wrong side of the blanket. When

Japanese legislators found that Boissonade's draft contained the same inauspicious provision, they again vigorously insisted that it be struck out. However, the learned professor finally convinced the legislators that the provision should be retained. Articles 73 to 76 of the Penal Code of 1907 also regulated offenses against the imperial household. These provisions were stricken out in 1946, this time on the ground that they were incompatible with the principle of equality before law declared by the new constitution. The present Penal Code, moreover, also deprives foreign monarchs, presidents, and their envoys of similar privileges.

The Penal Code of 1907

The Penal Code of 1880, which certainly was epoch-making legislation, had been in operation for some twenty-five years when it was radically revised by the 1907 code. Boissonade's project was not a mere translation of the French Penal Code of 1810. He took newer laws into account, introduced novel institutions such as parole, and also incorporated his own personal views on various points. The 1880 code was, however, guided by the old theory that punishment must exactly fit the offense. It adopted the French classification of offenses into *'crime'*, *'délit'*, and *'contravention'* and provided for each offense and its corresponding penalty in such a way as to leave as small a margin of judicial discretion as possible.

During the operation of the Penal Code of 1880 for over a quarter of a century, the influence of German legal science became more and more marked, even though the code itself was modeled on French law. Students of criminal law who went abroad spent most of their time in Germany. Franz von Liszt's seminar was a source of inspiration to many young Japanese scholars. The battles of various schools of thought, such as that between Birkmeyer and Liszt, were repeated in Japan. Not that French and Italian authors were entirely neglected; but the more systematic method of exposition and the philosophical way in which fundamental problems of punishment were discussed, characteristic of German legal science, deeply influenced Japanese students of criminal law. Out of such academic *Sturm und Drang* was born the 1907 code. In it, the subjective theory of punishment advocated by the newer school emerged victorious.

Compared with the former code's 430 articles, the new code was a shorter document consisting of only 264 articles. It abolished the old threefold classification (*crime, délit, contravention*) of criminal offenses. A wider margin was afforded judicial discretion in meting out punishment. Parole had already been recognized in the old code. The new code provided also for the suspension of the execution of sentence, though not yet for the indeterminate sentence.

The absence of a *nullum crimen* provision was conspicuous in the new code. Some Japanese jurists had considered the principle a nineteenth-century doctrine, inadequate for the twentieth-century administration of criminal justice – though they did not go so far as to condemn it as a 'bourgeois relic,' as Soviet jurists did in the 1920s. The general interpretation of the omission, however, was that an express formulation of the principle was unnecessary because Article 23 of the Meiji Constitution provided that 'no Japanese subject shall be arrested, detained, tried, or punished, unless according to law.' The doctrinal disputes between the old and the new schools thus continued to exist even after the coming into force of the new code, and their differences were reflected in the construction of specific provisions of the new code. The new school of jurists contributed greatly to the progress of criminology in Japan, but the practice of Japanese courts has still not been swayed by the new doctrines. Courts have been inclined, on the whole, to abide by the conservative doctrine, even though the code of 1907 embodied the new school's victory.

After World War I, an attempt was made, as in Germany and Switzerland, to effect a code revision, and a committee was set up for that purpose. But the attempt bore no fruit, nor have a few amendments after the Second World War affected in any fundamental way the character of the Penal Code of 1907. The deletion of the chapter on crimes against the imperial household has already been mentioned. The provisions respecting the offense of adultery were also amended in view of the constitutional requirements of sexual equality. Under the code of 1907, the wife and her paramour were punishable at the husband's request, while the husband who had intercourse with another woman was not punishable. The alternative for the legislators under the new constitution of 1946 was either to make husband and wife both punishable or to abolish the offense of adultery altogether. After long debates in the Diet, the latter alternative was chosen. Adultery, however, is now a ground for divorce for both the husband and the wife.

The Code of Criminal Instruction of 1880

The methods of criminal justice employed during the Tokugawa regime were radically changed by the enactment of the Code of Criminal Instruction of 1880, which came into operation simultaneously with the Penal Code on January 1, 1882. The code adopted the French semi-inquisitorial method which colored the Japanese administration of penal justice until the end of the Second World War.

If the administration of criminal justice in Western countries had not evolved so rapidly after the French Revolution, the method of administering criminal justice in feudal Japan might not have been so radically altered. The inquisitorial method, which had come into use in Europe under ecclesiastical influence, became more and more general in the period of absolute monarchy, during which the rights of the state were paramount. The inquisitorial system provided in the famous ordinance of Louis XIV, who identified himself with the state, is no less hideous to the modern mind than the similar method employed during the Tokugawa regime. The Code d'Instruction Criminelle of 1808 was influenced by the spirit of the revolution, and open trials and oral pleading were adopted. However, the essence of the traditional inquisitorial method was retained, and a marked contrast still seems to exist between the Anglo-Saxon accusatory method and the French inquisitorial method. It is well known that Englishmen have, from time to time, adversely criticized French criminal trials, especially during such *causes célèbres* as the Dreyfus case. Not a few learned essays have appeared in English and American legal journals, contrasting the French with the Anglo-American criminal procedure. It is also interesting that, in connection with the abolition of extraterritoriality in Japan. Harry Parkes, the British Minister to Japan, was not enthusiastic over the prospect of subjecting the English-speaking foreigners in Japan, who formed the great majority of the foreign colony, to laws which were mainly French and German in origin. He held that the English legal system should alone have been considered in preparing the new codes. Parkes's attitude was, perhaps, partially motivated by the traditional English prejudice against French criminal trials. In the 19205, the present writer often heard his American friends criticize Japanese administration of criminal justice. As a matter of fact, this criticism was generally directed against the French procedural institutions adopted by Japan in 1882.

Meiji statesmen early saw the necessity of reforming criminal law and procedure along Western lines. As early as 1869, Rinsho Mitsukuri translated the French Penal

Code by order of the government. Piecemeal reforms were achieved: the opening of the courts to representatives of the press (1872), separation of the courts from the procurator's office (1872), prohibition of the use of torture in civil cases (1872), abolition of class distinctions at court trials (1872), banning of vendettas (1873), restrictions on the use of physical torture (1874), organization of the judicial system along French lines (1875), recognition of appeal (*koso*) and revision (*jokoku*) appellate procedure (1875), introduction of the French system of *avocats* (1872) – who were, however, not allowed to appear in criminal cases until 1882 – and of *juges d'instruction* (1876), abolition of confession by the accused as a requisite for imposing punishment (1876), the adoption of bail (1877), and total banning of physical torture (1879). All these reforms were largely inspired by French models.

The Penal Code of 1880 and the Code of Criminal Instruction of 1880 were the first 'modern' Japanese codes. It is true that in the early years of the Meiji regime, two criminal codes, the Outline of the New Criminal Law (*Shinritsu Koryo*; 1870) and the Amended Criminal Regulations (*Kaitei Ritsurei*; 1873), had been enacted and were in force until 1881. They considerably humanized the old penalties, but they were largely based on criminal law of Chinese origin and cannot be styled 'modern'.

The Code of Criminal Instruction provided for the organization and jurisdiction of the criminal courts, as well as for criminal procedure proper. In dealing with the public trial the code adopted the procedure of the modern French type. Indeed, for the first time in Japan an advocate was permitted to appear to defend the accused. The advocate was theoretically on a par with the public procurator under this new procedure, but the latter kept his official dignity by sitting together with the judges on a raised platform as the French tradition of treating judges and public procurators as part of the magistrature was also introduced. (Only after the Second World War were procurators to sit at the same level as advocates.) The judge had to be very active at trials, behaving more like a confessor than an umpire. The advocate was allowed to cross-examine an adverse witness but only through the judge. Most important of all, the code contained elaborate provisions relative to 'preliminary investigation', which reminds one of the old inquisitorial methods. At this preliminary examination counsel was not allowed to assist the suspect; Boissonade, when drafting his project, was naturally unaware of the French law of 1897, which allowed the attendance of counsel at this stage. There were some Japanese critics of the system of preliminary investigation, but most Japanese jurists supported it as a more logical and scientific method for getting at the truth. It is quite natural that, after elaborate investigations by *juges d'instruction*, the accused was presumed in the public mind to be guilty, even if in the eye of the law he is presumed innocent until he is finally found guilty by the court. When an official, for instance, was committed to trial after preliminary investigation, it was customary for him to tender his resignation without waiting for the final judgment. Under this system, therefore, the function of the judge at the trial was to review the findings of the preliminary judge rather than to try the case de novo. The importance of this preliminary hearing continued for half a century until its abolition after the Second World War. However, the code contained many salutary provisions designed to guarantee a fair trial, such as the provision that supporting reasons must be given for all judgments, which provided a check on judicial arbitrariness.

Another point may be noted in connection with this code. The original Boissonade project contained provisions concerning the jury. He explained that it was important to adopt the jury system, in order to put the Japanese legal system on a par with that of other civilized nations. The code would eventually be applied to foreign residents in Japan, and it was desirable to have the jury system inasmuch as they would look upon it as a symbol of impartial justice. There were some Japanese legislators who supported him, but the relevant provisions were finally struck out, chiefly on the ground that it was premature for Japan to adopt the jury system. Boissonade was not satisfied with this decision, and, at the time of the making of the Meiji Constitution, he again advised the government to adopt the jury. Prince Ito, however, refused to accept his proposal.

The Code of Criminal Procedure of 1922

In 1890, after the promulgation of the Meiji Constitution providing for the separation of powers, a separate law relative to the constitution of the judiciary was enacted. Also the renamed Code of Criminal Procedure replaced, with minor changes, the old Code of Criminal Instruction. However, a more fundamental revision of criminal procedure was felt necessary. The reform committee set up for the purpose relied heavily on the German Code of Criminal Procedure of 1877 and on the 1908 and 1920 draft codes. Its work was completed in 1922, although a partial revision had been effected in 1899. The Code of Criminal Procedure of 1922, which came into effect on 1 January 1923, evinces the German influence in ample measure, especially as regards the arrangement of the Code, but the original French influence was not eliminated. The new code also reflected the liberalizing spirit of the 1920s by paying more attention to rights of the accused.

The spirit of the times was further reflected in the enactment of the Jury Law in 1923, which came into force on 1 October 1928. This law, providing for lay participation in criminal justice, took as a model the English jury system rather than the German assessor system. Like the English petit jury, the jury consisted of twelve persons, but the unanimity principle was rejected in favor of the majority principle. The jury had no power to say 'guilty' or 'not guilty', since this was barred by provisions of the Meiji Constitution guaranteeing the right of Japanese subjects to obtain justice from qualified professional judges. The function of the jury was confined to decisions on questions of fact put by the court. The verdict of a jury, moreover, was not finally binding on the court, which could change the panel as many times as it deemed proper, although the court could not render a judgment contrary to the verdict. If the court accepted the verdict of the jury, its judgment became final and conclusive and no appeal was to be allowed. The jury system did not prosper, although it was at first welcomed as the palladium of liberty. Particularly because of the expense involved and the absence of appeal, waiver of jury trial was the normal procedure. Jury trial was not congenial to the Japanese legal profession, trained in the inquisitorial system, and no serious endeavors were undertaken to make this modified Anglo-Saxon system a success in Japan. The Jury Law was suspended on 1 April 1943, and it has not yet been revived.

The American contribution to the world's legal science – the 'juvenile court', established in Chicago at the close of the nineteenth century – was transplanted to Japan by the enactment of the Juvenile Law of 1922. The juvenile court was administered by the Ministry of Justice for over two decades. After the Second World War, a new Juvenile Law replaced the prewar statute, and since 1949 the juvenile court has become part and parcel of Japan's judicial system. Unlike the jury system, this American innovation in criminal justice took firm root in Japan, as it has in many other lands.

The Code of Criminal Procedure of 1948

The new constitution of 1946 contains no less than nine articles directly affecting criminal procedure. A new Code of Criminal Procedure of 10 July 1948, was accordingly prepared and, supplemented by the Supreme Court Regulation of 1 December 1948, came into operation on 1 January 1949.

The postwar influence of Anglo-American law is most marked in the field of criminal procedure. Rights of suspected and accused persons from arrest to judgment are scrupulously protected, and the old preliminary investigation is now gone. The accusatory procedure replaced the former semi inquisitorial procedure at trials, though not to such an extent as to sweep away completely the old tradition. Many of the Anglo-American rules of evidence have been incorporated. The art of cross-examination has become the stock in trade of the public procurator as well as the defense counsel. This is not, however, the place to elaborate on those reforms and their practical operation.

...

The Civil Code of 1890

The Old Civil Code of 1890, which never came into effect, was in its arrangement based on the French code. Books II (Property in General), III (Acquisition of Property), IV (Security of Obligations), and V (Evidence) had been drafted by Boissonade. Their contents were mostly French law. Books I (Persons) and III (Inheritance) had been drafted by Japanese jurists. But the French legal influence was marked even in the part dealing with family and inheritance, although the original draft was radically revised prior to promulgation to preserve the old House system. Books II, IV, and V were promulgated on 27 April 1890; Books I and III on 7 October 1890. The entire code was to take effect on 1 January 1893. This was the first modern Japanese code in the field of private law. Since the code affected the social and economic life of the nation in all its aspects, it became a topic of earnest consideration among educated classes. There was heated discussion, especially among lawyers and politicians, as to its merits and demerits. The controversy developed into a dispute between the English and the French schools and finally into a political struggle between conservatives and progressives. The immediate result of this struggle was an eight-year postponement in the enforcement of a civil code.

A few paragraphs are in order to explain the condition of legal education at this period in Japan, since this proved to be an important factor in the factional clash that occurred in connection with acceptance of the Civil Code.

From early Meiji times there had been a law school attached to the Ministry of Justice in which French law was taught. Two or three private law schools also taught French law. Boissonade, who came to Japan in November 1873 and began to teach French law in 1874, was an outstanding figure. He was interested in natural law and lectured on that subject as well as on more technical subjects. In his days the *école d'exégese* was still dominant in France in the field of private law; the 'revival of natural law' in France, which took place at the close of the century, was not yet underway. Boissonade may have read Ahrens' *Cours de droit naturel*, which was first published in 1837 and ran through many editions; and, as is shown by his *Le nouveau code civil italien comparé au code Napoléon*, published in 1868, he had some interest in *législation comparée* before he came to Japan. However, his other works from this period indicate that his main interest lay in the historical aspects of various private-law institutions. Judging from his previous publications, one would suppose that he was a positivist interested in history. It seems that he first began to lecture on natural law in Japan. Was this motivated by his desire to expound his own *Weltanschauung* in the form of a lecture? Or did it arise from his newly assigned task of drafting modern codes for Japan and making her accept them as an embodiment of natural law? He considered that the system of positive law was, and ought to be, a reflection of natural law, which is in turn a universal idea of mankind and can be discovered by human reason. If there is any discrepancy between positive law and natural law, the positive law was no law but a corruption of law. Boissonade's theory, like Ahrens', is close to that expounded by the seventeenth- and eighteenth-century natural-law jurists. They, unlike the glossators and commentators, considered Roman law binding not because it was based on imperial authority but because it was an embodiment of universal human reason. As is well known, this idea of natural law inspired codification movements in Europe. Although such a theory perhaps served no practical purpose in France after the comprehensive Napoleonic codes had been completed, it could be eminently useful for the Japanese who had the task of codification before them. The natural law expounded by Boissonade seems to have appealed to the Japanese audience because it was very similar to the familiar concept of the Confucian 'Way of Heaven.' Many Japanese jurists who attended Boissonade's lectures naturally came to believe that the French code was not merely a French national product but an embodiment of natural law – a model of civilized law.

English law had been taught at the Tokyo Kaisei School, which subsequently became Tokyo Imperial University, since the year 1874 by American, English, and Japanese teachers, and it was taught in several other law schools. The methods of legal science in England in those days were analytical-historical, and the school of natural law was looked down upon as outmoded. Henry T Terry, an American lawyer who for a long time to come was to be familiar around the university as an eminent authority on Anglo-American law, also frowned on natural law. In *First Principles of Law*, published in 1878, his anti-natural-law sentiment is strongly expressed:

> The law of nature or natural law is a species of *pseudo* law which has occupied a great deal of the attention of writers on jurisprudence in the nations of continental Europe, and has been the source of no little confusion and obscurity in the law, and wild and foolish theorizing, and unfortunately of equally wild acting, in the politics of those countries. It is the very tap-root of communism. Fortunately it never took any strong hold of English and American legal thought, though it crops up in the 'glittering generalities' of the opening of the Declaration of Independence of the United States and it is the favorite appeal of demagogues of every time.

This book reached fifteen editions and was widely used as a textbook in Japan. His later works, *Leading Principles of Anglo-American Law* (1884) and *The Common Law* (second revised edition, 1898), and his lectures at the university on torts and equity evince, according to Albert Koeourek, an originality and analytic acuteness superior to that of John Austin. It was quite natural that, when the Hohfeldian system and the restatement-movement brought about a revival of analytical jurisprudence in the United States, his arrangement of the law and his original analysis of rights. drew the attention of American jurists. Terry was adept in analytical jurisprudence and, like Bentham and Austin, favored codification.

Another prominent American jurist who taught Anglo-American law in Japan was John H Wigmore. He, like Terry, did not uphold natural law. His lectures at Keio Gijuku, his monumental *Treatise on the Law of Evidence*, and his concise summary in *Cases on Torts* attest to his amazing analytic power. Unlike Terry, however, he was also interested in the dynamic aspect of law. His *Panorama of the World's Legal Systems*, the *Evolution of Law* series edited by him, and his highly original planetary theory of legal evolution may be regarded as the later developments of his interest in Tokugawa judicial decisions from the standpoint of comparative legal history. Wigmore was historical and analytical. He followed Henry Maine as well as John Austin.

Japanese jurists of the English school in this period studied not so much the reported cases as they did Bentham, Austin, and Maine and text writers such as Pollock, Holland, Anson, and Terry. They were interested in abstract positive rules and principles as expounded by those text writers. Unlike Savigny and his school, they were not opposed to codification, and, unlike the Germanist branch of the German historical school, they were not upholders of the indigenous law. They were no more 'nationalistic' than the jurists of the French school and, like the latter, held Western individualistic jurisprudence in high esteem.

The objection of the English school of jurists to the immediate enforcement of the Civil Code was scientific rather than political. The code was based exclusively on French Law. The English school did not consider French law the only civilized system of law and believed the English and German systems must also be taken into account. It may be noted in this connection that in 1887, three years before the promulgation of the Old Civil Code, a change had been made in the curriculum of the law department of Tokyo Imperial University. The law school of the Ministry of Justice was transferred to the university in 1885, and the German-law section was newly established in 1887. It may also be noted that German legal science was then acquiring an increased prestige in Japan as well as in other countries.

At first, the case for postponement of the enforcement of the Civil Code beyond 1893 was presented in a scientific spirit. When, however, the question of postponement or immediate enforcement developed into a fight between the two schools, the arguments for opposing immediate enforcement tended to run wild. It was an age of reaction against over-rapid westernization, and scholars sometimes appealed to patriotic sentiment. It is also true that some facets of the controversy took on aspects of the controversy between Thibaut and Savigny and of a struggle between the school of natural law and the historical school. However, it was not essentially a conflict of two philosophies, but a conflict of views based on expediency. Nobushige Hozumi, who was himself an English barrister of the Middle Temple and who had also studied at Berlin, was one of the leading champions of the postponement party. Masaaki Tomii, who was a *docteur en droit* of the University of Lyon and an eminent jurist of the French school, also belonged to the postponement group. Kenjiro Ume, who had studied law both at Lyon and Berlin, was a leading champion of the immediate-enforcement party. It is also interesting to note in this connection that in 1892 John Wigmore wrote an article, 'New Codes and Old Customs', in the *Japan Mail*, which gave aid and comfort to the enforcement group.

The New Civil Code of 1898

The postponement party won out. A bill to postpone the enforcement of the code was brought before the Lower House. After several heated debates, the bill passed both Houses, and the operation of the code was postponed until December 31, 1896. A new drafting committee of three, consisting of Hozumi, Ume, and Tomii, followed the policy first advocated by the English school and consulted many codes and drafts then available. The net result of their labors was that the arrangement of the new code became entirely German, adopting the Pandekten system rather than the institutional French system. Although its contents are of a composite nature, showing here and there the influence of French and English law as well as the native law, the influence of the first

(1887) and second (1896) drafts of the German Civil Code is clearly dominant. The new Civil Code of Japan came into operation on 16 July 1898. Although English, German, and French law continued to be taught at the Imperial University by foreign and Japanese professors, the predominance of German legal science continued down to the end of the Second World War. Subsequent legislation in other fields of law followed German models. Students of law went mostly to German universities, as German textbooks, commentaries, and court decisions could most conveniently be utilized for the interpretation and application of the codes and statutes in force in Japan.

After the coming into force of the Civil Code of 1898, many special laws were enacted to supplement or modify the provisions concerning real rights and obligations. A committee was set up in 1919 to revise the parts relating to the family and inheritance law, so as to bring them into accord with the 'old *boni mores* of our country' (*jumpu bizoku*). Despite the high-sounding proclamation smacking of political reaction, many of the thirty-four proposals for revision in the family law adopted by the committee in 1925, and the seventeen proposals for revising the inheritance law, adopted by it, in 1927, were in various aspects progressive in character. They served, therefore, as valuable material when the Civil Code was revised to bring it into accord with the spirit of the new constitution.

The Old and New Commercial Codes

As in the case of the Civil Code, there also were an Old Commercial Code and a New Commercial Code. The Old Code was based on a draft written by Hermann Roesler, a German adviser to the government and professor at the Imperial University. Roesler's draft was eclectic and not exclusively French, since German and English law were also taken into account. The Old Commercial Code was promulgated on 27 April 1890, but shared the fate of the Old Civil Code in the heat of the postponement controversy. However, unlike the Old Civil Code, which never came into force but only served as convenient material for the court in exercising 'reason,' some sections of the Old Commercial Code, especially those parts relating to companies, came into operation on 1 July 1893, and remained in force until the coming into effect of the New Commercial Code. Book III of the Old Commercial Code, which provided for bankruptcy of companies, also came into effect on 1 July 1893, and was in force until replaced by the Bankruptcy Law of 1922. These temporary measures were necessitated by a business panic. The New Commercial Code, drafted by a committee consisting of Ume, Okano, and Tabe, was promulgated on 9 March 1899, and took effect on 16 June of the same year.

The Commercial Code of 1899 consisted of five books: General Provisions, Companies, Commercial Acts, Bills, and Maritime Commerce. Book IV, dealing with bills of exchange, promissory notes, and checks, was stricken from the code simultaneously with the enactment of two statutes, one on bills of exchange and promissory notes (1932) and the other on checks (1933). These enactments followed the ratifications of two international treaties entered into at Geneva providing for uniform laws on those topics.

In view of the marked development of industry and commerce after World War I, the Commercial Code, especially Book II, was radically amended, and the amended code came into force on 1 January 1940. A separate statute providing for limited liability companies (*yugen kaisha*) came into force on the same date, thus amplifying the forms available for business enterprise. The law on companies was again radically revised during the Allied military occupation as one phase of the democratization of Japan, and in this process American corporation law was taken as a model.

Code of Civil Procedure and the Labor Laws

The Code of Civil Procedure was promulgated on April 21, 1890, and came into force on 1 January 1891. The code was almost a literal translation of the German *Zivilprozessordnung*; the translation of *Rechtshängigkeit* – 'pending in court' – as *'kenri-kosoku'* – 'fettered right' (in context a meaningless phrase which revealed that the translator thought that *Recht* in the German term *'Rechtshängigkeit'* had its ordinary sense of 'right' rather than the unusual sense of 'court') – was a famous laughing-stock among old lawyers, though it has now been deleted.

Important amendments to the Code of Civil Procedure were made on 24 April 1926. Unlike the case of the Code of Criminal Procedure, the new constitution did not necessitate revision of the Code of Civil Procedure. However, a few amendments were made modifying the mode of trial in the court of first instance, and here the Anglo-American influence is conspicuous.

After World War I, Japan's capitalistic economy made marked progress, and the interest of jurists was drawn to the law in relation to labor. Anton Menger's *Das bürgerliche Recht und die besitzlosen Klassen* (1903) was translated into Japanese by Tadahiko Mibuchi, then a young judge who after the Second World War became the first Chief Justice of the Supreme Court organized under the new constitution. Karl Rermer's more radical *Soziale Funktion der Rechtsinstitute besonders des Eigentums*, which appeared in 1904 in volume one of Marx Studien and was published in a revised edition in 1929 with the title *Die Rechtsinstitute des Privatrechts und die soziale Funktion*, was also studied with much sympathy by students of civil law. After Izutaro Suehiro returned from Europe, he sensed the coming importance of labor law in Japan, began his informal annual lectures on that subject, and published a number of articles in the field. He may indeed be regarded as the father of Japanese labor law. The Factory Law promulgated in 1911, which came into effect in 1916, was the first Japanese labor legislation. A series of social and labor legislation ensued – the Leased Land Law (1921), the Leased House Law (1921), the Leased Land and Leased House Mediation Law (1922), and the Tenant Farming Mediation Law (1924). The period of controlled economy under a series of laws enacted under the National General Mobilization Law of April 1938 can be passed over as an outcome of an extraordinary situation. During the military occupation, a trinity of labor laws – the Labor Relations Adjustment Law, the Labor Union Law, and the Labor Standards Law – enacted at the suggestion of American lawyers, brought Japanese labor legislation on a par with American labor law after the New Deal. Lawyers connected with the American occupation were influential in the drafting of labor legislation, as well as in the radical revision of the companies law mentioned above, and in the preparation of the antimonopoly law.

Akita, G, *Foundations of Constitutional Government in Modern Japan 1868–1900*, 1967, pp 58–66, Harvard University Press

In the years 1870–1880 the *Genro-in* proved that a constitution could be drafted in Japan which scholars later would consider to be creditable. The Meiji oligarchs, however, still felt it necessary to send one of their members abroad to sit at the feet of leading European constitutional specialists. This move was impelled in part by the peculiar nature of the threat posed by the outs, which now included the highly articulate Okuma partisans.

It has been argued that the movement for parliamentarism had but a peripheral role in the government's key decisions concerning the acceptance of a constitutional form of government and the timing of its establishment. In what may be regarded as the middle period of Meiji parliamentary history – the period of the actual preparations for parliamentary government – the premise that the outs had neither immediate nor direct influence on major issues and decisions in this area is still applicable.

The significance of the opposition to the government lay elsewhere. The one important early influence of the movement for parliamentarism was that its very existence served as a reminder to the oligarchs of the potential dangers of ignoring constitutionalism as the wave of the future. The pertinacious presence of the opposition in this period made the oligarchs uneasy because of the dangers it threatened once the constitution was promulgated. There were two ways in which the outs could cause mischief after 1890. One was to attack the constitution itself; the other was to act in an unrestrained and undisciplined manner once they became sharers of the public power. The constitution was drafted with these two possible threats in mind.

Perpetuation in power is the first law of politics, and the Meiji constitution predictably weighted power overwhelmingly in favor of the administration and against the Diet. Indeed, it would have been surprising had the reverse been the case, for the Meiji leaders from Satsuma and Choshu had what to them were excellent reasons in support of this axiom. The Meiji oligarchs, as revolutionaries in the truest sense of the word, were driven by a form of collective Messianic complex. They were thoroughly convinced that it was both their mission and responsibility to lead Japan out of the wilderness of backwardness and weakness toward the green pastures of civilization and power. Their contributions in bringing about the Restoration, they felt, fully justified their assumption of this role, and each successful step toward a stable and powerful Japan served to bolster this conviction. Kabayanla Sukenori, navy minister in the first Matsukata ministry, gave the most famous expression of this faith. 'Who would accuse us of defiling the national honor? ... The present government is the government which has succeeded in overcoming all external and internal difficulties the nation has confronted. Call it the Sat-Cho government, or designate it by whatever name you wish; but who would deny its achievement in maintaining the security and well-being of 40,000,000 souls?

A corollary of this Sat-Cho article of faith was the conviction of the Meiji oligarchs that the parties, the only other groups with the potential for eventually challenging their claim as directors and guardians of Japan's destiny, fully disqualified themselves by their conduct and avowed goals. An ideal party, according to Ito, was one that would conduct the affairs of the nation for all the people. It seemed to him, however, that the parties failed in this one basic requirement, and consistently sacrificed national interests for selfish party interests. This viewpoint is clearly expressed in Ito's bitter complaint about the members of the *Seiyukai*, a party formed by Ito himself. 'The one thing that drives me to distraction is that there is none among them who thinks of the nation above self ... I cannot visualize any one of them working out with any enthusiasm administrative plans and measures on the basis of true concern for the country.'

The oligarchs in the decade after the Rescript of 188I thus faced a real dilemma. On the one hand, they were impelled by their desire for Japan to become a modern and powerful state, and by their reading of Europe's history and experiences, to create a constitutional form of government; on the other hand, as enlightened and realistic men they realized that the ineluctable condition for the institution of such a regime was the sharing of power and responsibility with men and groups they believed lacked the qualifications for running the state. Furthermore, this sharing, as far as they were concerned, threatened to inject instability, disunity, and unseemly grasping for personal gains and benefits in the highest places. Such a state of affairs, they believed, would hinder and even subvert the very purpose for which constitutional government was to be established – the creation of a stable, powerful, and modern Japan. So the essential problem facing Ito in his task of drafting the constitution was to seek means of controlling and rendering as harmless as possible this encroachment into the public power area by the parties. This is the second special characteristic of the challenge posed by the outs to the Meiji government. But it was a danger and challenge that lay largely *in the future*.

Ito's trip to Europe to study constitutions can be explained partially on this basis. The fundamental elements of what was to be incorporated in the Meiji constitution were decided upon before the trip, the final product faithfully reflecting the stipulations contained in the Iwakura memoranda of 5 July 1881. The only mystery is why under the circumstances the oligarchs should have granted leave to the most powerful man in the government and permitted him a liberal expenditure of time and currency, both then in extremely short supply.

The constitution, after its promulgation, was to become 'public' property, in the same way that the private preserve in Tokyo that was the pre-1890 Meiji government was going to be opened for limited exploitation after 1890. The constitution, in a word, was going to be fair game, and, as Suzuki Yasuzo put it, 'if theoretically unsound, would enable the opposition to tear it apart or make fun of it'. And those in the government were keenly aware that they generally lacked the theoretical shield necessary to deflect the possible attacks on the constitution. Ito recalls: 'There were many types of constitutional governments ... I was completely at a loss as to what constitutional government, or whatever it was called, stood for. The situation was such that one classical scholar asked whether Shotoku Taishi's constitution would suffice.'

The leaders in the government were not only on uncertain theoretical footing; they were manning a lonely, embattled rampart. Ito Miyoji later recalled: 'Before the enactment of the constitution, in the days when the parliamentary government movement was vigorous, the French and English constitutional concept that sovereignty resided in the people or in the parliament was popular. The impact of those of us who said that sovereignty was located in the emperor or who advocated a strong monarchy was extremely weak, and it seemed that we were lonely and isolated voices.'

One way to forestall this future challenge to the constitution by the opposition was to link it with the emperor. 'If the constitution is known to the people as having been drafted by a given individual,' warned Ito, 'not only will this give rise to much public comment and criticism, but also the constitution will lose the people's respect. It may [even] come to be said that it would be better not to have a constitution than to have a constitution unrespected by the people.' At this time, however, there was no guarantee that coupling the emperor with the constitution would make the document automatically immune to attack. For if a tentative generalization about the role of the emperor may be permitted, it is that at least until some time after 1890 the emperor still had not become an unquestioned public symbol of reverence and awe. In the early 1880s, for example, the question of the locus of sovereignty was the object of a raging public controversy. And Dr Erwin Baelz, perhaps less biased than most Japanese reporters on this subject, was constrained to record in his diary even as late as 3 November 1880: 'The Emperor's birthday. It distresses me to see how little interest the populace take in their ruler. Only when the police insist on it are the houses decorated with flags. In default of this, house-owners do the minimum.'

Nothing less than a pilgrimage to the fountainhead of constitutionalism, then, with the prestige and theoretical fortification that would result from it, would suffice to silence the potential challenge from the outs. Ito's letters to colleagues remaining in Japan sometimes turned to the subject of acquiring theoretical support to counter the possible attacks by antigovernment forces. In a letter to Iwakura, he wrote:

> Thanks to the famous German scholars Gneist and Stein, I have come to understand the essential features of the structure and operation of states. In the most crucial matter of fixing the formations of our imperial system and of retaining the prerogatives belonging to it, I have already found sufficient substantiation ... The situation in our country is characterized by the erroneous belief that the words of English, American, and French liberals and radicals are eternal verities. This misplaced enthusiasm would practically lead to the overthrow of the nation. I have acquired arguments and principles to retrieve the situation ... I face the future with pleasant anticipation.

There are reasons to suspect that Ito felt that Okuma's group would be more formidable than Itagaki and his followers on the verbal front. For one thing, Ito and Inoue encouraged Itagaki to take a trip to Europe at this time. And the evidence is that Ito urged Goto, who also made the trip, to listen to lectures by Stein. Furthermore, Saionji Kimmochi, who was in Paris, sought to have Itagaki see as much of the political situation in France in the hope that Itagaki would thus be able to discern the difference in the theory and the practice of the French political system. Perhaps one of Ito's aims in supporting the Goto-Itagaki trip was that he believed he would be able to convert these two men to his political views.

Secondly, the Okuma faction enjoyed a widespread and justified reputation for wit and eloquence. The *Japan Weekly Mail*, for example, early in 1891 compared the Kaishinto and the Jiyuto in the following manner: 'In discipline, in intelligence, and in wealth, the Progressionists are upon the whole far ahead of their allies – the Radicals ... The Kaishinto journals, the *Mainichi*, the *Yomiuri*, and the *Hothi* occupy front rank in the press of the capital; while the single organ of the Jiyu-to, the *Jiyu*, is regarded at best as a second rate paper. The Kaishin-to organs write on the situation in a calm and confident tone, while the Jiyu-to paper resorts to childish displays of braggadocio and passion.' It is no wonder, then, that Ito, in a letter reminiscent of Inoue Kowashi's attacks against Fukuzawa, bitterly criticized both Okuma and the 'callow students' who surrounded him, as well as the English constitutional system.

One more possible motive exists for Ito's sojourn in Europe. Ito was well known among his contemporaries for his overweening and passionate drive for fame. Whether this striving stemmed from a feeling of insecurity, a sense of destiny, or both, is difficult to determine. Oka Yoshitake, however, has written a rather convincing article in which he attributes many of Ito's public acts to this personal trait. Ito's earnest application to his studies and the fantastic pace he set for himself throughout his stay in Europe indicate the seriousness with which he regarded his task of drafting a constitution that would at once be above criticism and remain a lasting and immutable monument to him.

The lessons learned in Europe were gratifying to Ito. Yet, it would be a mistake to lose sight of the crucial fact that he fully accepted a basic premise of constitutionalism: the sharing of power. 'Ito,' Kaneko remembers, 'sought rule by both the monarch and the people, the granting by the monarch to the people of the right to participate in government.' 'This,' Kaneko continues, 'was Ito's injunction to us in the writing of a constitution for a constitutional state.' Moreover, Ito may have been more liberal than Gneist on this point. In a rather intriguing passage of a letter to Matsukata, written shortly after he had met Gneist, Ito reported that the German professor's principles, at first glance at least, were 'extremely authoritarian' when viewed in the context of the situation existing in Japan.

On 23 June 1883, some thirteen months after they had arrived in Europe, Ito and his party left Rome for Japan. At Hong Kong Ito learned for the first time of Iwakura's death, which had occurred on 20 June. The party arrived at Yokohama on 3 August 1883, slightly over a year and a half after they had first turned toward Europe.

Three months after his return to Japan Ito established the Office for the Study of the Constitution (*Kempo torishirabe jo*). On 17 March 1884, the Bureau for the Study of Administrative Reforms (*Seido torishirabe kyoku*) was also established, and it absorbed the Office for the Study of the Constitution. The creation of these offices was not followed by serious work on the drafting of the constitution, for Ito, as the leading figure in the government, was occupied with other state matters, foreign and domestic. For example, he made a trip to China lasting two months to settle differences between Japan and China arising over their growing mutual interest in Korea. At home, Ito, as holder of three high administrative positions, undertook administrative reforms as necessary first steps toward constitutional government. On 7 July 1884, the Peerage Law was revised to establish the basis for the House of Peers. In December 1885 the *Dajokan* was abolished and replaced by a cabinet. Work on the constitution, however, was not entirely in abeyance. From March 1884 to the winter of 1885 Ito discussed in detail with Inoue Kowashi, Ito Miyoji, and Kaneko Kentaro his studies in Germany. From about the beginning of 1886, after the creation of the cabinet system, drafting the constitution was given top priority by Ito.

Much attention has been directed by scholars to the process of drafting the Meiji constitution. Hence it is sufficient here to note that the constitution was drafted essentially by five men – four Japanese and one foreigner: Ito, Inoue Kowashi, Ito Miyoji, Kaneko Kentaro, and Carl Friedrich Hermann Roesler. An aspect of the drafting process that seems to have been given less scrutiny is the constant pressure applied by those in the government to influence Ito's efforts – indeed, even to the extent of trying to undermine his efforts.

Ito took elaborate measures to safeguard his secrets and to forestall potential opposition attacks. The stringent security measures he took were more than ample to meet the 'danger' from without. In fact, the success of these measures was such that throughout the 1880s the outs, in their attacks against the government in this field, concentrated their efforts primarily on clandestine publications of what they asserted were drafts of the constitution. It is true that there was vigorous public opposition to Inoue's and Okuma's treaty revision attempts in the years 1887–89 which culminated in a bomb attack on Okuma. However, the failure to revise the treaties can be explained as much by looking at the conflicts within the government as by focusing on external pressure. In a word, it would be hazardous to gauge the strength of the political parties on the basis of the loudness of their opposition. It may be closer to the truth to say that Ito, while displaying some concern over the threats posed by the outs, was able without much difficulty to control and minimize these dangers, as he did in the Crisis of 1881. Until the day when the opposition was to partake of public power, through the Meiji constitution, Ito's primary concern was not the harassment by the outs but the demands of the various and constantly clashing factions composing the Meiji government. He attempted to keep these within manageable limits, by an adroit balance of compromise, firmness, and patronage.

The threat from the 'Left' in the government was personified by Terajima Munenori, head of the *Genro-in*. Terajima wanted to be named envoy to the United States in 1882 that he could duplicate Ito's efforts in Europe. He was named minister to the United States in July 1882, but was not able to fulfill his desire. The antagonism between those in the *Genro-in* and Ito is traceable, as we have seen, to the time when the *Genro-in* was commissioned to draft a constitution, an effort roundly criticized by Ito. Moreover, as mentioned earlier, it was the *Genro-in's* attempt to outdo Ito that had the unlooked-for result of bringing Ito and Kaneko together. This zeal for constitution-making remained undiminished even in 1887, when Ito was already deep in his work. Finally, one of the reasons for specifically creating the Privy Council to deliberate on the draft constitution, according to Osatake, was to bypass the *Genro-in*, which claimed the deliberative right. As Osatake puts it, 'The fate [of the Ito draft constitution] would have been a foregone conclusion if the *Genro-in* had been allowed to discuss it.'

Ito also expressed some concern about the charge made by still other proponents of parliamentarism that he was drafting a 'Bismarckian' constitution that would serve as the basis of an authoritarian regime. Okuma Shigenobu, for example, who was foreign minister at this time, in the company of Prime Minister Kuroda Kiyotaka one day personally called on Ito to make this charge and asked that certain elements of the English constitution be included in the draft.

However, it appears that what troubled Ito most were the attacks from the conservatives in the government. Imperial Household officials were especially vocal in their fears that Ito was a blind worshipper of the West and that he intended to establish the parliament-centered system of England. A leading figure in this group was Motoda Eifu, a scholar in Chinese learning. Ito later commented: 'In spite of the fact that in and out of [the Privy Council] there was an undercurrent of extreme conservatism, the emperor's wishes almost invariably were liberal and progressive.' And years after the enactment of the constitution Ito was still fighting this battle against the Chinese scholars. He described them as having 'narrow and limited' views on government because they insisted that the only form of government that conformed to Japan's polity was absolutism.

These internal pressures may have compelled Ito constantly to seek precedents for ideas that he sought to incorporate into the draft. Kaneko remembers once suggesting that representatives of the merchant, industrial, and farming classes be permitted to sit in the House of Peers. Ito agreed but told Kaneko that he did not relish facing later charges that this was a 'frivolous idea, typical of Ito.' To forestall such charges, Ito told Kaneko to find a precedent and was mightily pleased when Kaneko succeeded.

Ito successfully weathered most of the challenges from within the government, and the Meiji constitution bore Ito's unmistakable imprint. Needless to say, in no instance can any major concept or principle embodied in the constitution be said to have reflected the demands or pressures from the outs. Hence, just as Ito and the oligarchs had almost complete control over the questions of the *introduction* of constitutional government and the *timing* of the introduction, they exercised as firm a control over the *type* of constitutional government Meiji Japan finally adopted. Political phenomena, it is true, are not always susceptible to logical or even reasonable interpretations. Still, it is difficult to follow the widely accepted argument that in the matters of the introduction and timing of constitutionalism the government bowed to external pressure, but that in defining the substance of Meiji constitutional government the oligarchs were able to withstand and even ignore outside influence.

The attacks against the Meiji constitution by the outs were loud but not vigorously pressed. A reason that may be cited is that the opposition was fully aware of the immense number of theoretical arguments Ito could bring to bear in any debate. Another and more important reason may be that those in the opposition, after seeing the product, realized that the constitution offered it the opening to public power in Tokyo that they had been seeking, and the opportunities for later expanding and exploiting this wedge – a fact fully realized by the oligarchs themselves. Some years after the promulgation of the constitution, Kaneko asked Okuma why he did not attend the sessions in which the Privy Council deliberated on the draft constitution. Okuma's reply was that he felt that his presence was not necessary, for the draft contained three important provisions for the Diet: the right to petition the throne; the power to initiate legislation; and the guarantee that the budget would be presented to the House of Representatives before the House of Peers.

The measure of the enlightenment of the oligarchs is that they themselves accepted the fact of real participation in the government by the outs as an irreducible minimum for constitutional government, in spite of the fact that the revolutionary government was only twenty-two years old and they had very serious misgivings about the ability of both the opposition and the general public to handle public responsibilities. Given this premise, the Meiji constitution, through which the oligarchs hoped to control and soften this future challenge by the outs, should not, as is often the case, be construed as a symbol of illiberality and reaction, but rather as an expression of a clear-sighted leadership, willingly embarking on a bold and revolutionary experiment.

Kaino, M, 'Some Introductory Comments on the Historical Background of Japanese Civil Law' (1988) 16 *International Journal of Sociology of Law* 385–89

From the beginning of the Meiji period, French law was taught at the Law School of the Ministry of Justice. Among the law teachers from abroad at the School, Boissonade, who came to Japan in November 1873 and began to teach French law in 1874, was the most important figure. Boissonade was himself a leading natural-law jurist, and considered that the system of positive law was, and ought to be, a universal idea of human beings and could be discovered by natural reason. Like other natural-law jurists, he believed that the *Code Napoléon* was not merely a French national product, but the embodiment of natural law, in other words, a model of civilised law. Boissonade himself was the main author of what was eventually termed the Old Civil Code, which in its arrangements was based on the French Code.

However, English law had also been taught, since 1874, at the Kaisei School in Tokyo (the predecessor of the Tokyo Imperial University), by American, English and Japanese teachers. The methods of legal science in England during that period were analytical-historical, and the natural law school was looked down on by the English jurists as outmoded. Thus, the English school did not share Boissonade's belief that French law was the only civilized system of law, and claimed instead that English, as well as German law, should also be taken into account. Not surprisingly, the draft Civil Code based on French law was criticized by the English school.

At this point, German legal science quite rapidly acquired prestige in Japan. In 1885 the Law School of the Ministry of Justice was transferred to Tokyo Imperial University, and a German Law section was established there in 1887. The government showed open preference for things German, and in a subtle way a favourable climate was created for the Germanization of Japanese culture in general. When the Imperial edict decreeing the establishment of the Diet in 1890 was promulgated, and the government decided that the new constitution would be modelled on the Prussian constitution, the tide finally turned and the influence of French law was superseded by German law. As part of this process, the Old Civil Code, which had been opposed by both the German and English schools of jurists, was deferred: a Bill to defer its coming into force until 31 December 1886 was submitted and pushed by the postponement party, and passed by both Houses.

An important figure who should be mentioned at this point was Nobushige Hozumi, Professor at the Tokyo Imperial University, who was both a member of the English Bar and had also studied in Berlin. He could be called the true founder of Japanese comparative jurisprudence, if only for his pioneering work entitled *Horitsu Shinkaron* (Theory of the Evolution of Law). Although there was in general a lack of the comparative standpoint among contemporary Japanese jurists, Hozumi was fully conscious of Japan's peculiar cultural conditions, and pioneered methods for the reception of law as opposed to the mere copying of European law. Unfortunately however, his conception of Japanese society and culture was inevitably coloured by the tendency of the times, and his ideas on the preservation of the peculiarities of Japan effectively prevented the making place of a radical process of modernization, such as had occurred in France, as embodied in the provisions of the Napoleonic Code and reflected in its Japanese copy, the Old Civil Code (Noda 1972–73).

Therefore, the fight between the two schools was not essentially a fight between two philosophies, like the famous controversy between Thibaut and Savigny, but a conflict of views based on expediency, sometimes appealing to patriotic sentiment. At any rate, a new drafting committee was formed, consisting of Hozumi, Masaaki Tomii (an eminent jurist of the French school) and Kenjiro Ume (a champion of immediate enforcement), which followed the policy advocated by the English school and consulted many codes. The net result was that the arrangements of the new Code became entirely German, adopting the Pandekten system rather than the Institutional French system. This New Civil Code, or the Meiji Civil Code. came into operation on 16 July 1898 Although English, German and French law continued to be taught at the universities, the predominance of German legal science was securely established until the end of World War Two. Moreover, subsequent legislation in other fields of law followed German models.

Controversy over the Nature of Pre-War Capitalism in Japan

Thus the ancient styles of legal thought and codes that had been formed in Japan under Chinese influence were abandoned, and there emerged a new codified system based initially on French law. An outstanding example was the Criminal Code of 1882, based on a new notion of criminal justice, embodied in principles such as no retrospective provision and, in particular, equality before the law regardless of social status. As was discussed above, French law began to retreat from the high position it once held and German law increased in importance, especially after 1889 with the coming into force of the Meiji Constitution. This brought a rather backward trend into the political and legal development of Japan, since the Meiji Constitution, modelled on the Prussian constitution, was very undemocratic. This was especially the case with its provisions on the sovereignty of the Emperor (*Tenno*) and the broad imperial prerogatives it recognised. However, it should not be overlooked that the same period saw an advance in social and economic development. Under the Meiji Constitution Japanese capitalism built up to a certain extent a sound economic foundation based on modern legal principles, such as freedom of contract, absolute ownership, and individual responsibility.

What must be discussed is the relationship between the capitalist and precapitalist, or traditional forms of production in the mid-Meiji period. Although it can be assumed that, by about the year 1890, capitalist enterprise had generally attained the predominance required to control the whole of the Japanese political and legal superstructure, agriculture was still significantly influenced by pre-capitalistic elements. The remainder of this paper will try to survey how this situation expressed itself in the structure of Japanese society, and law, up to the Second World War.

There has been a well-known controversy among Japanese social science scholars concerning the nature of Japanese pre-war capitalism, as well as the features and structure of the pre-War Japanese state, known as the *Tenno Regime* (see Otsuka, 1966). One of the first influential works, by the late Professor Moritaro Yamada, put forward the view that the rapid progress of industrialization or modernization in the period after the Meiji restoration, expressed by the appearance of forms of capitalist enterprise in the urban areas, should be contrasted with the situation in the agricultural villages. There, with virtually no industrialization, small-scale agriculture and traditional social relations persisted strongly, particularly those of 'semi-feudal' landlordism and the family system. Furthermore, the two elements of urban capitalist and 'semi-feudal' rural relationships, did not merely co-exist but were interlinked, in that one constituted the precondition of the other. Essentially, the supply of cheap labour from the villages was being ensured by the preservation of the traditional social institutions there. So, the unique structure of the Japanese economy was formed, on the foundations of the strong persistence of village institutions in the agricultural villages, providing a basis for the expansion of modern industrial enterprise. In line with this view, it can be pointed out that traditional social institutions such as the hereditary form of the family enterprise (*Zaibatsu*), as well as the hierarchical organization of labour on the basis of seniority, cast their shadows even in today's enterprises.

Under the pre-war system, the primary unit of Japanese society was the family rather than the individual, and the relationship between parent and child as well as husband and wife, was that of superior and subordinate. This patriarchal order extended beyond domestic life, up to political organization, which was also hierarchically structured, a type of rule which the government had been attempting to strengthen in order to ensure the stability of the existing social order. This unique feature of the legal and political system was formally incorporated in the Meiji Civil Code of 1898, which replaced the more democratic provisions of the French-style Old Civil Code. The latter had moderated, to some extent, the excessive discrimination between men and women which was a traditional aspect of Japanese society, and placed some limitations on the patriarchal family system. This led a conservative lawyer such as Professor Yatsuka Hozumi to deplore the 'crisis of loyalty and filial piety', at about the time when the controversy over the Civil Code reached its climax.

Certainly, the political system established after the Meiji Restoration was very authoritarian, requiring the people to be uncritical as well as obedient. Government policy was to maintain the family system as the basis for its rule over the people. Therefore, especially in the rural districts, the village community known as the mura survived, and the lives of the peasants and farmers were controlled through the family. The mura was organized around its Houses, and the order of the mura was closely linked to the family. Similar relationships extended even to various spheres of town life: for instance, a company was likely to be considered as a sort of family, with the Managing Director as *paterfamilias*, and its employees as family members. Under this type of social structure, individual interests could be easily neglected in favour of the community, or of the interests of the 'generals'. I will discuss further, in broad outline, how these 'semi-feudal' relationships were expressed in legal forms.

Legal Expression of Semi-Feudalism

The ways in which the semi-feudal relationships were expressed in legal forms may be sketched out in broad outline as follows. The first resulted from the series of reforms centering around the revision of the land tax. These ensured free ownership rights in land, and completely abolished the restriction on the alienation of land which had existed under the feudal-lord system. Accordingly, the free circulation of land as a commodity was secured, while on the other hand the government was able to levy fixed land tax as a source of revenue. In order to ensure the efficiency of land tax collection, the land-deed system was established in 1872, and completed by the Old Recording Law of 1886. Further attempts were also made to develop land-management in a capitalist direction. This was illustrated by the proposal in 1887 for a draft Ordinance for secured tenancy, which however was never realised. Although the idea of land being accepted as an object of capital investment was never realised in pre-war Japanese society, it can perhaps be said that the very existence of such a draft law demonstrates the establishment of legally guaranteed private ownership rights in land on the one hand, and on the other the growth of a stable system of tenant farming. Indeed, the principles expressed in the draft Ordinance proposal were absorbed by the provisions on leases of the Old Civil Code and the Meiji Civil Code. This retained that peculiarity of pre-war Japanese society, the co-existence of pre-capitalistic agriculture and capitalist enterprise.

The second important area to mention is the controls over status and property relationships which evolved around the laws relating to the family system, especially those introduced by the Family Registration Law of 1871. The central problem was how to ensure the compatibility of private ownership with the restraints on disposition resulting from family relations. Although the restraints under the feudal-lord system had disappeared, those due to the House (*Ie*) system still remained. For this reason, strong opposition developed to the adoption of the principles of the Code Napoleon, which allowed the division of family property by divisible inheritance, allowing each individual family member full rights of disposition over their inherited portion. In both agriculture as well as industry it was considered necessary to maintain the unity of enterprises based on exclusive unified inheritance and prevent the division of capital. Therefore, the Meiji Civil Code adopted the system of unified inheritance by the eldest son, primogeniture. This enabled the continued concentration of the property of the House in the hands of the male Head of House.

Thirdly, we should emphasise the existence of specific laws regulating civil status, of a paternalistic character. In particular, the head of House had the right to approve certain acts of family members and to impose sanctions. These rights were closely linked with the concentration and stability of family property under control of the House Head, and his correlative duty to support family members. These status rights and obligations were no more than the expression of the rights of ownership of the House Head, which made his position absolute. In this way, private ownership and disposition of House property had skilfully interwoven with the requirements of the patriarchal or paternalistic ideology predominant in the period. Ultimately, the family registration system (*Koseki*) was revised and incorporated in the Civil Code. It was an indispensable element in the formation of Japan's civil law as well as providing some basis for various administrative institutions (Watanabe, 1963).

George, B, 'The Impact of the Past upon the Rights of the Accused in Japan' (1966) 14 *American Journal of Comparative Law* 672–78

THE DEVELOPMENT OF CRIMINAL PROCEDURE IN JAPAN

A. Prior to 1868

Like most aspects of Japanese law, the shape of ancient Japanese criminal proceedings is unknown, but granted the primitive clan-type structure which apparently characterized the early Japanese society, it was probably a simple group hearing with immediate imposition of sanctions. When in the 8th century Japan adopted various aspects of the superior Chinese culture of the time, it included among them the sophisticated Chinese criminal codes, with their formalized system of charges, proofs, and decrees. But after the close of the Heian period (794–1185), when the borrowed concepts of a centralized administration fell into disuse as feudalism developed, the relatively sophisticated procedures in the *Taiho* and *Yoro* codes disappeared from view. For nearly 700 years there was no clear distinction between administrative, legislative, and judicial functions, between law and custom, between substantive doctrines and procedural doctrines. Though a measure of specialization in fact manifested itself, so that certain offices or officials occupied much of their time in resolving disputes, this was a matter of degree only. Any official might in the course of his duties resolve matters, the modern counterpart of which would be classified as judicial rather than administrative. This being so, it is no wonder that there was no clear-cut line between civil and criminal problems and remedies. If a matter could not be settled locally by agreement, if agreement were possible, or by the imposition of penalties available under local customary law, then it was called to the attention of appropriate shogunate officials. If the controversy stemmed from a dispute over rights in property, there might be a shifting from 'civil' to 'criminal' proceedings, or the threat of criminal penalties might be used to promote agreement. Ordinary criminal matters probably did not occasion too much official activity at higher levels, in part because facts were promptly determined and sanctions summarily administered in each locality, and in part because appeals were for the convenience of the administrators and not for the benefit of the parties; local officials rarely bothered to raise a question about routine penalties for routine offenses.

B. 1868–1946

The Meiji Restoration of 1868 produced major changes. Many of them were in the substantive law. Perhaps more significant in the long run were those which created a delineation between police activity and judicial activity, between prosecuting functions and judicial functions, and between criminal procedure and civil procedure. That the process of creating categories which were unknown to the Tokugawa feudal system was not an easy one is evidenced by the sequence of procedural legislation itself. The first step was to create a Section of Criminal Affairs (*keiho jimuka*) within the first central governmental structure of 1868. This was followed by a succession of administrative offices, all of which attempted to develop regulations for the processing of criminal matters. At first these were intentionally patterned on the old 8th century codes, and therefore relied primarily on administrative activity designed to ferret out criminal conduct. In particular, torture was permitted as a formal part of the investigatory process. The most notable compilation of these regulations, promulgated in 1873, continued in effect until it was replaced by the first Code of Criminal Procedure (1881) patterned on French law. This Code, modified somewhat in 1890, provided the basic structure for criminal procedure until it was replaced by the Code of 1922, in effect from 1924, modeled on the more modern German law. What this evolution of procedural institutions signified, however, is best revealed by an examination of the evolution in the offices charged with administering procedural laws.

The police. Police functions prior to the Meiji Restoration were carried out at least in Edo, by the town magistrates and by special arson and theft inspectors. There were also a number of special secret agents who identified subversive activity as quickly as it arose. But the primary policing function was apparently achieved by citizens watching each other, particularly through the five-family groups (*gonin-gumi*) on which so much of Tokugawa administration ultimately rested.

With the Restoration in 1868, the initial responsibility for providing police protection for Edo was placed on the military; shortly thereafter, however, the actual supervision of the soldiers engaged in 'administrative' police duty was transferred to the Tokyo Metropolitan Office. However, 'judicial police officials', who helped prepare criminal cases, came almost immediately under the control of the government office concerned with criminal law administration generally. These police, therefore were under the direction of the procurator, of whom more will be said below. When civilian police replaced the military in 1872, they were first assigned to the Justice Department, but in 1874 the Home Department took over superintendence. Efforts were made to continue a clear distinction between judicial police and administrative police, but were never totally successful. Judicial police officials (*shiho keisatsu kanri*) were, and are, members of the police for purposes of police administration, but are under the close supervision of public prosecutors in the exercise of their functions. Furthermore, until 1940, local police command officials were empowered to impose disciplinary fines and punishment for contraventions without any participation by court or procurator. Police also carried out the primary censorship activities inherited from the Tokugawa administration, including supervision of newspapers and magazines. They regulated as well the circumstances under which public meetings might be held. These functions continued through the Pacific War; since police administration was directly controlled by the Cabinet, many of the repressive measures instituted by the prewar militarists were effectuated through the police.

The courts. It is at least implicit in the above that for a time after the Restoration there were no courts in the modern sense of the word, but only a specialized series of administrative agencies. The first use of the term *saibansho* for court occurred in 1872; the designated agency was a special office within the Justice Department charged with the responsibility of formally dispensing justice. Thereafter there was a gradual extension of the authority of this agency, both in terms of function and of geographical scope of function, as local and prefectural branches were established.

Though this might have led in time to a complete severance of the courts from the Justice Ministry, no strong figure appeared to ensure that this would be the case; the history of institutions in the Meiji era is often the history of the strong figures who founded them. As a result, the courts remained from that time on a part of the Justice Ministry. To be sure, the formal structure of the courts was embodied in statute law, beginning with the first Court Organization Law of 1886, so that significant changes could not be instituted solely by administrative regulation. Moreover, efforts were systematically made to ensure adequate training and tenure for judges so that political and economic pressures could not be effectively brought to bear on them as they decided specific cases. The seeds of judicial independence at least germinated. But the position of the court system as in form a part of a larger Justice Ministry, and the subjection of that Ministry in turn to the Cabinet, meant that courts could only implement, not create policy.

The procuracy. During the Japanese dynastic era (646–1192) the only office with specific prosecuting functions was the 'Imperial Prosecuting and Investigating Office' (*danjodai*) adapted from a T'ang Dynasty office. This office disappeared during the feudal era, and prosecuting functions were discharged in one sense by the complainant who brought a disputed matter to the attention of shogunate officials, and in another sense by those officials themselves, who discharged the responsibility of investigation as well as decision. There was at the Restoration, therefore, no surviving official on whom the office of public procurator or prosecutor might be patterned.

The inception of the office was in the Office Regulations for the Justice Department of 1872. The public procurator apparently was intended to discharge two functions. One was to supervise the judicial police. The procurator was not to supervise the administrative activity of the police directed at crime prevention, but he was to see that police investigations directed at an identified suspect were properly done. The other function was to check on the courts, or more correctly, judicial officials, to see that they did not stray to one extreme by treating defendants unfairly or to the other by discharging people who should be convicted. He clearly had no monopolistic control over the institution of prosecution; judicial officials could still initiate judicial proceedings on their own authority or on complaints received. This ambivalent function of the procurator is revealed in the language of the 1873 Regulations:

> The judge himself has the responsibility of conducting hearings, the clerk of the court is to record the oral statements and the procurator is to sit by the side of the judge and observe what transpires at the trial.

However, within ten years after the Restoration the procurator had begun to function as his Western-European counterpart did. In 1874, the revised Regulations for the Organization of the Justice Ministry provided that 'the procurator has the right to act as the complainant and to demand punishment, but does not have the right to conduct the trial'. By 1878, a Justice Ministry circular provided that 'all crimes except those committed in the courtroom or revealed incidentally to the trial of a case shall be adjudicated pursuant to formal charges brought by a procurator'. The 1881 Code of Criminal Procedure defined clearly the functions of the public procurator as chief investigator of the case against the accused; the voluminous file which he compiled formed the basis of the courtroom proceedings against the defendant, and the procurator was by far the most important figure in courtroom proceedings. His position of equality with, indeed at times of superiority to, the judge was underscored by the fact that both judges and procurators were within the jurisdiction of the Justice Ministry, and subject to the same requirements for appointment and tenure. This tradition continued strongly in force until 1946.

Lawyers. The lawyer was not known in feudal Japan. A rudimentary form of counsel was the head of the village who accompanied a townsman before an administrative official and the Edo innkeepers (*kujiyado*) who performed a like function for transient litigants presenting their cases to shogunate officials. Their formal training was nil, and the moral standing of the *kujiyado* abominable, so that they little resembled a Western advocate or lawyer. Furthermore, the heavy emphasis on mediation and conciliation in Japan meant that there was little litigation in the Western sense and therefore no function which an attorney could legitimately serve. There was, therefore, no socially-acceptable, adequately-trained body of men to serve as counselor and protector to those in trouble.

With the Meiji Restoration, however, a gradual interest developed in providing trained representatives to assist those engaging in litigation before the newly-developed courts, particularly criminal courts. Despite efforts to ensure adequate legal training for these attorneys, and despite a formal regulation of the legal profession through law from 1893 on, private practitioners played a relatively minor role in the administration of criminal justice. In part this was because the best minds went into the procuracy or judiciary. But in large measure it was also because the structure of criminal procedure v. as such that the important work was done by the procurator at a time when the attorney was not, and could not be, in attendance. By the time the decision was made to institute public prosecution, there was generally such a voluminous file of evidence against the accused that the lawyer could do little but seek leniency in treatment for his client. Therefore tradition and role combined to keep the attorney's impact on the criminal proceeding at a minimum.

C. Postwar Revision

Japan's defeat in the Pacific War led to a revision of the legal system which will perhaps prove in history to be as sweeping as that which occurred in the creation of that system from 1868 on. Three aspects of this revision are important to our topic. In looking at them, one should bear in mind that while in both outline and detail they were the results of substantial SCAP's pressure, they were capable of long-range effectuation only because there was much in modern Japanese history on which they could rest. SCAP reforms that lacked this base soon disappeared. It is a commonplace that efforts to regulate large industrial combines (*zaibatsu*) came to nothing after the signing of the peace treaty, and that the law regulating labor relations has proved relatively impotent because the aims of the Japanese labor movement appear to be more political than economic, at least in terms of wage–hour negotiations. Reforms in judicial practice would have quickly disappeared also if nothing but Occupation fiat supported them. What are these three aspects?

The first is the creation of an independent judiciary. Under the *Showa* Constitution of 1946, the whole of the judicial power is vested in a Supreme Court and inferior courts established by law. No agency in the executive branch can be given final judicial power, which ruled out of existence the separate Court of Administrative Litigation which had existed from 1890 on the pattern of the French *Conseil d'Etat*. Judges are bound only by the constitution and the law, and may not be disciplined by any executive organ or agency. Under this significant change in its power status, the judiciary has gradually established its position as the final arbiter on matters of constitutional doctrine, and has resisted efforts at intervention in judicial matters by either the executive or the legislative branch.

The second is the creation in the constitution itself of certain procedural guarantees to the citizen, guarantees which are not subject to legislative modification. The Meiji Constitution embodied a number of rights, including procedural rights, purporting to run in favor of the subject, but in each instance these were qualified by phrases like 'within the limit of the law'. While this might have restricted a single official from imposing *ad hoc* restrictions on exercise of these rights, it left the Diet free to make any changes in procedural law it saw fit. But the guarantees in the postwar constitution contain no such limitations. While the details of these guarantees will be mentioned later, it is clear that the 1946 Constitution fundamentally alters the traditional Japanese concept of individual constitutional rights, and precludes legislative impairment of them.

The third is the substantial revision of the Code of Criminal Procedure to transmute what was essentially a German-type proceeding into an adversary proceeding which borrows from the Anglo-American law system at key points. While significant details will be covered below, the net effect is to create more of a parity in position and power between public prosecutor and defense attorney than existed under the older law. Thus, by raising the judiciary to a position of independence in which it supervises the activities of both parties, and by strengthening the role of defense counsel in criminal trials, a tripartite adversary system has been created, at least in form, even though the public procuracy as such as not been directly the objective of legislative reform.

Oppler, AC, *Legal Reform in Occupied Japan. A Participant Looks Back*, 1976, pp 65, 74–76, 81–82, 111–15, 116–19, 120–22, 126–27, 128–29, 130–34, 136–37, 139–42, 146–48, Princeton University Press

The Courts and Law Division

A constitution is only a blueprint of pious principles and will remain ineffective as long as these are not implemented in the law of the land, which in Japan is codified, following the Continental system; and even the most progressive laws are of no avail unless they are willingly respected, vigorously enforced, and become an ingredient of the social fabric. Still, first things had to be done first, namely, the laying of the legal ground. While the constitution was deliberated in the Diet, I realized with some awe that the tremendous task of bringing the legal and judicial codes into accord with the new charter would, within the setup of the Occupation, be part of my duties, which included almost everything else connected with Japanese legal affairs. As indicated before, there was within headquarters a Legal Section under Colonel Carpenter, but it was charged only with advising on American and international law, and the prosecution of minor war criminals. Japanese law and legislation was, until 31 May 1948, the exclusive responsibility of the Government Section.

...

It did not take long until the Japanese representatives of the Ministry of Justice, the public procurators, and the men of the bar and the universities on the committees found out that we were not without understanding of their legal system, due to Blakemore's knowledge of Japanese law and my Continental legal background. Soon they felt free to express their opinions frankly. There was only one authoritative demand: compliance with the constitutional principles. Still, the question of compliance or violation was more often than not in twilight and open to discussion. It is astonishing in how few instances we had to resort to the fiat of the conqueror. The most sensational of these was SCAP's demand for the abolition of the lese majesty provisions in the Penal Code, which he considered contrary to the principle of equality before the law. The story will be told in Chapter 11; this demand was not made in the form of a SCAPIN, but, as pointed out before, by a letter from MacArthur to the prime minister. The demand was implemented in the Diet legislation, with the revision of the Penal Code by completely eliminating the lese majesty provisions.

Another less spectacular example, in which we insisted on a change in the law, pertained to the same Code, namely, its unequal treatment of the sexes in case of adultery. Here, the violation of the Constitution was so clear that it was even not necessary to bring the matter to the attention of SCAP. The existing law provided for punishment of the wife and of the other party to the adultery. A husband who was unfaithful with an unmarried woman was not subject to punishment. The principle of equality of the sexes, we told the Japanese, left them the alternative of either making adultery equally punishable for both sexes, or of abolishing it as a criminal offense. Characteristically enough, the Diet decided in favor of abolition. After all, it consisted mostly of males, and the habit of keeping a mistress was probably more customary in the case of Japan's married men than in other nations, since the choice of spouse was made by the family elders and often not based on mutual affection.

Our influence on the implementing legislation was exercised at various levels and in different forms. On the working level, we were consulted by ministerial officials in charge of the first drafting, and we had more or less informal conferences with members of cabinet committees and other committees that deliberated on the bills.

Article 98 of the constitution provided that all laws contrary to its principles would become null and void at the date of its enforcement. After the promulgation of the document on 3 November 1946, the Japanese government realized that a complete revision of the basic codes of law within the remaining six months was absolutely *ultra vires*. To fill the resulting legal vacuum, it was decided to submit to the Diet provisional bills 'For the Temporary Adjustment Pursuant to the Enforcement of the Constitution'. They contained only the most elementary changes required by the new constitutional principles. This emergency measure was used mainly for the Civil Code and the procedural codes.

Since it was to serve as a guideline for the courts in a transitional period, it was legislation in unusually broad and even intentionally vague terms, to leave much to judicial interpretation. A date for the expiration of these provisional laws was provided. They were subsequently replaced by regular legislation for the complete revision of the codes.

The device of temporary law was obviously not available for the implementation of the structural provisions of the constitution regarding the judiciary. Courts had to function immediately in their new setup after the enforcement of the instrument.

Therefore, the Court Organization Law had to be, and was indeed, passed within the six-month period between the enactment and coming into effect of the constitution on 3 May 1947. This was the first codification in which we resorted to the method of formal conferences with the Japanese. We did so because of the limited time available, which required intensive concentration, and the importance of implementing and strengthening the constitutional principle of independence of the judiciary. Blakemore and I, who alone represented the Occupation, frequently had to mediate between the representatives of the Ministry of Justice and the judges, among them President Hosono. The former were reluctant to give up the supervisory power of the executive branch of the government over the judges, while the latter occasionally went too far in their proposals. Among the younger officials of the ministry, several were in full sympathy with our democratization efforts, particularly Naito Yorihiro, who subsequently was transferred to the secretariat of the Supreme Court, and is now chief judge of a high court. Another was Higuchi Masaru, also a judge, and later a member of the Supreme Court Mission.

...

In the early period of my activity in Japan I frequently found it difficult to obtain the frank opinion of a Japanese in conversation because of his reluctance to disagree, which seemed to violate the ethical demand of politeness. It was our greatest satisfaction that we were able in these conferences to overcome the initial stiffness and restraint of our discussion partners, after they had realized that we not only wanted to give them a hearing, but were genuinely eager to learn from them. As chairman, I particularly enjoyed and encouraged debate between them, which put me into the welcome role of moderator. We Americans, far from playing the role of Occupation bosses who knew everything better, used persuasion rather than fiat. Soon we felt and acted as international colleagues in law. The debate was often vigorous, and occasionally witty. I even tried to submit controversial questions to voting, but the Japanese did not like that, lest the minority would lose face. Thus, since, we avoided imposing our view, results had to be reached patiently by compromise, and, indeed, we arrived at agreements or compromises in all the problems under discussion. It would be naive, however, to deny that two factors contributed to the auspicious atmosphere in these conferences: first, the traditional Japanese penchant for harmony and compromise; and, second, the awareness of all participants that reformatory action was necessary. At the risk of appearing overoptimistic, I may add that the majority of the Japanese even felt that it was desirable. Like all pioneers, we were optimistic with regard to the survival of our reforms after the end of the Occupation: but without this optimism, which at least up to the present has proved warranted, we would have been paralyzed.

...

Reform of Substantive Law

CIVIL CODE

The old Civil Code of 1898 was patterned on the Code Napoleon and on the German Civil Code, in the process of the adoption of Continental law after the Meiji Restoration. The objectives of the Occupation did not call for a change in the three first books of the Civil Code, namely, General Provisions, Real Property, and Obligations. They have remained unchanged, a fact that also disproves the assertion that the Occupation completely Americanized the Japanese law. It was only in the fields of family and inheritance law covered in the fourth and fifth books that fundamental changes were required to have constitutional principles such as dignity of the individual, equality of sexes, free choice of marriage partner, and freedom of movement implemented. Here the adoption of Western patterns had been carefully avoided in the Meiji reforms, and semifeudal customs had been retained, in spite of already remarkable opposition.

The family system under the old Code was characterized by the institution of the 'house,' that is, a clan unit distinguished from the Western type of nuclear family consisting of father, mother, and unmarried children. The head of the house, most often the oldest male of the clan, wielded important powers over the sometimes large number of other members, who did not necessarily live together with him. When they did, the customary 'three generation household,' as RP Dore terms it, 'would consist of the husband as head of the house and his wife; his eldest son and the latter's wife and children; his unmarried sons and daughters; and his unmarried younger brothers and sisters. When the brothers married, they sometimes also remained in their older brother's house, but more often they founded so-called branch families, which retain a certain deference to, if not economic dependence on, the main family. Daughters, when they married, left the house of their father and became members of their husband's house. Marriage was not considered the fulfillment of the partners' love, but rather as means for the preservation and perpetuation of the family. Neither the boy nor the girl could freely choose the partner, but the match was arranged by the parents through a go-between on the basis of considerations of the family's benefit rather than the happiness of the young couple. Seeking such happiness was frowned upon as egoism. The bride had to undergo a kind of apprenticeship under the frequently strict and unpleasant guidance of her mother-in-law, an apprenticeship called 'learning the ways of the family'. The *yome,* as the new daughter-in-law was named, had, in addition, often enough to suffer from the instruction and nagging of her unmarried sisters-in-law. Thus, from birth to death, a Japanese female had to be a patient servant, mostly to a male, be it her father or the head of his house, or her husband or the head of his house. Even as a widow, she remained a member of her husband's house and subject to control by its head. Of course, none of these dependencies were as hard to bear as the period of training by the mother in-law. After her eldest son had grown up and married, she would herself become a training mother-in-law of his bride, and one should assume that the remembrance of her own mother-in-law troubles should prevent her from using the same harsh methods. But according to all observation, this usually did not happen.

Here it may be mentioned briefly that the inequality of the wife extended to the legal arrangements for the administration of her property, divorce, and inheritance.

The 'head of the house' was, as a rule, a grandfather. When he died, his eldest son, to whom the younger children owed respect even before, succeeded him in the headship. Although emphasis is upon male superiority, widows – if childless or during the minority of their children – may become heads of the house, and so may daughters, although if they later marry the headship usually falls to their husbands. To have a male heir, a father may adopt a young man who is to marry his daughter, and who then takes the family name.

As for the powers of the head of the house, his approval was required for almost all important decisions in the lives of the members, such as change of residence, marriage, divorce, and adoption. Since property and inheritance were tied up with the house, a feature of particular importance in case of the agricultural farm, refusal to obey the head, which could lead to expulsion from the house, had serious economic implications, apart from the social ones. This was all the more notable as the powers of the head of the house were to some extent counterbalanced by his obligation to support needy members of the family. Incidentally, this economic cohesiveness might also benefit a retiring head of the house. When he grew very old or sick and needy, he would resign the headship in favor of his first-born son in the expectation of receiving support from him.

One may say, then, that the principal elements of the house system included primogeniture, male superiority, and social and economic cohesiveness. It is necessary to add respect for the ascendants, symbolized in ancestor worship and the demand of filial piety. This demand could lead to serious conflicts of loyalty, for instance, if the parents did not get along with their daughter-in-law and urged their son to divorce her. In the strict spirit of the house system, he was expected to give in to his parents' wish or command, even it he loved his wife.

All this was a reflection of Confucian philosophy, which neglects the individual and his 'inalienable rights' in favor of a hierarchical setup. In Japan, the imperial system itself was a product of this philosophy. At the top of the pyramid, the emperor towered as a kind of super-pater familias over the state, with the family below. The individual was far down, with duties to all levels of government and family, and with pitiably few rights. There existed a variety of personal dependencies, as we have seen, within the family unit, and, moreover, in the relationship between *sensei* (teacher) and pupil, or between *oyabun* (boss) and *kobun* (underling). These dependencies were praised by traditional-minded Japanese as 'beautiful' because of the corresponding mutual loyalties they engendered a remnant indeed of feudal attitudes, such as also prevailed in medieval Europe. The constitution laid the legal groundwork for liberating the Japanese people from what its Occupation drafters as well as many Japanese believed were antiquated bonds.

But this raises the sociological question: were they really antiquated? More specifically, was the house system still a vital ingredient of Japanese society, or was it already obsolete when we worked on the revision of the Civil Code? One of the most brilliant attempts to answer this question for the year 1958 has been Dore's book, *City Life in Japan*. The author, in introducing his description of the family system, makes the interesting remark that it 'is not a description of how most people behave today, nor even of how most (only some) people think people ought to behave today. It is rather a description of how most people think most people used to behave and everyone used to expect people to behave. To some extent, this observation was already true of the early Occupation period.

...

To return to the legal aspects, the existing Civil Code embodied the old house system and was obviously in sharp conflict with Article 24 of the constitution. After the latter had come into effect, that system was, at least legally doomed to elimination or emasculation. One may say that the real decision was already made with the enactment of the constitution. Still, when the very broad principles of Article 24 had to be implemented in the law of the land, particularly in a revised Civil Code, there remained definite possibilities of nuances. Realizing the sensitivity of this private family sphere, we assisted in the drafting of this aspect of the reforms in a carefully restrained manner, limiting ourselves to informative advice when such was requested. While we never urged the complete abolition of the house system, we watched with eager interest how the Japanese would adjust it to the principles of the constitution. They did a more thorough job than we had expected. The attempt to save at least the institution of the house, though deprived of features irreconcilable with the new individualism, was defeated in the committees in favor of its complete abolition as the family unit. We were told that this more radical solution was vigorously advocated by three women leaders. They had ample reason to fight, since women were the largest population group to benefit.

The principal and fundamental change enacted by the revised Code of 12 December 1947, lies, of course, in the replacement of the 'house' by the 'conjugal' Western family centered around father and mother with their unmarried young children. The powers of the head of the house disappeared with the abolition of the house system. There is, however, some sentimental remembrance of ancestor worship in Article 897 of the new Code, which exempts the ownership of genealogical records, of utensils for religious rites, and of tombs from the rules of succession, and provides that it devolves upon the person designated by the ancestor or by custom 'to hold as president the worship to the memory of the ancestors'.

The legal sanctions against a young man and woman who, in disobedience to their elders will, follow their own heart in choosing a spouse are gone. The new Code allows them to do so without any permission of a house head. The parents' consent formerly needed for the bride up to the age of twenty-five and for the bridegroom up to thirty years is now required only for minors. The customary go-between has certainly not vanished from the Japanese scene, but it is now easier for the daughter as well as the son to say no to the proposed engagement. The inferior position of the wife with regard to her legal capacity in the management of her property was also abolished. While formerly any important disposition she made of it without the approval of her husband could be voided, she is now free to manage her personal property and dispose of it.

Inequalities on account of sex have, moreover, been deleted in connection with divorce. In that area, the women suffered particular discrimination. The ancient custom permitting the husband to dismiss his wife by sending her a 'note of three and a half lines' must have been the source of much tragedy. Even when it came to judicial divorce, her position was inferior to that of her husband. The unequal treatment of adultery in the criminal law, which I have described before, had its parallel in the divorce law of the old Code. Adultery was always a ground for divorce when committed by the wife. She, however, could demand divorce only if the husband had been convicted of a sexual crime. Equalization has been adopted in this field, too. In consistency with our self-restraint with respect to domestic relations, we did not object to the retention of the traditional divorce by agreement, although we were aware of the danger that due to her subordinate position, which we did not expect to disappear overnight, this institution would continue to work to the disadvantage of the female partner. Even though she might not have been willing to choose the unenviable status of a divorcee, she more often than not agreed formally to the divorce, as we had found out, under the pressure of her husband and of her in-laws, with whom she usually, though now no longer necessarily, had to live. We saw to it, however, that a judicial check on the voluntary nature of the agreement was introduced in the revised law

As for inheritance, there was previously the distinction between succession into the house and succession into personal property. In succession into the house, which now no longer exists, the male was generally given preference over the female members. With regard to succession into personal property, the surviving spouse did not inherit anything as long as there were lineal descendants. Under the new Code, the wife as well as the husband, when succeeding with such descendants, are entitled to a legal share of one-third, a more generous rule than that provided in the German Civil Code, where the share is only one-fourth.

Parental power, previously exercised by the father, is, pursuant to the reform, in the hands of both parents. The family court, to which considerable authority is assigned, would decide if and when the parents could not come to an agreement in matters involving the welfare of the child.

These illustrations show that the radical revision of the Civil Code, with its sociological implications, represents a very important – if not the most important – part of the reform legislation, since it affects the intimate life of every Japanese man and woman. While not perfect, the reform surpassed our hopes, and appeared quite apt to open the way to a freer individual in a freer society. That does not mean that we expected collectivist attitudes to change rapidly into individualist ones, but we knew that this legal foundation would greatly help the progressive elements of the population to advance their ideas. The victory of these elements in the process of the legislative change encouraged us, and confirmed our previous impression that the traditional institution of the house was doomed, at least as a legally prescribed mode of life. Whoever wanted to stick to it as a 'beautiful' custom could, of course, do so, as long as others who rejected it were not forced into it by law. Up to now, twenty-five years later, reactionary attempts to restore the old family bonds have failed.

...

CRIMINAL CODE

The Criminal Code, which also leaned heavily on European models, did not require a thorough mending, since it was a relatively advanced piece of legislation. Although it was enacted as early as 1882 and needed some modernization, there were few provisions irreconcilable with the new constitutional principles. We have already mentioned that the revised version, enacted on 14 October 1947, adjusted the whole chapter called 'Crimes against the Imperial Family' to the principle of equality before the law as well as to the changed position of the Emperor as a symbol. The dramatic events leading to the abolition of these sanctions against lese majesty will be reported in a subsequent chapter. It has also been described how the unequal treatment of wives and husbands in cases of adultery was deleted in the Code. SCAP's insistence that nobody should enjoy privileged protection before the law resulted in our also approving the deletion of the provisions in the Code subjecting crimes against heads of state and envoys of a foreign power to more severe punishment than those against other people. While the retention of the lese majesty chapter would have been politically undesirable under the circumstances prevailing in the first years of the Occupation, the legal question of whether privileged protection in criminal law of a person or category of persons under specific conditions violates the constitutional principle of equality was subsequently under judicial review. In a famous patricide case, the Supreme Court had to deal with the articles of the Code prescribing more severe penalties for inflicting death or other bodily injury on lineal ascendants than for committing the same offenses against other persons. It might appear inconsistent that in spite of SCAP's abolition of lese majesty we left these provisions untouched. We did so out of the same consideration for the sensitive area of family relations that underlay our self-restraint in the revision of the Civil Code. As was to be expected, the majority of the court upheld the constitutionality of the unequal treatment on the basis of natural law, declaring the relations between close relatives 'the great fountainhead of human ethics', and also holding, among other points, that the requirement of equality applies to the subjects of rights rather than to the objects or victims of a crime. Justices Mano and Hozumi Shigeto, both later participants in the Supreme Court Mission, which I describe in Chapter 22, argued in courageous dissenting opinions in favor of invalidation of the provisions, criticizing the majority for confusing law and morality. In a concurring opinion, Justice Saito Yusuke vehemently attacked the two dissenters and the original judgment of the Fukuoka District Court, which had arrived at the same result as they did. Saito called the minority opinions 'conceited notions of ingratitude, lacking in understanding ... morality, and aimlessly chasing after innovations'. He expressed himself with special bitterness against Mano, writing: 'I find it unbearable to read the rest of the opinion for it develops an academically prostituted theory that is a national disgrace, a theory based on selfcentered egoism under the beautiful name of democracy.'

...

In light of my abomination of the death penalty, the question will be asked why I did not endeavor to bring about abolition in the Criminal Code of Japan. I raised, indeed, no objection to its retention because I had arrived at the conclusion that the overwhelming majority of the Japanese were still convinced of the deterring effect of capital punishment, which some of them also regarded necessary for the retributory satisfaction of the victim or his relatives. Since among us Americans, too, the adherents were more numerous than the opponents, I felt that merely on the basis of my personal aversion, I had no right to press for an innovation for which, as I saw it, neither the Japanese nor our own nation was ripe at that time. Soon after the enactment of the Code, namely, on March 12, 1948, the grand bench of the Supreme Court of Japan rejected an appeal from a death sentence in a murder case by holding that the penalty imposed did not violate the constitutional prohibition of 'cruel punishments'. The majority opinion emphasized that the threat of the death penalty may be a general preventive measure, its execution may be a means of cutting off at the root special social evils, and both may be used to protect society. The court suggested that its approval of capital punishment means 'giving supremacy to the concept of humanity as a whole rather than to the concept of humanity as individuals'. Ultimately, the majority resorted again to the magic formula in the constitution of public welfare, consideration of which, it held, limits the 'right to life', as all other civil liberties, and requires the retention of the death penalty. Interestingly enough, in a concurrent opinion four associate justices, who consider 'the feelings of the people decisive with regard to the question of cruelty of punishments' appear to share my opinion that the eventual trend, and I may add the desirable trend, is toward abolition. While recognizing that the people still favor capital punishment, their feelings are described as subject to change. The judges foresee the elimination of the death penalty 'as a nation's culture develops to a high degree and as a peaceful society is realized ... and if a time is reached when it is not felt to be necessary for the public welfare to prevent crime by the menace of the death penalty'.

...

There exists an essential difference between Western and Japanese ideology with regard to truth. While we believe, at least in theory, that truthfulness is an overriding ethical command, the Japanese, if I may generalize, are inclined to the attitude that to be polite is more important and decent than to say the truth if and when the latter would hurt the other fellow. It is, therefore, not astonishing that the old Criminal Code, in its chapter on defamation and libel, protected the reputation of a person regardless of the truth of publicly alleged damaging facts about that person. Such allegation was a criminal offense, and truth was no defense. This made adverse criticism of established powers within the state dangerous, if not impossible, and flagrantly violated the constitutional guarantee of freedom of speech. That had to be changed without doing away with the protection of people from false accusations and other forms of calumny. The revised Code, while increasing the penalties for libel, to a considerable extent admits evidence of truth as defense. Allegations injurious to the reputation of another person are not punishable now if made in the public interest and primarily for the public benefit, *and* if the alleged facts are found true. Two examples in which the public interest and the motivation for the public benefit can be assumed are listed: first, facts concerning the commission of a criminal offense as long as no prosecution has been initiated; and second, facts injurious to the reputation of a public official or a candidate for public office. The first illustration serves to promote the detection of crimes by the law-enforcement agencies, and the second emphasizes the principle, indispensable in any free nation, according to which he who holds public office or runs for it must be exposed to public criticism, inasmuch as a higher degree of integrity is expected of him than of others.

Among the more technical revisions, I may mention one correcting undesirable aspects of the police state: we increased the penalties for abuse of power by public officials in the process of prosecution or police investigation. More severe punishment was provided for the guard who treats a convicted prisoner with violence and cruelty. In light of the third-degree methods that prevailed among Japanese police and prison personnel, this was deemed imperative. We did not overlook the problem involved in fighting these methods, which also exist in our own country, namely, the reluctance of the cruelly treated person to complain and the inclination of the higher authority to refrain from taking action against the guilty official.

Minor offenses had not been dealt with previously in the Criminal Code, but under an ordinance, and were tried by the police courts, which were now abolished. The new constitution requires that penal provisions be enacted by Diet legislation unless explicit delegation is made to the cabinet. The Minor Offenses Law of 1 May 1948, replaces most of the regulations of the old ordinances by compiling a list of these insignificant offenses, carefully omitting those that could infringe on constitutional safeguards, such as freedom of assembly and speech.

...

Procedural Codes

CIVIL PROCEDURE

The existing Code of Civil Procedure of 1890 leaned heavily on its German model of 1877. There were not many provisions in this law that clearly violated principles of the new constitution. Although the constitutional requirement of a speedy and fair trial is restricted to criminal cases in the instrument, the changes in the Code, some of them purely technical, were also motivated by the desire to expedite the civil procedure and to relieve the courts from an excessive burden of work. The dominant role played by the single judge or the presiding judge of a collegiate court during the trial had manifold reasons. First, as we have seen, the training and prestige of lawyers had been inferior to those of judges. Pretrial procedures were unusual because the few lawyers who practiced in Japan had neither the time nor, often, the ability to examine witnesses – apart from the fact that such pretrial examination by the parties was regarded as unethical in light of the danger of coaching.

The public itself apparently looked at the lawyer less as one who acts within the framework of the process of achieving justice than as a private businessman whom the client had to pay. The judge, on the other hand, was respected and even trusted as bearer of governmental authority. No wonder that under such circumstances the forensic tradition we found in Japan was very like that in Germany (where the bar had reached higher prestige): the judge wielded almost complete power in conducting the trial, investigating, clarifying, taking evidence, and sentencing. He would always be the first one to examine the parties and witnesses, and he did it in an efficient and inquisitorial manner that many Japanese jurists now admit to have been paternalistic. The parties could ask supplemental questions, but this did not amount to much, since the thoroughness of the judge had usually exhausted the subject matter. The other side of the judge's domineering position was the overexertion of the courts, which resulted in postponements, piecemeal trials, piled-up case loads, and other forms of slow justice. The absence of a jury in Japanese law meant that the judge had the combined responsibilities of fact finding and sentencing, besides taking care of order in the court and conducting the trial.

Even the piecemeal trials have found their defenders. It has been argued, for instance, that the passing of considerable time between the several trial terms helps the parties better to understand each other's viewpoint, and also makes them more apt to settle their conflicts. I feel, however, that these arguments are rationalizations of the traditional Japanese reluctance to fight for one's rights in court, rather than convincing justifications.

Behind the few changes brought about by the amendment of the Code, dated 1 July 1948, were two main considerations: first, to relieve the courts, and second, to democratize the procedure by weakening judicial paternalism. We have already mentioned the limitation of appeals to three instances in those petty cases that start in the summary courts. The deletion of former Article 261, which authorized the presiding judge to take evidence *ex officio*, is now being interpreted as the most important innovation introducing the adversary system into the civil procedure. This change was certainly a step away from the inquisitorial conduct of the trial. The spirit of 'making the party win who should win' may be somewhat appealing, but independent evidence-taking by the judge in a civil procedure, which is, after all, a conflict between private parties, drives it to an extreme. This is the way we felt; and by deleting the article we also aimed at relieving the judge from a responsibility whose assumption added to his burden and slowed clown the procedure.

Was the deletion of Article 261 really the signal for the introduction of the adversary system? In answering this question, we must consider some other provisions of the amended Code. A new Article 294 provides that a witness shall first be examined by the parties, and that the presiding judge may do so after the examination by the parties has been concluded. While this appears to place the primary responsibility for the conduct of the trial and the main initiative on the litigants, some other articles of the old Code that strengthen the position of the presiding judge have remained unaltered. Article 336 authorized him to examine the parties themselves under oath, on application or ex officio if he thinks it proper, and Article 259 conferred power on him to disallow the taking of evidence tendered by a party if he finds it unnecessary to do so. In light of such seemingly contradictory arrangements, it may be correct to say that the revision did not constitute a categorical introduction of the adversary system. It still leaves open the possibility that an energetic or highhanded judge may dominate the trial by inquisitorial methods, even though he can no longer take evidence ex officio and may examine witnesses only after the parties have done so.

What, then, did we reformers have in mind? It was probably to be expected that my associates strongly favored the adversary system, as prevailed in the United States. But even I who, thanks to my German background, had a certain sympathy for the judicial endeavor to discover the truth in the trial, was inclined to move away from the rigidly inquisitorial Japanese system, particularly in civil procedure; I shall elaborate on my attitude toward the two systems in connection with the revision of the criminal procedure.

Both systems have their definite pros and cons. The Japanese societal and judicial tradition would have made the categorical introduction of the adversary system a hasty and unwise imposition. The revision was, therefore, designed to pave the way for an eventual adoption of the adversary system after a process of adaptation that could, possibly, last a long time. The enhanced prestige of the lawyers and their improved training, the disapproval by the young generation of jurists of judicial paternalism, and the increasing necessity of relieving the courts from excessive burdens of work – all that encouraged us in the belief that the civil procedure of Japan would move a significant step in the direction of an adversary system, but we did not anticipate a replica of the American practice. Here again, as in most of the legal and judicial reforms, the *leitmotif* has been to find what Judge Tanabe terms a 'midway position' or 'in a real sense a fusion of the Continental and Anglo-Saxon philosophies'.

As for the remaining changes in the Code, the penalties against non-cooperating witnesses were increased in view of the bad habit of ignoring summonses. This was all the more necessary since the Japanese were not yet ready to adopt some form of contempt of court along American lines. The abolition of the waiver of appeals previously permitted in advance of the judgment perhaps came nearest to requiring an amendment under the constitution, since it was looked upon as jeopardizing the guaranteed right of access to the courts. Sociologically interesting were the extensive immunities from the duty to testify in the old Code. They were based on concepts of loyalty and clan obligation, which not only the Occupation but also progressive groups among the Japanese regarded as incompatible with a democratic society. I refer particularly to the rights to refuse to testify against an employer and a relative within the sixth degree of blood. They were eliminated in the new Code to a considerable extent.

...

CRIMINAL PROCEDURE

It has already been pointed out that the amendment of the Code of Criminal Procedure, enacted on 10 July 1948, and in effect since 1 January 1949, was the most complicated and time-consuming legal reform. This was the consequence of the rich catalogue of safeguards in the new constitution for those entangled in criminal prosecution. Law-and-order champions of today may easily find them excessive, but for an Occupation resolved to introduce fundamental rights, it was necessary to provide the legal foundations for far-reaching rights in the very sphere where the individual's life and personal freedom are eminently involved.

Among the constitutional safeguards, I may mention the rule that no person shall be apprehended except upon warrant issued by a judicial officer that specifies the offense charged, unless the person is apprehended while committing the crime; the right to counsel; the right of all persons to be secure in their homes, papers, and effects against searches and seizures, except on judicial warrant or when apprehended while committing the offense; the absolute prohibition of the infliction of torture and cruel punishment; the right to a speedy and public trial by an impartial tribunal; the rule that no person shall be compelled to testify against himself, and that confessions made under compulsion, torture, or threat, or after prolonged detention shall not be admitted in evidence; moreover, the prohibition of conviction or punishment in cases where the only proof against the defendant is his own confession; the principle of *nulla poena sine lege* (no punishment may be inflicted unless provided by law); and exclusion of double jeopardy.

All these safeguards have been implemented and further developed in minute detail in the four hundred articles of the Code. Many changes have been made in the interest of expedition and efficiency of the criminal process as well as of humanization, and antiquated features of the old law have been deleted.

...

A significant innovation was the abolition of the preliminary investigation well known to me from Germany, and also traditional in France. It was conducted by a judge, and the idea behind it was that the investigation of grave offenses would be more impartial in the hands of a magistrate than if conducted by the prosecutor. In practice, it seldom worked this way either in Germany or in Japan, since the investigating judge was usually as eager as the procurator to prove the guilt of the accused in what amounted to a secret preparatory trial hardly reconcilable with the constitutional demand of publicity of a criminal trial. The device has, indeed, been compared to the medieval inquisition. Its abolition did not meet much opposition from our Japanese conference partners.

Unless very minor offenses are charged, the trial must take place in the presence of the accused; service by publication was formerly possible, so that a man could be convicted without his knowledge. Under the old procedure the first information that the trial court or single judge received of the facts of a case consisted of the records arid dossiers of the police and procurator. This inevitably influenced him in favor of the prosecution. The new law prohibits the submission of these papers. The evidence must be provided by testimony or documentary evidence in the presence of the parties and, apart from exceptional situations, in open court. As pointed out by Nagashima Atsushi, counselor in the Ministry of Justice, this change in connection with what he terms transition to the adversary system has caused much difficulty to the defense counsel in preparing the case. Formerly he had been given an opportunity to see the pretrial evidence that the procurator had submitted to the court. Due to the thoroughness of police and procuratorial investigation methods, this gave him a pretty good factual picture of the case before the trial, and spared him the burden of examining witnesses himself in pretrial procedures. Now, if he does not want to appear unprepared before the court, he must take evidence on his own initiative, something the Japanese lawyers are not yet fully equipped to do. The pretrial investigative records will and must, according to a Supreme Court decision, be disclosed to him only insofar as the prosecution makes use of them in the trial. I believe that these difficulties are unavoidable in the evolution from an inquisitorial to at least a partially accusatorial criminal process.' Unless the Supreme Court reverses its view and concedes the right of defense counsel to inspect without limitation the pretrial evidence, the development to larger lawyers' offices may be the answer. The junior law partners could then be given the task of preparing the case before the trial. This would also improve the ability of the defense counsel to examine and cross-examine witnesses.

Public procurator and defense counsel are now conceived as equal parties in the procedure, which is symbolized in the trial by the seating arrangements. Previously, the procurator, sharing in the governmental authority, sat on an elevated level together with the judges, while the counsel had his place next to or near the defendant. Their positions have now been symbolically equalized – to what extent in actuality, is hard to verify.

With regard to the system of trial, the tradition and the law were as inquisitorial and paternalistic as they were in civil procedure. Here again, the presiding judge was the sovereign master; he was the one who did the essential examining of the defendant as well as of the witnesses. Only when the parties had additional questions were they allowed to ask them. Some of the Occupation lawyers favored the complete adoption of the adversary system in which the initiative lies with the defense counsel and the prosecutor, while the judge towers over the parties as a detached umpire. Both systems have their advantages as well as disadvantages. In the Continental type, for which I have retained a certain inclination with respect to criminal procedure, the court, through the presiding judge, aims at finding out the truth. He may bring to light facts for or against the accused by taking *ex officio* additional evidence that a less conscientious counsel or procurator has overlooked or intentionally omitted. On the other hand, the presiding judge who conducts the taking of testimony is always in danger of growing inquisitorial, particularly if his concern for law and order overrides his consideration for the rights of the accused. Hence, apart from the difference that the trial is public, similar doubts can be raised as for preliminary investigations.

The adversary system avoids the danger that the judge may become prejudiced by his direct involvement, but, as far as I have observed, it has its own weaknesses, at least the way it has developed in the United States. Comparisons are, of course, precarious because the Japanese, unlike us, have no jury. While in our courts the parties are assured of having the opportunity of exhausting all means of proving the merit of their cause, their duel in the court has frequently degenerated to a kind of boxing match in which the stronger one prevails. In other words, especially in a jury trial, the greater efficiency, resourcefulness, and eloquence of the defense or the prosecution may – and too often does – influence the decision. While within the adversary system the cross-examination constitutes all effective means of finding the truth, the traditional reluctance of the American judge to interfere has also led to the bad habit of the parties intimidating and grilling the witnesses without being adequately restrained.

In view of these pros and cons, our 'experiment with the adversary system' again was not a radical one but moved along the middle road. The revised Code shows traits distinctively adversary as well as inquisitorial. The strengthening of the parties' position, especially that of the defense counsel, and of their role in the trial belong to the former; and so does the replacement of the principle of free judicial evaluation of the evidence by binding rules of evidence, that is, the exclusion of hearsay and of confession made under specific circumstances. Still, traditional elements of the presiding judge's power are evident in provisions such as Article 297, which authorizes the court to determine and change the scope, order, and method of the examination of evidence after hearing the opinion and suggestions of the litigants. According to subsequent rules of the Supreme Court, the presiding judge usually starts the examination of witnesses and is followed by the parties. This order may be changed. The parties may, however, now examine and cross-examine the witnesses by way of right. Several detailed provisions, some in the Code and others in Supreme Court rules, intensify their opportunity to challenge evidence.

...

Looking, in conclusion, at this all-important reform, one has only to remember which significant elements of American law have not been adopted by the new Japanese Code to realize that the Americanization was rather selective. We did not impose a jury system, neither the grand jury nor the petty one, although the latter is the darling of Anglo-Saxon people. A petty jury system, patterned again on the German model, existed in Japan from 1923–43, but never enjoyed much popularity during its short lifetime. Apparently, the majority of Japanese did not think too highly of the judicial competence of 'the people'. The reluctance to entrust to a jury the decision over their fate as defendants also indicates the general confidence in the professional judge, who, strangely enough, generally rendered more lenient verdicts than the jury. Actually, the Japanese jury system was even a watered-down edition of the German. The verdict did not bind the court. If the judges did not like it, they could rescind it and have the case retried. Since no appeal as to the factual evidence was allowed and the decision of the jury could be challenged by the parties only on legal grounds in the Supreme Court (Daishinin), it is understandable that in light of their past experiences our Japanese counterparts did not favor another jury experiment. My own view is that the jury system, as practiced in the United States, has its merits in criminal cases, which can frequently be decided by mere common sense, but that the same is not true of civil cases, which all too often involve extremely complex legal problems transcending the horizon of the average citizen. The jury serves as a beneficial counterpoise to the doctrinaire American objectivism in criminal law and courts. Such counterpoise is certainly less needed in Japan. I also believe that the grand jury system, which shifts the responsibility for indictment from the government prosecutor to the people, has proved its validity in our country. But we did not feel that we ought to adopt, against the opposition of the Japanese, institutions historically grown, after all, on a very different soil.

Neither did we urge the Japanese to follow the American pattern of pleading guilty or innocent, because we were afraid that the public procurator's customary predilection of obtaining a confession before taking public action, combined with the tendency of the Japanese people to avoid trial, would result in pleas of guilty by numerous innocent defendants. I personally was also afraid that such an innovation would soon be accompanied by plea bargaining and promises of immunity to co-defendants and witnesses, as practiced in the United States. While these institutions have their advantages for those involved, the prosecutor, and the court, I have always considered them as violating the principle of equality before the law and as basically unethical. One ought not to bargain with justice.

It may be argued, however, as our Anglo-Saxon lawyers did, that we did not go far enough in Americanizing the Japanese law, insofar as it protects the defendant in the trial to a perhaps excessive degree. I have in mind his right to lie. While in our country a defendant, if he does not prefer to remain silent, must testify as a witness under oath, the Japanese defendant never becomes a witness and may defend himself as ever he likes without the risk of perjuring himself. I do not think, however, that this 'permissiveness' is actually too dangerous, from the point of view of seeking the truth. Though not risking perjury if he lies, the defendant risks the loss of his credibility when the lie is discovered; and lies are usually short-lived. Moreover, the American transformation of defendant to sworn witness puts him into a precarious dilemma: if he remains silent, this will inevitably strengthen the suspicion that he is guilty; if, however, he decides to testify, his motivation to defend himself will, considering the frailty of human nature, continuously tempt him to deviate from the truth. He would then have added the prospect of a prosecution for perjury to his present tribulation.

These three important illustrations of restraint in Americanization on the part of the Occupation lawyers may suffice for our purpose, but they are not the only instances in which a change of the Code along American lines was considered unwise. What we have, then, as the product of the revision is sometimes characterized as a 'hybrid' law, a term easily understood as having a negative connotation. I prefer to write about a 'synthesis' of the American and Japanese systems. One may, indeed, ask: is not the culture of most nations, including their law, a combination of indigenous customs and imported concepts? Has not the Japanese law always been hybrid and adaptable to foreign influences, first Chinese and later continental European? If the imported goods satisfy a need – in other words, if the adopting nation is ripe for the innovation – the import will have staying power, regardless of whether or not the adoption was fully voluntary. The great codification of the law during the Meiji period, which survived half a century, was also born out of a considerable degree of international pressures, especially the strong desire of the Meiji rulers to get rid of the humiliating extraterritorial judicial rights of big powers by modernization of the Japanese law.

CHAPTER 3

SOURCES OF LAW

INTRODUCTION

This chapter will cover topics beyond those more traditionally associated with this area of legal theory. In addition to dealing with the hierarchy of written law, case law and legal theory, it is necessary to look behind those sources and deal with broader aspects of Japanese law. Modern Japanese law is drawn from a wide variety of legal sources, but to present it merely as a system of law developed over the last 120 years and consisting entirely of legal transplants, would be to ignore and misrepresent the structure and operation of law in Japanese society.[1] In spite of what might be considered massive injections of Western legal and cultural influences, there remain aspects of law and society which are fundamentally and uniquely Japanese, the strength and resilience of which affect the operation of the law.[2] Thus, the place of custom (*kanshu*) and equitable principles of common reason (*jori*) need to be considered, as does 'administrative guidance' (*gyosei shido*) which occupies a unique place in the Japanese legal system as what might be termed 'nonjusticiable law'. Issued by government departments it is an instrument of bureaucratic power which, whilst it is not 'law' in the strict sense, has a role and function beyond that of the mere bureaucratic circular.

The need to look at a broad spectrum of sources, justiciable and nonjusticiable law, written law and custom, is explained, in part, by the fact that the Japanese legal system is essentially a hybrid. It is an example of legal pluralism, a system which as a result of transplantation and adoption, combined with indigenous rules, identifies with no single tradition.[3] Thus,

---

1 One writer has commented that 'during a century of Japanese legal evolution we encounter, among other kinds of "law", unlimited official powers, status authority and privilege, family relations, natural law, village custom, customary law, and written law of several sorts: orders, decrees, case reports, statutes, ministerial regulations, and finally even constitutions and comprehensive codes.' Henderson, DF, 'Law and Political Modernisation' in Ward, RE (ed), *Political Development in Modern Japan*, 1968, Princeton University Press. For a more detailed account of Japanese legal history, see Chapter 2 and for a discussion on the nature of law in Japanese society see Chapter 1.

2 Whilst the current legal system and law in any country is the product of historical development, it is not a mere accumulation of rules and procedures, but must necessarily incorporate cultural and sociological features. Together with the fact that in Japan the function and operation of law in society might be considered somewhat different from that in other countries, this combination underlines the complexity of the situation. On the place of law in Japanese society see: Chapter 1; Noda, Y, *Introduction to Japanese Law*, 1976, Chapter 9, University of Tokyo Press; Upham, F, *Law and Social Change in Postwar Japan*, 1987, Chapter 6, pp 205–21, Harvard University Press; Fukutake, T, *The Japanese Social Structure*, 1989, Chapter 17, University of Tokyo Press; Haley, J, *Authority Without Power: Law and the Japanese Paradox*, 1991, Chapter 8, Oxford University Press.

3 The concept of 'tradition' in law is itself problematic and the term is used here in a broad and generalist manner. However, one explanation is that it is the presence of an authoritative past for present or future use; for this and a discussion on the theory of 'tradition' see Krygier, M, 'Law as Tradition' (1986) 5 *Law and Philosophy* 237. For an introduction to the various legal traditions/families/systems see: Merryman, JH, *The Civil Law Tradition*, 2nd edn, 1985, Stanford University Press; Watson, A, *Legal Transplants*, 1974, Scottish Academic Press; ...

although through its codes the Japanese legal system has elements of the civil law tradition and as a result of the Occupation it has absorbed something of the common law tradition, nevertheless, at the same time it has retained aspects of customary 'law'.[4] In a sense, the variety of sources of law, together with the social context and value system within which they operate, illustrate the dichotomy of identity and universality in Japanese law, the wish to maintain an element of uniqueness based on its history and culture, against the desire for a degree of universality in the context of the modern world.[5]

Whatever the theory, in practice Japanese law is a complex mosaic, a hall of mirrors, that is at once clear and yet elusive and where the apparent certainty of the written law can become less clear as a result of interpretation (*kaishaku*) or the meaning of the language itself.[6] The difficulties this raises will be more fully explored in the materials, but first it is important to establish the hierarchy of sources of Japanese law. At its simplest, the distinction is between written and unwritten law, thus enacted law (*seiteiho*) is the prime source of law.[7] Within this class of laws there is a sub-hierarchy consisting of the six codes (*roppo*) and statutes (*horitsu*).

However, there are other forms of written law. The Japanese term for written law is *horei*, which is made up of *ho*, meaning 'laws' and *rei* meaning 'orders'. Thus, in addition to the codes and statutes, written law also includes orders (*meirei*) issued by government agencies; foremost amongst these are Cabinet Orders (*seirei*), followed by Ministerial Orders (*furei* being an order issued by the Prime Minister and *shorei* issued by Ministers).[8] Also under this heading are

---

3 ... 2nd edn, 1993, University of Georgia Press; David, R and Brierley, JEC, *Major Legal Systems in the World Today*, 3rd edn, 1985, Stevens; Zweigert, K and Kötz, H, *An Introduction to Comparative Law*, 2nd edn, 1992, Clarendon, Oxford University Press.

4 In particular consider the rules of *giri*, a code of obligation and honour by which society was ordered and which continues to influence relationships, not least in business, and very often described simply as 'custom'; see Noda, *supra*, n 2, pp 174–83.

5 Toshitani, N, 'Identity and Universality of Japanese Law' in *Legal Culture: Encounters and Transformations* (Proceedings of the 1995 Annual Meeting of the Research Committee on Sociology of Law, International Sociological Association, Tokyo University). For background on Japanese social structure see: Fukutake, *supra*, n 2; Hendry, J, *Understanding Japanese Society*, 2nd edn, 1995, Routledge.

6 On aspects of judicial interpretation see: Itoh, H, 'How Judges Think in Japan' (1970) 18 *American Journal of Comparative Law* 775. For discussion of the difficulty in language and translation see: Agnello, AH, 'Thinking of Japanese Law – A Linguistic Primer' (1979) 12 *Comparative International Law Journal of South Africa* 83; Beer, LW and Tomatsu, H, 'A Guide to the Study of Japanese Law' (1975) 23 *American Journal of Comparative Law* 285; Henderson, DF, 'Japanese Law in English: Reflections on Translation' (1980) *Journal of Japanese Studies* 117; Kitamura, I, 'Problems of the Translation of Law in Japan' (1993) 23 *Victoria University of Wellington Law Review*, Appendix pp 1–40, originally published in French (1987) 28 *Les Cahiers de Droit* 747.

7 In general see: Ishii, G, 'Laws and Regulations in Japan' (1979) 7 *International Journal of Law Libraries* 155.

8 *Meirei* are orders issued by the Cabinet or government agencies, without approval of the Diet, therefore they are subordinate to Statute (*horitsu*). Cabinet Orders (*seirei*) are issued to detail rules necessary to make a Statute operative, or to deal with matters delegated by law. Ministerial Orders (*furei* and *shorei*) are issued to enforce Cabinet Orders or Statutes relating to the administrative responsibility of the particular ministry, as well as dealing with matters delegated by Cabinet Order or Law. See Ishii, *idem*, at pp 160–61; Pempel, T, 'The Bureaucratisation of Policymaking in Postwar Japan' (1974) 18 *American Journal of Political Science* 654.

rules (*kisoku*); these fall into three categories, (1) Rules of the Ministries, issued to supplement general statutes with detail; (2) Rules of the House of Representatives or the House of Councillors, which govern procedural and administrative matters and are made pursuant to Article 58(2) of the constitution; (3) Rules of the Supreme Court which detail the administration of justice, rules of practice and procedure in relation to the courts and profession, pursuant to Article 77(1) of the constitution. Although not technically law in this context, there are also Local Ordinances (*jorei*) which are issued by prefectural or city authorities pursuant to Article 94 of the constitution. Last, but by no means least, there are treaties (*joyaku*) which whilst no doubt a source of law, are the subject of debate amongst Japanese academics as to their effect on domestic law.[9]

CODES, STATUTES AND TREATIES

The six codes (*roppo*) are the prime sources of law and consist of the constitution (*kempo*), the Civil Code (*minpo*), the Commercial Code (*shoho*), the Code of Civil Procedure (*minjisosho ho*), the Criminal Code (*keiho*) and the Code of Criminal Procedure (*keijisosho ho*).[10] Article 98 of the constitution states that the constitution 'shall be the supreme law of the nation and no law, ordinance, imperial rescript or other act of government ... shall have legal force or validity', thereby setting it apart from other legislation as a supreme law. In a non federal system where there is no need to establish an order of priority as between federal and state laws, this Article could be seen as stating the obvious. However, it is argued that it, together with Articles 97 and 99 (titled Chapter 10 'Supreme Law'), rather than being a meaningless and unnecessary provision, are in fact 'stating that the "rule of law" is the fundamental principle of the constitution' and stands as a 'summation of the whole constitution'.[11] The other codes and laws are therefore subordinate to the constitution which, in accordance with its status as a higher law and together with the developing case law of the Supreme Court is considered in Chapter 7.

In addition to the constitution, the five other codes make up the basic law, though they may be complemented by a special statute which provides detailed support for the code provisions. However, there is an element of supplementation within the codes themselves which can then create a three tier hierarchy of reference. Thus, the Civil Code sets out general provisions in relation to civil matters, which is then particularised in the provisions of the more specialised Commercial Code. Since there are areas of commercial activity

9 Adams, JL, *Theory, Law and Policy of Contemporary Japanese Treaties*, 1974, Chapter 2, Oceana Publications/Sijthoff; Port, KL, 'The Japanese International Law "Revolution": International Human Rights Law and its Impact in Japan' (1991) 28 *Stanford Journal of International Law* 152–54.

10 The Six Codes are published as a single volume collection (*Roppo Zensho*) by the Codes Translation Institute (*Eibun-Horei-Sha*) with the title *EHS Law Bulletin Series* and prepared under the authority of the Ministry of Justice.

11 Ito, M, 'The Modern Development of Law and Constitution in Japan' in Beer, LW (ed), *Constitutional Systems in Late Twentieth Century Asia*, 1992, p 129, University of Washington Press.

which are too specialised to be covered by that Code, there are a number of laws which supplement the Commercial Code, eg the Bills of Exchange and Promissory Notes Law 1932 and the Cheques Law 1933. More than any of the other codes, the Commercial Code has undergone greater change and has more specialised laws associated with it than the others. It is also interesting that whereas the normal hierarchy of sources would place statute above custom, Article 1 of the Commercial Code reverses that and also illustrates the interrelationship between sources when it states that in commercial matters 'the commercial customary law shall apply if there are no provisions in this code; and the Civil Code shall apply, if there is no such law'.

As has already been mentioned in Chapter 2, the codes were introduced in the Meiji era and underwent a number of revisions, some of the most significant being during the Occupation.[12] The detail of their structure can be found elsewhere but essentially, as with codes based on the Continental civil law tradition, they are generally highly conceptual and very systematic.[13] Because of their highly systematic nature the codes 'speak to the courts directly', in that they are paramount, and although they may in certain areas need to be supplemented by 'special laws', they in fact act as a lexicon and a reservoir of basic principle thereby making the drafting of laws easier.[14] All laws enacted by parliament are referred to as *horitsu* and are the prime source of law, but the complex history of transplantation and adoption of law in Japan has resulted in greater space for other forms of law. Whereas in continental Europe Roman law could be said to have been 'received' and then undergone organic growth to become one of the civil law systems, the importation of the continental civilian tradition in Japan did not mean that it could either supplant customary law, or fill all the gaps.[15]

In placing written law at the top of the hierarchy the most important piece of legislation was the Great Council of State Decree No 103, 1875; entitled 'Directions for the Conduct of Judicial Affairs' (*Saiban Jimu Kokoroe*), Article 3 established written law as the prime source of law, but also recognised the place of custom and reason.[16] Given this fixed theory of sources, it is unsurprising to

12 There have been various revisions and attempted revisions since that time, but essentially the new constitution and modern codes were put in place then. For an account of the development of the codes prior to the Second World War see: Takayanagi, K, 'A Century of Innovation: The Development of Japanese Law 1868–1961' in von Mehren (ed), *Law in Japan*, 1963, Chapter 2, pp 15–33, Harvard University Press. On the Occupation reforms see: Oppler, AC, *Legal Reform in Occupied Japan: A Participant Looks Back*, 1976, Chapter 9 and 10, Princeton University Press.

13 Noda, Y, *supra*, n 2, pp 197–211.

14 Henderson, 1980, *supra*, n 6, pp 126 and 128. Seki, M, 'The Drafting Process for Cabinet Bills' (1986) 19 *Law in Japan* 168. An example is the relationship between the Family Registration Law 1947 and Book 4 of the Civil Code.

15 The importance and status of written law can be seen in situations where the advance of science has meant there is a new gap in the code. Thus, the Civil Code does not deal with intangible property, ie intellectual property rights, therefore it has been necessary to pass laws dealing with patent, design trademark and copyright.

16 Article 3, Decree No 103, 1875 'In civil trials, those matters for which there is no written law are governed by custom and those matters for which there is no custom shall be adjudicated by inference from reason *(jori)*.' Takayanagi, *supra*, n 12, p 25.

find that in later revisions of the Civil and Commercial Codes custom played a bigger role than might otherwise have been expected (see below). Moreover, even in a highly systematic legislative structure, interpretation plays an important role and whilst it is clear that non written sources can have an influence, the word for interpretation (*kaishaku*) also means 'construction', thereby rooting the process firmly in the written law.[17] In continental civil law systems, where deductive reasoning is the norm, divergence from written law is an accepted part of the process.[18] However, even where there is an acknowledged hierarchy, the multiplicity of sources of law in Japan makes that divergence 'more marked'.[19]

Against this background and as noted above, it is not surprising that the place of treaties in national law is very much a matter of debate. This arises from the fact that the constitution is silent as to the status of a properly signed and ratified treaty. Article 73(3) makes it clear that it is the Cabinet which concludes treaties, with the approval of the Diet and Article 98(2) states that treaties and established laws of nations 'shall be faithfully observed'. If the State is taken to be one and the same in both an international and a national context, then the concluding of a treaty is merely state decision-making and the treaty has the force of law. On the other hand the state is entering an international agreement which in order to become part of national law needs to be enacted in national law. Even if that is the case then there may be a distinction between those treaties which are self executing and those which are not.[20] Where the debate is more difficult is regarding the relationship with the constitution because Article 98(1) states that the constitution shall be the supreme law over *inter alia* an act of government, which includes the conclusion of treaties. There are strongly held views on either side, but as the leading (Western) commentary concludes after reviewing the various opinions a median position seems acceptable. In other words 'treaties occupy a middle position between the constitution, on the one hand, and ordinary legislation on the other. That is, the treaties are inferior in status to the constitution but are superior to legislation and laws of the state'.[21]

---

17 Tanaka, H, *The Japanese Legal System: Introductory Cases and Materials*, 1976, Chapter 2, University of Tokyo Press. In this chapter, Tanaka provides a variety of case examples based on statutory interpretation.

18 Merryman, *supra*, n 3, Chapter 7.

19 Takanayagi, *supra*, n 12, p 39.

20 For a discussion of these opposing views see Noda, *supra*, n 2, p 213; Tanaka, 1976, *supra*, n 17, p 57 and Adams, *supra*, n 9, Chapter 2. Also Sato, I, 'Treaties and the Constitution' in Henderson, DF (ed), *The Constitution of Japan. Its First Twenty Years 1947–1967*, 1968, University of Washington Press; Kyozuka, S, 'Internal Enforcement and Application of Treaties in Japan' (1968) 12 *Japanese Annual of International Law* 45.

21 Adams, *idem*, p 19. This position seems to be supported by a decision of the Supreme Court, (*Sunakawa Case*, 1959) but adds to the controversy by considering whether treaties are subject to judicial review under Article 81. In the end there seems to be a recognition and accommodation that these theoretical constitutional arguments should not interfere with what is essentially a matter of foreign policy, ie a question of political reality. See translation of this case in Maki, J, *Court and Constitution in Japan*, 1964, University of Washington Press. An extract can also be found in Tanaka, 1976, *supra*, n 17, p 709. For comment see Oppler, AC, '*Sunakawa Case*: Its Legal and Political Implications' (1961) 76 *Political Science Quarterly* 241.

CUSTOM AND *JORI*

As has already been mentioned, the place of custom (*kanshu*) in the hierarchy of sources of law is even enshrined in law; this is entirely in line with the civilian tradition which recognises custom as a source of law.[22] However, whilst this may be inconsistent with the authoritarian and positivist theories of the civilian lawmakers which hold that only the state can make law, it is clear that in practice there may be gaps which need filling.[23] This can happen through unrestricted judicial activism, or through a more structured recognition and application of secondary sources such as custom and, in the Japanese case, *jori* (see below). The fact that modern Japanese law was implanted into an existing set of codes and rules of conduct must have meant that in practical terms there were few who understood the new set of norms and fewer still who could apply them.[24] It is therefore natural to assume that in a wide variety of areas custom was more easy to apply and was more readily adhered to. This may account for the *de facto* recognition of custom in the hierarchy of sources both in the provision in Article 3 of the Directions for the Conduct of Judicial Affairs 1875 and Article 1 of the Commercial Code (see above). However, whereas Article 1 of the Commercial Code allows reference to custom only in the absence of code provisions, Article 92 of the Civil Code places an entirely different emphasis on custom; it states: 'if, in cases where there exists a custom which differs from any provisions of laws or ordinances which are not concerned with public policy, it is to be considered that the parties to a juristic act have intended to conform to such custom, that custom shall prevail.' Thus it is part of the legislative framework that in certain situations custom is of superior importance.

Whilst the historical explanation for the continued use of custom based on a 'familiarity and needs' argument applies easily to the 19th century situation, it might be expected that with the Occupation reform, less importance would be given to custom, but this was not the case. Successive revisions of the codes have retained the references to custom, in particular the Civil Code and Commercial Code; moreover, the 1947 revised version of the Law Concerning the Application of Law (No 10, 1898, revised Law No 233, 1947) maintained Article 2 and provides that customs which are not contrary to public order or good morals 'have the same force as law insofar as they are recognised by the provisions of the law and ordinances, or are related to matters which are not provided for by law or ordinances'. In other words custom is formalised as a source of reference to fill a gap where there is no legislation and provided it is not excluded by existing legislation. In the context of a discussion on civil and commercial law, Noda goes a stage further and comments that 'it is quite natural that the courts have often to accept customs *contra legem*, notwithstanding the prohibition on doing so, because a judge is not so much required to apply existing rules of law at any cost as to give a reasonable solution to the parties before him'.[25]

22 Merryman, *supra*, n 3, p 25.

23 *Idem*, p 24.

24 Noda, *supra*, n 2, p 223.

25 Noda, *idem*, p 221.

In a society, such as Japan, where law plays a limited role as a means of social ordering, it is not surprising that in certain areas custom has received acknowledgement in legislation and is formally recognised as a source of law.[26] However, Article 3 of the Directions for the Conduct of Judicial Affairs, 1875, which was so important in establishing written law as the prime source of law, not only recognised custom, but also stated that where no written law or custom existed, then cases should be adjudicated 'by way of deduction from *jori* (natural reason)'.[27] The word is said to have its origins in the word *dori* which was found in the laws and decisions of feudal Japan and meant common sense and ordinary reason, ie justice according to prevailing moral principles rather than the strict letter of the law.[28] In this sense it has much to do with notions of equity and explains what Noda was talking about (above) when saying it is for the judge to decide on a reasonable solution in the individual case; moreover, 'reliance upon *jori* in reaching a desirable conclusion has been both a cause and a result of the relatively flexible attitude of Japanese courts in interpreting statutes'.[29]

It is not unusual in any system of law to refer to some discretionary form of natural justice or common reason, although it goes against the principle of certainty inherent in a codified system in the civil law tradition.[30] General principles such as 'good faith' exist and are applied in civil law systems and are often to be found in the 'general provisions' of a code. Indeed, Article 1 of the Japanese Civil Code refers to public welfare, good faith and abuse of rights, which judges rely on to interpret codes and statutes.[31] Thus, whilst the idea of *jori* may at first seem strange, it is quite consistent with civil law tradition and is not dissimilar to the inherent equitable power exercised by English judges. However, it could be argued that *jori* should more accurately be described as a tool of interpretation rather than a source of law in the strict sense of a codified system.

---

26 Fukutake, *supra*, n 2; Upham, *supra*, n 2, Chapter 6. Also see Noda, *idem* on The Rules of *Giri* at pp 174–83.

27 Tanaka, *supra*, n 17, p 125.

28 Takayanagi, *supra*, n 12, p 25.

29 Tanaka, *supra*, n 17, p 125. He goes on to comment that 'it is to be questioned whether it makes sense to regard this extremely vague concept as a "source" of law'. On the other hand Noda, *supra*, n 2, p 223 states that 'whether or not *jori* is a source of law is a purely theoretical question, the answer to which depends upon the definition given to the term "source of law"'.

30 Merryman, *supra*, n 3, Chapter 8; Noda, *supra*, n 2, p 187 makes particular mention of Article 1 of the Swiss Civil Code which states that where a case is not covered by written law, the judge can decide the case according to his own sense of justice.

31 Tanaka comments on the tradition of code interpretation and the manner in which judges utilise these general provisions as a mechanism for reaching a 'desirable result' and goes on to observe: 'In most cases, Japanese judges reach a conclusion on the basis of policy considerations and then try to rationalise this conclusion by referring to one of these "general clauses" or to a more specific provision in the statute. Relatively few judges, however, openly reveal their policy considerations in their opinions. Judges usually prefer to pretend that the result has been reached by syllogism from the letters of a statute.' Tanaka, H, 'Legal Equality Among Family Members in Japan – The Impact of the Japanese Constitution of 1946 on the Traditional Family System' (1980) 53 *Southern California Law Review* 617–18.

CASE LAW AND COMMENTARIES

In strict civil law theory the only sources of law are statutes, regulations and custom.[32] However, in Japan, the importance of judicial decisions has been recognised for some time, particularly in the field of civil and commercial law.[33] Although lawyers traditionally preferred to rely on commentaries rather than case reports (*hanrei*), the influence of the American common law through the Occupation reforms and in particular the importance of Supreme Court decisions' means that there has been a change in emphasis.[34] Thus, case law might properly be considered a source of law, but it is in no way binding or authoritative as it is in a system where *stare decisis* operates. Instead, a lawyer will first seek authority from the codes and statute, then the commentaries and only at a later stage look at case reports.[35] Indeed, in an otherwise authoritative account of Japanese legal literature, the author omitted any discussion of collections of judicial decisions with the comment that 'the literature that reviews and analyses each judicial case is used widely in Japan, rather than the collections of judicial cases which are periodically issued by the courts'.[36]

The status of case law as a source of law is nowhere enshrined in law, save that Article 4 of the Court Organisation Law 1947 provides that 'a conclusion in a decision of a superior court shall bind courts below in respect of the case concerned'. Whilst a strict interpretation of this would mean that the decision of a superior court would only bind the lower court in the same case and not similar cases, in practice the judgments of superior courts are followed and courts at all levels try to follow their own decisions. Furthermore, this is recognised at a procedural level, since the Code of Criminal Procedure states that an appeal may be made where a decision is incompatible with established precedent of the Supreme Court or the High Court.[37] However, the meaning of 'precedent' in this context does not imply a system of binding authority, or some form of *stare decisis*. Instead, it is a system of case consistency rather than binding authority. Indeed, Article 76(3) of the constitution provides that judges 'shall be independent in the exercise of their conscience and shall be bound only by this constitution and the laws'. It would, therefore, be unconstitutional for a judge to fetter that freedom by adhering to notions of binding precedent, since strictly speaking cases are not 'law' within the meaning of the provision. This also applies to decisions of the Supreme Court, although in general it follows its

32 Merryman, *supra*, n 3.

33 Ishida, T, 'Case Law in Japan' (1979) 7 *International Journal of Law Libraries* 133.

34 Prior to 1947, there was no official reporting of lower court decisions, although some of the more important decisions did make it to 'Legal News'. Ishida, *idem*, p 137. On judicial decision making in the Supreme Court see Itoh, H, *The Japanese Supreme Court: Constitutional Policies*, 1989, Chapter 3, Markus Wiener.

35 Henderson, DF, *Foreign Enterprise in Japan*, 1973, p 187, University of North Carolina Press.

36 Yamamoto, N, 'Guide to Japanese Legal Literature' (1979) 7 *International Journal of Law Libraries* 177.

37 Article 405 (2) and (3) the Code of Criminal Procedure. The Code of Civil Procedure does not use the word precedent, but Article 394 refers to a 'misinterpretation or contravention of the Constitution' or a 'contravention of laws and orders' which affect a judgment and form the grounds for an appeal which is generally agreed to include decisions of superior courts.

own line of authority and has only rarely expressly reversed its own decisions.[38]

To talk of case 'law' may be misleading, first, because it is not a common law system in which judicial decisions form an authoritative source of law and second, the manner in which cases are reported is not consistent with it forming a body of law.[39] However, it is acknowledged that certain cases have a particular authoritative value which could loosely be defined as 'non-binding precedent'. This is to be expected in the Supreme Court and also applies to other courts, but the problem is that whereas reports of judicial decisions do exist, their content, method of selection and reporting style make them of limited practical value.[40] Moreover, whilst case law may be important in understanding the application and use of codes and statutes, the fact remains that 'judicial decisions are not the starting point for Japanese legal studies'.[41] Instead, much greater emphasis is placed upon the commentaries (*kaisetsu*), and although legal theory is not justiciable law, in line with the civil law tradition out of which the Japanese legal system grew, these writings have been given an authority in the hierarchy of sources of law which they are not accorded in common law systems such as England.

Commentaries and scholarly opinion (*gakusetsu*) are not sources of law in the strict sense, but have a 'great impact' on judicial decisions and lawmaking in general.[42] However, they are 'often abstract, philosophical, logical and ideological', mentioning judicial decisions 'to illustrate the application of an abstract interpretation, or to supplement theoretical analysis of principles and concepts'.[43] This is mainly the result of the German influence on early Japanese legal scholarship which gave a highly theoretical emphasis to scholarly writings and whilst these may be invaluable, even 'indispensable', to the practitioner,

38 Maki, JM, *Court and Constitution in Japan: Selected Supreme Court Decisions 1948–60*, 1964, University of Washington Press; Itoh, H and Beer, LW, *The Constitutional Case Law of Japan:Selected Supreme Court Decisions 1961–1970*, 1978, University of Washington Press; Itoh, H, *The Japanese Supreme Court: Constitutional Policies*, 1989, Chapter 3, Markus Wiener. For a detailed discussion of the Supreme Court see Chapter 7.

39 Although there is a sense in which the reporting of cases is systematised, particularly in the higher courts where cases for the *Collection of Superior Courts Cases* are chosen by a committee, the issue of selectivity and the principle of collegiality in court decisions makes the evaluation of the various collections of law reports a complex problem (Noda, *supra*, n 2, pp 236–41). Furthermore, although there is a paradigm of case report (Noda, *idem*, pp 232–35), very often the explanation of facts is incomplete since the important element is seen as the way in which a court interpreted and applied the law. Thus, although there seems to be a fairly wide selection of reports when looking at the various lists, they do not amount to the body of law in the manner of the common law; instead the work of academic commentators is more highly prized and comprehensive.

40 Henderson, 1980, *supra*, n 6, pp 140–41, comments: 'The nature of Japanese Supreme Court decisions is part of the problem. They are organised and written in a formal style which often makes than unintelligible without the lower court decision before the reader.' He goes on to refer to the 'evanescence and dilute authority of lower court decisions'. For an account of how Supreme Court decisions are arrived at see Danelski, DJ, 'The Supreme Court of Japan: An Exploratory Study' in Schubert, G and Danelski, D (eds), *Comparative Judicial Behaviour*, 1969, Oxford University Press; Itoh, *supra*, n 38.

41 Beer and Tomatsu, *supra*, n 6, p 306.

42 Yamamoto, *supra*, n 36, p 176.

43 Beer and Tomatsu, *supra*, n 6, p 304.

they are of limited use to others.[44] As one writer on the subject has commented: 'Most of these sources are valueless to the comparativist although they constitute probably the most authoritative source of Japanese law after the laws and administrative regulations themselves.'[45] Nevertheless, the importance of Japanese legal theory and the study of 'interpretative legal science' is fundamental to the whole legal system and whilst formally a secondary source has, in practice, attained a parity of importance with statute law.[46]

ADMINISTRATIVE GUIDANCE

The foregoing discussion has been concerned with what might be termed traditional sources of law but, as already indicated in the introduction, Japan has a class of nonjusticiable law which is unique, namely administrative guidance (*gyosei shido*). Strictly speaking this is not a legal term; it cannot be found in any of the general written laws and, as a concept, has no formal or fixed definition.[47] Instead it is used by central and local administrative authorities to describe a type of informal regulation of individuals, companies or associations. Generally, it is in the form of a request, of no legally coercive effect, made by an administrative authority asking for a party to take or avoid a particular course of action in pursuance of an administrative aim or policy

44 Beer and Tomatsu, *idem*, pp 127–28. That much Japanese legal thinking is dominated by German legal thought is acknowledged by Kawashima, who is nonetheless careful to state that 'this does not mean that the legal thinking of Japanese lawyers is completely western through and through. This is not the case. Upon examination, we can find significant elements which illustrate non-western ways of thinking. This "traditional way" of thinking permeates the doctrines of law, the decision making of the judges and the practice of law generally', Kawashima, T, 'Japanese Way of Legal Thinking' (1979) 7 *International Journal of Law Libraries* 127.

45 Stevens, C, 'Modern Japanese Law as an Instrument of Comparison' (1971) 19 *American Journal of Comparative Law* 683. He goes on to say 'To the comparativist they offer very little insight as to how the particular speciality functions in Japan or how or why Japanese law is different in its institutions and functions from the law of other industrialised states.'

46 Yamamoto, *supra*, n 36. Beer and Tomatsu, *supra*, n 6, pp 288–89, point out that Law Faculties are more important as centres of legal scholarship than as serving as a nursery for practitioners and that this focus on theory and jurisprudence is illustrated by the structure of Japanese law faculties as including the Department of Political Science. They also acknowledge the pressure to publish syndrome which has resulted in 'an excessive quantity of substandard work'. Nonetheless, the so-called leading commentaries tend to be generational and standard works acknowledged as outstanding in their field (Yamamoto, *idem*).

47 There are a variety of words which appear in statutes and are taken to refer to what is known as 'administrative guidance', eg instruction, advice, recommendation, encouragement and guidance. One example of this, away from the mainstream debate on administrative guidance and industrial policy, is the Basic Law for the Control of Environmental Control 1967 (Law No 132 as amended) which refers to measures, advice and recommendations. It is clear that what is known as administrative guidance is being referred to, but it is not specifically mentioned, though in effect forming a statutory basis for action. See Gresser, J, Fujikura, K and Morishima, A, *Environmental Protection Law in Japan*, 1981, Massachusetts Institute of Technology Press. More recently however, the Administrative Procedure Act 1993 (Law No 88) is the first piece of legislation to attempt a definition of the term, albeit very broad and abstract. See Ködderitzsch, L, 'Japan's New Administrative Procedure Law: Reasons for its Enactment and Likely Implications' (1991) 24 *Law in Japan* 105.

objective. Or, as it was once classically defined by the head of the Cabinet Legal Department:

> Administrative guidance is not legal compulsion restricting the rights of individuals and imposing obligations on citizens. It is a request or guidance on the part of the government within the limit of the task and administrative responsibility of each agency as provided for in the establishment laws, asking for a specific action or inaction for the purpose of achieving some administrative objective through cooperation on the part of parties who are the object of the administration.[48]

Described as 'at best alegal, and at worst illegal' it is the ultimate instrument of bureaucratic power.[49] However, it should be noted that much of the writing on this subject tends to be in the form of negative criticism from non-Japanese writers who have focused on the intervention of central government agencies in areas of international trade and finance and see this extremely powerful instrument of bureaucratic authority as a threat to the rule of law.[50] Instead, it is not limited to central government, but extends to local government. Although it is seen by Japanese writers as not without its problems, it is recognised as being part of the fabric of regulation which has advanced the economy and general well-being of the nation.[51] As one Japanese writer put it: 'Administrative guidance can be of a great value both to the government and to citizens and enterprises, and there is nothing inherently sinister about it.'[52]

---

48 Evidence to the House of Councillors Committee on Commerce and Industry (26 March 1974) cited in Matsushita, M and Schoenbaum, T, *Japanese International Trade and Investment Law*, 1989, p 32, University of Tokyo Press, also in Matsushita, M, 'The Legal Framework of Trade and Investment in Japan' (1986) 27 *Harvard International Law Review* 376.

49 Henderson, DF, 'Security Markets in the United States and Japan: Distinctive Aspects Moulded By Cultural, Social, Economic, and Political Differences' (1991) 14 *Hastings International and Comparative Law Review* 296.

50 Johnson, C, *MITI and the Japanese Miracle*, 1982, Stanford University Press; Haley, JO, *Authority Without Power*, 1991, Chapter 7, Oxford University Press; Narita, Y, 'Administrative Guidance' (1968) 2 *Law in Japan* 45; Yamanouchi, K, 'Administrative Guidance and The Rule of Law' (1974) 7 *Law in Japan* 22; Sanekata, K, 'Administrative Guidance and the Antimonopoly Law' (1977) 10 *Law in Japan* 65; Smith, M, 'Prices and Petroleum in Japan 1973–74 A Study of Administrative Guidance' (1977) 10 *Law in Japan* 81; Pape, W, '*Gyosei Shido* and the Antimonopoly Law' (1982) 15 *Law in Japan* 12; Sanekata, K, 'Administrative Guidance and the Antimonopoly Law – Another View of the Oil Cartel Criminal Decisions' (1982) 15 *Law in Japan* 95; Ramseyer, JM, 'The Costs of the Consensual Myth: Anti Trust Enforcement and Institutional Barriers to Litigation in Japan' (1985) 94 *Yale Law Journal* 604; Young, M, 'Judicial Review of Administrative Guidance: Governmentally Encouraged Consensual Dispute Resolution' (1984) 84 *Columbia Law Review* 923; Young, M, 'Administrative Guidance in the Courts: A Case Study in Doctrinal Adaptation' (1984) 17 *Law in Japan* 120; Matsushita, M, 'The Legal Framework of Trade and Investment in Japan' (1986) 27 *Special Issue Harvard International Law Journal* 361; Upham, F, 'The Legal Framework of Japan's Declining Industrial Policy' (1986) 27 *Special Issue Harvard International Law Journal* 425; Yeomans, RA, 'Administrative guidance: A Peregrine View' (1986) 19 *Law in Japan* 125; Dean, M, 'Administrative Guidance in Japanese Law: A Threat to the Rule of Law' (1991) *Journal of Business Law* 398.

51 For a more recent Japanese perspective on the subject see: Shindo, M, 'Administrative Guidance' (1992) 20 *Japanese Economic Studies* 69; also the use of administrative guidance as opposed to instituting criminal proceedings in environmental matters is taken as being positive; see Gresser *et al*, *supra*, n 47, pp 259–61.

52 Matsushita and Schoenbaum, *supra*, n 48, p 40.

The existence of administrative guidance may be seen as all the more curious in view of the fact that there are formal orders which can be used by administrative authorities, such as *meirei* and *jorei* (see the introduction above). However, whereas these orders are issued pursuant to some statutory authority and are therefore formal administrative acts, administrative guidance *per se* has no legal basis, although in some cases there may be power given to an authority to act in a certain way.[53] Attributed with preserving the 'often illusory values of harmony and consensus between government and industry', administrative guidance has also been recognised as a 'salient feature of the Japanese government-business relationship' and 'one important key to understanding the cooperative spirit between Japan's government and industry'.[54] And yet, defining the term and describing the limits of this powerful extralegal tool remains difficult, perhaps unusually so for something which has had such an obvious impact.

The description of administrative guidance given by a former director of the Cabinet Legislative Bureau places it firmly in the area of quasi-coercive, extra-legal cooperative consensus-making in that it 'refers to a practice by which administrative agencies attempt to get specific individuals, corporations, organisations, etc, to do their bidding in regard to the application or execution of law in a specific administrative area. This is done not by autocratically commanding or coercing them, or even by guiding, advising, or suggesting, on the basis of some legal rational, that they do something "voluntary". Rather, with no basis in law at all, it elicits spontaneous agreement and cooperation from the other party by letting it know what the administrative organ hopes or wishes to see done or realised'.[55] The reality of this remarkable statement is somewhat different to that which it implies, because in order that there is compliance with the 'hopes and wishes' of the administration, there can be informal and indirect threats of sanctions; these can take a variety of forms such as the withdrawal of government financing, the revocation of licences, the reduction of import quotas, or the withholding of subsidies.

The three main categories of administrative guidance are (1) regulatory; (2) promotional; and (3) conciliatory.[56] As already indicated, the emphasis has tended to be on the first of these, but it should not be forgotten that administrative guidance has a function in terms of dispute resolution. Conciliatory administrative guidance can be issued by a ministry or local government to mediate and resolve disputes between companies.[57]

53 See *supra*, n 47.

54 Matsushita and Schoenbaum, *supra*, n 48, p 31; Johnson, 1982, *supra*, n 50, p 273; Shindo, *supra*, n 51, p 78. For a discussion of the 'iron triangle' relationship between business, the bureaucracy and politicians see Chapter 4.

55 Cited in Abe, H, Shindo, M and Kawato, S, *The Government and Politics of Japan*, 1994, p 35, University of Tokyo Press.

56 Guidance can come in a variety of forms, ie directives (*shiji*), requests (*yobo*) warnings (*keikoku*), suggestions (*kankoku*) and encouragements (*kansho*) and although generally associated with a written form of communication, it can be oral thereby making any challenge all the more difficult.

57 Examples of the way this type of administrative guidance operates is given in Matsushita, M, 'Export Control and Export Cartels in Japan' (1979) 20 *Harvard International Law Journal* 123.

Furthermore, promotional advice is aimed at assisting enterprises in the operation of their businesses, whether on a technical basis, or in giving financial and management advice. However, it is regulatory administrative guidance which has caught the attention of writers, since government agencies have thereby been able to regulate business and, it is said, engineer the economic miracle.[58] Whatever the extent of its contribution, Japanese writers have recognised that it is perceived as problematic in the context of international trade. As one commentator put it: 'In a time of increasing economic friction between Japan and its traditional trading partners, administrative guidance is seen as a nontariff trade barrier and, as a type of government-business collusion, is severely criticised by foreign countries.'[59]

As already noted, administrative guidance *per se* has no basis in law, but there may be statutory authority upon which administrative agencies may exercise certain powers. In those situations, quasi-coercion is tantamount to compulsion.[60] However, the effect is described as 'factual' and not 'legal' because it does not create a legally enforceable right since the relationship is 'voluntary'.[61] In other situations administrative guidance 'permits agencies to regulate not only beyond the limits of the law, but also, on occasion, in direct contravention of the law. Such contravention is possible because any judicial inquiry into the propriety of the regulatory objectives will be limited'.[62] It is this aspect of administrative guidance which is a central concern of many Western writers, since the idea of an administration working beyond the limits of the law in a manner which is not realistically reviewable before the courts, is anathema. The fact that by its very nature administrative guidance is 'voluntary' makes a challenge difficult, if not unlikely, particularly in view of the coercive measures which may be applied. Moreover, there has been only a narrow band of cases where judicial review has taken place and the very idea has been slow to take root.[63] All of this means that the 'darker side' of administrative guidance, namely 'the absence of institutional review, the danger of arbitrary or discriminatory application, its vulnerability to political influence, the potential conflict with statutory objectives and its possible incompatibility with international commerce and foreign relations generally' will ensure that the subject remains at the heart of any consideration of the Japanese legal system.[64]

58 Johnson, 1982, *supra*, n 50.

59 Abe *et al*, *supra*, n 55, p 36.

60 Yamanouchi, *supra*, n 50.

61 Narita, *supra*, n 50, p 48.

62 Young, 1984, *supra*, n 50, p 936.

63 Young, *idem*, pp 953 and 958. The need for a more open system of review of administrative standards has been addressed in the Administrative Procedure Law 1993 and although the Act does not attempt to regulate administrative guidance it reiterates basic principles of administrative law derived from the Japanese concept of the rule of law and provides a procedural mechanism aimed at minimizing abuse by administrative authorities. See Ködderitzsch, *supra*, n 47, p 127.

64 Gresser, Fujikura and Morishima, *supra*, n 47, p 234.

In the materials which follow, various aspects of the topics discussed here will be examined. A more detailed account is given of some elements of the sources of law, but in all cases the material is intended to be illustrative rather than exhaustive. As indicated at the beginning of this chapter, it is the aim of both the text and materials to go beyond the strict limits of this area of legal theory. Thus, the importance of cultural factors is considered, particularly in relation to the translation of legal sources and the methodology of research.

I TRADITIONAL SOURCES OF LAW AND LEGAL THOUGHT

Angelo, A, 'Thinking of Japanese Law – A Linguistic Primer' (1979) 12 *Comparative International Law Journal of South Africa* 86–90

> With its thriving economy, sophisticated technology, bustling cities, traffic jams, fast trains, multi-storeyed hotels – and pollution, Japan is often cited as the first Asian nation to become Westernised.
>
> And so what we see becomes a matter of emphasis in our Western eyes; we see in Japan golf and baseball, but not sumo wrestling; in restaurants we note the whiskey, but not the *sake*; the smart Western-style clothes and Paris fashions, but not the *kimono*; the handshake but not the bow.
>
> But to treat the Japanese people in the same way as we do in this country, using well tried and trusted methods of negotiation and doing business, soon reveals that Westernisation is a myth ...
>
> The fact is that despite outward appearances, the Japanese have a lifestyle and codes of behaviour that are uniquely Japanese, and its essence flows from ideas, ethics, customs and institutions that stem from Japanese culture and history.

These sentiments are oft repeated ones and apply equally pertinently to the study of Japanese law. To study it from an ethnocentric point of view through the legislation might give some insights but it is questionable 'how useful such insights might be because they would tell us very little of the manner in which law is or is not a principle referent for behaviour in contemporary Japan ...'. This same warning is sounded by Noda in his *Introduction to Japanese Law*, 'The conflict between the legal structure and the actual life of the people is great, and as a result a great number of difficult and confusing problems, which European societies have not had to deal with ..., have arisen'. ...

...

General study should best precede specific study and in the case of Japanese law this is a virtual necessity. A consideration of religion provides a valuable example. Whether he is religious or not the Westerner and his law are deeply imbued with Christian principles. Just how deep the influence is is incalculable but in Japanese study that basic cultural influence on his life gives rise to false reaction and a failure to understand much that is seen. An assessment of divorce or abortion laws, for instance, must proceed in a totally different framework. It is not enough to know that in a given European context they would be regarded as liberal or strict. Such an assessment is meaningless for Japanese law. What is needed is an understanding of the cultural settings in which they were created and exist; only then can their nature be gauged. It will be found that the reasons given for the proscription of abortion in a common law system would make little sense to a Japanese. His law must be seen through his eyes.

A frequently stated theme of a leading scholar of comparative religion is that it is impossible to understand the West without its religions. He sees religion as the key to the Western character. Equally religion he says is a key to Japan, and it requires much study because Christianity and Japanese thought are not only historically antagonistic, but are also philosophical opposites. Western religion is premised on a qualitative difference between God and man. Japanese thought is polytheistic and there is no divine exclusivity or discontinuity between gods and men. The foreign students of Japanese law must acquire a knowledge and appreciation of Japanese religion and history. While those are strange to him he will find his Japanese studies unfulfilling ...

In the pre-Meiji era the characteristics of Japanese law were the public law emphasis and non-publication of its legislation, the strong influence of trade in the development of modern private law, the absence of private rights, a predilection for conciliation and compromise in dispute resolution and a great readiness to adapt foreign ideas to local needs. Throughout its history Japan has strongly maintained its traditions. Hearn likens these traditions to the carefully sculpted shapes of ancient trees in Japan which now even if left untrimmed would for a long time not change their shape much.

All this has led commentators to say things such as 'Japanese do not like the law' or 'Law exists in [Japan] but is not very important'. Warning enough surely to any researcher that the study of Japanese law will present some novel problems. Three well-documented examples will suffice to confirm the point.

Article 739 of the Japanese Civil Code provides the basic rule of the marriage law:

> A marriage becomes effective by notification thereof in accordance with the provisions of the Family Registration Law;
>
> The notification mentioned in the preceding paragraph must be made by both the parties and two or more witnesses of full age either orally, or by a document signed by them.

The immediate analogies are with the secular or registry office type marriage laws of Europe. The simple administrative form is perhaps a little different but the basic analogy is there. Social custom in Japan however admits a properly celebrated unregistered union as a valid marriage. According to Article 739 unregistered unions are not marriages yet the courts and the legislature, building on tradition, have given wide protections to the parties to what in positivist terms can only be a *de facto* union. The practice has even developed of granting *de facto* divorces. The legislation therefore does not have the effect its wording suggests, and only a knowledge of Japanese culture and a study of court and community practices will explain the true place of Article 739 in the life of the Japanese.

Article 723 of the Civil Code and Article 248 of the Criminal Procedure Code introduce another unexpected element in the operation of the legal system. This is sincere feelings of repentance and apology as factors which frequently mitigate responsibility or exonerate a defendant. In the civil law field the leading case of *Okuri v Kageyama* considered the nature of the apology as a method of redress in Japan and its relationship to the freedom of thought and conscience protected by Article 19 of the constitution. It was held that a court order under Article 723 of the Civil Code to a person guilty of defamation was both constitutional and a proper method of settling the case. There is no direct reference in Article 723 to apologies but they are nevertheless common in the civil law field. An investigation of the social reason for this phenomenon makes it clear in fact that suit, not apology, is the exception. In criminal law, again, there is no direct reference to apologies but the situation in practice is much as for civil cases.

Article 248 of the Criminal Procedure Code speaks of 'the circumstances which follow the commission of the offence' as a factor to be taken into account when a decision is being made on whether to prosecute or not. If for instance a person guilty of offensive driving or overstaying on a visitor's permit apologises to those he has inconvenienced, the prosecution may decide not to lay a charge. This test has by analogy also been used in relation to sentencing. Two possibilities therefore arise. A criminal suspect may avoid prosecution by a sincere expression of regret for what he did or by the tendering of an apology to his victim, and an accused may escape further sanction on his conduct in the same ways. It might be said that this is different from Western style laws only in degree. However, the use of the methods is so thoroughgoing as to refute any such explanation. Repentance and apology are deeply ingrained aspects of Japanese character and society. As Ishii said in commenting on the Meiji Criminal Code:

> For offenders surrendering themselves voluntarily to the law prior to the detection of their crime, the law specified that they would be exempt from punishment. This system of surrender and confession, based on the Oriental moral concept that corrected faults deserve no punishment, does not appear in the West.

Two extreme cases show the full significance of the custom. In the *Shimpuren* uprising, a samurai revolt of 1876, the dissidents attacked an army garrison committed to killing all civil and military officials. The *Shimpuren* manifesto added nevertheless that should junior officers who had come from outside Kumamoto 'repent their former crimes or ... surrender, they should, depending on the exact circumstances, be sent back to their own provinces'. The second example is the experience of Japan with its Peace Preservation Law of 1925. The purpose of the statute was to control thought and to suppress the holding or propagation of anti-governmental ideology. The law was most effective but owed that effectiveness to administrative rather than judicial action. The ratio of indictments to arrest was always very low and most of those convicted had their sentences suspended; administratively those arrested recanted of their behaviour and abandoned their criminal thoughts. Having fallen into step with society at large in this way punishment was seen as no longer having a purpose and so the guilty were released rather than indicted. In the 1930s the administration of the thought control legislation was developed to such a level of sophistication that 'a standard scale of degrees of *tenko*, ranging from total ideological conversion down to reluctant agreement to refrain from political activity' was developed. The success of this legislation depended fundamentally, upon cultural factors beyond the realm of the legal system factors peculiar to Japan and essential to an understanding of its legal system.

The third illustration is taken from the constitutional law field. In 1965 suit was filed against a local authority because it gave financial support to a Shinto sod-turning ceremony for a new building. Articles 20 and 89 of the constitution made it clear to the complainant that the use of public money in that way was unconstitutional. He lost his case at first instance but appealed and won. On final appeal to the Supreme Court however he lost with ten of the fifteen judges voting against him on the basis of the customary as distinct from religious nature of the ceremony.

A significant guide to the cultural influences at play in this, the most important case on the separation of state and religion in Japan, is found in the comments of a Shinto official who is reported to have said that the decision was a 'good ruling conforming to the general feeling of the Japanese people' and that 'a Shinto-style ground-breaking ceremony is a custom which has found a place in the life of the Japanese people through long tradition. Because of such a character, to subject the ceremony to a discussion of constitutionality and unconstitutionality itself is strange'.

Kawashima, T, 'Japanese Way of Legal Thinking' (1979) 7 *International Journal of Law Libraries* 127–31

As many of you already know, much of the law of contemporary Japan was originally imported from western society. Its initial influence came from French legal education and legal institutions. After the Meiji constitution was promulgated, the German school of legal thinking predominated the writing and thinking of Japanese lawyers and scholars. With the end of the Second World War and particularly during the post-war period of occupation, the ideas of Anglo-American law gradually came into our legal thinking. Despite these many influences, I would say, however, that the basic structure of the Japanese legal thinking of today is predominantly influenced by German legal thought. But this does not mean that the legal thinking of Japanese lawyers is completely western through and through. This is not the case. Upon examination, we can find significant elements which illustrate non-western ways of thinking. This 'traditional way' of thinking permeates the doctrines of law, the decision making of judges and the practice of law generally.

Today, I want to take up only one aspect of this subject which I would call the semantic tradition of Japanese language and law. There are, of course, numerous other aspects which I would say are specifically Japanese in their spirit and context. I might, for example, point to aspects such as the weakness of the notion of legal right, or the spirit of ideal harmony in human relationships, or the relationship between law and morality. Keep in mind that my topic represents only one aspect of the Japanese way of legal thinking.

In European society and in America, every word has a definite meaning. In western societies, it is presupposed, expected or even taken for granted that the meaning of every word should be clear, limited and fixed. If it were otherwise, communication would be confusing and our way of thinking would be disturbed. In Japan, however, the tradition is just the opposite. In Japan the traditional notion or expectation concerning language is that every word has some meaning which represents only the core of its many possible meanings. Around this core there lies rather an area of ambiguous meaning which fades away into zero through the process of interpretation. The meaning of a word is not expected to be definite, limited and fixed. It is intended to undergo change according to its use and application in a wide variety of possible situations. In this connection it is important to understand something about the correlation between non-normative assumptions or epistemology and legal ethical theory. It is also important to understand the contrast between the epistemology of naive realism and that of logical realism.

Naive realism is the special characteristic of the Japanese culture, while logical realism is much more characteristic of western thought. The naive realist views the images of man and society through his senses with a certain degree of empirical immediacy without resorting to abstractions. Ideas and feelings are suggested by concrete objects rather than being represented by abstract concepts. On the other hand, the logical realist construes the images of man and society through abstractions and concepts. For instance, in its beginnings, the aboriginal Japanese language itself did not have words through which an abstract idea or concept might be conveyed or communicated. When it was necessary, such words were borrowed from Chinese symbols and combined with Japanese characters. Thus, in contrast with contemporary western society is the fact that in the traditional culture of the Japanese, nature and society are accepted as they appear to the immediate empirical senses. The indeterminate quality of nature and society with its subtle and infinite variety is regarded as a welcome attribute. It is to be valued because by its very nature it is unlimited and contains infinite possibilities for development and expansion. This basic assumption not only permeates traditional Japanese culture, but is equally evidenced by the Japanese language which is not a suitable vehicle for detailed and determinate expression or precision in communication. For example, many of our writers have to be translated into English with much longer sentences than in the original Japanese, requiring numerous detailed expressions so as to make it understandable to western readers. In the English manner of writing, although the meaning of words is much clearer, at the same time such attempts at precise definition makes the language appear to be more limited and shallow. We do not make such an effort in our writing. The Japanese uses words which allow sufficient leeway to suggest various things and permit the reader to supplement the rest with that which is not expressed but only possibly suggested. The sentence of the westerner tries to restrict its meaning as narrowly and in such detail as possible so that there is no room at all for the imagination of the reader. In Japanese literature and in our daily communication the author or speaker tries to say something with very few words and with very vague meanings. The rest is supposed to be interpreted or supplemented by listeners and readers through associations. An example from Japanese literature is the very short form of poetry called *haiku*, which consists of three phrases with each phrase consisting of five syllables, seven syllables and five syllables respectively. In other words the whole poem consists of only seventeen syllables. An example might be translated as 'Frog, a frog jumped into an old pond'. My guess is that most western society people would not understand it. As a Japanese I feel to some extent that I can understand it, though I am not sure why it is considered a masterpiece. For the Japanese people it has greater meaning through the association it suggests or implies. For the Japanese, this *haiku* creates a rather mystic atmosphere which is completely quiet. Then the only sound is the splash made by the frog. The quietness comes back and the poet feels himself to be very lonely but spiritually purified. For the Japanese such associations are important. The only problem may be that such stimulus could cause too great a series of associations in the minds of readers of this poem. But if the western people read this, it is very likely that this kind of association would not occur.

Perhaps this explanation of the Japanese language has been too long, but I think it is important because language and words are very important elements of the law in civilized societies. In the legal traditions of western societies the law is made up of general norms or principles which are verbal statements consisting of terms artificially elaborated by logical reasoning or defined through a high degree of abstraction. It seems to me that is the very essence of the legal propositions or precepts expressed in European continental law. In its essence the law of Anglo-American society appears to be similar since it also represents logical thinking through words which have very specific and limited definitions. This creates some problems since very strictly stipulated definitions of legal terms appear to be incomprehensible to laymen in Anglo-American societies with the result that lawyers are blamed for using very strange jargon. I think this may be inevitable in European societies as well. For instance, the French are very proud of their *Code Civil* because it uses only words harmonious to laymen. Actually, the meanings of those words are not easily understandable by laymen even though most of the terms used are simply taken from daily images and a common vocabulary.

To me the question of legal thinking based on words with very strictly defined concepts is very interesting since in Japan legal reasoning is based on verbal propositions with ambiguous, changeable, and elastic meanings. In Japan the meaning of words used in legal principles or in statutes is taken for granted by Japanese people as being necessarily ambiguous and elastic. Here, the people would not be surprised to discover that the meaning of law sometimes is changed, shaped and sometimes distorted by policemen, prosecutors, lawyers and by judges during the legal process. It is inevitable, of course, in every society that lawyers and judges have to change the meaning of law in order to adjust the existing law to a new set of circumstances after the original legal norms have appeared. In European or Anglo-American societies, however, the scope and manner in which lawyers or judges can change or adapt the meaning of the law to a particular situation or set of circumstances is limited. However, in Japan it seems to me that the limit itself is not as clearly established. Let me give you an example which illustrates the Japanese legal mind or consciousness in this respect.

When I was in California the parking meters permitted parking only for five minutes for five cents or ten cents. During my visit, a policeman gave me a parking ticket even though the meter had registered a violation only by a minute or less. The policeman told me that the meter had passed the limited time and therefore, the fine had to be paid. When I told this story in Japan, my friend who is a prosecutor laughed. In Japan, if you apologized very, very politely, you would be dismissed from the violation. But if you were absolutely arrogant, then you would have to pay the fine. In Japan everything depends upon each particular situation and circumstance. While we have definite rules and limits in our laws, I think that the basic difference lies in our attitudes toward the language of the law and its enforcement. It is taken for granted by lawyers, prosecutors and judges that the meanings of words of law are subject to change by interpretation. As I stated earlier, in every society the interpretation of words of law or statutes is inevitable, particularly at a time of change. However, in western society, this kind of change through interpretation appears to be possible only as a last resort and not at the beginning of an instance or situation. In Japan it is understood from the beginning of a legal enactment that the meaning of law is changeable and not definite. This appears to be a peculiarly Japanese characteristic of legal thinking. Thus, when the parliament debates some legal enactment, often there are heated discussions about the meaning of terms. Yet, once the measure is enacted into law such debates lose their importance. This is due to the fact that traditionally Japanese lawyers and scholars do not regard the debates of legislators as being binding upon judges. In Japan the records of debate in the Diet have no particular meaning for retrospective interpretation.

Along the same lines, I should like to make one final point regarding the Japanese way of legal thinking and its relation to code revision. In Japan, once a measure is enacted into law, revision is very difficult and such instances are actually very rare. The reason for this is very simple. Code revision is not felt needed or to be desirable because change is always possible and accepted through interpretation. In this respect, I often like to say that the written provisions of Japanese law are just like the Cinderella story. Interpretation is the magic wand with which everything needed can be accomplished through some kind of semantic manipulation.

In summary, I would like to point out my belief that this semantic tradition in Japan is really contradictory to the basic values which are required for a modern, democratic society which needs predictable judicial decisions. Sooner or later we will have to change our traditional attitude toward the meaning of words, especially in our laws. Although our semantic tradition serves our literature well, it does not function with the needed precision and limits in our laws.

Noda, Y, *Introduction to Japanese Law*, 1976, pp 197–211, University of Tokyo Press

The Civil Code

The Civil Code is divided into five books: the general part, real rights, obligations, family law, and succession.

The general part, following the pattern advocated by the German pandectists, contains the rules common to all the other books. It is composed of the following six chapters: Chapter I, natural persons; Chapter II, legal persons; Chapter III, things; Chapter IV, legal acts; Chapter V, time limits; Chapter VI, prescription. The first chapter concerns the enjoyment of civil rights, capacity, domicile, and absence. Chapter II includes provisions relating to foundations, and the management and dissolution of corporate bodies. The third chapter contains general rules relating to those things which may be the object of private rights, and corresponds more or less to the title *'De la distinction des biens'* in Book II of the French Civil Code. Chapter IV contains, in theory, the rules applicable to all legal acts, but in reality acts affecting the legal status of individuals are regulated by rules quite different from those in this chapter. The articles in Chapter IV are therefore analogous to Articles 1108 to 1118 of the French Civil Code. The rules relating to defect of consent are found in the section dealing with declaration of intention.

A major difference between the French and Japanese codes is that the Japanese has a special part dealing with agency. This is section 3. Section 4 concerns the nullity and voidability of legal acts. Unlike the French civil law, which distinguishes between absolute and relative nullity, Japanese law divides defective acts into two classes: void and voidable. Voidable acts are valid until avoidance, but they are deemed void *ab initio* when they are avoided. Nullity can be claimed by any interested party, but only a restricted group of persons can bring an action for avoidance. Chapter V provides for the mode of computation of various time limits. Where there is no specific statutory provision, court order, or contractual term to the contrary, the provisions of this chapter apply. Chapter VI groups the provisions relating to acquisitive and extinctive prescription.

Book 2 regulates real rights and provides not only for property and the real rights related to it but also for possession and real securities. Chapter I contains some general rules. Article 175, for instance, declares that no real rights can exist except those provided for by legislation. Article 176 says the creation and transfer of all real rights is valid by the simple manifestation of the will of the parties. This article had its origin in Articles 1138 and 1583 of the French Civil Code. Inscription on the property register of a change relating to a real right is therefore not a condition of the validity of its transfer, but does, as Article 177 says, provide for protection of the right against third parties. On this point Japanese law has clearly followed the model of the French Civil Code and not that of the BGB. Though people are accustomed to thinking that the Japanese Civil Code is a faithful copy of the BGB, Article 177 should suffice to prove that such an opinion is ill-founded. Chapter II deals with possession; Chapter III with ownerships. Articles 209 to 238 relate to what the French call *servitudes*. The Japanese code deals with this matter in a section entitled 'Restrictions on Title', but it is studied under the rubric of 'relationships with adjoining properties' (*sorin kankei*). While the Code Napoléon is hostile to co-ownership, the Japanese code deals with the subject in detail in Articles 249–64. Article 208, which provides for co-ownership of apartments, has been replaced by a special law of 4 April 1962.

As divisions of ownership the Civil Code recognizes superficies, emphyteusis, and real servitudes. Superficies is a real right by which a person may use the land of another for planting or building; the right of emphyteusis permits an owner to cultivate land or to raise stock on it for a set fee. The economic effects of these two rights can be produced by a contract of lease, though a lease, of course, would not create a real right. Since a contract of lease is more favorable to an owner of land, it is very rare to find these real rights in practice. Non-owner cultivators are obliged to enter into leases to assure themselves of their rights to cultivate the land. The rules on real servitudes are similar to those in the French code. The right of usufruct, however, is unknown in Japan.

Real securities are regulated in the same book as real rights, but in spite of this the Japanese system is very close to that of the French code, save that the Japanese code provides in this part for the right of retention, which it treats as a sort of real right. Apart from the right of retention, the code provides for pledge, privilege, and hypothec, and all are modeled quite closely on French law.

Book 3 deals with the law of obligations. In Chapter I the general rules applicable to all obligations are set out, and these correspond to those provided in Chapter III of Book 3 of the French Civil Code. Chapter II deals with contract as the most important source of obligation. Having dealt with the rules common to all contracts in Articles 521–48, thirteen important contracts are covered: gift, sale, exchange, loan, bailment for use, hire of things, hire of services, labor contracts, agency, deposit, association, annuities, and compromise. Gifts *inter vivos* are considered one of the most important contracts, and legacies are dealt with in the provisions relating to wills in the book on succession. The other three chapters deal in turn with *negotiorum gestio*, unjust enrichment, and civil delict, that is, they deal with what Domat called non-contractually created obligations. The last chapter of this book bears the title 'Unlawful Acts', which undoubtedly comes from the *unerlaubte Handlung* of the BGB.

The last two books of the code were drawn up, taking particular account of Japanese family traditions. These books contain many rules which were already out of date at the time of the writing of the code. The ordinary family was already a nuclear one, composed of parents and children, except in remote areas where the concept of the large family still existed. Yet the code sought to maintain the extended family system headed by a head of the family (*koshu*) endowed with great power. Households which, in spite of their material independence, were noted on the civil status register as belonging to a given family were under the authority of the head of that family. Members of a family had to obtain the consent of their head of family to their marriage even after their majority. The head could arbitrarily determine the place of residence of members of his family, and those who did not obey him could be excluded from the family. Exclusion was equivalent to being disinherited!

The legal position of the head of the family was a privileged one. It was the object of a special succession, which meant principally that the eldest son of the head of the family succeeded. This succession (*katoku sozoku*) was monopolized by a single legitimate heir on whom devolved all the property, and the other members of the family could not participate. Brothers and sisters of the legitimate heir had to await the head's favor for a share in the succession. The system had the advantage of preventing the excessive subdivision of rural land, but the basic principle of this family-based organization had clearly fallen out of use by the time of the code. Just before the promulgation of the new constitution the complete reform of Books 4 and 5 was decided upon, and a committee instituted for the purpose drew up a new law to conform with the provisions of the constitution. In particular, it gave effect in the code to the principles of individual dignity and the legal equality of sexes. The books on the family and succession were thus completely rewritten and became law on 22 December 1947.

Book 4 is entitled *shinzoku*. According to Article 725 the *shinzoku* (the family) includes blood relatives to the sixth degree, spouse, and relatives by marriage to the third degree. In this book there are five chapters which deal respectively with marriage, filiation, paternal authority, guardianship, and the alimentary obligation. As in the draft for the revised French code, the matrimonial regime is dealt with in the chapter on marriage. The fact that this subject is dealt with in only eight articles reflects an important difference between the French and Japanese attitude toward law.

Book 5 deals with succession. The revised code has given up the system of *katoku sozoku*. It therefore deals with succession to all property and not just to moveables, and all heirs can participate in the succession. The book contains eight chapters. Chapter I contains four general articles, and Chapter II lists those who can succeed. In Chapter III, entitled 'The Effects of Succession', are found the rules relating to the hereditary shares and to the division of property. Subject to certain exceptions the division between co-heirs is usually on the basis of equality. When rural property is to be divided this principle, of course, brings with it the danger of fractionalization of the arable land, as the inevitable result of the suppression of the system of *katoku sozoku*. Several measures have been taken to deal with this problem of division but none has been satisfactory, and reactionaries would for this reason favor a return to the old system. But in practice there is no great problem. Heirs who do not want to live a rural life renounce their rights in favor of those who want the land, in return for an amount of money equal to the value of their share. Accepting and renouncing successions is dealt with in Chapter IV: acceptance can be simple, or subject to inventory. Chapter V deals with the separation of patrimonies. When there is no heir the succession is disposed of in accordance with the provisions of Chapter VI; Chapter VII relates to wills; and Chapter VIII deals with the reserved share.

Since the promulgation of the code, more than seventy years have passed. During this time the code has been supplemented by special statutes and by case law. The most important of the statutes are the law of 22 December 1947, relating to civil status, that of 24 February 1899, on registration of immoveable property, the law of 8 April 1921, on the leasing of building sites, and the law of 8 April 1921, concerning the leasing of houses.

The Commercial Code

Since coming into force, the Commercial Code has been the object of frequent reforms necessitated by the profound economic and social vicissitudes of a country which only a century ago began to modernize itself on the pattern of the economically advanced states. The many amendments attest the great efforts made by the Japanese people to adapt themselves to world economic developments. The reforms of 1911, 1938, and 1952 are particularly important.

The original code had five books. Book 4, however, which dealt with bills of exchange and cheques, was abrogated in 1933 as a result of signing the international conventions for unification of the law relating to bills of exchange and cheques concluded in 1931 and 1932 in Geneva. The present code thus has four books.

Book 1, completely redrafted in 1938, is the general part of the code. It includes the rules relating to merchants, Chapter II; the commercial register, Chapter III; trade names,

Chapter IV; commercial books, Chapter V; merchants' employees, Chapter VI; and commercial agents, Chapter VII. Book 2 deals with commercial associations. It too has undergone redrafting, in 1911, 1938, 1950, and 1974. The 1911 revision was made necessary by the great development of business in Japan following the Russo-Japanese War of 1905, and the 1938 revision was related to the radical transformation of economic conditions in Japanese society before the outbreak of the Second World War. Following a chapter of general provisions, three chapters deal with the three types of commercial corporations. The first two chapters provide for the first two types of association (partnerships) in almost exactly the same terms as the French law. Chapter III was drastically revised in 1950 on the advice of the Occupation authorities, and the influence of Anglo-American law in it is strong. The provisions on partnerships limited by shares which existed before the 1950 reform were abrogated because they were little used; private companies are regulated by a special law of 5 April 1938.

The third book deals with acts of commerce. In Chapter I three types of commercial acts are enumerated: absolute commercial acts (Article 501), professional commercial acts (Article 502), and accessory commercial acts (Article 503). Absolute commercial acts are those which are always such whether performed in the exercise of a profession or not. Professional commercial acts are those which are not so by their nature but which become commercial when they are performed professionally. Accessory commercial acts are all legal acts accomplished by merchants in order to advance their profession, whatever the nature of the act. The nine other chapters that make up this book deal with sale, current accounts, undisclosed partnership, brokerage, commission agents, forwarding agents, transport, deposit, and insurance.

Book 4, which was the fifth book at the time of the promulgation of the code, deals with maritime commerce. Its seven chapters are headed: ships and ship-owners, crew, transport, loss, salvage, insurance, and maritime lien creditors.

The most marked difference that exists between the French and Japanese commercial codes is that the Japanese code does not deal with bankruptcy or commercial courts. The rules on bankruptcy are in a separate law, the law on bankruptcy of 25 April 1922, which is applicable not only to merchants but to all persons.

Like the Civil Code, the Commercial Code is far from including within its pages all the rules that are relevant to commercial law. There are numerous complementary laws of which those of especial importance are the law on limited companies, the law of 15 July 1932, relating to bills of exchange, the law of 29 July 1933, relating to cheques, and the law of 13 June 1957, relating to the international transport of goods by sea.

The Code of Civil Procedure

The code is modeled almost exactly on the German code. No Japanese code has been less influenced by French law than this one, and until recent times Japanese procedural lawyers paid very little attention to the works of the French procedural lawyers. The code is divided into eight books. The first, the general part, has four chapters. Chapter I deals with the jurisdiction of the various courts and the exclusion, challenge, and withdrawal of judges and registrars. If any of the causes of exclusion set out in the law, whether raised by the parties or not, arises in connection with a judge called to hear a case, that judge cannot participate in the case, and anything done by him in the case is of no effect. Chapter II deals with parties to proceedings. Chapter III relates to costs, and Chapter IV contains a number of general rules for the hearing, time limits, notification of judgment, and adjourning of proceedings.

Book 2 is entitled 'Procedure at First Instance'. Of the four chapters of this book, the first deals with the statement of claim, the second with the hearing and preparation for it, the third with evidence, and the fourth with special rules for summary tribunals.

Book 3 deals with appeals, and Book 4 with retrial. The fifth book relates to the procedure on orders to pay. This procedure is aimed at facilitating the recovery of debts relating to sums of money, perishable goods, or incorporeal moveables. It is analogous to the procedure created in France for the same purpose by the law of 4 July 1957.

Book 6 contains the rules dealing with execution of judgment. It provides some general rules, then discusses methods of execution under three main heads. The first type concerns execution of obligations which have payment of a sum of money as their object, and separate procedures are provided for the seizure of moveables, the seizure of immoveables, and the seizure of ships. The second type concerns the execution of obligations which do not have a sum of money as their object. This mode of execution is used when the delivery of a certain piece of property, either moveable or immoveable, is required. The third type has to do with two measures preparatory to execution. One is provisional seizure and the other is *kari-shobun* (provisional disposition), which is similar in nature to an interim injunction. It follows the German *einstweilige Verfügung* and is very much like the French system of *référé*.

Book 7 deals with the procedure by which a court may at the request of an interested party give public notice to unknown creditors, calling on them to declare their rights or have their rights defeated. After this public notice the court can give an excluding judgment (*Ausschlussurteil*), the effect of which is to consolidate the legal position of the plaintiff to his advantage. Book 8 deals with arbitration.

The Code of Civil Procedure is a faithful imitation of the German code. However, the Civil Code, which contains the basic rules of private law, retains, in spite of the generally held belief that it too copies the BGB, a great number of rules of French origin. For this reason there exists between the two codes a certain lack of coherence which has given rise to many doctrinal controversies. The provisions of French origin obviously presuppose legal sanctions of a French type, and it is therefore a hopeless task to try to harmonize the rules of the two codes. As an example of the type of problem that arises, consider the law on possessory actions. The Civil Code provides, in Articles 197–202, rules relating to possessory actions. Subject to certain modifications which were not always fortunate in their result, the draftsmen of the Civil Code retained the French system of possessory actions, but they did not place the rules of procedure for these actions in the Civil Code because that was, according to them, a matter to be covered by the Code of Civil Procedure. However, the Code of Civil Procedure contains no provision relating to possessory actions, because the German law on which it was founded does not provide any special rules for possessory actions. Under the German code there are two methods of requiring the transfer of a thing: the owner of the property can get it back relying either on his possession or on his title. This is his choice, and he can even combine the proprietory action with the possessory action. The German law of 1898 abrogated a provision which had retained in a somewhat modified form the principle of *non-cumul* of actions borrowed from the French law. The system is therefore quite different from the French. The Japanese lawyers, if they wish to be faithful to the French system, must accept the solutions given by Articles 23–27 of the French Code of Civil Procedure. If on the other hand they support the German system they must at the same time accept the logical conclusions that follow from the German procedural system. For the moment, the law on the point is neither clear nor coherent.

The Code of Civil Procedure does not provide all the rules of civil procedure. There are many important laws outside it, ignorance of which would render an investigation of Japanese civil procedure imperfect and inaccurate. Apart from the Supreme Court rules of 1 March 1956, which are not in statutory form, there is the law of 16 May 1962, on administrative procedure, the law of 21 June 1898, on procedure in matters of civil status, the law of 21 June 1898, on procedure in non-contentious matters, the law of 6 December 1947, on family law procedure, the law of 25 April 1922, on bankruptcy, and the law of 9 June 1951, on conciliation in civil cases. This last law seeks to find equitable and practicable rather than legal solutions to civil cases, based on mutual concessions made by the parties. The Japanese do not like the solution of a dispute to be too decisive or contrary to their native sentiment of what is right, and therefore a large number of cases are dealt with by way of conciliation.

The Criminal Code

The first Penal Code was drawn up by Boissonade, and it introduced Japan to the principle of *nulla poena sine lege*. It had the great merit of causing the spirit of humanity to penetrate into penal institutions which previously had been utilized only as instruments of threat and intimidation on the part of those in power. However, under the influence of the new thinking in criminal law at the end of the last century, Japanese lawyers came to regard this code as imperfect from the theoretical point of view. In 1907 a new code was promulgated on 24 April to come into force on 1 October 1908. It is this criminal code which is in force today. It departed from the pattern of the former code in a number of important aspects. In the first place, the new code abandoned the French system of classification of offenses. Second, it extended considerably the power of judges to decide on the appropriate penalty to be imposed. The code allowed a reasonably extensive difference between the maximum and minimum penalties available for each crime, so the judge could within the prescribed limits choose a penalty appropriate to the degree of culpability of the accused, and individualization of penalty was thus much better realized. Third, the new code is more systematic than the earlier one. The provisions relating to self-defense, for example, which are applicable to all offenses, were placed in the old code in the part relating to homicide, assault, and wounding. The new code puts these rules in the first book, which contains general rules. Finally, the new code admits, to a large degree, stay of execution of penalties.

The new code has been amended several times since 1908. The most important of the reforms was that of 1947, when the law was reworked to a fairly large extent to bring it into line with the constitution. In conformity with the constitutional principles, the law of 26 October 1947, sought to make the code more democratic, more liberal, and more pacifist, and as a consequence of the constitutional postulate that war would be renounced, a large number of provisions relating to war were abrogated. The principle of individual dignity demanded the improvement and the extending of the system of stay of execution, and the laws relating to outrage were modified, too, so that personal honor would be better respected. Third, the principle of equality before the law made necessary the total abrogation of the provisions relating to offenses against the imperial family. The code is made up of two books. The first book has thirteen chapters in which are set out rules of a general nature which apply to all crimes: application of the code (Chapter I), penalties (Chapter II), calculation of time (Chapter III), stay of execution (Chapter IV), provisional release (Chapter V), prescription and extinction of penalties (Chapter VI), justification and exonerating circumstances (Chapter VII), attempts (Chapter VIII), concurrent crimes (Chapter IX), recidivism (Chapter X), accomplices (Chapter XI), mitigating circumstances (Chapter XII), reduction or increase of penalties (Chapter XIII).

Book 2, called by Japanese lawyers 'the part containing the special rules,' is called in the code 'Crimes.' It is divided into 40 chapters, each dealing with a particular class of crime.

Of the numerous special laws which complement the Criminal Code, the most important are the law on minor offenses (*Keihenzai ho*) of 1 May 1948, and the law of 21 July 1952, which seeks to prevent subversive activities (*hakai-katsudo boshiho*). This law was promulgated, in spite of lively opposition by intellectuals and the progressive political parties, to repress the violence of the Communist Party in an era when such violence was frequent. This law could undoubtedly be used to oppress freedom of expression in Japan, and the opposition succeeded in having the following clause inserted in it: 'This law, having as it does a very close relationship with the fundamental rights of the nation, must be applied in the most limited way possible considering the need to assure public order. Any broad interpretation of the law is strictly proscribed.' To date the law has been used – not as originally planned – principally to repress the violence of groups of the extreme right.

6. The Criminal Procedure Code

The Criminal Procedure Code (*Chizei ho*) drawn up by Boissonade remained in force until 1890. When the Constitution of 1889 was promulgated the code had to be revised, and a new law of October, 1890, was promulgated as the Code of Criminal Procedure (*Keijisosho ho*). The change of title preceded the change in France by 68 years. The new code, in spite of the change of title, was not very different from its predecessor and did not enjoy favor for long.

In 1922 a new Code of Criminal Procedure was introduced by the law of 5 May. This code retained many ideas of French origin, such as the *action civile*, *instruction préliminaire*, and *pourvoi dans l'intérêt de la loi*. The constitution of 1946 did introduce, however, in its chapter on fundamental rights, many rules of Anglo-American origin, destined to guarantee the liberty and dignity of suspected criminals; to keep in line with these rules it was necessary to revise the code again. From this revision came the law of 10 July 1948, a law presented as a revision of the earlier code but in fact a completely new code, which retained none of the former articles. The change of style alone is enough to show the degree of the change. Whereas the old code used literary style, the new code is written in familiar style.

In the new code the influence of Anglo-American law is predominant. A completely accusatorial type of procedure is adopted, and the accused is no longer an object of investigation but the subject of the proceedings. The preliminary investigation procedure, which had a bleak record, was suppressed, and the civil action was omitted because it was little used in practice.

The new code is in seven books. The first book deals with general matters: the jurisdiction of the courts (Chapter I), disqualification and challenge of judges (Chapter II), capacity (Chapter III), defense and legal aid (Chapter IV), preliminary hearing (Chapter V), procedural acts (Chapter VI), time limits (Chapter VII), summons, imprisonment, and preventive detention of accused persons (Chapter VIII), seizure and search (Chapter IX), viewing by the court (Chapter X), witnesses (Chapter XI), experts (Chapter XII), interpreters and translations (Chapter XIII), evidence (Chapter XIV), and costs (Chapter XV).

Book 2 is headed 'At First Instance.' It has three chapters which deal in turn with the inquiry, the prosecution, and procedure in court. Book 3 deals with appeals, Book 4 with retrial proceedings, Book 5 with cases stated for opinion by the court, Book 6 with summary proceedings, and Book 7 with the execution of judgment.

The laws complementing this code are numerous. Apart from the rules of the Supreme Court of 1 December 1948, relating to penal procedure, there is the law of 1 January 1950, relating to the indemnification of persons wrongly prosecuted, the law of 15 July 1948, on juvenile delinquents, that of 28 March 1908, on prisons, and the law of 1 April 1954, on probation.

The principal codes, of which a summary exposition has been given, constitute only a small part on the legislation of Japan. Of the remaining body of statute law it should be noted that there is no administrative code. Second, the importance of labor laws must be emphasized. Japanese workers did not really acquire legal independence from their employers until after the war, and so the laws that guarantee their legal position are very important. The three basic work laws are called *rodo sampo*. They are (1) the law of 7 April 1947, on work conditions, promulgated to give effect to Article 27 of the constitution: 'Work conditions, such as salary, length of time on the job, rest periods ... will be determined by law'; (2) the law of 1 June 1949, on trade unions, which with (3) the law of 27 September 1946, on the regulation of work disputes, aim at guaranteeing to workers the right to associate and to collective bargaining in accordance with the principle declared in Article 28 of the constitution. Thirdly, though the Japanese social security system is very backward, the laws in the field of social security are very important.

Ishii, G, 'Laws and Regulations in Japan' (1979) 7 *International Journal of Law Libraries* 164–68

THE PROMULGATION OF LAWS AND ORDERS (*HOREI*)

The promulgation of a law or an order is the publishing of a law or an order that has been established so that it may become publicly known. The Supreme Court in its decision of 28 December 1957, held, 'In order that enacted laws may become generally binding in reality on the people, it is a precondition that the content of the law be placed in a form available to the general public. In terms of the requirements of rule-of-law principle in a modern democratic state, this is indeed necessary.'

At the beginning of the Meiji period laws and orders were promulgated by public display and later distribution of the text, but from 1883 with the publication of *KAMPO* (Official Gazette), laws and orders became promulgated by printing in the Official Gazette. The Promulgation Procedures were established in 1886 and the Promulgation Procedure Order in 1907, and laws and orders in the prewar period were published in the Official Gazette in conformity with these, but the Promulgation Procedures Order was abolished simultaneously with the new postwar constitution's coming into effect. However, the Supreme Court ruled that 'One cannot go so far as to say that, in this day and age, promulgation of a law or order by means other than the Official Gazette shall not be recognized under any circumstances. However, with respect to actual practice after the abolition of the Promulgation Procedures Order, the promulgation of laws or orders has, as we have already noted, been conducted by the hitherto used means of the Official Gazette, and inasmuch as it is not apparent that the state promulgates laws or orders by any appropriate alternative means, it is reasonable to construe that laws or orders are promulgated by the hitherto used means of the Official Gazette.' (*Ibid* Decision.)

From what point of time are laws and orders said to be promulgated? The Supreme Court, in its decision of 15 October 1958, stated that if it is assumed that members of the general public who so desire will attempt to gain access to or purchase the Official Gazette, then a law or order should be understood as promulgated from the time the Official Gazette reaches the Official Gazette Section of the Printing Bureau of the Ministry of Finance or the outlets in the Tokyo metropolitan area where the Official Gazette is sold, these being the first places where the Official Gazette may be perused or purchased.

A number is attached to each law or order on promulgation. This is a number attached to law and order according to the kind of law or order, and its enactor in each year. Therefore, there is a Law No 1 and a Cabinet Order No 1 each year. In the case of Ministerial Orders, the number is headed by the issuer's name, ie Prime Minister's Office Order No 1, Ministry of Justice Order No 1, etc.

Where there has been an error in a promulgated law or order, this must be corrected by immediately publishing a correction notice in the Official Gazette. Even if a text that differs from the correct text is made public, the law or order itself is in no way affected. Certainly, once made public, it is easy to regard such law as published as the correct form of the law. When the law or order is violated, bona fide ignorance of the error without fault is construed as constituting not a reason for negation of the illegality, but a reason for the negation of liability blameworthiness.

THE DATE OF ENFORCEMENT

The date of enforcement of a law, when not fixed by the relevant law, is taken as being the day twenty days from the date of promulgation [Law Concerning the Application of Laws in General (1898, Law No 10) Article 1 Para 1], but all recent laws have specified a date of enforcement. Cabinet and Ministerial Orders invariably specify a date of enforcement. The date of enforcement of Supreme Court Rules is treated in the same way as that for laws. The date of enforcement for Ordinances and Regulations enacted by local public entities is the day ten days from the date of promulgation, unless otherwise provided for (Local Self-Government Law Article 16 Paras 3 and 5).

Moreover, retroactive application of a law or order to a certain date before the day of enforcement, may not generally be performed except when this would be in the public interest. Retroactive application of penal provisions is expressly forbidden (constitution Article 39).

THE CONSOLIDATION OF LAWS AND ORDERS

The total number of laws and orders in Japan in March, 1978 is said to be 6,830, including 1,610 laws, 1,946 Cabinet Orders and 2,607 Ministerial Orders. Laws and orders are constantly being enacted, amended, revised, or abolished. Even when a law is not revised or abolished, a law loses its effect where the law itself is planned to be limited in its application to one occasion only, or where the object of application no longer exists owing to changes in society. Moreover, old law that conflicts with new loses its effect. Whether a law has lost its effect or not in specific cases is not always apparent. However, as a corollary of rule of law, laws and orders must always be correctly and widely known by the people. In his work *HOTENRON* (Treatise on Legal Codes, 1890), Dr Nobushige Hozumi wrote, 'The question of whether or not the law of a nation is in fact written in clear and accurate language, and able to inform the people easily of their rights and duties, is one of such a magnitude that it should in no way be neglected.' Looking at examples in foreign nations, we find that in the United States in 1875 laws enacted over the previous eighty-five years were consolidated and reenacted as 'The Revised Statutes of the United States'. In 1926 these were revised and published as 'The United States Code'. 'The United States Code' continues to this day and it is said that 'The Statutes at Large' will eventually go out of use. In West Germany a law for the consolidation of federal laws (*Gesetz über die Sammlung des Bundesrechts*) was enacted in 1958 for the consolidation of German laws from the past hundred years. In Switzerland, consolidation of Federal Law was carried out as a Federal Centennial Project in 1948, and the '*Vereinigte Sammlung der Bundesgesetze und Verordnungen*' was published. In the United Kingdom, 'The Statutes Revised' has been published several times under the direction of the Statute Law Committee.

In the consolidation of laws in these countries, the three following methods appear to have been used.

(A) Codification

Editing of laws under a scientific system, working in court decisions and scholarly opinion.

(B) Revision

Consolidation of laws by correction of inadequate provisions so that the individual provisions of laws are mutually balanced and consistent.

(C) Compilation

Consolidation of laws by simple erasure of provisions that have been revised or abolished, or have lost effect through expiry, without any examination of consistency between individual provisions.

Civil, commercial, civil procedure, criminal and criminal procedure codes belong under codification. Belonging under revision are 'The Revised Statutes of the United States' and 'The United States Codes,' and under compilation may be found West Germany's '*Die Sammlung des Bundesrecht*' and Switzerland's '*Vereinigte Sammlung der Bundesgesetze und Verordnungen.*'

In Japan, the Civil, Commercial, Civil and Criminal Procedure and other Codes compiled from 1890 to 1907 come under the category of codification. Those coming under the category of compilation are:

Genko Ruiju Hoki (Anthology of Present Laws and Regulations) (ed) Ministry of Justice 1879–91.

Hoki Teiyo (Handbook of Laws and Regulations) (ed) Cabinet Legislation Bureau 1887–1906.

Genko Horei Shuran (Collected Present Laws and Orders) (ed) Cabinet Records Divisions, from 1907.

and the following, published after the Second World War.

Genko Hoki Soran (A Conspectus of Present Laws and Regulations) (ed) the Legislative Bureaus of both Houses of the Diet, from 1947.

Genko Nippon Hoki (Present Laws and Regulations of Japan) (ed) Ministry of Justice Secretariat from 1949.

The last three are commonly used for reference in Japanese law and, being viewed as being almost identical in content, it is thought these may be combined into one. Moreover, it should be noted that consolidation of laws and orders in Japan goes no further than the *de facto* compilation. In West Germany or Switzerland, laws not included in the law collections published after consolidation are deemed to be null and void, but in Japan, laws not thus included do not always lose their effect. Moreover, in the United States of America, laws included in the law collections published after consolidation are all deemed to be in effect, but in the case of Japan all of the laws thus included are not always in effect.

Beer, LW and Tomatsu, H, 'A Guide to the Study of Japanese Law' (1975) 23 *American Journal of Comparative Law* 306–08, 311–15

The Study of Japanese Judicial Decisions

Under the constitution of Japan of 1947, judges have had broad powers of judicial review for the first time, and the study of precedent has become an important part of legal studies. The doctrine of *stare decisis* is not accepted, and the Supreme Court has on rare occasions explicitly reversed itself; but consistency is duly honored in most cases. Some decisions of the pre-1945 supreme court, the Great Court of Cassation (*Daishin'in*) were reported, but their role in subsequent decision-making and especially in scholarship was of minor importance compared to systematic exegesis and legal theory. Under Art 4 of the *Rules for Conduct of Judicial Affairs* (Decree No 103, 8 June 1875), it was made explicit that court decisions would not be treated as law or precedent for future cases. Nevertheless, on occasion *Daishin'in* decisions have been used as precedent in the post-war Supreme Court.

A variety of sources give access to Japanese judicial decisions, but only a very few libraries in the United States, or anywhere outside Japan, have even one type of case reporter ... Moreover, Japanese case reporters publish only a fraction of the cases decided.

Although more decisions are included in the *Saikosaibansho Saibanshu* (Collection of Supreme Court Decisions), the most important official case reporters for the constitutional lawyer are the *Saikosaibansho Hanreishu* (Collection of Supreme Court Cases, since 1947) and the *Gyoseijiken Minji Hanreishu* (Collection of Judicial Decisions in Civil Administrative Cases) ... Each volume of the Supreme Court reporter contains first civil cases and then criminal cases; the division of each volume is indicated only by a piece of pink tissue paper, a detail that has caused waste of time and humorous frustration to beginners, both Japanese and foreign. The administrative case reporter contains many decisions of constitutional import handed down by courts of all levels.

The principal fast-service reporters of major decisions are the commercially published *Hanrei Jiho* (*The Case Review*), which comes out three times each month, and the monthly *Hanrei Taimuzu* (*The Case Times*). The former is especially recommended as the quickest and most economical way of keeping abreast of major constitutional decisions. By reference to the related *Hanrei Jiho Sosakuin* (*Complete Index to Hanrei Jiho*), one can easily determine whether a given case has been reported therein. *Hanrei Taikei* (*A Compendium of Decisions*) is an authoritative looseleaf reference tool, organized according to legal and constitutional provisions and subdivided into the fine points of related judicial doctrine; but in the past its case references have not been kept consistently current.

Background information and some commentary on major cases are normally carried by one or more of Japan's national newspapers (eg *Asahi Shimbun, Mainichi Shimbun, Yomiuri Shimbun, Nihon Keizai Shimbun*) for the days surrounding the date of the decision. Decision day for the Supreme Court of Japan is usually Wednesday; in contrast to the United States Supreme Court, this court is in session all through the year except for the peak of the summer heat. Supreme Court decisions tend to become more numerous toward the end of the calendar year, as the pivotal New Year's holiday season approaches and the felt-need to prepare by cleaning the ledger becomes stronger.

In good part due to the influence of Professor Itsutaro Suehiro in the immediate postwar period, a series of case law study groups focusing on different areas of law evolved and became well established at the University of Tokyo, Faculty of Law, thus constituting a notable source of in-depth analysis of individual cases. Various organized groups of legalists now study and discuss individual cases and publish the results of their analyses. Most important for the constitutional lawyer is the *Gyosei Hanrei Kenkyukai* (Administrative Case Study Association), composed of around 100 scholars, judges, lawyers, and government officials who meet every other Saturday and publish their analyses every month in *Jichi Kenkyu* (*Self-Government Studies*). The German law background of a large proportion of these influentials affects, in favor of bureaucratic interests, their interpretations of decisions in constitutional cases touching upon administrative law.

If a case has not been reported in any publication at the time of research, the most practical way to learn of it or about it may be to go to the Supreme Court library in Tokyo and ask for assistance. Attempting to deal with such situations by mail inquiries is usually inadvisable and impractical. Relying upon and imposing upon a Japanese scholar friend to go to the Supreme Court in one's place may be possible occasionally. (Unless one is well-versed in Japanese mores, such presumption on another's good will should be avoided, in part because travelling around Tokyo is time-consuming, and in part because the American lawyer may thus unintentionally offend or may misunderstand Japanese behavior.) The scholar will find library personnel competent, courteous, generous with their time, and imaginative in tracking down information not immediately available. Personal contact with Research Officers (*Chosakan*) in the Supreme Court with expertise in particular problem areas may also be helpful; and good relationships with Japanese judges at whatever level can facilitate prompt and full access to important judicial decisions, as well as to *Inyo Shorui* (Background Materials) on specific cases used by the judges themselves. Such materials may give the researcher not only a comprehensive picture of the documents, facts and Japanese law relevant to the case, but also the status of relevant law and policy in many other nations (mostly Western). For example, in the controversial *Ienaga Textbook Review Case* (Tokyo District Court, 1970), the judges had ready access to detailed information on the textbook approval systems, laws and policies of many democratic nations and of many States in the United States, before coming to their decision.

Other sources on cases are casebooks reproducing judicial decisions, in whole or in part (eg Isao Sato, *Kenpo Kihon Hanreishu*); books giving digests, without commentary, of court doctrine in all cases involving a specific question (eg defamation law) or problem area (eg rights of workers); and irregularly published special issues of Jurisuto with commentary on cases deemed most important (eg *Kenpo Hanrei Hyakusen-Shinpan*, 1968), or in a specific subject area (eg *Masu Komi Hanrei Hyakusen*, 1971) ...

Casebooks are relatively few, because law faculty students in Japan usually are not required to have detailed knowledge of judicial doctrine, in good part because judicial decisions are not the starting point for Japanese legal studies. Except for the work of Professor Takeo Hayakawa of Kobe University and a few others influenced by American political science, Japanese scholars show little interest in judicial processes and judicial behavior. Undoubtedly, the influence of Western legal systems on Japan motivates Japanese scholars in their study of American and German law; and the absence of Japanese impact on Western legal systems explains, in part, the paucity of Western studies of Japanese law. However, both historically and at present, the Japanese seem to have shown a greater intellectual curiosity and openness than Western jurists regarding foreign cases and diverse legal ideas, quite apart from the practical utility of such ideas.

...

A. The Citation of Japanese Judicial Decisions

Aspects of the Japanese citation system will be explained in the context of a few examples. The full citation will be given in Romanization, in the order and style it would appear in Japanese, except that in the original you would read from top to bottom, right to left. Numbers over the citation correspond to explanatory notes below.

Example I: citation of a criminal case decision:

1 2 3 4

Saikosai/ Showa 35nen 7gatsu 20nichi/ Daihotei/ Hanketsu./

5

Showa 35nen (a) Dai 112go/

6

Showa 25nen Tokyoto Jorei Dai 44go, Shukai-Shudan Koshin
oyobi Shudan Jiiundo ni kansuru Joreiihan Hikoku Jiken./

7

Keishu 14kan 9go 1143./

1) An abbreviation of *Saiko Saibansho*, the Supreme Court.
2) The date of the decision. The year is given according to the Japanese system; ie the name given to the reign of the current Emperor is presented first (*Showa* is the name of Emperor Hirohito's era), then the year of that Emperor's reign period (in this case, the 35th year of *Showa*). A simple method of calculating the *Showa* year in terms of the Christian calendar is to add 25. Thus, *Showa* 35 is 1960. The year is given first; then the month, which is named according to its ordinal place in the twelve months of the year; and finally the day of the month.
3) *Daihotei* means the Grand Bench; ie a quorum of the full membership (15 Justices) of the Supreme Court. See Example II for a contrast.
4) *Hanketsu* means 'a judgment,' one of a number of types of judicial decision (see Article 43, Law of Criminal Procedure).
5) The docket number of the case, assigned by the Supreme Court office.
6) The official name of the case. The names of parties are not given as a title; but the names of parties are discoverable between the title and the text of a decision. The official name of a case may be quite long, as in this case, where the name simply states that this is a case of alleged violation of a particular ordinance. Translation: 'An instance of alleged violation of Tokyo Ordinance No 44 of 1950, the

Ordinance concerning Assembly ...' In this, as in many cases, the name does not by itself adequately identify the case.

7) This most important part of the citation tells where to find the full text of the decision with all attendant opinions.

   a) *Keishu* is an abbreviation for *Saikosaibansho Keiki Hanreishu* (Collection of Supreme Court Decisions in Criminal Cases), unless *Keishu* is preceded by a modifying word such as *Kakyu* (or simply *Ka*; both referring to lower court decisions) or *Kosai* (High Court decisions). *Minshu* is the counterpart collection of decisions in civil cases (See Example II). There are many variations of these ready reference terms, but *Keishu* and *Minshu* are most common in the literature.

   b) Vol 14, No 9, p 1143. Note that No 9 is paginated both from page 1 and according to the pagination of volume 14; this citation gives the number of the volume page.

If you are citing a case in a Japanese-language article, you may omit 5) and 6), but must include 1), 4) and 7). See Example III.

Example II citation of a civil case decision:

1 2

Saikosai Showa 27nen 2gatsu 22 nichi/Dai-ni Shohotei Hanketsu/

3 4

Showa 25nen (o)/ Koyokeiyaku kaijo Muko Kakunin Hokyu

Shi-harai Seikyo Jiken./

5

Minshu 6kan 2go 258peiji./

1) and 3) correspond to 1), 2), and 5), in Example I; 5) to 7) in Example I.

2) *Dai-ni Shohotei* means Second Petty Bench. The Supreme Court, for some purposes, divides into three Petty Benches. Regarding the differences between the Supreme Court's Grand Bench and Petty Benches, see the Court Law, Articles 9 and 10. 4) The official name of most civil decisions spells out the subject matter of the case. Translation: A case demanding a declaratory judgment nullifying cancellation of an employment contract and (claiming) salary payment.

Example III: a sample of variations:

1 2

Iwayuru Wakayama Kyoso Jiken/Saikohan/Showa 40nen

3

7gatsu 14 nichi/ Daihotei/ Minshu l9kan 5go 1148peiji./

1) In this citation, the official name of the case appears first. Examples I and II showed that names of cases can be quite long. In part to obviate that inconvenience, and in part because of their fame, certain cases become known by a particular name which usually refers to a relevant place (eg the 'Matsukawa Case'), or to some characteristic of the case (eg 'One-Yen Case'), or to the name of a party in the dispute (eg 'the Asahi Case'). Even if a case does not have a brief proper name, its elongated official name is not always cited in Japanese works. All the parenthesized data should be given for clear identification; but not all Japanese authors do so.

2) An abbreviation of *Saikosaibansho Hanketsu* (judgment of the Supreme Court).

3) Note the word *Daihotei* (Grand Bench) is located at a point in the citation different from Examples I and II. In general, compare the order of data presentation in Examples I, II and III. Translation: The so-called Wakayama Kyoso Case (Supreme Court judgment, July 14, 1965, Grand Bench, Minshu, Vol. 19, No. 5, p. 1148).

Example IV: HANJI 500go.

Japanese authors' citations of decisions found in *Hanrei Jiho* at times provide no more than the number of the issue in which the case appears, with or without a page reference, and the name of the journal in abbreviated form. *Hanrei Jiho* (*Case Review*), No 500.

In light of the above examples and further variations which exist, and in light of the problems of recognition and consistency for the non-specialist reading an English-language article or book on Japanese constitutional law, the following citation form is suggested: (the parties names), 19 *Minshu* 1148 (Sup Ct, GB, 14 July 1965); other forms in use include: ——— v ——— (special name by which the case is commonly known in Japan, if such exists), Supreme Court, Grand Bench, 14 July 1965, 19 *Minshu* (No 5) 1148 (1965); and simply, 19 *Minshu* (No 5) 1148 (1965), when a case is more clearly identified in an author's text.

B. The Citation of Japanese Law Books and Periodicals

Since Japanese academic practice varies considerably, the following comments are only meant to be illustrative and suggestive.

Example I: citation of a Japanese legal article:

1 2

Ashibe Nobuyoshi,/ [Ikenshinsasei o meguru kadai]

3 4 5

Horitsu Jiho/ 39kan 9go 56peiji/ (1967)

1) The name of the author, family name first. The family name is not followed by a comma as in English. Even very well-educated Japanese find the reading of names quite difficult or impossible at times, because almost all names are written in kanji, which commonly have obscure readings in addition to frequently used readings. The more considerate periodicals will give the author's name in the Japanese syllabary at the end of an article; and book publishers sometimes give the proper reading of the author's name on the standard publishing data page found at the end of every book. The only other ways to learn the correct pronunciation are to consult the *Hogakusha Meibo*, or to ask someone who knows and to memorize the name. Should you meet an author and pronounce his name correctly, he will be quite pleased (sometimes shocked!) and well disposed to assist in research efforts. Upon receipt of a name card (*meishi*) it is helpful to write the donor's name on his card.

2) The title of an article is given in brackets, not in italics or quotation marks. Translation: Questions regarding the Institution of Judicial Review.

3) The name of a legal journal. Abbreviations are very commonly used, but there is not a single accepted abbreviation for each journal. The specialist needs to become familiar with a table of such abbreviations ... For example, one abbreviation of *Horitsu Jiho* is *Hoji*; *Kokka Gakkai Zasshi* becomes *Kokka*, and so on. Such abbreviations should be used only when writing for a Japanese-language journal.

4) The volume of the journal, followed by the number and page; Vol 39, No 9, p 56. Unlike American journals, most Japanese journals are paginated from the beginning of each issue (in contrast to the official Japanese case reporters), not from page 1 of the volume; so the issue number must be given in the citation. Also note that some important journals are numbered serially from the first issue of the periodical (excluding certain special issues and special series which may be separately numbered) to the present, without any annual or other division according to volumes. Although the month and day of the issue may be clear from a glance at the cover, only the fine print may reveal the year the issue came out.
5) The year of publication. Sometimes the year is not given, and sometimes the year given is that of the Imperial reign rather than of the Christian era (see IV, A, Example I, 2), above). As it should appear in an American publication: N Ashibe, title in Japanese (title in English), 39 *Horitsu Jiho* (No 9) 56 (1969).

Example II: citation of a Japanese book:

Ito Masami/ [*Genron-Shuppan No Jiyu*]/ 35peiji ika (1959).

1) The title of a book is also placed in brackets in Japanese.
2) Citation of a locus in the book; ika means 'from' page 35. There is less variation in citation styles for articles than for judicial decisions, and less for books than for articles. When citing a Japanese title in an English publication, reverse the author's name order, give the Japanese title, then a translation of the title in parentheses, the name of the publisher, and the year of publication, as follows: Masami Ito, *Genron-Shuppan No. Jiyu* (Freedom of Speech and Press Freedom), Iwanami Shoten, 1959. It is reasonable to assume that a book or journal was published in Tokyo unless otherwise indicated,

Ishida, T, 'Case Law in Japan' (1979) 7 *International Journal of Law Libraries* 135–48

... until early in the 20th century court decisions were disregarded by doctrinal Japanese scholars. However, even the attitude of such scholars toward judicial decisions began to change after World War I. They could not ignore an active role of the courts in the formation of law. It is impossible for legislation to make a perfect rule that will meet all changes in the society. Statutes provide no more than a framework and must be made more precise in their practical application. The legal scholars could not refuse any more to admit the effect of judicial decisions on the interpretation of law in the light of the rapid growth of Japanese industry. In 1923 Izutaro Suehiro, a law professor of the Tokyo Imperial University and one of the founders of the '*Hanrei Mimpo Kenkyu Kai*' (Study Group of Case Law in the Field of Civil Law), clarified the situation: 'If we observe the matter realistically, the legislature marks the outer boundaries of law and the court creates the contents to fill the inside space. Whether one will call the contents law or not is of minimal significance. As a matter of fact, the contents are nothing other than law. ... what is formulated by precedents is law in a certain sense, in that it affords the society with a standard of conduct. The court is not legislature. It is not, however, simply a tool for applying statutes. It is a peace-maker which tries to establish harmony between actual life and the statutes through constant creation.' There is no doubt that activities of this Study Group laid the foundation of today's nation-wide case study.

Mimpo Hanrei Kenkyu Kai, whose purpose was to study the law in its concrete form, tried to examine the facts of a case in detail. It seems to be undeniable that the official reports of the Great Court of Judicature were influenced by this method of study. By this time, the Great Court of Judicature had changed the title of its official reports from *TAISHIN-IN HANKETSU-ROKU* to *TAISHIN IN HANREI-SHU* (Collection of the Cases of the Great Court of Judicature), and turned over the publishing institute from Chuo University to '*Hoso Kai*' (the Bar Association). The influence of the Study Group's claims was shown when *TAISHIN-IN HANREI-SHU* began to publish the facts as determined by the court of first instance as well as the facts found and the reasons given by the court of second instance.

Briefly, we wish to touch on special court reports and lower court reports before 1947. Since the beginning of the establishment of the modern judicial system in 1890, the jurisdiction over litigation involving the government was totally excluded from the ordinary judicial courts jurisdiction. Under the Administrative Justice Law of 1890, administrative cases were handled exclusively in an Administrative Court composed of '*Hyojo-kan*' (councillors). The complete decisions of the administrative court, from its creation to its abolition, can be found in *GYOSEI SAIBANSHO HANKETSU-ROKU* (Records of the Judgments of the Administrative Court) published by three different publishers.

Prior to the judicial reform of 1947, there was no official source for publication of the lower courts' judgments. However, the important decisions of lower courts are included in the journal *HORITSU SHIMBUN* (the Legal News) which was published from 1900–44: Selected decisions of the Great Court of Judicature, highlights of major law developments, law news and comments are also included in this journal. At present, the Legal News is the only single source for reference to the decisions of the lower courts before 1947.

II. THE PRESENT SYSTEM OF LAW REPORTING

The democratic constitution of Japan was promulgated on 3 November 1946 and came into force on 3 May 1947. This new constitution and the new Court Organization Law, which was enforced with the constitution, radically changed the pre-existing judicial system. The whole judicial power was vested in a Supreme Court and ordinary inferior courts. The Administrative Court was abolished. No executive organ may be given final judicial powers. The power to exercise administrative supervision over the courts has been assumed by the Supreme Court. Although judges are appointed by the Cabinet, they must be appointed from a list of persons nominated by the Supreme Court. Moreover, the Supreme Court has been conferred the power to make rules. Thus the judiciary has acquired independence in real terms. It is needless to say that because the new system issued from one of the greatest case law countries, the United States of America, study of judicial precedents was expedited.

There are two other factors which have brought about notable reforms in the court reporting system; more particularly, in the reporting system of the Supreme Court decisions. The first is that under the new constitution the court has been vested with the power to determine the constitutionality of any law, order or regulation. Thus, the constitution itself has given the court, especially the Supreme Court, as one of its principal roles, the function to maintain uniform application of the law. This function can not be fulfilled without a stable case law. It is quite in the nature of things that the court reporters added their weights.

Secondly, the new constitution established the system of referendum of the Supreme Court justices. Under Article 79, the appointment of the justices of the Supreme Court is reviewed by the people. In order to help the judgment of the people, the Court

Organization Law requires that the opinion of every justice shall be expressed in written decisions. In rendering the judgment, the people will rely upon only those opinions of the justices that are published; thus the publication of the Supreme Court decisions has acquired an especially important meaning.

A. Supreme Court Decisions

The opinion of the court is always rendered by a *per curiam* form. What differs from the American cases is that the name of the specific judge writing the opinion of the court, regardless of a unanimous opinion, a majority opinion or a plurality opinion, is not shown. A member of the majority may write, under his own name, a concurring opinion which gives his reasons for the decision in addition to the reasons leading the opinion of the court. An opinion, in accord with the conclusion and result of the majority but disagreeing with its reasoning may be given as 'an Opinion of Justice so-and-so.' Dissenters to both the conclusion and reasoning express their dissenting opinions. Occasionally, concurring opinions, opinions and dissenting opinions are called collectively minority opinions by practitioners. However, on occasion only dissenting opinions are called minority opinions.

B. Official Reports of the Supreme Court

At present, two kinds of reports are compiled and published by the Supreme Court. One is *SAIKO-SAIBANSHO SAIBANSHU* (Collection of Decisions of the Supreme Court) and the other is *SAIKO-SAIBANSHO HANREISHU* (Supreme Court Reports). The Collection of Decisions of the Supreme Court publishes almost all decisions of the Supreme Court other than brief decisions of the whole court rendered by standardized forms in which the opinions are omitted. However this collection is for use only by judges and court officials.

The Supreme Court Reports publishes only decisions with precedential value. The number of decisions published in this series each year is strictly limited. We find that only about 100 cases out of about 2,000 annual civil decided cases, or about 5 percent, are published in the civil series and less than 30 cases out of about 3,000 annual criminal decided cases, or about 1%, are published in the criminal series of the Supreme Court Reports. This may be attributable to a characteristic of the Japanese appeal system which developed as a three instance trial system. Consequently, in Japan, the number of the total appeals shows an extremely high rate as compared with the Anglo-American legal system. In spite of this large number of appeal cases, the number determining constitutionality is very small. For the 10 years from 1967–76, the number of cases determining constitutionality was only 40 in civil and 103 in criminal, and only nine cases (two in civil and seven in criminal) were decided against the Government.

Judgments published in the Supreme Court Reports are chosen by a Case Law Committee set up within the Supreme Court. The Committee consists of not more than seven justices of the Supreme Court and holds a meeting monthly except August to decide whether or not the judgments rendered in the preceding month should be published. Standards for selecting cases to be printed are not provided by any rule. However, the Supreme Court has, as one of its principal functions, to insure the uniformity of judicial decisions; therefore, cases for inclusion are selected from this viewpoint. Thus the Supreme Court Reports publishes all decisions of the Grand Bench (*court en banc*) consisting of all 15 members, because cases proving to involve a constitutional question or to require a change in established precedents have to be decided by the Grand Bench. Where a decision of the Petty Bench (division) consisting of five members includes a new point of law, or indicates a new trend in legal thinking, or where a Petty Bench settles a point of law, opinions of which are divided among inferior courts, such decision is to be published.

At present, the Supreme Court Reports are generally issued in monthly parts by the General Secretariat of the Supreme Court.

C. Official Reports of Lower Courts and on Special Subjects

As may be seen elsewhere in this volume, numerous official reports of lower courts and on special subjects have been published since 1947.

KOTO-SAIBANSHO HANREICHU (High Courts Reports) contains selective cases of the eight High Courts.

KAKYU-SAIBANSHO MINJI SAIBANREISHU (Reports of Civil Decisions of Inferior Courts) is a reporter of selective civil cases of the High Courts and District Courts.

RODO-KANKEI MINJI SAIBANREISHU (Reports of Judgments in Civil Labor Cases) reports selective cases of lower courts on civil matters in the labor law field.

GYOSEI-JIKEN SAIBANREISHU (Reports of Judgments on Administrative Affairs) prints important cases in administrative matters. While the Supreme Court cases are not excluded, very few are included, because such cases which have already been published in the Supreme Court Reports are not included.

KEIJI SAIBAN GEPPO (Monthly Reports of Judgments on Criminal Relations) is a selective reporter of all lower court criminal decisions. It includes not only cases but also notices, questions and answers.

KATEI SAIBAN GEPPO (Monthly Reports of Judgments on Domestic Relations) publishes family and juvenile cases chosen from those that are sent by each Family Court to the Supreme Court on the basis of utility to judges and judicial officers. This reporter also includes articles, notices, questions and answers, statistics and other materials in the family and juvenile law fields.

MUTAIZAISAN-KANKEI MINJI-GYOSEI SAIBANREISHU (Reports of Civil and Administrative Judgments in the Field of Incorporated Property) includes patent, trade mark and copyright cases of lower courts.

All these serially published official reports are issued under the supervision of the Supreme Court.

D. Elements of Court Decisions

We should mention briefly the elements of Japanese court decisions. The title or case name is not identified by the names of the parties but by a brief description of the nature of the case such as a case claiming the right of entry to a house. Below the title, the docket number, the date of decision, the name of the court which rendered the decision and the disposition of the case as being affirmed or denied are indicated.

There follow the names of the parties, the plaintiff or the appellant and the defendant or the appellee. Names of counsels are also listed. If it is an appellate court decision, the name of the first instance court or the first appellate court is mentioned.

Next come the basic points at issue (*hanji jiko*) and the essential elements of the court's decision (*hanketsu yoshi*). '*Hanji jiko*' is an identification of the basic points at issue in the reported case and used merely as an index to the subjects. '*Hanketsu yoshi*' is a brief statement of the grounds of decision, or a brief summary of the law involved in the reported case. Thus *'hanketsu yoshi'* has a strong resemblance to the headnotes or syllabi of American law reports. *'Hanketsu yoshi'* is drafted by the case law committee or the reporter, and of course is not a part of the judgment.

There follows a list of the laws, orders and rules relevant to the reported case.

The substance of a judgment begins from the conclusion or main text with a heading *'shubun'*. The *'shubun'* is the actual disposition of the case by the court; thus, in the appellate court, the *'shubun'* is rendered with a form such as 'The decision below is reversed' or 'The appeal in the present case is denied'.

After the main text is the opinion of the court with the heading *'riyu'* (reasons). *'Riyu'* is the explanation of the court's decision. As already mentioned, in a Supreme Court decision there may be concurring opinions, separate opinions or dissenting opinions. However, in a lower court decision, there is only one opinion of the court. Although in a High Court cases are always handled through a collegiate court, and, in a District Court, some cases are handled by a collegiate court, a decision is rendered by a majority of opinions.

In the Supreme Court Reports and in the High Court Reports, judgments rendered in the first instance court or the second instance court are printed as reference.

E. Unofficial Reports

Besides the official law reports, private companies also publish judicial decisions. In these unofficial reports, cases are usually arranged by each article of law, rules and regulations. They are divided broadly into two main groups. In one group, cases in various fields of law are treated systematically and, in the other group, decisions relating to special and limited subjects are selected. The main law reports belonging to the former are *HANREI TAIKEI* (Systematic Treatment of Judicial Precedents), *SHIN HANREI TAIKEI* (New Systematic Collection of Judicial Precedents) and *KIHON HANREI* (Collection of Leading Precedents). Law reports belonging to the latter contain cases of copyright, criminal, damage, education, election, environment, housing, labor, land, medical malpractice, tax, trade regulation, traffic law and so on.

III. BINDING FORCES OF JAPANESE CASE LAW

Broadly speaking, in Japan, as a matter of law, judicial decisions are not a source of law. However, in the practical meaning, court decisions, especially precedents of the Supreme Court, have not only high persuasive authority but also strong binding force.

First, the Supreme Court is never required legally to follow its precedents, but it is equally true that the precedent of the Supreme Court, even if it is but a single decision, will not be reversed easily. The sole end of courts of justice is to enforce the laws uniformly and impartially, without respect of persons or times. Thus the Supreme Court has an important function to insure the uniformity of judicial decisions and to assure enforcement of the uniform application of the law. For this purpose, the new Court Organization Law provides that if the case proves to require a change in established precedents of the Supreme Court, it shall be heard by the Grand Bench comprised of all members of the court. There are a few examples where the Grand Bench reversed its precedents and precedents of Petty Benches, but they are very rare.

The Supreme Court is always sensitive to the need to maintain a stable case law and legal stability. Yet, there are two occupations when the court is compelled to overrule its precedents. One is a change in the sociological context of the problem involved in the case before the court. In the light of a rapid change in the condition of public life, solutions adequate a decade ago are not necessarily so now. In such a case, to the extent that the law can develop without a change of legislative texts, the court cannot help changing its precedents which are no longer acceptable for circumstances that have since changed. The other is a conflict of decisions between Petty Benches. As there are three Petty Benches each composed of five justices, one may take an opposing position on the point of law previously taken by the other Petty Bench. In such a case, the Grand Bench will reexamine and reverse one or the other's point of view.

Secondly, judges of lower courts are not required legally to follow precedents of higher courts, even those entered by the Grand Bench of the Supreme Court. A conclusion in a decision of a court of higher rank, of cause, binds the court below in deciding the case concerned after remand. However, it applies only to the particular case referred to the appellate court. When the lower courts decide other cases, neither the precedents of higher courts nor their own previous decisions have binding force. Thus the lower courts may reject even an opinion of the Grand Bench, especially when it cannot be accepted for circumstances that have since changed. However, except when departure from the precedents is justified by such manifest circumstances, a lower court judge cannot refuse to follow the established precedents of interpretation of law, because as the procedural laws provide that the parties may appeal on the grounds of an alleged conflict with a precedent of the Supreme Court or a High Court, an opposed opinion of a lower court will undoubtedly be reversed on appeal.

Besides the legal stability or the uniformity in statutory interpretation, there are some more reasons that case law has a binding force, used in the practical sense. One is to economize the time and labor of courts and parties. Since the losing party will appeal the decision contradicting a higher court's precedents and the appellate court will undoubtedly reverse it, vocational ethics of lower court judges make them avoid such a decision so that it might not inflict a loss of time and costs on the parties for such an appeal. The other is to meet expectations of the public. With regard to this Chancellor Kent's Commentaries said: 'If a decision has been made upon solemn argument and mature deliberation, the presumption is in favour of its correctness; and the community have a right to regard it as a just declaration or exposition of the law, and to regulate their actions and their contracts by it. It would therefore be extremely inconvenient to the public if precedents were not duly regarded, and pretty implicitly followed. The binding force in this sense is referred to as 'an informal sanction in the general public' by Professor Kawashima of the Tokyo University. Professor Tanaka of the Tokyo University mentions as 'a requirement of the equality' that once a decision has been made, it must be treated as binding upon courts which are subsequently called upon to determine similar issues, and he says the public requires such an equality in its original nature.

In this connection, I want to note that there are two opposing views as to the authority of the lower court decisions. Some commentators say that only decisions of the Supreme Court and the High Courts decided as the last resort courts have authority as judicial precedents, and the decisions of the lower courts have no such authority. However, other scholars comment that as the lower court decisions must be in conformity with the equality and the impartiality requirement of the public as well as the Supreme Court decisions, the lower court decisions may have the authority, especially where there are no established higher court precedents.

IV. CHANGES IN THE COURT MADE LAW THEORY

As already pointed out, up until the middle of the era of Taisho (the 1910s), few scholars acknowledged that law was made through cases. Most legal scholars thought that the role of the courts is to solve disputes brought before them, not to make laws. They thought the judge should shut his mind to the making of law because the principle of separation of powers prevents the creation of legal rules by the courts.

This tendency, however, changed radically in the 1920s. At the present, almost all scholars and practitioners believe that the courts perform the creative functions in a sense as Professor Suehiro stated in Preface to Case Law in the Field of Civil Law (the 1921 term): 'The court 'creates' law. The method which the court uses, and the law which is formulated by judicial precedents, are more subtle in nature than in the making of laws by the legislature.' The principle of separation of powers rather estimates than prevents the creative role of the courts to make legislative laws more precise in their practical application within the process to solve disputes before the courts.

Opinions are divided, however, as to whether the courts should perform this creative function with a sense of law making or not. Professor Suehiro stated that the Great Court of Judicature should dismiss its efforts to make law deliberately through cases. Several commentators in recent times, on the contrary, have published their views that the judges should perform their law making functions with awareness. Professor Tanaka stated that the courts should make certain that their tasks form a link in the chain of law making and should 'endeavor to express fully their substantial bases of conclusion', and Judge Nakamura said: 'The law making, since a legal rule ... must be performed on a forecast that it will be applied satisfactorily to similar cases and will meet with some excellent results, and further, it must be one which is able to be adjusted with other legal rules.'

There is no doubt that the function of the judges is to determine controversies between litigants. It is the province of a court to expound the law, not to make it. However, as Justice Frankfurter said: 'When the legislative will is clouded, what is called judicial construction has an inevitable element of judicial creation', and further as Justice Cardozo said: 'The judge interprets the social conscience, and gives effect to it in law.'

We believe the principle of separation of powers does not interfere with a judge in the performance of his creative function of the concrete legal rules inherent in the judicial adjudication maintaining intense consciousness that he is performing the law making task.

Needless to say, case law, although there is a difference between legislative enactment and judge made law, is fleshing out the enacted law, and a reversal in case law would have a similar effect as if the statute had changed. If judicial precedents were to be lightly changed, trust of the people in general who relied upon the precedents would be betrayed and the stability of rules of law established by the precedents would be lost. However, if the precedents were to be treated as binding absolutely as the decisions of the House of Lords before 1966, the creative function of the case law, the function to conform to the changing needs of successive generations, would be prevented.

The judges, so to speak, walk a tightrope stretched from the past to the future, balancing between stability of rules of law and needs of law making.

V. BINDING ELEMENT IN PRECEDENTS

The binding force of the judge made law is based upon the maintenance of equal treatment; that is, the court's statements of the principles of law applied to the legal problems raised by the facts of an earlier case shall be applied identically to those of the case before the subsequent court. Therefore, it will be in accord with the case law theory that the opinion of the court in an earlier case which has no or only remote relation to the settlement of that case shall not be regarded as binding to a subsequent case.

As already mentioned, every judgment contains two major parts: '*shubun*' (main text) and '*riyu*' (reasons). The '*shubun*' is the conclusion or the actual disposition of the case. The '*riyu*' is the explanation of the disposition and consists of findings of facts and statements of the principles of law applicable to those facts. The findings of facts consist of direct facts as found by the court which are based on the facts asserted by the parties and inferential facts which the court draws from them. Where a party asserts a certain fact, according to the circumstances, for instance, if the court wants to make a party listen to reason, the court does not omit it from the judgment even where that fact is not material for the statement of law which is needed essentially to draw a conclusion. Accordingly, for the purpose of the doctrine of precedent in Japan, on the lines of case law countries, attempts have been made to define the *ratio decidendi* to the statements of the principles of law applied to the legal problems raised by the material facts upon which the conclusion is based. The *ratio decidendi* shall be cited by a subsequent judge as an authority. Therefore, it must be an abstraction of the principle from the direct facts and arguments of the case.

The other statements of law are regarded as *obiter dicta* (*bo-ron*) and are not of binding authority but have only persuasive authority. Thus a statement of law either based on facts which are not found to be material or do not form the basis of the conclusion is regarded as an *obiter dictum*.

In Japan, however, the precedents even where they are the precedents of the Supreme Court, are not binding legally but are binding only in practice. As a matter of law, the lower courts may render a decision contrary to the precedents of the Supreme Court. Therefore, it is true that Japanese judges are not so deeply engaged in the laborious task of distinguishing between *ratio* and *dictum* as judges of common law countries.

Matsushita, M, *International Trade and Competition Law in Japan*, 1993, pp 27–32, 40–43, Oxford University Press

A. DIFFERENT KINDS OF INTERNATIONAL AGREEMENTS

In Japanese law, the most formal type of international agreements are treaties. Article 73(3) of the constitution declares that the Cabinet is vested with the power to conclude treaties with foreign nations. However, the Cabinet must obtain a prior, or if the circumstances demand, subsequent, approval of the National Diet when it concludes a treaty with a foreign nation. If an international agreement is a treaty, it enjoys, under Article 98(2) of the constitution, higher status than domestic laws. It is generally agreed that an international agreement is a treaty under Article 73(3) of the constitution if it affects the rights and obligations of private individuals in Japan. If, therefore, an international agreement contains provisions such as the restriction of an individual's conduct, it is a treaty and must be approved by the National Diet in order for it to have legal force domestically.

If an international agreement is concluded between the Japanese government and a foreign country but the agreement is not approved by the National Diet, then the agreement is regarded as an executive agreement. An executive agreement duly concluded by the Japanese government with a foreign country is part of the Japanese legal order and possesses a certain level of legal effect, even though the status and effect of an executive agreement is somewhat lower than those of a treaty. There will be a detailed discussion of the status and effect of treaties and executive agreements in a later section.

There are many types of international agreements to which the Japanese government is a party. They include: *johyaku* (treaty), *kyoyaku* (convention), *kyotei* (agreement), *torikime* (arrangement), *sengen* (declaration), *giteisho* (protocol), *ketteisho* (act), *kokanbunsho* (exchange of notes), *kokanshokan* (exchange of letters), and *oboegaki* (memorandum). Whether an agreement falls under the category of treaties as provided in Article 73(3) of the constitution or executive agreements depends on the substance of the agreement in question rather than the formal name for it.

Some important international trade agreements have been approved by the National Diet and are, therefore, international treaties. Prominent examples include the GATT, the IMF Treaty, and the World Bank Treaty. The Protocol of Terms of Accession of Japan to the GATT was drafted and signed on 7 June 1955 and approved by the National Diet on 29 July of the same year.

There is no need for an approval of the National Diet with regard to certain international trade agreements. They are: (1) an international agreement concerning technical details of diplomacy, (2) an international agreement concluded to provide for detailed rules of implementing a treaty that has already been approved by the National Diet, and (3) an international executive agreement within the scope of the powers authorized to the Cabinet by legislation.

Often the Executive Branch takes a relaxed interpretation of the requirement for obtaining approval of the National Diet and does not introduce international agreements into the National Diet for approval on the grounds that they belong to one or other of the categories mentioned above.

Also the Executive Branch takes a view that as long as an international agreement is not self-executing and requires domestic legislation to implement it, the Cabinet need not submit the agreement to the National Diet for approval since implementation takes place through domestic legislation enacted by the National Diet. In 1974, the United States and Japan entered into the United States-Japan Textile Agreement in which the Japanese government promised to impose a quantitative restriction on the export of textile products directed from Japan to the United States. The implementation of this agreement required the restriction of the export of textile products to the United States and, therefore, involved a restraint imposed on individuals' activities. However, this agreement was never submitted to the National Diet for approval.

Questions were posed by the opposition parties in the National Diet about why the agreement had not been submitted to the National Diet for approval. The Director General of the Cabinet Legislation Bureau answered the questions and stated that the agreement in question was no more than an executive agreement which did not directly impose obligations on private individuals and, therefore, there was no need to bring it before the National Diet. According to this rationale, the agreement would have no effects on Japanese exporters of textile products. However, in reality, the government invoked the export licensing requirement under the Control Law and imposed export restraint on the export of textile products to the United States. Again the rationale used by the government was that the government had been authorized by the Control Law to impose such restrictions.

B. TREATY-MAKING POWER

Treaty-Making Process

As stated earlier, the Cabinet has the power to conclude treaties with foreign nations under Article 73(3) of the constitution subject to the approval of the National Diet. In the language of Article 73(3), prior approval is required in principle and subsequent approval is permitted only exceptionally. In practice, however, international trade agreements are often submitted to the National Diet for approval subsequent to their conclusion. So far there have been eleven cases in which the Cabinet sought the subsequent approval of the National Diet including the Protocol of Terms of Accession of Japan to the GATT.

Under Article 61 of the constitution, in approving a treaty, the Lower House votes first, and, in cases of disagreement between the Lower House and the Upper House with regard to approving or not approving, the Lower House prevails.

As mentioned before, if an international agreement imposes restrictions on the rights and obligations of individuals, that is, if it changes an existing law, requires enactment of a new law, or abolishes an existing law, then it is necessary for the Cabinet to introduce it to the National Diet and obtain its approval.

Validity of a Treaty and Executive Agreement

The question of the validity of a treaty in Japanese law should be distinguished from that of the direct applicability. The question of validity is concerned with whether or not a treaty has the force of law in Japan whereas that of direct applicability is concerned with whether or not a treaty applies as a law without implementing legislation. Article 98(2) of the constitution declares: 'Treaties concluded by Japan and established laws of nations shall be faithfully observed.' This provision is couched in generalities and the exact content is not immediately clear. However, it states that the government and citizens are obligated to respect treaties. From this, it follows that treaties are part of Japanese law and have the force of law.

The natural interpretation is that an executive agreement also has the force of law under Article 98(2) of the constitution. This should be the correct interpretation of Article 98(2) which states that 'established laws of nations' shall be faithfully observed. Established laws of nations means customary international law and Article 98(2) requires that customary international law be faithfully observed. An executive agreement duly concluded by the Japanese government with a foreign nation should be at least equated with established customary international law which consists of cases, practices, understandings, and usages among nations. Compared with customary international law, an executive agreement provides for more formal and clear rights and obligations between the Japanese government and a foreign nation.

Direct Applicability of a Treaty

The question of whether or not treaties are directly applicable is separate from the question of their validity as discussed above. The validity question requires an inquiry into whether treaties are part of Japanese law and have the force of law in Japan. On the other hand, the question of direct applicability of treaties is that of whether treaties are self-executing or not. If a treaty is self-executing, then it can be applied without any implementing domestic legislation. However, if it is not self-executing, in order for it to be domestically applicable, it needs implementing domestic legislation.

Whether or not a treaty is self-executing is determined by the wording employed, the intent of the contracting parties, and the circumstances under which the treaty came into force. Generally speaking, it should be maintained that treaties are applicable as law in Japan since their observance is mandated by Article 98(2) of the constitution and, from this constitutional command, it can be inferred that treaties are applicable as law.

However, sometimes there are phrases in a treaty which can be interpreted as not having been intended to be self-executing. If so, the treaty in question should be held as not self-executing. A good example is the decision of the Supreme Court in the *Shiomi* case which was handed down in 1989. In this case, the petitioner was a disabled person who had been naturalized to Japan. She was born in Korea when Korea was part of Japan. Her naturalization took place in 1970. She applied for a welfare pension under the Welfare Pension Law which came into effect in 1959 but was denied for the reason that pensions could be granted only to Japanese citizens and when the law in question came into effect she was not a citizen of Japan. She argued that the International Covenant on Economic, Social, and Cultural Rights (ICESC), to which Japan was a party and which stated in Article 9: 'The State Parties ... recognize the right of everyone to social security', required the Japanese government to grant pension rights to her.

The Supreme Court rejected the argument of the petitioner on the ground that Article 2(1) of the Convention stated that the member states 'take steps with a view to achieving progressively the full realization of the rights ...'. This clause indicated that the Convention did not confer a right on individuals but merely imposed an obligation on the member states progressively to take steps to realize the content of the Convention.

In the ICESC, there were clauses which clearly stated that the member states were obligated progressively to take steps to realize the rights of individuals to social security. However, courts may rule that even an international agreement which contains no clear wording indicating that it is not self-executing has no direct applicability.

C. TREATIES AND DOMESTIC LAWS

An Overview

When the requirement under a treaty and that under a domestic law are in conflict, which prevails over the other? This question is directly related to that of the applicability of treaties, since no question arises as to whether a treaty or a domestic law prevails when they are in conflict if a treaty is not directly applicable because then there would be no clash between the two requirements or obligations to be reconciled. However if a treaty is directly applicable and provides for certain rights or obligations and if a law exists which carries conflicting rights and obligations, then one or the other should prevail.

Many commentators in Japan maintain that a treaty should override a conflicting domestic law. Among the reasons given by the commentators, that based on Article 98(2) of the constitution is probably the most important. Article 98(2) declares that treaties and the established laws of nations shall be faithfully observed. Under this article, treaties are given a special constitutional status as compared with regular domestic laws. From this constitutional provision, it follows that the National Diet is obligated to enact a law which would not conflict with the requirement of a treaty. If the National Diet did enact a law which conflicted with a treaty, then the legislation would be contrary to the constitutional requirement and should be overridden.

However, there is no court decision yet in which a domestic law which was in conflict with a treaty obligation was held invalid for that reason. In the *Jewellery Smuggling* case (1961), the Kobe District Court dealt with a violation of the Customs Law. A foreigner smuggled jewellery into Japan declaring that the jewellery he possessed was his 'personal effects' although in fact it was for sale in Japan. The court found him guilty of evasion of the Customs Law.

The defendant argued that Article 8(3) of the GATT, which stated that the Contracting Party shall not impose a penalty for minor breaches of customs regulations, restrained the Japanese government from imposing any penalty in this case. The court rejected the defence on the ground that the defendant's conduct was more than a minor offence. However, in referring to Article 98(2) of the constitution, the court stated: 'the principle of faithful observance of treaties ... is understood to proclaim superiority of treaties [over domestic law].'

...

D. TREATIES AND THE CONSTITUTION

An Overview (Two Schools of Thought)

The question here is whether the constitution is superior to treaties or the other way round. This question may look absurd. However, there have been some controversies with regard to this issue. In short, there are two schools of thought. One school, which may be termed 'the treaties supremacy school', holds that treaties are superior to provisions of the constitution. The school which may be termed 'the constitution supremacy school' maintains that the constitution is superior to treaties.

The treaties supremacy school was quite popular shortly after the Second World War and it brings up the following grounds for its validity. Article 98(1) of the constitution states the supremacy of the constitution over 'law, ordinance, imperial decree or other acts of the government' and that 'treaties' are not included in this wording. Article 98(2) of the constitution declares that treaties should be faithfully observed, and so if those two constitutional provisions are read together it would follow that treaties are superior to the provisions in the constitution. Article 81 of the constitution empowers the Supreme Court to review the constitutionality of 'law, order, regulation or official act', but here again treaties are not included. This school points out that the basic tenets of the constitution are 'internationalism' and that treaties which incorporate agreements and consensus should be regarded more highly than the constitution which incorporates only the consensus in one country.

On the other hand, the constitution supremacy school bases its beliefs on the following grounds. Article 81 of the constitution, which provides for the power of the Supreme Court to exercise judicial review on law, order, regulation, or official act, does not explicitly exclude treaties from its scope, and therefore there is reason to infer that treaties are included. Article 98(2) of the constitution, which declares the obligation faithfully to observe treaties, refers to the domestic legal order only. This may be taken to mean that treaties are supreme over domestic laws but it does not refer to the relationship between treaties and the constitution. Therefore, this provision does not necessarily exclude treaties from the scope of a judicial review to be exercised by the Supreme Court.

The treaty-making process is similar to the legislative process and, in this sense, treaties are equated with domestic laws. It follows, therefore, that treaties are subject to judicial review as much as regular domestic laws.

Also the amendment process of the constitution is much more stringent than the treaty-making process. In amending a provision of the constitution, there must be a National Diet initiative, approval by two-thirds or more votes of all members of the House of Representatives and the House of Councillors, and a referendum. On the other hand, a treaty can be made if the Cabinet concludes it with a foreign nation and the National Diet gives prior or subsequent approval to it – a much lighter requirement compared with the constitutional amendment.

If a treaty is given supremacy over the provisions of the constitution, then the requirement of a provision in the constitution can be *de facto* amended easily by concluding a treaty whose content is inconsistent with that of the constitutional provision without resorting to the constitutional amendment process provided for in the constitution. Important provisions in the constitution such as the basic human rights provisions could then be changed simply by making a treaty which denies them: an absurd proposition. The above is an outline of the arguments brought up by the school of thought which advocates the supremacy of the constitution over treaties.

The *Sunagawa* Case

There is no court decision yet in which a treaty was held void due to its conflict with the constitution. Nor is there any case in which a court exercised the power of judicial review over a treaty in light of the constitutional principles. However, the decision of the Supreme Court in the *Sunagawa* case is relevant here, and an account is made of this case below.

Based on the Security Treaty between the United States and Japan, the governments of both countries entered into the Administrative Agreement (the Status of Forces Agreement). To implement this agreement, the Japanese government enacted a law entitled the Criminal Special Measures Law which made it a criminal offence to trespass on the properties used by the United States Forces in Japan. There was an anti-American demonstration organized by a political group near the Sunagawa Air Base used by the United States Air Force, and some members of the demonstrating group broke into property used by the United States Air Force. They were arrested, tried under the Criminal Special Measures Law, and found guilty. An appeal was made by the defendants and the case was tried in the Supreme Court.

An argument was put forward by the defendants that the Security Treaty, which was the basis of the Administrative Agreement and the Criminal Special Measures Law, was contrary to Article 9 of the constitution, which renunciated war as a means of settling international disputes, and was void.

The Supreme Court held that it would not exercise its power of judicial review over the Security Treaty since this treaty was highly political in nature. Therefore, as far as the solution of this particular case was concerned, the Supreme Court relied on 'the political questions doctrine' and stated that the Supreme Court was barred from reviewing the treaty in light of its constitutionality. However, there is an important phrase in its decision which implied that the Supreme Court *would* in certain circumstances exercise its power of judicial review over the constitutionality of a treaty. It stated: 'The Security Treaty ... must be regarded as having a highly political nature. ... Consequently, the legal decision concerning its constitutionality has a character unsuitable in principle for review by the Supreme Court, *unless its unconstitutionality or invalidity is obvious'* (emphasis added).

It is generally understood that, in this decision, the Supreme Court admitted in the form of a dicta the possibility that a treaty could be reviewed regarding its unconstitutionality if its unconstitutionality or invalidity was obvious. What the circumstance is under which such a review can be made is not clear yet. This question is still open to future determination. However, this statement of the Supreme Court seems to reinforce the position of the constitution supremacy school as opposed to the Treaties supremacy school.

E. JUDICIAL REVIEW OF TREATIES

According to the preceding discussions, the Supreme Court and lower courts can exercise judicial review on treaties on certain occasions. Since in the judicial review process, treaties are equated with laws, the grounds for judicial review would be similar to those which are used in reviewing regular domestic laws. Generally speaking, therefore, courts examine whether provisions in a treaty violate constitutional principles. In the realm of economic regulation, the relevant constitutional principles include, *inter alia*, the freedom of business activities (Art 22(1)) and the guarantee of private property (Art 29). The same principles apply here as those which are applied when examining the relationship between the constitutional principles and domestic laws.

As we have already examined, there are two principles which have developed from previous Supreme Court decisions on this matter: when the domestic law in question is 'policy law type', then courts examine closely whether the law in question does not exceed the necessary minimum regulation and, if it does, courts do not hesitate to hold it as unconstitutional. On the other hand, if a law is 'policy law type', then courts in principle refrain from passing a judgment on the wisdom of the legislation and from holding it as unconstitutional, unless the law in question clearly provides an excessive control or the methods employed are unreasonable.

In treaties concerning international trade, it is possible to identify those two types of agreements. One of them is that type of international trade agreement in which measures based on socio-economic policies are incorporated and the other is where measures for public order, safety maintenance of health, and related matters are included. If a treaty belongs to the former type, then the scope for judicial review is rather limited, whereas courts can exercise wider powers on a treaty which incorporates measures of 'policy law type'.

II ADMINISTRATIVE GUIDANCE

Matsushita, M, *International Trade and Competition Law in Japan*, 1993, pp 59–73, Oxford University Press

Administrative Guidance

A. DEFINITION OF ADMINISTRATIVE GUIDANCE

... Although informal ways of carrying out government policies such as administrative guidance are not necessarily unique to Japan, the degree of pervasiveness and the importance of administrative guidance in the Japanese governmental process is probably unique to Japan. In Japan, economic regulations must ultimately be based on legislation as the source of their authority and legitimacy. However, government agencies in Japan often choose not to use laws directly to accomplish their policy goals but to utilize the more informal process of persuasion when they wish to control the conduct of private enterprises. This informal process of persuasion is often called 'administrative guidance'.

Administrative guidance is vague and flexible by its own nature, and, therefore, it is not easy to give a precise definition of administrative guidance. However, a high-ranking official of the Cabinet Legislation Bureau, when asked in the National Diet for the definition of administrative guidance, provided the following:

> [Administrative guidance] is not legal compulsion restricting the rights of individuals and imposing obligations on citizens. It is a request or guidance on the part of the government within the limit of the task and administrative responsibility of each agency as provided for in the establishment laws, asking for a specific action or inaction for the purpose of achieving some administrative objective through cooperation on the part of the parties who are the object of the administration.

The above statement is regarded as an official definition of administrative guidance by the Japanese government. Although this definition is abstract, hard to understand, and susceptible of different interpretations, it does contain several salient features in administrative guidance. (1) Compliance is voluntary. Administrative guidance is not a legal order with penalties for disobedience and, therefore, the party to whom it is addressed has the *legal* freedom of non-compliance. (2) Administrative guidance is a *de facto*, rather than *de jure*, directive issued by government officials and, even if an administrative guidance is issued, it does not make it automatically a legal order. (3) Administrative guidance should however, be distinguished from the personal conduct of government officials issuing it. It is often an expression of government policy of some kind. (4) In a broad sense, administrative guidance is a form of government regulation which imposes some kinds of rules of conduct on private individuals or enterprises. (5) Even though administrative guidance is informal and has no legally binding power, it is different from a request made by an individual to another individual. The relationship between the party requesting (the government) and the party to whom it is addressed is often not equal. In many cases, the government has more bargaining power, resources, and influence than the private individual or enterprise which has been made the object of administrative guidance. (6) In exercising administrative guidance to impose a rule of conduct on private enterprises, the government often represents the consensus of the industry in which the rule of conduct should be enforced. (7) Generally speaking, no precise procedure is required nor is a delineated scope defined. Often administrative guidance is made orally rather than in document form. (8) Administrative guidance is often used before a law is invoked in a situation when the government can invoke the law to impose discipline on the conduct in question. Used in this way, administrative guidance may be a preliminary stage of invoking a law.

B. TYPES OF ADMINISTRATIVE GUIDANCE

Administrative guidance can be classified into different types, among which the following three types seem to be most common: (1) promotional administrative guidance, (2) regulatory administrative guidance, and (3) adjudicatory or conciliatory administrative guidance.

Promotional Administrative Guidance

Often government agencies provide advice to enterprises in order to promote their business activities. In agriculture, the offices of the Ministry of Agriculture and of the prefectural governments operate governmental research institutes and disseminate agricultural technology produced by those institutes to farmers and, when necessary, officials give advice to farmers and assist them to improve production, storage, and processing of agricultural products.

Also, in small and medium enterprise areas, government agencies often render assistance to small enterprises to try to improve their production, management, transportation, research and development, and other matters. Often financial assistance through government financial institutions like the Medium and Small Enterprises Financial Bank, the Commerce and Industries Central Finance Bank, and the People's Bank is given. They issue loans at interest rates much lower than the market rates. Often government officials engage in advising the management personnel of small and medium enterprises, who have borrowed money from those institutions, how to improve their production and other business operations.

This type of administrative guidance can be called 'promotional' administrative guidance whose main function is to promote or protect enterprises or persons who are recipients of such advice.

Regulatory Administrative Guidance

Often government agencies use administrative guidance to regulate the conduct of enterprises and persons, and, when used in this way, it serves as a substitute for an order under law. There are many examples of administrative guidance of this type, particularly in the area of foreign trade, ie export and import controls. However, we will deal with examples of regulatory administrative guidance in export and import controls in a later chapter. Here we will limit ourselves to explaining regulatory administrative guidance in domestic regulation.

A well-known example is that of the *Sumitomo Metal* case in 1965, in which the MITI used administrative guidance to cut back production of steel. In 1965, there was an economic recession and there was a general agreement among the producers of steel to cut back production in order to avoid a further decline in prices. The MITI applied administrative guidance to the steel industry to reduce the amount of steel to a certain level. Most of the companies in the industry complied with this advice and agreed to reduce production. However, the Sumitomo Metal Company was dissatisfied with the quota of production which had been allocated to it and denied compliance.

In those days, the MITI had the power to allocate foreign currency to importers and, without such allocation it was impossible for the company to import the necessary coal and iron ore for production. The company stated that it would bring a legal action against the MITI if the MITI suspended its allocation of foreign currency.

The dispute was finally settled by a compromise between the company and the MITI to the effect that the company would comply with the MITI's request, with some reservations.

Another example is that of the *Price Control* case in 1973–74. In the year of the Oil Crisis prices in Japan sky-rocketed. The Cabinet decided to establish the price-reporting system in which each ministry would issue directives to enterprises producing products in its charge to report when they intended to raise prices. The ministries often pressured the enterprises to refrain from raising their prices or to reduce the level of price rises. Sometimes ministries set a maximum price above which enterprises could not raise their prices.

The government could have invoked the price control decree and fixed the price by law. However, the government decided not to use the price control order because of some questions about the interpretation of the order, and chose instead to use administrative guidance to deal with price hikes.

When used in this way, administrative guidance imposes rules of conduct on enterprises. As long as it is guidance, there is no compulsory power to enforce it in the event of non-compliance. However, government agencies try to utilize different types of persuasion techniques to secure compliance by enterprises.

There are several cases in which a regulatory administrative guidance caused the recipient enterprises to engage in collusive arrangements or cartels. There was an antitrust problem in those cases which will be touched on in a later chapter.

Adjudicatory Administrative Guidance

Government agencies sometimes use administrative guidance to help private enterprises settle disputes among themselves. Of course, legal disputes among enterprises must ultimately be settled by the courts. However, there are disputes which are not suitable for court proceedings and also there is a general desire among enterprises and among the public to avoid confrontation in the courts. For these and other reasons, there is a role for government agencies which belong to the Executive Branch to engage in dispute settlements.

A dispute between enterprises may have some impact on industrial policy matters too, and, in such a situation, the involvement of administrative agencies in mediating the dispute is probably justified as part of industrial policy.

Perhaps the best examples of the role of government agencies in dispute settlement are found in the solving of conflicts between large and small enterprises. As discussed in a later chapter, small and medium enterprises are given various types of protection and promotion due to their sheer number and their importance in the Japanese economy. However, because of a difference in scale of operations and in competitiveness between large and small enterprises, there are many conflicts and disputes between them when they are engaged in competition and also when they are in such transactional relationships as assemblers (like car manufacturers) and suppliers of parts and components (like subcontractors).

In the retail industry, there have been many disputes between supermarkets and small shopkeepers when a supermarket attempts to enter a local market. Small shopkeepers in the locality fear that their business will be seriously damaged when a larger supermarket enters the market. Similar disputes have arisen in the manufacturing and wholesale industries. For example, in some parts of the food industry such as bean curds and bean sprouts, the undertaking industry, and some light manufacturing industries which have been traditionally regarded as the areas for small and medium enterprises, disputes arise when large enterprises intend new entries.

There are several laws which are designed to deal with such problems. In the retail industry, the Large-Scale Retail Stores Law provides the mechanism for dispute settlements at the initiative of the government whereas, in the manufacturing and wholesale industries, it is the Medium and Small Business Areas Adjustment Law. Generally, in those laws, there is the provision for the government (in the form of the MITI and the prefectural governments) to issue recommendations to parties in dispute to come to terms. However, usually neither the MITI nor prefectural governments utilize this formal power for dispute settlement but engage in a more 'informal' persuasion. For example, the MITI or prefectural governments would informally urge a large supermarket intending to make a new entry into a local market to delay opening a new store or to reduce the floor space so as to mitigate its impact on the existing business of small retail stores in the locality.

In the above situations, the role of the government is that of an informal mediator, advising and suggesting to the parties in the controversy ways of resolving a dispute. This has proved to be effective and many disputes which the parties would never have solved themselves have been resolved without utilizing court proceedings.

C. LEGAL BASIS FOR ADMINISTRATIVE GUIDANCE

As explained earlier, administrative guidance is not a legal action and has no legally binding effect on the party to whom it is addressed. However, administrative guidance is sometimes based on a provision in a law. Sometimes it is authorized by a specific clause in a law and sometimes no such legal basis is found. As noted earlier, even though a law authorizes a government agency to engage in administrative guidance in the form of 'recommendation' and 'warning', the government agency often chooses not to utilize this power but engages in *de facto* advice to the recipient party.

Administrative Guidance without a Specific Statutory Authorization

Sometimes government agencies engage in administrative guidance without any specific statutory authorization. The *Sumitomo Metal* case, to which reference has been made, is one such case. In such cases, there is no wording in law which authorizes government agencies to render administrative guidance. Government agencies, especially the MITI, have emphasized that administrative guidance is allowed by 'establishment law' even though there is no specific provision in the authorization law. For example, the Law to Establish the MITI gives general powers and responsibilities to the MITI to supervise specified industries. The law, however, contains no wording which unequivocally sets out the power to give administrative guidance.

Even though administrative guidance is not based on a specific provision in a law authorizing the agency, it creates little problem when it is promotional administrative guidance. In such situations, the recipients of the guidance have little reason to complain since the nature of such guidance is to give benefit to the recipient by promoting its business, providing financial assistance, and so on.

However, if regulatory administrative guidance is utilized without any specific authorization by law, then the validity of it may be questionable since one inevitable aspect of regulatory administrative guidance is to impose a restriction on conduct or prohibition of conduct on the receiving party and, therefore, to infringe upon the rights and freedom of individuals.

Administrative Guidance based on Specific Statutory Language

There are laws which contain a provision that a government agency can issue administrative guidance. The terms used in those laws to describe administrative guidance vary from one law to another. Terms such as 'recommendation' (*kankoku*), 'warning' (*keikoku*), are used. If administrative guidance is issued on the basis of one of these laws, the administrative guidance is a legal act even though there is no power to enforce it by penalty.

The Marine Transportation Law authorizes the Ministry of Transportation to issue a recommendation to enterprises engaged in the ocean freight business to take the necessary measures when it deems that cut-throat competition exists and the sound development of the industry is likely to be impaired. Such measures include agreements among enterprises to limit competition. As we have seen already, in the Petroleum Business Law, there is a provision which states that the MITI can establish the standard price at which the petroleum companies are expected to sell petroleum products. The standard price has no binding power over the companies and is, therefore, a recommendation by the government.

As we have touched upon already, the National Life Stabilization Emergency Measures Law authorizes the government in a state of emergency to set the standard price for commodities designated by the government. Here again, the standard price has no binding effect on enterprises which sell the commodities. Non-compliance incurs only the publication of the names of the non-complying parties. In the Architects Law, the Ministry of Construction is authorized to announce a standard for the fees which architects charge to their clients and recommend it to them.

Administrative Guidance Combined with Other Promotional or Regulatory Measures

Sometimes, administrative guidance is not based on a provision of law but is combined with other measures to ensure its effectiveness. The Medium and Small Business Modernization Promotion Law and the Agricultural Products Price Stabilization law, which respectively authorize the government agency in charge to give advice to enterprises or farmers with regard to improving their management and operations, provide for financial assistance combined with such advice.

More importantly, however, regulatory guidance may be combined with some legal or extra-legal measures to ensure their effectiveness. The *Sumitomo Metal* case is a case in point. As we have seen, the administrative guidance of the MITI was backed by the power of the MITI to allocate foreign currency to importers. There are many cases in which the MITI advised exporters to engage in 'voluntary export restraint' by way of administrative guidance with the compulsory power incorporated in law as the background. References will be made to those cases later.

In the Large-Scale Retail Stores Law, there is a provision which states that the agency in charge (the MITI or the prefectural government, as the case may be) can issue an order to a large supermarket entering the local market to delay the opening of the store or to reduce the floor space after the agency has issued advice to the same effect and the advice has not been complied with. There is a similar provision in the Medium and Small Business Areas Adjustment Law. In such cases, the agency is required to use administrative guidance in the form of 'advice' before invoking compulsion by law.

As noted earlier, the agency, in enforcing those laws, often does not utilize even the provision authorizing it to engage in administrative guidance but exercises a *de facto* administrative guidance. However, even in such a situation, the fact that the government can ultimately resort to the provision in law which would achieve the same purpose if the *de facto* guidance is not respected enhances the effectiveness of the administrative guidance since the agency can utilize it as a tacit threat to make the party comply.

D. EFFECTIVENESS OF ADMINISTRATIVE GUIDANCE

Although the effectiveness of administrative guidance has somewhat declined compared with some decades ago, it is still an important policy tool for the Japanese government. Our enquiry turns to the reasons why guidance is effective. The effectiveness of administrative guidance depends on the types of administrative guidance and the circumstances under which it is made. However, as a general proposition, we can state the following.

When the government engages in administrative guidance, it often reflects the consensus in the industry to which the guidance is applied. An example is, again, the *Sumitomo Metal* case. Administrative guidance is never effective if the industry which is the object of the guidance opposes it as a whole. An important task for the government officials who exercise administrative guidance is to engage in effective persuasion and to create a spirit of co-operation among the recipients of the guidance. Often ex-officials of the government are in key positions in companies or trade associations of the industry to which the guidance is applied and they may play a crucial role in it.

There is a strong desire among the business community to avoid confrontation with the government even if the business community feels that the administrative agency has acted without legal authority in exercising *de facto* control by way of administrative guidance. This somewhat 'submissive attitude' of business communities towards the government may be a factor which makes administrative guidance effective.

When administrative guidance is supported by public opinion as in the cases of price control during the intensive inflation in the Oil Crisis, government agencies often publicize the fact that guidance has not been complied with in the event of non-compliance. In such a case, the effect of publicity is utilized as a technique of control. To give one example, consumer centres attached to local governments receive complaints from consumers regarding defects in commodities, and, when they think those complaints are not frivolous, they advise the manufacturers or vendors of such defective products to replace them with new goods or else take other appropriate measures to remedy the situation. This advice is not compulsory. However, if this advice is not respected, this is publicized. This has a considerable effect, and, whenever such advice is given, companies usually comply with it without questioning the legal authority behind it.

In view of this, some laws authorize recommendations to be issued by the administrative agencies and provide for publication as the sanction for non-compliance with such recommendations. The Law against Hoarding and Unreasonable Speculation, the Land Utilization Planning Law, and the National Life Stabilization Emergency Measures Law, *inter alia,* all provide for advice to be given by the agencies in charge and for publication of the fact of non-compliance.

The wide range of powers possessed by some agencies may account for the effectiveness of administrative guidance. Although the legal powers of the MITI have declined in recent decades, it still has powers in areas such as international trade, safety and other standards, pollution control, mining and petroleum, electricity supply, gas supply, and industrial properties. The MOF has the power, *inter alia,* to control banking, securities, and insurance as well as to impose taxes. An enterprise with a wide range of operations (which is a feature of enterprises today) is likely to be affected by one or other of those powers possessed by the agency which has the supervisory authority over its activities. The enterprise which has been made the subject of administrative guidance takes into consideration possible consequences at present or in the future of ignoring the administrative guidance and generally judges that to comply with the guidance is a wise business policy.

In foreign trade, enterprises often need assistance from the government when faced with trade conflicts with other nations. For example, if Japanese enterprises are challenged in the United States on account of a violation of United States antitrust laws, they need the support of the Japanese government when they argue in a United States court that the activities in question have been imposed upon them by the government. Also, if Japanese enterprises are unduly discriminated against in a foreign country, the enterprises may wish to complain to the Japanese government and request appropriate action (such as a complaint to the GATT) on the part of the government. Therefore, it is a good policy for enterprises to keep a good relationship with the government and avoid any confrontation with it. This type of consideration may be another reason why administrative guidance has worked relatively well in Japan.

E. EVALUATION OF ADMINISTRATIVE GUIDANCE

In spite of what has been said above, it must be emphasized that administrative guidance is by no means sacrosanct. It is often effective only if it is based on a consensus within the industry as regards the reasonableness of the guidance. In other cases it is effective only if it is backed up by law. Indeed, the effectiveness of administrative guidance is, in a sense, proportionate to the powerfulness of the agency exercising it. In the postwar period when the economy had been badly shattered by the war, enterprises needed help and assistance from the government, and, under such circumstances, administrative guidance could be very effective. However, now that many enterprises have acquired economic power and independence, they may not need assistance from the government any more. In this situation, the effectiveness of administrative guidance tends to decline. It is probably accurate to say that the golden age of administrative guidance has passed or, at least, is passing.

Administrative guidance can be of great value both to the government and to citizens and enterprises, and there is nothing inherently sinister about it. Administrative guidance, generally speaking, is more flexible than the formal enforcement of law. In emergencies like the Oil Crisis of 1973, economic regulation by law may be too inflexible; it may take too long before a law is invoked, and the scope of a law may be too limited to cope with changing situations. In contrast to the enforcement of law, administrative guidance is much more flexible, and the response of the government to the situation is much more prompt. This should be regarded as the advantage of administrative guidance. Usually negotiations and persuasion are used before administrative guidance is invoked, and economic regulation is accomplished in a more amicable way than unilateral imposition of a legal order by the government which may create tension between the government and business.

However, the advantages of administrative guidance, viewed from a different angle, are also its shortcomings. The flexibility of administrative guidance may mean that its exercise is not circumscribed by any limits. Since, as explained before, administrative guidance can put irresistible pressure upon the addressee, the lack of a clearly defined area within which it can operate may lead to an arbitrary and capricious exercise of *de facto* governmental power and to infringement of individual rights.

Another shortcoming of administrative guidance is a lack of transparency of the process through which it is executed. In enforcement of a law, the procedures are usually provided for in the law, and everyone can see the process of enforcement. In administrative guidance, however, there is no clearly defined procedure, and even if a compromise is reached between the government and the enterprise which has received the administrative guidance, it may adversely affect the interests of outsiders, and yet there is no standard procedure through which they can raise their objections. Also the general public is deprived of the opportunity of knowing what is under consideration by the government and of participating in the formulation of policy.

In the Structural Impediments Initiative (the SII), a bilateral trade negotiation between the United States government and the Japanese government concluded in 1990, the Japanese government promised to improve the process of administrative guidance by using written documents instead of just oral presentations. The idea involved here is to increase the transparency of the process. Perhaps a law should be enacted which generally provides for the process which the government must utilize when using administrative guidance and in which the rights of third parties to know the contents of administrative guidance and make their views known to the party receiving the guidance and to the government too are fixed.

F. REMEDY AGAINST ADMINISTRATIVE GUIDANCE

By definition, administrative guidance is an informal act of the government and has no binding power on the person receiving it. As such, compliance with administrative guidance is voluntary. As long as administrative guidance remains in such a pure form and non-compliance incurs no legal or *de facto* disadvantage, there is no legal remedy to it. Nor is it necessary to provide a remedy since non-compliance incurs no consequence. As we have seen already, however, administrative guidance is often a substitute for the enforcement of law. Sometimes the receiving party has little choice but to comply with it. If used in this way, it has almost the same effect as an order by law; In such a circumstance, it would be unjust and unreasonable to deny the party to whom it has been applied any relief even though the party has been seriously disadvantaged by it.

Under the Administrative Cases Litigation Law and the State Redress Law, the party whose interest has been adversely affected by the act of a government official can respectively seek for a cancellation of the act in question or for the recovery of damages caused by it. Under both laws, there must be an action by a state official in the exercise of the official power of the government which has caused a hardship on the party to whom it has been applied before the party can seek for a cancellation of the action or for the recovery of damages. An administrative guidance is by definition advice of a government official issuing it compliance to which is voluntary for the party receiving it and, to that extent, a legal action in the above laws is not possible, since it is not regarded as an action in the exercise of official power of the government.

However, in exceptional situations, administrative guidance can be regarded as an act of an official in the course of exercising the official power of the government and, therefore, a remedy is available. A case in point is the decision in the *Model Gun* case decided by the Tokyo District Court. Involved in this case was the following set of facts.

A person intended to import a model gun (a toy gun) and sell it. He imported and sold it. The police decided that the model gun in question was a weapon whose importation and sale was prohibited by the Law to Control Weapons. The police could have invoked this law and prohibited the importation and sale of the gun. However, the police chose not to invoke an order by this law but utilized an administrative guidance requesting the party not to import and sell the gun. The police sent the records of the case to the Public Prosecutor's Office and the Prosecutor's Office decided to indict the person for illegal importation and sale of a weapon.

The case was tried by the Tokyo District Court. The court held the defendant not guilty since, after a series of experiments, the court had come to the conclusion that the model gun in question was not powerful enough to be classified as a weapon and, therefore, the importation and sale of the gun did not amount to an importation and sale of a weapon.

Meanwhile the person (the defendant in the criminal trial) went bankrupt and brought an action against the government (the police) on the basis of the State Redress Law. The plaintiff argued that the business of the plaintiff was wrongfully damaged by the administrative guidance which had been based on a wrong assumption that the model gun was a weapon.

The Tokyo District Court held that the plaintiff could not recover damages since the plaintiff must prove the malicious intent or negligence on the part of the government official whose conduct had been alleged to cause the damage and there was no proof in this case that the act of the government official (the police officer) was done with malicious intent or negligence.

The Tokyo District Court, however, noted in a *dictum* that the administrative guidance in this case was an act in the course of exercising the official power of the government; that is to say, the administrative guidance in this case was a substitute of an official act in the from of legal order. This means that the court characterized the administrative guidance in the case in question as an official act of the government subject to the State Redress Law even if the guidance involved in this case was not an order by law at least as far as the form of it was concerned.

Judging from this case, we can conclude that a remedy in the form of recovery of damage caused by an administrative guidance is available under some specific circumstances. However, this is a limitation to such a remedy. First, in the *Model Gun* case, the administrative guidance was used in lieu of invoking a law when the administrative agency could have invoked the law to prohibit it. In this type of situation, there is a high degree of likelihood that there would be a legal action by the agency if the administrative guidance was not complied with.

As we have seen already, however, administrative guidance is often exercised without any law which would accomplish the same purpose. Often administrative guidance is merely informal advice from the agency. It may indeed have a *de facto* coercive impact on the party to whom it is applied. For example, a subsidy to a person may be withheld if the guidance is rejected by that person. This prospect of withholding a subsidy may be a strong incentive for the party to whom the guidance is applied to obey it. If a causal linkage is established between the rejection of the guidance and the withholding of the subsidy, it is possible for the person to bring a legal action utilizing the rationale stated by the Tokyo District Court in the *Model Gun* case under the State Redress Law that the guidance in question is an exercise of the official power of the government. Often, however, it is hard (or impossible) to establish that linkage and, as long as no such linkage is established, the administrative guidance is nothing but an informal admonition by the government no matter how strong a pressure it may have exerted in actuality, and is not subject to a legal remedy.

Furthermore, administrative guidance is often issued orally. For example, a government official merely announces the content of administrative guidance in a private meeting. In such a case, it is hard to prove that there was an administrative guidance.

Recently there have been growing criticisms against excessive use of administrative guidance. As we have touched upon already, one such example is the Structural

Impediments Initiative negotiated between the United States government and the Japanese government. The United States government raised an objection to administrative guidance to the effect that, because of its informality, it lacks transparency, and may lead to an infringement of the due process of law. The Japanese government promised to put administrative guidance in writing, to secure transparency.

In sum, administrative guidance is still a useful tool for the government to use for the variety of reasons mentioned above. However, it is perhaps necessary to bring in a little more 'legalism' in the process. To put it in writing in principle is an improvement in this respect since it increases transparency. It is also necessary to enact a law which establishes some rules for administrative guidance in general, such as the opportunity of third parties to be heard and the remedy which would be available. In Japan, there is no such law as the Administrative Procedure Act in the United States which provides general rules for actions by the United States government. Perhaps there is need for a law of this nature in which some rules on administrative guidance can be incorporated, such as those which require the government agency to publish administrative guidance to guarantee opportunities for third parties to participate in the process in some ways, including presenting their views on it and also to provide some procedure for remedy when the party which has been made the subject of administrative guidance is unreasonably disadvantaged.

Yamanouchi, K, 'Administrative Guidance and the Rule of Law' (1974) 7 *Law in Japan* 27–31

... the common view of scholars is that administrative guidance does not require a basis in an express statutory provision, and, even if there is no basis in an express statutory provision, administrative guidance may be effected. If one gathers the important elements of the scholarly theories, they are as follows:

(1) Professor Ogawa states the following: 'It is true that a problem of the kind you indicated exists, and, as I previously briefly suggested, there is the problem that a statutory basis in some form is probably necessary for taking these kinds of measures, whether they be administrative disposition or recommendation. In such event, there remains a problem as to whether [the requirement of] a statutory basis should be limited to cases expressly authorized by a specific law or ordinance. As Professor Narita said, the subjects for administration are changing minute by minute, and, if responsibility as an administrative agency must be discharged under these circumstances, there will probably be many cases in which the statutory measures will be inadequate to deal with the ever-changing situation. Speaking only from the standpoint of logic, it may be thought that it would be best if legislative measures are utilized. However, legislative measures cannot be adopted with that kind of ease, and, if individual legislative measures are adopted, the problem that the government cannot catch up nevertheless remains. Therefore, in present-day legal systems, in the event that an unforeseen problem appears, the question arises as to whether the administrative agency should refuse to deal with it saying that it bears no responsibility to the Diet or to the people because there is no way of handling it as a matter of law, or whether, as an administrative agency carrying out its responsibility to the Diet and the people, it can, and must, take the necessary measures to the extent that there is no conflict with existing laws and regulations.'

(2) Professor Narita states the following: 'Since, for the reasons already stated, I do not take the position that the activity of public administration abides totally by the 'reservation of law' (*horitsu no ryuho*) principle and that administrative authority should be authority undertaken only for enforcement of laws in the strict sense, I believe that administrative agencies, in effecting administrative guidance, do not, as a theoretical matter, require the authority of a specific law in the form of an express basic standard. Also, from the standpoint of reality, as long as there are reasons which affirm the existence of and necessity for administrative guidance, in cases in which there is no basis in an express provision of law, it does not conform to reality just to look on without taking any action regardless of what kind of situation arises. The establishment of standards and procedures may be a different matter, but the mere enactment of provisions to the effect that guidance, advice or recommendations can be given has very little meaning.' ...

Opposing this common view, there is a small minority opinion which holds that a statutory basis is necessary. The following assertion by Professor Yoshihiro Murakami is one example: 'A claim is sometimes made that, by virtue of the fact that administrative guidance takes as its premise the subjective intent of the recipient party, it is not necessary to think strictly (ie to require a statutory basis), but, as is seen from the example that I gave and from various other concrete cases, the more the scope of administrative action in the people's daily life is expanded, the greater is the concern regarding the damage which may be inflicted by administrative agencies in cases where guidance is not followed. Compliance or noncompliance is not something that can be readily determined by the people's free will. Moreover, how much resistance can be expected to guidance which is given by leaders who believe that they are able to comprehend even providence in the heavens, to say nothing of the national benefit and the public benefit, from the people, who have been familiar with this type of administrative system?' ...

The government's opinion naturally accords with the common view. This is made clear by the answer to a question of House of Representatives member, Mr Kazunori Tamaki. Mr Tamaki in his questions to the government takes the following position – 'The government, with a view to price controls, is considering setting prices through administrative guidance, but I don't think one can help but deny the legality thereof.' In response, it was stated that 'Since so-called administrative guidance does not have the coercive force of law in limiting the rights of the people or imposing obligations on the people, and it is carried out with the voluntary cooperation of the recipients in the performance by the administrative agencies of the functions given to them under their respective establishment laws and within the limits thereof, a problem of violation of law does not arise.' (Written reply to the questions concerning setting of prices through administrative guidance posed by representative Kazutoku Tamaoki, dated 22 March 1974.)

There are two reasons why the common view maintains that administrative guidance does not require a statutory basis. The first and principal reason is seen in the fact that administrative guidance is not accompanied by compulsion and that whether or not to follow it is completely up to the discretion of the recipient party. The second reason, which is based on the actual situation, is that if a statutory basis is required, administration could not cope with the constant changes.

I have the following criticism of the common view:

(1) First of all, apart from administrative guidance by request or factual precedent recommendation, with regard to general administrative guidance by official authority,

although whether or not it is followed is up to the discretion of the recipient party, this discretion exists only from a legal point of view. From a factual point of view, a constraint is exerted upon the discretion of the recipient, with the above-mentioned restrictive measures and encouraging measures as a background. Accordingly, administrative guidance – even if the substance thereof is objectively appropriate – must be viewed as having as one aspect intervention in the life of the recipient, and, if one focuses upon this aspect, I think that it may well be possible to believe that administrative guidance requires a statutory basis. I think that the fact that the common view maintains that because there is no compulsion in administrative guidance a statutory basis is not required adheres to the theory of *shingai ryuho* developed under the constitutional monarchy of the past and gives rise to the criticism that it is not something that is contemplated by the rule of law under the Japanese constitution.

(2) With regard to the second reason, which is based on the 'actual situation,' I would like to state that, as Professor Ogawa recognizes, 'there will be no difficulty whatsoever in having legislative measures enacted.' Some may say that it does not accord with the actual situation to require a statutory basis. I think that the situation is the same in the case of authoritative acts that are accompanied by coercive force (which require a statutory basis).

(3) It is needless to state that to require a statutory basis is more faithful to the concept of popular sovereignty.

Dean, M, 'Administrative Guidance in Japanese Law: A Threat to the Rule of Law' (1991) *Journal of Business Law* 398–99, 401–03

The Iraqi invasion of Kuwait resulted, amongst other things, in the freezing of Iraqi and Kuwaiti assets by the United States, Britain and other European Community countries. Japan, whilst declaring its support for such action claimed that the Government 'lacked a clear legal framework for imposing sanctions'. However, the Government did issue 'administrative guidance' preventing Iraq from withdrawing Kuwaiti assets from Japan. This took the form of a request to banks and securities companies to freeze Kuwait Government accounts. No further action was taken by Japan until the UN Security Council acted; only then did the Government announce full economic sanctions against Iraq and Kuwait in the form of a trade embargo and suspension of capital transactions, plus the freezing of aid to Iraq.

Whilst irritating the international community by apparent prevarication, the chain of events was a typical Japanese manoevre and illustrated the subtle and effective way in which the Government has power to control and regulate economic activity as well as its political position. It is, therefore, important to understand that apart from the basic laws and regulations governing business transactions, there is what some consider to be the secret weapon of the Japanese economic miracle ... administrative guidance (*gyosei-shido*). At best it can be seen as the triumph of expediency over principle, at worst it is economic protectionism as a form of national security ...

...

Statutory authority for administrative guidance in so far as it does exist really only provides the power to act. In strict legal terms a business cannot be compelled to abide by the guidance, neither can it be punished directly by the imposition of a statutory penalty. It is a system of voluntary co-operation in which the addressee is urged to – and invariably does co-operate. To understand how seemingly independent and powerful organisations are willing to follow such guidance is in part to understand the tight web of relationships binding politicians, bureaucrats and businessmen that is uniquely Japanese. As the Recruit scandal illustrated, it is no longer a mere joke to say that in Japan the businessmen control the politicians who control the bureaucrats who control the businessmen! This well established yet informal power relationship consists of an elaborate network of personal connections through which the triangle of economic power holders control internal and external policy. Thus the administrative and legal informality of administrative guidance derives its coercive power from governmental and administrative control over trade, foreign exchange and loan funds. Put simply, failure to comply could result in import quotas for raw materials being reduced, long term government financing for expansion being denied, or in the case of a foreign company, employees' visas being withheld. Alternatively, compliance can be rewarded by participation in government approved activities and loan funds being made available at favourable rates. It is a system of achieving indirectly that for which no direct legal power exists. A number of incidents serve to illustrate how the system works, often with devastating consequences ...

...

One recent and worrying example of its use was in the October 1989 stock market crash. The Ministry of Finance issued administrative guidance to all the banks involved in the United Airline's leveraged buyout deal. Japanese banks were known to have reservations about leveraged buyouts and that combined with administrative guidance from MOF on the particular deal was enough for the institutions to act. Whilst it is arguable that the extent of the effect on the markets of withdrawing from one deal could not have been foreseen and some would say it resulted in a timely re-adjustment of the markets, nevertheless it is of concern that administrative guidance can be used to such effect.

At about the same time a series of syndicated loans to China failed because Japanese banks refused to participate. Whereas they would normally have been keen to be involved in such deals, since 4 June 1989, the banks had been required to obtain 'approval.' In reality what this meant was that the Government had taken a particular stance since the Beijing massacre and issued administrative guidance to the banks concerning business with China. The result was that Japanese banks refused to approve lending to China thereby providing a simple and effective way of pursuing political ends through economic means.

More recently it was noted in Spring 1990 that Japan's institutional investors had altered their investment strategy in relation to United States Treasury Securities. During the third week of April, Japanese investors had been large sellers of all foreign bonds following a rumour of a Government directive: in particular the United States Treasuries Market collapsed over three-and-a-half points during the period. The following week, Dai-ichi Mutual Life Insurance, the second largest life assurance company in Japan, announced that it would be reducing expected purchase levels in the May United States Treasury auction. This was seen as clear confirmation that MOF was putting pressure on life insurance companies and institutional investors by means of administrative guidance in order to strengthen the yen against the dollar.

The new international standing of Japan's financial institutions has given renewed power to MOF; in their hands administration guidance can be used as a tool of economic power and to devastating effect. In a different situation and used by another ministry, administrative guidance is used to pursue political aims. Thus in November 1989 when Mr Yakolev of the Soviet Politburo visited Tokyo he was met with a blank refusal to discuss Japanese involvement in developing Siberia until the disputed Kuril Islands are returned to Japan. Behind this firm political stand by the Japanese was the fact that the relevant ministries had issued guidance advising against participation in joint ventures with Soviet companies and nobody has forgotten the Sumitomo incident!

The freezing of Iraqi and Kuwaiti assets in August 1990 is the most recent example of how administrative guidance can be used either as a tool or pure economic management, or as an economic adjunct to a political position. Whilst the debate as to the exact legal basis or characterisation of administrative guidance continues, it is interesting to note that its use in the initial move toward full sanctions against Iraq was justified precisely because a 'clear legal framework' for such action was said not to exist. Yet the use of administrative guidance in that situation was as effective as it was face-saving; protecting Japan's economic interests not least the Japanese operated Khafgi oil field, whilst maintaining its position in the international arena and moving cautiously toward full economic sanctions with other world powers. It also provided an insight into the tension and competing interests of various ministries. On the one hand there was MITI trying to protect Japanese business interests and opposed to sanctions which would damage exports, limit essential oil imports and jeopardise repayment of loans made to Iraq. On the other hand, the Foreign Ministry had to balance the consequences of not falling in line with world-wide condemnation, particularly remembering the political damage done when Japan was accused of breaking the 1979 sanctions against Iran. The issuing of administrative guidance in this situation was therefore a small victory for the Foreign Ministry whose spokesman added that 'there had been an evolution in the national consciousness and Japanese people seemed more prepared now to accept the risk of some economic damage in the cause of securing peace'.

The threat of the rule of law

At the heart of the issue of administrative guidance is the question of direct intervention in economic development. On the one hand it is possible to argue that administrative guidance is an example of effective government intervention in economic management; on the other hand it can be seen as a model of successful limited government action. Whichever view is subscribed to, it remains a fact that, as the 1981 survey by the Administrative Management Agency found, informal administrative guidance is the preferred administrative regulatory tool in both local and national government.

Shindo, M, 'Administrative Guidance: Securities Scandals Resulting from Administrative Guidelines' (1992) 20 *Japanese Economic Studies* 76–78, 81–86

There is room for all sorts of discussion regarding when it was that administrative guidance became an effective means of influencing industry and the economy. Chalmers Johnson, who wrote *MITI and the Japanese Miracle,* believes that 'administrative guidance became a salient feature of the Japanese government-business relationship only in the context of trade liberalization and MITI's failure to provide a new legal basis for its guidance activities' (p 273). (The legal basis here refers to the Special Measures Law for Promotion of Designated Industries.) Johnson cites the sixties as being the time when this took place.

While the conditions that Johnson describes cannot be overlooked, administrative guidance has been an important means of administering the economy and industry since the period of postwar economic revival. In the fifties, the government streamlined such important industries as steel and machinery while fostering the development of new ones such as the petrochemical and automobile industries by granting preferential fiscal, finance, and tax treatment. In order to regulate supply and demand during recessionary periods, administrative guidance was used to advise curtailment of operations and capital expenditure and as a measure to freeze inventories. Then, during the sixties, in order to develop the heavy and chemical industries, there were guidelines to regulate supply and demand and administrative guidance was used to establish joint ventures between corporations. Three Mitsubishi firms were regrouped into Mitsubishi Heavy Industries, and mergers of Nissan and Prince and of Yawata and Fuji Iron and Steel Works took place. In the seventies, Japan's industrial makeup was modified to be more knowledge-intensive and energy-efficient under guidelines known as the 'Planned Market Economy Model' (May 1971, Industrial Structure Council). Administrative guidance was the principal method used here as well.

Administrative guidelines, which were inseparable from this industrial administration, were acclaimed as a 'light-handed administrative method', not only among bureaucrats, but in some academic circles as well. But for whom was it light-handed and in what sense? Judging From the disgruntled reaction of the securities-firm executives after the scandal broke, one could imagine how it must have been for the securities firms to propose and execute business strategies that kept in line with a legally powerless Securities Bureau. In other words, the companies would get the necessary official certification from the supervisory agency according to each set of circumstances. This is not unique to the securities industry. Nearly all of Japan's basic industries operate using such official certification.

From a corporate point of view, the benefit from such a system would be significant. If, for example, corporate activities were always controlled using literal readings of every public law, then the flexibility of corporate activities would be necessarily restricted. Administrative protection would be preferable even if the system limits competition. At the same time, this point, which is advantageous to the corporation, is also good for the supervisory agency. If industrial reform is sought by making changes in the legal statutes, then the heavy administrative and political costs of amending laws in the Diet must be paid. It goes without saying that it would obey official certification.

I hasten to add, however, that this mutual 'enjoyment of advantage' for the supervisory agency and the industry is based on private discussions of which no public record is generally made. Though ostensibly 'for the good of the public', a perspective that emphasizes the narrow aims of two parties would necessarily fail to have far-reaching effects on society and the economy. This is only exacerbated by the fact that the citizens of Japan have no way of knowing what was actually discussed and agreed on even with the Diet and the media trying to supervise things more closely.

Secrecy of this kind is not entirely advantageous to a corporation. Since the firm 'voluntarily' has complied with the confidentially disclosed intention of a government agency, an unexpected change in the government agency's thinking would leave nothing to the firm on which it can base the 'appropriateness' of the earlier activity. You could therefore say that the company's awareness of the possibility of trouble like this sort could make them even more dependent on bureaucrats.

So then, why is it that this kind of system developed between the bureaucracy and industry? It is not sufficient to claim that administrative guidance brought it about. It is necessary to analyze closely Japan's administration, as well as its political and industrial organization, which make administrative guidance possible. That is one of the themes discussed throughout this book. Let us say that administrative guidance is one important key to understanding the cooperative spirit between Japan's government and industry ...

...

... Administrative guidance, now acquiring international currency as *'Gyosei shido'*, was evaluated in a positive light after the first oil shock among foreign economists and political scientists familiar with the term.

For instance, in EF Vogel's *Japan as Number One*, 1978, Harvard University Press, Japanese-style management and Japanese-style industrial policy, now considered terrible customs or systems that should be dismantled, were evaluated surprisingly highly. Vogel states: 'Whatever the issue, MITI officials do not approach their task legalistically. Their view is that rapidly changing conditions require the most adjustment to individual predilections and special circumstances than is permitted by relying on legal precedent' (p 78). Vogel states further that administrative guidance is an excellent method for effecting policy. He goes on to say that the United States should learn administrative guidance in order to develop industries that can compete in international markets.

In addition to Vogel, other comparatively young American political scientists in the late seventies and early eighties were involved with studies of MITI or industrial policy from a supportive perspective. With such favorable evaluations coming in from abroad, there was much discussion about the suitability of Japanese-style management and historical Japanese social customs for the rest of the world. One representative work would be Seizaburó Sato *et al*, *The Society as Civilization* (Chuo Koron, 1979).

Now, however, there are almost no favorable evaluations of a relationship between government and industry centering on administrative guidance. This became especially pronounced toward the end of the eighties when the so-called reformists and the Inaccessibility theory gained ground. In *The Enigma of Japanese Power* (Knopf, 1989), K van Wolferen believed that administrative guidelines were essentially a type of bureaucratic pressure or threat and says the following: '"Administrative guidance" is effective because of the leverage bureaucrats have over businesses. The power to withhold licenses is an obvious one. Government officials are responsible for approval of applications for almost every conceivable business activity. If they do not like an applicant, for whatever reason, they can hold off a decision on that person's applications. Although there is no legal obligation for a business to abide by the guidance, all abide by it simply because they want to continue to function. This is one of the keys to Japanese bureaucratic control. Official theory notwithstanding, administrative guidance is compulsory' (p 450).

Van Wolferen's comments on administrative guidance may sound a bit overstated in places, but international attitude toward and understanding of administrative guidance, as well as the relationship between Japan's bureaucracy and economy, are changing at a rapid pace. We Japanese must remain open-minded regarding these changes and criticism. Not only must we respond to foreign criticism, we must actively and voluntarily change this vague system and reform the broad range of inequities of the sort witnessed between the public and private sectors during the securities scandal.

The broadening base of administrative guidance

However you define the term administrative guidance, the central theme of the argument for administrative guidance is unquestionably that it evolved around the bureaucracy's influence on the business community. The principal consideration of this book is that of guidance employed in the administration of industry and the economy. Today, however, it is not only between the business community and bureaucracy that administrative guidance is developing. It is becoming the principal means of enacting policies in at least the two following areas as well.

One is the administrative guidance between the central government and municipalities. One of the best-known examples of the eighties was when the Ministry of Home Affairs suggested the lowering of the salaries of municipal employees and organizational and staff cuts of principal governments. The Ministry of Home Affairs issued guidelines for lowering the salaries of municipal employees to the levels of national civil servants based on the Laspeyres index. Models of the staff structure by type of municipality were created and, based on them, guidelines were made for rationalizing the municipal administrative system staff. The Ministry of Home Affairs is not the only central government agency that makes such guidelines for municipal bodies. The Ministry of Education makes them for municipal educational committees. One representative example is the 'National Anthem/Flag-Raising' guidelines. Also, although they work through huge profit-seeking collectives called agricultural groups, the 'Rice-Planting Adjustment and Acreage Reduction' program of the Ministry of Agriculture, Forestry, and Fisheries could be classified as administrative guidance between the central government and a self-governing body. This is because the Ministry of Agriculture, Forestry, and Fisheries gives prefectures very specific guidelines concerning rice-planting adjustment and then entrusts them with their execution.

Another example is the administrative guidance being developed by municipalities as 'Guidance Through Guidelines' (*Yoho gyosei*). Municipalities established 'General Guidelines for Housing and Development' during the late sixties and early seventies when faced with chaotic housing land development. They asked developers to pay a fee to provide for orderly development and urban maintenance. At the time, this was sometimes called 'administration without authority,' but what it amounted to was a collection of administrative desires covering extralegal areas. Developers were asked to voluntarily follow them. Such guidelines, started to organize housing land development, have covered a wide range of areas, including the preservation of the natural landscape, sunlight regulations, reduction of radiowave interference, golf course development, and insecticide use. Some legal experts are critical of such generalized administration, feeling that the practice has no legal basis.

The themes and organization of this book

The main focus of discussions on administrative guidance, principally from specialists of administrative law, has been on where the concept of administrative guidance fits into the system of legal thought, and how administrative guidance can be legally regulated. But there is no universally accepted view on, say, the concept of administrative guidance. While specialists of administrative law expect political science or policy science for its analysis, current thought in both fields says only that administrative guidance is an effective means for enacting policy and little has been done to clarify things further. In this way, administrative guidance has not yet moved beyond being an idiomatic expression or a vaguely described notion.

I will consider in detail the specialists' conceptual definition of administrative guidance in the first chapter, but keeping within its generally accepted definition, administrative guidance is not an administrative method that relies on the application of laws to achieve its objectives. For this reason, it is generally accepted that there is no authoritative relationship of command and compliance between the guiding and guided organizations. Just as the word *guidance* suggests, an administrative organization indicates a specific direction and then does no more than wait for a freely chosen and voluntary response and action.

This sort of administrative guidance 'discussion' owes much to Shuzo Hayashi (former director of the Cabinet Legislation Bureau), who gave it such conceptual definition. Mr Hayashi stated that administrative guidance was 'generally not the invocation or application of a law to give orders by force to specific individuals, corporations, or groups or to provide legally enforceable guidance, advice, or counsel to them on matters within its administrative area. It is rather the expression of not legally enforcing hopes or desires on specific individuals, corporations, or groups, and rather encouraging their realization ('Concerning So-Called Administrative Guidance', *Gyosei to Keiei* [Administration and management], No 4 [1962]). I have taken the liberty of outlining that part of Mr Hayashi's conceptual definition that mentions the administrative body's discussion or negotiation with, and persuasion of, a particular party.

But there is the question of what the intended limits of these 'hopes' or 'desires' expressed by the administrative body are. There are many examples, such as a traffic accident prevention campaign, where an administrative body offers a type of administrative guidance by making its intent known to an unspecified group, but the most controversial point in the discussion of administrative guidance is when the administration's 'hopes' or 'desires' are directed toward specific groups and specific activities. In that case, the content of that sort of notification of intent must be considered. In order to consider administrative guidance beyond a simple vaguely described notion or idiomatic expression, the range of activities to be included in administrative guidance must be specified.

One must also consider why these 'hopes' and 'desires' so often yield results. Earlier, in the section on securities scandals, I suggested that there were several 'advantages' to activities having an administrative body's 'official certification'. Even if there are such advantages in embracing administrative guidelines, however, it is necessary to consider what is behind these activities in order to contemplate administrative guidance beyond its being an idiomatic expression or vaguely described notion. Explaining this as being a psychological phenomenon unique to Japan's paternalism, vertical society, or interdependence is tantamount to saying nothing about its effectiveness. In the same way, describing administrative guidance as a fear of bureaucratic threats, as K van Wolferen did, is also highly inadequate. I want to believe that some sort of sanctions are possible when administrative guidance is not followed. Or that there is guidance that imposes sanctions. But before 'interdependence' or 'fear of sanctions', we must consider the relationship between the guiding and guided, as well as their respective psychology and thought, as preconditions to effective administrative guidance.

There is a danger that the expression 'administrative guidance' will become something of a 'curse word,' as the term receives more and more negative press. It is easy to cry 'administrative guidance' and criticize Japan's administration, but not only does that accomplish nothing in clarifying what it is, it also fails to specify any policies necessary for reform. It is precisely because international and domestic criticism is increasing that greater consideration is necessary.

Young, M, 'Judicial Review of Administrative Guidance: Governmentally Encouraged Consensual Dispute Resolution in Japan' (1984) 84 *Columbia Law Review* 926–31, 935–41, 953–59, 982–83

1. THE PRINCIPAL BUREAUCRATIC BEHAVIOR IN JAPAN: ADMINISTRATIVE GUIDANCE

A. Characteristics of Administrative Guidance

Administrative guidance (*gyosei shido*) is a common Japanese regulatory technique that, although generally nonbinding, seeks to conform the behavior of regulated parties to broad administrative goals. Two examples of administrative guidance clarify its scope. The first of these developed during late 1980 and early 1981, when the dispute between Japan and the United States over the import of Japanese automobiles reached crisis proportions. Threatened with the possibility of executive and legislative action restricting Japanese auto imports into the United States, the Japanese government agreed, in what is euphemistically known as an 'Orderly Marketing Agreement,' to restrict automobile imports 'voluntarily' for a three-year period. To implement this agreement, the principal ministry dealing with trade matters, the Ministry of International Trade and Industry (MITI), informed auto manufacturers that during each of the next three years they were to limit exports of passenger cars to the United States. In its notification letter, the MITI found authority for this action in its enabling legislation and in Article 48 of the Foreign Exchange and Foreign Trade Control Law (FEFTCL). To assure compliance, the MITI required each manufacturer to submit periodic reports on car exports. Falsification of such reports would be considered a violation of the reporting requirements under Article 67 of the FEFTCL and would subject firms to liability for punishment under Articles 72 and 73 of that same law.

The MITI also indicated that if any company threatened to exceed its export allotment, the Government would amend the Export Trade Control Order to subject car exports to the United States to export licensing, in accordance with Article 48 of the FEFTCL. The MITI would then be able to seek sanctions against any noncomplying company under Article 70 of the FEFTCL.

Another interesting, important and, at least within Japan, well-known example of administrative guidance involves local governments' attempts at land use planning. During the postwar period, Japan experienced tremendous urban growth, much of it concentrated in the Tokyo metropolitan area, where almost one-quarter of Japan's population resides. This rapid urban development seriously undermined the general living environment and placed tremendous strains on the ability of the government to provide adequate services.

While the national government undertook reasonably successful efforts to solve serious air pollution problems in Tokyo, additional concerns surfaced in the late sixties that were not directly addressed at the national level. Two areas became the particular focus of residents' energies. First, concerned parents began to focus on the dislocations this rapid urban development caused in the schools. To a large degree, education is the key to an individual's future in Japan. Even the slightest diminution in education opportunity evokes great concern. The strain placed on the school systems during this period threatened the quality of educational opportunities and parents were quick to demand solutions.

Second, residents became increasingly concerned about the effect of highrise buildings on ventilation and sunlight. This concern might strike Americans as odd, but

Japan's climate, especially the high humidity of the Tokyo area, and the relatively late advent of air-conditioning and central heating, elevated sunlight and air above mere aesthetic interest. To enhance ventilation, walls are thin, windows and doors large, and many rooms are cross-ventilated. Few dwelling places are without a small patio used for ventilation, drying laundry, and growing plants. To the growing alarm of residents, the construction of apartment buildings, even if only three stories high, undermined ventilation and its significant benefits. Moreover, while Japanese courts have created a right to sunlight (*Nisshoken*), thereby affording some minimal protection against undue interference, effective injunctive relief is rarely available and damages are usually low.

The national government addressed national standards for housing construction by adopting the Construction Standards Law. The Law establishes a basic construction permit process, requiring builders to submit a complex set of plans and blueprints to the construction supervisor, an employee of the local municipal government. The supervisor determines whether those plans conform to the requirements of the orders (*meirei*) and local ordinances (*jorei*) based upon it. Construction cannot lawfully proceed without a permit.

Despite this regulatory mechanism, the law attempts only to guarantee health and safety and not to assure the availability of adequate educational facilities or of sunlight and ventilation. Nothing expressly authorizes the construction supervisor to deny a permit because a building might block sunlight from surrounding buildings or because the increase in population resulting from the occupancy of the new building would put a strain on schools. Moreover, while the law allowed municipalities to establish additional building standards through local ordinances (*jorei*), no municipality enacted ordinances dealing with ventilation and local schools. Some commentators even doubted the legality of such ordinances, as they would arguably exceed the scope of the law. Indeed, given the specificity of the law's provisions, these regulations might directly conflict with it, a preemption problem. Moreover, while municipalities have a general mandate to enact local ordinances on matters within their jurisdictional ambit, direct, legally binding solutions – such as the requirement that developers donate land and money for the construction of educational facilities – would probably conflict with the takings clause of the Japanese constitution.

Despite these disabilities, local constituencies placed considerable pressure on local governments to safeguard education and ventilation. Local interest groups focused their energies on local solutions in part because they felt their needs and circumstances varied tremendously from area to area. The residential groups' resources would clearly be most effectively marshalled against the local – not national – government. Moreover, these groups refused to accept as an excuse for local-level nonaction the national government's failure to address their concerns adequately.

Municipalities initially responded to constituency pressure by urging national authorities either to undertake regulation of the incursions on sunlight and ventilation occasioned by housing construction, or to permit local regulation. The national authorities, however, were unresponsive and six concerned municipalities issued so-called 'guidelines', known more formally as Outline Guidance (*Yoko Shido*) ...

B. Prevalence of Administrative Guidance in Japan

Japanese administrative agencies turn to administrative guidance as the preferred regulatory technique with notable frequency. Administrative guidance enables agencies to avoid legal barriers such as constitutional prohibitions on action by statute and political difficulties such as local governments' inability to take action in certain areas. Administrative guidance further provides speed and flexibility. At the same time, administrative guidance is tolerable to regulated parties because they participate extensively in the formation of the regulation. The features of administrative guidance, essential to a strong administrative state, are consistent with Japan's historically activist approach to government.

1. *Enhancement of Bureaucratic Power Despite Legal Restrictions.* – While Japanese bureaucrats no doubt genuinely fear appearing too 'officious' and bureaucratic, a more plausible explanation for their enthusiasm for administrative guidance lies in its ability to extend regulatory activity beyond strictly legal limits. Because an agency exercising administrative guidance anticipates no direct legal enforcement, it is less constrained to base its regulatory activity on a specific statutory authorization. In the usual regulatory situation, the enforcing agency must demonstrate a clear statutory mandate in order to persuade the enforcement organ to marshal its resources against the regulated party. When the agency does not intend to seek direct legal enforcement, however, it need not pay the statute the same deference in defining the permissible scope of agency action.

Thus, in Japan, agencies frequently attempt to accomplish through administrative guidance what by most admissions they cannot achieve under the governing legal regime. Until very recently, for example, laws regulating drugs did not explicitly permit the government to force drug manufacturers to stop manufacturing and distributing drugs after permission was initially granted, even though subsequent data had proven them dangerous or capable of producing harmful side effects. The government has nevertheless continually taken the position, both in testimony before the Japanese parliament, or Diet, and in actual practice, that permission to manufacture a certain drug can be withdrawn in appropriate cases through administrative guidance. Evasion of possible legal limits also provided the motivation for instituting the Orderly Market Agreement regarding automobile exports and the Outline Guidance dealing with sunlight and ventilation.

Administrative guidance permits agencies to regulate not only beyond the limits of the law but also, on occasion, in direct contravention of the law. Such contravention is possible because any judicial inquiry into the propriety of the regulatory objectives will be limited. For example, during the oil crisis of 1973, the government strongly encouraged television stations to curtail late night broadcasts in an attempt to conserve energy. The government no doubt had the power to issue regulations regarding conservation of electricity. It is commonly suggested, however, that the measures directed against television stations took the form of administrative guidance because the government wanted to minimize the possibility of a direct legal challenge. Because these measures interfered with the editorial judgments of television stations, which enjoy some constitutional protection, their legal status was uncertain. Administrative guidance, by enabling the government to avoid a direct legal challenge to its action, may be understood as part of the inevitable and ever-present struggle between the governors and the governed to gain the upper hand – or at least coexist peacefully.

2. *Flexible Definition of Agency Mandate* – Administrative guidance also provides agencies in Japan with a flexible means of handling tasks that the current legal regime fails to accommodate. Because the use of administrative guidance frees an agency from the specific moorings of the governing statutory language, it may not only expand the scope of its activity, but also redefine the very nature of its regulatory mandate. Many

Japanese bureaucrats appear to view their enabling legislation not merely as establishing substantive areas over which they are to exercise regulatory control, but rather as descriptions of the various groups in society over which they have charge. The Ministry of Agriculture provides the best example of an agency redefining its jurisdiction in this way. The Ministry's enabling legislation only vests it with responsibility for agricultural development. Yet the Ministry generally interprets this legislation as placing under its purview all farmers and their families for almost any conceivable purpose. Thus, the Ministry has instituted programs that provide for medical examinations for farmers' wives, the maintenance of roads in farming areas, the construction of various public meeting facilities and recreational areas for farmers and their families, and the removal of sewage. Many of these activities encroach upon the domain of other ministries, but jurisdictional disputes rarely arise because the other ministries acknowledge the Ministry of Agriculture's prime responsibility for the welfare of the farmers.

The Ministry of Finance (MOF), though less explicit about its own inner workings, appears to take the same broad view of its jurisdictional mandate – to regulate banks and other financial institutions. Banking regulation thus extends as far as the establishment of energy conservation measures for banks, the encouragement of a five-day work week, and the provision of time off to permit bank employees to vote on election day. Other ministries do not quarrel with these intrusions into areas that fall within their substantive jurisdictional mandate because the MOF limits its regulatory activity to financial institutions.

When the Ministries of Agriculture and Finance redefine their regulatory mandate to embrace the regulated groups rather than merely to oversee certain types of activities, they gain considerable flexibility. The agencies can then use administrative guidance to implement a variety of substantive policies so long as they affect only the regulated groups' well-being.

3. *Collateral Enforcement* – Use of administrative guidance enables agencies to gain additional flexibility by resorting to collateral methods of enforcement to effectuate quite unrelated regulatory objectives. The MITI, for example, has been known to threaten restriction of the amount of coal a company could import if that company did not comply with the MITI's request to limit steel production. The flexibility provided by such covert pressures, as well as by expanding regulatory activity to groups, enables administrative agencies to go into areas not otherwise subject to regulation.

4. *Party Input* – At the same time, the flexibility that administrative guidance provides requires agencies to cooperate with the regulated parties. To assure voluntary compliance and substantial cooperation, agencies engage in practices designed to increase the informal, generally unreviewable input of parties into the regulatory process. Indeed, agencies that engage in administrative guidance undertake extensive consultations with regulated parties – who may include industry representatives – about the need for regulation and the form it will take.

The Ministry of Labor, for example, engaged in comprehensive discussions with various industry associations and labor representatives before it suggested that companies gradually phase in a five-day work week. Similarly, the Ministry of Construction encouraged construction firms and developers to form associations through which the Ministry then negotiated a series of reforms intended to strengthen and modernize the position and status of sub-contractors and other suppliers in the construction industry. In the Oil Cartel Cases, the MITI committed to the Petroleum

Federation, a major industry trade association, the task of allocating specific production shares among its members. The price for which the oil subsequently sold was also determined in all but one instance by agreement with industry officials. In an equally extreme example, evidence exists that the Ministry of Transportation committed to an informal industry council the task of dividing up coveted railroad routes for private railroad companies.

Consultation can take a variety of forms. All ministries have consultative and advisory committees comprised of industry representatives, academics, bureaucrats and representatives of other organizations, such as research institutes, the media and, on rare occasions, labor or consumer groups. Some of these councils, such as the MITI's Industrial Structure Council, are permanent. Others are formed on an *ad hoc* basis to deal with a specific problem and disbanded after agreeing upon the substance and form of the guidance. Depending on the nature of the problem and the agency's desired objective, the consultation may be more informal and loosely structured. The agency may initially approach only selected representatives of a particular industry or trade, hoping their support will be sufficient to elicit cooperation from the other potential targets of regulation. While the manner and extent of consultation may vary markedly from case to case, consultation almost always takes place.

Bureaucrats consult with involved parties before regulation both to build a consensus and, on occasion, to elicit the cooperation of the regulated parties. Administrative guidance issued without such consultation may meet with disobedience and, in rare instances, litigation. Agencies avoid this result by committing much of the actual formation and implementation of guidance to the regulated parties themselves. When the parties participate extensively in the design and execution of regulation, they can minimize the dislocations of particular regulatory burdens. They can also increase efficiency in accomplishing regulatory goals and introduce flexibility into the enforcement process, thereby ensuring that the regulations will not impose unnecessary, unfair or disproportionate burdens and compliance costs. They also may structure the compliance scheme to minimize the competitive disadvantages of regulation. If the parties are permitted genuine, regular, and unstructured input into the formation of administrative guidance, as it appears they necessarily are, it is no wonder they do not decry the frequency of its use. Indeed, in some instances, committing the formulation of policy to the parties results in regulation they consider not only less burdensome but also beneficial.

Thus, whether Japanese bureaucrats perceive the consultative process as mere accommodation or as a necessary prerequisite to action, most guidance undergoes noticeable and significant changes before it becomes official policy. The interactive consultation process that precedes the issuance of guidance is a significant and necessary step for the effective accomplishment of administrative goals and objectives ...

...

III. JUDICIAL REVIEW OF ADMINISTRATIVE GUIDANCE

The narrow class of cases in which administrative guidance is challenged judicially imposes a significant burden on Japanese courts. They must develop doctrine that allows adequate scope for this important and necessary mode of regulatory power, since the demands placed upon administrative organs in the Japanese state require a broader scope of regulatory power than anticipated under the imported doctrines of judicial review. At the same time, the very mode of behavior that permits agencies to accomplish their tasks – administrative guidance – increases the danger of excessive or unfair intrusions into the affairs of regulated parties.

Judicial review of administrative guidance is particularly challenging due to the theoretically voluntary nature of compliance with administrative guidance. In reality, however, noncompliance may significantly disadvantage regulated parties. Adhering too rigidly to a narrow concept of voluntariness would insulate from review much of the significant administrative activity in modern Japanese society, Yet once courts permit a direct challenge to administrative guidance, they must avoid the opposite extreme of placing severe limitations on the ability of agencies to use administrative guidance – which commentators estimate comprises over eighty percent of Japanese bureaucratic activity. Such a result would be equally unfortunate and would hamper the achievement of a variety of legitimate regulatory goals and objectives in Japan. Japanese courts' response to this dilemma has evolved from a blanket rejection of challenges to administrative guidance to full scale review, but review of a most interesting kind.

A. Traditional Approach to Reviewing Administrative Guidance

Japanese courts traditionally considered challenges to administrative guidance to be nonjusticiable. Thus the earliest cases dealing directly with administrative guidance accepted at face value the argument that compliance was voluntary and plaintiffs therefore had no claim for relief.

For example, in a 1963 decision, the Tokyo Court of Appeals rebuffed a challenge to administrative guidance issued by the Japanese Foreign Ministry. The plaintiffs were part of an organization that traditionally participated in the Biannual Festival of World Peace and Friendship for Students and Youths. In 1957, the Festival was to be held in Moscow and its sponsors invited the Japanese organization to send 500 participants. Plaintiffs were encouraged to attend by the Japanese organization, which entered into negotiations with the Foreign Ministry regarding the size of the group that would be permitted to participate. The Foreign Ministry initially insisted that no more than fifty could attend, citing the Ministry of Finance's inability to supply foreign currency to any larger group and Japan's general political alignment with the Western bloc nations. As the issue assumed political dimensions, the Ministry eventually permitted 155 people to attend the conference, requesting that no more apply for passports. The remaining 345 brought suit against the government, claiming monetary relief for the injury allegedly resulting from the refusal to issue passports. Plaintiffs argued, among other things, that the Ministry had acted in violation of both the constitution and the Passport Law by determining in a broad, generalized way that attendance at the conference would undermine the national interest. Rather, the plaintiffs argued, such a determination should have been made on narrow grounds, only after examining the merits of each individual applicant's situation. The court rejected this argument, however, on the ground that the 345 individuals did not apply for a passport and, as a result, the Foreign Ministry had not actually refused to grant passports. Thus, reasoned the court, the Ministry's failure to act on an individual basis could not be deemed illegal. The plaintiffs' voluntary compliance with the Ministry's instructions not to submit individual applications barred the success of plaintiffs' claim.

A 1969 case, arising when the prefectural governor gave a fishing cooperative permission to reclaim certain public shore lands apparently for the purpose of enhancing the ability of the cooperative members to engage in their trade, provides another example of this view of the legal status of administrative guidance. After the reclamation project was well under way, the fishermen received permission to change the purpose of the reclamation project from development of land for fishing to construction of a housing project, which had been the fishing cooperative's objective all along. A company that built and operated tourist hotels sought to obtain the land because of its particularly favorable view of the Inland Sea, but applications for reclamation by private companies were rarely successful. The company had thus persuaded the fishing cooperative, in exchange for a large contribution, to make the application, begin reclamation and then request the modification of purpose. Plaintiffs, owners and operators of *ryokan* or Japanese-style inns on the Inland Sea, sued the prefectural governor under the Administrative Case Litigation Law (ACLL) for rescission of both the initial approval and the subsequent permission to change purposes. The ACLL's one-year statute of limitations had run on the challenge to the initial approval, however, so the success of their case turned on whether they could challenge the subsequent grant of permission for a change in purpose. The court found the subsequent permission for a change in purpose merely advisory. Thus, the court reasoned, the grant of permission must have been achieved through administrative guidance, which was not a legal act or administrative disposition (*shobun*) that could be challenged by plaintiffs under the ACLL.

The courts' formalistic reasoning in both these cases ignores the real impact of the administrative determinations. In the first case, plaintiffs did not make a passport application because they were told in no uncertain terms their applications would be rejected. In the second case, only the subsequent grant of permission for a change in the purpose of the reclamation project revealed to plaintiffs the real danger the project posed to their livelihood. Indeed, everyone but the court agreed that a hotel could not have been built on the land except for the subsequent grant of permission. Nevertheless, the courts reasoned in both these cases, obedience to administrative guidance is voluntary and a regulated party that complies cannot come into court and challenge the governmental action that induced or encouraged compliance. Neither can an aggrieved party challenge administrative guidance given to others because ultimate compliance with that administrative advice is purely voluntary.

Courts' insistence that compliance was voluntary insulated from meaningful judicial review a significant amount of administrative activity with a pronounced impact on the affairs of the regulated parties. Indeed, in many instances, administrative guidance places regulated parties at the mercy of administrative agencies – in a practical, if not legal, sense. As the dimension of this problem grew more apparent, courts became increasingly unwilling to use formalistic reasoning about the voluntary nature of compliance to preclude them from exercising even minimal oversight of administrative activity or from providing any protection for the rights and interests of regulated parties. The inadequacies of the strict conceptual approach to administrative determinations that fall under the rubric of administrative guidance led courts to search for ways to review this kind of administrative activity.

B. Recognition of the Need for Administrative Accountability

Although unable to resolve fully the doctrinal difficulty inherent in judicial review of administrative guidance, Japanese courts began as early as 1971 to permit direct challenges to administrative guidance. In that year, the Tokyo District Court permitted a suit challenging a notice (*tsutatsu*) issued by the MITI. The plaintiff in this case manufactured and sold plastic rulers that measured in centimeters, inches, and even the traditional Japanese measurement standard. The MITI issued a notice that plaintiff's ruler was a measuring device under Article 12 of the Weights and Measurements Law and thus must contain only the authorized units of measurement – centimeters. The notice also directed the local prefectural authorities to deal with the matter and report back to the MITI. Based on this notice, the prefectural authorities issued a warning (*kankoku*) to halt production of the ruler. The plaintiff lodged an objection (*igimoshitate sho*) with the MITI, which was denied. Plaintiff then sued the MITI and the local prefectural authorities, seeking invalidation of both the notice and warning.

The court held that plaintiff could challenge the notice but not the warning. The court reasoned, in the traditional manner, that the warning merely sought to gain plaintiff's voluntary cooperation and thus did not affect his rights and duties in a legal sense. The court also explicitly recognized that the notice was nothing more than an internal directive and did not change the concrete rights and duties of an individual. Moreover, the court acknowledged, a regulated party normally could bring an action against a specific administrative disposition based upon a notice, thereby adequately protecting his rights. Nevertheless, the court reasoned, in the reality of administrative affairs, notices play an important role and in practice can strongly affect the concrete rights and duties of individuals. Thus, in the rare case where an individual cannot obtain relief without directly disputing the validity of the notice, the court held a direct judicial challenge against the notice itself would be permissible. Although the court ruled against the plaintiff on the merits of his challenge, the significance of this opinion lies in its explicit acknowledgement that strict adherence to the notion that administrative guidance does not change legal relationships may insulate from meaningful judicial review significant administrative action.

The following year, 1972, the Kyoto District Court also allowed a judicial challenge to administrative guidance. The plaintiff, a company that owned and operated gasoline stations throughout Japan, had secured an option on land in a part of Kyoto that was designated a special area of scenic beauty (*fuchi chiku*). The city's Planning Bureau informed plaintiff that any gasoline station it built would have to conform to extremely restrictive aesthetic specifications, which the plaintiff determined would make the venture unprofitable. Plaintiff thus let the option on the land lapse, after which someone else purchased the land and built a gasoline station that did not conform to any of the requirements that had been presented to plaintiff. Plaintiff sued the city for damages under the National Compensation Law. The court held that the city's actions, though administrative guidance, amounted to an 'exercise of public authority' (*kokenryoku no koshi*) under Article 1 of the National Compensation Law, entitling plaintiff to damages if the action was illegal. Although the court found that defendant's actions were not illegal under the circumstances, the significance of its holding lies in the determination that even actions that do not directly change legal relationships and that involve at least theoretically voluntary compliance can be 'exercises of public authority' and thus reviewed in court. The court was probably the first to construe 'exercises of public authority' broadly enough to include many of those administrative activities that fall within the rubric of administrative guidance.

In these two transition cases, the courts were clearly troubled by the prospect of dismissing a plaintiff's complaint when it was clear dismissal would leave a genuinely aggrieved party without legal recourse. Given the frequent resort to administrative guidance as a regulatory technique in Japan, strict adherence to the narrow conception of an administrative disposition as the sole object of judicial review would leave entirely unreviewable the vast bulk of administrative determinations. The traditional doctrine regarding voluntary compliance simply could not provide the degree of flexibility necessary to assure some role for the judiciary in Japan's system of regulatory behavior. Thus, the courts were motivated to recognize the right of the aggrieved party to challenge the administrative directives and guidelines, despite the fact that these directives and guidelines had not yet crystallized into formal administrative determinations ...

...

CONCLUSION

Administrative guidance, an administrative technique frequently used in Japan, is nonbinding administrative action that encourages regulated parties to act in a way that furthers an administrative aim. Although compliance with administrative guidance is technically voluntary, Japanese administrators rely on informal pressure and other means of enforcement to persuade regulated parties to comply. This reliance on informal encouragement as opposed to legal coercion permits the bureaucracy to expand the areas into which it may intrude. It simultaneously limits the extent of those intrusions, however, and requires the bureaucracy to consult and negotiate extensively with the regulated parties. Indeed, administrators often leave largely to the parties the task of determining many of the details of the regulatory scheme and, on occasion, even the appropriate degree of regulation. Frequently, regulation amounts to little more than administrative organs' structuring of a bargaining situation in which the parties are compelled to negotiate with each other over the proper allocation of the benefits and burdens of regulation.

The absence of any legal compulsion in administrative guidance also initially deterred Japanese courts from reviewing such action, thereby insulating from judicial scrutiny a significant portion of Japanese regulatory conduct. More recently, however, courts have addressed the proper scope of review, particularly in cases involving municipalities' Outline Guidance – regulation designed to resolve informally disputes between building developers and residents over sunlight and ventilation.

From these more recent cases, this Article has distilled an approach to judicial review of administrative guidance. This approach directs courts to focus primarily on the agencies' attempt to restructure the bargaining situation. Courts accomplish this task by rearticulating the agencies' mandate and refusing to determine the priority of competing claims of right. Through use of traditional and sometimes not so traditional doctrines of judicial review the courts are then able to limit the extent to which agencies can compel negotiation. These doctrinal constructs, while perhaps appealing to traditional Japanese attitudes toward consensual dispute resolution, nevertheless offer important advantages that have little to do with culture or tradition; they enable the courts to strike a balance between protection of regulated parties and agency flexibility in a modern, industrialized state in which citizens place high demands on their bureaucracy. While not without potential pitfalls, the Japanese experience with administrative guidance offers Western legal systems a promising model for regulation and the resolution of certain kinds of disputes in a postindustrial era.

CHAPTER 4

GOVERNMENT AND THE LAW

INTRODUCTION

When Japan formally surrendered to the Allied Powers on 2 September 1945, the Imperial Japanese Government was still intact, if politically impotent.[1] Instead of establishing a military government, as had been done in Germany, the Occupation forces exercised supervisory authority through the Supreme Commander for the Allied Powers (SCAP).[2] In theory this left the Japanese government to continue governing the country, but in practice there is little doubt that the real power and authority rested with SCAP, which immediately set about enforcing the terms of the Potsdam Declaration.[3] This was done by issuing directives (known as SCAPINs) to the Japanese government for implementation.[4] Through these provisions the Allied Powers sought to bring about far reaching reforms, but central to achieving these aims was the drafting of a new constitution which, in short, was to achieve demilitarisation, democratisation and decentralisation.[5]

---

1 For an account of the surrender and the Occupation see Maki, JM, *Government and Politics in Japan. The Road to Democracy*, 1962, Chapter 2, Thames & Hudson; McNelly, T, *Contemporary Government of Japan*, 1963, Chapter 2, Allen & Unwin; Storry, R, *A History of Modern Japan*, 1982, Chapter 10, Penguin; Beasley, WG, *The Rise of Modern Japan: Political, Economic and Social Change Since 1850*, 2nd edn, 1995, Weidenfeld & Nicolson.

2 Supreme Commander for the Allied Powers. The abbreviation SCAP is used to indicate either General MacArthur personally, or, more often, the Headquarters of the Occupation forces. SCAP Headquarters was divided into 13 sections, see Oppler, AC, *Legal Reform in Occupied Japan: A Participant Looks Back*, 1976, p 18, Princeton University Press. Another interesting personal account of the work of SCAP is provided in Williams, J, *Japan's Political Revolution under MacArthur: A Participant's Account*, 1979, University of Georgia. Also see van Staaveren, J, *An American in Japan 1945–1948*, 1994, University of Washington Press, which deals with the civilian bureaucracy administration of the Occupation.

3 Proclamation Defining Terms for Japanese Surrender, 26 July 1945; Maki, *supra*, n 1, p 40. At Potsdam, the American and British delegations agreed, on behalf of all countries at war with Japan, on a declaration calling upon Japan to surrender 'unconditionally'. Following the 26 July publication of the Declaration atomic bombs were dropped on Hiroshima and Nagasaki on 6 and 9 August. On 10 August the Americans received Japan's acceptance of the terms of the Declaration; however, it was conditional upon the Allies agreeing that the prerogatives of the Emperor as sovereign ruler were not prejudiced. On 11 August the Americans replied that the Emperor would be subject to the Supreme Commander and that, in accordance with the Declaration, the ultimate form of government would be established by the freely expressed will of the people. Japan surrendered on these terms on 14 August and the formal instrument of surrender was signed on 2 September.

4 SCAPIN's were 'supraconstitutional' and not subject to any other Japanese law, thus it was a system of 'indirect military government through the indigenous authorities' Oppler, *supra*, n 2, p 41. During the Occupation, which ended on 28 April 1952, around 520 of these so-called Potsdam Ordinances were issued to the government, see NcNelly, *supra*, n 1, p 28 and Beer, LW, 'The Present Constitutional System of Japan' in Beer, LW (ed), *Constitutional Systems in Late Twentieth Century Asia*, 1992, pp 176–82, University of Washington Press.

5 The new Constitution was promulgated on 3 November 1946 and came into effect on 3 May 1947. Although the Occupation authorities had not immediately embarked on preparing a new Constitution, by early 1946 SCAP officials had drafted what was to become known as the MacArthur Draft. This was presented to a Cabinet committee for consideration, but their suggestions did not go far enough. The Draft was eventually presented to the Cabinet with ...

Under the Meiji Constitution, sovereignty resided with the Emperor who, according to Article 3 was 'sacred and inviolable' and was 'head of the Empire, combining in Himself the rights of sovereignty' (Article 4). The most important change brought about by the 1946 Constitution was establishing the sovereignty of the people and giving the Emperor a purely symbolic role.[6] Furthermore, in setting up a constitutional government based upon parliamentary democracy, it was essential to establish a governing structure based upon the principle of separation of powers. This was achieved under the new constitution by dividing state power amongst three independent branches of authority: legislative power was given to the Diet (Article 41), executive power conferred upon the Cabinet (Article 65) and judicial power on the courts (Article 76).[7]

What follows is a discussion of the institutions of government in Japan today. However, it should be borne in mind that a greater part of the function of governing in Japan, perhaps more so than in any other democratic country, takes place outside the formal structures and regulations normally ascribed to that process. In fact, the operation of the formal institutions of government relies heavily on informal or extra-legal mechanisms such as the interrelationship between politicians, bureaucrats, business and other interest groups, and on the device of 'administrative guidance'.[8] Much work has been carried out by

5 ... the threat that if it was rejected the Supreme Commander would put it to the Japanese people before the planned general elections in 1946. Thus it was that by 7 October 1946 the new constitution had passed both houses of the Diet and in effect the MacArthur Draft became the Japanese constitution. Although it is referred to as the new constitution, from the Japanese point of view it was of vital importance that it be seen as a 'revision' of the Meiji Constitution. However, a view often expressed is that the 1946 Constitution was 'imposed' and in support of this is the fact that some have argued that the process was completed with what could be described as undue haste (NcNelly, *supra,* n 1). See also Chapter 7; Burks, AW, *The Government of Japan*, 1964, Chapter 2, Thomas Crowell; Storry, *supra,* n 1, Chapter 10; Stockwin, JAA, *Japan: Divided Politics in a Growth Economy*, 2nd edn, 1982, Chapter 10, Weidenfeld & Nicolson; Ward, RE, 'Reflections on the Allied Occupation and Planned Political Change in Japan' in Ward, RE (ed), *Political Development in Modern Japan*, 1968, Princeton University Press; Kades, CL, 'The American Role in Revising Japan's Imperial Constitution' (1989) 104 *Political Science Quarterly* 215; Higuchi, Y, 'The Constitution and the Emperor System: Is Revisionism Alive?' (1990) 53, No 1 *Law and Contemporary Problems* 51; Beer, 1992, *idem.*

6 The Preamble states *inter alia* 'We, the Japanese people, acting through our duly elected representatives in the National Diet ... do proclaim that sovereign power resides with the people ... Government is a sacred trust of the people, the authority for which is derived from the people, the powers of which are exercised by the representatives of the people, and the benefits of which are enjoyed by the people'. and Article 1 provides that 'The Emperor shall be the symbol of the State and of the unity of the people, deriving his position from the will of the people with whom resides sovereign power'.

7 Since the executive (Cabinet) consists almost entirely of members of the legislature and is responsible to parliament, it is perhaps more accurate to talk of a fusion of powers than an absolute separation. In fact given the American authorship, it is interesting that the end product is closer to the British parliamentary-cabinet system, although the relationship between the legislature and the judiciary (ie the power of parliament to impeach judges and the Supreme Court's power to decide on the constitutionality of legislation) remains closer to the American system. Nevertheless, the independence of the three branches of government is secured and the checks and balances upon which a parliamentary democracy is predicated clearly set out in the Constitution, Oppler, *supra,* n 2, p 57.

8 On administrative guidance (*Gyosei Shido*) see Chapter 3. For an overview of its use see: Narita, Y, 'Administrative Guidance' (1968) 2 *Law in Japan* 45; Yamanouchi, K, 'Administrative Guidance and The Rule of Law' (1974) 7 *Law in Japan* 22; ...

political scientists in an attempt to understand the functioning of the process of government in Japan; the materials later in this chapter draw upon that work, whereas the text concentrates more on form than function.[9]

THE EMPEROR SYSTEM

The death of Emperor Hirohito in January 1989 once more focused attention on the role of the Emperor in government.[10] The decision of the Allied Powers to preserve and reform the monarchy was a compromise between opposing views on all sides, but one which meant that the Emperor could reign, although no longer rule.[11] If, as was maintained at the time, the new constitution was only a revision of the Meiji Constitution, then further revision was possible and the ascendancy of a new Emperor presented an opportunity to rekindle that debate.[12] In the event the enthronement of Emperor Akihito, although not entirely uncontroversial, did not seem to generate a lasting movement toward constitutional revisionism.[13] Indeed, as one writer has concluded 'rational discussion of real improvements is hardly possible in a climate produced by reactionaries, still a part of public life, whose dreams of Japan are all in the past'.[14]

---

8 ... Pape, W, '*Gyosei Shido* and the Antimonopoly Law' (1982) 15 *Law in Japan* 12; Young, M, 'Judicial Review of Administrative Guidance: Governmentally Encouraged Consensual Dispute Resolution' (1984) 84 *Columbia Law Review* 923; Young, M, 'Administrative Guidance in the Courts: A Case Study in Doctrinal Adaptation' (1984) 17 *Law in Japan* 120; Yeomans, RA, 'Administrative Guidance' (1986) 19 *Law in Japan* 125; Dean, M, 'Administrative Guidance in Japanese Law: A Threat to the Rule of Law' (1991) *Journal of Business Law* 398.

9 Maruyama, M, *Thought and Behaviour in Modern Japanese Politics*, 1963, Oxford University Press; Vogel, E (ed), *Modern Japanese Organization and Decision-Making*, 1975, University of California Press; Johnson, C, *MITI and the Japanese Miracle*, 1982, Stanford University Press; Stockwin, JAA, *Japan: Divided Politics in a Growth Economy* 2nd edn, 1982, Weidenfeld and Nicolson; Ishida, T and Krauss, ES (eds), *Democracy in Japan*, 1989, University of Pittsburgh Press; van Wolferen, K, *The Enigma of Japanese Power: People and Politics in a Stateless Nation*, 1990, Macmillan; Ramsayer, JM and Rosenbluth, F, *Japan's Political Marketplace*, 1993, Harvard University Press; Abe, H, Shindo, M and Kawato, S, *The Government and Politics of Japan*, 1994, University of Tokyo Press; Williams, D, *Japan: Beyond the End of History*, 1994, Routledge; Beasley, WG, *The Rise of Modern Japan*, 2nd edn, 1995, Weidenfeld & Nicolson; Johnson, C, *Japan, Who Governs?*, 1995, Norton.

10 Beasley, WG, *idem*, p 279; Higuchi, *supra*, n 5. For an overview of the Emperor system see Hall, JW, 'A Monarch for Modern Japan' in Ward, *supra*, n 5, Chapter 2; Haley, JO, *Authority Without Power: Law and the Japanese Paradox*, 1991, Oxford University Press.

11 Chapter 1 (Articles 1–8) Constitution of Japan 1946; see Oppler, *supra*, n 2, Chapter 5.

12 Constitutional reform had been discussed since the 1950s and in 1957 the Commission on the Constitution was set up. It reported in 1964 and concluded that the constitution was functioning effectively and in particular undermined the two most powerful arguments in favour of revision; first that the constitution was imposed from outside and was not the result of the freely expressed will of the Japanese people; second that it ran counter to Japanese history, culture and values. See Maki, JM, *Japan's Commission on the Constitution: The Final Report*, 1980, University of Washington Press. During the 1980s there was a revival of constitutional revisionism, spurred on by the then Prime Minister, Yasuhiro Nakasone, so it was hardly surprising that the death of Emperor Hirohito provided a timely vehicle for further debate. However, the likelihood of a constitutional revision at a time of short term, coalition governments seems remote.

13 Higuchi, *supra*, n 5, p 57.

14 Henderson, DF, 'Comment' (1990) 53 No 1 *Law and Contemporary Problems* 94.

Article 1 of the constitution states that 'The Emperor shall be the symbol of the State and unity of the people, deriving his position from the will of the people with whom resides sovereign power', thereby establishing that the Emperor (*Tenno*) reigns by popular sovereignty and not divine right. Underlining that symbolic role is Article 4 which states that the Emperor 'shall not have powers related to government'. Although the Emperor has no power, he does have certain duties. These are set out in Articles 6 and 7 but must be read in the light of a clear statement in Article 3 that such matters of state are subject to the advice and approval of the Cabinet, which bears the responsibility for them.[15]

The use of the word 'symbol' in Article 1 was in some ways controversial. The drafters of the constitution would seem to have been attempting to use an abstract term to describe a role; this was to ensure that the Emperor was perceived still to lead his people, thereby avoiding civil unrest against the Occupation, yet depriving him of political power.[16] It is argued that this is not such a departure from either feudal or Meiji Japan where the Emperor was head of the nation, but political power lay elsewhere. All that had happened was a move from divine to secular authority.[17] It could also be argued that all constitutional monarchies are symbolic and in the case of the Emperor system (*tennosei*), merely the role has changed with the transfer of sovereign power to the people.[18] The idea of an historical continuity is both important and powerful in popular opinion as well as constitutional theory and the Emperor as symbol, rather than ruler, preserves his authority to act as head of state, albeit without political power.[19]

Article 2 of the constitution sets out that the Imperial Throne is hereditary and is 'succeeded to in accordance with the Imperial House Law passed by the Diet'. This provision further illustrates the change from divine right to popular sovereignty, with the Imperial Family having lost its autonomy and become subject to a law passed by parliament. Whereas the Imperial House Law 1947 has the status of any other law, the 1889 Law of the same title was not subject to

---

15 Article 6 and 7 assign to the Emperor the duties *inter alia* of appointing the Prime Minister and Chief Justice, appointing ministers of state and ambassadors, promulgation of laws, proclaiming a general election, the calling of a Parliament and the Dissolution of the house of representatives.

16 Titus, D, 'The Making of the "Symbol Emperor System" in Postwar Japan' (1980) 14 *Modern Asian Studies* 529; Oppler, *supra*, n 2, pp 49–55.

17 Takayanagi, K, 'A Century of Innovation: The Development of Japanese Law, 1868–1961' in von Mehren (ed), *Law in Japan*, 1963, pp 11–13, Harvard University Press. The views of Takayanagi on this point are particularly interesting in view of the fact that he was Chairman of the Commission on the Constitution (see Maki, *supra*, n 12).

18 Noda, Y, *Introduction to Japanese Law*, 1976, p 66, University of Tokyo Press.

19 One interesting insight into the Japanese perspective on this matter can be seen in Abe, H *et al*, *supra*, n 9, p 11 '... although the abolition of the prewar emperor system and creation of a new polity with a merely symbolic throne clearly marked a major transition, the fact that the emperor system was retained, even if only as a symbol, represented continuity with the prewar period. At the very least, this facilitated the survival of archaic and unreconstructed popular attitudes and facilitated the continuation of old ideas of domination within a democratic institutional framework'. (Note, this view was expressed as part of a comment on the limitations of the process of democratisation under the Occupation.)

parliament and could be amended only by the Emperor on the advice of the Imperial Family Council and Privy Council. Indeed, since 1947 the Imperial Family is, in theory, subject to the laws of the land, although in practice there is a body of laws and regulations which somewhat mitigates the rigour of these provisions.[20]

To underline further the place of the Emperor in the government structure, the Imperial Household Agency, is placed under the control of the Prime Minister's Office and is 'responsible for the affairs of State concerning the Imperial House and those affairs concerning the Emperor's acts in matters of State which shall be provided for by Cabinet Order'.[21] Despite the apparently anachronistic or paradoxical position of the Emperor within the modern Japanese system of government, for the moment it remains a symbol of secure democratic government.[22]

THE LEGISLATURE

The Japanese parliament, known as the Diet (*Kokkai*), is a bicameral institution which celebrated its centenary in 1990. Under the Meiji Constitution of 1889, and in accordance with the Law on the Election of Members of the House of Representatives of the same year, elections were held in July 1890 and the first Japanese parliament inaugurated in November. Referred to as the Imperial Diet, it consisted of two houses, the House of Peers and the House of Representatives (Article 33). The former was composed of members of the Imperial Family, 'of orders of nobility, and of those who have been nominated by the Emperor' (Article 34), whereas the latter was composed of members 'elected by the people' (Article 35). However, the electorate was initially limited to men over the age of 25 who paid a certain level of taxes and not until 1925 were all male citizens over the age of 25 enfranchised.[23]

The preamble to the 1946 Constitution asserts that the principle of representative democracy is one of its fundamental principles. It states that 'Government is a sacred trust of the people, the authority for which is derived from the people, the powers of which are exercised by the representatives of the

20 Imperial House Law 1947; Imperial House Economy Law; Law Concerning Family Registration of Person who has Lost or Acquired Membership of Imperial Family.

21 *Organization of the Government of Japan* (Prime Minister's Office, 1992); see also Table 1 on p 239 and Table 2, p 240.

22 Noda, *supra*, n 18, pp 68–69 illustrates the difficulty thus: 'The legal position of the *tenno* under the new constitution is unique. He is neither to be compared with an ordinary monarch or a president of the republican system, nor can he be said to be the head of state as it is not he but the cabinet who represents the Japanese state in foreign affairs ... It is an institution born of efforts made to harmonize a long monarchic tradition with the requirement of a modern democratic republic'. Noda goes on to point out that since Japan is no longer an empire, it is inaccurate to translate tenno as Emperor. This is further supported by the fact that the Meiji Constitution was titled the constitution of the Empire of Japan, whereas the 1946 Constitution is titled the constitution of the State of Japan.

23 Although limited to male citizens the legislation was entitled the Universal Suffrage Law 1925! In fact the first opportunity for universal manhood to exercise its new found right was at the 1928 election. Women had to wait until April 1946 before they could vote for the first time in accordance with the revised Election Law 1945, which also lowered the age for voting to 20.

people, and the benefits of which are enjoyed by the people.' In accordance with this, the Diet now consists of two elected chambers, the House of Representatives (*Shugi-in*) and the House of Councillors (*Sangi-in*).[24] This is all the more interesting since Article 41 of the MacArthur Draft provided that the legislature was to be unicameral and composed of between 300 and 500 elected members. The Japanese government argued for a bicameral system in order to act as a check on precipitate actions or measures supported by a majority party in the lower house.[25] In the event this turned out to be one of the few changes agreed to by SCAP; there were to be two elected houses and no discrimination based on 'social status, family origin, education property or income'.[26]

Although the 1946 Constitution was technically a revision of the Meiji Constitution, the shift in content and character was so fundamental that it has to be seen as something entirely new.[27] Not only was the Emperor reduced to the status of a symbol, but the Diet was transformed into the 'highest organ of state power' and the 'sole law-making organ of the State' (Article 41).[28] Thus whilst the legislature has supremacy over the executive and the judiciary, the checks and balances inherent in any system of parliamentary democracy which has embraced the idea of separation of powers, are likewise present, eg dissolution by the executive and the power of judicial review.[29]

As the 'highest organ of state' the Diet has a variety of powers commensurate with that status. These include such things as deciding on the budget (Articles 60 and 86); approving treaties (Article 61); the power to conduct investigations into government and to require the presence of

24 Articles 42 and 43.

25 NcNelly, *supra*, n 1, p 101.

26 Article 44.

27 The 1946 Constitution was introduced, in accordance with Article 73 of the Meiji Constitution, as an amendment to the old constitution. Subsequent academic discussion has disputed the validity of the 1946 Constitution as a legitimate amendment under Article 73. Instead it has been described as a part of a legal revolution brought about by Japan's surrender in 1945. See Beer, LW, 'Constitutional Revolution in Japanese Law, Society and Politics' (1982) 16 *Modern Asian Studies* 33. A Japanese scholar has concluded that 'Japan's surrender substantially modified the Meiji Constitution, though it did not abolish it' and that the Potsdam Declaration was the first step of the transition from the Meiji Constitution to the present one. He goes on to note that although the 1946 Constitution was introduced as an amendment to the Meiji Constitution 'it has rightly been referred to as the "new constitution" and not as the "amended constitution"'. Miyazawa, T, 'Constitutional Law' (rev edn 1962) translated extract in Tanaka, H (ed), *The Japanese Legal System*, 1976, pp 682–84, University of Tokyo Press. On the constitutional framework see Chapter 7.

28 Noda, *supra*, n 18, p 73, n 1 makes an interesting etymological observation about the use of the word Diet. The word for legislature is *kokkai*, which is translated as Diet. However, the word Diet was used in the translations of the Imperial Constitution and therefore has connotations of imperial power and for that reason Noda uses the word Parliament and not Diet.

29 The supremacy of the Diet is also seen in order of the constitutional provisions, ie the Legislature (Chapter IV, the Diet) precedes the Executive (Chapter V, the Cabinet) which is followed by the Judiciary (Chapter VI). This can be seen as an example of the idea that the order of constitutional provisions is a reflection of the priorities, theories and values of the authors. Indeed the priority of SCAP in securing the position of the Emperor, ensuring peace and the protection of fundamental rights is seen in that Chapter I deals with the Emperor, Chapter II the Renunciation of War and Chapter III, the Rights and Duties of the People. See Okudaira, Y, 'Forty Years of the Constitution and its Various Influences' (1990) 53 No 1 *Law and Contemporary Problems* 17.

witnesses (Article 62); the power to impeach judges (Article 64) and to designate the Prime Minister (Article 67). The Diet was also given the role of 'sole law-making organ of the State' which meant that the parallel system of imperial ordinances which prevailed under the Meiji Constitution ceased to exist, and legislative acts of the Executive became limited to orders, such as decrees for administering laws passed by the Diet. However, Article 95 contains a limited exception to the Diet as sole law-making body. It states that a law applicable in only one locality cannot be passed by the Diet without a local referendum to approve such a law. Furthermore, Article 58(2) allows for each house to establish its own rules of procedure and Article 77(1) gives the Supreme Court the power to determine the rules of procedure and practice relating to the legal profession and the courts.

Decisions of the Diet require the approval of both the House of Representatives and the House of Councillors. Thus, in relation to legislation, Article 59(1) states that before a bill becomes law, it must be passed by both houses. However, whereas the Meiji Constitution upheld the principle of equality of power between the two houses, under the present constitution it is clear that the House of Representatives occupies a superior position. Article 59(2) provides that when a bill is passed by the lower house, but fails to pass through the upper house, the bill will nevertheless become law if it passes through the lower house again, with a two thirds majority. Article 59(4) goes on to provide that where the House of Councillors fails within 60 days to take final action on a bill already passed by the House of Representatives, the bill is deemed to have been rejected and the lower house may exercise its right to pass it a second time under Article 59(2).

The supremacy of the House of Representatives is illustrated further in relation to the budget, the approval of treaties and the appointment of the Prime Minister. Under Article 86 of the constitution it is for the Cabinet to prepare the budget and submit it to the Diet and in accordance with Article 60(1), the budget bill is submitted first to the House of Representatives. If the decision of the House of Councillors differs from that of the lower house and no agreement can be reached by a joint committee of both houses, or if the upper house fails to act within 30 days of receiving the budget then, in accordance with Article 60(2), the decision of the House of Representatives becomes the decision of the Diet.[30] Similarly in relation to the approval of treaties, Article 61 provides that where the two houses do not agree, the Article 60(2) procedure applies. However, since there is no requirement to submit a treaty to the House of Representatives first, if the Cabinet submits it to the House of Councillors, the Article 60(2) procedure cannot be instituted, thereby giving the upper house a notionally stronger position than in relation to other legislation.

Finally, in line with the parliamentary cabinet system, the Prime Minister is selected by the Diet, in contrast to the procedure under the Meiji Constitution. The process for 'designation' of the Prime Minister is set out in Article 67, but again, in a case where the two houses fail to agree on the same candidate, the

30 When passing the budget under Article 60(2), it is referred to as automatic passage. The 1989 budget was the first to receive automatic passage in 35 years, but it then happened again in 1990 and 1993 after the budget was rejected by the upper house.

decision of the House of Representatives becomes the decision of the Diet.[31] All Prime Ministers have, so far, been members of the House of Representatives and men. In 1989, one of the two occasions when both houses failed to nominate the same candidate, the person put forward by the House of Councillors was the Chairwoman of the Japan Socialist Party, Takako Doi. In the event a joint committee decided upon the House of Representatives' candidate. However, in 1993 the House of Representatives elected Takako Doi as their Speaker, the first woman to hold that office in the history of the Japanese Parliament.

The term of office for members of the Diet is set out in the constitution. For the House of Representatives, Article 45 states that it is four years, unless there is a lower house dissolution. Article 46 provides that the term of office for members of the House of Councillors is six years. This longer period of time, combined with the indissolubility of the upper house, was intended to provide continuity and stability in what could have been, and in fact became, a turbulent lower house. On average, there have been general elections every two and a half years since 1946 and except for the House of Representatives elected in 1972, every term has ended in a dissolution. Not only has factionalism of party politics disrupted the life of the lower house, but party politics have played an increasingly important role in the upper house. As a result it has become less of a check on the lower house than was originally anticipated and may even have led to a loss of independence.[32]

Dissolution may occur in one of two ways, either by means of Article 7, or Article 69. The former is where the Emperor, with the advice and approval of the Cabinet, dissolves the House of Representatives as a matter of state, whereas the latter is consequent upon the House having passed a resolution of no confidence, or having rejected a confidence resolution. Thus, it is clear that Article 7 is the method used by the government, and Article 69 by the opposition. Since the House of Councillors cannot be dissolved, Article 54(2) provides that it shall be closed at the same time, but that in times of national emergency, the Cabinet may recall the House for an emergency session. This is an unique exception to the principle of bicameralism, but although unicameral

31 The two houses have failed to agree on only two occasions. In 1948, both houses having nominated different people, in accordance with Article 67(2) a joint committee was set up and when this failed to agree, the decision of the House of Representatives became the decision of the Diet. In 1989 the two houses nominated different candidates, but on this occasion the joint committee reached a decision and in fact approved the candidate designated by the House of Representatives.

32 Abe *et al*, *supra*, n 9, p 16. Until 1993, Japan had been ruled by one party, the Liberal Democratic Party (LDP), which came to power for the first time in 1955 as a result of an amalgamation of two conservative parties. In 1993 Prime Minister Hosokawa, a former LDP member who founded a new political party, the Japan New Party, led the first non LDP coalition of the postwar years. However, in January 1996, following the resignation of the first socialist Prime Minister in 46 years, Tomiichi Murayama, a return to conservative dominated politics was heralded with the appointment to that office of Ryutaro Hashimoto, the LDP leader. The next general election, which must take place no later than July 1997, will be a more substantive indication of whether there is a real LDP revival or whether, together with the effect of the new electoral system, this is part of a new political map. For an assessment of this period see Todokoro, M, 'The End of Japan's 'Non-Decision' Politics' (1994) 34 *Asian Survey* 1002. [Note: the general election took place on 20 October 1996 during the preparation of this book. A full analysis of the new electoral system is not possible in this edition but it should be noted that the LDP failed to gain a majority of the lower house seats. It won 239 seats, 12 short of the 251 needed to govern and whilst still the dominant party in a ruling coalition, the fragmentation and factionalism of lower house politics looks set to continue.]

decision-making can take place during an emergency session, Article 54(3) provides that measures taken at such sessions will become null and void unless they are agreed to by the House of Representatives within 10 days after the opening of the next session of the Diet.

Election to one of the 511 seats in the House of Representatives traditionally has been based on a medium-sized multimember district system which is 'unlike that of any other Western democracy'.[33] Members were elected from one of the 129 electoral districts where, on average, there were three to five seats and voting was by single non-transferable vote. Thus it was neither a preference voting system, nor a proper system of proportional representation, although it did prove relatively advantageous to smaller political parties.[34] However, in order to win the 256 seats necessary to obtain the majority, a party had to have two or more of its candidates running against each other in the same district. The consequence of this was that where a party put forward a number of candidates, the campaign was run on an individual basis, thereby turning candidates into rivals, causing party infighting and resulting in factional politics.[35] Indeed, it became clear that the difficulties encountered in postwar politics could be attributed directly to the factionalism born of the multi-seat system.[36] Furthermore, since through the individualisation of campaigns, the candidates were encouraged to promote special interests, a national consensus on major issues often seemed to remain elusive.[37] The factionalism and money politics that was to tear successive governments and the ruling Liberal Democratic Party (LDP) apart started in 1976, following the Lockheed scandal.[38] Throughout the next few years the politics of irregular political financing continued, as did the setbacks for the LDP, but it was not until the Recruit scandal of 1988 that any genuine attempt was made to initiate reform to the system.[39]

The loss of public confidence forced Prime Minister Takeshita to set up a number of committees of inquiry aimed at political reform. At party level, the LDP produced various proposals for internal restructuring and made specific recommendations in relation to political funding. However, it was recognised that one of the root causes of the problems lay in the electoral process itself and

---

33 Krauss, ES, 'Politics and the Policymaking Process' in Ishida and Krauss (eds), *supra*, n 9, p 41.

34 Stockwin, *supra*, n 5, p 98.

35 Abe *et al*, *supra*, n 9, p 141.

36 For an account of party factions see Ramsayer and Rosenbluth, *supra*, n 9, Chapter 4.

37 Stockwin, *supra*, n 5, pp 103–05.

38 At the time, the allegation was that Prime Minister Tanaka received bribes from the Lockheed Corporation, but it was not until 1983 that the Tokyo District Court found him guilty. In general see Krauss, *supra*, n 33, p 47.

39 The Recruit scandal involved the offer and sale of shares in a property company to politicians before they were available to the public. When the shares went on open sale, the price rose and those who had bought them were able to make substantial gains. When the story broke, those involved claimed that dealing in unlisted shares was a purely private matter. However, it lead to a number of people in the political, bureaucratic and industrial elites being arrested and charged with bribery. More importantly, the situation developed from yet another scandal about money politics, to a broader debate about the defects of the political system and electoral system in particular.

it was recommended that this be one of the major objects of a broader programme of political reforms. In the event, an Election System Council, an advisory body to the Prime Minister, was established in 1989 and the two reports it published formed the basis of the reforms which, following a number of unsuccessful attempts to implement them, became law in 1994.[40] In consequence, after the next general election (which must take place before July 1997), there will be 500 members of the lower house. These will consist of 300 members drawn from single seat constituencies, plus 200 members elected by a fixed list proportional representation system, drawn from 11 regional blocs.[41]

Whereas reform of the House of Representatives was the main purpose of the debate, one of the two reports of the Election System Council did address itself to reform of the House of Councillors.[42] Traditionally, this House had 252 members elected on a two tier system; 100 were elected through proportional representation and 152 from electoral districts. Since, according to Article 46, members are elected for a term of six years, but election for half the members takes place every three years, only 126 members are chosen on each occasion. Thus 50 are elected from the single national constituency, using proportional representation and 76 are elected from regional (ie prefectural) districts which have up to four seats. In the event, no major reforms of the House of Councillors took place and it therefore retained the system described, with the result that the voting systems for both houses are now very similar. The one major difference is that whereas the upper house system of proportional representation draws from a single, national constituency, that of the lower house is divided into 11 regional blocs.

Each House has a number of special and standing committees; at the moment there are 20 standing committees in the House of Representatives and 17 in the House of Councillors. Save for the audit, budget, steering and disciplinary measures committees, the standing committees mirror cabinet ministerial responsibility. The membership of these committees is determined according to party strength and is intended to reflect the balance of the House, but with the chairmanship, in the case of the lower house, usually going to members of the ruling party.[43] A bill, whether proposed by a Diet member, the Cabinet, or received from the other house, is referred to the relevant committee.[44] Whatever the consequences of the new election programme, it is

40 Abe, *et al*, *supra*, n 9, pp 148–53. By this time the LDP had lost power in the 1993 elections (see n 31).

41 Christensen, RV, 'Electoral Reform in Japan. How it was Enacted and Changes it may Bring' (1994) 34 *Asian Survey* 589.

42 The reports were wide ranging and covered all aspects of the election process, from funding to campaigning as well as size and structure. These matters are beyond the scope of this book, but some of the materials touch upon these issues. In addition, see Ramsayer and Rosenbluth, *supra*, n 9, Chapters 2 and 5, and Johnson, 1995, *supra*, n 9, Chapter 10.

43 Abe *et al*, *supra*, n 9, pp 18–20.

44 Stockwin, *supra*, n 5, p 93 states 'Whereas a bill may be sponsored by private members in either House, most bills are now proposed by Cabinet'. He goes on to note that whilst private members' bills are not uncommon, they will invariably have originated from a ministry and the member simply 'pilots' the bill. For a detailed account of cabinet bills see Seki, M, 'The Drafting Process for Cabinet Bills' (1986) 19 *Law in Japan* 168.

clear that the committee system will remain an essential feature of the legislative process.

THE EXECUTIVE

Article 65 of the Constitution states that executive power is vested in the Cabinet (*Naikaku*), but it is evident that the Prime Minister (*Naikaku Sori Daijin*) has a superior status within the parliamentary cabinet system. Whilst he is chosen from among members of the Diet and appointed by the Emperor (Articles 67 and 6), once he is in office he has considerable powers. First among these is the power to appoint and to remove Ministers (Article 68), the majority of whom must come from the House of Representatives. However, in the context of factional politics, as mentioned above, this is more complex and important than this simple statement might suggest; as one commentator has written 'the art of cabinet-making in Japan consists of being able to distribute just the right number and type of posts to satisfy one's factional allies, one's own faction, and opposing factions in the party'.[45]

All this is in contrast to the Meiji Constitution under which the Prime Minister was a first among equals and the words 'Prime Minister' and 'Cabinet' did not appear in the document at all. Thus the only mention of ministerial authority was in Article 55 which said that Ministers of State gave advice to the Emperor and were responsible for such advice. The Cabinet, at that time, was established and organised by Imperial Ordinance, with ministers responsible to the Emperor and therefore the exercise of independent executive authority was impossible. Under the new constitution, the Executive is answerable to Parliament. Indeed, whereas a minister in the United Kingdom is ultimately responsible to the Crown, in Japan, to underline the nature of the parliamentary cabinet responsibility, ministers are answerable to the Prime Minister and ultimately, in accordance with Article 66(3), to the Diet. However, as part of the checks and balances in any system, the Cabinet is not totally subservient to Parliament since, in accordance with Article 7(3), it can recommend the dissolution of the House of Representatives.

In addition to the constitutional provisions in Chapter 5, the Cabinet is governed by the Cabinet Law of 1947.[46] This states that the Cabinet shall be headed by the Prime Minister and consist of not more than 20 Ministers of State.[47] Although the Cabinet must consist of a majority of lower house members, the more interesting qualification is contained in Article 66(2) of the Constitution which states that the Prime Minister and Ministers of State must be civilians. One interpretation of this is that since the Renunciation of War clause in Article 9 of the Constitution also prohibits the formation of 'land, sea, and air

45 Krauss, ES, 'Politics and the Policymaking Process' in Ishida and Krauss (eds), *supra*, n 9, p 49.

46 Law No 5, 1947. See p 242 below. This is supplemented by the National Government Organisation Law (No 120), 1948. See p 244 below.

47 This means those ministers who head the 12 ministries, plus those who head various non-ministerial government agencies which aid the Cabinet in its executive function. It is also possible for a minister to head more than one agency, but the Cabinet must not exceed 20, plus the Prime Minister. See Table 1, p 239 and Table 2, p 240 below and Tanaka H, *The Japanese Legal System*, 1976, p 42, University of Tokyo Press.

forces, as well as other war potential', Article 66(2) can apply only to people who have previously been military personnel.[48] However, Article 9 did leave open the option of the use of armed forces for defensive purposes and thus it is that Japan has developed Self Defence Forces, since 1954, which have recently started to contribute to United Nations peacekeeping activities.[49] Japan now has one of the largest defence spending budgets in the world, leading to substantial standing armed forces, but at what point these become 'military' as opposed to 'defensive' is debatable.[50] Furthermore, the Defence Agency, whilst organisationally under the authority of the Prime Minister's Office, is nevertheless an external body headed by a Minister of State.

In view of these factors and the frequently discussed possibility of amending Article 9, the additional safeguard afforded by Article 66(2) cannot be underestimated.[51]

The powers of the Cabinet are set out in Article 73 of the Constitution. These include the administration of the law; the conduct of affairs of state; the management of foreign affairs; the conclusion of treaties, with the approval of the Diet; the administration of the civil service; the preparation of the budget; the issuing of Cabinet orders (*seirei*); and the right to grant general amnesty, special amnesty, commutation of punishment, reprieve and restoration of rights. Article 4 of the Cabinet Law states the Cabinet shall perform its functions through Cabinet meetings presided over by the Prime Minister and Article 74 of the Constitution provides that all laws and Cabinet orders must be signed by the competent Minister of State and countersigned by the Prime Minister. A potential contradiction might appear to have arisen in that the Cabinet can issue orders in order to execute the provisions of the Constitution and of the law and yet Article 41 states that the Diet is the sole law-making organ of the State. However, these orders are more correctly to be considered as administrative regulations rather than constituting any higher form of legal instrument such as would conflict with Article 41.[52]

Within the Cabinet structure, mention must be made of one particular office, namely that of the Prime Minister. As can be seen in Table 2 (p 240) this is much more than a private office since it contains 12 agencies or commissions, most of which are headed by a Minister of State. Whilst at one level it performs what might be characterised as an essential administrative housekeeping function,

48 Noda, *supra*, n 18, p 94, n 4.

49 The participation in UN peacekeeping was only approved in 1992 with the Law on Co-operation with UN Peace-keeping Operations which came into force on 10 August 1992. For a review of Article 9 and the use of the Self Defence Force see: Hamura, S and Shiu, E, 'Renunciation of War as a Universal Principle of Mankind – A look at the Gulf War and the Japanese Constitution' (1995) 44 *International and Comparative Law Quarterly* 426. On Article 9 see McNelly, T, 'The Renunciation of War in the Japanese Constitution' (1962) 77 *Political Science Quarterly* 350.

50 McKean, M, 'Comment' (1990) 53 No 2 *Law and Contemporary Problems* 197.

51 For a discussion of the current conflict between Article 9 and defence spending see Auer, JE, 'Article Nine of Japan's Constitution: From Renunciation of Armed Force "Forever" to the Third Largest Defense Budget in the World' (1990) 52 No 2 *Law and Contemporary Problems* 171.

52 Noda, *supra*, n 18, p 96.

contained within this structure are some of the organs responsible for the development and administration of Japan's postwar economic success and security. Thus, in many ways, the Prime Minister's office is the embodiment of the administrative state, which in the postwar years experienced rapid growth and development.[53] To achieve this it was necessary to have a highly organised and efficient bureaucracy.

Although a study of the bureaucracy in Japan is beyond the scope of this work, mention must be made of its unique place and influence on Japanese government and politics. Following the Meiji Restoration in 1867, Japan established a strong bureaucratic administrative structure. A ruling elite was put in place which, whilst providing an essential continuity in the process of government, has also, in effect, controlled the country for more than a century.[54] The pre-eminence of administrative elites, rather than being something new, was very much in line with the Confucian tradition of bestowing high prestige upon government officials.[55] However, the transformation of the bureaucracy at that time involved a move from a regional to national institution and from a system based on birth and ascription to one based on merit and achievement.[56]

The introduction of the cabinet system in 1885 meant that the bureaucracy was, in theory, responsible through the Cabinet to the Emperor, although the reality was somewhat different. Civil servants were appointed by the Emperor and acted in his name. However, since the competence of the Cabinet was limited to assisting the Emperor, it was unable to control the day-to-day activities of government by bureaucratic means and was reduced to being 'a link between seen and unseen organs of government'.[57] Operating under a system of imperial sovereignty meant that there was no sense in which bureaucrats were public servants and the word used to describe civil servants was *kanri*, 'government official' which in effect meant that this privileged class were servants of the Emperor and not the people.[58] Moreover in such circumstances there was little attempt to control abuse of power by officials and the arrogant and non-egalitarian ethos was summarised by the phrase *kanson minpi* – 'respect for officials and scorn for the people'.[59]

---

53 The National Government Organisation Law, 1948 provides for the structural liaison between the various ministries, agencies and commissions under the authority of the Cabinet and Prime Minister. See Table 2, p 240 below and Table 3, p 241 below.

54 Wilson, RA, *Genesis of the Meiji Government in Japan 1868–1871*, 1957, University of California Press; Ishii, R, *A History of Political Institutions in Japan*, 1980, The Japan Foundation; Hackett, RF, 'Political Modernisation and the Meiji *Genro*' in Ward, RE (ed), *Political Development in Modern Japan*, 1968, Princeton University Press; Rothacher, A, *The Japanese Power Elite* , 1993, Macmillan; Silberman, BS, 'Bureaucratic Development and the Structure of Decision-Making in the Meiji Period' (1967) 27 *Journal of Asian Studies* 81; Silberman 'Bureaucratic Development and the Structure of Decision-Making in Japan: 1868–1925' (1970) 29 *Journal of Asian Studies* 347.

55 Storry, *supra*, n 1, pp 80–82; Beasley, *supra*, n 1, p 16.

56 Lehmann, JP, *The Roots of Modern Japan*, 1982, p 199, Macmillan; Abe *et al*, *supra*, n 9, p 33.

57 Burks, *supra*, n 5, p 101.

58 Noda, *supra*, n 18, p 103.

59 NcNelly, *supra*, n 1, p 93. In general see, Silberman, BS, 'The Bureaucratic Role in Japan, 1900–1945: The Bureaucrat as Politician' in Silberman, BS and Harootunin, HD (eds), *Japan in Crisis: Essays in Taisho Democracy*, 1974, Princeton University Press.

One of the key successes of the Occupation was to democratise the bureaucracy, first and foremost by making it clear that government officials were 'public servants', ie *komuin*. This is underlined by Article 15(2) of the constitution which states that public officials are servants 'of the whole community – and not any group thereof'. It also makes clear that since 'the people have an inalienable right to choose their public servants and dismiss them' that the civil service is in effect subject to popular control through the Diet. Article 73(4) further strengthens the idea of accountability by stating that the Cabinet shall 'administer the civil service, in accordance with standards established by law'. To this end the National Public Service Law 1947 was introduced to regulate all aspects of government service. It is administered by the National Personnel Authority (*Jinjiin*) which is an autonomous organisation with the status of an advisory bureau to the Cabinet (see Table 3 (p 241)).[60] The fact that the National Personnel Authority puts all matters related to the civil service beyond the control of the ministries, is as important for accountability as it is frustrating to the ambitions of the ministries. Nevertheless, it has withstood attempts to dispense with it and has survived with its independence intact.[61]

The task of reform which the Occupation had set itself necessarily relied upon the existence of an administrative infrastructure to put the plans into effect. The prewar bureaucracy was well placed to preserve itself and, save for the initial moves to make it democratically accountable, received very little attention in relation to its own reform and reorganisation. Since the civil service was not the prime object of the occupation purges, the old style elite survived, along with the attitudes and management style of prewar times.[62] By co-operating with and implementing Occupation reforms the bureaucrats maintained their position of influence in the structures of government and were able successfully to pursue the national policy of economic recovery and industrial growth with which they have rightly been credited.[63] Furthermore, the fact that institutional structures changed as a result of the Occupation did not alter the position of the bureaucratic elite in terms of authority or power.[64]

Whatever the power of the bureaucracy, it is part of an interdependent triangle, a set of interlocking elites consisting of politicians, big business and bureaucrats.[65] This 'iron triangle' or, as some writers term it, the 'ruling triad' works on a system of mutually beneficial activities which both secure and perpetuate the structure of government which has run Japan for the last 50 years.[66] In many ways it mirrors what one writer identified as the 'system of

60 Noda, *supra*, n 18, p 101.

61 Stockwin, *supra*, n 5, p 145.

62 McNelly, *supra*, n 1, pp 31–33.

63 Johnson, 1982, *supra*, n 9.

64 Koh, BC, *Japan's Administrative Elite*, 1989, p 257, University of California Press; Pempel, TJ, 'The Bureaucratisation of Policymaking in Postwar Japan' (1974) 18 *American Journal of Political Science* 647; Keehn, EB, 'Managing Interests in the Japanese Bureaucracy' (1990) 30 *Asian Survey* 1021.

65 Haley, *supra*, n 10, Chapter 7; Johnson, 1982, *supra*, n 9; Johnson, 1995, *supra*, n 9, Chapter 6; van Wolferen, *supra*, n 9, Chapter 14.

66 Muramatsu, M and Krauss, ES, 'Bureaucrats and Politicians in Policymaking: The Case of Japan' (1984) 78 *American Political Science Review* 126; Campbell JC, 'Democracy and Bureaucracy in Japan' in Ishida and Krauss (eds), *supra*, n 9.

irresponsibilities' based on a tripartite hierarchy of mutual responsibilities which prevailed in Imperial Japan.[67] Nowadays the beneficial mutuality operates in the following manner: bureaucrats assist corporations through the granting of licences and issuing of administrative guidance; the corporations assist the politicians through financial support for election campaigns and the politicians assist the bureaucrats through the allocation of budgets, or more importantly, following retirement as a civil servant, by offering them candidacy in elections or a post in the party hierarchy.[68] Furthermore, on retirement, the bureaucrats are offered posts in corporations; the corporations are watched over and benefit from their politician advocates in the Diet and the politicians receive support from the bureaucrats in policymaking.

In many ways the role of the bureaucrat is pivotal in this structure, not least because very often he will be dealing with a former colleague who is now a politician or in the company hierarchy. Certainly he is at the apex of the iron triangle in terms of power over the politicians and corporations, all of which further underlines the important distinction between power and authority in the structures of modern Japanese government.[69] The move of a bureaucrat from the apex of the triangle is so institutionalised that it has a word to describe it, namely *amakudari*; literally translated as 'the descent from heaven' it conveys much about the role of bureaucracy in modern Japan.[70] The move is more than a mere sinecure. It is intended that the bureaucrat utilise his contacts with former colleagues and by moving around the triangle he is merely taking up another role in the power structure as well as fostering the next generation of the ruling elite. Although Article 103(2) of the National Public Service Law prohibits a national government employee from obtaining a job closely connected with his administrative post for a period of two years after retirement, in practice Article 103(3) provides a 'let out' whereby a job may be taken as long as the move is approved by the National Personnel Authority as not contrary to the spirit of the law. In practice this means that the process appears to be 'lightly controlled'.[71] The process of *amakudari* is not limited to

67 Maruyama, *supra*, n 9. In his essay 'Thought and Behaviour Patterns of Japan's Wartime Leaders', Professor Maruyama identifies three basic types of political personality vested with power, authority and violence who through a structure of mutual relationships create a 'system of irresponsibilities'. Although he used this device to explain the fascist period, in particular wartime activities, he also acknowledges that the structural relationship applies to 'the entire political world of Imperial Japan' pp 128–31.

68 The beneficial relationships of the 'iron triangle' were the subject of a paper by Professor Takashi Maruta, presented to the symposium on 'Japanese Law in a Comparative Cultural Perspective' at the 1995 Meeting of the Research Committee on the Sociology of Law, International Sociological Association in Tokyo and titled 'In the Same Boat: Legal and Political Structure of the Japanese Authority'. He concludes that the 'iron triangle' has three major benefits. (1) It enables long-term planning of national economic policy. (2) It protects domestic industry against foreign competitors. (3) It contributes to an integrated economic policy. However, whilst there is little doubt that the 'iron triangle' contributed to 38 years' of government by a single, conservative party, Maruta poses the question as to whether it can survive the post-LDP era.

69 Maruyama, *supra*, n 9, p 128.

70 Johnson, C, 'The Reemployment of Retired Government Bureaucrats in Japanese Big Business' (1974) 14 *Asian Survey* 953; Blumenthal, T, 'The Practice of *Amakudari* within the Japanese Employment System' (1985) 25 *Asian Survey* 310.

71 Stockwin, *supra*, n 5, p 149.

central government and is very much part of local government where, however, legal restrictions such as apply to *amakudari* in central government do not exist.[72]

As far as the process of government is concerned, the influence of the bureaucracy is twofold; first, the effect of bureaucratic power on policymaking and second, the control it has over policy implementation.[73] As one writer has commented, bureaucrats 'make most major decisions, draft virtually all legislation, control the budget and are the source of all major policy innovations in the system'.[74] If this is seen within the context of the control exercised over the implementation of policy through the use, amongst other things, of administrative guidance, it becomes clear that within the ruling triangle there is, at the very least, a concentration of power in the bureaucracy. Furthermore, just as with the Emperor, there was an important distinction to be made between 'reigning' and 'ruling', the same analysis may apply to the process of government. There may be discussion about the exact balance of power, but 'political scientists who ignore the bureaucratic dimension are likely to misconceive the true capabilities and limitations of the Japanese government'.[75] In essence the clear distinction which has to be made is between those who have power and those who merely exercise authority.

72 The importance of local government in modern Japan cannot be overlooked. Whereas the Meiji Constitution made no mention of local government, as part of the process of democratisation, the new constitution put in place the decentralised system of local autonomy; an entire chapter (Articles 92–95) is devoted to securing the authority of local government: see Abe *et al, supra,* n 9, Chapter 7; MacDougall, TE, 'Democracy and Local Government in Postwar Japan' in Ishida and Krauss (eds), *supra,* n 9; Yoshida,Y, 'Authority of the National and Local Governments under the Constitution' (1990) 53 *Law and Contemporary Politics* 123.

73 Ramsayer and Rosenbluth, *supra,* n 9, Chapter 6; Haley, 1991, *supra,* n 10, Chapter 7; Campbell, J, 'Democracy and Bureaucracy in Japan' in Ishida and Krauss (eds), *supra,* n 9, Chapter 6.

74 Johnson, 1982, *supra,* n 9, p 20.

75 Johnson, 1995, *supra,* n 9, p 140.

I THE STRUCTURE OF JAPANESE GOVERNMENT

Table 1

Source: Organisation of the Government of Japan, Institute of Administrative Management, Management & Co-ordination Agency, Prime Minister's Office, 1992

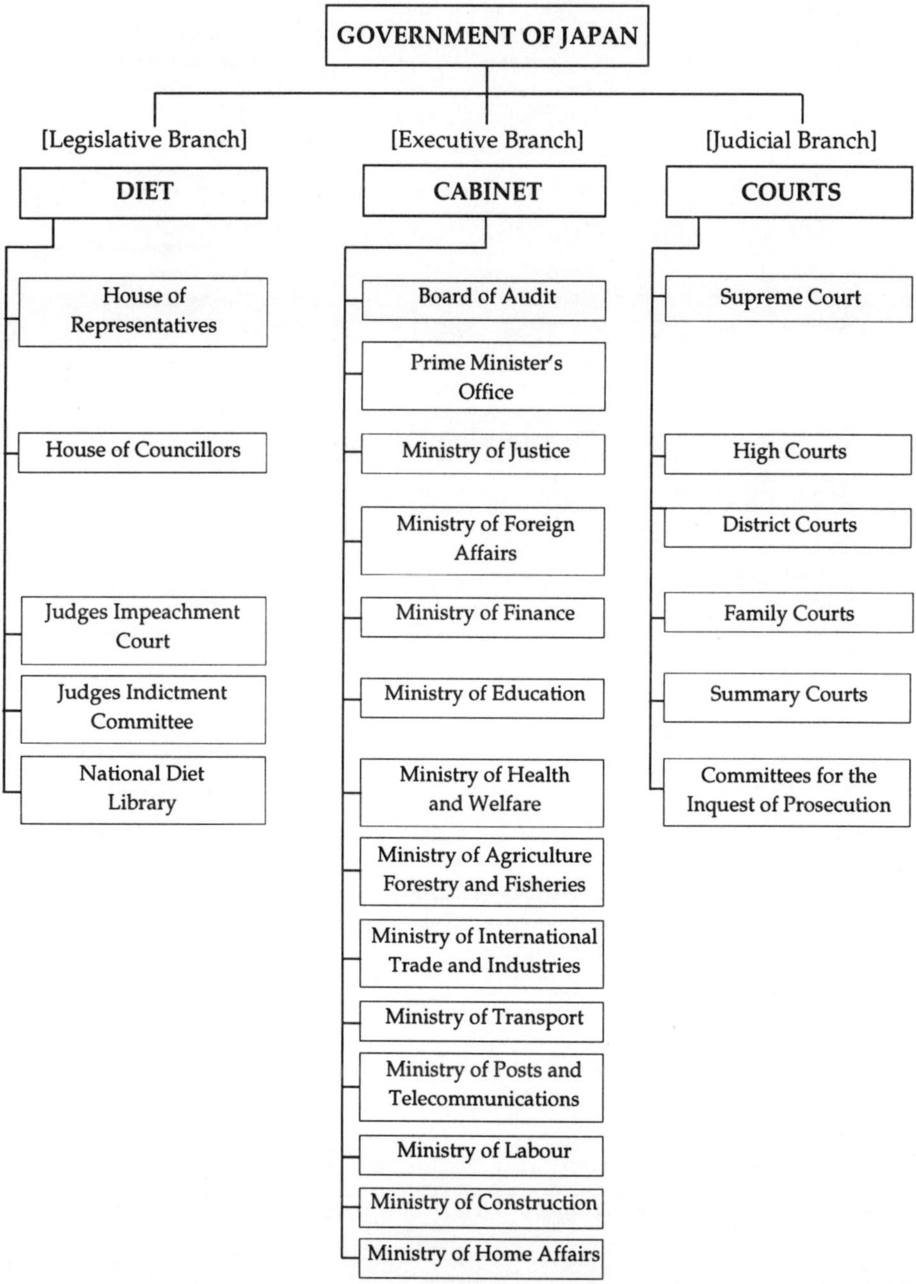

Table 2

Source: Organisation of the Government of Japan, Institute of Administrative Management, Management & Co-ordination Agency, Prime Minister's Office, 1992

Office on the Ministerial Level or Ministry	Commission	Agency
Prime Minister's Office	Fair Trade Commission National Public Safety Commission Environmental Disputes Coordination Commission	Imperial Household Agency Management and Coordination Agency Hokkaido Development Agency Defence Agency Economic Planning Agency Science and Technology Agency Environment Agency Okinawa Development Agency National Land Agency Defence Facilities Administration Agency
Ministry of Justice	National Bar Examination Administration Commission Public Security Examination Commission	Public Security Investigation Agency
Ministry of Foreign Affairs		
Ministry of Finance		National Tax Administration Agency
Ministry of Education		Agency for Cultural Affairs
Ministry of Health and Welfare		Social Insurance Agency
Ministry of Agriculture Forestry and Fisheries		Food Agency Forestry Agency Fisheries Agency
Ministry of International Trade and Industry		Agency of Natural Resources and Energy Patent Office Small and Medium Enterprise Agency
Ministry of Transport	Central Labour Relations Commission for Seafarers	Maritime Safety Agency Marine Accidents Inquiry Agency Meteorological Agency
Ministry of Posts and Telecommunications		
Ministry of Labour	Central Labour Relations Commission	
Ministry of Construction		
Ministry of Home Affairs		Fire-Defence Agency

Note: Defence Facilities Administration Agency shall be set up in Defence Agency

Table 3

Source: Organisation of the Government of Japan, Institute of Administrative Management, Management & Co-ordination Agency, Prime Minister's Office, 1992

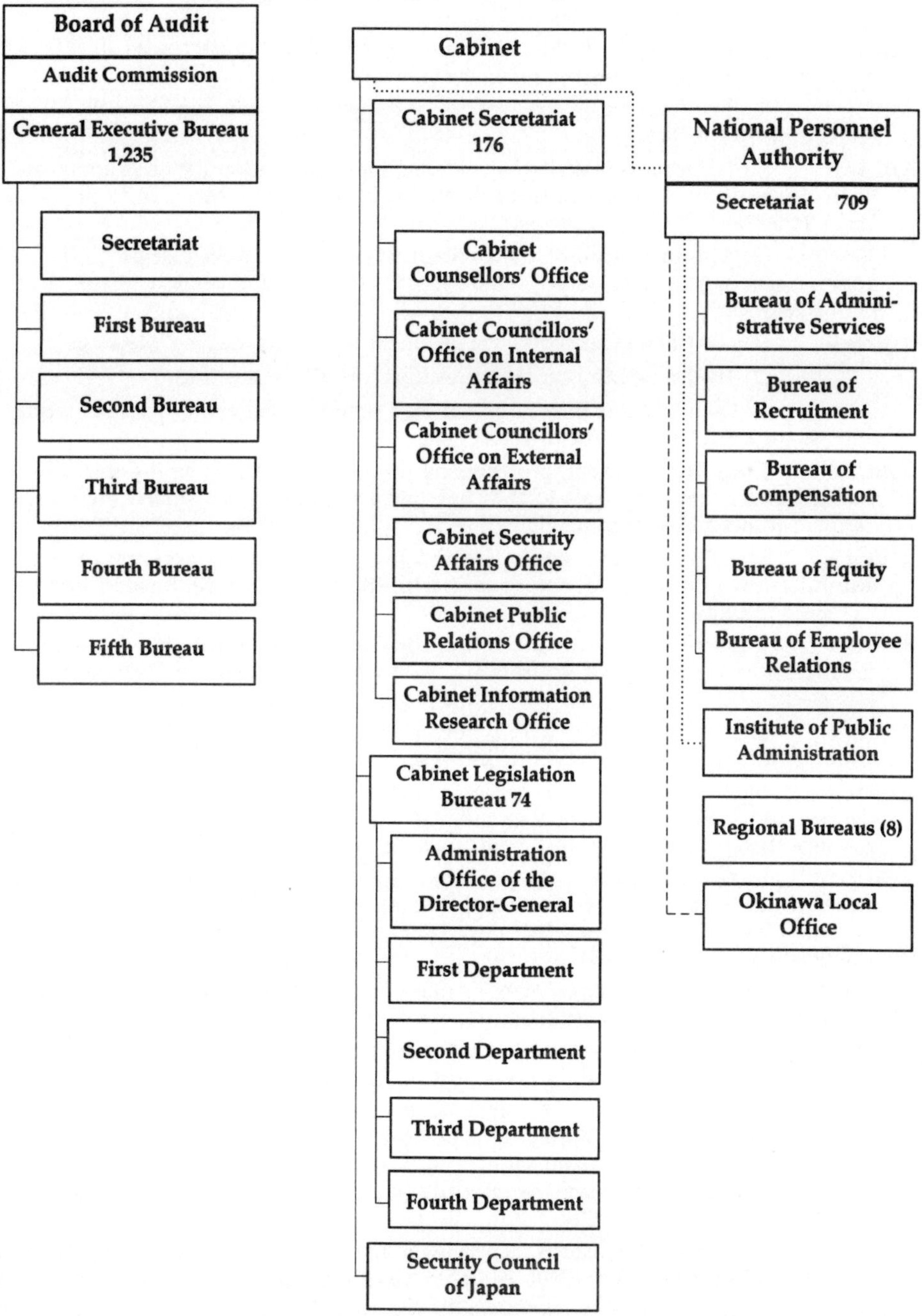

THE CABINET LAW

(Law No 5 of 1947, as amended)

Article 1. The Cabinet shall perform functions provided for in Article 73 and other articles of the constitution of Japan.

Article 2. (1) The Cabinet shall be composed of the Prime Minister, who shall be its head, and not more than twenty Ministers of State.

(2) The Cabinet, in the exercise of executive power, shall be collectively responsible to the Diet.

Article 3. (1) The Ministers shall divide among themselves administrative affairs and be in charge of their respective share thereof as the competent Minister, as provided for by other law.

(2) The provision of the preceding paragraph does not preclude the appointment of Ministers who have no specific share of administrative affairs under their charge.

Article 4. (1) The Cabinet shall perform its functions through Cabinet Meetings.

(2) The Prime Minister shall preside over Cabinet Meetings.

(3) Each Minister may submit to the Prime Minister any question or matter and ask for a Cabinet Meeting therefore.

Article 5. The Prime Minister, representing the Cabinet, shall submit Cabinet bills, budgets and other proposals to the Diet, and shall report to the Diet on general national affairs and foreign relations.

Article 6. The Prime Minister shall exercise control and supervision over the administrative branches in accordance with the policies to be decided upon at Cabinet Meetings.

Article 7. The Prime Minister shall, following consultation at Cabinet Meetings, decide on any point of doubt relating to jurisdiction between the competent Ministers.

Article 8. The Prime Minister may suspend the official measures or orders of any administrative office, pending action by the Cabinet.

Article 9. In case the Prime Minister is prevented from discharging his functions, or the post of the Prime Minister is vacant, the Minister of State designated by him in advance shall perform temporarily the functions of the Prime Minister.

Article 10. In case a competent Minister of State is prevented from discharging his functions, or the post of such Minister is vacant. the Prime Minister, or the Minister of State designated by him, shall perform temporarily the functions of the said competent Minister of State.

Article 11. No provisions imposing obligations or restricting rights can be made in a Cabinet Order unless authorized by law.

Article 12. (1) There shall be set up in the Cabinet a Secretariat.

(2) The Cabinet Secretariat shall be in charge of general affairs such as arrangement of the agenda of Cabinet Meetings, be in charge of the coordination necessary for keeping integration of the policies of administrative offices such as the coordination of important matters for decision by Cabinet Meetings, and be in charge of the collection and researches of information concerning important policies of the Cabinet.

(3) Besides the matters mentioned in the preceding paragraph, the Cabinet Secretariat shall assist the work of the Cabinet as provided for by a Cabinet Order.

(4) Besides the Secretariat there shall be set up in the Cabinet necessary offices which shall assist the work of the Cabinet, as provided for by law.

Article 13. (1) The Cabinet Secretariat shall have one Chief Cabinet Secretary.

(2) The post of the Chief Cabinet Secretary shall be filled by a Minister of State.

(3) The Chief Cabinet Secretary shall preside over the affairs of the Cabinet Secretariat and shall control and supervise the personnel thereof in regard to the performance of their duties.

Article 14. (1) The Cabinet Secretariat shall have two Deputy Chief Cabinet Secretaries.

(2) The Deputy Chief Cabinet Secretaries shall assist the Chief Cabinet Secretary.

Article 14–2. (1) The Cabinet Secretariat shall have Cabinet Councillors, Cabinet Deliberators, Cabinet Researchers, Cabinet Officials and other necessary personnel.

(2) The Cabinet Councillors shall, by order, be in charge of general affairs such as arrangement of the agenda of Cabinet Meetings.

(3) The Cabinet Deliberators shall, by order, be in charge of the coordination necessary for keeping integration of the policies of administrative offices such as the coordination of important matters for decision by Cabinet Meetings.

(4) The Cabinet Researchers shall, by order, be in charge of the collection and researches of information relating to important policies of the Cabinet.

(5) The Cabinet Officials shall, by order, perform the affairs of the Cabinet Secretariat.

(6) The fixed number of the Cabinet Councillors, Cabinet Deliberators and Cabinet Researchers shall be prescribed by a Cabinet Order.

Article 15. (1) In the Cabinet Secretariat there shall be three Confidential Secretaries assigned to the Prime Minister, and one Confidential Secretary each assigned to the Ministers of State other than the Prime Minister and the competent Ministers.

(2) The Confidential Secretaries mentioned in the preceding paragraph shall, by order of the Prime Minister or of the Minister of State to whom they are respectively assigned, take charge of confidential matters or shall assist temporarily in the affairs of the administrative organs concerned including the Cabinet Secretariat.

Article 16. Deleted

Article 17. The internal organization necessary for the discharge of the affairs coming under the charge of the Cabinet Secretariat shall be prescribed by a Cabinet Order.

Article 18. So far as the affairs coming under the jurisdiction of the Cabinet Secretariat are concerned, the competent Minister as referred to in this Law shall be the Prime Minister.

THE NATIONAL GOVERNMENT ORGANIZATION LAW

(Law No 120 of 1948, as amended)

(General Provisions)

Article 1. The object of this law is to determine the national government organization necessary for the efficient prosecution of national administrative affairs by establishing standards for the organization of administrative organs under the control and jurisdiction of the Cabinet.

Article 2. (1) The national government organization shall, under the control and jurisdiction of the Cabinet, be made up of a system of administrative organs having a well-defined scope of authority and responsibility and specific functions.

(2) The national administrative organs shall, under the control and jurisdiction of the Cabinet, maintain liaison with one another so that they may consummate their administrative functions as an organic whole.

(Establishment and Abolition of Administrative Organs, Then Specific Functions, etc)

Article 3. (1) The national government organization shall be determined in this law.

(2) The national administrative organs to be established for the purpose of administrative organization shall be Office on the Ministerial Level, Ministry, Commission, and Agency. The establishment and abolition of such administrative organs shall be provided for by other law.

(3) An office on the Ministerial Level and a Ministry shall be set up as organs which takes charge of administrative affairs under the control and jurisdiction of the Cabinet. Commissions and Agencies shall be set up as independent organs of an Office on the Ministerial Level or of a Ministry; provided that, in case of special necessity, Commissions and Agencies may be set up in a Commission or Agency, of which the head is a Minister of State as provided for by law.

(4) The administrative organs established in accordance with the provisions of paragraph 2 of this Article are listed in Appendix 1 [see Table 2, p 240].

Article 4. The scope of the functions and powers of the respective administrative organs referred to in the preceding Article shall be provided for by other law.

(Heads of Administrative Organs)

Article 5. (1) The Heads of the Prime Minister's Office and of each Ministry shall be, respectively, the Prime Minister and the Minister of each Ministry (hereinafter referred to as 'each Minister'), who as competent Ministers referred to in the Cabinet Law (Law No 5 of 1947), shall have charge and control of their respective administrative affairs.

(2) Each Minister shall be appointed by the Prime Minister from among the Ministers of State. This shall not, however, preclude the Prime Minister from assuming any of these posts.

Article 6. The head of a Commission shall be called Chairman and the head of an Agency shall be called Director-General.

(Internal Subdivisions)

Article 7. (1) An Office on the Ministerial Level and a Ministry shall, for the purpose of administering its own functions have a Secretariat and Bureaus.

(2) The Secretariat and Bureaus referred to in the preceding paragraph may, in case of special necessity, have Departments.

(3) For the purpose of administering its functions, an Agency may have a Secretariat and Departments.

(4) Notwithstanding the provision of the preceding paragraph, Agencies, of which the head is a Minister of State as provided for by law, have Bureaus instead of Departments. The provision of paragraph 2 of the present article shall apply correspondingly to the Secretariat and Bureaus of the Agency which has Bureaus instead of Departments.

(5) The establishment of the Secretariat, Bureaus and Departments, and their respective jurisdiction shall be provided for by Cabinet Order.

(6) An Agency, Secretariat, Bureau and Department may have Divisions, and Offices which are equivalent to Divisions. The establishment of such Divisions and Offices and their jurisdiction shall be determined by a Cabinet Order within the limits of applicable laws.

(7) A commission may have an Executive Office as authorized by law. The provisions of paragraphs 3, 5 and 6 of this Article shall apply correspondingly to the internal organization of the Executive Office.

(Councils)

Article 8. Each administrative organ referred to in Article 3 may establish by law or Cabinet Order collegial bodies to be in charge of deliberation of important matters, review of administrative appeals or other affairs deemed proper to be dealt with by conference of men of learning and knowledge and the like within the scope of its jurisdiction as provided for by law.

(Facilities)

Article 8–2. Each administrative organ referred to in Article 3 may establish by law or Cabinet Order Experimental Laboratories, Examination or Research Institutes, Educational or Training Facilities (including facilities or organizations similar to these), Medical or Rehabilitation Facilities, Correctional or Internment Facilities and Work Facilities within the scope of its jurisdiction as provided for by law.

(Extraordinary organizations)

Article 8–3. In addition to the organizations provided for in the preceding two articles, each administrative organ may, in case of special necessity, establish by law extraordinary organizations within the scope of its jurisdiction as provided for by law.

(Local Branch Offices)

Article 9. Each administrative organ referred to in Article 3 may, as authorized by law, establish local branch offices, in case they are necessary for carrying out its functions.

(Authority and Responsibility of the Heads of Administrative Organs)

Article 10. Each Minister, Chairman of each Commission, and Director-General of each Agency, shall preside over the affairs of his organization and control and supervise its personnel in regard to the performance of its duties.

Article 11. When each Minister considers it necessary to enact, amend or abrogate any law or Cabinet Order in respect of administrative affairs under his charge, he shall submit a draft proposal to that effect to the Prime Minister for Cabinet decision.

Article 12. (1) For the purpose of implementing any law or Cabinet Order or under special authorization by law or Cabinet Order, each Minister may issue ordinances of his respective office (ordinances of the Prime Minister's Office or ministerial ordinances) in respect of administrative affairs under his charge.

(2) The head of an independent organ may submit to the competent Minister a draft of the ordinance referred to in the preceding paragraph in respect of the affairs under the jurisdiction of his organization and ask for its issuance.

(3) The Chairman of a Commission and the Director-General of an Agency, other than the heads of independent organs, may submit to the competent Minister a draft of the ordinance referred to in paragraph 1 in respect of the affairs under the jurisdiction of the Commission or the Agency, and ask for its issuance, as provided for by other law.

(4) Unless authorized by law, no penal clauses nor any provisions which impose obligations or restrict the rights of individuals may be included in ordinances referred to in paragraph 1.

Article 13. (1) Each Commission and the head of each Agency may, as provided for by other law, issue on his own initiative rules and special orders other than Cabinet Orders and orders prescribed in paragraph 1 of the preceding Article.

(2) The provision of paragraph 4 of the preceding Article shall apply correspondingly to the orders referred to in the preceding paragraph.

Article 14. (1) Each Minister, Commission or the head of each Agency may, in case it is necessary to make any public announcement in respect of the affairs under the jurisdiction of his organization, issue a Notice to that effect.

(2) Each Minister, Commission, or the head of each Agency may, for the purpose of giving orders or conveying directions in respect of the affairs under jurisdiction of his organization issue instructions or circular notices to the organizations and personnel under his jurisdiction.

Article 15. (1) Each Minister may, in accordance with the provisions of Article 150 of the Local Autonomy Law (Law No 67 of 1947), direct and supervise the heads of local public entities in their capacity as organs of the national government with respect to the execution by them of those national administrative affairs which fall under the charge of each Minister.

(2) In the case in which the control or execution of national affairs that fall within the sphere of competence of the governor of To, Do, Fu or Ken in his capacity as an organ of the national Government, is deemed to be contrary to the provisions of law or order or to the actions of each competent Minister, or if he is negligent in the control or execution of such national affairs as mentioned above, if it is difficult to correct it except by the measures provided for by Article 151–52 of the Local Autonomy Law and if it is obvious public interests will be seriously injured to leave it as it is, each competent Minister may, in accordance with the provision of the same Article, such governor to correct the said contrariness in, or the negligence of, the control or execution of the said national affairs; order him to do so; or ask for a trial by law court, and proceed to take such action on behalf of the said governor.

(3) Each Minister may request the Prime Minister that the latter shall, in accordance with the provisions of Article 246–42 of the Local Autonomy Law, ask ordinary local public entities or their heads to take measures necessary for correction of violations or improvement in respect of performance of or control and execution of the affairs which come under the charge of each Minister.

(4) On the basis of requests made by each Minister in accordance with the provision of the preceding paragraph, the Prime Minister may take necessary measures.

Article 16. (1) When the head of a local public entity finds that an ordinance of an Office on the Ministerial Level, a ministerial ordinance, or an order or direction issued or action taken in accordance with the provisions of the preceding Article by each Minister to the head of a local public entity is contrary to the principles of local autonomy, he may make due representation to that effect to the Prime Minister. If the Prime Minister finds the representation well-founded, he shall make investigation of the matter within thirty days, give the Ministers concerned necessary instructions and take other adequate measures. If he finds the representation unfounded, he shall so notify the head of the local public entity stating the reason therefor.

(2) The representation referred to in the preceding paragraph shall not thereby affect the validity of an order, direction or other action of the Minister concerned.

(Parliamentary Vice-Minister)

Article 17. (1) Each Ministry and each Agency, of which the head is a Minister of State as provided for by law, shall have one Parliamentary Vice-Minister.

(2) Notwithstanding the provision of the preceding paragraph, the Ministries enumerated in Appendix II [Ministry of Finance; Ministry of Agriculture; Ministry of Forestry and Fisheries; Ministry of International Trade and Industry] may have two Parliamentary Vice-Ministers.

(3) The Parliamentary Vice-Minister shall assist the Minister heading the Ministry or Agency, participate in the formation of policies and in programme planning, conduct the political affairs; and, under prior orders of the Minister heading the Ministry or Agency, perform the Minister's functions on his behalf in the absence of the Minister.

(4) As regards the Ministries where two parliamentary Vice-Ministers are assigned, the scope of the functions as referred to in the preceding paragraph to be carried out by each of the Parliamentary Vice-Ministers and the order whereby each Parliamentary Vice-Minister perform Minister's functions on his behalf shall be determined by the Minister heading the Ministry.

(5) Appointment and dismissal of the Parliamentary Vice-Minister shall be effected by the Cabinet upon request of the Minister heading the Ministry or Agency.

(6) In the event of the resignation en masse of the Cabinet, the Parliamentary Vice-Minister shall lose his position simultaneously with the resignation of the Prime Minister and all the other Ministers of State.

(Administrative Vice-Minister, Deputy Director-General of Agency, etc)

Article 17–2. (1) Each Ministry and each Agency, of which the head is a Minister of State as provided for by law, Article 3 shall have one Administrative Vice-Minister.

(2) The Administrative Vice-Minister shall assist the Minister heading the Ministry or Agency in such a way as to keep in order the affairs of Ministry or Agency and to supervise the working of respective Bureaus and Departments and of the organizations provided for in Articles 8 and 9.

(3) In case of special necessity, the Agencies other than those of which the head is a Minister of State as provided for by law may have a Deputy Director-General as a position to assist the Director-General and to keep in order the affairs of the Agency. The establishment of such a Deputy Director-General shall be provided for by Cabinet Order.

(4) In case of special necessity, the Prime Minister's Office, each Ministry and Agency may have positions in charge of partial coordination of the affairs thereof. The establishment and the duties of such positions shall be provided for by law (by Cabinet Order in case of Agencies other than those of which the head is a Minister of State as provided for by law).

(Confidential Secretary)

Article 18. (1) Each Ministry shall have one Confidential Secretary.

(2) The Confidential Secretary shall, under orders by the Minister, take charge of confidential matters and assist temporarily in the affairs of respective administrative organs.

(Positions in Internal Subdivisions)

Article 19. (1) An Executive Office of a Commission, Bureau, Department, Division and Office equal to Division shall have respectively Director of Executive Office, Chief of Bureau, Chief of Department, Chief of Division and Chief of Office.

(2) Establishment and duties of the positions of Chief of a Secretariat, Deputy Chief of a Bureau or Department, or Deputy Director in the Executive Office of a Commission shall be effected by Cabinet Order.

(3) The establishment, duties and fixed number of positions which may be created to take charge of partial coordination of affairs, or of positions equal to the Chiefs of Divisions which may be created to take charge of affairs which do not fall under the charge of any Division (including Offices equal to Divisions) in a Secretariat, Bureau, Department or Executive Office of a Commission respectively, shall be provided for by a Cabinet Order. The same applies to the establishment of positions equivalent to these in an Agency which do not have a Secretariat, Bureau, or Department.

(Special Provision for Administrative Organs charged with Government Enterprises)

Article 20. Regardless of the provisions of Article 7 and of the preceding Article, provisions may be made otherwise by law in respect of the administrative organs charged with government enterprises.

(Organizational Title of Position)

Article 21. Each of the positions provided for in this Law shall have an organizational title in addition to its official class title prescribed by the position classification plan.

(Report to the Diet and Publication)

Article 22. (1) The Government shall report to the Diet any establishment, reorganization or abolition of the organizations to be provided for by Cabinet Order pursuant to the provisions of paragraph 5 of Article 7 (including the case where it is applicable as provided for by paragraph 7), Article 8, Article 8–2, paragraph 3 or 4 of Article 17 or paragraph 2 of Article 19 and other organizations of equal importance during the session to be convoked at a proximate date.

(2) The Government shall publish by the official gazette, a list of organizations of the national administrative organs at least once a year.

Additional Rules

1 The date of enforcement and other matters necessary to enforce this law shall be provided for by separate law.

2 The Government shall, after the lapse of five years from the date of enforcement of this law, conduct without delay a comprehensive review of organizations prescribed in paragraph 1 of Article 22 and the ceiling prescribed in Article 25, and take necessary measures based on the results.

Additional Rules

Article 25. The ceiling of the number of Secretariats (in case of Secretariats of Agencies, limited to those established in Agencies which the head is a Minister of State as provided for by law) and Bureaus established pursuant to the provisions of paragraphs 1, 3 or 4 of Article 7 shall be 128 for the time being.

II THE EMPEROR SYSTEM

Hall, J, 'A Monarch for Modern Japan' in Ward, RE (ed), *Political Development in Modern Japan*, 1968, pp 11–19, 57–58, 59–64, Princeton University Press

Central to Japan's history of political modernization has been the role of the monarch – the *tenno* – and the institutions and ideas adhering to the imperial tradition. No aspect of the Japanese political system has proved so controversial and so little understood, for as with the English monarch, constitutional definitions of powers and functions reveal but a narrow range of the manifold sensibilities which the emperor was able to touch in the lives and minds of his subjects. The very diffuseness and mysteriousness of the imperial presence has frustrated systematic or objective analysis. The emperor has been many things to many people. In fact he has often seemed to hold contradictory meanings for the same individual who might rationally disapprove of, yet emotionally admire, the deep feelings of national pride which the monarchy stirred within him. The Emperor Meiji has been extolled as the father of progress in modern Japan, and yet his memory has at the same time been maligned as the ultimate source of the destructive forces of imperialism and militarism which nearly destroyed his country.

After the end of the Second World War, when the taboos against criticism of the monarchy were lifted in Japan, the emperor was subjected to a deluge of disparaging literature which heaped upon the '*tenno* system' blame for centuries of suffering by the Japanese people, for the recent failure of democracy, and for the drift toward disastrous war in the Pacific. In much of this literature of disenchantment and resentment, Japanese writers took refuge in the unhappy though self-comforting claim that they had faced unique handicaps as a nation because of the unmatched virility of reactionary forces which oppressed their country through the agency of the emperor system. Modern Japan, they have implied, was a victim of its monarchy.

Granted that from the point of view of its history and cultural context the Japanese monarchy has had features quite distinct from the monarchies of the Western world, yet taken in broad perspective, in terms of the many interrelated processes of political change out of which modern nation states have evolved, the relationship of the Japanese emperor to the problem of nation building has not been so unique as some have claimed. The fact that Japan, unlike China or Indonesia, carried its monarch into modern times is an index to one of the most obvious and significant differences separating Japan's political history from that of other Asian states, making it in reality more nearly comparable to those of the Western democracies today. 'The stability of any given democracy,' Martin Lipset has observed, has depended 'not only on economic development but also upon the effectiveness and the legitimacy of its political system'. And monarchies have proved sufficiently useful as legitimizing devices that today 'we have the absurd fact that ten out of twelve stable European and English-speaking democracies are monarchies'.

Of course these Western monarchies are not the only 'modern' states in the world today, and many a Japanese will opt for the greater openness of an America or the social policies of a Russia. But if we are inclined to place value upon the factor or stability during the process of political modernization, monarchy has been able to play a crucial and not altogether negative role. If Japan has achieved in outcome a condition comparable to the 'stable democracies', she also shared at the outset many of the problems which confront the late modernizers in the world today. And though the

Japanese may look back upon the last hundred years of their history to decry the burden of state authoritarianism which weighed upon them, one wonders whether they are prepared to exchange those conditions for the prospect of national disintegration which could have resulted from a society warring upon itself or under a headless political anarchy. It is possible, then, that the monarchy helped carry Japan through certain phases of modernization that would have proved difficult under a less controlled political system.

In their study of the challenges faced by Japan and Turkey in achieving the transition between traditional and modern national organization, Ward and Rustow have observed a typology of crises and necessary responses. These nations – and they suggest others fit the pattern as well – were faced first with the crises of national identity, then with the critical need of self-defense against external enemies, then with the need for adequate development (chiefly economic), and ultimately with the need to achieve a satisfying internal political adjustment – the problem of popular relationship to the political process. Unquestionably in the case of Japan the emperor played a decisive role in getting Japan through the first several crises on the path toward modernization. As an embodiment of Japan's sense of national identity, as the bridge linking traditional sources of legitimacy to the new state authority, as the father figure which justified his subjects' self-discipline and sacrifice, the monarch became both a rallying point for his people and a means of concentrating authority behind the emerging national leadership. In the first decades after 1868 the emperor came to symbolize all the forces of self-control and enforced stability which combined to channel the prime energies of the Japanese toward meeting the foreign challenge and toward adopting essential social and economic reforms.

Yet if the emperor served the Japanese people well in the initial stages of the forced march toward modernization, the same cannot be said for all that followed. No thinking Japanese who lived through the 1930s and 1940s can easily forget the extremes to which the Japanese people were driven in the name of the emperor. (And the fact that the same individual continues on the Japanese throne perpetuates to this day a lingering fear that the spirit which once made him the agent for nationalist excesses may still lie latent beneath the benign exterior of the postwar polity.) It is understandable too that thinking Japanese, who had been obliged to make their settlement with the dogmas of the imperial polity (*kokutai*) and the public ritualism of emperor veneration during the prewar decades should live in horror of a repetition of that experience. Outsiders who have come upon Japan in her second modern incarnation, reborn out of the ashes of war and defeat, have sometimes dismissed too casually those black years. Yet they need only refresh their memory of the literature of hatred and denunciation in the West which accused Japan so vehemently of a 'crime against herself and against civilization.

What went wrong? Why was it that an institution which seemed so appropriate to the problems of Meiji Japan should have failed so disastrously in the age of *Showa*? Our typology of political modernization suggests that the answer lay in the area of adjustment between the mass needs of the modern state and the political process as a whole. With respect to the monarchy this involved essentially the related problems of the transfer of sovereignty from out of the hands of the emperor into those of the people and of relinquishing the mythological belief surrounding the throne. The conversion of transcendental monarchy into a modern representative government, of whatever political orientation, has never been smooth, and it may well be that it has never been achieved without violence or at least the generation of a great deal of social heat.

Nonetheless, the eventual change from monarchal to popular sovereignty has been a necessary prelude to the formation of the modern state, and the alternative routes which Japan might have used to achieve a government responsible to the people were perhaps more limited than we care to admit. The question even suggests itself whether, if the transfer of sovereignty had been accomplished without the experience of the totalitarian 1940s, it could have been done without an equal and compensating trauma of another sort. Was Japan's recent war simply the direction outward of the violence of the social and ideological revolutions which Japan had avoided by its conservative resolution of its first steps in the modernization process? Or was there a more moderate alternative?

It would be hard to deny that the initial form that the modern Japanese monarchy took proved resistant to the changes which might have permitted an easy transition to popular sovereignty. The present status of the emperor, though perhaps anticipated in the hidden desires of the Japanese during the tragic years of wartime suffering, was brought about only as a result of defeat and occupation directive. The constitution of 1946, in giving legal form to a government of the people with whom resides sovereign power' and in which the emperor assumed the position of a 'symbol of the state and of the unity of the people,' has completed the long transition of the monarchy from absolute sovereign to popular symbol. Has Japan, then, at last entered the ranks of the 'stable democracies'? Have the Japanese attained a state of affairs in which they feel secure in their own sense of achievement and control over their political destinies and sufficiently affluent that they can support without begrudging it a family-man monarch and a tennis-playing crown prince? Or is the emperor still a lingering threat to popular sovereignty and democratic life in Japan? The masses, who are so often evoked in regard to questions of this kind, seem to forget the past more readily than do their interrogators. The recent acts of right-wing violence which have struck terror into the hearts of the intellectual keepers of the Japanese conscience have not stirred many to demand the total eradication of the emperor system. And certainly the framers of the new constitution have made it most difficult to return the emperor to the center of a virile ultranationalist movement without the most obvious tampering with the legal foundations of the state. Time may indeed have fashioned a safe monarch for modern Japan.

But among the Japanese people some are apt to be sceptical. After having succumbed to the myth of imperial omnipotence during the years of wartime hysteria, they find it hard to believe that the imperial institution can be easily restructured. And although the literature of polemic criticism of the 'emperor system' has begun to subside, Japanese writers are still inclined to question whether the emperor has been safely democratized and whether on historical grounds the monarchy can justly be admired. To follow this critical literature too closely would distract us unduly from the effort to bring impartial judgment to bear on the problem of the emperor's role in the modernization of Japanese politics, yet it is of some use to put it on the record so as to identify one extreme in the range of interpretations to which serious scholars subscribe. It is hard, furthermore, to attempt any discourse on the Japanese monarchy without implicit engagement with this literature because of its continued prevalence.

Let us take for example the works of Inoue Kiyoshi, not because he is necessarily a representative writer, but because he is respected as an historian, and is in fact rather moderate among those who have written to 'expose the *tenno* myth' since the war. His 1953 paperback publication entitled *The Emperor System* (*Tennosei*) brings together articles published by him from 1946–52, and features his 'History of the Emperor System' which had served as the lead article in the important volume edited by the *Rekishigaku*

Kenkyukai in 1946 entitled *How Do Historians Look at the Emperor System?* Inoue's history of the emperor in Japan has little good to say for the monarchy. 'The line of emperors, unbroken for ages eternal', he begins, 'was able to perpetuate itself only because it served as the apex of an unbroken condition of suffering for the people'. There was, of course, a prior condition, before the appearance of the emperor, 'when the Japanese people inhabited the islands enjoying a democratic society in perfect peace and freedom. All land was owned communally and there was neither ruler nor subject.' But thereafter, with the appearance of social class distinctions, the tenno emerged to serve as the legitimizing element behind an elite power hierarchy. The climax to the long line of exploitation of the people perpetrated in the name of the emperor came with the Meiji Restoration. By the middle of the nineteenth century, Inoue claims, evidence of a popular desire for a 'people's state' had begun to manifest itself, but before this could be achieved, the samurai leadership, utilizing the revolutionary energies of the people, had carried out a counterrevolutionary movement.

The people, betrayed by their leaders, traded the domination of feudal rulers for a modern absolutism. And so, 'Japan put into practice an absolute monarchy of the kind that France had discarded a hundred years before, an absolutism much more colored by pure feudalism than that which had prevailed in France, in other words a "Japanese variety" of absolutism'. With the promulgation of the Meiji Constitution this system was legitimized and the modern emperor system was created. What this *tenno* system represented was a feudalistic control mechanism in which the bureaucracy and military using the police and the armed forces and in complete accord with the *zaibatsu* capitalists and landlords carried out a policy of domination over the workers at home and of militarism abroad. The emperor stood at the head of this state, at the point at which the bureaucracy, military, *zaibatsu,* and landlords came together, serving as their pivot. He himself was the greatest of the feudal landlords, the greatest of the *zaibatsu,* the highest bureaucrat, and the highest military officer.

There are many variations on this line of interpretation, differing chiefly in the manner in which the Meiji Restoration is handled. But it is not the bias which needs to concern us so much as certain viewpoints of a more general nature which these and other writings take for granted. Inoue has in fact made four basic assumptions which take him beyond pure polemic or historical dogma and serve to define a recurring set of questions which appear in nearly every treatment of the emperor in Japan today. These are, first, that the emperor system in premodern times had a notoriously bad influence on Japan's historical development and should be evaluated chiefly as a force for political conservatism in Japan. Second, that the emperor system of Meiji times was not a direct legacy from this earlier tradition but was an entirely new and reactionary creation. Third, that the modern monarchy was essentially antidemocratic and bears the responsibility for bringing the era of fascism and war into being. And fourth, that the present emperor represents a continuation of the prewar system. These four assumptions which characterize what might be called the 'antiestablishment' approach to the imperial institution are not necessarily new with the present generation of Japanese scholars. They have commonly been voiced by critical writers outside of Japan who had no reason to be bound by the taboos which hampered free discussion of the emperor within Japan. ...

As it turned out, the Meiji constitution had its defects. Not only did it institutionalize sovereignty in the person of a divine emperor, it gave a cloak of credibility to the myths and dogmas of sanctification which had historically supported the Japanese monarchy. It added to the Japanese monarchal tradition, in other words, the legal magic and imperial ritualism of the modern Prussian system. But were there voices which might have been raised against this in the days before the principles of popular rule were fully understood or before the doctrine of socialism had touched many minds? Figuratively and emotionally the emperor remained the most cherished symbol of national identity to Japanese from Iwakura to Uchimura Kanzo. However clearly the issues may have been drawn over the question of monopoly of power by the 'clan clique', there were certainly few who foresaw in 1889 the problems created by carrying 'Japan's particular form of monarchy' into modern times. The constitution also perpetuated that particular form of Japanese political decision-making which obscured the locus of responsibility behind an 'irresponsible' sovereign who spoke for the consensus of his political advisors. The combination of imperial absolutism and undefined responsibility continued a practice of government which was second nature to the Japanese leadership. That it passed so easily into the clauses of the Meiji constitution is to some extent the result of the failure of the German advisors to the Japanese drafters of the constitution to appreciate fully the practical differences between the Prussian and Japanese monarchies ...

...

The Emperor Today

In the end it took defeat in war and the intercession of an occupation force to explode the imperial myth and to wrest sovereignty from the inviolable emperor and grant it to the people. The new constitution not only limited the emperor to the status of national symbol but drastically stripped from him the means of maintaining himself independently of the peoples' representatives. The emperor's disavowal of his divinity, the discrediting of nationalist myths, the withdrawal of state support from Shinto, the abolition of a separate imperial military command, the elimination of the emperor's private wealth were all significant subtractions, each devised to remedy a major source of danger in the prewar system and to prevent the emperor from again being used either by an irresponsible leadership or an irrepressible people for ultranationalist purposes.

But if the institutionalization of the Meiji monarch had the full force of Japanese historical tradition behind it, the postwar establishment of a shadowy symbol devoid of power had a ring of artificiality about it. The logical result of military defeat for a Japan which had gone to war behind its sacred emperor would have been the destruction of the imperial system. Not only was it clear to the Japanese that the victorious forces after the Second World War could just as well have abolished the emperor, but they also took into the postwar period their own private aversion to the institution for which they had so recently been ready to give their all. For once the war was lost, the emperor inevitably became a victim in the effort of the Japanese to fix the blame for their wartime experience. And despite the spread of the word that the emperor had been opposed to the war and the confirming judgment of the Tokyo Trials absolving the emperor of war guilt, the thought was to persist that he should have abdicated, or even committed suicide, in 1945 and that the new constitution should have abolished the institution once and for all. The knowledge that prior to the Japanese surrender there were strong voices raised in the Allied councils which demanded the elimination of the emperor as a necessary corollary to 'unconditional surrender' served as a reminder that the institution was saved only by the decision of a conquering enemy. The presurrender disagreement among the Allies on what to do with the emperor had brought out all of the questions which still remain unresolved in the minds of the Japanese: the questions of the necessary relationship between emperor and emperor system, between emperor and aggressive militarism, and between emperor and the capacity of the Japanese to achieve political democracy. And many Japanese were unconvinced of the wisdom of the ultimate American decision and refused to believe that the emperor could be 'democratized', that a knife could be inserted between the emperor as symbol of national unity and his rampant other being, the emperor as champion of conservatism and ultranationalism. For such sceptics it was no comfort to know that retention of the emperor was in part agreed upon as an occupation expediency.

The early years of the Occupation during which the Japanese awoke to their first freedom to attack the emperor produced a flood of critical literature which questioned the intentions of the Americans in retaining the emperor and refuted the possibility that the 'emperor system' had been destroyed. Inoue Kiyoshi, for instance, put the entire subject into the context of America's desire to use Japan as a base of operations against Soviet Russia. 'In keeping with this ultimate objective,' he wrote 'America, making superficial concessions to the forces of international democracy and to democratic forces in Japan, carried out "a colonization of Japan in the name of democratization." The emperor and the emperor system were part of this same design. And so, enacting a phoney land reform and *zaibatsu* dissolution, they laid the economic foundations for a continuation of the *tenno* system.'

But as Ishida Takeshi has shown in his study of postwar Japanese opinion toward the emperor, this hypercritical attitude ultimately faded. The relative stability of postwar politics, the growing economic prosperity, and the new public image of the imperial family all contributed to the acceptance of the new constitutional formula and a return of the monarch to a position of popularity of a vastly different sort from the prewar style. The new popularity retained little of the fanatic nationalist fervor of prewar days but took delight in a sense of familiarity and intimacy. The great outpouring of interest in the wedding of the crown prince, the new ease with which the Japanese have turned back to the prewar years without rancor, taking pride in the 'great men of Meiji' or in the figure of Emperor Meiji, the ability to look with clinical objectivity at movies depicting the patriotic excesses of Japanese wartime behavior, all indicate a new maturity of the popular mind. And although there are still cynics who warn of the danger inherent in the emperor's continued existence, the behavior of the Japanese in recent years would seem to indicate otherwise. The emperor today stands as symbol, not of some irrational 'superiority' of the Japanese race, but rather as a projection of their own pride in their own achievements as a modern people; not as a reminder of the terrors of war and humiliation of defeat but rather as symbol of Japan's purity of intent to lead the world in working for peace.

Perhaps it was in the ceremonies attending the 1964 Olympics that the new popular sovereignty and the status of the emperor were most clearly displayed to the rest of the world. For amid the frenzied efforts to bring order out of the chaos which was Tokyo and in the excitement of the opening-day pageantry, the mild-mannered *Showa Tenno* belied the fact that he had once served as the mystical center of every national ritual and the rationale for every major national effort. As he stood before his countrymen in the great Olympic Stadium, it seemed no longer that it was simply through him that the fiercest feelings of pride were drawn from the hearts of the Japanese. Rather it was in the physical surroundings themselves, in the bold sweep of prestressed concrete, in the visions of superhighways arched over central Tokyo, and in the thought that the athletes of the world had been assembled with unprecedented efficiency and hospitality that the majority seemed to find their deepest satisfaction. To an observer of that moment it appeared that for the Japanese their knowledge of what they had wrought was sufficient to the occasion; through their own works they were speaking to the world in a language more direct and universal than that which could have been expressed symbolically through a sacred emperor. Clearly, a basic change in the relationship between monarch and people was being ritualized.

For the historian, the Japanese monarch today stands as both a symbol of national unity and a reminder of the vicissitudes through which the institutions of national sovereignty have passed in modern times. Few Asian nations entered the modern world by strengthening a monarchal system rather than destroying it. For Japan in its period of crisis between 1853 and 1871 the monarchy served the essential functions of assuring national unity and impressing a sense of responsibility upon the nation's leaders. Thereafter the emperor became a symbol of Japan's determination to modernize and to gain a place among the nations of the world. Japan's modern monarchy was a direct institutional and functional inheritance from the Japanese past, yet it served as a receptacle for new national aims. As the sovereign who presided over Japan's early steps toward modernization, Meiji Tenno became an inspiration to his people in their struggle to create a strong independent state. The person of the emperor linked both past and future, giving the Japanese a sense of security and identity while encouraging their dedication to the difficult tasks of reforming their social and economic institutions. But the government he stood for remained shrouded from public view by its transcendental nature and remained resistant to the kinds of modern change which were affecting the rest of the culture. If history could ask more of the Meiji leaders, it would be that they might have built into their constitution a broader vision of political tutelage which would have looked forward to both the material development of the country and to its political evolution toward fuller representation. For without such enlightened guidance the Japanese people as a whole, overwhelmed perhaps by manifold domestic and international problems, found the further reform of their government beyond their capacity. Increasingly they heaped upon their emperor the burden of their frustrated aims until they found themselves caught in the mythology of the most traditional and irrational inheritances which the emperor had brought with him out of the Japanese past.

Reborn out of the ashes of military defeat and wartime disillusionment, the *Showa* Emperor, by virtue of retaining the same body under a new constitutional system, has again become the symbol of continuity despite drastic change. And by virtue of the new myth which depicts the emperor as the symbol of Japan's good conscience which suffered silently during the war, he has literally come to embody the new determination of the Japanese to remain a peaceful democracy. Thus in its second modern transmutation the monarchy has passed still further into the realm of symbolic meaning, hopefully leaving behind those many irrational inheritances from the past which proved so dangerous when taken literally by the modern nationalist. Stripped today of power and sovereignty, the emperor serves only in the most disembodied of the manifestations with which he was historically endowed, as symbol of his country's moral consciousness. Yet behind this symbol there burns as fierce a fire of determination that Japan shall be first – this time in peace, not in war.

Higuchi, Y, 'The Constitution and the Emperor System: Is Revisionism Alive?' (1990) 53, No 1 *Law and Contemporary Problems* 55–60

CONCEALED REVISIONISM: A CERTAIN CONTINUITY IN THE STATUS OF THE EMPEROR BETWEEN THE TWO FUNDAMENTAL LAWS

A. More than a 'Symbol': The Problem of Contra Constitutionem *Practices*

In Japanese juridical culture, interpretation is greatly favored over legislation. This statement applies more on the level of the fixed constitution than on that of parliamentary laws. The Imperial Charter of 1889 underwent no revisions in its 55-year lifetime.

Thus, in order to measure exactly the real political and social repercussions of the revisionists' demands, one must consider the issue of constitutional interpretation in practice. In effect, the revisionists often achieve in practice what they have been unable to realize through explicit textual revision.

At issue is what I call 'concealed revision.' Before analyzing two typical examples of this practice, I would like to re-examine, with regard to the question of the status of the emperor, the two opposing propositions argued at the time of the drafting and implementation of the 1947 Constitution. One thesis emphasized the continuity that its proponents held should exist between the fundamental law of 1889 and the new Constitution of 1947. The second thesis called for a clean break between the two constitutions. The revisionist movement, despite its occasionally nuanced statements, seems to want to establish a certain continuity with pre-1945 practices.

As I have already suggested, the Japanese government finally accepted the constitution in 1945–46 only in order to preserve the Imperial system and to protect the person of the emperor, who risked accusation as a war criminal. One minister of the time even called the new constitution a 'lightning rod' to protect the Imperial regime.

Of which Imperial regime was he speaking? The government had at first resisted the initiatives of General MacArthur's team in the name of that which it felt to be the very essence of the Imperial regime, that is, the *kokutai*. Yet the government finally accepted the constitution in the name of the same *kokutai*.

This paradox was rendered possible by the ambiguous nature of the word *kokutai*. Indeed, the word may signify either imperial sovereignty in the juridical sense of the term, or the national belief, of a moral or sentimental order, in the emperor. Preservation of the *kokutai* in its latter sense ultimately involved a renunciation of the former sense of the term.

The *kokutai* in its juridical sense was indeed incompatible with the constitution of 1947, which proclaims the sovereignty of the people, and which defines the role of the emperor as being the 'symbol of the Japanese State and of the unity of the Japanese people'. Nevertheless, a few impassioned debates were required to clarify matters. Two fundamental lines of argument can in effect be distinguished.

On the one hand was the continuity thesis upheld by Tomoo Otah, a legal philosopher who hoped to minimize the extent of the changes caused by the promulgation of the constitution of 1947. Otah emphasized the notion that there is a certain continuity of the 'sovereignty of *nomos* (law)', and that this continuity bridges the apparent fissure between the old and new constitutions.

On the other hand was the rupture thesis of Toshiyoshi Miyazawa, constitutionalist and successor of Minobe. Criticizing Otah's thesis, Miyazawa developed his theory of the 'August Revolution', according to which Japan had already in August 1945 renounced the juridical interpretation of *kokutai* by accepting the Potsdam Declaration, which demanded Japan's adherence to the universal principle of democracy.

Otah's doctrine supports those who do not wish to recognize the abolition of the *kokutai* in the juridical sense of the word, and who hope to consolidate their position by emphasizing the continuity of the 'sovereignty of *nomos*', Miyazawa's doctrine, on the contrary, bears the great distinction of having stood for the establishment of popular sovereignty for its own sake; such popular sovereignty signified by definition the pure and simple negation of the juridical *kokutai.*

One can and must ascertain, upon reading the text of the constitution of 1947, that the *kokutai* in its juridical sense has been abolished. It remains to be verified whether the *kokutai* in its moral sense has also been changed. I shall later return to this problem, which, due to the events of 1988–89, has assumed a highly topical character. But before doing so, I would like to insist upon the juridical aspect of the problem and show how, forty years after the implementation of the constitution, the continuity thesis has reappeared to justify practices whose constitutionality has been called into question by specialists in constitutional law. I will cite but two examples. The first concerns the idea of the head of state. Is the symbolic emperor no longer the head of state? Or, on the contrary, is he still the head of state, although his role as such has become merely honorary?

In order to be characterized as a head of state, a monarch or president must have the competence, be it real or nominal, to represent his state in its external relations. We have already taken note of one example of proposed constitutional revision in this domain. The constitution stipulates, in the eighth phrase of Article 7, that the emperor is to attest to the instrument of ratification of international treaties. However, the function of 'concluding international treaties', and consequently of ratifying them is assigned to the cabinet of ministers by the second phrase of Article 7. A clear distinction has been drawn between 'ratification' itself and the 'attestation' to that ratification.

The constitution was hence designed to depict the image of a monarch whose competences have been reduced to a minimum. The text thus clearly stresses the break with the imperial regime consecrated by the Charter of 1889: A symbolic emperor based upon the principle of popular sovereignty has replaced the sovereign emperor who was termed a living god.

However, the situation is different in practice. The government insists upon a very careful wording of various diplomatic instrument. For example, the emperor only 'attests' to an ambassador's letters of accreditation, which are issued by the cabinet of ministers. Yet such letters are all the same so skillfully drafted as to lead the foreign head of state who receives them to think that they were issued by the emperor himself. Thus, in practice, attempts are made to have the emperor play the role of head of state.

Let us now consider the second example, which concerns the problem of the separation of church and state. The divorce of Shintoism from the state, one of the major objectives of the postwar democratization process, was effected in order to eliminate the specter of that political-military-ideological giant, the 'Great Empire of Japan'. It is in light of this that debate has been focused on the government's decisions concerning the series of ceremonies that took place (and that will continue until the official celebration of the new Emperor's accession to the throne, scheduled for the autumn of 1990) in the wake of the death of Emperor Hirohito.

The problem concerns mainly the official funeral services for the late Emperor. According to critical observers, these services violated the 'principle of the separation of religion and state' by inadequately distinguishing between the official rites and the imperial family's Shinto rites. The Communist members of parliament and the representatives of the Japanese Federation of Bar Associations boycotted the official services, which were attended by the representatives of 159 countries. The majority of the Socialist members of parliament avoided the Shinto rites and took part in only the nonreligious services.

A similarly heated debate is certain to occur with respect to the new Emperor's rites of accession, planned for the autumn of 1990. The government has yet to announce any official decisions concerning the administration of the ceremonies. But it is said that the government intends to observe the traditional Shinto rites, in keeping with the precedent established in 1927, when Emperor Hirohito succeeded his father on the throne. The enthronement ritual of the new Emperor Akihito was held on 12 November 1990 as an official ceremony of state, enumerated by the tenth phrase of Article 7 of the Constitution. The traditional and secret Shinto ritual of *Daijosai* was performed at midnight on 22 November 1990. The debate occurred on the constitutionality of the decision of the government to finance this rite through the state budget.

The question of constitutionality proves highly troublesome in the case of the funeral services, which may to a certain degree accommodate the personal religious beliefs of the deceased. However, to ascend the throne is a purely official act. The constitutional principle of the separation of church and state must in this instance be strictly observed. We are now faced with the possibility of a reestablishment of continuity with the pre-1945 era in a very significant sphere of constitutional life.

B. The Social Function of the Symbolic Emperor: The Question of Praeter Constitutionem *Practices*

This question concerns the social effects generated by the very presence of the symbolic emperor. Of course, the constitution does not treat this subject. Article 1 defines the emperor as 'the symbol of the Japanese state and of the unity of the Japanese people.' The word 'unity,' however, is understood to be devoid of any concrete juridical meaning. Furthermore, contrary to Rudolf Smend's doctrine of integration type unity, the word possesses no specific political character. Yet it remains no less true that in Japan the very presence itself of the emperor creates an atmosphere of integration, unity, and conformity within society, and that this *praeter constitutionem* phenomenon has a considerable effect upon constitutional life.

A remark is required concerning the drama created by the long illness and subsequent death of Emperor Hirohito, events that occurred from 17 September 1988, to 7 January 1989. A conformist attitude of a political nature spread astonishingly throughout Japanese society, particularly during the period of the emperor's illness. This phenomenon was due in large part to the amplifying effect produced by the mass media. Indeed, one witnessed a flood of inscription (*kicho*): Over 10 million women and men rushed to sign the registers placed throughout the country to express their wishes for the emperor's recovery, and, later, their grief at his death. A wave of self-restraint (*jishuku*) disrupted daily life. The cancellation of countless sporting and cultural events, the postponement of several celebrities' wedding feasts, and the removal from broadcast of an automobile commercial beginning with the words 'do you feel well' are but a few examples of this trend.

It would be wrong to interpret these gestures as signs of a renaissance of the cult of emperor worship. At issue rather is apolitical conformity that leads citizens to act in accordance with the mood of submissiveness and mourning systematically projected by the media. We are thus certainly not confronted with the revival of the *kokutai* in the moral sense of the word. However, it was precisely because they concerned the emperor that the media's initiatives were able to evoke such a considerable response from the citizens. Hence, it is possible to speak, while not in the strictly moral sense, at least in a psychosociological sense, of the continued existence of the *kokutai*.

This conformist behavior is not necessarily passive may be accompanied by a consciousness, be it false or not, of participation. One weekly magazine quotes a twenty-two-year-old worker as saying, 'This is a historic event ... I have lived this moment ... I signed the register in order to attest to that fact.'

Within this climate of consensus occurred several incidents of major concern from a constitutional point of view. I will cite but one example. The mayor of Nagasaki, the city that along with Hiroshima was the victim of nuclear attack, was divested of his honorary functions in the local branch of the LDP because he asserted, in response to a question posed during debate in the municipal assembly, that Emperor Hirohito bore responsibility for the events of the Second World War. More serious is the fact that this conservative mayor had also to face the threats of right-wing extremists, who for several months surrounded the city hall with armored trucks whose loudspeakers blared deafening messages.

As John Stuart Mill aptly indicated in his essay 'On Liberty, social tyranny (in which society itself becomes conformist) is an even greater threat to individuals' autonomy than are the visible constraints of political oppression. The unfolding of events in the highly industrialized East Asian archipelago threatens to confirm, after an interval of 130 years, the foresight of that unshakable Victorian liberal.

This observation, which from a constitutional perspective is essentially pessimistic, should all the same be tempered by the following remark. The wearing thin, if one may call it that, of the mood of premature mourning that lasted nearly four months finally permitted the appearance of more or less open debate. Curiously, the atmosphere was markedly less conformist during the official funeral services than it had been in the preceding months.

I will here dose my remarks concerning the social conformism generated by the presence itself of the symbolic emperor. What will be the situation under the new emperor? I would like in closing to draw your attention to a particular aspect of the problem, namely, the role that the emperor himself might play with regard to constitutional revisionism.

CONCLUSION

It is significant that, on 9 January 1989, during the solemn rite of succession, the new Emperor Akihito expressed to the representatives of the three branches of the state his desire to 'defend the constitution with [them]'. Theoretically, one may not interpret the emperor's statements as expressions of his *personal* will, since, according to Articles 3 and 7 of the Constitution, all of his official acts require the 'advice and consent' of the cabinet of ministers, under whose responsibility he is placed. The emperor's comments were greeted with much commotion, even more so in light of the fact that successive governments have been little given to expressing their respect for the nation's fundamental law, under which Japan has nonetheless achieved unprecedented economic growth, social stability, and also a measure of international credibility. The revisionists of the extreme right thus find themselves in a quandary and are struggling to reestablish their identity.

Will the emperor henceforth become the 'symbol' of the defense of the constitution without exceeding the limits imposed on him by that constitution, which states that the emperor shall have no political character? The future will tell.

III THE LEGISLATURE, POLITICAL PARTIES AND ELECTIONS

Abe, H, Shindo, M and Kawato, S, *The Government and Politics of Japan*, 1994, pp 17–23, University of Tokyo Press

One defining characteristic of a democratic legislature is that it is composed of representatives elected by the people. But what, or who, do the legislators actually represent?

The dominant view in contemporary democratic societies, including Japan, is that legislators represent the interests of the people as a whole. Accordingly, the fact that a member of parliament (MP) was elected from one constituency or another is simply coincidental – what the MP should represent in parliament is not simply the interests of the people in his or her constituency but those of the people as a whole. Of course, it is not necessarily clear exactly what the interests of the people as a whole are, but ideally it is the duty of the legislator to imagine that such a general public interest does exist and to try to recognize and articulate it. This view of the representative as 'trustee' of the entire national interest predominates in Japan and the industrial democracies of Western Europe.

Opposed to this view is the ideal of the representative as a 'delegate' who is sent to parliament with the sole duty of representing directly the interests of the voters in his or her constituency. In the United States, where the tradition of direct democracy is strong, the original legislative principle – epitomized in the New England town meeting – was one of universal participation in collective decisions. In this tradition, representation is only an expedient adopted when large populations make direct democracy impossible. The duty of a representative is to act faithfully on behalf of the demands of those who elected him or her. Thus, the United States is the exception in that it has a system in which the representative as delegate reflects the dominant view.

In so far as a legislature attempts to seek generally acceptable and beneficial policies through its debates, it may well be easier for an assemblage of trustees, seeking to define and pursue a common national interest, to reach unity than an assemblage of delegates, each of whom is likely to insist on local interests. This may be the reason trusteeship is the ideal in most democracies outside the United States. The Japanese constitution's stipulation that 'both Houses shall consist of elected members, representative of *all the people*' (Article 43; emphasis added) accords with this idea.

It probably comes as no surprise to learn, however, that in fact, behind the principle of trusteeship, there are many MPs who operate more according to the ideal of the local delegate. This tendency is especially strong in contemporary Japan. Certainly, even beyond the fact that one of an MP's paramount interests is his or her own reelection, it is inevitable that every MP will at times act as a delegate. When legislators focus exclusively on local interests, however, parliament loses its ability to agree or to lead, and it becomes impossible to give coherent direction to affairs of state through parliamentary deliberations. Therefore, it is important to recognize that an MP should not exclusively follow one principle or the other but, rather, must pursue both of these two potentially contradictory paths.

PARLIAMENT AS A LEGISLATIVE BODY

A legislature performs multiple functions; among them, the most important are the *integrative* function and the *legislative* function. In the past, these two functions were closely intertwined: it was expected that parliament as a legislative body would, through its legislative debates, serve to resolve conflicts, temper opposition, and integrate the body politic. The legislative function has been transformed today, and this transformation has influenced the integrative function. In today's Japanese parliament, how is the legislative function performed?

First, both MPs and the cabinet are empowered to introduce legislation. The Constitution makes no provision for the cabinet to introduce legislation, but Article 5 of the Cabinet Law states that the prime minister, as the representative of the cabinet, may introduce legislation to parliament. Bills may be introduced by individual MPs or by the cabinet into either house of parliament. Upon submission, the speaker of that house sends the bill to the appropriate standing or special committee. Either house's steering committee, however, may designate a bill as especially important and introduce it directly into a plenary session; moreover, in emergencies, by decision of the house, the stage of committee deliberation may be bypassed.

Presently, there are 20 standing committees in the House of Representatives and 17 in the House of Councillors, as shown in Table 2.1. The standing committees, with the exception of the budget, audit, steering, and house discipline committees, correspond to the ministries of the cabinet. For example, the jurisdiction of the House of Representatives' Cabinet Committee includes all matters pertaining to the cabinet, the National Personnel Authority, the Imperial Household Agency, the Management and Coordination Agency (formerly the Prime Minister's Office), the Hokkaido Development Agency, the Defense Agency, and the Okinawa Development Agency; that

TABLE 2.1 Standing Committees of the Diet

	Number of members	
Committee	House of Representatives	House of Councillors
Cabinet	30	19
Local Administration	30	19
Judicial Affairs	30	19
Foreign Affairs	30	19
Finance	40	22
Education	30	19
Health and Welfare	40	19
Agriculture, Forestry, and Fisheries	40	21
Commerce and Industry	40	19
Transportation	30	19
Communications	30	19
Labor	30	19
Construction	30	19

National Security	40	–
Budget	50	45
Audit	25	30
Steering	25	25
Disciplinary Measures	20	10
Science and Technology	25	–
Environment	25	–

of the Foreign Affairs Committee covers everything concerning the Foreign Ministry; and that of the Committee on Commerce and Industry includes the Ministry of International Trade and Industry (MITI), the Economic Planning Agency (EPA), and the Fair Trade Commission (FTC). The number, size, and functions of special committees are determined at the time of their establishment.

Committee deliberations begin with an explanation of the major features of proposed legislation and continue with interpellation of government and other witnesses, debate, and revision, after which bills are voted on. Presentation of the government's position on bills is the task of the relevant cabinet minister, assisted by ministry officials. In fact, it is these officials who provide most of the substance of the government's replies to committee interpellations. Public hearings are a common part of committee deliberations, but they are not utilized as fully in Japan as they are in the United States or Germany, where they are a key component of committee operations. Bills not brought to a vote in committee during a session of parliament expire with the end of that session.

Bills passed by committee are reported to the full house by the committee chair. In the full house they are again the subject of interpellation, debate, and revision, and then voted on. There are three forms of voting in parliament: unanimous voice vote, standing vote, and roll call. Bills passed by one house of parliament are sent to the other for consideration; when a bill is passed by one but not the other, it can still become law in one of three ways. First, when the House of Councillors revises and then passes a bill previously passed by the House of Representatives, the bill becomes law if the lower house passes the revised version during the same session of parliament. Second, if the upper house rejects, revises, or fails within 60 days to vote on a bill, it becomes law if passed again in the original version by the lower house by a two-thirds' majority. Third, the bill becomes law if passed by a joint committee of both houses. Such joint committees were never convened between 1953 and 1989; since the LDP lost control of the upper house in 1989, however, they have been convened a number of times.

After a bill becomes law, the speaker of the house that last passed it sends it via the cabinet to the emperor for promulgation. Promulgation is reported in the official gazette within 30 days, and at that point it assumes the force of law.

CHARACTERISTICS OF THE LEGISLATIVE PROCESS

Among the special characteristics of Japan's legislative process, the first to note is that bills submitted to parliament by the cabinet account for the great majority of proposed legislation. Between the first postwar session of parliament in 1947 and the 112th in 1988, cabinet submissions accounted for 68 percent of all bills submitted, with members' bills accounting for 32 percent. Moreover, when one looks only at bills passed, fully 85 percent were cabinet submissions and only 15 percent were members' bills.

Not only do cabinet-proposed bills outnumber members' bills – qualitatively, too, they account for most of the important legislation. In parliamentary systems such as Japan's, it is normal for the executive branch to play this sort of leading role in the legislative process. Although few laws result from members' bills, one should note that they have included some very important legislation. Not only were the Diet Law, the Public Office Election Law, and other laws governing parliament itself the result of members' bills, but so also were many laws promoting regional development for the purpose of either correcting interregional socioeconomic disparities or eliminating the harmful effects of the administrative standardization so dear to the hearts of central government planners and bureaucrats. Such acts as the Northwest Coast Development Promotion Law, the Central Japan Regional Development Law, the Remote Islands Promotion Law, the Mountain Villages Promotion Law, and the Law for Special Measures for Promoting Underpopulated Regions – all of whose names indicate their purpose – were the result of members' bills. One should also note that a number of laws addressing new social problems, such as parental leave legislation and regulation of the consumer loan industry, were the result of members' bills.

The second characteristic of the legislative process is that committee proceedings have become the heart of the process, with house plenary sessions losing much of their meaning. In many European and North American legislatures, bills are 'read' multiple times to the full house, with the aim of making house deliberations important, but, in Japan, bills are presented but once. In a 'three-reading' system, for example, upon its first submission to the legislature, a bill is presented and its major features explained in general outline; at the second reading, the bill is debated in general terms and accepted or rejected for committee consideration. If it is accepted, it goes through the committee process; if voted out of committee, it returns to the full house for a third 'reading,' or debate and decisive vote. Under the prewar constitution, the three-reading system was used in the Japanese parliament. Under this system, discussion of each bill in the full house is quite time consuming, but it is hoped that serious deliberation will result. Under the one-reading system, one can expect speedier deliberations, but the full house is less able to restrain or countermand the deliberations of the committees, which are far more susceptible to influence from special-interest and pressure groups.

The sharp imbalance between Japan's parliamentary committees and plenary sessions becomes clearer in comparison with other countries. Between 1970 and 1974, the House of Representatives met in plenary session 50 times per year on the average, for a total of 82 hours; the House of Councillors met 34 times for 63 hours. During the same time, the British House of Commons met 167 times per year for 1,528 hours and the House of Lords 112 times for 730 hours, while the US House of Representatives met 164 times annually for 766 hours and the Senate 183 times for 1,146 hours. The number of committee meetings and the time thus spent were far greater in Japan: between December 1981 and December 1982 the House of Representatives met 45 times for a total of 47 hours, while 352 standing committee sessions consumed 1,170 hours. The House of Councillors met 35 times in plenary session, for a total of 46 hours; at the same time, its standing committees convened 291 times for a total of 878 hours. From such data one can see how full house sessions are becoming little more than a shadow of the legislative ideal.

ROLE OF BUREAUCRATS IN THE LEGISLATIVE PROCESS

The third characteristic of the legislative process is the historical influence of executive-branch civil servants, which continues to this day. What is the manner in which civil servants exercise this influence? For our purposes it is sufficient to note that their influence is conspicuous at three different legislative stages: drafting, deliberation, and implementation.

First, although some important legislation is drafted by MPs, the majority of laws are based on cabinet-submitted bills, and such bills are ordinarily drafted by civil servants. The procedure varies considerably, but most such bills originate in discussions within government ministries and agencies – specifically, in discussions among department heads and their assistants and the chief clerks in that branch of the agency. As a concrete proposal is worked out, the matter also becomes the subject of discussion with the bureau head and other administrative officials, and is eventually formalized in the form of a draft proposal (*ringi-sho*). Once this draft has been agreed on by the whole agency, the next step is to negotiate the agreement of other concerned ministries. Subsequently, the proposal is considered by the Cabinet Legislative Bureau, which drafts it into the legally proper form of a legislative proposal. After a proposal has thus been formalized, it is presented to the ruling party for examination; once approved there it is submitted to the cabinet and finally adopted as a government-sponsored bill. Along the way, deliberation by advisory councils (*shingikai*) may also occur; nevertheless, it is clear that the greatest influence on the preparation of legislation is exercised by the bureaucrats.

As for legislative deliberation, one can also see the influence of civil servants at work in many aspects of the parliamentary process. First, the functional jurisdictions of the standing committees of both houses of parliament correspond to those of the ministries and agencies of the executive branch. This correspondence serves to promote mutual understanding, coordination, and communication between government bureaucrats and their parliamentary counterparts on corresponding committees. Of course, these relationships can also become paths of reciprocal influence, lobbying, and logrolling among MPs and civil servants. Needless to say, the participation of civil servants as assistants to the minister in responding to committee questioning works to strengthen their influence. The influence of executive-branch civil servants is, in fact, demonstrated most clearly during committee deliberations, although it is a minor factor in full sessions of the house. In other words, the centrality of parliamentary committees to the legislative process enhances the influence of the bureaucracy in that process.

Finally, at the implementation stage of the legislative process, the civil servants of the executive branch do not stop at simply applying laws passed by parliament: under the pretext of 'fleshing out' the law, they, in fact, make rules themselves. These rules take the concrete form of ordinances (*seirei*), announcements (*kokuji*), notifications (*tsutatsu*), and so forth. Ordinances are orders issued by the cabinet for the purpose of enforcing the provisions of laws, and are of two types: executive orders, which spell out in detail the procedures for enforcing laws, and delegatory orders, which specify details of the actual content of laws. The latter form of ordinance is also known as 'delegatory legislation,' reflecting the fact that, as administrative functions have grown, there has been a trend for parliament simply to legislate the main points of a law, with the elaboration of concrete detail left to the cabinet. In Japanese law, wholesale delegation of legislative authority is not permitted, but in specified and limited circumstances it is permissible. In addition to cabinet ordinances (and for the purpose of implementation of both laws and ordinances), there are ministerial ordinances, but they are subordinate to cabinet actions. it is clear, however, that, as forms of administrative legislation, they too serve to supplement, and thus in effect to make, laws.

Announcements and notifications were not originally designed to be directly binding upon the citizenry; announcements formally publicized the particulars of ministerial and agency decisions, while notifications were orders or instructions from high-level agencies to lower-level ones that interpreted laws regarding the exercise of authority. They were thus intended to set standards internal to government, but in fact they have a great impact on the lives of the people. Thus, contemporary Japanese law as a parliamentary product simply sets forth basic frameworks, purposes, and goals, entrusting the determination of the details essential to enforcement to cabinet and ministerial ordinances, announcements, and notifications. By performing this 'administrative legislation,' the bureaucrats of the executive branch shape and control basic policy, and should they so desire, can on occasion even render it wholly ineffectual.

Seki, M, 'The Drafting Process for Cabinet Bills' (1969) 19 *Law in Japan* 171, 172–77, 179–80, 185–87

In a Diet-cabinet system, the political parties have the leadership in determining policy. The following three factors, however, support recognition of the executive branch's right to introduce legislation:

(1) First, the executive, through its role in enforcing and applying existing law, is in a position to acquire information regarding problems in meeting changes in social and economic conditions and to recognize and deal with social demand for measures requiring new legislation. It only makes sense to allow those in such a position to present concrete proposals directly to the legislative branch.

(2) The process of drafting laws calls for gathering analyses by experts in various fields, based upon statistics and materials compiled from the sorts of information accumulated by the administration; accommodating a variety of demands, some of which may at times be in direct conflict: assembling from these various materials a single plan; and then using drafting skills to formulate the text of the bill. Thus, an organization that might appropriately be referred to as a 'bill-drafting factory' is needed. A suitable organization of this sort already exists within the executive branch, and that organization should be utilized.

(3) The cabinet possesses the right to prepare the budget, which ranks with lawmaking as a key instrument of policy. Many policies call for both legislation and budgetary allowances, and many bills require substantial expenditures. In light of the need for consistency between the budget and legislation, it would be irrational to deny the cabinet the right to introduce bills related to the budget.

For these reasons, the introduction of legislation by the executive branch has positive advantages. Still, the executive branch is organized sector-by-sector in a vertical structure, so the drafting of bills by the executive branch may not proceed smoothly for matters requiring integrated handling. Furthermore, administrative bodies can easily fall into slavish adherence to precedent, and thus may be unreceptive to proposals for legislation that do not follow existing patterns. These matters call for our attention and reassessment.

With respect to the participation of the executive in the legislative process, the mass media and scholars have voiced the criticism that such participation, taken together with the other major component of policy execution, the drafting of the budget, may lead to evils of bureaucratic government ...

...

The majority of bills introduced by the cabinet are submitted at an ordinary session of the Diet. In the typical case, when a ministry or agency draws up plans with regard to policies involving matters that will require legislation, investigations are undertaken with an eye toward the ordinary sessions of the Diet. Normally, the aim is to have the bill ready for introduction at either the next ordinary session of the Diet or at some other specified ordinary session.

Ordinary sessions are normally convened 'during December of every year' (Article 2 of the Diet Law) and are ordinarily reconvened in late January of the following year, after a recess for formulation of the budget and for the year-end and New Year holidays. In anticipation of this, the Cabinet Secretariat and the Cabinet Legislation Bureau jointly convene a meeting with the heads of the Legal Affairs Divisions [*bunshoka*] of all ministries and certain other persons by early January in order to prepare the list of bills to be introduced during that session. In theory, the Councillors [*sanjikan*] from the Cabinet Legislation Bureau begin their preliminary review [*shitashinsa*] of the bills *en masse* on that date. In fact, however, the preliminary review of fundamental laws with numerous provisions may take over a year, or may have commenced during the preceding summer.

As to matters requiring expert opinions or the views of interested parties, a deliberative council [*shingikai*] or similar body is utilized, and the legislative process usually proceeds on the basis of that body's report. In theory, harmonization with other ministries and agencies is supposed to occur before the Cabinet Legislation Bureau commences review, but in some cases that harmonization occurs concurrently with the Bureau's review.

Explanations to and necessary arrangements [*nemawashi*] with the majority party take place after the Cabinet Legislation Bureau's review has reached a certain level. Thereafter, such discussions also go on concurrently with the continuing review. While a draft is being firmed up, it is not unusual for the responsible official to receive directions from the majority party or to have conferences with members of the majority party with responsibility for the issues in question.

The formal review by the majority party usually commences a week or ten days prior to the cabinet determination. Throughout the preceding process and the subsequent handling in the Diet, the responsible ministry or agency is at all times in charge of managing and promoting the bill.

Information Necessary for Drafting Bills and the Impetus behind Bills

The information necessary for drafting bills is normally obtained through one of several typical routes. In turn, the flow of information through these routes usually provides the impetus behind the drafting of new legislation. Those routes include the following:

(1) Questions Raised in the Course of Routine Work: In the course of their routine work, the various ministries and agencies learn about the actual manner in which existing law is applied and about social demand for new legislation in a number of ways. These include inquiries from the regional bodies (including the responsible departments within the metropolitan areas and prefectures) charged with the actual enforcement of the law, questions raised at various types of meetings, and statistics and other materials concerning the application of the law. This type of information represents the basic source of cabinet bills.

(2) Questions Raised in the Diet: In numerous cases, members of the Diet, through their contact with the electorate, have a more complete understanding of the precise

manner in which the existing law actually operates than do those responsible for applying the law. These Diet members often point out problems in the course of deliberations by committees of the Diet, and this represents another important source of information that often results in the introduction of legislation by the cabinet.

(3) Raising of Issues by the Mass Media and Journalists: By raising issues, the mass media may both prompt questions by Diet members at committee meetings in the Diet (questions of the type discussed in the preceding paragraph) and directly stimulate the drafting of bills by the government authorities. Coverage by the media also aids in clarifying the reactions of various segments of society during the drafting process.

(4) Proposals by Deliberative Councils and Gather Bodies: On occasion, deliberative councils and other such bodies begin drawing up plans at their own initiative, rather than in response to requests from the government.

(5) Appeals from Interest Groups, Local Public Bodies, and Others: Among interest groups in Japan, business and industry bodies and occupational groups are well organized and may appeal either through political parties or directly to the responsible departments within the government. In addition, their members may make proposals at deliberative councils or other bodies. Recently, consumer and other groups have also increased in strength. Local public bodies are also able to raise issues forcefully.

(6) Recommendations from Other Government offices: Recommendations from the National Personnel Authority naturally often lead to proposals to amend the General Government Service Salary Law [*Ippanshoku kyuyoho*]. From time to time, reports and recommendations stemming from administrative review also serve as the impetus for new legislation.

Internal Studies by Ministries and Agencies

Work on developing legislation commences with conferences among the division head, deputy division head, and chief clerks in the division responsible for the matter in question within the relevant ministry or agency. In some cases, the minister, the vice-minister, or the bureau director will issue instructions with regard to the matter. Whatever the case, however, the initial work is centered on the key personnel within the responsible division of the ministry or agency. When the new legislation involves broad topics exceeding the jurisdiction of any single section, though, a bureau-wide, agency-wide, or even ministry-wide project team is assembled.

Once the work has progressed to a certain level, the situation is explained to the bureau director and other responsible officials and a conference is convened. At this stage efforts are made to accommodate existing legal conceptions and political demands. To accomplish this the conference may last for several days and carry over late into the night. In the drafting of legislation, the so-called ringi system (in which one staff member formulates a draft and then circulates it to the other members and officials for their approval) is not followed: rather much rewriting of drafts occurs at these conferences.

Before the basic review by the Cabinet Legislation Bureau the responsible ministry, often through the legal affairs division of the ministry secretariat, carries out an internal review and harmonizes views within the ministry. Once the process has reached a certain point the matter is explained to the minister and vice-minister of that ministry. Finally when the Cabinet Legislation Bureau's basic review is complete and the bill is ready for discussion by the cabinet approval is obtained through the *ringi* system.

Deliberative Councils

When the topic is complicated and difficult or the interests of various segments of society are in opposition and harmonization would not be easy the matter is submitted to a deliberative council for consideration. In some cases the law requires that the drafting of certain statutes be referred to deliberative councils. In other cases temporary deliberative councils may be established for the purpose of preparing new sets of laws in particular fields. The deliberative councils are composed of 'persons of learning and experience,' and include academic experts in the particular field representatives of the industry that would be affected, and others. The deliberative councils have often been criticized as being a 'soft dark cloak' that conceals the exercise of important powers. Leaving aside problems with the actual operation of the deliberative councils, ultimately the government is responsible for whatever decisions are made so this criticism is unwarranted the value of the work by deliberative councils in the process of drafting bills should not be denied.

Negotiations with Ministries

Negotiations with the various ministries are one of the most troublesome tasks for those responsible for drafting a bill. These negotiations begin with the presentation of the draft to each ministry. Where necessary a meeting may be held to explain the draft. Thereafter the process consists of gradually clarifying points of contention at the lower levels and then moving on to negotiations with higher-ranking officials.

It is essential to persevere in negotiations with each ministry until a compromise can be worked out. In certain cases however one ministry or agency may express views about the draft that are directly opposite to the views of one or more other ministries or agencies and in other cases one ministry or agency may delay by waiting to state its views until after it sees what position some other ministry or agency is taking. In such cases it is sometimes necessary for the Councillor's Office of the Prime Minister's Secretariat [*soridaijin kanbo shingishitsu*] to harmonize these views basing its authority on the Cabinet Secretariat's right of harmonization [*choseiken*]. A notable recent example of this is the vigorous harmonization efforts that took place during the course of drafting the 1980 Environmental Impact Assessment bill. On that occasion deliberations by officials at the bureau director [*kyokucho*] and councillor [*shingikan*] level lasted for several days often going late into the night or even all night long.

In the normal situation these negotiations with the ministries and agencies take place concurrently with internal consideration by the ministries and agencies – and in some cases at the same time as the basic review by the Cabinet Legislation Bureau. ...

...

In theory the review of bills by the Cabinet Legislation Bureau is to begin only after the responsible ministry or agency (all outside agencies under the Prime Minister's Office report in the name of the prime minister) has sent a formal application to the Cabinet [*kakugi seigisho*], addressed to the prime minister. It appears that such a method may actually have been followed at one time but at present review proceeds through a preliminary stage (referred to as the 'preliminary review' [*shitashinsa*] pursuant to a 1961 memorandum from the Chief Cabinet Secretary). As previously explained the time limit for submission of bills submitted by the cabinet is fixed so a thorough review would be difficult if the preliminary review did not commence until after receipt of the cabinet notification. Moreover review by the councillor normally results in major revisions which are often followed by further changes by the department director deputy director-general and director-general of the Legislation Bureau. The paperwork involved in these revisions would become incredibly complicated if the review did not commence until after the formal application to the cabinet.

Preliminary review by the Cabinet Legislation Bureau proceeds through a series of readings. Each of these readings consists of a cycle in which the draft is first explained to the responsible councillor in the Cabinet Legislation Bureau. This explanation is followed by questions and answers regarding the draft discussions and reexamination by the responsible official in the particular ministry or agency. Finally the cycle ends with revision of the draft.

The first reading begins with a consideration of whether the proposed new enactment or revision is truly necessary and of how the proposed legislation would fit into the existing legal order. In cases involving constitutional questions – for example, questions relating to the balance and consistency between the policy objectives and the measures for implementation or to the requirements for and scope of delegation of decree authority – those questions are considered at the first reading stage. In addition, the arrangement of the specific provisions and other broad matters relating to the organization and structure of the bill as a whole are examined at this stage.

Problems remaining after the first reading are referred back to the responsible ministry or agency for reconsideration: At the same time however a detailed examination is conducted within the Legislation Bureau with the department director and other councillors also taking part. In addition in cases where the views of the various ministries and agencies have not been sufficiently harmonized and in cases where as a result of examination and revisions at the first reading stage it becomes necessary to work out matters with other ministries and agencies considerable periods of time must be set aside on occasion for examination by such other ministries and agencies after the first reading. In such cases the councillor responsible for reviewing that bill often begins the review of some other bill during that period ...

...

When review by the Cabinet Legislation Bureau has entered the final stage where all that remains is to check minor points of wording and legal terminology the responsible ministry or agency requests review of the draft by the appropriate section of the ruling Liberal Democratic Party's Policy Board [*seimu chosakai*]. In this case a ministry official at the bureau director level with responsibility for the draft provides the responsible department head within the Policy Board with a detailed advance briefing on the contents of the draft. The middle and upper-ranking personnel of the bureau responsible for the draft divide up the names of other interested legislators among themselves and begin the *nemawashi* process of briefing those legislators and obtaining their approval for the draft. Diet members belonging to the section of the Policy Board with responsibility for that particular issue possess considerable expert knowledge and have received extensive information on the matter. Thus, scrupulous preparation and considerable persuasive powers may be needed to convince them and win their approval.

Once the draft has made it past the responsible section of the Policy Board it is submitted to the Inquiry Committee of the Policy Board [*seimu chosakai-shingikai*, an upper-level body within the Policy Board] and then to the General Committee [*somukai*]. The chairman of the relevant subcommittee within the Policy Committee is responsible for explaining the draft at the meetings of these two committees. At the meeting of the inquiry Committee that explanation may be supplemented by answers from the Inquiry

Committee that explanation may be supplemented by answers from the director of the responsible bureau and other officials within the appropriate ministry or agency in response to questions from members of that Committee In principle, however personnel of the administrative agencies are not permitted to attend the meeting of the General Committee. The Inquiry Committee of the Policy Board meets regularly on Tuesdays and Thursdays and the General Committee on Tuesdays and Fridays. Approval of the General Committee must normally be obtained at the last meeting before the scheduled date for submission to the cabinet (which also meets on Tuesdays and Fridays). In very rare cases, however, the draft may be submitted to the cabinet as a non-agenda item 'not cleared by the Party' [*to-michosei*] on the understanding that the draft will be approved at the General Committee meeting on the same day as the cabinet meeting. In recent years, for only a summary of the draft legislation rather than the entire draft itself to be submitted to the Policy Board – and especially to the Inquiry and the general committees – has almost never been permitted. For this reason as a practical matter the amount of time spent on review within the administrative sector has been reduced.

Frequently when negative or non-supportive views go unaddressed during either review within the ruling party or the *nemawashi* process the legislation ends up not being enacted even if it is submitted to the Diet. After all the ones truly responsible for pushing the legislation through the relevant committee at the Diet are the Diet members who belong to the responsible section within the ruling party. If they do not take responsibility for the legislation discussion will not move forward.

Responsible personnel at the ministry or agency may also decide to undertake *nemawashi* with the opposition parties or may explain the legislation at the request of the opposition parties. Contacts of this sort are treated on a case-by-case basis, however.

I will leave the process of consideration by the Diet for some other paper. It would appear though that the key to the success or failure of the legislation lies not only in the committee deliberations which are given such glowing coverage in the mass media for their 'pursuit' of the government but even more importantly in the discussions of the majority and minority party members on the steering subcommittees. Moreover credit must be given to the efforts of the responsible officials in the concerned ministries or agencies, who run from party to party during those negotiations providing groundwork in an attempt to ensure that the bills to which they have devoted such care will see the light of day.

Stockwin, JAA, 'Political Parties and Political Opposition' in Ishida, T and Krauss, ES (eds), *Democracy in Japan*, 1989, pp 89–90, 93–95, 104–09, University of Pittsburgh Press

Can a predominant party system like that of Japan sit easily within the category of 'parliamentary democracy' or should it be a matter of serious complaint that the party in power does not change over several decades? If parties in opposition never take office, does this mean that the system ceases to be genuinely democratic?

Two contrasting kinds of answers may be given to these questions. The first would deny that a predominant party system is necessarily undemocratic: even though the same party always takes power, this occurs on the basis of the freely expressed will of the electorate, which has the freedom to dismiss the government and replace it with the opposition should it so wish. The electorate, however, has not so chosen, and this ought to be interpreted as indicating electoral satisfaction, rather than a defect in the system. Reinforcing this argument is the suggestion that continuity in power creates continuity, and thus consistency, in administration. Government based on one-party dominance may thus plan from a long-term perspective, without having to adjust traumatically to elections which change the party or parties in power.

The opposite kind of answer is that predominant party politics fails to provide access to power (or the prospect of access to power) for those parties and their supporters which are permanently out of office. Thus a very substantial part of the electorate, and a major segment of those who enter politics, are deprived of the opportunity to participate – or elect those who participate – in the control of government. The argument is reinforced by the more empirical consideration that predominant party politics may lack the stimulus provided by fairly regular alternation in power. Alternating politics – according to this argument – is rather like the effect of the tide on a beach: by a regular tidal process of flushing and cleansing, the beach is kept pristine, fresh, and free of detritus and jetsam. A beach not subject to tidal action needs cleansing by other mechanisms if it is to stay pure and function properly as a beach ...

...

During the late 1950s and early 1960s many political observers within Japan believed that Japanese politics were likely to travel down a road leading to alternating politics and that such a system as it operated in Britain and elsewhere had merits that were readily transferable to Japan. Today in contrast, it has become quite fashionable to present Japan as an example demonstrating the merits of nonalternating politics. Several factors appear to be at the root of this remarkable change in approach.

From a Japanese point of view, lack of appeal in British-style alternating politics (whatever it may have meant in practice) reflected in part the perception that the British economy was in relative decline. A common belief in Japan about the British (and other European) politicoeconomic systems was that conflict between antagonistic and well-organized social classes served to inhibit economic progress. Alternating government therefore was seen as essentially the political reflection of (or at best, an attempt to manage) a fundamentally class-divided society from which Japan is happily distinct.

The other side of this coin was that domestic criticism of Japan's own politicoeconomic arrangements declined as belief in Japan as an economic success story capable of overtaking in economic competitiveness regions such as Europe, became widespread. Political continuity and stability, allied with social discipline, diligence, resourcefulness, and communal striving for group goals on the part of a technologically educated work force were seen as highly desirable features of the system.

The specifically political part of this evaluation contains some interesting nuances. Defenders of the system are perfectly prepared to criticize (often in forthright terms) particular politicians or decisions or even institutions, but assume as a matter virtually beyond argument that the LDP will and should continue more or less to monopolize the right to form cabinets. The opposition parties are dismissed as incapable of governing in their own right, although it is conceded that one or other of the smaller middle-of-the-road parties might be brought into government as a junior partner. (This has already happened with the New Liberal Club (NLC) that in 1986 was reabsorbed into the LDP from which it defected, in a protest over corruption, in 1976.)

There are certain tacit assumptions here of great importance. One is that there is no point in upsetting the channels of communication that have been built up over a long period between the LDP government ministries and a range of interest groups. In the main, these relationships are thought to work well and result in policy outcomes which are both realistic and forward-looking. Another is that the opposition parties have shown little evidence of their capacity to undertake responsible government. They are badly fragmented and do not effectively cooperate because each is seeking increased parliamentary representation at the expense of the others. The quality of their leadership is generally low and they lack the depth and extent of contacts and experience that the LDP possesses. Third, and at a deeper level of analysis (or rather, feeling), the concept of alternation of power, or even the idea that the opposition parties might have a realistic chance of governing at rare intervals, runs counter to the sense of a unified Japanese polity, in which so far as possible a patron-client relationship is maintained between the central government and other elements within the system, whether these be interest groups (other than those semi-incorporated into central government), local government authorities, or political parties in opposition.

The opposition parties themselves are taking on some of the characteristics of government clients. Essentially this is because a party permanently out of office is still faced with the necessity of effectively representing its supporters, even though it has no chance of doing so by attaining office and seeking to put its proposals into law. Except in the case of parties whose ideological opposition to the established government is uncompromising, parties in permanent opposition must over a long period be strongly tempted to be drawn into a client role *vis-à-vis* government, including the party in office. There is evidence that faction leaders in the LDP actively pursue contacts for their own purposes with leaders of some opposition parties, which have been developing a relationship with the LDP smacking of clientelism. In any case, the parties in opposition occupy a largely peripheral position in the political system, and this has come to be widely accepted as their natural situation. The LDP, by contrast, has become a kind of 'Japan-party,' in other words, the party whose natural role it is to run Japan ...

...

The Opposition's Role in Japanese Politics

The stable equilibrium of Japanese politics (which should not be confused with illusory 'metastability') favors the LDP at the expense of the opposition and excludes the opposition from most meaningful participation in policymaking. On the other hand, the opposition since the 1950s has managed to exercise a certain degree of veto power, the results of which are to be seen in particular in defense policy. The 'no war' clause (Article 9) of the 1946 Constitution would seem, according to a literal interpretation, to render armed forces ('military potential') illegal. Although the LDP has patently not been inhibited by this article from building up the quite impressive military force euphemistically described as the Self-Defense Forces, it has never been able to revise the article (nor any other article in the constitution) because the opposition has blocked the two-thirds majority of both houses of the Diet required before a proposal for constitutional revision can be put to a referendum of the people. So far as actual defense policy is concerned, the fact that it has been developed in an atmosphere of controversy about the legal status of the Self-Defense Forces may be seen as some measure of the opposition's effectiveness. The LDP itself, however, has been divided on defense matters, with some influential groups being strongly in favor of restraint. On the other hand, there has been some erosion of antidefense thinking on the part of opposition parties.

The National Diet has been a forum for the exercise of a limited amount of opposition influence though the manner of its exercise has changed over time. During the 1950s and 1960s there were set-piece confrontations over contentious issues, in which the opposition (at that time largely the JSP) would resort to filibustering and boycotts in order to block government legislation. The filibuster was used because the government lacked complete control of the parliamentary timetable. The opposition was sometimes able to force a delay to the point where contentious legislation would lapse at the end of the session. There was a limit to the extent to which extraordinary sessions of the Diet could defeat these tactics. Boycotting the Diet (or its committees) also had some success because the LDP was at times inhibited from resorting to the 'forced vote', where it would pass the legislation on its own votes in the absence of the opposition.

For several years during the 1970s, known as the *hakuchu* or 'parity' period, the opposition parties had sufficient parliamentary strength to deny the LDP control of key committees of both houses. This was a time of greater give and take in relations between government and opposition, partly because of changes within the opposition itself: it was now not one party but several, with the small centrist parties favoring a conciliatory approach. It is doubtful whether the fragmented opposition parties even during the *hakuchu* period, with their narrow clienteles, were ever able to make much of a *positive* impact on policy. Since the end of the *hakuchu* period in 1980, government-opposition relationships have still been notably less confrontational than in the 1960s. The LDP is able to buy off the opposition with minor concessions on many issues, which makes less surprising the frequency with most of the opposition parties vote with the government. The publicity given to noisy confrontation on certain issues ought not to obscure the backstage deals on many others.

All this, however, is less important than the overwhelming fact that the opposition remains a weak and rather minor force in political decision making. It has faced the unenviable dilemma of other longterm oppositions – whether to adopt a strategy of confrontation or assimilation. In postwar Japan, confrontation used to be crucially important, but has tended to give way to assimilation. The tendency is aided and abetted by the mechanisms of clientelism, put into operation by sections of the LDP with a view to 'subverting' sections of the opposition. Most of the opposition parties, but not the Communists, have virtually opted out of serious policy formulation on 'hard' issues of economic choice. Civil servants admit that they only take serious note of policy proposals emanating from the LDP and are able to forget about most of what comes from the opposition, which they would say is hardly 'policy' in any case.

Conclusion

In conclusion, let us return to the principal questions posed by the 'predominant party' character of Japanese politics since the 1950s, and the weakness of the opposition faced with the impressive political success of the LDP.

Why the system has evolved in this way is a question best answered by comparison with other nations. Where something approaching the alternating politics model has operated, the major parties have been able to stay reasonably close to the 'middle ground' of political opinion. Also, related to this, they have continued to represent the interests of broad sections of the community, rather than confining their appeal to narrow groups. This in turn has contributed to their general moderation of approach. They have for the most part avoided severe polarization based on region, religion, class, or ideology, even though these factors have played some part. In addition, the major parties have remained reasonably intact and have avoided excessive fragmentation.

In Japan, from the late 1950s onward, one major party, the JSP, rather than following the 'aggregative' path of the German Social Democrats or the British Labour party, turned inward on itself and sought to appeal to the ideologically committed and to what the party itself defined, somewhat unrealistically, as the working class of Japan. This led to various evils from the party's point of view. Talented people of moderate views were forced out of the party, its base of support narrowed, and much of its electoral support, especially in the cities, was eroded by minor parties, notably the *Komeito*, the DSP, and the JCP.

To an extent this would have been understandable had Japan been a society severely divided along class lines. It was difficult, however, to view the nation in the 1960s and 1970s in this way, and indeed many commentators have noted that contemporary Japan appears to be remarkably homogeneous. While not accepting the more extreme versions of this view, it is nevertheless difficult to understand the rationale behind the direction of the JSP appeal in that period. Minor parties were able to erode its support as a result, though it is worth noting that none of them succeeded in aggregating widely different sources of support and evolving into major parties. It is true that rapid economic growth tended to erode the JSP's appeal, but that ought to have dictated evolution toward the more mundane and practical concerns of the electorate, rather than a retreat to narrow Marxist rhetoric. However we state the problem, the rationale behind the JSP approach in the 1960s and 1970s is difficult to understand. The net effect of JSP failure combined with limited success by the minor parties has been to weaken the opposition, even though, as we have seen, it is not entirely impotent.

Our final concern, raised in the introduction to this chapter, is whether the weakness of the opposition has really mattered. A respectable case can be made for the view that it has not. Essentially the argument is that the LDP has brought good government to Japan. In face of this one salient fact, what some might regard as blemishes, such as factional struggle, corrupt dealings, personality rather than party voting, opposition clientelism, and so on, pale into insignificance. Politics in Japan has developed in such a way as to avoid for the most part the economically debilitating effects of strong horizontally organized unions confronting employers. The governability problem besetting European politics in the 1970s has been rather less salient in Japan. The Japanese way of conducting politics has evolved in the direction of strong central government able to stay in control without stifling local and private initiative. It is true that some decision making is characterized by immobilism, though there are subtle ways in which immobility is paraded as an argument against foreign pressure in issues of trade and defense. Indeed it is quite possible to construct an argument that policy immobilism has actually contributed to the national interest, in particular by slowing down foreign-induced change in ways that enable the domestic economy to adjust to them more easily.

On the other hand, a largely impotent, fragmented, and in part clientelist opposition is a feature of the Japanese system of politics which is difficult to reconcile with notions of democracy as generally understood. It is true that there are pluralistic as well as corporatist features of the system, irrespective of weak political opposition. To some extent factions in the LDP provide opposition, but their operation has a personalistic and money-centered, rather than policy-oriented, character.

Governments before 1940 changed frequently in a kaleidoscopic process of competing elites, none of which had sufficient power to dominate. The occupation reforms provided greater clarity and simplicity in the location both of sovereignty and of power. This had the salutary effect of enabling the political system to evolve in the direction of 'fusion-of-power' politics where power and responsibility were fairly clearly located. It is also true that the establishment of political stability and accountability was facilitated by the formation and consolidation of the LDP.

The system, however, as it has evolved in the three decades since 1955, shows distinct signs of stagnation and self-satisfaction. In the words of Robert Dahl:

> If high consensus societies can profit from the advantages of incremental change, they run an opposite danger. Where there is little dissent, both political leaders and citizens escape the compulsion to weigh the relative advantages offered by a comprehensive, large-scale change, even when a large-scale change might prove less costly in the long run than either the status quo or a series of incremental changes. The history of politics is writ large with the results of costly timidities that have produced too little too late.

Dahl, it is true, goes on to warn against 'ideological' conflict as in postwar France and Italy, but the essential point still stands.

It is obvious that for a range of reasons it would be difficult to create a viable opposition in Japan, capable of responsibly taking power. Many observers, Japanese and foreign, will remain unconvinced of the desirability of trying.

Nevertheless, we conclude with three points. The first is that changes of government do not necessarily mean loss of national 'consensus'. To an extent the belief that a loss of 'consensus' would ensue derives from European and other class-conflict models that are largely inappropriate for Japanese conditions. Second, the assumption that the present electoral system is 'natural' for Japan needs to be subjected to close scrutiny. I have suggested in this chapter that in several crucial respects it is an outdated and inefficient system that serves to perpetuate without much intellectual justification a status quo that strongly favors the present political establishment. Finally, no real change in the system is likely to occur unless the opposition parties themselves will it (though a change in the electoral system may be required to help them rethink).

Healthy democratic politics for Japan depends on a willingness on the part of government and opposition alike to rethink the system creatively and with a long-term perspective. Many aspects of Japanese life since the war have proved extraordinarily creative and successful. Why should this not happen in politics also?

Ramsayer, J and Rosenbluth, F, *Japan's Political Marketplace*, 1993, pp 80–84, Harvard University Press

Party Organization

'The Liberal Democratic Party,' Marxists were fond of saying, 'is neither liberal, democratic, nor a party.' We have argued that the LDP does in fact compete within a democratic system, though its policies may seem illiberal to the Left. In describing how the LDP functions as a party, we found that while factions weaken its ability to function as a unit, they do not destroy it. One question to be discussed is why LDP members delegate crucial party-management functions to a collective, transfactional leadership.

Japan's multi-member district electoral system, as we explained, gives individual LDP backbenchers a powerful incentive to provide constituency services so as to enhance their reelection. The LDP's extra-parliamentary policymaking apparatus is a device to facilitate the provision of these constituency services. While the inevitable intra-party competition for election is organized along factional lines, neither constituency service nor factional organization assures the election of LDP members. The

LDP has an additional layer of organization that contributes importantly to the electoral success of party members. A central party leadership, drawn from factions but transcending factional leadership, coordinates policymaking among the PARC committees and brokers differences among factions.

LDP backbenchers entrust party leaders with a variety of powers for reasons similar to those motivating the coolies on the Yangtze to hire overseers to beat them. In cases of multiple principals, the principals need to constrain themselves and each other in order to provide themselves with collective goods. LDP backbenchers and factions, acting independently, would face classic prisoners' dilemmas in the provision of collective goods. Lacking a means to coordinate their actions, they would most likely act myopically and self-destructively.

This chapter outlines who the LDP leaders are and how they provide party backbenchers with collective goods. For members of the LDP, the collective goods are the party's reputation for delivering promised services, the party's policy platform, and limits on the dishing out of pork. To provide these collective goods, LDP leaders establish the basic policy direction of the party and restrain wayward LDP backbenchers.

Any principal-agent relationship also harbors the danger of agent opportunism. We will thus examine the means by which LDP backbenchers keep their leaders – and agents – constrained. If LDP backbenchers have put their leaders on a long leash, it is not because they lack the means to rein them in.

Why Party Leadership?

We have already established that Japanese politics is highly particularistic; in that sense factional organization helps individual LDP Diet members provide particular favors to their constituents. Many people vote on the basis of personal favors they receive from politicians. But even the provision of private goods requires the collective action of party members. Legislators must decide which favors to fund, at what levels, and with what resources. The party also must maintain a credible party reputation that attracts campaign contributions, and it must monitor bureaucratic behavior. But each legislator or each faction is inclined only to take credit for the provision of favors, not to be associated with the costs of the favors. The single nontransferable vote electoral system with its large built-in bias toward particularism thus creates major collective-action obstacles to any group of legislators who must cooperate in order to maintain a legislative majority.

The problems LDP members face are compounded by their need to provide some public goods to the general voting public in order to get elected. The LDP cannot reach all voters with private favors: a large group of 'floating voters' – typically urban, educated, white-collar workers – is harder to incorporate into the LDP's traditional support networks. There is some evidence that these voters make their electoral choices on the basis of, among other things, general economic indicators that provide clues about their expected earnings (Miyake, 1989; Arai, 1990). Lavish favors at the expense of inflation or large government budget deficits might tilt the electoral balance away from the LDP. The LDP must therefore calculate and maintain a balance among the private goods it provides to groups of supporters, the public goods with which it woos harder-to-catch floating voters, and the tax cost of both kinds of benefits. Even if the balance between private and public goods is, say, 65 or 70 percent in favor of private goods, the LDP has to make tough choices in setting spending ceilings and distributing the tax burden.

The Electoral Imperative and LDP Organization

Despite the broad similarities among democratic systems, what politicians must do to get elected varies by electoral system. In a single-member-district, parliamentary system such as Britain's, a politician's electoral fate is determined largely by the popularity of his or her party's platform in the district. It comes as no surprise to learn that in such a system the party's backbenchers delegate considerable powers to party leaders.

In Japan, as we have seen, politicians need to deliver a far higher level of particular services. But even in Japan's LDP, where politicians compete for election with members of their own party and therefore work assiduously to build a personal following with factional help, party members recognize advantages in delegating certain tasks to a collective party leadership. The delegation is not as complete as in Britain, to be sure. LDP Diet members insist on more involvement in policymaking, and we have seen that factions undertake most personnel matters for the LDP.

Nonetheless, the strong party organization helps Japanese legislators avoid potentially suboptimal behavior. While unaffiliated politicians would have difficulty raising campaign contributions because the contributor has little reason to believe the politician's pledge to provide policy favors in return, parties are inter-generational, ongoing concerns with a long-term reputation to protect. Parties can therefore more readily make credible promises about favors in exchange for contributions.

Political parties also institutionalize a particular portfolio of policy choices that allow legislators to diversify the product they offer. Although each legislator can specialize in only a few types of policy areas, party affiliation gives voters cues about what range of favors the legislator can deliver with the help of his or her party. Without a party label, it would be impossible for individual legislators to take credit, with any degree of credibility, for favors other than those in their own areas of jurisdiction.

Furthermore, a party label may include a commitment to provide certain public goods. An unaffiliated politician cannot make credible promises regarding public goods, since the provision of these requires the agreement of a legislative majority. Finally, parties reduce the transactions costs of forging minimum winning coalitions on every issue. All political parties cannot, by definition, win a majority every time. But they are the primary unit of competition for forming majorities. The costs to legislators in terms of reduced flexibility of partners may be more than offset by reduced bargaining costs.

Factions in the LDP only incompletely solve these problems. Although they do help members with fundraising, factions do not represent alternative portfolios of policy choices for either private or public goods. As we have discussed, policy differentiation along factional lines would cause more problems than it would solve. Nor do factions eliminate the transactions costs for members of forming permanent coalitions. No faction has ever been close to forming a Diet majority on its own. LDP members overcome these prisoners' dilemmas and coordination problems by delegating powers to a transfactional party leadership.

Who the Party Leaders Are

Our discussion so far has suggested a sharp line between party leaders and backbenchers. The distinction is in fact more blurred, because many Diet members are on their way up the LDP organizational ladder. It is probably best to think of LDP leadership in terms of concentric circles. The smallest circle of LDP leaders includes only the heads of the five or so LDP factions. The Prime Minister is often, though not always, one of this inner group. It is not uncommon, in fact, for heads of factions not to hold any formal position within the party organization, though it is well understood that all important personnel decisions must meet with their approval.

It is the second tier of LDP leadership that is most responsible for the routine management of the party. This group includes the party president (who is also Prime Minister), in the event that he is not the head of a faction. Also in this group are the party secretary (*Kanjicho*), chairman of the PARC (*Seicho kaicho*), and chairman of the Executive Council (*Somu kaicho*), who together make up the party's Committee of Three (*Tosanyaku*). The Committee of Three is effectively an executive committee of the party that is consulted when there are disagreements within the party that neither the PARC nor the Executive Council can iron out. They often bring into their executive meetings lower-ranking LDP leaders, depending on the nature of the problem. During their tenure as party leaders, they refrain from holding factional posts or even from attending their respective faction's business meetings.

The broader leadership circle – senior party members awaiting further advancement – holds many positions, including chairmanships of PARC committees, administrative posts at the LDP's headquarters, and cabinet jobs. As we will discuss later, seniority is the first criterion for advancement up the ladder. Political savvy is also rewarded. But a willingness to work with the top leadership is essential to promotion beyond a certain point.

Party Management

LDP leaders contribute to their members' electoral prospects in several ways. First of all, they protect the party's brand-name capital by formulating the party's stance on public goods and maintaining a ceiling on the private goods that backbenchers dispense; and they broker the interests of factions when they impinge on the party's overall electoral performance and policy choices. They play a smaller role in two areas one might expect to place within their jurisdiction: fundraising and party discipline.

Krauss, ES, 'Politics and the Policymaking Process' in Ishida, T and Krauss, ES (eds), *Democracy in Japan*, 1989, pp 45–46, 48–50, University of Pittsburgh Press

Legally, the prime minister of Japan has powers and limitations similar to leaders of other parliamentary democracies. He is the chief executive elected by members of the Diet (but in case of disagreement between the two houses, the decision of the House of Representatives is the determining vote). He has the power to dissolve the House of Representatives and call an election and to select the cabinet, without having to have his choices confirmed by the Diet. Within the prime minister's office, further, are located various agencies, ranging from relatively insignificant information gathering ones such as the Statistics Agency to more important ones such as the Economic Planning Agency and the Defense Agency.

The prime minister, his cabinet, or an individual minister is responsible to the Diet through the device of no confidence' resolutions; a successful vote necessitates within ten days either the calling of a new election or the resignation of the cabinet. In addition, to avoid the prewar situation in which prime ministers or cabinet ministers were military or ex-military men, the prime minister and a majority of the cabinet, must be Diet members, and all must be civilians. The prime minister's chief aide is the chief cabinet secretary, who serves as something equivalent to a combination of head of the White House staff, chief press secretary, liaison to the party, and political advisor.

The major limitations on the otherwise legally powerful office of prime minister are political, not constitutional. It is the way the prime minister is selected and the nature of the perpetually ruling LDP that limit the power of the office. No politician can become prime minister unless he is a leader of one of the major factions in the party and forms alliances with other faction leaders. The prevalence of factionalism in the party has many origins, including the multi-member district electoral system which encourages members of the same party to run against each other and to give loyalty to a faction leader in exchange for support at election time. But as Nathaniel Thayer has pointed out, perhaps the chief cause of factionalism is the way in which the prime minister has been selected.

...

Because factions are based on personal loyalty and political self-interest, distinctions among the factions usually are not significant in deciding policy matters (although there have been some exceptions). But factions are crucial in other respects. First, the coalitions and relations among them obviously determine who becomes prime minister. Second, the necessity to make political deals and gain the support of other faction leaders in order to win office limits the independence of the prime minister. He must always consult and reach agreement with his allies and their factions lest he jeopardize his majority coalition within the party. Despite the inherent powers of his office, therefore, the prime minister politically is like the head of a rather collective leadership. Furthermore, the factions that were not part of the coalition that put him in office are constantly trying to manoeuver against him, criticize him, and create an opportunity for one of their own leaders to take his place. For these reasons, although it is something of an exaggeration, some LDP politicians and students of Japanese politics say that the real limitations on the ruling party and the most effective 'opposition' in the Japanese system comes from *within* the LDP, rather than from the other parties. Factions thus provide a check on monolithic power, partially substituting for the lack of alternation of parties in government.

Finally, factions are important because they have a great deal of influence on who is selected for the cabinet. The cabinet consists of about twenty people: the heads of the twelve ministries and eight other ministers who are usually given posts as heads of some of the various agencies in the prime minister's office. There is no real difference between the heads of ministries and the heads of agencies – all are considered of cabinet rank.

The ultimate aim of most Diet members is to attain that rank, where a post provides prestige and the opportunity to do something for one's constituency. Here, too, factions are important if not decisive. When the new prime minister forms his cabinet, one of the primary considerations in the distribution of portfolios is factional politics. Cabinet positions are used to reward a few members of one's own faction, and they provide another incentive for faction members to remain loyal and work hard for their leader through the years. But more important, they also are used to reward the leaders of factions that supported the prime minister in his successful bid to capture the prize and may also be seen as a 'down payment' on continued support in the next race. In effect, cabinet posts are an integral part of the exchange relationship within factions and among the factional coalitions.

A wise prime minister will also distribute a few posts in his cabinet even to the factions that opposed his candidacy. Such largesse may help to convince enemy factions to switch sides next time and in the interim may help to mitigate their manoeuvering and dampen their criticism. After all, it is hard for factions to criticize the actions of a cabinet in which they hold office. The art of cabinet-making in Japan consists of being able to distribute just the right number and type of posts to satisfy one's factional allies, one's own faction, and opposing factions in the party.

If factional balance is so important in who gets a cabinet post, then one may wonder how qualified Japan's cabinet ministers are to govern the country and preside over the specialized ministries they head. The truth is that some may not be 'qualified' in the narrow sense of having detailed expertise in a particular policy area. But some are, perhaps being senior Diet politicians with long careers on Diet and party committees in that area. Expertise is not as necessary for a cabinet post in the Japanese system where, as we shall see below, a highly skilled career bureaucracy can manage the details of administration and policy. The job of a cabinet minister has less to do with detailed administration and policymaking than it does with approving bills that are hammered out in the party and bureaucracy, representing the interest and view of one's ministry *vis-à-vis* the other agencies of government, and managing conflicts that arise within the party and the government. For these tasks, the skills of a senior politician are more useful than those of a technocrat.

Even if the cabinet member wanted to learn the details of administration of his ministry or agency, he would hardly have time. Cabinets are typically shuffled by the prime minister about once a year (he doesn't need the approval of the Diet for cabinet appointments). This frequent shuffling gives the prime minister that many more posts at his disposal during his tenure in office to distribute as part of the factional game. It also allows that many more LDP Diet members to take their turn in the cabinet, a not unimportant means of providing incentive to them to continue to do their best for the party and their factions. The rapid turnover of cabinet ministers has allowed a large number of LDP Diet members in the postwar period to be part of the government.

Tadokoro, M, 'The End of Japan's "Non-Decision" Politics' (1994) 34 *Asian Survey* 1002–05

Japanese politics is in total confusion, and has been since the conservative Liberal Democratic Party (LDP) lost power in July 1993 after 38 years of stable rule. Within a year, the country had seen four prime ministers, and it is widely believed that the current government will fall sooner rather than later. Morihiro Hosokawa, who came into power with both political and economic reforms as his top agenda, enjoyed unusually strong popular support. After four decades of LDP rule, filled with scandal and corruption, the Japanese public had become quite cynical about politics, but the advent of Hosokawa's new reform government had raised expectations that long-overdue and serious changes would finally be made. Yet, despite his enormous popularity and high public expectations, the Hosokawa government collapsed after only eight months. The irony is that the self-proclaimed reformer was forced to resign because of financial improprieties; this, in turn, has deepened popular cynicism about Japanese politics.

A successor government was difficult to form. After long and laborious negotiations, the coalition parties worked out a consensus on key policies. The new Hata government, however, was even more fragile than its predecessor, as the Japan Socialist Party (JSP) bolted from the coalition despite a thorough policy discussion before its formation. The Socialists' dissatisfaction did not stem from differences over policy but simply from factional strife within the coalition. The minority government did not last long. Shortly after the Diet passed the budget bill, the LDP, not surprisingly, tried to regain power. The surprise came when the Socialists and the Liberal Democrats, who had been arch-rivals in postwar Japanese politics, now agreed to form a new grand coalition government. The Socialists' official platform is obviously inconsistent with that of the LDP but these two parties, which had battled each other on almost every major issue on the Diet floor over the last four decades, announced no change in their basic policies to the public.

To the astonishment of many Japanese, they are now in the same cabinet under the new Socialist prime minister, Tomiichi Murayama, a typical country politician with no idea whatsoever about international relations. What motivated the two parties to get together is their hostility toward Ichiro Ozawa, the political strategist who triggered the previous series of political changes. The Liberal Democrats were furious about his betrayal of the party, which resulted in its fall from power. The Socialists were angry because they correctly saw through Ozawa's intention to encourage a split in the JSP. Thus, the rising public expectations at the inauguration of the Hosokawa government have now turned into political cynicism. Although politics has been closely covered by the mass media, the Japanese are watching the series of political games as if they were professional wrestling matches rather than a matter of serious concern that affects the fate of themselves and their children, to say nothing of their Asian neighbors and the world. The Japanese may enjoy abusing those whom they have elected to office but they never seriously worry that these corrupt politicians could destroy their daily lives.

Is Japanese politics really an endless and meaningless series of factional power struggles? And can the Japanese afford a continuing stalemate in politics? The answer is no because there are serious political issues to which the Japanese people must respond in one way or another. The old framework of politics characterized by 'conservatives' vs 'left-wing' and 'pro-American vs anti-American' have become entirely obsolete. In fact, the present political turmoil in Japan is integral to the transitional process leading to a new Japanese political framework through splits and realignments. Based on the current changes, this article presents four possible future courses that Japan could take.

The Reality of the 1955 System

The confrontation between the LDP and the JSP, which characterized the so-called 1955 system, was at its initial stage a more serious and meaningful political struggle than mere competition for power. The Socialist call for neutrality and cutting off security relations with the United States may now sound totally out of tune with reality. But during the early part of the postwar period and during the Vietnam War, the concern expressed by the Socialists that Japan might be dragged into a military confrontation through US global strategy was highly appealing to the Japanese public, and it was not totally unrealistic. On the domestic side also, when the Japanese were still suffering from poverty, many socialist economic programs aimed at protecting weak economic sectors from merciless capitalist competition appeared both attractive and realistic. Better protection of labor rights, a stronger emphasis on national welfare, and an antipollution policy were popular not only among the masses but also among intellectuals.

In contrast, the LDP obviously supported an anticommunist and anti-Soviet foreign policy, and during the Cold War its foreign policy was strongly pro-American. However, in the early stages of the 1955 system, a significant number of its members were more nationalistic than simply pro-American. Some major LDP members had been closely related to the prewar Japanese military, and it is not surprising that the party's charter explicitly mentioned the revision of the constitution to legitimize military forces. On the domestic front, the LDP's attitude was obviously pro-business, and its policies emphasized economic growth rather than equal distribution, industrial prosperity rather than national welfare. But as Japan's high growth continued and the two parties confronted each other in Diet debates, an implicit convergence of basic policies developed between them. First, the LDP, though it never officially gave up its goal of revising the constitution, practically shelved the issue, and its basic foreign policy stance became less right-wing nationalistic. As it actively pursued Japan's economic interests, LDP foreign policy became 'dovish' or passive with a minimum commitment to risky power politics.

This foreign policy line was basically consistent with that of the Socialists, who were unhappy with the pro-American elements in the LDP and frequently embarrassed LDP governments by pointing out the inevitable contradictions between the 'peace' clause of the constitution and Japan's security policy, particularly regarding US-Japan security relations. But the role of the Socialists here was negative at best because they could not come up with any feasible alternative. In other words, the Socialists could serve as a brake on the LDP's possible over-commitment to power politics but they did not have a realistic foreign policy alternative, and as long as LDP policies were not too hawkish, the Socialists could live with an LDP government.

While the convergence between the two became clearer in the diplomatic strategic aspects of foreign relations, their differences in domestic affairs grew smaller as well. When the failure of socialism in the Soviet Union and Japan's economic success became unquestionable realities, the Socialists ceased to take their ideology seriously. Although they kept using socialist rhetoric, they became satisfied with material goals; they sought a better distribution of economic benefits for their clients, such as organized trade unions within the LDP-dominated capitalist system, rather than challenging the system itself. It was easy for the LDP to accommodate the JSP because the former was far from the believer in laissez faire that its name suggests. While the LDP was anticommunist, it was anything but liberal and had no philosophical difficulties in granting favors to special interests and subsidizing selected groups. Conflicts between the Socialists and the LDP, therefore, became manageable and negotiable.

Thus, the latter stage of the 1955 system was characterized by strong consensus on the combination of a passive or 'dovish' foreign policy and corporatist economic policies. It is no coincidence that the LDP-Socialist coalition in 1994 is talking about preservation of the constitution and a dovish foreign policy in order to distance itself from the activist foreign policy advocated by the 'reformers' represented by Ichiro Ozawa. It is also symbolic that the first major economic policy decision of the LDP-JSP government was to increase subsidies for rice farmers, who under the 1955 system were amply protected and given stronger political voice due to their formidable lobbying power and the over-representation of rural votes in the Japanese electoral system. Now, it has become totally clear that the LDP and the JSP were actually partners within the 1955 system instead of its defenders and challengers, respectively.

Christensen, R, 'Electoral Reform in Japan: How it Was Enacted and Changes it May Bring' (1994) 34 *Asian Survey* 589–91, 602–05

On the last day of an extended session, the two houses of the Japanese Diet met together and, by a standing vote, approved political reform legislation. The legislation changed the Japanese electoral system, put greater restriction on political fundraising, and introduced government subsidizing of political parties. These changes would be unremarkable if they did not represent five years of debate and a history of failed attempts to change the electoral system dating back to the 1950s. Why did such legislation finally pass on 29 January 1994, and what distinguished this successful effort?

Some explanations spring quickly to mind but upon closer inspection prove inadequate. For example, the recent string of campaign financing scandals, beginning with the Recruit affair, would seem to explain the public outcry for reform and the legislative response. But scandals are endemic in Japanese politics; they have occurred with regularity in the postwar period, and much of what is considered fodder for scandals now was the accepted norm of political behavior in the past. The timing of scandals does not explain why past reform efforts failed or why reforms passed in 1994 rather than two, three, or four years earlier.

The present reforms are closely associated with the 1993 political earthquake in Japan, which fragmented the ruling Liberal Democratic Party (LDP) and brought down the government after a vote of no confidence. Elections were held, and LDP defectors formed a coalition government with the non-communist opposition parties. The coalition, led by Morihiro Hosokawa, pledged to enact reform legislation by the year's end. It might be argued, therefore, that political reform succeeded in 1994 because the LDP was no longer in power. However, the new coalition government was led and run primarily by former LDP politicians, and further, the reforms passed only after the government struck a compromise with the LDP. Hosokawa's government did not have any numerical advantages in passing legislation that previous LDP governments did not also have.

A third explanation might point to the commitment of Prime Minister Hosokawa, whose coalition took shape around the issue of reform and who staked his career on a promise to enact political reform legislation. But Prime Ministers Kaifu and Miyazawa had made similar commitments in 1991 and 1993, respectively, and these were unfulfilled. Indeed, when passage of the reforms appeared in doubt, Hosokawa began to back away from a previous threat to step down. A committed leader does not appear to be the crucial explanatory factor in understanding the recent success of reform efforts.

A fourth explanation focuses on the loss of control of the House of Councillors by the LDP in 1989. This forced the LDP to work with the centrist opposition parties to pass legislation. It could be argued that opposition control of the upper house prevented the LDP from sidestepping the issue of reapportionment through a minimal shifting of seats. Though this strategy had worked in the past, another reapportionment became necessary by the early 1990s, and the opposition in control of the House of Councillors demanded broader changes. If the boundaries of many electoral districts were to be jumbled by such a broad reapportionment, then by comparison it would not seem as disruptive to install a completely new electoral system. However, contrary to this scenario, opposition parties did cooperate with the LDP in passing a limited reapportionment in late 1992. They were unable or unwilling to force a more significant measure.

In contrast to other failed attempts, political reform succeeded in 1994 for two reasons. First, the preferences of individual politicians and support organizations had changed, which increased the number and intensity of supporters of reform efforts. These changed preferences were closely related to a renewed interest in political realignment in Japan, a movement distinct from the contemporaneous anticorruption initiatives. Prorealignment activists wanted to combine moderate elements of the non-communist Japanese opposition with defectors from the LDP. They hoped to create two moderate political parties that could alternate in power, and their goal was largely accomplished by the LDP defections and the new coalition government of 1993.

Second, the frequency of campaign contribution scandals created strong public sentiment in support of legislation to control corruption. Prorealignment forces were able to ally with anticorruption forces to create the large support base needed to pass reform legislation. An atmosphere existed in which no politician could publicly oppose political reform. Politicians were forced to express their opposition in the context of competing reform proposals, and thus could only delay legislation or urge the passage of partial or weaker versions of bills under consideration ...

...

Promises and Predictions of the Reforms

The most important feature of the new bill is its influence on realignment. The Japanese seem to be fervent believers in Duverger's law that single-seat districts lead to two-party systems. However, there is no assurance that the new electoral system will produce two main political parties, as it does not create the iron-clad incentives for multiple parties to coalesce into two that a straight, single-seat plurality system would do. Two hundred of the 500 seats in the House of Representatives will be elected in eleven regional proportional representation districts, which vary in size from seven to 33 seats. Therefore, small parties will still have a chance to win some seats in the PR districts; in fact, simulations show that the Communist Party will actually win two additional seats under the new system.

An additional hurdle in the realignment scenario is the inability of all the competing political groups to come to terms with their potential coalition allies. The Communists have been written off as coalition partners; if the Socialist Party splits, its left wing would form a new political group; the prorealignment camp is also divided between Ozawa and his close allies and those who are uncomfortable with Ozawa's leadership and tactics; and the LDP is similarly divided between those who are potential allies of Ozawa and those who are working with his opponents. It is quite possible that Japan would end up with five political parties (communist, left-wing socialist, and three centrist) competing in the first post-reform election, unchanged from the five major parties that existed prior to the events of 1993.

A third factor that works against party consolidation is the tendency of Japanese voters to choose politicians based on local popularity. Though the reform is intended to make elections more issue-oriented, nothing in the Ozawa-engineered realignment suggests any greater agreement on significant political issues within each political grouping than between groupings. The nascent political parties that are forming and reforming are based much more on strategic considerations, personality, and loyalty to a leader than they are on genuine policy differences. Furthermore, campaign laws have not been changed to give candidates better access to voters. In last minute compromise negotiations, the LDP managed to retain the ban on door-to-door campaigning, and the tried and true methods of reaching voters through personal support networks may remain a candidate's best hope. Future campaigns may still turn on local alliances and personalities rather than party platforms. Such local stability in the single-seal districts coupled with the stability of a proportional representation vote could make it easier for small parties to remain viable political actors.

A second feature of the electoral reforms that deserves attention is the introduction of a separate proportional representation (PR) ballot. Previous Japanese experience in the upper house has shown that a separate PR ballot encourages and allows a greater protest vote. A PR list attracts minor parties that otherwise would not run candidates in single-seat districts. Voters now may cast a variety of protest votes, an option they lack in district elections; the split vote allows them to express a more sophisticated preference: for a major party in the numerically superior district races and for a protest party in the PR race. Proportional representation could also affect the type of person elected to the Diet. Typically, PR lists allow room for nonpoliticians such as bureaucrats, academics, or media personalities, and make it easier for parties to put up candidates from historically underrepresented groups, such as women. This feature, however, is counteracted by the ability to joint list candidates on the PR and district lists. Under this system, it is likely that most party candidates in district races will simultaneously be listed on the PR list. The degree to which these district politicians take precedence over candidates who appear only on the PR list will determine the extent to which the PR system becomes a means of diversifying the membership of the lower house. Ultimately, the effect of PR candidates on diversity will depend on whether national/factional party leaders control access to party nominations and can overrule local, parochial interests and nominate significant numbers of nontraditional candidates.

It is asserted that this new electoral system will weaken political factions in Japan's large parties. The intraparty competition created by the multimember districts of the former system is given as one reason for the existence of factions in Japanese politics. Similarly, the centralization in the political parties of campaign funding and nominating procedures is also seen as strengthening the hand of the party *vis-à-vis* the factions by placing limits on how much money can be transferred among politicians, thereby hampering the ability of faction leaders to disburse funds to their followers. However, factionalism may not disappear from Japanese politics; there are loopholes in campaign financing laws that will still allow faction leaders to help out their followers, and the powers that are being concentrated in the party leadership will still have to be exercised by someone. It is quite possible that faction leaders will disburse nominations and funds in the name of the party just as they have in the past.

Finally, there is the consideration of the effect of reforms on rampant corruption and money politics in Japan. On paper, the reforms fight corruption in several ways. They limit the number of fund raising groups and lower the limits on the amount an organization can contribute annually to each fundraising group. The clear intent is to force corporate donations into party coffers rather than those controlled by faction leaders or individual politicians, but it is likely that the reforms will just make more circuitous the route such contributions follow. Politicians and analysts have been quick to point out that politicians will rename their local support organizations as local party organizations, and money could then flow into them even though they are dominated by an individual candidate. Similarly, it is expected that even contributions to the national party will be made with informal strings attached. Donors will ask that the money be given to a certain politician or group of politicians. A second anticorruption measure provides for government funding to replace the anticipated decline in corporate contributions. This measure attracted very little controversy as all parties are amenable to augmenting their campaign war chests with supplemental government funding. However, the limits on corporate contributions are still so weak that it is unlikely that government funding will affect money politics or corruption in Japan.

A third reform beefs up penalties for violations of these measures. Culpability is extended to a candidate's immediate relatives and campaign managers, and a violation by any one of this group will result in annulment of the victory and leave the candidate ineligible to run for office from that district for five years. Though this last reform is a step in the right direction in terms of anticorruption, it also could be easily evaded. Politicians point out that the likely effect of the measure will be the appointment of figurehead campaign managers, while the real political operatives will be given lesser titles that put them beyond the reach of the law. These operatives will still be prosecuted for their own electoral law violations but their guilt will have no effect on the politicians for whom they work. Perhaps the greatest threat to corrupt politicians is simply the switch to single-seat districts. In the past, a convicted politician could easily be reelected because victory required only 15% to 30% of the vote in any one district; now the threshold for victory is closer to 50%.

Though it is easy to conclude from the momentous battle for electoral reform that Japanese politics will never be the same, one must be careful before assuming that the predicted changes will occur. It is clear that the alliances formed to pass electoral reform and the new system will encourage a realignment of political parties in Japan. However, beyond this assured change, the new legislation has sufficient mixed incentives and loopholes to make any additional claims questionable. Though a coalescence into two major political parties is quite possible, it is equally possible that it won't happen. Similarly, claims about the demise of money politics, factional politics, and personal support networks are questionable. The only sure change, political realignment, was predictable, given that the bill from its inception was designed for political realignment despite its anticorruption masquerade.

IV THE EXECUTIVE

Abe, H, Shindo, M and Kawato, S, *The Government and Politics of Japan*, 1994, pp 28–32, University of Tokyo Press

CABINET GOVERNMENT IN A PREDOMINANT-PARTY SYSTEM

Party politics in postwar Japan began as a competitive party system. From the merger of the conservative parties in 1955 until 1993, however, the party system was consistently dominated by the LDP. Party systems have been classified into seven types. In the 'predominant-party' type of system, 'parties other than the major one not only are permitted to exist, but do exist as legal and legitimate – if not necessarily effective – competitors of the predominant party ... A predominant-party system is such to the extent that, and as long as, its major party is consistently supported by a winning majority ... of the voters'. This description neatly fits the Japanese party system between 1955 and 1993.

The permeation of the ruling party by corruption became increasingly apparent in the late 1980s, however, epitomized by the Recruit scandal of 1989, to which the public reacted with outrage. Support for the LDP plummeted in the House of Councillors election of July 1989, and it lost a majority of seats there for the first time since the founding of the party. Nevertheless, the LDP managed to maintain a majority of seats in the more powerful House of Representatives in the general election of February 1990. Although the LDP's control was seriously diluted, it is fair to say, however, that the Japanese party system still fit the model of a predominant-party system until the LDP lost control of the lower house in July 1993. Throughout, cabinet government in Japan was to a large extent controlled by the internal politics of the ruling party, in addition to parliamentary politics. Let us look now at this situation with reference to several aspects of cabinet government in the post-1955 period.

From the first House of Representatives election in April 1946 to the most recent, in July 1993, there have been 19 general elections in postwar Japan, with 13 since the conservative merger in 1955. Of these 13, the general election of 1976 came as the result of the house fulfilling its entire four-year term; all the others came as the result of dissolutions of the house.

Article 69 of the constitution specifies dissolution of the lower house as one response the cabinet can make to passage of a motion of no confidence by that house. With a single predominant party, however, it was rare for the terms of Article 69 to be applied, since no opposition party or parties held enough seats to pass such a motion. Most postwar dissolutions have invoked, rather, Article 7, which allows the emperor to dissolve parliament with the advice and consent of the cabinet.

In 1948, during the tenure of the second Yoshida cabinet – which enjoyed only minority support in the House of Representatives – one constitutional scholar argued that the *cabinet* had the power, under Article 7, to dissolve parliament without need of a parliamentary vote of no confidence. This interpretation set off a vigorous debate about whose prerogative parliamentary dissolution really was. Even today there is disagreement as to the constitutionality of such a dissolution, but under the terms of Article 7, dissolution of parliament has in fact become standard practice. Thus, even when major political confrontation like that caused by the Recruit scandal or the 1988–89 debate over tax reform erupts and the opposition parties call for a dissolution and new elections 'to seek a judgment by the people', they actually appeal to the cabinet on the basis of Article 7.

Our aim here is not to debate further the constitutional propriety of parliamentary dissolution under the terms of Article 7. One could say that the flexible utilization of this type of dissolution introduces a healthy, plebiscitary element into policy debate. On the other hand, as the terms 'consultative dissolution', 'collusive dissolution', and 'snap dissolution' suggest, dissolution has on occasion been used as a technique of ruling and opposition party wheeling and dealing or of ruling party coercion *vis-à-vis* the opposition. The people, therefore, unsurprisingly, no longer see a prime minister and cabinet as being electorally 'purified' or legitimated when they dissolve parliament and are then reelected. To the extent that the people are aware of these compromises and deals, this tendency will become stronger.

Moreover, the cabinet's exercise of the power of dissolution has thus far been governed by the internal political dynamics of the ruling party. In a predominant-party system, where the president of the LDP became prime minister with little concern for the attitudes of parliament, dissolution was a move in the drama of prime ministerial succession. If the prime minister and his allies tried to strengthen their intraparty legitimacy with a dissolution followed by an electoral 'appeal to the people', other intraparty forces tried to obstruct the move. Conversely, intraparty groups that did not support the prime minister tried to create a situation in which he had to resign by pushing him to dissolve parliament when they knew the party stood to lose parliamentary seats in the election to follow (even though the LDP would remain in power). Moreover, some of the opposition parties on occasion became participants in these stratagems. On the other hand, whenever a situation emerged in which the legitimacy of the ruling party was really called into question, the LDP simply installed a new prime minister and cabinet without dissolving parliament, thus hoping to clean up after the party's political failures and restore its image. Such 'political cosmetic surgery' made the continuation of one-party dominance possible until the early 1990s, when an unprecedented string of scandals and the LDP refusal to implement meaningful political reforms finally cost the party its parliamentary majority.

Some of the pathologies of cabinet government under one-party predominance are reflected in the selection and terms of office of cabinet ministers. Since 1955 the average term of office of a cabinet minister has been only one year. On one or more occasions during his own term of office the typical prime minister has used his powers of appointment and dismissal of ministers to 'reorganize' his cabinet. Needless to say, the reason for frequent cabinet reshuffles is simply to strengthen the intraparty base of the party president-cum-prime minister; they are unrelated to the parliamentary process. Until 1993 cabinet selections were made on the principle of factional balance among the major factions within the LDP. This procedure, which developed under prime ministers Ikeda Hayato and Sato Eisaku in the 1960s and early 1970s, called for each faction, regardless of whether it supported the prime minister, to receive cabinet posts equivalent to the number of MPs in it. A comparison of the actual number of portfolios awarded to each faction in each cabinet since Ikeda's time with the predicted number of portfolios that would be awarded if cabinets were formed in proportion to the size of each faction has demonstrated a precise correspondence between the two.

The frequency with which cabinets are reshuffled and the interfactional and interparty equity with which portfolios are awarded spread the opportunities for access to prestige and authority (and indebtedness to the prime minister) widely and evenly, thus preventing division within the ruling party or coalition. As this process of cabinet selection has become institutionalized, however, a very clear precedent of experience and prior posts has been created within which any MP who wishes to attain a cabinet post must proceed. No matter how superior one's qualities, it is extremely rare for a freshman MP – at least under LDP rule – to become a cabinet minister. It can be argued that the institutionalization of this intraparty seniority system has hurt the party's ability to make maximum use of MPs of talent and capability, and has sapped the vitality of the cabinet as well.

CABINET GOVERNMENT AND THE ADMINISTRATIVE BUREAUCRACY

Under a predominant-party system, cabinet government largely reflected the internal politics of the ruling party. Such a situation gave rise to a variety of problems in the relationships between both the cabinet as an institution and individual ministers, on the one hand, and the civil service on the other. As already noted, in a predominant-party system the cabinet does not derive its authority and legitimacy from having won the mantle of rule in electoral battle with its partisan competitors. This makes it very difficult to control the bureaucracy by wielding the symbolic political weapon of a popular mandate, a weapon that the current ruling coalition does have at its disposal. Moreover, in that the appointment, dismissal, and tenure of ministers are as capricious as described above, it is inevitable that ministerial control of the civil service, whose members are in office for life, is severely restricted. Ministers come and go so fast that bureaucratic wits refer to them as 'Minister What's-his-name'. And this transience may offset the power of the ruling coalition's mandate.

Of course, the bureaucrats cannot ignore the importance of either ministers or the cabinet. For this reason civil servants provide frequent briefings for ministers, hoping that by so doing the influence of their own agency will be enhanced. For their part, ministers attempt to realize the interests of their own factions, their constituents, and their favorite interest groups, by communicating them to the civil service – backed, of course, by the political clout of their ministerial position. This sort of collusive, mutually manipulative, apolitical process may make life easier for both politicians and bureaucrats, but, as economic friction with foreign countries increases, it raises the anxiety and mistrust with which Japan is regarded internationally. It may be that one of the reasons Japanese politics is seen as having deteriorated into a parochial fixation with domestic issues, with an utterly inadequate international perspective, is that the cabinet system, in the absence of alternation between ruling parties, simply fell victim to intraparty rivalry, party-bureaucracy collusion, and interest-group politics.

Lehmann, JP, *The Roots of Modern Japan*, 1982, pp 199–203, Macmillan

... in 1885 a major reorganisation of the government apparatus took place with the introduction of the Cabinet system. This was a move taken in preparation for the new constitutional structure which the country was to obtain at the end of the decade, but also involved a rationalisation of the procedure of government affairs. Ministries and ministerial responsibilities became more clearly defined. In turn however this organisational change was also a reflection of the growing complexity of state affairs – whether finance, agriculture, military, diplomatic and so on – and hence a corresponding demand for professional specialists rather than simply inspired amateurs. Given the reforms and innovations in the field of education it was now possible to select from a pool of qualified candidates. It is, therefore, in the mid-eighties that the modern Japanese bureaucracy was officially born.

The first Imperial University had been established in 1877. What is known today as Tokyo University – and remains to this day and will undoubtedly remain in the future the prestigious educational institution *par excellence* – was originally simply designated as the Imperial University. When an Imperial University was created in Kyoto in 1897, and subsequently in Sendai, Sapporo, Fukuoka, Osaka, Nagoya and in due course Keijo (Seoul) and Taipei, the first Imperial University became Tokyo Imperial University; since the Second World War the designation 'Imperial' has been dropped. In 1886 the Imperial University Ordinance was promulgated and Tokyo University combined the faculties of law, medicine, engineering, literature and natural sciences. The original *raison d'être* of this national university, as opposed to a number of private institutes of secondary and tertiary learning, was to serve the state directly. In consequence, in the following year civil service examinations were introduced. These applied mainly, however, to the lower echelons of the bureaucracy. Further reform was introduced in 1893 with the Civil Service Appointment Ordinance. Although a degree of nepotism was retained, nevertheless on the whole by the end of the century Japan had a fully-fledged modern professional civil service.

With modernity the phenomenon of *kanryo-shugi* was not only alive and well, but indeed probably far healthier than it had ever been. The Edo period motto of *kanson-minpi* ('revere officials – despise the masses') could also, accepting certain modifications, be said to have remained operative. Bureaucrats came to form a highly privileged, quasi-sacrosanct elite. Legislation was passed to ensure that they were well beyond the control of the Diet and the tumultuous political parties. Indeed, not only were bureaucrats beyond the control of the parties, but the parties can be said to have fallen under the control of the bureaucrats. As will be seen in the following chapter, shortly after the establishment of the Diet the parties changed considerably in character once they began actually exercising a degree of power – from being hitherto popular parties, namely responsive to the populace and the issues which excited them, to becoming institutionalised, or entrenched, parties, namely absorbed into the establishment. Part of this scenario, indeed a fundamental dénouement in it, consisted of bureaucrats joining the parties and being invited to high offices in them. In the twentieth century, with only a very few exceptions, practically every prime minister came from either a civil or military bureaucratic background. Similarly, throughout the modern era the power of the bureaucracy, independently of government office, has been extensive. This remains true today. Extensive, however, does not mean absolute.

The bureaucracy came to be divided between upper and lower echelons. Entry into one or the other was determined by examination. The dividing line between the two was clear: lower-ranking civil servants were second-class citizens within the bureaucratic order. A strict regime of apartheid was maintained: the lower did not join the ranks of the upper. Upper-ranking bureaucrats were almost exclusively from Tokyo Imperial University and also almost exclusively from the Law Faculty of that institution. The prestige of Law Faculty graduates from Tokyo especially, but also from the other former Imperial Universities – except of course, Keijo (Seoul) and Taipei – remains a marked feature of contemporary Japan. In fact, it would not be too much of an exaggeration to state that they constitute a caste, the Brahmins of modern Japan. For this reason, a few points should be made clear. Although Law Faculties do produce lawyers and judges, this is by no means their primary function. The lawyer in Japan is not the omnipresent factor, both in the private and public sectors, in the manner of his American colleague; there are, in fact, few lawyers in Japan. The establishment of Tokyo Imperial University and recruitment into the top grades of the civil service took place at a time when Japanese affairs of state were still very much dominated by considerations regarding the revision of the treaties in particular, but also Western-imposed international relations in general. The syllabus of the Law Faculty took account of the contemporary realities and the bias necessary in the formation of the country's bureaucratic elite. Thus while jurisprudence was studied, including civil and penal law, constitutional law and, of course, international law, modern European history, international relations, political science and philosophy were equally important elements in the curriculum. Entrance to the Law Faculty included an examination in a European language. A Law Faculty degree was also generally complemented, especially for those who joined the diplomatic service, by a stint in a European or American university: to polish up linguistic abilities, to gather further knowledge at closer quarters of Euro/American institutions and to establish contacts with the Western élites.

Bureaucracies are, of course, a feature of all societies. In Japan it is held that while the government provides the head of the body politic, the bureaucracy is the backbone. This comment, however, could equally apply to many other societies, but the calibre and competence of Japan's bureaucracy ensured a particularly strong backbone – especially necessary in view of the comparative instability of governments throughout most of the period of transformation; indeed up to recent times very few governments lasted more than two years in office. Another interesting feature of modern Japan is that after the retirement into the background of the great architects of Meiji Japan, the country can boast hardly any statesmen of not just international, but even national standing. It is probable that one of the many causes for the failure of democracy in pre-war Japan is precisely this absence of powerful political figures emanating from the parties. The absence of a strong political movement made the bureaucracy's role in the administration of the affairs of state and the direction of government policy all the more significant. In comparison with other modern societies, therefore, one can underline the degree of power and initiative exercised by the bureaucracy. This reality and the ethic of public service, as opposed to private gain, inherited from *bushido*, also no doubt account for the fact that the civil service has remained throughout the modern period the most prestigious career.

It was claimed in the former chapter that in the course of the transformation to modernity the prestige attached to samurai status rapidly declined, while the key to political, social and financial success lay securely in the hands of university graduates, the *crème de la crème* emanating from Tokyo Imperial University. It was also claimed that the decades in the immediate aftermath of the 1868 revolution witnessed a comparatively high degree of social mobility, both upwards and downwards. Was the selection process into the universities and recruitment into the elevated civil service based on entirely meritocratic principles? The answer must be no. It is true that entrance into Tokyo University, and others, was conditional on passing a highly competitive examination. On the other hand, it was only at the turn of the century that primary education was made not only compulsory but also free of tuition charges; secondary and tertiary education remained fee-paying. Most secondary and all tertiary educational institutions were concentrated in the big cities, which, as we have seen, accounted for only a small percentage of the population. There were occasional examples of poor country boys – Tokyo Imperial University was closed to female candidates – rising in meteoric fashion up the meritocratic/bureaucratic ladder: perhaps the most striking illustration being Hirota Koki (1878–1948), variously foreign minister, prime minister, and one of the very few civilians to have been executed under orders from the Allied Military Tribunal for the Far East after the Second World War. In general terms, however, from geographical, economic and academic perspectives, the system was clearly biased in favour of the urban upper-middle classes. While it remains true that in comparison with Western European countries there was probably a higher degree of social mobility – and the élite Japanese universities never adopted or encouraged the social pretentiousness of Oxbridge or the American Ivy League colleges – in Japan, so far as the bulk of the native population was concerned, and, especially in contrast with the post-war situation, by the twentieth century this mobility was marginal. A similar trend can be discerned in the world of industry. While entrepreneurs were often parvenus, sons of their own works, the managers who succeeded them in the leadership of industry were almost invariably products of the new middle classes. By the early 20th century the bureaucracy, as well as the other leading sectors of society, tended to issue from what increasingly became a self-perpetuating social élite.

van Wolferen, K, *The Enigma of Japanese Power*, 1989, pp 348–50, 351–53, 357–58, 360–62, Macmillan

Luckiest survivors of the war

The most momentous decision the occupation authorities made when they set about transforming Japan's political leadership was to leave practically the entire bureaucracy intact. The usual explanation for this is that SCAP had no choice but to work through the existing organs of state. But as a specialist on Japanese politics points out, this overstressing of United States dependence ignores the realities of power. The vast majority of those involved in occupation policies were not even aware that any significant decision had been made. The Americans in charge simply assumed that bureaucrats everywhere behaved as they did in the USA, that is to say, as apolitical technicians.

The occupation purge eliminated the defeated military organisations, removed fifteen hundred highly placed businessmen, barred a few party politicians from holding public office and dissolved ultra-nationalist organisations. It did not go beyond this to tackle the mainspring of Japan's governing system. The aims of the purge, to some extent contradictory, were neither clearly outlined nor attainable under the circumstances. Moreover the strong incentive to preserve, for political reasons, the 'tranquillity' of the occupation led the US reformers to keep to a minimum interference in areas outside the military and ultra-nationalist organisations. Thus the purge of the bureaucracy was, in its details, left to the bureaucrats themselves, who soon realised that they were free to use a large variety of loopholes; they often simply ignored SCAP instructions.

By 1950, when the return to public life of depurged bureaucrats coincided with the 'Red Purge' (in which more than one thousand government officials and almost eleven thousand company employees suspected of communism or 'communistic-type' thinking lost their jobs), the effects of the occupation purge on Japan's officialdom had been reduced to almost nil.

Reform bureaucrats and the 'new order'

SCAP's ignorance of the true power of Japanese bureaucrats gave the latter the opportunity to develop and integrate further economic institutions they had experimented with, in the context of the wartime industrial effort, from the early 1930s until 1945. This postwar effort was better organised; the bureaucrats had learned from experience and, more important, had been given powers by SCAP that they never had before.

Many of the most prominent figures associated with post-war industrial policy had been known in pre-war and wartime Japan as 'reform bureaucrats', strongly influenced by the ideas of Hitler's Germany and by Mussolini's corporatism. This does not mean that they were converts to Nazism, but that they sponsored the application of German methods to problems of the economy and social control in Japan. Nazi and fascist theory are not generally associated in the Western mind with the Japanese 'economic miracle', but it is doubtful whether this could have occurred without the inspiration of these theories supporting totalitarian state control. In fact, the reform bureaucrats and their apprentices dominated the postwar leadership of the economic ministries, the central bank and the large business federations ...

...

Bureaucratic institutions and personnel fitted smoothly into the new Japan that was being 'defeudalised'. One of the closest associates of Tojo Hideki, reform bureaucrat Kishi Nobusuke, who as the most powerful official in the wartime Ministry of Munitions was the central figure among executors of Japan's wartime industrial policy, became the dominant figure of postwar industrial policy. We have noted how Kishi, after a stint in Sugamo prison as a war criminal suspect (never brought to trial), became first one of

Japan's best-known prime ministers, then, until his death in 1987, Japan's most influential *eminence grise.*

Second only to Kishi as a shaper of post-war industrial policy was Shiina Etsusaburo, a Manchurian reform bureaucrat, who had the timely idea, between the surrender and the arrival of the first United States troops, of re-baptising the Ministry of Munitions so that it became the Ministry of Commerce and Industry once more. He himself became MITI minister after the war, and remained a powerful force behind the scenes at the ministry, as well as one of the most prominent leaders of the LDP, until his death in 1979.

The leader of the Ministry of Finance group in Manchuria was Hoshino Naoki, who was president of the wartime CPB. After the war he became a prominent member of the Keizai Kenkyukai, the study group established to re examine postwar economic policy, which produced the blueprint for policies of economic high growth in the shape of Prime Minister Ikeda's 'income doubling plan'. He was also chairman of the Tokyo Hotel and Trading Group, and of Diamond Publishing, a firm specialising in business publications.

The main architects of wartime financial controls had originally come from the foreign exchange section, established in 1933, of the Ministry of Finance, and were found in its secretariat and the Finance Bureau, an extraordinary ministerial group with great discretionary powers in designing state policy. Pre eminent among them was the reform bureaucrat Sakomizu Hisatsune, who became head of the Economic Planning Agency and postal minister after the war.

Another prominent Ministry of Finance official associated with this wartime planning, Morinaga Teiichiro, was to become vice minister of finance in 1957–59 and governor of the Bank of Japan during the second half of the 1970s. A third, Shimomura Osamu, determined the pricing policies of the crucial postwar Economic Stabilisation Board, and was later one of the main brains behind Prime Minister Ikeda's 'income doubling plan'.

Many of the crucial wartime controls over lending were co-ordinated in a bureau whose chief, Ichimanda Hisato, was to become governor of the Bank of Japan in 1946, a position he held for eight and a half crucial years before being appointed finance minister. Under his governorship the central bank was popularly known as 'the Vatican'.

The bureaucrats survived the purges with the added advantage of being freed from their sometimes troublesome military associates. Moreover, the occupation authorities, believing that big business had been 'active' exponents of militant nationalism and aggression', ordered the dissolution of the *zaibatsu* conglomerates and disbanded the holding companies, which meant that the bureaucrats no longer faced troublesome rivals for power in the business world. The bureau chiefs of each ministry began to attend cabinet meetings, a practice unknown before the war. They became go-betweens between MacArthur's headquarters and government ministers, and their utterances gained significantly in weight.

When, after the war, Japanese intellectuals and commentators began to refer to the bureaucrats as 'subcontractors of the occupation', they missed the essential fact that the tail was wagging the dog. Perhaps the biggest present bestowed on the postwar MITI bureaucrats by SCAP was the power to form cartels, an essential instrument of Japanese industrial policy that had earlier been the monopoly of the wartime 'control associations'. These associations, created in 1941 after much friction among the various bureaucratic cliques involved and much business opposition, were meant to co-ordinate activities, production targets and the allocation of materials in the various sectors of wartime industry. But the bureaucrats never gained an effective grip on them, since business had made sure that they were headed by the top executive of the largest firm in each sector, thus putting them under effective control of the *zaibatsu*. In disbanding the *zaibatsu*, SCAP forbade any further private cartelisation. To the economic officials of what was to become MITI it suddenly seemed 'as if they had arrived in the bureaucratic promised land'.

Talkative officials have publicly acknowledged that, whereas, formally, Japan underwent a great transformation after the war, the economic system and especially the institutional base for financial controls were retained in the forms they had taken during the war. Two former Ministry of Finance bureaucrats have contrasted the two 'realities', the formal and the substantial, and asserted that this duality was essential in the shaping of the postwar 'miracle'. As they put it, the ideology of democratic equal opportunity caused an explosion of energy in favour of economic growth, while the high growth itself was actually achieved through the reality of strict financial controls. Writing thirty-two years after the war, they noted that the basic law governing the activities of the central bank was still the same as the original law that had reflected the totalitarian economic purposes of the Nazi Reichsbank. They also argued that the creation of the post-war Japan Development Bank, Export-Import Bank and Long-Term Credit Bank can be viewed as a strengthening of the role the Industrial Bank of Japan (which survived) played during the war ...

...

While very kind to the economic-control bureaucrats, the occupation authorities placed bureaucrats steeped in pre-war and wartime *social*-control methods in a frightful predicament. 'Democratised' education meant teachers organising under Marxist inspired leadership, and the loss of a whole arsenal of indoctrination methods. Justice Ministry officials had to cope with idealists who actually believed that the law was situated above everyone, including officials; it took at least a decade and a half before they regained control through the secretariat of the Supreme Court. The *Naimusho* was broken up, and the police were reorganised. While the devastated economy and dire living conditions warranted much economic planning and thus control, the new start with 'democracy' hardly warranted a 'thought police'.

But, by bestowing a constitution upon Japan, General MacArthur, without realising it, did the social control bureaucrats at least one great favour. The constitution was not wrested from the power holders by the people. The latter, therefore, were not encouraged to believe that they had the *right* to wrest anything from the ruling elite; and the theory of ultimate benevolence could be maintained. Also as the occupation period reached its midpoint it was gradually becoming clear that the 'damage' the US reformers were inflicting could be contained. By 1949 a popular movement towards genuine reform of the civil service and its selection methods, originating among lower echelon bureaucrats, engineering bureaucrats and more liberal elements in the higher bureaucracy, had petered out for lack of SCAP support.

The main hazard to the administrators was the new democratic legislature, which could easily undermine social-control mechanisms. The threat was averted thanks to a massive influx into the Diet of veterans of the disbanded *Naimusho* – the major social control ministry – that in 1960 was represented by 54 of its former officials. The majority of these had been 'purged'. This 'descent' of retired bureaucrats into the pre-LDP conservative parties had begun shortly after the war, aided by the room made for them by the occupation purge of wartime politicians. Some thirty elite bureaucrats joined the Liberal Party ranks for the 1949 elections, and in subsequent elections their number grew to roughly a quarter of the Diet membership, providing Japan with the crucial Yoshida, Kishi, Ikeda and Sato cabinets – during whose tenure the postwar System was consolidated as well as a majority of the prime ministers following them ...

...

The influential postwar careers of these wartime bureaucrats are only part of the story. No less important is the phenomenal institutional memory of the System's components. Japanese bureaucrats, like their counterparts everywhere, constantly seek to minimise their personal responsibility for anything they do. But they differ from their counterparts in the West or Asia in the extraordinary sense of responsibility they are expected to feel towards their organisation. As we have seen in various contexts, Japanese socio-political circumstances leave members of an organisation little choice but to identify strongly with it, and this is especially true of elite groups. Members of MITI, the prosecutors' office, *Nikkeiren* and all the institutions that guide and control Japan are continually aware of the experiences of their predecessors and the seriousness of their tasks. Institutional memory and institutional motivation go together, because collective experience gives a keen edge to a collective purpose, as well as to passionate partisanship. In Japanese government agencies they are strong, vivid and sharply etched into the minds of the officials. For comparable instances outside Japan, one could point to the Kremlin specialists who deal with the capitalist world; to, possibly, some intelligence organisations; and to churches and secret societies. These special institutions are like ordinary Japanese administrator institutions in the sense that membership can never be a casual or short-term affair (as it is in many US government agencies). Another similarity is that they operate largely under conditions in which the laws of mainstream society hardly affect them, or even bring their own set of 'laws' to their task.

No ministry of the interior of any Western country could, for example, be compared to the *Naimusho* in its dictatorial powers over the ordinary public. The occupation officials who disbanded it in December 1947 had no inkling of the breadth and depth of its institutional memory and of the force it would remain after its demise. Besides providing the abovementioned Diet members and vice-ministers, as well as many of the prefectural vice-governors who were key figures at the regional level in postwar Japan, this Hydra-like institution lives on through its social bureau, which became the postwar Ministry of Labour and Ministry of Health and Welfare; its civil engineering bureau, which was turned into the Ministry of Construction and the National Land Agency; its police bureau, which became the National Police Agency; and its local bureau, which after an interim period as a special agency renewed itself as the Ministry of Home Affairs (*Jichisho*). The last-mentioned institution is generally considered to be the chief heir of its pre-1947 antecedent,[58] but officials from all the offshoots share, in varying degrees, the '*Naimusho* spirit'.

In the 1980s several of the *Naimusho's* descendants are thought to be increasing their relative power. This is certainly true of the Ministry of Home Affairs, whose former bureaucrats already occupy about one-third of the prefectural governorships, as well as prominent positions in municipal governments, so that it has gradually become the most formidable rival to the Ministry of Finance. Most relevant in the context of social control are special committees set up by the Ministry of Home Affairs in local governments to collect information on inhabitants and their *jinmyaku*. The ministry has the advantage of not being attractive to politicians who use cabinet portfolios to expand their 'political fund' resources, so it is not much bothered by the LDP.

There are also traces of the *Naimusho* tradition in less obvious places. For example, Shoriki Matsutaro, the powerful postwar boss of the *Yomiuri Shimbun*, Japan's largest newspaper, was in the *Naimusho* before becoming the newspaper's president in 1924. He exerted himself on behalf of the bureaucrats in the 1936 merger of the news agencies into one government propaganda organ, Domei Tsushinsha. After a stint in prison as a war criminal suspect, he established Nippon Television and became a Diet member and director-general of the Science and Technology Agency.

After the Second World War the military ceased to be a factor, and the police lost their more drastic means of compelling compliance. The education and justice ministries were obliged to give themselves a 'democratic' appearance, which inevitably had an inhibiting effect on the overbearing attitudes of pre-occupation days. But an essential element in the attitude of administrators in the civil service, the notion that they must always control the people, has remained.

Japan's social control bureaucrats have always believed that their mission goes far beyond the enforcement of regulations that is the normal task of civil servants in most Western nations. With or without support from their military allies, they have always been interested in social engineering, and have viewed such active and inventive interference in civil society as necessary to prevent instability. The Japanese ruling elite had before the war and still has today an overpowering 'daddy knows best' attitude, while, as we have seen throughout this book, the people have been kept under permanent political tutelage. It is this continuity through the pre-war, wartime and postwar periods, rather than the undoubted modification of elitist demeanour and the gains in personal freedom, that most significantly determines the character of the Japanese political system today.

Ramsayer, J and Rosenbluth, F, *Japan's Political Marketplace*, 1993, pp 99–100, 103–05, 110–12, Harvard University Press

Political Structure and Bureaucratic Incentives

Several years ago, one of us attended regularly a research group sponsored by MITI. During the meetings, the organizers customarily supplied tea. Most of the organizers were young fast-track bureaucrats who had joined MITI from the preeminent University of Tokyo (*Todai*). When the scheduled outside speaker brought his personal secretary to one of these meetings, she could not have been happier. Here, with a dash of sarcasm, she flavored the awe that Japanese routinely save for their bureaucrats: 'Wow. I've never been poured tea by a *Todai* grad at MITI before.'

It is an awe American scholars have shared, though it is not necessarily justly earned. Many observers routinely exaggerate the power and autonomy of Japanese bureaucrats. When most modern scholars describe the world of these men and women, they stress the control and independence they wield. In fact, however, that control and independence may be mere appearance. Basic principal-agent theory suggests that they are more likely just implementing LDP preferences.

Accordingly, we turn to the possibility that LDP leaders rationally delegate power to bureaucrats – and for good reasons. We then investigate the institutional constraints that the leaders have developed to monitor and police their bureaucratic agents.

How well does this monitoring system work? Monitoring is not free in the United States. Neither is it free in Japan – and given positive monitoring costs, one would expect positive agency slack. Nonetheless, modern theories of institutional change do suggest that political organizations should evolve in ways that enable them to exploit the tactical opportunities created by the institutional shape of government (North, 1990, Chapter 1). More simply, through political evolution, political actors should come to structure their organizations and manipulate the institutional framework in ways that maximize their political returns. Unless agency slack increases those returns, therefore, they should come to develop ways to minimize it. LDP legislators have been doing just that.

Bureaucrats and Professors

In locating the source of Japanese policy, most observers point to bureaucrats rather than to legislators. Legislators do not much matter, they suggest, while bureaucrats largely do as they please. A few writers insist that Japanese legislators do have some power, and many speculate that legislators have more power now than they had twenty years ago. But most students of Japan locate policymaking in the bureaucracy. According to this orthodoxy, policy is less a function of a distinctly political logic than it is a projection of a peculiarly bureaucratic vision. As Bernard Silberman (1982, p 231) elegantly put it, bureaucrats ran the country before the Second World War, and bureaucrats still do: in the prewar years, 'the bureaucracy continued to enjoy the highest status and most powerful place in the formation of public policy, a place it continues to enjoy today under a quite different structure of authority.' Apparently, that the institutional structure of politics changed radically after the War matters not at all.

More than any other American scholar, TJ Pempel (1974, 1978) pioneered this analysis.' In this early work, Pempel first asked who drafted the bills that the Diet passed. He found that bills drafted by ministries passed overwhelmingly, while bills drafted by legislators almost never did. If bureaucrats are writing the statutes (a point confirmed by Table 7.3), Pempel reasoned, then politicians must not be making policy. Second, Pempel examined the use of ministerial regulations. He found that bureaucrats increasingly relied on regulatory measures to implement policy, and concluded: 'The emerging picture is of an increasing proportion of the serious political policymaking in Japan taking place outside the public arena of the Diet and under the increasing control of a democratically unresponsible bureaucracy' (1974, p 656) ...

...

Although orthodox Japanologists note how bureaucrats take initiative and exercise discretion, they miss the role initiative and discretion play within principal-agent relationships. Legislators need not shift the locus of power by letting bureaucrats take initiative or exercise discretion. For reasons we have seen, LDP leaders may rationally instruct bureaucrats to draft designated bills. They may even find it advantageous to instruct the bureaucrats (explicitly or implicitly) to draft any bills they think the LDP would find politically advantageous. The leaders do so because they can relatively cheaply police their bureaucratic agents. If the LDP leaders do so delegate, the power will appear to lie with the bureaucracy, for the legislators will appear to 'rubber-stamp' the bureaucrats' bills. But the appearances will be deceptive. Legislators will be rubber-stamping them only because the bureaucrats wrote bills the leaders liked.

The Data to Date

Students of Japan have yet to test this hypothesis of relatively faithful bureaucratic agents. Take Pempel's pioneering early work described above. If Japanese bureaucrats will draft the statutes that LDP leaders want, the leaders may rationally delegate those drafting jobs to them. The Diet will then pass the statutes that the bureaucrats draft, but only because the bureaucrats drafted the statutes the LDP leaders wanted anyway. Similarly, suppose that regulations are cheaper than statutes in transactions and organizational costs. If bureaucrats can implement the desired policies through regulation, then LDP leaders may rationally relegate policymaking to the regulatory (rather than statutory) process. The Diet will let stand any regulations that the bureaucrats draft, but only because the bureaucrats draft the regulations the LDP leaders want in the first place. By themselves, neither the percentage of cabinet bills passed nor the ratio of regulations to statutes discloses the relative power of legislators and bureaucrats.

That Japanese bureaucrats draft and regulate in the shadow of the Diet also explains what Johnson and others saw at the ministries. At MITI, Johnson rightly found smart and hardworking bureaucrats discussing policy, drafting statutes and regulations, and doing all this with scarcely a wink from the Diet. But if the MITI bureaucrats were implementing LDP policy preferences, LDP leaders had no reason to interfere. Such bureaucrats would appear autonomous, but in effect they were doing what LDP leaders wanted them to do.

Much the same conclusion follows from Campbell's careful work on the budget. MOF, he nicely notes, 'can maintain its power (or its reputation for power) only by refraining from using it; if Finance officials were to attempt, say, a major transfer of funds from one ministry or policy area to another ... opposition sufficient to veto the move [would] quickly arise'. But power one cannot exercise is not power, and all this is not a word game. By Campbell's own description, MOF bureaucrats do not independently make policy. Rather, they operate in the shadow of the LDP. They work on their own, but according to a distinctly political logic ...

...

Legislators can also determine bureaucratic careers. In the United States they appoint, promote, and fire senior bureaucrats. Knowing this, senior bureaucrats appoint, promote, and (where civil service rules do not intervene) fire subordinate bureaucrats in ways that advance legislative preferences since, by doing so, they also advance their own careers. By monitoring and disciplining bureaucrats at the apex, legislators monitor much of the entire bureaucracy.

LDP leaders have the same power over bureaucratic careers. They head the bureaucracy as ministers, ministers control promotions, and the senior bureaucrats heed this. To be sure, it is far from clear how often LDP leaders actually punish renegade bureaucrats. Some scholars argue that 'political leaders get involved only rarely in making personnel decisions within the bureaucracy.' Others disagree. Yung Chul Park (1986, pp 61–77) explains in elaborate detail the way politicians, particularly those affiliated with a ministry's PARC, dominate personnel matters. Pempel (1974, p 653) argues that bureaucrats who push policies contrary to LDP preferences seldom advance beyond bureau chief. BC Koh cites a recent study finding 'that bureaucrats in ... top-level positions could lose their jobs should they antagonize key politicians in the ruling political party.' Kent Calder (1982, p 10) notes that Kakuei Tanaka self-consciously manipulated 'intraministerial personnel selection policies in a systematic way'. Muramatsu and Krauss (1984, p 143) write that the LDP leaders may even contact private-sector employers to insure that deviant bureaucrats do not find good jobs when they leave the ministry. And one eight-term LDP politician categorically assured us: 'People who are not popular with the LDP don't get promoted.'

Whatever the case, the quarrel over how often LDP leaders punish bureaucrats bears less on bureaucratic control than one might think: in equilibrium, one would not observe many penalties anyway. LDP leaders can – potentially – punish bureaucrats. Indeed, one agriculture minister began his tenure with a speech to his subordinate bureaucrats (Park, 1986, p 66): 'It is said that art is long and life is short. You must think that "agriculture lasts long and the minister's life is short." You fellows don't last long either. My term is at most one year, but I can fire you through evaluations of your work performance. The truth is that "agriculture is long and the bureaucrat's life is short".' Bureaucrats know they serve at the pleasure of party leaders and will seldom ignore them. Some bureaucrats even help legislators raise political contributions from corporate constituents, while others threaten regional officials with reduced pork unless they raise votes for the LDP (Sone and Kanazashi, 1989, p 136; Takeuchi, 1988, pp 56–68).

Likewise, the bright seniors at the elite national universities who constitute the pool of potential bureaucrats also know that LDP leaders can make or break bureaucratic careers. Students hostile to LDP policies will therefore generally shun bureaucratic careers. Notwithstanding the Marxist domination of Japanese social science faculties, the young people who do join the ministries disproportionately share LDP policy preferences. According to one survey (Koh, 1989, p 169), 73 percent of the students entering the University of Tokyo law faculty in 1977 identified themselves as 'progressive' or 'somewhat progressive', as did 40 percent of the freshmen six years later. The poll did not test whether liberal students joined ministries and became conservative, or conservative students chose ministerial jobs; neither did it compare Tokyo graduates in the ministries with other Tokyo graduates of the same age. But it did find that only 16 percent of the graduates of the Tokyo law faculty who worked as bureaucrats labeled themselves as at least 'somewhat progressive'.

With conservatives disproportionately staffing the bureaucracies, bureaucrats have a self-interest in seeing the LDP maintain its control over the Diet. For if the bureaucrats who staff the ministries largely share LDP policy preferences themselves, they would not enjoy working for a Socialist cabinet. In short, Japanese bureaucrats, like the LDP leaders for whom they work, have a *personal* interest in their party's electoral success.

Usui, C and Colignon, R, 'Government Elites and *Amakudari* in Japan 1963–1992' (1995) 35 *Asian Survey* 684–89, 696–97

Amakudari: *The Institution*

There is increasing recognition that much of the governance in Japan is not done by politicians but by bureaucrats. The sources of bureaucracy's power are its legislative and administrative roles, its experience, and mechanisms of 'guidance' of the private sector. These sources of power may be summarized in the following way.

First, bureaucrats write most legislation, give it to politicians to pass, then (the same bureaucrats) interpret and apply that same legislation. In Japan, politicians and Diet members do not have their own policy-making staff but rely on the civil servants. As the ministries that write legislation are also the ministries that enforce it, these laws are often written in a vague manner in order to permit wide flexibility in interpreting and applying them. In contrast, US, politicians draw heavily on large staffs and groups of experts who are independent of the government bureaucracy, to initiate legislation. Once passed, a law is turned over to the bureaucrats to carry out.

Second, vice-ministers have life-long career experience as bureaucratic officials with the most seniority in a particular ministry. Their training experience and extensive knowledge of the ministry, as well as the loyalty of thousands of bureaucratic officials working under them endow them with extraordinary influence. In contrast to these 'career bureaucrats,' the cabinet ministers, formally superior to the vice-ministers, are temporary political appointees with far less administrative experience.

Third, 'administrative guidance' of the private sector rests on Japanese law, which gives ministries the authority to issue directives, regulations, requests, warnings, suggestions, and encouragement to private organizations. These direct mechanisms encourage private corporations to operate in a manner consistent with ministry planning. Although government regulation of some markets recently has opened up somewhat (eg citrus, supercomputers, beef), the number of regulations actually has risen.

Fourth, 'economic guidance' is the form of control ministries have over commercial loans. In contrast to the US, corporations in Japan are more likely to expand through bank loans than new stock issues. Ministries target certain industries for development and carry out their plans by directly influencing which corporations secure capital for growth. In addition, they indirectly influence the access to capital of target industries through 'administrative guidance' to private banks and their control over the Japan Development Bank and the Bank of Japan, both government agencies.

Several studies contend that *amakudari* is fed by pressures arising out of the logic of the seniority system within ministries. Johnson and Okimoto, for example, discuss the process of *amakudari* within the Ministry of International Trade and Industry (MITI), and Horne and Kerbo and McKinstry in the Ministry of Finance. It works as follows: (1) entering bureaucrats, upon passing the civil service examination (type 1) and being selected for a ministry, go through extensive training and advance together as a cohort; (2) by the time these bureaucrats reach their 40s, their career mobility options begin to narrow, as there are few section chief positions, fewer bureau chief positions, and only one vice-ministership for each ministry; (3) those who are promoted to bureau chief are still in the running for vice-minister, and those who are not promoted are compelled to resign and seek a lucrative job in a private industry or public corporation; (4) ultimately, everyone must 'descend' because of the unrelenting pressure from cohorts advancing from below. The usual retirement age for a vice-minister is slightly over fifty.

Not everyone competes for the vice-ministership, and many bureaucrats retire before they reach the level of bureau chief. The process of separating those who will resign early and those who will stay in the ministry is called *kata-tataki* (the tap on the shoulder) or *mabiki* (thinning out). Nevertheless, the final weeding out comes at the vice-ministerial level. One man from one cohort is chosen by the outgoing vice-minister as his own replacement, and all members of the new vice-minister's cohort must resign to ensure that he has absolute seniority in the ministry. He and the chief of the ministry's secretariat are responsible for finding the retiring officials (who are fellow classmates) good positions in the private sector.

At this point, retirement may take one of several forms. Retiring government officials obtain new careers along one of three general paths:

1. They move into profit-making enterprises. The movement from ministry or agency to a private business is a strict definition of 'descent from heaven' (*amakudari*) and is subject to legal restrictions.
2. Bureaucrats move into public corporations or 'special legal entities.' These public corporations are established by law and financed in part from public funds. Re-employment by such an organization is called 'sideslip' (*yokosuberi*) and is not subject to legal restrictions.
3. Some bureaucrats move into the political world, chiefly by becoming a candidate for election to the Diet, most commonly as a member of the House of Councillors (upper house). This post-retirement career is called 'position exploitation' (*chii riyo*), and is usually open only to bureaucrats who served in choice national or regional posts that are suitable for building general political support.

The literature on the political economy of Japan is vague on the exact definition of *amakudari*. In general, it refers to a career movement of a bureaucrat from ministry or agency to private business. However, *amakudari* also refers to employment in both private and public organizations. For example, Okimoto defines it as: 'leaving the bureaucracy [to] 'descend from heaven' into high-level posts in public corporations, industrial associations, and private industry. Still others define *amakudari* as re-employment of bureaucrats in private and public organizations, as well as political positions. Aoki defines it as: 'bureaucrats who quit the bureaucracy after attaining positions higher than that of section director in the administrative hierarchy 'descend from the heaven' (*amakudari*) of the elite bureaucracy ... become available as human resources for national and local politics, business management in private and public corporations, and other consulting activities.

The retirement pattern of top bureaucrats is made interesting and complex by the visibility and distribution of these alternative paths out of government service. Some authors note the number and unusual visibility of ex-bureaucrats elected to the Diet, others see the explosive growth of public nonprofit companies since the mid-1980s as the emerging and prevailing destination of retired ministry officials. Both avenues of retirement merit extensive examination to illuminate the relationships binding the Japanese state and society. In this article, however, we use Johnson's first definition of *amakudari*, that is, a career movement of retiring bureaucrats to the private sector, leaving the questions of career movements to public and political sectors for later studies.

Perspectives on Amakudari

Recent literature on the political economy of Japan suggests three perspectives on the nature of *amakudari*: (1) Japanese insulation and regulation; (2) institutional imperative; and (3) government control.

Japanese insulation and regulation. This perspective contends that *amakudari* developed out of Japan's need for insulation and regulation during its rapid industrialization. Although it implies a strong element of free market, the argument in this perspective takes several forms all suggesting that *amakudari* is in decline. One variation contends that after the rapid economic growth of the 1950s and 1960s, strict insulation was no longer needed and retired bureaucrats thus lost much of their usefulness to business. A second variation contends that *amakudari* is a form of corruption that operates to enrich certain elite groups by excluding others from Japanese markets. A final variation is that *amakudari* operates between government and business as a hidden barrier to entry into lucrative Japanese markets and thus is 'a hindrance to the opening up of Japan'.

This perspective suggests that recent trade disputes and continuing foreign pressures to bring down trade barriers and deregulate domestic markets will reduce the linkage between government bureaucracy and domestic markets. It predicts the decline of *amakudari* as Japan is increasingly pressured by international trade partners to reduce its trade surplus, ease inspection and certification rules for foreign goods, and shin from a producer-oriented to a more consumer-oriented society. One analyst shows the decline in the number of *amakudari* positions since the mid-1980s as evidence for this perspective. However, this short period does not represent the overall pattern, nor does the study by do Rosario offer a substantive interpretation of how 'external pressures' should have affected the number of *amakudari* after the mid-1980s and not other periods.

> *Proposition* 1: *Amakudari* had been in a decline since the mid-1980s due to outside pressures for open markets and deregulation.

Institutional imperative. This perspective contends that as ministries achieved success over time, *amakudari* became institutionalized as an integral mechanism for maintaining a 'ministerial fortress' and replenishing their bureaucratic ranks with talent. The assurance of postretirement careers for top bureaucrats is critical in recruiting and motivating the most talented and the brightest, who otherwise would seek more lucrative careers in the private industry. Upon retirement, a bureaucrat's knowledge and connections are valued by business for absorbing the uncertainties of markets and government contract allocations.

In Japan, civil servants are powerful and accorded high respect, but they receive modest incomes. Respect follows from their education at the best universities and their screening through demanding training and testing. They become career bureaucrats, in part, because of career certainty, and the assurance of lucrative postretirement jobs makes the civil service even more attractive. In short the institutional perspective suggests that the assurance of 'descent' to high-profile positions in private industry becomes increasingly necessary to attract the requisite talent. This perspective implies that uncertainty is positively related to *amakudari* placements, and that market, technology, and political uncertainties affect the process. In view of international trade pressures, emerging global markets, and political scandals such as those that led to the fall of the Liberal Democratic Party in 1992, one would expect the bureaucratic elite to become more important and the talent requirements of business all the more pressing. This perspective suggests a general increase in *amakudari* placement over time.

> *Proposition* 2: There is a general increase in *amakudari* over time as global uncertainty increases and ministries attempt to maintain their continued success by attracting the brightest and most talented.

Government control. To many authors, *amakudari* is an important mechanism of government control over private industry. The private sector participates because of the extensive licensing and approval authority (*kyoninkaken*) held by the ministries, although some firms and industries are more receptive to *amakudari* placements than others. According to this perspective, there is greater receptivity of *amakudari* placements in industries and firms that are subject to 'administrative guidance' by the government. The ministries do not give direct orders to businesses but those firms that listen and respond to the signals coming from a ministry are favored with easy access to capital, tax breaks, and approval of plans to import foreign technology or establish joint ventures. Thus, the government-control perspective suggests that the absolute number of *amakudari* is a measure of the extent of government control over the economy.

This perspective is rooted in a recognition of the unique political economy of Japan – that is, the institutional configuration of Japan as a state-directed economy that is nonsocialist. War and industrial development are viewed as having created an 'organic interdependence,' but an interdependence controlled by the state'. In this sense, the number of *relationships* between each ministry and the private sector is the most appropriate measure of ministry power, and a measure of the degree of government control of the economy is the number of *amakudari* placements. Variations of this perspective speculate on the waxing or waning of this bureaucratic control, but in the aggregate, this perspective simply identifies annual *amakudari* as a measure of that control.

> *Proposition 3*: *Amakudari* placements are a measure of the degree of bureaucratic control of the private sector.

Data and Results

Our data derive from the annual reports of *amakudari* published by the National Personnel Agency for the period 1963-92 for all ministries and agencies. The initial publication year on a systematic basis was 1963 after the Diet had amended Article 103 of the Government Employee Act (*Kokka Komuin Ho* 103) and mandated the public disclosure of *amakudari* reports in 1962. Each annual publication contains information on ministry positions of bureaucrats in the last five years of service and the description of new positions in the private sector for all the ministries and agencies (about 40) that had *amakudari*. Japanese law prohibits bureaucrats from accepting positions in private enterprises regulated by their ministry for two years after leaving the civil service. The National Personnel Agency has the power to approve or disapprove *amakudari* of retiring bureaucrats at the level of section chief and above.

Overall Trend

The total number of *amakudari* ranged from a low of 123 in 1967 to a high of 320 in 1985, with a mean average of 205 over the 30-year period, 1963–92. ...

...

Our examination of *amakudari* placements over a 30-year period makes several important points. First, a complex causal dynamic underlies the pattern of *amakudari* placements; second, there appears to be evidence for the institutionalization of MoF's penetration of the economy, and third, the MoF's dominated the other ministries in this respect for almost the entire period.

The first perspective – Japanese insulation and regulation – is partially supported in our analysis. It suggests that *amakudari* will decline due to outside pressures for open trade and deregulation. The data show[s] that the number of *amakudari* rose until the mid-1980s, indicating the increasing interpenetration of the government and corporate worlds. However, starting in 1985, the trend came to a halt and reversed its direction, suggesting that the political economy may have shifted in the mid-1980s as Japan initiated deregulation of some industries. However, scholars advocating this insulation and regulation perspective need to show more clearly the linkage between deregulation and *amakudari* decline.

The second outcome of our analysis lends support to the institutional imperative perspective, suggesting a strengthening of the institution of *amakudari*. An overall increase in *amakudari* placements from 1963–92 suggests *amakudari* is an institutionalized form of government-business cooperation that will, in turn, contribute to increasing placements. More importantly, the analysis shows the steady institutionalization of the MoF. This evidence is consistent with the general impression that MoF recruits the best and most talented and that the financial sector is less pressured for deregulation. Further, a growing number of *amakudari* placements implies that finance is a strategic sector of the economy and a key link between ministry and central financial and industrial sectors. We might anticipate MoF's continued importance in controlling the damage of the bubble economy that burst in 1989. The government control perspective suggests that the shifts in *amakudari* indicate the changing influence of different government ministries over the economy. In particular, the relative change in *amakudari* placements suggests the decline of MITI's influence and the rise by MoF. Our data indicate that MITI exceeded MoF *amakudari* placements only once – in the early 1960s. MoF has shown continuous rise in *amakudari* placements over the period. Thus, to the extent that amakudari placements are a measure of a ministry's power, this analysis raises doubts about MITI's celebrated ministry dominance.

We conceptualized ministry power as a relational concept measured by the actual number of bureaucrats placed in private corporations. This measure reflects the actual number of *relationships* between a particular ministry and the private sector. The more relationships a ministry actually operates, the more powerful that ministry. A ratio measure or measure controlling for other variables (eg the ratio of *amakudari* to the size of a ministry) reflects an attribute of a ministry, possibly reflecting efficient placement of bureaucrats. However, large ministries that are inefficient at placing their bureaucrats may still be more powerful in our sense because they operate a greater number of relationships with the private sector. The relative decline of MITI is supported by the data. MITI was no longer the top ministry in *amakudari* placements by the mid-1960s, though it retained the second or the third position consistently, along with the Ministries of Construction and Transport. In contrast to MITI, MoF outpaced other ministries in the placement of retiring bureaucrats in the private industry. Since 1981, MoF had 50 or more *amakudari* per year, which is almost twice the number of the second-highest ministry, the Ministry of Construction.

Amakudari appears to be a historically sensitive process linked to complex causal operations. It does not appear necessarily to operate in the same manner across different ministries. This feature is demonstrated by the exceptional pattern of the MoF, noted earlier. In addition, the number of *amakudari* placements does not operate in a simple linear manner over time. The indication of three distinct periods suggests different, nontransitive features are in effect. Thus, the selection of any one segment of time or one ministry may distort the interpretation of the nature and future of *amakudari* – that it is one type of relationship in the multiplex network society of Japan that has important spatial and temporal distinctions that should be incorporated into future analyses.

CHAPTER 5

THE LEGAL PROFESSION

The Japanese legal profession is a relatively recent phenomenon. In the same way that Japanese law 'did not develop along with, and as a part of, the whole society and culture' and was 'not the product of an organic evolution', the modern legal profession was imported in the 19th century.[1] Before this, based on the Chinese model, Japan had developed a centralised government under the Emperor and adopted legal codes, incorporating Confucian ideas. Although the Emperor's power was weakened by the rise of the military class, Japan remained a feudal society strongly influenced by traditional Chinese thinking until the middle of the 19th century.[2] Against this background governmental authorities in Tokugawa Japan (1603–1867) were of the view that they should handle legal matters. Since there was no theory of separation of judicial and executive authority it followed that administrative officials carried out judicial functions. Furthermore, in the absence of a developed theory of individual rights, where conciliation was the preferred method of resolving disputes, the idea of legal representation was anathema.[3] In cases where it was inappropriate for a litigant to attend by reason of age or infirmity, an exception to the prohibition on legal representation could be made, but this was more likely to be a relative or the equivalent of a *McKenzie friend* than a true legal representative.[4] Since, in the normal course of events, the feudal rulers did not allow representation in court, the nearest thing to official contact or intervention by the court was that a commoner would be accompanied to court by an

---

1 von Mehren, AT, 'Some Reflections on Japanese Law' (1958) 71 *Harvard Law Review* 1491 and 1493.

2 Hall, J and Jansen, M (eds), *Studies in the Institutional History of Early Modern Japan*, 1968, Princeton University Press; Ishii, R, *A History of Political Institutions in Japan*, 1980, in particular Chapters 2–4, University of Tokyo Press; Ch'en, P, *The Formation of the Early Meiji Legal Order*, 1981, Oxford University Press. For a simple overview see Wren, HG, 'The Legal System of Pre-Western Japan' (1968) 20 *Hastings Law Journal* 217; Luney, PR, 'Traditions and Foreign Influences: Systems of Law in China and Japan' (1989) 52 *Law and Contemporary Problems* 129. On the general historical background see Chapter 2.

3 See Chapter 1 on the importance of the group in Japanese society. On conciliation in Japan see Henderson, 1965, *infra*, n 7. The absence of a rights based society is underlined by the fact that the word for right (*kenri*) had to be 'invented' in the 19th century. In fact the words *kenri* and *gimu* (obligation) are said to have been borrowed from Chinese words used in the translation of an English book. See Chapter 7, n 5 and Noda, *infra*, n 14, p 44.

4 A 'McKenzie friend' is someone who accompanies a party to proceedings before a tribunal or court and helps in the conduct of the case by means of suggestions or advice. The term arose from the decision in *McKenzie v McKenzie* (1971) Ch 33. In the same way that representation was not allowed before the Tokugawa courts, except in these exceptional situations, it has been established that there is no *right* to a McKenzie friend (see *R v Leicester City JJ, ex p Barrow, The Times*, 9 January 1991), indeed the words relied on in *McKenzie* came from the judgment of Lord Tenterden CJ in *Collier v Hicks* (1831) 2 BA 663 at 669 where he stated that 'Any person, whether he be a professional man or not, may attend as a friend of either party, may take notes, may quietly make suggestions, and give advice; but no one can demand to take part in the proceedings as an advocate, contrary to the regulations of the court as settled by the discretion of the justices'.

administrative official from the place of residence.[5] Although these officials may have acted in some minor way as advisers, this was not a full-time occupation but part of a broader administrative role.[6]

Some legal historians have suggested that in pre-modern Japan the *kujishi* performed the role of a lawyer.[7] These were innkeepers who due to their proximity to the Administrative and Tax offices gained some knowledge of relevant procedures and over a period of time started to advise potential litigants. The *kujishi* did not, indeed could not, act as representatives, but performed advisory and administrative functions. They drew up documentation, dealt with the administration of court dates and although the government tried to suppress their activities because they were seen to be encouraging litigation, they nevertheless had a recognised function, not least since the inn was often used as a place of detention pending trial.[8] In so far as the *kujishi* acted as counsellors and advisers there is a similarity with some aspects of the role of a modern lawyer. This is particularly so in the context of the debate as to whether the Japanese are litigious or not and in particular the role of conciliation in the modern Japanese legal system.[9] Viewed in this light, there is a closer analogy than at first might appear. However, the detail concerning the role and status of the *kujishi* is such that it would be stretching the analogy rather far to suggest that they were the model for the modern legal profession. Indeed it is generally accepted that 'a legal profession as such did not exist in premodern Japan'.[10] Whereas the western lawyer inherits a time honoured profession borne of centuries of organic change and growth '[t]he Japanese lawyer lacks a tradition. His role is a new one, one not part of traditional society. When the role was introduced in the early modern period there was lacking an indigenous model of significance or importance'.[11]

In a general historical context, the Tokugawa era is seen as having been a period of 'incubation' during which 'the foundations for the transformation to modernity were being laid'.[12] Certainly by the time the last Shogun (Keiki) surrendered his remaining powers to the Emperor in 1867, Japan had developed

5 Rabinowitz, RW 'The Historical Development of the Japanese Bar' (1956) 70 *Harvard Law Review* 62; Hall, JC, 'Japanese Feudal Laws: Tokugawa Legislation' (1913) 41 *Transactions of the Asiatic Society of Japan* 683; Hiramatsu, Y, 'Tokugawa Law' (1981) 14 *Law in Japan* 1.

6 Wigmore, JH, *Law and Justice in Tokugawa Japan, Introduction*, Parts I–IX, 1967–86, University of Tokyo Press; Henderson, DF, 'Law and Political Modernisation' in Ward, RE (ed), *Political Development in Modern Japan*, 1968, pp 387–411, Princeton University Press; Hall and Jansen (eds), *supra*, n 2.

7 Ch'en, *supra*, n 2, p 73; Henderson, DF, *Conciliation and Japanese Law: Tokugawa and Modern*, 2 vols, 1965, University of Washington Press, see Vol 1 for a detailed discussion, in particular Chapter 6.

8 Rabinowitz, *supra*, n 5, pp 61–64; Henderson, DF, 'Contracts in Tokugawa Villages' (1974) 1 *Journal of Japanese Studies* 51.

9 See n 73 below and discussion in Chapter 1 and Chapter 6. In general see Henderson, 1965, *supra*, n 7, Vol 2.

10 Hattori, T, 'The Legal Profession in Japan: Its Historical development and Present State' in von Mehren (ed), *Law in Japan*, 1963, p 111 at p 112, Harvard University Press.

11 Rabinowitz, *supra*, n 5, p 79.

12 Lehmann, J-P, *The Roots of Modern Japan*, 1982, London: Macmillan.

a legal system based on customary law, suffused with Confucianism.[13] There was an independent, judicially created system of dispute resolution but, as a feudal system, it was there as a means of constraint. It existed to uphold the prevailing social structures and enforce government authority; there was no room for individual rights in a system where the people were merely expected to obey.[14] The Meiji era (1868–1912) was a period of change and adjustment; it is also known as the Meiji ishin – *ishin* meaning 'here are new things'.[15] Although the Emperor's government struggled to strike a balance between maintaining independence whilst needing to adapt to a new situation, the restructuring of the legal system was undertaken without any real reference to the foundations provided by the indigenous structures. Instead of adaptation of those structures, the response to the challenge of the new took the form of adoption; Western ideas and institutions were simply transplanted.[16] This was particularly true of the legal profession.[17]

Before 1867 there was no mention of what might accurately be referred to as a lawyer in the modern sense of that term.[18] However, the first Minister of Justice, Shinpei Eto, was strongly influenced by Western legal systems, in particular the French, and in 1872 drafted the first regulations governing lawyers.[19] The most important feature of these Regulations was that they provided for the establishment of local courts and in particular for legal officers, thus establishing judicial institutions and professionals separate from the administrative organisation and officials of former times. Although a step in the right direction, this did not go as far as establishing the principle of separation of powers, since the Minister of Justice was in overall control of all aspects of courts and legal appointments.[20] Furthermore, local courts continued to be

13 In general see Chapter 2. On the Chinese influence see Ch'en, *supra*, n 2. The general background to the period is discussed in various essays in *The Cambridge History of Japan*, Vol 5, 1989, Cambridge University Press; in particular see Chapter 1, Jansen, M, 'Japan in the Early Nineteenth Century'; Chapter 5 Jansen, M, 'The Meiji Restoration'; Chapter 7 Hirakawa, S, 'Japan's Turn to the West'; Chapter 10 Beasley, WG, 'Meiji Political Institutions'.

14 Henderson, 1965, *supra*, n 7, Vol 2; Noda, Y, *Introduction to Japanese Law*, 1976, pp 31–39, University of Tokyo Press; Ishii, *supra*, n 2, Chapter 4. On the general political background see Ward, RE (ed), *Political Development in Modern Japan*, 1968, Princeton University Press.

15 Noda, *idem*, p 42; Beasley, WG, *The Rise of Modern Japan: Political, Economic and Social Change Since 1850*, 2nd edn, 1995, Chapters 3–6, Weidenfeld and Nicolson.

16 This is something of a generalisation. For a fuller discussion see Chapter 2. See also Hirakawa, *supra*, n 13 on Western influence at this time. On Chinese and indigenous influences see Ch'en, *supra*, n 2.

17 The development of the modern Japanese legal profession is divided into four main periods, the Daigennin period (1872–93), the Lawyers Law 1893 (1893–1933), the Lawyers Law 1933 (1933–49) and the Lawyers Law 1949 (1949 to the present).

18 Rabinowitz, *supra*, n 5, p 62, notes that in 1854 a lawyer was described as 'one who accompanied stupid people to court and wrote documents for them'.

19 *Shiho Shokusei Narabi ni Jimu Shotei* (Justice Staff and Operating Regulations) 1872. See also the Court Organisation Law 1890 (*Saibansho Kosei ho*) Law No 6 1890 which was of particular importance in regulating the judiciary.

20 The power of the Ministry of Justice and in particular its position of influence within the overall Japanese power structure is well illustrated in Yasko, R 'Bribery Cases and the Rise of the Justice Ministry in Late Meiji-Early Taisho Japan' (1979) 12 *Law in Japan* 57. In relation to the appointment of the judiciary see Haley, JO, 'Judicial Independence in Japan Revisited' (1995) 25 *Law in Japan* 3–8.

presided over by administrative officials, though this was put down to the fact that there was an insufficient number of trained legal personnel.[21] However, this need for trained legal professionals was to some extent anticipated by the establishment of an institution called the *Meihoryo*, the literal meaning of which was 'Bureau for Illuminating the Law'.[22]

Set up in 1871 under the auspices of the Ministry of Justice, the Bureau started to train students in drafting, the giving of advice and aspects of law in particular French law. Indeed, the medium of study was French. To this extent the idea of the Tokugawa era as a period of incubation and laying of foundations certainly rings true. The government of the time had maintained diplomatic relations with France and even sent a number of officials from the Ministry of Justice to study law in Paris.[23] The Bureau continued to train officials of the Ministry of Justice, judges and prosecutors until it was abolished in 1875 when it was replaced by the Ministry of Justice Law School (*Shoho-sho Ho Gakko*).[24] In 1876, led by Georges Bousquet and Gustave Boissonade, the School offered four year courses in law and legal training.[25] In 1884 the School transferred to the Ministry of Education and was amalgamated with Tokyo University as *Tokyo Ho Gakko*. In 1885, it was established as the French Law Section of the Tokyo University Department of Law (*Tokyo Daigaku Hoka Bu Futsuho Ka*).[26]

In line with the tradition of the universities of continental Europe, the role of the law faculty was seen to be the provision of 'recruits for government and business bureaucracies'.[27] The creation of an elite body of judicial officials who graduated from Tokyo Imperial University, as opposed to those who studied law at other universities, was to set the pattern of a 'twin track' system that was

21 Hattori, *supra*, n 10, p 114.

22 For an account of the etymology of the word see Mukai, K and Toshitani, N, 'The Progress and Problems of Compiling the Civil Code in the Early Meiji Era' (1967) 1 *Law in Japan* 39, n 27.

23 Hattori, *supra*, n 10, p 114, n 8. See also Chapter 2.

24 Public prosecutors are sometimes referred as public 'procurators'. This term, still used today by some writers, was a Japanese adaptation from the French, *procureurs*.

25 In 1872 Bousquet had been invited to Japan as legal adviser to the government and it was on his advice that the School of Law was established. The government had likewise invited Boissonade in 1873 to advise on the new legal system. Both are credited with founding the modern Japanese legal system and in establishing the foundations of legal education. See Chapter 2 and Noda, *supra*, n 14, p 45.

26 In 1886 the name of the university was changed to the Tokyo Imperial University and the Department of Law changed to the College of Law, thus becoming *Tokyo Teikoku Daigaku Hoka Daigaku*. See Mukai and Toshitani, *supra*, n 22. The Department of Law also had German Law and Common Law sections. Since graduates of the Imperial University went on to fill the senior posts in government, their exposure to these different systems of law has been seen as one of the reasons that there was not an immediate acceptance of the work done by Boissonade. Furthermore, the committee charged with preparing a new draft consisted of two members of the French School and one of the Common Law School; the latter and one of his French School colleagues had studied German Law in Berlin, thus leading to a far greater German influence, particularly in the compilation of the Civil Code, than might have been anticipated on the basis of the French jurists' work (see von Mehren, *supra*, n 1, p 1488). The German jurists Hermann Roesler and Hermann Techow also had a significant influence. See also Chapter 2.

27 Rabinowitz, *supra*, n 5, p 81.

a feature of the pre-war period. The clear separation between 'legal officials', ie judges and prosecutors as opposed to 'lawyers' was mirrored in the destination of university graduates.[28] Whilst the 'elite' became government officials, judges and prosecutors, it was the graduates of other universities that made up the body of practising lawyers.[29] The relative inferiority of lawyers is seen in the provisions of the 1893 Lawyers Law. Admission to the legal profession was to be by exam, except for those who were graduates of the Imperial University (or the former Ministry of Justice Law School and Tokyo University Department of Law), those who held the equivalent of a doctorate and those who were qualified as judges or prosecutors. Even the exam itself was conducted by a committee made up of officials from the Ministry of Justice, judges and prosecutors.[30] However, with so many exceptions to those needing to take the exam before being placed on the Lawyers Roll, the status of lawyers remained inferior. Any attempt to establish an independent and well respected profession was frustrated at every turn. Even the development of Bar Associations, as provided under the 1893 Law, did little to help; their early history was punctuated by ideological differences between French and English law factions, leading in some cases to physical violence.[31]

After the examination, the twin track system was maintained during the apprenticeship period. Judges and prosecutors were selected by the Ministry of Justice from those who obtained high marks in the Law Examinations; they then undertook a training period of 18 months. As salaried public officials they were placed in District Courts and given practical training in various departments, with particular emphasis on drafting indictments and judgments. These probationary legal officials were placed under the guidance of individual judges and prosecutors, much in the manner of pupillage and articles in the modern English legal system, except that it extended to the judicial role. Meanwhile, practising lawyers received little by way of systematic training; instead they would enter the office of a senior lawyer and, after an indeterminate number of years, would set up on their own. Whilst in theory a person who had passed the qualifying exams could set up as an independent practitioner immediately, few chose to do this; it was not until 1936 that a formal probationary system of 18 months was established.[32] The clear structure and organisation of training for judges and prosecutors was taken a step further in 1939 when, under the auspices of the Ministry of Justice, an Institute of Legal Research was established. Its role was supplementary to the judicial or prosecutorial apprenticeship; the candidates were simply drawn together a few months

28 This duality is seen in the language used to describe the various parts of the profession. *Zaicho hoso* (lawyers in office) was for judges and prosecutors, whereas *zaiya hoso* (lawyers out of office) referred to practising lawyers. See Tanaka, H, *The Japanese Legal System*, 1976, p 550, University of Tokyo Press.

29 Haley, 1995, *supra*, n 20 has concluded that: 'Japan's judiciary has almost from its inception been organised as a remarkably autonomous elite bureaucracy', p 3.

30 Rabinowitz, *supra*, n 5, p 70.

31 *Idem*.

32 Abe, H, 'Education of the Legal Profession in Japan' in von Mehren, AT (ed), *Law in Japan*, 1963, p 154, Harvard University Press.

before the final exam in order to iron out any differences in their practical training.[33]

No such institutional training or structures existed for practising lawyers, their status remaining inferior to that of judges and prosecutors. Although apprenticeship for lawyers was provided for in the revised Lawyers Law of 1933 the system was to be administered by the Bar Associations, but failed to become fully operational before the outbreak of the Second World War. Although this could be seen as the first step in establishing the autonomy of the Bar away from the control of the Ministry of Justice, in truth the reason the scheme was in their control in the first place was that there were budgetary problems which prevented the Ministry from obtaining the control it wanted.[34] It was not until the reforms of the American Occupation that there was a unification of the training process. The new constitution of 1946 changed the role of law in society; the administration of justice was now to be in the hands of the courts, headed by the Supreme Court, with judges, prosecutors and lawyers acting as a unified profession.[35] To the extent that legal training was unified by the provision of a single post graduate legal apprenticeship provided by the newly formed Legal Training and Research Institute, unification could be said to have been achieved. The reality is somewhat different.

The task of reforming the legal system after 1945 was entrusted to the Courts and Law Division of the Government Section, Supreme Command Allied Powers.[36] As Oppler observed, 'the legal profession enjoyed little social prestige in Japan, even less than the judges, and was subject to tight supervision by the Ministry of Justice, exercised by the procurators over the bar associations'.[37] Since the position of the judiciary had been transformed under the new constitution, it was recognised that in order to ensure the modern and effective administration of justice the status of lawyers would have to be raised and they would need to be freed from government control and supervision. Having created an independent judiciary, the issue was whether, or to what extent, the Bar Associations should be independent. The Supreme Court wished to retain total control of the profession whilst the Attorney General was willing to accept a limited supervisory role. In the event the Bar Association's desire to achieve

33 *Idem*, p 154.

34 Rabinowitz, *supra*, n 5, p 77.

35 Oppler, *infra*, n 36, Chapter 8. A general overview of the role of the judiciary under the 'new' 1946 Constitution is given by Luney, P, 'The Judiciary: Its Organisation and Status in the Parliamentary System' (1990) 53 *Law and Contemporary Problems* 135. See also Itoh, H, *The Japanese Supreme Court: Constitutional Policies*, 1989, Chapter 1, Markus Wiener; Ramsayer, JM and Rosenbluth, F, *Japan's Political Marketplace*, 1993, Chapter 8, Harvard University Press. On the Supreme Court in particular Itoh, *idem*; Danelski, D, 'The Political Impact of the Japanese Supreme Court' (1974) 49 *Notre Dame Lawyer* 955. For a more detailed consideration of the subject see Chapter 7.

36 The section was headed by Alfred C Oppler, a German jurist who had held various positions in the Prussian judiciary. The various accounts of his work for SCAP give an invaluable insight into the reform process. See Oppler, AC, *Legal Reform in Occupied Japan. A Participant Looks Back*, 1976, Princeton University Press; Oppler, AC, 'The Reform of Japan's Legal and Judicial System Under Allied Occupation' (1949) 24 *Washington Law Review* 290 reprinted in 1977 (Special Issue) *Washington Law Review* 1.

37 Oppler, 1976, *idem*, p 107.

full autonomy was realised.[38] Under the Lawyer's Law 1949,[39] a Bar Association was established within the jurisdiction of each District Court. The Japan Federation of Bar Associations (*Nihon Bengoshi Rengokai*) would be the national, umbrella organisation, of which each district association, as well as individual lawyers, would be members. In addition it would have responsibility for registration and regulation of practising lawyers. Any idea of unification of the profession at this level did not succeed, since judges, prosecutors and academic lawyers were precluded from membership. However, in the spirit of union, it was felt that the training of all three branches of the profession should be brought together under a single, post graduate apprenticeship, to be provided by the newly established Legal Training and Research Institute. The Institute was established under the Courts Organisation Law 1947[40] which, together with the National Law Examination Law[41] and Lawyers Law of 1949 formed the structure upon which the education and regulation of the modern legal profession is established.

Legal education in Japan takes three stages, which are common to all lawyers, whichever branch of the profession they eventually follow. First there is the university degree, followed by the national law examination and finally, a period of apprenticeship at the Legal Training and Research Institute. Following this unified education process, three career paths are open to successful candidates; they may become judges, prosecutors, or practising lawyers. After graduation from the Institute, any notion of a unified profession is misleading.[42] At best it consists of two discreet sections, those who are effectively the old style 'judicial officials' (judges and prosecutors) and those in private practice. Therefore, to talk of a 'legal profession' as if it were a homogenous group would seem to be inaccurate.

The Occupation reformers had set out to ensure independence and equality of status across the profession and the idea of an integrated or unified profession (*hoso ichigen*) was the cornerstone of these reforms.[43] The word *hoso* is often used to denote the legal profession, or *hosokai*, meaning the community of jurists.[44] However, it more correctly refers to a distinct social group comprising judges (*hanji*), prosecutors (*kenji*) and practising lawyers (*bengoshi*). They are members of the same profession in that they have completed the same training, but little more. As one commentator observed, 'even today, almost a

38 Oppler, 1977, *supra*, n 36, p 26.

39 Law No 205, 1949.

40 Law No 59, 1947.

41 Law No 140, 1949.

42 See Kato, M, 'The Role of Law and Lawyers in Japan and the United States' (1987) *Brigham Young University Law Review* 627, Table 2, p 639.

43 Oppler, 1976, *supra*, n 36, p 110 recorded that he 'professed belief in the basic brotherhood of all those who serve the law' and that he had visualised that 'future bar associations would include judges, prosecutor, and legal scholars in their membership'.

44 Whilst the term *hoso* was used to describe the broad class of legal professionals, meaning judges prosecutors and lawyers, it was more usual to refer to the first two groups as *zaicho hoso* (legal professionals in office) and the latter as *zaiya hoso* (legal professional not in office). This linguistic distinction served further to underline the inferior status of practising lawyers.

generation after the new judicial system started, there is still a sharp line dividing the profession. For a typical Japanese lawyer, the feeling that he belongs to one of the three branches of the profession is much stronger than his sense of being a member of the whole legal profession'.[45] However, it remains a matter of debate whether the reformers' vision of *hoso ichigen* has, to any great measure, been achieved or whether in reality the tripartite division of the legal profession has remained entrenched.[46]

The Japanese legal profession is relatively small in size when compared to other countries.[47] In April 1995 there were 15,450 lawyers registered with the Japan Federation of Bar Associations, giving a ratio of one lawyer for every 8,000 people.[48] In addition there were 2,092 Public Prosecutors and 2,864 judges.[49] The National Law Examination is notoriously difficult and with an average pass rate of approximately 2% it has been described as the most difficult examination in the world.[50] Although there is no limit to the number of times it may be attempted (many try five or six times) it remains a rigorous and effective filter ensuring that only the most exceptionally bright candidates go on to the Institute.[51] Following this, whilst graduation from the Institute is in no way guaranteed, the failure rate is negligible.[52] Given the comparatively small number of lawyers, it is interesting to note that their geographical distribution throughout Japan is very uneven. The majority are to be found in the major cities; 7,150 in Tokyo; 2,184 in Osaka; 725 in Nagoya; 587 Yokohama and 502 in Fukuoka. In other words, the number of lawyers practising in Tokyo and Osaka account for 72% of the total, whereas in contrast, some areas of the country have no lawyers at all. In 1993 out of the 201 District Courts in Japan, 50 had no lawyer within their jurisdiction and 24 had only one.[53] Furthermore, in a 1990 study carried out by the Japan Federation of Bar Associations, it was found that the overwhelming majority of law firms in Japan are run by sole practitioners;

---

45 Tanaka, *supra*, n 28, p 553. In some respects this is closer to the position in England and Wales where, without a fused profession, there is a distinct sense of being a solicitor, a barrister, or a member of the judiciary, whereas in the United States and therefore in the minds of the Occupation, the term lawyer was seen as including all branches of the legal profession.

46 See Abe, *supra*, n 32, p 167; Chen, I, 'The National Law Examination of Japan' (1989) 39 *Journal of Legal Education* 1; Kato, *supra*, n 42.

47 See Kato, *supra*, n 42, Table 6, p 648. For an account of the role of lawyers in modern Japanese society see Haley, JO, *Authority Without Power*, 1991, Chapter 5, Oxford University Press.

48 Source, Supreme Court of Japan. For further details see Table 1, p 349.

49 *Idem*.

50 Chen, *supra*, n 46, p 9, Table 2.

51 It is significant that 58% of those who pass come from three universities (Tokyo, Chuo and Waseda) with the remainder usually being drawn from the same 12 universities each year. More than half of all Japanese law faculties have never had a student who has passed the exam. See Chen, *supra*, n 46, p 11. For an analysis of the pass rate for the national law examination 1949–83 see Kato, *supra*, n 42, p 645, Table 4. On the significance of these institutions in the judiciary see Haley, 1990, *supra*, n 20, pp 15–17.

52 See Table 3 below, p 351.

53 Japan Federation of Bar Associations, 1995.

even in Tokyo and Osaka it would be unusual to find a firm with 10 or more lawyers.[54]

The figures used to illustrate the relatively small size of the legal profession are somewhat misleading when viewed in the broader context. Each year there are approximately 40,000 law graduates, of which around 95% do not attempt to enter the legal profession.[55] Most will try and obtain a job in the civil service or in the legal department of a company.[56] Compared to the comparatively small numbers of practising lawyers, it is interesting to note the relatively recent and somewhat rapid growth in company legal departments. In a 1990 poll, 35.5% of the companies which responded had established their legal departments since 1985, whereas between 1975 and 1984 the figure was 13.85%; with continuing growth in international business combined with revision of the Commercial Code in 1993, it is expected that the potential for in-house legal activity will continue to increase with more companies setting up legal departments.[57] The poll further revealed that over 30% of staff in company legal departments had no legal education at all and the remaining 70% were graduates of Law Departments, but not qualified licensed practitioners; in fact out of the sample of 547 companies, there were only a total of seven qualified lawyers employed. However, in addition to this growth sector, there are a range of other legal professionals performing much the same, or similar, jobs as those described as lawyers in other countries.[58] These quasi lawyers, or para legals, are very often people who have completed law degrees and then joined a profession which has its own examinations, or have received 'in house training'.[59]

First amongst these are the judicial scriveners (*shiho-shoshi*) whose main responsibility is the drafting of legal documents to be filed with the courts, Public Prosecutor's Office, or regional offices of the Ministry of Justice.[60] In

54 An inside look at the work of Japanese lawyers is provided by four articles published in (1995) 25 *Law in Japan* 104–34 (translated by Daniel H Foote). Although they are written by reporters and freelance writers, rather than lawyers, they provide interesting insights into the work of 'ordinary' lawyers (as opposed to those in the large firms in Tokyo and Osaka): Nishimura, K, 'Want to Win Disputes? He'll Show You How' pp 104–10; Ishii, Y, 'All this for a Retainer of Just ¥50,000 a Month' pp 111–14; Yonemoto, K, 'The Shimane Bar Association: All Twenty-One Members Strong' pp 115–24' Miya, Y. 'Twenty-Eight and Single: Occupation: Secret' pp 125–34.

55 Supreme Court of Japan, The Legal Training and Research Institute, 1990, Tokyo.

56 In so far as there may be a legal section in a company, in smaller enterprises it is often found in the general affairs section (*somuka*). In large companies there might be a separate legal department (*hokika or homuka*) which is staffed by law trained personnel who have not obtained the formal qualifications to be a registered *bengoshi*. See Henderson, DF, *Foreign Enterprise in Japan*, 1973, p 179, University of North Carolina Press.

57 Report of *Keiei Hoyukai* and *Shoji-homu-kenkyukai* cited in Kosugi, T, 'The Legal Profession in Japan – Focusing on the Practitioner' presented to a symposium on 'Japanese Law in a Comparative Cultural Perspective' at the 1995 Meeting of the Research Committee on the Sociology of Law, International Sociological Association in Tokyo.

58 Much family and inheritance law does not require the use of a lawyer and can be conducted through the registration of documentation.

59 An analysis of the various groups of professionals engaged in legal work is provided by Kato, *supra*, n 42, Table 9, p 654.

60 Judicial scriveners number around 16,000 and need to be distinguished from administrative scriveners (*gyosei shoshi*) who are closer to 35,000 and who draft papers for submission to government offices alone and do not give 'advice' of any sort.

carrying out this task a judicial scrivener will also give advice to members of the public, though formally, the Lawyers Law 1949 states that nobody other than a practising attorney may handle legal business and there is certainly no question of them appearing as representatives in court. Judicial scriveners are also responsible for title registration and this has lead to their being described as *de facto* lawyers. There is a National Association of Judicial Scriveners which, until the recent introduction of a state examination, administered the qualifying examination. Unlike the Bar Association it is much more closely controlled by the Ministry of Justice, particularly concerning rules, regulations and disciplinary proceedings. In terms of cost and convenience it is better to see a judicial scrivener than a lawyer; furthermore, in areas where there is a dearth of lawyers, they effectively operate as such and public perception is that they are an inferior class of lawyer. This, in turn, has led to suggestions that their role as quasi-lawyers be formalised so that they might also represent clients in the lower courts. Although the provisions of the Lawyers Law 1949 remain an obstacle, in an appeal decision in 1979 the court, whilst reinforcing the view that a judicial scrivener had no right to provide general legal advice, nevertheless acknowledged that scriveners could advise clients on some issues and provide guidance on the handling of cases in court, but fell short of allowing appearance in court.[61]

The next significant group of quasi lawyers is the patent and tax attorneys. The patent attorneys (*benrishi*) can give advise to clients, or act on their behalf in matters of patent, trademark and design. There is a national examination which, like the National Law Examination, has a low pass rate, in this case less than 3%.[62] Practising lawyers who have worked for over seven years in the Patent Office are exempt from this exam, but all are governed by the Patent Attorneys Law 1921. Whereas there are approximately 3,000 patent attorneys, tax attorneys (*zeirishi*) number some 48,000 although the national examination is no less demanding and has an overall pass rate of between 3% and 5%.[63] In addition to preparing documents, calculating taxes and giving general advice on tax matters, tax attorneys may act as representatives before tribunals. An alternative route is to qualify to become a certified public accountant (*konin kaikeishi*). The pass rate is around 5%, but there are only approximately 7,000 certified public accountants; they, like practising lawyers, are *ipso facto* qualified tax attorneys. Given the difficulty of the examinations and the pass rate, it is unsurprising to find that most tax attorneys are former civil servants who have worked in government tax offices. The burgeoning numbers in this field were the result of the postwar introduction of an American style tax reporting system, in consequence of which two new laws were introduced, the Certified Public Accountants Law 1948 and the Tax Attorneys Law 1951.

Finally, it is necessary to consider the position of the foreign lawyer in Japan. The number has never been great, but the history surrounding their admission to practice gives an insight into the complex relationship between Japan and the

61 Judgment of the Takamatsu Appellate Court, 11 June 1979.

62 Brown, R, 'A Lawyer by Any Other Name' in *Legal Aspects of Doing Business in Japan*, 1983, p 403.

63 *Idem*, p 403.

outside world, as well as the complexities of operating an open market in legal services. Prior to the Lawyers Law 1933 there was no regulation of practice by foreign lawyers; the Advocate Regulations 1876 (*Daigennin Kisoku*) specifically provided that foreign lawyers could participate in civil actions where a foreign party was involved.[64] However, whilst the regulations provided for Japanese to pass an examination, there was no such requirement for foreign lawyers. The Lawyers Law 1893 was similarly silent on the matter, with the consequence that foreign lawyers continued to represent non Japanese in civil actions and in matters of international transactions. The rationale for this situation was said to be that the presence of foreign lawyers was convenient to Japanese lawyers and 'it was believed that they would introduce the fairness and justice of the Japanese judicial system abroad'.[65]

By the time the Lawyers Law 1933 was introduced, Japan had entered a period of rising nationalism and imperialist expansion; there was a desire to be seen, not as subservient to Western ideas, but as equal in all matters.[66] This was expressed through the principle of reciprocity; Article 6 provided that a person qualified as a lawyer in their own country could practice provided a Japanese lawyer was accorded the same right in that foreign country. The foreign lawyer could still only deal with matters involving foreigners, or international transactions, but was now allowed to maintain offices.[67] However, heightened tensions resulting from the Manchurian Incident and leading up to the outbreak of the Second World War meant that in reality few foreign lawyers worked in Japan; those that did were mainly confined to aiding Japanese lawyers in international matters.[68] When the Lawyers Law 1949 was enacted it was seen as being open and liberal minded in its approach to foreign lawyers practising in Japan.[69] The reciprocity requirement was dropped, as was the need to hold Japanese nationality, and instead it provided that a person who was qualified in a foreign country and had adequate knowledge of Japanese law could apply to the Supreme Court for recognition as a lawyer; furthermore, if they passed a special exam, foreign lawyers could practice in Japanese law.[70] However, this was something of a honeymoon period generated by the Occupation reformers, for in 1955 the barriers went up. The Lawyers Law was amended to prevent foreign lawyers from practising in Japan, unless they were already doing so.[71]

---

64 Since defendants in criminal cases were not allowed representation in court, it was not necessary for the Regulations to refer to criminal matters.

65 Fukuhara, T, 'The Status of Foreign Lawyers in Japan' (1973) 17 *Japanese Annual of International Law* 22.

66 On the background to this period of expansionism see Lehmann, *supra*, n 12, Chapter 9; Beasley, WG, *supra*, n 15, Chapter 11.

67 In the late 1920s there were reported to be four foreign lawyers practising in Kobe and Yokohama. See Fukuhara, *supra*, n 65, p 25.

68 *Idem*, p 26. On the Manchurian Incident and the period 1931–41, see Storry, RA, *History of Modern Japan*, 1982, Chapter 8, Penguin; Beasley, *supra*, n 15, pp 169–75.

69 Article 7 set out the provisions related to foreign lawyers who wished to practise.

70 Only one foreigner achieved this, an American called Thomas Blakemore. He had studied law in Japan before the Second World War and became a member of the Courts and Law Division of SCAP during the Occupation. See Chapter 2, n 93.

71 Law Amending Part of the Lawyers Law (*Bengoshi Ho No Ichibu O Kaisei Sunu Horitsu*) No 155 of 1955.

With the recognition provision gone, the only route into the closed market for legal services was as a trainee for a Japanese law firm and under strict regulations administered by the Japan Federation of Bar Associations. It was not until the 1970s that access to the legal services market became a major issue of dispute, at first between Japan and the United States, but followed by various members of the European Community. There ensued a 15 year battle for improved rights of access culminating in what became known as the Foreign Lawyers Law (*Gaikoku Bengoshi Ho*) which came into effect on 1 April 1987.[72]

Even when the various groups of quasi lawyers are taken into account, there is still a remarkably low number of lawyers in Japan. This has traditionally been explained by the litigation averse theory of Japanese society.[73] However, it is doubtful whether the status quo will be sufficient to meet the needs of Japanese society into the 21st century. Discussions have taken place between the Ministry of Justice and the Japan Federation of Bar Associations about the possibility of increasing the number of places at the Legal Research and Training Institute, but proposals have yet to be adopted. In a situation where there are vested interests in maintaining a small elitist monopoly over certain legal activities, there may be some resistance to such a move; however, the indications are that the legal profession, whilst not undergoing a dramatic change, may nevertheless be in the process of a small, but significant transformation.[74]

72 The Law Providing Special Measures for the Handling of Legal Business by Foreign Lawyers 1986 (*Gaikoku Bengoshi niyoru Horitsujimu no Toriatsukai ni kanseru Tokubetsusochi Ho*) No 66. See Ramsayer, JM, 'Lawyers, Foreign Lawyers, and Lawyers Substitutes: The Market for Regulation in Japan' (1986) 27 *Special Issue Harvard International Law Journal* 499. For a full account of all aspects of the debate surrounding the new law, see the papers and articles presented to the Japan-America Society/ABA Seminar 'Symposium on American Lawyers in Japan' published together with supporting information in (1988) 21 *Law in Japan* 19–193.

73 The debate as to whether the Japanese are litigious or not and, if so, to what extent is a complex one. See Chapter 1. It is centred on the work of Kawashima and Haley. For the main viewpoints and comparisons see Kawashima,T, 'Dispute Resolution in Contemporary Japan' in von Mehren, AT (ed), *Law in Japan*, 1963, Harvard University Press; Haley, JO, 'The Myth of the Reluctant Litigant' (1978) *Journal of Japanese Studies* 359; Kim, C and Lawson, C, 'The Law of the Subtle Mind: the Traditional Japanese Conception of Law' (1979) 28 *International and Comparative Law Quarterly* 491; Haley, JO, 'Sheathing the Sword of Justice in Japan: An Essay on Law Without Sanctions' (1982) *Journal of Japanese Studies* 265; Miyazawa, S, 'Taking Kawashima Seriously: A Review of Research on Japanese Legal Consciousness and Dispute Resolution' (1987) 21 *Law and Society Review* 219; Ramseyer, JM, 'Reluctant Litigant Revisited: Rationality and Disputes in Japan' (1988) *Journal of Japanese Studies* 111; Maruta, T, 'Japanese Claims Consciousness: Are the Japanese Still Reluctant Litigants?' in Bankenburg, E, Commaille, J and Galanter, M (eds), *Disputes and Litigation* (Oñati Proceedings, No 12, 1991). On the role of lawyers in a non litigious society see Haley, 1991, *supra*, n 47, Chapter 5.

74 Kosugi, T, 'The Legal Profession in Japan – Focusing on the Practitioner' presented to a symposium on 'Japanese Law from a Comparative Perspective' at the 1995 Meeting of the Research Committee on Sociology of Law, International Sociological Association in Tokyo.

I HISTORY

Hattori, T, 'The Legal Profession in Japan: Its Historical Development and Present State' in von Mehren, AT (ed), *Law in Japan: The Legal Order in a Changing Society*, 1963, pp 111–14, 115–19, 119–26, Harvard University Press

Until the collapse of the national policy of isolation toward the end of the Tokugawa regime, when Western civilization began to be introduced into Japan, no thought had been given in Japanese political philosophy to the separation of judicial institutions from general executive authority. The traditional principle, based upon Chinese thinking, was that governmental authorities should also handle judicial matters; as a logical consequence, judicial officers, as distinguished from administrative officials, did not exist. Additionally, in part because a negative attitude in the society toward civil litigation was coupled with an extremely inquisitorial criminal procedure, the feudal regime did not permit representation, at least on a professional basis, in either civil or criminal proceedings. Thus, a legal profession as such did not exist in premodern Japan.

THE PROFESSION IN THE FORMATIVE ERA

Shortly after it came to power in 1867, the new national government proclaimed its intention of adhering to the principle of the separation of powers. However, the system of government actually established in 1869 followed the *Ritsuryo* institutions, which had existed in Japan many centuries before and were based upon T'ang Chinese models. These were completely inconsistent with the doctrine of Montesquieu which the government had enunciated only two years earlier. One explanation for this apparently surprising reversal is that power came into the hands of conservative leaders who were influenced by traditional Sino-Japanese political ideals; they also desired a general revival of classical traditions, one element of which was the 'return' of administrative power to the imperial throne.

However, shortly after he was appointed Minister of Justice, Shimpei Eto, who had a comparatively good understanding of Western judicial systems as well as an unusual enthusiasm for legal reform, and who probably was stimulated to some extent by personal ambition, drafted the *Shiho Shokumu Teisei* (Justice Staff Regulations and Operating Rules, hereafter called Regulations) along quite liberal lines. These Regulations were promulgated into law in 1872. They constituted the first Japanese judicial code and provided not only for the organization of the courts but also dealt with other matters relating to the administration of justice. Particularly to be noted is the fact that they contained provisions for the establishment of local courts as separate and distinct judicial institutions and provided for legal officers, both judges and procurators, whose functions were distinguished from those of general administrative officials. The Regulations also authorized so-called *daigennin* or advocates to represent parties in civil actions, thus casting aside the traditional principle that a litigant could not appear in court through a professional representative.

Although the reforms contemplated by the Regulations represented a drastic ideological departure from the traditional ideas briefly noted above, they did not provide for a complete separation of powers. This is most clearly seen in the fact that the Minister of Justice was the presiding judge of the Ministry of Justice Court, the court prescribed in the Regulations as the highest tribunal in the land. Additionally, the Minister of Justice was given complete authority over the appointment and removal of judges, and judgment could not be rendered in criminal cases involving political crimes such as treason until the Minister's approval had been obtained. Finally, the power to supervise the trial of grave crimes was reserved to the cabinet. In practice the situation was made worse by the fact that the local courts, which had been established pursuant to the Regulations, were as a rule presided over by local administrative officials, just as the premodern courts had been, because of an insufficiency of adequately trained personnel. Additionally, there were no provisions in the Regulations or elsewhere prescribing qualifications for judges and procurators. Thus, even full-time judges were appointed principally from among administrative officials who had not been educated in the law.

...

Although the institutional structure of the judicial system was worked out through the series of reforms discussed above, the judiciary and the procuracy of the day may well have been staffed by individuals without sufficient capabilities or training; it is understandable then that many trials were improperly conducted and mishandled. Perhaps the major reason is that the reforms were pushed through too hastily, without adequate modification of the social structure and culture, because of zeal to free the country from extraterritoriality. Tsuyoshi Inoue, an able assistant of Hirobumi Ito (frequently regarded as the greatest statesman in the Meiji era), criticized the judges and procurators in the following manner:

> A glance at the courts ... of today in our country reveals that decisions are not rendered very quickly. They are unable to maintain fair trials ... This is probably because the courts are not independent; the judges often do not realize the nature of their position and responsibility, they take into account personal considerations and play politics, they are moved by favoritism and attempt to patch up the mistakes of the police and officials, they do not render judgments in accordance with whether or not a fact exists, and many rely upon the mistaken belief that the way to make one's fame and fortune is to give judgments which will ingratiate oneself with the government ... procurators, too, do not handle a defendant's case pursuant to their beliefs, but are inclined strongly to pressure judges in compliance with the directions of the police.

Another indication of the low repute in which the judiciary and the procuracy were held, and of the failure fully to appreciate the significance of the legal process, was the proposal seriously made in 1887 to appoint foreign lawyers as judges and procurators in Japanese courts in cases involving foreign nationals. True, the measure was an unambiguous expedient to deal with the problem of extraterritoriality, but it could not have been proposed if Japan's leaders, so sensitive to infringements upon national sovereignty in other spheres, had considered the administration of justice an essential part of that national sovereignty.

It should be noted also that most leading figures in the judiciary and the procuracy at that time either had taken legal training abroad, usually in France, or had been trained in Japan by foreign lawyers. This fact, coupled with the inadequacy of the statutes, on occasion resulted in judicial determinations strongly influenced by foreign legal concepts that were not in accord with circumstances prevailing in Japan.

The development of the bar in Japan followed a different course. While the government was very active in stimulating the development of soundly trained judges and procurators, it did little to develop the advocates (*daigennin*), who were not authorized to represent litigants until 1872 and then only in civil cases. This passive attitude toward the advocates may have derived in part from the poor reputation of the *kujishi* the precursor of the modern lawyer, as well as from the general tendency during the long feudal period to esteem official position over private occupations. An additional factor was that advocates were less important to the national policy of breaking down extraterritoriality than were judges and procurators.

About the time of the Meiji Restoration, the Western concept of the lawyer was introduced to Japan by observers who went abroad. In 1872, recognition was given for the first time to the principle of representation in civil litigation through advocates. The *Soto Bunrei* (Forms for Pleadings) of 1873, regulations which were the precursor of a modern code of civil procedure, provided for some procedures which envisaged the use of advocates. However, qualifications were not established, and any person, except a minor or one under other disability, could act as advocate. As a result, advocates had no privileges and were dealt with by the courts in the same manner as the litigants themselves. In principle, they were subject to close supervision by the courts; thus they could be fined if they delayed a court session and reprimanded or suspended if they were disrespectful toward the courts. According to available data, they were viewed with substantially the same lack of esteem as had been shown the *kujishi* in the feudal period.

The creation of the advocate role without the requirement of professional qualifications resulted in entry into the bar of many individuals who were deficient in knowledge of the law or very unethical in their behaviour. In 1876, the Ministry of Justice prescribed the *Daigennin Kisoku* (Advocate Regulations), which for the first time required applicants to pass an examination and obtain the permission of the Minister of Justice as prerequisites to practice. It is worthy of note that, although this examination was required before one was prescribed for judges and procurators, its objective was not to inquire into the knowledge of the law but to exclude persons on grounds of poor character or general lack of education. The very fact that an examination of this type was given is a reflection of the fact that the quality of the advocates was extremely low and that not much was expected from them. Moreover, the examination system did not contribute substantially to improvement in the quality of advocates because the examinations were administered by regional groups and by local administrative officials who were totally unfamiliar with the lawyer's role. In 1880, the examination system was revised in order to make it uniform throughout the country. At the same time, advocates were required to organize into associations in each judicial district for the avowed purpose of raising professional ethics but also perhaps in order to permit the government to exercise control over their activities. Significantly, these associations were responsible to the chief district procurators; they were not autonomous bodies.

While advocates were allowed to act in civil matters, they had not been authorized to defend in criminal cases. However, after the government in 1875 had designated two officials of the Ministry of Justice as *bengokan* (something similar in nature to public defenders), in a case arising out of the assassination of a high government official, it could not continue indefinitely to refuse to extend the same principle to other cases. Thus, under the new Code of Criminal Instruction of 1880, all accused were given the right of counsel ...

...

THE PROFESSION UNDER THE CONSTITUTION OF 1889

The positions of judge and procurator, which had been developed through frequent but fragmentary reforms, were recognized in the Imperial Constitution of 1889 and the Court Organization Law of 1890, one of the items of legislation that implemented the constitution.

Upon the recommendation of Hirobumi Ito, who had studied the operation of the constitutions of Western countries for a considerable period of time and had concluded that it was most desirable for Japan to follow the example of the absolute monarchy in Prussia, the Constitution of 1889 was drafted on the Prussian model. As a result, the government also determined to adopt Prussian principles in drafting the Court Organization Law, casting away the previous French models. Thus, Otto Rudorff, then a lecturer on German law at Tokyo University, was ordered to draft an organization law on the model of the *Gerichtsverfassungsgesetz* of 27 January 1877. This shift to German models, however, did not bring about any significant alteration in either the technical functions of Japanese judges and procurators, which had been set in earlier legislation, or in their social status. Both the German and the French systems were within the Continental system of jurisprudence, and, moreover, Boissonade, the French professor and the draftsman of the earlier laws, collaborated with Rudorff in drafting the new organization law. It might have been quite different if there had been a shift to Anglo-American models.

Under the Constitution of 1889 and the Court Organization Law, a judge was guaranteed tenure, and he was required to have knowledge of law and also to have received professional training. Tenure was ensured by the fact that a judge could not be removed, assigned to other courts, suspended, or penalized by reduction in salary unless: (1) he had been convicted of a criminal offense or punished in proceedings as specified in the Judge Disciplinary Law; (2) he had been adjudged incapable of performing his duties because of mental or physical incompetence by the Ministry of Justice, upon a resolution of the judges of the Great Court of Judicature or of the judges of a Court of Appeals sitting in an administrative capacity. Professional competence was required in that an individual could not be appointed a judge until he had passed an examination and successfully completed three years of professional training as a probationary legal official in the courts and the procurators' offices. The new system did not provide for judicial autonomy because the power of general administrative supervision over the judiciary remained in the hands of the Minister of Justice, although he had no authority over the judges in the exercise of their judicial functions.

It can be said that the structure of the Japanese judiciary, both in its favorable and unfavorable aspects, was stabilized by the Constitution of 1889 and the Court Organization Law. Since that time, by and large, the judiciary has been composed of individuals who entered judicial service immediately after completing their university education, passing the legal examination and taking apprentice training. Thereafter, in the normal course of events, they served until retirement. Thus, the judicial career, quite distinct from other careers in law, came into existence. Both the tradition of complete independence from political influence, which is generally considered to have been established through the famous *Otsu* case, and a strong sense of professional integrity are manifestations of a consciousness of identity as members of a distinct professional group. The fact that there is not a single recorded instance of judicial corruption, while many bribery cases were reported in the legislative and executive branches particularly at the beginning of this century, and the fact that the judiciary did not yield completely under militaristic and ultranationalistic pressure, even in the critical years of the Second World War, are further manifestations of this consciousness. In fact, one Japanese authority has called the Japanese judiciary 'the most reliable among the branches of government and administrative organizations'.

However, one must not evaluate the prewar judiciary and its position too highly. In the first place, as a result of the retention by the Minister of Justice of the power of general administrative supervision over the judiciary, personnel administration within the judiciary inevitably was influenced by the government. Particularly noteworthy is the fact that the Minister of Justice, by offering greater opportunity of promotion, could induce promising judges and procurators to enter the Ministry to perform general administrative functions. This practice not only resulted in competent jurists leaving the judiciary but also led people to think of the relationship between the Ministry of Justice and the courts in much the same light as that between a central administrative organ and its regional offices. This tendency reinforced by the traditional concept of the judiciary discussed in the preceding section, led to a general evaluation of the status of the judge as inferior to that of the administrative official assigned to a Ministry's head office (though not to a regional office). This in turn led to the view that the judge did not have to be treated as well as the higher administrative official. The Minister of Justice, who had the power to assign judges to particular courts, also sometimes urged them to accept new assignments for the convenience of the government. Furthermore, the judge's status guarantee within the context of a bureaucratic system was accompanied by an unexpected and undesirable result. Whereas the administrative official enjoyed quick promotion and could look forward to a better-paying position in either a public enterprise or a private corporation after relatively early retirement, the judge who remained in the judiciary could reach the highest salary grade only by a slow and gradual process over a comparatively long period of time, with relatively late retirement. This factor probably tended, as it still does, to discourage some young and able individuals from entering the judiciary, though it cannot be denied that security of assured lifelong work on the bench was an attraction to others.

Secondly, in considering the prewar judiciary one must recognize that the system of the career judiciary, and particularly the exercise of judicial authority by younger men, sometimes met with popular dissatisfaction because of the purported inexperience and immaturity of judges. This dissatisfaction was probably increased by a tendency to expand the number of so-called *Generalklauseln* (statutory provisions cast in broad and highly generalized terms), which required greater maturity of outlook for interpretation than did statutes cast in fairly specific terms. Needless to say, both the requirement of training for three years (since 1908, only one and a half years) before going on the bench and the requirement of a collegiate court composed of at least three judges – except in minor civil and criminal cases where a single judge could preside – was designed and actually served to some extent to reduce this dissatisfaction. Nevertheless, there were many sharp criticisms concerning the 'fossilization' or *Weltfremdheit* of the judiciary.

Turning to the procurators, their most notable characteristic under the Court Organization Law of 1890 was the similarity of their status to that of judges. Of course, the procurator differed from the judge in that, as a matter of law, he was subordinate to his superior in performing his duties. However, there was no clear prescription of law determining whether the Minister of Justice, who was not a procurator, could issue instructions to a procurator with respect to the disposition of a particular case. Some people who attached special importance to the integrity of the procuracy, were of the opinion that such attempted exercise of power was illegal. The Minister never tried to exercise this directive power in the prewar days, so the matter remained largely academic. In this sense, the prewar procuracy enjoyed independence similar to that of the judiciary, at least as far as political or other outside pressure was concerned. This comparatively strong guarantee of independence is one of the most important reasons why the procuracy in prewar Japan had a reputation for impartiality and proved itself highly capable in dealing with numerous scandals in political circles – an ability which won it much support from the general public around 1930.

It should be noted, however, that the strong procuracy later was criticized for *kensatsu fassho* (fascism by the procuracy), though it has never been made clear in any objective study whether *kensatsu fassho* really existed or, if it did, exactly what it was.

With regard to professional independence, procurators were selected in a manner substantially similar to judges. Candidates for the procuracy, after passing the same examination as that given the candidates for the judiciary, were appointed probationary legal officials and received the same training as those going on the bench. Procurators were on the same salary scale as judges and probably enjoyed the same prestige.

Notwithstanding the similarity between these two branches of the profession, movement between them was rare because of specialization in function. It is also worthy of note that procurators enjoyed better opportunities for promotion than judges because, though the procuracy was smaller in size, the number of higher-paying positions was about the same in both branches. Some people have suggested further that public procurators enjoyed greater possibilities of selection as members of the House of Peers or appointment to the position of Minister of Justice. During this period, leadership in the administration of justice reportedly was in the hands of the procuracy.

Rabinowitz, R, 'The Historical Development of the Bar' (1956–57) 70 *Harvard Law Review* 64–78

THE *DAIGENNIN* PERIOD

Though they did not go so far as to provide for a legal profession, the first modern regulations dealing with the practice of law, those of 1872, when set against the background of the Tokugawa system which we have just described, appear as a radical departure from tradition. In these regulations general recognition was given for the first time to the principle of representation in civil litigation. It should be noted, however, that qualifications were not established and anyone was free to act as a representative. Although the regulations were modified in the following year to distinguish between general and limited powers of representation, qualifications still were not set for the performance of either type. Anyone could go into court as a representative (*daigennin*).

In 1873 more detailed regulations were issued which provided for a formal appearance by the *daigennin* by the filing of a document signed jointly by the *daigennin* and the party. Use of a *daigennin* at trial was at the discretion of the party, but all documents had to be prepared by a judicial scribe (*daishonin*). There were still no restrictions placed on the performance of either of these roles, and a single individual could function in both capacities provided he did not do so in one case. This purely formal, nonfunctional differentiation seems to have resulted from imperfect comprehension of relevant provisions of the French Civil Code, which was being introduced in Japan at the time. Because the French Civil Code distinguished between these two functions, a formal dichotomy appeared in the Japanese law, even though the respective functions were but imperfectly understood.

Professionalization of the role of representative dates from 1876, when the Ministry of Justice issued detailed regulations concerning *daigennin* for the first time. Competence to practice, as demonstrated in examinations drawn up and administered by officials who, as it turned out, were themselves without legal education, was a prerequisite to admission to the bar of a district court or a high court. As a result of the unfamiliarity of these officials with the lawyer role, the examinations were so difficult that the first two times they were given only 56 candidates, a number patently insufficient to handle the legal affairs of the entire nation, succeeded in passing them.

Because of the paucity of lawyers, individuals who had not passed the examinations and who were therefore not licensed to practice continued to appear as general or special representatives. The regulations did not prevent them from doing so, for all the regulations did was limit the right to use the title *daigennin* to those who had passed the examinations. Anyone at all could be a representative so long as he did not use the title. The consequence was that the role of the lawyer continued to be performed by individuals who had no formal legal education and who had not manifested by examination their competence to practice.

In 1877 a special category of *daigennin*, '*daigennin* to the Ministry of Justice', was established. This was done in order to deal with the case of Hoshi Toru, an official of the Ministry of Finance who had become Japan's first barrister after being educated at the Middle Temple. Upon his return home Hoshi made the unprecedented decision of withdrawing from public service to enter the bar. His decision was viewed with great disfavor by government officials, and the case was ultimately disposed of by creating a special category of *daigennin* on the model of Queen's Counsel, as Hoshi himself suggested. In this status it was possible for Hoshi to handle litigation for private parties as well as for the government.

A thoroughgoing revision in the structure of the profession was made in May 1880. For the first time systematic and comprehensive legislation dealing with the profession was provided. No doubt this change was a reflection of the fact that knowledge of the function and the organization of the profession in Europe and America had increased. Among the more important provisions of this legislation were the following: the examination system was put entirely under the control of the Ministry of Justice; the system of admission to the bar of a single court was abolished and admission carried with it the right to appear before any court in the land; formal organization of the bar was required, and a bar association was established within the jurisdiction of each district court.

It should be noted that so far we have been dealing with an occupation whose recognized function was that of representation in civil litigation only. Extension of this principle to criminal litigation was not an easy matter. As early as January 1873, the idea had been advanced that representation should be permitted in criminal matters. The notion was rejected at that time on the ground that there was a shortage of *daigennin* of sufficient competence to handle criminal litigation. Representation was permitted for the first time in 1875, when the position of *bengokan* was created in connection with the Hirosawa Sangi assassination case. The *bengokan* was in some sense a defense lawyer, but he was appointed by the court, not retained by the defendant, and his function was limited to that of eliciting facts; he was not permitted to argue law. In the following year the government announced that counsel would be permitted to participate in actions in which foreign nationals were defendants. Having gone this far, it was difficult not to extend the principle to Japanese nationals. Accordingly, in June 1876 the Ministry of Justice announced that Japanese defendants could request counsel, a request which could be granted or denied at the discretion of the Ministry. A month later the government modified this position by announcing that henceforth all requests for counsel by criminal defendants would be granted. This still was not recognition of right to counsel *per se*.

The first person actively to advocate the right to counsel qua right was Isobe Shiro, one of the first Japanese to obtain a French law degree. He drew up a bill to this effect in 1879 and argued for it before the committee engaged in drafting the codes which were to become the basis of the new legal system. Eight of the ten members of the committee opposed the proposition. Some idea of the grounds for opposition may be gleaned from the contents of one of the documents drawn up by those antagonistic to the idea. It was stated, for example, that it was inconceivable to propose using *daigennin* in criminal cases when it was well known that even in civil litigation they were cunning and greedy and 'given to turning black into white'. The feeling against granting the right to counsel in criminal cases was so strong that even many of those favorably disposed to the general idea of the introduction of foreign legal systems drew the line at this proposition.

In spite of the opposition, the right to counsel was incorporated in the Criminal Code of 1880. This surprising turn of events is attributed to the fact that Boissonade, a French legal scholar who had come to Japan as adviser on code drafting, gave very strong support to Isobe's position. After the general principle of representation had been established in 1882, when the Criminal Code took effect, no major institutional changes were made in the formal structure until 1893.

As a consequence of the historical connection with the *kujishi* and the lack of formal recognition of the occupation, the status and reputation of the *daigennin*, at least at the beginning of the early modern period, was as low as that of the *kujishi* during the Tokugawa Period. Indeed, so poor was their reputation that a special term of opprobrium, *sambyaku daigen*, a term which it has been suggested might best be translated as 'shyster' or 'pettifogger', gained currency. Scholars who have sought to discover the origin of the term, which literally is translated '300 spokesmen', are inclined to accept various explanations, but all are in agreement that, regardless of its origin, the term has been used as a term of opprobrium directed at the lawyer whose services could be purchased inexpensively and who could not be relied upon to act in the most forthright manner.

In the early modern period, when the *daigennin* role still had not been recognized as an occupation, the individual who undertook to perform these functions was treated merely as another petitioner coming before the court. Those who have studied the history of the legal profession at this period inevitably refer to the treatment received by the *daigennin* at the hands of the courts with a kind of morbid fascination. The *daigennin* suffered the humiliation of being subjected to the same vexatious controls over entry to and egress from the courtroom as the petitioners. No special waiting room was provided for him, and, perhaps worst of all, all court personnel, even mere gatemen and clerks, addressed him without using honorifics. To add to his woes, he had a most unfavorable press, and several celebrated instances of friction between press and bar are on record.

Gradually conditions improved. Separate waiting rooms were provided and the system of admission to the courtroom was simplified. Not only did court personnel begin to use a respectful term of address (*dono*) when speaking to the *daigennin*, but also the custom developed of calling him from his waiting room rather than shouting for him from the hall. The spread of such practices did much to increase the prestige of the lawyer.

A factor not calculated to enhance the reputation of the *daigennin* was the persistent dissension within the bar. The very formation of an organized bar in Tokyo was marked by strife so bitter that the public procurator had to intervene. Time and time again from 1887 on the procurator was forced to deal with disputes within the bar. Dissension was so severe that in May of 1889 the procurator finally authorized the Tokyo *Daigennin* association to break up, and its members were permitted to enter either one of the two associations formed at that time.

Even this drastic action did not terminate the conflicts among the warring factions. In one of the new organizations, the Tokyo *Shinkumiai Daigennin Kai*, a dispute over leadership broke out and appeal was made once more to the procurator. Three years. later elections of officials occasioned such violent quarreling that a very unfavorable impression was made on the public at large. The fact that the procurator had to be called in with such frequency to restore order within the organized bar was a constant reminder of the immaturity of this occupational group and of its inability to handle its own affairs.

While it is true that the main thrust of development in the profession was not in the direction of enhancing the status of its members, it is also true that there were some favorable elements in the situation. In an age of 'superiority of the official and inferiority of the citizen', or 'omnipotence of the official', anything which served to assimilate the *daigennin* role to that of the official, or at least to make the *daigennin* appear of status equal to that of the official, was a major improvement. This explains why so much importance was attached to the right of representation in criminal litigation. The *daigennin* was thereby placed upon equal footing with the procurator and was able to address the official without using elaborate language of respect. The same longing for prestige explains the importance attached to entry into the bar of ex-officials. Such action was invariably commented upon and was considered tangible proof of the increasing respectability of the occupation.

Hara, one of the outstanding authorities on the subject of the legal profession, has cited participation in the Peoples' Rights movement, innovations in trial practice introduced by the bar, and activities related to penal reform as other factors important in the establishment of appropriate prestige for the occupation. Perhaps more relevant to improvement in the prestige of the lawyer at this time was the fact that there was a rapid increase in the volume of litigation and a consequent improvement in the financial position of the practitioner.

III. THE LAWYERS LAW OF 1893

Modern Japanese law dates from the nineties. The adoption of modern legal codes which took place at this time was part of a general revamping of governmental structure in connection with the promulgation of the constitution of 1889. The changes were made in order to bring an end to discriminatory treaties under which the nation was prevented from exercising full sovereignty. The Lawyers Law of 1893 was but one relatively minor aspect of this general reform.

As finally passed the law was a comprehensive regulation of the legal profession. Admission was limited to Japanese males of legal capacity over twenty years of age. As a general principle it was to be by examination. There were, however, several important exceptions to this principle; those who were qualified as judges or procurators, those who held a *hakushi* degree (equivalent to a doctorate) in law, and those who were graduates of law faculties in imperial universities, the former Tokyo University, and the former Ministry of Justice law schools all could be admitted without examination. A supplementary provision permitted those who had been enrolled in the register of *daigennin* also to be admitted without examination. A lawyer could not engage in any business activity without the express permission of his bar association. Admission to practice was gained by transmitting an application to the Minister of Justice through the chief procurator of the district in which the petitioner sought to practice. Only those in practice for at least three years were permitted to practice at the bar of the supreme court. An integrated bar under the supervision and control of the chief district procurator was to be established in each district.

The Lawyers Examination Regulations, issued a little later in the same year, provided for annual examinations given by a committee made up of judges, procurators, and officials of the Ministry of Justice. Lawyers were excluded from this committee. Candidates were to be examined in the fields of civil, criminal, and commercial substantive law, and civil and criminal procedure.

From the point of view of the historical development of the profession, the most important features of this law were those which placed control over the bar in the hands of the procuracy, thus effectively preventing autonomy of the bar, and those setting up numerous exceptions to the requirement of examination. Examinations had been waived as early as 1879, when three graduates of Tokyo University were admitted to practice without examination on the ground that they were manifestly better qualified for practice than were *daigennin* in general who had no legal education. The examination problem, as we shall see, has remained a persistent one throughout the history of the profession.

Another point of considerable importance is that *daigennin* were permitted to transfer their registration to the Lawyers Roll. This had the effect of permitting *kujishi,* who had become *daigennin* without examination, to continue in practice as lawyers without any demonstration of competence whatsoever. This could only have a deleterious effect on the reputation of the lawyer.

IV. PROBLEMS OF LAWYER STATUS AFTER 1893

Formal status inferiority came to an end in 1893, and though the bar might complain of a lack of consideration shown the practitioners by judicial officials, as happened in 1893, or undertake investigation of the 'unfriendly' attitude of bailiffs and the 'haughtiness' of officials, as was done in 1907, the situation on the whole seems to have improved. Lawyers began to fill important positions in government, an occasional official entered the bar, and social contact between lawyers and high-ranking officials occurred from time to time. Especially impressive was the fact that a private practitioner carried through to a successful conclusion litigation entered into by the Japanese government before the Privy Council in England.

Political prominence, social contact with high officials, and successful conduct of important international litigation could not change the fact that the prestige of the profession continued to be severely damaged by internecine conflict within the bar. There was nothing which so frustrated efforts of the bar to improve its status as the almost incredible conduct associated with the formation and development of the bar associations provided for by the Lawyers Law of 1893.

Under that law the two Tokyo groups which had separated in 1885 were required to reunite. The ensuing turmoil was even more intense than the earlier confusion. Physical violence at meetings was not unknown and on more than one occasion police had to be called in.

Bitter feeling between the so-called 'French law' and 'English law' factions in the bar seems to have been one of the principal causes of the demand for a national bar organization free of government control. This demand was made by the 'English law' faction, the minority group in the Tokyo association, and in 1897 a private association, the Japan Bar Association (*Nihon Bengoshi Kyokai*) was founded. This organization soon began publication of a journal and issued the first national directory of the bar.

In 1907 and 1909 violence occurred once more in meetings of the Tokyo Bar Association when a reform faction took over from the 'French law' group. Except for some trouble in 1916, the reform faction managed to remain in control without further violence until 1922, when the reform faction itself broke up and another private group, the *Tokyo Bengoshi Kyokai*, came into existence. When insurgents took control of the Japan Bar Association, the deposed faction introduced a bill in the Diet to permit more than one public bar association per district. This measure became law in 1923, and soon thereafter the old 'English law' faction withdrew from the Tokyo Bar Association en masse and formed the First Bar Association of Tokyo. In a parallel move, another nationwide private association, the Imperial Bar Association (*Teikoki Bengoshi Kai*), came into existence under the domination of substantially the same group.

The last major division in the Japanese bar came in 1926 when the Second Bar Association of Tokyo was formed as an offshoot of the First Bar Association. At this point, then, there were two national bar associations of a private character, one official association in each district except Tokyo, where there were three, and no official national body. This situation remained unchanged until the end of the Second World War.

One reading this history might conclude that the organized bar consisted of men who did nothing but conduct sniper raids against rival factions. This seems not to have been entirely true. The bar became increasingly articulate concerning matters relating to organization of the legal system, though it is impossible to determine how influential its views were in the determination of policy. Hara has stated that the first expression of opinion by the organized bar concerning a matter not directly relating to its internal affairs was a protest against the removal of a judge from one district to another district without obtaining his prior consent. In 1899 the judiciary called upon the organized bar for an expression of opinion concerning an aspect of the administration of justice, the first time such a step had been taken. There are cases on record in which bar associations protested against poor judicial administration, and the bar frequently formed committees to consider drafts of legislation submitted to it by the Ministry of Justice or to draft bills to be submitted on its behalf to the Ministry.

Viewing this entire period, it seems fairly clear that the bar was called upon with increasing frequency to participate in activities relating to the development of the legal system as a whole. In this regard the contrast with the early modern period is striking. However, the evidence of constructive activity is, on the whole, relatively scant, and one is left with the impression that the influence of the bar was minor. Efforts to increase prestige appear to have been seriously hampered by the divisive activity, the quarreling, and the violence which all too frequently were characteristic of the activity of the organized bar.

V. THE LAWYERS LAW OF 1933

From 1893 to 1933 no complete revision of the Lawyers Law was undertaken, though several important changes were made. For example, in 1900 the requirement of a minimum period of practice for admission to the Supreme Court bar was discontinued, and provision was made in 1923 for revocation of the privilege granted graduates of the law faculties of imperial universities to enter the bar without examination.

Interest in revision became especially strong in the twenties because many considered the profession to be in a state of acute crisis. The number of lawyers had increased sharply during the twenties, and a survey undertaken by the Japan Bar Association indicated that the profession was in truly alarming economic circumstances. According to this survey, more than 2,400 lawyers out of 4,100 reporting indicated that they failed to meet living expenses, and 240 had not even managed to pay ordinary office expenses.

The report was greeted with dismay by the bar. One lawyer wrote regretfully in 1929 that the prestige of the profession still seemed somewhat higher than it had been during the age of the *kujishi* and the *daigennin*, but that there was no doubt in his mind that it had declined rapidly in the decade immediately preceding his writing. It was asserted that unethical and criminal acts were being committed under the pressure of economic need. Some felt the problem was caused by high fees. Others asserted that fees were too low. There was only one point on which all were agreed: the status of the lawyer was gravely endangered.

While various solutions were proposed to meet this crisis, the one most frequently advanced was, as might be expected, that the number of lawyers should be cut. It was asserted that there were too many members of the bar, and too many nonmembers doing work properly within the sphere of special competence of the lawyer.

Lively debate took place in the journals on the question of the oversupply of practitioners. Whether or not the bar was in fact overcrowded, and apart from the question of the exact number of nonmembers, or *sambyaku daigen*, the fact remains that these two problems were inextricably bound together in the minds of those concerned with the condition of the profession. Bills to make unauthorized practice illegal were introduced in the Diet in 1912, 1921, and 1925. Surprising as it may seem, these proposals were invariably greeted by strong opposition based on two grounds that it was difficult to define the sphere of practice of law once a narrow definition of advocacy was departed from, and that people needed to be able to turn to someone other than the lawyer to handle minor problems because the expense of engaging a lawyer would be too great.

The Ministry of Justice invariably opposed inclusion of provisions for the control of unauthorized practice in the Lawyers Law. If legislation was to be passed on the subject the Ministry wanted it in a separate bill. It was primarily because the bar wanted a clear prohibition spelled out in the Lawyers Law itself that a draft proposed in 1930 never got to the floor of the Diet. The Ministry of Justice persisted and in 1933 a separate piece of legislation, the Law of Control of Unauthorized Practice, was passed over the opposition of the bar. The lawyers opposed this bill, even though one article prohibited representation in litigation by nonlawyers unless the activity were performed without fee for public benefit by one who possessed the qualifications of a lawyer, because another article gave the Minister of Justice control of the enforcement machinery. The bar feared that this discretionary power would be used to permit the *sambyaku daigen* to continue his activities.

The lawyers objected to other features of the proposed Lawyers Law, in addition to its failure to prohibit unauthorized practice. They felt, for example, that it was insulting to require an oath of the lawyer when a similar oath was not required of judges and officials. They also found certain features of the apprentice system which was to be instituted not to their liking. Some of the strongest criticism was directed at the fact that the Minister of Justice was to retain control over the profession, which was not to be permitted to organize as a juristic person. Many commentators criticized the lack of provision for nationwide organization of the profession. Some felt this was done because of a fear of domination by Tokyo and Osaka. Others, however, felt that nationwide organization was undesirable because the hostility between the existing private nationwide organizations would also be reflected in a national body of a public nature. Unfavorable comment was also directed to those provisions which would permit certain categories of individuals to enter the bar without examination. And there was some criticism of the fact that the right of practice was not to be limited territorially or by type of court.

When the bill finally went to the floor of the Diet, the Minister of Justice asserted that its principal features were recognition that the lawyer role extended beyond the courtroom; raising of qualifications to the same level as those for judges and procurators through the lawyer-apprentice system; admission of women to practice; and recognition of bar associations as juristic persons. As finally passed, the Lawyers Law of 1933 contained these features as well as most of those which the bar found objectionable.

Perhaps the most significant omission in the law was the lack of a specific prohibition against practice by nonlawyers. As noted above, lawyers felt that the ancillary law designed to meet this situation was wholly inadequate. One writer has suggested that the *sambyaku daigen* were such political powers in the countryside that the Ministry did not want to antagonize them.

VI. POSTWAR REVISION OF THE LAWYERS LAW

In common with many other phases of Japanese law, the Lawyers Law was revised during the American occupation. Three different bills were drawn up by interested groups. The principal problems raised in connection with the proposed revision were admission without examination; admission to practice of former members of the judiciary in a district in which the jurist had been sitting immediately prior to seeking admission to the bar; supervision and control over lawyers and bar associations; structure and power of bar associations; and practice by foreign attorneys. The revision was passed in 1949, and it is this law under which the legal profession operates at the present time. The outstanding feature of the revision was that the bar associations for the first time were freed from government control. General supervision was to be exercised by the Japan Federation of Bar Associations (*Nihon Bengoshi Rengokai*), an independent juristic person. To say that the legal profession became free of administrative supervision is not to say that it became completely self-governing, for under the constitutional grant of rule-making power to the Supreme Court it is clear that the court, if it so desired, might formulate appropriate regulations for the profession. To date the Supreme Court has not exercised this power and the profession itself now plays an important role in admission and disciplinary proceedings formerly entrusted to the Ministry of Justice.

Another change of considerable importance was the unification of the lawyer- and judicial-apprentice systems. This was the culmination of a movement dating back to 1893, for in that year the draft of the Lawyers Law contained a provision, later deleted, for apprentice training comparable to that of judges and procurators. Periodically thereafter provision for apprentice training was included in draft bills, but it was not until 1933 that apprenticeship was included in a bill which became law. Control over the program was placed in the bar associations because budgetary difficulties prevented the Ministry of Justice from taking control as it desired. The system never got into full operation before the war, and in the postwar period it was decided that this apprentice system should be combined with the Ministry of Justice training program for officials. A Judicial Research and Training Institute was established as an agency of the Supreme Court. The first class entered the Institute in 1946, and at present a class enters each April for a two-year period of training.

Although the bar has won its historic struggle for autonomy from the Ministry of Justice, other important problems hold the attention of the profession. Of these the most important is that which is subsumed under the rubric 'integration of the legal profession' (*hoso ichigen ron*), a phrase difficult to interpret, but meaning in its broadest sense the integration of all segments of the profession – the bar, the judiciary, and the procuracy – and in a narrower sense the selection of members of the judiciary from the bar rather than directly from among graduates of the Judicial Research and Training Institute. While great support has been given *hoso ichigen ron* by members of the bar, other segments of the profession are markedly less enthusiastic about the idea.

The unification of the apprentice-training systems and the establishment of the Association of the Japanese Legal Profession (*Nihon Horitsu Kyokai*) an unofficial organization with the specific objective of bringing about closer relations among the branches of the profession, are generally considered steps in the direction of integration. The fact that the lawyer now plays a more prominent part in the criminal trial than he did in the past, and the fact that a nationwide bar association now has considerable responsibility for the profession are considered by some to have improved the status of the lawyer.

Undercurrents of dissatisfaction are still to be observed. As late as 1952, a writer noted that the phrase *sambyaku daigen* still had currency, and a lawyer has written a small book on the profession for the layman which is highly critical of the bar. Such complaints are of minor importance compared to the criticism that genuine integration of the profession seems far off. Judges are not being selected from the bar in significant numbers, and prospects for the future, from the point of view of the bar, are not encouraging. One would guess that, at least in the near future, there will be increasing contact between lawyers and other members of the legal profession without any significant alteration in the pattern of recruitment into the judiciary.

Oppler, AC, *Legal Reforms in Occupied Japan: A Participant Looks Back*, 1976, pp 104–10, Princeton University Press

The separation of the judiciary from the executive branch of the government affected both the procurators and the Ministry of Justice. The changed position of the former is reflected in the Public Procurators Office Law, which was enacted simultaneously with the Court Organization Law. The procurators, whose education corresponds to those of the judges, as we have seen, are now strictly administrative officials under the Ministry of Justice. Their function before the courts is the public action or indictment in criminal cases. In the trial they represent the state as a party on a level equal to the defence attorney. They also act for the public interest in certain domestic relations cases. The organization of the procurators' offices parallels that of the courts, with supreme, high, district, and local procurators' offices. Heading the Supreme Procurators' Office is the procurator general who, in his relationship to the ministry, enjoys a great deal of independence. Thus, the ministry may not directly give orders to a procurator, but must do this through the procurator general.

The procurators are also appointed officials. Here again, some check on their appointment and continuation in office was considered advisable. A Committee for the Examination of Qualifications of Public Procurators, consisting of members of both Houses of the Diet, the procurator general, and representatives of the ministry, the Supreme Court, the bar associations, and the law schools, serves this purpose by periodic examinations that could result in the removal of a procurator found unsuitable. Besides this personal check, a functional one was set up by the Law for the Inquest of Prosecution, in the form of a popular investigation of cases in which the procurator has failed to prosecute. The inquest has been characterized as a mild or embryonic form of grand jury; it has in practice played only a modest role in terms of percentages, but has served as a relatively effective check. Although its finding does not constitute a true bill of indictment, but is of an advisory nature, it could, if unfavorable, have undesirable consequences for the procurator's career, in as much as it is publicly posted and brought to the knowledge of his superior and of the Qualifications Committee. One of the reasons for establishing this check was the latitude given the procurator by the Code of Criminal Procedure to dispense with the indictment because of the character, age, and situation of the offender, the nature of the offense, the circumstances under which it was committed, and the conditions subsequent to the commission. This provision, which will be discussed in connection with the Code of Criminal Procedure, lends itself to favoritism – discovering which was thought to be the main purpose of the inquest.

The change brought about by rendering the judiciary independent from the Ministry of Justice altered the nature of the latter. The conclusion from this change was drawn by the law of 17 December 1947, establishing the Attorney General's Office (AGO), which was enacted simultaneously with the new Police Law Pursuant to a 'suggestion' of the Supreme Commander in form of a letter to the prime minister. It replaced the minister of justice by an attorney general, who is a member of the cabinet serving as its supreme legal advisor. As such, he took over the functions of drafting and editing legislation and cabinet orders, which were previously exercised by the Cabinet Bureau of Legislation. This Bureau was abolished 'in the interest of governmental efficiency and economy.' Actually, the efficiency of its staff did not leave anything to be desired, at least from the point of view of the pre-occupation regime. It consisted mostly of jurists trained in the law school of the Imperial University. The reason that SCAP took exception to the bureau was rather that it had developed the habit of checking not only on the formulation and legal correctness, but also on the policy of proposed legislation, thereby exercising an influence incompatible with the principles of the new constitution and the position of the Diet under it.

Within the Attorney General's Office several bureaus, each headed by an assistant attorney general, reflected the various responsibilities of that authority. They were concerned with legislation, prosecution, research and opinion, litigation, and execution.

It is obvious that this reorganization along American lines not only constituted a modernization, and drew the logical consequences from the independence of the judiciary, but beyond that was of high political importance. With the abolition of the Home Ministry and the democratization and decentralization of the police, it did away with two powerful agents of the former police state. The emphasis in the law on civil liberties gives expression to the idea that the state, besides controlling its citizens, has the obligation to protect their rights. Awareness of this obligation was shown by the initiative of the first attorney general, Suzuki Yoshio, in establishing a Civil Liberties Bureau within his office. This bureau works in the field through civil liberties commissioners.

LAWYERS

Although not without political influence, the legal profession enjoyed little social prestige in Japan, even less than the judges, and was subject to tight supervision by the Ministry of Justice, exercised by the procurators over the Bar associations. While disbarment and other disciplinary punishment of lawyers were entrusted to a disciplinary court connected with the appellate courts, the minister of justice could open the procedure. I have already mentioned the shockingly small number of lawyers in Japan, a phenomenon caused mainly by the aversion of the people to litigation and by their preference for compromise and out-of-court settlement. In court trials the customary role of lawyers was not that of courageous fighters for the rights of their clients. In criminal cases, their advice to the defendant was often, even in doubtful instances, not to deny guilt, but to plead mitigating circumstances in order not to irritate the presiding judge. It was clear to us from the beginning that the liberation from governmental control of the bar had to follow the creation of an independent judiciary. Our contacts with the leaders of the bar associations made us see the potentiality of an eventual development of Japan's bar to a protagonist of civil rights.

The revision of the Lawyers' Law was, however, delayed until 10 June 1949, and thus turned out to be the last important reform within the jurisdiction of my division. The reason for the delay was that the question of the degree of independence to be granted the bar was for a lengthy period a controversial subject among the leading bar associations, the Attorney General's Office, and the Supreme Court. Here we did not have to push anything, since the bar associations themselves showed a gratifying zeal to achieve the greatest possible degree of independence. We had, however, the satisfaction of being continuously consulted by their leaders, who were interested in the American system of an integrated bar. We restricted ourselves to information, and in this function MacCormick proved particularly useful. The Lawyers' Law was introduced as a member bill by a lawyer, who was a member of the Diet. Without going into any detail, it may be pointed out that the position of the bar associations was finally accepted. The law provided that a bar association be established within the area of each district court. A Japan Federation of Bar Associations was to be the nationwide top organization, with the various bar associations as well as the individual lawyers throughout the country as its members. Admission to the bar must be made through the local bar association that the candidate wants to join. The application is then forwarded to the federation, which keeps a name list of all lawyers. Registration in this list is a prerequisite for admission to the bar. If, however, the local bar association refuses to forward the application, the candidate may complain to the federation, which decides on the merits of the case. Against its finding, the person adversely affected may appeal to the high court. The only function left to the Supreme Court is the admission of foreign lawyers.

In September 1951, a representative of the Japan Bar Association asked me to write an article on the future of the Japanese bar in the Peace edition of *Hoso Koron* (Legal Review). In this article, I pointed out that, although Japan's lawyers had enjoyed the status of full autonomy for only two years, they had, under the guidance of the Federation of Bar Associations, given proof that freedom from outside control means increased responsibilities. The federation, I wrote, had worked out a code of ethics for the legal profession; created a Civil Liberties Committee, and shown considerable initiative in the protection of civil rights; expressed opinions on legislation and judicial administration; promoted legal aid to the poor; encouraged the establishment of Practicing Law Institutes to train lawyers in the revised law and procedure; and engaged in many other significant activities. Women lawyers had organized their own bar association and specialized in family law and those legal aspects that affect women's status. Moving on to the future, I professed belief in the basic brotherhood of all those who serve the law. I somewhat sanguinely visualized future bar associations that would include judges, procurators, and legal scholars in their membership.

II EDUCATION

Abe, H, 'Education of the Legal Profession in Japan' in von Mehren, AT (ed), ***Law in Japan: The Legal Order in a Changing Society*****, 1963, pp 159–63, Harvard University Press**

LEGAL PROFESSIONAL EDUCATION UNDER THE POSTWAR EDUCATION SYSTEM

Education in the University Law Departments and the National Legal Examination

... the law departments of the Japanese universities are unlike the American law schools in that they do not have as their principal objective the training of persons who will enter the legal profession. The departments of law, even though called by that name, ordinarily give instruction in political science, administration, and economics, as well as law; and most graduates of the law departments have expected from the beginning of their studies to enter government or to find employment with private companies. In 1959, 36 universities in Japan gave instruction in law; their law or similar departments in that year graduated 13,165 students In the same year about 8,000 persons took the national legal examination, and 319 qualified. In 1961 only eight universities sent more than ten legal apprentices to the institute. Thus, most of the universities in Japan which offer instruction in the law send none or at most a few of their students into the professional legal world, and, even in those universities that have a fair number of graduates who become legal apprentices, these represent only a small portion of all their graduates. As a result, legal education in the universities resembles that of American undergraduate political-science departments rather than American law schools and must be limited to the fundamentals necessary for students considering positions in government or industry.

The universities, using chiefly the lecture method, explain the principal academic views relating to the legislative bases, the interpretation, and the structure of the fundamental codes and the constitution. From this instruction the student can acquire a general knowledge of the content and interpretation of these codes and become familiar with the method of interpretation of legal rules and the processes of legal reasoning. However, because of the insufficient length of university education, because of the low proportion of professors to students, and because of the necessary assumption that most students will not become professionals, detailed examination and study based on analysis of the facts of individual decisions and specific cases are generally not attempted. There is rather a tendency to emphasize the systematic development of theory from a certain academic viewpoint, particularly that of the professor lecturing. It is also unusual to discuss in much detail the social background of changes in decisional and statutory law.

However, since the war, under the influence of Anglo-American law, there has been a tendency among the university scholars also to emphasize the explanation of cases and to conduct case-method study and criticism of decisions in seminars or other small classes. However, since there is limited capacity to handle such seminars, not all students can participate in them, and resort to the lecture system, with a content as described above, apparently continues to be the prevailing tendency. As a matter of fact, one cannot say that such a legal education is entirely inadequate for the majority of students, who will not enter the formal legal profession but will, in government and in companies, acquire skill in general legal matters not involving litigation, such as the drafting of contracts and the handling of business relating to taxes and stock transactions. The fundamental legal knowledge necessary for such quasi-lawyers is taught very efficiently in a short time along with courses in administration, government, economics, and other fields. Since case law is not yet well established in such fields as commercial acts, taxes, and company law, matters of practice are frequently carried out by such graduates in accordance with the particular academic views learned at the universities. For these students who will not spend their lives working within the profession, a more complete grasp of law may not be necessary. To American lawyers it is a surprising fact that procedure is frequently an elective course and that many students who have not studied procedure are graduated from the law departments.

It is thus clear that in Japan graduation from the law department of a university does not at all imply legal knowledge at a professional level or a capacity for legal thinking of a professional character. Furthermore, the postwar reform of the educational system has lowered the level of scholarly attainment. Before the war, the university law faculty gave a legal education of three years' duration to students who had completed a preparatory general education consisting of six years of primary, five years of middle, and three years of high-school training. Under the new postwar system, however, the university must include in a four-year course both general and specialized education, including law. The distribution of this four-year period between general and specialized training varies somewhat from university to university, but, because of the shortened period of education prior to entrance into the universities, the preparation of the entering students is less adequate than before the war, and the universities must devote some time to the teaching of language and other general subjects. As a result, the time which the law departments can allocate to specialized legal study is in practice normally about two and a half years. When one considers that, in addition to this reduction in the period of training, the content of law has become more complex and varied since the war, the level of legal knowledge transmitted to the students is most certainly lower than in the prewar period.

It is difficult to avoid concluding that there is a gap between the standard of legal knowledge which should naturally be demanded of the professional apprentices and the level of legal knowledge imparted by the universities. However, since one must qualify in the national legal examination to become a legal apprentice, it may be that this gap is in fact narrowed to some degree by the special study of law undertaken by students in preparing for the examination. This, however, is accompanied by some undesirable consequences. Since the examination covers the major codes, the candidate must begin rather early to emphasize the courses relating to them if he wishes to qualify before leaving the university. Many begin such study even before attending the relevant lectures. Because this is a heavy burden on the student, there is a tendency to concentrate on courses preparatory to the examination at the sacrifice of courses in social sciences and the liberal arts. However, since the examination is difficult, requiring about the same high level of knowledge of law as before the war, most students are unable to qualify before graduation from their universities and a rather large number of *ronin* (masterless scholars) study for the legal examination. The average age of the 333 persons who became legal apprentices in 1961 was 27.1 years (if one progresses normally in his education, he might graduate from a university at 22), and among them only 65 (18.8% of the total) had qualified while university students. Not a few of these 'masterless scholars' take the examination a third and a fourth time, and many study for it while working as clerks in law offices or as secretaries to the courts.

It is certainly true that this laborious preparation for the national legal examination enlarges to some degree the student's knowledge of law, but one may doubt whether it actually assists the development of either a good legal sense or a capacity for legal thinking. The questions in the examination are of the type found in the examinations of the various courses of the university law departments, and, since they are chiefly essay questions, the candidates tend to prepare by memorizing academic interpretations and theory to be able to get down a good outline in a short time. Accordingly, one must question to what extent the depth of the candidate's knowledge of law and his capacity for legal thinking are developed by this sort of preparation, particularly if it is repeated for several years. Furthermore, the fundamental function of university education is distorted by this sort of study for the examination: students are deprived of a grounding in general culture and in other social sciences.

Of course it must be recognized that the existence of the national legal examination maintains the capacity of the legal apprentices at a rather high level. Recently, particularly since a number of practitioners have been named as examiners and the proportion of simple hypothetical case problems requiring a legal solution has increased, the kind of preparation required is tending to develop that ability in legal analysis which is not always sufficiently nourished in the universities. It is also true that, because of the examination, a good many young men with a capacity for serious and diligent study and who are able to undergo this long trial are entering the legal profession. Nevertheless, since the sort of study they pursue is not conducted in a planned manner under good teachers and, moreover, is often repeated with the same content each year for several years, it clearly constitutes irrational and inefficient work.

In view of these circumstances, and particularly in order to draw a larger number of talented persons into the legal profession, the Legal Examination Law was amended in 1958 with the objective, among others, of making it possible for students to qualify for the examination while still in the universities. The amendment became effective on 1 January 1961. It eliminates from the subjects formerly required either civil or criminal procedure, as the candidate may elect, and permits the candidate to elect any one of several specified nonlegal subjects, such as political science or economics. Such changes effect an important reformation of the examination method. Yet the modifications have been criticized as failing to reach the heart of the problem since there is no change in the basic method of study. Moreover, they present one important difficulty in that legal apprentices can now enter the institute without having been examined in civil procedure or, alternatively, in criminal procedure. Given the importance of procedure to the professional in law, it cannot be denied that in one sense the gap between university and professional training has been widened. It is expected, as a consequence, that the institute will be compelled to give much more systematic instruction in procedural law.

Chen, E, 'The National Law Examination of Japan' (1989) 39 *Journal of Legal Education* 4–7, 10–15, 18–21

The Lawyers Law of 1949 (1949 to Present)

The Allied Occupation, following the defeat of Japan in 1945, ushered in sweeping judicial reform. The new constitution, implemented in 1947 and still in force, declares that the people of Japan, not the Emperor, are sovereign, and that the fundamental human rights of the people guaranteed in the constitution are 'eternal and inviolate'. The constitution also insures the independence of the judiciary, and gives the Supreme Court the power to determine 'the rules of procedure and of practice, and of matters relating to attorneys, the internal discipline of the courts and the administration of judicial affairs'. Prosecutors remain under the supervision of the Ministry of Justice (still in the executive branch), although they, too, are subject to the rule-making power of the Supreme Court. Thus, the constitution transformed the Japanese judicial system from one patterned after the prewar German model to the American model based on respect for human rights and democracy.

To implement the spirit of the new constitution, the Organic Law of the Courts of 1947, the Lawyers Law of 1949, and the National Law Examination Law of 1949 were enacted. They all adhere to two principles insisted upon by the occupation authorities: (1) that lawyers be free from the supervision of the government, and (2) that the status of lawyers be elevated to a level equal to that of judges and prosecutors.

The first principle was embodied in the new Lawyers Law, which mandated the creation of an independent legal entity, the Japan Federation of Bar Associations, with which all lawyers were required to register through their local bar associations. The national federation and local bar associations, not the Ministry of Justice, were charged with the responsibility of determining the eligibility of lawyers and of disciplining those who violate the law or the rules of the federation or local bar associations. As the primary enforcer of the Lawyers Law, the federation is considered a coequal of the Supreme Court, which administers the affairs of courts and the Ministry of Justice, which supervises prosecutors.

The second principle, raising the status of lawyers to that of judges and prosecutors, is recognized in the Organic Law of Courts and the law establishing the National Law Examination. The new Organic Law departed from the practice of the old law by making lawyers eligible for appointment to the bench. Judges are now appointed from among judges of lower-level courts and prosecutors as well as attorneys (and law professors) with a stipulated number of years of experience in legal practice or teaching. In an effort to achieve uniform qualification among the three branches of the legal profession, the National Law Examination Law established a single system of examination for testing 'the legal knowledge and the ability to apply such knowledge' of all three groups. Further, everyone who passes the National Law Examination is required by the new Organic Law to receive two years of practical training at the Legal Training and Research Institute under the general supervision of the Supreme Court. Nearly 40 years after the implementation of the new Lawyers Law and the National Law Examination Law, virtually all Japanese lawyers, judges, and prosecutors are products of the same examination and the same process of training. The principle of *Hoso Ichigen* (uniformity of the three branches of the legal profession) is now a reality.

II. The Examination

A. Supervisory Commission

The Ministry of Justice is authorised to appoint a supervisory commission charged with the overall responsibility of supervising the administration of the examination. Although the commission has broad authority to resolve problems arising from the management of the examination, its most important function is to nominate examiners from among law professors as well as members of the three branches of the legal profession. The examiners (in 1984 there were 92 of them) compose and grade the tests and collectively determine who passes. To minimize the chance of undue outside influence, their appointment is limited to a single examination. All examiners are paid for their services, with 23,956 applicants in 1984, each examiner graded an average of 220 tests.

B. Eligibility of Applicants

The examination is divided into two parts. The first part, in essence a qualifying test, may be taken by anyone without regard to age or educational background. Applicants are tested only on the subjects normally found in the first and second years of a college curriculum. Those who pass are allowed to take the second part of the examination. Several categories of persons, however, are exempted from the first part of the examination, and only a small number of those required to take the first part ultimately pass the main examination.

C. Methods, Subjects, Times, and Places

In the second part of the examination, applicants take both written and oral tests. The written portion consists of multiple choice and essay questions. The multiple choice examination is given in May, and covers constitutional law and the civil and criminal codes. The essay examination (for the 10–20% who pass the multiple choice examination) is held for four days in July and covers constitutional law, the civil, commercial, and criminal codes, and either civil or criminal procedure as selected by the candidate. In addition, candidates must choose one subject from each of two other lists: (1) civil or criminal procedure (whichever was not chosen earlier), administrative law, bankruptcy, labor law, public or private international law, or criminal policy; and (2) political science, principles of economics, public finance, accounting, psychology, economic policy, or social policy.

As can be seen, the examination covers both a broader and narrower range of subjects than bar examinations in the United States. The examination in Japan is designed essentially to test the knowledge in basic areas: constitution law and the civil, commercial, and criminal codes. All other subjects are elective. Evidence and such areas as taxation, commercial paper, secured transaction, trusts, wills, and other areas covered by bar examinations in the United States are conspicuous by their absence. Evidence and other 'practice' oriented areas are studied in the Legal Training and Research Institute by those who pass the examination. All applicants are required to elect a liberal arts subject in part because almost all participants in the examination have only an undergraduate-level education, and because the examiners recognize that a good legal education is grounded in a good liberal education.

The oral examination, open to those who pass the essay examination, is held in Tokyo during a ten-day period in late September and early October. It covers the four basic areas and the same three subjects the candidates elected for the essay examination. The examiners, in teams of two, take turn quizzing applicants for fifteen to twenty minutes on each of the seven areas. The applicant is expected to respond instantly and accurately to each question. The oral examination has the reputation of being an exhausting experience.

D. Admitting No More Than Five Hundred

From the perspective of American lawyers, the most striking feature of the process is the apparently deliberate effort to limit the number of successful applicants to approximately five hundred. Although there is no explicit provision of law limiting the number, the practice of the last thirty years has established the ceiling as the widely understood unwritten rule. Some believe that such a limitation is necessary because of the limited capacity of the Legal Training and Research Institute. Others attribute it to the pressure of the Japan Federation of Bar Associations. Still others express genuine concern that to allow the number to increase would mean reducing the quality of the legal profession. The director of the Legal Training and Research Institute said in 1980: 'To increase the number (of trainees) means commercialization of legal training.'

... the multiple choice examination prevents between 80–90% of the applicants from taking the essay examination which, in turn, further disqualifies more than 80% of the remaining applicants from taking part in the oral examination. Thus, after the essay examination is completed, the number of the successful applicants dwindles to slightly more than five hundred or, as has been the case in recent years, somewhat below five hundred. In contrast, only a handful of applicants fail the oral examination, making it statistically the easiest part of the three-part examination. The limitation goal is further aided by a rule that applicants who pass the multiple choice but fail the essay portion must retake both examinations if they wish to try the examination again. In contrast, an applicant who passes both the multiple choice and essay parts but fails the oral examination may take the oral examination again the following year without retaking the other two ...

...

Selecting a University

Of the 457 four-year colleges and universities in Japan in 1984, seventy-six have a faculty of law (either as an independent unit or as a joint entity in combination with a cognate discipline, such as economics or literature). Because of the sharp disparity in the success rates of bar applicants from different schools, students in Japan who are serious about practicing law seek admission to schools with a high pass rate on the examination. (With fewer than 2% of the applicants passing, of course, no school has a high pass rate in American terms.) Table 4 lists the 15 universities with more successful applicants than other universities during the 10 year period starting in 1975. They are listed in order of the number of successful applicants from each of the schools in 1984.

TABLE 4

Successful Applicants Categorized by University Affiliation 1975–1984

	1975	1976	1977	1978	1979	1980	1981	1982	1983	1984
Tokyo (N)*	108	101	88	94	90	89	101	78	83	102
Chuo	77	69	71	87	83	86	58	90	63	84
Waseda	52	45	58	68	75	61	56	72	88	76
Kyoto (N)	42	48	28	33	44	42	44	29	36	25
Keio	13	15	19	27	31	28	19	31	23	24
Meiji	19	12	20	16	23	17	12	15	8	18
Hitotsubashi (N)	16	13	15	16	18	7	17	20	17	16
Kyushu (N)	11	7	11	15	12	9	6	6	10	15
Osaka (N)	16	13	16	11	11	13	13	14	13	10
Soka	2	1	2	3	2	2	3	5	3	9
Ritsumeikan	5	5	7	7	9	7	6	4	4	8
Nagoya (N)	10	10	7	9	11	10	9	12	12	6
Kobe (N)	5	5	5	5	5	6	8	5	3	4
Osaka (M)**	11	7	6	8	12	6	7	7	3	4
Doshisha	8	5	4	2	6	8	7	5	4	3
Others	77	109	108	74	71	95	80	64	47	49
Total	472	465	465	485	503	486	446	457	448	453

*(N) denotes national university

**(M) denotes municipal university

Source: Mimeographed leaflets distributed by the Ministry of Justice, 1985

In 1984 more than 89% of successful applicants were affiliated with the fifteen universities. The success of the top three universities, Tokyo, Chuo, and Waseda, is striking. Their applicants accounted for nearly 58% of the total, and their record as 'the top three' is consistent. In contrast, the share of 'others' in 1984 was less than 11%, and their share had declined steadily since 1975. More than one half of all university law faculties have apparently never been successful in helping a student or a graduate to pass the examination.

The message is clear. High school graduates who want careers in the legal profession have a better chance of success if these gain admission to one of the 'top three' or at least to one of the fifteen it is not easy. Every year tens of thousands of bright and ambitious high-school graduates compete by means of entrance examinations in an effort to secure admission to one of the choice university law faculties. Many of those who fail remain as *ronin* for a year or more (*ronin* is the Japanese term for masterless warriors of feudal times awaiting employment), waiting to try again for admission to one of the choice universities rather than seeking admission elsewhere.

C Purposes of Legal Education

What, then, is the purpose of legal education in Japan, especially for those law faculties not listed in Table 4? (Could an American law school justify its *raison d'être* if none of its graduates pass a bar examination?) Preparing students to practice law, of course, is not the exclusive purpose of any of the law faculties in Japan. Their principal purpose is to provide a general background in law for students who seek careers in government, international organizations, or industry. In 1979 in an opinion poll conducted among

2,329 law professors and other professionals, some 70% expressed the view that the purpose of the legal education at the university level should be to 'provide our future citizens ... with general legal culture.' Only about 15% insisted that it should be aimed at educating specialists for the legal profession. In fact, most students admitted to the law faculty of various universities have no intention of taking the examination. They want a BA in Law in order to help them find a job in civil service or private corporations. In an average year, only one-seventh of the 37,000 or so law graduates take the examination.

The problem facing the law faculty is how to educate a large number of students who lack a professional orientation while simultaneously providing a professional education to the one seventh who wish to take the examination. The answer lies in the creation of two curricula: one required of all and an additional (extracurricular) one for those who wish to pass the examination. The latter group must carry both curricula at the same time.

D Educational Programs at Tokyo, Chuo, and Waseda Universities

1. Degree Programs

Founded in 1869 as a part of Kaisei Gakko, a school of Western learning, the Faculty of Law of the University of Tokyo has the longest tradition in Japan and enjoys broad recognition as the best law faculty in the country. It is divided into three divisions: Private Law, Public Law, and Political Science. Each offers its own curriculum. Students who wish to prepare for the examination are enrolled in the private law division, which offers all the courses covered by the examination. A student must accumulate a minimum of ninety credits of specialized courses to graduate (in addition to a minimum of fifty-four credits of general education courses).

At Tokyo all students are required to spend the first two years (four semesters) attending the College of General Education located on a separate campus. During the first three semesters they take nothing but general education courses. In the fourth semester they are permitted to take up to two subject-matter law courses. At the end of the fourth semester, they transfer to the main campus, at which they are officially recognized as the students of the Faculty of Law.

Tokyo's policy of compelling its students to complete all required general education courses before allowing them to take law courses is based on the conviction that a good legal education can only be built on the foundation of a good liberal arts education. It means, however, that students must complete the bulk of the ninety credits of specialized courses in the two years before their graduation. Students are advised not to regard the aim of their education as mere preparation for the examination.

Chuo University was founded in 1885 as 'The English Law School' and was authorised to become a university in 1949, A mammoth private university today, as of April 1984 its Faculty of Law had 306 members and a student body of 7,616, including 1,800 evening students. It has law and political science divisions, each offering a separate curriculum. In the Division of Law, a minimum of 132 credits, including 44 credits of general education courses, are required to graduate.

There are no required courses. Students, however, must earn credits in six groups of specialized courses to meet the graduation requirements. Nor is there a requirement that specific courses be taken in a specific year. Thus at Chuo, students who intend to take the examination have the flexibility to mold their own programs to fit the needs for both a college degree and preparation for the examination. By postponing some of the general education courses and by focusing on courses covered by the examination, they can concentrate on study programs outside the regular curriculum. In contrast with Tokyo, Chuo openly acknowledges that preparing students for the examination is an important goal.

Waseda University, founded in 1889 by the famed statesman, Okuma Shigenobu, enjoys the reputation of being one of the best private universities of Japan. Its Faculty of Law has a long distinguished history of devotion to legal education. Unlike Tokyo and Chuo, Waseda's Faculty of Law is not subdivided. All subjects related to political science are taught under a separate Faculty of Political Science and Economics. The Faculty of Law, therefore, has a single curriculum. It requires a minimum of 160 credits for graduation, with not less than 48 nor more than 64 credits of general education courses. Unlike Chuo, Waseda requires its students to take a fixed number of designated courses in each of the four years. Electives are chosen within the maximum number of credits allowed for each year. Further, students must complete all required general education courses in the initial two years. Unlike Tokyo, however, they are allowed to take up to two specialized law courses during their first year, which eases somewhat for them the tension their counterparts at Tokyo experience in their last two years.

At all three universities, the credit system approximates that in the United States, ie one credit represents one hour of class every week for 15 weeks and two credits are given for a course meeting two hours (which customarily means ninety minutes) per week for 15 weeks.

2. Extracurricular Study Programs (Bar Reviews)

With the exception of Tokyo, most universities included in Table 4 provide extracurricular study programs designed to help students prepare for the examination. Normally the programs consist of a series of lectures, seminars, and trial examinations held in the evenings. Students pay additional fees but receive no credit toward graduation. In short, although courses taught under an extracurricular study program carry identical subject titles with those offered under the regular curriculum on the same campus, they are separate financially, administratively, and often in teaching personnel.

Tokyo takes a strong position against extracurricular study programs and insists that it is not a preparatory school for the National Law Examination. It declares that the aim of the legal education is to help students develop, through their knowledge of law, politics, and economics, an understanding of the totality of human life,' and to acquire decision-making ability based on such an integrated knowledge (as opposed to knowledge of law only, which Tokyo seems to fear students would seek under the pressure of preparation for the examination). It is argued that, in the final analysis, 'the shortest path to success in the examination is for students to study diligently the courses provided in the regular curriculum based on the true understanding of the aim of the legal education. As a result, however, many Tokyo students seek extracurricular assistance from privately operated review schools, often paying fees higher than the tuition they pay to their university.

Chuo and Waseda are more pragmatic. They view preparing students for the examination as an important goal of legal education. A key to ultimate success on the examination is seen as early exposure of students to specialized legal courses, even before the completion of general education courses. Many students opt to attend Chuo or Waseda because of the opportunity to participate in the extracurricular study programs. Because they are private universities, Chuo and Waseda probably feel less restricted than

Tokyo by a Ministry of Education requirement that students complete their general education courses within the first two years of a university curriculum ...

...

IV. Post-examination Training

The most immediate reward for passing the examination is automatic admission to the Legal Training and Research Institute in Tokyo. Upon admission students attain the status of 'legal apprentice' and are entitled to a monthly stipend equal to the salary of first-year civil servants fresh out of a university. They also receive family support and are barred from taking a concurrent position in the government or engaging in any profit-generating enterprise.

The Institute, established in 1947, is an agency of the Supreme Court of Japan and has a faculty consisting of experienced judges, prosecutors, and practicing attorneys. The judges and prosecutors are employed as full-time teachers, while attorneys serve part time. The Institute is Japan's one-and-only agency of its kind and, as such, it is sometimes referred to by American writers as 'Japan's only Law School'.

The training period is divided into three terms: initial (four months), field or clinical (sixteen months), and final (four months). During the first and final four months, all apprentices attend classes at the Institute. During the intervening sixteen months, they are assigned for eight months to the civil and criminal sections of various district courts, and for four months each to district prosecutors' offices and to offices of the selected practicing attorneys. After completing the two-year training period, the apprentices are subjected to another round of examinations, both written and oral. Few fail, however, and those who do are permitted to retake the examinations after staying at the Institute for another year.

After completing the examinations. apprentices have the choice, depending on available vacancies, of becoming assistant judges or assistant prosecutors, or registering as practicing attorneys. In recent years, as shown in Table 6, most opt to become practicing attorneys. The favoring of private practice is a reversal – before the Second World War judges and prosecutors were viewed as holding the choice positions – that has caused a shortage of judges and public prosecutors.

TABLE 6

Career Choices of the Legal Apprentices Legal Training and Research Institute, 1980–1985

Year	Graduates	Judges	Prosecutors	Attorneys	Others
1980	454	64	50	336	4
1981	484	61	39	378	6
1982	499	62	53	383	1
1983	483	58	53	370	2
1984	436	58	50	325	3
1985	444	52	49	337	6

Source: Statistics prepared by Department of Personnel Affairs, Ministry of Justice, 1985

The requirement since 1947 that all judges, prosecutors, and attorneys take the same examination and undergo the same training is credited with improving the image of attorneys. The Institute has been the sole supplier of personnel to the Japanese legal profession since 1947. In 1961 more than 30% of the entire legal profession was reported to be comprised of Institute graduates; the number grew to 77% in 1979 and 84% in 1983.

At present, virtually the entire profession is composed of persons trained at the Institute.

V. Conclusion

The National Law Examination is more than a competency test. It is, in essence, the entrance examination to the Institute, which limits its capacity to five hundred persons. Inevitably, the examination process deliberately fails thousands of well-qualified applicants who almost certainly have the capacity to be productive, able members of the legal profession. It is a waste of talent for people to study the same subjects over again (as many as four or five times) in what is usually a futile attempt to gain entry into the profession. The process clearly is exceedingly painful for the applicants, a heavy financial burden on their families, and a loss of human talent for the entire society. There can be no relief as long as completion of the Institute course remains the sole method of entering the profession.

A proposal is reportedly being considered to restrict to two or three the number of times students will be permitted to take the examination. The rationale is that the government should put an end to the vain hope of so many repeat applicants and force them to seek careers in other professions. Although adoption of the proposal would permit applicants to get on with their lives, it would perpetuate a system that makes less than optimal use of the talents of many in Japanese society.

The highly selective examination has important international ramifications. Japan has the lowest lawyer/population ratio among all the industrialized nations of the world. In 1979, for example, Japan had an attorney for every 9,970 persons, while the number for France was 6,263; West Germany, 1,970; Italy, 1,448; Britain, 1,398; and the United States, 531. Although cultural reasons may explain Japan's apparent lack of need for as many lawyers as other industrialized nations, it cannot be denied that the examination process has contributed directly to the disparity.

Although there may be enough Japanese lawyers (12,000 in 1985) to serve her own population (115 million), there are too few to serve adequately Japan's ever-expanding foreign trade. Moreover, there are few Japanese lawyers trained in international business transaction, and fewer still who comprehend English well enough to assist foreign merchants. But until April 1987, foreign lawyers were prohibited from practicing law in Japan unless they were licensed to do so by the Ministry of Justice (which means that they must pass the examination and undertake two years of training at the Institute).

The enactment of Foreign Lawyers Law in the spring of 1987 appears to have solved the shortage of competent lawyers for foreigners in Japan by allowing foreign lawyers to advise on foreign laws. But what Japan needs is more of its own lawyers competent to give advice to foreign merchants on Japanese laws as well as to its own merchants on foreign laws.

Japan is now the second largest economic power in the noncommunist world. In the past ten or so years, Tokyo has become a major international trade center with a large number of foreign corporations engaged in joint ventures. The Japanese themselves have also experienced various effects of rapid industrialization and urbanization and have been profoundly affected by the swift introduction of the Western way of life. It is likely that these changes have created the need for a greater number of lawyers in Japan. Some serious consideration should be given to a very substantial modification of the current examination system to accommodate the needs of Japanese society, both domestic and international.

Feldman, E, 'Mirroring Minds: Recruitment and Promotion in Japan's Law Faculties' (1993) 41 *American Journal of Comparative Law* 466–74

II. AN OVERVIEW OF LAW FACULTIES IN JAPAN

Universities in Japan are both public and private, with public being further divided between the imperial institutions, operational prior to the Second World War, and national, what were once known as primarily as technical schools. Every imperial university maintains a law faculty, but there are some national universities in which law teaching is subsumed under the Faculty of Economics or another faculty. While some of these schools would like to have separate legal departments (Chiba and Yokohama, for example), they are tightly controlled by the Ministry of Education, and are unable to amass the necessary funding and administrative largesse.

The remainder of the more than 100 law faculties, most with at least 500 students, are private. These are roughly divisible between older, elite institutions and newer, less prestigious ones. Most private universities with well-respected law faculties, such as Keio, Waseda, Meiji, Chuo and Hosei, were founded in the late nineteenth and early twentieth centuries, when Japan was ending several hundred years of isolation and following the Meiji Restoration. Legal codes were being rewritten, and Japanese scholars were returning from Europe advocating various approaches to the law. Chuo University was started as a school for English law, Hosei and Meiji for French law, with other schools also reflecting the learning and inclinations of their founders.

In addition to law faculties that exist as academic departments at four-year universities, there is one school that oversees the education of all practicing attorneys, judges, and prosecutors. It is the Legal Training and Research Institute, under the control of the Supreme Court and fully funded by the government. The Institute, started during the American Occupation of Japan (1945–52), was founded on the day the postwar constitution became effective. It provides two years of training to the approximately 2.7% of 23,000 people who pass the National Jurist Exam each year. Divided between classroom and clinical work, the curriculum fosters a strong sense of cohesion between students, who spend both their study and leisure time with their classmates. This camaraderie carries over to the cozy relationship between attorneys, judges, and prosecutors, though relations between these groups are often tense.

Selected by the Supreme Court from among practicing professionals, instructors at the institute generally serve for only three or four years. They may be fired at any time by the court but seem to require little disciplining. Since the Institute is in the business of producing practitioners, not academics, and the faculty is rotated on a regular basis, it is an exception to the system of recruitment and promotion at university law faculties.

While there is room to argue the merits and flaws of particular Japanese universities, there is no disagreement as to which one is the most desirable and difficult to enter, provides the greatest professional options after graduation, and offers the most prestigious teaching positions. The University of Tokyo, known by its Japanese abbreviation '*Todai*,' holds a firm place at the top of the academic hierarchy. *Todai's* faculties of literature, medicine, engineering, and others are considered the nation's best, but the Faculty of Law is in a class by itself. Its graduates dominate the upper echelons of the corporate hierarchy, inhabit the world of the political elite, and make up the core of the administrative authorities who operate Japan's bureaucratic agencies.

Of the 24 recent graduates to enter the elite track at the Ministry of Finance this year, for example, 22 were from *Todai*. Other powerful ministries, such as the Ministry of International Trade and Industry the Ministry of Posts and Telecommunications, and the National Police Agency also recruit a disproportionate number of *Todai* law graduates. Former Prime Minister Kiichi Miyazawa, *Todai* class of 1941, suggested that the number of elite government jobs open to *Todai* law graduates be limited to 50%, exclaiming that 'a healthy society has a variety of values'. Not surprisingly, the reaction of senior officials at the ministries, also *Todai* graduates, amounted to the Japanese equivalent of 'who does that guy think he is, anyway?' If change is on the way at all, it will not come quickly.

III. BECOMING A LAW FACULTY PROFESSOR: *JYOSHU*

A student who is interested in teaching at a top law faculty must first endure what is known as 'examination hell,' the period when high school students sit the exams required for entrance to the school of their choice. There are far more applicants than openings at high quality universities, and students intent on studying at a particular place must often re-take the exam over a period of many years. Such students are known as *ronin*, a word formerly used to describe masterless samurai who roamed the countryside of feudal Japan in search of lords to employ them. Since the rank of one's university determines one's future possibilities, the exams are taken very seriously, and there are annual reports of suicides by students who failed.

Students hoping to teach know that where they gain admittance is critical to where they may eventually work. Of the 54 full time teaching staff members of *Todai's* faculty of law, for example, 49 of them are University of Tokyo graduates. The numbers are similar at Kyoto, Keio and other top universities. Other sorts of diversity are also lacking – *Todai* has only one woman professor and just one who was not born a Japanese citizen – and the appointments of both were controversial. American-style discussions of faculty diversity are completely unknown.

In stark contrast to examination hell is the work that is expected once one is matriculating. Professors and students alike view the four years of education as a resting period between the competitive high school years and a career. Everyone is expected to pass, even students who miss every lecture and put in a mediocre performance on the final exam. Students admitted to a faculty of law will spend their entire first year, and a significant part of their second, in general education courses. This limits their study of law to between two and three years, during which students are divided among the public law, private law, and political science departments of the law faculty. Large lecture classes are the norm, case analysis is rare, and student participation is minimal. This system has been criticized by some law professors because it results in graduates who are not well schooled in the law. But as one expert on the legal system has pointed out, 'most law students only seek a degree that will assure them of a good position and are not much concerned with an appropriate knowledge of law, [so] it would be difficult to require them to do any extensive professional training'. Those who are interested in learning more details of the law must enter graduate school or become trainees at the Legal Training and Research Institute.

It is during the third or fourth year of one's undergraduate years, when many are fully enjoying the leisure life of the university, that the critical match of professor and student occurs. Students interested in teaching careers must do somewhat better than their peers, with a high percentage of 'A' grades necessary to demonstrate academic promise. Such students will attend seminars in their field of interest, sometimes conducted by a professor with whom they hope to link their future. But most frequently it is the professor who must survey the students in a seminar in search of an able successor. If a suitable candidate is found, the professor will discuss with him (again, rarely her) the possibility of becoming a *jyoshu*. *Jyoshu* is written with two Chinese characters, one meaning help or rescue, the other hand or arm. It is usually translated as assistant, though 'right-hand man' better captures the nuance of the professional and personal closeness to the professor.

There are no written requirements outlining the necessary qualities of a *jyoshu*, but a student's analytical skills carry some weight. Beyond the threshold requirement of good grades, personal and social skills become critical. They are summarized by one professor as 'the need to be easy-going, to be at peace with others, the ability to discuss issues in friendly terms, and a willingness to listen to the ideas of other people.'

One difficulty immediately encountered by many faculty members is the possibility that students with whom they hope to pair are more interested in other career options. Teaching at a top university is an attractive life, but no more so than working at an elite ministry, which holds great social status, or taking a job with a prominent corporation, which promises a lucrative salary. Professors therefore must sometimes use their power, or at least their power of persuasion, to convince top candidates to accept the position of researcher, and still many of those considered prime for the job are lost.

Once a suitable candidate is identified and expresses interest in the *jyoshu* post, the formal procedure begins. The host professor must attend a faculty meeting at which an application from the candidate is presented, a short written paper is sometimes submitted, and a five member faculty selection committee is appointed. Unless the candidate makes an unimaginable mess of the interview – a situation no one I spoke to could recall – he will be approved.

Those who accept the position of *jyoshu* are committed to spending three years as civil servants in the case of public universities, or as university employees in the case of private ones. Formally, they are required to write a lengthy thesis on a topic selected by, or at least approved by, their professor. Other duties may include helping the professor in applying for grants and designing budgets, auditing and lending assistance in the professor's seminar, making copies or going to the post office, and doing whatever else is necessary to fulfill the role of apprentice.

By most accounts, the *jyoshu* is not abused or neglected, but is rather taken under the wing of the professor and expected to emulate his professional and personal being. Professors must nurture and coddle them, for they will eventually grow into a sort of mirror image of the teacher himself. This means that the *jyoshu* must be prepared to surrender a great deal of privacy, because even intimate aspects of life are fair game for the attention of the professor. During evenings of eating and drinking together, the bonds between apprentice and master will be strengthened, as intimacies are shared and the secrets of academic life are revealed.

There are other pleasures in the life of a *jyoshu*. One has plenty of time to read, think, or just relax, without the responsibility of having a demanding full-time job within or outside the university. Some professors will make efforts to include the *jyoshu* in research meetings, study trips, and other professional activities, which can be intellectually stimulating and lead to important professional contacts. And a close relationship with a professor, if that professor is competent and willing to share his information, can be a good entry into the academic world.

Because professors exert a powerful influence in persuading students to become *jyoshu*, they feel a strong sense of responsibility in ensuring the *jyoshu* find suitable employment. This means that as the three-year research period draws to a close, the professor will begin to search for suitable employment for his charge, largely without regard to the completion of the *jyoshu's* thesis. The job being sought is that of assistant professor (or lecturer), an appointment that carries job security and ensures a long, though not necessarily fruitful, career in academia.

Those fortunate enough to come of age at a time when there is a faculty opening may remain at the school where they were undergraduates and *jyoshu*. The majority, however, will be sent to other universities, which announce they are looking for professors by quietly informing those privy to the 'grapevine'. Mentors respond by advocating for the job candidate they feel is most qualified, inevitably their *jyoshu*. The most powerful professor from the most prestigious university wins, and his protégé will take up residence at the school of the mentor's choice without having been interviewed or scrutinized in any systematic way – no job talk, no one-on-one interviews, no teaching observation. If written work is requested at all, it is used only retrospectively by the hiring committee to justify the appointment to the rest of the faculty.

Recently, some faculties of law with job openings have begun to make posters announcing vacant positions. But these are just a token bow towards egalitarianism, since there is little intention of actually finding an employee in this manner. Even the most naive aspiring professor knows that it would be fruitless, no less inappropriate, to rely on such an advertisement, and that if one's professor does not have the necessary contacts, a job offer will never be made.

Academic job candidates have some, but very little, input into where they will be employed. After putting in time teaching at a university where they did not study, those considered most desirable will sometimes be invited to return to their home faculties, where they will be in the company of other professors who followed an almost identical career path. Some prestigious universities that produce more professors than can be rehired colonize other law faculties. For example, Rikkyo and Nagoya Universities are dominated by University of Tokyo graduates who were not 'called home'.

Having been selected to complement a professor at age 23, and living in the shadow of that professor for three years, a *jyoshu* will have become a lifetime employee of Japan's legal academy at 26, and the seeker of a new generation to match the intellectual and personal qualities that have been so handsomely rewarded.

IV. BECOMING A LAW FACULTY PROFESSOR: GRADUATE STUDENTS

While entering academia after being a *jyoshu*, particularly at *Todai*, is considered the most elite route, there is an increasing number of people who become academics after pursuing graduate studies. One reason for this is that the *jyoshu* system is most common at places long devoted to producing legal scholars. Many other universities with excellent law departments do not have a *jyoshu* system, or they use the budget allotted to hiring entry-level staff for administrative assistants (*jimu jyoshu*) rather than researchers (*kenkyu jyoshu*). In addition, there are some students who, despite their wishes, are not selected as *jyoshu*, but have strong enough academic backgrounds to enter graduate school.

Most graduate students remain at their undergraduate institutions. At *Todai*, for example, more than 90% of law graduate students were law faculty undergraduates in most years. All prospective graduate students are required to pass a difficult examination, though being graduated from the undergraduate program and making oneself known to the faculty may increase one's chances of admission because the examination is written by professors from the department. Everyone who enrolls in graduate school must enter as either a two-year MA (*shushi*) or five-year PhD (*hakushi*) candidate, except in those institution that only have PhD programs. Degree candidates are required to pursue a mix of coursework and research like that of many other systems.

Occasionally, exceptional graduate students will be rescued from their studies by an offer to become researchers (*jyoshu*) for three years when they complete their Masters degrees. The selection process of such students is similar to that of choosing undergraduate *jyoshu*. However, their status is somewhat lower, and they are designated as graduate student researchers (*daigakuin sotsugyo jyoshu*, or *insotsu jyoshu*) in contrast to those recruited directly after completing undergraduate studies (*gakubu sotsugyo jyoshu*, or *gakusotsu jyoshu*). Nonetheless, such students form strong bonds with their mentors and generally find a job with an ease similar to that of undergraduate *jyoshu*.

Other graduate students will be left to toil over their studies. Workloads vary depending upon the field of study, with constitutional law considered a difficult field and international law a relatively easy one. Some will actually finish their PhD dissertations before finding a job, a distinction that makes them the most well-educated and least valued people on the job market. Others will decide, or rather their professors will decide, that they have had enough of graduate school before their dissertations are completed, or even started. This will generally occur after two or three years of study in the PhD program, once all course requirements are satisfied and perhaps a publication or two has appeared. Suitable employment will then be found by the same word-of-mouth fashion as was used to place *jyoshu*. Particularly motivated professors can submit their dissertations within several years of leaving the program, but given that a job has been secured, the value of the PhD degree will be purely ornamental, and many never file.

For both *jyoshu* and graduate students, the relationship with their professor is the most important determinant of their future careers. The professor functions as a teacher, role model, employment agency, parent, inspiration, and source of status, but will never become a colleague. The word used to address one's professor, *sensei*, translates not only as teacher/master, but also functions as a general term of respect used by those of inferior social status to address a superior. No matter how successful and influential one becomes, *sensei* remains *sensei* forever. In turn, the professor will do everything he can to ensure that his disciples enjoy rewarding careers.

There are two critical differences between *jyoshu* and graduate students with regard to their employability in Japanese law faculties. One is that graduate students, because they must attend numerous seminars and write longer theses than *jyoshu*, are more easily evaluated for future academic promise and better prepared as researchers. The other is that the allegiance of professors rests squarely with *jyoshu*, and hiring committees internalize this mentality by viewing *jyoshu* as the top job candidates. This is most acutely true in departments that have a supply of both types of candidates. But even when universities without *jyoshu* are hiring, and where ties between graduate students and teachers are similar to those between *jyoshu* and teacher, there remains a bias that *jyoshu* have higher status and are more attractive job candidates than graduate students. Consequently, while there may be parallel tracks for entering law department faculties, the rails ridden by *jyoshu* are markedly more swift.

Still, finding a job after graduate school may not be remembered as one of life's most challenging tasks. One former graduate student, whose PhD thesis would remain incomplete for several years, describes receiving a letter from his advisor while studying abroad that informed him that he had been recommended for a job. An interview was set up in Tokyo, which turned out to be a friendly chat with the hiring professor that did not once drift into talk about the law. The decision to make him a job offer was finalized, a resumé and writing samples were requested to pass around at the next faculty meeting, and the process was quickly concluded. In this case, the department relied on a well-respected professor to suggest a job candidate, and was fortunate to have found a serious young scholar. But there are many instances when the results are not as encouraging, and amiable but mediocre candidates are offered jobs based exclusively on personal connections, to the exclusion of less personable but more talented researchers.

III THE MODERN LEGAL PROFESSION

(i) Legal professionals

Table 1

The Legal Profession in Japan 1995

Practising Lawyers	15,540
Public Prosecutors	2,092
Judges	2,864

Judges of the Supreme Court	15
Presidents of the High Courts	8
High Court & District Judges	1,385
Assistant Judges	650
Summary Court Judges	806
Total	2,864

Source: Supreme Court of Japan

Table 2

Pass Rate for the National Law Exam in Japan

Year	Persons Taking	Persons Passing	Pass Rate
1949	2,514	265	10.5
1950	2,755	269	9.8
1951	3,648	272	7.5
1952	4,765	253	5.3
1953	5,141	224	4.4
1954	5,172	250	4.8
1955	6,306	264	4.2
1956	6,714	297	4.4
1957	6,920	286	4.1
1958	7,074	346	4.9
1959	7,819	319	4.1
1960	8,302	345	4.2
1961	10,921	380	3.5
1962	10,802	459	4.2
1963	11,725	456	3.9
1964	12,728	508	4.0
1965	13,681	528	3.9
1966	14,867	554	3.7
1967	16,460	537	3.3
1968	17,727	525	3.0
1969	18,453	501	2.7
1970	20,160	507	2.5
1971	22,336	533	2.4
1972	23,425	537	2.3
1973	25,259	537	2.1
1974	26,622	491	1.8
1975	27,791	472	1.7
1976	29,088	465	1.6
1977	29,214	465	1.6
1978	29,390	485	1.7
1979	28,622	503	1.8
1980	28,656	486	1.7
1981	27,816	446	1.6
1982	26,317	457	1.7
1983	25,138	448	1.8

Source: The Legal Training and Research Institute of Japan, Supreme Court of Japan (1984)

Table 3

Number of Adopters and Graduates

Adopted Year	Number of the Admitted	Graduation Year	Number of Graduates
1984	451	1986	450
1985	450	1987	448
1986	482	1988	482
1987	473	1989	470
1988	492	1990	489
1989	511	1991	506
1990	509	1992	508
1991	507	1993	506
1992	596	1994	594
1993	635	1995	633
1994	703		
1995	724		

Source: Supreme Court of Japan, Tokyo

Table 4

Career Destination of the Legal Training and Research Institute Graduates

Year	Number of Graduates	Assistant Judges	Public Prosecutors	Practising Lawyers	Others
1949	134	72	44	18	–
1950	240	106	54	78	2
1951	284	84	77	113	10
1952	246	57	79	97	13
1953	215	51	67	84	13
1954	226	45	48	131	2
1955	236	67	59	109	1
1956	216	73	50	89	4
1957	267	77	45	143	2
1958	256	65	45	144	2
1959	282	69	51	157	5
1960	291	81	44	166	–
1961	349	84	48	216	1
1962	319	75	42	202	–
1963	334	88	40	202	4
1964	365	57	45	261	2
1965	441	72	52	316	1

Table 4 continued

1966	478	66	47	359	6
1967	484	73	49	356	6
1968	511	85	49	369	8
1969	516	84	53	374	5
1970	512	64	38	405	5
1971	506	65	47	388	6
1972	495	58	59	370	8
1973	493	66	50	371	6
1974	506	85	47	367	7
1975	543	84	38	416	5
1976	537	79	74	376	8
1977	487	72	50	363	2
1978	463	78	58	325	2
1979	465	64	49	350	2
1980	454	64	50	336	4
1981	484	61	38	378	7
1982	499	62	53	383	1
1983	483	58	53	370	2
1984	436	58	50	325	3
1985	444	52	49	337	6
1986	450	70	34	342	4
1987	448	62	37	347	2
1988	482	73	41	367	1
1989	470	58	51	360	1
1990	489	81	28	376	4
1991	506	96	46	359	5
1992	508	65	50	378	15
1993	506	98	49	356	3
1994	594	104	75	406	9
1995	633	99	86	438	10

Source: Supreme Court of Japan

Table 5

Ratio of Lawyers to Population in Six Countries

	POPULATION	JUDGES (Numbers in parentheses exclude Summary Court Judges & Justices of the Peace)	PROSECUTING ATTORNEYS	LAWYERS	Ratio of Population to Members of Legal Profession			
					JUDGES	PROSECUTORS	LAWYERS	ENTIRE LEGAL PROFN
JAPAN	1 15,174,000	2,731 (1,940)	2,092 (1,173 excluding Ass't Prosecutors)	11,552	42,173 (59,368)	55,054 (98,187)	9,970	7,034 (7,854)
US	218,100,000	Approx 45,000 (7,845)	Fed 1,513 State 8,739	424,980	4,847 (27,801)	21,274	513	454
UK	49,119,000	24,802 (819)		35,131	1,980 (59,974)		1,398	820
WEST GERM.	61,400,000	14,765	3,233	31,167	4,158	18,992	1,970	1,249
FRANCE	53,080,000	3,590	1,062	8,475	14,786	49,981	6,263	4,044
ITALY	49,904,000	5,739	993	34,461	8,696	50,256	1,448	1,211

This table is based on materials from the Supreme Court of Japan and was published in 700 Jurisuto 206

Ramsayer, J, 'Lawyers, Foreign Lawyers and Lawyer Substitutes: The Market for Regulation in Japan' (1986) 27 (Special Issue) *Harvard International Law Journal* 507–09, 513–15

THE JAPANESE LEGAL SERVICES INDUSTRY

A The Contours of the Cartel

Of all aspects of the regulatory program in the Japanese legal services industry, the entry barriers, advertising restrictions, and fee schedules potentially carry the most severe consequences. Among these three, perhaps the most Draconian are the barriers to entry. The government rather than the bar controls these barriers and prosecutes those who attempt to circumvent them.

One who aspires to join the bar in Japan generally majors in law as an undergraduate. He or she must then, however, be admitted to the Legal Training and Research Institute in Tokyo. The Institute operates as the sole law school in Japan and has consistently limited the number of entrants, and therefore the number of potential new lawyers, to about 500 per year. This it has done by maintaining the pass rate on the entrance examination at less than 2%. As a result, barely 12,500 lawyers practice in Japan while 620,000 practice in the United States. Except for the approximately 500 Tokyo attorneys who specialize in international business transactions, most of these lawyers spend the bulk of their time in litigation.

Although the government authorizes several categories of attorney-substitutes, it severely limits entry into these fields as well. Tax matters are often handled by tax agents or certified public accountants. Yet to become a tax agent, one must pass a battery of five tests for which the overall pass rate has been about 3–5%. In becoming a certified public accountant, one faces examinations with a combined pass rate of 4–6%. Consequently, there are scarcely 36,000 tax agents and 6,800 certified public accountants in Japan. Patent and trademark work may be done by patent agents. Yet these specialists have passed a special examination with a pass rate of less than 3%. As of 1982, there were only 2,430 patent agents in Japan. Two groups of personnel draft documents for clients to submit to courts and various administrative agencies. Generally called judicial and administrative scriveners, some apparently do the type of routine work that lawyers do in the United States, while others do work done by paralegals and skilled legal secretaries. Examinations, however, are ubiquitous. The pass rate for the judicial scrivener's examination is less than 3%, and for that of the administrative scriveners about 30%. Although in 1982 there were 14,800 judicial scriveners and 30,300 administrative scriveners, many scriveners were licensed under both categories.

Under the pretext of regulating ethics, the JFBA and local bar associations have established fee schedules and prohibited advertising. The schedules generally key attorney fees to the size of a litigated claim or the value of the property involved in a matter and are determined independently of any government agency. Tax agents, patent agents, judicial scriveners, and administrative scriveners have also promulgated fee schedules, but tax agents negotiate their schedules with the Ministry of Finance, patent agents with the Ministry of International Trade and Industry (MITI), and the scriveners with the Ministry of Justice. Whether any of these schedules are legal is another matter.

...

The crux of the problem is the apparent informational asymmetry in the legal services industry. Because legal services are inherently complex and infrequently purchased, consumers find it hard to judge their quality. Not only do they find it difficult to determine in advance the worth of the service they are about to purchase, they are often unable to judge its value afterward.

As a 'cure', the anticompetitive restraints in the Japanese legal services industry threaten to be more painful than the disease. A 98% failure rate on the Institute examination is a formidable entry barrier indeed. Advertising restrictions reduce rather than increase the information available to the public, and fee schedules simply make legal services less accessible. If informational asymmetry were a problem, one could solve it simply by providing more information. But in any case, the extent of the actual asymmetry is far from clear. Any asymmetry is partially self-correcting: sellers of high quality services have an incentive to demonstrate that quality to consumers and consumers have an incentive to search for information about quality. And lawyers develop reputations for high or low quality work. Those reputations, as a form of information, offset the asymmetry and enhance the ability of consumers to choose the quality of service they wish to purchase.

C. The Consequences of the Cartel

The regulatory scheme in the Japanese legal services industry thus constitutes a classic cartel: a framework for excluding competitive outsiders and charging monopoly prices. Japanese lawyers have not been unaware of this point. As former Supreme Court Chief Justice Takaaki Hattori noted, lawyers themselves often have opposed, or at least have been reluctant to see, an increase in the size of the bar for fear of 'excessive' competition. Unfortunately for those lawyers, the regulatory framework may not have enabled many of them to charge what its structure might otherwise suggest. This possible inability to capitalize on the cartel's potential derives from at least three sources: (a) institutional disincentives to the use of the courts, (b) the success of non-lawyer sellers of legal services, and (c) the ability of Japanese consumers to structure their transactions and to handle their disputes in ways that minimize the value of a lawyer's contribution.

The relation between attorney prices and these barriers to full exploitation of the cartel is straightforward. Institutional disincentives to litigation represent factors that reduce the marginal utility of the courts to disputants. In so doing, they reduce the demand for an attorney's services and reduce the price an attorney can successfully charge. If attorney-substitutes can perform the work of an attorney and consumers can fashion extralegal arrangements that replicate legal arrangements, these factors, too, prevent lawyers from raising their prices much above competitive levels.

Yonemoto, K, 'The Simane Bar Association: All Twenty-One Members Strong' (trans Daniel H Foote) (1995) 25 *Law in Japan* 117–19, 120–22

When there are few lawyers, what sorts of things happen?

What might be 'coincidence' in a big city turns into 'inevitability' in the country. For example, in a big city the same lawyer seldom comes into contact with the same judge But in Shimane, the same lawyers argue before the same judges day after day.

At the district court level, in the main district court in Matsue, there are a total of five judges in the civil and criminal divisions combined, apart from the chief judge; in the Hamada Branch there is only one judge. A total of six judges in the prefecture. In Izumo, and in the Saigo and Masuda Branches, there are no judges at all. When they conduct trials in those locations, judges go from Matsue to Izumo and Saigo, and from Hamada to Masuda. When the 18 lawyers go to court, they're bound to meet up with one of the six judges.

In fact, they meet more than that. That's because each attorney handles many cases. There are times when one attorney is handling a different trial before each of the six judges at the same time. It's only natural for attorneys to remark that, 'When I go to Matsue District Court, I meet all five judges there every day'. What's more, the one attorney in Masuda ends up arguing before the same judge all the time.

You'd think this might mean that they're all good friends, working together in a jovial atmosphere, sort of like children playing a game of judges and lawyers. But that doesn't seem to be the case.

'Back in the old days, we used to play mah-jongg together, but not any more. Although they didn't take place here in this prefecture, there were some scandals involving judges. Whether it was to maintain official discipline or not, I can't say, but thereafter judges stopped associating with lawyers and other non-judges.'

'They may be even more strict about that here than in large cities. This is a small town, and the chances of meeting a defendant somewhere around town are high. So it seems that the judges are following very prudent lifestyles. We hardly ever see them around town. They may drink sake at official gatherings, but they never attend the parties afterward (*nijikai*).'

Even if there aren't personal get-togethers, there are some good points to this situation. Ago continued his account:

'We know where the judges come from and what they're like. This is really beneficial. Because we don't have to speculate about what sort of judge they are. We understand how they'll approach cases. On top of that, they show understanding for the position we attorneys are in, and they are quite accommodating.

For example, in big cities there are often times when evidentiary investigation is cut off for very formalistic reasons. Here that doesn't happen. If you make a request for examination of evidence, the judges will grant it. They're more warmhearted (*yori ningenteki*).'

But there is also a downside to meeting every day. You can't get into quarrels with the judges. If you end one trial with bad feelings, they can easily carry over to the next one. And it goes further than that. The relationship is so close that, the day after a quarrel, you're bound to face the same judge in another case. It's not as though the judges and attorneys are in collusion, but the attorneys can't afford to get themselves worked up over little things. They have to take a more mature attitude. And the same goes for the judges.

Laughing Inside

The same attorneys sometimes represent the man in one divorce proceeding and the woman in another. They approach the cases differently and present different arguments, depending on which side they're on.

The same thing can happen in big cities, of course, but it occurs more frequently in the country. Moreover, in a place like Shimane, the odds are high that the attorney will have to present such contrasting arguments before the same judge. The judge is probably thinking, 'What's this? This attorney was just arguing for a man, but now he's taking the woman's side.' With a laugh, Ago said:

'I've got a good example for you.

The rule is that the blameworthy spouse cannot demand a divorce. In other words, if one spouse takes a lover, that spouse is not permitted to demand a divorce.

On the other hand, there are cases where the family unit has already weakened and the marital relationship has completely collapsed. One view is that divorce should be recognized in that situation. So, depending on the position of my client, sometimes I find myself arguing against divorce and other times arguing that the family had already collapsed. I can only imagine that the judge must be laughing inside.'

There are many situations where legal theories conflict – not just in divorce law. Thus, sometimes an attorney is arguing for a 'sword' (*hoko*), other times for a 'shield' (*tate*). It might seem that the lawyers have no integrity, no convictions. When you stop to think about it, though, this is their job. Lawyers are pros at representing clients. In big cities, some attorneys transcend the interests of their clients in staking out positions – by arguing, for example, for the rights of spouses to keep their own names; and some of them become the darlings of the mass media. In the city you might be able to make a living that way, but it won't work in the country. If all you do is talk about justice, the residents won't take you seriously. What they really want is a pro at representing their interests.

It's a common sight for one trial to end and the attorneys simply to switch places for the next one. In other words, the plaintiff's attorney moves over to the defense side for the next trial, and the defendant's attorney shifts to the plaintiff's side. The judge doesn't change, so the three main members are all the same. Only the plaintiff and defendant are different.

'So, I guess I move over there [for example, the plaintiff's side] this time, right?'

'Come to think of it, you do. You were tough on me last time, but I'm the defendant this time, so go easy on me, will you?'

The attorneys may never say these things aloud, but they have to be thinking similar thoughts. And if they ever did say such things aloud, it could only help give the public a feeling of greater familiarity with attorneys and the courts ...

Disputes in a Country Town

Fairly often, an attorney gets consulted by both parties in a case.

' Once, when I was listening to a client who came to consult about a divorce, I began thinking that I'd heard a similar story before. When I checked, I discovered that his wife had already come to consult me about the case. That sort of thing happens quite a lot.'

Naturally, the same attorney can't represent both sides, so it's not rare for the attorney to introduce the party that came in later to another attorney.

The attorney who moved to Masuda has requested anonymity, so I'll refer to him as Yoshida. Shortly after he arrived, he had the following experience:

'At a free legal aid clinic that I offered, a husband whose wife had been stolen away by another man came in. He asked what he could do to collect damages. Some time later, another man came to consult me at my office. This time it was a paying client. He'd received a claim for damages and wanted to know what he should do. When I asked the circumstances, I discovered that he was the man who'd stolen the wife.'

Free legal aid sessions undoubtedly are not unique to Shimane, but the number of times per attorney is very high there, with each attorney taking on sixteen or seventeen sessions each year. With only 18 practicing attorneys, they can't just stick their noses in the air and act haughty; and they all take their fair share of the burden.

In addition to the scarcity of lawyers, another reason for the frequency of the free consultation sessions is that the practice of visiting lawyers' offices has not yet caught on in Shimane. In past years, the functions now provided by attorneys were performed by, for example, the chief priest of the temple, the teacher at the school, or the officer at the local police station. Even today, that same atmosphere persists in some areas.

'When there's a dispute, I sometimes send a content-certified letter. In some of those cases, the head of the community will come to see me. He'll say that the village is in a tizzy because one of the residents got a letter from a lawyer. And he'll ask whether someone in the village did something so awful (*hidoi*) as to have to trouble an attorney. Since another one of the villagers delivers the mail, the word spreads right away. For that reason, some people request that, when I send letters, I not use an envelope that shows I'm an attorney. The same thing is true for summons sent by the courts.'

There's no custom of visiting a lawyer's office – just to be safe – whenever anything happens, so by the time someone comes in to consult a lawyer, the situation has become rather serious.

'Both sides have worried over the case and have thought hard about it. It's only when they can't come up with any other way of resolving it that they come to a lawyer. By then, though, the situation inevitably has gotten complicated', one lawyer commented.

Society is no longer so simple that a temple priest can resolve disputes, but it will still be a long time before the atmosphere will be such that people can readily consult with an attorney. This inevitably means that the soil remains fertile for the flourishing of fixers who help people settle their cases (*jidanya*). Times have changed enough that most such people no longer advertise their services publicly, with signs that make them sound like lawyers, but there is still one such person in Masuda.

The stated occupation of this man, whom I will call O, is money lending. When there is a dispute over a debt, O will himself lend the creditor money, and thus he will in effect take over the creditor's claim. Then he files suit. O doesn't use a lawyer, instead asserting his claims for repayment himself. Word has it that O is the plaintiff in half of the civil actions in the Masuda Branch District Court. This is a violation of the prohibition in the Lawyers Act against 'the business of obtaining the transfer to oneself of the rights of any other person and enforcing such rights' [s 73 of the Act]. Reportedly, one of O's claims was rejected on this basis in January of this year, and the police are said to be keeping an eye on him.

A Major Undertaking Just to Get Around

When there wasn't even a single attorney in Masuda, attorneys would go from Matsue and Izumo to cover. In civil cases, parties could request services from attorneys in the neighboring prefectures of Hiroshima or Yamaguchi, but that was not the case for state-appointed lawyers in criminal matters. That is because the prefectural bar association bears responsibility for such representation.

The overall national rate for representation by state-appointed counsel in district and summary courts is 65%; but in Shimane the rate is much higher, standing at 90%. Thus, when one talks about representation in criminal cases in Shimane, it is safe to assume that counsel is state-appointed.

At a minimum, there are three tasks that state-appointed counsel must perform: read the file in the case, meet the defendant who is being held in custody, and appear at trial.

Yet, as mentioned earlier, it's a long way from Matsue to Masuda – fully 100 miles ... By car, the round trip takes ten hours, and even by limited express train it takes three hours each way. By plane, using the airport in Izumo, one can get from Matsue to Tokyo in the same amount of time. To make it to Masuda by the early afternoon, one has to take either the 8 am or 10 am limited express. ... The last limited express of the day back to Matsue leaves at 4.30 pm. If you miss that, you have to take a regular train and won't make it back till after 10 pm. In other words, just getting to Masuda is a job in itself.

Furthermore, the rate of compensation for appointed counsel cases at the district court level is about ¥70,000. For that reason, attorneys are reluctant to do each of the three tasks mentioned above on separate days. To do so would be physically tiring, as well. Three round trips would amount to eighteen hours on a rolling train. The attorneys can't go two or three times, even if it's for meetings with the defendant.

'For that reason, while it depends on the nature of the case, we try to accomplish everything in one day. We read the file in the morning, then we meet with the defendant, and then in the afternoon we go in for the trial. It doesn't give you time to really think through the defense. I haven't ever received a complaint directly from a defendant, but I suspect that defendants harbor some resentment. After all, they've been confined and questioned for twenty days, and then the meeting with the defense counsel ends quickly. It's unfortunate, but there's an inevitable disparity between the work of appointed counsel for cases in Matsue and for cases in Masuda', said Ago.

The courts take into consideration both the amount of compensation and the time it takes for attorneys to get there.

'When a date has been fixed for a hearing in a civil case, the judge will ask whether I'd like to handle the trial of a criminal case in which I'm serving as appointed counsel on the same day.'

This doesn't mean that Ago and the others are shirking in their representation in appointed counsel cases. Shimane had a case of wrongful prosecution (in the case of the rape and murder of a young girl) and, despite prosecution demands for a life sentence, the defense bar fought the case in court for eight years and won an acquittal. That was in 1990. The victory resulted from the efforts of a team of five lawyers, but the starting point was Ago's appointment as state-appointed counsel.

(ii) The judiciary

Haley, JO, 'Judicial Independence in Japan Revisited' (1995) 25 *Law in Japan* 3–18

Historical themes

Japan's judiciary has almost from its inception been organized as a remarkably autonomous elite bureaucracy within the civil law tradition. In that tradition, as career government officials, judges neither enjoy the degree of individual autonomy nor the overtly political role of common law judges. They form a highly specialized, elite corps responsible for the administration of justice and the interpretation and enforcement of legislated rules. Without powers taken for granted in common law systems – such as equity and contempt – they depend far more on public confidence in their nonpartisan professionalism and expertise than their common law counterparts. Without juries they function under the burden of ultimate responsibility for determinations of fact and law in every case they decide. They are also subject to the predominant values of the civil law tradition, which include an emphasis on legal certainty and uniformity in the application of law. The result is greater caution and passivity in the exercise of judicial authority than their counterparts in the common law tradition.

By the late 19th century in Japan, judicial independence in terms of a separation of powers, insulation from intervention in the adjudication of particular cases, and the personal security of judges had been largely secured by constitution and statute. The 1889 constitution provided (Article 57) that the courts exercised their authority 'in the name of the emperor' (*tenno no na ni oite*), thereby insulating the courts from any direct political intervention in the adjudication of cases by either legislative or administrative organs. Like the military's plea that the 'supreme command' of the emperor precluded legislative or executive civilian control, the inscription 'in the name of the emperor,' placed prominently in all courtrooms, served as a meaningful reminder to imperial officials and subjects alike that the emperor's judges were not subject to political direction. The security of judges was also guaranteed under the express provisions of Article 58. Japan's first comprehensive court law, enacted pursuant to the constitution in 1890, established the structure of Japan's contemporary career judiciary. Judges were to be appointed by the emperor with life tenure. However, unless physically or mentally unable to carry out their duties or pursuant to a criminal conviction or disciplinary sanction, no judges could against their will be removed to a different office or court, nor could they be suspended or dismissed or have their salaries reduced. These protections were not perfect. For example, the authority over appointment was delegated to the Minister of Justice and judges were made subject to mandatory retirement from active judicial service at age 65. Judges also could be persuaded to resign. The protections did, however, give judges a significant degree of formal security.

Judicial independence meant more than protection against outside political intervention. Of equal importance were statutory requirements to prevent political activity by judges. The political neutrality and professional integrity of the career judiciary was a critical aspect of judicial independence as understood by the makers of Japan's modern state. The 1890 Court Organization Law prohibited judges 'on the active list of the judicial service' from engaging in the following activities:

1. To publicly interest themselves in political affairs.
2. To become members of any political party or association or of any local, municipal, or district assembly.
3. To occupy any public office to which a salary is attached or which has for its object pecuniary gain.
4. To carry on any commercial business or to do any other business prohibited by administrative ordinance.

By the end of the 19th century all judges in Japan were selected by examination. The 1890 Court Organization Law provided that judges and prosecutors had to pass two successive tests. Between the two, a three year period of practical training in the courts was required. Graduates of an imperial university were exempted from the first but not the second examination. Imperial university professors were eligible after three years without examination. By 1900 Japan's judiciary comprised 1244 career judges, most of whom had been selected through this process.

In practice the independence of Japan's prewar judiciary from direct political control does not appear to be in doubt. Although in the 1930s judges like other government officials were subject to the increasing pressures of military and ultra-nationalist forces and many shared prevailing conservative nationalist views, there is little in the record to show any significant change in the direction of the courts. Richard Mitchell's exhaustive studies of censorship, thought control, and political repression in prewar Japan confirm former Chief Justice Takaaki Hattori's observation that judicial independence remained intact and judges were considered the most trustworthy of all government officials. Inasmuch as the pool of qualified judges was limited by the examination system – in 1936 there were still only 1391 career judges, whatever informal pressures might have persuaded particular judges to resign or retire early could not lead to any massive change in the composition of the judiciary. The examination imposed severe limits on the pool of judges from which politically acceptable candidates could possibly have been chosen. Nonetheless, judges were not totally insulated from politics.

Some Japanese scholars view the issue of prewar judicial independence in Japan more in terms of the long-term influence on both the procuracy and judiciary of two of Japan's most important ultra-conservative prewar political leaders, both of whom began their careers in the Ministry of Justice. The first was Kiichiro Hiranuma, who entered the Ministry of Justice in 1888. He was Procurator-General from 1912–21 and then briefly Chief Justice of the Great Court of Cassation. In 1922, as Vice Minister of Justice, Hiranuma reached the pinnacle of his career as a government official. Late that year he entered politics to become Justice Minister. Subsequently, he served as Vice President of the Privy Council from 1926–36, President of the Privy Council from 1936–39, and Prime Minister in 1939. The second figure was Hiranuma's ally, Kisaburo Suzuki, who also began his career in the Ministry of Justice, in 1891. By 1907 he had become Chief Judge of the Tokyo District Court and he later served as a justice on the Great Court of Cassation. In 1912 Suzuki was appointed procurator of the Great Court of Cassation and in 1921 served as Procurator-General. Suzuki followed Hiranuma in politics and also became Minister of Justice (1924). He later served as Home Minister (1928) and president of the *Seiyukai* political party. The commanding political presence of both men throughout the prewar period was a telling reminder of the nexus between politics and justice officials – procurators and judges. Their ardently conservative views were unquestionably felt within both the procuracy and judiciary. Their careers indicate, however, less the intrusion of politicians on the career justice officials than the reverse. Such political activities by former prosecutors and Justice Ministry officials may help to explain why the *Seiyukai's* political rivals in the Minseito were among the most vocal critics of the Justice Ministry's administrative control over the judiciary.

Others also voiced concern over Ministry of Justice dominance of the judiciary. The Japanese bar was especially active in seeking a change. The close identification of judges with the procuracy was considered an unjust obstacle for defense attorneys and they were galled by their inferior status relative to both procurator and judge.

For the judiciary the problem of the prewar scheme was lack of full autonomy. The administrative authority of the Ministry of Justice meant that the procuracy had an often determinative voice in the assignment of judges, including appointment of the Chief Justice of Japan's highest court, and also could claim equality of status. Since judges were equals within the ministry bureaucracy, it should be emphasized, they did exercise a significant degree of influence over the administration of justice in general and predominant influence over the administration of the courts. Nonetheless, conflicts were bound to occur and when they did the potential for prosecutorial influence was unavoidable. Thus it seems likely that among the postwar reforms desired by the judiciary itself was to gain as much autonomy as possible.

Japanese concerns over judicial independence echoed within the small group of Japan specialists assembled in the United States Department of State in the early war years to begin preparations for a military occupation of a defeated Japan. Judicial reforms were hardly their first priority, however; the transfer of administrative control of the judiciary from the Ministry of Justice was the only reform related directly to the legal system that appears in their early planning documents. The first mention of any need for judicial reforms in available presurrender planning documents is a May 9, 1944 revision of a preliminary memo on 'Japan: Abolition of Militarism and Strengthening Democratic Processes,' dated five days earlier and drafted by Hugh Borton, who directed the effort. The revised version recommended changes in the process for appointing judges by the Ministry of Justice. In July 1944 the planning group prepared a separate memo on the judicial reforms. Entitled 'Japan: Treatment of Courts in Japan during Military Government', the document commended the high professional standards of Japanese judges, who received appointment, in the words of the memo, 'after rigorous qualifying examinations'. The memo suggested no reforms in the existing system except the elimination of the administrative court and some provision to assure the 'independence of judges' from the Ministry of Justice.

The presurrender American proposal to protect judicial independence by transferring administrative authority from the Ministry of Justice was implemented by the Occupation authorities. The constitutional revisions proposed initially by the committee headed by Minister of State Joji Matsumoto, which the Supreme Commander for the Allied Powers (SCAP) rejected outright, included only one reform related to the courts: the abolition of the administrative court and transfer to the regular judiciary of competence to adjudicate direct appeals from administrative decisions. In the end this change would be enthusiastically endorsed by the Occupation authorities who, like the presurrender planners, were not comfortable with the European dichotomy between administrative and regular courts. But US policy demanded more fundamental reforms. A committee headed by Col Charles L Kades, Deputy Chief of Government Section, was formed in February 1946 to draft a model constitution to be presented to the Japanese officials responsible for constitutional revision. The point of major contention within the SCAP drafting committee was the transfer of administrative authority to administrative organs of the proposed Supreme Court. The views of the majority coincided with concerns of postwar Japanese progressives who urged the removal of jurisdiction over judicial administration from the Ministry of Justice. Kades, however, repeatedly questioned the powers the committee on the judiciary had proposed for the courts, arguing with perceptive foresight that the 'kind of Supreme Court established in this draft might develop into a judicial oligarchy'. The solution, which did not fully satisfy Kades, was to provide for cabinet appointment of all judges and electoral review with potential dismissal of Supreme Court justices. By these means some assurance of political accountability would balance the implicit powers of judicial review.

No record was kept of the discussions during the marathon 32 hour conference held on the 4th and 5th of March 1946 among the Americans who submitted the model draft and the Japanese who translated its provisions. The result, however, was acceptance of nearly all of the American proposals on the judiciary. Japan's postwar constitution, as revised by a joint American and Japanese effort and later during deliberations in the

Diet, includes nearly all of the provisions and much of the language related to the judiciary of the original SCAP model. The provisions for judicial independence were almost identical. The constitution of Japan provides:

> Article 76.
>
> All judges shall be independent in the exercise of their conscience and shall be bound only by this constitution and the laws.
>
> Article 80. The judges of the inferior courts shall be appointed by the Cabinet from a list of persons nominated by the Supreme Court. All such judges shall hold office for a term of ten (10) years with privilege of reappointment, provided that they shall be retired upon the attainment of the age as fixed by law.
>
> The judges of inferior courts shall receive, at regular fixed intervals, adequate compensation, which shall not be decreased during their terms of office.

Several themes emerge from the events and concerns that led to the particular institutional structure of Japan's independent judiciary. A judiciary free from direct political direction and control was institutionalized from the beginning. The postwar reforms from both American and Japanese perspectives were intended to preserve this independence but also to end administrative – particularly procuratorial – influence and to elevate the status of judges over the procuracy. Balancing judicial autonomy with political accountability was more of an American concern. Less apparent but still evident was the underlying emphasis on the need for public trust in a professional judiciary. In combination with events in the early 1970s these themes reinforced the tendency toward even greater judicial autonomy.

Judicial Autonomy

Despite the attempt to assure a degree of political accountability, Japan's new constitutional structure has operated to ensure greater not less judicial autonomy and political insulation. At least to this extent, Kades' fears of a judicial oligarchy have been realized, albeit without the powers that would have given them cause. Yet the political checks remain and do influence judicial administration. Those who administer the career judiciary are mindful that their autonomy depends on the trust of political leadership in their ability to maintain a corps of effective and competent judges whose decisions are within predictable and generally accepted parameters. Individual judges also function within the shadow of potential political intrusion. They cannot help but be aware that in adjudicating highly publicized, politically sensitive cases, they can be held professionally accountable for their decisions. Nevertheless, direct oversight is exercised by judges themselves. The response of the judiciary, particularly senior judges in charge of its administration, to the potential politicization of the courts in the 1970s, secured the necessary political and arguably public confidence for them to continue to claim immunity from politics. In the end, however, the judiciary, not the political branches of the Japanese government, determines the parameters of responsible judicial behaviour. This conclusion is best understood through close examination of the process for appointment and promotion of career judges as well as Supreme Court justices, the career judiciary's influence on the court, and the mechanisms for judicial socialization. These are among the principal factors that help to explain the cohesion of the judiciary and its autonomy.

Appointment and Promotion

Japanese judges generally spend a professional life of thirty to forty years within a nationwide or unitary court structure that they themselves as judges administer. They begin their professional lives usually in their mid- to late twenties upon graduation from the court-administered Legal Training and Research Institute, spend the first 10 years as assistant judges until their appointment as full judges for 10 year terms. Reappointment has been routine and more than half continue to serve until they reach retirement age at 65. (Mandatory retirement for both Supreme Court justices and summary court judges is at age 70.)

The selection of assistant judges begins with entry to the Legal Training and Research Institute on the basis of what is widely recognized as Japan's most competitive national examination. Although formally appointed by the cabinet from a list of nominees presented by the Supreme Court, the selection is actually made by the personnel bureau of the Supreme Court, which prepares the list. Assistant judges are formally appointed to 10 year terms. At the end of the 10 year term, they are eligible for appointment as full judges, again for a term of 10 years. Nearly all are promoted. In each instance that reappointment has been denied, the personnel office of the Supreme Court made the decision. The judge was not included on the list presented to the cabinet for appointment.

Despite the greater potential for at least indirect influence on the Supreme Court by political leaders and the electorate, it remains in fact one of the most autonomous highest courts in the industrial world. Appointments to the court are formally among Japan's most politically significant. The Chief Justice is nominated by the cabinet with ceremonial appointment by the emperor and is accorded the same rank and salary as the prime minister. The other fourteen justices have equal rank and salary as ministers of state and are appointed by the cabinet. The statutory requirements for appointment to the Supreme Court are rather broad. Article 41 of the 1947 Court Organization Law provides:

> Justices of the Supreme Court shall be appointed from among persons of broad vision and extensive knowledge of law, who are not less than forty years of age. At least 10 of them shall be persons who have held one or two of the positions mentioned in item (1) or (2) for not less than 10 years, or one or more of the positions mentioned in the following items for a total period of 20 years or more:
>
> (1) Chief judge of a high court
> (2) Judge
> (3) Summary court judge
> (4) Public procurator
> (5) Lawyer
> (6) Professor or assistant professor of jurisprudence in a statutorily designated university.

Hence the potential for political appointments is rather great.

In fact, however, since the first justices were selected, rarely if ever have purely political considerations influenced even the appointment of the Chief Justice. In a paper on the administrative control of the Supreme Court's General Secretariat over individual judges, Setsuo Miyazawa notes that the promotion of Justice Kazuto Ishida as Chief Justice in 1969 was the result of the advice to Prime Minister Eisaku Sato by a conservative politician, former Justice Minister Tokutaro Kimura. Although Miyazawa suggests that the recommendation of Ishida over Justice Jiro Tanaka, a former University of Tokyo law professor, was motivated by concerns over a series of liberal decisions, Kimura was, as Miyazawa emphasizes, a long time friend and former colleague of

Ishida. In any event, such incidents have been rare certainly since 1969. Who becomes a Supreme Court justice or the Chief Justice has been largely determined by the judges who administer the judiciary. More typical than the Ishida appointment is the *Mainichi Shimbun* Social Affairs Bureau account of the appointment of Ryohachi Kusaba as Japan's twelfth Chief Justice in February 1990. Two months before the appointment, soon-to-retire Chief Justice Kyoichi Yaguchi visited the official residence of then-Prime Minister Kaifu. The purpose was to inform the Prime Minister of the judiciary's choice for his replacement, a choice made with the participation of the principal administrators of the judicial branch – all career judges themselves. Kaifu did not object. As one official is quoted to have said (translated into idiomatic English): 'We wouldn't have the vaguest idea who anyone they might suggest was, and we wouldn't have any way of finding out whether they would be suitable. The Supreme Court people have researched this. We trust their judgment.' A similar procedure has been followed in the appointment of every Chief Justice for a quarter of a century. Trust counts.

Prime Minister Kaifu's trust had context. Since 1971 the judiciary has denied promotion and reappointment as full judge to only one assistant judge. That year Assistant Judge Yasuaki Miyamoto was excluded from the list submitted to the cabinet. No reason was given, but the cause was widely acknowledged: Miyamoto's membership in the leftist *Seihokyo* (Young Lawyers Association, *Seinen Horitsuka Kyokai*), which had been formed in the early 1950s. By 1971 about 230 judges had joined, many during the late 1960s at the height of radical student activity in Japan. The senior judiciary was clearly concerned and began to take a variety of steps to prevent the *Seihokyo* influence. Nearly two-thirds of the Legal Training and Research Institute apprentices denied appointment as assistant judges between 1970 and 1976 were *Seihokyo* members. Career judges who belonged were subject to discriminatory treatment in court assignments and promotions. Still, denial of reappointment was an extreme measure, and the response to Miyamoto's denial was immediate. Nearly a third of Japan's judiciary protested in one form or another. Articles and books denouncing the case poured forth.

For many the independence of individual judges from the judiciary itself was the issue. In the words of Tohoku University law professor Toshiki Odanaka, 'From the perspective of judicial democracy (*minshushugi shiho*) ... active associations of judges are to be welcomed, for through them democratic movements of various forms and organizations must develop within the courts.' And, as Odanaka noted, judges also enjoy basic civil rights and freedoms. New consideration was given to the ambiguous words of Article 76, originating in the American draft of the constitution, that judges were to be 'independent in the exercise of their conscience.' There was no question, however, that the decisions on appointments, reappointments, and assignments were made by judges, not politicians.

We need to recall first their broader context in evaluating the importance of these events. They occurred in the midst of a decade of global radical student activity. Paris, Berkeley, and Prague no less than Tokyo witnessed student protests against those in authority. Beginning in 1966 students in Tokyo began to occupy university buildings. The general education campus at Kyoto University remained occupied for nearly a decade. Demonstrations were so violent at the University of Tokyo that in 1968, for the first and only time in its history, entrance examinations were cancelled. Consequently, there was no graduating class from the *Todai* law faculty in 1972.

Other countries experienced similar challenges. The experience of the Italian judiciary during this period, as described by Frederic Spotts and Theodore Wieser, is especially relevant:

> The problem began in the Fascist era when the Piedmontese model of a politically neutral judiciary was increasingly compromised. By 1945 Italy was in the hands of a judiciary that was deeply conservative in its approach to the law and the role of the courts. The senior judges, being at the top of a tightly organized judicial system, tacitly imposed their own points of view on the new judges as they rose through the ranks. But when they lost control of promotions, they lost their hold on the subordinate judges. A sense of intellectual liberation swept through the judiciary. Younger judges in particular began to challenge both their superiors' authority and their theory of law.
>
> This disagreement coincided with the wave of student and worker unrest in 1968–69, which radicalized a large number of judges, especially the younger ones in the North, driving many of them to the extreme left. By the end of the 1960s the judiciary was split from top to bottom over issues as basic as the nature of law and the role of judges. The consequence was a political polarization that fractured the unity of the judiciary and has impeded the administration of justice.

Spotts and Wieser conclude that the Italian judiciary's loss of political immunity also led to a loss of independence as the Italian judicial system increasingly became 'prey' to government and other external pressures on individual judges intended 'to cajole or intimidate magistrates into redirecting their activities or dropping a case'.

The parallels to Japan are striking, and the contrasts even more striking. In Japan, the Miyamoto incident had two apparent if somewhat paradoxical consequences. First, it affirmed the trust of conservative political leadership in the judiciary's self-policing mechanisms to prevent ideological shifts leftward. Without belaboring the obvious, prior to 1970 senior judges in Japan, in contrast to Italy, had not lost control over judicial promotions and the attitudes and activities of younger judges. Nor in exercising that control did the Japanese judiciary lose the confidence of either the government or the public. Instead the career judiciary in Japan strengthened its influence on Japan's highest and most political court.

Second, however, the embarrassing outcry it produced among scholars, lawyers and, more importantly, judges themselves made it difficult for any future judicial administrators ever again to deny reappointment and promotion to assistant judges for political reasons. As a result the judiciary as an institution gained both greater political trust and more secure judicial tenure. In any event the stakes were high, particularly with respect to the character of constitutional decisions. This is best understood in terms of the career judiciary's influence on Japan's highest and most political court.

The Career Judiciary's Influence on the Court

All but four of Japan's 12 chief justices have themselves been career judges. Only one lawyer (Fujibayashi), appointed in 1976, followed the next year by the one prosecutor (Okahara), have held the office. Two University of Tokyo law professors (Kotaro Tanaka and Kisaburo Yokota) were appointed back to back as the second and third Chief Justices in 1950 and 1960. The remaining eight were all career judges, five of whom had previously held the position of *Saikosai jimu socho*, the judiciary's highest administrative post.

Similarly, by convention a third of all Supreme Court justices are appointed from the career judiciary, with another third from the practicing bar and the remaining five of the fifteen justices other persons of 'attainment in their profession with a knowledge of law'. Thus at least five of the fifteen justices at any one time have spent their entire professional lives, usually from their mid-twenties, as judges. Between 1947 and 1992, for example, 107 persons served as justices. Excluding the first appointments in 1947, which included three former Great Court of Cassation justices and one former Councillor of the Administrative Court, of these 107, 35 held a high judicial post at the time of their appointment, and all but one of the 35 were in fact career judges. Four others had begun their professional lives as judges.

Equally significant are the career paths of the justices selected from the judiciary. Of the 35 judges who have been appointed to the Supreme Court, 32 were serving as chief judge of a high court at the time of appointment: 15 from the Tokyo High Court, 10 from the Osaka High Court, 4 from the Nagoya High Court, and 2 from the Fukuoka High Court, with the most recent appointment from the Sapporo High Court. A justiceship is thus the highest rung of a career ladder that has been consistently determined first by the judge's seniors and at the finish by his or her judicial peers, not agencies, political or otherwise, outside of the courts.

The relative lack of ruling party or other political influence on Supreme Court appointments is also indicated by the non-career judge appointees. Since the appointments of the first justices in 1947, 29 lawyers, 10 prosecutors, 9 legal scholars, 4 diplomats and only 5 administrative officials have been appointed. Of the lawyers, a third (10) were bar presidents and 3 were vice presidents at the time of their appointment. In addition, Shunzo Kobayashi, who was serving as Chief Judge of the Tokyo High Court at the time of his appointment, had spent most of his professional life as a practicing attorney, having also served as president of the Second Tokyo Bar Association. The predominance of former bar officials exemplifies the influence of the bar itself, rather than political leaders, on which attorneys are selected to become justices. One of the nine legal scholars and two of the five former administrative officials were also former judges, and one of the legal scholars was a former attorney. Moreover, all of the five former administrative officials were serving in one of Japan's most politically neutral administrative posts as head of the Cabinet Legislation Bureau or its Diet equivalent at the time of appointment. Even in the case of the four diplomats appointed to the Supreme Court, all of whom were former ambassadors who rose through the ranks of the Foreign Affairs Ministry, political considerations appear to have been secondary to a purely bureaucratic concern to reward members who have served well.

One of the most striking features of the composition of Japan's Supreme Court is the age of the justices. Since 1952 only two persons under sixty years of age have ever been appointed to the court, Jiro Tanaka and Kenichi Okuno, both of whom were 58. Only one justice was sixty. No one born after 1929 has ever served on Japan's highest court, and all but three of the 108 postwar justices have served less than 10 years. Not until 1990 was anyone appointed who received legal education in postwar Japan.

Japan's career judges staff all of Japan's district and high courts as well as the principal administrative offices necessary for the management of the entire judicial branch. In addition, about thirty *chosakan* (or research judges) are appointed from the senior ranks of the career judiciary to assist the Supreme Court. As a result, the influence of Japan's career judges extends throughout the judicial system from the Supreme Court through the summary courts. No governmental organ in Japan enjoys such extensive autonomy or freedom from political control or influence.

Itoh, H, *The Japanese Supreme Court: Constitutional Policies*, 1989, pp 19–30, Markus Wiener

Regarding the question of how the initial fifteen members of the Supreme Court were appointed, the 1947 Constitution stipulates that the Emperor shall appoint a Chief Justice of the Supreme Court as designated by the Cabinet (Article 6, Paragraph 2) and that associate justices shall be appointed by the Cabinet (Article 79). The Court Code, enacted to implement the constitutional provisions on the courts, elaborates in Article 41 the qualifications of the Supreme Court justices as follows:

> The Supreme Court justices shall be appointed from among persons, not less than forty years of age, who possess broad vision and extensive knowledge of law. At least 10 of them should have held either one or both of the positions mentioned in Items (1) and (2) below for not less than 10 years, or one or more of the positions in the following items for the total period of 20 years or more: Items (1) high court presidents, (2) judges, (3) summary court judges, (4) prosecutors, (5) private attorneys, and (6) university professors of legal science ... If positions such as assistant judge, *chosakan*, court secretary, Judicial Research and Training Institute instructor, or vice-minister, secretary, or educational official of the justice ministry have also been held by persons who have held the positions in Items (1) and (2) above for at least five years, or by persons who have held, for not less than 10 years, one or more of the positions in Items (3) to (6) above, such positions shall be deemed to be equivalent to those mentioned in Items (3) to (6) above.

Pursuant to the provisions above, Prime Minister Shigeru Yoshida, with the advice of Justice Minister Tokutaro Kimura, issued Cabinet Ordinance No 14 of 16 April 1947, creating the Advisory Committee for the Nomination of Supreme Court Justices. The following were selected to serve on the committee: the Chief Justice of the Great Court of Cassation, one lower court judge, the Chief Justice of the administrative court, the vice-minister of the justice ministry, the speakers of both Houses, the chief of the first department of the Imperial Academy, the president of Tokyo Imperial University, and the chairmen of the three major bar associations. The committee set out immediately to nominate thirty candidates, including three candidates for the chief justiceship, and reported their nominations to the Cabinet. From the list of candidates thus recommended, the Cabinet selected one Chief Justice and fourteen associate justices and was ready to have them formally appointed on 3 May 1947.

However, the proposed appointments were unexpectedly delayed by General MacArthur who instructed Prime Minister Yoshida to postpone the appointments until the first elections for the Diet had been held under the new constitution. One, for the House of Councillors, was slated for 20 April, and another, for the House of Representatives, for 25 April 1947. MacArthur might have echoed a strong feeling among many Japanese that the new Supreme Court justices should be appointed by a new Cabinet which would be selected by both Houses after the first election, rather than by the transitional caretaker Cabinet operating under the old constitution. Yoshida was expected to be reelected and appoint the Supreme Court justices from among the candidates recommended by the advisory committee during the previous term of his Cabinet. However, the unexpected victory of Tetsu Katayama of the Socialist Party over

Shigeru Yoshida (the Liberal Party) in the general election had a great impact on the subsequent selection of the justices.

Immediately after the elections, the new Prime Minister Katayama told the public of the significance of appointing Supreme Court justices who would reflect a new constitutional spirit, and appointed Yoshio Suzuki as the new minister of justice, who would be given overall supervisory power over the selection process. Suzuki decided to rely on a similar type of advisory body which had existed under the Yoshida Cabinet in order to avoid any appearance of singlehanded appointment by the Cabinet. Convinced that the new Supreme Court should be built on a broad consensus of both legal professionals and the public, he convened a meeting of all legal professionals to select the members of the advisory body. He also added the chairmen of both Houses, and other men of knowledge and experience to its membership. Finally, in the light of the old animosity between the Great Court of Cassation and the minister of justice who used to appoint all judges, including the justices of the Great Court of Cassation, he made it explicit that the selection was the collective action of the Katayama Cabinet, and he was merely assisting the Prime Minister and other Cabinet members in his capacity as a state minister without portfolio. In order to stress this point he personally drafted many proposals for the selection of candidates and had the personnel bureau of the Prime Minister's Office rather than the ministry of justice handle all the work of judicial selection.

Between 5 June and 17 June 1947, a large number of people presented various suggestions and petitions concerning the composition and the function of the Advisory Committee. On 17 June the Cabinet promulgated the Advisory Committee Regulations for the Appointment of Supreme Court Justices (Cabinet Ordinance No. 83) which provided that: (1) the committee would have sixteen members with the speaker of the House of Representatives serving as the committee chairman; the committee would include the speaker of the House of Councillors, four judges, one prosecutor, the Chief Justice of the administrative court, one assessor, four practicing attorneys, three law professors, and one person of knowledge and experience to be appointed by the Prime Minister; (2) each committee member would submit in writing to the committee a list of fifteen to thirty candidates; (3) the committee would choose thirty candidates from the list thus submitted and report their selections to the Cabinet; and (4) that any candidate should report his unwillingness to serve to the committee within one week of the first recommendation. This last provision was inserted in the light of the large number of people who had declined recommendations by the Yoshida Cabinet.

An election for the advisory committee was held by mail between 10 July and 18 July 1947, in an atmosphere that was tense and competitive, so much so that the election among the judges resulted in a Great Court of Cassation justice suing a district court judge for an alleged smear campaign. Finally, a double-ballot election returned the following delegates to the advisory committee. Representing the judges were Tamotsu Shima, (former justice of the Great Court of Cassation), Katsumi Tarumi (president of the Sendai High Court), Hachiro Fujita (president of the Osaka Court of Appeals), and Saburo Iwamatsu (president of the Fukuoka High Court). One thousand one hundred and thirteen votes were cast altogether with seven invalid votes and 38 abstentions. Minoru Miyagi (former justice of the Great Court of Cassation) was a runner-up.

Representing the prosecutors was Attorney General Morita Fukui. There were 633 votes cast, of which 111 were cast by prosecutors of the former Administrative Court, with 6 invalid votes and 11 abstentions. The runner-up was Yoshihiro Kishimoto, chief prosecutor of the Sapporo High Prosecutors' Office.

Elected from among the lawyers were Naoyoshi Tsukasaki, chairman of the Tokyo Bar Association, Yoshio Konishi, chairman of the Osaka Bar Association, Ichiro Hasegawa, chairman of the First Tokyo Bar Association, and Kunisuke Nagano, member of the Tokyo Bar Association. Tsuyoshi Mano, chairman of the Second Tokyo Bar Association, was the runner-up. A total of 4,590 votes was cast, with 16 invalid votes and 1,702 abstentions.

The Cabinet appointed Sakae Wagatsuma, chairman of the faculty of law at Tokyo University, Koshin Takigawa, chairman of the faculty of law at Kyoto University, Rikisaburo Imamura, president of Senshu University, and Koichi Shimada, president of Waseda University, to represent law professors and 'the men of knowledge and experience' in the advisory committee. Under the chairmanship of Komakichi Matsuoka, speaker of the House of Representatives, the committee held its first meeting where the names of eighty candidates were submitted for consideration of a Supreme Court justiceship. Justice Minister Suzuki seemed to have initially hoped that the committee would refrain from recommending its members for the post, but later dropped such an idea when he saw the names of the committee members who were just as well qualified for justiceships as those recommended. Indeed, several committee members were eventually appointed to the Supreme Court. On 22 July, at its second meeting, as many as 139 additional names were submitted including those of Kotaro Tanaka, Tadaichiro Tanimura, and Shunzo Kobayashi. The committee finally managed to reduce the list to thirty candidates and submit their names to the Cabinet.

Prime Minister Kayatama and other Cabinet members showed a keen interest in the selection process. Heated discussions ensued at several Cabinet meetings reviewing the background, personality, and expertise of each of the thirty nominees. A few names were mentioned as possible candidates for the Chief Justiceship, and eventually Tadahiko Mibuchi was unanimously chosen for the post. The selection of Seiichi Shimoyama, former Chief Justice of the Great Court of Cassation, was apparently motivated by the government's desire that his nomination might add to the prestige of the new court. On 4 August 1947, exactly three months after the creation of the Supreme Court, a Chief Justice and fourteen associate justices were finally sworn in.

Chief Justice Mibuchi was appointed at the recommendation of the advisory body who believed that the strong-willed Mibuchi would not become a yes-man to the occupation authorities, and would help enhance judicial independence. Subsequently, GHQ, SCAP and the Japanese government apparently felt that an advisory body might stand in the way of the discretionary power of the Cabinet to appoint justices. They quickly abolished it on the grounds that the constitutional provision which gave the executive branch the power to appoint Supreme Court justices might be violated by the use of the advisory committee. A bill to revive the advisory committee was submitted to the Diet in 1947, but was tabled indefinitely.

Thus, except for the initial fifteen justices placed on the court by the Socialist Cabinet, all the justices who succeeded them were appointed by Prime Ministers of the ruling Liberal Democratic Party (LDP) or its predecessors. Although the process of nominating and appointing justices after 1947 remains unclear, it appears that a Prime Minister and a handful of advisors, including an incumbent Chief Justice of the Court, are directly responsible for the selection of final candidates.

An analysis of the fifteen justices appointed by the Katayama Socialist Cabinet in 1947 reveals the following major occupational backgrounds: six career judges (Inoue, Iwamatsu, Shima, Fujita, Shimoyama, Mibuchi), five private attorneys (Shono, Tsukasaki, Hasegawa, Mano, Kotani), one prosecutor (Y Saito), one law professor (M Kawamura), one judicial administrator (Sawada), and one diplomat (Kuriyama). Some observers classify Mibuchi, Sawada, and Shimoyama along with Kawamura and Kuriyama, both of whom are classified as 'intellectuals', and see the 1947 Supreme Court membership as consisting of five practicing attorneys, five judicial officials (ie four career judges and one prosecutor), and five intellectuals.

Analyzing prior occupations of justices appointed after 1947 by the LDP and other conservative parties, these court observers deplore the fact that the equal ratio of 5:5:5 among these three groups has been abandoned at the expense of non-legal intellectuals who have broad vision and political ideals, and that career judges and prosecutors have come to outnumber other groups. In response, former Justice Minister Suzuki recalls in his memoirs that each candidate's qualifications were the single most important factor for selection, and that if such equal ratios among practicing attorneys, judicial officials, and intellectuals, had existed, it must have been a mere coincidence.

Be that as it may, the equal ratio among these groups came to be seen almost as a vested right of each group. Whenever a vacancy arose, the group which had lost the position acted as if it were entitled to have one of its men fill the vacancy. For instance, the Eisaku Sato government decided to appoint Tsuda, former vice-justice minister, to succeed retiring Chief Justice Kazuto Ishida. However, Ishida and a new Chief Justice Tomokazu Murakami reportedly pushed for the appointment of Judge Yutaka Yoshida on the grounds that with the retirement of Ishida and the promotion of Murakami to the Chief Justiceship, the second petty bench would be left with only ex-lawyers and prosecutors and that the vacancy should be filled by a career judge. This argument prevailed and Yoshida, after serving only three months as President of Osaka High Court, was appointed a Supreme Court justice.

By the end of 1980 the LDP's 10 Prime Ministers, starting with Prime Minister Yoshida, appointed a total of sixty-three justices to the court. The major occupational backgrounds of these justices are listed as follows: twenty-four career judges, twenty practicing attorneys, seven prosecutors, seven law professors, three judicial administrators and two diplomats. Furthermore, at the time of this review in 1980, the court consisted of six career judges, four private attorneys, two professors, two prosecutors, and one diplomat. Compared with the Socialist Court of 1947, the categories of prosecutors and professors each gained one additional position, and the categories of attorneys and judicial administrators each lost one. This meant a ratio of 8:4:3 among the judicial officials (ie career judges and prosecutors, private attorneys, and the intellectuals.

A further analysis of the backgrounds of the seventy-eight justices appointed between 1947 and 1980 produces the following patterns of judicial recruitments. First, a total of thirty justices included career judges of the following lower courts: nine presidents and two judges of the Tokyo high court, eight presidents of the Osaka high court, two presidents of the Nagoya high court, one president of the Fukuoka high court, one director of the Tokyo district court, one Chief Justice and four associate justices of the former Great Court of Cassation, and two presidents of former courts of appeals. Second, a total of 26 practicing attorneys appointed to the court included 16 attorneys who had served as either president or vice-president of the following bar associations:

five from the Tokyo Bar Association, three from the First Tokyo Bar Association, two from the Second Tokyo Bar Association, two from the Japan Federation of Bar Associations, two from the Osaka Bar Association, and one each from the Nagoya Bar Association and the Kobe Bar Association. Third, a total of eight prosecutors appointed to the Supreme Court included the following: one from the Supreme Prosecutors' Office, three from the Osaka High Prosecutors' Office, one each from the Nagoya and Tokyo High Prosecutors' Offices, and two prosecutors from the former Great Court of Cassation. Fourth, six law professors of Tokyo Imperial University, one law professor from Kyoto Imperial University and one from Kyushu Imperial University have been recruited to the Supreme Court so far. Fifth, three judicial administrators appointed to the Supreme Court had served in the former administrative court, in the legislative bureaus of the two Houses, or the Cabinet. Sixth, three former ambassadors (to the United States, the Netherlands, and French Indochina) have been appointed to the bench.

Thus, presidents of the Tokyo and Osaka high courts, presidents of the Tokyo and Osaka bar associations, Tokyo Imperial University law professors, Osaka high prosecutors and heads of legislative bureaus of the Diet or the Cabinet seem to have a very high chance of becoming Supreme Court justices. Indeed, a promotion to the position of secretary general of the Supreme Court, then a chief judgeship of a high court, especially in Tokyo, Osaka, and Nagoya, seems almost to assure an appointment to a Supreme Court justiceship and has come to be regarded in judicial circles as being 'the elite' road to success.

In tune with the principle of recalling public officials, the popular review of Supreme Court justices has been institutionalized (Article 79, Paragraph 2 of the Constitution). A newly appointed justice is reviewed by the voting public in the first general election for the House of Representatives following his initial appointment, and is subsequently reviewed in a similar manner every 10 years thereafter. He is subject to dismissal by a majority of voters, provided the total votes cast are no less than 1% of all registered voters. The Supreme Court, referring to the popular review system, was of the opinion in *Sasaki v Yamashita, Chairman of the Popular Review Control Commission for the Supreme Court Justices* (1950) that the voting public does not directly select justices but can remove justices who are appointed by the Cabinet.

In the first popular review in which about 74% of the eligible voters participated, the justices reviewed received, on the average, a non-confidence vote of less than 5%. Chief Justice Mibuchi received the highest percentage (5.5%) of non-confidence votes while Justice Sawada got the lowest (4.0%). In the second review of 1952 the votes of non-confidence climbed a little bit, averaging around 8–9%. No record was made available to the voters about the judicial behaviour of the justices at the first review: the electorate probably trusted the Cabinet's appointment of these justices. By the second review, however, the court had handed down many decisions that drew some public criticism, which was reflected in an increased number of non-confidence votes.

Takezo Shimoda's 15.2% of non-confidence votes was the highest any individual justice has ever received. Of 10 justices reviewed in 1976, Dando received the highest non-confidence vote (13.2%) while Motobayashi received the lowest (11.2%). The 25 June 1980, popular review of four justices produced the highest average rate (14.4%) of disapproval so far. But no justice has ever been recalled as a result of popular reviews conducted between 1949 and 1987. In reality, popular review of the Supreme Court justices has not affected the LDP-influenced judicial selection in the slightest degree.

Next, legal education, training, and judicial appointment of lower court judges will be briefly described. Legal education in Japan has always started at the university level. The faculties of law at major universities offer the law courses necessary to prepare for the national bar examination. Virtually all justices who have ever served on the highest bench graduated from the schools of law at major universities, specializing in German or French law, while judges of the postwar generation have focused on Anglo-American common law. Post-university legal training is given at JRTI to those who pass the bar examination. If one passes the bar examination before university graduation and starts two years of training immediately afterward, one can be a judge at the age of 23. However, the bar examination is so hard that most university graduates must spend five to seven years after graduation studying to pass it. JRTI admits fewer than 500 people each year. Only 465, or less than 1.6% of 29,088 applicants, for instance, passed the bar examination in 1975. The average age of first-year students attending the institute is approximately 28.

Trainees must choose one of three legal careers, ie judge, prosecutor, or private practice, during their two years of training at the institute. Upon graduation legal apprentices can apply for a position of judge or prosecutor or can be admitted to the bar to practice. Aspirants to be judges are often separated from those trainees who opt for prosecutorial positions or private practice. They receive intensive training, the rationale being that the judges are a special breed of government servant and require a high caliber of legal professionalism and a special sense of dedication to justice and the public interest. Top students at the institute are often persuaded to become judges rather than pursue other legal careers. A judge-aspirant becomes a freshman judge, on the average, at the age of thirty, which is still younger than either a new prosecutor or lawyer.

A new judge is normally appointed for 10 years to the post of assistant judge, and sits on the left side of the presiding judge on a three-judge bench. Since 1972 a newly appointed assistant judge receives job training at the Tokyo district court, and also studies at JRTI for four months. Under the supervision of a presiding judge, he participates in collegiate decision making and assists in analyzing legal issues, the facts of a case, sentencing, and opinion writing. Also, since 1974 an assistant judge of less than five years of service has been assigned to a single bench in order to learn how to read trial records, sort out disputed points, deliberate, and draft a court opinion. However, he does not participate in decision making. In both instances the objectives of the job training have been to learn how to speedily handle cases and to acquire the techniques of writing court opinions that would withstand review by a higher court.

At the end of 10 years, or approximately at age forty, the assistant judge is up for reappointment and promotion to full judge, and sits on the right side of the presiding judge or sits alone in a one-man court. In the early postwar years the number of litigations grew tremendously and there was an acute shortage of judges. The government encouraged prosecutors and lawyers to become judges. Some did, but after the mid-1950s only a few lawyers made such a switch. Only four lawyers responded in 1961 when the Supreme Court requested various bar associations to urge their members with the minimum of 10 years of legal experience to become judges. Even fewer public prosecutors have switched to judges. The reason for such a low rate of career change from lawyers and prosecutors to judges, seems to be not so much the low salaries of judges as their heavy work load. Judges' salaries have been fixed higher than those of prosecutors, but because of the relatively small number of judges and the large number of litigations, their work load is the heaviest of the three legal professions and has been more than the salary can compensate for.

Consequently, the limited number of newly available recruits affected the judicial assignment to lower courts. An assistant judge after the initial five years is expected to work as a full judge, five years later is made a full judge. Then he may be appointed as an acting high court judge to sit on the left side of a presiding judge; after another five years he may be promoted to the position of a regular high court judge. When the first twenty years of service have passed, the seniority system is replaced by a merit system under which younger able judges pass over some older judges. Subject to reappointments at 10-year intervals, a judge becomes a lifelong career judge serving various district courts and high courts of both remote rural places and urban metropolitan areas. He may also serve in administrative posts throughout the country The compulsory retirement age is 70 for the Supreme Court justices and summary court judges, and 65 for career judges of both the high courts and district courts.

Ramsayer, J and Rosenbluth, F, *Japan's Political Marketplace*, 1993, pp 151–59, 162–68, Harvard University Press

... The constitution guarantees independence: 'All judges shall be independent in the exercise of their conscience and shall be bound only by this constitution and the laws.' It promises them 'adequate compensation which shall not be decreased during their term of office.' And the courts remain administratively distinct from the bureaucracy and seemingly impervious to anyone in the cabinet or legislature. As Bradley Richardson and Scott Flanagan (1984, p 59) put it, '[t]he postwar constitution completely transformed the judiciary into an independent coequal branch of government'.

Despite this nominal independence, Japanese judges are not as free as, for example, their American federal peers. Like senior American politicians, LDP leaders decide who will become a judge. Unlike American politicians, they can also manipulate the system to reward and punish those they have made judges. More specifically, they mitigate the agency slack that would otherwise inhere in the judiciary through the following ploys:

1. They appoint to the Supreme Court only those judges whose policies are consistent with their own, and appoint them late enough in life (close enough to their mandatory retirement age) to prevent their growing substantially more independent over time.

2. They assign their Supreme Court appointees the job of monitoring the performance of lower-court judges, and of rewarding and punishing them appropriately. In practice, these justices delegate much of this administrative task to the Secretariat (the courts' administrative offices). To ensure that the Secretariat itself remains responsive, however, party leaders maintain on the Supreme Court at least one justice who has headed the Secretariat and understands closely how the system works. Thus:

(a) Party leaders appoint to the lower courts only those people whom their Supreme Court nominees (using the Secretariat) recommend to them as appropriate.

(b) They assign their Supreme Court justices the job of stacking the Secretariat with politically reliable judges.

(c) They then assign the judges in the Secretariat the job of manipulating the careers of the other lower court judges in a way that minimizes agency slack.

(d) Less frequently, they also let the Secretariat judges generate the desired decisions by manipulating case assignments.

The Supreme Court

The cabinet directly appoints Japanese Supreme Court justices. By tradition, it appoints several of the fifteen justices from the career judiciary. It usually appoints as justice at least one person who has served as Secretary General of the Secretariat. The rest of the justices it names from the bar, the university law faculties, the prosecutorial ranks, and the career bureaucracy. The justices face a popular referendum at the first lower-house election after their appointment, and every 10 years thereafter. No one has ever failed one of these popular votes. Only 4–15.17% of the people voting at these referenda have ever voted to dismiss a justice.

Despite security of tenure, Japanese Supreme Court justices do not last long on the job. Because the LDP holds solid control over the legislature, it can afford, as American presidents cannot, to appoint quite elderly justices – even though the law forces justices to retire by age 70 (*Saibansho ho*, §50). By so doing, it avoids the risk of the Earl Warren type of agency-slack: the chance that a politically reliable appointee will shift, over time, to very different positions. Justice Matasuke Kawamura served the longest tenure of any Japanese Supreme Court justice. Appointed in 1947, when he was a 54-year-old university professor, by the first and last Socialist cabinet, he served until age 70. By contrast, among the last 20 justices appointed, the age at appointment has ranged from 60–67. The mean appointment age has been 64.

The Lower Courts

The cabinet appoints lower-court judges from a list of nominees prepared by the Supreme Court and Secretariat. Almost all appointees are young men (and a few women) who have decided to become judges immediately upon graduating from the national law school, the Legal Research and Training Institute (the LRTI). For Japanese lower-court judges, the decision to join the bench is thus made early in their career. This transforms the court system into an institution very different from the federal court system in the United States and closer to the model of continental Europe. Although federal judges also obtain their jobs through politicians, they generally join the bench in middle age. Some federal trial judges hope to obtain an appellate post, others a Supreme Court spot (Cohen 1991). But most federal judges' initial post is their last, and they know it. Their position is one they can keep for the rest of their working lives.

Tenure apart, whether Japanese judges live well or live humbly depends on their status with the LDP leaders in the cabinet and the LDP agents in the Secretariat. Basically, the judges serve 10-year terms, which the cabinet can freely decide to renew (*Kenpo*, art 80; *Saibansho ho*, §40). Generally, that decision will depend on the judges in the Secretariat. If renewed, a judge may work until his or her sixty-fifth birthday, though some retire earlier (Table 8.1).

On some of the minute details of job assignment, the Secretariat may defer to High Court presidents and district court chief judges (Tsukahara, 1990, p 27). With each assignment, for example, a judge also takes a post in a division within the local court. Each such division is composed of three to five judges, one of whom chairs the division and handles administrative matters. The local court then allocates cases to these divisions according to its own internal rules.

Most important, the issues of when judges receive promotions, where they work, and what they do are all decided by the judges at the Secretariat. In theory, these assignments are something the LDP appointees to the Supreme Court determine (*Saibansho ho*, §47). In practice, the justices delegate the task to the judges in the Secretariat, who then determine the basic assignments. Crucial to agency slack is thus the composition of the Secretariat: by appointing politically reliable justices to the Supreme Court (including at least one who knows first-hand how the Secretariat works), and by having these justices pick reliable judges for the Secretariat, LDP leaders can keep considerable control over the entire judiciary.

Table 8.1 Age of retirement for judges who began their careers in 1951

Age	Number retiring	Age	Number retiring
64	26	55	1
63	5	54	2
62	4	53	0
61	14	52	1
60	5	51	0
59	4	50	0
58	0	40–49	4
57	4	30–39	11
56	1	20–29	0

Source: Nihon minshu horitsuka kyokai (1990, pp 38–45)

Note: The table excludes the 14 members who either died in office, were still working at the end of 1990, or whose birth dates were unavailable.

Table 8.2 Monthly salaries of judges (in yen)

Supreme Court Chief Justice	1,892,000
Supreme Court Associate Justice	1,319,000
Tokyo High Court president	1,222,000
Other high court presidents	1,125,000
Full judge (high end)	1,115,000
Full judge (low end)	494,000
Assistant judge (high end)	405,000
Assistant judge (low end)	190,600

Source: Nihon minshu horitsuka kyokai (1990, p 471)

Note: Current as of 1 April 1989, when $1.00 equalled ¥132.5. To allow for the customary Japanese bonuses, assume a 17-month year (Hattori and Henderson, 1983, pp 3–35).

How much money Japanese judges make depends on how highly the Secretariat judges regard their work. As Table 8.2 shows, the pay scale ranges from ¥190,600 per month to ¥1,892,000. These are relatively good wages for a professional ...

More important for issues of judicial independence, the Secretariat can use this pay scale to reward and punish judges. Judicial pay is not a matter of lock-step seniority. A judge's place on the pay scale depends on the Secretariat, and considerable variance within each age cohort develops over time. From top to bottom of the pay scale, judges face a pay multiple of 9.93. Of course, as Table 8.3 shows, Supreme Court appointments and High Court presidencies are not realistic goals for most judges. Even the full-judge pay scale has a pay multiple of 2.26.

Table 8.3 Highest judicial positions attained by class of 1951

Position	Number attaining
Supreme Court Justice	1
President (high court)	2
Chief judge (district court or family court)	50
High court judge	9
District court judge	13
Family court judge	4
District court branch office head	1

Source: Nihon rninshu horitsuka kyokai (1990, pp 38–45)

Note: The table shows the highest judicial (non-administrative) position held by judges who began their career in 1951 and remained in their job for at least 20 years.

Job prestige and geographical location also matter to judges, and the Secretariat can use its control over these issues to punish and reward. Indeed, the Secretariat can probably use this power *more* effectively than its power over the purse, for it can *de*mote. By Article 80 of the Constitution it is not permitted to lower a judge's pay. Nothing, however, prevents it from transferring a Tokyo High Court judge to a small branch office or a back-mountain family court.

Most judges share basic preferences about the type of appointment they want. Granted, a few judges will prefer small-town life and some will dislike appellate work. In general, though, most Japanese judges prefer an urban post to a rural post. They prefer a family court to a branch court, a district court to a family court, and a high court to a district court. They prefer a chief judgeship to associate judge status. And they hope for an occasional administrative position in the Secretariat or at one of the ministries. According to Table 8.3, most judges can realistically hope for at least one stint as a chief judge in a district or family court. Generally, they will obtain it near the end of their career. As 58 of the judges in this class of 1951 also served at least once on a High Court, they can also realistically hope for an appellate position.

Although the lengths of assignment vary, judges generally work for three years in each post. Before reassignment, they can request preferred appointments (Tsukahara, 1990, p 27). Nominally, they can even refuse transfers they do not want (*Saibansho ho*,

§48). In fact, however, they refuse them at their peril. By 1969, Judge Shigeharu Hasegawa had worked in Hiroshima for 17 years, and his wife was sick. When he declined an out-of-town transfer that year, he was out of a job: the cabinet refused to reappoint him to his next 10-year term. ...

...

Conclusion

An independent judge might do several things. For example, an independent judge might help self-interested legislators increase their rent-extracting potential by enforcing their legislative deals An independent judge might even help legislators monitor and constrain their bureaucratic agents.

None of these potential virtues flowing from judicial independence matters much in Japan. LDP legislators make their promises credible by delegating broad powers to party leaders, who stand to lose large rents if the LDP reneges on its deals. Party backbenchers monitor bureaucrats to win votes, and assign any residual monitoring to their party leaders. And the Japanese governmental structure – a stable parliamentary system run by a centralized and disciplined party – helps legislators constrain bureaucrats.

To the extent judges are independent, they introduce enormous problems of agency slack of their own. Accordingly, where – as in Japan – legislators can devise extra-judicial ways to make their commitments credible and to constrain their bureaucratic agents, one would expect them to limit the independence of their judicial agents. The LDP leaders have fashioned a judicial organization that is susceptible to such control. Lower-court judges join the court at a young age, and stay for most of their working lives. Where they work, what they earn, and what cases they decide all depend on what their superiors at the Secretariat think of their work. In turn, judges at the Secretariat answer to the Supreme Court. And the Supreme Court includes only recent LDP appointees.

Through all this the LDP could – if it chose – maintain tight control over the ways judges decide cases. We predict that, as an organization that competes successfully in a volatile political market, it does choose to keep control. In due course we will investigate just how tight a control it maintains. ...

...

The Fukushima Incident

According to many observers, it was not until the late 1960s that the LDP began to manipulate judicial careers toward political ends. Before then few judges asserted any political independence, so the Secretariat could assign them to judicial posts without considering their politics (*Zadankai*, 1959, pp 13, 16; Shioya, 1991).

Most scholars of the Japanese judiciary locate a judicial 'crisis' in the late 1960s. Right-wing ideologues, they argue, began attacking judges for their leftist bias (Saito, 1971, p 66; Hanada, 1970, p 5). Eager to placate these conservative constituents, the LDP launched a witchhunt. It criticized recent court decisions, and urged the cabinet to make independent judges pay for their independence (Saito, 1971, p 66). By March 1969 the Minister of Justice could declare that the time had come to jam the cogs of the courts' (Hanada, 1970, p 5).

The man who would take center stage in this controversy was one Shigeo Fukushima, a Sapporo district judge born in 1930. He had joined the judiciary in 1959, and had just begun his second 10-year term in 1969 when he found an explosive issue on his docket. Nearly 200 local citizens had sued the Japanese government over a planned missile base. Article 9 of the constitution banned military force, they claimed, and the base was thus unconstitutional.

Fukushima was a leader in a leftist organization of lawyers, law professors, and judges called the Young Jurists' League (YJL). By its own terms, the group was dedicated to preserving the 1947 Constitution (Seinen, 1969, p 58). Given the LDP's persistent attempts to remove Article 9, this slogan was code for fighting the Japanese military. The implications worried local chief judge Kenta Hiraga. Lest Fukushima ban the proposed base, Hiraga wrote him a letter explaining why, were *he* deciding the case, he would refuse the injunction. But to no avail. Fukushima ignored the letter and enjoined the base.

Although Japanese academics vilified Hiraga, he followed a noble tradition. The man considered to be the patron saint of judicial independence, prewar Justice Iken Kojima, often told lower-court judges how to decide their cases (Kusunoki, 1989, p 2). Even when he fought the Ministry of Justice over executing Tsuda, for example, the issue was not properly his – for he was not on the panel hearing the case. To him, and apparently to Hiraga, 'judicial independence' meant that judges judged independently of the executive and legislative branches. It did not mean that they did so independently of other judges *within* the judiciary.

Fukushima did not keep Hiraga's efforts quiet. Instead, he circulated copies of Hiraga's letter to his friends in the YJL, and some of them circulated copies to the press. Within a few days, the letter was in the newspapers. The press and professoriate accused Hiraga of subverting judicial independence, and the Diet launched impeachment proceedings. Nonetheless, Hiraga emerged relatively unscathed. On 19 October 1970, the impeachment committee reprimanded him but dismissed the charges. After additional reprimands from the Sapporo District Court and Supreme Court, he joined the Tokyo High Court.

Fukushima fared worse. He too faced impeachment proceedings, for leaking the letter to the press. But where the committee dismissed Hiraga's charges, it ruled against Fukushima. It did let Fukushima stay on the Sapporo bench, however, and Fukushima himself remained adamantly 'independent'. He railed against the judicial bureaucracy in public (see Fukushima, 1971). And notwithstanding Supreme Court decisions to the contrary, in 1973 he held the entire Japanese military unconstitutional. Although the Secretariat eventually brought him to the Tokyo District Court for a time, it soon dispatched him to the Fukushima and later the Fukui family courts. By 1989, he was 59 years old and had served without relief in provincial family courts for over 12 years. Rather than continue, he quit (ZSKS, 1990, pp 86–87).

The Young Jurists' League

What happened to the other YJL members is just as controversial. Academic writers persistently claim that the LDP and its politically reliable judges in the Supreme Court and Secretariat launched an anti-leftist crusade. Because the League had over 200 judges on its rolls (Table 9.1), they say, the Court and Secretariat fought desperately to eliminate it from the courts. To be sure, the LDP had made ominous statements: Japan, 'as a constitutional nation, could never allow' its judges to join the League (quoted in Ushiomi, 1971, p 3). The secretary general of the Secretariat himself declared that judges should not join activist political organizations. And the chief justice of the Supreme Court announced that the judiciary should exclude political extremists of all sorts (quoted in *Zadankai*, 1971b, p 69).

But talk is cheap. More interesting is what the judges at the Supreme Court and Secretariat did. In 1970, they refused to hire several League members who wanted judicial jobs. While they never explained their refusal, they did hire other League members. But most observers accused them of violating the candidates' civil rights. In turn, the frustrated applicants railed against the 'Gestapo tactics' of the Supreme Court in legal journals, extolled the plans they had made to revolutionize the judiciary, and criticized the pressure on young judges to avoid red-light districts and pinball parlors (judges would thereby lose touch with the common man; see Saibankan, 1971, p 12). None of this moved the Supreme Court, of course. It continued to hire selectively, and by 1979 had rejected 34 graduates; 24 of them were members of the League.

Equally controversially, in April 1971 the cabinet and Supreme Court refused to reappoint League member Yasuaki Miyamoto. Critics immediately accused the LDP of politicizing the courts. Miyamoto had been an assistant judge on the Kumamoto District Court, and had served on panels that issued several mildly left-leaning opinions. Yet they were hardly so aberrant as to warrant this unusually draconian treatment. In contrast to the critics, some observers suggested that Miyamoto was simply a mediocre and slow judge. After all, not every slight is political harassment. As Freud put it, sometimes a cigar is just a cigar.

Because the court steadfastly refused to explain why it did not reappoint Miyamoto, the public can only speculate about its reasons. Lawyers and law professors claimed political harassment, but to no avail. The court insisted that 10-year contracts were 10-year contracts: it could offer judges another term or it could let their contracts expire, and in either case it owed no one an explanation. The next year, League member Toshio Konno of the Nagoya Family Court heard that the court might not reappoint him either. Rather than risk that fate, he resigned.

Contrary to almost all accounts of the subject, however, the Supreme Court did not generally punish leftist judges for joining the League. Its message seems instead to have been: 'Think whatever you want, but don't let personal politics interfere with your work.' Table 9.1, which describes the composition of the League's judicial branch in 1969, shows that most members had begun their career in the 1960s. Theirs was a generation radicalized by the massive 1960 riots over the United States-Japan security treaty negotiations. Joining the League was not much of a nonconformist act, for close to a third of them had joined.

According to Table 9.2, listing the highest jobs attained by 1990 for the judges in the classes of 1960 and 1961, the Secretariat judges promoted League members as high as their non-League colleagues. If by joining the League a judge showed serious ideological heterodoxy, then the judges in the Secretariat might also have hesitated to assign League members to the sensitive administrative jobs in the Secretariat or the Ministry of Justice.

Table 9.1 1969 Young Jurists League membership, by entering class (percentages in parentheses)

Class	League members		Class	League members	
1950	3	(2.70)	1960	31	(35.2)
1951	0	(0)	1961	20	(22.7)
1952	2	(2.94)	1962	26	(34.2)
1953	0	(0)	1963	28	(30.8)
1954	0	(0)	1964	28	(44.4)
1955	1	(1.41)	1965	25	(32.9)
1956	0	(0)	1966	20	(27.8)
1957	8	(9.76)	1967	5	(6.49)
1958	7	(10.4)	1968	10	(11.6)
1959	10	(13.2)			

Sources: Biographical data: Nihon minshu horitsuka kyokai (1990, pp 30–143). League membership roster: Shiso undo kenkyu sho (1969, pp 61–70)

Table 9.2 Highest judicial positions attained by classes of 1960 and 1961 (percentages in parentheses)

Position	Non-League class member		League member	
President (high court)	1	(1.27)	1	(2.63)
Chief judge (district or family court)	6	(7.59)	4	(10.5)
High court judge	48	(60.8)	24	(63.2)
District court judge	22	(27.8)	7	(18.4)
Family court judge	2	(2.53)	2	(5.26)
Total	79	(100)	38	(100)

Sources: Biographical data: Nihon minshu horitsuka kyokai (1990, pp 72–77)

Note: the table shows the highest judicial (non-administrative) position held by judges who began their careers in 1960 or 1961 and remained in their job for at least 20 years. The two classes are aggregated because of the relatively small numbers of League members.

Again, however, they showed no such hesitation. By late 1990, 42.1% of the League members in the classes of 1960 and 1961 and 41.7% of the others had held administrative jobs (*ZSKS*, 1990, pp 90–101). Moreover, some League members had held extraordinarily important positions: Kozo Tanaka had headed the Ministry of Justice's litigation bureaus for Fukuoka and Osaka; Naoyuki Kuroda had headed the litigation bureaus for Hiroshima and Nagoya; Akira Machida had served in the Cabinet's Legal Affairs Bureau; and Yoshio Osaka had held two chief judgeships and the presidency of the Osaka High Court (*ZSKS*, 1990, pp 90–101).

Although Table 9.2 suggests League members did well in the long run, we wanted to find out whether the Secretariat penalized them at its first chance after the 'crisis' of the late 1960s. To test for such a penalty, we graded judicial positions by status and geography, and compared judicial jobs on September 1969 (when a conservative group published the League's membership roster [Shiso, 1969]) with those held two years later. These calculations yield the results in Table 9.3; a positive figure indicates a net promotion, a negative number a net demotion. At least by this crude index, League members did not suffer. Members of the class of 1960 did mildly worse than their non-League colleagues, but that difference is less than the amount by which 1961 and 1962 members did *better* than their colleagues. Because of the arbitrariness of the index and the large variance involved, Table 9.3 does not prove the Secretariat was partial toward League members. The message is more basic: the calculations yield no evidence of any bias against them.

Table 9.3 Mean promotion index from September 1969 to September 1971 for classes of 1960–62

Class of 1960	
Non-League members	+.178
League members	0
Class of 1961	
Non-League members	+.240
League members	+.429
Class of 1962	
Non-League members	-.700
League members	+.560

Sources: Biographical data: Nihon minshu horitsuka kyokai (1990, pp 90–107). League membership roster: Shisho undo kenkyu sho (1969, pp 61–70).

Note: We graded judgeships as follows: high court appointments and administrative positions – 8 points; district court judgeships – 6 points; family court judgeships and district court or family court branch office headships – 4 points; branch office judgeships – 2 points. In addition, we added 1 point for moves into Tokyo or Osaka and subtracted 1 point for moves out of the two cities.

The evidence also shows the extent to which the LDP targets the median voter rather than right-wing voters. To test how closely the Secretariat sympathized with fringe right groups, we compiled biographies for the 21 League members named in a prominent 1969 right-wing book as having participated in 'problematic' panels (Shiso, 1969, pp 246–50). Of these, two had bad careers: Miyamoto, fired in 1971, and one eccentric Haruhiko Abe, described below. Of the other 19 judges, only two among the 16 who served at least 20 years in the courts had not had a high court appointment, a chief judgeship, or a series of fast-track administrative jobs by 1990 (*ZSKS*, 1990, pp 30–131). In short, only four had done poorly. The fraction is higher than the analogous rates for the entire class of 1951 (see Table 8.3), but not by much.

More to the point, some of the 21 judges fingered by the ultra-rightists did spectacularly well. Yoshio Okada took a chief judgeship at age 55, Tatsunori Shishido at the unusually young age of 53, and Takeo Kojima retired after four chief judgeships and two high court presidencies (*ZSKS*, 1990, pp 96–97, 104–05, 32–33). Of the 21 judges, two had participated in more than one 'problematic' opinion: Yasuhisa Tanaka (eight such opinions) and Akira Takayama (nine opinions) (Shiso, 1969, pp 249–50). Yet Tanaka spent 13 years with the Ministry of Justice, then took an administrative position with the cabinet before returning to the Tokyo District Court. Takayama spent 10 years in high court appointments, including four with the Tokyo High Court and three with the Osaka High Court (*ZSKS*, 1990, pp 122–23, 80–81). Fundamentally, the evidence confirms the middle-of-the-road character of the LDP. Complaints from the fringe-right in fact counted for very little.

(iii) Foreign lawyers

Kigawa, S, 'Foreign Lawyers in Japan: The Dynamics Behind the Law No 66' (1989) 62 *Southern California Law Review* 1490–99, 1503–06

1. THE HISTORY OF JAPANESE REGULATION OF FOREIGN LAWYERS: 1876–1955

The status of foreign lawyers in Japan has gone through several changes from the first promulgation of a law regulating foreign lawyer practice and the laws of today.

A. HISTORY

Daigennin Kisoku, the Advocate Regulations of 1876, were the first Japanese statutes regulating foreign lawyer practice. Under these statutes, foreign lawyers could participate in civil litigation only when foreign parties were involved. The Advocate Regulations may have been created in response to the need for disposing of civil cases which foreigners had filed in Japanese courts. In 1893, the first *Bengoshi Ho*, Lawyers Law, introduced the term *bengoshi* in an attempt to coin a translation for the English term 'barrister'. The law, however, was silent concerning foreign lawyers; thus, they continued to handle cases involving aliens and international transactions.

The first statute to effectively regulate the practice of foreign lawyers was Lawyers Law, Law No 53 of 1933. Foreign lawyers were allowed to maintain offices and handle cases involving foreigners or international matters provided the lawyers came from countries recognizing reciprocity. This law also required *bengoshi* to pass an exam and meet citizenship requirements, just as judges and prosecutors were required to do.

In the post-Second World War era, Lawyers Law, Law No 205 of 1949, reflected a 'broad international viewpoint and extremely open approach'. The law eliminated the citizenship requirement for bar admission and created the *Nichibenren* as the organization for screening, registering, and disciplining *bengoshi*. Article 7 of the law allowed qualified foreign lawyers to practice in matters related to Japanese law, foreign law, or cases involving aliens without requiring reciprocity. Foreign lawyers had to receive approval from the Japanese Supreme Court in order to practice.

As a result of this liberal admissions policy and the need for foreign lawyers in the International Military Affairs Trials, Japan experienced an influx of foreign attorneys. Article 48(1) of the Rules of the *Nichibenren* classified these foreign lawyers as *junkaiin* and established rules regulating their practice of law. In the postwar period, the *junkaiin* system played a very important role:

> So-called 'foreign trade legal activities', with few exceptions, were outside the realm of a lawyer's [*bengoshi*] work. For this reason, the foreign *junkaiin* in the post-war period filled a gap, and a proper assessment should be made of their contribution to the development of international transactions in Japan and of the fact that many of the persons who today specialize in such international business matters were once employed by and received their training in the offices of these *junkaiin*.

In 1955, Law No 155, an amendment to the Lawyers Law, instituted strict regulation of the legal services market. Prospective *bengoshi* had to meet specific requirements, and the legal market was completely closed to foreign lawyers not already established in Japan. The repeal of Article 7, which had previously allowed foreign lawyers free access to the Japanese legal market, had two important consequences: (1) it allowed the *junkaiin* to remain as practicing lawyers', and (2) it allowed all other foreign lawyers to access the legal market only by serving as legal trainees for Japanese law firms.

B. LAW NO 155: THE TRAINING AND LICENSING OF *BENGOSHI*

Law No 155 established the current system of specific licensing requirements for *bengoshi*. All persons wishing to become *bengoshi* must pass the National Legal Examination, the equivalent to the 'law school' entrance exam. Students passing the exam are admitted to the Legal Training and Research Institute (the 'Institute'). Since the Institute accepts a class of only 500 students each year, the passage rate is less than 2% for Japanese nationals taking the exam. Many who pass are repeat takers.

Once admitted to the Institute, students are trained largely in litigation skills. During their two years at the Institute, students are paid salaries out of the National Treasury. They become *bengoshi* upon passing the 'Second Examination', the Institute's final exam. This exam is not used to further screen prospective *bengoshi*, and it is rare for anyone to fail.

A person also may become a *bengoshi* by serving as a professor or an assistant professor in a graduate school law department for at least five years. It is rare, however, for people to be admitted to the Japanese bar by this process.

II. THE 'CLOSED DOOR' YEARS – 1955–86

PRELIMINARY ATTEMPTS TO BROADEN AMERICAN PRACTICE IN JAPAN

Law No 155 of 1955 ended a period in which foreign lawyers enjoyed relatively unrestricted access to the Japanese legal services sectors. American lawyers and other legal personnel, displeased with this result, believed that they needed direct access to the Japanese legal services market in order to better serve their clients in Japan. The existing system of legal trainees was insufficient. Americans sought access to the market through two means: (1) under the rights which were interpreted to exist under Article VIII of the Treaty of Friendship, Commerce and Navigation and (2) through direct pressure on the Japanese government.

A. US-JAPAN TREATY OF FRIENDSHIP, COMMERCE AND NAVIGATION

The Japanese constitution is the supreme law of the land and supersedes any law, ordinance or other act of government. Article 98(2) states: 'The treaties concluded by Japan and established laws of nations shall be faithfully observed.' Commentators have interpreted Article 98(2) to mean that a Japanese treaty provision takes precedence over other laws. Thus, the Treaty of Friendship, Commerce and Navigation (the 'Treaty of Friendship') may grant American lawyers some basis for practicing in Japan despite the prohibitions of Law No 155 Article VIII of the Treaty of Friendship states:

> 1. Nationals and companies of either Party shall be permitted to engage, within the territories of the other Party, accountants and other technical experts, executive personnel, *attorneys*, agents and other specialists of their choice. Moreover, such nationals and companies *shall be permitted to engage accountants and other technical experts regardless of the extent to which they may have qualified for the practice of a profession within the territories of such other Party*, for the particular purpose of making examinations, audits and technical investigations exclusively for, and rendering reports to, such nationals and companies in connection with the planning and operation of their enterprises, and enterprises in which they have a financial interest, within such territories.
>
> 2. *Nationals of either Party shall not be barred from practicing the professions within the territories of the other Party merely by reason of their alienage*, but they shall be permitted to engage in professional activities therein upon compliance with the requirements regarding qualifications, residence and competence that are applicable to nationals of such other Party.

If the term 'technical experts' in the second sentence of Article VIII(1) included attorneys, then attorneys may have been able to practice in Japan despite Law No 155 prohibitions. American companies and nationals could employ American lawyers to help with the planning and operation of businesses in Japan; however, such lawyers would be limited to giving general business advice in the internal affairs of a client. An American attorney would not be able to engage in outside representation or function in any manner other than in-house counsel. Thus, American lawyers would be limited to giving general business advice in the internal affairs of a client corporation.

The *Nichibenren* has accepted no part of the above analysis. The *Nichibenren* holds that any foreign lawyer wishing to draft agreements, express legal opinions, or meet with clients for legal consultation must become a bar member; they must pass the National Legal Examination and attend the Institute.

At best, the Article VIII arguments supporting the right of American lawyers to practice in Japan are weak. The United States has numerous treaties of friendship with a variety of countries. The actual force of these treaties as a basis of established rights is not very strong. According to at least one source, neither the US nor Japan have made any conclusive decisions regarding the force of the Treaty of Friendship. Thus, the Treaty of Friendship, which has never been clearly interpreted, currently appears to be of little importance in light of the enactment of Law No. 66 and the United States Supreme Court holding in *In Re Griffiths*.

B. US–JAPAN NEGOTIATIONS

Even though the foreign lawyer issue has existed since the 1970s, it was not until 1986 that American legal interests finally saw some results from the pressure exerted on the Japanese government. One reason for the long delay in resolving the issues was the disparate American and Japanese viewpoints concerning the problem. Japan views the foreign lawyers issue as one concerning a sovereign nation's right to set professional standards. In contrast, the United States views the issue as one concerning trade in services.

Although the ABA was first to initiate pressure towards accessing the Japanese legal market, the Office of the United States Trade Representative (USTR) has played a very active, ongoing role in negotiations. In March 1982, the United States listed the foreign lawyer issue as a nontariff barrier to entry into the Japanese legal services market.

A second, weightier reason why the foreign lawyer dispute was not easily settled was that American legal interests had no uniform proposal; American interests were fractionated. As Professor Ramseyer discovered, '[t]he US Trade Representative's office tried to coordinate the American attack – but what it would propose seemed to depend solely on which law firm could muster the greatest political pressure. By the very nature of the United States legal services industry, there could be no neutral 'American' position. Although Japan appeared to be closer to a consensus position, the Japanese factions also had conflicting interests'.

Initial progress towards a resolution began when the Prime Minister Nakasone suggested to the *Nichibenren* that it take some action to resolve the issue. On 9 December 1984, the *Nichibenren* voted to develop an 'acceptable framework for practice by foreigners'. Even before this, the *Nichibenren* had begun to react to the combination of American and domestic pressure.

The initial draft of Law No 66 contained several points which were unacceptable to American interests:

1. Foreign lawyers must come from a nation that recognized reciprocity. If the nation had a federal system, then a majority of the states must have reciprocity provisions which would allow Japanese lawyers to practice in the state without passing the state's bar.
2. Compulsory *Nichibenren* membership which would place all foreign lawyers directly under the disciplinary power of the *Nichibenren*.
3. Foreign lawyers were prohibited from hiring or forming partnerships with *bengoshi*.
4. Foreign lawyers would not be allowed to show any indication that they were affiliated with any foreign law firm. They would be limited to advising in the law of their home country.
5. All applicants must have had five years of experience as a practicing lawyer in the country or state in which they were licensed.
6. Each licensed foreign legal consultant was limited to employing one legal trainee.

The ABA's section of international law and practice responded quickly to the *Nichibenren*'s proposed draft, and, in December of 1984, it sent a 'strongly worded' letter to Nobuo Matsunaga, the Japanese ambassador to the United States, calling the proposals unacceptable. American interests wanted (1) the Ministry of Justice, rather than the *Nichibenren*, to have jurisdiction over foreign lawyers, (2) reciprocity on a state-by-state basis, (3) foreign lawyers admitted under the proposed law to be able to practice American law and the law of any other foreign jurisdiction so long as they were qualified, (4) the ability to hire or form partnerships with *bengoshi*, and (5) no restrictions on the number of legal trainees that could work for a foreign legal consultant.

The American lawyers serving as legal trainees were angered by the proposed requirement that at least five of the last seven years of an applicant's practice be in the country of licensing. This requirement effectively barred many trainees from becoming licensed. A group of dissatisfied legal trainees filed a section 301 petition, under the U.S. Trade Act of 1974, seeking retaliation against Japan for unfair trade practices. The USTR did not act on this petition; however, when another legal trainee filed a second section 301 petition, the USTR took the petition more seriously and used it as a means to pressure the *Nichibenren* for concessions.

After considerable negotiations, Japan ultimately agreed to accept reciprocity on a state-by-state basis, to allow qualified applicants to practice American business law and the business law of another jurisdiction, and to remove restrictions on the number of legal trainees a foreign legal consultant could hire. However, the *Nichibenren* membership remained mandatory, no foreign legal consultant could employ or form a partnership with any *bengoshi*, and the five-year experience requirement remained in force ...

LAW NO 66 OF 1986

Currently, the Ministry of Justice (MOJ) and the *Nichibenren* are implementing the terms of Law No 66 cautiously; the terms are neither being strictly enforced, effectively keeping foreign lawyers from entering the Japanese legal market, nor are they being construed liberally, granting broad access to the legal market. Generally, the law is structured to allow Japanese interests the greatest freedom to interpret it in the manner that best suits the nation's needs at any given time. The next three sections present an overview of the new law's application and registration processes and discuss the scope of foreign attorney practice that it allows.

A. THE APPLICATION PROCESS

Article 9 of Law No 66 requires a foreign applicant to submit a written application to the MOJ for approval and to pay an application fee.

The criteria for approval are:

1. Applicants must have practiced as lawyers in the foreign jurisdiction in which they were originally licensed for more than five years;
2. Applicants must not have been sentenced to imprisonment or a graver punishment by the law of their own country or have failed other ethical or competency standards; and
3. Applicants must have sufficient financial resources to establish themselves as foreign legal consultants and must be capable of indemnifying their clients against loss or damage arising from their performance.

The MOJ is empowered to approve the applications. However, the *Nichibenren* provides the MOJ with opinions concerning which applications to approve. The MOJ also has the power to cancel a foreign legal consultant's approval under specified circumstances.

B. THE REGISTRATION PROCESS

Once approved, all foreign legal consultants must submit applications for registration with the *Nichibenren* through a local bar association in the area in which they wish to practice. The *Nichibenren* may refuse an applicant's registration for specified reasons or because the applicant 'is likely to be unsuitable in practicing law as a foreign law business lawyer'.

If applicants successfully register with the *Nichibenren*, they must observe all bar association rules. As bar members, they should be able to attend, express opinions, and vote at *Nichibenren* and local bar association general meetings pertaining to specified issues. The *Nichibenren* is also responsible for carrying out disciplinary actions. To this end, they have the sole power to cancel a foreign lawyer's registration. The *Nichibenren* works in conjunction with the local bar associations to promulgate rules regulating foreign legal consultant practice.

C. SCOPE OF PRACTICE

Foreign legal consultants may advise clients in the business law of the foreign jurisdiction in which they were originally licensed. They may also advise clients in the business law of a second foreign country provided that they are qualified to give such advice. However, a foreign legal consultant admitted under Law No 66 may not advise a client regarding Japanese law.

Several other restrictions limit a foreign legal consultant's activities. Consultants may not represent clients in any proceedings before a court, government, or public agency, nor may they prepare or serve documents for submission to such entities. They may not act as counsel in any transaction which is meant to change Japanese property rights or in any matter which involves marital rights of Japanese nationals. Furthermore, foreign legal consultants are prohibited from participating in criminal cases. If any of the prohibited areas of legal practice overlap into areas of practice open to foreign legal consultants, the consultants must seek the advice of *bengoshi*.

Foreign legal consultants must reside in Japan more than 180 days each year. However, if they must leave the country due to 'unavoidable circumstances', the period for which they are away may be counted as part of their residency term. There is no explicit definition in Law No 66 regarding what would be considered an 'unavoidable circumstance'.

Foreign legal consultants may not form partnerships with or employ *bengoshi*. They may maintain only one office in which there must be a posted, visible sign identifying the foreign legal consultants' country of original licensing and the foreign business law which they are designated to practice. The name of any legal entities to which these lawyers belong in their country of original qualification may be used provided there is no other office using the same name.

All foreign legal consultants must be originally licensed in a jurisdiction which recognizes reciprocity – that is, from a jurisdiction which allows *bengoshi* to practice law within its territory without passing a state bar exam. Under Law No 66, Japan has accepted reciprocity from the United States on a state-by-state basis.

Finn, A, 'Foreign Lawyers: Regulation of Foreign Lawyers in Japan' (1987) 28 *Harvard International Law Journal* 126–30

The Japanese Diet passed the Foreign Lawyers Law in response to pressure from American firms eager to enter the market for legal services in Japan. Pressure to open the Japanese legal market had been growing in recent years, mainly because of the expansion of Japanese investment in the United States and the emergence of Tokyo as a major financial center. American law firms feel that they must have direct access to the Japanese legal services industry in order to represent adequately their clients who do business in Japan In March 1982, the United Stares listed the foreign lawyers issue as a nontariff barrier to entry into the Japanese market. The United States government argued that in order to make other trade concessions meaningful Japan must afford American companies in Japan access to American lawyers who can facilitate trade.

This pressure from the United States created domestic pressure in Japan for the Ministry of Justice to propose changes in the laws pertaining to foreign lawyers. It is widely believed that the JFBA's previously strict stance regarding foreign lawyers had been maintained out of deference to the economic motives of a group of some 400

Japanese attorneys who handle international business transactions. The remaining 97% of Japanese lawyers were ambivalent regarding whether foreign lawyers should be allowed to practice in Japan. New pressure from the United States on the Japanese government, however, posed a threat that the JFBA would lose some of its autonomy if it did not modify its position. With this threat in mind, in December 1984, the JFBA proposed the initial draft of the new law governing foreign attorneys in Japan.

While the new law applies to all foreign lawyers, the American lawyers were the most involved in the negotiations regarding the law. Following the original proposal from the JFBA, the negotiations focused on four main issues. The first was whether partnerships of foreign lawyers and Japanese lawyers would be allowed. The Japanese side did not want to allow partnerships out of concern that US-based firms would dominate the international legal market in Japan by hiring the Japanese attorneys who do international business transactions. The American side argued on the other hand that most international legal questions involve both Japanese and American law, and that the right to associate is therefore essential.

The second issue was the extent to which reciprocity would be required. The Japanese side argued that all states, or at least some key states, in the United States should admit Japanese lawyers without examination. In response, the American side argued that an open legal market already exists in the United States, since it is so much easier for Japanese to pass United States bar examinations than it is for Americans to pass the Japanese bar examination. Also, the American negotiators pointed out that New York, arguably the major center for international transactions in the United States, already admits foreign attorneys as 'foreign legal consultants'.

The third issue was the extent of the experience requirement. The Japanese site originally proposed a five-year requirement. But, many of the foreign lawyers who are interested in practicing in Japan are young attorneys already working in Japan as trainees. Lacking lengthy experience in the United States, they preferred a shorter requirement.

The fourth issue was whether the JFBA or the Ministry of Justice would have jurisdiction over the foreign attorneys. The American side argued that the Ministry of Justice should have jurisdiction over foreign law business lawyers since foreign law business lawyers will be engaged in types of practice which are very different from those engaged in by Japanese attorneys. Moreover, some were opposed to any new regulations at all. Instead, they argued that the United States-Japan Treaty of Friendship, Commerce and Navigation, whose purpose was to promote trade between Japan and the United States, and the 1949 Attorneys Law allow foreign attorneys to provide clients with the same type of general business advice as Japanese banks, trading companies and other enterprises offer.

The Japanese themselves act as trade facilitators in negotiating and drafting contracts and in giving legal advice without being licensed to practice law. Therefore, the new law may be interpreted as expanding the definition of 'practice of law' to cover the activities of foreign attorneys but not their Japanese counterparts. In light of this, and in view of the argument that the Treaty of Friendship, Commerce and Navigation allows foreign attorneys to give general business advice to promote trade, the Foreign Lawyers Law may further restrict, rather than expand, the scope of practice permitted foreign lawyers in Japan.

The Foreign Lawyers Law may also reduce the privileges and constrain the practice of foreign lawyers already operating in Japan. The firms that currently have Japanese offices could lose some of their rights. For instance, Baker & McKenzie, which maintains a liaison office in Tokyo based on the argument that foreign lawyers who provide counselling services unrelated to litigation are not engaged in 'case-like legal affairs' as defined under the 1949 Attorneys Law, may no longer be able to continue its partnership with Japanese lawyers. Moreover, depending on how the term 'unavoidable circumstances' in the provision regarding the 180-day-residency requirement is interpreted, some foreign attorneys may not be able to retain their visas to practice in Japan. For foreign law firms with established offices in Japan, added to these restrictive changes is the new law's most threatening aspect – greater competition from other firms.

The legal trainees also may not gain from the new law. Despite the greater demand for trainees among foreign firms as firms entering Japan seek to hire lawyers with some experience in the Japanese legal services industry, trainees still will not be able to form partnerships with Japanese lawyers. Many trainees will have difficulty meeting the requirement that they have five years of domestic legal experience before being able to practice in Japan as foreign law business lawyers.

While imposing these restrictions on foreign lawyers already working in Japan, the new law will benefit those foreign firms that have been trying to enter the heretofore closed Japanese market. The Foreign Lawyers Law will finally permit those firms to open offices in Japan, albeit with some restrictions. The reciprocity requirement should not prove troubling for those firms, since most of them are based in New York. And, the five-year-experience requirement will not pose a problem for the associates and partners of those firms who have practiced that long in New York. While these firms may wish to associate with Japanese lawyers, a law allowing access without association may be better than no law at all.

At least for the near future, it is probably the Japanese lawyers who will benefit most from this new law. Since Japanese lawyers will remain the sole qualified practitioners of both Japanese and international law, they will be able to maintain their monopoly. Moreover, with more foreign lawyers working in Japan, there will be more work involving Japanese law. In addition to the benefits in the domestic market that this new law will have for Japanese lawyers, there will be derivative benefits for them in foreign jurisdictions, because the reciprocity requirement may prompt more foreign jurisdictions to admit Japanese lawyers without examination. Ironically, while the foreign Lawyers Law will probably not open the Japanese legal services industry very much, and may in fact prohibit foreign attorneys from providing trade counselling services, it may expand even further the opportunities for Japanese attorneys in what is already a relatively open market for legal services in the US.

The new law could perhaps become the foundation for future progress. Hopefully, as more foreign attorneys work in Japan as foreign law business lawyers, the benefits of allowing foreign attorneys to practice in Japan will be realized. In turn, the usefulness of foreign law business lawyers may demonstrate the need for a more open system that will allow partnerships between American and Japanese lawyers.

CHAPTER 6

THE COURT SYSTEM AND ALTERNATIVE DISPUTE RESOLUTION

ORGANISATION OF THE COURT SYSTEM

The postwar constitution established a unitary court system for civil, criminal and administrative cases, with the Supreme Court at its head.[1] Article 76 states: 'The whole judicial power is vested in the Supreme Court and in such inferior courts as are established by law.' The Court Organisation Law 1947 provided for four types of inferior courts, Summary Courts, District and Family Courts and the High Courts.[2] There is no distinction between civil and criminal courts, or courts of first and second instance. Instead, all courts are called *saibansho*, with the only difference being that of jurisdiction (see Table 1, p 405). Two appeals are allowed against an original judgment thereby establishing a three-tiered court structure, but the only real distinction drawn is that indicated in the Constitution as between the Supreme Court and inferior courts (see Table 3, p 409).[3]

The current unitary system is in contrast to that under the Meiji Constitution which distinguished not only between courts of appeal, but had a separate administrative court (see Table 1(a), p 406). The Court Organisation Law 1890 provided for a Great Court of Judicature, sometimes referred to as the Great Court of Cassation (*Daishinin*) and seven Courts of Appeal (*Kosoin*). Below these were the District Courts (*Chiho Saibansho*) and Ward Courts (*Ku Saibansho*). Alongside these courts was the Administrative Court (*Gyosei Saibansho*) set up according to Article 61 of the Meiji Constitution and the Administrative Justice Act 1890.[4] The separateness of this court was both geographical (it sat in Tokyo) and administrative (it was staffed not by judges but by specially appointed officials (*hyojokan*)).[5] Although the judicial courts had no competence to hear

---

1 Some authors refer to the 1946 Constitution, others the 1947 Constitution. This disparity arises from the fact that it was adopted on 3 November 1946 and came into effect on 3 May 1947. Further terminological differences occur between references to the 'old' or Meiji Constitution and the 'new' or Showa Constitution.

2 Law No 59, 1947. Under the unitary system established by the new Constitution, it could be argued that the Family Courts are somewhat paradoxical; they are a form of special court which, like the Meiji Constitution administrative courts, have no place in a unitary system. Furthermore, Article 76(2) prohibits the establishment of *'tokubestsu saibansho'*. Translated strictly, this could mean special courts; in fact the official translation of the section states that 'no extraordinary tribunal shall be established' thereby leading to the conclusion that the Family Courts are not unconstitutional. However, they remain unique as the only specialist courts in the structure, there being no administrative, commercial or labour courts.

3 Article 81 states that the Supreme Court is the court of last resort on constitutional issues, so that where a court other than the Supreme Court is the court of last resort, a further special appeal is allowed to the Supreme Court on a constitutional issue, eg the High Court is the court of last resort for minor civil matters which have originated in the summary courts, but a special appeal to the Supreme Court would be allowed if a constitutional issue arose.

4 Article 61 stated: 'Litigation alleging an infringement of the rights through an illegal disposition by the administrative authorities shall come under the judgement of the administrative court separately prescribed by law, does not come within the purview of the courts of justice.'

5 For a general discussion of the Meiji Administrative Court see Hashimoto, K, 'The Rule of Law: Some Aspects of Judicial Review of Administrative Action' in von Mehren, AT (ed), *Law in Japan*, 1963, p 239, Harvard University Press.

administrative cases, not every detrimental or illegal administrative act was subject to action before the administrative court, only those provided for by statute. The jurisdictional limitations of that court have led to the view that there was 'a dangerous tendency toward arbitrary exercise of administrative power'.[6]

The 1946 Constitution makes no separate provision for an administrative court and although it does not prohibit such an entity in express terms, the clear purpose of Article 76 was the establishment of a unitary system.[7] At the lowest level are the Summary Courts (*Kan-i Saibansho*) whose jurisdiction is determined in civil cases, by a monetary amount (claims not exceeding ¥900,000) and in criminal cases, by the classification of the offence as 'minor'.[8] These courts were an essentially Anglo-American idea based on a cross between small claims and magistrates' courts and replaced the Ward Courts (*Ku Saibansho*) which had existed previously. They were intended to provide quick and easy access to the courts as well as introducing an element of lay participation by having adjudicators who were not professionally trained judges.[9] This latter idea was not fully developed, for although Summary Court judges need not be qualified as such, they do tend to be legally trained in some way or other.[10] However, lay participation was effected within the system, by the provision of Judicial Commissioners (*Shihoin*), who can be called upon by the judge to advise or assist, but who are not formal members of the court process like jurors or lay assessors. There are also Conciliation Commissioners (*Chotei-in*) who sit on a committee in conciliation proceedings before the Summary Courts as well as the District and Family Courts. The committee consists of a judge and not less than two lay persons (conciliation commissioners) and deals with civil and domestic disputes as provided for by statute.[11]

In 1994 there were 448 Summary Courts staffed by 806 judges (*Kani saibansho hanji*) (see Table 2, p 407).[12] These courts are spread throughout Japan and in addition to mainstream civil and criminal cases, handle certain pre-litigation

---

6 *Idem*, p 241. See also Wada, H, 'The Administrative Court under the Meiji Constitution' (1977) 10 *Law in Japan* 1.

7 Article 76(2) states: 'No extraordinary tribunal shall be established, nor shall any organ or agency of the Executive be given final judicial power.' This, together with the establishment of a system of judicial review, has made it unlikely that an administrative court structure would be either necessary or likely under the present system. On judicial review see Chapter 7.

8 In general these are crimes carrying fines or a short period of detention; however if a lengthy custodial sentence is necessary, the case must be transferred to the District Court.

9 Oppler, AC, *Legal Reform in Occupied Japan: A Participant Looks Back*, 1976, Chapter 8, Princeton University Press.

10 Apart from practising lawyers and prosecutors, other persons such as experienced court clerks, family court investigators, conciliators and prosecution clerks would be considered. They are selected by competitive examination and nominated by the Supreme Court to be appointed by the Cabinet, in accordance with Article 80 of the Constitution.

11 Kawashima, T, 'Dispute Resolution in Contemporary Japan' in von Mehren, AT (ed), *Law in Japan*, 1963, p 41, Harvard University Press. In general see Tanaka, H, 'Legal Equality Among Family Members in Japan – The Impact of the Japanese Constitution of 1946 on the Traditional Family System' (1980) 53 *Southern California Law Review* 611.

12 Summary Court judges retire at 70.

conciliation procedures.[13] By reducing pressure on the District Courts, the Summary Courts have, to a certain extent, provided easier access to the court system. Speedy disposal of cases which would otherwise have queued for the District Court is achieved by the need for only one judge in all cases. However, for two reasons, easy access may not have been achieved in the manner anticipated by the Occupation reformers.[14] First, the rules of procedure and conduct of cases varies little from the District Courts and still needs the advice and assistance of a lawyer. Second, there is a strong tradition and preference for various forms of alternative dispute resolution which runs parallel to and in a complimentary manner with the court structure.[15]

Nevertheless, there are three pre-trial summary procedures which, whilst not depriving a person of the right to trial should they so demand, do allow a judge to decide a case on the basis of documentary evidence alone and thereby lead to a speedier disposal of certain cases. First, in cases where the fine is not more than ¥500,000, a judge may adjudicate solely on the basis of documentary evidence and before the defendant has any hearing or trial. Second, in cases involving traffic offences a judge may impose a fine up to ¥500,000 after examining the documentary evidence and hearing the defendant's statement in court. Finally, there is a procedure whereby a creditor may make an application to the court for an order that a debtor must pay the sum owed and that may be granted without a hearing. However, Article 33 of the Court Organisation Law 1947 preserves the right of a defendant to demand a trial even in these types of cases. Thus whilst on the same jurisdictional level, the Summary Courts are 'lesser' District Courts in that the type of case is determined by lower monetary or sentencing limits. Furthermore, although the numerical caseloads of both types of courts are not dissimilar (Table 7, p 413) it should be remembered that the District Courts also hear appeals from the Summary Courts in civil cases,

13 For a full account of the history and background to conciliation in Japan see Henderson, DF, *Conciliation and Japanese Law, Tokugawa and Modern*, 2 Vols, 1965, University of Washington Press. See also Tanaka, H, *Introduction to Positive Law*, pp 289–94 extract translated and cited in Tanaka, H (ed), *The Japanese Legal System*, 1976, p 492, University of Tokyo Press.

14 Oppler, *supra*, n 9. The Occupation reformers were those working for the Courts and Law Division of the Government Section of SCAP (see Oppler, p 18). This section was headed by Alfred C Oppler whose book (*supra*, n 9) is the leading account of the process of law reform during the Allied Occupation.

15 Kawashima, *supra*, n 11; Haley, JO, 'The Politics of Informal Justice': The Japanese Experience 1922–1942' in Abel, R (ed), *The Politics of Informal Justice*, Vol 2, 1982, Academic Press; Bryant, T, 'Marital Dissolution in Japan: Legal Obstacles and their Impact' (1984) 17 *Law in Japan* 73; Iwasaki, K, 'Japanese Experience with Conciliation' (1994) 10 *Arbitration International* 91; Ohta, T and Hozumi, T, 'Compromise in the Course of Litigation' (1973) 6 *Law in Japan* 97; Rosch, J, 'Institutionalizing Mediation: The Evolution of the Civil Liberties Bureau in Japan' (1987) 21 *Law & Society Review* 243; See, H, 'The Judiciary and Dispute Resolution in Japan: A Survey' (1982) 10 *Florida State University Law Review* 339; Tanase, T, 'The Management of Disputes: Automobile Accident Compensation in Japan' (1990) 24 *Law & Society Review* 651.

whilst the Summary Courts dispose of some cases without trial by means of the pre-trial summary procedures outlined above.[16]

There are 50 District Courts (*Chiho Saibansho*) with territorial jurisdiction over judicial districts which match the prefectural areas (see Table 2, p 407).[17] In addition there are 203 branch offices throughout the country staffed by around 910 judges (*hanji*) and 460 assistant judges (*hanji-ho*).[18] The District Courts have both original and appellate jurisdiction and are the courts of original jurisdiction for all cases not under that of another court, ie Family Courts or Summary Courts. Where the court is acting as a court of appeal for civil matters from the Summary Courts, there must be a panel of three judges.[19] However, where the District Courts exercise original jurisdiction, cases may be handled by a single judge or by a collegiate court consisting of three judges. The majority of cases are dealt with by a single judge, but in three classes of case, other than when carrying out its appellate function, there must be a three judge court; first, when hearing cases where the sentence is death, life imprisonment, or where the minimum period of imprisonment is not less than one year;[20] second, where the court itself determines that the case is of such importance or seriousness that it must be heard by three judges, and third, where a case is designated a collegiate court case by virtue of a statute other than the Court Organisation Law 1947.

The number of judges and assistant judges assigned to the District Courts is determined by the Supreme Court.[21] Assistant judges may not hear cases sitting alone unless there are exceptional circumstances, such as a shortage of judges. In such situations the assistant judge must have completed five years training and have been designated by the Supreme Court as entitled to exercise full judicial power. What is particularly interesting is that where there is a panel of three judges, individual judgments are not given, furthermore there are no dissenting opinions. Instead, where dissenting opinion exists, a judgment is agreed and given on the basis of the 'majority'. This collegial consensus is

---

16 Appeals are divided into two types, *koso* (the first appeal) and *jokoku* (the second appeal). Where the final court of appeal is not the Supreme Court, in order to comply with Article 81 of the constitution, which says the Supreme Court must always decide on constitutional issues, a special appeal process allows for an additional opportunity on that issue. There is also a '*kokoku* appeal' (Book III, Chapter III Code of Civil Procedure and Book III Chapter IV Code of Criminal Procedure) which could more accurately be referred to as a procedural complaint, or *kokoku* procedure (see below, pp 418–20 and pp 437–40).

17 Except Hokkaido which is divided into four judicial districts, thus there is a District Court for each of the 47 prefectures, plus the three extra for the Hokkaido area.

18 Supreme Court of Japan, Outline of the Japanese Judicial System, 1992.

19 Article 26 Court Organisation Law 1947. Following the Occupation reforms and introduction in 1948 of a new Code of Criminal Procedure, appeals from the Summary Courts in criminal cases go direct to the High Courts.

20 Various exceptions exist in relation to cases of robbery, theft and attempts to commit these crimes.

21 Article 80 of the Constitution states: 'The judges of the inferior courts shall be appointed by the Cabinet from a list of persons nominated by the Supreme Court. All judges shall hold office for a term of ten years with privilege of reappointment, provided that they shall be retired upon the attainment of the age fixed by law.' At the moment all judges of the inferior courts retire at 65, although summary court judges retire at 70. Judges of the Supreme Court also retire at 70.

preserved and perpetuated by the Court Organisation Law which states that a judgment must be signed by all three judges.[22]

The Family Courts (*Katei Saibansho*) occupy a unique position in the court structure in that they are the only specialist courts; they are independent from, but nevertheless equal to, the District Courts. There are 50 Family Courts with territorial jurisdiction matching that of the District Courts (see Table 2, p 407).[23] In addition there are 203 branch offices and 77 sub-branches staffed by 350 judges and assistant judges.[24] Judges of the Family Courts are selected on the same basis as those in the District Courts, ie from a list supplied by the Supreme Court to the Cabinet for approval and for a (renewable) period of 10 years. However, unlike the District Court, cases are always heard by a single judge, although they work closely with the 1,500 Family Court Probation Officers as well as the 50 Medical Officers who have specialist psychiatric training.

The unique and somewhat paradoxical position of the Family Courts stems from Article 24 of the Constitution which necessitated a major reform in family law.[25] In particular Article 24(2) states that 'with regard to choice of spouse, property rights, inheritance, choice of domicile, divorce and other matters pertaining to marriage and the family, laws shall be enacted from the standpoint of individual dignity and the essential equality of the sexes'. The introduction of this article was controversial in that it went against the history and tradition of Japanese society enshrined in the 1898 Civil Code and the Household Registration (*Koseki*) Law 1915, which laid down that all aspects of family life were based on the (male) head of the household.[26] It was proposed by the Occupation reformers against opposition from the Japanese government, but by introducing the concept of equality into family law Article 24 necessitated revision of the Civil Code.[27] It further focused on what were seen by the Occupation reformers as 'poorly coordinated nonjudiciary agencies' which had previously handled juvenile and family matters.[28]

22 Article 191 Code of Civil Procedure, Articles 26 and 77 Court Organisation Law. For a discussion of case law in Japan see Chapter 3, 'Sources of Law'.

23 *Supra*, n 17.

24 Supreme Court of Japan, *Guide to the Family Court of Japan*, 1995.

25 Article 24(1) Marriage shall be based only on the mutual consent of both sexes and it shall be maintained through mutual cooperation with equal rights of husband and wife as a basis. In general see Kawashima, Y, 'Americanisation of Japanese Family Law, 1945–1975' (1983) 16 *Law in Japan* 54.

26 *Ko*, meaning house and *seki* meaning registration is translated as Household Registration Law 1915. Before 1947 the concept of 'the House' was fundamental to Japanese family law, so much so that it has led one writer to comment that the postwar changes meant that the 'family system of Japan has been abolished'. Watanabe, Y, 'The Family and the Law: The Individualistic Premise and Modern Japanese Family Law' in von Mehren, AT (ed), *Law in Japan*, 1963, p 377, Harvard University Press. For a discussion of the process of reform and its impact on family law see: Steiner, K, 'The Revision of the Civil Code of Japan: Provisions Affecting the Family' (1950) 9 *The Far Eastern Quarterly* 169; Steiner, K, 'Postwar Changes in the Japanese Civil Code' (1950) 25 *Washington Law Review* 286; Bryant, T, 'The Oppressive Impact of Family Registration on Women and Minorities in Japan' (1991) 39 *UCLA Law Review* 109.

27 Law No 222, 1947; For a comparison of the Meiji system of family law based on structural inequality and the postwar system see Coleman, J, 'Japanese Family Law' (1956) 9 *Stanford Law Review* 132.

28 Oppler, *supra*, n 9, p 149.

The history of juvenile and domestic proceedings from the Civil Codes of 1890 and 1898 up to the postwar reforms demonstrates the difficulty of superimposing alien ideologies and unfamiliar forms of dispute resolution.[29] It has also been suggested that 'the biggest source of friction which ensued from the introduction of a modern legal system in Japan was legal control of family life'.[30] This process of legal transplantation created difficulties in reconciling traditional family structures and values with the modern, Western, court based methods of dispute resolution and issues of equality.[31] The resulting 'tension' between these differing systems goes some way to explaining why the Occupation reformers thought that the system for dealing with domestic and juvenile matters was poorly co-ordinated .[32]

Following the introduction of Article 24, Books IV and V of the Civil Code were revised and law introduced to deal with domestic and juvenile matters.[33] The Family Courts were established on 1 January 1949 and given a dual jurisdiction to deal with domestic and juvenile matters. Apart from their uniqueness as the only 'special' courts, they also differ in the extent of their jurisdiction and the scope of the work undertaken by quasi legal or specialist officers of the court (Tables 10 and 11, pp 416–17). The Law on the Adjudication of Family Affairs 1947 divides the jurisdiction of the courts over family matters into three types: (1) cases which can be disposed of only by judgment of the court, eg an amendment to the family register; (2) matters which could be litigated but are dealt with by conciliation proceedings, eg divorce; (3) matters which should *prima facie* be dealt with through conciliation proceedings, but in the event that these fail, can be subject to the judgment of the court. The importance and extent of conciliation work in the Family Courts is illustrated by the fact that whereas proceedings for judicial divorce may be instituted in the District Court, the majority of divorce cases are settled at the conciliation stage through the Family Courts.[34]

---

29 The traditional Japanese family system was lineal and based on the principle of primogeniture. It is described as the *'ie'* system and is translated as home, household, or family. Some writers refer to the concept of 'the House' under the Meiji Constitution, others talk of the 'family system' but the concept of *ie* is broader than the strict meaning of family or household. It is a concept which transcends the sum of the individuals which make up that unit. For a discussion of the *'ie'* system see Fukutake, T, *The Japanese Social Structure*, 1989, Chapters 3 and 15, University of Tokyo Press.

30 Mikazuki, A, 'Problems in the Japanese Judicial System' in Tanaka, H (ed), *The Japanese Legal System*, 1976, p 455, University of Tokyo Press. Fukutake, *idem*, p 125 comments that 'it is no exaggeration to say that the revision of the Civil Code after the war was a direct challenge to the uniquely Japanese system and its long standing traditions. Of course, legal change did not immediately mean a change in reality, and as social custom the system lives on today. But the change in the legally embodied system of values relating to the family could not fail to have an effect on the reality of family life'.

31 During this period juvenile matters were dealt with by the Juvenile Determination Office set up under the Juvenile Law 1922; this was an administrative office under the authority of the Ministry of Justice.

32 Mikazuki, *supra*, n 30, Fukutake, *supra*, n 29, p 125, Oppler, *supra*, n 28.

33 Law No 152, 1947 on the Adjudication of Family Affairs and the Juvenile Law 1948, Law No 168.

34 A summary of these procedures can be found in the *Guide to the Family Court of Japan*, *supra*, n 24, pp 18–25.

The jurisdiction of the Family Courts in juvenile matters is divided into cases involving 'delinquent juveniles under 20' and those where the juvenile is under 14. The latter type of case is often dealt with by the Child Guidance Centre and comes under the provisions of the Child Welfare Law.[35] There is an additional jurisdiction over adults accused of causing harm to children, eg under the Labour Standards Law.[36] Alternatively the Child Welfare Law makes provision for specific offences to be dealt with by the Family Courts. The rationale of the juvenile jurisdiction is prevention and protection, hence the emphasis on treatment rather than punishment.[37] However, if the minor is over 16 and the view is taken that the offence is so serious that it can only be treated as a criminal matter under the criminal law, the judge may transfer the case to the Public Prosecutors Office for proceedings to be started before the Summary Court or District Court.[38]

There are eight High Courts (*Koto Saibansho*) exercising territorial jurisdiction over designated areas and which sit in the major cities of Tokyo, Osaka, Nagoya, Hiroshima, Fukuoka, Sendai, Sapporo and Takamatsu. These are geographically large areas, so the Supreme Court has used its power to create six branch offices; these territorial divisions are in the jurisdictional areas of Nagoya, Fukuoka, Sendai and Sapporo, with two in Hiroshima. Each High Court has a President (*Chokan*) appointed by the Cabinet and approved by the Emperor. There are currently 280 High Court judges, including the eight Presidents, but in certain highly populated areas District Court judges may be assigned to assist in the High Court (see Table 2, p 407).[39]

This second tier jurisdiction corresponds to the former Court of Appeals (*Kosoin*) in the Meiji era, but differs in that it has an original jurisdiction over certain classes of case.[40] Thus the eight High Courts have original jurisdiction over what can be broadly classified as administrative cases which include election disputes, insurrection cases, *mandamus* proceedings and petitions for *habeas corpus*.[41] In addition, the Tokyo High Court has exclusive original jurisdiction to review decisions of certain quasi-judicial agencies such as the Fair Trade Commission, the Patent Office and the Marine Accident Agency, as well as deciding extradition applications. However, the main function of the High Court is as an appellate court. This is not restricted simply to a court of second instance, since in civil cases brought before the Summary Courts, there is an appeal first to the District Court and then a second and final appeal to the High Court, although with the consent of both parties a 'leap-frog' appeal from the Summary Court straight to the High Court is possible. Appeals from criminal cases before the Summary Courts go directly to the High Court as do appeals

35 Law No 164, 1947.

36 Law No 49, 1945.

37 Abe, H, 'The Accused and Society: Therapeutic and Preventative Aspects of Criminal Justice in Japan' in von Mehren (ed), *supra*, n 5, p 324. On juvenile crime in particular see p 354.

38 The *Guide to the Family Court of Japan*, *supra*, n 24, pp 20–27 provides a summary of the procedures.

39 Supreme Court of Japan, *Outline of the Japanese Judicial System*, 1992.

40 Articles 16–18 Courts Organization Law 1948.

41 Article 4 *Habeus Corpus* Act 1948; Law No 199, 1948.

from all cases originating in the District and Family Courts. All appeals in the High Courts are heard before a panel of three judges, although in insurrection cases and review decisions of the Fair Trade Commission, a panel of five judges is required. The judgment of the court is 'unanimous' and as with the District Courts, there is no dissenting opinion.

Finally the Supreme Court (*Saiko Saibansho*) sits in Tokyo and has territorial jurisdiction over the whole of the country. Article 76 of the constitution states that the whole judicial power is vested in the Supreme Court and inferior courts, but it is Article 81 which sets out its place and function within the judicial system. This states that 'the Supreme Court is the court of last resort with power to determine the constitutionality of any law, order, regulation or official act'. In other words, it exercises an exclusively appellate jurisdiction; this may take the form of a *jokoku* or *kokoku* appeal.[42]

There are five broad categories of *jokoku* appeal.[43] (1) an appeal against a first or second instance decision of the High Court; (2) the leap-frog, or direct appeal against a first instance decision of the District or Family Court, or first instance decision of the Summary Court; (3) an appeal which was to be heard by the High Court, but for special reasons is transferred to the Supreme Court; (4) special appeals against decisions of the High Court as a court of third instance; and (5) extraordinary appeals brought by the Prosecutor-General against a final judgment in a criminal case. In criminal cases a *jokoku* appeal is limited to matters where a constitutional question arises, or where there is a conflict with previous decisions of the Supreme Court, or in the absence of such decisions, those of the High Court. In civil and administrative cases the appeal is slightly broader in that it can be on grounds of a violation of the constitution, or any other law or ordinance relevant to the decision (see Table 3, p 409).

A *kokoku* appeal can be classified as an appeal on a point of procedure and is provided for generally in the Codes of Procedure.[44] However, Article 419-2 Code of Civil Procedure and Article 433 Code of Criminal Procedure provide for special *kokoku* appeals to the Supreme Court and deal with decisions where there has been a misinterpretation of the constitution, or other forms of 'constitutional inconsistency', eg an error of interpretation. However the majority of appeals before the court will be straightforward appeals from the judgments of the High Courts.

42 The Supreme Court does have other very limited jurisdiction, eg under Article 22 *Habeus Corpus* Law 1948 the Supreme Court may 'when deemed especially necessary' ... 'order the transfer of a case pending in an inferior court, regardless of its degree of progress, and handle the case on its own'. Article 43 *Habeus Corpus* Rules (Supreme Court Rules No 22, 1948) sets out the procedure for the order for transfer of the case. In general see Itoh, H, *The Japanese Supreme Court: Constitutional Policies*, 1989, Markus Wiener.

43 Whereas a *koso* appeal is the first appeal (*supra*, n 16 and Articles 360–92 Code of Civil Procedure, Articles 372–404 Code of Criminal Procedure) *jokoku* appeal is a second, or final appeal and is likewise provided for in each of the Codes of Procedure. (Articles 393–409 Code of Civil Procedure and Articles 405–18 Code of Criminal Procedure.)

44 Articles 419–34 Code of Criminal Procedure and Articles 410–19 Code of Civil Procedure. As an appeal on a point of procedure the *kokoku* appeal is less formal and quicker than the normal first or second appeal from the decision of a court.

The Supreme Court consists of 14 judges and the Chief Justice. Under Article 79 of the constitution all judges are appointed by the Cabinet, although in accordance with Article 6(2) of the Constitution, the Chief Justice is appointed by the Emperor.[45] This contrasts with the Great Court of Judicature (*Daishinin*) of the Meiji era which had between 30 and 50 judges at various times in its history and was part of the executive, rather than an independent branch of government.[46] That the Supreme Court is more than a reformed Great Court of Judicature is clear from the structure and organisation of the court, as well as the new responsibilities and prerogatives invested in it under the constitution.[47] The Great Court of Judicature sat in chambers, either criminal or civil, consisting of five judges, and except for a small number of special situations, it reviewed questions only of law and did not deal with constitutional or administrative matters.[48] The Supreme Court sits as a full court of 15, or in a division of five judges. These divisions, or Petty Benches (*sho hotei*), of which there are three, are the norm, but in exceptional cases the judges must sit together as a Grand Bench (*dai hotei*), with the Chief Justice presiding.[49] These exceptional cases fall into four categories: (1) an appeal on a constitutional issue where there is no Supreme Court precedent; (2) an appeal on a non-constitutional point of law, where a Petty Bench wishes to overrule a Supreme Court precedent; (3) cases referred to the Grand Bench by a Petty Bench on the grounds of their importance; and (4) cases where the Petty Bench does not reach a majority view (see Table 2(a), p 408 and Tables 4 and 5, pp 410–11).

Every appeal case is assigned to one of the three Petty Benches and, save for these exceptional cases involving constitutionality and precedent, will be determined by that Bench without the necessity of an oral hearing. Although the majority of decisions are rendered on the basis of the documentary evidence alone, oral statements from the parties may, on occasion, be heard. When the court announces its judgment, it usually does so without giving its reasons. The text of the decision is given to the parties later, as well as being made available to the public. Unlike decisions of the other courts, those of the Supreme Court must include the decision of each judge.[50] In a culture where homogeneity is the norm and expressions of dissent undesirable, when introduced, this was a significant departure from tradition. In the Great Court of Judicature decisions

45 This puts him on a par with the Prime Minister and is said by Oppler, *supra*, n 9, p 89, to have been 'for reasons of prestige' as well as forming the constitutional safeguard inherent in the separation of powers.

46 Oppler, *idem*, states that 'considerations of prestige, as well as the intention to avoid the clumsiness resulting from too large a decision-making body motivated the preference for a smaller number'.

47 Oppler, *supra*, n 9, p 100.

48 Although the figure varied, there were generally four criminal and five civil chambers. Under Article 49 of the Organization of the Courts Act 1890, where a chamber determined that a previous decision of the court was to be overruled, the case had to be heard either by all the criminal or all the civil chambers. In exceptional cases the case was heard by all the chambers, both criminal and civil (Tanaka, *supra*, n 13, p 53).

49 To be quorate the Grand Bench must have nine judges and the Petty Benches, three. In order for a law to be declared unconstitutional there must be a Grand Bench majority of eight.

50 Article 11 Court Organization Law 1947 states that 'the opinion of every Supreme Court justice shall be expressed in written decisions'.

were unanimous, in that there were no *open* expressions of dissent.[51] The use of the dissenting judgment has taken time to develop and its impact, not surprisingly, has been slow to have effect.[52] Nonetheless it remains 'an almost revolutionary innovation', and one which clearly defined the new orthodoxy of the postwar constitutional legal system.[53]

Article 41 of the Court Organisation Law 1947 introduced another reform which was a significant departure from practice in the Meiji era. Judges of the Great Court of Judicature had been chosen from the ranks of lower court judges and prosecutors. In the new Supreme Court, judges were to be chosen not just from the career judiciary, but from among lawyers, public prosecutors, law professors and those not in these categories but who are 'of broad vision and well grounded in law'.[54] The article also lays down that Supreme Court judges must be over the age of 40 and not less than 10 of them must have been High Court presidents or judges for at least 10 years or have 20 years experience as a lower court judge, public prosecutor, practising lawyer or law professor. In reality this has meant that the court has had a tripartite division consisting of five judges, five practising lawyers and a further five from the other categories. Although these categories have necessarily been flexible due to the timetable of recruitment over the years, the basic ethos of a broad based membership has been maintained. The diversification of recruitment and the introduction of the dissenting opinion have led to a small but perceptible increase in judicial individualism in the Supreme Court.[55] This may be considered all the more remarkable in view of the effect that the system for reviewing appointments could have. The occupation reformers felt that a check on the appointment of Supreme Court judges was needed and decided on a system of popular review.[56] Article 79(2) of the constitution provides that the appointment of Supreme Court judges shall be reviewed at a general election and from time to

---

51 In fact it has been said that when a judge of the Great Court of Judicature did not agree with the opinion of the court, he would place his seal upside down on the Court's judgment, Danelski, D, 'The Supreme Court of Japan: An Exploratory Study' in Schubert, G and Danelski, D (eds), *Comparative Judicial Behaviour: Cross-Cultural Studies of Political Decision-Making in the East and West*, 1969, Chapter 6, p 137, Oxford University Press.

52 See discussion in Chapter 3, Sources of Law and Chapter 7, Constitutional Framework.

53 Oppler, *supra*, n 9, p 103.

54 This rather vague turn of phrase had the intention of widening further the categories of persons eligible to sit in the Supreme Court. Persons who have been recruited to the Supreme Court under this category have included those who have worked in the Diplomatic service, members of the Legislative Bureau of the Cabinet, or the Legislative Bureau in either House of the Diet. See Tanaka, H, *The Japanese Legal System*, 1976, p 555, University of Tokyo Press.

55 Kawashima, T, 'Individualism in Decision-Making in the Supreme Court of Japan' in Schubert, G and Danelski, D (eds), *supra*, n 51, p 103; Danelski, D, 'The Supreme Court of Japan; An Exploratory Study' in Schubert and Danelski, *idem*, p 121; Tanaka, H, 'The Appointments of Supreme Court Justices and the Popular Review of Appointments' (1978) 11 *Law in Japan* 25; For further discussion of judicial activism as a source of law and in the Supreme Court see Chapters 3 and 7 and Itoh, *supra*, n 42.

56 Oppler, AC, 'The Reform of Japan's Legal and Judicial System under the Occupation' (1949) 24 *Washington Law Review* 290, see pp 311–12; reprinted in 1977 *Washington Law Review* (Special Edition 'Legal Reforms in Japan During the Allied Occupation') pp 1–35, see pp 20–21.

time thereafter.[57] This provision was also seen as a way of emphasising the sovereignty of the people. However, in practice, the idea of popular review by democratic means has proved to be more symbolic than real since it is all too evident that at general elections the voters are more concerned with the election of representatives than considering the performance of rather remote judges in the Supreme Court.[58]

A judge of the Supreme Court is usually appointed at around the age of 60 and will remain in office until the age of 70.[59] He (for there have been no women appointed to the court) may be removed, following either the Article 79 review procedure, or by impeachment.[60] In addition to the judges, there are a number of 'research officials' (*chosakan*) who have themselves been judges in the lower courts. Whereas in the United States law clerks in the Supreme Court are appointed to serve a particular judge, in the Japanese Supreme Court, they act for the court as a whole.[61]

ALTERNATIVE DISPUTE RESOLUTION

Perhaps more than any other area of the Japanese legal system, the subject of alternative dispute resolution has caught the attention of those from other legal cultures. As a result, there is an easily available literature, making it one of the more accessible parts of the Japanese legal system.[62] A widely held view is that

---

57 Article 79(2) states 'The appointment of the judges of the Supreme Court shall be reviewed by the people at the first general election of members of the House of Representatives following their appointment, and shall be reviewed again at the first general election of members of the House of Representatives after a lapse of ten years, and in the same manner thereafter'.

58 Luney, P, 'The Judiciary: Its Organization and Status in the Parliamentary System' in Luney, P and Takahashi, K (eds), *Japanese Constitutional Law*, 1993, p 136, University of Tokyo Press; Tanaka, *supra*, n 13, p 28; Ramsayer, JM and Rosenbluth, F, *Japan's Political Marketplace*, 1993, Chapters 8 and 9, Harvard University Press.

59 Article 50 Court Organization Law, 1947. Judges of the Summary Courts also retire at 70, whereas all other judges retire at 65.

60 Impeachment of Judges Law 1947 (Law No 137).

61 There are between 20–30 research officials in the Supreme Court, as well as those who work in the District and High Courts. See Itoh, *supra*, n 42. Whereas all those in the Supreme Court are judges who retain that status during their appointment, those in the High Court are not necessarily so and those in the District Courts only work on certain categories of cases, eg taxation. As for the Family Court, almost none of the research staff are or have been judges. In general see Court Organization Law 1947.

62 See Chapter 3. For an account of Japanese attitudes to law and litigation in a cultural context see Noda, Y, *Introduction to Japanese Law*, 1976, Chapter IX, University of Tokyo Press. The most influential works on the theoretical background to this subject are: Haley, JO, *Authority Without Power: Law and the Japanese Paradox*, 1991, Chapter 8, Oxford University Press; Kawashima, T, 'Dispute Resolution in Contemporary Japan' in von Mehren, AT (ed), *Law in Japan*, 1963, Harvard University Press; Haley, JO, 'The Myth of the Reluctant Litigant' (1978) *Journal of Japanese Studies* 359; Kim, C and Lawson C, 'The Law of the Subtle Mind: The Traditional Japanese Conception of Law' (1979) 28 *International and Comparative Law Quarterly* 491; Haley, JO, 'Sheathing the Sword of Justice in Japan: An Essay on Law Without Sanctions' (1982) 8 *Journal of Japanese Studies* 265; Wagatsuma, H and Rosett, A, 'The Implications of Apology: Law and Culture in Japan and the United States' (1986) 20 *Law and Society Review* 461; Ramsayer, JM, 'Reluctant Litigant Revisited: Rationality and Disputes in Japan (1988) *Journal of Japanese Studies* 111.

the Japanese are by nature non litigious, a fact which has been attributed to 'an unusual and deeply rooted cultural preference for informal, mediated settlement of private disputes and a corollary aversion to the formal mechanisms of judicial adjudication'.[63] Although recent scholarship, discussed elsewhere in this book, has sought to re-evaluate this view, the fact remains that the structures for alternative dispute resolution in Japan are long established, entrenched and well used within the modern legal system.[64]

The origins of the various ideas and forms of dispute resolution are found in Tokugawa Japan (1603–1867).[65] It was based on Confucian ideas of harmony and a recognition of the natural, hierarchical order of society, reinforced by feudal ideas of loyalty to the family and community. Helped by the fact that Japan was geographically and historically isolated and therefore maintained a unique level of homogeneity, social order was maintained and upheld by adherence to a traditional code, the rules of *giri*.[66] An interesting observation is provided by the leading writer on this subject who notes that the majority of (Tokugawa) civil disputes were settled by 'didactic conciliation' on the village level, without resort to the court, indeed, without a right to sue. Moreover, when trials did take place they were usually little more than a series of hearings in which the judge pressurised the parties to reach compromise settlement. However, 'the coercive character of the didactic conciliation resulting from the social differences between the parties and between parties and officials and conciliators, plus the lack of appeals and other alternative remedies, makes us wonder if this conciliation process did not serve well the established authority of the community and tend to perpetuate tradition'.[67] Nevertheless, a tradition

63 Haley, 1978, *idem*, p 359. Haley comments that this view is 'remarkably pervasive' amongst commentators both Japanese and foreign, but the article itself dissented from this view, sought to dispel the 'myth' and was the start of a debate re-evaluating this view.

64 Haley, 1978, *idem*, p 389 concluded that 'few misconceptions about Japan have been more widespread or as pernicious as the myth of the special reluctance of the Japanese to litigate'. It is also argued that the 'myth' has been perpetuated as a politically convenient tool of the power elites in order to suppress outward, public signs of conflict. Furthermore and more recently that it is a means of perpetuating the mystery of and the monopoly enjoyed by, a limited number of legal professionals. Thus in earlier texts dealing with Japanese government, the courts are often dismissed as politically insignificant due to the perceived unwillingness of citizens to litigate, eg Burks, AW, *The Government of Japan*, 1964, p 173, Thomas Crowell; 'the processes for the settlement of disputes often have little or nothing to do with the law as such and are often effected completely outside the formal court structure. In this sense, the Japanese judicature remains a remote administrative arm of the state, impersonal, alien and suspect'. And, Ward, RE, *Japan's Political System*, 1967, p 102, Prentice Hall. For a fundamental reappraisal of these views see: Upham, FK, *Law and Social Change in Postwar Japan*, 1987, Harvard University Press.

65 Henderson, 1965, *supra*, n 13; Henderson, 'Some Aspects of Tokugawa Law' (1952) 27 *Washington Law Review* 85.

66 Noda, *supra*, n 62, p 174–83. Difficult to define, *giri* encompasses ideas of obligation and duty to the community to which one belongs and involves a reciprocity in pursuit of harmony. Various descriptions can be found of the context and function of *giri*: Fukutake, *supra*, n 29, Chapter 17; Benedict, R, *The Chrysanthemum and the Sword*, 1946, Houghton Mifflin; 1967, Chapter 5, Routledge; van Wolferen, K, *The Enigma of Japanese Power*, 1989, Chapter 7, Macmillan. See also Chapter 1.

67 Henderson, DF, 'Law and Political Modernisation' in Ward, RE (ed), *Political Development in Modern Japan*, 1968, p 410, Princeton University Press; Henderson, 1965, *supra*, n 13 (Vol 2) at p 183 notes the importance in the character of modern Japanese conciliation which has moved from 'pre-war, didactic to present-day, voluntary Conciliation'.

it was, and the transplantation of continental European codes during the Meiji Restoration did little to undermine these structures of dispute resolution.[68] Since the modern laws were based on 'rational principles incompatible with the idea of *giri*' most conflicts appeared to be regulated and resolved outside of the state law system, with the courts, when used, operating 'less as instruments of judgment than as organs of conciliation'.[69] Resort to litigation of disputes in the courts was viewed as a sign of the disintegrating social order and a threat to a part of Japanese culture.

In response, and as if to reinforce the traditional custom of non court dispute resolution, the government during the Taisho democracy enacted a series of laws which provided for formal conciliation.[70] The Leased Land and Leased House Conciliation Law 1922 was the first in a series of statutes which introduced formal conciliation (*chotei*) into certain areas of law through legislative intervention.[71] This was followed by the Farm Tenancy Conciliation Law 1924 and in 1926, the Commercial Affairs Conciliation Law and the Labour Disputes Conciliation Law.[72] Whether as a positive response to the effects of rapid industrialisation and urbanisation, with its consequential disturbance of established social structures, or as a symptom of the collapse of traditional

68 Ishimura, Z, 'Empirical Jurisprudence in Japan' in Schubert and Danelski (eds), *supra*, n 51, Chapter 3 observes that the continental laws introduced in the Meiji period did not suit the prevailing Japanese social conditions. As a consequence people resorted to what were less expensive and more convenient forms of informal dispute settlement which were rooted in the feudal system, but nonetheless familiar and effective.

69 Noda, *supra*, n 62, p 180.

70 The Taisho period was from 1912–26 and is one about which commentators have widely differing views and which are beyond the scope of this book. In broad terms it is seen as something of a golden era for social and political change in Japan. This was characterised by 'liberal' developments such as a more pluralist approach to party politics, including, in 1925, extending the right to vote to all adult males. On the other hand the notorious Peace Preservation Law was introduced in 1925 and represents the more sinister side of state control which presaged the rise of militarism and nationalism. Silberman, B and Harootunian, H (eds), *Japan in Crisis: Essays in Taisho Democracy*, 1974, Princeton University Press; Storry, R, *A History of Modern Japan*, rev edn, 1982, Chapters 6 and 7, Penguin; Hane, M, *Modern Japan*, 1992, Chapters 10 and 11, Westview Press; Kato, S, 'Taisho Democracy as the Pre Stage for Japanese Militarism' in Silberman and Harootunian (eds), *idem*.

71 Correctly translated as 'conciliation', *chotei* is also used by some writers to describe 'mediation' or 'arbitration'. Thus, although they have a different meaning, mediation and conciliation are sometimes used interchangeably to describe the same process, or as meaning 'non lawsuit' cases. In an analysis of this subject, Kawashima, *supra*, n 62 translates *chotei* as mediation, thereby reserving the terms 'reconcilement', or 'conciliation' for extra judicial activity, whereas mediation and arbitration refer to formalised, structured or statutory procedures for dispute resolution. Henderson, 1965, *supra* n 13 (Vol 2) at pp 185–86 notes the official translation of *chotei* as 'conciliation' but accepts mediation as 'an acceptable rendition'. He states that modern dispute resolution in Japan has three aspects: (1) Informal Conciliation (*jidan*); (2) Conciliation (*chotei*); and (3) Code Compromises (*wakai*), which include arbitration (*chusai*) under the Code of Civil Procedure. However, confusion may still arise as a result of imprecision and the interchangeability of the terms which some writers adopt.

72 On the background which led to this series of laws see: Waso, A, 'The Origins of Tenant Unrest' in Silberman and Harootunian (eds), *supra*, n 70 and Henderson, 1965, *supra*, n 13, Vol 2, p 212. A detailed discussion of the development of extra judicial dispute resolution is given by Haley, JO, 'The Politics of Informal Justice: The Japanese Experience, 1922–1942' in Abel (ed), *supra*, n 15.

Japanese society brought about by the adoption of 'foreign' ideas, the history of alternative dispute resolution is a paradigm of the tension between indigenous and transplanted law.[73] Nowadays, even if a matter is litigated before the courts, there is, in civil cases, the possibility of compromise in the course of litigation.[74] However, the growth and formalisation of procedures for mediation, conciliation and arbitration has meant that the modern Japanese legal system has the most advanced set of structures for dispute resolution in the world. This, in spite of the fact that the whole idea of conciliation runs contrary to the traditional idea of enforcement of rights inherent in a (Western) private law system.

The way in which this tension is resolved represents an interesting insight into the transplantation, or adoption of 'alien' ideas against a background of traditional social structures.[75] Just as in the 1920s conciliation was the immediate response of the government to landlord and tenant disputes, so too in the 1960s and 70s the government responded to claims by conciliation rather than immediately resorting to litigation.[76] Likewise, in more recent years the government response to other rights issues such as equality has been to cocoon

73 Family law provides a good example of the tension between traditional and 'foreign' ideas and is discussed in Tanaka, H, 'Legal Equality among family Members in Japan – The Impact of the Japanese Constitution of 1946 on the Traditional Family System' (1980) 53 *Southern California Law Review* 611; Kawashima, Y, 'Americanization of Japanese Family Law 1945–1975' (1983) 16 *Law in Japan* 54; Bryant, T, 'Marital Dissolution in Japan: Legal Obstacles and their Impact' in Haley, JO (ed), *Law and Society in Contemporary Japan*, 1988, Kendall Hunt, also printed in (1984) 7 *Law in Japan* 73.

74 As noted by Henderson, 1968, *supra*, n 67, conciliation in the course of litigation has a long history; it is now enshrined in Article 136 Code of Civil Procedure; see Ohta, T and Hozumi, T, 'Compromise in the Course of Litigation' (1973) 6 *Law in Japan* 97; Muto, S, 'Concerning Trial Leadership in Civil Litigation: Focusing on the Trial Judge's Inquiry and Compromise' (1979) 12 *Law in Japan* 23; Kusano, Y, 'A Discussion of Compromise Techniques' (1991) 24 *Law in Japan* 138.

75 The 1946 Constitution is generally agreed to be a rights based document, Article 14 of which states that all people are equal under the law and will not be discriminated against, *inter alia* on grounds of sex. However, the Labour Standards Law 1947 failed adequately to address discrimination against women other than in the area of wages. Not until the 1972 Law Respecting the Improvement of the Welfare of Women Workers (Law No 113, 1972) was any direct attention given to the issue; this was more exhortation than an implementation and established an Equal Opportunity Mediation Commission to conduct mediation in areas of dispute. Much was expected of the Equal Employment Opportunity Law 1985 (Law No 45) in terms of enforcing rights, but again the emphasis was on mediation (Article 15 states that any disputes shall be referred for mediation to the Equal Opportunity Mediation Commission). This is a classic example of 'rights' transplanted from one culture and enforced in the social culture of the host, ie through mediation rather than the courts. For a commentary on this and other 'rights' based issues in modern Japanese society see Upham, 1987, *supra*, n 64. On the Equal Employment Opportunities Law (Act) Upham comments at p163 'There seems little doubt that the EEOA is part of a government attempt to follow the time-honoured Japanese pattern of dealing with social conflict by simultaneously ameliorating its causes and incorporating the antagonists into government-controlled mediation machinery.'

76 This was particularly true in the area of environmental issues, see; Gresser, J, Fujikura, K and Morishima, A, *Environmental Law in Japan*, 1981, The Massachusetts Institute of Technology, in particular Chapter 7, 'The Uses of Conciliation, Mediation and Arbitration in the Settlement of Environmental Disputes'. For an account of the way environmental matters have been dealt with more recently see Jones, C, 'Narita Airport and the Japanese Constitution: A Case Study' (1991) 24 *Law in Japan* 39.

the issue in the processes of mediation.[77] Nevertheless, the last 30 years have seen a small but significant shift in the balance from conciliation and mediation on the one hand, to litigation on the other.[78] Where litigation has been resorted to, it may have been the result of a growing frustration, or necessity, but it also represents a greater willingness to resolve matters through the courts than was the case in former times. However, whilst there may be a shift in balance, the essential structures of alternative dispute resolution remain and are used in a wide variety of circumstances as illustrated in the following materials.[79]

I ORGANISATION OF THE COURT SYSTEM

Table 1. Court Structure and Jurisdiction

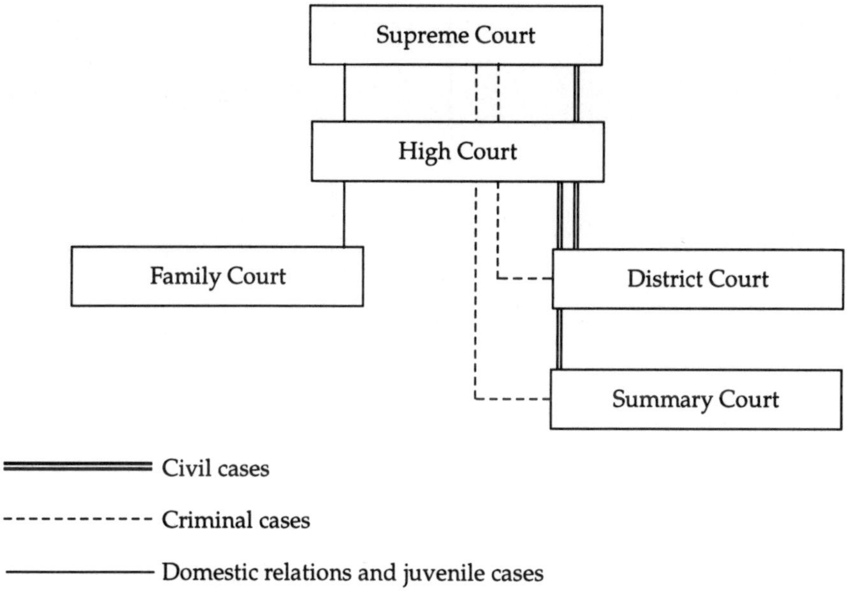

Source: Supreme Court of Japan, 1995

77 Upham, *supra*, n 64.

78 For a more detailed discussion see Chapter 1.

79 Matsuda, Y, 'Conflict Resolution in Japanese Industrial Relations' in Shirai, T (ed), *Contemporary Industrial Relations in Japan*, 1983, University of Wisconsin Press; Rosch J, 'Institutionalizing Mediation: The Evolution of the Civil Liberties Bureau in Japan' (1987) 21 *Law and Society Review* 243; Bryant, T, 'Marital Dissolution in Japan: Legal Obstacles and their Impact' in Haley, JO (ed), *Law and Society in Contemporary Japan*, 1988, Kendall Hunt; Ramsayer JM and Nakazato, M, 'The Rational Litigant: Settlement Amounts and Verdict Rates in Japan' (1989) 18 *Journal of Legal Studies* 263; Tanase, T, 'The Management of Disputes: Automobile Accident Compensation in Japan' (1990) 24 *Law and Society Review* 651; Iwasaki, K, 'Japanese Experience with Conciliation' (1994) 10 *Arbitration International* 91; Foote, DH, 'Resolution of Traffic Accident Disputes and Judicial Activism in Japan' (1995) 25 *Law in Japan* 19.

Table 1a. Court Structure Before 1947

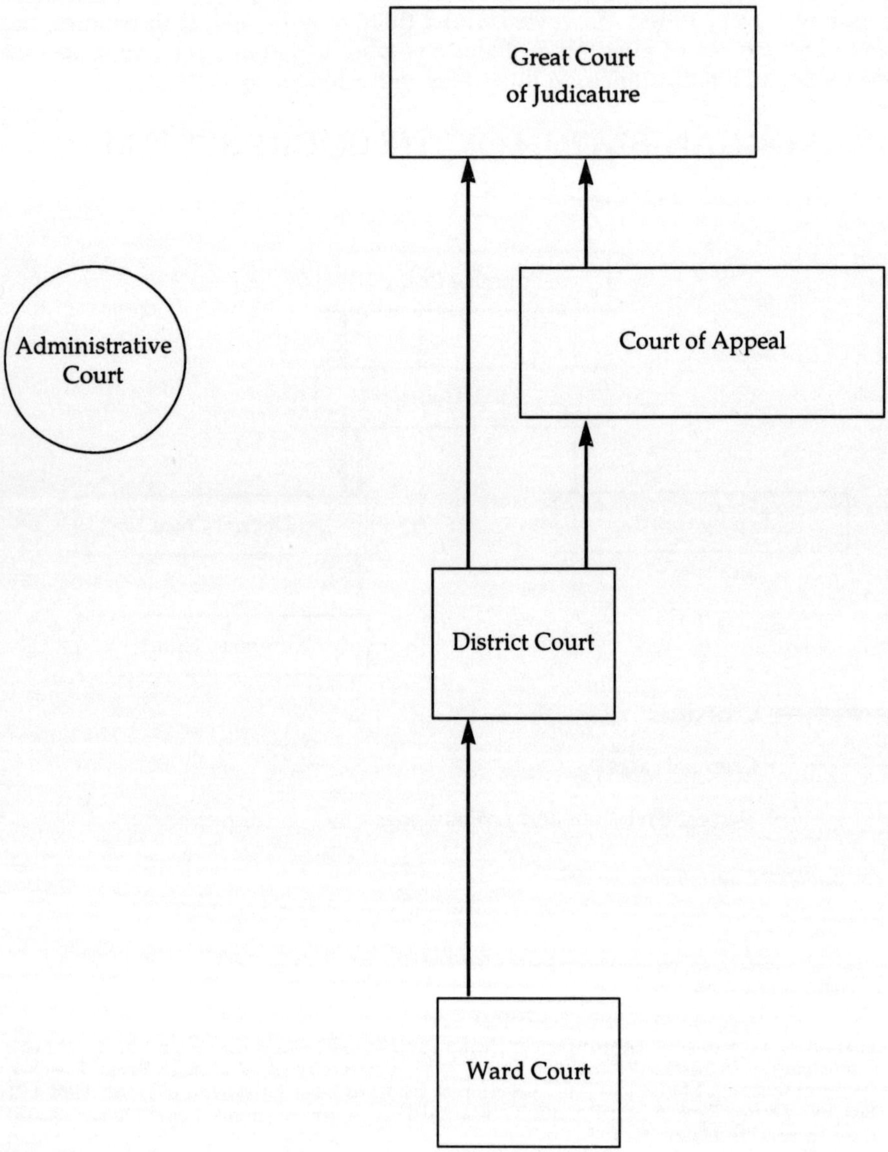

Table 2. Court Organisation and Staff

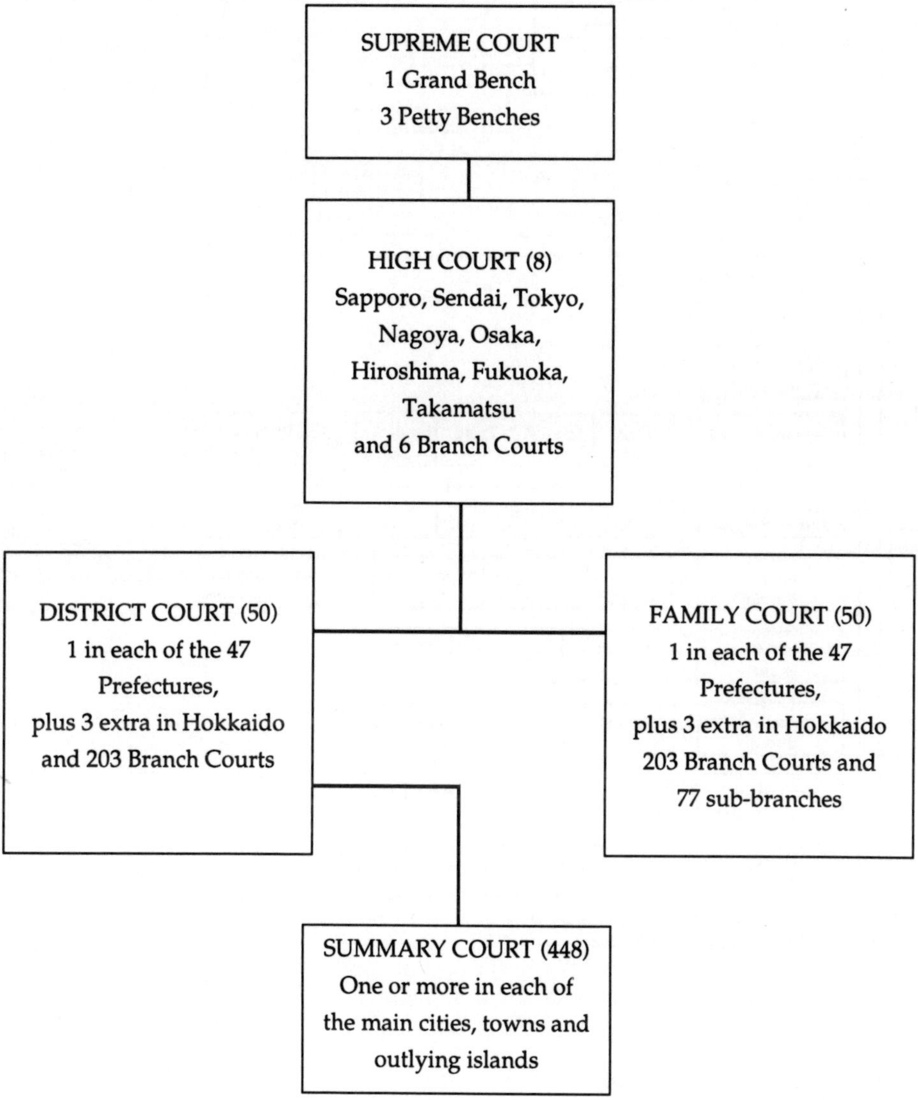

Source: Supreme Court of Japan, 1995

Table 2a. Organisation Chart of the Supreme Court

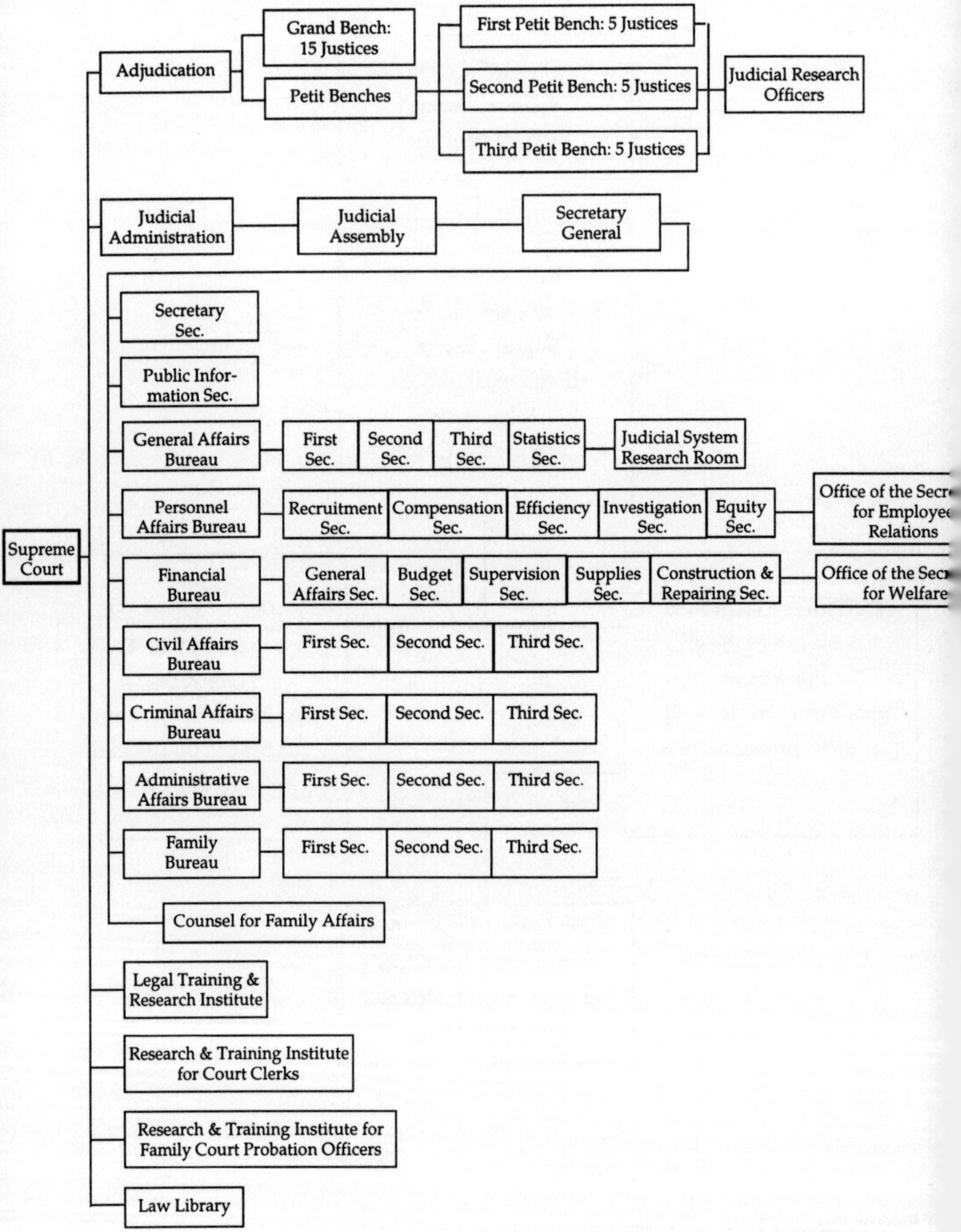

Source: Supreme Court of Japan, 1995

Table 3. Illustration of Appeal System

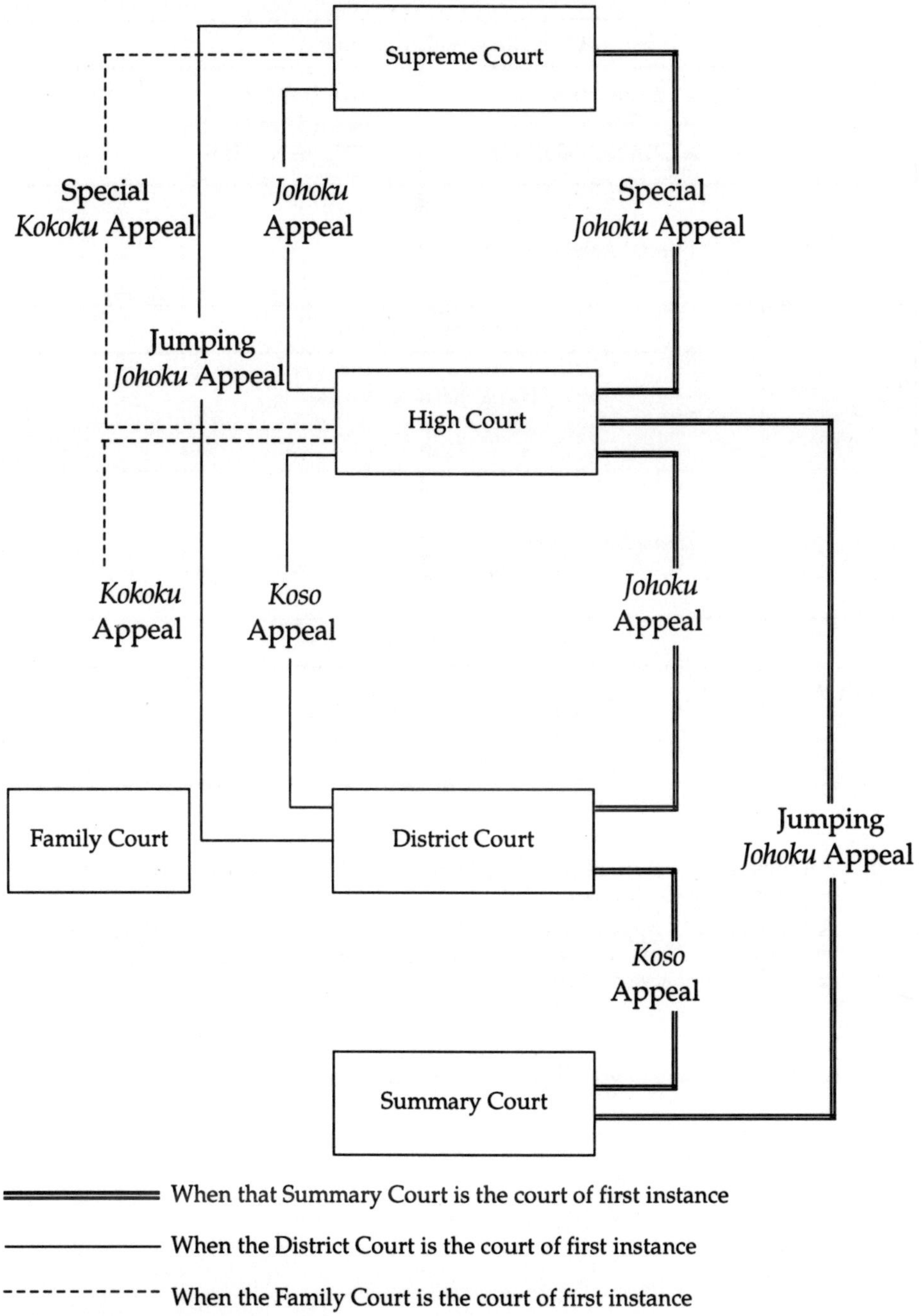

Source: Supreme Court of Japan, 1995

Table 4. Flow of Family Affairs Determinaton Cases

SUPREME COURT	Appellate Jurisdiction only	
	PETTY BENCHES All cases (Some are referred to the GRAND BENCH)	GRAND BENCH Cases referred by the PETTY BENCHES

↑ Special *Kokoku* Appeal

HIGH COURT	Appellate Jurisdiction only
	by a THREE-JUDGE COURT

↑ Immediate *Kokoku* Appeal

FAMILY COURT	Appellate Jurisdiction only
	by a SINGLE-JUDGE COURT

Note: An immediate *Kokoku* appeal may be made within two weeks only when the Supreme Court Rules permit.

A special *Kokoku* appeal may be made to the Supreme Court from a judgment of the High Court or the Family Court when the appellant claims the unconstitutionality of the judgment.

Source: Guide to the Family Court of Japan, Supreme Court of Japan, 1995

Table 5. Flow of Juvenile Delinquency Cases

SUPREME COURT	Appellate Jurisdiction only	
	PETTY BENCHES All cases (Some are referred to the GRAND BENCH)	GRAND BENCH Cases referred by the PETTY BENCHES

↑ Second *Kokoku* Appeal

HIGH COURT	Appellate Jurisdiction only
	by a THREE-JUDGE COURT

↑ *Kokoku* Appeal

FAMILY COURT	Appellate Jurisdiction only
	by a SINGLE-JUDGE COURT

Note: Second *Kokoku* appeals may be made to the Supreme Court within two weeks from an order dismissing an appeal, but only on the ground that the order is in violation of the provisions of the constitution or that the order is erroneous in the interpretation of the constitution or that the order contains judgment inconsistent with the judicial precedents rendered by the Supreme Court or by High Courts in the appellate instance.

Source: Guide to the Family Court of Japan, Supreme Court of Japan, 1995

Table 6. Statistical Tables

Civil and Criminal Litigation Cases disposed of in the Supreme Court, the High Courts, the District Courts and the Summary Courts of Japan.

Courts	Year	Civil Cases			Criminal Cases		
		Commenced	Terminated	Pending	Commenced	Terminated	Pending
Supreme Court	1986	1,931	2,171	1,467	1,671	1,781	709
	1987	2,024	2,048	1,443	1,611	1,591	729
	1988	2, 249	2, 285	1,407	1,626	1,625	730
	1989	2,240	2,300	1,347	1,507	1,552	685
	1990	2,288	2,224	1,411	1,401	1,446	640
High Courts	1986	13,756	13,819	12,390	6,352	6,139	2,199
	1987	14,030	14,310	12,110	6,062	6,189	2,072
	1988	14,329	14,377	12,062	5,576	5,820	1,828
	1989	14,978	14,931	12,109	5,178	5,165	1,841
	1990	15,673	15,369	12,413	4,982	5,078	1,745
District Courts	1986	132,679	133,723	120,167	85,276	86,355	23,774
	1987	131,818	133,533	118,452	82,734	83,592	22,916
	1988	128,905	130,349	117,008	75,638	78,146	20,408
	1989	119,435	124,702	111,741	69,738	70,870	19,276
	1990	114,402	120,030	106, 113	63,763	65,862	17,177
Summary Courts	1986	214,144	222,565	47,516	24,852	24,845	4,058
	1987	190,132	195,909	41,739	22,807	23,502	3,363
	1988	147,504	159,162	30,081	19,781	20,235	2,909
	1989	113,673	119,409	24,345	18,160	18,329	2,740
	1990	97,355	100,362	21,338	16,087	16,776	2,051

Number of Cases disposed of in the Family Courts

Courts	Year	Domestic Relations			Juvenile Cases		
		Commenced	Terminated	Pending	Commenced	Terminated	Pending
Family Courts	1986	403,992	401,793	50,725	671,973	674,405	119,938
	1987	389,480	388,731	51,474	574,467	597,891	96,514
	1988	382,814	379,358	54,930	538,919	538,832	96,601
	1989	350,542	349,837	55,635	505,226	503,462	98,365
	1990	342,998	340,232	58,401	483,442	494,136	87 ,671

Note: The statistics of civil and domestic relations cases show the number of cases, while those of criminal and juvenile cases show the number of defendants and juveniles.

Source: Outline of the Japanese Judicial System, Supreme Court of Japan, 1992

Table 7. Number of Civil Cases in 1983–1992

Court	Year	Received			Disposed of	Pending
		Total	Old	New		
All Courts	1983	3,043,660	533,666	2,509,994	2,441,833	601,827
	1984	3,564,941	601,827	2,963,114	2,891,175	673,766
	1985	3,625,581	673,766	2,951,815	2,934,862	690,719
	1986	3,528,538	690,719	2,837,819	2,824,725	703,813
	1987	3,422,971	703,813	2,719,158	2,739,55	683,416
	1988	3,183,526	683,416	2,500,110	2,545,236	638,290
	1989	2,863,665	683,290	2,180,375	2,236,247	582,418
	1990	2,640,609	582,418	2,058,191	2,119,501	521,108
	1991	2,725,294	521,108	2,204,186	2,182,874	542,420
	1992	3,085,112	542,420	2,542,692	2,445,695	639,417
Supreme Court	1983	3,915	1,473	2,442	2,189	1,726
	1984	4,370	1,726	2,644	2,499	1,871
	1985	4,661	1,871	2,790	2,874	1,787
	1986	4,544	1,787	2,757	2,939	1,605
	1987	4,349	1,605	2,744	2,820	1,529
	1988	4,773	1,529	3,244	3,113	1,660
	1989	4,794	1,660	3,134	3,264	1,530
	1990	4,639	1,530	3,109	3,050	1,589
	1991	4,901	1,589	3,312	3,020	1,881
	1992	5,404	1,881	3,523	3,406	1,998
High Court	1983	33,909	14,118	19,791	19,765	14,144
	1984	34,462	14,144	20,318	20,696	13,766
	1985	34,902	13,766	21,136	21,212	13,690
	1986	34,964	13,690	21,274	21,143	13,821
	1987	35,480	13,821	21,659	21,775	13,705
	1988	36,106	13,705	22,401	22,297	13,809
	1989	36,694	13,809	22,885	23,079	13,615
	1990	36,799	13,615	23,184	22,767	14,032
	1991	38,031	14,032	23,999	23,957	14,074
	1992	39,338	14,074	25,264	24,492	14,846
District Court	1983	1,010,911	375,641	635,270	609,355	401,556
	1984	1,153,947	401,556	752,391	691,010	462,937
	1985	1,222,666	462,937	759,729	717,780	504,886
	1986	1,247,953	504,886	743,067	713,161	534,792
	1987	1,260,362	534,792	725,570	741,985	518,377
	1988	1,217,975	518,377	699,598	730,163	487,812
	1989	1,139,217	487,812	651,405	700,027	439,190
	1990	1,050,656	439,190	611,466	671,753	378,903
	1991	1,007,046	378,903	628,143	619,235	387,811
	1992	1,120,213	387,811	732,402	666,091	454,122
Family Court	1983	447,857	50,544	397,313	398,651	49,206
	1984	459,389	49,206	410,183	411,055	48,334
	1985	451,564	48,334	403,230	403,038	48,526
	1986	452,518	48,526	403,992	401,793	50,725
	1987	440,205	50,725	389,480	388,731	51,474
	1988	434,288	51,474	382,814	379,358	54,930
	1989	405,472	54,930	350,542	349,837	55,635
	1990	398,633	55,635	342,998	340,232	58,401
	1991	410,503	58,401	352,102	352,056	58,447
	1992	429,364	58,447	370,917	365,032	64,332
Summary Court	1983	1,547,068	91,890	1,455,178	1,411,873	135,195
	1984	1,912,773	135,195	1,777,578	1,765,915	146,858
	1985	1,911,788	146,858	1,764,930	1,789,958	121,830
	1986	1,788,559	121,830	1,666,729	1,685,689	102,870
	1987	1,682,575	102,870	1,579,705	1,584,244	98,331
	1988	1,490,384	98,331	1,392,053	1,410,305	80,079
	1989	1,232,488	80,079	1,152,409	1,160,040	72,448
	1990	1,149,882	72,448	1,077,434	1,081,699	68,183
	1991	1,264,813	68,183	1,196,630	1,184,606	80,207
	1992	1,490,793	80,207	1,410,586	1,386,674	104,119

Source: *Outline of Civil Trial in Japan*, Supreme Court of Japan, 1993

Table 8. Proceedings of Civil Case

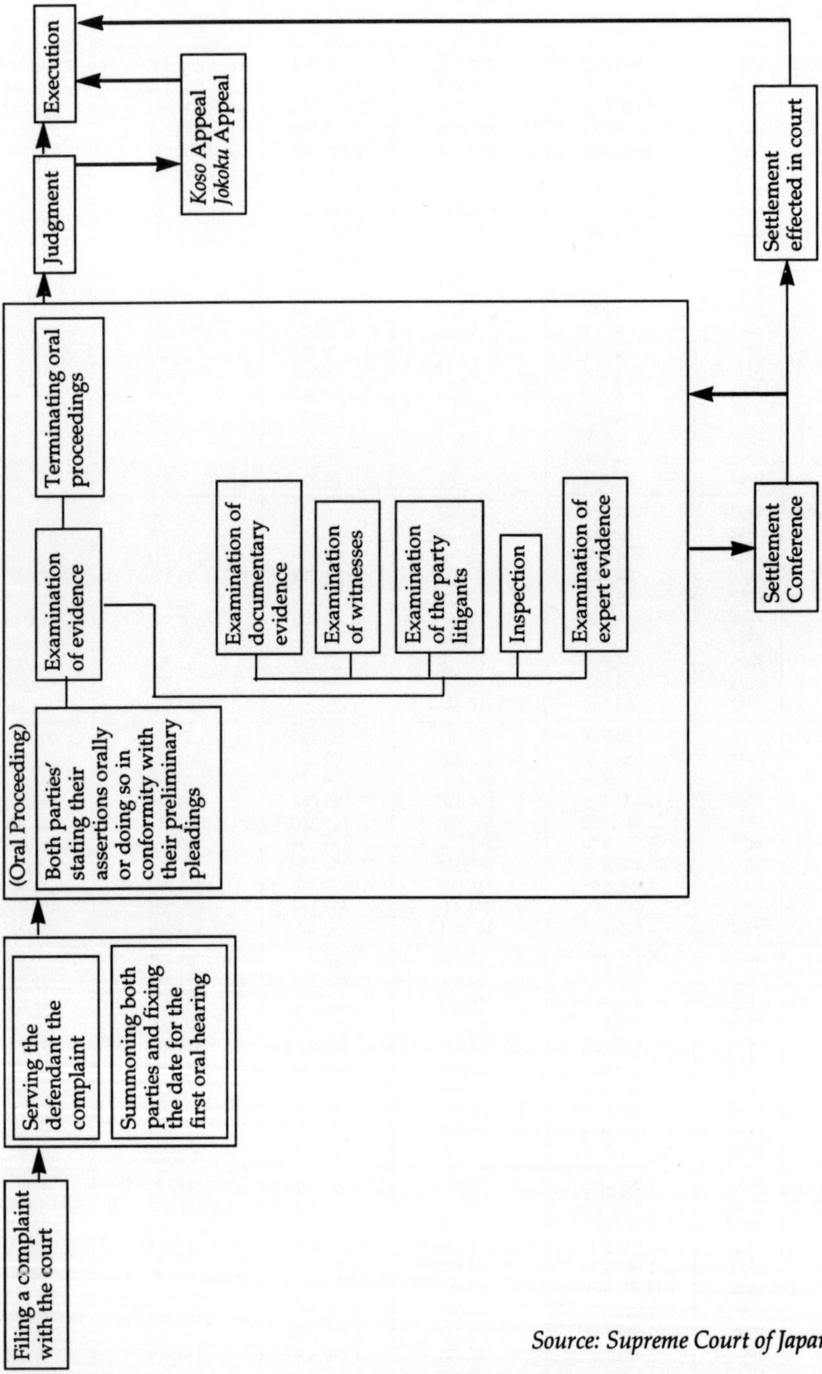

Source: Supreme Court of Japan, 1994

Table 9. Proceedings of Criminal Case

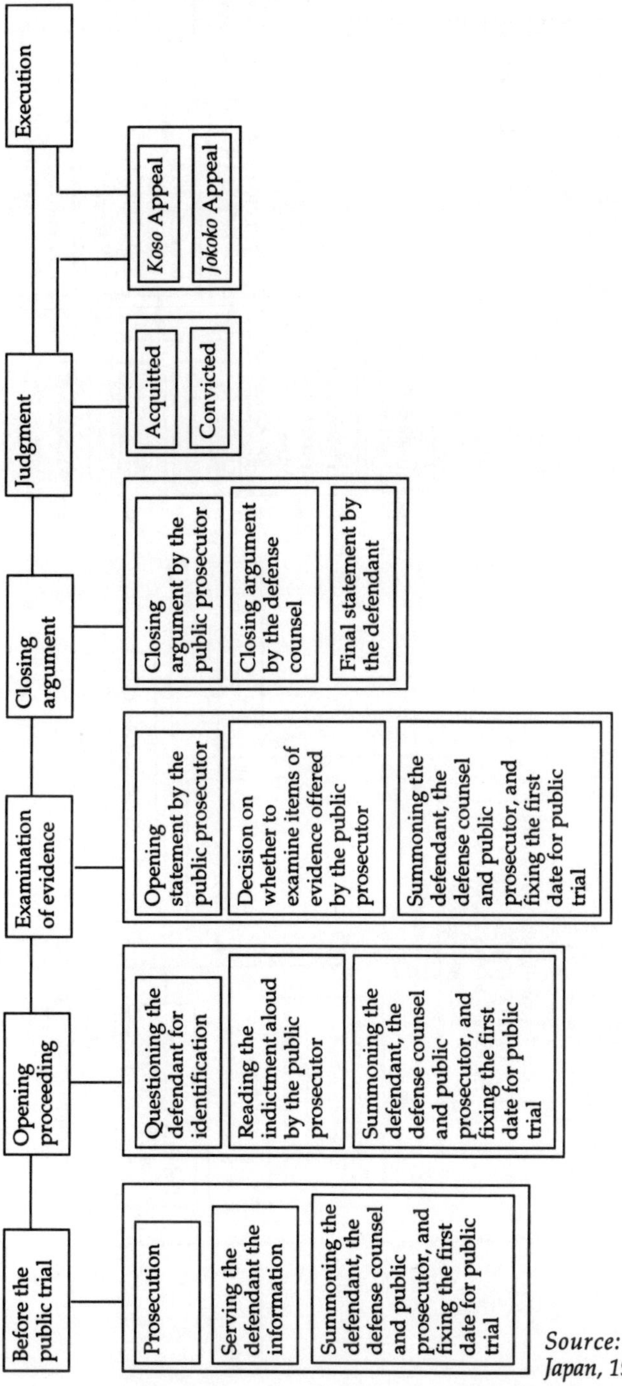

Source: Supreme Court of Japan, 1994

Table 10. Proceedings of Domestic Case

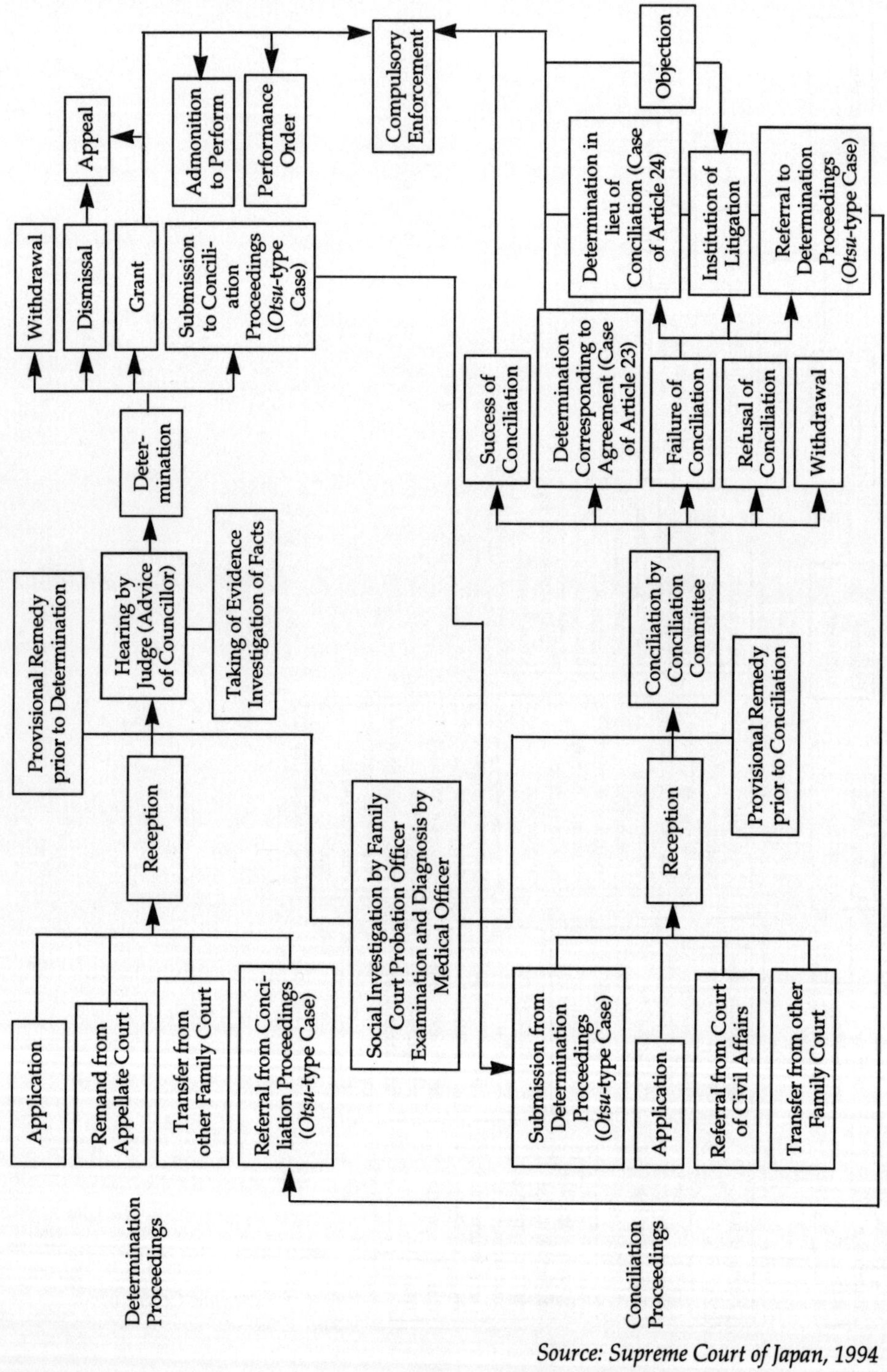

Source: Supreme Court of Japan, 1994

Table 11. Proceedings of Juvenile Case

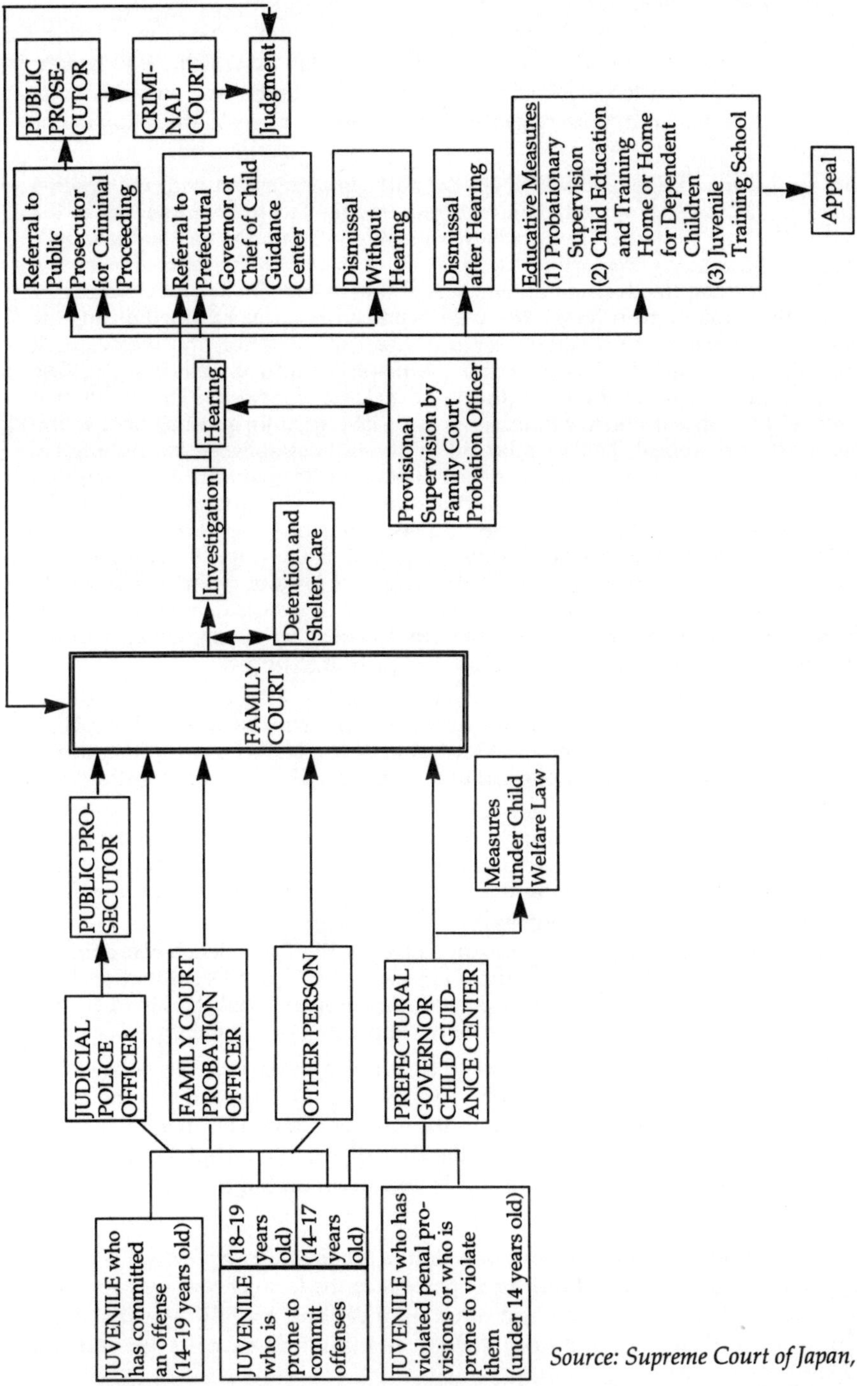

Source: Supreme Court of Japan, 1994

***Outline of Civil Trial in Japan*, 1995, pp 13–16, Supreme Court of Japan**

Appeal from Decision – Koso *Appeal and* Jokoku *Appeal* [See Table 3, p 409]

The party dissatisfied with the judgment of the court of first instance may lodge *Koso* appeal with a higher court within two weeks from the day on which the judgment has been served; and further lodge *Jokoku* appeal if he is still dissatisfied with the judgment in the second *Koso* instance. With regard to *Koso* and *Jokoku* appeals, the following points may be noted.

(a) *Koso* appeal may be lodged whenever the party is dissatisfied with the original judgment. In the *Koso* appeal, the Court goes into the fact in the same way as the trial in the first instance. The appellate court inquires into the fact and law once more to the extent necessary to ascertain the reasons for dissatisfaction by the parties regarding the decision of the court of first instance. The oral proceedings are continuation of the original trial and the procedures accomplished during the first trial continues to maintain force in the *Koso* instance; the materials of proceedings of the first instance and the materials added newly in the *Koso* instance form the basis of the judgment of the Court of Appeals. The situation at the *Jokoku* instance is entirely different. It is a trial regarding question of law, and the court of re-appeal (*Jokoku*) is bound by the facts established by the original judgment. In principle, the propriety of facts established by the original judgment is outside the jurisdiction of the court. It inquires only into the correctness of application of laws and orders. Therefore, the *Jokoku* appeal may be lodged only on the ground that the judgment of the original court contains unconstitutional questions, or is in contravention of laws or orders which would probably affect the conclusion of the judgment. So, in the *Jokoku* appeal, the court of original instance is vested with authority to reject, by ruling, the application for appeal on the ground that the form is irregular or improper.

(b) A judgment of a Summary Court may be appealed to a District Court, and the judgment of the District Court in the second instance may be appealed to a High Court of competent jurisdiction. The decision of the High Court, setting in the third instance may again be appealed to the Supreme Court where constitutional question is involved.

(c) A party may lodge a *Jokoku* appeal directly with a competent court from the judgment of the court of first instance with the consent of the other party, in case he is dissatisfied with the judgment only in regard to question of law. This appeal is called a 'jumping *Jokoku* appeal' (*Hiyaku Jokoku*).

(d) In the Supreme Court, cases are usually heard by the Petty Bench consisting of five justices of the Supreme Court. However, the Court Organization Law provides that the cases involving constitutional issues shall be heard by the Grand Bench comprised of all justices of the Supreme Court numbering 15.

Generally speaking, the average period of time spent in various levels of courts for ordinary types of cases may be set forth as follows: about 2.5 months in the Summary Court; 10.9 months in the first instance in the District Court; 11.5 months for the *Koso* appeal in the same court; 11.3 months for the *Koso* appeal in the High Court; 9.3 months for the *Jokoku* appeal in the same court; and 7.6 months in the Supreme Court.

Legal Aid to Indigent Litigants

As a matter of basic rule, such costs of litigation as are provided by law are borne by the losing party. It consists of court cost made payable in the form of revenue stamps which are to be affixed to the petition and other applications; travelling expenses, daily allowances, etc for a witness and so on. It does not include all the costs necessary for the prosecution of proceedings in a lawsuit, such as the lawyer's fee which amounts to a considerable sum.

With respect to the relief in litigation for the impoverished, there are provisions regarding 'Aid in Litigation' to satisfy the right of access to the courts. This aid applies to the case in which the chance of winning is not against the claimant.

However, there is an opinion that lawyer's fee should be included in the costs of suit. This opinion is based on the fact that the Japanese system concerning lawyer's fee appears to be contrary to the trend of legislation in many other countries. So this is one of the problems to be resolved in the future at the field of civil procedure in our country.

It is reported that the work of legal aid in our country was first started by the Private Affairs Consultation Office established by the Tokyo YMCA in 1892. In the prewar days this organization grew gradually with the support of private volunteers, but it failed to attain sufficient maturity. In the postwar days, however, with the upsurge in the sentiment of protection of human rights, there arose a strong demand for the establishment of a system of legal aid in a more solid basis. As a result, under the leadership of the Japan Federation of Bar Associations and supported by the Civil Liberties Bureau of the Ministry of Justice, preparations for the establishment of a private organization were pushed and finally in 1952, a foundation called the Legal Aid Association was established. This Association affords assistance in matters relating to the costs of suit and lawyer's fee. In the beginning necessary funds were raised from donations made by public organizations, and private persons, etc, and since 1957, grants were made by the government to enhance the offer, but we cannot say such are quite satisfactory yet. Further efforts in this field are desired in the future.

***Outline of Criminal Justice in Japan*, 1995, pp 26–28, Supreme Court of Japan**

APPEALS

1 *KOSO* APPEAL (FIRST APPEAL) [See Table 3, p 409]

A party who is not content with judgment rendered at the court of the first instance may file an appeal, which is called *Koso*, to a High Court for its review alleging an error exists. It must be noted that public prosecutor can appeal as well as defendant.

Grounds for *Koso* appeal are not only (i) non-compliance with procedural law in the trial proceedings, (ii) an error in the interpretation of or the application of law in the judgment, but (iii) excessive severity or leniency of the sentence, (iv) an error in fact-finding.

The *Koso* appeal proceedings are not new trials in which all issues of facts are tried again, but subsequent proceedings in which a High Court reviews the proceedings and the judgment of the court of the first instance by examining the written record of what happened at the original court. Therefore, the procedure of public trial, if any, in most of the *Koso* appeal cases are limited to such procedure as the public prosecutor and the defense counsel present oral argument whether the original judgment erred or not. In principle, a High Court, unlike the court of the first instance, does not examine witnesses and other evidences. However, it is exceptionally allowed for the court of *Koso* appeal to examine a witness who was examined during the first instance trial or a witness who could not be examined for various reasons, when it is necessary to inquire into factual matters that remain uncertain, notwithstanding the examination of the original court record.

If the High Court finds no error in the original judgment after reviewing the original court record and examining the factual matters, the court has to render a judgment to dismiss the appeal. On the other hand, if the court finds a reversible error in the original judgment, the court by a judgment has to quash the original judgment. If the High Court finds that the court of the first instance should make further examination of evidence or render a corrected judgment, the High Court by a judgment should remand the case to the court of first instance. When this occurs, the case will be tried again by the court of the first instance. However, the High Court may enter a new judgment immediately, if it is possible, on the basis of the record of proceedings and of the evidence examined at the court and at the original court.

In either case, no penalty heavier than that imposed by the original judgment can be pronounced if the appeal was filed only by defendant. It goes without saying that, in a retrial of the case, the decision of the High Court is binding the court of the first instance.

2 *JOKOKU* APPEAL (SECOND APPEAL)

The party may also file a statement of objection against the judgment of the court of *Koso* appeal, which is called *Jokoku* appeal, to the Supreme Court for its review. The grounds for *Jokoku* appeal are limited to (i) a violation of the constitution or an error in its interpretation, or (ii) an alleged conflict with precedent of the Supreme Court or High Courts. Considering that the Supreme Court, as being 'the Guardian of the Constitution', is the court of the last resort with the power to determine the constitutionality of any law, order, regulation or official act (Article 81 of the Constitution), the grounds for *Jokoku* appeal mentioned above are provided to empower the Supreme Court to exercise this power and perform the function of the final court in promoting uniformity in interpretation of law.

Thus, the main objective of the *Jokoku* appeal system, which is to secure proper interpretation of the constitution and the law, distinguishes the proceedings of the *Jokoku* appeal court, in which the examination of a witness never takes place, from that of the first instance or of the *Koso* appeal. However, considering that the Supreme Court is the final court of resort in Japan, it has the discretion to reverse such original judgments that has convicted an innocent, or that has exercised extreme impropriety in sentencing, if it deems that it is manifestly unjust not to do so.

The mode of adjudications on *Jokoku* appeal such as dismissing the *Jokoku* appeal when the Supreme Court finds no error in the original judgment or as remanding the case when the Supreme Court quashes the original judgment are nearly the same as those of *Koso* appeal. However, when quashing the original judgment, the Supreme Court sometimes remands the case not to the court of *Koso* appeal but to the court of the first instance. The Supreme Court can still enter its own independent judgment immediately as an exception.

***Guide to the Family Court of Japan*, 1995, pp 18–23, 26–31, Supreme Court of Japan**

IV JURISDICTION OF THE FAMILY COURT

1 Jurisdiction over Family Affairs Cases

The Family Court has a very broad jurisdiction encompassing all disputes and conflicts within the family as well as all related domestic affairs which are of legal significance. The Law for Determination of Family Affairs divides these problems into three kinds: ie (a) matters which by nature can only be disposed by a court's judgment such as a declaration of incompetency, a declaration of disappearance, or a correction of the family registers (These are called *Ko*-type matters.); (b) matters which should be disposed in accord with the agreement of the parties such as divorce (These are litigation matters.); and (c) matters which may be disposed either by agreement of the parties or by a court's decision such as share of expenses arising from marriage or partition of a decedent's estate (These are called *Otsu*-type matters.). The law provides that (a) will be governed exclusively by the determination procedure and (b) will follow exclusively the conciliation proceedings while (c) will be governed in the first instance by the conciliation proceedings and, in the event of failure of conciliation, by the determination procedure.

Though a judicial divorce may be sought in Japan under an action in a regular court, proceedings must first be commenced in the Family Court. Here an attempt is made through the conciliation proceedings to eliminate difficulties and to reconcile the parties, or where reconciliation is impossible, to have the parties agree to an equitable termination of the matrimonial state. Since divorce by mutual agreement is possible in Japan, unlike the situation in Europe and America, there is no conceptual difficulty such as the requirement of a court's judgment. Most divorce cases are settled in the conciliation stage of the Family Court. Only when it is not possible to reach any agreement and one of the spouses still wants a divorce, will an action for cause be brought in the District Court.

The new provisional remedy system came into force in the determination procedure in 1981. This is a means whereby the party who invokes it successfully prevents the adverse party from taking steps which would thwart the enforcement of the final determination during the course of the determination procedure. For instance, in case where a divorced wife applies for a determination of distribution of matrimonial property due to divorce and her husband is likely to dispose the property, the Family Court may issue an order of provisional attachment prohibiting him from disposing the property until the final determination shall have been entered. The new provisional remedy system also enables the party to overcome the impending difficulty or prevent imminent danger during the determination procedure. For instance, in case where an applicant for a determination of support is too poor to buy the daily necessities, the Family Court may issue an order of provisional disposition forcing the adverse party to pay money temporarily until the final determination shall have been entered. These orders of the Family Court are enforceable.

Although the conventional procedure (often costly and troublesome) of compulsory execution is available for the enforcement of performance of obligations decided upon or agreed upon in the disposition of family affairs cases, the Family Court has power to take, upon application by a party, certain measures for ensuring the performance of such obligations. The Family Court will investigate, upon petition of the party concerned, to see if an obligation to pay money imposed by it has been performed. If not, the court will issue a warning notice to perform the obligation which, in turn, if neglected will result in an enforcement order. Failure to obey the enforcement order produces a non-penal fine against the offending party. Also, where it is inconvenient for the parties to make payments directly each other or payments are to be made in installments, the Family Court may intervene between them requiring the obligor to make deposits of money with the court which the court in turn pays to the obligee. Not only does this help the recipient party to obtain what he or she is entitled much more easily, but also saves him or her the awkwardness and uncomfortableness that often accompany even the voluntary performances of such obligations.

Information and Advising service for domestic affairs at the Family Court is a service accompanied with the filing procedure, rendered by competent members of the personnel in response to the request of the general public. When any citizen with various family troubles steps in the inquiry office of the Family Court, the adviser on duty listens to him and help him to find what his problems really are. If necessary, as is often the case, he informs of the detail of the filing procedure. This practice provides a way of easier access to the regular services of the Family Courts (and of other social welfare agencies, too), and is very popular as the fact that 321,649 people ask for such advice in 1993 shows.

2 Jurisdiction over Juvenile Delinquency Cases

The Family Court handles cases involving delinquent juveniles under 20 years of age. 'Delinquent juveniles' include not only minors who have committed criminal offenses under the penal laws but juveniles whose tendencies indicate that they might commit offenses in future as well. The court has primary jurisdiction in regard to all juvenile offenses, whether they are felonies such as homicides or arsons, or misdemeanors such as traffic offenses. Thus, all criminal cases concerning minors must primarily be sent to the Family Court as juvenile delinquency cases for investigation and hearing.

The present Juvenile Law provides that the Family Court has jurisdiction over such a minor as (a) habitually disobeys the proper control of his custodian, (b) repeatedly deserts his home without proper reason, (c) associates with persons having a criminal tendency or offense or who are of immoral character, or immoral persons, or frequents places of dubious reputation, or (d) habitually acts so as to injure or endanger his own morals or those of others, provided that from his character or environment there is a strong likelihood that the minor involved will become an offender.

Children under 14 years of age are primarily handled by the Child Guidance Center, as provided by the Child Welfare Law when they have committed acts which, if committed by a person over 13, would constitute an offense under the penal laws. These young children come under the jurisdiction of the Family Court only when the Prefectural Governor or the Chief of the Child Guidance Center refer them to the Family Court.

The Family Court has ordinarily jurisdiction over any juvenile under 20 years of age, but has exceptionally jurisdiction over the following persons over 20 years of age: (1) any probationer of whom the Family Court is informed by the Director of the Probation Office on the ground of his tendency of delinquency beyond control by probationary supervision; (2) any parolee who does not keep the conditions to be observed and is applied for the necessity of his recommitment to the Juvenile and Training School by the Regional Parole Board; and (3) any inmate of the Juvenile Training School who is applied for the extension of the term of his commitment by the Superintendent of the School on the ground of the necessity of continuance of his reform education.

3 Jurisdiction over Adult Criminal Cases

Adults who have committed acts injurious to the welfare of juveniles are also subject to the Family Court's jurisdiction. Various specific offenses are set down in the Child Welfare Law, the Labor Standards Law, and the School Education Law, etc. Such offenses as the inducement of obscene acts, cruel treatment, and employment of children at extremely late hours are examples. The foundation of the jurisdiction over the offenses is the protection of juveniles and the maintenance of their basic human rights. However, neither desertion nor neglect of the duty of support by parents or guardians constitutes an offense under the jurisdiction of the Family Court. Support is considered to be family law problem and therefore is subject to determination and conciliation procedure of the family affairs division, while desertion, if sufficient to constitute an offense under the Penal Code, is handled by a regular criminal court.

V THE FAMILY COURT'S PROCEDURES

Procedures for Family Affairs Cases

(a) Both determination and conciliation proceedings are commenced upon application of the person concerned. The application may be either written or oral. All hearings involved are non-public and informal, which are quite different from litigation in a regular civil court.

(b) After the application for the determination proceedings is filed, the Family Court summons the parties and conducts a hearing, if proper, in the presence of Family Court Councillors. Where necessary the judge may order an investigation by the Family Court Probation Officer, may seek the diagnostic services of the Family Court Clinic or may require the production of evidence.

When a determination is issued by the judge, it may be appealed to the High Court, if the Supreme Court Rules permit. Once the determination becomes binding, personal relationships are fixed in accord therewith. If the decision orders payment of money or transfer of property, it may immediately be enforced.

(c) Conciliation seeks to settle a family dispute through the intervention of a court facilitating a compromise between the parties. The conciliation proceedings are conducted by a conciliation committee which is normally composed of one judge and two Conciliation Commissioners of Family Affairs, one of whom is usually a woman. As mentioned above, the parties are ordinarily summoned to the Family Court for a hearing. An attempt is then made through expert advice to guide the parties to reach a compromise which is just and fitted to the welfare of both parties and the interested persons.

When the parties in the conciliation proceedings reach an agreement approved of by the conciliation committee, the agreement is entered in the court's case record and it has the same binding force as an absolute judgment or an order of determination. Cases most frequently subjected to conciliation are those involving divorce, designation of the parent to exercise parental power, partition of a decedent's estate, compensation on termination of *de facto* marriage, and support. Applications for divorce are submitted principally by wives, constituting over 70 percent of the total.

Since divorce can be accomplished merely by a simple registration of an agreement between the spouses in Japan, only a portion of divorces reach the Family Court. Most of the divorce cases brought before the Family Court are settled there and only a very small number go on to the District Court's judicial divorce procedure. Though many of the divorce cases in the Family Court attain their aim, not a few number ends in reconciliation and rehabilitation of the matrimonial relationship. If a divorce is effected, such matters as consolation money, support, distribution of matrimonial property, and the custody of children are also determined by the conciliation proceedings.

2 Procedures for Juvenile Delinquency Cases

(1) Family Court proceedings involving juveniles are generally commenced when:

(i) the police officer or the Public Prosecutor sends a juvenile case to the court (Cases involving minor offenses are sent directly to the Family Court by the police officer while the other cases must pass through the Public Prosecutor.);

(ii) the Prefectural Governor or the Chief of the Child Guidance Center refers a juvenile case to the court;

(iii) the Family Court Probation Officer who has is covered a delinquent juvenile reports the case to the court;

(iv) one charged with the protection of the juvenile, a school teacher, or any other person inform the Family court of the case;

(2) When a case is filed in the Family Court, the judge in charge of the particular action assigns the Family Court Probation Officer giving him directions for his investigation. The officer then undertakes a thorough and precise social inquiry into the personality, personal history, family background, and environment of the juvenile. When the juvenile needs to be taken into protective custody the judge may detain him into the Juvenile Detention and Classification Home up to four weeks.

We have the system of an Attendant, which is similar to the system of a defence counsel for a criminal defendant. A juvenile and his parents or guardians may appoint one or more Attendants with the permission of the Family Court. If a lawyer is to be appointed as the Attendant, however, no permission of the Family Court is required.

Upon completion of his inquiry, the Family Court Probation Officer sets down the minor's social record and his opinion as to the case with his recommendations for its disposition, and submits this as a report to the judge. Taking this report into consideration, the judge sets a time and place for a hearing. The hearing is non-public, and no person other than the judge, the court clerk, the juvenile, the persons charged with the protection of the juvenile (parents or guardians), the Family Court Probation Officer, the Attendant, persons specially permitted by the judge may be present.

(3) If the judge feels that it is improper to take any of the above courses immediately or that further and more thorough investigation must be necessary before a determination can be made, the juvenile may be placed under the supervision of the Family Court Probation Officer. During this period of supervision, the juvenile may continue to live with the person who is charged with his protection (his parents or guardians) under conditions imposed by the Family Court or he may be placed under the guidance of a suitable institution, agency or individual. This intermediate disposition, taken while the final determination is held in suspension, is called tentative probationary supervision (*Shiken-kansatsu*) and is one of the most important responsibilities of Family Court Probation Officers.

(4) The Family Court judge renders his decision and issues his determination in accord with his own wisdom after considering the investigation of the Family Court Probation Officers involved, the mental and physical examinations required, and the testimony at the hearing. Where necessary for the determination of facts, witnesses may be examined including expert witnesses – under the Code of Criminal Procedure in so far as the provisions of the Code do not conflict with the nature of juvenile proceedings.

(5) The determination of the judge may take one of several forms. It is made on the basis of the Family Court Probation Officer's report, the judge's own study and inquiry, and the results of the hearing. The possible forms are as follows:

(i) A decision to refer the case to the competent Prefectural Governor or, Chief of the Child Guidance Center. This action is taken when it is deemed that the minor should be dealt with under the Child Welfare Law rather than be placed under protective control.

(ii) A decision to dismiss the case. Such a decision is reached when the Court finds it is unnecessary to make any particular disposition of the child. Actually, though, often a considerable amount of casework is carried on prior to the final determination. In case the court finds it lacks in jurisdiction, or is not satisfied that the case is proved beyond reasonable doubt, the same decision shall be entered.

(iii) A decision to refer the case to the Public Prosecutor. The basis of this decision is the view that the minor should be subjected to normal criminal procedure due to the serious nature of the offense or the circumstances of the case, only when a juvenile is 16 years of age and over. The court also refers the case to the Public Prosecutor when it finds the person is over 19.

(iv) A decision to place the juvenile under protective control (educative measures). There are three kinds of protective control.

(i) The juvenile is placed under the probationary supervision of the Probation Office. This is an organ of the Ministry of Justice with one office located in the district of each Family Court. The actual supervision over juveniles is undertaken by the Probation Officer of the district office and he is aided in his work by volunteers from among the public who are called Volunteer Probation Officers.

(ii) The juvenile is placed in the Child Education and Training Home (*Kyogo-in*) or the Home for Dependent Children (*Yogo-shisetsu*). Both of these institutions are provided for under the Child Welfare Law. The Child Education and Training Homes are established by the National or Prefectural Governments, or private persons to take care of children who are delinquents or are likely to become delinquents, while the Homes for Dependent Children are private or prefectural institutions designed to care for dependent, abused or neglected children.

(iii) The juvenile is placed in the Juvenile Training School (*Shonen-in*). This is an institution of the Ministry of Justice to give corrective education to juveniles committed to it by the Family Courts. The Juvenile Training Schools are divided into four groups: Primary – which care for juveniles 14–15 without necessity of medical care, Middle – which care for juveniles over 15 without aggravated criminal tendencies, Advanced – which care for juveniles 16–22 with aggravated criminal tendencies, and Medical – which care for all juveniles 14–25 who need medical treatment physically or mentally.

(6) In his order of determination the judge writes out the reasons for his decision and the disposition of the juvenile to be taken. A copy of the order then is attached to the social records and forwarded to the particular agency charged with its execution, such as the Probation Office or the Juvenile Training School to provide a reference for the minor's treatment.

Even after the notice of the decision to place the juvenile under protective control was given, because of the protective nature of the disposition of the juvenile and the concern of the family court involved with his future development, the judge and the Family Court Probation Officers may visit the juvenile under protective control for observation and necessary recommendations to the agency involved. Further, if an inmate of the Juvenile Training School is to be kept there after he has attained his majority or the term he can be detained by original decision has expired, in order to continue his corrective education, a petition to the Family Court must be made by the Superintendent of the Juvenile Training School and the approval of the judge obtained, if proper.

(7) If the juvenile himself or his legal representative or Attendant objects to the Family Court's decision to place the juvenile under protective control, they may file a *Kokoku* appeal in the High Court. The Attendant, however, may not appeal against the clearly expressed intention of the custodian who appointed him. In addition to that, they may make a second Kokoku appeal to the Supreme Court from an order dismissing an appeal only on the limited ground.

Miyazaki, A, 'The Judicial System' (1966) edited translated extract from Tanaka, H, *The Japanese Legal System*, 1976, pp 446–47, 453–71, University of Tokyo Press

First of all, our judicial system had to be created within a short span of time 'from above,' so to speak. Establishment of a new judicial system as a measure in the creation of a new legal system [along Western lines] was one of the necessary preconditions to Japan's demand for revision of the unequal treaties [that had been concluded with Western nations in the 1850s and 1860s], which was one of the most urgent tasks of the Meiji government. Unlike the situation in most foreign nations, there was little inherent need to create and develop a judicial system in Japan at that time. The judicial system was created instantaneously on the sole initiative of the bureaucrats without much pressure from the general populace. Thus it was possible in Japan for a modern judicial system to be created in the most easily understandable form without any opposition. This indeed did take place, just as if a picture had been drawn on a blank sheet of paper, while in most other countries modern court systems were created only after serious efforts to unify the existing court systems which, reflecting the hierarchical divisions in the populace in the feudal era, had several independent layers with no reasonable division of functions. This means that the Japanese judicial system at its birth achieved the goal of a simplified system with schematic consistency, a goal still to be achieved in other countries even after decades of hard effort to sever the links with the past. If we look at judicial systems throughout the world in this period [ie in the last quarter of the nineteenth century], it would be impossible to find a system to rival the Japanese judicial system in terms of uniformity and simplicity.

This peculiarity in the way the [modern] judicial system in Japan emerged brought about its second peculiarity, the extreme degree of stagnation once the system was established. There was nothing to serve as a force to counteract the newly introduced idea of the judiciary. Nor had the Japanese people perceived any real inherent need to establish a new judicial system [except as a means to revise the unequal treaties]. Under these circumstances it was almost inevitable that a mental attitude of inertia developed, even among those closely related to the administration of justice, ... which tacitly assumed that the judicial system which had been established was the only possible system. Thus there was an inherent danger from the outset that future reform of the judicial system would be neglected, since no one among the lawyers or among those in power, and much less in the general populace, ever thought that such a reform was an urgent problem.

If we consider these peculiarities of the Japanese judicial system together with the general proposition that the courts are the central mechanism of the law, it may be easy to fathom the cause-effect relationships between the lack of significant reform in the Japanese judicial system and the stagnation of Japanese law. As a corollary to this, one would also notice that the placing of greater emphasis on the role of law in Japan and the making of efforts to improve the judicial system, the central mechanism of law, are inseparably related. It would be absurd to neglect the latter task and emphasize the need for the former through a sort of sermon on morals. What is most necessary in discussing Japan's judicial system is to reconfirm these self-evident propositions, to disclose the distortions in the Japanese court system which have emerged in the past, to gauge the disparity between the Japanese system and the universal trends seen in present-day foreign systems, to determine the direction that should be followed in the future, and to make continuous efforts to strengthen our judicial system in those directions. ...

...

If we look at the Japanese court system in reference to the above-mentioned general trends, we will find that our system is peculiar in its attitude toward special courts. In the early [Meiji] period when Japan tried to model her court system after the French system, hardly any part of the system of special courts was adopted because it was thought that special courts were out of tune with the schematic plan of courts as then contemplated. Though it was in the French tradition to establish commercial courts and labor courts as special courts, neither was introduced to Japan. This tendency was maintained even after the Organization of Courts Act (*Saibansho Kosei Ho*), modeled on the German pattern, was enacted under the Meiji Constitution.) ... One phenomenon which should be noted here was the fact that the Outlines of the Proposed Amendment to the Book on Relatives; of the Civil Code (*Mimpo Shinzoku Hen chu Kaisei no Yoko*) [1925] and the Outlines of the Proposed Amendment to the Book on Succession of the Civil Code (*Mimpo Sozoku Hen chu Kaisei no Yoko*) [1927] proposed the establishment of 'domestic relations courts' (*kaji shimpansho*). This formed part of the undercurrent which brought about the establishment of family courts (*katei saibansho*) after the Second World War.

Respect for the ideal of maximum simplification of the court system, which meant refusal to establish special courts unless absolutely necessary, was carried one step further under the new constitution. The constitution of Japan set as its ideal the integration of judicial power into a single system of [ordinary] judicial courts, by explicitly prohibiting the establishment of 'extraordinary tribunals' (*tokubetsu saibansho*) in Article 76, Paragraph 2. In spite of this, there is a paradoxical phenomenon that a number of institutions which are substantially the same in nature as special courts have developed under the new constitution. One example is the establishment of family courts. Another is the introduction of the system of administrative commissions vested with quasijudicial functions which are modeled after the American pattern. According to the interpretation of the above provision of the constitution, these institutions are not *tokubetsu saibansho* (extraordinary tribunals). [Since *tokubetsu saibansho* can also mean 'special courts,' discussions on special courts in Japan have been unnecessarily confused. I believe that the meaning of the term '*tokubetsu saibansho*,' officially translated as 'extraordinary tribunal,' is limited to entirely unusual tribunals established to meet unusual situations.]

The above observations seem to reveal the unfavorable attitude displayed by the Japanese court system toward special courts. ... The establishment of family courts is, therefore, conspicuous. We have now to consider why the special courts movement has not been strong in Japan and why only family courts have been institutionalized despite the general trends in other countries. This will help to reveal the hidden idiosyncrasies of the Japanese court system.

(1) The biggest source of friction which ensued from the introduction of a modern legal system in Japan was legal control of family life. The fact that the old Civil Code [of 1890 drafted by Boissonade] was never put into effect tells the story [of this friction] in a dramatic way. Those who opposed putting the old Civil Code into effect carried the banner of protection of the traditional 'good morals and beautiful manners' (*jumpu bizoku*). ... This friction was papered over by the enactment of Books IV and V of the Civil Code in 1898 after the 'Code Disputes' (*Hoten Ronso*) However, a sense of incompatibility between tradition and the new law remained. One of the expressions of this feeling was the repeatedly expressed doubt cast on the wisdom of solving disputes about domestic relations by way of formal adjudication in courts. Proposals for establishing domestic relations courts made in the Taisho period had their roots in this feeling. The enactment of the Conciliation of Personal Affairs Act (*Jinji Chotei Ho*) in 1939, which was favorably received, was an extension of that idea.

This persistent tension between [the necessity of settling] domestic relations disputes [by paying respect to tradition] and the Western style judicial structure developed further after the Second World War, and took a different shape. The family law was completely changed in a direction which generally denied tradition. What was desired was establishment of a special machinery which would carry out the task of making the new law permeate everyday life on the one hand and on the other hand would deal with various conflicts which could arise because of the gap between the revised law, which changed the ideals of family law in a rather hasty manner, and the realities of people's lives. It was therefore desired to establish an institution which would be somewhat different from other institutions dealing with ordinary types of cases – an institution which would handle cases in a way more familiar to the people and which is more flexible in its procedure and structure. It was natural that the proposal for the establishment of domestic relations courts was placed on the table again, albeit reflecting a new viewpoint. The domestic relations courts were thus established in 1948. They were then amalgamated with the juvenile courts (*shonen shimpansho*), an institution established in 1922 during what was then a new wave in penal policy. The juvenile court was, in substance, of the nature of a special court. The two institutions formed the family courts (*katei saibansho*). Thus a system of courts which bases its jurisdiction on two seemingly dissimilar areas – ie civil cases covering domestic relations and juvenile cases, which are criminal in substance – was established.

The family court movement has existed as an undercurrent on the Continent as well. What has been envisaged in Germany, however, is somewhat different from the picture of the Japanese family courts. Japanese family courts emerged under the strong influence of the family court movement in America, which advocated putting domestic relations cases and juvenile cases under the jurisdiction of the same court. In fact this proposal had been experimented with in several American states, but there was no direct connection with the family court movement on the Continent. The family court system is truly unique within the Japanese court system, in that it is completely of American origin and in that it is the only court which clearly is in substance a special court.

(2) The fact that family courts have taken root in the Japanese court system is a good illustration of what I have described as the rationale of special courts. It shows that what

in substance are special courts can be established even in Japan, despite the prohibition against *tokubetsu saibansho* in the constitution, if there is a strong desire for the establishment of a particular sort of special court. It should also be noted that Japanese family courts, just like special courts in any other country, are placed in the position of being continually required to assert their distinctive characteristics *vis-à-vis* ordinary courts and to prove their efficacy. So long as they pursue their original ideals, family courts have to try to make themselves distinct in terms of their personnel and procedure. In that sense they must play the role of continually bringing to light the hidden problems of ordinary courts. Family courts, which are situated at the tip of the glacier-slow movement in the evolution of judicial courts, are destined to act as agents introducing diversity into the court system.

(3) Only after an investigation of the causal relationship between the fact that family life in Japan creates a tension with the court system and the fact that family courts are practically the only kind of special courts, can we understand why no serious desire has arisen in other fields for the establishment of machinery which in substance is similar to special courts. Of course we must note the fact that the role which special courts are expected to play in other countries has been shouldered in Japan by the American-type administrative commissions. The primary reason why we don't see serious efforts to establish special courts in other areas, however, lies in the fact that there was, and is, no seriously felt need. ... The matter is not peculiar to special courts in this sense. There has been no serious concern about courts in general, since contact with this institution of the state has been minimal in fields other than family law. The problem is indeed one aspect of the general problem concerning the function and efficiency of the whole machinery of law. So long as the situation remains as it is there will naturally be no serious criticisms made about the efficiency and manner of operation of the ordinary courts. Much less is there a basis in Japan from which a strong desire for the establishment of special courts could emerge. ...

To discuss the merits and demerits of special courts in an abstract manner without paying due regard to this fundamental problem [ie the lack of concern about the judicial system as a whole] is meaningless. ... Thus I believe that proposals for the establishment of special courts in Japan lack any support in society at the present stage. What we should do now is to face squarely the fact that even ordinary courts, the main stream of the judicial system, are not fully performing their function, and to try to strengthen them. If we try to strengthen the secondary stream without having first strengthened the main stream, there will be little hope of success. Even if special courts are created in a high-handed way, it can only result in drying up both the main stream and the secondary stream, so long as the main stream is left as it is.

IV. SOME PROBLEMS OF THE JAPANESE COURT SYSTEM

The Japanese court system has not faced the problem of multiplicity and diversity inherent in a federal system. Neither has it experienced serious conflict between ordinary courts and special courts. Thus various problems, which might have been perceived if there had been such sharp conflicts, have been ignored. As a result there has been an inclination toward excessive attachment to, and complacency toward, the existing system, which after all was not established by a spontaneous development but was handed down from above. Side by side with this inclination, there has been a tendency for a schematic and formalistic way of thinking to prevail even among those who are professionally concerned with the adjudicative process. This attitude reflects the schematic uniformity of the Japanese court system as described above.

What I wish to discuss here is whether such a mentality has been subconsciously carried over to the solution of various problems concerning ordinary courts, resulting in a blurred division of functions among various courts as well as a perverted equality between courts, thereby shaping a latent characteristic of Japanese courts as contrasted with systems in foreign countries. There are three major points to be discussed from this angle. The first is whether or not such a mental attitude among lawyers has hindered the adoption of drastic measures for the settlement of cases where only small claims are involved. The second is related to the first, namely, whether or not our appellate system has been marred by formalistic thinking to an extent unseen in foreign countries. The third is whether or not the predominance of an excessively schematic way of thinking about the geographical distribution of courts has resulted in our system ignoring the differences in local conditions.

A. On Courts at the Lowest Level

... Japanese courts at the lowest level were at first created upon the French pattern. Even though Japan took on the name and the form of *justice de paix*, however, it was an utter impossibility for her to create more than two thousand justice of the peace courts throughout the country [as France did], as she had to create an entirely new judicial system without having any tradition to base it on. Neither was it possible for her to fill benches in courts at the lowest level with laymen. There was no necessary precondition for her doing so because her situation was different from that in France where the *justice de paix* system was created during a revolution carried out by *citoyens*. Therefore the Japanese 'justice of the peace courts' (*chian saibansho*) emerged as part of the regular court system, manned by career judges, though one may suspect that their legal training, by contemporary standards, was not substantially different from that of laymen. This created the tendency to try to assimilate justice of the peace courts with other kinds of ordinary courts as far as possible rather than to stress their peculiarities . . . as had been the case in France. In other words, though the Japanese justice of the peace court appeared in form as the equivalent of the French *justice de paix*, it was in substance nearer to the German *Amtsgericht*, even at the outset. Consequently, when the court system was reorganized along German lines by the Organization of Courts Act [of 1890], justice of the peace courts were smoothly absorbed into the new system [as ward courts (*ku saibansho*)] without any of the psychological tension experienced in France during the more than one hundred years of history of *justice de paix* before they were finally reorganized into *tribunal d'instance*. Even compared with the German *Amtsgericht*, Japanese [ward] courts in substance had little of the character of summary courts which [in theory should] stand close to the populace. In fact, if we look at the procedure followed in ward courts and the system of appeal therefrom, we cannot help thinking that they had more in common with courts of first instance exercising general jurisdiction, than did the German *Amtsgericht*.

After the Second World War, substantial changes were made in courts at the lowest level. The familiar name of 'ward courts' was deliberately changed to 'summary courts' (*kan'i saibansho*). The position of 'summary court judge' (*kan'i saibansho hanji*) was created with the expectation that it would be filled by those who would follow a career different from that of ordinary judges. The number of summary courts was set at twice that of the old ward courts. All these decisions reveal the deliberate efforts made to change the position of courts at the lowest level. Here we can clearly perceive an intention to give summary courts a position demonstrably different from that of district courts, which are courts of first instance with general jurisdiction. It is not hard to surmise that what was intended was to approximate them to justices of the peace and small claims courts in America.

The question to be asked here is whether the ideal which lay behind the establishment of summary courts is taking root in reality or whether these courts are moving to assimilate themselves with courts of first instance exercising general jurisdiction, as was the case in the past. To my regret I am unable to say that summary courts are steadily marching toward the achievement of their original ideal.

(1) The primary reason for this is that when summary courts were first organized inadequate consideration was given to [the development of special] procedural rules to be followed in them. It is obvious that summary courts cannot adequately demonstrate any special advantages in performing their functions so long as the ordinary procedural rules have not been modified to meet their new task, no matter how much the special nature of their personnel is emphasized. Indeed almost all the measures taken in other countries to handle small claims effectively give much more weight to the problem of adjusting procedural rules. Procedures to be followed in summary courts are different from those in district courts only to the same extent as procedures in ward courts differed from those in district courts under the old system. This, together with other shortcomings in our court system and lack of adequate understanding about [the significance of affording efficient machinery for adjudicating] small claims, has created the tendency, as in the past, to model the method of disposing of litigation in summary courts after the pattern of procedure in courts of first instance with general jurisdiction. This tendency is further strengthened by the following factors: namely, the maximum amount at issue in the claims which may be filed in the summary courts has been increased with the purpose of decreasing the number of civil *jokoku* appeals to the Supreme Court, and summary courts have had to bear the burden of the problems which emerged from the awkward assistant judgeship system.

We should also point out the following phenomenon in relation to the problem discussed above. Traditionally the procedures for handling civil cases have been judged by certain criteria [which have developed with the adjudicative process in courts of general jurisdiction in mind]. These traditional criteria have been so firmly embedded [in the minds of Japanese lawyers] that they assume that no other procedures would ever be imagined. Judged by such criteria, the procedures in summary courts often appear to them to be untrustworthy. Inadvertent expressions of this distrust of summary courts tend further to drive summary courts to try to assimilate their practice with that in district courts.

In order to achieve their goals as originally perceived, summary courts should have developed new forms of procedure and new methods of disposing of cases, and departed from the traditional road. It was, however, not to be expected that summary courts would achieve by themselves such a goal which would have necessitated a number of new experiments, because they were, and still are, surrounded by an atmosphere [created by the tradition described above] which was critical of any experimentation. What was needed for the development of a truly summary procedure was encouragement by career judges, by those responsible for the 'administration of the judiciary' and by practicing attorneys. But such encouragement was given only rarely, if at all.

(2) The above comment also points up the mental processes which Japanese lawyers tend to follow.

The court system, by its nature, must cope with an extremely wide range of demands. On the one hand it must accept cases involving an enormous amount of money, which involve highly complicated issues of law. On the other hand it must dispose of minor cases and small claims in an appropriate manner. From the standpoint of strengthening the court's ties with the people and thereby broadening the base of the judicial system, the latter may in one respect exert a larger influence. The American small claims court movement, which seeks to dispose of minor cases appropriately in accordance with the principle 'litigation is for the people and not for lawyers,' gives an accurate insight into this truth. What is desired for the Japanese judicial system at this stage is not so much the creation of elaborate and complicated procedures as the establishment of adequate measures to meet the latter problem [concerning disposition of small claims] by throwing away the traditional way of thinking. This latter problem has been almost completely neglected since the establishment of the modern judicial system, reflecting the peculiarities of the circumstances surrounding its birth. Such neglect has been one of the reasons why the people have been driven far from the reach of the judicial system.

The Japanese legal profession has tended to emphasize the summit and neglect the foundation. I am afraid that this is causing the further alienation of the people from the judicial system. I cannot help thinking that it is extremely important for us to face seriously the problems concerning small claims courts and to reflect deeply upon the outcome of our neglect.

B. On the Appellate System

The failure to give adequate consideration to the problems concerning the system of handling small claims thus seems to depict a pattern of thought peculiar to Japanese lawyers. In close correlation with this point, I would like to explore next whether or not the formalistic way of thinking which derives from the same roots has been reflected in our structuring of the appellate system. If we look at the Japanese appellate system objectively, keeping the above question in mind, we will readily discover a tendency, or a psychology, characteristic of Japanese lawyers. Unlike the problems concerning those small claims courts, the appellate system is one of the oft-discussed problems in relation to the judicial system. ... I therefore wish to limit my writing to the extent necessary to point out the problems concerning this topic in a pretty general manner. To express it straightforwardly, what is characteristic of the Japanese lawyers' view on the appellate system is the almost blind adherence to the scheme of three levels of adjudication with one chance for trial de novo at the second level and another chance for full review of issues of law at the third. The most faithful observance of this formula is to be found in the structure of the courts under the Organization of Courts Act. The Courts Act [of 1947] had somewhat destroyed the symmetry of this scheme. Yet the above formula of three levels of adjudication has been retained for civil litigation. The above scheme was modified for criminal procedure as a part of the over-all reform of criminal procedure made pursuant to strong suggestions by the occupation authorities. This has created an imbalance between civil and criminal procedure. Yet [it is noteworthy that] there has been a persistent trend among lawyers, particularly among practicing attorneys, to try to dissolve the imbalance by restoring the *status quo ante* in relation to criminal procedure.)

The ideal of the appellate system is to maintain a balance between the demand for correcting possible errors in the original judgment and the demand for uniformity in statutory interpretation in as simple a form as possible, without causing unreasonable delay. From this standpoint the system of three levels of adjudication in the form described above can certainly be regarded as one of the ideal types which the wisdom and experience of the legal profession has produced. However, we must not forget that it is nothing more than an ideal form. One should bear in mind that a literal application of this ideal may possibly bring about a result repugnant to the ideal of the appellate system as described above. In fact a comparative study of appellate systems reveals that few countries have ever built up their appellate systems by the rigid and literal application of this ideal form. Most countries have modified this ideal form so as to match their own traditions.

(1) The first modification which appears universally is to provide for differences in the grounds of appeal to correspond with the seriousness of each case. Of particular interest is the appellate system for small claim cases. There are two kinds of systems which at first sight appear to go in entirely opposite directions. One is to restrict the grounds of appeal very narrowly on the theory that it is in fact an imbalance to allow appeals in relation to small claim cases as liberally as in relation to complicated cases or cases with a large sum of money at stake. The appellate systems on the Continent are more or less based on this notion. The other is to allow a trial *de novo* (as if it were a newly instituted case) when the loser in small claims court files an appeal. This is coupled with structuring the procedure in small claims courts in an extremely summary way. This system is followed in relation to appeals from judgments of justice of the peace courts in some states in America. This makes a great contrast with the general appellate system in America where a trial *de novo* or 'supplementary trial' (*zokushin*) [ie trial of facts to supplement the trial made in the court of first instance] is almost never held in the appellate court when the appeal is from any other court than a court dealing with small claims. There is a close correlation between the very summary procedure in small claims courts and trial *de novo* when an appeal is brought against the judgment entered therein.

Compared with these appellate systems in other countries, the Japanese system constitutes a marked exception, in that it provides for three levels of adjudication in relation to minor cases with a small amount of money at stake as well as in relation to complicated cases and cases where a large sum of money is at stake. This hints that this point may be one of the most serious problems concerning our court system.

(2) As to the review of facts, there again are two different systems. One tries to guarantee a second trial of the facts in the appellate court by as far as possible trying all issues of fact again. The other tries to limit the function of the appellate court to reviewing the findings of fact made by the court of first instance. The appellate system under the old Code of Criminal Procedure which allowed trial *de novo* was one of the typical examples of the former. ... Typical of the latter system is the American appellate system and the present Japanese system of criminal appeals. The systems of civil appeal in Japan, Germany and Austria are situated between these two. The Japanese system can be regarded as a variation of the former, as additional evidence can be freely introduced at the appellate stage. The Austrian appellate system goes the other way as it allows the introduction of additional evidence only in highly exceptional cases. The German system stands between the Japanese and the Austrian.

The second problem concerning the appellate system is whether to let courts of first instance of general jurisdiction also hear appeals from courts of limited jurisdiction ... The French system of civil appeals after the 1958 reform is negative on this point. So is the Japanese system of criminal appeals [by providing that all *koso* appeals in criminal cases shall be heard by high courts]. The German system, the Japanese system of civil appeals [under which civil appeals from summary courts are heard at district courts] and the old French system are positive. Here again the Japanese system follows different principles in civil cases and in criminal cases.

As have been described, there are many different ways of delimiting the functions of courts at the second level ... A general principle can hardly be drawn from our comparative study. Consequently we cannot really say that the Japanese system demonstrates marked peculiarities. Such an observation shows that it is inappropriate for us to criticize the fact that the Japanese appellate system has lost its former schematic symmetry by following different principles in civil cases and in criminal cases [under the present system established in 1947] ... The machinery of criminal justice need not be identical with the machinery of civil justice. There are many countries which provide for two kinds of appellate systems. Though the present system of criminal appeals is different from the traditional scheme, it is rather nearer to systems adopted by many other countries. One may well wonder whether it is not indeed our system of civil appeals that is peculiar. We should note ... that the present system of civil appeals may bring about an undesirable tendency among district courts to divert their primary concern to the handling of appellate cases rather than to trying cases originally filed therein. In this connection it should be pointed out that from the comparative viewpoint it is very peculiar that our courts freely allow the introduction of additional evidence. As the expression of complaints about delays in obtaining justice becomes louder in the future these problems will have to be faced more squarely.

(3) We also find many problems which are peculiar to our court system in relation to 'courts with power to decide finally on issues of law' (*horitsu-shin*). The first relates to the question discussed above. That is the fact that even a minor case with a small amount of money at stake can be taken on appeal to the court at the highest level. The second relates to the fact that, because of the first problem, we have a very peculiar system where two sets of courts have power to decide finally on issues of law [ie high courts and the Supreme Court]. The third relates to the fact that there is a qualitative difference between the Supreme Court and other courts to an extent unseen in other countries. Our Supreme Court lies at the summit of the judicial system as a court which is considerably different in nature from other courts. Yet almost no consideration has been given to its special functions, primarily because of the traditional conception of *jokoku* appeals. This conception had been based upon a different court structure where the Great Court of Judicature was at the apex [a court whose functions were different from those of the present Supreme Court]. For the highest court of the land this presents a very odd picture.

In relation to the first problem, the German system adopts very clearly the position of disallowing second appeals for those minor cases which are handled by the *Amtsgericht*. In France no ordinary appeal can be filed in relation to minor cases, while motion for cassation may be filed [to *Cour de Cassation* on specified grounds]. The systems are not identical but they are common in not adhering to the principle of guaranteeing two chances of appeals. Moreover Germany has provided that cases where the amount in controversy is less than a set limit can be appealed a second time only after obtaining leave from the court of second instance. In France a fairly large fine may be imposed when the court finds that the second appeal was filed on frivolous grounds. None of these measures has been adopted in Japan. Consequently Japanese *jokoku* appeals in civil cases follow a very peculiar system. A second appeal is open in all cases without regard to the amount in controversy and with few conditions other than the requirement that there be an allegation of error in law. The only sanction against a groundless appeal is that the losing party must bear the 'costs' [which are not very large in amount]. ... This is an extreme expression of the schematic, formalistic way of thinking which the Japanese people are apt to follow. It should also be noticed that the Japanese legal profession has shown a strong inclination in favor of maintaining the *status quo* on this point. ...

Secondly, as a result of achieving such schematic symmetry in the appellate system, a huge number of *jokoku* appeals are filed. It is clearly impossible for the Supreme Court with a limited number of justices to dispose of all of them. Therefore a typically Japanese device has been adopted: vesting high courts with jurisdiction to hear *jokoku* appeals in those civil cases in which summary courts have heard the case as courts of first instance. Few other countries which have a system of second appeal, or which allow a motion for cassation that is conceptually distinct from the first appeal, have more than one court hearing cases on the second appeal or on motion for cassation. The rationale of having a court with power to decide finally on issues of law can only be adequately satisfied by giving that power exclusively to a single court. The abnormal system described above only shows that we have paid more respect to the schematic design of the appellate system with three levels of adjudication than to the function to be performed by the court at the third level, namely, maintaining uniformity in the interpretation of statutes.

The third problem relates to the fact that our Supreme Court must perform the function of the final court in deciding on the constitutionality of statutes as well as the function of deciding finally on issues of law, this latter function being shared with high courts. ... The former responsibility requires that the number of justices of the Supreme Court be small enough to perform this function properly, and that the justices be chosen in a manner different from that employed in choosing judges of other courts. Thus the Supreme Court differs in its composition from those other courts which share the function of deciding finally on issues of law [ie high courts]. The court with power to decide finally on issues of law stands in principle at the top of the hierarchical structure of courts. Therefore, its justices are usually recruited from among the same human resources from which judges of inferior courts are drawn. In a judiciary with a career judge system they are recruited from among those who stand at the top of the career judiciary. In the United States [which has a different method of selecting judges] also, judges of the lower courts are appointed in basically the same manner as the Supreme Court justices ... The composition of the Japanese Supreme Court is in this sense exceptional [as only about one-third of the justices are chosen from among career judges] ... Though such a case is rare indeed in other countries, it may still be regarded as reasonable if the function of the Supreme Court is centered on its special position as the final arbiter of constitutional questions. The fact is that the Supreme Court must also hear *jokoku* appeals on non-constitutional grounds (in those cases that originated in district courts) without any means being afforded to restrict the number of these appeals ... If this latter function be emphasized, the composition of the Supreme Court should have been set up differently from the way it is at present.

If the ideal of the US Supreme Court is to be pursued, we should be ready to accept the idea that our Supreme Court's Continental type function as the final arbiter of all issues of law will decline ... For instance, we would have to adopt a system which gives wide discretion to the Supreme Court as to whether to allow appeals to it, as under the American system of the writ of *certiorari*. So long as we expect the Supreme Court to perform the two functions mentioned above, we will have to develop a special system since vesting the highest court with these two functions is unique indeed. ... Such a system must necessarily be complicated. It can only be devised by adopting a resolutely flexible way of thinking which not only has to break through the traditional schematism in Japanese thought but also go beyond the commonly accepted view of the judicial system held by lawyers throughout the world.

... As I have repeatedly pointed out, the Japanese appellate system suffers from a conspicuous lack of consideration of the peculiarities of the functions of courts at each level and a strong adherence, either conscious or subconscious, to the system of three levels of adjudication. ... This has resulted in the following: an increase in opportunities for parties to use the appellate system as a device for making a deal; more serious delays in justice, as under our system the center of litigation often moves to the court of second or third instance rather than being the first; the creation of a chronic state of bankruptcy in the operation of the Supreme Court due to an excessive caseload; and serious damage to the prestige and the proper functioning of the courts with power to decide finally on issues of law. ... The first premise for overcoming such institutional deficiencies is, I believe, to throw away fixed ideas among lawyers. It is especially desirable in this field for one to probe the peculiarities of our own system by an in-depth comparative analysis. ...

Itoh, H, *The Japanese Supreme Court: Constitutional Policies*, 1989, pp 30–37, 75–83, 93–96, 102–05, Markus Wiener

One Supreme Court, fifteen high courts, 292 district courts, 388 family courts, and 575 summary courts comprise the Japanese court system. Fifteen Supreme Court justices, 278 high court judges, 805 judges and 399 assistant judges of the district courts, 193 judges and 148 assistant judges of the family courts, and 767 summary court judges fill the benches of the Japanese courts. Two thousand six hundred and five judges serve the nation's population of over 121 million. All cases are channelled through either a civil or criminal court structure. Constitutional and administrative cases are disposed of in either a civil or criminal proceeding.

A criminal case deals with an offense against the state in a proceeding to which the state becomes a party, such as a theft which is criminally prosecuted by the state. The functions of the prosecutor are to conduct criminal investigations, initiate public prosecutions, and supervise the execution of judicial decisions. The system of the prosecutor's office is hierarchically structured. There are four levels, with each office located at the level of a corresponding court: the supreme prosecutor's office is parallel with the Supreme Court, the high prosecutor's office is parallel with the high court, the district prosecutor's office is parallel with the district court, and the ward prosecutor's office is parallel with the summary court. The supreme prosecutor's office is headed by the attorney general (*kenji socho*) and below him by the solicitor general (*kenji jicho*). A prosecutor at each level is assigned functions related to the level of his court. The public prosecutor submits his charge in the form of an affidavit of evidence, supported by sworn statements, and conducts a preliminary examination. A prosecutor lacks the inquisitorial power of the grand jury and cannot compel attendance or testimony.

A civil case deals with an offense against a private person at the suit of the injured person; a trespasser, for instance, is sued by those whose rights he has violated. But note that while a refusal to pay tax is an offense against the state and is dealt with at the suit of the state, it is handled as a civil case just as is a refusal to repay money lent to a private person. Likewise, an action by the state for damages is civil, although the 'person' injured is the state.

The three-tiered court system adopted under the Meiji Constitution has been preserved in the form of trial *de novo* used in criminal procedure; the function of the first two levels of courts is primarily to find facts, while that of a third level of court is mostly to review questions of law. Continuous trial as practiced in civil procedure is one variation of the same idea.

For the purpose of criminal trials, the courts are divided into three levels: 1) the district court, the summary court and the family court, 2) the high court, and 3) the Supreme Court. For the purpose of civil cases, the courts are divided into four levels: 1) the summary court, 2) the district court and the family court, 3) the high court, and 4) the Supreme Court. Summary courts, which used to be called local courts, constitute the lowest echelon of courts, and their number has increased to twice that of the former local courts. Each summary court has three judges, distinct from career judges. They are similar to the justices of peace or judges of small claims courts in the United States. Jurisdictions of lower courts over both civil and criminal matters are as follows: the summary court handles claims of less than 300,000 yen; crimes such as gambling, theft, or attempted theft (against which a penalty of a fine or less is optional); embezzlement; and transactions involving stolen goods. A single judge always sits on the bench at a summary court level. Decisions rendered by a summary court can be appealed to no higher than a high court.

The family court conducts an adjustment (*shimpan*) or conciliation (*chotei*) in family matters, and a protective adjustment (*kajishimpan*) of juvenile delinquents. An adjustment is conducted by a court-designated officer in the presence of, or on the advice of, a counsellor with whom the family court can dispense. A domestic conciliation (*kajichotei*) is conducted by a commission composed of a domestic conciliation officer and conciliation committee members, also with whom the family court can dispense. Neither a conciliation nor an adjustment is required to follow litigious procedures such as an open trial and a confrontation of witnesses. The family court can also act as a first instance trial court on matters related to an adjustment or conciliation of family matters, and a protective measure of juvenile smoking, drinking, or other delinquencies. As a rule, only one judge sits at a family court. If otherwise stipulated by law, three judges act *en banc*.

A district court becomes a first instance court on a claim of not less than 300,000 yen or one based on an administrative suit excluding the crime of domestic disturbance. It is ordinarily presided over by one judge. However, a three-judge panel can take up these cases at its own discretion and is needed to conduct a trial involving capital punishment or imprisonment of an indefinite, or no less than one-year term.

Judges render three types of decisions at a district court level and up. *Hanketsu* is a court decision rendered after an oral hearing. *Kettei* is a court decision without an oral hearing, and is used in cases in which objection is made either to the way a judge conducts a trial or the qualification of a judge to hear a case. *Meirei* is a ruling of a judge (often a presiding judge) or judges regarding a courtroom procedure such as the time limit for oral argument or permission to excuse the defendant from a courtroom. Whereas a *koso* appeal challenges a decision of a first instance court on questions of fact-finding, a *jokoku* appeal is confined to the question of legal interpretation and application made by a second instance court. Whereas a *koso* appeal is made against a *hanketsu* form of decision, a *kokoku* appeal is made against *kettei* or *meirei* form.

A high court accepts a *koso* appeal challenging fact-findings contained in the *hanketsu* decision of a district court, a family court, or a summary court on criminal matters. It also accepts a *kokoku* appeal and reviews *kettei* or *meirei* of a district court, a family court, or a summary court on criminal matters. Finally, it accepts a *jokoku* appeal made against *hanketsu* of a district court or *kettei* of a summary court on non-criminal matters. In each of the above three instances, the high court conducts a trial as a three-judge panel. Otherwise it conducts a trial as a first instance court in a case involving a crime of national disturbance with five judges *en banc*. There are few restrictions on the right to review in appellate courts in Japan. *Jokoku* appeal on civil matters is open to any kind of summary case, as long as a contention is based on the breach of law or ordinance.

There is no practice of gatekeeping which enables the Supreme Court to screen and reject appeals on purely procedural grounds at its own discretion. Even a frivolous appeal automatically placed on the Court's docket receives a pro forma review before being dismissed. Five different avenues are open to seek a review by the Supreme Court as the court of last resort. Routes that may be taken in civil cases include: 1) *jokoku* appeal against a high court which adjudicated special administrative cases; 2) *jokoku* appeal against a high court which has decided on an appeal coming from a district court in an ordinary administrative case involving a claim of more than 300,000 yen; 3) special *jokoku* appeal against a high court which decided on an appeal coming from a summary court through a district court in a case involving a claim of less than 300,000 yen; 4) special *kokoku* appeal against a high court which ruled on an appeal lodged against a district court; and finally 5) jumping appeal directly to the Supreme Court against a district court which acted as a first instance court. A jumping appeal can be made even by a party to a case, challenging a first instance court decision despite its contract with the other party to forsake his right to *koso* appeal.

There are also five different avenues for an appeal to the Supreme Court in criminal cases: 1) *jokoku* appeal against a high court decision; 2) special *kokoku* appeal against a high court, a district court, a family court, or a summary court or judges thereof on the ground of an alleged violation of the constitution or a judicial precedent; 3) a jumping *jokoku* appeal by either a prosecutor or defendant challenging a decision of a first instance court, which holds that a law, order, regulation, or official act violates the constitution or that ordinances or regulations of a local government violate law; this can also be lodged by the prosecutor who challenges the judgment upholding the constitutionality or lawfulness of an ordinance or regulation passed by a local government as in the *Sunagawa* case (1959); 4) a transfer from a high court on a *hanketsu* decision; and 5) quasi-*jokoku* against a Supreme Court justice(s) who dismiss(es) a petition seeking disqualification of a judge, and against a disposition by a prosecutor and judicial officer regarding a defendant's right to legal counsel or lawful search and seizure.

The Great Court of Cassation (five civil divisions and four criminal divisions with each division having five judges) handled all *jokoku* appeals in both criminal and civil matters. Despite the fact that the 1947 Constitution greatly enlarged the functions of the Supreme Court compared with the Great Court of Cassation, the number of justices was reduced from 45 to 15. In less than five years after its inception the Supreme Court accumulated more than 7,000 cases pending in its docket. Alarmed by the delay of trial and the familiar public outcry of 'justice delayed is justice denied,' the Japan Bar

Association and the Court itself made various reform plans. The Japan Bar Association proposed that: 1) the number of the Supreme Court justices be doubled to 30; 2) the Court be composed of a grand bench (one Chief Justice and eight associate justices, all appointed by the Cabinet) and several petty benches with each petty bench having one grand bench justice and no fewer than two justices; and 3) only the grand bench be empowered to decide constitutional issues while petty benches be confined to the function of reviewing judicial precedents.

In May 1956 the non-partisan Council on the Legal System proposed that: 1) grand bench justices and a presiding justice from each of the six petty benches be appointed by the Cabinet; 2) grand bench justices be nominated by a selection committee composed of judges, prosecutors, private attorneys, and intellectuals appointed by the Cabinet, and be popularly reviewed at regular intervals thereafter; and 3) thirty judges be appointed to six petty benches.

Whereas the Japan Bar Association sought to alleviate the court's overload by increasing the number of judges while decreasing the jurisdiction of the petty benches, the Supreme Court attempted to solve the same problems by proposing that 1) the Supreme Court have only one bench with either nine or eleven justices; 2) the jurisdiction of the Supreme Court be expanded to encompass not only the questions of unconstitutionality and inconsistency with judicial precedent, but also the interpretation and application of socially important laws and ordinances; and 3) an additional court be established to dispose of *jokoku* appeals involving alleged violations of laws and ordinances of ordinary importance. The proposal of the council on the legal system was introduced by the justice ministry to the twenty-eighth session of the Diet in December 1957, but was never legislated. As the total of pending cases decreased from the peak of 7,000 to 2,000, all reform plans died and to date no action has been taken.

Emergency control measures were enacted at the same time in both criminal and civil areas to mitigate the impact of a flood of appeals to the Supreme Court. The Civil Procedure Emergency Control Code (*minji okyu sochiho*) conferred upon the high courts jurisdiction over appeals from summary courts. Likewise, the Criminal Procedure Emergency Control Code (*keiji okyu sochiho*) prohibited those appeals to the Supreme Court that would challenge only a fact-finding or the propriety of penalties imposed by a trial court. With these measures designed to ease its increased workload, the Supreme Court has come to perform two main functions. The first is to review, as the court of last appeal, the constitutionality of a law, order, regulation or official act; and, second, to supervise the uniformity of judicial interpretation and application of law.

In civil cases, the rapidly increasing number of appeals excessively overloaded the Supreme Court and it became necessary to remove an alleged violation of a law or regulation as a proper ground for appeal available to the court. In December 1949, the Commission to Investigate the Legal System advised the justice minister to revise the grounds for *jokoku* appeals to the Supreme Court. It proposed to give the court mandatory jurisdiction over cases involving constitutional questions or an incompatibility of a lower court decision with Supreme Court precedents, and a discretionary power to review those cases which the court holds to involve an important interpretation of a law or ordinance. The Commission also advised establishment of a special court to dispose of cases involving a violation of statutory law. Although the idea of a special court met opposition from GHQ, SCAP, other recommendations of the commission were adopted as a temporary measure effective for two years beginning 1 June 1950. After extending the measure for another two years in 1952, the commission, in its subcommittee on civil litigation, made an interim report in January 1954 advising a further restriction of *jokoku* appeals by: 1) expanding the summary court's jurisdiction to cover civil matters involving claims up to 100,000 yen (the amount was raised to 300,000 yen in 1970; 2) by conferring the finality of judgment on high court review of an appeal coming from a summary court in cases involving these issues; and 3) by restricting cases not involving a constitutional issue from *jokoku* appeal to the Supreme Court.

The present Code of Civil Procedure, which was passed at the nineteenth session of Diet in 1954, consequently allows a special *jokoku* appeal (*tokubetsu jokoku*) from a high court only if constitutional issues are involved. In the field of criminal cases, the Code of Criminal Procedure, which became effective on 1 January 1949, had the same effect of greatly reducing the number of *jokoku* appeals to the Supreme Court. Article 405 therein limits grounds for *jokoku* appeal to: 1) alleged violations of the constitution or an error in the interpretation or application; 2) an alleged incompatibility of a lower court decision with Supreme Court decisions; and 3) a case which the court deems to involve an important interpretation of law. An emergency *jokoku* appeal (*hijo jokoku*) can be lodged by the attorney general with the Supreme Court on the contention of a gross violation of laws and regulations. Further, in both civil and criminal cases, a reference to a specific constitutional provision is required in challenging the court decision. ...

...

All the cases coming to the Supreme Court are first referred to a petty bench for judicial screening, except for those appeals which are required by law to be decided by the grand bench. Approximately 4,500 appeals come to the Supreme Court each year. Roughly 1,500 appeals forwarded to each petty bench are assigned equally among the five petty bench justices, excluding the Chief Justice who does not normally participate in petty bench deliberations. This would mean that a little over 100 civil and 200 criminal cases are assigned to each justice on a rotation basis. While no clear guidelines exist, difficult cases which may create new precedents or which involve constitutional or other important issues are distinguished from relatively easy and clear-cut cases, which number over 90% of criminal and 50–60% of civil cases.

Each justice assumes responsibility for his own cases and presides over a group discussion of his cases. With the assistance of a *chosakan*, he examines both the substance and the procedure of an appeal to determine whether or not it warrants the court's review. He clarifies disputed points, prepares necessary materials, and drafts a proposed decision for a consideration of other justices at a group discussion. Thus, the role of a presiding judge clearly becomes one of great significance. The petty bench can dispose of detention, relief, bail, and suspension of compulsory execution. While discussions take place freely, confidentiality is required of all justices concerning what transpires at a group discussion. Indeed, Justice Shima later destroyed all his trial materials and his personal notes. Strict secrecy is observed during judicial group discussion, with no one else allowed in the conference chambers except for two groups: *chosakan* who may be called in to the grand and petty benches at the request of justices, and trainees of JRTI who, at the discretion of the justices, may be allowed in the chambers in order to observe deliberation processes.

In the case of the second petty bench, *chosakan* are called in all cases, but in the first and third petty benches, they are called in only when needed. *Chosakan* can stay even while justices are deliberating a case. The petty benches convened their first meeting on 1 October 1947. The first petty bench meets on Mondays and Thursdays, the second petty bench on Mondays and Fridays, and the third petty bench on Tuesdays and Fridays.

Judicial group discussion provides a forum for an exchange of opinions in which justices attempt to influence one another and settle their differences. Usually when a case is remanded to a petty bench with a grand bench's instructions on important issues, the petty bench proceeds to decide less important issues with the same presiding judge. Overall, cases have become more difficult and complex than before, and require detailed research. Justices usually read the transcript of the first and second instances' decisions, the appeal brief and rebuttals and the research report prepared by their *chosakan*. They may also read various records and evidence if they determine it to be necessary. The work load has been so heavy, with each justice assigned as many as a dozen cases at a time, that most justices call spare little time for research on cases assigned to other judges, thereby increasing their dependence upon a presiding justice and *chosakan* for the formation of their opinions.

The legal culture of Japan has long encouraged informal, non-litigious types of conflict resolution among people. Thus, direct accommodation by negotiation takes place from time to time at the level of lower courts, but conciliation at the Supreme Court level is rare between private parties who are determined to fight to the end. Prosecutors may withdraw their appeals in criminal cases to the Supreme Court by failing to contest petitions by opposing counsels. Conciliation by the court in civil cases has grown from a few to more than 30 cases per annum in recent years. The legal basis of conciliation is unclear, but justices rely on the provision of Article 130 of the Civil Procedural Code, which enables a presiding judge to handle a court mandate, and even commission another judge. An individual justice initiates conciliation and most of the actual conciliation process is done by a *chosakan*. Pre-trial conferences are conducted to secure agreements and concessions on the question of facts that are not substantially in dispute, to narrow and simplify the disputed points, and dispense with unnecessary witnesses that may impede a shortened but fair and adequate trial. They are also designed to settle disputes with a minimum of trouble and court time, while both parties feel that they have had a fair hearing.

Conciliation is preferred when a judge tries to circumvent a judicial precedent which he feels should not bind the present dispute. Through the prestige and influence of his office a justice could conciliate an increased number of disputes to the satisfaction of both parties, but he would not normally encourage conciliation at this level lest he should deprive the court of a chance to deliberate issues in a dispute and make a new precedent.

All appeals made to the Supreme Court are first reviewed by *chosakan*. Article 57 of the Court Code provides that a *chosakan* engage in the research necessary for justices to dispose of cases at their group discussions. Twenty-nine *chosakan*, including one chief *chosakan*, work for an average of five years for the Supreme Court, and are mostly recruited from among relatively young and able lower court judges. Unlike the justices who handle all kinds of cases, *chosakan* specialize in types of cases. Twelve *chosakan* take assignments in criminal cases, another 12 in civil cases, and the remaining four in administrative cases. The chief *chosakan* is not assigned to any type of case. In order to avoid a situation in which justices can pick and choose any *chosakan*, they, unlike their American law clerk counterparts, are not attached to any particular justice.

In the criminal section, 12 *chosakan* are divided into three groups, with each group assigned to one of three petty benches. Judicial socialization is facilitated by the composition of each group in which a senior *chosakan* with over 20 years of experience as a trial judge assists a junior *chosakan* who may have about 10 years of experience as a trial judge. They receive assignments from any of the five justices in the petty bench and stay with their petty bench for four months, rotating among all three in 12 months. Cases are assigned to each *chosakan* on a case-by-case basis. The *chosakan* in the civil section are divided into three groups and the remaining four *chosakan* form one group in the administrative section. They do not rotate in either the civil or administrative sections but each case gets assigned by rotation. In a criminal case proceedings of the first and second instance courts and appeal briefs need not be typed up. They are given to all five members of a petty bench, and a *chosakan* in charge of a given case.

A *chosakan*'s work in the criminal section starts with careful readings of the briefs and proceedings of lower courts. He familiarizes himself with the facts of a case, past criminal records of the accused, and other circumstantial factors. If, for instance, an appellant contends that a judgment below has violated a statute or a judicial precedent, a *chosakan* goes back to the statute or the precedent to compare it with the present case, and then may point out any fine differences in factual relations in the two cases. In rare instances he may want to contact administrative agencies in order to know the administrative background of a law under dispute. Furthermore, he may consult with a *chosakan* who handled the precedent case.

Since 1954, *chosakan* have annually published for future reference a volume of their comments on the Supreme Court decisions they handled, which is also reprinted in the law journal *Horitsu Jiho*. As a rule, all *chosakan* hold a weekly study meeting where they exchange their opinions about each other's cases. If a *chosakan* feels that his court may be inclined to overturn the precedent, he cites all relevant cases, scholars' opinions, legislative backgrounds, and foreign case laws. If he feels, however, that an appellant lacks procedural grounds, he so reports by filling out a fixed form for dismissal. A *chosakan* submits his report not only to the presiding judge, but also to all four others one week before a scheduled group discussion. He advises his justice not to decide in his petty bench those cases which should be transferred to the grand bench.

In a civil case proceedings of all lower courts and appeal briefs are printed and distributed to all five justices and a *chosakan* in charge of a given case. After a *chosakan* submits his case report a date is fixed for a group discussion among the five justices. If a presiding justice feels that the case report is insufficient or that a group discussion raises further questions to be clarified, a *chosakan* continues his work.

Considering the fact that many *chosakan* are among the most able career judges of 10–20 years of experience and expertise as trial judges, it is not difficult to assume that their case reports are more than mechanical, value-free research, and often reflect their own policy preferences. Also, considering the relatively advanced ages of most justices and their very heavy work load, many justices, especially those justices who have little prior judicial experience, are likely to rely heavily on *chosakan* for important input on their decision making. Former Justice Fujita once referred to such influence in creating the Supreme Court decisions which guide all lower courts in the country.

The grand bench is a collegiate body composed of all fifteen justices. A quorum is nine, and unless a judge is excused on grounds of illness, official trip, expulsion, restraint, or challenge, he is required to participate in both grand and petty benches. A Chief Justice always serves as a presiding judge of the grand bench; in his absence his authority and duties are delegated to one of the associate justices according to an order established at a judicial conference. Since the petty bench exercises the judicial power delegated to it by the grand bench, the latter can order a referral of cases whenever it wishes. A petty bench usually decides by a simple majority vote whether or not to forward a case to the grand bench. Initially, the grand bench was called on to decide all issues, constitutional or otherwise, raised in a case, but now only relevant issues and not the whole case are forwarded to the grand bench.

As a rule a petty bench first examines the formal aspects of a case and then refers it to the grand bench whenever an appeal involves the following issues, as provided for in Article 10 of the Court Code: 1) When constitutionality is challenged either by an appellant or a petty bench itself, except regarding an issue which was already decided by the grand bench; 2) when an interpretation and/or application of law and regulation by a petty bench contradict those of the grand bench; 3) when the petty bench is equally divided; and 4) when a petty bench decides that an appeal raises legal issues that are so important as to have a great social impact.

The grand bench first met on 21 November 1947, and has scheduled itself to meet on Wednesdays ever since. There were initially some difficulties in creating common grounds for group discussions among the first 15 justices due to their different backgrounds and experiences. Justice Saburo Iwamatsu critically recalls that some ex-lawyers and ex-scholars were not accustomed to listening to and accommodating opinions of other justices and kept insisting on their views to the end. Discussions were unnecessarily prolonged, he continues, because many opinions were irrelevant to a solution of disputed points, and the debates were often carried out in the form of formal speeches rather than a free exchange of opinions, but it all gradually improved and became more orderly. Justice Daisuke Kawamura describes what transpired at those initial sessions of the court:

> Very rarely at the outset of group discussion was there consensus on a case. Disagreements arose very often and a compromise was worked out only after a considerable amount of deliberation. It is not difficult to imagine the development of heated discussion. But when the time was ripe to reach a decision, all the justices felt relieved and left no grudges.

Acknowledging the effect of judicial group discussion upon individual judicial behavior, Justices Iwamatsu and Shima in *Suzuki v Ishigaki* (1956) recall that they were defeated on the question of the constitutionality of conciliation in lieu of a judicial trial, and subsequently changed their opinion to conform to the majority.

Usually a presiding judge of a petty bench, which refers a case to the grand bench, continues in charge of the case in the grand bench by briefing his colleagues on disputed points in a case, and often drafts the opinion of the court whenever he is in the majority. Justice Mano recalls his influence on other justices at the grand bench deliberation of *Japan v Murakami* (1948), a case involving manslaughter, as follows:

> There were occasions when my concurring opinions became the majority opinion of the court. One such occasion was the reviewing of an appeal challenging the constitutionality of capital punishment in the Criminal Code. No justice on the grand bench held a provision in question unconstitutional and seemed to have agreed to the opinion drafted by the presiding justice. But I felt the draft to be too simplistic and insufficient. So I decided to write a concurring opinion of my own. Strangely enough, when I presented my opinion at a group discussion, one colleague after another changed his opinion and eventually all of them came to agree with my concurring opinion which eventually was adopted as the majority opinion of the court without modification.

Justice Mano also recalls the stifling effect of the practice in which many justices heavily rely on the information provided by a presiding justice and simply follow the majority opinion with little or no discussion. Justice Jiro Tanaka wanted to have all his colleagues express their opinion in each case, but Chief Justice Kisaburo Yokota rejected this proposal for fear of slowing down the work. It seems that even now only about one-third of the justices present at the grand bench deliberations express their opinions and engage in substantive discussion.

As far as the power of the Chief Justice is concerned, he has only one vote in a grand bench discussion and his role as the presiding judge in the grand bench does not seem to have any overt effect upon an outcome of a case. As a rule, unless his presence is required to meet a quorum, a Chief Justice does not participate in proceedings in his petty bench. Chief Justice Hattori was an exception to the rule. He took upon himself about one-half of the normal work load and participated in petty bench deliberations. When Saburo Ienaga attributed certain court decisions to the personal influence of Chief Justice Kotaro Tanaka, Justice Noboru Inoue refuted such influence and described the role of a Chief Justice in judicial decision making as follows:

> The judiciary has always been a place where a Chief Justice never exerts pressure on his associate justices, no pressure at all as far as judicial process is concerned. I think the public has misunderstood this. Those intellectuals who have been criticizing the *Lady Chatterley's Lover* decision as a religious trial influenced by Chief Justice Tanaka are wrong and naive. Each justice who participated in that case expressed what he believed to be a right opinion and the Chief Justice never exerted any pressure on him. Many justices have been on the bench longer than the Chief Justice and each of them claims to be an expert in his own field. Many critics ludicrously disregard this. It is true that an opinion of the court which I presume was written by Chief Justice Tanaka smacked somewhat of religion but that was all.

This view of Justice Inoue has been widely shared. A Chief Justice in Japan does not seem to wield power influencing the Supreme Court decision making comparable to his counterpart in the United States Supreme Court.

The court very rarely holds an open hearing which enables the litigants to persuade justices directly. The majority of the cases that come before the court are decided on the basis of examinations of the written records like proceedings of lower courts, appeal briefs, and the reports of the *chosakan*. In criminal cases, however, there are three types of situations in which the court holds open hearings in accordance with either its own custom or statutory requirements. First, the court holds an open hearing when the justices believe that a judgment below should be reversed. When informed of a hearing, an attorney of a litigant whose interests may be favorably affected by a Supreme Court review, tends to suspect that the judgment below may be reversed and gets busy in preparing for an open hearing. The court invites the appellee to submit his response in writing. Second, the Supreme Court is likely to hold a hearing when reviewing capital punishment. It is not clear when and how this practice began, but Justice Mano made the following remarks concerning its origin in the Supreme Court:

> With the *Mitaka* case [*Iida et al v Japan* (1955)] as turning point, the grand bench began to hold it unconstitutional for a second instance court to sustain without oral hearing the first instance court's conviction. I do not know if this change was due to the criticism I made a few months after the *Mitaka* trial but we can regard this as a by-product of the case. Thereafter, both the grand and petty benches began to hold oral arguments whenever they dealt with an appeal involving capital punishment.

Third, the court tends to hold an open hearing when it reviews public security incidents as in the *Matsukawa* (1959) or *Sunagawa* (1959) cases. Whereas Article 408 of the Code of Criminal Procedure provides that when the court of last resort believes, on the basis of the appeal briefs or other documents, that the motion for appeal is not supported by reason, it may dismiss such an appeal by judgment without an oral argument. The court apparently feels itself obliged to give a thorough review of such socially important issues as public security by holding open hearings. Furthermore, these cases often receive a great deal of publicity by mass media. If no hearing was held, the litigants might begin to speculate that the court was going to dismiss an appeal on the grounds of Article 408 of the Criminal Procedural Code and such speculation might promptly spread to the public before a court announcement. The court, therefore, may feel obliged to hold an oral argument partly to keep the mass media from guessing at the outcome of a trial.

An oral argument at open hearing is often characterized by an absence of lively questions and answers. Since the function of attorney is to advocate his client's legal interests before judges and to convince them that his client's interests deserve the protection of the legal system, poor oral presentation among Japanese attorneys tends to reduce this function. ...

...

Group discussions and mutual persuasions are followed by decision making and opinion writing. On most occasions formal voting by either ballot or show of hands is not necessary nor practiced. Nodding or some form of implicit expression of decision is all it takes to reach a collective decision in both petty and grand benches. In the case of the grand bench a Chief Justice ranks the highest and each associate justice ranks according to his formal seniority. Seniority is determined by the date of appointment to the bench or, in the event two judges have the same appointment date, according to age. However, because a presiding judge changes from one case to another there is apparently no predetermined order to follow in expressing opinions or decision making at a petty bench group discussion. Neither does there seem to be any power advantage inherent in the discussion and voting sequence. This practice of the Japanese Supreme Court is in contrast with that of the United States Supreme Court where the Chief Justice states his opinion first, followed by the other justices in order of their seniority. Then the justices formally vote, also beginning with the Chief Justice and working down the seniority scale.

The Great Court of Cassation used a type of deliberation and voting patterned after the German method. Judicial voting proceeds, according to this method, from one disputed point to another, and each disputed point was usually arranged by the parties to a case in such a way as to contain one question of law or fact. The court ordinarily followed the order arranged by a party in deciding each disputed point. When all the judges exhausted their opinions on each issue, they took a vote and differences were resolved by a majority vote. If they agreed on the disposition of an issue, however, they could omit voting and proceed to the next issue. A justice whose opinion was defeated in the voting had to conform to that of the majority of the court and decide the next issue by accepting the premises favored by the majority. As the collegiate body of the Great Court of Cassation moved from one issue to another it eliminated minority opinions on each issue, so that when it finished its deliberations on all the points raised in a case, a decision was made on a final issue. Out of this came a single decision and a single opinion of the court for the case, with no dissenting opinions recorded. Under this method, therefore, there is no way of knowing the voting behavior of the justices nor is there a record of any dissenting opinion of the court.

Today the Court Code in Article 77, Paragraph 1 requires that the Supreme Court decide a case by a 'majority opinion,' unless otherwise stipulated in a Supreme Court regulation; Article 76 requires that each justice express his decision at a group discussion. Although a simple majority is generally sufficient to dispose of a case, both at petty and grand benches, the Supreme Court Business Disposition Rules (*ji-mushorikisoku*), in Article 12 stipulates that whenever the grand bench holds any law, ordinance, regulation, or official act to be unconstitutional, at least eight justices must agree. But since the quorum of the grand bench is nine, a vote of five to four can render a law or ordinance unconstitutional. Typically, an opinion of the court in a case which is decided by a divided opinion ends with a statement that the present judgment is made with the agreement of all the justices except for the dissenting opinions of Justices So-and-So.

So long as a case involves only one issue, a judicial decision on the particular issue will determine the outcome of the case as a whole. A decision made on the issue at the end of all the deliberations on such a case is expected to reflect a judicial attitude on the single issue in an unadulterated manner. For instance, if a decision is made on the issue of equality under law, the single issue involved in the case, judicial attitudes toward that particular issue will be the determinant.

However, where more than one issue is raised in a case, there has been a disagreement as to how the case should be decided. Justice Mano, favoring the method practiced by the United States Supreme Court, advocated making only one decision on the case as a whole. Since different judges employ different logical constructions and legal interpretations to arrive at different judgments, he argued, the spirit of a collegiate type of decision making will be reflected best by a decision made at the end of all deliberations to determine the judgment reached by a majority of the justices on the case as a whole, regardless of their different opinions on some issues in the case. Accordingly, he construed the provision of Article 11 of the Court Code which requires a written court judgment to state each justice's opinions to mean that a concurring opinion refers to an opinion of those justices who agree with the majority's judgment of the case but not with the majority's reasoning, in whole or in part, and that a dissenting opinion is an opinion of a justice who disagrees with both the holding and the reasoning of the majority.

According to some scholars, both constitutional and criminal cases should be decided by the votes on the conclusion whereas civil cases should be decided by the votes on each disputed point. For example, a three-judge panel is divided three ways. Judge A holds the defendant committed no crime; Judge B feels that the defendant committed a crime but should be acquitted on the grounds of insanity; Judge C feels that the defendant's crime was an act of self defense. Thus, none of the three judges feels that the defendant should be convicted and go to jail if votes are taken on the conclusion of this case. But if votes are taken on the question of whether a crime was committed, Judge A would be outvoted by Judges B and C who believe that a crime was committed. Then the three judges would proceed to the next question of guilt or innocence. If there is no majority vote on either the insanity or self defense of the defendant, however; the accused may be convicted and sent to jail despite the fact that all three judges feel that he is not guilty.

It seems to be a settled practice of the Japanese Supreme Court to decide on each issue raised by the parties to a case, and not on the case as a whole. According to this method a separate decision made on each issue, when put together, will comprise the judgment of the court on that case, provided each issue is independent of every other one. …

…

An analysis of the abridged Supreme Court reports reveals that a little over a quarter of constitutional cases were decided by divided opinions during the first decade of the court. Studying a justice's ratio of concurring and dissenting opinions to his total participation in divided decisions, Takeyoshi Kawashima found that there was a steadily increasing number of dissenting and concurring opinions voiced from 1947 through 1962, and that after the mid-1960s a tendency to write dissenting opinions decreased considerably. According to the same study, justices were inclined to dissent nearly twice as often as they concurred. In regard to the specialization of justices, Kawashima confirmed, both criminal and civil specialists were more prone to write concurring and dissenting opinions than their counterpart non-specialists in cases involving their specialty. Further, criminal specialists had a higher dissenting rate in criminal cases than civil cases, and civil specialists had a higher concurring rate in civil cases than criminal cases. Finally, it was found that criminal specialists were twice as likely to write their own opinions as civil specialists, especially in expressing concurring opinions.

The practice of writing concurring and dissenting opinions was introduced from the United States after the Second World War, since under the Meiji Constitution the Great Court of Cassation followed the German practice of writing and publishing only the majority opinion. Some well-known opinions were attributed to Chief Justice Hideo Yokota (1862-1937) of the Great Court of Cassation, on the basis of their style and wording, but, as a rule, it was impossible to associate judicial attitudes with judicial behavior. An underlying assumption of the old practice was that publishing any opinion other than the majority opinion would decrease a popular trust in legal stability and authority and would encourage more unnecessary litigation. The Meiji practice still persists in the provision of Article 75, Paragraph 2 of the Court Code which reads in part that, except as otherwise provided for in the law, strict secrecy shall be observed with respect to the proceeding of deliberation, the opinion of each judge, and the number of opinions.

The lower courts continue to publish only the majority opinion and do so anonymously. The rationales behind the Supreme Court practice of publishing both dissenting and concurring opinions are several. It is contended that concurring and dissenting opinions will further clarify legal issues and judicial policies in the case. Further, a dissenting opinion, once made known, might gain an increased acceptance in the society and perhaps become a majority opinion later. Also, it is hoped that publishing concurring and dissenting opinions would enable a voting public to know the views of individual justices at the time of popular review of Supreme Court justices.

It should be pointed out, however, that although Article 11 of the Court Code requires a written court judgment to state each justice's opinions, each judge is not required to write his own opinion. Except for a few majority opinions of which Justice Mano identified himself as a writer in 1948, there is no way of knowing who drafts the majority opinion of the court. The majority opinion is supposed to be the statement of rationales for the decision acceptable to each justice in the majority group. However, when the majority is large and diversified in its reasoning, an initial draft is so modified and adulterated by other members of the same group, the final draft of the court and personal views of each justice tend to lack clarity and logical cohesion.

Exchanges of written opinions among some justices sometimes become amusing. Dissenting in *Oda v Japan* (1952), Justice Yusuke Saito complained about the clarity of the majority opinion, did not believe the majority to have agreed among themselves, and construed the majority to base its holding on the alleged unconstitutionality of the provision of Article 45 of the Weaponry and Powder Control Ordinance of 1911. Then Justices Kawamura and Irie wrote their joint concurring opinion on the ground that they joined the majority group, but not for the reason Saito had attributed to the majority.

When more than one justice concurs with or dissents from the majority, both abridged and unabridged Supreme Court reports simply state that the 'following is the concurring or dissenting opinion of Justices A, B, and C.' What is worse, the reports failed to cite the dissenting opinion of Naoyoshi Tsukazaki in *Asano v Japan* (1952). Thus, dissenting and concurring opinions when written jointly tend to suffer from the same problem of a lack of clarity and logical consistency as the majority opinion, thereby weakening the objectives of publishing various judicial opinions.

The Supreme Court decisions are announced in three different ways. In a small number of cases the court hears an oral argument and renders its *hanketsu* judgment in an open court. Usually the court announces its decision in the *hanketsu* form when it reverses a decision below. The court reads its holding and reasons at open court and/or mails it to the litigants. If the court does not hold oral hearings it need not specify the date of announcing its decision. In reversing a decision below, however, the date of announcement must be given to both parties to a case. A large majority of appeals made to the Supreme Court lack proper grounds and are dismissed in the form of *kettei*, which require neither open hearing nor open court announcement, in accordance with Article 381, Paragraph 1, Item 3 of the Code of Criminal Procedure. Only the first petty bench has traditionally announced its *kettei* judgment at open court. While *kettei* is rendered by a petty bench itself, *meirei* is issued by a justice(s) in his (their) individual capacity.

The court need not give its opinion in dismissing a defense motion that a public prosecution is unconstitutional. The court is also regarded to have upheld the constitutionality of a law or ordinance being challenged when it cites that law or ordinance in its opinion upholding the conviction.

The Supreme Court passes several judgments. It may uphold the decision below and dismiss an appeal, it may reverse the decision below and remand the case for further review in accordance with its own instruction, or it may reverse the decision below and pass its own judgment.

II ALTERNATIVE DISPUTE RESOLUTION

Henderson, DF, *Conciliation and Japanese Law: Tokugawa and Modern*, Vol 2, 1965, pp 183–92, University of Washington Press

The modern skyscraper is not the necessary lineal descendant of the prehistoric mud hut, but by analogy the functional similarities between Tokugawa conciliation (*atsukai* and *naisai*) and three aspects of modern dispute resolution in Japan – (1) Informal Conciliation (sometimes called *jidan*), (2) Conciliation (*chotei*), and (3) some of the code Compromises (*wakai*) – suggest considerable continuity in the Japanese approach to law, lawsuits, and lawyers. But the changes in the character of Japanese conciliation itself, in moving from pre-war, didactic to present-day, voluntary Conciliation (*chotei*), are quite as important as the continuity, and both aspects will be given close scrutiny in this chapter.

TERMINOLOGY AND DEFINITIONS FOR TOKUGAWA AND MODERN TYPES

In following the growth of modern conciliation from its Tokugawa antecedents, some specific preliminary attention must be given to definitions and language equivalence.

There is not only the awkward problem of selecting English terms suitable for labeling novel Japanese institutions, but also the Tokugawa and the modern Japanese conciliation practices themselves, as well as their respective Japanese terminology, are quite distinguishable from each other. Since their distinguishing characteristics are important parts of our story, the terminology must reflect both the historical distinctions and the different types of modern conciliatory practice.

Informal conciliation: What we have called the first stage of didactic conciliation (*atsukai* or *naisai*) in the Tokugawa period – the informal settlement discussion on the local level – persists in Japan today as a social practice outside of the courts, unfettered by technicalities and conducted in much the same way as it was centuries earlier, except, as we shall see, lawyers and police officers now have significant roles as conciliators. We shall refer to this modern usage as 'Informal Conciliation.' With reference to its volitional aspects in the bargaining stage, it may still be in some degree didactic even today, depending on how practicable litigation may appear to the parties as an alternative in any particular case. For if the parties are legally minded, either of them can go to court at his option, or once an informal agreement has been reached, it is accorded the formal, legal status of an enforceable contract under the modern Japanese Civil Code, Articles 695-96.

Conciliation (*chotei*): At this point then it is sufficient to know that it is primarily a prelitigation procedure, conducted in the regular courts by a three-man conciliation committee composed of two laymen and a judge appointed for each case. Conciliation proceedings as such may be voluntarily filed by either of the parties to a dispute; the parties may legally discontinue conciliation and start a lawsuit at their option.

The term *chotei* is used in at least five different technical senses in the Japanese legal material:

1. The institution or whole system of conciliation.
2. The conciliation procedure.
3. The act of conciliating itself.
4. The substance of the agreement or compromise embodied in writing.
5. The 'meeting of the minds' in making the agreement (like Compromise, *wakai*).

Hereafter we will use the term *chotei* to indicate the entire institution, as in number one listed above, and other Japanese usages will be distinguished as necessary in the context. *Chotei* is similar to some of the practices in the United States called 'conciliation'; however, as mentioned ... , there is little uniformity in the American usage, and mediation would also be an acceptable rendition perhaps.

Compromise (*wakai*): For us the most important meaning of the multipurpose, modern Japanese legal word, *wakai*, is the process whereby the judge encourages the parties to a lawsuit to compromise the dispute which is being tried before him in the court. But like *chotei*, *wakai* is used in a number of different ways in the modern Japanese law. For example, as mentioned above, *wakai* is a contractual agreement embodying a private compromise, as provided for in the Civil Code (Article 695). *Wakai*, in the Code of Civil Procedure (hereafter CCP) Article 136, is also a method used by the judge to induce compromise in a lawsuit being tried before him. Such a compromise agreement when written into the protocol of the court is given the force of a final judgment (CCP Article 203). Disputants may also apply to a summary court (CCP Article 356) to make a compromise, even without having a lawsuit pending before the court, and if such a compromise agreement is concluded and embodied in a protocol of the court, it becomes effective as a final judgment. Hereafter we will use 'compromise' to indicate the process wherein the judge attempts to settle cases before him in court, and the other usages will be explained in context where required.

How precisely do these modern conciliatory practices Informal Conciliation (*jidan*), Compromise (*wakai*), and Conciliation (*chotei*) – relate to the Tokugawa conciliation [*naisai* and *atsukai*]? Certainly the present-day informal conciliation, however different its milieu, is a lineal descendant of the Tokugawa village practices, although the relative accessibility of the courts as an alternative today is indeed significant ... . Current compromise and *chotei* legal procedures are, however, quite distinguishable from the Tokugawa practices in the Shogunate courts. Compromise is a German borrowing apparently; *chotei* was devised in Japan piecemeal during the 1920s and 1930s. Despite the differences, however, we suggest that there is a strong functional similarity between these procedures and the Shogunate court practices ... .

The earlier Japanese jurists writing about modern *chotei* seem to have given little attention to the possible underlying continuity of these modern conciliatory practices. Several of the recent legal historians, however – Kobayakawa Kingo, Kaneda Heiichiro, Maki Kenji, and Ishii Ryosuke – have mentioned in passing the significance of a study of the continuity between modern and Tokugawa conciliation practices. The continuity is sometimes particularly difficult for a modern Japanese lawyer to see because the conciliatory tendency is largely of social origin, and its present legislative embodiment tends to prevent inquiring for its origins beyond the date of enactment. Nor should we overlook the developmental significance of the legislative embodiment; this sort of conciliation is now in court.

The massive reconstruction of the Japanese legal system along foreign lines between 1868 and 1900 tended to preoccupy the Japanese jurists with exegetical tasks and to obscure the functioning of the continuing conciliation process, especially until the 1920s, and to some extent obscures the informal conciliation even now. So far apart were the social practices and the new Meiji legal codes, which presumed to change them at the turn of the century; that in order to fathom the reasons for this continuing hiatus, it is worthwhile to consider briefly the way the massive reception of foreign legal institutions came about.

MEIJI RECEPTION

It is well known that the Meiji reception of western law was inspired as much by diplomacy and oligarchic pride as by popular zeal for legal codification on the part of any substantial Japanese social group at the time. In the crucial Treaty of Amity and Commerce between the United States and Japan (signed 1858), Townsend Harris reluctantly included a provision extending extraterritoriality to United States citizens in Japan in order to get the treaty ratified by the Senate. This provision was preceded by a similar one in the Dutch treaty (1856). It is fair to assume that few Japanese understood at the time the reasoning behind the foreigners' demand for extraterritoriality, which derived from the vast differences between the Tokugawa and western legal systems. Nevertheless, the Meiji political authorities resented this feature in the early treaties, and by the late 1870s it had become a major goal of successive Japanese foreign ministers to negotiate new treaties in which the western nations would relinquish their extraterritorial rights. Before the western nations would agree to subject their nationals to the Japanese law and courts, it was necessary for Japan to reconstruct its whole formal legal system; eschewing the details, one can say that the reconstruction was accomplished by 1899, and in the same year the new western treaties relinquishing extraterritoriality became effective.

The resulting statutory changes amounted to a monumental reception of foreign codified law, mostly German. A new Meiji Constitution (1889) and five new codes (criminal, 1882; civil, 1898; commercial, 1899; criminal procedure, 1882; civil procedure, 1891), modeled mostly after the German and French codes, were enforced. A judiciary was established which was to a degree independent from the administration; a German-type system of multiple appeals on both the law and facts was provided in a highly centralized hierarchy of courts, composed of summary courts, district courts, high courts, and a Supreme Court; a rudimentary professional bar was recognized; criminal and civil jurisdictions and procedures were distinguished; torture was abolished; and a token system of judicial review of official action was provided through a separate administrative court.

The contrast between the new code system and the Tokugawa legal system – generally decentralized, with only the beginnings of a recognized bar, with no separate bench, and with a fusion of civil and criminal procedures – was indeed striking. Therefore, without detracting from the magnitude of these Meiji accomplishments, it is enough to recognize that the reception of foreign law was to a large extent externally inspired and that the social efficacy of the alien codes has been understandably gradual and only partial among the populace.

As might be expected, it was several decades after 1900 before sufficient jurisprudence had been accumulated by the courts and jurists to make the system a thoroughly indigenous product. During this period of concentrated exegesis of the new codes, a working understanding of the internal consistency of the codes as a system was achieved by the universities and jurists, but the populace at large was slower to understand and even slower to act in accordance with the new legislation. The social efficacy of the law was difficult to appraise because penetrating academic studies of social compliance with the codes or empirical inquiries into the jural life of the people were rare. But it is no doubt a fair assumption that the people went about their affairs for some time after the enactment of the Code of Civil Procedure in much the same way that they had before 1890.

Fortunately, since 1945 Japanese interest in the sociological aspects of the law has increased at an encouraging rate. In the meantime, the interaction between the code system and the society has also had its effect on both. Yet, as we shall see, lawsuits based upon the codes are still a relatively small part of social control or dispute settlement in Japan even today.

Informal conciliation practices continued to function underground immediately after the codes were adopted, but conciliation procedures began to appear in the legislation to an increasing extent after 1920. In order to see their total effect, we will examine the several conciliatory methods of settling civil disputes – informal conciliation, *chotei*, and compromise – as they have come to operate in present-day Japan since the enactment of the Law for Adjustment of Domestic Affairs (1948) and the Civil Conciliation Law (1951). It is important to understand not only their relationship to each other but also their relationship to formal Arbitration (*chusai*) and Lawsuits (*sosho*). Together, these several types of procedures constitute the major methods for resolution of civil disputes in Japan, and we will seek to identify the combined quantity of disputes settled by the various conciliatory practices as opposed to lawsuits in contemporary Japan.

INFORMAL CONCILIATION

Although few experienced observers would doubt that the Japanese have an unusually pronounced tendency to avoid litigation and, conversely, an equally pronounced tendency to obtain settlements informally, nevertheless the informal and confidential handling itself makes such a process very illusive to the investigator. We cannot measure the extent of this phenomenon by direct statistics, but indirectly and inferentially we can get an inkling of its magnitude and importance by the following types of evidence.

Police counseling: It has become quite common for Japanese police officers to act informally as conciliators in civil disputes arising within their area, and the larger police offices usually maintain facilities for conciliating disputes brought to them voluntarily in the context of a disturbance. National statistics are not available, but in 1958, there were 21,596 civil disputes brought to the Tokyo police for conciliation, and 39% of them were apparently settled in one way or another. In the Tokyo district court area there were only 6,815 cases filed for formal conciliation. Hence it seems that for Tokyo the police alone received more cases for informal conciliation than the courts handled by formal, *chotei* proceedings.

Divorce by agreement (*kyogi rikan*): Article 763 of the Japanese Civil Code authorizes married couples to divorce themselves by registering their signed divorce agreement at the proper registry office. No court action is required. Most significantly, the vast majority of Japanese divorces are accomplished in this manner. For example, in 1955, over 90% (68,514 out of 75,267) of all divorces which became effective in Japan were divorces by agreement. We cannot say with precision how many of these divorces were arranged by informal conciliation, especially since Japanese marital relationships are changing rapidly in the postwar period in accordance with changing social conditions and the individualism expressed in the 1947 Constitution. No one, however, would doubt that many divorces by agreement still occur only after inter-family conciliation involving also the go-betweens, who customarily assist in the marriage arrangements in the first place and who are often consulted regarding subsequent marital storms. We can assume that, through the go-between, family members, and friends of both spouses, the informal conciliation process operates extensively in the arrangement of these numerous divorces by agreement, quite outside of the judicial process.

Kawashima, T, 'Dispute Resolution in Contemporary Japan' in von Mehren, AT (ed), ***Law in Japan. The Legal Order in a Changing Society*****, 1963, pp 50–59, Harvard University Press**

INFORMAL MEANS OF DISPUTE RESOLUTION: RECONCILEMENT AND CONCILIATION

The prevailing forms of settling disputes in Japan are the extrajudicial means of reconcilement and conciliation. By *reconcilement* is meant the process by which parties in the dispute confer with each other and reach a point at which they can come to terms and restore or create harmonious relationships. As stated above, social groups or contractual relationships of the traditional nature presuppose situational changes depending on their members' needs and demands and on the existing power balance; the process of conferring with each other permits this adjustment. Particularly in a patriarchal relationship the superior (*oyabun*) who has the status of a patriarch is expected to exercise his power for the best interests of his inferior (*kobun*), and consequently his decision is, in principle, more or less accepted as the basis for reconcilement even though the decision might in reality be imposed on the inferior. Reconcilement is the basic form of dispute resolution in the traditional culture of Japan. *Conciliation*, a modified form of reconcilement, is reconcilement through a third person.

In the legal systems of Western countries as well as of Japan, dispute resolution through a third person as intermediary includes two categories: mediation and arbitration. In mediation a third party offers his good offices to help the others reach an agreement; the mediator offers suggestions which have no binding force. In contrast, a third party acting as arbitrator renders a decision on the merits of the dispute. In the traditional culture of Japan, however, mediation and arbitration have not been differentiated; in principle, the third person who intervenes to settle a dispute, the go-between, is supposed to be a man of higher status than the disputants. When such a person suggests conditions for reconcilement, his prestige and authority ordinarily are sufficient to persuade the two parties to accept the settlement. Consequently, in the case of mediation also, the conditions for reconcilement which he suggests are in a sense imposed, and the difference between mediation and arbitration is nothing but a question of the degree of the go-between's power. Generally speaking, the higher the prestige and the authority of the go-between, the stronger is the actual influence on the parties in dispute, and in the same proportion conciliation takes on the coloration of arbitration or of mediation. The settlement of a dispute aims to maintain, restore, or create a harmonious 'particularistic' relationship, and for that purpose not only mediation but also arbitration must avoid the principles implicit in a judicial settlement: the go-between should not make any clear-cut decision on who is right or wrong or inquire into the existence and scope of the rights of the parties. Consequently the principle of *kenka ryo-seibai* (both disputants are to be punished) is applied in both mediation and arbitration.

If a dispute is very likely to arise and the parties thereto are more or less equal in their status (in other words, the power balance is not sufficient to settle an eventual dispute), they normally agree in advance on a third person as mediator or arbitrator. For example, when marriage takes place, it is a common custom in Japan to have a go-between (sometimes each of the marrying families appoints its respective go-between) witness the marriage and play the role of mediator or arbitrator if serious troubles arise later. Or, when a man is employed (not only as a domestic servant or apprentice of a carpenter, painter, or merchant, but also as a clerk in such business enterprises as steel mills, chemical plants, and banks), it is still common practice for the employer to demand from the employee an instrument of surety signed by a *mimoto hikiukenin* or *mimoto hoshonin* (literally translated, a person who ensures the antecedents of the employee). Originally this man had to undertake the role of mediator or arbitrator in case of sickness, breach of trust of the employee, or other eventual troubles; in recent years he simply undertakes the obligation as a surety. The reason that a very small portion of disputes are brought to court is to be found, as stated above, in the fact that most of the disputes are settled through these informal means.

Kankai

Very soon after the Meiji Restoration, the government was forced to make concessions to this centuries-old practice and accordingly legalized conciliation; in 1876 the government initiated *kankai* (literally, invitation to reconcilement) as a legal court procedure and provided for its preferred usage prior to a regular judicial proceeding. In 1883 the Ministry of Justice issued a directive that *kankai* should be a compulsory procedure prior to regular judicial process in all except commercial cases.

Kankai – the Japanese word gives the impression that it is a recommendation favoring reconcilement – was actually the imposition of a settlement under authority of the court with the litigants often being in no position to refuse the proposal. A scene of a famous Kabuki drama, *Suitengu Megumi no Fukagawa* (first performance in 1885), by Mokuami presents a very realistic description of the image of *kankai* then held by the people. The usurer Kimbei comes, accompanied by Yasuzo, a pettifogger, to the home of his debtor Kobei, an indigent former samurai. In front of the debtor's home Yasuzo says to his client: 'If the debtor is not likely to pay the debt, let's intimidate him by saying that we will resort to *kankai* in case he does not deliver a pledge.' They enter the house and demand that Kobei deliver them pledges as a substitute for the payment of his debt: 'If you are delayed in delivering them, I will bring the case to *kankai*, have them arrest you and let you enjoy a cool breeze.'

Table 10 shows how frequently *kankai* was resorted to and what an important function it had. Probably this was due to the fact that, in the social chaos of the early Meiji era, the traditional extrajudicial means such as reconcilement and conciliation were insufficient for settling disputes. In 1890 the institution of *kankai* was abolished by the Code of Civil Procedure. This was but one of the codes promulgated during the 1890s as preparatory measures to bring to an end the privileges of extraterritoriality for alien residents in Japan; and it was with this aim in mind that the government strove to follow the pattern of Western nations in its recognition of judicial institutions. The reactions to the reform can be inferred from the comments on it given 30 years later by members of the House of Representatives when the reinstitution of mediation was under debate.

> Shotoku Taishi, who drafted the 'Constitution of Japan', wrote in Article 17 that harmony is to be honored. Japan, unlike other countries where rights and duties prevail, must strive to solve interpersonal cases by harmony and compromise. Since Japan does not settle everything by law as in the West but rather must determine matters, for the most part, in accordance with morality and human sentiment (*ninjo*), the doctrine of mediation is a doctrine indigenous to Japan ... The great three hundred year peace of the Tokugawa was preserved because disputes between citizens were resolved harmoniously through their own autonomous administration, avoiding, so far as possible, resort to court procedure ... However, later the justice bureaucrats, assuming upon the appearance of the Code of Civil Procedure that the bureaucracy should attempt to settle all problems in dispute, extremely perverted the thought of the people.

Even after 1945, a leading lawyer, Yoshikata Mizoguchi, now Chief Judge of the Tokyo Family Court, declared in the preface to *Chotei Tokuhon*, (Mediation Reader; published by the Japanese Federation of Mediation Associations in 1954): 'Needless to say, the basic idea of *chotei* [mediation] is harmony and since, as Crown Prince Shotoku revealed to us in Article 1 of his Constitution of Seventeen Articles enacted 1,350 years ago which stated that 'harmony is to be honored,' respect for harmony is a national trait, the development of the *chotei* institution in our country seems natural.' We can imagine, then, the popular reaction which followed the abolition of *kankai*.

Chotei

During World War I the industrialization and urbanization of Japan developed rapidly and upset the traditional social structure. In such a time of social unrest, the trust in those traditionally in positions of authority, such as employers or landlords, was weakened; and those who had been in an inferior position began to assert their legal rights. The traditional authority and prestige of superiors was no longer effective to prevent, much less to solve, disputes with inferiors. Lawsuits by landlords or lessors against their tenants or lessees, which had been quite rare in the past, were becoming frequent, thus sharpening the antagonism between parties who were supposed to be friendly toward each other. What the government attempted, facing this dissolution of the social structure upon which the political regime had been based since the Meiji Restoration, is interesting from our point of view. Instead of coordinating the conflicting vested interests by legislation, the government reinstituted *chotei,* with which the disputes themselves were to be 'washed away' (*mizu ni nagasu*) by reconcilement; the emerging individualistic interests of lessees, tenants, and employees were to be kept from being converted into firmly established vested interests independent of the will of their superiors.

A member of the House of Representatives urged, when the Leased Land and Leased House Mediation Law was under debate: 'By endeavoring to be sympathetic and by expressing harmony, we amicably reap rights which are not actually rights in themselves.' Another member argued:

> Handling this matter as merely a determination of the problem of the rights of a lessee of land or a tenant of a house so that the owner may assert his own rights even to the point of rapacity, in a period such as that of today when a shift in society in the harmony of supply and demand brings only shortages, with anyone being able to assert his own rights exclusively, makes it quite difficult, in the final analysis, to obtain true stability of rights. Therefore, the establishment of the Mediation Law is not so that someone by sticking to the law can determine the relationship of rights among the parties. That is, the relationship between a tenant and a house owner, a land lessee and a landowner differs from that between complete strangers. Therein is the personal expression of sympathy; therein is morality. And in the sense that it attempts to base settlement on these things exists the *raison d'être* of mediation.

The institution of *chotei* was to replace the informal mediators of the past who had been mostly men of 'face' – for instance, village elders and sometimes even policemen – by mediation committees (consisting of laymen and a judge) and to have parties reach agreement under the psychological pressure derived from the 'halo' of a state court. This attempt was quite successful. A large number of disputes arising out of leases were brought to *chotei* procedure and not to regular judicial proceedings. ...

The number of mediation cases concerning land and house leases, farm tenancies, pecuniary debts, and domestic relations increased surprisingly after the institution of mediation, but, remarkably enough, the number of regular judicial cases underwent no significant decrease. In other words, a large number of disputes which had been solved outside of the court or left unsolved were now brought to *chotei,* which meant that (1) *chotei* was much preferred to regular judicial proceedings, (2) traditional informal means of dispute resolution already had lost their function in this sector of personal relations, and (3) society needed control by a governmental agency of some kind during a period of social disorganization.

The tendency to settle disputes by compromise is also illustrated by the number of suits withdrawn or formally compromised and the number of mediation cases withdrawn. ... Such a termination takes place when the need for a judicial decision or *chotei* disappears; in most such instances, this occurs because the parties have settled the dispute themselves. ... the court takes an active role in encouraging settlement at stages short of a final decision. In Summary Courts the number of cases settled by judicial compromise entered in the official record is approximately equal to the number settled without the formal aid of the court and with drawn. In District Courts, the ratio is lower, but the number of judicial compromises is only a little less than half that of the cases settled privately. Practicing attorneys report that, in a large number of cases, the judge urges the parties to compromise at least once during the course of the trial. Both the tendency of parties to settle and the court's practice of encouraging compromise reflect the general attitude of the people.

In addition to *chotei*, there is a long tradition of police intervention in disputes between citizens. Officers act as mediators on the basis of their authority, particularly when another man with sufficient prestige and authority is not available. *Chotei*, as legalized by the series of mediation statutes, may in a sense be a modified, perhaps rationalized, form of the type of mediation performed by police officers. But even after *chotei* was legalized, mediation by the police did not lessen. With their authority and psychological dominance, particularly under the authoritarian regime of the old constitution, police mediators were by and large effective and efficient. The total number of cases brought to police officers for mediation is presumed to be still very great, though the exact figures are kept secret ... . A certain portion of the cases in which solutions were not reported presumably were resolved by party agreement based on the recommendations made. If these are taken into account, the number of cases solved by the police is indeed quite sizable. In my own investigations, I have found that a rather large number of cases in the Family Courts were first brought to police officers for mediation and came to court only after mediation proved futile. Presumably the same may be true for *chotei* cases in other courts.

Arbitration

It is characteristic of Japanese culture that arbitration has been a kind of reconcilement. For this very reason, arbitration in the sense of contemporary Western law is alien to Japan. Despite the fact that the Code of Civil Procedure contains provisions for an arbitration procedure, it is seldom used. Clauses specifying that a dispute arising out of a contract shall be settled through arbitration are normally not employed except in agreements with foreign business firms.

The Construction Industry Law provides both arbitration and mediation procedures for disputes arising out of construction contracts, in order to promote the legal disposition of these disputes instead of leaving their resolution to traditional extrajudicial reconcilement. Nevertheless, very few cases of arbitration have been initiated since these provisions came into effect, only two applications for arbitration having been filed with the Ministry of Construction during the period between October 1956 and April 1961, as compared with fourteen applications for mediation. Although the Ministry of Construction is encouraging the use of an arbitration clause in construction contracts (the standard contract stipulations drafted and recommended by the ministry contain a clause of this type), few contracts have made use of it. Contractors and owners have told me that they feel insecure under the provision, since arbitrators might render unfair decisions. Presumably the underlying basis for this feeling of insecurity is not that arbitrators are in fact unfair, but rather that they might make decisions in accordance with universalistic standards; the contractors and owners prefer to settle disputes in accordance with the prevalent psychological climate and the subtle power balance existing between the two parties.

Statistics of labor disputes present an even more interesting picture. Compared to the mediation cases, the number of arbitration cases is surprisingly low. ... Furthermore, it is worthy of note that, out of five arbitration cases filed with the Central Labor Relations Commission, three were withdrawn because the disputes had been settled outside of the administrative proceeding. This again shows that even in the process of arbitration parties are ready, and prefer, to enter into informal reconcilement.

At the same time, however, collective-bargaining agreements, in contrast to construction contracts, apparently tend to familiarize the disputants with arbitration as a means of dispute resolution. According to an investigation by the Ministry of Labor in 1958, 57 labor agreements from a sample of 532 contained arbitration clauses. In 1961 the Central Labor Relations Commission conducted an investigation of collective labor agreements, and its interim report shows that, from a sample of 280 collective agreements, approximately 20% contained arbitration clauses. The sampling methods employed in these surveys were not identical, but indications are that the number of collective agreements containing arbitration clauses nearly doubled over the three years. This figure is indeed impressive, especially in comparison with the extremely few construction contracts or contracts of sale between Japanese citizens containing arbitration clauses (though no supporting statistical figures are currently available). This striking difference is probably due to the fact that the relationship between employer and employee is, unlike most other contractual relationships, more individualistic, each party insisting upon his own interests.

These figures should be compared with those of the international commercial arbitrations administered by the Japan Commercial Arbitration Association. In 1960 there were filed with the association 78 cases of mediation and 93 cases of arbitration. The ratio of arbitration cases to mediation cases is thus 1:19; the ratio of arbitration cases in the Ministry of Construction for the three and a half years between October 1956 and April 1960 is only 0:09, and that in the Central Labor Relations Commission for the entire period from 1946–60 only 0:0027.

RECENT CHANGES

I have tried to show the main features of various forms of dispute resolution, with particular emphasis on their specifically Japanese aspects. However, there are indications of gradual change. Some of these have been touched on above. Since the Meiji Restoration, Japan has been in the process of rapid transition from a premodern, collectivistic, and nonindustrial society. The traditional forms of dispute resolution were appropriate to the old society, whereas judicial decision and arbitration as contemplated in the provisions of the Code of Civil Procedure are alien to it. But all modern societies, including Japanese society, are characterized by citizens with equal status and, consequently, by a kind of check and balance of individual power. It is against this background that traditional relationships serving to make a proposed settlement acceptable have been disrupted and that the need for decisions in accordance with universalistic standards has arisen.

Furthermore, there is another aspect specific to the modern industrialized society: the economic value of calculability (*Berechenbarkeit*, as Max Weber calls it) or foreseeability of rights and duties, without which the rational operation of capital enterprise would be seriously endangered. As industrialization proceeds, the need for perfection of the judicial system and of legal precepts becomes both more extensive and more intensive; and the traditional informal means of dispute resolution are found to be disruptive to capital enterprises. In the latter years of World War I, the outward signs of this change were the increase in collective transactions, the growing number of lawsuits involving immovable property, and the development of a new form of labor relations. Though further changes were not apparent under the strong control of the totalitarian regime during the thirties and forties, the large-scale industrialization necessitated by the war in China and later with the Allied powers undoubtedly accelerated the transition. During the whole period of the war, Japanese family life was gradually disorganized, accompanied by dissolution of the social controls exercised by the family. The result was a large number of serious conflicts within families and kinship groups which the traditional means of social control (patriarchal power and the family council) could no longer effectively resolve. The traditional family system being the very basis of the official ideology (*shushin*) and the power structure of the state, the government adopted chotei to settle disputes arising from the disorganization of the family. Rather than adjustment through a system of legal rights, disputes were to be 'washed away' in order that the family might be strengthened and preserved.

With the collapse of government through the Emperor, the authority of the traditional social institutions as a vehicle of social control was lost or at least greatly weakened. Although various 'superiors' still survive to some degree, they are no longer so influential as to be able to solve all controversies arising out of their relationships with their 'inferiors.' The most conspicuous of these changes is in the area of family disputes. Today neither the authority of the head of the family, the family council, nor the marriage go-between is capable of settling all family disputes. The large number of such disputes brought to the Family Courts in the postwar era suggests this fact.

In 1950 the Ministry of Labor made a very interesting nationwide survey of social attitudes. Among questions on family solidarity, parental authority, selection of a marriage partner, primogeniture, equality of the sexes, and the like, there was this one: 'If you checked the weight of rationed sugar [in those days sugar was tightly rationed] and found a shortage, would you notify the merchant or not?' This question was designed allegedly to determine the extent to which people would uphold their rights. From a sample of 2808 (randomly selected), 90% of the men and 82% of the women replied 'I would notify him,' 9% of the men and 16% of the women replied 'I would not,' and 1% of the men and 2% of the women replied 'I don't know.' Perhaps this particular question was not entirely appropriate to probe the attitude sought because a deficit in the weight of rationed sugar was of vital importance to everyone in those days of food shortages; thus, while important, one should not overgeneralize from this response. In 1952, the National Public Opinion Institute conducted a nationwide survey, a part of which bears upon our problem. The institute investigated the reaction to the following question: 'There is a saying, "yield to a superior force" [*nagai mono ni wa makarero*: literally, allow oneself to be enveloped by a long object]. Have you ever heard of this?' Those who replied affirmatively were then asked: 'Do you think that the attitude expressed in that saying should be approved and that nothing else can be done?' Purportedly these questions were designed to measure the extent to which people yield to authority or power. Out of 3000 random samples, 51% of the men and 30% of the women replied that such an attitude should not be approved. Of course, this question simply pertained to the attitude toward authority and did not cover the exact problem under consideration, but it indirectly reveals the attitude of people toward informal means of dispute resolution in which the authority of the go-between plays a significant role.

Probably of greater significance is a change which seems to be taking place in *chotei* cases, particularly in the Family Courts of large cities such as Tokyo or Osaka; it is not at all rare for parties to be aware of their legal rights and to insist upon them so strongly that reconcilement becomes at times quite difficult. Parties to *chotei* cases have frequently complained that lay mediators did not pay sufficient attention to their rights under the law. From time to time various political leaders complain of the people's awareness of their rights and of the decay of harmony-minded traditions. Whatever their feelings about this may be, the legal institution of *chotei* no longer functions to maintain the precarious nature of the interests involved in the traditional social and contractual relationships. The transition is irretrievably in process, and the outcome is clear.

Iwasaki, K, 'ADR: Japanese Experience with Conciliation' (1994) 10 *Arbitration International* 91–96

CONCILIATION BEFORE THE COURT

In 1951 the Civil Conciliation Act (Law No 222, 1951; 'CCA') was enacted to integrate several similar statutes relating to conciliation or civil and commercial disputes. The earliest statute was enacted in 1922 for conciliating disputes arising out of continuous relationships such as land-leases, house-leases or farm-tenancies. Article 1 of the CCA stipulates that its purpose is to settle amicably a civil or commercial dispute not by strictly applying law but by applying the general principles of justice and fairness as befitting the actual circumstances of the dispute. A conciliation under the CCA is called a conciliation before the court since the conciliation is conducted by a conciliation committee organised by the court. In this regard it is distinguishable from a conciliation outside the court which is carried out by the conciliators appointed by the parties or by a conciliation institute.

Conciliation before the court is commenced either on application by a party to a dispute or by a court order if the court finds that the dispute brought before the court is suitable for conciliation. A party can make an application for conciliation either before starting litigation or even while litigation is pending. If the party's application or the court's order is made while litigation is pending, the pending litigation is suspended until the termination of the conciliation process. Upon the party's oral or written application for conciliation or the court order submitting the case to conciliation, a conciliation committee is appointed by the court. If the court considers it appropriate, the conciliation committee can be composed of judges, but if the party requests it, a judge and not less than two commissioners arc appointed outside the court under Article 5 of the CCA. If the committee deems preliminary conservatory measures to be necessary, the committee can order the party or any related person not to transfer the right or items disputed or not to change its status quo under Article 12 of the CCA.

The committee fixes a date for conciliation and summons the parties and the persons concerned or having an interest in the dispute. Where the summonsed party or person fails to appear on the date without any justification, the court can impose a non-penal fine under Article 34 of the CCA. The conciliation process is usually held in the court, but the committee can select a suitable place outside the court if necessary, but in principle the conciliation process is not open to the public. The parties and interested persons can appear in the conciliation process in person with or without their counsel. In addition to hearing the parties' statements the committee can (on its own authority) investigate facts and take evidence from the parties, experts and administrative agencies, and summon witnesses. The committee attempts to identify the true nature of the dispute, makes clear the points at issue; and confers with the parties so as to lead the dispute towards an amicable settlement.

Where an amicable settlement is reached between the parties and the committee decides the settlement is appropriate, the settlement is put on record by the court and becomes a compromise before the court. If the committee deems the parties' settlement inappropriate, or if there is no possibility for the parties to reach an amicable settlement, the committee can terminate the conciliation process, unless the parties agree in advance and in writing to accept the committee's determination. If the parties' agreement is available, the committee notes the terms of conciliation. which terms are put on record by the court and then become a compromise before the court. The conciliation process is then terminated. Even where the conciliation process is terminated without a successful result, the court can render upon its authority such ruling which it thinks necessary for the settlement of the dispute after consultation with the committee members. Any party or interested person can file an objection to the court's ruling within two weeks from the date when the party has been notified of the ruling by the court. If an objection is filed within the period, the ruling loses its effect; but if no objection is filed within the period, the ruling becomes final as a compromise before the court. A compromise before the court has the same legal effect as a final and binding agreement under Article 203 of the Code of Civil Procedure (Law No 29, 1890); and it is enforceable by the court under Article 22 item 1 of the Civil Execution Act (Law No 4, 1979).

Where the conciliation process is terminated without the court's ruling or the court's ruling loses its effect, the pending court litigation will start again. If the party brings an action with respect to the dispute to the competent court, the action is deemed to have been brought to the court on the date when the conciliation process started.

Conciliation before the court is a simple, speedy, private and cost effective method of ADR; and it is the most popular and effective means of ADR in Japan. In 1991 the number of newly-filed cases of conciliation before the court was about 74,000; and this number has increased gradually in the 45 years since the Second World War. (On average, this number is equivalent to about 30% of the civil cases newly-filed in the courts). About 55% of the cases of conciliation before the court have been successfully settled by the parties' compromise. The average duration of a case of conciliation before the court is 8–9 months, which is shorter than 12 months required for a district court hearing in case of litigation. The fee for conciliation before the court, which is paid to the court, is determined according to the amount of dispute, but roughly speaking is about 60% of the amount required in litigation.

The problems of conciliation before the court are that (i) the parties cannot appoint the conciliator(s) by their agreement; (ii) the quality of a conciliation committee member is not always suitable for a commercial dispute since their fee is nominal and too small for appointing an able businessman or business lawyer as a conciliation committee member; and (iii) the compromise before the court resulting from conciliation before the court has legal effect as a judgment in Japan but is not directly enforceable in foreign jurisdictions since it is not a court judgment.

CONCILIATION OUTSIDE THE COURT

Conciliation outside the court is further divided into (a) ad hoc conciliation and (b) institutional conciliation. In Ad-hoc conciliation, one or more conciliators are appointed by the parties agreement and mediate between the parties with or without proposing their own idea for settlement. If the parties succeed in agreeing upon an amicable settlement under the guidance of the conciliators, it legally becomes a compromise outside the court. If the parties fail, they are free to refer their dispute to arbitration or litigation. Ad hoc conciliation has not been popular for the resolution of commercial disputes in Japan since it is not easy for the parties to find appropriate conciliators and for the conciliator or the parties to manage the conciliation procedure effectively.

Institutional conciliation: the Japan Shipping Exchange, Inc. (JSE), the Japan Commercial Arbitration Association (JCA) and the International Chamber of Commerce (ICC) offer institutional services for managing the conciliation of international or domestic business disputes under their respective conciliation rules. These institutions offer important assistance to the parties in the appointment of conciliation. Under the ICC's Conciliation Rules, the conciliator is always appointed by the ICC and the parties cannot appoint their conciliator by their agreement. On the contrary, in case of the JSE or the JCA the parties can appoint the conciliation by agreement, and the institution can appoint the conciliation only if the parties request it or fail to appoint the conciliators by agreement. The conciliator's function and the legal result of conciliation are almost identical to those of an ad-hoc conciliation.

An amicable settlement which arises from a conciliation outside the court is a compromise outside the court and has legal effect as a contract under Article 659 of the Civil Code (Law No 89, 1896 and Law No 9, 1898), as well as conclusive evidence of the legal relations between the parties under Article 696 of the Civil Code. If the parties agree to submit their amicable settlement to the court for registration on the court's record, the amicable settlement can become a compromise before the court under Article 356(2) of the Code of Civil Procedure. Conciliation outside the court is a simple, speedy private and cost-effective method of ADR. The conciliator can flexibly adopt appropriate and practical means of resolution according to the particular nature of the dispute, since the conciliator has no obligation to apply any law to the substance of the dispute or to follow any procedural law in the conciliation process. On the other hand, the conciliator cannot have such power as the conciliator is given in case of a conciliation before the court under the CCA, nor can the conciliator expect any assistance from the court even if a person concerned refuses to submit evidence to the conciliator or to appear before the conciliator as a witness. Litigation is also necessary if one of the parties to the conciliation does not voluntarily perform its obligations under the amicable settlement (unless the amicable settlement was converted into an enforceable compromise before the court).

RELATIVE SUCCESS

The reasons why conciliation before the court has been so successful in Japan are submitted to be as follows:

1. The enactment of The Civil Conciliation Act: It is notable that this statute was enacted in 1951, and annexed conciliation to the court system more than 40 years ago. It could be said that this statute has promoted conciliation before the court and built up a court-supporting system for conciliation before the court for over 40 years.

2. Practical and non-legalistic conclusion or conciliation: This is a marked contrast to a judgment in a court case. In the case of conciliation, even if it is conciliation before the court, conciliation are not required to apply the law strictly, but required to apply the general principles of justice and fairness which befit the actual circumstances of the dispute. In contrast a judge is required strictly to apply the law and cannot help making an all-or-nothing conclusion even if it is not befitting to the actual circumstances of the dispute.
3. Non-binding character of the conciliation process but binding character of the parties' agreed settlement: The parties can reject the conciliators suggestion or proposal. Only where an amicable settlement agreement is reached between the parties under the guidance of the conciliator the settlement is put on record by the court and obtains the legal effect to bind the parties. This non-binding character of the conciliation process and binding character of the parties agreed settlement make conciliation before the court very attractive for the parties. These characteristics guarantee the parties satisfaction with the conclusion in conciliation. Such satisfaction is not guaranteed in the case of litigation or arbitration.
4. The conciliator's power to summon the parties and others: The conciliator is given a strong power to summon the parties and persons concerned or having an interest in the dispute; and the court guarantees this power of the conciliator by imposing a fine against the summonsed party or person who fails to appear timeously without justification. This power of the conciliator makes it possible for the actual parties to be involved in the dispute directly but not through their legal advisers and to control the dispute. In the case of litigation or arbitration, legal advisers tend to move to centre stage and the actual parties lose control of the dispute. This phenomenon often disturbs a equitable resolution of the underlying dispute.
5. The fact that conciliation procedure is simple, speedy, private and cost effective: All of these peculiar features of conciliation are lacking in court litigation although they are required for resolving commercial disputes.
6. Enforceability of the amicable settlement: The parties' amicable settlement agreement resulting from the conciliation before the court and put on the court's record, has the same legal effect as a final and binding judgment of the court. This enforceability makes it possible for the parties to a commercial dispute to finally settle their dispute by conciliation before the court.

Yet there remain certain problems. In spite of the successful track record of conciliation before the court, it cannot be denied that conciliation before the court is facing some new difficulties at this stage. First, there can be difficulty in appointing suitable conciliation for complicated, international or highly technical disputes. Recently parts of commercial disputes have become more complicated, international or highly technical. In the case of conciliation before the court a judge who is in charge of the case has to appoint conciliation committee members who will mediate the dispute. It is very difficult however for the judge to find suitable committee members for these complicated disputes. As the members' daily fee is fixed by court regulation to a comparatively low level (about US $60 per day, such amount is not sufficient to attract an experienced expert's consent to be appointed to the committee. Secondly, there can be hesitation by the parties to express frankly their views. Parties to a dispute often hesitate to make suggestions or proposals for a settlement during the process of conciliation before the court. This is because it is not fully guaranteed that the parties' views, suggestions or proposals will never be introduced into future judicial proceedings as evidence or to create an unfavourable impression with the judge when the conciliation proceeding is unsuccessfully terminated and litigation is started. The third difficulty is that an amicable settlement resulting from conciliation before the court has the same legal effect as a final and binding judgment in Japan, but it is not enforceable in foreign jurisdictions without great difficulties.

Tanase, T, 'The Management of Disputes: Automobile Accident Compensation in Japan' (1990) 24 *Law & Society Review* 660–67, 675–82

THE NONCONFRONTATIONAL COMPENSATION SYSTEM

To manage the disputes so that legal services are not used, or to stimulate people to say, 'I will not use a lawyer (or court) for I do not need it,' three interrelated measures are necessary; (1) the system must enhance the capability of the victims to prosecute the claims on their own; (2) it must simplify the law so that professional services are not needed; and (3) it must provide alternative forums in which the unresolved disputes can be settled short of full legal war. Concretely, the first measure is taken in Japan by providing extensive free legal consultation, the second, by standardizing the compensation scheme, and the third, by establishing court-annexed mediation and a special forum.

These measures are bolstered by the norm in Japanese society, which demands that the insurer take a personal responsibility for the accident. When attention is diverted from strictly legal arguments to moral concerns, the lawyer offers less specialized authority in obtaining restitution. In the following section, I look in detail at how these techniques are used to manage the compensation disputes in Japan.

A. Legal Consultation

When legal knowledge exists as a system of abstract rules, persons extracting relevant rules from such a system and applying them to specific situations provide an indispensable service. While these services are supplied almost exclusively by private practitioners in the United States, in Japan they are provided extensively by free legal consultations. Consequently, the disputants need not retain lawyers in Japan to obtain legal information.

Although in sheer numbers the insurance companies and the police are the most conspicuous providers, in terms of the quality of the information provided the two most important consultation centers are the local government centers and the bar association centers. The government consultation centers provide free consultation by special traffic accident counselors (there are 361 such counselors in Japan; they are nonlawyers and most are retired governmental officials) (Sori-fu, 1988: 278). These centers are usually located at government office buildings and, in large cities, are open daily. The consultation, lasting typically 40 minutes to an hour, covers all aspects of compensation. When a complex legal issue arises, clients are referred to a lawyer of the general legal consultation center usually located in the same building. The local bar association's consultation center provides consultations exclusively with lawyers, and in addition it offers mediation services in which the consulting lawyer contacts the other party on behalf of the client and tries to resolve the dispute. (In 1986, 723 cases, or 4% of all consultation sessions, led to mediation services, and two-thirds of these were resolved by the mediation.) In addition, the Legal Aid Society and the Traffic Accident Dispute Resolution Center together provided 3,000 consultations by lawyers. In all, these four organizations offered close to 180,000 consultations, 13% of which were provided by lawyers. Since lawyers are retained privately by the injured in approximately 3% (about 18,000 cases) of the accidents involving death or injury, these specialized organizations provided 10 times as many consultations as did private practitioners. Lawyers working in these consultation centers provided 30% more consultations than did those in private legal services.

Some government bodies also give free consultations regarding automobile accidents in connection with services they regularly provide. The police also give extensive consultations. As many as 230,000 drivers or victims sought such services. Moreover, insurance companies offer free consultation as a consumer service. Two quasi-public organizations in the insurance business provided 95,000 consultations, while insurance companies provided 450,000 such consultations. In total, these services offer an enormous amount of information, almost two consultations per accident, free of charge so as to meet the disputant's need for individually tailored information.

1. *Function of Legal Consultations*. Each center assumes a partly overlapping but slightly different role. Typically a police officer is the first person the victim is likely to contact concerning an accident, and thus is the person who gives overall guidance as to how to proceed in handling the accident. But the police do not usually provide specific legal information. Such information is provided by both local government and bar association centers. Here, we should note that lay consultants are viewed as sufficiently competent to give an independent opinion concerning such legal issues as the liability of the parties and the proper amount of damages. Although this trust is related to the fact that the Japanese in general have great confidence in government and its officials, the standardization of compensation payments (discussed in the next section) plays an important part. Timing is also important: 45% of all visits to these centers take place within a month of an accident, and 65% within three months (Kyoto City Government, 1984: 4). So, as the authority first contacted for specific legal advice, these centers have a great deal of influence on the course the dispute will take.

There are no readily available data on the total cost of these consultation services. However, if we tentatively assume that one consultation session with a lawyer costs 5,000 yen, and with a nonlawyer 2,000 yen, the expenses born by public organizations and insurance companies add up to 2 billion yen, which is 0.2% of the total amount paid to the injured. Although we do not know exactly how much these free consultations cut the demand for private legal services, certainly they account at least partly for the relatively insignificant earnings of Japanese lawyers in representing the disputants in automobile accident cases; legal fees comprised only 2% of the total compensation paid to the injured. If we compare this with the US figure (legal fees amounting to 47% of the net compensation received by the injured), the savings of potential costs are enormous. Even if all the consultations are with lawyers, still their involvement is limited and their expertise is offered at a discounted price within the consultation system; thus their active participation in the system hardly contributes to an overall increase in the demand for legal services.

Conceivably, however, the consultation system could act as a springboard to more intense involvement of lawyers at a later stage. An injured party informed of his legal rights at a consultation center could as a result define the dispute essentially as legal matter and begin seeking full legal recourse by retaining counsel. In fact, to encourage this development, some local bar associations have lifted the traditional ban on taking a private case directly from a public consultation session. However, this channeling function of consultation has not yet materialized. In fact, the norm is to divert disputes away from the legal system. For example, in Osaka, where the bar association is most aggressive in promoting the program, in only 2% of the free legal consultations was the consulting lawyer later retained privately. In a society in which lawyers do not yet handle a significant portion of such traffic accident disputes, the extensive legal consultation system fills the information gap and thus reinforces the tendency of people to do without lawyers. As a survey on pre- and post-consultation behavior reveals one-third of disputants who visited one of the bar association's fee-charging, general legal consultations had already received free legal consultations (on average 1.5 sessions per person). After the consultation, 30% planned to or did attend yet another consultation session. Apparently disputants were not inclined to seek full legal recourse merely on receiving advice about their legal rights. Rather, disputants returned to consultation at successive stages of their negotiations, or visited several institutions to shop around for information to enhance their bargaining positions or, more modestly, to guard against losing entitlements at the hands of a shrewd opponent. Note that many of these disputants themselves read law books. They seemed to view legal consultations essentially as a means of enabling them to resolve the dispute by themselves.

2. *Consensual Nature of Legal Consultations*. Because consultations provide information that is consensual in nature, they contribute to the diverting function of the system. Generally speaking, two types of legal information for the pursuit of rights can be provided: partisan and consensual. The former attempts to provide a person with legal weapons to further his interests, while the latter attempts to promote agreement between the parties by providing both with the same legal information. When the information assumes a strong partisan character, the assertions of one party are more likely to conflict with those of the other and an intervening third party may be requested to adjudicate the conflicting claims. On the other hand, when the information is less partisan and more consensual, it moves the parties toward a middle ground and thus facilitates autonomous agreement.

The consultation in automobile accident compensation has a consensual character in a double sense. First, since most consultations are provided by the government or insurance companies, they inevitably reflect the bias of their providers against legal action. As nonlawyers committed to the efficient handling of claims, government officials and insurance agents often express the view that lawyers unnecessarily complicate the case and, for the victim's sake, are to be dispensed with. But more important, the very nature of free consultations predisposes them to assume the consensual character. Since the consultant cannot do an independent investigation and relies entirely on information provided by a party, he naturally becomes cautious in giving legal advice too aggressively. Even if the consultant is a lawyer and does recommend aggressive legal action, he cannot provide close follow-up. The burden to put the legal strategy into effect falls on the lay party, and thus the consultation counselor is discouraged from becoming a true partisan advocate. As a result, the consultation center, whether government or bar association, tends to provide consensual information to all parties, the injured and the injuring alike, and thus promotes consensual solutions among the parties.

Yet consensual consultation cannot work effectively unless the whole compensation system is constructed to keep partisan conflicts to a minimum. Otherwise, the information meant to provide a common legal framework would simply be discarded by disputants as being ineffective for their legal fights or would encourage them to pick only opportunistically favorable bits of information, lessening the integrity of negotiations. Therefore, we should expect the proliferation of consultation services in Japan as a way of managing disputes to be complemented by an effort to create a nonconfrontational compensation system. ...

...

Nonjudicial Forum

In spite of these efforts, some claims do erupt into full-fledged disputes. But even in these cases, a lawsuit is rarely instituted or a lawyer called in, for there is another buffer. Extrajudicial machinery often settles the dispute before it escalates into a full-scale legal war.

1. *Court-annexed Mediation.* The most important extrajudicial machinery is the court-annexed mediation (*chotei*). At its peak in 1971, 16,396 disputes were submitted to it; and in 1986, 5,374 were submitted, accounting for 0.9% of the total number of automobile accident cases. Lawyer participation in mediation has increased in recent years to about 46% for plaintiffs and 23% for defendants. Still, in most cases, the parties are not represented and mediation is used by parties who have attempted in vain to settle the matter of compensation by themselves, and continue to try to resolve it without resorting to litigation or to lawyers.

On the average, it takes 6 months to conclude a case by mediation, in contrast to 14 months for litigation. Furthermore, since a lawyer's average fee is less in a mediation case, more than half of the mediation claimants are not represented by a lawyer, and the amount claimed as compensation also smaller in mediation, the total costs borne by a disputant in mediation are one-seventh those of litigation. But mediation carries its own costs – the risk of not being able to reach a settlement and the likelihood of compromising a legitimate claim for the sake of settlement. These risks are reflected in two measures: the settlement/win ratio (the percentage of cases settled or found for plaintiff), and the recovery ratio (the amount awarded divided by the amount claimed). Here mediation naturally trails behind litigation. Moreover, in every type of injury the amount awarded in litigation is higher than that awarded in mediation. It is difficult, however, to determine whether these costs are balanced by the greater efficiency of mediation. If we consider the interest that would accrue on a mediation award (between the time of filing and that of settlement in litigation) as well as the difference in costs (court costs plus lawyers' fees), the difference in awards between litigation and mediation decreases. If mediation is pursued without the help of lawyers, the financial advantage of litigation, except in serious injury cases, almost disappears. In such cases when an injury involves permanent disability, aggressive use of the law produces a higher settlement because of the uncertainty involved, while in the rest of the cases, mediation pursued by the claimant himself produces as satisfactory a result as litigation.

2. *Traffic Accident Dispute Resolution Center.* An additional institution, the Traffic Accident Dispute Resolution Center, deals exclusively with automobile accident disputes in Japan and offers mediation outside the official court setting. It was first established; in 1974 as a nonprofit corporation, financed by investment profits from compulsory insurance. It now has eight branch offices in major cities. As it is a new, private institution, it lacks to some degree; the authority and acceptance by the public that court-annexed mediation enjoys. However, by tactful management, and by assuming a

quasi-public character, it has gained a strong foothold within the automobile accident compensation system. Annually more than 4,000 disputes are brought before the center (4,166 cases in 1986), and approximately 40% of them are settled there. Although it focuses on mediation, the center is unique in that it incorporates elements of legal consultation and of adjudication in order to cater to individual needs as well as to facilitate a settlement.

In about two-thirds of the cases, serious efforts are not made by center consultation lawyers to settle disputes, because the time is not ripe for conciliation (eg the injured party is still in the hospital, or substantial negotiation has not yet taken place with the other party) or because the center was visited only to obtain advice on how to proceed with a claim or to get an objective, third-party estimate of damages. The center's ability to offer such consultation services nonetheless contributes to its overall effectiveness by enabling it to become involved in diverse cases at early stages. In that way the still relatively weak center can carefully cultivate a clientele among the general public, as well as acquire cases for its mediation services.

The center is unique in furnishing adjudicatory services. In difficult cases in which the parties cannot reach agreement even with the help of a lawyer-mediator, the center refers the case to adjudication by its own panel of legal experts. For example, in 1981, mediation was attempted in 1,181 cases (37% of the new cases), out of which 751 cases (64%) reached agreement (typically involving multiple sessions, an average of 4.9 sessions per settled case, before an agreement was reached). In addition, 91 cases (8%) were referred to adjudication. Although the judgment rendered by the center's panel is not legally binding, it is regularly honored by insurance companies as a matter of courtesy. Furthermore, claimants very seldom challenge decisions, for the decision rendered by the tripartite panel of a retired judge, a lawyer, and a legal scholar seems to have, at least in the eyes of the lay disputants, the authenticity of a 'correct' legal decision, and hence to be impervious to lay challenge. In fact, this aura of authenticity is the very policy of the center. In order to reproduce a judicial decision as accurately as possible, the center not only tries to apply legal standards meticulously but also to update its judgment standard by systematically collecting judicial decisions and holding periodic conferences with judges working in the traffic section of the courts. As this effort to simulate a judicial decision is completed, any net gain to be derived from full-scale litigation diminishes rapidly so that an incentive for pursuing formal litigation is lost. Through this center injured parties can obtain at low cost (ie without a lawyer) the benefits which the judiciary would otherwise be called on to provide at a higher cost.

Thus, in Japan, not only is confrontation between injured parties and insurance companies kept to a minimum, but the occasional confrontation that arises between the parties themselves is mostly absorbed by these extrajudicial institutions, leaving only a few cases to be resolved by full legal measures.

D. Moral Confrontation

Paradoxically, however, there remains deep-rooted confrontation between the injured party and the injurer over the moral responsibility for the accident (ie the injured trying to hold the injurer morally accountable for the accident), which further biases the parties against bringing lawyers into the dispute.

This unique type of confrontation comes from the sense of justice or moral reasoning held by the Japanese. In Japan, where the maintenance of good social relationship is given the highest consideration, 'giving trouble to others' is in itself considered a serious offense. Therefore, a person who has inconvenienced another, for whatever reason, by his own fault or not, is obliged to fulfill his moral duty to make up for the inconvenience independent of his legal obligation to do so. This duty, above all, requires the inconveniencing party to repeatedly express his sincere apologies for the inconvenience. In automobile accidents, this necessity to apologize is best represented by the frequent use of the word 'sincerity.' For example, if an injurer takes an 'insincere' attitude by failing to inquire after the insured party at the hospital or fails to offer condolences to the deceased's relatives, the injured party or his relatives will harden their attitude, and negotiations will become very difficult or may even deadlock.

In this respect, Japan contrasts sharply with the United States, where the insurance company literally acts as a proxy for the injurer in attempting to reach a settlement. Since insurance companies in the United States take charge of handling all the injurer's responsibility, including not only liability for compensation but also the responsibility of carrying out negotiations, the injurer usually remains completely uninvolved in the dispute over compensation. It is not at all unusual for the injurer to be unaware of the final outcome of his own dispute (Conard *et al*, 1964: 297). The injured party himself regards the dispute purely as a matter of monetary compensation, and while allowing the injurer to remain completely uninvolved in the negotiations, he entrusts his own part of the negotiation to an attorney who has no emotional involvement in the accident.

On the other hand, in Japan, strong resentment toward the injurer on the part of the injured party, which is refueled by a moralistic interpretation of responsibility for the accident, makes it difficult for the injurer to remove himself from personal involvement in the negotiations. The injured party himself is anxious to take part in negotiations and keeps demanding the injurer to express his 'sincere' apologies for the accident. Of course, in compensation disputes where a large monetary stake is involved, the demand for sincerity does not simply mean a verbal apology. In practice, it also means 'show your sincerity through generous compensation,' requiring that the insurance company, sharing the moral burden of the original injurer, add a little to the standard payment, or as is quite often the case, requiring the injurer himself to pay in addition some consolation money out of his own pocket. But no matter how calculating a motive may underlie the demand for sincerity, as long as the process of negotiations is couched in terms of moral responsibility, lawyers cannot satisfactorily take over the role of the disputants. Or to put it differently, lawyers' special expertise can have little relevance in these highly moralistic negotiations.

IV. A PARADOX MANAGEMENT

A. The Successes and Failures

The nonlitigious society of Japan has not developed spontaneously. Instead, it has been cultivated by well-planned management. Under the ostensibly efficient Japanese compensation system, the people seem content with what they get and do not resort to law to recover damages. Moreover, the myth of functionalism prevails; people apparently believe in the benevolence of the system, and have not seriously challenged it in courts or in legislature. They have even looked down on the occasional campaign against the system waged by Japanese lawyers, suspecting it to be motivated by their parochial interests. In view of the apparently satisfied public, the system is not likely to change its basic structure in the near future.

In fact, the automobile accident compensation system has been applied to other disputes as well. For example, in medical malpractice, where the number of disputes has sharply increased, a third-party reviewing panel was recently established. A doctor against whom a complaint is lodged must report the complaint to the local medical association, which reviews the complaint and recommends whether the insurance should be paid. If either party or the insurance company is not satisfied with the local association's finding, the case is referred to a central reviewing panel, the Medical Dispute Investigation Council, which consists of representative members of the Japan Medical Association and the insurance companies along with members of the bar. Although the findings of this panel are not legally binding, insurance companies regularly honor them. Interestingly the panels, both in local associations, and in the central body, review the case in closed sessions, based, not on the adversary arguments of both parties but only on a report compiled by the special staff of the medical association. Furthermore, in view of the strong supervisory power of the Ministry of Finance over insurance companies and that of the Ministry of Public Welfare over the medical associations, this seemingly private panel in reality assumes a semiofficial character. In other areas as well, such as product liability, construction disputes, environmental pollutions, real estate transactions, and unpaid wages, similar dispute management has been designed and sanctioned by the government, although implementation has not been uniformly successful.

Note that these nonconfrontational systems are also consonant with the cultural heritage of Japan. Two cultural themes especially recur throughout dispute management: authority and morality. Although in the United States authority often carries a negative connotation, in Japan it has an intrinsic value; it breeds a sense of orderliness in an otherwise chaotic social world. While an authoritarian person is disliked in Japan just as in any other society, the authority figure can expect respect so long as he cares for and guides subordinates properly. The resulting hierarchical order makes the nonconfrontational system work. The government, through administrative guidance, directs insurance companies; the judiciary, which is itself hierarchically organised, unifies the interpretation of the law; and the police authoritatively determine the facts on the spot. The third-party neutrals also rely implicitly on this hierarchical control when they set forth the just resolution to the parties.

Morality is also important. In the United States, because morality is left entirely to individuals and cut off from meaningful community sanctions, it has lost much of its binding force. Moreover, as people are overwhelmed by the legal consequences, they are discouraged from showing such fundamental human concern for the victims by, for example, expressing sincere apologies for their fault. By contrast, in Japan, not only is the moral dimension of the accident clearly retained, but also all actors in the system are mutually bound by moral obligations. If the insurance companies did not genuinely honor, or at least, appear to value, morality above legality, and hence live up to the people's expectations, the liability insurance could not have been transformed into the quasi-public system. Judges also activate moral concerns. Although committed to maintaining the standardized compensation system, judges nevertheless step beyond the neutral umpire role and urge insurance companies to settle at higher levels when the standardized compensation would work a hardship in a particular case. Otherwise, the rigidity and unconcern for individual plight often associated with bureaucratic justice would strain the system too much. Morality, then, adds a touch of 'social justice,' if not individual justice, to an otherwise efficient but rigid bureaucratic justice, encouraging support for the system from the people of Japan.

Behind the appearance of consensus and stability, however, one can detect some inherent structural weaknesses in the compensation system. The very effort to create a nonconfrontational system produces problems, for a system which does not employ legal resources is defenseless against overly aggressive parties. The result is a series of irregular payments when persistent claimants wield undue influence or, more troubling, when innocent claimants are subtly induced to accept lower than standard payments. Moreover, the very paucity of litigation weakens the legal system. Only daily experience with law, testing its premises under different circumstances through vigorous, partisan advocacy, can invigorate the law, adapting it to an ever changing society. As the standardized compensation system itself stands on the principle of tort law, this stagnation of the law may in the long run diminish the public support for the system.

Although at the moment only a few critics have noted these systemic defects, if the nonconfrontational system harbors the seeds of its decay, it is possible that in the future, when the underpinnings of cultural consensus further erode, and when people with an emerging law consciousness deem the system less satisfactory, the system may collapse or evolve into another form. It is too early to predict any major change, but the recent upward turn of litigiousness may reflect the growth of this divergent consciousness. Since 1983, the litigation rate has continued to climb, and mediation is increasingly legalized; the claimants are represented more often, and their cases are less likely to result in settlement. If the problems of unjust compensation and the weakening of the law, which inhere in the system of management, do in fact explain these developments, dispute management has an insoluble contradiction in it; as the management is perfected, it creates the problems that undermine the very foundation of management.

Rosch, J, 'Institutionalizing Mediation: The Evolution of the Civil Liberties Bureau in Japan' (1987) 21 *Law & Society Review* 243–48, 252–56, 260–63

I. INTRODUCTION

The Civil Liberties Bureau (CLB; *Jinken yogo kyoku*) was established on 5 February 1948 during the American occupation of Japan as part of the Japanese Ministry of Justice (at the time the Attorney General's Office). Originally modeled after the Civil Rights Section of the United States Justice Department, the CLB has evolved into an institution that in 1984 heard over 315,000 cases. Much of what has been written in both Japan and the United States about the CLB concerns its role as either a protector of civil rights or an ombudsman. Although the bureau performs both functions, with the ombudsman role bringing it some of its most rationally significant cases, together they represent less than 5% of the CLB's caseload. The other 95% reflect the agency's evolution into a place for hearing disputes that in the United States and many Western European countries would be settled through mediation by the police or a therapeutically oriented social service agency or would 'fall between the cracks.'

Why did an institution designed to protect civil rights become a place where people bring cases for mediation? How does a government agency handling 375,000 disputes per year coexist with popularly held ideas about the limited role that public means of dispute resolution play in Japanese society? In attempts to explain why the Japanese so infrequently use formal adjudication, too much attention has been given to Japanese culture and tradition and not enough to institutions such as the CLB.

II. THE ROLE OF THE CLB

Most of the 375,000 CLB cases in 1984 involved problems that the complainants believed raised questions about fundamental human rights. This represented only a slight increase over previous years. This number of cases would be high even for places like South Africa or the Soviet Union, where many violations of human rights have often been alleged. But in Japan, the numbers in no way reflect the extent of the human rights problem.

In the vast majority of its cases the CLB's function is best described as mediation. Most cases involve what can be called social rights rather than individual rights. When asked about the cases in his office, for example, the director of the bureau in Hiroshima, a city of close to one million people, first mentioned those involving social ostracism and family disputes. The CLB tries to help people who are having such problems to reach mutually acceptable solutions.

Less than 1% of the cases involve public officials. Although the bureau hears allegations of misconduct by individual police officers, it has consciously avoided general questions about the rights of defendants because CLB officials believe that other organizations can best deal with those issues. Groups traditionally discriminated against, such as Koreans, women, and *burakumin* (descendants of Tokugawa period outcasts), do not find the CLB especially useful (see Upham, 1984; Tsurushima, 1984). The CLB has likewise not been involved in any of the major controversies involving censorship or the separation of church and state.

Other avenues are open to those concerned with what Americans would call civil liberties. The Japan Civil Liberties Union, also set up and encouraged under the American occupation, addresses such issues. More importantly, however, the Japan Federation of Bar Associations obligates lawyers to play an active role in the protection of civil rights in the Western sense (Horiuchi, 1968: 80). Contrary to the popular notion that Japan is a peaceful society with little conflict, civil disobedience, mass demonstrations, and even violent protest have proved successful for a variety of groups interested in civil rights (Upham, forthcoming).

The type of cases that the CLB can hear is limited only by the cases brought to it and by the judgment of the Civil Liberties Commissioners (Ministry of Justice, 1985: 6–8). Less than 5% of the cases require more than counseling by the commissioners. Cases arise from complaints about neighbors, family members, and minor public officials. A great many involve public nuisances, such as dogs, loud music, noisy children, bad odors, and noise or vibrations from trains, planes, construction, or business activity. People also bring complaints about newspaper articles, movies, television shows, and even neighborhood rumors that they feel are damaging their good names. Many of the family disputes involve complaints by older citizens who feel that their children or grandchildren are not treating them properly.

A peculiarly Japanese complaint centers on ostracism (*mura-hachibu*) (Haley, 1982b: 277). Although social intercourse is not usually regarded as a human right, in traditional Japanese society people were supposed to be entitled to belong to a group for religious and economic reasons. Those who feel they are being ostracized from a certain group continue to bring complaints to the CLB (Horiuchi 1968: 72; Ministry of Justice, 1985).

According to agency documents, over 360,000 of the more than 375,000 cases brought to the CLB in 1984 were handled by consultation with the parties involved. Of the remaining cases, 14,500 were deemed too serious to be resolved by routine consultation and were consequently investigated. Usually a little more than half are found to involve actual violations of human rights. Only 243 of this smaller group involved public officials (the usual source of alleged human rights violations in the West), who in most years are judged to be at fault in a little less than half the cases (Ministry of Justice, 1985: 7-8).

Because the majority of cases are handled quickly and quietly through consultation with the parties involved, few records are kept. The following sampling of cases shows how the CLB defines civil rights violations and why mediation is used to protect these rights:

Case 1. A farmer's wife was mentally ill. Her mother applied the usual home remedies: binding her hands and feet, scorching her face with hot incense, and feeding her hot peppers. The husband asked the CLB to intervene and let his mother-in-law and neighbors know that he was not acting improperly by stopping the home remedies and placing his wife in a mental hospital (Gellhorn, 1966: 725, n 65).

Case 2. A rural family was ostracized by their neighbors for being uncooperative; they were not invited to any weddings or funerals, and their children were bullied at school. CLB officials convinced the community that its behavior was inappropriate (Horiuchi, 1968: 72).

Case 3. An elderly gentleman was unable to sleep because of noise in a business adjoining his apartment. The CLB showed both parties how to mute the noise (Beer and Weeramantry, 1979: 12).

Case 4. A woman was falsely accused of stealing from a store. Even though she was acquitted and the real culprit was caught, news of her arrest caused her, her son, and her husband great embarrassment. For example, children at her son's school would have nothing to do with him. The CLB distributed handbills explaining the mistake all over her neighborhood. Everyone was said to have lived 'happily ever after' (Gellhorn, 1906: 725).

Case 5. The family of a patient who had been treated for a serious illness complained that the patient had received the wrong blood type during a transfusion Although the mistake was corrected, the patient did suffer some unnecessary discomfort. The patient died a few days later, but an investigation showed that the error was not the cause of death. The CLB persuaded the doctor to publicly recognize his mistake and apologize to the family (Horiuchi, 1968: 75).

Case 6. An elderly woman was very lonely and felt that she did not see her son, daughter, and grandchildren enough. A Civil Liberties Commissioner contacted the offending relatives. The elderly woman was not satisfied with the results, but did stay in contact with the commissioner who had tried to help her.

Case 7. The CLB was able to stop the private publication of a list of *burakumin* who lived in and around a large city, which would have made it easier for people to discriminate against this group.

Case 8. A home was damaged by vibrations from nearby construction. The CLB persuaded the private company to pay damages (Gellhorn, 1968: 720).

Case 9. People living hear the Shimida River in Tokyo claimed that noxious odors from the river were threatening their health and making their homes unusable. After some hesitation, the CLB helped persuade the local and national governments to do something about the pollution. The river now has fish living in it. The CLB takes credit for assisting in establishing the notion of environmental rights, publicizing the problem, and applying pressure for change (*ibid*, 719; Horiuchi, 1968: 74).

Case 10. A railroad policeman stopped a railroad worker from bathing in a public rest room and forced him to walk half-naked through a crowded train station. The CLB persuaded the policeman's superior to make sure that the worker received an apology and that the policeman was given a reprimand (Horiuchi, 1968: 58).

Case 11. Workers at a drug company were forced to take a drug the company wanted to test. A number became ill, and one died. The CLB persuaded the company to cease such practices and compensate the insured parties (*ibid*).

Case 12. The CLB has often intervened after citizens complained that fictionalized accounts of real events in movies or on television would embarrass them and damage their good names. The CLB report a success in obtaining clearer disclaimers on such movies and programs and even in stopping some proposed projects (Ministry of Justice, 1960: 8).

The interviews with CLB officials and the various CLB publications that were a source for the above examples reveal the agency's particular pride in achieving a substantial reduction in the amount of cruel corporal punishment in Japanese public schools, helping to foster the concept of environmental rights, making it more difficult for companies to search their employees and reducing the amount of rude behavior by public officials (Horiuchi, 1988; Ministry of Justice, 1985: 8).

At its inception, the CLB was charged with a number of missions, including to investigate and collect information about violations of human rights, to disseminate information about human rights, to sponsor programs to promote human rights, and to prod other governmental and nongovernmental organizations to respect the fundamental rights of individuals (Horiuchi, 1968: 54). Although virtually no limits are placed on the kinds of cases it hears, the CLB is supposed to avoid hearing cases that are currently being litigated, have already been heard in a civil or criminal court, or would clearly be more appropriate for other government agencies (*ibid*, p 75). The above examples show that even these minimal guidelines are not followed very closely. ...

...

B. Social Rights

While the Japanese may have had a weak conception of civil liberties and individual rights as they are defined in the West, they had and continue to have a strong sense of what are best called social rights. Although this strong sense is certainly not unique to Japan, Japan may be unique among highly urbanized, complex capitalist societies in having public institutions like the CLB that both recognize and protect these rights. Included as social rights are ideas about how group members ought to treat each other and how people of higher status ought to treat those of lower status.

The social rights protected by the CLB are more consistent with the traditional Japanese self-conception than with the individualistic notions that the postwar reformers were trying to encourage. In traditional Japan 'justice was relational ... [as] superiors as well as inferiors were only important as parts of a group which legitimately claimed their complete dedication. Duty, not right, was the emphasis' (Henderson, 1985: 174). Although notions of reciprocal duties among family, social group, community, and country have always been strong in Japan, Japanese scholars have argued that if there were anything like the Western idea of rights in Japan, it involved the concepts of group membership (Kawashima, 1963: 44–45) and group rather than individual entitlements (Kawashima, 1975: 264–265).

During the formative Tokugawa shogunate (1603–1868), the legal remedies available to an individual, as well as one's legal status, were the result of membership in a family, clan or village group (Henderson, 1965: 25–28). In this rigidly hierarchical society, disputes between group members were to be settled through conciliation by the leader of the group, whether it be the family head, the five-man group chief, the village headman, or the lord of the fief. Family or status group officials responsible for conciliation had considerable resources to coerce compliance or at least to guide it to serve the interests of social harmony that they were supposed to maintain (*ibid*, pp 174–77). The greater the social distance between disputants, the larger the group involved and the higher status and the greater the resources of the official responsible for conciliation (*ibid*, p 174).

It would be wrong, however, to characterize traditional Japanese society as quiescent, with few claims being made against officialdom. Although under Tokugawa rule individuals had to overcome formidable obstacles to claim their social rights against those of higher status, many still did (Haley, 1978: 371). Such claims were usually stated in group rather than individual terms (Upham, 1976). People could also bring claims about essentially private matters to public officials. This is very different from the Western, Lockean notion that views rights as protections from government (Flathman, 1976).

In part because of its language, which calls for the protection of 'the right to maintain the minimum standards of wholesome and cultured living' (*Kenpo*, art 25), the right to individual dignity and equality in marriage (*Kenpo*, art 24), and the right to be 'respected as individuals' (*Kenpo*, art 13), the Japanese constitution has been interpreted as protecting a range of rights, including these social rights, broader than those protected in the West. These rights are as likely or more likely to be read as adjurations to the public (covering largely private activities) as to government officials (Gellhorn, 1966: 719; Ministry of Justice, 1985: 7–8). That this notion of group or social rights is still prevalent in Japan helps explain why the CLB, an institution that Westerners believed would protect individuals from government, is used so extensively to mediate problems between individuals.

C. Conciliation

Japan has a long tradition of providing public means to mediate essentially private disputes. Traditional law in Japan, as elsewhere, stressed conciliation (Henderson, 1965: 183–84; Kawashima, 1963: 44, 46–47). Like the mediation practiced by the CLB, conciliation in Tokugawa Japan focused on the facts unique to each dispute as opposed to the universal notions of rights and duties. For the Japanese equity has always been a more important component of justice than consistency and predictability (Henderson, 1968: 409–10, esp nn 42 and 43; Kawashima, 1975). 'The notion that a justice measured by universal standards can exist independent of the wills of the disputants is apparently alien to the traditional habit of the Japanese people' (Kawashima, 1963: 50). Some commentators see the tendency of the Japanese to rely on institutions that individualize disputes as an important obstacle to the growth of rights consciousness and the rule of law envisioned by the framers of the postwar legal system (Henderson, 1968: 448–54; Haley, 1982b).

Whether the tendency of the Japanese people to avoid litigation can be explained by their inherent nature, the system of discipline set up by the Tokugawa shogunate clearly reinforced conciliatory attitudes (Henderson, 1965: 174). During this period every effort was made to see that interpersonal disputes at the local level were handled by conciliation. While the shogunate developed a system of courts to hear cases that crossed status lines and feudal boundaries, these courts had little relevance for the average citizen, whose disputes were handled through conciliation by family or status officials within the household village. 'The thought was that if people must live permanently in close association with others, they must compromise their differences and not to be too contentious about their interests' (*ibid*). Even when cases went to court, it was felt that reason and the particulars of each case should override custom and precedent (Henderson, 1968: 409).

Local officials responsible for maintaining the peace were given a high degree of autonomy and could impose criminal penalties in any case (Henderson, 1965: 92–98, 123–29). In addition to local officials, every community also had unofficial mediators of considerable prestige and status who had developed reputations for their skill in resolving disputes. Once a local official or one of these other mediators was brought into a dispute, the parties were under considerable pressure to settle their differences. 'One suspects that the "conciliation" principle was not that it was better to agree, but rather "You had better agree!" – a principle more like adjudication' (*ibid*, p 236). Individuals had no real choice about where to bring their disputes and no effective appeal from the decisions.

Henderson (1965) has argued that the principal difference between the traditional forms of conciliation in Tokugawa Japan (*atsukai* and *naisai*) and the nonadjudicatory forms of dispute settlement in contemporary Japan (*chotei*, *wakai*, and *jidan*) is that the latter are voluntary. *Chotei* and *wakai*, which he refers to as formal conciliation, are curious blends of informal justice and adjudication. Although they are voluntary and not guided by formal rules and precedents, they take place in court. Under the Japanese Code of Civil Procedure (*Minji sosho ho*, arts 203, 695, 696), the settlements can have the force of a final judgment. Court-sponsored mediation has been the subject of considerable scholarly analysis (Tanaka and Smith, 1976: 492–94; Henderson and Haley, 1978: 649–73). *Jidan*, which Henderson calls informal conciliation, is practiced outside the courts and is used to characterize the activities of institutions like the CLB (Henderson, 1965: 184).

Those who facilitate conciliation outside the courts are no longer traditional authority figures such as village chiefs and local Tokugawa officials. Their place has been taken by institutions like the CLB, the police, and the myriad of public conciliation organizations set up by the courts and local governments. Although the family and neighborhood dignitaries used by these organizations can be heavy-handed, relying on a strong normative sense of what it means to be Japanese, *jidan* as practiced by the CLB is considerably different from Tokugawa conciliation. It involves no formal sanctions, its use is voluntary, and there are a variety of forums to which the Japanese can bring their disputes. Disputants also retain their right to bring cases to the courts for formal adjudication. The number of cases heard by the CLB demonstrates that the notion that individuals can bring private disputes to public institutions continues to affect how the Japanese deal with their disputes even if those institutions have dramatically changed.

The ability of an agency like the CLB to function effectively in a complex, urban society should not be attributed to uniquely Japanese traditions alone. Examples of social rights and a preference for informal ways to settle disputes abound in both historical studies of Western law and anthropological accounts of dispute-processing in third world countries (Merry, 1982; McThenia and Shaffer, 1985; Felstiner, 1974; Auerbach, 1983). However much it has been clothed in traditional symbols, the voluntary aspects of mediation practiced by the CLB stand in marked contrast to traditional forms of conciliation in Japan.

The movement from what Henderson has called didactic conciliation under the Tokugawa to voluntary mediation was one of the many changes the Japanese made after their increased contact with the West (Henderson, 1965: 187–91; Haley, 1982a). It has been argued that voluntary mediation was encouraged by the traditional elite in Japan in response to the growing number of lawsuits during the turbulent period following World War I (Haley, 1982a; Cole, 1979: 127). The Japanese have been particularly adept at attaching traditional symbols to institutions they borrow from abroad. Like the development of permanent employment and quality circles, which likewise arose from exposure to the West, the adoption of voluntary forms of mediation came to be attributed to unique Japanese culture and traditions (Cole, 1979:12–14). Rather than being a static barrier to the development of modern institutions, Japanese tradition has been flexible enough to facilitate the creation of new institutions and practices that have later been seen as distinctly Japanese ways of handling problems (White, 1974: 419–22). The evolution of the CLB and its ability to attract a large number of cases demonstrates both the adaptability and persistence of those traditions. ...

...

Legal scholars in the United States and elsewhere have raised a number of questions about the pernicious effects of informal justice. Some ask whether informal institutions are really able to help people in complex, modern societies (Felstiner, 1974), while others worry about the modern state's growing use of agencies of informal justice to delegalize and depoliticize conflict (Mathiesen, 1980; Cain and Kulcsar, 1981–82: 392–94). Law does more than help people settle disputes. When legal systems apply general rules to new situations, they help to clarify, articulate, and define basic norms. However desirable it is to have institutions that promote social harmony by allowing individuals to settle disputes as amicably as possible, when cases are settled informally there is less opportunity to explore the normative underpinnings of society.

Although the ability of the Japanese to avoid formal litigation is often viewed as a positive attribute of their unique character and culture (Kawashima, 1963; Noda, 1976; Vogel, 1979), some take a more critical view of this phenomenon. Several scholars believe that the persistence of informal dispute resolution has retarded the growth of law and the development of rights consciousness in Japan (*cf* Henderson, 1968; Haley, 1982b; Ramseyer, 1985). For example, Henderson (1965: 241) has written that:

> the excessive use of conciliation stunts the growth and refinement of the body of rules necessary to sustain complex community life; it dulls the citizens' sense of right, essential to the vindication of the law. It may also allow old rules and social prejudices, which new legislation has sought to abolish, to influence the outcomes of disputes; or it may allow a new regime to ignore the law in favor of its new policy, as happened in Japan in the 1930s. In other words, conciliation is neither conservative nor progressive in principle; it is simply unprincipled.

Institutions like the CLB may contribute to the low litigation rate in Japanese society by providing an attractive alternative to the courts, which, in addition to being slow and expensive, offer few benefits even to those who win cases (Haley, 1978: 362–64; 1982b). With few people using the courts there is little pressure on the government either to make more attorneys available or to allow the courts to offer litigants a wider range of remedies. Because litigation has the potential to generate new rules and either vindicate or challenge the viability of old ones, there are cases in which both the individuals involved and society as a whole might be better served by formal litigation. This cannot happen when a dispute goes to the CLB. Informal institutions in Japan rely on existing norms and by their actions reinforce those norms (Bryant, 1984: 86).

In recent years the idea that the Japanese have little need for lawyers, litigation, and effective legal remedies has come under attack by a number of Western legal scholars (Haley, 1982b; Ramseyer, 1985; Bryant, 1984) who assert that the Japanese would be no less likely to litigate than anyone else if their government allowed more lawyers to be trained and if the courts were able to offer more effective remedies to litigants (Haley, 1982b). Some argue that the 'myth of the reluctant litigant' (Haley, 1978) is manipulated by political elites to encourage the Japanese to believe that they are by nature nonlitigious, thereby perpetuating the status quo by discouraging litigation that could directly challenge widely held norms (Ramseyer, 1985: 637–43; Haley, 1982b). 'The larger the number of Japanese who went to court, the harder each individual would find it to believe that such conduct was unethical and to define a Japanese as someone who does not sue' (Ramseyer, 1985: 610). By providing an attractive alternative to litigation the CLB may reinforce a normative climate that delegitimizes conflict and inhibits democracy (*ibid*, pp 637–43). The growth of alternatives to courts was encouraged in the 1920s for just such purposes (Haley, 1978; 1982a).

Whatever informal justice institutions may contribute to the low litigation rate in Japan, individual citizens seem to have access to a wider variety of useful alternative agencies for resolving their disputes than do citizens in most other industrialized societies (Hayden, 1986: 244–47). The CLB has transformed some of the negative externalities normally experienced by large numbers of powerless people, including damage to the environment, unfriendly neighbors, automobile accidents, noise from airports, ungrateful children, corporal punishment in the schools, and intrusive media, into injuries for which people actively seek a remedy. Whatever else it may do, the CLB seems to support those values in Japanese society that discourage exploitation and encourage social solidarity. It is hard to imagine that the life of the average Japanese would be better without it.

Because the courts are perceived as weak, the Japanese are less likely to see them as the solution to as wide a range of problems as Americans do. While institutions like the CLB may defuse cases in which both the individual and the society could benefit from litigation, Japanese groups interested in social change, such as environmentalists and *burakumin*, are also less likely to become involved in litigation and more inclined to take direct collective action (White, 1984) to protect their existing rights and at times to create new ones. It is not at all clear whether they have been less successful than comparable groups in the United States that have relied heavily on the courts (*cf* Scheingold, 1974; Upham, forthcoming).

Whether normative criticisms of informal justice apply to the CLB depends in part on what one sees as the proper role of law and litigation in a modern society. Although the Japanese have created a variety of useful mechanisms to help people settle disputes quickly, quietly, and amicably, this may have occurred at the expense of the system's ability to resolve or clarify larger normative issues. While the CLB and other agencies of informal justice cannot alter the distribution of wealth and power in Japanese society, it is doubtful that formal litigation could, or should, be very effective in achieving this goal even in the United States with its active judiciary (*cf* Horowitz, 1977; Fiss, 1979; 1984).

Ohta, T and Hozumi, T, 'Compromise in the Course of Litigation' (1973) 6 *Law in Japan* 99–102

II–1 Cultural Elements

a. Japanese Legal Attitudes and Compromise

One reason why many civil suits are settled by compromise is a so-called love for compromise – the feeling that exists among the Japanese that, if one has reluctantly become enmeshed in a lawsuit, one should settle it as quickly as possible through compromise. This attitude is probably common to a greater or lesser extent to all the parties involved in a lawsuit.

If one compares judgment and compromise from the standpoint of legal attitudes, the result is as follows: The essence of dispute resolution through judgment is that a third party (the judge) first determines the facts and then applies to these facts impartial legal standards that have been set in advance without regard to the relative strengths of the litigants. In this manner the existence and scope of the respective rights and duties of the litigants is determined. On the other hand, the essence of dispute resolution by compromise is the cessation (smooth adjustment) of a dispute by virtue of the mutual agreement of the parties. Moreover, in the case of compromise it is possible to achieve a resolution by 'washing away' the matter itself without clarifying the respective rights and duties of the parties (without assigning blame) and in actual practice this is the way that disputes are frequently settled. Of course in so far as settlement of a dispute is involved, the respective rights and duties of the parties are clarified in the sense that the actions that are required of them are specified under the terms of the compromise and the matters so specified are safeguarded as legally recognized rights and duties. However, the relationship of the rights and duties in dispute – in other words, whether or not the rights asserted by the plaintiff exist – does not have to be determined. (Accordingly, the findings of fact that serve as a premise for such determination also are unnecessary). And in most cases no determination is made. The conflict is ended without clarifying who is right and who is wrong.

In addition, since compromise requires mutual concessions (Civil Code Article 695), it is possible to have a settlement in which both parties are losers, and in actual practice there are settlements of this kind. The 'concessions' in this situation do not take the form of first determining the extent of the parties' rights and duties and then deciding to what extent each party should yield. Ordinarily, their rights and duties are left indefinite and only their assertions themselves are given up to a certain extent.

The reason the Japanese are fond of compromise is related to the fact that in their social relations the boundary of one's rights and duties are only vaguely defined (Professor Kawashima's so-called 'indefinite rights').' Stated otherwise, social relations are not conducted in light of the abstract rules known as law. Since the resolution of a dispute is essentially something that restores *the (harmonious) situation*, ie *the social relations that existed before the occurrence of the dispute*; if one assumes that social relations before the dispute were as stated above, then Japanese favor a means of resolution that 'washes away' the dispute without clarifying rights and duties.

In contrast, judgment is favored as a means of dispute resolution in societies in which rights and duties are clearly defined from the start (or, it is thought, should have been clearly defined) since the objective of resolution of disputes is to return to a situation in which rights and duties are clearly defined. (Even if compromise is considered desirable in such a society, it is not for the reasons related above.)

In Japanese society a means of dispute resolution that clarifies rights and obligations (since it creates relations that differ from those that existed prior to the dispute) will not produce a smooth settlement. Japanese feel that 'the settlement is not amicable' (*kado ga tatsu*) or 'afterwards a stiffness remains' (*ato ni shikori o nokosu*) between the parties. (However, as stated below, it is said that this attitude is changing at the present time.)

b. Settlement without Loss of Face

As has already been pointed out by Ruth Benedict, the Japanese are very sensitive about loss of face. And Japanese frequently feel that they suffer impairment of honor, a loss of face, by losing a lawsuit. Since compromise does not involve an assessment of right and wrong, the actual loser can escape impairment of his honor. Thus in situations where it appears likely that the lawsuit will be lost in addition to where the economic considerations discussed below are applicable, the party bearing this in mind will seek to protect his honor through compromise.

To avoid the dishonor of losing a lawsuit is not merely the concern of the parties themselves, it is also in part a concern of their lawyers. A lawyer who accepts a case where there is not much chance of victory can through closing the case by a compromise preserve his reputation as a 'lawyer who never loses.'

In addition to losing a lawsuit, withdrawing a suit can also cause certain litigants to feel dishonor. Accordingly, in situations where a dispute has already lost its meaning (from the standpoint of face as well as the prevention of relitigation), one might select compromise in lieu of withdrawal.

II-2 The Nature of Litigation

Judge Tanabe has pointed out that there are two different types of civil litigation, a justice-seeking suit and a money-seeking suit. The former is a lawsuit for the purpose of 'having the wrongfulness of the other party's act personally condemned and then publicly censured by an instrumentality of the state,' while the latter is a suit in which the plaintiff 'wants to obtain prompt judgment or actual performance of an obligation.' Besides a 'justice-seeking suit,' which aims at 'cleansing the muddied name' (*omei o sosogu*) of an individual or satisfying a desire for revenge, we think that there is a suit of this type by which the plaintiff reveals the problem to society and socially indicts the wrongful act of the other party. In such a suit, personal advantage is a secondary motive or is not in issue at all. For example, within this category fall the so-called 'textbook case', shareholders' suits demanding return to the company of political contributions, and so-called 'salaryman suits' attacking irrationalities in the tax system. Pollution cases also have similar natures even though the direct objective of the plaintiffs is to obtain compensation for damages. This type of lawsuit will be referred to as a public justice-seeking suit. We will consider below the relationships between these two types lawsuits and compromise.

Muto, S, 'Concerning Trial Leadership in Civil Litigation: Focusing on the Judge's Inquiry and Compromise' (1979) 12 *Law in Japan* 24–28

COMPROMISE (*Wakai*)

Compromise, together with the judge's inquiry and the court decision, is important work for judges. There is no mistaking that the great majority of litigants usually desire a compromise. When I was an assistant judge, as you all are now, I thought that since the parties brought the dispute to court they naturally wanted a court decision and that naturally a court should respond to this and decide the case; so I promptly made a decision with almost no effort at reaching a compromise. However at that time I once was told by a lawyer that 'You reach a decision too quickly. Even if a party wants a compromise he is embarrassed to broach the matter by himself.' I thought 'that might well be so,' and from that time on I said 'How about a compromise?' at the conclusion of the case. When I did so there were in fact litigants who took an interest, and at that time I came to think that 'Compromise might be good, at that.' Thus, although for several years I have taught only the technique of decisions here at the Institute, when I went back to Division 25 of the Tokyo District Court for the first time in quite a while there were nearly 800 cases awaiting me. When due to this backlog efforts at compromise were made, during one day of closed court sessions, the number steadily declined. I well understood that the parties desired a compromise. However, this is natural if you think about it.

Litigants come to the court requesting a resolution of the dispute, and one that is a final resolution, not a tentative one. A trial court decision is only a tentative resolution, and furthermore considerable time is required until there is a decision of the highest court; the defeated party is dissatisfied and successful execution of the judgment is doubtful. In contrast to this, compromise requires only a few concessions, obtains a final resolution, no antagonism (between the parties) remains and execution is prompt and certain so that it is the best way. It is often said that there are some cases appropriate for compromise and some inappropriate for compromise, but I think that the overwhelming number of cases belong to the former category.

Therefore, the court must not neglect the effort to achieve a compromise at every opportunity. I will be speaking about various things, but if courts make appropriate efforts a large majority of cases can be resolved through compromise. Speaking in a somewhat exaggerated manner, I've come to think that rendering a court decision indicates an inadequacy in the persuasive powers of the judge. In the past I had thought that for a judge to make efforts at reaching a compromise was an indication of an inadequate ability to render a court decision and I occasionally stated this publicly. I have now changed my mind 180°. In any case, I think that the court decision and compromise are the two vehicles for handling cases. However even if I say to strive for a compromise, of course it is useless to do so haphazardly. Here, the timing and method are important.

First taking timing, the first opportunity is after the definition of issues and prior to beginning the examination of witnesses. If it is a simple case where the facts are understood by glancing at the complaint and answer without any definition of issues it is proper to begin compromise procedures immediately, as long as it is the wish of the parties. But in the usual case I think it is better not to initiate compromise procedures before the definition of issues is completed. This is because when both parties say they want a compromise and compromise procedure is immediately entered into under the urging of the parties, the arguments of the parties will not be clarified and accordingly neither the court nor the parties have a clear outlook concerning the case. This can easily result in wasting time without making any progress. Therefore, compromise must be initiated following the definition of issues when it is understood by all where the controversial issues lie and when they hold a tentative outlook concerning the case. Thus, when issue definition is completed, documents have been presented, and the court has come to hold a tentative view concerning the case, this view should be frankly stated to both parties. For example, one might speak about the state of the case saying, 'In this lawsuit if this point is proven it will probably turn out like this. If that point is proven there is a strong possibility it will turn out like that, but it may well be difficult to prove that point in the light of this documentation. In spite of that if Mr. X gives some money some solution may possibly be achieved. What if we call in Mr. X and try talking it over?'

However, when the parties do not wish to initiate a compromise at this stage, unreasonable efforts should not be made since there is not yet any belief concerning the merits on my part, and even if compromise is initiated material for persuasion is meager. In this case I make an attempt at compromise once again at the stage when useful witnesses have been examined concerning the important issues and I have formed a tentative belief about the case. When you have come this far, very often one of the parties desires a compromise, but thinks that if he speaks out by himself it will cause him some loss, and in many cases he secretly hopes for an initiative by the court.

Finally, another opportunity for compromise occurs following the examination of evidence prior to concluding the trial. At this stage the court already has a belief (concerning the case) and the parties are predicting their respective chances of winning. It is the final chance for compromise in the trial court. Therefore, it is easy to reach a compromise by advancing the discussion premised on this fact. However, since no compromise was possible up to this stage it can also be said that it will be as difficult to obtain a compromise as before. Also, in a rare case there may be an attempt at compromise after conclusion of the trial. In this case I make an exception and postpone assignment of a date for the announcement of the decision, and if the compromise attempt fails I immediately assign a date for announcement of the decision.

Next, taking the method of attempting a compromise, I always have the litigants themselves come to court. This is because first hand information can be obtained from the litigants and because only they can make the final decision. Few litigants are audacious enough to entrust everything to their attorneys. As a place for compromise, I try not to use the judges' rooms, where other people are present, but rather to pick an isolated room such as a compromise room. In this so-called secret room there will be only the judge, the litigant and his attorney, and I hear information directly from the litigant. I have the litigant repeat what he told his attorney at his attorney's office and I listen to this. It seems that when people are separated from others and you have a heart-to-heart talk they generally tell the truth. Especially when considering that the other person is a judge, it seems that litigants who meet a judge for the first time often reveal the whole truth. Sometimes the attorney says 'I haven't heard that' concerning what the litigant is saying and the litigant says, 'I haven't even told this to my attorney ...' and proceeds to discuss even facts which hurt his position. Indeed, it may be that he speaks the truth since he feels that even if he tells a lie it will be discovered by the opposing litigant who is also in the courtroom at my request.

Another benefit is that the litigant apparently has a sense of satisfaction in having the judge listen to him. Sometimes there are simple people who are satisfied just by having the judge listen to their entire story and who don't care what happens afterwards, so that a compromise can be reached on the spot. Therefore even if I think the litigant keeps harping on the same trivial subject I endure and listen to it without interrupting to demand that he end his story and quickly state his terms. And thus if I listen for about ten minutes the litigant is satisfied, and even from a seemingly trivial story the true situation of the case often emerges.

Another by-product of listening to the stories of both the litigants in their own words is that even if compromise negotiations stall and it is suggested that we return to oral arguments, *de facto* examination of the litigants has already been completed. This is a powerful trump card for the court; the likelihood is that, since there are no other valid witnesses to question, the compromise procedure continues and easily achieves success.

After listening to the litigant's story, I next hold a discussion with the litigant and his attorney. This discussion is not fundamentally different from that with the attorney at the time of the initial judge's inquiry. For example, I say something like 'Your argument goes like this, but considering it from the viewpoint of general common sense it is strange that this conclusion should be reached despite the existence of this and this fact. And although these documents are evidence for this point they probably can't be said to be evidence for that point.' In this way I explain my outlook on the case. It is best if the litigant says 'I see, that makes sense,' but even if it doesn't go that far it will certainly reach the point where he thinks 'if that's what the court thinks about it, it can't be helped.' If by this time witnesses have been examined and a tentative belief about the case has been formed, I think this may be expressed after explaining that it is only a tentative belief. Also, when the discussion makes no progress because only hypothetical arguments are produced concerning some point, I sometimes suspend the compromise discussion and examine witnesses on only that point. Doing it this way shows sincerity and zeal on the part of the judge, and in any case if you persuade them with reasoning based on the evidence many of the litigants are persuaded.

Thus, when the court and both parties come to have some level of common perception of the case, at this point the terms first emerge. Of course depending on the case a litigant may first state terms and then provide an explanation. In either case I discuss it with the litigant; I must understand why this proposal is put forward. It serves no purpose to simply transmit a proposal from one party to the other or to strive to split the difference between the proposals from both sides. Therefore even when I listen to proposals from both sides I do not take them whole to the other side, rather I examine them based on the discussion up to the point reached and transmit them to the opposing party after increasing or reducing them to an appropriate point as much as possible.

Also, you must be determined not just to take up more time, but to come nearer to your goal at the next session than was possible this time. Therefore, I indicate what matters and terms should be investigated by each party prior to the next session. Occasionally there are unscrupulous litigants who come and feign ignorance saying 'Did you really say something like that last time?' or who think nothing of presenting a lower amount than was discussed before. In such a case I am indignant and say 'Don't trifle with the court!' Ultimately, many of the cases turn out unfavorably for a litigant who does something like that.

When the proposals of the plaintiff and defendant are far apart it is probably best for the court to put forward its own proposal. Also in this situation there is no splitting the difference (between the parties' proposals). Unless it is a proposal which can be explained on a clear basis the parties will not be satisfied. For example, when deciding compensation for eviction I might say 'The current price of land according to the published price is this much, let's consider a lease to be worth 70% of that. Since we have not yet investigated evidence on this point let's put the chance of the existence of a lease being recognized at 1/2. Money initially paid as Key money would now be worth this much, so adding that, how would a total of about this much be?' Also, I put forward proposals based on the strength of my belief about the case. For example, I might say 'In this claim for repayment I think you have a 60–40 advantage. Therefore, if a judgment is made in the trial court you will win everything, but in the appellate court you have a 40% chance of losing everything, so how about accepting 60% of the amount of money claimed?' However when finally working out the terms it is no time for theory; it is necessary to appeal to emotion. Also, when there is a difference of 100,000 yen or so it is necessary to press for a resolution which splits the difference down the middle. In either case, once a proposal of the court has been put forward it must not be changed unnecessarily. Changing the proposal in favor of one party because he is intransigent negates the purpose of the court's proposal. Since all the various facts of the case were fully considered by the time the court proposal was produced, you must have the intention to break off the compromise procedure if the court's proposal is unacceptable. Also, when you show such a resolve an agreement is often reached. I think that a method which centers on logic and evidence and which adds to this an appropriate appeal to emotion is the most satisfactory for all including the court itself.

In this way, I think the court should strive for a compromise with zeal, but never force things unreasonably. If you think of imposing a compromise on the parties it will never work out well. Even when with great pains and effort you enter into compromise procedure, if there is no progress because the parties lack enthusiasm or are obstinate and won't concede anything it is best to immediately call a halt. As a principle I hold three or possibly up to five sessions and if there is still no hope I discontinue. You must not make further efforts which would lead the parties to believe that you are attempting to achieve a compromise because you do not wish to render a judgment. In this case I sometimes renew efforts at compromise after completing the examination of evidence if it has not yet been finished, but when the parties are obstinate and there is no hope I instead quickly render a decision. If the examination of evidence has been completed, I immediately set a date for announcement of the decision and always render a judgment on that date. Also, when compromise procedure is initiated following conclusion of the trial, I have sometimes completed a rough draft of a decision, told this to the parties and then achieved a compromise. In this case, the contents of the decision must be the same as the belief concerning the case expressed during compromise proceedings. Thus, I display an attitude that 'The court never imposes a compromise. It is quite simple to write a judgment. I attempted a compromise for the sake of the parties, and I frankly expressed my belief about the case.' When you do this, at the very least the lawyers understand the attitude of the court and will become very cooperative in the next case, and they also convey this to other lawyers. Also, I hear from lawyers and appellate judges that when you strive for a compromise and considerable concessions are made, even if a court judgment should result in the trial court it is easy to achieve a compromise in the appellate court, so it is not a waste to make efforts at a compromise. Occasionally I receive reports that even after compromise procedure was discontinued and a judgment was rendered the case was then settled along the lines of the court's proposal without being appealed.

Considerable time is required in carrying out the above method of compromise. I allocate from 3:00 to 5:00 of the opening day of court to compromise and handle three cases. One case is allotted an average of 40 minutes, but usually this is insufficient and the session lasts until past 5:00. However I never handle two compromises at the same time. This is based on the same reasoning as not calling two witnesses and hoping that one of them will be late or will not come to the court. There also is a philosophy that if two come together, while the court is taking care of one it's good to have the parties of the other discuss matters by themselves, but that doesn't work well. If they can discuss things easily without a judge it means that it already is easy to reach a compromise. Also, I never handle cases during lunchtime for the protection of health. However I do occasionally handle cases at such a time when the terms of compromise are almost complete and are scheduled to be finished at the next session.

Saying a word about the terms of a compromise, of course the clauses cannot be vague, and it is important to pay attention so that there are no contradictions among the terms. When it is completed you must be careful when dictating the terms to the clerk and must not neglect to examine it closely once more when the written agreement is signed.

Kusano, Y, 'A Discussion of Compromise Techniques' (1991) 24 *Law in Japan* 140–57

Compromise as a Means of Dispute Resolution

Judgment and Compromise

Though I use the phrase 'A Discussion of Compromise Techniques,' we must be very sure to understand at the start the special features and advantages of compromise. Judgment and compromise are both available as means of resolving a dispute that takes place at the level of civil procedure. But the special feature of judgment lies, in a word, in its syllogistic character. Judgment applies the law to facts that lie in the past and produces a conclusion. The objective of judgment is the realization of the law, ie justice, and it is the special feature of judgment that the procedure can be concluded forcibly even if the parties disagree or are absent. Although nearly all the provisions of the Code of Civil Procedure concern the procedure for rendering judgment, arriving at the judgment which necessitates so very many provisions is a long and arduous journey.

As against this, the special feature of compromise is that it aims at an appropriate resolution through mutual concessions (*gojo*) between the parties. The meaning of 'appropriate' is problematic, but I believe that it is synonymous with Article 1 of the Civil Affairs Conciliation Law (*Minji chotei ho*): 'A resolution befitting the case and consistent with reason' (*jori ni kanai jitsujo ni soku shita kaiketsu*). Compromise aims for a resolution befitting the case and consistent with reason, yet what ensures the contents of compromise is not justice but rather the agreement of the parties. There are only two important provisions in the Code of Civil Procedure that deal with compromise. One is Article 136, which provides that the court may encourage compromise at any stage of litigation. The other is Article 203, which provides that once a compromise is reached and entered in the record (*chosho*), it has the same effect as a final judgment (*kakutei hanketsu*). So long as the parties agree, a resolution of the dispute is possible even without taking the long and arduous journey to judgment.

The Judgment Faction and the Compromise Faction

When it comes to resolving cases, the judge has at his disposal two means, judgment and compromise; and I believe that judges can be divided up according to which of these two they stress. I call the former the 'judgment faction' and the latter the 'compromise faction.' There are, indeed, many judges who view both means as important and on a par, but it seems to me that even they incline in some measure toward one or the other. Further, to some extent it is easier to understand an explanation that emphasizes the differences between the two factions. As a consequence, I will continue to use the terms 'judgment faction' and 'compromise faction.'

The judgment faction consists of traditional judges who take the view that parties seek out the court precisely because they are unable to resolve their differences by themselves. Once the parties are in court, on this view, it is perfectly natural for the judge to render a judgment. Those in the compromise faction, by contrast, take the view that because autonomous resolution by the parties is the basis of civil litigation, the basis of resolution is first to facilitate compromise between the parties and to render judgment only when compromise is out of the question. In the past, the judgment faction overwhelmingly predominated, and when I joined the bench I was often told, by way of instruction, 'Don't be the kind of judge who reaches compromise' (*wakai hanji to naru nakare*). What people meant by this was that a judge who reaches compromise does so because he is incapable of rendering a judgment and that I mustn't become that sort of judge. On the other hand, there were also those who said that compromise was the best resolution of a civil case. The latter, however, had little voice, and spoke in a sort of muttering tone.

These days, though, the importance of compromise has come to be recognized, and I do not believe there is anyone even in the judgment faction who ignores compromise. Examining the breakdown of the disposition of ordinary civil cases in district courts in 1984, 46.6% were disposed of judgment, 18.9% by withdrawal of the case, and 31.2% by compromise. Given the fact that 45% of the judgments were default judgments (*kesseki hanketsu*) and some of the withdrawals were essentially compromises, there can be no doubt that more cases are now resolved by compromise than by judgment. As a result, compromise is important even for those in the judgment faction – just as preparing judgments is important even for those in the compromise faction. Thus, compromise techniques are important for all judges, and from this perspective as well they must become the common property of the courts.

The Advantages of Compromise

When a judge actually seeks to encourage compromise, he must have a thorough understanding of its advantages. For in encouraging the parties to resolve their dispute by compromise, a judge will lack persuasive power unless he himself believes that compromise is in the parties' best interests.

The first such advantage is that, unlike judgment, which is a provisional means of resolution premised on appeal, compromise is a means of resolving the dispute once and for all. If compromise is reached it represents a final resolution of the dispute, and for this reason is unquestionably superior to the provisional means of resolution provided by judgment.

The second advantage is that while judgment often produces formulaic 'all or nothing' resolutions in an attempt to slice through the problem by means of the law, in the case of compromise it is possible to make a proposal for resolution that befits the case and is consistent with reason.

For example, judgment can resolve only the specific case between the parties. In contrast, compromise makes it possible to include other disputes that are not the object of the litigation and to bring in at the appropriate time third persons who are not parties before the court. Further, judgment can do no more than decide whether a fact existed in the past depending on which side bears the burden of proof, and thus can only resolve matters that have already occurred. In the case of compromise, however, it is possible to produce an appropriate proposal for resolution that takes into account the impact on the parties' futures. In other words, the special advantage of compromise as compared to judgment is the markedly greater extent to which the former can respond to the desires of the parties.

Third, even when a judgment orders a party to perform a duty, the loser in litigation may turn obstinate; and the chances that the party will actually perform the duty are poor. Instead, the loser will seek to avoid compulsory enforcement that would require him, for example, to turn over title to property. In compromise, by contrast, because the party himself has promised performance to the judge, he will make an effort to perform of his own accord. The difference between the two becomes perfectly clear when one considers that if a party to compromise lacks money he will go so far as to borrow from another person in an effort to pay. Reaching a satisfactory resolution of the dispute naturally exerts a more positive influence on the future relations of the parties as well, and this is all the more true in disputes between neighbors or relatives. Similarly, in labor disputes, the satisfactory return of discharged employees to the workplace is possible only through compromise.

Fourth, judgment in the courts entails three levels of decision – the original judgment followed by two levels of appeal, so reaching a decision takes time. In contrast, compromise enables a speedy resolution. Emphasizing this point, however, amounts to little more than acquiescing in an undesirable situation marked by delays in litigation; if the judge seeks to make use of this point, the parties may come to have doubts about the court's attitude. This point therefore requires careful attention.

Fifth and finally, while rendering a judgment takes considerable time and effort on the part of the judge and the clerk of the court, compromise requires less time and helps to save labor. Yet since this benefits solely the court and not the parties, it must be considered strictly a secondary matter.

Criticism and Dissatisfaction Directed at Compromise

Although there are very considerable advantages to compromise as discussed above, I often hear criticism and dissatisfaction directed at compromise, as well. For example, there are those who say that compromise produces only proposals for resolution that involve splitting the difference, that compromise is imposed on the parties by threats, that forcing the prospective winner in litigation to make concessions limits and obscures the people's sense of their own rights, that compromise benefits only those who refuse to give up, and that my attention is fixated exclusively on getting rid of cases. Thus, I hear a wide variety of complaints. I am well aware that such complaints must be carefully considered. Still, in my view, these criticisms are aimed at the methods and contents of compromise, without denying compromise's importance Within compromise there is, if you will permit me to say so, good compromise, in which the parties give their consent, and bad compromise, in which the parties are left feeling dissatisfied. I believe that criticism of the sort described above is aimed at bad compromise. The judge's goal must not be compromise for its own sake but rather good compromise that manages to please both parties. As I go about my work of encouraging compromise, I tell myself that the above criticism is warm encouragement for those judges who make good compromise their goal.

The Time to Encourage Compromise

The text of Article 136 of the Code of Civil Procedure indicates when and at what stages the judge may encourage compromise, but in actual practice there is a difference of opinion on the appropriate time for compromise. The ordinary case progresses in stages: filing of the complaint, statement of the complaint, clarification of the issues, taking of evidence, conclusion of oral argument, and judgment. Professor Akira Ishikawa asserts that in principle compromise must be conducted after either the clarification of the issues or the close of the taking of evidence. It is commonly thought that even a significant number of judges share this opinion. But in my experience there is a chance to encourage compromise at every stage of litigation – precisely, I feel, as provided for in the Code.

Nevertheless, I have never conducted compromise at a stage earlier than statement of the complaint (though I have heard of others doing so with success). The reason for this is bound up with the way I understand oral argument and the first court date (*dai-ikkai kijitsu*). Because the cases are divided up into so many different types – some headed for default judgments, some in which the parties desire compromise, some in which issues need to be clarified, and so on – I run my court with the thought that I will try to use the first court date to sort the cases out, and so I do not seek compromise before that time. Once the first court date has passed, however, and after I have confirmed the intentions of the parties, I will often enter into compromise discussions right away or do so while clarifying the issues. In addition, I often conduct compromise in the midst of taking evidence or after the conclusion of oral argument. Particularly in *pro se* cases, I make an effort to listen to what the parties have to say not in compromise negotiations but out of court. While I'm asking both parties about the nature of their grievances and what they want from the other side, quite often compromise just naturally occurs. Sometimes, of course, the parties cannot reach compromise, but in these cases I seek to begin taking evidence having arranged the parties' allegations in my own way, summarized them, and put them in the record.

There is some question as to the basis for engaging in this sort of endeavor out of court. I customarily refer to it as 'preparatory compromise-type argumentation' (*junbiteki wakaiteki benron*), but I cannot deny that there is a concern in relation to the principle of public access to the courts. Still, this method has been infused with an energy quite unlike that of the argumentation that goes on in the arid atmosphere of the courtroom, and I myself intend to go on using it as living procedural law.

Because the judge ordinarily has not formed a personal opinion of the case (*shinsho*) prior to the stage at which evidence is taken, there is a problem as to the basis on which he should encourage compromise. On this point, Professor Ishikawa asserts that compromise must take place on a party-directed rather than a judge-directed basis. Attorney Toichiro Kigawa further states that in Germany the judge's encouragement of compromise prior to taking evidence follows a party-directed model, and in cases where the allegations of the plaintiff and defendant are consistent Kigawa professes amazement at the absence of persuasive power in the judge and the readiness (compared to Japan) with which the judge gives up. There is thought to be a deep-rooted opinion among Japanese judges, as well, that if the judge cannot form a personal opinion of the case then he cannot responsibly encourage compromise. I cannot agree with this view. It is possible for the judge to encourage compromise even if he has no personal opinion of the case. I, too, adopt a party-directed model, but I find no direct connection between this model and weakness in the judge's persuasive power.

You may now be wondering, 'Well how *does* he do it?,' yet this is not a difficult question. It is quite sufficient if the judge facilitates dialogue between the parties. Surely there are numerous cases in which resolution of a dispute without resort to litigation has become possible once both parties have exhausted their dialogue. Therefore, in cases where resolution would be considered possible if both parties could exhaust their dialogue, if the judge strives to ascertain the cause of the parties' failure to communicate and removes this obstacle, thus facilitating true dialogue, compromise naturally falls into place. The important thing is to draw out the natural rejuvenative power that lies within the parties themselves. Of course, there are cases in which the judge forms a personal opinion of the case in taking evidence and must then add this opinion later on. But I believe that such cases are, rather, the exception, and cases in which the parties can reach compromise by exhausting their own dialogue are more numerous and more the norm.

Methods of Persuading the Parties

*The One-by-One (*kogo*) Persuasion Method and the Both-at-Once (*taiseki*) Persuasion Method*

Although it is said that there are two methods of persuading the parties to reach compromise, one-by-one and both-at-once, in Japanese courts compromise is almost always achieved through the one-by-one persuasion method. According to Attorney Kigawa, in West Germany the one-by-one persuasion method raises doubts about the fairness of the judge's actions. This method, it is believed, results in the acceptance of underhanded bargaining and is a dubious way to recommend compromise. In discussing this method, Kigawa goes so far as to say that it should never be used.

I, however, think that the one-by-one persuasion method has an outstanding feature; there are invariably virtues in a method that continues to be employed in actual practice. Since the opponent is not present in the one-by-one persuasion method, a party can candidly tell the judge about the contents of the case, his own feelings, complaints, hopes, and so on. The judge, for his part, can enter into the feelings of the party and consider how to resolve the case as though he stands in that person's shoes. The judge then listens to what the opponent says and this time in the same fashion puts himself in the opponent's shoes and considers a resolution. My experience is that when the judge shuttles back and forth in this spirit a good proposal for resolution generally arises, giving birth to a compromise proposal that both parties can accept. In the both-at-once persuasion method the judge cannot engage in separate dialogue with the parties. He has no choice but to discuss his personal opinion of the case or, when he has formed no such opinion, to say to both parties, 'Can't you work something out?' The one-by-one persuasion method must be retained so that the judge can come up with good compromise proposals on behalf of the parties. I do think, however, that the judge must try to avoid the sort of persuasion method whereby he tells both parties that their chances of losing are great, so that they think he is demanding concessions.

Joint Attendance by the Attorney and the Party Himself as a General Rule

In actual practice, the general rule is to make the attorney and the party attend together and then go about persuading them. But there are many other ways of pursuing compromise. Sometimes the judge calls in the attorneys for the plaintiff and the defendant together, sits them down facing each other, and produces a compromise proposal through discussion. The judge has the attorneys persuade the parties and calls in for a second attempt at persuasion only those parties who remain unconvinced. This method only works, however, when the attorneys and the judge see the case in the same way.

A method that is an exception to the exceptions consists of getting rid of the attorneys and conducting direct negotiations. But since this method occasionally results in a loss of trust between the attorneys and the judge, it should be used only when there is no alternative and when, moreover, the attorneys give their genuine consent. I was once involved in a case in which dispute activity at a certain company had gone on for 300 days and every means of resolution had been exhausted. At this point I obtained the consent of the attorneys and held repeated high-level meetings with the company president and the labor union committee chairman, through which a compromise was reached. The compromise resulted in a normalization of labor-management relations and earned me the thanks of both parties. It was a case I shall never forget.

Techniques of Persuasion

The Basic Types

While I believe that there are many techniques of compromise, I think of the whole as divided into two categories: the types that are basic (basic types) and the types that apply the basic types (applied types). No matter what the nature of the case, the judge must make his first approach through the basic types. Only when the basic types have proven unsuccessful does it become possible to use the applied types. The basic types have no special therapeutic effect but their adaptive range is broad and they pose little risk of adverse side effects. The applied types, by comparison, have a narrow adaptive range, demonstrate a special therapeutic effect in a limited number of cases, and carry serious side effects.

a. Listen Carefully to What the Parties Say

This is the supreme principle. When the judge listens carefully to what the parties say, he understands what they want. And if he can achieve this, a compromise proposal will emerge.

In the book *Getting to Yes*, there appears the story of two sisters who quarreled over an orange. After the sisters decided to split the orange in half, the first sister ate the fruit and threw away the peel, while the second sister used the peel to make a cake and threw away the fruit. If a third person had asked the sisters why they wanted the orange, they would have found out that the second sister wanted the peel to make a cake and the first sister wanted the fruit to eat. Thus, a compromise proposal giving the peel to the second sister and the fruit to the first sister would have emerged naturally, and both sisters would most likely have been happy to accept it. If the judge were to turn this situation into a compromise on the basis of his personal opinion, I think he would come up with a proposal to cut the orange and give most of it to the first sister if she seemed likely to win, give most of it to the second sister if she seemed likely to win, and split the orange in half if the case were evenly divided. But viewed from my perspective, which dictates that I focus on the parties' dialogue and conduct compromise unconstrained by my personal opinion of the case, the good compromise proposal would give – quite apart from the judge's own opinion – the whole peel to the second sister and the whole fruit to the first sister.

b. Communicate with Sincerity

Every party thinks of himself as unhappy. Basically, nobody wants to reveal his dispute before a third party, and continuing with litigation is very stressful. It is important to sympathise with feelings such as these on the part of litigants and to communicate with them with sincerity. As I try to communicate with the parties, my attitude is this: 'Right now this dispute of yours is in an unhappy and unsatisfactory state. As luck would have it, I am going to be participating in this dispute, and I'd like to do everything I can to make a bad situation even a little bit better.' In my experience, when the judge does this he can generally make an impression on the parties.

c. Stick to it with Persistence and Enthusiasm

The judge can't simply conjure up compromise with a word. The emotional antagonism between the parties won't dissolve overnight. But the judge mustn't give up easily, and even if he should fail, it is important to seek second, third, and fourth chances, and to make every effort he can.

d. Strive to Resolve the Parties' Mutual Mistrust

There is a great deal of mistrust between parties involved in litigation. Because this mutual mistrust continues to supply the parties with energy, the judge must cut it off at the source. In a case in which misunderstanding, needless worry or the like forms the basis for a party's mistrust of his opponent, when the party becomes aware of this on his own the feeling of mistrust dissipates naturally. I listen carefully to what the parties say and when I think that one party has misunderstood the other, I explain this to the party and try to resolve the misunderstanding. The party then says, 'Oh, so I misunderstood. That guy isn't like that after all,' and a crack appears in the wall of mistrust toward his opponent. The remainder of the wall collapses instantly, and a feeling of trust is restored. Civil cases (apart from cases like traffic accidents) seldom occur between strangers; most occur between parties who have trusted in each other. Because most people won't lend money to or serve as surety for someone they don't trust, disputes don't occur between people who don't trust each other. Resolving the parties' mutual mistrust and restoring their sense of trust therefore occupies an important place among techniques of persuasion.

e. Consider a Party's Psychological State from His Own Perspective

When encouraging compromise, the judge must carefully consider how the parties feel. When the judge considers the situation from their perspective, a good proposal will occur to him. Disputes don't happen unless there are at least two people involved, and so there can be no dispute resolution without considering human psychology. In my experience, parties by and large have fallen into the following psychological states.

First, they feel more upset about a small hurt that lies in the future than about a big hurt that lies in the past. So when the judge makes a proposal that takes care of the future hurt, it becomes possible to extract far-reaching concessions on matters that are already over.

Second, as I said earlier, every party feels that he alone is unhappy. Thus, when a party realizes that other people as well – all of them – are miserable, he relaxes and can calmly consider a proposal for resolving the dispute.

Third, because Japanese dislike disputes, before going to court they feel a desire to avoid court even if it means making hefty conclusions. Once in court, however, the feeling becomes one of resisting to a greater degree than is necessary and refusing to make concessions. But since the parties fundamentally don't like to dispute, they desire resolution at an appropriate time. Consequently, there are times when it is necessary for the judge to keep working in the belief that deep down, even if they show resistance, the parties want a speedy resolution. If the judge does this, the parties are sometimes impressed by his enthusiasm and will happily accept the court's compromise proposal. I conduct compromise thinking that I will do my best to reach this point.

f. Look for the Real Cause of the Dispute and Seek to Resolve it

The judge must always consider why the dispute arose and why it has continued to the present, without getting caught up in the contents of the complaint and reply statements. There is no guarantee that what is revealed in the statement of the case will correspond to the aim of the person bringing the suit. When the real aim of the plaintiff is altogether different, it is virtually impossible to resolve the case unless the plaintiff realizes that aim.

This situation often arises in disputes between neighbors, such as suits to settle boundaries. For example, suppose that someone can't stand the racket caused by his neighbor's piano. The person wants to go to his neighbor and say, 'Would you quit playing the piano?' If his neighbor should reply, 'Is there a law against playing the piano?,' then, he thinks, he could argue back. Should he be unable to argue to the contrary, he would end up sadly heading for home, yet staying silent would do nothing to eliminate what's bugging him. Now the person may remember being told that he owns a piece of land in the middle of land that his neighbor has occupied for two generations. When he first heard about this, he thought that bringing up the matter of the land and quarreling over it would just be unpleasant, so he decided to keep things as they were. But he can't stand the situation any longer. Thinking that because he has proof of the boundary line it will be an open-and-shut case, he resolves to take his neighbor to court.

A scenario like this is relatively common, and in cases where litigation abruptly breaks out despite long-term, stable relations between neighbors, the real aim, as we have seen, must be thought to lie elsewhere. When the judge listens carefully to what the parties say he wilt perceive their real aims, and so in a case like that above, if the judge adds a proviso stating that there shall be no piano playing after 8:00 pm, he can reach agreement satisfactorily on the boundary line as well.

g. Take Pains to Make Your Speech Concrete

Taking pains in how you speak to the parties is also important. Appearing before a judge is a source of great anxiety for the parties; it is essential to remove this anxiety and to take steps to ease, their minds. I say things like, 'Nice day today, isn't it?' or 'You've come an awfully long way to be here,' sometimes starting off with matters that have nothing to do with the case. Since this works to relax nervous parties, it is far from idle chatter.

It is also important to explain things in a way that is easy to understand. Proverbs, colloquialisms, allegories and the like are effective means of persuasion. Each party and case has its own individual character, and it's necessary to look at the personalities and the plot of the case and respond in a manner suited to the circumstances. I write down in a notebook the phrases I've used that have proven successful and introduce them in conversation at places like assistant judges' meetings. Because it would be overly technical, however, I'll cut short my discussion of this topic.

h. Explain the Advantages of Compromise and Make a Good Compromise Proposal

When parties are encouraged to compromise by the judge, they vacillate between accepting and rejecting the suggestion. In such cases, the judge must persuade the parties why reaching compromise is good and why it will be to their benefit. It is necessary to explain fully the differences between compromise and judgment, the methods of enforcement should there be a failure to perform – the things that make the parties feel uneasy. When the judge has become thoroughly familiar with the advantages of compromise that I stated at the start, his ability to persuade the parties will increase.

Further, the judge must not only explain the virtues of compromise in abstract terms, but must also make proposals that are outstanding in content. The important thing is to listen carefully to what both parties say and come up with a proposal that will, insofar as is possible, give both of them what they want. You'd have to say that the proposal I mentioned earlier to give out the orange by dividing it into peel and fruit was an outstanding one. I have arranged into types those compromises I have tried that worked well, and I'd like to explain them in detail a bit later when I speak of types of compromise proposals.

i. Leave the Other Person an Escape Route and Don't Corner Him

In conducting compromise, the judge must not corner the parties. It is vital that he always seek to leave the parties an escape route and that he not cause them to lose face. Sun Tzu's The Art of War states: 'Always leave open an escape route for an encircled enemy; do not harass an enemy driven into a corner. This is a rule of war. Since the parties aren't hostile armies, it is all the more true that the judge absolutely must not do things to corner them. In my experience it is largely undesirable to, for example, tell a party that I find myself unable to trust him. Instead, I think it's better to say that the truth may be as he's telling me but that, in view of the allegations and evidence on the other side, in my capacity as judge, I can't very well take him at his word.

j. Inspect the Site in Real Estate Cases

They say that seeing is believing, and in real estate cases this adage is very apt. Inspecting the site enables the judge to understand the parties' allegations and gather materials for making a good compromise proposal. Moreover, parties won't trust a judge who hasn't inspected the site, for they suspect that he doesn't know what's really going on. They think that unless he has seen the site, the judge won't know the truth and won't be able to render a correct judgment. Consequently, whether as an inspection (*kensho*), examination of the location (*shozai jinmon*), on-site conciliation (*genchi chotei*), or whatever the case may be, if the judge inspects the site, the parties will trust him and ultimately listen to him.

The Applied Types

The above are the basic types of persuasion techniques, but when the judge thoroughly attempts the basic types and still doesn't succeed, it becomes necessary to use the applied types. However, the judge must absolutely never forget that the applied types materialize only when he has thoroughly attempted the basic types. The applied types produce results precisely because they follow upon the judge's sheer hard work – his enthusiasm and his sincerity. The basic types always make up the basis of compromise, while the applied types are something like spices that bring out the flavor of the basic types. And using the applied types right from the start is like eating spice by itself: not only bad tasting, but bad for you.

a. Use the Reverse Version of the Basic Types

The most simple applied type involves using a reverse version of the basic type. 'If pushing doesn't work, try pulling, ' as the saying goes. We judges have come to learn by experience that if methods are tried and prove fruitless, trying the opposite sometimes works well. If the basic type is to listen carefully to what the parties say, then the applied type is to not listen. But this method is only meaningful once the judge has listened carefully to the parties; it doesn't imply that the judge need not listen from the beginning. Failure to understand this distinction would lead to serious problems.

b. Assert Yourself Forcefully by Emphasizing Your Judicial Duty

Some litigants violently pummel the judge with the resistance and mistrust they feel toward their opponent. In these cases, the party's energy is so fierce that it's difficult for the judge to handle; but the judge can't possibly persuade anyone if he's getting pushed around like this. On these occasions, I assert myself more forcefully than usual and state flat out that since the party's allegations and my judicial duty cannot be reconciled, 'In order to carry out my duty as a judge I refuse to adopt your view.'

For example, in one case a wife divorced her husband because he had been unfaithful and then demanded compensation from her husband's lover for mental suffering (*isharyo*). The lover, herself now separated from the husband and married to a third party, was embarrassed at the serving of the complaint; she offered an apology and wanted to compromise. But the wife rejected compromise, objecting furiously that, 'This woman wrecked my home. Is someone like her entitled to be happy?' I told the wife in no uncertain terms: 'You're going too far when you say she's not entitled to be happy. That's an affront to me. No matter how awful the crime, if the criminal defendant makes amends for it the role of the judge is to consider how he can be happy in the future. As a judge, I must protect the right of this woman to be happy. Remarks like yours are regrettable.' The wife then said, 'My words were excessive,' and withdrew. Thereafter, a compromise quickly came together.

Earlier, I brought up the case in which we succeeded by getting rid of the attorneys and holding repeated top-level meetings between the company president and the labor union committee chairman. The reason this dispute grew so large and lasted for 300 days had to do with the fierce antagonism between the two unions at the company, affiliated with the General Council of Trade Unions (*Sohyo*) and the Japanese Federation of Labor (*Domei*), respectively. The dispute began when each union demanded the dismissal of the other's leader and the company's former president promised – to both unions – that he would grant the request. When the company dismissed the Federation union leader, the leader's retention of his position was recognized by a court under a provisional disposition (*karishobun*), and the company withdrew the dismissal and acknowledged the leader's reinstatement. But the General Council union pressed the company hard on this issue, claiming that the company's actions amounted to reneging on its promise.

The General Council union insisted that the company, having broken its promise, was at fault, and fiercely struggled on. I said very forcefully to this union: 'Interfering in the affairs of another union is taboo. If the Federation said they wanted a union member of the General Council fired, I'd put myself on the line to protect you. But if you're saying you want a Federation union member fired, then by the same token I'll put myself on the line to protect them. The company promise you're making so much of has absolutely no legal effect, just like a contract to maintain a mistress (*mekake keiyaku*).' At this point a union member said in amazement, 'Have we been fighting for 300 days over something like a contract to maintain a mistress?' With this, the energy that had been so fierce vanished, and the beginnings of a compromise took hold. When, as in this instance, the energy of the party before him is fierce, there is a great difference between the judge getting pushed around and the judge getting the party to back down. It's the turning point between victory and defeat. Like the other methods, this method won't produce results if it is misused Precisely because he has already thoroughly attempted the basic types and has gotten the parties to see his enthusiasm and his sincerity, the judge won't arouse the parties' antipathy even if he strongly asserts himself by emphasizing his judicial duty.

c. Point out Problems of Which the Parties are Unaware

This is a somewhat unusual method of persuasion. A proverb says that 'Ignorance is bliss' (*shiranu ga hotoke*), ie an unknowing person is a strong person. But once the person learns of a future danger, he can't stand the anxiety and becomes a weakling. Although the person is happier not knowing, there is a question as to whether telling him of the danger and making him worry is really a kindness or is rather pushing kindness altogether too far. Thus, I try to use this method only on a party who is putting up more of a fight than necessary.

For example, when the manager of a small to mid-sized company refuses to agree to pay a sum of money that seems reasonable, I say:

> Aren't you borrowing money from the bank? If you are, it may be tough on you, but you'd better not push your point too far. There's a condition attached to your loan from the bank, right? When you're subject to attachment by a third party the time term on the loan accelerates (*kigen no rieki o ushinau*) and you have to pay off the entire debt all at once. Sometimes in a case like yours, people go bankrupt because they're subject to attachment and the bank demands full payment. If I were you, tough as it may be, I'd pretend I didn't know about all this and pay up.

When I say this, most people see how difficult such a situation would be, and compromise comes together.

d. Give the Parties Room

Should the judge's efforts at persuasion not go as intended, giving the parties room is a very good method of persuasion. When you talk with a person and he just won't agree, you may feel like using logic to push him around and wrestle him to the ground. But you can't persuade anyone that way. If you pursue the person and he has to tell you 'no,' it's all over. Once the person has gone so far as to say 'no,' it's not likely, in view of what's happened, that he's going to shift and tell you 'yes.'

In cases like this, it is essential to stop halfway. Even in a competitive game, the skillful player doesn't hurry towards a conclusion, and it's the same with compromise. In the midst of persuasion, it's fine for the judge to stop and have one party think things over for a while, bringing in his opponent to trade places with him. While the party is waiting, he'll be thinking that maybe he ought to do as the judge said. It also works to break off compromise talks for the moment and proceed to the taking of evidence or some other procedure.

In short, the important thing is for the parties to want to compromise of their own accord. When the judge gives the parties room, they cool down and are able to consider what he has said; thereafter if efforts at persuasion are resumed the probability of success increases.

e. Switch the Way You Conceive of the Problem

Even the judge who uses all the methods of persuasion I've stated won't be able to reach compromise in all cases. But he mustn't give up. There's still hope, and it lies in switching the way he conceives of the problem. Toward that end, the judge has to be flexible. As I said earlier, 'If pushing doesn't work, try pulling,' but even if neither pushing nor pulling works, the judge still mustn't give up. Even though the judge finds the door locked and gets nowhere by pushing or pulling, if he switches the way he conceives of the problem – if he breaks the door down, climbs over the top of it, or digs a hole underneath it, there are lots of things he could do – there's got to be a means of resolution. The judge must fight on in the spirit that there's always an answer, he just hasn't been able to discover it yet.

Within what I'm talking about as the applied types, there are numerous examples of succeeding by switching the way of conceiving of the problem, and here I'd like to introduce one of them. There was a case in which the wife had an affair and left home, the couple divorced, and the husband sought compensation from her for mental suffering. The facts were largely undisputed, and, leaving aside the amount in damages, the husband was certain to win. I tried to reach a compromise on the amount of money the defendant should pay in damages, but she said, 'I didn't do anything wrong. On the contrary, I'm the one who ought to be getting compensation for mental suffering.' She resisted fiercely and simply would not agree to compromise. Then she said, 'Even though I threw away everything and left, the only reason he's suing me is to make me suffer.' When I heard these words it struck me that rendering a judgment would be no resolution of the case at all, for the wife would merely hate and scorn the husband all the more. Was there no way to resolve the matter without rendering a judgment?

It then occurred to me that if compromise wouldn't work, the only thing to do was to withdraw the case. So I said to the defendant, 'Let me ask the plaintiff to withdraw the case unconditionally. If he says he'll withdraw the case and you express your heartfelt thanks, please understand that he's not going to court just to make you suffer.' When I asked the plaintiff to withdraw the case, he willingly agreed. The moment I told her that the plaintiff had agreed to withdraw the case, the defendant started sobbing uncontrollably and said, 'It's my fault. ' As I looked at her, I wondered whether by withdrawing the case the plaintiff hadn't achieved supreme victory in the form of his ex-wife's tears. Watching the former couple showing kindness to each other, even I was moved.

How to Make Compromise Proposals

The Basic Type

Listen Carefully to Each Party's Wishes, Relay these to the Other Side and Make Mutual Adjustments. But When Even This Doesn't Work, Make a Proposal on the Judge's Own Authority (shokken'an)

The basic approach is to listen carefully to each party's wishes, relay these to the other side and make mutual adjustments. The ideal is for a compromise to fall into place naturally while the judge is repeating his game of catch with the parties. Of course, since compromise takes place at court, the judge will form his own views about a compromise proposal as he considers his personal opinion of the case after taking evidence and reviewing the case law, scholarly opinion, and so on. But it's best if the judge doesn't force his views on the parties. Rather, in the course of repeating their own dialogue, the parties should be led along by an unseen hand so that they approach naturally the appropriate compromise that the judge has in mind.

In cases in which agreement is not reached between the parties even though the judge does what I've just said, it's important for the judge next to vigorously advance a compromise proposal on his own authority. There are, however, many cases in which simply making a proposal doesn't work, and the judge needs to take pains also as to how he makes the proposal. What I've sought to take pains on are the following applied types.

The Applied Types

a. Try to Make a Broad Proposal without Deciding on its Shape

When the judge makes his proposal to the parties and tries to draw close to what he has in mind, a concretely fixed proposal won't work well. For example, if the question is the amount of money, it's important to present a broad proposal such as one ranging from

1,000,000–2,000,000 yen. Also, with respect to the manner of conducting compromise, I think that the judge's frame of mind at the moment he hammers in the nails of his proposal is important. When he hammers four nails into four corners, the work won't go well unless he hammers in all the nails little by little and in just the same fashion. If he hammers in one nail all the way, then later when he hammers in the other nails the board will crack. It's the same with compromise: the judge mustn't decide on its shape. The important thing is to start to the greatest extent possible with a loose proposal.

In what I've named 'the theory of 1 versus 2,' if the difference between the parties is within the range of 1 versus 2 say, 1,000,000 yen versus 2,000,000 yen – the case will likely settle should the court make a proposal on its own authority. It's difficult, however, when the difference between the parties increases to more than 1 versus 2, so in such cases the key is dogged persuasion of the parties to reduce the difference to 1 versus 2.

b. Try to Make Multiple Proposals and Let the Parties Choose

Rather than making a single proposal, when proposing compromise to the parties a good method is to prepare multiple proposals and let the parties choose among them. For in the course of selecting one from among multiple proposals, the parties become aware of their own autonomy, and this eliminates the feeling that a proposal is being forced upon them by the court.

In one case, for example, the plaintiff demanded 8,000,000 yen while the defendant wanted to pay 4,000,000 yen. Using 'the theory of splitting the difference' (*tashite ni de waru riron*) would have produced a compromise recommendation of 6,000,000 yen, but I prepared one proposal for 7,000,000 yen in installment payments and another for 5,000,000 yen to be paid immediately. The plaintiff chose the former while the defendant chose the latter; later through continued discussion the parties settled on the proposal for 7,000,000 yen in installments. In this situation, since each party could plausibly have chosen either one, there was little difference in substance between the two proposals. There would not have been a great difference in substance had I made a proposal for payment of 6,000,000 yen. Yet, as a consequence of my having prepared two choices and having introduced a process by which the parties sought to choose a proposal while considering which one was better, I made the parties aware of their autonomy, and this had the effect of promoting substantive dialogue.

In addition, making multiple proposals causes the parties to see that several proposals are possible. This enables the parties themselves to start thinking of a variety of proposals, and ultimately they come closer to genuine dialogue. In contrast to this, when there is only one compromise proposal on the table, the parties feel not only passive but intensely concerned that they are being pressured as to whether to accept it, and this makes genuine dialogue impossible. Of course, there are cases in which the judge has to present the parties with a fixed, single proposal and get them to consider it seriously, but I believe that in ordinary cases it more often works better to have flexible dialogue from multiple points of view. In dismissal cases, as well, I sometimes prepare multiple proposals – a proposal for return to work and a proposal for retirement – and involve them reciprocally as I push along compromise procedure.

c When the Parties Don't Accept Your Proposal Don't Press Them; Make the Same Sort of Proposal in the Form of an Alternate Proposal

Even if the parties fail to agree to a proposal by the court, the judge mustn't press them. Right away he must make the same sort of proposal in the form of an alternate proposal. Because the second proposal is of the same sort as the first, it doesn't have a great effect on the case as a whole. And from the standpoint of the party who rejected the first proposal, a complicated mixture of feelings occurs: the party feels some satisfaction in that the court has recognized his sentiments by withdrawing its original proposal, and yet he feels sorry for rejecting the court that has worked so hard for him. Thus, when the second proposal is made, it becomes possible for the party to accept it comfortably.

Above all, as I will explain next, when the judge has made a written proposal to the parties he must not (barring a change in circumstances) alter it.

d. Make the Compromise Proposal in Writing

When the court makes a proposal on its own authority, it is sometimes effective to make the compromise proposal in writing. The reason for this is that since both parties receive identical documents, they see that there is no danger of unfair bargaining, and since the court's view is clear they won't misunderstand it.

This method is also effective in dealing with blue-chip businesses and insurance companies. With these companies, whether or not to agree to compromise is examined back at the head office primarily on the basis of whether compromise will influence other cases; the appropriateness of the resolution in individual cases is not much considered. consequently, the judge won't get very far no matter how much he tries to persuade the company attorney who appears in court, for the attorney is not in a position to make the decision, which ultimately will be made at the head office. The attorney, for his part, finds writing a memorandum (*ringisho*) and presenting it to the company to be a nuisance, so he doesn't feel like going along with the compromise negotiations. But a written proposal eases internal decision-making and reduces the time and labor of writing a memorandum. When the judge makes a proposal to the company in writing, he can easily and accurately transmit his thoughts, and so the attorney, too, is inclined to cooperate.

There is no particular form for the writing, but if the compromise proposal needs to look impressive the judge can indicate his proposal as a compromise recommendation (*wakai kankoku*) on either the record of oral argument (*benron chosho*) or the record of the date of compromise (*wakai kijitsu chosho*). If he gets the parties to request these formally as certified transcripts (*tohon*), he can hand out the compromise proposal in the form of an official document (*kobunsho*) stamped with the authentication of the clerk of the court. Since these are official documents, the side receiving them feels a certain weight attached to the compromise proposal, and my feeling is that in some cases this makes the proposal easier to accept.

e. Provisional Compromise Proposals

Depending on the case, the antagonism between the parties may become so serious that it extends all the way to everyday life. Labor cases are particularly notable in this regard. In such cases, because there is often continuous antagonism in everyday life and in the workplace, merely trying to persuade the parties when they come to court is of no effect. So there's no way around this, right? Not at all. There's always a way, and the judge must set about finding it by switching the way he conceives of the problem.

The method I've come up with is the provisional compromise. For the period that both parties are attempting compromise they provisionally agree, by way of a truce, on a fixed number of provisions. For example, in the dispute I mentioned earlier that went on for 300 days and in which we succeeded by holding repeated top-level meetings between the company president and the labor union committee chairman, antagonism between the two sides was at first exceedingly serious. The company was in a very difficult position because the union members refused to come to work early or work overtime. I therefore proposed a provisional compromise by which, for the duration of compromise negotiations, the union members would come to work early and work overtime. Of course the company agreed to this, and the union agreed as well, since by coming to work early and working overtime the members would sharply increase their wages. Even parties who strongly mistrusted each other could accept that this was of a provisional nature during compromise negotiations. Both parties cooperated in accepting the provisional compromise, both found that they benefitted when the union members came to work early and worked overtime, and it naturally developed that both felt a desire not to return to the previous quagmire. By emphasizing the judge's enthusiasm and duty I caught hold of the beginnings of a compromise; by proposing a provisional compromise I eased the antagonism and emotions of the parties. Through a series of spirited top-level meetings, the president, labor union committee chairman and I were able to reach agreement. Because this was such a difficult case one I'll never forget – I did my best to combine various ways of conceiving of the problem.

My next example is also a labor case. In this case the union accused the employer, a medical corporation, of wrongful practices (*fusei*), and from this the dispute grew to include problems of dismissal and transfer as well as a claim for damage compensation made by the employer against the union, producing severe antagonism in labor-management relations. Relations between the two sides were extremely tense when I entered into compromise negotiations. The employer refused to give work to the employees, who had returned to their former workplace under a provisional disposition that voided their transfer. The employer also issued an order that prohibited the employees from doing anything, even when seated at their desks, and that regarded movement of even two meters away from the desks (apart from going to the rest room) as an abandonment of work. The labor union filed suit alleging violation of human rights.

My thinking was that a compromise was very unlikely and that I had to make the employer get rid of the no-work order alone. I submitted to both parties the following proposal for a provisional compromise that would last for the duration of compromise negotiations with me: 'The no-work order is lifted. Union members may do their jobs together with others. However, even if union members work together with others, payment of their preexisting wage shall suffice and the company need provide no special [premium pay] work allowance (*tokubetsu teate*).' Both sides accepted this proposal. The labor union thus refrained from protest activity, the employer responded by stopping its use of coercive methods, and the antagonism gradually relaxed. After I submitted the provisional compromise there were many twists and turns and it took almost a full year, but we finally managed to resolve the case completely.

In cases in which antagonism persists because the parties contest not the facts but merely the method of payment (the number and amount of installment payments), I sometimes try to persuade the debtor to make, even before compromise materializes, just those payments he has already shown a willingness to make. For the creditor this is no doubt more reassuring than receiving nothing while compromise negotiations continue, and even if compromise never comes about, the debtor suffers no loss because the creditor will recognize as repayment the amount that the debtor has voluntarily paid.

As we have seen, provisional compromise is tentative and is for that reason easy for the parties to accept. If the contents of the provisional compromise can be realized both parties will be benefitted, and hence this relaxes the antagonism on both sides. And once the antagonism is relaxed, the effect is to arouse a feeling of not wanting to return to the original quagmire. I will put the provisional compromise to use often in the future.

CHAPTER 7

THE CONSTITUTIONAL FRAMEWORK

The recent constitutional history of Japan can be divided into two main periods, the modern and the contemporary. The modern spans the period of monarchical constitutionalism from the mid-19th century to the Second World War, including the Meiji Restoration and the introduction of a Western inspired constitution in 1889. The contemporary is from the promulgation of the 'new' constitution in 1946 to the present and has been a period of constitutional democracy.[1] Both periods have been characterised by a leading commentator as 'constitutional revolutions' and were 'assimilative reactions to Western legal traditions' rather than responses to internal growth and organic development.[2]

The revolutionary nature of the first period is illustrated by the issues surrounding the introduction of individual rights. In the neo-Confucian society of 19th century Japan, such a concept did not exist; instead there was a complex system of obligation, loyalty and benevolence which was based on the (natural) hierarchical order of society and thereby rooted in status.[3] Thus, the idea of rights contained in Articles 18–32 of the Meiji Constitution was indeed revolutionary, although some Japanese legal historians have noted that during the Heian period (810–1185 AD) there was a concept and term corresponding to that of right.[4] However, it is generally acknowledged that a new Japanese term for 'rights' had to be invented and Rinsho Mitsukuri, a leading scholar of the Meiji period who translated the French Codes, is credited with having done so.[5] Even so, the view that the term is a 'modern fabrication, extraneously derived, neither understood, nor digested, nor entirely trusted' seems an accurate description; it is also an apposite assessment of the Meiji Constitution itself.[6]

Although introducing Western ideas, the Meiji Constitution preserved many of the hierarchical and societal norms embodied in a system of monarchical constitutionalism. In short, it was 'nothing less than the transplantation of a

---

1 The Meiji Constitution was promulgated in 1889 and came into effect in 1890 (see Appendix I, p 609). The *Showa* or 'new' constitution was promulgated in 1946 and came into effect in 1947; it is also referred to as the 'peace constitution' because of the renunciation of war clause in Article 9 (see Appendix II, p 617). Although practice varies, throughout this book the date of promulgation is used. In general see: Ito, M, 'The Modern Development of Law and Constitution in Japan' in Beer, LW (ed), *Constitutional Systems in Late Twentieth Century Asia*, 1992, University of Washington Press; Ward, RE, 'The Origins of the Present Japanese Constitution' (1956) 50 *American Political Science Review* 980.

2 Beer, LW, 'Constitutional Revolution in Japanese Law, Society and Politics' (1982) 16 *Modern Asian Studies* 33.

3 Noda, Y, *Introduction to Japanese Law*, 1976, Chapter 9, University of Tokyo Press.

4 Takayanagi, K, 'A Century of Innovation: The Development of Japanese Law 1868–1961' in von Mehren, AT (ed), *Law in Japan*, 1963, p 24, Harvard University Press.

5 Noda, *supra*, n 3, p 44. The words *kenri* (right) and *gimu* (obligation) are said to have been borrowed from Chinese words used in WA Martin's translation into Chinese of an English book by Henry Wheaton entitled *Elements of International Law*, 1863, see Blacker, C, *The Japanese Enlightenment: A Study of the Writings of Fukuzawa Yukichi*, 1964, p 105, Cambridge University Press.

6 Lehmann, J-P, *The Roots of Modern Japan*, 1982, p 254, Macmillan.

Western legal heart into the Japanese body'.[7] However, during the early 20th century, as a result of a complex interplay of sociological and political forces within that 'body', there was a growing awareness of new norms and ideas, although not the development of a coherent tradition. This period, often referred to as the Taisho democracy (1912–26), was one during which there were developments suggesting the potential for lasting structural and political change, not least of which could have been the establishment of parliamentary democracy.[8] In the event, the rise of nationalism, combined with the military ambitions and exploits of the 1930s and 1940s, was to overwhelm any attempts at liberalisation and democratisation.[9] Somewhat ironically, it was this same nationalism and militarism which ultimately led to the downfall of the old order and the creation of a new one. In fact, as one writer has observed:

> The present widespread acceptance of the constitution in Japan rests in part on a continuing reaction against a pre-war system that failed in the mind-numbing defeat of the Second World War. It does not seem probable that Japan would soon have become a constitutional democracy without the shock of losing the Pacific War and without massive Occupation support for Japan's liberal forces.[10]

The Meiji Constitution had been a bridge between the semi-feudal Tokugawa heritage and the new, centralised authoritarian government. Heavily influenced by Western thinking, it nevertheless retained the Emperor as the embodiment of national identity, thus linking traditional legitimacy to the new state authority.[11] In a similar manner the 1946 Constitution could not divest itself completely of

---

7 *Idem*, p 254. Though said in the context of the reception of Western law in general it remains true of the constitution in particular.

8 In the field of legal theory, the democratic liberal tendency was represented by a Tokyo University professor of constitutional law, Tatsukichi Minobe. Together with others he was particularly attracted by the British parliamentary system. However, he and his group of liberal constitutionalists were suppressed by the government in the 1930s and early 1940s. See Takayanagi, *supra*, n 4, p 11 and Miller, FO, *Minobe Tatsukichi: Interpreter of Constitutionalism in Japan*, 1965, University of California Press. A full account of this period is given in Silberman, BS and Harootuniun, HD, *Japan in Crisis: Essays in Taisho Democracy*, 1974, Princeton University Press.

9 Although there may have been an indigenous nationalism at the start of the Meiji period, in the view of some, the political strength of that may be 'overstated'. Craig A, 'Fukuzawa Yukichi: The Philosophical Foundations of Meiji Nationalism' in Ward, R (ed), *Political Development in Modern Japan*, 1968, p 100, Princeton University Press; see also, Maruyama, M, *Thought and Behaviour in Modern Japanese Politics*, 1963, Oxford University Press, Chapter 4, 'Nationalism in Japan: Its Theoretical Background and Prospects'. Beasley argues that 'there already existed by 1868 a set of assumptions about what constituted 'Japaneseness' – a Japanese self-image – which Meiji nationalism was to incorporate and extend.' Beasley, WG, 'The Edo Experience and Japanese Nationalism' (1984) 18 *Modern Asian Studies* 556. However, the origins of modern nationalism and the rise of fascism were in a sense, 'formalised' by the Meiji Constitution. Maruyama, *idem*, Chapter 2, 'The Ideology and Dynamics of Japanese Fascism'. Furthermore, the formalised relationship between the armed forces and the Emperor was no less significant: see Ike, N, 'War and Modernisation' in Ward, *idem*. See also Kato, S, 'Taisho Democracy as the Pre-Stage for Japanese Militarism' and Crowley, J, 'A New Asian Order: Some Notes on Pre-war Japanese Nationalism' in Silberman and Harootunian, *idem*. For further reading on nationalism in general see: Storry, R, *The Double Patriots: A Study of Japanese Nationalism*, 1957, Chatto.

10 Beer, 1982, *supra*, n 2, p 35.

11 Akita, G, *Foundations of Constitutional Government in Modern Japan, 1868–1900*, 1967, Harvard University Press.

the Meiji heritage; instead, inspired in the main by the American Occupation reformers, the old apparatus of state authority was transformed and a foundation for a new democratic constitutionalism established.[12] The link between the two was Article 73 of the Meiji Constitution which enabled the reformers to present the new constitution as an amendment to the old one.[13] Furthermore, albeit of necessity, the Emperor was preserved as a symbol of the state who could reign but not rule, thus providing a certain and, at the time, essential continuity between monarchical constitutionalism and constitutional democracy.[14]

Thus, one of the important features of the second 'revolution' was to convert the Emperor's subjects from objects of the constitution to citizens of a new democratic order. Inherent in this process was the notion of democracy and accountability in government and the law, as well as the protection of the individual through the creation of fundamental rights. The inspiration for the new framework was the Potsdam Declaration of 26 July 1945, which had set out the terms for the Japanese surrender. Its stated purpose was to 'remove all obstacles to the revival and strengthening of democratic tendencies among the Japanese people' and to establish 'freedom of speech, of religion, and of

---

12 Although it was an allied occupation, the American influence was paramount; Beer, LW, 'The Present Constitutional System of Japan' in Beer (ed), 1992, *supra*, n 1, p 176 'Other nations, such as Australia and the United Kingdom, participated in Japan's occupation, but the United States' influence was dominant from start to finish.' However, Roger Buckley is deeply critical of this neglect of the allied contribution, references to which he describes as 'perfunctory'; he goes on to state that both American (and Japanese) scholars seem 'reluctant to recognise that in name and sometimes reality the occupation was an allied venture, since this goes against the grain of American unilateralism'. See 'The British Model: Institutional Reform in Occupied Japan' (1982) 16 *Modern Asian Studies* 233. One recent and notable exception to this is a contribution from a Japanese scholar who recognises the influence of the British Constitution, see Ito, M, 'The Modern Development of Law and Constitution in Japan' in Beer (ed), 1992, *supra* n 1, p 149. An interesting personal account, but one which underlines the essentially American influence, is provided by Williams, J, *Japan's Political Revolution Under MacArthur: A Participant's Account*, 1979, University of Georgia Press.

13 There is a considerable amount of debate concerning this point, together with whether the constitution was 'imposed' by the Americans. One view put forward is that the surrender of Japan in 1945 'substantially modified' the Meiji Constitution, but did not abolish it, Miyazawa, T, 'Constitutional Law' extract cited in Tanaka, H, *The Japanese Legal System*, 1976, p 682, University of Tokyo Press. However, he goes on to conclude that although the Article 73 procedure was used to introduce the 1946 Constitution, 'it has rightly been referred to as the "new constitution" not as the "amended constitution".' *idem*, p 684. On the 'imposition' debate see Oppler, AC, *Legal Reform in Occupied Japan: A Participant Looks Back*, 1976, Chapter 5 'The New Constitution: Imposed by the Victor?', Princeton University Press; Maki, JM, *Japan's Commission on the Constitution: The Final Report*, 1980, p 375, University of Washington Press; Stockwin, JAA, *Japan: Divided Politics in a Growth Economy*, 1982, p 202, Weidenfeld and Nicolson; Ward, 1956, *supra*, n 1; Williams, J, 'Making the Japanese Constitution: A Further Look' (1965) 59 *American Political Science Review* 665; Kades, C, 'The American Role in Revising Japan's Imperial Constitution' (1989) 104 *Political Science Quarterly* 215.

14 See Chapter 4; Titus, D, 'The Making of the "Symbol Emperor System" in Post-war Japan' (1980) 14 *Modern Asian Studies* 529; Buckley, R, 'Britain and the Emperor: The Foreign Office and Constitutional Reform in Japan, 1945–46' (1978) 12 *Modern Asian Studies* 553; Inoue, *infra*, n 15, Chapter 5 makes some interesting observations on the American-Japanese attitudes towards the role of the Emperor in postwar Japan and even ventures that the Americans 'apparently did not understand or appreciate the actual position of the Emperor', at p 168.

thought, as well as respect for fundamental human rights'. However, these were predicated upon the removal of the old order and the establishment of a new order to secure peace, preserve security and provide justice.

In pursuance of these objectives and following the redesignation of the Emperor as symbol and instrument of constitutional government in Chapter 1 of the 1946 Constitution, the next chapter consists of Article 9 alone, the renunciation of war clause. Next comes Chapter 3 which sets out the 'Rights and Duties of the People' and only after these provisions are the institutions of democratic government, parliamentary democracy and justice dealt with. This order reflects the framework imposed by the allies through the Potsdam Declaration and the essentially American origins of the constitution (see Appendix II, p 617). Furthermore, it reinforces the notion that the constitutional ideas, theories and value system of such documents tend to reflect the drafters' own predilections and priorities, if not prejudices.[15]

Although it is usual to speak of the 1946 Constitution as the 'new' constitution, this is in the context of Japanese history. In a global context, it is one of the more long-lived and enduring, as well as one of the few which since its inception has not been amended.[16] Almost 10 years after it had come into effect, a 'Commission on the Constitution' was set up on 13 August 1957 under the Chairmanship of Professor Kenzo Takayanagi. The Commission carried out a thoroughgoing investigation into all aspects of the constitution, from its enactment under military occupation, through its practical operation, to an analysis of problems relating to all 99 articles (the supplementary provisions of Article 100–03 were excluded). The work of the Commission was to last for seven years with the final report published on 3 July 1964.[17] It was a massive undertaking involving 131 plenary sessions, 325 committee meetings, 418 expert witnesses, a series of reports totalling 40,000 pages and a final report of some 1,161 pages.[18] And yet at the end of the process constitutional revision, which

15 Ward, 1956, *supra*, n 1 refers to the 'clandestine American influence on the style, content and adoption of the Japanese constitution'. However, in a recent innovative study, Kyoko Inoue argues that there was a block in the cross-cultural communication between the Japanese and American representatives which resulted in the Japanese making changes which the Americans did not notice and thereby shifting the emphasis and impact of the text, in short, 'neither side realised the differences in meaning between the two versions' *MacArthur's Japanese Constitution: A Linguistic and Cultural Study of Its Making*, 1991, p 267, University of Chicago Press.

16 Luney notes that 'of the nearly 160 nations possessing written constitutions, only thirty-two were in effect prior to 1960' see Luney, P and Takahashi K (eds), *Japanese Constitutional Law*, 1993, p xiv, University of Tokyo Press. *Note*: this book is an edited version of 1990 Vol 53 Nos 1&2 *Law and Contemporary Problems*, referred to in other chapters; the materials are slightly different in each publication, which on occasion may account for the different citation. In 1988 the Constitution of Japan was one of only 22 out of 165 constitutions which dated from the 1940s or earlier. See Beer, LW, 'Law and Liberty' in Ishida, T and Krauss, ES (eds), *Democracy in Japan*, 1989, p 69, University of Pittsburgh Press.

17 See Takayanagi, K, 'Some Reminiscences of Japan's Commission on the Constitution' in Henderson, DF (ed), *The Constitution of Japan: Its First Twenty Years, 1947–67*, 1968, University of Washington Press; Maki, 1980, *supra*, n 13.

18 *Idem*, p 4.

had been a central issue for the Commission enquiry, did not take place and no serious attempt to revise the constitution has since been forthcoming.[19]

Since promulgation there have been periods of constitutional controversy, but the essential constitutional order has not been found defective or wanting in any fundamental manner; no amendment has been proposed and hitherto there has been no real constitutional crisis.[20] However, notwithstanding the benefits of such stability, the key concerns of the revisionist movement, namely the emperor system and the renunciation of war clause, have maintained a place at the centre of the debate on constitutional reform and, approaching the 50th anniversary of the constitution, are once more in the headlines.[21] Even so, the general consensus is that there is little likelihood of amendment or revision in

19 In fact, although the report was submitted to the Prime Minister, who said it would be studied by the Cabinet and forward to the Diet, it was never formally forwarded to the Diet and there was no government reaction or report in response. Thus 'the movement to revise the constitution has for all intents and purposes come to an end'. See Maki, *idem*, p 8.

20 Maki, JM, *Court and Constitution in Japan: Selected Supreme Court Decisions, 1948–1960*, 1964, University of Washington Press; Itoh, H and Beer, LW, *The Constitutional Case Law of Japan: Selected Supreme Court Decisions 1961–1978*, 1978, University of Washington Press; Luney and Takahashi (eds), *supra*, n 16. For a background study see Sato, S, 'Debate on Constitutional Amendment: Origins and Status' (1979) 12 *Law in Japan* 1.

21 Whereas the death in 1989 of Emperor Hirohito prompted debate over the Emperor system and constitutional revisionism, the 1995 anniversary of the end of the Pacific War generated a renewed debate on the renunciation of war clause (Article 9) and its ramifications for Japan in the new world order. The number of territorial disputes between Japan and her neighbours has increased, eg over the Kuril Islands with Russia, the Takeshima Islands with Korea and the Senkaku islets with China. The escalation of these disputes can be seen as a consequence of the growing perception that America no longer maintains its role as power broker or peace keeper in the region and that Japan therefore needs to be seen as able and willing to assert herself. This position is underlined by Japan's economic strength in the world, a concomitant of which has been the increased pressure for a greater role in the United Nations, not least a seat on the Security Council. The complexities of the Japan-America relationship were highlighted during the Spring of 1996, first by the sentencing of three American servicemen for the rape of a 12 year old schoolgirl on Okinawa and the subsequent calls for American bases to be closed (*The Times*, London 8 March 1996); second, by the China-Taiwan 'war games' which prompted America to send two aircraft carriers to the region, and third, the Korean border crisis. (*The Times*, London 6 April 1996). Following these events the US-Japan Security Treaty was renegotiated, in which America promised to reduce its bases whilst maintaining the overall level of its forces in East Asia and Japan pledged to take an active role in the defence of the Asia-Pacific region. (*The Times*, London 16 April and 18 April 1996). It remains to be seen whether this is a prelude to the development of a new revisionist movement within Japan aimed at effecting changes in the constitution, and in particular amending or removing Article 9. The increasing awareness of China's imposing presence in the region, together with the Taiwan-Korea crisis has certainly provided some politicians with an opportunity to debate the possibility of a 'watering-down' of the constitution on the grounds that a failure to support the US in any regional conflict would 'incur world censure'. *idem*. In general see Beasley, WG, *The Rise of Modern Japan*, 2nd edn, 1995, Chapters 16 and 17, Weidenfeld and Nicolson; Fukui, H, 'Twenty Years of Revisionism' in Henderson (ed), *supra*, n 17; Higuchi, Y, 'The Constitution and the Emperor System: Is Revisionism Alive?' in Luney and Takahashi (eds), *supra*, n 16; Kasuya, T, 'Constitutional Transformation and the Ninth Article of the Constitution' (1985) 18 *Law in Japan* 1; Auer, J, 'Article Nine: Renunciation of War' in Luney and Takahashi (eds), *idem*; Brown, E, 'Japanese Security Policy in the Post Cold-War Era' (1994) 34 *Asian Survey* 430; Egami, T, 'Politics in Okinawa Since the Reversion of Sovereignty' (1994) 34 *Asian Survey* 828; Hamura, S and Shui, E, 'Renunciation of War as a Universal Principle of Mankind – A Look at the Gulf War and the Japanese Constitution' (1995) 44 *International and Comparative Law Quarterly* 426.

the near future.[22] In fact the conclusion of Noda some 20 years ago still holds true. He said: 'The present constitution is not so defective that it ought to be recast immediately. The experience of almost thirty years of application reveals no serious problem other than a lively controversy of an ideological nature concerning a few provisions. Its style and construction are far from perfect, but this sort of defect is not the monopoly of the Japanese constitution.'[23]

The three pillars of the present constitutional framework, popular sovereignty, pacifism and protection of fundamental human rights, are based upon the foundation of respect for the rule of law and are guaranteed by the Supreme Court through the use of judicial review. Although the constitution does not make specific mention of the rule of law, it is clear that the relationship between law and government was to be predicated upon that basis.[24] This is demonstrated by the fact that fundamental human rights are protected against the arbitrary exercise of government power and by the use of judicial review, introduced in Article 81, which represents 'the most universally typical institution embodying the rule of law'.[25] However, there is what might seem to be something of an inconsistency between the concept of parliamentary supremacy based on popular sovereignty and the idea of judicial supremacy embodied in judicial review.[26] This alleged inconsistency arises from Article 41 which designates the Diet as the 'highest organ of state power' and thereby seems to give the legislature some kind of superiority.[27] The ambiguity can be explained by characterising the situation as one of 'dual supremacy' and the result of a 'confluence of English and American ideas'.[28] Moreover, even if the superiority of the Diet is of 'symbolic rather than legal significance', it may be one explanation for the apparent reluctance of the Supreme Court to invalidate laws as unconstitutional.[29] Certainly in the 50 year history of the constitution, the Supreme Court has declared a law unconstitutional on only five occasions

22 Ito, *supra*, n 12; Luney and Takahashi (eds), *supra*, n 16; Stockwin, 1982, *supra*, n 13.

23 Noda, *supra*, n 3, p 192.

24 A number of features in the constitution support this. First, Chapter 10 entitled 'Supreme Law' is a coherent expression of the concept of the rule of law. Article 97 confirms the historical antecedents of human rights and their inviolability; Article 98 expressly provides that the constitution is the supreme law and Article 99 obliges those who exercise power to respect and uphold the constitution. Second, the guarantee of human rights in Chapter 3, which cannot be restricted by enactments of the Diet, is evidence of a higher law. Another feature is the manner in which judicial power is enshrined (see Appendix II, p 617).

25 Ito, M, 'The Rule of Law: Constitutional Developments' in von Mehren, AT (ed), *Law in Japan*, 1963, Harvard University Press. See also Hashimoto, K, 'The Rule of Law: Some Aspects of Judicial Review of Administrative Action' in von Mehren (ed), *idem*; Takayanagi, K, 'Opinion on Some Constitutional Problems – The Rule of Law' in Henderson (ed), 1968, *supra*, n 17; Urabe, N, 'Rule of Law and Due Process: A Comparative View of the United States and Japan' Luney and Takahashi (eds), *supra*, n 16.

26 Stockwin, 1982, *supra*, n 13, p 50.

27 Maki, 1980, *supra*, n 13, p xxxviii states that this 'clearly ... places the Diet over the Court'.

28 Henderson, DF, 'Law and Political Modernisation' in Ward, RE (ed), *Political Development in Modern Japan*, 1968, p 441, Princeton University Press.

29 Oppler, 1976, *supra*, n 13, p 88.

and invalidated the legislation in just four of the five cases.[30] Given the volume of legislation during the period, this may be considered as something of a triumph for the process of legislative drafting in the Diet.[31] On the other hand, there is considerable support for the view that the Supreme Court is self restraining and that 'negativism in judicial review is one of the most characteristic features of the Japanese Supreme Court'.[32]

With the move from the authoritarian Meiji era of rule by law, to the new postwar constitution based on the rule of law, the second 'revolution' was complete. How it has been sustained will be examined in the materials, but first a number of issues will be highlighted, in particular the role of the Supreme Court and the use of judicial review. Article 76 of the Constitution states that 'the whole judicial power' is vested in the Supreme Court and Article 77 provides that it is 'vested with the rule-making power under which it determines the rules of procedure and practice' for the courts, profession and administration of justice. In addition Article 81 states that the Supreme Court 'is the court of last resort with power to determine the constitutionality of any law, order, regulation or official act'.[33] Thus, not only is it a court of last resort with

30 *Aizawa* (Supreme Court, 4 April 1973) Article 200 of the Criminal Code which imposed a heavier penalty for patricide than murder was declared unconstitutional and a violation of the equal protection provision in Article 14 of the Constitution. *KK Sumiyoshi* – The Pharmacy Case (Supreme Court 30 April 1975) the regulation determining the location of new pharmacies was declared contrary to Article 22 (1) and an unconstitutional violation of the freedom to choose an occupation. *Kurokawa* (Supreme Court 14 April 1976) concerned the distribution of parliamentary seats. Although the court found that the provision of the Election Law violated the equal protection clause, in this case it did not invalidate the law, but simply declared the election unconstitutional, without nullifying the result. *Kaneo* (Supreme Court 17 July 1985) A correction in the disparities arising from the apportionment of Diet seats under the Election Law had not occurred within a reasonable time (as relied on by the Supreme Court in the previous case) and the court therefore declared the provision unconstitutional. *Hiraguchi* (Supreme Court 22 April 1987) Provisions of the Forestry Law were declared unconstitutional and a violation of the guarantee of property rights in Article 29 (1) of the constitution. For a discussion of these cases see: Ashibe, N, 'Human Rights and Judicial Power' in Beer, LW (ed), *supra*, n 1, pp 239–42; Haley, JO, 'Recent Developments: Constitutionality of Penalty under Article 200 of the Penal Code for Killing a Lineal Ascendant' (1973) 6 *Law in Japan* 173; Haley, JO, 'The Freedom to Choose an Occupation and the Constitutional Limits of Legislative Discretion – *KK Sumiyoshi v Governor of Hiroshima Prefecture*' (1975) 8 *Law in Japan* 188; Emi, H, 'Summary of the Supreme Court Grand Bench Decision on the Number of Members of the House of Representatives' (1985) 18 *Law in Japan* 134.

31 Seki, M, 'The Drafting Process for Cabinet Bills' (1986) 19 *Law in Japan* 168.

32 Okudaira, Y, 'Forty Years of the Constitution and Its Various Influences: Japanese, American and European' in Luney and Takahashi (eds), *supra*, n 16, p 20.

33 The introduction of judicial review is modelled on American constitutional practice developed from *Marbury v Madison* 1 Cranch (5 US) 137 (1803). In that case, Chief Justice John Marshall found that judicial review was implicit in the nature of a written constitution and particularly in the supremacy clause and the grant of judicial power. In other words that the constitution was law and must be followed; that the supremacy clause made the constitution the supreme law of the land and that the judges having been accorded 'judicial power' had the authority to say what the law was in each case. Given the relative paucity of cases where the Japanese Supreme Court has held a law unconstitutional and the fact that the first such case was 26 years after the constitution came into effect (*supra*, n 30), it is interesting to note that after *Marbury v Madison* it was not until over 50 years later in *Dred Scott v Sandford* 19 (How 60 US) 393 (1857) that the US Supreme Court held another congressional act unconstitutional.

powers of constitutional review, but it is also seized with responsibility for the administration and management of the profession. Taking the judiciary into the independent sphere and away from the bureaucracy was an important innovation. Whereas in the Meiji era the judiciary was subordinated to the will of the Ministry of Justice, under the new constitution the relationship was determined by the theory of separation of powers. However, in spite of its position as guardian of the constitution, the Supreme Court is not a constitutional court in the mould of continental European models, a fact that was made clear in a Supreme Court decision in 1952.[34] In that case, whilst upholding the power of judicial review, the Supreme Court made the following statement clarifying the position:

> Under the system prevailing in our country, a judgment may be sought in the courts only when there exists a concrete legal dispute between specific parties. The argument that courts have the power to determine in the abstract the constitutionality of laws, orders, and the like, in the absence of a concrete case, has no foundation in the constitution itself, or any statute.[35]

This is in line with the essentially American antecedents of Article 81, in that judicial review arises out of a particular case involving parties with standing rather than any broad based authority to determine constitutionality in abstract. Following the introduction of the power of judicial review, some Japanese scholars interpreted Article 81 as conferring powers on the Supreme Court which were consistent with that of a constitutional court such as that in West Germany.[36] Although that view was dispelled by the Supreme Court in 1952, there are still those who, whilst recognising that Article 81 does not confer the power of a constitutional court on the Japanese Supreme Court, nevertheless claim that since the granting of such power is not prohibited by law, if the relevant procedures were to be established by law, the Supreme Court could indeed act as a constitutional court and determine constitutionality in abstract.[37] However, to date there has been neither the need nor the desire for such a move, either within the Supreme Court or elsewhere.[38]

The democratic nature of the constitution and the principle of popular sovereignty is illustrated further by Article 79(2) which provides that the appointment of Supreme Court judges shall be reviewed by the people at the first general election following their appointment and every 10 years thereafter. In the view of one writer this provision 'seems to carry the principle of popular sovereignty to an almost ridiculous extreme'.[39] Whilst it was merely one more manifestation of the desire of the Occupation reformers to ensure a democratic framework, it is also an illustration of the mismatch between ideas born in a federal system and superimposed on an essentially civil law and non federal

34 *Suzuki* (Supreme Court 8 October 1952) See Maki, *supra*, n 20, pp 362–66.

35 *Idem*.

36 See Okudaira, *supra*, n 32, p 16, n 38.

37 Ashibe, *supra*, n 30, p 238 notes this debate, as does Ogawa, I, 'Judicial Review of Administrative Actions in Japan' in Henderson (ed), *supra*, n 17.

38 Itoh, H, *The Japanese Supreme Court: Constitutional Policies*, 1989, Markus Wiener.

39 Maki, 1964, *supra*, n 20, p xx.

structure.[40] Experience to date would seem to suggest that it has had little practical effect since there has rarely been even 5% of voters in favour of dismissal and the chances of a majority in favour seem highly remote.[41]

As a formal gesture in the direction of popular sovereignty it would seem to be both harmless and meaningless. Only if it could be shown that it had the effect of introducing bias because judges were concerned about the review, could it be seen as dangerous. This would seem to be unlikely in view of the fact that the current average age of appointment to the Supreme Court is 64, so even with a retirement age of 70, tenure is short enough for popular review to be of little relevance.[42] However, recent research suggests that judicial independence is 'nominal', due to the control which the Liberal Democratic Party exerts over all aspects of judicial appointments, up to and including the Supreme Court.[43] Although this is a view rebutted by another author, if it is true, it means that the suggestion that Article 79 (2) is 'of symbolic rather than practical significance' now has a double meaning.[44] In other words, not only is popular review a theoretical nicety and little more than a democratic decoration, but even if it had

---

40 This system of popular review was taken from the American state of Missouri. See Ito, *supra*, n 12, p 158. It is a system which really only makes practical sense where, as in the United States, judges are elected.

41 To date, no judge has been dismissed. During the first popular review in 1949, Justice Sawada received a 4% negative vote and Chief Justice Mibuchi received the highest negative vote of 5.5%. In 1972, Justice Shimodo, a former ambassador to the US and a well-known conservative, received the highest ever negative vote of 15.2%. However, in 1980 when the popular review of four judges took place, the highest average disapproval rate of 14.4% was recorded. See Itoh, H, *The Japanese Supreme Court: Constitutional Policies*, 1989, p 27, Markus Wiener; also see Ramsayer, JM and Rosenbluth, F, *Japan's Political Marketplace*, 1993, p 153, n 13, Harvard University Press. However, Tanaka argues that the system of popular review is an 'emergency exit' and to say that it serves no purpose because no justice has yet been removed 'is like saying that since there has been no fire and no one has had to escape by the emergency exit, the emergency exit is useless'. Tanaka, H, 'The Appointment of Supreme Court Justices and the Popular Review of Appointments' (1978) 11 *Law in Japan* 25 at p 33. This theoretical justification of the constitutional guarantee needs to be seen against the political background provided in the more recent work of Ramsayer and Rosenbluth, *idem*, Chapter 9

42 Since 1952 only two judges under the age of 60 have been appointed to the Supreme Court (both were 58) and one aged 60. More importantly, all but three of the 108 postwar judges of the Supreme Court have served less than 10 years. Haley, JO, 'Judicial Independence in Japan Revisited' (1995) 25 *Law in Japan*, 14.

43 Ramsayer and Rosenbluth, *supra*, n 41 argue that the guarantee of judicial independence in the constitution is 'nominal' when set against the grip the Liberal Democratic Party (LDP) has over all matters relating to the appointment of judges. Thus Supreme Court judges are appointed because their views are consistent with LDP policy and they are appointed late in their careers so as to prevent the possibility of growing independence during a lengthy tenure. The Supreme Court judges also monitor lower court judges and only recommend 'suitable' judges for appointment to the lower courts, ie those who are politically reliable. *idem*, p 152.

44 Haley, 1995, *supra*, n 42, p 18 rebuts the views of Ramsayer and Rosenbluth concluding that: 'The Japanese judiciary has in fact maintained a remarkable degree of cohesion and autonomy within the shadow of potential political control. Those who argue to the contrary that politicians in Japan direct the courts and its decisions distort the facts and profoundly mislead.' Oppler, *supra*, n 13, p 91 argues that the check on the appointment of Supreme Court judges as provided in Article 79 is symbolic rather than practical and 'encourages reverence for the sovereignty of the people, to which even the members of the highest tribunal should be subject'.

substance, it could not operate effectively due to the alleged political stranglehold on the process of judicial appointment.[45]

This impacts upon the operation of judicial review. Whereas earlier writers spoke of the novelty of judicial review and the 'constant alteration in the membership of the court due to the preference for elderly men' as factors affecting Supreme Court decisions, more recent commentators see caution verging on timidity in such cases.[46] Since the 1970s the use of the power of judicial review could best be described as sparing, though willing, but certainly not robust. This is a situation which is characterised more generally by the comment that 'although the Japanese judiciary has a long and well deserved reputation for political independence and a willingness to make decisions unpopular with the government, this political independence has not developed into an effective judicial review of administrative decisions, even or perhaps especially those with important distributive or political consequences'.[47] As far as the Supreme Court is concerned, it may not strike a powerful blow at the heart of the government or executive, but neither is it the subject of bitter criticism or derision. Particularly in the area of protection for fundamental human rights, it has experienced a relatively lengthy and steady period of development.[48] Even if it were to try and take on a more robust role as defender of human rights, for sociolegal, cultural and political reasons it would not achieve the same stature as the United States Supreme Court or the German Federal Constitutional Court because, in what has been referred to as a 'communitarian feudal democracy', mutual respect and understanding is more highly prized and effective, whilst the enforcement of individual rights still remains something of anathema.[49]

---

45 Ramsayer and Rosenbluth *supra*, n 41. Compare with the analysis Danelski D, 'The Political Impact of the Japanese Supreme Court' (1974) 49 *Notre Dame Lawyer* 955. For an earlier comment on this see Yokata, K, 'Political Questions and Judicial Review' in Henderson (ed), *supra*, n 17. More recently one Japanese author has concluded as follows: 'In reality, popular review of Supreme Court Justices has not affected the LDP influenced judicial selection in the slightest degree.' Itoh, 1989, *supra*, n 41, p 27.

46 *Idem*, p 321; Ashibe, *supra*, n 30, p 261 states that 'Judicial passivity has been too great in Japan. Too much modesty has been shown and too much deference has been paid to the policy makers of the legislative and executive branches'.

47 Upham, F, *Law and Social Change in Post-war Japan*, 1987, p 15, Harvard University Press. See also Beer, LW, *Freedom of Expression in Japan: A Study in Comparative Law, Politics, and Society*, 1984, Kodansha International.

48 Although the emphasis in this chapter is on the protection of fundamental rights, the issue of judicial review in other areas is important and in particular in relation to Administrative Guidance (see Chapter 3) and industrial policy. See, Upham, *idem*, Chapter 5; Matsushita, M, *International Trade and Competition Law*, 1993, pp 110–11, Oxford University Press; Young, M, 'Judicial Review of Administrative Guidance: Governmentally Encouraged Consensual Dispute Resolution in Japan' (1984) 84 *Columbia Law Review* 923; Haley, JO, 'Introduction [To Japanese Administrative Law]' (1986) 19 *Law in Japan* 1; Matsushita, M, 'The Legal Framework of Trade and Investment in Japan' (1986) 27 Special Issue *Harvard International Law Journal* 361; Young, 1988, *infra*, n 54.

49 Beer, LW, 'Law and Liberty' in Ishida and Krauss (eds), *supra*, n 16, p 85. Beer goes on to comment 'that a mutualist understanding may more adequately protect the individuality and the rights of each person than a self-centred individualism blind to the rights and needs of other individuals and the community', p 86. These views are particularly interesting in the context of libel where loss of personal reputation may not be as important as loss of face, which has familial implications, but which may not constitute a libel and all of which has to be set in the context of the freedom of expression provision in Article 21 of the Constitution. See Youm, KH, 'Libel Law and the Press in Japan' (1990) 67 *Journalism Quarterly* 1103.

Whilst some observers may be tempted to emphasise judicial reluctance or negativism and would wish the Supreme Court to take a more active role in implementing constitutional values, in general, where it has been possible to act, the court has done so with a creditable if unspectacular record.[50] At the same time it should not be forgotten that the potential for judicial review can be limited in a number of ways, not least by restricting the standing of an individual to sue and by so limiting the definition of reviewable administrative actions that few can come within the narrow band of reviewable acts.[51] Thus, it is not entirely fair to criticise a judiciary which, in certain areas, has neither the capacity to exercise the power of judicial review, nor the range of remedies available to it which would alleviate the situation.[52] Where a matter might have been reviewable, the Supreme Court has limited its use by deciding that some constitutional questions are either political or matters of legislative discretion and cannot be interfered with.[53] Furthermore, Article 17 of the Constitution can

50 Beer, LW, 'Freedom of Expression: The Continuing Revolution' in Luney and Takahashi (eds), *supra*, n 16, p 221; Nakamura, M, 'Freedom of Economic Activities and the Right to Property', *idem*, p 255; Osuka, A, 'Welfare Rights' *idem*, p 269; Tomatsu, H, 'Equal Protection of the Law', *idem*, p 187; Osuka, A, 'Constitutional Protection and Guarantee of Rights and Freedoms: The Case of Japan' (1986) 7 *Waseda Bulletin of Comparative Law* 1; Matsui, S, 'Freedom of Expression in Japan' (1991) 38 *Osaka University Law Review* 13.

51 The concept of standing (*uttae no rieki*) has been used very effectively in Japan to restrict the right of citizens to review administrative action. Thus it is necessary for an individual to show that he has a right recognised by statute and that there is a causal link between the alleged defective administrative action and the individual's legal interest. Furthermore, Japanese law distinguishes between 'legal interests' and 'factual interests', ie those interests shared with the general public which are affected by the administrative action. These 'factual interests' usually have not been recognised by the courts as the basis for an individual's standing; in other words the courts have restricted standing to the narrow definition of personal and legal interest. See *Sakamoto* (Supreme Court 19 January 1962), known as the *Bathhouse Case*, where the court considered standing. Maki, *supra*, n 20, p 293. In that case the lower court adopted the strict interpretation and denied standing, but the Supreme Court took a more liberal approach and whilst still insisting on direct legal interest, nevertheless marked the start of a broadening of the standing doctrine. In fact as one writer has observed: 'In the fifteen years that followed *Sakamoto* the lower courts appeared to loosen standing requirements somewhat, particularly in the second-generation environmental suits that followed the Big Four.' Upham, *supra*, n 47, p 172; See also Tanaka, H, *The Japanese Legal System*, 1976, Chapter 8, University of Tokyo Press; Ogawa, I, 'Judicial Review of Administrative Actions in Japan' (1968) 43 *Washington Law Review* 1075. On the background to environmental cases see Gresser, J, Fujikura, K and Morishima, A, *Environmental Law in Japan*, 1981, Massachusetts Institute of Technology Press. In general see: Hashimoto, K, 'The Rule of Law: Some Aspects of Judicial Review of Administrative Action' in von Mehren, AT (ed), *Law in Japan*, 1963, Harvard University Press; Slomanson, W, 'Judicial Review of War Renunciation in the Naganuma Nike Case; Juggling the Constitutional Crisis in Japan' (1975) 9 *Cornell International Law Journal* 24; Wada H, 'Decisions Under Article 9 of the Constitution: The *Sunakawa, Eniwa, Naganuma* Decisions' (1976) 9 *Law in Japan* 117.

52 Although not restricted to judicial review and fundamental rights, note the following interesting empirical works: Kawashima, T, 'Individualism in Decision-Making in the Supreme Court' in Schubert, G and Danelski, D (eds), *Comparative Judicial Behaviour. Cross Cultural Studies of Political Decision-Making in the East and West*, 1969, Chapter 5, Oxford University Press; Danelski, D, 'The Supreme Court of Japan: An Exploratory Study', *idem*, Chapter 6.

53 Kamata, T, 'Adjudication and the Governing Process: Political Questions and Legislative Discretion' in Luney and Takahashi (eds), *supra*, n 16; Tokikuni Y, 'Procedures for Constitutional Litigation and Judgments of Constitutionality' (1980) 13 *Law in Japan* 1.

provide an alternative route for redress and thereby siphon off a certain number of cases which might otherwise be the subject of judicial review. This article provides that anyone can sue the state or a public entity, 'as provided by law', in a situation where damage has occurred through the illegal act of a public official, ie an action in tort brought in accordance with the State Compensation Law 1947 which gives individuals an effective remedy in damages.[54] An interesting aspect of this law is that not only are damages recoverable when an official is negligent, but also if an official tries to enforce a law or regulation which conflicts with a constitutional obligation.[55] However, if the decision is based on government discretion then, as already noted, the courts will decline jurisdiction. Another alternative to judicial review, where an individual believes that the action of an administrative agency has adversely affected his interests, is to bring an action under the Administrative Cases Litigation Law 1962.[56]

These indirect forms of judicial review should not be seen as undermining or diminishing the importance of Article 81.[57] Moreover, the relative paucity of cases before the Supreme Court is not a sign of weakness or failure. The constitution is sufficiently new to have taken account of some matters which the older constitutions, in countries where a Supreme Court or Constitutional Court is said to be more active, did not provide for, eg social rights. Also, the administrative bureaus and Cabinet Legislative Bureau are meticulous in the drafting process and keen to avoid unconstitutionality, thereby possibly filtering out some potential areas of conflict.[58] On the other hand, some writers recognise the difficulties encountered by the Supreme Court in relation to judicial review, but argue that it results 'from the conflict and interaction between the new judicial system that Japan received from abroad in the late

54 Article 1(1) of the State Compensation Law (No 125, 1947) states: 'The State and public corporation (including local governments) shall be responsible for the damage unlawfully inflicted upon third parties by the intentional or negligent acts of responsible public officials during the exercise of their public duties.' For a comment of the tortious remedy as a route to judicial review in place of the direct appeal see Young, M, 'Administrative Guidance in the Courts: A Case Study in Doctrinal Adaptation' in Haley, JO (ed), *Law and Society in Contemporary Japan: American Perspectives*, 1988, Kendall/Hunt.

55 In 1979 damages were recovered in a case where an unconstitutional regulation abolishing home voting for the disabled was enforced. *Hanrei Jiho* No 762, p 34, cited in Matsushita, M and Schoenbaum, T, *Japanese International Trade and Investment Law*, 1989, p 43, University of Tokyo Press.

56 Article 9 of the Administrative Cases Litigation Law (No 139, 1962) keeps to the narrow definition of standing in that the individual must have a legal interest and not just a mere factual interest. However, standing remains a difficult point to overcome. See *Shufu Rengokai v Fair Trade Commission* – The Juice Case (Supreme Court 14 March 1976) in which the Supreme Court reaffirmed the view that there must be a direct legal interest and not just a factual, ie indirect or third party interest. See Matsushita, 1993, *supra*, n 48, p 58.

57 Haley argues that whatever the detractors might say, judicial review is a crucial factor in achieving political solutions through the democratic process. 'Introduction: Legal vs Social Controls' in Haley (ed), 1988, *supra*, n 54.

58 Seki, *supra*, n 31.

1940s and the Japanese legal tradition'.[59] Perhaps with the appointment in 1990 of the first Supreme Court judge to have received a postwar legal education, the scene is set for the start of the next phase of development in Japan's constitutional history.[60]

The 50 year history of the constitution and the activity of the Supreme Court in particular could be characterised as a period of cautious conservatism. This is not in any sense a pejorative evaluation. Indeed, as was stated earlier, the view of one Japanese writer was that the Supreme Court is self-restraining and displays considerable negativism in judicial review.[61] The fact that the Supreme Court has held a law unconstitutional on five occasions, could be read either as a sign of success, because the constitution is widely respected and upheld, or of weakness, because the courts are unwilling to enforce constitutional principles and are particularly negative in their approach to judicial review. Statistics alone cannot provide the whole picture, but given that the constitutional framework of the United States was the role model for Japan, it is interesting to compare the history of the United States Supreme Court in this area. Thus in the 75 years from 1789 to 1864 the court held only two Acts of Congress unconstitutional; in the 164 years from 1789 to 1953 the number was 76. However, from 1953 to 1991 the Supreme Court held 66 Acts of Congress unconstitutional, in other words almost two a year.[62] On that basis the Japanese constitutional framework could be said to have been resilient and enduring and the Supreme Court relatively active in its short life. This is particularly so bearing in mind the sociolegal and political factors which mitigate against bringing a case to court in the first place and considering the size of population and number of laws in force in Japan as compared with the United States.

59 Tanaka, H, 'Legal Equality Among Family Members in Japan – The Impact of the Japanese Constitution of 1946 on the Traditional Family System' (1980) 53 *Southern California Law Review* 619. Certainly 'the relative absence of a means for effective after-the-fact judicial review' is seen by some as a weakness of existing Japanese law. Ködderitzsch, L, 'Japan's New Administrative Procedure Law: Reasons for its Enactment and Likely Implications' (1991) 24 *Law in Japan* 108. The author goes on to state that the continental European approach, as best illustrated by Germany, avoids such difficulties by concentrating on detailed legislation on substantive issues which the courts then have the task of checking to see if the administration has applied properly. Known as *Rechtsstaatsprinzip* this approach 'stresses the review of after-the-fact outcomes rather than the procedures followed.' *idem*, p 106. By enacting the new Administrative Procedure Law (Law No 88, 1993) the importance attached to procedure has been reinforced and opportunities for judicial review remain on the same narrow basis as before, a fact which in relation to administrative guidance is perhaps unfortunate. For a full text of the new Law see (1995) 25 *Law in Japan* 141.

60 Haley, JO, 'Judicial Independence in Japan Revisited', 1995, *supra*, n 42, p 14. Haley also notes that no one born after 1929 has ever served on the Supreme Court. It should also be noted that no woman has sat on the Supreme Court. The same is true for the United Kingdom House of Lords, though not of the United States Supreme Court, which has had one woman member.

61 *Supra*, n 38.

62 O'Brien D, *Storm Centre: The Supreme Court in American Politics*, 3rd edn, 1993, Norton. Although not strictly relevant for comparative purposes, a similar trend occurred in relation to state laws. The Supreme Court invalidated 79 state laws during the first 100 years of the constitution and 840 in the second 100 years, but what is interesting is that 398 invalidations took place after 1953.

A further matter to reflect upon is that in the United States the increase in cases declaring acts unconstitutional emerged from what is generally characterised as the 'liberal' Supreme Court of 1953 to 1969.[63] The likely change in the Japanese Supreme Court over the next five to 10 years during which the 'old school' will be replaced by the new postwar educated judges, could raise a number of interesting questions. Foremost among these is whether, in spite of the innate conservatism and alleged 'political' control over the judiciary, the Supreme Court will move to a more active and positive approach to constitutional issues. Certainly since the 1970s there has been an increase in attention focused on constitutional issues in general and individual rights in particular.[64] On the other hand, are the deeply ingrained sociolegal and cultural traditions of Japanese law and lawyers such that, together with the strength of the constitutional document itself, little dramatic change will be experienced?

The natural conservatism and controlled legal education provided by the Legal Training and Research Institute might still 'educate out' what are perceived to be liberal or unorthodox tendencies. However, contemporary Japanese lawyers and scholars have had considerably greater exposure to, and experience of, other legal traditions, particularly in the area of human rights and civil liberties, than their predecessors. In a period where constitutional issues play an increasingly important role in many areas of the law, in a 'rights' oriented climate, both nationally and internationally, the precise dynamics and development of the constitutional framework of Japan in the next 50 years and into the 21st century are difficult to predict. To say that trends in other countries will be mirrored in Japan is to deny the uniqueness of the Japanese approach to the law and the social order; equally so, it is no longer the hermetically sealed nation of the mid-19th century. Instead Japan is a major player on the international stage and open to the influences of other and different traditions and cultures, as well as being subject to international obligations and standards. Any constitution goes to the heart of a nation's being and in many ways a major test of its democratic health is its treatment of fundamental rights and freedoms. In this regard the patient is healthy but has, not unusually, certain weaknesses such as judicial passivity and excessive deference to the legislative and executive.[65] Nevertheless the core values are secure and unshakeable and nothing short of a revolution will displace the firmly entrenched structure and ideas which, whilst transplanted, have now firmly taken root.[66]

63 Farber, D, Eskridge W and Frickley, P, *Constitutional Law: Themes for the Constitution's Third Century*, 1993, West. The periods of Supreme Court history have traditionally been referred to by the name of the Supreme Court Chief Justice. Hence, the Warren Court of 1953–69 invalidated 25 Acts, the Burger Court (1969–86), which was said to be more conservative, invalidated 34 and the Rehnquist Court invalidated seven in the years 1986–92 (see O'Brien, *supra*, n 62).

64 Upham, *supra*, n 47, Gresser *et al*, *supra*, n 51.

65 Ashibe, *supra*, n 30, p 261.

66 As Okudaira puts it: 'I am somehow rather more optimistic than pessimistic about the healthy development of modern constitutionalism in Japan – on the condition that it will not confront an unexpected, extraordinary crisis, either political or economic, in or out of the country's domain.' *supra*, n 32, p 32.

I HISTORY

Ito, M, 'The Modern Development of Law and Constitution in Japan', in Beer, LW (ed), *Constitutional Systems in Late Twentieth Century Asia*, 1992, pp 135–40, 142–49, University of Washington Press

Making of the 1889 Constitution

Japan always had a constitution in the substantive sense of a fundamental law of the realm; but it was not until the Meiji Revolution (*Meiji Ishin*) that she had a constitution in the normal sense, ie a written constitution. During the Meiji Period (1868–1912), demand arose for a modern constitution, a fundamental law based on constitutionalism and restricting the powers of the state by law.

By the Imperial Restoration (*Osei Fukko*, 1869) and the Abolition of Fiefs and the Establishment of Prefectures (*Haihan Chiken*, 1871), the feudal political system was dissolved, and Japan started to organize itself as a modern state. Opportunities for participating in politics and governance were increased backed by theories of politics responsive to public opinion. This led to calls for a national assembly under a constitutionalism similar to that in the developed countries of the West. The Petition to Establish an Elected Assembly (*Minsen Giin Setsuritsu Kenpakusho of 1874*) by Taisuke Itagaki and other influential politicians is a well-known example. The Meiji Government eventually issued the Edict to Hold Councils of Local Officers (*Chihokan Kaigi Kaisai no Fukoku*) in 1874, and later enacted the Rules and Regulations for Prefectural Assemblies (*Fukenkai Kisoku*) of 1878 and the Local Assembly Law (*Kuchosonkai Ho*) of 1880, all as means to provide for elected local assemblies.

The Government also began to draft a written constitution. In 1873, the task of drafting a constitution was assigned to the *Sa-in* [a deliberative body to discuss and report on legislation to the *Sei-in*, the main department of government. When the *Sa-in* was abolished in 1875, the Emperor issued an edict ordering the chairman of the *Genroin* (Council of Elders) to draft a constitution (1876). Within that Council, Research Members for Constitutional Law (*Kokken Torishirabe Iin*) wrote drafts. The first was titled a Constitutional Proposal for Japan (*Nihonkoku Ken-an*) and the second, the National Constitution (*Kokken*). Both were rejected by Tomomi Iwakura and other prominent leaders as too democratic. At that time, various privately drafted constitutions were also made public. Many recommended adoption of a parliamentary cabinet system and guaranteed rights and liberties for the people, due to the influence of the then-active People's Rights Movement (*Jiyu Minken Undo*). Their declarations stood clearly for the basic principles of democratic government. The government responded by toughening its attitude and suppressing the freedom of political activities under the Assembly Ordinance (*Shukai Jorei*) of 1880. At the same time, this conflict accelerated the urgent efforts to make a constitution.

In 1881, the Emperor issued the Edict to Establish a National Assembly announcing that a Diet [parliament] would be held by 1890 and that a constitution would be promulgated by them. The next year, Hirobumi Ito was sent to Europe to conduct the research necessary to serve as the basis for writing a constitution. He studied mainly German constitutional law under Rudolf von Gneist and Lorenz von Stein. The German constitutional monarchy, rather than the British parliamentary system, was considered most appropriate by those controlling the Government at that time. Although the German monarchical system allowed an elected legislative body, it limited the powers of that body. Such a system supported a powerful and centralized executive branch which would maximize the power and authority of the Emperor at its apex. After Ito's return to Japan, the enactment of the Peerage Ordinance (1884) and the establishment of the Cabinet (1885) and the Privy Council (1888) prepared the stage for the coming constitution and the national assembly. Ito, with the help of Kowashi Inoue, Hermann Roesler and a few others, drafted the constitution – often called the Meiji Constitution – which the reigning Emperor (*Tenno*) Meiji promulgated on 11 February 1889. At the same time, the Rules of the Imperial Household (*Koshitsu Tenpan*) of 1889, which were considered part of the constitution, also came into effect. Japan thus came to have a modern constitution and began to live under constitutional government.

The Duality of the Meiji Constitution

The Meiji Constitution adopted both the absolutistic theory that the sovereignty of the Emperor is based on the divine will of a god similar in theory to the divine right of kings on the one hand, and various principles of modern constitutionalism on the other. The Meiji Constitution may be unique in that it was a mixture of two contradictory momenta. In the background explaining this dualistic nature were the aims of the mainstream of the ruling elite, during the period between the Meiji Restoration and the making of the constitution, to strengthen the rights of sovereignty, to establish a powerful central government whose authority was based on those rights of sovereignty, and to pursue the basic policy of enriching and strengthening the nation as a whole. The underlying purpose of all these measures was to bring Japan even with the Western powers. Furthermore, the constitution was made with a Government inclined towards absolutism.

Nevertheless, the Government could not simply ignore the public opinion which strongly supported constitutionalism; it had to present at least the appearance of a modern political and legal system comparable to those of Western countries. The former was evidenced by the rise of the people's rights movement. The latter was necessitated by the wish to revise the unequal treaties with Western Powers. A more fundamental factor was that Japan could not spare the time to go through the long historical process of development that the European nations had experienced, a process during which absolute monarchy did away with feudal regimes, and then the citizens overthrew the monarchy to establish modern constitutionalism upholding freedom and equality. Instead, Japan had to establish an absolutist structure of authority which would wipe out the feudal fiefdoms and, at the same time, introduce modern constitutional principles. Thus, the Meiji Constitution allowed the democratic elements of modern constitutionalism and the feudal and anti-democratic elements to co-exist. This duality made it possible for future politics under the same constitution to be contradictory in tendency at different times. Politics under the Meiji Constitution (1889–1947) depended very much on which features were highlighted in the interpretation and application of the constitution.

The Meiji Constitution and the British and American Constitutions

Prior to the making of the Meiji Constitution, the British and American constitutions, especially that of the United Kingdom, were introduced as examples of constitutions of developed and democratic countries. This is illustrated by the fact that the works of Sir Maurice Sheldon Amos, Walter Bagehot, Jean Louis De Lolme and Albert Venn Dicey, which are known as the representative authorities on the British constitution at that time, were translated into Japanese quite early. The 'Constitution of England' was among the lectures included in the curriculum of the Faculty of Law at the University of Tokyo when it was established in 1877. It should also be noted that, at that time, there was an active movement for an elected assembly. The fact that the works of Sir Thomas Erskine May and Hadley on the parliament of the United Kingdom, the mother country of parliamentary systems were translated shows the degree of interest that people had in a parliamentary system.

Once the Meiji Constitution modeled after the German constitution was promulgated, studies of the British and American constitutions were never employed for interpretation or application. Generally speaking, there was no noticeable influence from the British and American constitutions. During the Taisho period (1912-1926), the majority party of the House of Representatives began to control the Cabinet under 'regular procedures of a constitutional government.' As this type of polity was in part modeled after British parliamentary democracy, the British constitution may well have been referred to from time to time, but with no implication that studies of the British and American constitutions were used as a basis for interpreting and applying the Meiji Constitution. Before the Second World War, scholarly studies by Japanese academics on British and American constitutional laws did not have much influence.

The Rise and Decline of Constitutionalism

Within the Meiji Constitution, the contradictory principles of absolutism and modern constitutionalism co-existed. The Meiji Constitution had relatively few and briefly worded provisions, which allowed a wide variety of interpretations. Conflicts appeared between 'the theory of the Emperor as an organ of the state' (*Tenno Kikan Setsu*) and 'the theory of imperial sovereignty' (*Tenno Shuken Setsu*). The former adopted and modified a theory then prevalent among German public lawyers that sovereignty resides in or is incorporated into the state with the monarch as its highest organ. The latter was associated with militant nationalism. Tatsukichi Minobe was the representative scholar propounding the Emperor-as-Organ Theory, maintaining that the state is a legal entity capable of exercising its rights, and that the Emperor is one of its organs and capable of performing acts prescribed for it in the constitution. This theory denied that the imperial prerogatives were unlimited and interpreted the constitution so as to stress the importance of the Diet, especially the House of Representatives, as the organ representing the subjects. In contrast, according to the Imperial Sovereignty Theory, with Yatsuka Hozumi as the representative scholar, the most fundamental principle of the Meiji Constitution was that the Emperor possessed the highest authority and the power of the state. Because the sovereignty of the Emperor derived from the will of the gods, it was absolute and could not possibly be limited.

This conflict was not merely a theoretical issue of legal interpretation. The choice of theory and its application to the constitution had tremendous impact on the course of politics. Whenever the democratic elements of constitutionalism were considered important, the status of the Diet, especially the elected House of Representatives, was enhanced. Whenever the antidemocratic factor of absolutism was emphasized, the authority of the Diet was weakened and the powers of the Emperor increased—in practice, the power of the executive branch which ruled in his name. The course of politics under the Meiji Constitution was determined by the weight placed upon one or the other of these two conflicting aspects of the constitution.

Between the period of promulgation and the Sino-Japanese War (1894–95), the intent of the authors of the constitution, who endorsed a weak elected assembly, prevailed. The

Government was the Emperor's, independent from all political parties and factions, and not to be influenced by the Diet. This was referred to as the period of *'Chozen Shugi'* or 'Transcendentalism.' However, this caused confrontation between the various political parties in the House of Representatives and the Government, and the Government was forced to compromise. After victory in the Sino-Japanese War, the Transcendentalists tended to soften their stand. The Government began to cooperate, in varying degrees, with one or the other of the influential parties in the House of Representatives. This gradually led to increased Diet power and implementation of a system similar to that of the British parliamentary cabinet. The short-lived first term of the [*shigenobu*] Okuma Government (1898) was the first party cabinet in Japan.

During the Taisho period (in 1912 and in 1924), there was a movement to promote constitutional government by establishing a party cabinet system. Efforts to modernize politics in line with the rise of capitalism took the form of reinforcing the authority and powers of the Diet. In the second wave of the movement, the Kato Government was formed and from that time on the majority party in the House of Representatives formed the government. One of the defects of the Meiji constitutional system was that the Imperial Household and the military were beyond the control of the Diet and political parties. Nevertheless, the democratic elements in the constitution were influential during the period of Taisho Democracy (1912–1925). During this time, political scientist Sakuzo Yoshino's theory of the sovereignty of the Japanese people (*Minponshugi*) and the constitutional theory of Tatsukichi Minobe that the Emperor was a state organ (*Tenno Kikansetsu*) were respected by many as authoritative.

From 1926 on, political tensions rose in the international atmosphere of East Asia and uncertainty in Japan's domestic economy. None of the political parties were effective in dealing with the situation, and some politicians were attacked as corrupt. The people lost trust in party politics, and reform movements emerged from both ends of the ideological spectrum. Due to governmental suppression, the reformism of the Left never had much impact, but the totalitarian vanguard of the Right took control of politics by making the most of the anti-democratic elements of the Meiji Constitution. Thus, parliamentary politics, which stood on shaky democratic legs, went into decline. The Manchurian Incident (September, 1931) was the turning point; thereafter, the military and militarism dominated politics. The constitutionalist elements in the Meiji Constitution were almost totally overshadowed. The suppression of Minobe's Emperor-as-Organ Theory in the 1930s illustrates this trend. With the surrender of 1945, the Meiji Constitution was forcibly changed in character.

...

The Making of the Constitution of Japan of 1946 and the British and American Constitutions

Since the constitution was drafted in an extremely brief period primarily by SCAP American lawyers, one might reasonably suppose that most of it was a direct translation and importation of American (federal and state) constitutions with which they were very familiar. Indeed, the provisions about those accused of crime are very similar to provisions of the United States Constitution. But on the whole, the draft constitution included many elements which are not in American law, in contrast to some other legislation during the Occupation (for example, the Securities Exchange Law). Longer was spent in enacting some legislation considered a direct importation of American law than in writing the constitution. The drafters understood that a constitution is the fundamental law of the state and did not think it appropriate to impose American law.

They paid much attention to the likelihood of its acceptance by the Japanese people, because it would determine the future direction of Japan. They also were aware that the making of an appropriate constitution was a serious concern to many outside Japan, such as the member nations of the Far Eastern Commission (FEC).

Here are some of the factors which affected the drafting of the constitution.

(1) General Douglas MacArthur gave notes (the so-called 'MacArthur Notes') to the drafters on a few basic principles not to be ignored in the drafting process: maintenance of the Emperor institution (he had explicitly written that the Emperor was to be at the head of the state and that succession was to be dynastic); renunciation of war; and abolition of aristocracy and feudalism. These principles revealed Occupation policies, conditions peculiar to Japan, and General MacArthur's idealism in making the constitution. In fact, apart from reference to adoption of the British budgetary system, one cannot find any linkage in the Notes with the British or American constitutions.

(2) The draft reflected the strong influence of political theories underlying American federal and state constitutions. The political theory behind the U.S. Declaration of Independence, the Preamble to the United States Constitution, the Federalist Papers, addresses of Abraham Lincoln and others – the modern theory of natural law and the theory of democracy based on the idea of social contract – was alive throughout the whole draft. Although these ideas may seem to some a little dated in a contemporary constitution, they appealed to the Japanese people as refreshing after the dominance of anti-democratic elements at the end of the Meiji Constitution regime.

(3) The draft also paid some attention to Japan's traditional system. It is well documented that the strengths as well as the weaknesses of the Meiji Constitution were analyzed in the drafting process. The fact that the draft followed the Meiji Constitution with respect to the formal structure of the whole constitution, the titles of each chapter, their sequence, and the wording of the text, may be due to the attempts to maintain continuity. Such respect for the Meiji Constitution may be counted as one of the factors which prevented any direct importation of the British and American constitutions in substance. Retention of the Emperor institution and hereditary succession is a prominent example. Other illustrations may be the rejection of a presidency and continuation of a parliamentary cabinet as the executive branch. Moreover, SCAP wished to implement Occupation policies without inviting obstruction or more radical suggestions for reform.

(4) Attention was paid to recent European constitutions, such as the German Weimar Constitution (1919). During the drafting process, comparisons were made between constitutions. In particular, the inclusion of explicit provisions to guarantee social rights was influenced by constitutions of Europe, though strong and influential opposition felt that these rights should be guaranteed by Diet legislation and not by the constitution.

(5) From the time SCAP indicated the need to revise the constitution, each political party published its own proposal for a draft constitution. Private citizens and groups also came out with numerous proposals and drafts. SCAP seems to have paid some attention to these private drafts, as well as to revisions by the Government task force, as expressions of ideas of the Japanese people. Among these, the one published on 26 December 1945 by the Study Group on the Constitution (*Kempo Kenkyukai*), composed of Iwasaburo Takano and six others, contained epoch-making provisions for that time, proposing that sovereignty should reside with the people, that the Emperor should perform only ceremonial

acts, and that the people should have the 'right to maintain standards of living which are wholesome and decent,' as well as other social rights. These proposals significantly influenced SCAP's draft.

(6) The Charter of the United Nations came into effect in October, 1945 shortly before the writing of the draft constitution. It was considered the primary document providing for a new international order. The Constitution of Japan presupposes this international order. Before the actual drafting began, the drafters were told that the principles of the Charter should be kept in mind, but that the Charter need not be explicitly referred to.

The Adoption of British and American Constitutionalism in the (1947) Constitution

Some factors dissuaded SCAP in the drafting process from simply transplanting British or American constitutionalism, while others favored consideration of other constitutions. Nothing was impossible for SCAP at that time, including the direct import of American federal and state constitutional ideas. However, SCAP actually took a broad view in order to integrate all factors and their impacts, and avoided direct induction during the drafting process. It was exactly the attitude an occupation force should take in making the constitution or the basic law of an occupied country. Even though it was drafted by foreigners, the constitution of 1947 has enjoyed the general support of the public and is considered the most suitable post-war constitution for Japan, preferable to all the other constitutional drafts by Japanese, including that of the Japanese Government. With the consent of the people, it has survived without being amended even once until this day. Under this constitutional regime, Japan has managed to rise from the ruins of war and defeat, and to achieve high international status. Considering all these facts, one cannot but be struck by the wisdom of the drafters. Had they been forced by time pressures to hastily draft a direct importation of British or American constitutionalism, the resulting document would most likely have had a different fate from that of the present constitution.

Undeniably, in the Preamble, in the theoretical background of the fundamental provisions and principles of the constitution, and in the text, the institutions and principles of British and American constitutionalism had tremendous influence. My first impression of the draft was that one could trace back the origins of many of the provisions to British or American constitutionalism. Here is an attempt to see the relationship between specific provisions of the constitution of Japan and the British and American constitutions.

Constitutionalism

The Concept of a Higher Law

Broadly speaking, constitutionalism means that a state is restricted by constitutional law in the use of its powers, and that government is conducted in accordance with the constitution and all pursuant laws and orders. In earlier times, absolute monarchs were not bound by law, but constitutionalism has come to be accepted as the fundamental principle for governance of a modern state. The modern era has been marked by popular overthrow of various forms of despotism in recognition of the individual's dignity. Citizens have gained political power and civil liberties have become a prevailing social value in the West. A constitution not based on constitutionalism is not considered a true constitution. Moreover, constitutions based on constitutionalism have become widely accepted among countries outside Europe and America.

The historical and social circumstances of a state when its constitution is made seriously affect the actual state of its constitutionalism. For example, the Meiji Constitution embodied modern constitutionalism only partially and inconclusively. The following are a few features of a modern constitution which restrains state power.

(1) Popular participation in politics and government. Citizens are not merely the object of governance. Many people actively participate directly or indirectly in the formation of the national will [eg voting] and take part in government.

(2) Separation of powers. The effective way to combat abuse or arbitrary exercise of power is to prevent the concentration of power in one entity. Power should be divided among different authorities so that each restrains the others from abuse and misuse, as among the legislature, the executive and the judiciary, or between federal authority and the authority of states, or between central and local offices of government.

(3) The guarantee of human rights. In modern constitutionalism, it is essential to prevent state power from interfering with the rights and liberties of individuals and to place some limits on the exercise of rights. One might even say that this guarantee of human rights is the central feature of constitutionalism.

Compared with the Meiji Constitution, the constitution of 1947 is more thorough in the embodiment of constitutionalism as outlined above. Such constitutionalism manifests common characteristics of a modern constitution rather than the influence of the British and American constitutions.

A modern constitution guarantees the rule 'by government' not 'by a person.' The constitutions of the common law countries and the civil law countries do not differ on this point. In the European civil law countries, it is the principle of *'Rechtsstaat'* or constitutional state, especially *'Gesetzmassigkeit der Verwaltung'* or administration according to law. The principle is based on liberalism, as opposed to the absolutism of a police state. A statute enacted by a legislature representing the people binds the operation of the state through its executive and judiciary. An executive, however despotic it attempts to be, must base its administration on law and execute its policies according to law. This sign of constitutionalism, a liberal principle of government, was important in Germany and elsewhere, including Japan under the Meiji Constitution. Here, it is precisely the legislative body and its judgment which controls the content and adequacy of legislation. When a legislature is dominated by despotic elements, there is danger of an empty constitutionalism. Under the Meiji Constitution, the history of oppression of the freedoms of thought and expression with the Peace Preservation Law (*Chian Iji Ho*) well illustrates the point.

The words of Bracton in the English middle ages that 'The King should not be under the authority of man, but of God and the law' illustrates the essence of the rule of law. This principle – which is also called the 'supremacy of law,' a 'higher law' or 'government according to law' – is the core of the British and American constitutions as handed down to this day. The Bractonian rule of medieval law, which was also that of natural law, became the rule of common law with the words of Sir Edward Coke. Those rules served as the harbinger of modern revolution and were eventually incorporated into the various American constitutions. In 19th-century Great Britain, under Whig dominance, Albert Venn Dicey analyzed the rule of law as a constitutional principle. The importance of the constitutional principle of 'rule of law' rests not only on the rule that legislation enacted by Parliament restricts all state functions, but also on the furtherance of constitutionalism. That is to say, there is a higher law which binds parliamentary statutes. Although this principle was transformed in Great Britain by the establishment of the principle of parliamentary sovereignty, it still is part of the jurisprudence which forms the basis for British and American constitutionalism and common law in general.

Three concrete examples can be used as standards to judge whether the 'rule of law' is incorporated in a specific constitution: (1) a thorough guarantee of the individual's human rights; (2) a legitimacy in the procedures and content of law, what is called due process of law in the United States and natural justice in Great Britain; (3) respect for the judiciary which gives institutional expression to the rule of law by restricting state operations.

The Constitution of Japan and the Rule of Law

The concepts of constitutionalism and the state under the Meiji Constitution did not include the 'rule of law,' as described above. The rule of law is not explicated as such in the text of the 1947 Constitution – that would be inappropriate. Nevertheless, the rule of law is fundamental to the whole constitution and serves as the basis for important institutions such as the following:

(1) Chapter 10 of the Constitution is entitled the 'Supreme Law.' In the United States, because of federalism, it is necessary to determine the relationship between federal and state laws. The Supremacy Clause of Article VI of the United States Constitution plays a significant role as the keystone of federalism. Some people consider the three articles [Articles 97–99] of Chapter 10 in Japan's Constitution legally meaningless and unnecessary, as they only state obvious legal and moral obligation. However, it is more appropriate to read them as clearly stating that the 'rule of law' is the fundamental principle of the constitution, probably placed at the very end, just before the supplementary provisions, as a summation of the whole constitution. Here one may see the influence of the long history of the British and American constitutions.

The three articles of Chapter 10 are a coherent expression of the 'rule of law.' Article 97 reconfirms the eternity, the inviolability, and the historical origin of human rights. The fact that this article is placed at the head of the chapter on supreme law makes clear that the guarantee of human rights is at the core of this constitution. Human rights under Article 97 are central to the 'rule of law.' Article 98 explicitly states the supremacy of the constitution; based on the idea of the supremacy of law, all acts of state power in violation of this higher law shall be null and void, and all acts of the state are to comply with the constitution. Article 99 declares the obligation of all those who exercise the powers of the state to respect and uphold the constitution. This is also a straightforward expression of British and American constitutionalism and the rule of law, not man.

(2) Chapter 3 of the Constitution of Japan provides for the guarantee of human rights. It fully responds to the demands of the 'rule of law' to guarantee human rights in both substance and form. Most of the guaranteed human rights are, like those in the United States Constitution, unaccompanied by any qualification which allows restrictions by law. In most cases, human rights are guaranteed absolutely. The text does not necessarily mean that human rights should not be limited in any way. The idea is that even legislation enacted by the Diet, representing the people, may not restrict human rights, which are an expression of a higher law.

The constitution does not have any provisions regarding martial law or emergency powers, and does not recognize any exceptional restriction of human rights in times of emergency. This leaves open the issue of how to apply the constitution in an extraordinary situation. The lack of any emergency provisions is noteworthy as an indication of the rule of 'ordinary law.'

(3) There is controversy as to whether or not Article 31 of the Constitution is modeled after the due process of law, an American expression for the 'rule of law.' Because it is worded 'except according to procedure established by law,' and is different from 'without due process of law' in the United States Constitution, the drafters of the constitution, in all likelihood intended to avoid a direct importation of the American concept of the due process of law. The activist interpretation of the American due process clause by the United States Supreme Court, especially in order to secure economic freedom and property rights, had a number of times held social legislation and New Deal legislation unconstitutional. In my opinion, the basic idea contained in the concept of American due process is incorporated in Article 31. This has been recognized subsequently in principle, by court decisions and scholarly opinion. This point will be touched on later; suffice it to state here that the concept of due process of law was brought into the constitution and that it adds life to the 'rule of law.'

(4) A clear institutional indication of the 'rule of law' is strong judicial power. The judiciary under the Meiji Constitution was supposedly independent, but had far less power and a lower status than the courts under the Constitution of Japan. The new constitution gives the judiciary enlarged powers, institutionalizing the 'rule of law' of British and American constitutionalism. Under the Court Organization Law, the judicial power now is not limited to civil and criminal proceedings, but extends to all kinds of cases and controversies in law, including administrative law. The whole judicial power is concentrated in the judiciary. No extraordinary tribunal may be established. An executive agency may exercise an adjudicative function but cannot have the final judicial power. There must always be means provided for resort to courts from decisions of an executive organ.

Under the Meiji Constitution, the Administrative Tribunal (*Gyosei Saibansha*) belonging to the executive branch, not courts of general jurisdiction, had jurisdiction over litigation between the executive and subjects. Moreover, controversies defined as administrative cases were narrowly limited. That is not compatible with the concept of the 'rule of law.' Under the Constitution of 1947, the Administrative tribunals was abolished and all administrative cases now come under the jurisdiction of the courts. Of course, numerous problems remain, such as defining the scope and extent or special procedures of judicial review of administrative acts. In a welfare state, a wide variety of acts comes under administrative discretion, raising questions about strict judicial review and the control of administrative acts. (The issue is not unfamiliar to common law countries.) Only a 'rule of law' basis enables the courts to substantially guarantee compliance of the state to law.

Even statutes enacted by the Diet, the highest organ of state power, are subject to the power of courts to review for constitutionality. The ultimate manifestation of the 'rule of law' is to entrust to the ordinary courts of law the role of substantially guaranteeing the supremacy of the constitution. The forerunner was an attempt by Sir Edward Coke to apply the 'rule of law' to a particular case. In the United States, this claim, under the influence of natural law and higher law, bore fruit as judicial review of unconstitutional legislation. Instead of adopting the constitutional court system that prevailed in the European continent, the Constitution of 1947 follows the American model, directly following the tradition of the 'rule of law' and British and American constitutionalism.

The Influence of the British Constitution

I will now note examples of influence on the 1947 Constitution, first of the British Constitution and then of the American Constitution. Although the principal drafters of the constitution were American lawyers, the text and the institutions suggest more elements derive from the British Constitution than from the various American Constitutions. Of course, many rules of the British Constitution are, like constitutional conventions, unwritten and this allows flexibility. Many of these same rules are spelled out in the Constitution of Japan, and in statutes and orders enacted and issued under the Constitution. On the whole, the influence of the British Constitution is significant. The main reasons for this may be that the United States Constitution has many provisions peculiar to a federal system, and that both the United Kingdom and Japan are unitary states, making it easier for Japan to use British institutions as a model. In some respects, the constitutional structure under the Meiji Constitution honored democracy and a parliamentary cabinet system similar to that of the United Kingdom. Where appropriate, the drafters wanted to maintain continuity with the Meiji regime.

Buckley, R, 'The British Model: Institutional Reform and Occupied Japan' (1982) 16 *Modern Asian Studies* 234–40

The fate of the Emperor was debated at length by American and British diplomats and commentators during the later stages of the Second World War. In the United States the administration was deeply divided over the question of whether the Emperor should be permitted to remain on the throne. In Britain the question aroused less passion and greater unanimity. British officials, led by the Foreign Office's far east specialists, were convinced that retention of the Emperor was essential for the stability of post-surrender Japan and central to any planning how the allies might administer the defeated nation. The British contribution to the thesis that the Emperor ought to be retained and then employed in the service of the occupation proved important but hardly crucial. Sir George Sansom and his colleagues provided additional support to Joseph Crew's group in the State Department who had campaigned so insistently for safeguarding the throne. Yet the struggle was essentially an American one, fought out in Washington between American politicians and diplomats.

The monarchists were vindicated when the nonviolent reaction to the Imperial rescript on Japan's surrender permitted the occupation to begin without the widely predicted resistance. The military bands and press photographers who were on hand to welcome and record General MacArthur's arrival at Atsugi symbolized the non-hostile, plastic framework under which the allied occupation fortunately began. The success of the first weeks of the occupation, when combined with MacArthur's own royalism, seemed certain to secure some future for the Emperor. MacArthur's regard for the British and Dutch households made it probable that a limited, constitutional monarchy would be required of Japan. The opposition, however, to any such scheme was formidable. The Japanese establishment was reluctant to defer to SCAP's Government Section over the extensive reduction of the Emperor's powers. Prime minister Shidehara's cabinet was badly split over the issue. One version of events on the genesis of the new constitution claimed that SCAP threatened to publish both its constitutional proposals and the more timid Shidehara amendments.

> Faced with this ultimatum, the Japanese government produced in ten days a draft which was in substance the constitution now in force. The cabinet were, however, by

> no means agreed upon the draft, about half of the members being opposed to it. Baron Shidehara informed General MacArthur privately of his dilemma and asked for advice. General MacArthur advised him to consult the Emperor, since the Meiji Constitution provided that all amendments to the constitution had to be proposed to the Diet by the Emperor himself. Shidehara then consulted the Emperor who gave the draft his unqualified approval.

This would tend to suggest considerable cordiality between MacArthur the Emperor and discount the theory that Shidehara's cabinet only accepted the new constitution out of concern that the Emperor might be arraigned before the International Military Tribunal for the Far East.

The outcome of these negotiations was to leave the Emperor as little more than a cypher. Already by 1948 the British mission in Tokyo was voicing its disagreement at what it regarded as an unsatisfactory state of affairs divorced from the supposed British example on which MacArthur claimed to have based his constitutional monarchy. The British mission in Tokyo produced a lengthy analysis of the 1947 Constitution which was critical of SCAP GHQ, Sir Alvary Gascoigne's staff canvassed the opinions of Yoshida, Ashida and Katayama and reported that all three political leaders felt that the Emperor was 'almost entirely ignorant of the political situation and of the problems facing his ministers.' UKLIM noted that it appeared to be the American view 'that the role of a constitutional Monarch should be that of a royal rubber stamp.' It concluded that 'if the Emperor has neither power nor knowledge, it is surely impossible for him toe a constitutional monarch as those words are generally understood, and if he is not a constitutional monarch there can be no justification for his remaining on the throne.' The American abolitionists, if they were still following events in Japan, could hardly complain of his non-role. They had lost a battle in 1945 but by 1948 had won the war by default.

Britain disliked the manner in which the Emperor was managed by SCAP. MacArthur kept the palace in almost total isolation and refused to permit contacts with allied diplomats. It was not until January 1948 that the British Special Commissioner for Southeast Asia, Lord Killearn, became the first British official to have visited the Emperor since 1941. Killearn, in the course of what he afterwards described as 'a "matey" reception', felt that the Emperor had been 'excessively friendly' and had 'most sincerely and humbly expressed his regret for the terrible suffering and damage inflicted by "the Japanese".' Killearn concluded by claiming that

> the Emperor was delighted at the opportunity of a little real outside air. Though he did not say so, he gave the very clear feeling (and I am sure purposely) that he entertains strong pro-British contact; and he seemed pathetically anxious to show his genuine and profound regret for Japan's outrageous part in the last war.

The British mission's criticism of MacArthur's control of the Emperor was probably excessive. The need for caution to prevent future exploitation of the Emperor's position had been conceded by British diplomats in 1947. UKLIM had noted in its report of the Emperor's visit to the Kansai in June 1947 that 'it was amply clear during this tour that, while the Emperor may have been attempting to do his best to comport himself as a democratic monarch, his subjects still regarded him with the reverence and awe of former days.' Under these circumstances it was wiser to limit the Emperor's functions and display patience. MacArthur moved slower than the Foreign Office had hoped over encouraging the evolution of a limited monarchy in occupied Japan but, given the political uncertainties of the period, American policy was sensible. While British diplomats might see the Emperor as a strong defender of the 1947 Constitution they, too, held ambivalent opinions over his future. The Foreign Office Research Department could criticize E.H Norman, the head of the Canadian mission in Tokyo, for his unenthusiastic views on the retention of the Emperor. Yet it warned that though the Emperor has moreover shown sufficient, if embarrassed, conviction to play the very small part allowed him by the Americans since 1945 in a straightforward manner. 'It is too early yet to be sure that this worm will never turn.'

British diplomats kept private their reservations over American and Japanese understanding of constitutional monarchy. There was a similar British refusal to comment at length on the functioning of Japan's postwar parliamentary system. It was tempting at times to point out the faults of SCAP's rule and the irresponsibility of Japanese politicians, but any such criticism could easily become counter-productive. It was safer for UKLIM to desist from lecturing SCAP on how the Westminster textbooks might have improved matters since MacArthur regarded the 1947 Constitution as holy writ. Gascoigne warned the Foreign Office that 'the Supreme Commander himself is inordinately proud of his handiwork and so is likely to resist any suggestion for amendment.' The Foreign Office prepared an article-by-article analysis of the constitution, in case the Far Eastern Commission was called upon to exercise its right to review the document, but made no effort to press its views on American officials. There was concern that 'the English cabinet system, which would appear well suited to Japan, had not been entirely followed' and predictions that the no-war clauses of Article 9 of the Constitution were certain to be deleted once the peace settlement had been secured, but still little diplomatic action. Additional doubts over the independence of the judiciary (created by the popular review scheme) and fears over possible civil rights infringements of foreign residents in Japan were hardly issues to warrant causing certain offense to MacArthur.

Yet British doubts on Japan's conversion to parliamentary democracy persisted. Gascoigne contended that 'the most, I feel, that we can hope from this great experiment of democratizing Japan is that the Japanese will, after the peace, retain their hold upon some of the foundations of our democratic system; I do not think they will ever fully take to themselves democracy as it is practised in the West.' As with its misgivings over the Japanese monarchy, British scepticism was directed at both American master and Japanese pupil. UKLIM found SCAP's frequent press releases on the continual success of Japan's democratic revolution particularly hard to swallow. It was difficult to accept statements from MacArthur that 'in no land are men more free or more safe and secure. A serenity of calm has enveloped the Japanese islands.' MacArthur's rhetoric was known to British officials to conceal severe private unease over Japan's democratic progress. In conversations with British diplomats MacArthur admitted to sharing many of the same fears as the Foreign Office over the performance of Japanese politicians. MacArthur noted disappointedly in December 1947 that

> since the end of the war no great Japanese leader or leaders of the Japanese people had appeared who could co-operate with him in his efforts to bring about better economic and social conditions in Japan. He had interviewed numerous Japanese who had been prominent in civil life before the war, both men who had since been 'purged' and men who had not, and others who occupied important positions at the present time. He was prepared to work with any Japanese who had the qualities of leadership, but so far he had found no one of the requisite calibre.

UKLIM ascribed the blame for this situation to inexperienced Japanese politicians and SCAP's Government Section Gascoigne was hardly exaggerating when he wrote in his headmasterly style that 'the Japanese have not as yet any clear idea of the meaning and responsibilities of parliamentary democracy.' He reported that the first session of the Diet in December 1947 had been 'characterized by rowdy heckling in the place of serious debate, and during the most turbulent week, when the temporary Coal Mining Control Bill was being debated in the House of Representatives, there were displays of fisticuffs.' *The Nippon Times* more bluntly described the scene as 'Diet or Zoo'. Yet even Gascoigne was obliged to note that the mining bill was passed, despite the Liberal party's rapid mastery of the filibuster. Doubtless Gascoigne would have seen such parliamentary imports as derived from southern senators rather than upright MPs.

There was also an occasional modicum of sympathy for Japanese politicians when Government Section's hidden, or at times barely undisguised, hand controlled Japanese political life. Shortly before Ashida Hitoshi look office in 1948 the outgoing premier, Katayama Tetsu, told the British mission's information officer that the new cabinet would only last 'as long as General Whitney would let it,' Yet the more usual Foreign Office view was to note the intrigues behind attempts to form stable Japanese coalitions and to argue as Esler Dening did in February 1948 after hearing of the resignation of the Katayama cabinet that 'it is all a little unreal while the occupation lasts.' British criticism was double-edged. It saw chicanery from Japanese political groupings and a most undemocratic pressure from SCAP officials to funnel reform into channels acceptable to the United States.

Once again UKLIM displayed caution over conveying its misgivings to MacArthur. Only when it was apparent that SCAP held approximately the same views as the British mission did Gascoigne express anything but a guarded opinion. Both men, for example, were sympathetic towards the Socialist leader Katayama and had reservations over the suitability of Yoshida for the premiership. Gascoigne informed the Foreign Office in February 1948 that 'I agree with General MacArthur that the only useful form of "puppet" government during this period of occupation is a coalition.' Such tactics might have restored Katayama to power but the constantly shifting political groups were hard for outsiders to manipulate. Even after the formation of Yoshida's third cabinet, following his resounding victory in the January 1949 general election, the Foreign Office continued to doubt Yoshida's abilities. Gascoigne acknowledged that the new premier headed 'incomparably the strongest government' since the surrender but feared for factionalism. There remained the 'regrettable tendency of Japanese politicians to follow an individual leader rather than to regard themselves as members of a party' which retarded 'the growth of healthy parliamentary convention, and so of stable government.'

An equal danger after 1949 proved, however, to be the weakness of the opposition groups and the emergence of what was later to be termed 'a one and one half party system.' The Foreign Office for all its many reservations over Yoshida had to concede that there was no viable alternative government in the making. It was for UKLIM a decidedly gloomy picture with which to end the occupation. The lack of an effective opposition, the problem of splintering parties and predictions that extremist groups were waiting off-stage combined to contrast sharply with SCAP's public hopes for the success of parliamentary democracy in Japan.

Beer, LW, 'The Present Constitutional System of Japan', in Beer, LW (ed), *Constitutional Systems in Late Twentieth Century Asia*, 1992, pp 175–82, University of Washington Press

The Establishment Process, 1945–47

During her period of ultranationalist militarism – especially between 1936 and 1945 – Japan inflicted great suffering upon many peoples in East and Southeast Asia, but also broke the back of European colonialism in Asia. At her surrender to the Allied Powers on 14 August 1945, Japan was a numb, defeated and devastated nation while the rest of the world rejoiced at the end of the Second World War. The humiliating shock of unprecedented defeat gave way to preoccupation with food and other survival needs, as rubble was cleared away, as millions of overseas Japanese military and colonial personnel came home to stay, as the leadership of war collapsed. In the aftermath, upheaval continued in China, Korea, and other Asian nations with the end of colonialism and the remaking of the political order. Japan's last war to date ended in 1945.

With help in the early days from the remarkably benevolent American victors, Japan has rebuilt in peace her political and economic structures and has risen to a high position among democratic leaders of the world. To this writer, it seems probable that Japan's constitutional revolution towards freedom, individual rights, and democratic government would not have occurred without the catalytic effect of reforms instigated by Americans in the Occupation apparatus. (In the quite separate area of economy, Japan's current leadership was attainable in good part because of partnership with the United States.) Historical origins are not in themselves important as a determinant of the legitimacy of a country's constitution and its pursuant systems of law and government. Thus, what is crucial is not that the 1947 'Constitution of Japan' (the formal title of the constitution; *Nihonkohu Kempo*) was to some degree a result of American insistence upon certain constitutional principles in 1945 and 1946, but that the document and its spirit have enjoyed free and overwhelming popular support, at its Occupation-period inception, upon the return to independence in 1952, and today. Perhaps no constitutional arrangement in Japanese history, and relatively few constitutional systems in the world today have been so strongly supported by the general citizenry of a country as the present constitution of Japan.

Constitutional principles such as popular sovereignty, self-government, the rule of law, limited and divided governmental power, and individual rights had not been preoccupations of Japan's ruling elite at any time before 1945. The revolutionary changes that occurred between the signing of the surrender documents on 2 September 1945, and the coming into effect of the Constitution of Japan on 3 May 1947, were momentous and the attendant processes historically unique.

The Law and Process of Establishment

The Allied Powers assumed indirect control of Japan's government and law in early September, 1945, with the arrival in Tokyo of General MacArthur, Supreme Commander of the Allied Powers (SCAP), and the establishment of his General Headquarters (GHQ) and other institutions of the Occupation period (2 September 1945–28 April 1952). As a defeated and occupied nation-state, Japan was subject to the Occupation's will under international law and the terms of surrender in the Potsdam Declaration (26 July 1945) accepted by Japan. SCAP ruled through the Japanese government leadership and apparatus rather than governing the nation directly as in Germany and Southern Korea.

Other nations, such as Australia and the United Kingdom, participated in Japan's occupation, but the United States' influence was dominant from start to finish.

Very few in the American apparatus were fluent in Japanese or knowledgeable about Japan's law and institutions. The United States relied heavily upon the competence of functionaries in the Japanese Government for implementation of its policies and used the Emperor to legitimize early Occupation law and a new constitution. While thousands were accused of ultranationalist taint and purged, in general, Japan's leaders, government personnel and general population cooperated in reforms with less SCAP coercion than might reasonably have been expected; there was no armed resistance. It is easy to underestimate the improbability of Occupation success, in part because there is no clear precedent or sequel elsewhere for Japan's constitutional transformation, the most impressive accomplishment of the Allied Occupation.

On 29 August 1945, General MacArthur received general instructions from President Harry S Truman, 'the United States Initial Post-Surrender Policy for Japan' [hereinafter, the Policy]. How to transform this Policy into Japanese law? Into law that the generality of Japanese would comprehend and Japan's government comply with? The Policy stated that Japan should be governed by SCAP directives, called 'SCAPIN.' SCAPIN were issued to the Imperial Japanese Government which converted them into indigenous law, by administrative action and statute, but often by means of 'imperial ordinances' (*chokurei*). Since the late 19th century, Japan's oligarchic leaders had at times found imperial ordinances promulgated in the name of the Emperor faster and politically more expedient than reliance on statutes passed by the Diet. Imperial Ordinance No 542 of 20 September 1945, provided the umbrella under which SCAPIN were implemented; it reads, in part:

> In accordance with the acceptance of the Potsdam Declaration, in order to carry out items based on the demands made by SCAP, the Government may, when especially necessary, take the necessary steps through ordinances, and may establish necessary penal regulations.

In all, some 520 such 'Potsdam Orders' (*Potsudamu meirei*) were issued by the Japanese government. Imperial ordinances as a form of law ceased to exist when the 1947 Constitution came into effect; and the name of existing imperial ordinances and subsequent orders was changed to 'Cabinet Orders' (*seirei*).

Japan's constitutional revolution – its fundamental shift in legally legitimized sociopolitical values and government institutions toward peaceable democracy – began with the issuance of many SCAPIN in September and October, 1945. In substance, the Potsdam Declaration required that Japan start down a new road of peace, freedom and popular sovereignty. The Policy called for a broad range of individual rights and freedoms, demilitarization, punishment of war criminals, and general democratization of government and economics. SCAPIN 1 of 2 September started the process of dismantling Japan's armed forces and defense industries, while other directives insisted on freedom of expression and other individual rights. Inevitably, as SCAP participated in the governance of Japan and pulled it away from chauvinistic authoritarianism, anti-democratic expression was censored; so was criticism of the Occupation and discussion of its role in constitutional change. But censorship and other restraints were exceptions in the new environment of radically increased freedom and respect for individual rights.

Initially, Japan's leaders balked at freedom and popular sovereignty. Illustrative of the revolutionary circumstances was the confrontation between SCAP and the Japanese

Government over the publication in newspapers of a photograph of the sovereign Emperor Hirohito standing alongside the more imposing figure of General MacArthur during his visit to GHQ on 27 September 1945. Strict *lese majeste* law was still in force; the demystification of the Emperor had not yet begun, though SCAPIN requiring press freedom had already been transmitted to the government. Japan attempted to ban the national newspapers carrying the photo. On the same day, 27 September, SCAPIN 66, on 'Further Steps Toward Freedom of Press and Speech,' forbade all but 'such restrictions as are specifically approved by the Supreme Commander' and ordered the repeal of parts of twelve contrary laws. Nevertheless, Home Minister Yamazaki continued to instruct Japanese newsmen to comply with the Peace Preservation Law which severely restricted discussion of the Emperor. On 4 October SCAPIN 93 responded to this test of SCAP resolve; the Higashikuni Cabinet resigned the next day.

SCAPIN 93 concerned the 'Removal of Restrictions on Political, Civil and Religious Liberties.' It ordered the Government to release and restore rights to all political prisoners, to abrogate all law contrary to freedom of expression, 'including unrestricted discussion of the Emperor, the Imperial Institution' and the government system, and to 'abolish all organizations and agencies' of a repressive nature (the Police Bureau, the Special Higher Police, the Protection and Surveillance Commission, and all 'secret police').

With American urging, the Japanese government then began serious consideration of constitutional change in October, 1945 in order to bring Japan's system into compliance with terms of the Potsdam Declaration and thus set the stage for withdrawal of the occupying forces. Prime Minister Kijuro Shidehara's Cabinet established the conservative 'Matsumoto Committee' (Constitutional Problem Investigation Committee; *Naikaku Kempo Mondai Chosa Iinkai*), under the distinguished scholar-official Joji Matsumoto. While the Committee worked, SCAP pushed ahead with reforms on many other fronts and awaited Japan's proposals for constitutional reform. For example, on 11 October SCAP called for Five Great Reforms: the liberation of women, the promotion of labor unions, the democratization of education, the end of repression, and more democratic economic structures. SCAPIN 448 of 15 December 1945, gave all religions equal legal footing while separating government from Emperor-centered Shinto, and banned dissemination of the ultranationalist ideology. For his part, Emperor Hirohito quite willingly announced on 1 January 1946, that he is an ordinary human being, not a quasi-god as modern propaganda had insisted for many decades. One of the most momentous official acts taken under SCAP prodding was the revision of the House of Representatives Election Law on 17 December 1945, to confer on women for the first time the right to vote and to lower the voting age for all from 25 to 20.

From December 1945 through the following February, political parties, private organizations and individuals came forth with proposals for constitutional change. On 1 February, without authorization, the *Mainichi Shinbun* newspaper published a draft constitution drawn up by the Matsumoto committee. Like the proposals of the ruling Liberal and Progressive Parties, the draft manifested little intent to substantially democratize the Meiji Constitution. To SCAP readers, it seemed to be at variance with the Potsdam Declaration, with the thrust of reforms since September, 1945, and with the reform guidelines provided by the State-War-Navy Coordinating Committee in Washington through a confidential January communication to SCAP, SWNCC 228. Particularly critical to subsequent events, under the Matsumoto Draft the sovereignty of the Emperor was retained and the traditional neglect of individual rights and freedoms continued.

At this point, General MacArthur and his staff despaired of the government's capacity to break cleanly with its authoritarian past and secretly drafted a new constitution. MacArthur assigned the task of writing a model constitution to the Government Section of GHQ, which was headed by his confidant, General Courtney Whitney. Whitney and his staff, not MacArthur, authored the 'MacArthur Draft' constitution. However, either on his own initiative or by approval of Whitney's ideas, the General set three requirements in the 'MacArthur Notes': (1) retain the Emperor system but make it subject to the will of the people; (2) include a renunciation of the nation's right of belligerency; and (3) eliminate all forms of feudalism and aristocracy.

On 3 February, Colonel Charles L Kades, Whitney's Deputy Chief in the Government Section, formed a Steering Committee with two other lawyers, Alfred R Hussey and Milo E Rowell, to set the ground rules and divide the work of drafting different sections among small staff groups. None of the drafters was a specialist in American constitutional law or knowledgeable about Japanese public law; but all were educated and able people. The Steering Committee was of central importance during the short drafting period of 4 February to 12 February.

> They, individually and collectively wrote many of the provisions of the draft and rewrote, revised, or vetoed most of the provisions drawn up by their colleagues on the legislative, executive, judiciary, civil rights, local government, and finance committees into which the staff were divided.

Kades, the most influential co-author of the constitution, reports that the drafting process 'was a group project with group thinking and group ideas'; it involved 21 Americans. On 13 February, General Whitney and the Steering Committee presented a completed draft constitution in English to Matsumoto and other Japanese leaders at Foreign Minister Shigeru Yoshida's residence. Matsumoto had assumed the purpose of the visit was to discuss the Matsumoto Draft, as part of a long deliberative process looking toward modest amendments. All were stunned when Whitney said that draft was 'wholly unacceptable to the Supreme Commander as a document of freedom and democracy,' and insisted upon quick preparation of a new Japanese draft based on SCAP's. Flabbergasted at this boldness—of which even Washington was unaware at the time—the Japanese government sought reconsideration in the days that followed, in vain. The Shidehara Cabinet then ordered the Bureau of Legislation to prepare a new draft constitution, in consultation with the Government Section. On wording and detail and regarding a few major issues, the Japanese influence at this and later stages was substantial. For example, SCAP accepted proposals that parliament have two Houses rather than one, and that the courts' power of judicial review not be limited to civil rights cases. Following intense, sometimes bitter discussion between SCAP and Japanese representatives from 10 am 4 March to 4 pm 5 March, Japan's new 'General Outline of Draft Revision of the Constitution' was released to the public along with a supportive imperial rescript. Then, as later, the constitution met with an enthusiastic welcome. While feigning uninvolvement in its drafting, SCAP publicly expressed satisfaction and exuded high praise for the document.

The amending processes of Article 73 of the Meiji Constitution and a related imperial ordinance on the Privy Council were then followed: the Emperor through his Cabinet presented the proposed change to the Privy Council, which approved the document on June 8 and sent it on to the House of Representatives for action. The House of

Representatives which debated the new constitution was elected on 10 April in the first post-war election. Eighty-one per cent of the victors were new to Diet office; women voted and held seats in parliament for the first time. On 24 August 1946, the lower House approved the Constitution of Japan by a vote of 421 to 8; on 6 October, the amended-Constitutional Revision Bill was passed overwhelmingly (298 to 2, according to Whitney) by the House of Peers; the House of Representatives passed the slightly amended bill without debate on 7 October; and on 29 October, the Privy Council in the presence of the Emperor also approved. With the issuance of the Emperor's edict of promulgation and the constitution, the ratification process ended. Six months later, on 3 May 1947, the Constitution of Japan came into effect and stands unchanged in 1991.

A fair number of Americans and Japanese made noteworthy contributions to the making of Japan's constitution in its final form; a few examples will be mentioned in relation to specific provisions. Hussey was the principal author of the Preamble, which eloquently advocates popular sovereignty, peace, and freedom. General Whitney wrote Article 97: 'The fundamental human rights by this constitution guaranteed to the people of Japan are fruits of the age-old struggle to be free; they ... are conferred upon this and future generations in trust, to be held for all time inviolate.' Rowell and Hussey were principal drafters of provisions establishing for the first time a separate judicial branch of government with power to determine the constitutionality of laws and other official acts. Beate Sirota, Pieter K Roest and Harry Emerson Wildes constituted the committee working on individual rights. Sirota deserves special credit for the inclusion of women's rights in the constitution (Arts 14 and 24) and the inception of a process of radical improvement in women's status in law and society. Sirota was a young woman of twenty-two who had grown up in Japan and was fluent in the language. Along with her future husband, Joseph Gordon, she also played a major role in reconciling Japanese and English texts (eg at the March 4 and 5 meetings), and in searching out reference materials on other nations' constitutions for the drafters.

Kades wrote Article 9, which renounces war and Japan's right of belligerency; Kades also seems to have initiated the idea of having such a provision. 'Shidehara's reported suggestion to MacArthur that the Japanese constitution renounce war may have stemmed indirectly from Kades' initiative. In any event, it is clear that key figures [notably Kades, MacArthur, Shidehara, and Whitney] were thinking along very similar lines.' McNelly argues that, since Japan had repeatedly violated the Kellog-Briand Pact renouncing war, one purpose of Article 9 was to blunt Allied and opposition Japanese demands that the militaristic imperial institution be abolished and the Emperor put on trial, as sovereign, for war crimes. Militarism was abolished instead, and sovereignty transferred to the people, with the Emperor's cooperation and approval.

Among distinguished Japanese drafters in the Bureau of Legislation were Tatsuo Sato and Toshio Irie. Sato later became head of the National Personnel Authority and Irie served longest of anyone ever on the Supreme Court of Japan, 1952–70. Learned constitutional lawyers, like Tatsukichi Minobe, were involved in government discussions but often not supportive of fundamental change in the Meiji Constitution. With respect to specific provisions, Socialists were responsible for amendments guaranteeing 'minimum standards of wholesome and cultured living' (Art 25) and worker rights (Arts 27 and 28). Kades and many of his colleagues shared these positions as quite congruent with New Deal ideas and with mainstream European constitutionalism. Although the role of the Far Eastern Commission was severely constrained, it was responsible for a few amendments during the ratification process, such as the requirement that the majority of Cabinet members be members of the Diet (Art. 68).

Before the constitution became law in 1947, the monumental task began of making, amending and abolishing laws to conform with its requirements. Provisions in the basic Codes had to be modified: the Civil Code (*Mimpo*), the Code of Civil Procedure (*Mimjisoshoho*), the Criminal Code (*Keiho*), the Code of Criminal Procedure (*Keijisoshoho*), and the Commercial Code (*Shoho*). These codes, under the constitution, enjoy almost quasi-constitutional status in the vast civil law world of which Japan had been a part since the late 19th century. Few American occupationnaires had any competence in this oldest and most widespread of the world's legal traditions. Thomas Blakemore from Oklahoma was the only trained specialist in Japanese law. Kades continued a major role. Fortunately, Alfred Oppler, a refugee judge from Germany, arrived in Tokyo on 23 February 1946, and presided over the Courts and Law Division of the Government Section:

> Oppler will long be remembered for his revision of the Japanese codes of law along democratic lines. It was he who brought about the sweeping reforms of the Civil, Criminal, and Procedural Codes and the enactment of the Court Organization Law, innovations that breathed life into the new constitution ...

As during the constitution ratification process, SCAP retained some veto power during the remaining years of the Occupation; but cooperative lawmaking characterized processes, with the Japanese Government assuming an ever larger responsibility for implementing the revolutionary constitution of Japan. Cold War and Korean War realities did occasion SCAP interventions at times; but more symbolic may be the effect of a 1947 Conversation between Oppler and Yoshio Suzuki, the Justice Minister, about individual rights. Oppler mentioned the new Civil Rights Section (now the Civil Rights Division) of the US Department of Justice; Suzuki 'enthusiastically adopted the idea and established such a bureau in his ministry.' The Civil Liberties Bureau has developed into an effective instrument for human rights education and protection with the help of its many thousands of carefully selected lay Civil Rights Commissioners (*Jinken Yogo Iin*; literally, human rights protectors). Like other laws and systems introduced under the Constitution of Japan during the Occupation period, this democratic institution evolved to fit Japanese preferences, needs and mores. Japan has been responsible for the great accomplishments of constitutional democracy, as well as its weaknesses, since 1952.

Kades, C, 'The American Role in Revising Japan's Imperial Constitution' (1989) 104 *Political Science Quarterly* 215–19, 227–28, 234–35, 241–45

Unlike the Constitution of the Empire of Japan, commonly called the Meiji Constitution after the Meiji emperor, the current Japanese constitution was not produced by an elite group of clan oligarchs and then octroyed or issued in 1889 by the emperor as a *fait accompli*. Neither was the current constitution produced by a learned constitutional commission or a national or constituent assembly convened as a result of a popular vote or otherwise selected for the purpose of drafting a constitution, submitting it to the electorate for ratification, with or without power to govern in the meantime, and then dissolving when and if the new constitution was approved by the electorate. On the contrary, the national legislature that adopted the current constitution consisted of one house chosen under the Meiji Constitution by direct popular vote and another house composed of nobles, peers, and persons appointed by the emperor and others elected by the biggest taxpayers. The legislature continued to sit with an equally obsolescent privy council for the primary purpose of enacting a series of vitally important statutes designed to conform the law codes of the land to the principles of the new fundamental law.

Men of letters, journalists, and one national commission of inquiry have concluded that the current constitution was imposed by the Americans upon the Japanese, and have condemned the constitutional process that was followed as coercive and undemocratic. For example, such a scholarly historian as Ray A Moore of Amherst College has written:

> In revising the constitution ... SCAP [Supreme Commander for the Allied Powers] committed flagrant violations of normal democratic procedure, imposed stringent controls on discussion and revision of the American draft, and intervened actively in the Japanese political process, all the while professing complete commitment to democratic principles. SCAP rejected Japanese efforts to rewrite their own constitution, ignored arguments that a new constitution, to be sound, should be based on achievements in democratic government since the Meiji period, and imposed radical ideas copied virtually verbatim from foreign constitutions that reflected personal concerns of their authors.

This article merely revisits the extraordinary process by which the current constitution came into being and in the light of that process examines briefly why it has continued to exist without formal change. Nothing herein is not already known, but the circumstances are viewed by the somewhat different and possibly biased perspective of one who shared in the process.

THE UNILATERAL MAKING OF THE MODEL FOR A CONSTITUTION

In mid-July 1945, the American, British, and Soviet leaders met for the last of their Second World War conferences in the Berlin suburb of Potsdam. It was President Harry Truman's first meeting with Marshal Joseph Stalin and Prime Minister Winston Churchill. Churchill departed during the conference for the British general election and did not return because of the defeat of his Conservative Party; his place was taken by the new Prime Minister Clement Attlee. On 21 July, Truman learned that the test of an atomic bomb on 16 July had not only been successful but that it was even more powerful than had been expected and that it would soon be ready for use. On 26 July, Truman and Attlee, with the concurrence of the absent Chiang Kai-Shek – but without that of Stalin, because the USSR had not yet entered the war against Japan – set forth their terms for the surrender of Japan in the awesome document known as the Potsdam Declaration.

Constitutional Reform as an Occupation Objective

The stated purpose of the Potsdam Declaration was to eliminate the authority and influence of the old order in Japan that had misled the Japanese people into a war of conquest, with a view to establishing a new order of peace, security, and justice. Accordingly, the declaration required the Japanese government to 'remove all obstacles to the revival and strengthening of democratic tendencies among the Japanese people' and to establish 'freedom of speech, of religion, and of thought, as well as respect for fundamental human rights.' The declaration also stated that after the objectives of the declaration had been accomplished 'and there has been established in accordance with the freely expressed will of the Japanese people a peacefully inclined and responsible government,' occupying forces of the Allies would be withdrawn.

On 29 August 1945, the US government announced the 'United States Initial Post-Surrender Policy for Japan,' a document approved by the president and drafted by the

State-War-Navy Coordinating Committee, an interdepartmental group engaged in planning postwar policies for occupied areas. That policy declared

> The ultimate objectives of the United States in regard to Japan, to which policies in the initial period must conform, are
>
> (a) To insure that Japan will not again become a menace to the United States or to the peace and security of the world.
>
> (b) To bring about the eventual establishment of a peaceful and responsible government
>
> [which]
>
> should conform as closely as may be to principles of democratic self-government but it is not the responsibility of the Allied Powers to impose upon Japan any form of government not supported by the freely expressed will of the people.

About the middle of January the Far Eastern Advisory Commission (FEAC) came to Tokyo. The commission, which had been organized in October 1945 under the auspices of the US State Department, consisted of representatives of ten of the eleven nations that had been at war with Japan; the USSR had declined to join. The FEAC was about to become the Far Eastern Commission (FEC), which had been created by the Moscow Agreement of 27 December 1945 between the foreign ministers of the United States, the United Kingdom, and the USSR, and was to have its headquarters in Washington. The FEC included the Soviet Union as well as the ten members of the FEAC and acted by majority vote with the US, the UK, the USSR, and China having the power to veto any action. The Moscow Agreement provided that the FEC would formulate 'policies, principles and standards in conformity with which the fulfillment by Japan of its obligations under the Terms of Surrender may be accomplished' and it was entrusted with power to review 'any directive issued to the Supreme Commander for the Allied Powers or any action taken by the Supreme Commander involving policy decisions' within its jurisdiction.

At a meeting in Tokyo on 30 January 1946 with the FEAC, General of the Army Douglas MacArthur, Supreme Commander for the Allied Powers (SCAP), stated that it was his hope that whatever might be done about constitutional reform in Japan should be done in such a way as to permit the Japanese to look upon the resulting document as a Japanese product. He felt that only in this way could the work be permanent. He stated that it was his belief and conviction that a constitution, no matter how good or well-written, forced upon the Japanese by bayonet, would last just as long as bayonets were present. He was certain that the moment force was withdrawn and the Japanese left to their own devices, they would get rid of that constitution. Thus, it is clear that MacArthur believed that he should not direct the specific constitutional reforms to be made, but that they should be initiated by the Japanese.

Nevertheless, MacArthur put a high priority on the revision of the Meiji Constitution. Less than six weeks after the signing of the Instrument of Surrender aboard the USS *Missouri* in Tokyo harbor, he initiated the process of constitutional reform. On 5 October 1945, the day after the issuance by SCAP of a civil liberties directive to the Japanese government, the cabinet under Prince Higashikuni as prime minister resigned. Immediately after Baron Kijuro Shidehara succeeded him as prime minister, MacArthur emphasized that reformation of the constitution was an essential prerequisite to compliance with the Potsdam Declaration. According to Theodore McNelly, professor of political science at the University of Maryland, MacArthur had earlier suggested on 4

October 1945 to Prince Fumimaro Konoe of the Higashikuni cabinet that he undertake constitutional reform. Commander Alfred R Hussey of SCAP's staff puts the date even earlier, saying that in September Prince Higashikuni was informed that MacArthur regarded revision of the Meiji Constitution as a 'matter of first importance.'

Unaware of either the approach to Higashikuni or to Konoe, I was informed of MacArthur's discussion with Shidehara, which became public on 11 October 1945, when MacArthur dispatched a 'Statement' to the Japanese government, the first paragraph of which said:

> In the achievement of the Potsdam Declaration, the traditional social order under which the Japanese people for centuries haw been subjugated will be corrected. This will unquestionably involve a liberalization of the constitution.

The statement then gave examples of what 'liberalization' meant. After saying that the Japanese people must be freed from 'all forms of control which seek to suppress freedom of thought, freedom of speech or freedom of religion, the statement called for the 'emancipation of the women of Japan through their enfranchisement,' the 'encouragement of the unionization of labor,' the 'opening of the schools to more liberal education,' the 'abolition of systems which through secret inquisition and abuse have held the people in constant fear,' the 'democratization of Japanese economic institutions to the end that monopolistic industrial controls be revised through the development of methods which tend to insure a wide distribution of income and ownership of the means of production and trade,' and the 'full employment in useful work of everyone.' ...

...

Sources of the Model for a Constitution

It should be emphasized that the Government Section did not draft the model constitution in one week from scratch; by no means was the draft a Pantagruel emerging full grown from a Gargantuan Government Section. Quite the contrary: Japanese sources were most useful. Used to good advantage were outlines of draft constitutions that had been published by the Progressive, Liberal, and Socialist Parties; and other draft revisions which had been prepared by private groups and individuals – such as that of the Constitutional Research Group headed by Iwasaburo Takano, Tsunego Baba, and Tatsuo Morito on which Rowell had written his 11 January memorandum and also the *Kempo Kondankai*, or Constitutional Discussion Group, headed by the venerable Yukio Ozaki, who had been elected to every House of Representatives from the first one convened in 1890. Although it has been said that the decision to introduce judicial review in the Constitution of 1946 'appears to be a fairly direct response to the pressures and counsel of the American military occupation officials,' not only Ozaki's Constitutional Discussion Group but also the Progressive Party proposed a specific constitutional statement vesting in a court the power of judicial review. The Constitutional Research Group and various lawyers' groups, as well as the Liberal and Socialist Parties, all supported the principle of an independent judiciary. In addition to the availability of various indigenous drafts, Lieutenant Esman and Beate Sirota separately collected from various libraries in Tokyo constitutions of about a dozen other countries.

Drawing on all these sources as well as their remembrance of state constitutions, the paradigm for a new constitution of Japan did not follow in the footsteps of the Founding Fathers of the US Constitution. Rather it beat a new path in the direction of a Japanese constitutional structure consistent with Japanese liberal traditions, which had persisted throughout the more than six decades that followed the founding of the *Kaishinto* or

Reform Party by Yukio Ozaki and his colleagues in 1881. Not only the Reform Party, but also the *Jiyuto* or Liberal Party founded in 1882, adhered to the principle that 'all men ought to be equal in respect of their rights' and drew inspiration from the American Declaration of Independence and the French Declaration of the Rights of Man and the Citizen. It is sometimes forgotten that the Japanese, though homogeneous in their physical characteristics, have heterogeneous ideas; and it was the Japanese intellectual successors to their democratically inclined leaders of the nineteenth century who contributed many of the concepts which under MacArthur's and Whitney's leadership became principles embodied in the new constitution. Not entirely a voluntary; enactment, the Constitution of 1946 was a product of Potsdam, prodding by MacArthur and Whitney, and pressures emanating from forward-looking Japanese political leaders, the press, and academicians; neither potential force nor covert coercion brought about the metamorphosis of the Government Section's model into the current constitution. After the initial phase of the drafting process described above, the revised constitution became the creation of a joint enterprise of Japanese and Americans working together under the inauspicious circumstances of a foreign occupation to establish a political and social system which could be the prelude to a treaty of peace. ...

...

The Language Gulf

In reviewing the 17 April Privy Council Bill, the Government Section noticed that, though the English translation remained almost the same as the 6 March Cabinet Outline, in some instances different Japanese words had been substituted for those agreed upon at the all day/all night/all day session of 4-5 March. Rizzo, Gordon, and I met with Sato and a few assistants. We pointed out the discrepancies, which Sato attributed to using colloquial Japanese and discarding archaic words, the use of which the press had criticized. Although we too favored using colloquial Japanese, the colloquial ideographs had connotations inconsistent with the concepts accepted at the 4-5 March meeting. For example, to express the 'advice and approval' required by Article 3 as a condition precedent for all 'acts of the emperor in matters of state,' it was manifest from the Japanese term that the Cabinet's function amounted to something less than an authorization for the emperor to act.

It was crucial that the emperor's role under the new constitution should be clear and unambiguous. Under the Meiji Constitution it had not been. Many Japanese constitutional lawyers, including Matsumoto and Sato, maintained that the emperor was powerless to act except by virtue of and pursuant to the advice of his ministers. Others maintained the emperor was an organ of government whose powers had been usurped by clan, oligarchic, and militaristic cliques. Apparently the Japanese government had not viewed him as an impotent figurehead. In its so-called qualified acceptance of the Potsdam Declaration on 10 August, rejected by implication the next day by the Allied reply, the Japanese had stated their readiness to accept the declaration 'upon the understanding that the said [Potsdam] declaration does not comprise any demand which prejudices the prerogatives of His Majesty as a Sovereign Ruler.' Any notion that the emperor retained residual sovereign power to rule would have vitiated the underlying purpose of constitutional revision and returned the process to Matsumoto's original proposals in February. Accordingly, it was agreed that the Privy Council would amend the Bill for Revision to use colloquial words not susceptible to equivocation. Nevertheless, new and other problems of language clarity arose during the debates in both the House of Representatives and the House of Peers. Those problems were resolved in a friendly atmosphere, even though a military occupation is by its nature coercive. It cannot be gainsaid that the ultimate choice of words and phrases was left to the Japanese, who may have well believed that receptivity would accelerate their regaining the independence for which they had to wait six more years.

After the Privy Council acted, the emperor on 20 June sent it to the Diet in accordance with his exclusive power under Article LXXIII of the Meiji Constitution to initiate amendments. Had it not been for Whitney's wide decision to omit from the 'model' at Matsumoto's request at the 22 February meeting the article on ratification, legal continuity of the new with the old constitution might have otherwise been breached. ...

...

IN THE WAKE OF THE PASSAGE OF THE CONSTITUTION

Once the basic principles of the model constitution were accepted by the Cabinet, MacArthur's policy in furthering constitutional revision could be accurately described as that of monitoring the Japanese enactment process to the degree necessary to assure that the American objective of fundamental constitutional reform was not subverted by intransigent imperialist zealots.

As Tetsu Katayama, later to be prime minister, told a plenary session of the House of Representatives on 26 August, the reason why the Socialist Party, whose votes in the House of Representatives were indispensable to the adoption of the constitution, endorsed the new constitution is because 'sovereign power is in the hands of the people.' It was also because of Article 9 renouncing war and arms which, Katayama continued, 'has by no means been given or dictated from outside but is an expression of a strong current of thought which has been running in the hearts of the Japanese people.'

More to the point perhaps is the testimony of Tatsuo Sato, who was present from the beginning to the end of the joint drafting and deliberative process. He wrote in his memoirs:

> They [GHQ staff] were very strict about the Preface [sic] and the chapter on the Emperor. They would make no concessions. Only a few minor wording changes were allowed. But they granted a great many of our points and objections about other parts of the draft ... unlike their attitude at the stage when we were preparing the government draft [based upon the GHQ draft] the GHQ applied hardly any direct pressure on the Diet's deliberations on the constitution. Indeed they seemed to have great respect for the Diet as the supreme representative of the people. With the revisions as well they needed SCAP's approval, but 80 or 90 percent of our changes were allowed to stand.

Even with respect to the preamble, mentioned by Sato as if it were untouchable, amendments were made in the House of Representatives. Preambles proposed in the House of Peers by Kenzo Takayanagi and Eiichi Makino would have been acceptable, but were never referred to the Government Section. It is worthy of note that each of those preambles began, as does the enacted preamble with the words, 'We, the Japanese people ... '

The House of Peers did actually make a significant alteration in the thrust of the preamble. Apparently not satisfied that the Ashida amendment to Article 9 codified the constitutional right of self-preservation, the peers tried to clarify any ambiguity in the text of Article 9 by inserting in the preamble to demonstrate their intention the clause: 'and we have determined to preserve our security and existence.'

Reluctance of the Diet to Review the Constitution

In the interim between the promulgation of the constitution and its effective date, MacArthur wrote the prime minister that 'between the first and second years of its effectivity, it [the constitution] should again be subject to their [the Japanese people's] formal review and that of the Japanese Diet' because 'the Allied Powers feel that there should be no future doubt that the constitution expresses both the free and considered will of the Japanese people.' When neither the Cabinet nor the Diet moved toward a review of the constitution, the Government Section called MacArthur's letter to the attention of Yoshio Suzuki, attorney general in the Katayama and Ashida Cabinets. Suzuki passed on the suggestion for such a study to the Speakers of the House of Representatives and of the House of Councillors.

The matter was dropped when Shigeru Yoshida became prime minister after the election in January 1949, and was not revived until the Commission on the Constitution was created in June 1956 by a Diet statute. Marlene Mayo of the University of Maryland has attributed 'the constitution's continuing popularity and staying power' to three reasons: 'First, it owes much to lessons learned during Japan's prior experience, both good and bad, under the Meiji Constitution of 1889. ... Second, the present document. benefited from the support of the Showa Emperor who in effect legitimated the process of revision. ...' Third, and crucial to 'the success of the document was a massive campaign of political education and popularization' undertaken by the American occupation authorities and Japanese leaders.

In his penetrating introduction to *Japan's Commission on the Constitution: The Final Report*, John M Maki of the University of Massachusetts concluded that the Commission on the constitution (according to Maki, after 131 plenary sessions, 325 committee and subcommittee sessions, 56 public hearings at which over 418 expert witnesses testified and 487 representatives of the public appeared, over a period of seven years) had created a new and special framework within which revision would have to be carried out and that the components of that framework preclude revision. Those components, which Maki describes with deep discernment, are: *first*, the commission unanimously affirmed the three basic principles of the constitution: – popular sovereignty, pacifism, and the guarantee of fundamental human rights; *second*, no single potentially crippling defect in the constitution has surfaced; *third*, the constitution is functioning effectively in practice as a fundamental law for Japanese society based on general principles of democracy; *fourth*, no matter what the outcome on the question of revision, one inevitable result would be a deep scarring of the body politic; and *fifth*, no revision, whether on a large scale or small scale, would be quick or easy.

There may be other reasons for the constitution's stability. The first is that the constitution accurately caught the spirit and aspirations of the Japanese people. The people were heartsick and weary with war; they were resentful of military adventures abroad and police repression and thought control at home; they longed for peace and liberty and governmental recognition of the sanctity of life and the dignity of the individual. The constitution struck a responsive chord and answered those yearnings with its renunciation of war, with its declaration of both political and economic rights of both men and women (as well as boys and girls), with its establishment of an independent judiciary to safeguard those rights, and with its proclamation that the people are sovereign. Although the people continued to respect the emperor, their respect ceased to be rigid subservience to a sacred sovereign.

The second is that the constitution contained provisions aimed at the liberation not only of individuals but also of congeries of individuals, such as women, labor unions, local governmental entities with their limited home rule powers, the academic community, the press and other information media, and the previously underprivileged. Because any movement to amend the constitution in any one respect risks opening the door to amendments in other respects, a consensus seems to have developed among all groups that this overall risk outweighs any specific advantage from any particular amendment.

The third is that without any formal constitutional amendment there has been a 'gap between the constitutional law-in-books and the constitutional law-inaction.' The constitution enjoins equality of treatment for 'All of the people' in Article 14 and for both of 'the sexes' in Article 24. Although after over 40 years the gap may have narrowed (but has by no means closed) with respect to the inequality of women with men, unequal treatment of others by both men and women continues in Japan. Lawrence W. Beer of Lafayette College has pointed out the discrimination with respect to various classes, including (among others):

> the *dowa* or *burakumin* ... ethnic Japanese descended from traditional outcasts ... ethnic Koreans in Japan as a result of Japan's prewar possession of the Korean peninsula ... Chinese ... Okinawans ... who returned to citizenship with the 1972 reversion of the United States to Japan; a small proto-caucasian group, the Ainu of Hokkaido ...

Another such gap relates to the electoral system. Disparities in population of election districts in Japan debase the weight of electors' votes in such a way that a representative from one district often represents several times as many voters as a representative from another district. The Supreme Court of Japan recognizes that the election law contravenes constitutional provisions that provide for equality under the law (Article 14), guarantee universal adult suffrage (Article 15), and prohibit discrimination against membership in the Diet and their electors (Article 44). Although the Diet has taken some remedial action, its reluctance to enact more drastic electoral reform, which would equalize the weight of all votes, calls to mind how long it has taken the United States to rid itself of the 'rotten apportionment' statutes of some state legislatures (reminiscent of the 'rotten boroughs' of England) which contract the value of some votes and expand that of others.

The constitution's form of parliamentary government has also been modified without a formal amendment to conform to parliamentary practice in western democracies, such as England and France. When Prime Minister Yoshida in 1952 secured from the emperor a rescript to dissolve the House of Representatives without the passage of a non-confidence resolution or the rejection of a confidence resolution – as Article 69 provides – he established a precedent effectively expanding the power of the Cabinet vis-à-vis the Diet.

II CONSTITUTIONAL REVISION

Maki, JM, *Japan's Commission on the Constitution. The Final Report*, 1980, pp 372–73, 374–77, 378–81, 382–88, University of Washington Press

Views on the necessity for constitutional revision fall into two broad groups: those supporting it and those opposing it. The revisionist opinion was in the majority, and the antirevisionist opinion in the minority. This classification of opinions is based on the conclusions held by each commissioner. The revisionists were not in agreement on all points and the same was true of antirevisionists. In both groups there were numerous differences both in basic thinking and in reasons offered for and against revision; and on certain problems both groups shared common opinions. Even where there was agreement on the necessity for revision, there were differences on whether it should be broad, covering many sections, or narrow, limited to only one. However, the specific content of views in favor of revision (the majority) and views opposed to revision cannot be classified with absolute clarity and simplicity into two opposing groups on all points.

GENERAL TRENDS IN THE OPPOSING VIEWS

As it is used here, 'revision' refers to the general alteration of the express language of the preamble and all chapters of the constitution. On the whole, the two views on revision differed simply on whether it is necessary to undertake such a modification of both the text and the form of the constitution. The view holding it to be necessary supported revision as here defined, while the opposing view, not infrequent in the commission, argued that the objective of revision could be achieved by means of the interpretation and application of the constitution as it stands. Some commissioners, while opposing the view that interpretation and application would be sufficient, were also against general revision but in actual fact agreed with the demands of the revisionists on specific constitutional points. However, in this regard, 'revision' as here used must be regarded as a general revision of the text, as pointed out above. However, this results in a confusion in the distinction between the two basic views, because some of those opposing general revision (and thus to be classified as antirevisionist) also supported amendment of certain specific points (and thus to be regarded as revisionist). Although the revisionist view was in the majority, it was also not uniform; it can be split into many groupings on a variety of grounds. ...

...

REASONS FOR THE OPPOSING VIEWS ON REVISION

Out of what did the confrontation of views on the necessity for revision arise? The sources of difference among the members of the commission lay in their basic thinking in relation to the three fundamental problems that the commission confronted in its reexamination of the constitution, namely: (1) its ideal form; (2) the evaluation of the process of enactment; and (3) the basic attitudes toward its application and interpretation.

On the ideal form of the Constitution of Japan it was evident that the commissioners were all agreed that it should be freely enacted by the Japanese people, in accord with Japan's history and tradition as well as the principle of universal human rights, and realistic, effective, and in harmony with world trends. But what separated the revisionist view from the antirevisionist view was not necessarily disagreement over the concrete content of such words and phrases as 'independent,' 'principle of universal human rights,' 'Japan's history and tradition,' 'world trends,' and 'realistic and effective'; rather, it was based on differing views of possible defects and shortcomings in Japan's constitution as measured against the ideal form described above. The majority revisionist view arose from the feeling that there are such shortcomings and defects, and the opposing view that there are not. But not all those who recognized such shortcomings and defects could be classified as revisionists for some believed that they could be dealt with through legislation, court decisions, and the operation of government itself without constitutional revision.

Among the revisionists the assertion was frequently made that the texts of all constitutions should precisely and adequately set forth both their ideals and the means to achieve them in an unmistakable fashion and that the present constitution is defective in this regard. In opposition, it was maintained that in general the ideals of a constitution cannot be realized simply by means of textual provisions, but rather the point of emphasis should be on what was termed a 'living constitution' and thus the discussion of the ideal form of the constitution should avoid excessive concentration on textual provisions. This latter view further argued that it is probable that the history and tradition of Japan would naturally be woven into such a living constitution and, equally importantly, the ideals of the present constitution would actually be realized if it really is a living constitution and that revision is not needed.

It was the majority opinion in the commission that the present constitution was not enacted on the basis of the freely expressed will of the Japanese people. This led directly in many cases to the view that revision is necessary for this reason as well as because of problems relating to the content of the constitution. On the other hand, the minority view against revision stemmed in part from the point that the absence of the popular will in the process of enactment was not necessarily improper under the circumstances at the time. A special point bearing on the timing of revision among those opposing revision was that those of the generation which bears both direct and indirect responsibility for the lost war under the old constitution are particularly unsuited to discuss revision of the present constitution. Therefore, it was argued, the decision on the need for revision should be left to the coming generation.

In regard to the evaluation of the interpretation and application of the present constitution, it was the majority view in the commission that revision is needed, because there are necessary limitations on the application and interpretation of all constitutions, and because the stage has been reached where it is no longer possible to deal with the shortcomings and defects of the present constitution by means of application and interpretation alone. The opposition view that revision is not needed held that even though there are limitations on the application and interpretation of all constitutions, at the same time their scope should be recognized as being as broad as possible and that, consequently, the variety of problems apparent in the present constitution can be solved through elastic interpretation and application.

There was also the revisionist view in this connection that as a matter of both legal methodology and constitutional process the texts of all constitutions in theory should be precisely set forth so that there is no room for doubts in interpretation. Consequently, since the wording of the present constitution has led to numerous disputes in both interpretation and academic theory, and since this is an obvious defect, revision is necessary in order to close off the areas producing such disputes as much as possible.

In opposition it was argued that the thinking is improper which holds that revision is necessary in order to unify both academic theory and interpretation and to eliminate disputes on the technical legal grounds that constitutional processes must be strictly honored. All constitutions no matter how perfectly drafted in theory are nothing more than blueprints or plans, and consequently the function of application and interpretation is to make it possible for the documents to operate as 'living constitutions.' It was further argued that when a constitution's actual operation is offered as a reason for the need for revision, that view is improper which holds that points which can be decided by means of interpretation, legislation, and court decision should be dealt with by means of constitutional revision. Behind the confrontation between these two views there is a difference in fundamental thinking in regard to constitutions, namely, whether they should be regarded as static or dynamic instruments.

Here too the opposition of views was not a simple and well-defined one. The source of this difficulty was that the conflict was not produced over general and abstract questions as might be gathered from the above account, but over concrete problems of the application and interpretation of specific constitutional provisions. For example, some revisionists held that certain problems could be dealt with by application and interpretation and thus did not require revision.

There were also fundamental differences in thinking on the problem of the timing of revision. For example, the attitude was expressed that even as of today it cannot be said that the people's understanding and awareness of the constitution have been sufficiently nurtured and firmly established, and as a result to undertake revision under such conditions would have to be regarded as not necessarily being based on the true will of the people. Thus, a decision on revision should be left to the future when the development and the establishment of the people's understanding and consciousness of the constitution can be counted on.

On the question of timing it was also argued that constitutional revision should be decided on purely theoretical grounds, removed from political considerations such as the possibility of foreign and domestic consequences of an attempt at revision. Some felt that such consequences, though to be expected, should not be feared. But some revisionists held what was called the 'cautious revision opinion,' namely, that the time and method of revision should be treated with care because of the possible foreign and domestic consequences, thus ending in a position close to that of those who held that revision is unnecessary.

In general, antirevisionist commissioners opposed each specific argument of the revisionists, primarily on the grounds that they approved of the actual state of the application of the constitution, that is to say, the administrative actions, the court decisions, and the legislation in existence. As an example, in regard to the various provisions of Chapter 3 relating to the rights and duties of the people, they opposed the revisionist claim that revision is necessary in order to make clear certain limitations on fundamental human rights. At the same time they approved existing legislation limiting fundamental human rights in the name of the public welfare as being constitutionally justified.

Thus, many antirevisionist commissioners approved the actual state of the functioning of the present constitution, since the actions already undertaken by the Diet, the cabinet, and the courts are permissible within the limits of application and interpretation of the constitution as it stands. This view differs from the antirevisionist position expressed outside the commission that attacks some existing legislation and other acts involving the application of the constitution as being unconstitutional. Also some commissioners holding the above view did not clearly express an opinion as to whether, for example, the Self-Defense Forces Law should be recognized as falling within the limits of the application and interpretation of the present constitution. …

…

Problems Relating to Basic Thinking on the Constitution

EVALUATION OF THE PROCESS OF ENACTMENT OF THE PRESENT CONSTITUTION. One majority view on the evaluation of the process of enactment of the present constitution can be summarized as follows. The present constitution was not enacted on the basis of the freely expressed will of the Japanese people; the enactment was an expression of Allied occupation policy for Japan; General Headquarters presented to the Japanese government a draft which was in reality an order; the draft of the Japanese government's version was based on GHQ's and the revisions made in the Diet were all under the direction and supervision of GHQ. In addition, even in those situations where the wishes of the Japanese side were adopted, it happened only to the extent that they were in agreement with occupation policy, that is to say, within the limits of GHQ's basic policy.

A second view was that the present constitution should be revised if only because the process of enactment prevented the free expression of the will of the Japanese people. Also, because there are a number of defects and shortcomings in its content, revision is necessary from the standpoint of both content and enactment.

The minority view simply held that the opinion that the process of enactment of the present constitution was not based on the directly expressed will of the Japanese people is incorrect. In reality the enactment was carried out as a responsibility based on the acceptance of the Potsdam Declaration which resulted from the lost war. Although it is admitted that the constitution was enacted under the occupation and within the ambit of occupation policy and that the wishes of the Japanese side were accepted only to the extent that they were in agreement with the basic policy of GHQ, both the international and domestic situations at the time were complicated, and the conclusion should not be reached that the enactment took place only under compulsion from GHQ or the Allied powers. In addition, it should be accepted as a fact that the will of the Japanese government and people was reflected in the constitution in no small degree. This minority view therefore held that the necessity for the revision of the constitution should be decided not on the basis of the process of enactment, but on the basis of its content and actual functioning.

However, there were several special variations on the majority view. One held that it cannot be said that the constitution was necessarily not enacted on the basis of the freely expressed will of the people. At the time of enactment the constitution was not far removed from the will of the people and in this regard it is necessary to evaluate both the free efforts and the desires of the Japanese people. Another view held that the various elements in the process of enactment were extremely complicated and it is impossible to make a simple and incisive judgment as to whether it was or was not based on the free will of the people.

In addition, there was a special minority opinion which held that revision of the constitution is unnecessary because of the welcome nature of its content, even though it be admitted that it cannot be termed as having been enacted on the basis of the freely expressed will of the people.

THE IDEAL CONSTITUTION FOR JAPAN. Japan's constitution, in the majority view, should be one which has been freely enacted by the Japanese people; is in accord with the history, tradition, individuality, and national character of Japan as well as the universal principle of fundamental human rights; and is realistic, effective, and in harmony with world trends. In addition, all constitutions should provide, both adequately and precisely enough to leave no room for doubt, for an approach to their ideals and the realization thereof. If the present constitution is viewed from the above standpoint, the following conclusions must be reached: its rationale does not accord with the ideal of what Japan's constitution should be; it is visionary in nature and is not only lacking in sufficient indications of the means for its realization, but its processes are both illogical and ambiguous; and there are many doubtful points of interpretation.

The minority view accepted the above three characteristics of an ideal constitution for Japan. However, it held that the present constitution does not fall so far short of the ideal that there are shortcomings and defects that absolutely must be revised now. Another minority view held that it is impossible to arrive at agreement on the definition of such phrases as 'principle of universal human rights,' 'Japanese history and tradition,' 'world trends,' and 'realistic and effective,' as set forth by the revisionists in their demands for the revision of the preamble and various chapters of the constitution. A third view was that emphasis should not be placed on how the ideal of a constitution should be embodied in the instrument but rather on the 'living constitution' and the problem of what legislation and social conditions can give birth to constitutional ideals. Thus, the thinking of the revisionists who believe it necessary to revise the constitution completely in order to make it an ideal one is not correct. The present constitution should be considered on the basis of whether in actual fact its operation has created difficulties which must somehow be eliminated.

Some revisionists did not accept the views on the ideal constitution as set forth in the majority view above. One held that a constitution should not be thought of as simply a written document and it should not be discussed only in light of whether or not what are called its ideals have or have not been written into it. Another view was that although the text of the constitution should naturally be the foundation, the accumulation of authoritative interpretations, legislation, judicial precedent, and its actual application form a living constitutional order, resulting in a situation where it is not absolutely necessary that there be strict adherence to the provisions of the text of the constitution. Another view asserted that the necessity for a uniquely Japanese constitution should not be emphasized to the point where it might lead to a diminishing of the principle of universal human rights, thus leading to a collapse into the so-called reverse course away from democracy; rather, that universal principles should be used as to add flavor to the special Japanese characteristics and individuality in the constitution.

THE APPLICATION AND INTERPRETATION OF THE PRESENT CONSTITUTION. A majority view held that in the application and interpretation of all written constitutions there are specific limits and to recognize too broadly the scope of such application and interpretation will lead to the negation of the constitution. A second view was that the present constitution has a number of shortcomings which have already gone beyond the point where they can be dealt with by interpretation and application; therefore, elimination of these shortcomings through revision is necessary

In opposition, the minority held that although there are various problems relating to the present constitution, they should be handled through its application and interpretation and since this is already being done by legislation, court precedents, and administrative action there is no reason for revision. It was also argued that since there should be elastic interpretation of all constitutions, the scope of both application and interpretation should be recognized as being as broad as possible. Another view was that what are cited as evils in the present constitution should not be regarded as having necessarily been produced by its imperfections and shortcomings and in addition it does not necessarily follow that these evils will be immediately remedied by revision.

A special view among those who held that the application and interpretation of the present constitution indicate no necessity for revision was that the special nature of the present constitution is in its style which is not in accord with the classical constitutional methodology which sets great store on logical rigidity. Therefore, interpretation should be approached flexibly in accord with that special character.

Within the majority view there was also the opinion that held that contradictions, lack of clarity, and imperfections in the constitution can be handled to a suitable degree by means of application and interpretation, especially by means of Supreme Court decisions, although there are natural limitations on interpretations of this kind. However, it should be recognized that the three branches of the government do possess certain special authority in respect to constitutional interpretation and therefore it is impossible to agree with the revisionist view that calls for a broad revision of the text in order to eliminate doubts in interpretation by means of logical exactitude. But if through actual observation it is determined that there are irregular points, then it is appropriate to eliminate them by revision.

Another view in this category was that what can be taken care of under the actual application of the constitution should be excluded from the scope of revision, while at the same time the written constitution should not be allowed to become a dead letter through the accumulation of interpretations in judicial precedents, administrative practice, and Diet legislation. ...

...

THE EMPEROR. Among the revisionists a majority view held that the ideal form of the emperor system must be in accord with popular sovereignty and, therefore, the emperor system as established in the present constitution on the basis of popular sovereignty must be preserved. Also it was asserted that the position of the emperor as a 'Symbol' under the present constitution is appropriate, but it is also necessary to set forth his position clearly as 'the head of state' in terms of his functions. Therefore, the provisions relating to the emperor's role in affairs of state should be completed by a reference to his role in foreign relations where, as 'head of state,' he would represent the state in general matters in its foreign relations.

The minority antirevisionist view was in agreement with the first view regarding the ideal emperor system indicated above. However, the fear was expressed that if the emperor did enjoy the functions and the position of a formal head of state there might be the possibility of a reversion to the emperor system as it was under the old constitution and that should not be. It was further pointed out that in his capacity as 'symbol' the emperor has in actual fact represented the people of Japan in their external relations and that consequently the idea that he must be explicitly termed the 'head of state' through constitutional revision is unacceptable.

However, there were a number of special opinions relating to the position of the emperor which differed from the majority view of the revisionists. One view held that the emperor system provides the spiritual foundation of the nation, thereby giving fruit to the unity of the people. The present constitution has adopted the principle of popular sovereignty and has made the emperor a mere 'symbol,' denying his legal authority as the center of the unity of the people of Japan. Therefore, not only should the phrase 'popular sovereignty' be eliminated, but the emperor should be placed in a position of legal authority arising from the unity of the people and should be provided with a mediating function permitting him to resolve possible conflicts among the organs of state.

It was also argued that popular sovereignty by its very nature is incompatible with the emperor system and that Japan's democracy must be a democracy under a sovereign emperor. Therefore, it is necessary to change the idea, as adopted by the present constitution, of an emperor system based on the sovereignty of the people.

Another view held that it is acceptable to retain the emperor's position as a symbol, but both his domestic and foreign functions must be broadened to make clear that he is actually the head of state. Others held both that his foreign and domestic functions should be broadened and that he should explicitly be made the head of state. Another argument was that although it is acceptable to retain the emperor as a symbol, his functions in affairs of state should be further reduced while he is given a more active role in nonpolitical cultural and social affairs. A final view was that no term such as symbol or head of state should be applied to the emperor, and his functions in national affairs should be reduced even more than are his present acts in matters of state.

THE RENUNCIATION OF WAR. Naturally, there was a wide variety of opinions regarding the possible revision of Article 9. They are summarized below.

The views approving the revision of Article 9 were as follows:

1. The ideal of pacifism must be supported as a matter of course and it absolutely must be preserved.
2. As an ideal, pacifism in itself is proper, but Article 9, particularly the nonmaintenance of war potential, is unrealistic, idealistic, and visionary at the present stage both of international politics and of the structure of international peace.
3. Japan's self-defense structure today must be based on the concept of the right of self-defense possessed by all independent countries.
4. Article 9 raises difficulties in respect to Japan's self-defense. That is to say, because of doubts about the interpretation of Article 9, certain problems and abuses have developed.
5. It is necessary to revise Article 9 and to clarify the issue of the maintenance of a self-defense army both in terms of national defense itself and in terms of cooperation with international peace-keeping organizations, particularly the United Nations and other systems of collective security. Civilian supremacy must be maintained as well as democratic control over the self-defense army. If such a revision is carried out, it will be possible to unity national opinion in respect to Japan's defense and basic policy in foreign affairs.

Special opinions favoring revision of Article 9 were as follows:

1. It is argued that the Self-Defense Forces are not unconstitutional but they must be regarded as clearly being so. Consequently, Article 9 must be amended to make the SDF constitutional.
2. Since constitutional provisions should not go beyond statements of general principle, there should be only a provision permitting the maintenance of an army for self-defense, and such matters as its organization and functions and the system of civilian control should be provided for only by law.
3. Since the ideals of Article 9 must be highly valued, that article should be maintained even today just as it is. Because it is difficult today to realize those ideals, necessary concrete measures must be devised to guarantee Japan's

security. Accordingly, while Article 9 should be continued unchanged, another part should be added to it relating to 'measures to guarantee the security of the nation,' thus providing a constitutional basis for the existing defense structure.

Views holding revision of Article 9 to be unnecessary were as follows:

1. The ideal of pacifism as set forth in the present constitution must, of course, be preserved. In addition, the defense of Japan while providing for the national security must be directed toward the ideal of pacifism and at the same time must contribute to both national security and to world peace by participation in systems of collective self-defense such as the United Nations and others.
2. Under Article 9 as it presently exists, the defense system already adopted, including the Self-Defense Forces, participation in the United Nations, and the Japanese-American security treaty, is not unconstitutional.
3. Article 9, particularly its second paragraph, should not be regarded as unrealistic, visionary, and idealistic, but the principle of the renunciation of war potential should be regarded as possessing a new and realistic meaning, particularly in view of the movement today toward the achievement of complete disarmament.
4. Today the concept of the right of self-defense residing in individual nations is undergoing change, and for one country to offer it as the reason for its defense possesses the danger of harm to the general achievement of peace.
5. Even under the present Article 9, a defense structure has already been created without being confronted with insurmountable obstacles.
6. It cannot be said that through a revision of Article 9 a unification of national policy on defense and the defense structure will be realized. On the other hand, the undesirable effects, both foreign and domestic, that will accompany attempts at such revision must be taken into account.

A special opinion on the renunciation of war was also given. It is possible to interpret Article 9 as being a political declaration or the statement of a constitutional standard setting forth an ideal impossible of immediate realization at the present stage of international society. Under this view it has still been possible to maintain a self-defense army, notwithstanding the wording of the second paragraph of Article 9. Even though the establishment of a self-defense army and other matters cannot be approved under a strict interpretation of Article 9, revision should not for that reason be considered necessary. In other words, the problem of our national defense is not a constitutional one; it must be debated as one of national policy.

THE RIGHTS AND DUTIES OF THE PEOPLE. Some who favored the revision of Chapter 3 argued that it is prejudiced in favor of the rights and freedoms of the people and against their duties and responsibilities, stating that therein the evil of making light of the social order and the welfare of all the people is strikingly made manifest. Also the thinking favoring freedom runs counter to the principles of the contemporary welfare state, which stands on the concept of social solidarity.

Another view was that the concept of 'the public welfare' which is set forth in the present constitution as a limitation on the fundamental human rights of the people is a vague one. On the one hand, there is the fear that fundamental human rights might be improperly limited by law in the name of the public welfare; and on the other hand, proper laws establishing limitations on fundamental human rights under the public welfare doctrine might be held to be unconstitutional, thus leading to possible abuses of those rights. Therefore, a provision should be added clarifying the degree to which fundamental human rights may be limited.

It was also argued that the provisions relating to rights and duties should be supplemented and fully completed in order to bring them into accord with the principles of the contemporary welfare state. Expanding on this view was another which held that since the present title of Chapter 3 is based on the old concepts of 'rights and duties' it should be changed to 'The Welfare and Obligations of the People' in order more clearly to indicate the new concepts of the contemporary welfare state.

Among those who felt there is no necessity to revise Chapter 3 were some who argued that any problem arising out of the possible conflict between fundamental human rights and the public welfare or out of the development of the concepts of the welfare state can be taken care of by the application and interpretation of the constitution and should consequently be left to legislation and court precedents.

It was also argued that the present constitution should not be regarded as being behind the times because it is not directly in accord with the principles of the contemporary welfare state, the requirements of which can be met under the constitution as it stands. It was further declared that what is asserted to be a basic principle of the welfare state, namely, that the responsibility for the guarantee in actual fact of the rights and freedoms of the people is placed on the state, has already been adopted in Article 25 of the present constitution. Thus, a preferable course of action is to emphasize Article 25 rather than to strengthen limitations on the rights and freedoms of the people in the name of the principles of the contemporary welfare state.

THE NATIONAL DIET. The majority of commissioners, even those who believed that the provisions relating to the National Diet should be revised, also held that such basic principles as popular sovereignty, the representative system, the separation of powers, and the parliamentary cabinet system should be preserved. However, it was also asserted that the provision of Article 41 which states that 'the National Diet is the highest organ of state power' runs counter both to the principle of separation of powers and the present trend toward the strengthening and stabilization of the executive branch. In addition, this provision gives the impression of the absolute omnipotence of the Diet, thereby leading to possible abuse of power to the legislative branch. For these reasons this provision should be changed.

In addition, it was argued that although the bicameral system should be preserved, it is necessary to change the structure of the House of Councilors by some means such as the addition of nonelected members in order to differentiate it in character from the House of Representatives.

Among the opinions favoring revision of the provisions relating to the Diet was the special opinion that the present parliamentary cabinet system should be abolished and replaced by the system of an elective prime minister. In regard to the structure of the Diet, another view was that it will be impossible to preserve a difference in character between the two houses if both are to be composed of popularly elected members. Therefore, a start should be made toward a unicameral system. It was also asserted that perhaps the House of Representatives should be organized under the party system while the House of Councilors should be made nonpartisan, with the latter undergoing a broad change in both structure and functions. This same view also advocated the granting of special and exclusive powers to the House of Councilors relating to important matters of state requiring particular impartiality.

Some of those believing revision of the Diet provisions to be unnecessary held that the Diet should continue to be 'the highest organ of state power.' This view was based on the attitude that the present constitution recognizes the separation of powers and checks and balances and thus, viewing the constitution as a whole, there is no contradiction between Article 41 and other provisions such as those relating to judicial review. It was also pointed out that the 'highest organ of state power' provision eliminates the subordinate position of the Imperial Diet under the Meiji Constitution.

It was also held that although Article 41 gives rise to the impression of the absolute omnipotence of the Diet and thus may lead to such evils as the abuse of power, those evils arise from problems of the political parties and the attitudes of Diet members; this provision is not the cause. The argument was also put forth that the bicameral system should be preserved. However, the achievement of the goal of giving the House of Councilors a character different from that of the House of Representatives can be realized through a revision of the Election Law while preserving the elective nature of the upper house.

THE CABINET. The majority of those supporting revision of the cabinet provisions felt that the parliamentary cabinet system must be preserved and the system of an elective prime minister must be rejected. However, to preserve the parliamentary cabinet system it is necessary to correct the excessively subordinate position of the cabinet in relation to the Diet, and to strengthen its authority in order to strive for a stabilization of its position, while revising the 'highest organ of state power' provision.

Of course, the view supporting the system of an elective prime minister included the idea of developing a powerful executive branch based on a foundation of popular support.

Those holding revision of the cabinet provisions to be unnecessary argued that the present system should be continued without changing the position of the Diet as the highest organ of state power, and without strengthening the authority of the cabinet (and thus weakening the Diet). Likewise, the system of an elective prime minister should not be considered because Japan is lacking in the conditions under which the election of the prime minister should be carried out, and accordingly the system would not only be ineffective in eliminating problems of Japanese politics, but also would be dangerous.

THE JUDICIARY. Most of those supporting revision in the judiciary asserted that the basic principle adopted in the present constitution of broadening and strengthening the judicial power must be preserved. It was also argued that the present system of judicial review should not be changed; that a constitutional court should not be established; and that the Supreme Court should not be given the character of a constitutional court. This group concentrated on the method of appointment of Supreme Court justices and the revision of the system of popular review of their appointment and dismissal. The argument was that the present systems of appointment and popular review are not adequate for preventing the intervention of political and party considerations. Therefore, a consultative commission on appointments should be established and the system of popular review of Supreme Court justices should be abolished. The emphasis in this view was on the necessity for the selection of well-qualified justices for the Supreme Court.

However, among those favoring revision of the provisions relating to the judiciary the following special opinions were expressed. Military and administrative courts, as special tribunals lying outside the system of regular judicial courts, should be established. A constitutional court should be created or the Supreme Court given the character of a constitutional court. The system of judicial review of laws should be abolished. Abstract judicial review of laws should be carried out by the National Diet itself as a part of the legislative process and to that end a committee for the review of constitutional problems should be set up in the Diet.

Those holding revision of the judiciary provisions to be unnecessary naturally supported the basic constitutional approach of broadening and strengthening the judicial power. However, it was also felt that there is no need to strengthen the system of judicial review beyond what it is at present. The view was also expressed that a consultative commission on Supreme Court appointments could be established by law without constitutional revision. The system of popular review of Supreme Court justices was also supported as being an element of the ideal form of judicial power as based on the principle of popular sovereignty and also as a means to insure a concurrence between the Court and public opinion.

Sato, L, 'Revisionism During the Forty Years of the Constitution of Japan' (1990) 53, No 1 *Law and Contemporary Problems* 98–103

FOUR PERIODS OF THE DEVELOPMENT OF REVISIONISM

A. The 1950s

The Korean War broke out in June 1950. As that war escalated, peace negotiations between the Allied Powers and Japan progressed. In October 1951, both the peace treaty and the Japan-US security treaty were concluded. At the same time, Japan was establishing its defense power under Article 9 of the constitution, which prohibited the maintenance of war powers. In July 1952, the Allied Occupation came to an end. Just prior to the end of the Occupation, the movement to revise the so-called 'imposed Constitution under Occupation' began.

The revisionists advocated the amendment of Article 9, which provides for the renunciation of war and nonmaintenance of war powers, and also sought constitutional provisions establishing a symbolic emperor system and the unrestricted protection of fundamental rights and freedoms of the people. In October and November 1955, the two factions within the Socialist Party were reintegrated and the two conservative parties organized a new LDP. The point of confrontation between these two new parties was the issue of constitutional revisionism.

The Hatoyama Cabinet had declared in 1954 that one of its fundamental policies was the realization of the overall constitutional amendment. However, the revisionist policy of the Hatoyama Cabinet did not succeed. In both the general election for the House of Representatives in February 1955 and the ordinary election for the House of Councillors in July 1956, the governing party failed to obtain the two-thirds voting majority necessary for a constitutional amendment. The debates in these years marked the highest peak in the development of revisionism. After that time, the debate on this issue gradually subsided and disappeared – at least from the surface of politics in Japan.

B. The 1960s

This period saw the height of activity of the Commission on the Constitution. This Commission was established by law in 1957 as a governmental body whose purpose was to investigate constitutional problems. The Socialist Party was against its creation and refused to participate in the Commission. The original intent of the Commission's promoters was to prepare a draft amendment of the constitution. However, the final report submitted in 1964 did not state a majority opinion for revising the constitution but stated various opinions expressed in the Commission, together with their respective arguments for and against revision. The Commission report was offered as a basis for a judgment by the Cabinet, the Diet, and the people. After this report, constitutional debates on revisionism diminished.

The proceedings of the Commission reflected the political and constitutional activities in this period. After the Hatoyama Cabinet ended, the new Kishi Cabinet expressed an intention to revise the Japan-US security treaty and provoked the so-called 'security treaty struggle,' a huge, turbulent opposition movement. The Socialist Party and other opposition parties asserted the unconstitutionality of the security treaty. Amid this turbulence, the Kishi Cabinet resigned and the new Ikeda Cabinet took steps to avoid another violent clash with the opposition parties on this issue. Prime Minister Ikeda said, 'We do not push the constitutional revision, even if we can obtain the two-thirds majority in both Houses.' For the Ikeda Cabinet, constitutional revision became an issue of decreasing significance.

In addition to cabinet reforms, the December 1959 Supreme Court decision in the *Sunakawa* case hastened the decline of the constitutional debates on revisionism. The Supreme Court avoided deciding the constitutionality of the security treaty by using the political question doctrine. Even so, this decision had the effect of approving both the security treaty system and the view that it was not necessary to amend Article 9 for the maintenance of the security and defense system. In this context, this decision contributed to the decline of the constitutional revision debates.

C. The 1970s

The constitutional revision issue remained quiet during the 1970s. During this period, the percentage of seats held by the LDP and opposition parties in both Houses became close. There was minimal activity by the Constitution Investigation Committee of the LDP. Furthermore, in this period, litigation relating to the constitutionality of the Self-Defense Forces was settled. Courts avoided deciding the issue of constitutionality by using the political question doctrine or by using statutory interpretation techniques to avoid addressing questions involving provisions of the constitution. The decisions also had the effect of legitimizing the Self-Defense Force Law and contributed to a downturn in revisionist activity.

D. The 1980s

In this period, the perceived 'threat of the Soviet Union' and the policy of strengthening Japan's joint defense responsibility pushed the Article 9 debate back into the spotlight. However, the Nakasone Cabinet declared in November 1982 that the Cabinet did not intend to establish a timetable for constitutional revision, even though Prime Minister Nakasone was well-known as a militant revisionist.

The Constitution Investigation Committee of the LDP submitted an interim report in 1982. However, there are striking differences in basic tone and content between this report and similar reports prepared by the same committee in earlier periods. Particularly, as I mention later, on the areas of the emperor system, Article 9, and fundamental human rights, the tone and attitude of this new report is very passive and moderate. Moreover, in 1989, after the heavy defeat of the LDP in the ordinary election for the House of Councillors, the coming general election for the House of Representatives presents the possibility of a win by the opposition parties and of a coalition cabinet led by the Socialist Party. If this possibility could be realized, the political situation surrounding the issue of constitutional revision would be fundamentally changed for the first time in the history of this constitution. Now, in such a process as mentioned above, how has revisionism in the areas of the emperor system, Article 9, and fundamental human rights been developed? I would like next to review this point.

III CHANGES IN REVISIONISM

The political process and events previously described evidence a decline of revisionism. Today, it looks almost impossible, in the near future, to revive the old prewar constitutional regime. Even though the LDP keeps its platform policy proclaiming as a goal the overall revision of the present constitution established under Allied Occupation, the underlying policy and attitude of the party on this issue is strikingly changed. The basic tone of the LDP's position on revision of the constitution has been weakened and the existence of strong opinions against revision is recognized therein. In a word, the revisionism movement has stagnated.

A. The Emperor System

To the report of Professor Higuchi, 'The Constitution and the Emperor System: Is Revisionism Still Alive?,' I would like to add only three points. First, in the early periods, the revisionists strongly advocated that Article 1, which provides that 'The Emperor shall be the symbol of the State and of the unity of the people,' should be amended in accordance with the history and tradition of the emperor system to read 'The Emperor is the Head of State.' More recently, however, the 1982 interim report stated that it was not necessary to amend Article 1, but included a minority opinion favoring the replacement of the word 'symbol' with the phrase 'Head of State.' As a background for this debate, surveys of the constitutional consciousness of the Japanese people in these periods continuously illustrated strong support of the symbolic emperor system.

Second, before and after the passing of Emperor Hirohito, there was much discussion about the new rise of revisionism. I also was often requested by the foreign press to give my opinion about the increased possibility of constitutional revision. Speaking in all candor, such a question gave me a strange impression. I used to answer: 'You think too much about it. The question indicates to me that you are overly concerned with the possibility of revision.' There is no reason to believe that the situation I previously described will be changed by the accession of the new Emperor Akihito. There is no possibility that the government of the LDP will propose a constitutional revision aimed at reviving the prewar emperor system. Such a possibility is equally unlikely under a coalition government with the Socialist Party as leader.

In my opinion, the so-called 'fever phenomenon,' which was characterized by long processions of millions of people praying and mourning for the emperor, was only the expression of human affection for Emperor Hirohito. Moreover, the so-called 'self-restraint' displayed at various social events, such as the autumn festivals in villages, musical concerts, athletic meets, year-end parties, and New Year's greetings, illustrated the conformism of the Japanese people, but should not be interpreted as an expression of sentiment or opinion supporting the revival of the prewar emperor regime.

Third, the following point should be mentioned. At the audience with the representatives of the people after the accession (*Choken no gi*), the new Emperor Akihito stated in his speech, 'I have succeeded to the Imperial Throne in accordance with the Constitution of Japan and the Imperial House Law .... I swear to uphold the Constitution of Japan together with you and to accomplish my duty.' In contrast, when the late Emperor Hirohito originally succeeded to the throne in 1927, he stated in his speech, 'I have succeeded to the Imperial Throne in accordance with the divine will of my Imperial ancestors, and as the descendant of sole Imperial dynasty unbroken for ages eternal.' This contrast illustrates clearly that the position of the emperor and the foundation for the emperor system are fundamentally changed. With the accession of the new emperor, the symbolic emperor system entered into its second period. But, I think, at the beginning of this second period, the symbolic emperor system under the present constitution is perfectly realized for the first time, and the above-quoted statement of Emperor Akihito is broadly and strongly supported by Japanese people.

B. Article 9

In the early periods, the revisionists strongly advocated that the inherent right of self-defense should be clearly stated and that the Self-Defense Force should be authorized for self-defense and for participation in a collective security system. In contrast, the 1982 interim report of the LDP offered only one tentative draft amendment to Article 9.

It is worth mentioning that the following comments were added:

> Against this tentative draft there is an opinion stating: (1) The present constitution played a great role for the peace and prosperity of our country and it has obtained stability in the consciousness of Japanese people. (2) If Article g were amended, many … foreign countries, especially the Asian countries, would be more cautious regarding the renewed development of [a militarized] Japan.

Then, this interim report states conclusively: 'Thinking over the existence of such an opinion, we recognize that the revision of Article 9 needs careful and composite consideration.' The attitude of this report relating to the revision of Article 9 looks, as a whole, rather cautious; at least, it does not actively propose a revision.

C. Fundamental Human Rights

In the early periods, the revisionists strongly advocated that the provisions of the constitution relating to the unrestricted protection of fundamental human rights placed too much emphasis on the rights and freedoms of individuals and neglected the importance of the duties of the people. On this point, the revisionists believed that the present constitution was out of date with the realities of the mid-20th century, the era of the Social Service State, which demand cooperation between the state and governed individuals. They advocated that the duties of the people should be enlarged and that the foundation for restricting individual rights and freedoms by law should be stated clearly. Again, in contrast, the 1982 interim report of the LDP moderated this position in a section entitled 'General Understanding,' which reads as follows:

> The present constitution was drafted in [a very short time during] the period of confusion immediately after the war … Accordingly, there are many points to be improved in wording and terminology. All of the members agreed that the more simple and adequate expression should be demanded. However, the provisions of the present constitution upon the fundamental rights of the people are, comparatively speaking, excellent and have been [applied] carefully in response to the needs of [the] time by the wisdom of [the] Japanese people and many of the points debated before [have been settled or] will be settled in [the] future [by] the process of legislation and by the consideration [of] practical [application]. [On] this point all of the members agreed.

In my opinion, this statement comes rather close to opposing directly constitutional revision of provisions protecting fundamental human rights This statement also implies evaluation and approval of court decisions involving these provisions.

IV CONCLUSION

The reason for the decline of revisionism mentioned above is fundamentally that the original revisionism of the early periods could not gain broad public support, particularly because (1) the revisionists, in overemphasizing the constitution's origins in the Occupation, did not consider the constitutional consciousness of the people, and (2) the contents of the revisionists' draft amendments evoked the fear of significantly altering the fundamental values and principles of the constitution. Furthermore, I would like to point out that this constitution redefines the status of modern citizenship in Japan. This constitution aims not only at the reconstruction of the governmental structure of Japan, but also at the total reorientation of the traditional social order of Japan.

Now, I call to mind the first suggestion of General MacArthur to Prime Minister Shidehara in October 1945 as the first step in the process of establishing a new constitution. He said: 'In fulfillment of [the] Potsdam Declaration, the traditional social order under which the Japanese people have been for centuries subordinated should be reformed and this will unquestionably involve the revision of the constitution.' He stressed four issues of concern for which reform was urgently needed: (1) the emancipation of women, (2) the liberalization of education, (3) the democratization of the economy, and (4) the promotion of organization of labor unions. All four points concern social reform, not governmental reform. Thus, the scope of the constitutional change envisioned was broad indeed. Great changes were sought in law, society, labor organization, education, family life, and other areas of national life. Such a reorientation of the traditional social order meant sweeping away feudalistic institutions and the traditional social structure, emancipating individuals, and creating the status of modern citizenship.

I believe these objectives have been successfully accomplished in the process of modernizing Japanese society and the Japanese way of thinking during these last forty years. The revisionism which intends to revive the traditional social order cannot appeal to the people today. The dignified emperor system, the predominance of militarism, and the predominance of state interest constituted the traditional social order in prewar Japan. The revisionism that aims at the revival of such a social order will not be supported by the people. If revisionism is to survive, it is necessary to construct a new philosophy based on the new social order in Japan, and this task is very difficult. This is, I believe, the achievement and lesson from these last forty years.

III THE SUPREME COURT

Danelski, DJ, 'The Supreme Court of Japan: An Exploratory Study', in Schubert, G and Danelski, D (eds), *Comparative Judicial Behaviour: Cross Cultural Studies of Political Decision-making in the East and West*, 1969, pp 132–37, Oxford University Press

Each year approximately 4500 cases are appealed to the Supreme Court of Japan. All cases come before one of the court's three divisions, which are designated Petty Benches I, II, and III. Each division usually consists of five justices, three of whom constitute a quorum. If a case is found to involve a constitutional question not already settled by the court or by some other issue that is important or complicated, it will be referred to the Grand Bench, which is the entire court sitting *en banc*. Nine court members constitute a quorum of the Grand Bench, and, if a law, regulation, or executive action is declared unconstitutional, a majority of the Grand Bench (eight members) must so agree. Cases are not transferred between divisions.

Research officials (*chosakan*) play an important role in the disposition of cases. There are presently thirty of them assigned to the court. Their functions are analogous to those of the law clerks in the US Supreme Court, but there the similarity ends. American law clerks are usually recent graduates of leading law schools chosen by the justices to assist them for a year or two. Research officials, on the other hand, are themselves judges who have had from ten to twenty years' trial or appellate experience. Presently the chief research official is a high court judge; all of the others are district judges. Chosen for their ability, they are likely to rise high in the judicial hierarchy after serving the usual four or five years with the Supreme Court. Indeed, one of the present justices – Makoto Iwata – was formerly a research official. There is some specialization among research officials: fourteen handle only civil cases; another fourteen handle only criminal cases; and two are specialists in administrative law. Unlike law clerks in the US Supreme Court, research officials are not assigned to particular justices. The civil and administrative research officials are assigned cases in the order they are docketed and work with the justices to whom they have been assigned on the same basis. Research officials who specialize in criminal law are divided into three groups – each group working with one of the petty benches for a period of four months, after which it is assigned to another petty bench. Criminal cases assigned to justices of a given petty bench are assigned by rotation to research officials then working with that petty bench. Since cases are also assigned to the justices in sequence according to the order in which they are docketed, each of the research officials has an opportunity to work with each of the justices.

After counsel has been appointed in certain criminal cases and briefs have been printed, the typical case in the Supreme Court goes to the research official who has been assigned to it. He is referred to as the 'research official in charge of the case.' His first task is to determine whether it is an 'important case,' that is, one worthy of extensive research and careful consideration by the justices, or a 'simple case,' usually a frivolous appeal. If it is the latter, he will stamp an 'X' on it, which means, as a practical matter, dismissal. Since approximately 80% of the civil cases and 90% of the criminal cases fall into the latter category, he spends a good part of his time sifting appeals to find those that are meritorious. When he determines a case to be important, he often does exhaustive research – reading and digesting voluminous records and depositions and briefing the relevant statutes and precedents. His report, which is printed, sometimes attains the size of a large book. The report is usually objective; if there is more than one plausible decision for a case, the basis for each is given in the report. Sometimes the research official gives his opinions, although this is said to be infrequent. In working on research reports, it is common for research officials to consult one another, and such consultation is officially encouraged. It is, in fact, institutionalized in the 'joint meeting' of research officials that is held several times a month for the purpose of studying common problems and ensuring uniformity of decisions in cases involving identical or similar issues before different petty benches. A research official typically devotes about ten days to an important case.

When the research report is completed, it goes to the justice who has been assigned the case, and his assignment, like the research official's, is based on rotation. He is referred to as the 'justice in charge of the case.' After studying the report, and perhaps consulting with the research official, he sets a date for its consideration at a petty bench conference. These conferences are held weekly, and twice a month there is a special conference. At the conference, the justice in charge of the case presides over its discussion. Although the conferences are secret, the research official, unlike his counterpart in the US Supreme Court, may be present to give further information or to clarify some aspects of his report. Discussion usually proceeds in light of the report, which all of the justices have received and read before the conference. Informality is the rule in the conference: there is no prescribed order in regard to speaking or voting. Sometimes the positions of the justices are so clear from the discussion that no vote is taken. If it is evident that the appeal cannot be sustained, the action of the petty bench will be to dismiss, but if it looks as though reversal is possible, the appellee will be asked to file a brief and the case will be set for oral argument. When an appellant is informed that the court desires to hear argument, he knows that he has at least a fifty-fifty chance of winning, for about 80% of the civil cases and 50% of the criminal cases that go to oral argument are reversed. The rate of reversal is lower in the criminal cases because if they involve a capital offense or a serious disturbance of the public peace, oral argument is ordered as a matter of course.

The amount of time allotted for oral argument of a case depends upon its importance. Sometimes many hours are given to a single case. Oral argument in Japan is not like it is in the United States. There is less questioning by the justices and practically no give-and-take between counsel and the court. As one Tokyo University professor put it, 'The justices sit like Buddha until the lawyer finishes.'

After the case has been argued, there is another conference for further discussion and decision. Unless the justice in charge dissents, which is rare, he writes the court's opinion. If he does dissent, then the majority justices decide among themselves who will write the opinion, often choosing the justice who was most vocal in conference. Although it seldom happens, sometimes a justice is assigned an opinion because of his expertise in a particular area of the law.

The principal differences between the Grand Bench and petty bench consideration of cases are livelier discussions in conference and greater manifestation of dissent. The Grand Bench conferences, like those of the petty benches, are held each week, but they tend to last longer, and it is not uncommon to carry the discussion of a case over from one meeting to another. The justices discuss the case without any time limitation, and in this respect, according to former Chief Justice Tanaka, they are perhaps unique among collegial bodies in Japanese government. It is almost impossible, said Tanaka, to control the free speech of the justices. Although the chief justice presides, the justice in charge of the case plays a leading role in its discussion, for usually his opinion is the basis for it. Discussion again is informal and so is voting.

Because a great number of the cases before the Grand Bench involve constitutional questions, the values of the justices are inevitably manifested in conference discussion and later in their written opinions, especially dissenting and supplementary opinions. In conference, attempts are made at persuasion, and at times they are successful. This may be viewed as task-leadership behavior. The concept of task leadership must, however, be understood in a Japanese context. Such leadership in the court is far more subtle and less aggressive than it is in the Supreme Court of the United States. What is involved is complex interpersonal communication that operates at a non-verbal as well as at a verbal level. In discussing this matter in more general terms, Ike has written that many Japanese 'are prevented by training and social custom from saying what they think and of revealing their real and innermost feelings and thoughts. The pressure for social harmony and for outward unanimity is too strong. Individuals who grow to maturity in such an environment must learn to fathom another's thoughts, feelings, and intentions by reading between the lines, by observing indirect signs, and by resorting to a kind of intuitive process.' When disagreements among justices come to the surface in conference, their colleagues characteristically seek to reconcile opposing positions, thus manifesting social-leadership behavior. As one retired justice told me, 'We collaborated to harmonize our views; that is what we all wanted.' Despite the high value placed on harmony, the right to dissent is highly respected in the court. In cases involving matters of principle, at least, there is no expectation of compromise.

After the Grand Bench reaches a decision the research official in charge of the case usually assists in writing the court's opinion, but the amount of work he does depends on the justice in charge. Justice Mano, for example, seldom availed himself of the research official's service. On the other hand, some justices are said to have relied so heavily on the research official that he was virtually author of the court's opinion. A number of the research officials have taken graduate work in law in Europe or the United States, and thus many of the references to foreign precedents may be attributed to them. The authors of the court's opinion are usually not identified, but after retirement, justices are willing to acknowledge their authorship.

The right to express individual views in the form of dissenting and supplementary opinions is highly prized by members of the court. The dissenting opinion was a remarkable post-war innovation in view of the previous Continental practice of announcing only unanimous court decisions. It also runs counter to the value placed on consensus in Japanese society: Japanese cabinet decision-making still proceeds in terms of consensus without votes being taken, and there is no right to dissent in the district and high courts. At first, some members of the career judiciary in the court doubted the wisdom of the expression of dissent, but after coming to the Supreme Court, they were persuaded of the usefulness of the practice. One justice said the right to individual expression of views makes for greater alertness and responsibility on the part of the court. Another said that if he had not the right to dissent, he could not in good conscience have remained on the court after his first disagreement with the majority. In preparing a dissenting opinion in a very important case in which the court was sharply divided, one justice worked so hard that he became ill, and when he finished the opinion, he had to be taken to the hospital. In the same case, another justice devoted similar effort in writing his dissenting opinion, and when he finished he was moved to write a *haiku* about the case, the first he had ever written.

Reference individual and reference group behavior appears to be present in the Japanese Supreme Court, as it does in the US Supreme Court, especially when justices are writing dissenting opinions. In view of the selection of justices in terms of occupations – career judge, lawyer, procurator, professor – it is not surprising that the justices would wonder what their former colleagues would think of their positions in certain cases. One justice – a former professor – said that he had dissented by himself in a certain case and was gratified to learn that another professor, to whom he had sent his opinion, fully agreed with him. I was told by a venerable Japanese scholar that in the old *Daishin-in*, where public expression of dissent was prohibited, dissenting judges would sometimes put their seals upside down on the court's opinion so that they could later prove to former colleagues that they did not agree with the judgment. This is an excellent example of reference group behavior.

After the opinions are written, they are circulated and sometimes elicit further opinions – usually supplementary opinions that take issue with the views of the dissenters. When the opinion writing is completed and the court's judgment is finally approved in conference, the justices place their personal seals on the opinions that represent their views, and the opinions are publicly announced by the Chief Justice.

Tanaka, H, 'The Appointment of Supreme Court Justices and the Popular Review of Appointments' (1978) 11 *Law in Japan* 33–36

(1) The Purpose of the System

We saw earlier that the Supreme Court was intended to assume much more important responsibilities than those assumed by the Great Court of Judicature. The reason why the Constitution of Japan adopted the system of popular review of the appointment and performance of justices by the electorate may be explained as an attempt to ensure that the Supreme Court is ultimately responsible to the people in whom resides sovereign power.

It is, of course, true that if the judicial branch is swayed by the will of the people in every case, it may not fulfill its role, in particular, the protection of the rights of the minority. However, in consideration of the principle that sovereign power resides in the people, it is also undesirable that the judicial branch be isolated from the will of the people for any long period of time in view of the fact that the Constitution of Japan empowers the courts to review the constitutionality of any legislation enacted by the Diet, whose members are elected by the voters. The constitution attempts to bring the judicial branch closer to the people through the system of popular review.

In other words, if a deadlock situation arises between the judicial branch and the executive and/or the legislative branch, the popular review system would serve as an 'emergency exit.' There is a view that, since there is no case of a justice being removed from office by the electorate, the review system is useless. However, this is like saying that since there has been no fire and no one has had to escape by the emergency exit, the emergency exit is useless.

A question sometimes raised about the review system, is whether ordinary people have the qualifications to examine the abilities of justices who are legal professionals. As may be understood from the abovementioned nature of the review system, voters are not required to review – to use the words in the Courts Act – whether a justice has 'legal knowledge' but are required to review whether there is any definite gap between the will of the people and the justices' approach to political and social issues. Therefore this is not a reason for questioning the system.

(2) Nature of the System

The question has been asked whether the nature of the popular review system is to let the electorate rule on the appropriateness of an appointment or to give the electorate the chance to remove a justice from office on the basis of his record on the bench. Depending on the time of the appointment it is possible that a justice may be reviewed by the voters either immediately after his appointment or after a long lapse of time. Indeed the first review can take place up to four years after the appointment and the second review will occur after another ten years. Under the existing system, therefore, it must be said that the review serves two functions. It could only be definitely said that the popular review system was solely for the purposes of removal, if Japan only screened justices who had held office for more than a specified period after their appointment, as is the case in ten of the fifteen states in America which adopt the review system.

(3) Details of the System

In the initial stages the purpose of the review system was not fully recognized. The removal of a justice from office as the result of a vote was beyond the realms of possibility in the traditional concept of the judiciary which evolved in the era of the Great Court of Cassation. In view of this, the popular review system was probably designed to make removals from office very difficult in practice. In addition, the system was set up within a very limited period of time and the actualities of judicial appointments have been quite different from the ideas of those who drafted the Constitution of Japan. Looking at things today, there seem to be several defects – at least there is room for improvement in the present systems.

(a) Voting Method Used in Review

Under the voting system used in Japan, a voter puts an X sign (*batsu jirushi*) against the name or the justice to be dismissed and all other votes (ie those ballot papers which are not filled in) are taken to mean that dismissal is not necessary. This method was held constitutional by the Supreme Court. Nevertheless, as has often been pointed out, it has the following defects. In the first place, all blank ballot papers returned, that is, those without an X, are regarded as signifying that dismissal is not necessary. In particular, where several justices are under review by the electorate, as occurs in most cases, if a voter wishes to cast a vote against one or more justices he cannot abstain from voting for the rest of the justices (because in the existing method, a voter receives a copy of a ballot paper on which all the names of the justices to be reviewed are listed). Secondly, when a ballot paper for the review of the justices is not issued at the same time as a ballot paper for a candidate for the House of Representatives, there seems to be a great danger of violation of the secrecy of the ballot. The danger arises because those people who do not intend to cast a negative vote tend to go directly to the ballot box and lodge the paper. It is therefore possible to guess which way the vote has been cast.

In the light of these circumstances, there have been several proposals that an O sign (*maru jirushi*) should be placed against the name of a justice not to be dismissed in addition to an X sign against the name of a judge to be dismissed, and that blank ballot papers should be regarded as an abstention from voting. In this connection the Supreme Court decision in *Sasaki v Administrative Committee for the Electoral Review of Supreme Court Justices* took the view that the purpose of the existing review method is to ask voters whether or not justices should be removed from office. and held that the existing voting method was a corollary of that purpose. However, I do not think that the court was correct as a matter of theory. As a matter of fact, in all the American states where the popular review system has been adopted, the ballot paper is worded 'Shall Judge ... of the ... court be retained in office?' and voters are asked to reply 'yes' or 'no' in the relevant box.

(b) Minimum Votes Necessary to Continue in Office

Under the existing system, it is provided that a justice will not be dismissed, where 'the total number of votes does not reach one-hundredth of the total number of voters registered in the electoral rolls on the day of their closing,' even though the votes for dismissal are greater in number than the votes in favor of continuing in office. If the existing voting system were improved by the adoption of the choice between an X and an O as outlined above, the existing ratio would seem to be too low as there would be a possibility of dismissal by the will of a minimal number of people. Among the various proposals for the reform of the review system of justices, the proposal by the Tokyo

Practicing Attorneys' Association suggested the ratio of one-fifth and the other proposals one-tenth. I believe that one-fifth or one-fourth would be reasonable.

(c) The Time for Review

Article 79(2) of the Constitution of Japan provides that the appointment of justices 'shall be reviewed by the people at the first general election of members of the House of Representatives following their appointment'. Thereafter their performance is reviewed periodically by the people at the first election following each 10 years of service.

With regard to the time for the review, there are three main problems. First of all, since the review is carried out at a general election for the House of Representatives, the people tend to be more concerned with the general election than with the review of the appointment of the justices. This might be one of the reasons for the lack of interest by the electorate in the review process. Therefore it would seem to be better if the constitution had directed that the review be held at the time of the elections for the House of Councillors. In this regard it should be noted that the draft of the constitution prepared by the GHQ proposed a unicameral system, but, in accordance with a proposal from the Japanese a bicameral system was finally adopted. At the time when the draft was changed from the original GHQ proposal, under which the review of justices was to be carried out concurrently with the election for the only House, the House of Representatives, to the bicameral system, consideration should have been given to conducting the review with the elections for the House of Councillors.

Secondly, the 10 year interval between each review is rather too long. Probably it would have been better to establish a six-year term, in parallel with the election of the House of Councillors. Under the present practice of judicial appointments, it is quite rare that a justice is subjected to popular review twice. There is no opportunity to screen most justices after their ability as a Supreme Court justice actually becomes clearer, because of this ten-year interval. This seems to be one main factor in both the deterioration of the effectiveness of the existing review system and the increase in voters' indifference to the system.

Thirdly, it would be much more desirable if it were stipulated that at least one year should elapse between the initial appointment and the first review of the justice. If one sees the purpose of the review as being to ask the voters' approval of the appointment *ex post facto* then the existing review system would not necessarily be illogical. However, considering the fact that there is not always enough information available to examine the fitness of a justice, it would be more realistic to set up a fixed term from the time of appointment to the time of review so that voters would be able to reach a more informed decision.

IV. CONCLUSION

As American constitutional history shows, the strength of the judicial power, particularly the grant of the right to review the constitutionality of legislation, necessarily draws the Supreme Court into the political process. Therefore under the principle that sovereignty resides in the people, it naturally is required that the selection of justices must be in some way controlled by the democratic process. Democratic control could be carried out not only by the Diet or the Cabinet, but also more directly by the people themselves, by way of popular review of the appointments of justices or by public election as may be seen in the majority of states in the United States. The method or methods to be adopted should be decided according to each country's political system and the position accorded to judges under the particular constitutional structure. Therefore the selection of our justices must always be examined in the light of the authority conferred by the constitution on the Supreme Court. In addition, it is necessary to be consistent in weighing views about the system of popular review of judicial appointments.

Itoh, H, *The Japanese Supreme Court: Constitutional Policies*, 1989, pp 204–12, Markus Wiener

The Meiji constitution provided for the proper qualification, tenure, and discipline of judges in accordance with the law (Article 58). The constitutional guarantee for judicial independence was also stated in the Court Organization Code of 1890. Tenure for life was established, and then it was later changed to compulsory retirement at sixty-three years of age. Judges were selected for legal expertise, and their salaries were excluded from a general official cut in 1931. Their dismissal was possible only after criminal conviction or formal disciplinary action stipulated by law. These legislations reflected a great improvement over the Tokugawa practice, and contributed to generating the tradition in which Japanese judges could perform their duties relatively independent of political fluctuations in the subsequent era.

A review of judicial history, however, reveals instances of politically motivated onslaughts on judicial independence. The executive not only exerted undue pressure on judicial decision making in a courtroom but also attempted to replace judges for political reasons. Vice-Justice Minister Kikuomi Yokota, taking advantage of a newly appointed justice minister, attempted to force the resignation of ten elder judges to be replaced by those judges who were affiliated with Yokota's political party in 1898. This attempt was stopped by the new minister at the very last minute. The famous test case of the *Otsu* trial (1891) is often cited as exemplary of an effort to secure judicial independence under the Meiji constitution. This was a criminal trial of Japanese politician Sanzo Tsuda who wounded the Russian crown prince Nicholas II with a sword in an assassination attempt at Otsu in 1891. The Japanese government, for diplomatic reasons, wanted the death penalty, but the Criminal Code provided only life imprisonment for an attempted murder unless the victim was a member of the Japanese imperial family. Chief Justice Ikken Kojima of the Great Court of Cassation refused to give in to political pressure and the five man criminal division of the court sentenced Tsuda to life imprisonment in accordance with the law.

The wartime Prime Minister Hideki Tojo's attack on liberal judges and his demand for their cooperation with the Japanese war effort eventually led to what Otto Kirchheimer would call political justice, in which a judge collaborated with or at least works for the interest of the regime of the day and attempted to suppress its opponents. There were some Japanese judges who tried to withstand the political pressure. Nagayoshi Hosono, chief judge of the Hiroshima Court of Appeals, in 1944 protested Tojo's speech that threatened judicial independence. Likewise, Shotaro Miyake of the Great Court of Cassation acquitted Godo Ozaki on 27 June 1944, of the prosecution's charge that Ozaki committed the crime of *lese majesty* during an election campaign speech he made on behalf of liberal candidate Daikichi Togawa when he compared the Meiji, Taisho, and Showa Emperors. Shuichi Ishizaka of Tokyo district court acquitted Professor Eijiro Kawai who was charged with the violation of the Publication Code. Hisashi Yoshida of the Great Court of Cassation nullified the 1 March 1945, election victory in the Kagoshima second district, claimed by Tojo's Imperial Rule Assistance Association. But, some judges probably could not have been expected to resist the military government's attempts to suppress anti-war liberal thoughts, or even such basic rights as the freedom of speech and religion.

Based on his findings that 4,119 of 4,208, or 98 percent, of all those prosecuted were formally placed on trial after a preliminary hearing between 1936 and 1940 while 1.1 percent of them were dismissed and 0.9 percent were dropped, Eigoro Aoki suspects that judges accepted testimony by the police and prosecution without much examination and proceeded to place their charges on trial. Under such circumstances, judicial independence might have been a hollow principle, yet no recorded account offers any evidence of wholesale distorted trials. If there had been any, a miscarriage of justice would not have been so large as to lead to the total collapse of judicial independence.

During the allied occupation of Japan there was no judicial independence in the political sense, because GHQ, SCAP functioned outside the constitutional framework in the Japanese judicial decision making. Many orders and directives issued by GHQ, SCAP were binding above and beyond the Japanese constitution. The judicial attempt to reinstate a former Cabinet member showed a peculiar feature of the Japanese judicial independence under the occupation. Rikizo Hirano, then minister of agriculture, was dismissed by Premier Tetsu Katayama because of his disagreement with the Cabinet. Hirano, who was also purged as a suspected war criminal, requested the Tokyo district court to rescind his dismissal from the Cabinet. The court in *Hirano v Premier Katayama* (1948) granted an injunction on 2 February 1948, but GHQ, SCAP ordered the retraction of this injunction on the grounds that the Japanese courts did not have a jurisdiction over such a purgee case. Three days later the Supreme Court, in compliance with the GHQ directive, ordered the district court to reverse the judgment. Former Justice Tamotsu Shima denies GHQ, SCAP's interference with other trials while others argue that GHQ, SCAP openly directed trials involving occupation policies. An ever-present possibility of a court's decision being overruled by the occupation government made Japanese judges in the early period very uncertain and cautious.

Judicial independence under the present constitutional system is insured in a number of ways. The courts are independent of the ministry of justice. The judges are not removable except by public impeachment. No disciplinary action against judges may be taken by the executive (Article 78), and judicial salaries shall not be decreased during their terms of office (Article 78). Nevertheless, political involvement in trials have not been absent.

Diet was criticized for having interfered with judicial independence during an ongoing trial in 1948. On 6 April 1948, Urawa poisoned and strangled to death her three children after she was abandoned by her husband and could not take the hardship of supporting her family. After an abortive suicide, she turned herself in to nearby police, upon which the public prosecutor charged her with manslaughter and sought a three-year imprisonment. The Urawa district court of Saitama prefecture sentenced her to a three-year imprisonment, but granted her a three-year stay of execution. When the prosecutor decided not to appeal, she was immediately released.

Then the House of Councillors' Legal Committee invoked the constitutional power (Article 62) to investigate government affairs and criticized the court's decision by arguing that the sentence was allegedly based on the feudalistic notion which viewed children as mere possessions of their parents. There was also an unproven assumption that the defendant's hardship drove her to an abortive suicide with her children. The committee held the court's sentencing unreasonably light. Against the protest by the

Supreme Court, the committee defended this investigation of the ongoing case by stating that the power of investigating government affairs extended equally to all three branches of government and might demand the testimony of witnesses and a transcript of judicial proceedings. The reaction of Diet to the Urawa trial stirred up wide criticism from many quarters as political interference in judicial independence.

Judges have also been subject to criticism from both the prosecutor and defense counsel in criminal trials. On 19 November 1963, 103 defense attorneys of the *Matsukawa* case (1950) and the *Shiratori* case (1952) filed in vain a petition which the Diet Judge Impeachment Committee sought the dismissal of Supreme Court Justice Masuo Shimoiizaka on the grounds of improper judicial conduct. Likewise in 1966, prosecuting attorney Ichiro Osawa of the Osaka district prosecutor's office criticized at a press conference the lack of severity in a penalty imposed by two judges of the Osaka summary court in a traffic violation case. While the judicial conference of the Osaka district court held the criticism to be improper, it later transferred the two summary court judges. Thereupon, the Osaka Bar Association requested the Osaka district court and the prosecutor's office to insure the judicial independence of the two judges.

The Meiji constitution did not have any notion of judicial review of overseeing the constitutionality of governmental acts or actions. Although the view was persuasively set forth by many people that a court was empowered to invalidate a law which conflicted with the Meiji constitution, both the Great Court of Cassation and the mainstream of lawyers refused to recognize judicial review of the law.

As recently as 1937 the court ruled in *Sato et al v Japan* (1937) that it could not reject the application of a constitutionally dubious law as long as such a law met the formal requirements of legislative procedure. Hirobumi Ito, the first Prime Minister and an important framer of the Meiji constitution, argued along the line of the unitary imperial sovereign power that the judiciary was a part of the executive and might not review the constitutionality of actions taken by the legislature, which was ranked equal to the executive. Tatsukichi Minobe, a prominent public law scholar, based his case against the judicial review of law on the principle of separation of powers, as he understood it from the European legal experiences in the 19th century. Although the parliamentary-cabinet system in Japan has modified the 'rigid compartmentalization' of the separation of powers by harmonizing the executive and legislative powers, Minobe concludes, each branch of government should be left free to judge for itself its own constitutional competence and responsibilities. Furthermore, there was no centralized court system in Japan until 1875. Justice Minister Shimpei Ito's efforts toward judicial independence were first directed toward a separation of judicial function from the local administration rather than the political branches of the national government.

The judicial power of the Great Court of Cassation was restricted by political forces of the day as well. The provision of Article 57 of the Meiji constitution required the judicial courts to perform their duties 'according to law in the name of the Emperor.' Under this provision the privy council was entrusted with the function of providing the Emperor with the most authoritative interpretations of the constitution, laws, and imperial ordinances. Whenever the Diet requested the Emperor's judgment over disagreements between the two Houses of Diet, or between the Cabinet and the Diet, the Cabinet was obliged to refer the matter to the privy council. Yet due to the lack of a clear separation between the government and the privy council, as exemplified by the overlapping membership between the two, the council's advisory opinions had a dubious binding force on the government. Also, because the privy council could meet only upon the Emperor's request and was not held responsible to Diet, it remained inactive and was by no means an effective institution to examine the government's legal interpretations. In reality, key policies were made by a handful of oligarchical leaders who invoked the Emperor's name mainly to legitimize their own decisions. In turn, judicial efforts to conform to the imperial will or the national polity often caused him to follow the oligarchical leaders.

Judicial control did not extend over administrative disputes, either. Article 61 of the Meiji constitution conferred on the administrative court the competency to deal with the rights allegedly infringed by the illegal measures of the administrative authorities. Yet adjudication by the administrative court was far from satisfactory. Influenced by German positivism, administrative codes were legislated in such a way as to confer upon bureaucrats rather restricted discretionary powers. Yet whatever administrative discretion existed gained finality in a wide range of matters, and administrative interpretation and application of law and regulation tended to overshadow those by the administrative court. An alleged misapplication of law by a public official was heard by successive levels including a competent minister, and then, if a judicial hearing was granted, a suit could be brought to the administrative court. However, the administrative court was not structured to handle a large number of cases. The Administrative Court Code restricted the jurisdiction of the court to only a limited list of narrowly and specifically enumerated claims, and a person adversely affected by an illegal administrative action could bring a charge only when a statute permitted him to do so.

Commenting on Article 61 of the constitution, Hirobumi Ito stated that individuals were free to petition the court but not to resort to any legal suit against an administrative action. On the average, less than 300 administrative cases were filed annually between 1890 and 1930, and inadequate procedural safeguards in the proceedings of the administrative court often adversely affected the substantive rights of the injured individual. Whenever the administrative court turned to the Code of Civil Procedure to fill a procedural gap, it, too, was often ill-equipped to handle such a need. Finally, many administrative judges tended to be favorably disposed toward bureaucratic actions, and many complaints, including wages and other public law-related claims brought before it, were dismissed as being immaterial.

There were occasional jurisdictional disputes between the administrative court and the Great Court of Cassation, and two different decisions were sometimes rendered on virtually identical cases. Although no administrative court decisions were appealable to the judicial courts for review, some government actions in private law like contract and tort were challenged in separate suits before a judicial court. This created, in turn, the need for a uniform interpretation between the Great Court of Cassation and the administrative court on the same public policy problems. The administrative court in *Ouchi Village Mayor v Aomori Prefecture, Obayashi District Forestry Bureau Chief* (1914), held irrevocable any mistake made by administrators in their assessment of boundary lines between public and private lands. The Great Court of Cassation, however, ruled in *Omiya et al v Japan* (1917) that such a wrong boundary could and should be corrected. Tatsukichi Minobe attributed such conflicting decisions to the practice of the judicial court to determine the applicability of administrative laws in civil actions.

Whereas many scholars, including Minobe, favored substantive review of ordinances, the Great Court of Cassation initially limited judicial influence to the form of law and orders, and not the substance. In *Japan v Shimada* (1913) the court, upholding an order for the police criminal investigation which led to the conviction of Shimada, gave the opinion that the term 'law,' as used in Article 23 of the constitution, included the order which was sublegislated to carry out the imperial rescript. After 1916 the court began unmistakably to review the substance of ordinances and orders under challenge in criminal cases, and between 1900 and 1939 the court reviewed and sustained government orders in sixteen cases. Only in *Sato et al v Japan* (1937) did the court invalidate the provision of Article 1 of the Foreign Exchange Control Ordinance prohibiting preparation for smuggling on the grounds that restrictions imposed therein exceeded the authorization delegated by Diet. Only a few civil cases involving ordinances were reviewed and upheld by the court, and then no reference was made to any specific provisions of the constitution.

The Commission on the Constitution was created in 1956 to investigate the background of the present constitution and advise any need for constitutional revision. It debated judicial review more heatedly than any other aspect of the judiciary. The majority of the committee members felt that the present scope of judicial review should not be changed, while some members felt that the power of judicial review gives the Supreme Court too much of an edge over Diet. In the opinion of the opponents, it is contrary to the principle of democracy for the fifteen members of the Supreme Court, who are not chosen by the public, to pass a judgment on the constitutionality of a law enacted by the majority of the popularly elected Diet members. They also cited the MacArthur draft constitution which proposed that judicial review on matters other than fundamental human rights should not be final but might be overruled by a two-thirds majority vote of a unicameral Diet.

In short, precarious judicial independence and absence of judicial review in relation to political branches conditioned the judicial environment in prewar Japan. While judicial independence and judicial review are now firmly established, the judicial self-restraint remains pervasive in Japan, and some Supreme Court justices who were trained and worked under the old judicial system cannot be expected to behave otherwise. Furthermore, they feel strongly that the judiciary should not declare acts and actions of political branches unconstitutional and invalid unless it is absolutely necessary. This feeling is especially strong on constitutional policies which often require high levels of political discretion.

Where a given law or ordinance is amenable to more than one interpretation, a court tends to adopt an interpretation that would uphold its constitutionality. For example, according to the majority opinion in *Hasegawa et al v Japan* (1969), the basic rights of labor are extended to local public employees as a rule, and if provisions of the Local Public Employees Code are interpreted to prohibit any and all kinds of labor disputes waged by local public employees and also penalize those who conspire, incite, and instigate these disputes, such a provision would violate Article 39 of the constitution. However legal provisions should be interpreted in harmony with the constitutional spirit as much as possible. Thus these provisions, despite their wording, should not necessarily be interpreted as unconstitutional.

Danelski, D, 'The Political Impact of the Japanese Supreme Court' (1974) 49 *Notre Dame Lawyer* 958–68

A. The Emperor

The Supreme Court's impact on the Emperor has been negligible. One of the first cases before the court concerned the Emperor Matsutaro Mahushima, a former Chuo University law student, had been convicted of the crime of *lèse-majesté* for carrying a placard criticizing the Emperor at a Communist demonstration in front of the Imperial Palace. Since amnesty had been declared in such cases, the Tokyo High Court ordered dismissal of the indictment (*menso*). Believing the effect of the High Court's action left him still convicted of *lèse-majesté*, Matsushima, seeking an acquittal (*muzai*), appealed to the Supreme Court. The court rejected his appeal, but two justices – Shimoyama and Sawada – indicated in a dictum that they thought the crime of *lèse-majesté* had not been completely abolished in Japan. To the contrary, Justice Shono argued that when the Emperor's status had been changed with Japan's acceptance of the Potsdam Declaration, the crime of *lèse-majesté* had been completely abolished. Today slander of the Emperor may be punished as ordinary defamation, but the prime minister must make the complaint. No complaint was made against Fukasawa when his novel, *Furyu Yume Monogatari* (The Tale of an Elegant Dream), describing the beheading of the Emperor and his family, was published in 1960. This stirred the ire of right-wing groups, and in 1961 a young extremist murdered the maid and wounded the wife of the novel's publisher.

About the time the court decided the *Placard* case (May 1948) Chief Justice Mibuchi participated in a round-table conference on the Emperor's responsibility for the war, and he was reported as saying that the Emperor should abdicate. When this statement was published in the *Shukan Asahi*, Mibuchi claimed he had been misquoted or misinterpreted. 'At the time,' he told reporters later, 'I said I thought it would have had a better effect on the morality of the people in general if the Emperor at the time of surrender had issued an Imperial Rescript morally blaming his own self.' The effect of Mibuchi's statements cannot be gauged, but they reflected and supported a view held by many Japanese.

B. The Diet

During the first two years of its existence, the Supreme Court faced a Diet challenge to judicial independence. The Judiciary Committee of the House of Councillors began an investigation of a criminal case decided by a district court in which the defendant had been convicted of killing her three children and given a light sentence. On 20 May 1949, acting Chief Justice Tsukazaki wrote to the Speaker of the House of Councillors stating that the Committee's action was 'absolutely unpardonable from the standpoint of the constitution.' 'The constitution is the supreme law of the State,' he added, 'and it is needless to say that the Diet should respect it.' Tsukazaki's final words in behalf of the Supreme Court were: 'We hereby ask you to reflect seriously on the matter.' The Judiciary Committee did not capitulate and made counter-constitutional arguments, but eventually the matter was settled in the court's favor.

In the years that followed the Supreme Court viewed its power of judicial review with caution and exercised it with restraint. It managed to avoid passing on the constitutionality of important statutes and treaties by invoking the doctrine of political questions and by refusing to decide cases unless they involved concrete legal disputes. The most important example of judicial restraint was the court's decision in the *Sunakawa* case in which it held that the constitutionality of the United States-Japan Security Treaty was a political question it could not answer. Some have argued that the court's early timidity in exercising judicial review was necessary because the court was still in the process of legitimation. Others argued that restraint was appropriate because the rule of law is better realized through the political process rather than the judicial process. Chief Justice Tanaka, who served on the court from 1950 to 1960, felt that even though the court had not exercised judicial review in an important case during his tenure, 'the very power of judicial review would have a psychological effect in persuading the legislature to respect the constitution,' a conclusion many scholars found dubious.

The court has exercised judicial review only four times – in 1953, 1960, 1962, and 1973. The first case involved Cabinet Order 325, which had been issued during the Occupation, and two transitional statutes covering the period immediately preceding the 1952 peace treaty. At the time the court declared the statutes unconstitutional, they were no longer in effect. 'The statute declared unconstitutional in 1960 was likewise not in effect when it was struck down.'

In 1962 the court held unconstitutional Article 118 (1) of the Customs Law in *Nakamura v Japan*. Nakamura and others attempted to smuggle from Japan to Korea a large quantity of textiles belonging to a third party. They were caught, and under Article 118 (1) the textiles were confiscated. On appeal the owner of the textiles argued that the property had been confiscated unconstitutionally because the procedure used under Article 118 (1) did not provide notice and hearing as required by the constitution. The Supreme Court agreed, declared Article 118 (1) to be in violation of Articles 29 and 31 of the constitution and, as required by law, notified the Cabinet of its action. As a result of the court's decision, new rules governing confiscation of third parties' property were established in 1963; and those rules require notice and hearing before confiscation.

Although the *Nakamura* decision was a clear exercise of judicial review, it was not regarded as important. The *Asahi Shimbun* devoted only 35 lines to it, and in 1973, when the court declared Article 200 of the Penal Law unconstitutional in the *Parricide* cases, some newspapers reported that as the court's first exercise of judicial review. Certainly it was the first important exercise of judicial review in regard to a statute still in effect.

The defendants in the *Parricide* cases were women. One killed her father who had forced her to have sexual relations with him when she was 14. After 20 years of intimate relations with him and five children by him, she decided to leave him and marry a man she met at her place of employment. When her father objected, she strangled him in his sleep. The second woman strangled her foster father to death because she could not stand his excessive drinking. The third woman, perturbed by her mother-in-law's incessant criticism, attempted to kill her by serving her poison in some rice balls. The women were charged with violating Article 200 of the Penal Code, which makes mandatory more severe penalties in parricide cases. In one of the cases the trial court declared the statute unconstitutional. The Supreme Court, by a vote of 14 to 1, overruled a 1950 decision in which two justices – Mano and Hozumi – had dissented and held that Article 200 violated Section 14 of the constitution, which provides that all persons are equal under the law.

Reaction to the decision was generally favorable. Professor Takeyoshij Kawashima of Tokyo University praised the decision saying that Article 200 reflected old feudal notions. Professors Seiichi Isono of Tokyo Educational University and Jiro Kamijima of Rikkyo University also praised the decision. The latter said it shows the Supreme Court is following the principles of the constitution. Dr Inada Nada, the physician-novelist, said that 'even the judges who are always behind the times' this time could not help seeing the contradiction in the parricide statute. Justice Mano, now retired and in his mid-80s, said that the decision points to the 'true flow of history.' His former conservative colleague, Yusuke Saito, was annoyed with the decision. He said that it seemed to him that justices had lost their qualifications for the Supreme Court. 'The new decision,' he added with some exaggeration, 'is ruining the whole penal system of the country.' There was also some popular criticism. The writer, Ayako Sono, said that the penalties for parricide should be more severe because there is greater regret in such crimes and so the heavier penalty allows for special atonement. The popular entertainer Sanyutei said with all the talk about fundamental human rights and equality, social life has become abnormal. 'The existence of the special penalty for parricide is a reasonable thing.'

Justice Minister Isaji Tanaka told a Diet committee in answer to a question by a Komeito member that he would 'respect' the *Parricide* decision. Daizo Yokoi, director of the trial section of the Supreme Public Procurator's office, said that sentences in 36 parricide cases now before the courts would be determined by the penalty provisions for regular crimes. In addition, he said the sentences in previous parricide convictions would be reviewed because of the Supreme Court decision.

Some newspapers saw the *Parricide* decision as a sign of the court's willingness to act vigorously in defense of the constitution. The *Asahi Shimbun* pointed out that since 1966 the court had been moving in this direction as evidenced by its decisions granting public workers the right to strike and by insisting that persons accused of crimes be given prompt trials. The observation may be accurate and indicate a willingness of the court to be more activist. A recently retired justice who participated in the decision of the *Parricide* cases told a group of students at the Harvard Law School that he had hoped there would be at least one case in which the court would exercise judicial review before he retired, and he got his wish.

A similar sequence of activity led to the exercise of judicial review in the *Parricide* and *Nakamura* cases:

1) Each involved constitutional issues that had been decided earlier by a divided court.
2) The earlier decisions had been criticized by scholars.
3) Lawyers continued to raise constitutional objections to statutes upheld earlier, and sometimes lower court judges declared the statutes unconstitutional.
4) The issues continued to return to the court, and chances of over-ruling the statutes became better because of changes in personnel on the court and a different climate of constitutional opinion.

This suggests that sometimes dissenting opinions – such as Mano's and Hozumi's in the 1950 *Parricide* case – have impact, particularly in the scholarly and judicial communities. Mano, for example, believed that the dissenting opinions in the 1950 *Parricide* case may have influenced the drafters of the proposed Revised Penal Code to delete Article 200 in 1961. The work of scholars like Professor Shigemitsu Dando is read with respect, and his belief that Article 118 (1) of the Customs Law was constitutionally suspect probably played some role in the court's decision in the *Nakamura* case. Whether the sequence described indicates a pattern is something that will not be known until the court exercises judicial review in a number of cases.

The exercise of judicial review in the *Parricide* cases is a reminder to members of the Diet that they must follow the constitution or run the risk of being reversed by the courts. But judicial review is not the only means of Supreme Court impact on the Diet. Court interpretations of statutes and ordinances have been known to influence the legislative process in the Diet. What influence the court has with the Impeachment Committee of the Diet is not known, but Chief Justices Tanaka and Ishida easily survived attempts to impeach them.

C. The Cabinet

The Supreme Court has influenced the Cabinet chiefly in the area of judicial appointments. The court plays a crucial role in the appointment of lower-court judges because the constitution requires the Cabinet to appoint judges from a list of persons nominated by the court, and the practice has been for the Supreme Court to nominate the exact number of judges for the available positions, thus leaving no choice to the Cabinet. Constitutionally, the power to select Supreme Court justices is entirely the Cabinet's, but court members, especially the chief justice, have influenced the selection of their own colleagues. During the Ashida administration – circa 1949 – Chief Justice Mibuchi asked that he be consulted when appointments to the court were made. The reason for his request was to assure that the Cabinet selected persons who were compatible with other members of the court. The request was granted, and the practice of consulting the chief justice on appointments to the court has continued. Consultation is informal. The chief justice and the prime minister often meet at ceremonial functions – for example, at an Imperial garden party or in the waiting room of the Diet just before its opening ceremony. The views expressed by the chief justice are his own, not the court's, because as a former chief justice said, '[i]t would be a grave matter if the court's opinion were rejected.' The last consultation for a chief justice concerns the choice of his successor. How frequently the advice of the various chief justices was followed by the prime ministers will probably never be known, but one former chief justice told me that his advice was almost invariably followed.

In the early 1950s there was some feeling in the court that a person selected by the Cabinet for the Supreme Court was too young. Because others in the judiciary who had graduated from the university the same year were still in much lower positions, some judges and judicial administrators believed that his appointment was highly premature. As a result, two justices called on the justice minister in an effort to persuade him that the appointment should be withdrawn. They were unsuccessful. Recently, however, Liberal-Democratic governments have been unsuccessful in countering the court in the selection process. Both Sato and Tanaka wanted to appoint Minoru Tsuda, a justice ministry official, to the court, the former in 1971 and the latter in 1973; but Chief Justice Ishida was able to prevail with his candidates in both instances. In 1971 Seiichi Kishi, secretary general of the court and 'Ishida's right arm,' was appointed. In 1973 Yutaka Yoshida, Kishi's successor as secretary general, was appointed. And when Ishida retired from the chief justiceship in 1973, he supported his colleague, Tomokazu Murakami, as his successor, and Murakami was named chief justice.

Some decisions of the Supreme Court have impact on the policies of the government and its ministries. In 1969, for example, when the court decided public workers could strike without incurring criminal penalties, Prime Minister Sato directed that the government's coordinated position on the ruling be put in writing, and ministers immediately began a review of policies in relation to the decision. Another example is the court's 1971 decision that held the Ministry of Transport's procedure for screening applicants for owner-driver taxi licenses was illegal. Soon after the decision, a spokesman for the Ministry said that the policy in question had changed and no similar trouble would arise in the future.

D. The Judiciary

The Supreme Court has had a substantial impact on the judiciary. The main reason for its influence over lower-court judges is that it plays a crucial role in their nomination, assignment, and promotion; but it would be a mistake to generalize about Supreme Court influence over the entire 25 years of its existence because the makeup of the lower judiciary has changed considerably during that period.

The typical judge from the late 1940s to the early 1960s cautiously decided cases with expectations of his superiors in mind. If he believed the Supreme Court would decide a case a certain way, he would feel constrained to decide it that way, and he was aware that his seniors tended to be conservative and that their views on him might well be reflected in his dossier in the personnel section of the Supreme Court. During most of this period Kotaro Tanaka, a conservative and a militant anti-communist, was chief justice; and he frequently gave his views at judicial conferences and to the press. He is often quoted as having said that communists should not be treated by the courts as law-abiding citizens but as criminals by conviction. Some judges were undoubtedly influenced by such statements. During this period, however, some judges were atypical. One of them, Tokyo District Judge Akio Date, declared the United States-Japanese Security Treaty unconstitutional in the *Sunakawa* case and thereafter resigned his judgeship. In his writings he urged judges to be more independent, to think for themselves, and to decide cases according to their best judgment without worrying about the Supreme Court. It has been said that he resigned because the Supreme Court reversed his decision in the *Sunakawa* case. When I asked him about this in 1969, he denied it, saying he had made up his mind to leave the bench before he decided the case. He had been a Supreme Court research official (*chosakan*) before he returned to the Tokyo District Court, and hence he knew the Chief Justice and justices fairly well. Because of that, he believed that they would know that he had been sincere in his decision; hence he was not concerned about their criticism of him. He was however, surprised that when the court announced its decision not a single justice agreed with him. If Date did not resign because of a Supreme Court decision, at least one judge during this period did. He was Eigoro Aoki, who resigned in 1962 in protest of the Supreme Court's decision in the *Yakai* case that year.

By the middle 1960s a generation gap had developed in the judiciary. Older judges tended to be conservative and younger judges progressive; a few younger judges perhaps even saw themselves as radical. The more radical students at the Legal Training and Research Institute during this period almost invariably chose to become lawyers, refusing to become a part of the conservative establishment by becoming judges or procurators. Thus there were few if any radical judges but to their older colleagues, some of the young judges seemed radical. As confirmation, the older judges pointed to the fact that many young judges (about 200) belonged to the Young Jurists Association (*Seinen Horitsuka Kyokai*, generally known in abbreviated form as *Seihokyo*), which has been described by some as a group of anti-government, leftist lawyers and judges. In 1968 and 1969 I talked to a number of judges in Japan about the developing generation gap, and the major portion of a meeting I had with judges of the Sapporo District and High Courts was devoted to it. Several judges under 40 spoke openly about differences of attitude between younger and older judges. The senior judges present said nothing but asked to talk to me privately later. At that meeting they expressed their concern about the developing polarization in the judiciary. They did not see themselves, they said, as conservatives. Judging to them was not ideological; rather it was something requiring technical skill and experience. By the fall of 1969 the tensions between the two groups of judges erupted in a series of incidents, the first of which occurred in Sapporo.

On 14 August 1969, Kenta Hiraga, Chief Judge of the Sapporo District Court, wrote a private letter of 'advice' to District Judge Shigeo Fukushima, a 39-year-old Kyoto graduate, giving his views on the merits of a controversial case that Fukushima had before him in which 173 local citizens sought to enjoin the building of a missile base of the Self-Defense Forces on the ground that this action violated Article 9 of the constitution. Fukushima ignored Hiraga's advice, granted the injunction, and Fukushima's friends gave a copy of Hiraga's letter to reporters. Thereupon the judicial conference of Hiraga's own court disciplined him for his action, and less than a week later Chief Justice Ishida convened a judicial conference of the Supreme Court which also disciplined Hiraga and transferred him to the Tokyo High Court. Soon thereafter, Chief Judge Shigeto Iimori of the Kagoshima District Court, the younger brother of Kotaro Tanaka and an ultra-rightist, came to Hiraga's defense contending that the whole incident had been engineered by judges who were members of the 'subversive' Young Jurists Association. For this he was reprimanded by the Fukuoka High Court. In late October Chief Justice Ishida, troubled by the matter and probably with Fukushima in mind, told an assembly of Kanto area judges that in a case involving the propriety or impropriety of the exercise of governmental power, 'it is desirable that each judge avoid falling into self-righteousness. ... I hope I can expect that you will mutually exchange acquired experience and knowledge in a spirit of modesty.' The court's secretary general, Seiichi Kishi, said on 8 April 1970: 'If judges join groups that are vested with political color this will give rise to public doubts as to the probity of the courts; judges should not join [such] groups.' Less than a month later Chief Justice Ishida told reporters at a press conference on the eve of Constitution Day, May 2: 'As a matter of ethics, it is undesirable that ultranationalists, militarists, and clearly not communists should be judges.' Proceedings were brought against Fukushima, Hiraga, and Ishida in the Diet's Impeachment Committee. It ruled that proceedings could be brought against Fukushima but suspended them during his good behavior. The petitions against Ishida and Hiraga were rejected. On 28 October, the Sapporo High Court, apparently influenced by the Impeachment Committee's action, orally reprimanded Fukushima for permitting Hiraga's letter to become public. The next day, the Supreme Court announced it supported the High Court's action. Fukushima resigned the same day, criticizing the High Court for being subservient to political power. On the following day he had a change of heart and asked if he might withdraw his resignation. His request was granted. He was reprimanded again for his critical remarks, he formally apologized, and he resumed his work on the bench.

In April, 1970, the Supreme Court refused to nominate three graduates of the Legal Training and Research Institute as assistant judges. No reason was given for its action, but two of the three were known to be members of the Young Jurists Association.

On 22 December 1970, Chief Judge Iimori sent a letter to his young colleagues in Kagoshima District Court, asking them if they were members of the Young Jurists Association. Upon being summoned to the Fukuoka High Court for discipline he withdrew his questionnaire. Immediately the Supreme Court also acted. On 25 December, it transferred Iimori to the Tokyo High Court. When he refused to come to Tokyo, he was demoted to the position of regular judge in his court. As a result of the court's tough action, he resigned.

In April, 1971, the Supreme Court refused to nominate seven judicial trainees at the Legal Training and Research Institute for posts as assistant judges. The secretary general of the Supreme Court insisted there had been no discrimination, but six of the persons rejected were members of the Young Jurists Association, and one was a sympathizer. When the president of the Japan Federated Bar Association, Kijuro Watabe, criticized the court for its failure to nominate the seven Institute trainees, the court's secretary general, Yoshida, wrote an angry rebuttal, saying Watabe 'threatened to damage the independence of the judiciary.' The Federated Bar, the latter continued, should act with restraint and stop interfering in matters that were entirely in the province of the court.

During the graduation ceremony at the Legal Training and Research Institute on 5 April 1971, one of the graduating students, Tokuo Sakaguchi, grabbed the microphone from Director Tadashi Morita and started to protest what he thought was discriminatory action of the Supreme Court in denying judicial nomination to seven of his fellow students and pleaded that the seven be given a chance to speak. The ceremony ended at that point, and Sakaguchi was dismissed from the Institute by the Supreme Court the same day. Despite considerable political pressure directed toward the court to reverse itself, it refused to do so. Graduation ceremonies were held a few days later, but the press was barred. A court public relations officer later quoted Chief Justice Ishida as telling the graduating students: 'I wish all of you to act with confidence and pride but try not to be too over-confident or self-conceited.'

In January, 1971, the chief judges and senior judges from four high courts and 36 district and family courts throughout Japan met for six hours at the Supreme Court to discuss the propriety of judges' membership in *Seihokyo*. 'According to the secretariat of the Supreme Court,' the *Japan Times* reported on 23 January 'it was unanimously agreed at the meeting to hold that membership in the association was undesirable from the standpoint of fairness and the neutral stand that judges have to maintain.' About this time, a controversy about Assistant Judge Yasuaki Miyamoto of the Kumamoto District Court was just getting under way. Like Fukushima, he was a member of the Young Jurists Association but, unlike Fukushima, he was just completing ten years in the judiciary, which meant his record would be reviewed by the Supreme Court and a decision would be made whether to reappoint him. The decision was negative, and the Supreme Court did not explain its action even though several persons and groups sought an explanation. On 7 April and 9 April, two assistant judges who were also up for reappointment – Etsuru Suzuki, 37, and Keikichi Hirasawa, 35 – resigned in protest. On 15 April, Miyamoto went to Tokyo and asked the director of the personnel bureau of the Supreme Court, Koichi Yaguchi, why he had not been reappointed; but Yaguchi would not tell him. All the Supreme Court would say about the matter was that Miyamoto was not rejected because he was a member of the Young Jurists Association. Its official position in 1971 was that it did not discriminate against members of the Young Jurists Association. When Yaguchi was asked by a Socialist Diet member during a House Audit Committee hearing whether the court discriminated on the basis of sex or ideology in nominating judges, he answered it did not. 'We never use anyone's ideology as criteria for adoption or reappointment of judges,' he said, 'and we will not do so in the future.

And we have never checked on whether a judge is a member of *Seihokyo*, nor have we ever discriminated against a judge because of that affiliation.' Despite a campaign by scholars, lawyers, and judges who argued that the court was violating judicial independence and freedom of conscience, the court held fast in its decision not to reappoint Miyamoto or to tell why it would not do so. Miyamoto also held an appointment as summary court judge and served in Kumamoto in that capacity until March of 1973 when he resigned. He said he had remained in that post so that he could better manifest his resistance to the Supreme Court. Miyamoto told reporters that he would continue as a citizen fighting for reinstatement.

When the Supreme Court was faced with the decision to reappoint judges in March, 1972, there was a report that five of the 62 judges being reviewed were in limbo. All were members of the Young Jurists Association. One of them was Toshio Konno, an assistant judge in the Nagoya District Court. When he had served in the district courts of Nagano and Gifu he had ruled 11 times that a provision of the Road Traffic Law was unconstitutional because it required anyone who was responsible for a traffic accident to report it to the police. In 1970, he was arrested for speeding in Nagano Prefecture and failed to identify himself as a judge, saying he was a businessman. He did this, he said, because if he had identified himself correctly he might not have been fined. When he learned that there were problems in Tokyo concerning his application for reappointment, he withdrew it. He told reporters that he did not have confidence in his work as a judge; obviously he did not think about legal matters like the Supreme Court justices did; so perhaps he should not be a judge. The court recommended reappointment of the remaining 61 judges, including the four members of the Young Jurists Association.

The Supreme Court's impact on the lower judiciary in the past few years has been great. Its confrontation with the Young Jurists Association and its supporters appears to have enhanced its power over the judiciary because (1) it has driven some independent-minded judges from the bench, (2) it has brought would-be recalcitrants into line, (3) it has indicated that membership in the Young Jurists Association is suspect, and as a result membership in the Association has declined among judges, (4) it has shown that it will act against the right as well as the left if its authority is challenged, (5) it has discouraged persons with strong ideological views from choosing the judiciary as a career, and (6) it has shown that as long as it has the support of the government, as clearly shown in the incidents described above, it cannot be successfully challenged by bar associations and other groups.

In exercising power over lower courts, the Supreme Court is constantly creating the judiciary in its own image or, more accurately, in the image of the court's secretariat, which has been controlled from the beginning by bureaucratic career judges like Ishida, Kishi, and Yoshida. Although the generation gap led to a crisis in the Japanese judiciary in the past few years, Ushiomi predicted that the Supreme Court would have prevailed anyway because of the bureaucratic nature of judicial life in Japan. As today's young, fresh, independent-minded judges grow older, he wrote, they will turn out much like their seniors because they lead isolated lives, they must 'breathe old bureaucratic air' while they wait many years for promotion to important posts, and little by little they conform until they too fit the Supreme Court secretariat's bureaucratic mold.

Perhaps Ushiomi is correct, but it is too early to tell. This much is clear: the Supreme Court has had great impact on the judiciary and quite likely will continue to have such impact for the indefinite future.

IV THE RULE OF LAW AND JUDICIAL REVIEW

Urabe, N, 'Rule of Law and Due Process: A Comparative View of the United States and Japan', in Luney, P and Takahashi, K (eds), *Japanese Constitutional Law*, 1993, pp 174–78, 180–83, University of Tokyo Press

In contrast to the Anglo-American idea of the rule of law, which regards the law as protecting individual rights and liberties, the German idea of *Rechtsstaat*, established in the nineteenth century, is unconcerned with the content of the law. It means only that administrative action should be based on a law – 'administration by law.' *Rechtsstaat* assumes the superiority of the administrative power over the people and controls this superior administration through legislative statutes providing the grounds and framework of administration. The law applied to administration is distinguished from the ordinary law applicable to the people and is regarded as a special law peculiar to administration, or administrative law. Therefore, in the traditional *Rechtsstaat*, administrative action is not subject to the judicial review of the ordinary courts, whose task is to administer the ordinary law. Only the administrative court, which itself is considered an administrative organ, can review administrative actions. In this sense, despite a superficial resemblance to the English rule of law, the *Rechtsstaat* is very different, due to its emphasis on the idea of administration by law. The *Rechtsstaat*, when combined with the legal positivism that regards the law as an order of the ruling authority, represents no more than the self-restraint of the state power. Indeed, the *Rechtsstaat* in nineteenth-century Germany was merely a concession of the monarch. The *Rechtsstaat* did not require that the law itself should protect individual rights and liberties. It was only the basis for administrative action. Insofar as the *Rechtsstaat* forbids arbitrary activity by the administrative power, it protects the individual's right to know what the law is and how it will be applied. But, unlike the rule of law, it is by no means a principle for protecting individual rights and liberties.

In summary, the major distinction between the rule of law underlying traditional Western constitutionalism and the *Rechtsstaat* or rule by law of German and Japanese origin is where power and rights are vested. The Western rule of law holds that powers and rights vest naturally in individuals, and that government is limited in its power to infringe upon these rights. On the contrary, the *Rechtsstaat*, a more hierarchical tradition, holds that all powers and rights naturally vest in government, which then allocates rights and powers to its citizens. *Rechtsstaat* does not recognize any individual rights as fundamental; government and not nature is the source of individual rights. This distinction is generally discussed in the Japanese academic world of jurisprudence. This is because the Meiji Constitution of 1890 surely stood on the German concept of the *Rechtsstaat*.

Rule of Law and the Constitution

The Rechtsstaat *in the Meiji Constitution and the Rule of Law in the Constitution of Japan*

The Meiji Constitution was modelled after the Prussian Constitution and introduced the German *Rechtsstaat* principle. The guarantee of the 'rights of the subject' in the Meiji Constitution was limited by a provision securing these rights only 'according to law,' and therefore any kind of restriction on the 'rights of the subject' was allowed so long as it had a statutory basis. In short, the Meiji Constitution required only that administration be based on statute, but it imposed no limitation on the contents of the statutes.

Furthermore, the whole governing power under the Meiji Constitution belonged to the Emperor. The Parliament was not the representative organ of the people but an organ supporting the legislative power of the Emperor. All law was regarded as an order of the Emperor. Therefore, the Emperor was able to issue an order without the participation of the Parliament in certain situations. Thus, there existed an important exception even to the formal administration by law, or *Rechtsstaat*, principle.

The central meaning of the *Rechtsstaat* in the Meiji Constitution was that the people should obey the orders of the Emperor. It was rule by law, which was far from the rule of law. And, as a matter of course, judicial control of administrative and legislative action was denied. The legality of administrative action was only reviewed by the administrative court, which was regarded as an administrative organ. But even the administrative court's review of administrative action was limited to certain matters defined by statute. *Rechtsstaat* in the Meiji Constitution was by no means for the purpose of protecting people's rights and liberties. That is because the constitution itself was given by the Emperor to the people and asked the people to assume the 'duty of allegiance.' The Imperial Rescript for the Promulgation of the Constitution of 1890 said as follows: 'My Ministries should be responsible for putting this constitution in operation on my behalf, and my present and future subjects should assume the duty of eternal allegiance to this constitution.'

On the other hand, the fundamental principle underlying the 1947 Constitution is that the constitution is established by the Japanese people, and the National Diet, the representative organ of the people, monopolizes the legislative power. Therefore, in principle, both the constitution and the law are the manifestations of the will of the people instead of the order of the ruling authority. In this way, the constitution has established the notion of binding the governmental power by the will of the people. The constitution also establishes the concept of fundamental human rights, together with the system of judicial review for assuring the protection of these rights. These characteristics have led to a general view in Japanese jurisprudence that the basic principle of the 1947 Constitution is the rule of law, as distinguished from the *Rechtsstaat* of the Meiji Constitution.

How is the Rule of Law Incorporated in the Constitution:

Like the US Constitution, the Constitution of Japan has no express provision for the rule of law. But it is understood to express the rule of law in the following ways. The first way is by the concept of the supreme law. Chapter 10 of the constitution is titled 'Supreme Law' and implies the rule of law. Article 98 provides that 'no law, ordinance, imperial rescript or other act of government, or part thereof, contrary to the provisions hereof, shall have legal force or validity.' This provision could be seen merely as a statement of a natural attribute of a 'rigid constitution,' that is, that the constitution is simply the highest level in a system of positive law. If so, the supreme law would embody the legal positivistic concept rather than be an expression of the rule of law. Indeed, the Meiji Constitution too was deemed the supreme law in this sense. However, as long as Article 98 is construed as stating that all governmental actions should be ruled by the constitution, one could say that this provision alone reflects the idea of the supremacy of law or the rule of law. But Article 98 says nothing about the substantive contents of the law that is to be the rule. A similar provision would make any constitution the rule of law, whether it protected rights or not.

The Japanese constitution goes further than this. The first article of Chapter 10 confirms the perpetuity and inviolability of fundamental human rights. This means that fundamental human rights are the supreme law of Japan. Therefore, the concept of the supreme law in the constitution is to be understood not only as a legal positivistic and formalistic concept but as a concept with the substantive content of protecting fundamental human rights. It is for this reason that the concept of the supreme law in the constitution is deemed to be an expression of the rule of law.

The second way the constitution incorporates the rule of law is by guaranteeing fundamental human rights under Chapter 3. If the protection of individual rights and liberties is the kernel of the rule of law, Chapter 3 of the constitution, which guarantees people's rights unconditionally, must be regarded as a direct expression of the rule of law. Under the 1947 Constitution, even the National Diet, the representative organ of the people, cannot restrict the fundamental rights of the people. In other words, the fundamental rights of the people bind the legislative power. This represents the most important difference between the Meiji Constitution and the 1947 Constitution.

Requiring due process of law under Article 31 is the third way in which the constitution incorporates the rule of law. The rule of law as an Anglo-American constitutional principle has its roots in the Magna Carta of 1215, and the phrase 'except by the law of the land' in the thirty-ninth clause of that instrument has been read as 'without due process of law.' The rule of law and due process have continued to be closely related in Anglo-American law. As for Article 31 of the constitution, there are some arguments as to whether it has the same meaning as the due process clauses of the fifth and fourteenth amendments of the United States Constitution because those due process clauses are concerned both with procedure and substance. But it is understood almost unanimously that Article 31 requires at least 'procedural due process' in restricting the people's rights and liberties. From this point of view, Article 31 is also deemed to be an expression of the rule of law.

The fourth expression of the rule of law in the constitution is that the whole judicial power is vested in the Supreme Court and lower courts under Article 76. Contrary to the Meiji Constitution, in which the judiciary could not handle administrative cases, the 1947 Constitution vests ordinary courts with jurisdiction over administrative cases and prohibits the establishment of any extraordinary court, such as an administrative court. Administrative action is subject to the judicial review of the ordinary courts, and the superiority of the judiciary over the administrative bureaucracy is a constitutional principle. Needless to say, this is an important element of the Anglo-American rule of law.

Finally, Article 81 of the constitution establishes the system of judicial review. Although the rule of law in England does not include the system of judicial review of constitutionality of legislation, one can say that the Japanese system of judicial review is an expression of the American rule of law or stands on the principle of the American rule of law.

We can recognize the establishment of the principle of the rule of law in the constitution in the above-mentioned points. But the problem is whether this constitutional principle is realized in practice. ...

...

Some Arguments on the Rule of Law in Japan

In Japan, the meaning of the rule of law was extensively debated for a couple of years before and after 1960. The most enthusiastic advocates of what they called the rule of law in those years were the then Chief Justices of the Supreme Court, Tanaka Kotaro and

Yokota Kisaburo. To them, the central meaning of the rule of law was that the people should obey the law. According to Tanaka, 'rule of law' was the antithesis of 'rule of force.' He said that a state of disorder in postwar Japan had misled people into justifying the use of force.

> It has started from the labor dispute, in which the use of force has been legalized within a strict limitation. Beyond this limitation, justification of the use of force has been widely extended to political movements or some other ways to secure one's own interest. This tendency has been growing greater and greater, and in an extreme case it takes the form of a mass movement, by which the normal functioning of the Diet or of the court is obstructed.

Tanaka insisted that 'it is the people in general who are subject to the rule of law, including both the individual person and private groups, and hence the most important thing is to exclude the use of private force, which invades the rule of law.'

Yokota, who was Tanaka's successor as Chief Justice, spoke the same way but more clearly. He said that 'the rule of law today means that the law rules the people, and that the people should obey the law and should act as the law ordains.' Although Yokota admitted that this rule of law was somewhat different from the Anglo-American rule of law, in his opinion this difference was of little importance, because to him the rule of law meant the exclusion of unlawful force of any kind. Hence, whether this 'force' was governmental power or private force was a matter of no importance. According to Yokota, the reason that the notion of the rule of law as a limit on governmental power had been established in England was that the autocratic government had potentially unbounded power in those days. But in 1962, he said, 'there is no autocratic government at all,' and so 'it is hard to imagine that the government shall exercise an arbitrary power. [Therefore,] to make the law superior to governmental power ... is not important. On the other hand, there are still many cases in which the people do not obey the law or do not act as the law ordains.' Yokota further said that mass movements advocating certain political ideologies often exercised violent force, disregarding the law. Therefore, the most important purpose of the rule of law was not to bind governmental power but to exclude the use of force by the people and to require the people to obey the law.

Tanaka and Yokota shared the perception that there existed a dangerous tendency in those days in Japan to resort to violence and to ignore the law. They found this tendency in contemporary labor movements and political mass movements, specifically in the huge mass movement against the revision of the US-Japan Security Treaty from 1959–60.

The understanding of the rule of law articulated by these two former Chief Justices shows that prewar *Rechtsstaat* thinking still remains strong in Japan. Furthermore, the fact that Tanaka and Yokota were not only Chief Justices of the Supreme Court but also prominent law professors who understood the rule of law in this way is enough to give an idea of the actualities of the rule of law in Japan. In practice, the rule of law in Japan does not work as a principle to protect the rights and liberties of the people. Rather, it is no more than ideology to legitimize domination.

If the rule of law in Japan has such a meaning as Tanaka and Yokota asserted, it is natural that the constitution, which is the direct expression of the supremacy of law over governmental power, plays no important role in Japanese society. Of course, I do not intend to say that the constitution is treated entirely as a trivial instrument. On the contrary, I would say that the constitution is given much importance in Japan as a matter of form or theory. For instance, in Japan, in order to acquire a schoolteacher's certificate, one must have credit for a university level course on the Constitution of Japan. Moreover, constitutional law is a required subject, not only on the bar exam but also on the civil service and diplomatic service examinations. In short, as a matter of theory, anyone who is going to be a teacher, a jurist, a civil servant, or a diplomat should have an accurate understanding of the constitution. But this knowledge is useful only on the examination. Once one passes the examination and engages in a job, employers tell one, 'Forget all you have studied at the university.' In Japan, the constitution is in most cases treated as important in principle, but of little importance in practice. This situation is typified by the fact that the majority of the Japanese people are opposed to amending Article 9 of the constitution while they are in favor of the Self-Defense Forces. For them, the constitution is a kind of ornament rather than an enforceable law.

The Rule of Law and Due Process in Some Decisions of the Supreme Court

The Supreme Court of Japan does not seem to consider it important to sustain the rule of law against governmental power. In the past forty or more years of history, there have been only five cases in which the Supreme Court has declared a statute unconstitutional. As there is no evidence that the Japanese legislature is particularly faithful to the constitution, only five cases in forty years is too small a number. This fact proves that the Supreme Court of Japan has almost no idea that government action should be bound strictly by the constitution. If the core of the rule of law is that governmental power be bound by law, and if the rule of law is to be realized through the judicial process, the scarcity of court decisions that have ruled statutes unconstitutional indicates that the rule of law is not realized in practice in Japan.

Moreover, these five decisions have had little impact on Japanese political and social life. Two decisions ruling malapportionment unconstitutional would have great impact on politics if the Supreme Court were to nullify the contested elections. But the Supreme Court did not invalidate the elections, and this rendered the decisions ineffective. Even in the patricide case, which involved important problems of equal protection, the Supreme Court ruled the criminal code provision unconstitutional only on a technical ground. The other two cases in which the Supreme Court declared statutes unconstitutional were both concerned with economic liberty or property rights, and the constitutional issues in these cases had no significant meaning for public life. In short, the Supreme Court of Japan has never said nay to the Government in a serious manner.

When looking at individual decisions, there are many that are doubtful from the point of view of the rule of law and due process. In the *Nishiyama* case, the Supreme Court decided that the newsgathering activity at issue, whereby a reporter had taken advantage of a love affair to obtain a confidential telegram of the Ministry of Foreign Activity from a woman official, was illegal in light of the 'spirit of [the] whole legal order.' Of course, there is no law that prohibits a reporter from gathering news from his or her lover. This decision, which restricted freedom not by law but by such a vague concept as the spirit of the whole legal order, paid no attention at all to the rule of law or due process.

In a case in which the exclusion of illegally seized evidence was the key issue, the Supreme Court said that unlawful procedures of search and seizure alone would not exclude evidence because the value of material evidence for arriving at truth would be unchanged whether the procedure for securing it was lawful or not. To exclude evidence by reason of unlawful procedure is, according to the Supreme Court, an 'improper way to investigate the truth of the case.' In spite of the detailed constitutional provisions requiring due process of law, the Supreme Court deemed the substantive truth more important than the procedure.

The idea of a strict distinction between 'public law' and 'private law,' which has been a legal tradition in Japan since the Meiji era, is still strong. Although it is said in Japan that the constitution stands on the Anglo-American idea of the rule of law, the Administrative Case Procedure Law provides a special procedure peculiar to administrative cases. Thus, the Japanese legal system is constructed on the premise of a distinction between public law and private law, which does not quite correspond with the Anglo-American rule of law. This is not wrong in itself, but if the distinction between public law and private law becomes a reason to reject the protection of people's rights, it results in the superiority of administration over the people.

A typical example of this is the Supreme Court decision in the *Osaka Airport* case, in which the Supreme Court said that a suit to enjoin airplane landings and takeoffs at night was unlawful as civil litigation because it was nothing but a demand to change an operational decision of the aeronautic administrative power. The Supreme Court refused to consider the claims of the residents around the airport by saying that people could not lodge an objection against the administrative power through a civil procedure.

In the *Hyakuri Base* case, a contract that the Government made with a private party to acquire a base site for the Self-Defense Forces was alleged to be invalid because the existence of the Self-Defense Forces violated Article 9 of the constitution. The Supreme Court declared that the constitution does not limit government action done according to private law. According to the court, because the constitution is a public law and hence does not limit the actions of private parties, it does not limit government action when the Government acts as a private party. Here, the formalistic distinction between public law and private law overrides the demand that all government action should be consistent with the constitution.

Okudaira, Y, 'Forty Years of the Constitution and Its Various Influences' in Luney, P and Takahashi, K (eds), *Japanese Constitutional Law*, 1963, pp 13–23, University of Tokyo Press

The Concept of Due Process

The process by which foreign law was incorporated into the Japanese constitution can also be seen through the constitution's treatment of the concept of due process of law. It is almost certain that the draftsmen of SCAP deliberately avoided using the term 'due process of law' in the text of the Japanese constitution. There is no due process clause identical to that which Americans have in the fifth and fourteenth amendments to their constitution. Article 31 of the Japanese constitution is similar to the due process clause. It says: 'No person shall be deprived of life or liberty, nor shall any other criminal penalty be imposed, except according to procedure established by law.' It was generally maintained in the early days of the constitution that however similar Article 31 might appear to be to its American cousin, it did not constitute a due process clause. The reasons were that, first, unlike the American model, Article 31 states, 'No person shall be deprived of life or liberty' without mentioning 'property.' And, second, instead of the American phraseology, 'without due process of law,' Article 31 used the wording 'except according to procedure established by law.' A majority of SCAP legal officers were New Dealers, and it is reasonable to assume that they hated the 'substantive due process' analysis that invalidated much early New Deal legislation. Perhaps it is true that these

Americans did not desire to introduce into postwar Japan the due process jurisprudence that had existed in the 1930s in the United States.

In connection with this topic, the Indian experience is illuminating. Article 22 of the Indian Constitution of 1949 provides: 'No citizen shall be deprived of his personal liberty except according to procedure established by law.' This article was, as an Indian professor proves, written under the influence of Article 31 of the Japanese constitution. It is reported that during the framing of the Indian constitution, BN Rau, who was the constitutional advisor to the Constituent Assembly, visited North America for discussions with eminent persons in the field of constitutional law and was advised by Justice Felix Frankfurter not to include the due process clause in the Indian constitution. Justice Frankfurter's position was 'that the power of review implied in the "due process" clause was not only undemocratic but also threw an unfair burden on the judiciary.' It seems that in order to eliminate the possibility of a judicial activist interpretation, the constitutional founders in both Japan and India took care not to introduce a due process clause.

The scope of the American concept of due process of law is wide, and it has various meanings. 'Substantive due process' is not the only meaning of the due process clause. Above all, it connotes procedural safeguards in criminal proceedings. As discussed above, this aspect of due process is reasonably well covered by the Constitution of Japan in Articles 32–39. Thus, in contrast to the American concept, due process was institutionalized in the Constitution of Japan as a narrower concept, especially concerned with criminal justice.

The American concept of due process of law implies procedural safeguards not only in criminal proceedings, but also in every phase of the governmental process, including administrative proceedings. The Japanese, who had been influenced by German law, were utterly unfamiliar with the concept of procedural due process. Articles 32–39 enable the Japanese to enjoy due process protection within the field of criminal proceedings. But what about procedural due process in other areas of state power?

Twenty years ago – coincidentally twenty years after the promulgation of the Constitution of Japan – Walter Gellhorn of Columbia Law School was asked at a session of the Cabinet Committee of Investigation of the constitution to give his comments on the Constitution of Japan. He stated, 'I have no hesitancy in expressing the belief that Japan has not yet sufficiently concerned itself with procedures.' He continued, 'I believe this [change regarding due process] to be one of the areas that most urgently deserves continuing study and reflection, lest the high aspirations of the constitution be set at naught by crude methods of law administration.' He criticized the lack of respect for procedural safeguards in general, but his bitter comment was specifically concerned with the field of administrative process. There was no serious attempt to provide a citizen with procedural protections against an administrative agency. Such terms as the 'right to notice' and the 'right to have an opportunity for a hearing' were scarcely known to the Japanese at that time.

Many factors contributed to such an underdeveloped situation regarding procedural protection. The most important of all was the traditional lack of awareness on the part of the Japanese regarding procedural due process. If an explicit due process clause had been adopted, the new constitution might have changed the way of thinking in this respect. But in actuality, the due process clause was deliberately excluded from the new constitution. Though some institutions for due process were adopted in the area of criminal justice, their adoption was done in such a localized way that it was not enough to create a new sense of procedural due process with broader implications that might have been similar to American ideas.

Gellhorn's observation was totally correct then, and still is so today to a great extent. However, a sign of a slowly emerging Japanese sense of procedural due process was shown in court decisions in the early 1960s. In 1962 the Supreme Court announced for the first time that in some situations Articles 29 and 31 of the constitution required that 'notice and opportunity of explanation and defense' be given to a person whose rights have been invaded. In 1963 the Tokyo District Court held for the first time that the court would reverse an administrative agency's denial of a license to become a taxi driver because the applicant had not been given notice and the opportunity for a hearing. A few months later, the same Tokyo District Court handed down a similar decision in the case of a bus route license. These two cases finally reached the Supreme Court, and in both cases the court substantially affirmed the district court's position that the applicants should have been provided with notice and an opportunity to be heard. Interestingly, however, the court held so as a matter of statutory interpretation, without mentioning constitutional law at all. Awareness regarding procedural due process has increased considerably, especially since the 1970s when the demand for participatory democracy increased.

As mentioned above, the adoption of 'due process of law' in an explicit way was deliberately avoided by the drafters of the present constitution. And, partly because of this lack of textual support, the development of the concept of 'due process of law' was retarded and remained only in a narrow field. However, as modern constitutionalism and constitutional institutions, including the system of judicial review, have become more prevalent, the value of 'due process of law' has been gradually recognized; we now can say that it has become part of our constitution – without an explicit clause to guarantee that concept.

The Concept of Judicial Review

Arguments About Article 81. Article 81 of the Constitution of Japan provides that '[t]he Supreme Court is the court of last resort with power to determine the constitutionality of any law, order, regulation or official act.' Against the general background of American influence in the drafting and subsequent deliberations attending the enactment of the Japanese constitution, it was reasonable to assume that Article 81 was intended to introduce the American system of judicial review developed from *Marbury v Madison*. This assumption finally prevailed, but not without some opposition. Some legal scholars took the position that Article 81 should be interpreted as conferring upon the Supreme Court a special power so that it would become a constitutional court as well as the highest court of appeal. Standing on the traditional legal viewpoint, they invoked Article 81. Under the prewar system, judicial review was utterly unthinkable; the Japanese could go only so far in accepting an institution such as a constitutional court or a constitutional review board of the European type. In 1948, however, in judging a criminal case, the Supreme Court declared: 'Article 81 of our constitution should be characterized as an explicit provision adopting the type of judicial review which has been established in the [United States] by way of the mere interpretation of the constitution.' That statement was obiter dictum. The elaboration of this point remained for another occasion.

Another question concerning the interpretation of Article 81 was whether the lower courts were also entitled to review the constitutionality of legislation. If put to an American, an affirmative answer would come back almost automatically. By contrast, through Western European eyes, the text of Article 81 looks as if only the Supreme Court was granted special power to review the constitutionality of state actions. In 1950, the court decided in favor of the lower courts. This is another indication of the adoption of the American model.

In October 1952, the court elaborated on this issue in a case in which the chairman of the left-wing section of the Socialist Party was the plaintiff. The chairman filed suit against the state directly with the Supreme Court without first going through the screening of the lower courts. In his suit, the chairman asked the court to deciare that an ordinance establishing the Police Force Reserve, which was enacted only by the Cabinet, was a violation of Article 9, the pacifist clause, and was therefore invalid. The Supreme Court declined to review the merits of his arguments and instead held that litigation like this could not be sustained because there were only abstract arguments and no concrete case. The plaintiff had no standing to file an action. It is generally understood that, in so holding, the Supreme Court considered whether there existed a 'case or controversy,' which is required by the United States Constitution as a prerequisite to constitutional litigation.

Transformation of Judicial Power. The purpose of the introduction of judicial review by Article 81 was to revolutionize the traditional concept of the judiciary. This change was not clearly recognized for a period after the constitution's enactment, and, most likely, the revolutionary process remains unfinished even today.

According to the prewar concept of judicial power, based on German constitutional doctrine, judicial courts were used only for solving legal disputes among citizens and for dealing with criminal sanctions. All other litigation was outside the jurisdiction of judicial courts. Thus, for example, administrative law litigation could be handled only by a special tribunal within the administrative branch. This concept of the judiciary was closely related to the peculiarly German idea of the dualism of state and society. Judicial courts should be concerned with matters within society, and the government (or the crown) should be responsible for state affairs involving matters of the relationship between the state and society.

Article 81 of the new constitution provides judicial courts with the power to review an act's constitutionality, a concept that had been absolutely foreign to the traditional concept of the judiciary. Furthermore, it is almost an established interpretation that under Article 76, clauses 1 and 2, no administrative court, as existed in prewar Japan, shall be maintained. Against the backdrop of these two constitutional provisions and of the general character of the whole constitution, it seemed rather natural to assume that the framers were creating a brand new concept of judicial power. But the process of its creation has not proven to be an easy one.

In 1953, the Japan Association of Public Law published issue number 8 of *Koho Kenkyu*. The journal is divided into three parts, one of which is entitled, [*The*] *Relationship Between the Administrative Power and the Judicial Power*. The leading article is entitled *Prerogatives of Administrative Authorities Against Judicial Review* and was written by Tagami Joji, professor of Hitotsubashi University. Tagami emphasized the limitations on judicial power in relation to administrative activities. He seemed particularly interested in narrowing judicial judgments based on the merit of administrative decisions by stressing the discretionary power of administrative agencies. He also argued that both declaratory judgments and *mandamus* were generally impermissible against administrative authorities.

An article by Yanase Yoshimoto appears in the same journal section. Yanase firmly adhered to the traditional, narrow concept of judicial power in spite of the constitutional change. He maintained that the jurisdiction of the judiciary covered only civil and criminal litigation and that, therefore, disputes concerning administrative law belonged intrinsically to an area outside (*fremdes Gebiet*) of the judicial power. Further, he insisted that there was an essential limit on judicial intervention in the field of administrative law. The reader will notice in the articles appearing in *Koho Kenkyu* the frequent repetition of terms such as 'independence of administrative authorities from the judiciary' and 'supremacy of the administrative power.'

The articles and essays contained in the journal were representative of the then-prevailing concept of judicial power. About that time, I graduated from law school and started my apprenticeship to an academic career. While reading these articles and essays, I felt much irritation. But I must confess that I did not know how to overcome it; the authors were so confident. This was the doctrinal situation that confronted the new concept of the judiciary.

The doctrinal atmosphere surrounding the concept of judicial power in relation to administrative authorities has changed slowly since then. Now, no scholar seems to stick to the traditional narrow concept, and judicial power is interpreted as extending to suits against administrative agencies as well as to civil and criminal proceedings. Judicial control over administrative discretion has thus greatly expanded, and such expressions as 'independence of administrative authorities from the judiciary' and 'supremacy of the administrative power (over the judiciary)' are rarely heard.

It appears, however, that elements of the traditional, limited concept of judicial power remain and control both the judiciary's way of thinking and its way of operation. One of the most conspicuous indications is the insufficiency of judicial remedies against administrative authorities. First, the Administrative Litigation Law strictly limits the opportunity to issue preventive injunctions against administrative decisions and makes explicitly impermissible provisional dispositions of any administrative actions. Second, there are no provisions for declaratory judgments or mandamus. For these reasons, the prevailing opinion is that judicial courts can neither make declaratory judgments nor issue writs of mandamus against administrative bodies. These limitations on judicial remedies provoke various arguments about administrative law proceedings at large. Needless to say, however, in the case of constitutional litigation, these limitations are more problematic, since the infringement of a citizen's fundamental right is involved more frequently than in other cases.

For instance, in a case concerning the constitutionality of the apportionment of seats for the House of Representatives, the Supreme Court declared for the first time that the seat allocation for the House of Representatives provided in the Public Officials Election Act violated the constitutional guarantee of equality under the law. The Supreme Court first took the opportunity to consider an apportionment controversy in 1964, in a case concerning the House of Councillors. In this case, the issue was more delicate than in the later House of Representatives' case since, in the former, the controversy revolved around the particular issue of how to consider prefectures as constituency units. The Supreme Court made a great deal of the Diet's ability to frame constituency units, and emphasizing the broad extent of legislative discretion, upheld the constitutionality of the law under attack. Thus, the court relied upon the legislature's wide discretion, not upon the American doctrine of 'political questions.' By contrast, in his separate supplemental opinion, Justice Saito Kitaro argued that the case was nonjusticiable, adopting arguments similar to those in Justice Frankfurter's 1962 dissenting opinion in *Baker v Carr*.

No immediate remedy in the plaintiff's favor was expected from the court's holding the disputed law unconstitutional. This was not necessarily due to the Supreme Court, but primarily due to what I would submit is the defective system of constitutional litigation.

In accordance with Article 204 of the Public Officials Election Act, which enables any voter to file a suit to invalidate a recent election, the plaintiff instituted this suit against the Chairman of the Chiba Election Supervision Commission. There is no doubt that the original intention of Article 204 was to make it possible for the voters to ask that an election of specific candidates be nullified for technical reasons. With regard to malapportionment suits, a specific ease is not necessarily concerned with the particular candidate's fate but rather with the whole system of seat allocation. Moreover, plaintiffs in malapportionment cases do not always request to invalidate the particular election already held, but seek to make it impossible to apply the current seat allocation law to any future elections. For the purpose of malapportionment disputes, the most appropriate remedies are declaratory judgments, preventive injunctive relief, or both. However, there is no law that supports the permissibility of such judicial remedies in Japan.

Irrespective of the lack of legislative support, the courts may create a remedy that will prevent the invasion of a citizen's constitutional right. But the prevailing opinion of administrative law takes the position that neither declaratory judgments nor preventive injunctions are within the realm of judicial power. It is unlikely that in the near future the courts will invent a remedy so that plaintiffs may question the validity of a seat allocation law before an election has actually taken place.

Thus, at present, Article 204 is regarded as the only route available for plaintiffs in malapportionment litigation. Article 204 litigation is concerned with the validity of an election already completed. It is almost impossible for the Supreme Court to nullify a nationwide election as a whole, because the invalidation of the election may invite the invalidation of all of the important political decisions made by the Diet, such as the appointment of the Prime Minister, legislative or budget matters, and treaty enactments. Therefore, as the Supreme Court showed in its 1976 holding, it is practically forced to avoid invalidation of an election, despite its judgment of the unconstitutionality of a law under attack. The political status quo is almost always strong enough to nullify whatever action the Court may want to take. Not only because of Japanese adherence to the narrow concept of the judicial power in relation to state powers, but also perhaps because of the lack of equitable institutions, no attempt has been made to renovate the system of remedies for constitutional litigation. It is now time to do so.

A General View of Judicial Review in Operation. During the past 40 years, there have been five occasions on which the Supreme Court denied the validity of legislation on constitutional grounds. Opinions will vary as to whether the figure, five, constitutes a good or bad record as an indicator of the function of our judicial review system. Against the countless number of enactments during the same period, the figure five is undoubtedly small. Is it the excellent nature of draftsmanship that prevents the Diet from making bad laws? Or, rather, is it the negativist, or self-restraining, approach of the Supreme Court that makes the court apt to respect legislative determinations? It would not be unfair to say that most scholars and lawyers share the opinion that negativism in judicial review is one of the most characteristic features of the Japanese Supreme Court.

Throughout the history of the present constitution, the expression 'wide legislative discretion' has been employed by the courts in one way or another. Even in the field of freedom of expression, the Supreme Court is willing to speak about 'legislative discretion.'

Perhaps it should be noted here that the Supreme Court has never held unconstitutional any regulation on freedom of expression. The court once suggested that freedom of expression deserves more protection than freedom of economic activities and that, therefore, court examinations should be more strict in the field of free expression. In practice, however, the court has never strictly scrutinized regulations on free expression. Considering that the court has twice declared economic regulations unconstitutional, it appears that the court treats freedom of economic activities more seriously than freedom of expression.

There is a general tendency for the Supreme Court to avoid constitutional judgments as much as possible. In 1971 the Supreme Court affirmed the decision of the lower court concerning an application for a taxi driver's license, saying that the administrative agency had denied the application for the license without first providing the applicant with proper notice and an opportunity for hearings. For the first time, the Supreme Court was speaking about a citizen's right to procedural due process in an administrative proceeding. While the Tokyo High Court as well as the Tokyo District Court based a citizen's right on Articles 13 and/or 31 of the constitution itself, the Supreme Court did not rely upon any constitutional provisions. The court established the right as if it existed as a necessary result of the interpretation of the Road Transportation Law.

To the court, this was not constitutional litigation but a regular case of administrative law. However, it should be noted that the reason the agency denied the application without complying with the procedural requirements was that there was no explicit provision in the law conferring upon an applicant the right to notice and the opportunity for a hearing. Therefore, it is fair to say that the court invented a new interpretation of the law so that for the first time, applicants were able to enjoy procedural safeguards with respect to administrative agencies. It is almost certain that in so doing the Supreme Court was guided by the liberal, democratic spirit of the constitution. Without relying on the constitution, it would have been impossible for the court to have invented such a right.

Why, then, did the court not mention anything of a constitutional nature? The reason seems rather simple: If the court had relied upon constitutional law, the coverage of a citizen's right to notice and opportunity for a hearing would extend to various administrative processes other than the one concerned in the instant case. On the other hand, if confined by the narrow framework of statutory interpretation, the recognized right is only applicable to cases within the same framework. By failing to acknowledge constitutional questions, the Japanese Supreme Court seems to want to decide constitutional issues on a case-by-case basis.

Another example indicating the same tendency to operate on a case-by-case basis is contained in one of the court's most recent decisions. The case concerned the lawfulness of a judge's order prohibiting those in attendance from taking notes during courtroom proceedings. Theoretically, this kind of restraint order is made on the basis of the discretionary, disciplinary powers of the individual judge presiding over the court; in practice, however, almost all trial courts have adopted a similar rule of general prohibition. A few years ago, an American lawyer filed a suit against this type of prohibition. The Tokyo District Court dismissed the action and held that the prohibition order was within the discretionary powers of the presiding judge, and that there was nothing unlawful about such an order. This holding was affirmed by the Tokyo High Court. The plaintiff appealed to the Supreme Court. Surprisingly, the Supreme Court reversed the judgment of the lower court in substance and declared that, in spite of a judge's wide disciplinary powers, the presiding judge was not allowed to prohibit those in attendance from taking notes, irrespective of the type of case.

The issue presented was related to a citizen's right to attend, inspect, and record court proceedings, and as such it was very much similar to the issue that the United States Supreme Court confronted in *Richmond Newspapers, Inc v Virginia* and similar cases. In those cases, the United States Supreme Court dealt, without the slightest hesitation, with the issue at the constitutional level as a problem regarding First Amendment rights. In contrast, however, the Japanese Supreme Court solved the case simply on the basis of the scope of a judge's discretionary and disciplinary powers. Evidently our court would not like to make any affirmative statements about the people's right to know, because, once open to that direction, constitutional claims would extend from the right to take notes in the courtroom to the right to inspect various government institutions, as well as to the right to have access to government records.

One additional example is helpful. The top leader of one of Japan's largest and most influential religious organizations charged a magazine publisher with the crime of defamation and claimed that his reputation had seriously been harmed by the defendant's publication. The publisher was indicted. The issue presented was precisely the freedom of expression versus a person's right to enjoy his reputation. The questions asked were whether the publisher's constitutional right was more important than the leader's personal claim and, if so, why and to what extent? Borrowing the American terminology, the court was dealing with the concept of a 'public figure.' Needless to say, in the United States, that concept belongs within the area of constitutional law. The First Amendment is the starting point: The concept of 'public figure' has been created and clarified by the courts in order to uphold the First Amendment and to accommodate other interests, such as personal reputation or privacy.

The same must apply to Japanese jurisprudence when dealing with the concept of 'public figure.' In contrast, however, in the defamation case of the religious leader mentioned above, the Supreme Court spoke little about constitutional law or the guarantee of freedom of the press. The court solved the case almost exclusively within the framework of statutory interpretation. The resolution of the case was correct – I have no serious objection with it. What is annoying is the way the court resolved the issue.

The court introduced a kind of 'public figure' concept by setting three requirements to establish defamation. The court did this by merely interpreting the defamation law. A young American lawyer, a postgraduate student who was studying in Japan, remarked 'I have recently examined the Supreme Court decision carefully. But one thing puzzles me very much. The court does not say much about the constitution. It talks only about statutory construction. Is statutory law predominant over the constitution in Japan?' It is not clear why the Supreme Court preferred to rely on statutory construction rather than on Article 21 of the constitution. However, one thing is certain: If you are successful in establishing such a doctrine on constitutional grounds rather than on a mere statutory basis, the position of the doctrine will be stronger because it would be invulnerable to any change in the law concerned.

Ashibe, N, 'Human Rights and Judicial Power', in Beer, LW (ed), ***Constitutional Systems in Late Twentieth Century Asia*****, 1992, pp 235–37, 239–47, University of Washington Press**

Under the Meiji Constitution, the judicial power extended only to criminal and civil cases, and not to administrative cases. Administrative cases were tried within the executive branch in an Administrative Court separate from the ordinary courts. These were trials of disputes concerning rights and duties in public law between an administrative organ and a person whose rights or interests had been illegally damaged by an administrative disposition. This system had been adopted by continental European countries such as France and Germany.

In contrast, the present constitution of Japan, after the model of Anglo-American law, includes the trial of administrative cases among the functions of the regular courts. Article 76, paragraphs 1 and 2, provide: 'The whole judicial power is vested in the Supreme Court and in such inferior courts as are established by law. No extraordinary tribunal shall be established, nor shall any organ or agency of the Executive be given final judicial power.'

Article 76 marks a major change in the Japanese court system from a continental law model to the Anglo-American model. The judicial power in Japan is almost the same as that under the US Constitution, in spite of the fact that the Constitution of Japan lacks a 'cases and controversies' clause as found in Article 3, section 2 of the US Constitution. The Supreme Court has said: 'The permissible function of the courts is limited to conclusively resolving, pursuant to legal interpretation, those disputes related to the existence of legal relationships or the concrete rights and duties of the parties concerned, that is "legal disputes" (Article 3 of the Court Organization Law).'

A 'concrete dispute' is an indispensable condition for any trial under the above provision. However, we must keep in mind the following points:

Included within the Japanese concept of a *judiciary* is its independence (as well as the need for a concrete dispute), together with the requirement of fair procedures as under traditional principles of fairness, ie oral arguments and a public hearing.

The constitution of Japan expressly guarantees access to the courts as a human right (Art. 32). This differs from the guarantee of trial rights which the US Constitution establishes in Article 2, section 2 regarding the object of court deliberations, in the Sixth and Seventh Amendments guaranteeing trial by jury, and in the due process clauses. In Japan, the right of access to the courts is understood in case law and scholarly exegesis to require procedural guarantees, with rigorous provisions for due process set forth under Article 82: 'Trials shall be conducted and judgment declared publicly' with few exceptions, and 'trials of political offenses, offenses involving the press, or in cases wherein the rights of the people as guaranteed in Chapter III of this constitution are in question shall always be conducted publicly.'

Since the time of the Meiji Constitution, litigation other than cases involving the rights and interests of the litigants alone has been recognized. Litigation to protect a public interest and to assure the lawfulness of administrative acts has been established in positive law; such suits are usually referred to as 'a people's action' ('*minshu sosho*') or 'an objective action' ('*kyakken sosho*'). An example is a suit in which voters challenge the validity of an election or its results. The prevailing view is that, strictly speaking, such a suit does not come under the normal judicial function, but is *an exception recognized pursuant to legislative policy*.

If such objective suits are recognized, and if they are permitted as under implied judicial powers, there will be arguments on whether this goes against the concept of judicial power, or again whether a broader understanding of plaintiff standing than is traditional should be permitted in consumer suits and environmental litigation. This would happen even if the Supreme Court were given a German-style constitutional court power by law.

In the United States, such litigation exists in taxpayers' suits and citizens' suits; but the relationship between the constitutional requisite of 'case and controversy' and the rule of standing is unclear, whether it is to be considered a matter of constitutional requirement or a prudential rule of judicial self-restraint.

The questions of 'institutional reform litigation' or 'public law litigation' and American legal theory are being hotly debated; clarification of related issues is a matter of serious concern in current Japanese legal discourse. However, Japanese case law has been rather negative about strengthening the idea of objective action or expanding the traditional understanding of the judicial function. Great importance is attached to requiring a controversy, so a liberalization of the conditions necessary for standing has not taken place to the extent found in US case law. The American model of public law litigation and institutional reform litigation has come under heavy criticism in Japan, even from influential scholars.

Undoubtedly, there are limits to the liberalization of plaintiff standing requirements. Also, many problems arise with the present model of litigation recognizing direct judicial intervention into matters of public policy and politics. However, together with Archibald Cox, I think that 'the hard question is one of degree.' With the focus on requiring a controversy while opening the door of justice as wide as possible, especially in the area of remedial law, this approach meshes with judicial power under the Constitution of Japan and is worthy of positive consideration. ...

...

Judicial Review and Its Function of Guaranteeing the Constitution

As in the United States, there are two ways of declaring a law unconstitutional in Japan: the law itself may be considered unconstitutional, or the application of the law to a certain case may be unconstitutional. In the forty-three years since the birth of the constitution, Supreme Court decisions have declared a law provision unconstitutional in only four cases.

The first case dealt with the killing of a parent (a lineal ascendant) and the severe penalty imposed for such a crime by Article 200 of the Criminal Code. While the gratitude and respect owed to one's direct ascendant is recognized as one of the most basic moral principles in society, and its protection by the criminal law is valued as a reasonable legislative purpose, Article 200 was declared unconstitutional by the Grand Bench of the Supreme Court in a 1973 decision. The court held that the method used to achieve this purpose was discriminatory and a violation of the 'equal protection' clause (Art. 14), in that the penalty was unreasonably harsh when compared with that for ordinary homicide (a minimum three-year sentence with the possibility of a suspended sentence). Six of the liberal judges took the position that the legislature's intent was itself unconstitutional. However, the majority held the degree of disparity between the two penalties unconstitutional, while a minority felt that any disparity between the provisions should be deemed unconstitutional.

The second case concerned the licensing and opening of a new pharmacy in Hiroshima. On 30 April 1975, the Grand Bench unanimously held that a regulation requiring a certain distance between two pharmacies under the Pharmaceuticals Law was an unconstitutional violation of the freedom to choose an occupation (Art. 22(1)).

Then, in 1985 the Grand Bench held unconstitutional Table #1 of the Annex to the Public Offices Election Law, a provision which fixed the apportionment of Diet seats among election districts. When the 1980 general election for the House of Representatives was held, the disparity in the value of a vote in different election districts ranged up to 1 to 4.40. Since the 1975 revision to the Public Offices Election Law, correction of disparities within a reasonable period has been required. In the absence of such a correction, this present lawsuit occurred.

In the fourth case, the Supreme Court voided in April, 1987 Article 186 of the Forestry Law (*Shinrin Ho*) as counter to Article 29, paragraph 2 of the constitution ('Property rights shall be defined by law, in conformity with the public welfare') in its treatment of jointly or communally owned forests. Article 186 negated an owner's right of petition for a division of property under Article 256, paragraph 1 of the Civil Code in cases where a joint owner has less than a half interest in the forest property. The court held that such a limitation of rights has no reasonable connection with the legislative purposes of Article 186 of the Forestry Law to strive for stable forest management and to prevent excessive dividing up of forest lands, and exceeds the bounds of necessary regulation. Soon after this decision, the Diet took steps to abolish Article 186.

On the same day the decision on the Pharmaceuticals Law was handed down, the Welfare Ministry issued a notice to each prefectural governor which stated, 'We kindly ask you, effective immediately, not to apply the proper site requirement of the ordinance when granting a license for a pharmacy.' This was done as an exercise of administrative guidance (*gyosei shido*). On 29 May, a bill was introduced in the Diet to delete the site location provision from the Pharmaceuticals Law. After passing both Houses, the bill took effect on 13 June. On 28 June, the Welfare Ministry sent a notice to each prefectural governor, recommending that they take appropriate measures to promptly abolish ordinance provisions imposing a placement restriction on pharmacies, due to the revised law which stemmed from the Supreme Court's decision.

In Japan the effect of a decision holding a law to be unconstitutional is generally thought to have individual effect applicable only to the case in question. However, in light of what happened after the Pharmaceutical Law was held unconstitutional, we can say that Supreme Court decisions in fact have binding power actually affecting all future decisions. In the case of the unconstitutionally heavy penalty for patricide, the authorities quickly took corrective measures. There was, however, some negative reaction from the Diet. Immediately after the 1973 decision, the Supreme Public Prosecutor's Office sent a notice to all prosecutors directing them to use Article 199, the provision on ordinary murder, when prosecuting someone for the killing of a lineal ascendant. In addition, the Ministry of Justice issued a notification on April 18, 1973 requesting all related agencies of the government to consider granting pardons (reduction of penalty or remission of sentence) to all those who were serving time in prison as a result of conviction under Article 200. These government agencies were to take these steps even without application from the prisoners themselves. Reasonable amnesty would be recognized, and prompt special corrective actions were to be taken. However, in the Diet there was no consensus as to whether or not Article 200 was still in effect. No one knew if it had been abolished or revised, and if revised, then in what form. [The debate remains unsettled].

The 1985 case, dealing with unconstitutional malapportionment of Diet seats, is more complex. The validity of an election was questioned after it was held pursuant to the Public Offices Election Law. In Japan, a request for an injunction or a declaratory judgment finding unconstitutional malapportionment, as in the US, is not allowed. Moreover, for a long time legal precedent hesitated over the question of whether the right to vote carries with it a right to have votes equally valued. The decision in *Baker v Carr* on reapportionment had a great influence on scholarly opinion in Japan. Accordingly, the question of equal vote values has been considered a subject for constitutional litigation. In 1976, the Japanese Supreme Court, in a Grand Bench decision, first recognized that equality in vote values was constitutionally demanded:

> If the degree of the inequality can in no way generally be considered reasonable, then there can be no special reason which would justify it, and if there was no correction within a reasonable period of time, as demanded by the constitution, the apportionment in its entirety would become unconstitutional.

The 1976 decision only declared that the election was unconstitutional; it did not nullify the results of the election, for to do so would have given rise to various inconvenient results not anticipated by the constitution. Article 31 of the Administrative Case Litigation Law recognizes the so-called principle of 'special circumstances' (*jijo hanketsu*). It provides, in part:

> In the event an administrative agency's disposition or ruling is illegal, the court may, nevertheless, turn down a request which seeks to quash said disposition or ruling, when to do otherwise would be incompatible with the public welfare. In such a case, the court's judgment must contain a statement that the agency's disposition or ruling was illegal.

Invoking this principle as a 'basic principle of general law,' the court did not invalidate the election, but merely held it to be unconstitutional. There are problems with the application of the principle of 'special circumstances' to election-type litigation, and with the Supreme Court's view concerning the equality of vote values. Nevertheless, the above decision is compared to the *Baker* case, and has been highly regarded as of epoch-making significance.

The solution to the apportionment problem lies with the Diet; it is their duty to take remedial measures when a situation has been declared unconstitutional. The use of the principle of special circumstances is not the final solution to the dilemma. Actually, the Diet has been very slow to react and to pass a reapportionment bill. After the 1976 decision, people groped for a method which would elicit a new decision declaring the present malapportionment unconstitutional. Two views are: (a) Even though there is no tradition of equity law in Japan, the court itself should reapportion the electoral seats until the Diet does so, for this is a problem of remedial law, not primary law. (b) Have an election enjoined and if the Diet does not immediately correct the situation, then let the court hold the election based on its own reapportionment.

In the 1985 decision mentioned above, Chief Justice Jiro Terada, along with four other Justices, argued in a concurring opinion: 'Elections held without taking corrective measures after a judgment of special circumstances *(jijo hanketsu)* has declared the previous election's appointment unconstitutional should be held invalid. However, such a judgment would not take effect until after a certain period of time had elapsed.' For some time, this has been the position advocated by scholars. It is noteworthy that this approach, using decisions with prospective effect, was employed in a Supreme Court judgment, though in a concurring opinion.

As the above cases illustrate, many unanswered questions remain regarding the effect of and method for obtaining decisions which hold a law or governmental act unconstitutional. Nevertheless, the actualization of human rights guarantees through the power of judicial review clearly occupies an important role in preserving the constitution and establishing the 'rule of law.'

We must not overlook the fact that Japan's system of judicial review is the same as that of the state supreme courts in the United States. They are courts which exercise not only powers of judicial review, but as the highest legal organs they must also promote consistent legal interpretation. The distinguishing feature about the Japanese court system is that judges are all career judges, except for the Supreme Court. Supreme Court Justices come under Article 41 of the Court Organization Law: 'Justices of the Supreme Court shall be appointed from among persons of broad vision and extensive knowledge of the law, who are not less than forty years of age.' Though prosecutors, lawyers, and law professors also enter the Supreme Court, the strong tendency is to fill many positions with career judges, and this has had a significant effect on judicial review. ...

Avoiding Constitutional Decisions

Assuming there is a case or controversy, the system of judicial review does not have as its direct purpose constitutional decision-making itself constitutional decision making is for the purpose of solving a specific dispute. Controlled by the rule of strict necessity 'constitutional decision making is limited to the unavoidable.'

In the 1967 *Eniwa* case this rule was the subject of much debate. Originating in the Eniwa district of Hokkaido, the case was the first to deal with the constitutionality of the Self-Defense Forces (SDF). Many dairy farmers complained of injury to their livestock resulting from explosions, the shooting of live shells, and other effects of military exercises conducted near their property boundaries. The farmers protested the continuation of the exercises by cutting the communication lines to the practice area. Some of the farmers were prosecuted for violating Article 121 of the Self-Defense Forces Law which provides: 'Any person who damages or destroys any possession or weapon, ammunition, aircraft, or other device used for defense shall be punished by a sentence of not more than 5 years or a fine of not more than 50,000 yen.' In the course of a three-and-a-half-year prosecution, the constitutionality under Article 9 of the Constitution of the activities of the Self-Defense Forces was an important issue. However, side-stepping the constitutional question, the Sapporo District Court found the defendant not guilty as hereafter summarized:

> Article 121 of the Self-Defense Force Law provides for punishment of a destructive act against 'or other devices used for defense.' The same Article refers to 'weapon ammunition, or aircraft,' which implies that to be legally punishable an act must be similar in kind and in quality to these. The SDF's communication lines during training are not to be included, and the act of cutting the wire does not come within the prohibition of the statute. Consequently, there is no need to decide the constitutionality of the SDF itself

Excluding the statutory construction issue, the technique used by the court here is the same as that used in Justice Brandeis' opinion in *Ashwander v T.VA.* in 1936.

In Japan, there are three views on when to invoke constitutional issues: a) when it is possible to solve the case with a statutory interpretation, a court should not resort to constitutional decision-making; b) the question of the constitutionality of a statute should first be addressed before ruling on its application; or c) even where a constitutional judgment can be avoided with statutory construction, a court can boldly make a decision on constitutionality when it finds sufficient reason after comprehensively examining the following conditions: the degree of unconstitutionality and the scope of its influence; the importance of the case and the nature of the rights involved; the reasons for deciding on constitutional grounds outweigh those for using statutory construction upon examination of the different effects of the two approaches. The third view (c) conforms with a view of the judicial review power as a system for upholding the constitution, and this is the dominant view in the academic world. Here we see the great influence of American judicial theory.

Legal construction provides two ways of avoiding constitutional problems. The first way, used in the *Eniwa* case, is to leave unanswered the question of constitutionality and decide the case on other grounds, that is the construction of a statute. The other way is to restrict the meaning of a statute so as to exclude the unconstitutional aspects from application, usually referred to as 'a constitutionally restricted construction.' The use of constitutionally restrictive construction raises many serious questions.

In 1969 the Supreme Court handed down two landmark cases known as the *Sendai Court Workers Union Incitement* case (*Sendai Zenshiho Jiken*), and the *Tokyo Teachers Union* case (*Tokyoso Jiken*). The cases involved the constitutionality of the National Public Employees Law (Art. 98 and Article 110, paragraph 1, item 17), and the Local Public Employees Law (Art. 37 and Article 61, number 4). These laws prohibit strikes or the instigation thereof by government workers. The Supreme Court in restricting the meaning of the term 'instigate,' said, 'If these provisions are interpreted literally to prohibit all strike-related activities and to penalize anyone who conspires to effect, instigate or incite,' there would be doubts about their constitutionality. Therefore, 'insofar as possible the provisions should be interpreted reasonably as conforming to and capable of harmony with the spirit of the constitution.' The court attempted to limit the meaning of strike-related activities and their instigation to those cases where there was a strong showing of illegality. That is to say, the prohibition and punishment of strike-related activities was limited to cases wherein

> the related activities themselves were strongly tainted with illegality, by deviating from the essential purposes of the employees' organization, by attendant violence or otherwise improper pressures similar in kind, or by seriously interfering with the daily life of the people by improper delays and other means contrary to the common sense of the community.

Regarding the term 'instigation,' the court interpreted it so as to exclude 'those activities ordinarily incidental to strikes,' activities like the transmission and distribution of information concerning the aims of the strike and instructions for carrying out the strike itself. In this way, the court avoided having to declare the statute unconstitutional. By using the narrow interpretation approach, the court was able to uphold the constitutionality of the statute. The court reversed the appellate court's conviction, taking the liberal position of acquitting the defendants.

However, in a 1973 decision known as the *Zennorin* (National Union for Agriculture and Forestry Workers) case, the Supreme Court overruled the 1969 decision, and held that the statute in question prohibited *all* strikes. The court said that a narrow construction of the law was contrary to the principle of Article 31 of the constitution that criminal penalties be prescribed in law (*zaikeihoteishugi*). In this decision we see a shift in the court, with the minority opinion in the 1969 decision becoming the majority opinion in *Zennorin.* With much debate, this case drastically changed the course of constitutional law in Japan.

If we disregard the actual result in this case and look only at the use of the narrow construction approach, the statute undoubtedly lacks clarity, as noted in the reasoning of the 1969 decision. I wonder if it may not be appropriate for the legislature to establish a specific standard providing something less than a complete and absolute ban on strikes by public employees, thus restoring purpose and meaning to the guarantee of basic labor rights (Art. 28). However, under substantive due process, the court overlooked the closely related problem of how narrowing construction of a statute's language is compatible with the purpose and meaning of individual human right guarantees. The court maintained that a complete and absolute ban on strikes was a natural limitation on the rights of labor, and emphasized the clarity of the statutory definition of a violation. Decisions using the narrow-interpretation approach have caused many problems with respect to legislation regulating freedom of expression, where especially careful construction is required. For example, in 1975 when the Supreme Court upheld the constitutionality of the Tokushima City Public Safety Ordinance regulating group activities in public places, the justices said that the phrase 'to maintain orderly traffic' (*kotsu chitsujo o iji suru koto*) could be read 'as a standard related to interference with ordinary traffic.' The court reversed both the trial and high court decisions which had held the ordinance to be excessively vague criminal law.

There may be serious difference of opinion on whether or not the Supreme Court's ruling could be said to conform with the doctrines of 'void for vagueness or overbreadth'. The problem with language in this case did not involve the content of speech, but the manner of regulating expression of ideas through a demonstration. However, as the court pointed out: 'Although it is quite possible to clarify obligations in an ordinance with examples of acts that would be likely to interfere with orderly traffic, no thought was given to that.' 'As a piece of legislation it is notably lacking.' Without doubt, 'the charge that its language is too abstract is inescapable.' If one takes seriously the implications for law of regulating a 'preferred freedom,' one can say there were solid grounds for the high court's judgment that the language was too vague for an interpretation upholding its constitutionality.

A 1984 Supreme Court, Grand Bench decision on obscenity sparked serious debate when it held constitutional Article 21 of the Customs Standards Law which prohibits the import of 'written materials, pictures, statues, and other articles harmful to public order and good morals.' The case involved imported magazines with pictures of nude females. The majority opinion held that concern about harming 'good morals' should be limited to 'obscene' items; and with that, the law cannot be considered invalid and unconstitutional because unclear or overly broad.

However, Justice Masami Ito and three other Justices dissented on this point, reasoning: 'A statute regulating freedom of expression is subject to stricter standards of narrow interpretation than other law. Its use is limited to cases where restraints can be shown to be reasonably related to its regulatory purpose and content, and to other statutory provisions. The term (good morals) is multivocal; to confine its interpretation to mean good sexual morals goes beyond such bounds.' The minority opinion is very sound; in it, we can see the influence of the doctrine of 'overbreadth' found in the United States.

Itoh, H, *The Japanese Supreme Court: Constitutional Policies*, 1989, pp 37–38, 186–97, Markus Wiener

The introduction of an American type of judicial review raised a host of questions concerning constitutional litigation in Japan. Such questions range from the standing to sue, the ripeness of a case, and estoppel, to legislative facts and political questions. In the absence of any separate procedural code governing constitutional litigation, constitutional disputes must take the form of civil, criminal, or administrative cases. There are several requirements which the Supreme Court imposes on constitutional decision making. It seems that the following judicial restraint rules set forth by Justice Brandeis' concurring opinion in *Ashwander v T.V.A.* (297 US 288: 1936) have formed the *modus operandi* of the Japanese Supreme Court: 1) the court will not pass upon the constitutionality in a friendly, non-adversarial proceeding; 2) the court will not anticipate a question of constitutional law in advance of the necessity for deciding it; 3) the court will not formulate a rule of law broader than the facts of the case require; 4) if possible, the court will dispose of a case on nonconstitutional grounds; 5) the court will not pass upon the validity of a statute on complaint of one who fails to show injury to person or property; 6) the court will not pass upon the constitutionality of a statute at the insistence of one who has accepted its benefits; and 7) whenever possible, statutes will be construed so as to avoid a constitutional issue.

In 1952 shortly after the end of the American occupation, Mosaburo Suzuki, secretary general of the Social Democratic Party, filed a suit directly to the Supreme Court on the original jurisdiction against the state, seeking a judicial judgment declaring the National Police Reserve unconstitutional in contravention of Article 9 of the constitution. Declining to issue any advisory judgment in *Suzuki v Japan* (1952), the court ruled that the present judicial power is not capable of abstract pronouncements on constitutional issues. In the opinion of the court, 'If anyone could bring before the court suits claiming unconstitutionality, the validity of laws, orders, and the like, would be frequently assailed and there would be a danger of the court's assuming the appearance of an organ superior to all other powers in the land, thereby running counter to the basic principle of democratic government that the three powers are independent, equal, and immune from each other's interference.'

This decision was to eliminate from the Supreme Court any attribute of a 'constitutional court,' as was expounded by such scholars as Soichi Sasaki. According to him, while all and any courts are empowered to determine the constitutionality of a law as a premise for disposing of concrete and actual disputes, the Supreme Court can review the constitutionality of law even in an abstract manner. The dictum of the *Suzuki* case, which was unanimously reached, was followed in *Tomabechi v Japan* (1953) in which Dietman Tomabechi appealed to the Supreme Court to issue an advisory judgment making the House dissolution void. In dismissing his appeal, the court ruled that an advisory judgment pronouncing such a dissolution null and void would not be in conformity with law in the absence of any concrete legal dispute between the two parties to the suit.

The court also refuses to hear an appeal which becomes moot. For instance, a labor union applied to the government for a permit to hold a rally at the Imperial Palace plaza on the occasion of May Day in 1952. Because of the time it took the case to reach the Supreme Court for review, the date of the scheduled rally had passed. In *The General Council of Japanese Labor Unions v Welfare Minister* (1953), the Supreme Court dismissed the appeal and gave its opinion that since 1 May 1952, the date for which the appellant had applied for a permit to hold a rally, had passed while an appeal was pending, the appellant had lost a legal interest. These and other court decisions have become important procedural rules, which regulate not only access to a court, but also an outcome of the litigant's substantive rights and duties. ...

...

Three Types of Judicial Activism

There are three types of constitutional issues which give rise to all activist Supreme Court in relation to the political branches: 1) The Supreme Court follows its own judicial policy according to the working principle of *stare decisis* in spite of a policy change on the side of political branches; 2) both the Supreme Court and political branches change their policies respectively, but either in opposite directions or at an unequal rate of change; and 3) the Supreme Court changes its policy in spite of the status quo adhered to by the political branches. In each instance above, the Supreme Court comes into conflict with the political branch over a constitutional issue and results in judicial activism.

The first type of judicial activism manifests itself very rarely. It did happen when the Supreme Court struck down legislative policy changes as a violation of the constitutional freedom of occupation. In *Kakukichi Co v Governor, Hiroshima Prefecture* (1975), the plaintiff applied for a new license to open a drug store in Fukuyama city, Hiroshima prefecture in 1963. While its application was pending in the governor's office, the Pharmaceutical Code of 1960 was amended in 1964 so as to empower the governor to deny a license if the location of the new drug store was too close to existing stores. In January 1964, the plaintiff was denied a license after having found the existence of many drug stores in the vicinity of the proposed site.

The Hiroshima district court first upheld the plaintiff's suit seeking revocation of the governor's action and held that the respondent erred in basing his judgment on the amended provisions which came into force after the application for the new license instead of the law which was in effect on the day of the application. Upon appeal, the Hiroshima high court reversed the district court's judgment on two accounts. First, the governor was correct in applying the law in effect at the time of his disposition, not the law at the time of the plaintiff's application. Second, the amendment to the law does not violate the freedom of occupation guaranteed in Article 22, Paragraph 2 of the constitution because without such a regulation on the location of pharmacies, proper dispensation of medical supplies cannot be assured, and an excessive number of pharmacies might cause a dispensation of substandard drugs.

Upon appeal, the Supreme Court grand bench unanimously reversed the judgment below and held that the provision of the Pharmaceutical Code as amended and the Hiroshima prefectural ordinance were both in violation of the constitutional guarantee of the freedom of occupation. In the opinion of the court, there was no evidence of prevalent abuse of dispensing substandard drugs so as to necessitate the application of geographical regulations to the licensing of new pharmacies. Granted the legislative intent to eliminate the maldistribution of pharmacies and to prevent public health hazards caused by substandard drugs, the court concluded, the present restrictions on geographic locations of new pharmacies are neither reasonable nor necessary, and exceeded legislative discretion. Thus, the court and Diet came in conflict with each other. Yet, Diet soon revised the unconstitutional portion of the law, thereby restoring harmony with the court.

Similarly, in relation to the Cabinet and the local government, the Supreme Court has passed judgments on several occasions, narrowly constructing the scope and extent of the power of the executive as well as the local assembly.

One such occasion arose when the Aomori prefectural assembly in 1952 expelled its member, Giichiro Yoneuchiyama, on the ground that his remarks at a general assembly meeting violated the assembly's code of ethics. The Aomori district court first granted a temporary injunction against the expulsion order, and then after substantive review, declared that the local assembly exceeded its disciplinary power in expelling Yoneuchiyama. The court ruling was immediately followed by Prime Minister Yoshida's objection thereto. Following the district court's judgment that the Prime Minister's objection was unsubstantial, the prefectural assembly filed special appeal to the Supreme Court contending in part that a local assembly should be granted the same degree of autonomy to manage its own affairs as the Diet.

In *Yoneuchiyama v Aomori Prefectural Assembly* (1953) the Supreme Court, sustaining the judgment below by twelve to two, construed the provision of the Special Code for Administrative Litigation Procedure to require that the Prime Minister's objection be lodged before the district court issued its injunction. Justice Mano, in his concurring opinion, even held the provision in the Special Code to be in contravention of the principle of separation of powers. Denying the discretionary power of a local assembly to expel members, as in the present instance, Mano reasoned that the assembly, which makes ordinances and regulations, does not become a legislative organ any more than does the Supreme Court which makes rules and regulations, and the expulsion order which immediately affects rights and duties of injured members becomes subject to judicial review. Dissenting justices K Tanaka and Kuriyama argued that except where an assembly's disciplinary action becomes unconstitutional, such as in violation of the equality clause, a local assembly is just as final an arbiter as the Diet in disciplining its own members for misconduct, and the propriety of an expulsion remains a political matter beyond judicial remedy.

The first type of activist Supreme Court is likely to emerge because of the time lag between changes in the composition of the court and more rapid changes in the political branches of government. In the context of the Japanese government in which personnel and policies have remained essentially the same under the long reign of the LDP administration, the first type of activist Supreme Court seldom emerges. Major policy changes are likely to come only when opposition political parties succeed in reversing the LDP's razor-thin majority control in the Diet and institute significantly different policies, while the Supreme Court adheres to the precedents it has created during the LDP rule.

Next, turning to the second type of activist Supreme Court, it is little surprise that the court and the political branches should seldom set forth policies that oppose each other or supplement each other but at an uneven rate. The Supreme Court decisions in two reapportionment cases and the subsequent corrective measures taken on the side of Diet are probably the only instances of this type of activist court in Japan.

Koshiyama, a voter in Tokyo, brought suit in vain before the Tokyo high court after the 1962 election for the House of Councillors, challenging the validity of the election result which, in his opinion, grossly violated the constitutional principle of 'one man, one vote.' The Supreme Court, in dismissing the plaintiff's contention in *Koshiyama v Chairman, Tokyo Election Control Commission* (1964), ruled that apportionment in a national election had been left 'to the discretionary authority of Diet' and that only in cases of extreme inequality 'in the enjoyment of the elector's rights' could a court declare an election void in contravention of the equality clause in the constitution Inequality to the extent it exists today, the court continues, is still only a problem of the propriety of legislation; the problem of unconstitutionality cannot be recognized.

On the question of whether or not malapportionment is even a subject for judicial review, Justice S Saito wrote a concurring opinion which reflected judicial restraint more strongly than the rest of his colleagues. In his opinion a court should not render a judgment even in cases of gross malapportionment because confusion might arise out of different judgments between Diet and the court in determining the extent of malapportionment. He also expressed strong doubt about the legality of a suit, as in the present case, seeking judicial nullification of all election.

Despite the fact that the court dismissed Koshiyama's contention, the Diet went ahead and initiated a partial reapportionment in 1964 by adding five new electoral districts and nineteen new seats to five of the most underrepresented metropolitan areas. With this new policy a chance of major conflict between Diet and the Supreme Court seemed to have been averted on the issue of malapportionment.

Meanwhile, the Supreme Court changed by a narrow margin of eight to seven its policy in 1976 when it reviewed the appeal challenging the general election for the House of Representatives held on 10 December 1972, in the first electoral district of Chiba prefecture. In *Kurokawa v Chiba Prefecture Election Control Commission* (1976) the court declared an election unconstitutional on the grounds that Article 13 of the Public Office Election Code, Accompanying Table I (prior to the 1975 revision) and Supplementary Rule (Articles 7 and 9) on Apportionment of Representatives in Each Election District violated constitutional provisions of Article 14, Paragraph 1, Article 15, Paragraphs 1 and 3, and Article 44, Proviso, all requiring political equality in an election. However, conceding that a judicial nullification of the election results would not correct any error already committed, the court dismissed the portion of the appeal which sought nullification of the allegedly unlawful election result. Only Justice Amano favored dismissing the present suit entirely, because, as he saw it, there was no judicial remedy for malapportionment.

A series of events surrounding the *Koshiyama* decision, a subsequent move by the Diet, and the *Kurokawa* decision suggest that the Diet tried to correct malapportionment by redistricting and partially updating apportionments in some election districts; that the Supreme Court in the *Kurokawa* case demanded a more thorough practice of the 'one man one vote' principle; and that the Diet and the Supreme Court moved in the same direction of correcting malapportionment, but at different paces. Hence, the second type of judicial activism.

Next, the Supreme Court reveals a third type of judicial activism when it changes its policy in spite of the status quo maintained on the side of the political branches. Here the court becomes a proponent of policy making while policy makers in the political branches of government stand pat. The Japanese Supreme Court, which has a little over four decades of constitutional policy-making history, has changed considerably fewer of its own policies when compared with the United States Supreme Court which has over two hundred years of history behind it. Yet, there have been several instances in which the Japanese Supreme Court has acted as a catalyst by invalidating some statutory and administrative acts as being unconstitutional.

One of the earliest examples involved the Customs Code. In *Fujikawa et al v Japan* (1955) a seven-member majority of the Supreme Court ruled that a penalty against a crime committed in violation of the Customs Code in all area which at the time of the crime was still foreign territory, should not be construed to have been abolished on the ground that the area was later incorporated into Japanese territory and that the penalties had been abolished by a law after the crime. Six justices dissented by stating that 'Government Ordinance 407 concerning the Temporary Measure in the application of Regulations Related National Taxes Following the Return of the Amami Archipelago' of 24 December 1953, incorporated this territory into Japan, abolishing a license required by the Customs Code to import and export to the region; that the provision of Article 76 of the Code Setting Forth the Penalties of Violation of the Customs Code lost its applicability, and that the accused should be acquitted by analogy to the abolition of penalty after conviction.

The *Fujikawa* precedent made by a one-vote margin was followed in seven other cases, but was reversed in *Miyazaki v Japan* (1957) in which nine justices adopted the dissenting opinion of the *Fujikawa* case while six adhered to the majority opinion of the same case. Thus, in the *Fujikawa* case the Supreme Court upheld the law enforcement agency's action by convicting the accused. But in the *Miyazaki* case the court came in conflict with the law enforcement body by acquitting the accused, thereby becoming an activist court of the third type. This change in precedent was a direct result of the new membership of the court and not vote switching by any incumbent members. Iwamatsu, Motomura, Inoue, and Kuriyama, who all voted against the abolition of the penalty in the Customs Code, and Tanimura, who voted for such abolition, retired and were replaced by four liberals (D Kawamura, Shimoiizaka, Okuno, and Tarumi) and one conservative (Takahashi). Fujita, M Kawamura, Kobayashi, Kotani, Mano, Y Saito, Shima, and Tanaka voted the same way in each case, respectively, while Ikeda and Irie who were absent in the *Fujikawa* case, voted conservatively in the *Miyazaki* case, all resulting in the reversal of the *Fujikawa* ruling by nine to six.

The third type of judicial activism is also found in a series of cases which dealt with the constitutional provisions of property rights (Article 29) and due process (Article 31), invoked in conjunction with a confiscation of ships and their cargoes used in smuggling. First, in *Omachi v Japan* (1960), in which some smuggled goods and a motorboat were confiscated in accordance with Article 83, Paragraph 1 of the old Customs Code, the Supreme Court dismissed, by the narrow margin of eight to seven, an appeal against the Fukuoka high court, Miyazaki branch. Upholding the constitutionality of the confiscation by the government, eight majority justices were of the opinion that the accused was not allowed to seek remedy by challenging the confiscation of a third party's property used in a crime. Especially, Justice Takagi stressed that confiscation in this instance serves the function of preventing future crimes and that since an innocent owner of the confiscated property could later seek a judicial remedy, the accused should not be allowed to claim innocence.

Five of the dissenting justices argued that it violates Article 31 of the constitution to confiscate a boat belonging to a third party to a crime without giving him such protections as notice, a hearing, and claim of self-defense in a criminal proceeding. Vaisuke Kawamura even went so far as to say that Article 83, Paragraph 1 of the old Customs Code itself violated Article 31 of the constitution in allowing confiscation of a property possessed by the accused.

However, two years later the Supreme Court changed its own policy established in the *Omachi* case when it decided *Nakamura et al v Japan* (1962). The accused in this case attempted to smuggle contraband goods to South Korea in a motorboat, but failed to transfer the shipment to a fishing boat off the coast of Hakata (Fukuoka, Kyushu) because of stormy seas. The Fukuoka district court, sustained by the Fukuoka high court, convicted the accused for their attempted violation of the Customs Code, and confiscated the motorboat and cargo. However, since the cargo confiscated included that of a third party, the accused appealed to the Supreme Court contending that an unknown person to whom the cargo belonged was unaware of the commission of the alleged crime and yet had his property confiscated without redress. The fourteen-member grand bench reversed the *Omachi* precedent by the vote of nine to five. Nine justices agreed with the defense contention that the accused in possession of the third party's property to be confiscated can appeal to the Supreme Court, challenging the constitutionality thereof and that confiscating, on the strength of Article 118, Paragraph 1 of the Customs Code (corresponding to Article 83, Paragraph 1 of the old Customs Code), without safeguards, the property of a third party to a crime violated Articles 29 and 31 of the constitution. Justice Okuno expressed his concern that an owner, who has more at stake than the accused, may not be able to seek remedy, civil or criminal, once the confiscation of his property is finalized.

After the *Omachi* decision, two liberals (Kotani and Shima) and two conservatives (Kotani and Y Saito) retired. Of the four new justices, K Yokota, Gokijyo, and M Yokota decided against such a confiscation while only Yamada adhered to the *Omachi* decision. Switching Tarumi's decision in the two cases also aided the proponent of the new policy on this issue. Five justices who were among the majority in the *Omachi* case became a minority group in the present case, and repeated the same arguments in the earlier case.

Thus the *Nakamura* decision rendered the Supreme Court an activist in relation to the Diet, but no sooner had conflict emerged between the court and the Diet than the latter enacted on 12 July 1963, an emergency measure (Code 138) providing a third party whose property is being confiscated with notice, a hearing, and other safeguards in a criminal proceeding.

In view of this new legislation the Supreme Court began upholding once again the constitutionality of confiscation, while maintaining its vigilance. In *Tokunaga v Japan* (1963) the Supreme Court stressed that an appellate court, in reversing and remanding a first instance court decision, should instruct the latter to follow the new statutory requirements. Likewise, in *Yoshida v Japan* (1965) 43 the court ruled that the court below violated Articles 29 and 31 of the constitution to order, in accordance with Article 197-4 of the Criminal Code (prior to revision in 1958), a third party to a crime to pay the price of a bribe. Finding that the third party was questioned merely as a witness in the lower court's hearing and was denied the opportunity to defend his property right with due process, the court denied the state the power to order a third party to a crime in a case in which he was judged to have received a bribe, to repay a sum equal to that of his bribe.

Finally, in *Japan v Che et al* (1966) the court ruled that confiscation, without notice, hearing, or self defense, of property belonging to an unindicted co-owner violates Articles 29 and 31 of the constitution. It is not clear from the reading of the *Nakamura* decision whether the court declared unconstitutional the provision of Article 112, Paragraph 1 of the Customs Code itself, the administrative action of confiscation, or both. Nonetheless, the Supreme Court sent a copy of its decision to the Diet as reference.

Thereupon the Diet acted to remove what the Supreme Court considered to be an unconstitutional portion of the law, restoring harmony with the *Nakamura* decision.

If the *Nakamura* ruling left some ambiguity on the question of whether the court declared unconstitutional a provision of the Customs Code, the administrative action of confiscation, or both, the Supreme Court was explicit in declaring Article 200 of the Criminal Code unconstitutional in the 1973 patricide cases.

The accused in *Fukuoka District Prosecutors' Office v Yamato* (1950) beat and killed his father and was subsequently charged with inflicting bodily injury on his father resulting in death. The Fukuoka district court found him guilty and sentenced him to three years at forced labor with a stay of execution for three years. The same court, however, found the provision of Article 205 of the Criminal Code, which imposed much severer punishments on those guilty of inflicting bodily harm on lineal ascendants than on others, unconstitutional in violation of the constitutional principle of equality under law (Article 14).

Upon appeal, the Supreme Court grand bench reversed and remanded the verdict of the first instance court, upholding the constitutionality of Article 205 of the law. The thirteen-member majority (Tsukasaki, Hasegawa, Sawada, Shimoyama, Inoue, Kuriyama, Iwamatsu, Kotani, Shima, Y Saito, Fujita, M Kawamura and K Tanaka) held that since the rationale underlying the provision incorporated the eternal natural law which attached special importance to the moral duties of the child toward his parents, ancestor worship, unity of loyalty, and filial piety which constituted the moral and social backbone of Japanese society, the deviation from such would be a travesty of the Japanese social fabric. Only Mano and Hozumi dissented. Justice Hozumi regarded punishing ascendant manslaughter by a heavier penalty as unreasonable and unnecessary. Tsuyoshi Mano was the only justice who declared the discriminatory provision to be a violation of the equality clause.

It took more than two decades for the Supreme Court to change the *Yamato* policy when it reviewed *Aizawa v Japan* (1973). The Utsunomiya district court (Tochigi prefecture) in this case acquitted the accused, a daughter, who killed her father after having been forced to live with him as a common law wife. In the opinion of the district court, Article 200 of the Criminal Code, which imposes a severe penalty only upon a lineal descendant who kills a direct lineal ascendant by stressing the socially harmful and unethical nature of killing a lineal ascendant, unreasonably discriminates against lineal descendants. In contrast to a husband who kills his wife, or a lineal ascendant who kills a lineal descendant, the court continued, the provision puts the parent-child relationships above matrimonial ones. This discriminatory provision stems from the notion of the old family system based on the supremacy of parental (especially paternal) authority, and on the authority-obedience, hierarchical relationship between lineal ascendants and descendants, rather than on a status of legal equality between spouses and one between a parent and a child. The court concluded that the provision in question is unreasonable and should be declared invalid.

Eight members of the Supreme Court, by this time having been composed of entirely new members, basically accepted the opinion of the district court that the intent of punishing lineal ascendant manslaughter by a penalty heavier than other types of manslaughter may be a reasonable discrimination, but that Article 200 of the Criminal Code by far exceeds the necessary limit to achieve this legislative objective by restricting the choice of such heavier penalty only to capital punishment or life imprisonment at hard labor. In comparison with Article 199 of the same law, dealing with manslaughter of all other types, the court concluded, Article 200 is unreasonably harsh and violates Article 14, Paragraph 1 of the constitution and Article 199 should be, henceforth, applicable to the manslaughter of lineal ascendancy. Six concurring Justices (Ogawa, Sakamoto, Shimomura, Irokawa, Osumi, J Tanaka) held that distinguishing the manslaughter of lineal ascendant from other types of manslaughter while penalizing the former more stiffly than the latter is against Article 14, Paragraph 1 of the constitution.

Justice Shimoda, the sole dissenter, was of the opinion that a distinction between lineal ascendants and lineal descendants does not fall under a social distinction prohibited in Article 14, Paragraph 1 of the constitution and that however discriminatory, Article 200 of the Criminal Code is not unconstitutional. The Supreme Court formally sent a copy of its decision to both the Cabinet and Diet, while announcing it in the government gazette of 16 April 1973.

The present Criminal Code was adopted in 1907 under the Meiji constitution. Much of the Criminal Code was revised in 1947 to better accord with the spirit of the new constitution, but Article 200 was not touched then or later. Most leading Japanese constitutional lawyers hailed this landmark *Aizawa* decision, but feel with the concurring opinions that the majority might have gone further in bringing the Criminal Code into line with the constitutional principle of equality under the law. The entire Criminal Code was under deliberation for some years. The Criminal Code Revision Preparatory Committee deleted from its draft proposal the heavier penalty against patricide in line with the dissenting opinion of Justice Mano in the Yamato case, which now commands a majority among the Supreme Court justices, but the Diet has yet to delete either Article 200 or Article 205, Paragraph 2.

Tanaka, H, 'Legal Equality Among Family Members in Japan – the Impact of the Japanese Constitution of 1946 on the Traditional Family System' (1980) 53 *Southern California Law Review* 634–38

Because the requirements of the constitution concerning family law were so faithfully implemented through revisions of the Code and other statutes enacted since 1947, there have been no constitutional challenges before the Japanese Supreme Court in this area. There have been, however, two constitutional cases concerning the penal provisions for patricide that illustrate the changing attitude toward traditional values.

The Japanese Penal Code was partially amended in 1947. The most important amendments were those abolishing the crime of adultery and crimes against the Imperial household. Articles 200 and 205, however, which provided heavier penalties for killing one's lineal ascendants remained unchanged. This gave rise to several constitutional cases that drew public attention because they questioned the validity of the traditional concept of filial piety.

In 1950, the Supreme Court in *Japan v Yamato* upheld Article 205, paragraph 2, which provided that a person who inflicts bodily injury upon the offender's or the offender's spouse's lineal ascendants shall be punished by imprisonment at forced labor for life or for a term of not less than three years, while the punishment for killing an unrelated person is imprisonment with labor for a fixed term of not less than two years. Two weeks after that decision, the Supreme Court also upheld the constitutionality of Article 200, which provided that a person who killed the offender's or the offender's spouse's lineal ascendants shall be punished with death or imprisonment at forced labor for life. In contrast, the provision in Article 199 provided that the punishment for killing an unrelated person is death or imprisonment at forced labor for life or for a term not less than three years. This second decision was relatively brief and referred in most pan to their opinions in the first decision.

The majority in the first decision wrote:

> [M]orality, controlling such relations as those between husband and wife, parent and child, or brother and sister, is the great fountainhead of human ethics, a universal moral principle recognized by all mankind without regard to past or present or East and West. In other words, it must be said that this principle belongs to what in theory is called natural law.
>
> ...
>
> ... [I]t is reasonable to interpret the main object of the legislation [Articles 200 and 205 of the Penal Code] as not being focused on the protection of the lineal ascendant who is the victim, but rather on a special consideration of the antimoral character of the descendant who is the assailant, the occasional greater protection thus given to lineal ascendants being merely a reflection of this.

Justices Shigeto Hozumi and Tsuyoshi Mano dissented. Justice Mano, being the more critical of the majority's philosophy, argued that:

> The majority opinion repeatedly emphasizes morality between parents and children, and this may easily appeal to those among the masses who do not understand democracy. But what would remain if we subtract from the morality of children toward parents ... the proper democratic morality based on the dignity of man and the respect of personality? ... [F]ilial piety is a relationship between parents, who hold a superior status, and children, who hold an inferior status in the social organization; in other words, it is a relationship between persons unequal in status and not a relationship between equal individuals. Thus what was called filial piety in the past was the basis of the [old] family system, the foundation of a system of patriarchy that was a kind of relationship of authoritarian control and at the same time had a strong feudalistic coloration. ... The new filial piety should be a truly voluntary, free, uncoerced, and sound morality based on the principle of equality of personality.
>
> ...
>
> ... [T]o differentiate between degrees of protection according to differences of object [ie victim] is in violation of the principle of equality; is this not clear from the circumstances and developments that arose when offenses against the Imperial House[hold] were abolished ... ? Was not the fact that this naturally gave greater protection to the object as compared with ordinary cases treated as inequality under democracy?

This statement led to an emotional outburst by Justice Yusuke Saito who was unable to refrain from using expressions that clearly exceeded the acceptable standards of judicial conduct:

> It must be stated that to go this far [as Justice Mano and the court below did] is democratic infantilism, which cannot but be surprising, and a deplorable idea of civil liberties. Why is it feudalistic to respect in the [Criminal] Code the great fountainhead of human ethics and a universal principle of mankind?
>
> ...
>
> ... We should remember over and over again that every work or phrase we use, the very mouths and lips that form those words, and even [the existence of] you and I are the heritage of our ancestors. We must reject completely such ideas as

> those of the original judgment and of the minority opinions, which must be called conceited notions of ingratitude, lacking in understanding of this morality, and aimlessly chasing after innovations.
>
> ... I find it unbearable to read the rest of the [dissenting] opinion for it develops an academically prostituted theory that is a national disgrace – a theory based on self-centered egoism under the beautiful name of democracy.

In another patricide case that came before the supreme court in 1973, *Aizawa v Japan*, it was held that Article 200 of the Penal Code was an unconstitutional violation of the principle of equality under the law. The opinions of this case clearly reflect the basic change of philosophy during this period of nearly a quarter of a century. In *Aizawa*, six of the fourteen justices who concurred in the result flatly denied the constitutionality of a penal statute that imposed a heavier penalty on the assailant because of the status of the victim. These concurring justices stated:

> Article 200 ... stands on the moral principle of a hierarchical society holding that a lineal ascendant should be respected ... simply because he or she is a lineal ascendant. ... A moral principle to govern parent-child relationships is not fit for enforcement by law. Moreover, to enforce the above-mentioned moral principle by law ... is tantamount to creating an unreasonable discrimination based upon one's status [by Justice Osumi].
>
> It is natural that a child feels gratitude for his or her parents' efforts in protecting and bringing him or her up. But to call this feeling 'moral indebtedness' (on) as the majority does, and to hold a child's requirement of such moral indebtedness to be 'a fundamental principle of morals' and 'universal ethics 'whose violation shall be heavily reprehended legally as well as socially ... just shows that the justices in the majority are still haunted by the conventional concept of filial piety (ko). ... Filial piety was the most admired virtue under Confucianism. ... It was a virtue nurtured under a special family system during a certain period of history, which in turn served as an ideological pillar for this system. It is not a principle of natural law applicable to all ages and countries. ... The concept of filial piety which demands blind, absolute subordination to parents is dearly incompatible with democratic ethics based upon the principle of individual dignity and equality [by Justice Irokawa].
>
> 'To respect the dignity of each individual and to protect equality and individuals as human beings is the first principle of democracy. ... Article 14, Paragraph I is meant to invalidate every sort of differential treatment that conflicts with this fundamental principle of the constitution. The enumeration of grounds for differential treatment therein should be understood as merely exemplary [by Justice Jiro Tanaka].

The majority paid more respect to traditional values. They stated:

> It is true that members of a family are united together by mutual respect and natural affection. ... It is also true, however, that there is a certain order among them due to the fact that the younger give precedence to their elders and each member assumes different kinds of responsibility. Ordinarily, descendants are brought up under the custody of parents or grandparents. These lineal ascendants are held legally or morally responsible for the acts of their descendants. That descendants pay respect to, and feel obliged to require 'moral indebtedness' (on) to, their lineal ascendants is indeed a fundamental principle of morals in our social life. The maintenance of such natural feelings and universal ethics is appropriately to be regarded as one of the legitimate objectives of penal law. ...

> It is, therefore, not unreasonable to have the high degree of reprehensibility which attaches to the act reflected in the provision prescribing the punishment to be inflicted ... The fact that the victim was a lineal ascendant of the offender is certainly a factor to be taken into consideration when a judge determines the extent of the penalty to be imposed in a particular case. The legislature may go a step
>
> further to categorize this by enacting a provision prescribing a heavier penalty for murder of the offender's lineal ascendants than for ordinary murder. ... This is not ipso facto repugnant to Article 14, Paragraph I of the constitution.
>
> But if the extent of the penalty is augmented to such an extent ... that it loses sight of the above legislative purpose ..., the distinction in penalties should be held clearly unreasonable and repugnant to Article 14.
>
> The penalty prescribed for murder of the offender's lineal ascendant under Article 200 of the Penal Code is too heavy in that it provides only for the death penalty or life imprisonment. This is much heavier than the penalty prescribed for ordinary murder under Article 199 [which provides for the death penalty or imprisonment for life or for a term of not less than three years]. Such a difference cannot be justified as being necessary to achieve the above-mentioned policy of law, namely, to honor natural affection for one's lineal ascendant and to preserve the universal principle of ethics we have just described. Article 200 is void as against Article 14 of the constitution in making such a clearly unreasonable discrimination between ordinary murder and murder of one's lineal ascendant.

Subsequent decisions of the petty benches of the Supreme Court (consisting of five justices out of the total of fifteen) followed this moderate line by holding that Article 205, paragraph 2 was constitutional. The majority in these decisions emphasized the fact that the lower limit of penalties provided for intentionally inflicting bodily injury upon one's lineal ascendant was not unreasonably more severe than that for a comparable crime committed against an unrelated person.

Beer, LW, 'Law and Liberty' in Ishida, T and Krauss, ES (eds), *Democracy in Japan*, 1989, pp 73–76, University of Pittsburgh Press

As a civil-law country, prewar Japan had courts as units administered by the Justice Ministry and staffed by judges who were a type of higher civil servant; the judiciary was not constitutionally separate and had only limited jurisdiction, especially with respect to civil rights and liberties. In democratic civil-law jurisdictions generally, the function of judges is to faithfully and fairly apply the written statutory law passed by democratically elected parliaments, with deference to the constitution and the codes; but judges are not supposed to make law or policy – as they occasionally do in the United States – with inventive legal interpretations in decisions which may serve as binding precedents in future cases. Furthermore, European constitutional history from before the French Revolution of 1789 established a long-lasting bias in civil-law countries against viewing courts as defenders of individual rights.

The view of the law and of the limited role of the judiciary had been absorbed by most democratically inclined legal professionals in 1946 Japan. Into this world view came the quite different American notion that the judiciary should be an independent branch of government with broad powers. Ever since, judges in Japan have been deciding legal disputes guided by a mixture of civil law and American theory, judicial precedent, and their sense of duty as custodians of individual rights. In this perception, law and constitutional principle are best sought not in neat codes or in the results of sometimes tumultuous parliamentary debates, but in the context of judicial decisions on real controversies brought before a court. Thus, within Japan's constitutional law, two democratic conceptions of judicial role have vied for influence since 1947, with a modified American plan regarding the judiciary gradually attaining full integration into the civil-law framework. Neither civil law nor common law is inherently more democratic. Had Japan's postwar revolution of freedom been instigated by a democratic European conqueror, for example, the role of the courts and judicial review might be much less important than they are today, and arguably at least, without a loss of democratic thrust.

However, under the Constitution of Japan (chapter 6), an institutionally independent Supreme Court has authority over all other courts, comprehensive jurisdiction, and the judicial review 'power to determine the constitutionality of any law, order, regulation or official act' (Article 81). The Supreme Court contains fifteen justices who divide into three Petty Benches in deciding most cases. Only occasionally, as for major constitutional cases, do all justices join in deliberation as the Grand Bench. Today the courts enjoy their increased autonomy and influence as settlers of disputes and, in effect, as participants in societal policymaking. Precedent is not binding as law in future cases, but judges pay due regard to the substantial body of accumulated prior decisions, and the mass media and- scholars have, by their reports and comments on cases, vastly expanded public awareness of the courts and democratic legal issues in the past forty years. Judges are major actors in some human rights dramas; but some critics fault some courts, especially the Supreme Court, for being too deferential at times to law passed by democratically elected legislatures.

The scope of justiciable constitutional rights in Japan is quite broad under chapter 3, Articles 11-40. Article 97 proclaims: 'The fundamental human rights by this constitution guaranteed to the people of Japan are fruits of the age-old struggle of man to be free; they have survived the many exacting tests for durability and are conferred upon this and future generations in trust, to be held for all time inviolate.'

In broad terms, Chapter 3 provides a more adequate constitutional basis for theoretical discourse on human rights law and policy than the Constitution of the United States with its amendments; but the American authors of chapter 3 may well have been setting forth what they considered an appropriate understanding of *American Constitutionalism* in 1946. The enumeration of rights in Japan's document reflects well-integrated views of the rights many Americans felt should be explicitly honored in American constitutional law. In the idealistic days after the New Deal and the Second World War, a year and half before the United Nations adopted (with major American input) the rather comprehensive Universal Declaration of Human Rights, Americans wrote into a historic and lasting foreign constitution an understanding of American constitutional rights which American scholars and lawyers might well look to for perspective when interpreting related law in the United States. The extensive Japanese case law on constitutional rights accumulated since 1947 in a quasi-common-law manner, and the solid knowledge of American constitutional law which many Japanese legal professionals bring to their consideration of a case, make Japan's experience in this area an apt object of American attention. Moreover, since Japanese law may integrate European civil-law approaches with Anglo-American common law and constitutionalism more systematically than any civil-law or common-law country, Japan serves as a laboratory of living non-Western comparative law and a possible bridge for better mutual understanding between nations of civil-law and common-law legalism and constitutionalism, particularly with respect to human rights.

Japan's learned and large corps of constitutional lawyers has written voluminous commentary – too little of it known outside Japan – on the constitution and on each important judicial decision. They commonly categorize different sets of human rights as follows:

1. Equality of rights under the law. Article 14 prohibits 'discrimination in political, economic, or social relations because of race, creed, sex, social status, or family origin,' as well as inherited honors or nobility (except in the case of the powerless dynastic monarchy). Article 24 recognizes 'the equal rights of husband and wife' in all matters. The governing interpretive principle of private law is 'the dignity of individuals and the essential equality of the sexes' (Civil Code, Article 1-2).
2. Economic freedoms and property rights (Articles 22 and 29). Japanese have the freedom to choose their occupations and to engage in business, and the right to use property within limits 'in conformity with the public welfare.'
3. Rights related to the quality of socioeconomic life (*shakaiken*). This category includes rights to welfare assistance, social medicine, compulsory education (Article 26), 'minimum standards of wholesome and cultured living' (Article 25), and workers' rights. Workers have the right to work under laws that set reasonable conditions of wages, hours, rest, and working environment (Article 27), and 'to organize and to bargain and act collectively' (Article 28), unless they fall within the broad category of public employee.
4. The right to participate in election politics (*sanseiken*) by standing as a candidate, campaigning, or voting (Article 15). Articles 44 and 14 ban discrimination in connection with a person's candidacy and election to office. Japan's most serious constitutional problem seems to be malapportionment of seats in the House of Representatives. In the face of recent Supreme Court findings of unconstitutionality, the Diet may be moving, ever so hesitantly and reluctantly, toward a reassignment of seats to constituencies which will assure the citizen of densely populated areas that his or her vote has more than one-third the value of a vote in sparsely populated election districts, the very modest standard discussed by the Supreme Court.
5. Procedural rights (Articles 31-40). A full array of such rights is guaranteed by law and generally assured by highly professional judges, prosecutors, and police. Article 31 sets the basis: 'No person shall be deprived of life or liberty, nor shall any other criminal penalty be imposed, except according to procedure established by law.'
6. Rights and freedoms of the spirit (*seishinteki jiyuken*), such as thought, conscience (Article 19), religion (Article 20), expressions (Article 21), and professional academic activity, the world's first such provision (Article 23); and the right to choose occupation and place of residence (Article 22). All the above exist within the limits of and with the expressed civic duty to further 'the public welfare' (Articles 12 and 13), which has been judicially defined as the maintenance of public order and human rights.

Although some of these rights may seem only glowing guidelines without legal bite, such is not the case; they have proved justiciable in court. Japan's system of constitutionally guaranteed human rights and democratic government does measure up to the transcultural criteria suggested earlier. And, in general comparative terms, its human rights record emerges as rather strong, especially perhaps in the areas of civil liberties and criminal justice.

APPENDIX I

THE CONSTITUTION OF THE EMPIRE OF JAPAN 1889 (THE MEIJI CONSTITUTION)

Promulgated on 11 February 1889; Put into effect on 29 November 1890

IMPERIAL OATH SWORN IN THE SANCTUARY IN THE IMPERIAL PALACE

We, the Successor to the prosperous Throne of Our Predecessors, do humbly and solemnly swear to the Imperial Founder of Our House and to Our other Imperial Ancestors that, in pursuance of a great policy co-extensive with the Heavens and with the Earth, We shall maintain and secure from decline the ancient form of government.

In consideration of the progressive tendency of the course of human affairs and in parallel with the advance of civilization, We deem it expedient, in order to give clearness and distinctness to the instructions bequeathed by the Imperial Founder of Our House and by Our other Imperial Ancestors, to establish fundamental laws formulated into express provisions of law, so that, on the one hand, Our Imperial posterity may possess an express guide for the course they are to follow, and that, on the other, Our subjects shall thereby be enabled to enjoy a wider range of action in giving Us their support, and that the observance of Our laws shall continue to the remotest ages of time. We will thereby to give greater firmness to the stability of Our country and to promote the welfare of all the people within the boundaries of Our dominions; and We now establish the Imperial House Law and the Constitution. These Laws come to only an exposition of grand precepts for the conduct of the government, bequeathed by the Imperial Founder of Our House and by Our other Imperial Ancestors. That we have been so fortunate in Our reign, in keeping with the tendency of the times, as to accomplish this work, We owe to the glorious Spirits of the Imperial Founder of Our House and of Our other Imperial Ancestors.

We now reverently make Our prayer to Them and to Our Illustrious Father, and implore the help of Their Sacred Spirits, and make to Them solemn oath never at this time nor in the future to fail to be an example to Our subjects in the observance of the Laws hereby established.

May the heavenly Spirits witness this Our solemn Oath.

IMPERIAL RESCRIPT ON THE PROMULGATION OF THE CONSTITUTION

Whereas We make it the joy and glory of Our heart to behold the prosperity of Our country, and the welfare of Our subjects, We do hereby, in virtue of the supreme power We inherit from Our Imperial Ancestors, promulgate the present immutable fundamental law, for the sake of Our present subjects and their descendants.

The Imperial Founder of Our House and Our other Imperial Ancestors, by the help and support of the forefathers of Our subjects, laid the foundation of Our Empire upon a basis, which is to last forever. That this brilliant achievement embellishes the annals of Our country, is due to the glorious virtues of Our Sacred Imperial Ancestors, and to the loyalty and bravery of Our subjects, their love of their country and their public spirit. Considering that Our subjects are the descendants of the loyal and good subjects of Our Imperial Ancestors, We doubt not but that Our subjects will be guided by Our views, and will sympathize with all Our endeavours, and that, harmoniously cooperating together, they will share with Us Our hope of making manifest the glory of Our country, both at home and abroad, and of securing forever the stability of the work bequeathed to Us by Our Imperial Ancestors.

PREAMBLE

Having, by virtue of the glories of Our Ancestors, ascended the Throne of a lineal succession unbroken for ages eternal; desiring to promote the welfare of, and to give development to the moral and intellectual faculties of Our beloved subjects, the very same that have been favoured with the benevolent care and affectionate vigilance of Our Ancestors; and hoping to maintain the prosperity of the State, in concert with Our people and with their support, We hereby promulgate, in pursuance of Our Imperial Rescript of the 12th day of the 10th month Or the 14th year of Meiji, a fundamental law of the State, to exhibit the principles, by which We are guided in Our conduct, and to point out to what Our descendants and Our subjects and their descendants are forever to conform.

The right of sovereignty of the State, We have inherited from Our Ancestors, and We shall bequeath them to Our descendants. Neither We nor they shall in the future fail to wield them, in accordance with the provisions of the Constitution hereby granted.

We now declare to respect and protect the security of the rights and of the property of Our people, and to secure to them the complete enjoyment of the same, within the extent of the provisions of the present Constitution and of the law.

The Imperial Diet shall first be convoked for the 23rd year of Meiji and the time of its opening shall be the date, when the present Constitution comes into force.

When in the future it may become necessary to amend any of the provisions of the present Constitution, We or Our successors shall assume the initiative right, and submit a project for the same to the Imperial Diet. The Imperial Diet shall pass its vote upon it, according to the conditions imposed by the present Constitution, and in no otherwise shall Our descendants or Our subjects be permitted to attempt any alteration thereof.

Our Ministers of State, on Our behalf, shall be held responsible for the carrying out of the present Constitution, and Our present and future subjects shall forever assume the duty of allegiance to the present Constitution.

CHAPTER I. THE EMPEROR

Article 1. The Empire of Japan shall be reigned over and governed by a line of Emperors unbroken for ages eternal.

Article 2. The Imperial Throne shall be succeeded to by Imperial male descendants, according to the provisions of the Imperial House Law.

Article 3. The Emperor is sacred and inviolable.

Article 4. The Emperor is the head of the Empire, combining in Himself the rights of sovereignty, and exercises them, according to the provisions of the present Constitutions.

Article 5. The Emperor exercises the legislative power with the consent of the Imperial Diet.

Article 6. The Emperor gives sanction to laws, and orders them to be promulgated and executed.

Article 7. The Emperor convokes the Imperial Diet, opens, closes, and prorogues it, and dissolves the House of Representatives.

Article 8. The Emperor, in consequence of an urgent necessity to maintain public safety or to avert public calamities, issues, when the Imperial Diet is not sitting, Imperial Ordinances in the place of law.

(2) Such Imperial Ordinances are to be laid before the Imperial Diet at its next session, and when the Diet does not approve the said Ordinances, the Government shall declare them to be invalid for the future.

Article 9. The Emperor issues or causes to be issued, the Ordinances necessary for the carrying out of the laws, or for the maintenance of the public peace and order, and for the promotion of the welfare of the subjects. But no Ordinance shall in any way alter any of the existing laws.

Article 10. The Emperor determines the organization of the different branches of the administration, and salaries of all civil and military officers, and appoints and dismisses the same. Exceptions especially provided for in the present Constitution or in other laws, shall be in accordance with the respective provisions (bearing thereon).

Article 11. The Emperor has the supreme command of the Army and Navy.

Article 12. The Emperor determines the organisation and peace standing of the Army and Navy.

Article 13. The Emperor declares war, makes peace, and concludes treaties.

Article 14. The Emperor declares a state of siege.

(2) The conditions and effects of a state of siege shall be determined by law.

Article 15. The Emperor confers titles of nobility, rank, orders and other marks of honor.

Article 16. The Emperor orders amnesty, pardon, commutation of punishments and rehabilitation.

Article 17. A Regency shall be instituted in conformity with the provisions of the Imperial House Law.

(2) The Regent shall exercise the powers appertaining to the Emperor in His name.

CHAPTER II. RIGHTS AND DUTIES OF SUBJECTS

Article 18. The conditions necessary for being a Japanese subject shall be determined by law.

Article 19. Japanese subjects may, according to qualifications determined in laws or ordinances, be appointed to civil or military or any other public offices equally.

Article 20. Japanese subjects are amenable to service in the Army or Navy, according to the provisions of law.

Article 21. Japanese subjects are amenable to the duty of paying taxes, according to the provisions of law.

Article 22. Japanese subjects shall have the liberty of abode and of changing the same within the limits of the law.

Article 23. No Japanese subject shall be arrested, detained, tried or punished, unless according to law.

Article 24. No Japanese subject shall be deprived of his right of being tried by the judges determined by law.

Article 25. Except in the cases provided for in the law, the house of no Japanese subject shall be entered or searched without his consent.

Article 26. Except in the cases mentioned in the law, the secrecy of the letters of every Japanese subject shall remain inviolate.

Article 27. The right of property of every Japanese subject shall remain inviolate.

(2) Measures necessary to be taken for the public benefit shall be provided for by law.

Article 28. Japanese subjects shall, within limits not prejudicial to peace and order, and not antagonistic to their duties as subjects, enjoy freedom of religious belief.

Article 29. Japanese subjects shall, within the limits of law, enjoy the liberty of speech, writing, publication, public meetings and associations.

Article 30. Japanese subjects may present petitions, by observing the proper forms of respect, and by complying with the rules specially provided for the same.

Article 31. The provisions contained in the present Chapter shall not affect the exercise of the powers appertaining to the Emperor, in times of war or in cases of a national emergency.

Article 32. Each and every one of the provisions contained in the preceding Articles of the present Chapter, that are not in conflict with the laws or the rules and discipline of the Army and Navy, shall apply to the officers and men of the Army and of the Navy.

CHAPTER III. THE IMPERIAL DIET

Article 33. The Imperial Diet shall consist of two Houses, a House of Peers and a House of Representatives.

Article 34. The House of Peers shall, in accordance with the Ordinance concerning the House of Peers, be composed of the members of the Imperial Family, of the orders of nobility, and of those who have been nominated thereto by the Emperor.

Article 35. The House of Representatives shall be composed of Members elected by the people, according to the provisions of the Law of Election.

Article 36. No one can at one and the same time be a Member of both Houses.

Article 37. Every law requires the consent of the Imperial Diet.

Article 38. Both Houses shall vote upon projects of law submitted to it by the Government, and may respectively initiate projects of law.

Article 39. A Bill, which has been rejected by either the one or the other of the two Houses, shall not be brought in again during the same session.

Article 40. Both Houses can make representations to the Government, as to laws or upon any other subject. When, however, such representations are not accepted, they cannot be made a second time during the same session.

Article 41. The Imperial Diet shall be convoked every year.

Article 42. A session of the Imperial Diet shall last during three months. In case of necessity, the duration of a session may be prolonged by the Imperial Order.

Article 43. When urgent necessity arises, an extraordinary session may be convoked in addition to the ordinary one.

(2) The duration of an extraordinary session shall be determined by Imperial Order.

Article 44. The opening, closing, prolongation of session and prorogation of the Imperial Diet, shall be effected simultaneously for both Houses.

(2) In case the House of Representatives has been ordered to dissolve, the House of Peers shall at the same time be prorogued.

Article 45. When the House of Representatives has been ordered to dissolve, Members shall be caused by Imperial Order to be newly elected, and the new House shall be convoked within five months from the day of dissolution.

Article 46. No debate can be opened and no vote can be taken in either House of the Imperial Diet, unless not less than one-third of the whole number of Members thereof is present.

Article 47. Votes shall be taken in both Houses by absolute majority. In the case of a tied vote, the President shall have the casting vote.

Article 48. The deliberations of both Houses shall be held in public. The deliberations may, however, upon demand of the Government or by resolution of the House, be held in secret sitting.

Article 49. Both Houses of the Imperial Diet may respectively present addresses to the Emperor.

Article 50. Both Houses may receive petitions presented by subjects.

Article 51. Both Houses may enact, besides what is provided for in the present Constitution and in the Law of the Houses, rules necessary for the management of their internal affairs.

Article 52. No Member of either House shall be held responsible outside the respective Houses, for any opinion uttered or for any vote given in the House. When, however, a Member himself has given publicity to his opinions by public speech, by documents in print or in writing, or by any other similar means, he shall, in the matter, be amenable to the general law.

Article 53. The Members of both Houses shall, during the session, be free from arrest, unless with the consent of the House, except in cases of flagrant delicts, or of offences connected with a state of internal commotion or with a foreign trouble.

Article 54. The Ministers of State and the Delegates of the Government may, at any time, take seats and speak in either House.

CHAPTER IV. THE MINISTERS OF STATE AND THE PRIVY COUNCIL

Article 55. The respective Ministers of State shall give their advice to the Emperor, and be responsible for it.

(2) All Laws, Imperial Ordinances, and Imperial Rescripts of whatever kind, that relate to the affairs of the State, require the countersignature of a Minister of State.

Article 56. The Privy Councillors shall, in accordance with the provisions for the organisation of the Privy Council, deliberate upon important matters of State, when they have been consulted by the Emperor.

CHAPTER V. THE JUDICATURE

Article 57. The Judicature shall be exercised by the Courts of Law according to law, in the name of the Emperor.

(2) The organisation of the Courts of Law shall be determined by law.

Article 58. The judges shall be appointed from among those, who possess proper qualifications according to law.

(2) No judge shall be deprived of his position, unless by way of criminal sentence or disciplinary punishment.

(3) Rules for disciplinary punishment shall be determined by law.

Article 59. Trials and judgments of a Court shall be conducted publicly. When, however, there exists any fear, that such publicity may be prejudicial to peace and order, or to the maintenance of public morality, the public trial may be suspended by provisions of law or by the decision of the Court of Law.

Article 60. All matters, that fall within the competency of a special Court, shall be specially provided for by law.

Article 61. No suit at law, which relates to rights alleged to have been infringed by the illegal measures of the administrative authorities, and which shall come within the competency of the Court of Administrative Litigation specially established by law, shall be taken cognisance of by a Court of Law.

CHAPTER VI. FINANCE

Article 62. The imposition of a new tax or the modification of the rates (of an existing one) shall be determined by law.

(2) However, all such administrative fees or other revenue having the nature of compensation shall not fall within the category of the above clause.

(3) The raising of national loans and the contracting of other liabilities to the charge of the National Treasury, except those that are provided in the Budget, shall require the consent of the Imperial Diet.

Article 63. The taxes levied at present shall, in so far as they are not remodelled by a new law, be collected according to the old system.

Article 64. The expenditure and revenue of the State require the consent of the Imperial Diet by means of an annual Budget.

(2) Any and all expenditures overpassing the appropriations set forth in the Titles and Paragraphs of the Budget, or that are not provided for in the Budget, shall subsequently require the approbation of the Imperial Diet.

Article 65. The Budget shall be first laid before the House of Representatives.

Article 66. The expenditures of the Imperial House shall be defrayed every year out of the National Treasury, according to the present fixed amount for the same, and shall not require the consent thereto of the Imperial Diet, except in case an increase thereof is found necessary.

Article 67. Those already fixed expenditures based by the Constitution upon the powers appertaining to the Emperor, and such expenditures as may have arisen by the effect of law, or that appertain to the legal obligations of the Government, shall be neither rejected nor reduced by the Imperial Diet, without the concurrence of the Government.

Article 68. In order to meet special requirements, the Government may ask the consent of the Imperial Diet to a certain amount as a Continuing Expenditure Fund, for a previously fixed number of years.

Article 69. In order to supply deficiencies, which are unavoidable, in the Budget, and to meet requirements unprovided for in the same, a Reserve Fund shall be provided in the Budget.

Article 70. When the Imperial Diet cannot be convoked, owing to the external or internal condition of the country, in case of urgent need for the maintenance of public safety, the Government may take all necessary financial measures, by means of an Imperial Ordinance.

(2) In the case mentioned in the preceding clause, the matter shall be submitted to the Imperial Diet at its next session, and its approbation shall be obtained thereto.

Article 71. When the Imperial Diet has not voted on the Budget, or when the Budget has not been brought into actual existence, the Government shall carry out the Budget of the preceding year.

Article 72. The final account of the expenditures and revenues of the State shall be verified and confirmed by the Board of Audit, and it shall be submitted by the Government to the Imperial Diet, together with the report of verification of the said Board.

(2) The organisation and competency of the Board of Audit shall be determined by law separately.

CHAPTER VII. SUPPLEMENTARY RULES

Article 73. When it has become necessary in future to amend the provisions of the present Constitution, a project to the effect shall be submitted to the Imperial Diet by Imperial Order.

(2) In the above case, neither House can open the debate, unless not less than two-thirds of the whole number of Members are present, and no amendment can be passed, unless a majority of not less than two-thirds of the Members present is obtained.

Article 74. No modification of the Imperial House Law shall be required to be submitted to the deliberation of the Imperial Diet.

(2) No provision of the present Constitution can be modified by the Imperial House Law.

Article 75. No modification can be introduced into the Constitution, or into the Imperial House Law, during the time of a Regency.

Article 76. Existing legal enactments, such as laws, regulations, Ordinances, or by whatever names they may be called, shall, so far as they do not conflict with the present Constitution, continue in force.

(2) All existing contracts or orders, that entail obligations upon the Government, and that are connected with expenditure, shall come within the scope of Article 67.

APPENDIX II

THE CONSTITUTION OF JAPAN 1946

Promulgated on 3 November 1946; Put into effect on 3 May 1947

We, the Japanese people, acting through our duly elected representatives in the National Diet, determined that we shall secure for ourselves and our posterity the fruits of peaceful cooperation with all nations and the blessings of liberty throughout this land, and resolved that never again shall we be visited with the horrors of war through the action of government, do proclaim that sovereign power resides with the people and do firmly establish this Constitution. Government is a sacred trust of the people, the authority for which is derived from the people, the powers of which are exercised by the representatives of the people, and the benefits of which are enjoyed by the people. This is a universal principle of mankind upon which this Constitution is founded. We reject and revoke all constitutions, laws, ordinances, and rescripts in conflict herewith.

We, the Japanese people, desire peace for all time and are deeply conscious of the high ideals controlling human relationship, and we have determined to preserve our security and existence, trusting in the justice and faith of the peace-loving peoples of the world. We desire to occupy an honoured place in an international society striving for the preservation of peace, and the banishment of tyranny and slavery, oppression and intolerance for all time from the earth. We recognise that all peoples of the world have the right to live in peace, free from fear and want.

We believe that no nation is responsible to itself alone, but that laws of political morality are universal; and that obedience to such laws is incumbent upon all nations who would sustain their own sovereignty and justify their sovereign relationship with other nations.

We, the Japanese people, pledge our national honour to accomplish these high ideals and purposes with all our resources.

CHAPTER I. THE EMPEROR

Article 1. The Emperor shall be the symbol of the State and of the unity of the people, deriving his position from the will of the people with whom resides sovereign power.

Article 2. The Imperial Throne shall be dynastic and succeeded to in accordance with the Imperial House Law passed by the Diet.

Article 3. The advice and approval of the Cabinet shall be required for all acts of the Emperor in matters of state, and the Cabinet shall be responsible therefor.

Article 4. The Emperor shall perform only such acts in matters of state as are provided for in this Constitution and he shall not have powers related to government.

(2) The Emperor may delegate the performance of his acts in matters of state as may be provided by law.

Article 5. When, in accordance with the Imperial House Law, a Regency is established, the Regent shall perform his acts in matters of state in the Emperor's name. In this case, paragraph one of the preceding article will be applicable.

Article 6. The Emperor shall appoint the Prime Minister as designated by the Diet.

(2) The Emperor shall appoint the Chief Judge of the Supreme Court as designated by the Cabinet.

Article 7. The Emperor, with the advice and approval of the Cabinet, shall perform the following acts in matters of state on behalf of the people:

(i) Promulgation of amendments of the constitution, laws, cabinet orders and treaties;

(ii) Convocation of the Diet;

(iii) Dissolution of the House of Representatives;

(iv) Proclamation of general election of members of the Diet;

(v) Attestation of the appointment and dismissal of Ministers of State and other officials as provided for by law, and of full powers and credentials of Ambassadors and Ministers;

(vi) Attestation of general and special amnesty, commutation of punishment, reprieve, and restoration of rights;

(vii) Awarding of honours;

(viii) Attestation of instruments of ratification and other diplomatic documents as provided for by law;

(ix) Receiving foreign ambassadors and ministers;

(x) Performance of ceremonial functions.

Article 8. No property can be given to, or received by, the Imperial House, nor can any gifts be made therefrom, without the authorisation of the Diet.

CHAPTER II. RENUNCIATION OF WAR

Article 9. Aspiring sincerely to an international peace based on justice and order, the Japanese people forever renounce war as a sovereign right of the nation and the threat or use of force as a means of settling international disputes.

(2) In order to accomplish the aim of the preceding paragraph, land, sea, and air forces, as well as other war potential, will never be maintained. The right of belligerency of the state will not be recognised.

CHAPTER III. RIGHTS AND DUTIES OF THE PEOPLE

Article 10. The conditions necessary for being a Japanese national shall be determined by law.

Article 11. The people shall not be prevented from enjoying any of the fundamental human rights. These fundamental human rights guaranteed to the people by this Constitution shall be conferred upon the people of this and future generations as eternal and in. violate rights.

Article 12. The freedoms and rights guaranteed to the people by this Constitution shall be maintained by the constant endeavor of the people, who shall refrain from any abuse of these freedoms and rights and shall always be responsible for utilising them for the public welfare.

Article 13. All of the people shall be respected as individuals. Their right to life, liberty, and the pursuit of happiness shall, to the extent that it does not interfere with the public welfare, be the supreme consideration in legislation and in other governmental affairs.

Article 14. All of the people are equal under the law and there shall be no discrimination in political, economic or social relations because of race, creed, sex, social status or family origin.

(2) Peers and peerage shall not be recognised.

(3) No privilege shall accompany any award of honour, decoration or any distinction, nor shall any such award be valid beyond the lifetime of the individual who now holds or hereafter may receive it.

Article 15. The people have the inalienable right to choose their public officials and to dismiss them.

(2) All public officials are servants of the whole community and not of any group thereof.

(3) Universal adult suffrage is guaranteed with regard to the election of public officials.

(4) In all elections, secrecy of the ballot shall not be violated. A voter shall not be answerable, publicly or privately, for the choice he has made.

Article 16. Every person shall have the right of peaceful petition for the redress of damage, for the removal of public officials, for the enactment, repeal or amendment of laws, ordinances or regulations and for other matters, nor shall any person be in any way discriminated against for sponsoring such a petition.

Article 17. Every person may sue for redress as provided by law from the State or a public entity, in case he has suffered damage through illegal act of any public official.

Article 18. No person shall be held in bondage of any kind. Involuntary servitude, except as punishment for crime, is prohibited.

Article 19. Freedom of thought and conscience shall not be violated.

Article 20. Freedom of religion is guaranteed to all. No religious organisation shall receive any privileges from the State nor exercise any political authority.

(2) No person shall be compelled to take part in any religious acts, celebration, rite or practice.

(3) The State and its organs shall refrain from religious education or any other religious activity.

Article 21. Freedom of assembly and association as well as speech, press and all other forms of expression are guaranteed.

(2) No censorship shall be maintained, nor shall the secrecy of any means of communication be violated.

Article 22. Every person shall have freedom to choose and change his residence and to choose his occupation to the extent that it does not interfere with the public welfare.

(2) Freedom of all persons to move to a foreign country and to divest themselves of their nationality shall be inviolate.

Article 23. Academic freedom is guaranteed.

Article 24. Marriage shall be based only on the mutual consent of both sexes and it shall be maintained through mutual cooperation with the equal rights of husband and wife as a basis.

(2) With regard to choice of spouse, property rights, inheritance, choice of domicile, divorce and other matters pertaining to marriage and the family, laws shall be enacted from the standpoint of individual dignity and the essential equality of the sexes.

Article 25. All people shall have the right to maintain the minimum standards of wholesome and cultured living.

(2) In all spheres of life, the State shall use its endeavors for the promotion and extension of social welfare and security, and of public health.

Article 26. All people shall have the right to receive an equal education correspondent to their ability, as provided by law.

(2) All people shall be obligated to have all boys and girls under their protection receive ordinary educations as provided for by law. Such compulsory education shall be free.

Article 27. All people shall have the right and the obligation to work.

(2) Standards for wages, hours, rest and other working conditions shall be fixed by law.

(3) Children shall not be exploited.

Article 28. The right of workers to organise and to bargain and act collectively is guaranteed.

Article 29. The right to own or to hold property is inviolable.

(2) Property rights shall be defined by law, in conformity with the public welfare.

(3) Private property may be taken for public use upon just compensation therefor.

Article 30. The people shall be liable to taxation as provided by law.

Article 31. No person shall be deprived of life or liberty, nor shall any other criminal penalty be imposed, except according to procedure established by law.

Article 32. No person shall be denied the right of access to the courts.

Article 33. No person shall be apprehended except upon warrant issued by a competent judicial officer which specifies the offence with which the person is charged, unless he is apprehended, the offense being committed.

Article 34. No person shall be arrested or detained without being at once informed of the charges against him or without the immediate privilege of counsel; nor shall he be detained without adequate cause; and upon demand of any person such cause must be immediately shown in open court in his presence and the presence of his counsel.

Article 35. The right of all persons to be secure in their homes, papers and effects against entries, searches and seizures shall not be impaired except upon warrant issued for adequate cause and particularly describing the place to be searched and things to be seized, or except as provided by Article 33.

(2) Each search or seizure shall be made upon separate warrant issued by a competent judicial officer.

Article 36. The infliction of torture by any public officer and cruel punishments are absolutely forbidden.

Article 37. In all criminal cases the accused shall enjoy the right to a speedy and public trial by an impartial tribunal.

(2) He shall be permitted full opportunity to examine all witnesses, and he shall have the right of compulsory process for obtaining witnesses on his behalf at public expense.

(3) At all times the accused shall have the assistance of competent counsel who shall, if the accused is unable to secure the same by his own efforts, be assigned to his use by the State.

Article 38. No person shall be compelled to testify against himself.

(2) Confession made under compulsion, torture or threat, or after prolonged arrest or detention shall not be admitted in evidence.

(3) No person shall be convicted or punished in cases where the only proof against him is his own confession.

Article 39. No person shall be held criminally liable for an act which was lawful at the time it was committed, or of which he has been acquitted, nor shall he be placed in double jeopardy.

Article 40. Any person, in case he is acquitted after he has been arrested or detained, may sue the State for redress as provided by law.

CHAPTER IV. THE DIET

Article 41. The Diet shall be the highest organ of state power, and shall be the sole law-making organ of the State.

Article 42. The Diet shall consist of two Houses, namely the House of Representatives and the House of Councillors.

Article 43. Both Houses shall consist of elected members, representative of all the people.

(2) The number of the members of each House shall be fixed by law.

Article 44. The qualifications of members of both Houses and their electors shall be fixed by law. However, there shall be no discrimination because of race, creed, sex, social status, family origin, education, property or income.

Article 45. The term of office of members of the House of Representatives shall be four years. However, the term shall be terminated before the full term is up in case the House of Representatives is dissolved.

Article 46. The term of office of members of the House of Councillors shall be six years, and election for half the members shall take place every three years.

Article 47. Electoral districts, method of voting and other matters pertaining to the method of election of members of both Houses shall be fixed by law.

Article 48. No person shall be permitted to be a member of both Houses simultaneously.

Article 49. Members of both Houses shall receive appropriate annual payment from the national treasury in accordance with law.

Article 50. Except in cases provided by law, members of both Houses shall be exempt from apprehension while the Diet is in session, and any members apprehended before the opening of the session shall be freed during the term of the session upon demand of the House.

Article 51. Members of both Houses shall not be held liable outside the House for speeches, debates or votes cast inside the House.

Article 52. An ordinary session of the Diet shall be convoked once per year.

Article 53. The Cabinet may determine to convoke extraordinary sessions of the Diet. When a quarter or more of the total members of either House makes the demand, the Cabinet must determine on such convocation.

Article 54. When the House of Representatives is dissolved, there must be a general election of members of the House of Representatives within forty (40) days from the date of dissolution, and the Diet must be convoked within thirty (30) days from the date of the election.

(2) When the House of Representatives is dissolved, the House of Councillors is closed at the same time. However, the Cabinet may in time of national emergency convoke the House of Councillors in emergency session.

(3) Measures taken at such session as mentioned in the proviso of the preceding paragraph shall be provisional and shall become null and void unless agreed to by the House of Representatives within a period of ten (10) days after the opening of the next session of the Diet.

Article 55. Each House shall judge disputes related to qualifications of its members. However, in order to deny a seat to any member, it is necessary to pass a resolution by a majority of two-thirds or more of the members present.

Article 56. Business cannot be transacted in either House unless one-third or more of total membership is present.

(2) All matters shall be decided, in each House, by a majority of those present, except as elsewhere provided in the Constitution, and in case of a tie, the presiding officer shall decide the issue.

Article 57. Deliberation in each House shall be public. However, a secret meeting may be held where a majority of two-thirds or more of those members present passes a resolution therefor.

(2) Each House shall keep a record of proceedings. This record shall be published and given general circulation, excepting such parts of proceedings of secret session as may be deemed to require secrecy.

(3) Upon demand of one-fifth or more of the members present, votes of the members on any matter shall be recorded in the minutes.

Article 58. Each House shall select its own president and other officials.

(2) Each House shall establish its rules pertaining to meetings, proceedings and internal discipline, and may punish members for disorderly conduct. However, in order to expel a member, a majority of two-thirds or more of those members present must pass a resolution thereon.

Article 59. A bill becomes a law on passage by both Houses, except as otherwise provided by the Constitution.

(2) A bill which is passed by the House of Representatives, and upon which the House of Councillors makes a decision different from that of the House of Representatives, becomes a law when passed a second time by the House of Representatives by a majority of two-thirds or more of the members present.

(3) The provision of the preceding paragraph does not preclude the House of Representatives from calling for the meeting of a joint committee of both Houses, provided for by law.

(4) Failure by the House of Councillors to take final action within sixty (60) days after receipt of a bill passed by the House of Representatives, time in recess excepted, may be determined by the House of Representatives to constitute a rejection of the said bill by the House of Councillors.

Article 60. The Budget must first be submitted to the House of Representatives.

(2) Upon consideration of the budget, when the House of Councillors makes a decision different from that of the House of Representatives, and when no agreement can be reached even through a joint committee of both Houses, provided for by law, or in the case of failure by the House of Councillors to take final action within thirty (30) days, the period of recess excluded, after the receipt of the budget passed by the House of Representatives, the decision of the House of Representatives shall be the decision of the Diet.

Article 61. The second paragraph of the preceding article applies also to the Diet approval required for the conclusion of treaties.

Article 62. Each House may conduct investigations in relation to government, and may demand the presence and testimony of witnesses, and the production of records.

Article 63. The Prime Minister and other Ministers of State may, at any time, appear in either House for the purpose of speaking on bills, regardless of whether they are members of the House or not. They must appear when their presence is required in order to give answers or explanations.

Article 64. The Diet shall set up an impeachment court from among the members of both Houses for the purpose of trying those judges against whom removal proceedings have been instituted.

(2) Matters relating to impeachment shall be provided by law.

CHAPTER V. THE CABINET

Article 65. Executive power shall be vested in the Cabinet.

Article 66. The Cabinet shall consist of the Prime Minister, who shall be its head, and other Ministers of State, as provided for by law.

(2) The Prime Minister and other Ministers of State must be civilians.

(3) The Cabinet, in the exercise of executive power, shall be collectively responsible to the Diet.

Article 67. The Prime Minister shall be designated from among the members of the Diet by a resolution of the Diet. This designation shall precede all other business.

(2) If the House of Representatives and the House of Councillors disagrees and if no agreement can be reached even through a joint committee of both Houses, provided for by law, or the House of Councillors fails to make designation within ten (10) days, exclusive of the period of recess, after the House of Representatives has made designation, the decision of the House of Representatives shall be the decision of the Diet.

Article 68. The Prime Minister shall appoint the Ministers of State. However, a majority of their number must be chosen from among the members of the Diet.

(2) The Prime Minister may remove the Ministers of State as he chooses.

Article 69. If the House of Representatives passes a non-confidence resolution, or rejects a confidence resolution, the Cabinet shall resign en masse, unless the House of Representatives is dissolved with ten (10) days.

Article 70. When there is a vacancy in the post of Prime Minister, or upon the first convocation of the Diet after a general election of members of the House of Representatives, the Cabinet shall resign en masse.

Article 71. In the cases mentioned in the two preceding articles, the Cabinet shall continue its functions until the time when a new Prime Minister is appointed.

Article 72. The Prime Minister, representing the Cabinet, submits bills, reports on general national affairs and foreign relations to the Diet and exercises control and supervision over various administrative branches.

Article 73. The Cabinet, in addition to other general administrative functions, shall perform the following functions:

(i) Administer the law faithfully; conduct affairs of state;

(ii) Manage foreign affairs;

(iii) Conclude treaties. However, it shall obtain prior or, depending on circumstances, subsequent approval of the Diet;

(iv) Administer the civil service, in accordance with standards established by law;

(v) Prepare the budget, and present it to the Diet;

(vi) Enact cabinet orders in order to execute the provisions of this Constitution and of the law. However, it cannot include penal provisions in such cabinet orders unless authorised by such law.

(vii) Decide on general amnesty, special amnesty, commutation of punishment, reprieve, and restoration of rights.

Article 74. All laws and cabinet orders shall be signed by the competent Minister of State and countersigned by the Prime Minister.

Article 75. The Ministers of State, during their tenure of office, shall not be subject to legal action without the consent of the Prime Minister. However, the right to take that action is not impaired hereby.

CHAPTER VI. JUDICIARY

Article 76. The whole judicial power is vested in a Supreme Court and in such inferior courts as are established by law.

(2) No extraordinary tribunal shall be established, nor shall any organ or agency of the Executive be given final judicial power.

(3) All judges shall be independent in the exercise of their conscience and shall be bound only by this Constitution and the laws.

Article 77. The Supreme Court is vested with the rule-making power under which it determines the rules of procedure and of practice, and of matters relating to attorneys, the internal discipline of the courts and the administration of judicial affairs.

(2) Public procurators shall be subject to the rule-making power of the Supreme Court.

(3) The Supreme Court may delegate the power to make rules for inferior courts to such courts.

Article 78. Judges shall not be removed except by public impeachment unless judicially declared mentally or physically incompetent to perform official duties. No disciplinary action against judges shall be administered by any executive organ or agency.

Article 79. The Supreme Court shall consist of a Chief Judge and such number of judges as may be determined by law; all such judges excepting the Chief Judge shall be appointed by the Cabinet.

(2) The appointment of the judges of the Supreme Court shall be reviewed by the people at the first general election of members of the House of Representatives following their appointment, and shall be reviewed again at the first general election of members of the House of Representatives after a lapse of ten (10) years, and in the same manner thereafter.

(3) In cases mentioned in the foregoing paragraph, when the majority of the voters favors the dismissal of a judge, he shall be dismissed.

(4) Matters pertaining to review shall be prescribed by law.

(5) The judges of the Supreme Court shall be retired upon the attainment of the age as fixed by law.

(6) All such judges shall receive, at regular stated intervals, adequate compensation which shall not be decreased during their terms of office.

Article 80. The judges of the inferior courts shall be appointed by the Cabinet from a list of persons nominated by the Supreme Court. All such judges shall hold office for a term of ten (10) years with privilege of reappointment, provided that they shall be retired upon the attainment of the age as fixed by law.

(2) The judges of the inferior courts shall receive, at regular stated intervals, adequate compensation which shall not be decreased during their terms of office.

Article 81. The Supreme Court is the court of last resort with power to determine the constitutionality of any law, order, regulation or official act.

Article 82. Trials shall be conducted and judgment declared publicly.

(2) Where a court unanimously determines publicity to be dangerous to public order or morals, a trial may be conducted privately, but trials of political offenses, offenses involving the press or cases wherein the rights of people as guaranteed in Chapter III of this Constitution are in question shall always be conducted publicly.

CHAPTER VII. FINANCE

Article 83. The power to administer national finances shall be exercised as the Diet shall determine.

Article 84. No new taxes shall be imposed or existing ones modified except by law or under such conditions as law may prescribe.

Article 85. No money shall be expended, nor shall the State obligate itself, except as authorised by the Diet.

Article 86. The Cabinet shall prepare and submit to the Diet for its consideration and decision a budget for each fiscal year.

Article 87. In order to provide for unforeseen deficiencies in the budget, a reserve fund may be authorised by the Diet to be expended upon the responsibility of the Cabinet.

(2) The Cabinet must get subsequent approval of the Diet for all payments from the reserve fund.

Article 88. All property of the Imperial Household shall belong to the State. All expenses of the Imperial Household shall be appropriated by the Diet in the budget.

Article 89. No public money or other property shall be expended or appropriated for the use, benefit or maintenance of any religious institution or association, or for any charitable, educational or benevolent enterprises not under the control of public authority.

Article 90. Final accounts of the expenditures and revenues of the State shall be audited annually by a Board of Audit and submitted by the Cabinet to the Diet, together with the statement of audit, during the fiscal year immediately following the period covered.

(2) The organisation and competency of the Board of Audit shall be determined by law.

Article 91. At regular intervals and at least annually the Cabinet shall report to the Diet and the people on the state of national finances.

CHAPTER VIII. LOCAL SELF-GOVERNMENT

Article 92. Regulations concerning organisation and operations of local public entities shall be fixed by law in accordance with the principle of local autonomy.

Article 93. The local public entities shall establish assemblies as their deliberative organs, in accordance with law.

(2) The chief executive officers of all local public entities, the members of their assemblies, and such other local officials as may be determined by law shall be elected by direct popular vote within their several communities.

Article 94. Local public entities shall have the right to manage their property, affairs and administration and to enact their own regulations within law.

Article 95. A special law, applicable only to one local public entity, cannot be enacted by the Diet without the consent of the majority of the voters of the local public entity concerned, obtained in accordance with law.

CHAPTER IX. AMENDMENTS

Article 96. Amendments to this Constitution shall be initiated by the Diet, through a concurring vote of two-thirds or more of all the members of each House and shall thereupon be submitted to the people for ratification, which shall require the affirmative vote of a majority of all votes cast thereon, at a special referendum or at such election as the Diet shall specify.

(2) Amendments when so ratified shall immediately be promulgated by the Emperor in the name of the people, as an integral part of this Constitution.

CHAPTER X. SUPREME LAW

Article 97. The fundamental human rights by this Constitution guaranteed to the people of Japan are fruits of the age-old struggle of man to be free; they have survived the many exacting tests for durability and are conferred upon this and future generations in trust, to be held for all time inviolate.

Article 98. This Constitution shall be the supreme law of the nation and no law, ordinance, imperial rescript or other act of government, or part thereof, contrary to the provisions hereof, shall have legal force or validity.

(2) The treaties concluded by Japan and established laws of nations shall be faithfully observed.

Article 99. The Emperor or the Regent as well as Ministers of State, members of the Diet, judges, and all other public officials have the obligation to respect and uphold this Constitution.

CHAPTER XI. SUPPLEMENTARY PROVISIONS

Article 100. This Constitution shall be enforced as from the day when the period of six months will have elapsed counting from the day of its promulgation.

(2) The enactment of laws necessary for the enforcement of this Constitution, the election of members of the House of Councillors and the procedure

for the convocation of the Diet and other preparatory procedures for the enforcement of this Constitution may be executed before the day prescribed in the preceding paragraph.

Article 101. If the House of Councillors is not constituted before the effective date of this Constitution, the House of Representatives shall function as the Diet until such time as the House of Councillors shall be constituted.

Article 102. The term of office for half the members of the House of Councillors serving in the first term under this Constitution shall be three years. Members falling under this category shall be determined in accordance with law.

Article 103. The Ministers of State, members of the House of Representatives, and judges in office on the effective date of this Constitution, and all other public officials, who occupy positions corresponding to such positions as are recognised by this Constitution shall not forfeit their positions automatically on account of the enforcement of this Constitution unless otherwise specified by law. When, however, successors are elected or appointed under the provisions of this Constitution, they shall forfeit their positions as a matter of course.

INDEX